(63-7657) 8-4-67

American Ideas

Source Readings in the Intellectual History
of the United States

Volume I: Foundations (1629-1865)

Volume II: Dilemmas of Maturity

(1865-1962)

Edited by GERALD N. GROB and ROBERT N. BECK

The Free Press of Glencoe
Collier-Macmillan Ltd., London

For Our Parents

Preface

LIKE MOST PEOPLES, Americans have wondered about the nature and meaning of their national existence. Unlike other peoples, however, their questioning has been complicated by a number of unique circumstances, particularly the diversified national origins of the American people and their dependence on European traditions. Thus they have been led to ask whether America has an independent and indigenous intellectual tradition of its own, or whether American thought is simply a derivative by-product of a larger and older European tradition, or, in either case, whether there is an indentifiable American national purpose and goal.

This book is an attempt to deal with these important problems by presenting lengthy excerpts from major American intellectual figures arranged in such a manner as to relate their ideas to the development of a native intellectual tradition. In addition, extensive introductions, connective commentaries, and headnotes provide the reader with the historical perspective and background that are so necessary to an understanding of America's intellectual heritage. The general point of view presented is that while America has borrowed much from Europe, it has always modified these borrowings in the light of its own experiences. The result has been the unique synthesis of ideas and attitudes that has characterized the American mind.

To illustrate the movement of American thought we have distinguished five major periods in the intellectual history of the United States: the Puritan era, the age of the Enlightenment, the Romantic period of the early nineteenth century, the reaction to industrialism, and finally the dilemmas of American society since the 1930's. We have conceived of our task in a broad manner and have attempted to take a representative cross section of the American heritage, including theologians, philosophers, men of letters, political theorists, educators, statesmen, reformers, economists, jurists, and historians, in order to illustrate the predominant modes of thought in given historical epochs. Each generation has sought to give meaning and significance to its existence, and the way in which this has been accomplished has varied with the problems faced.

From the time of the Puritans until the coming of the Civil War, Americans looked to the future with optimism and eager expectation, firmly committed to the vision of a constantly improving society. They tended to interpret their experiences in religious terms, whether borrowed from the Puritan vocabulary, the creed of the Enlightenment, or the evangelical version of religious truth. Had not America been divinely blessed with abundant resources as well as immunization from a more corrupt and decadent Europe? Was not America destined to serve as a haven and model for all mankind, offering to the rest of the world a shining example of what human society could accomplish under the aegis of a generous Deity?

Indeed, the vision of a new society under a beneficent Deity provided much of the drive that constantly impelled Americans to improve their position and to build a better world. The Puritans underwent great hardships and deprivations in order to establish a society based on divine law, a society that would truly embody a religious ideal and serve as a beacon to all mankind. In many ways the Puritans set the tone for much of America's subsequent development, especially in the intellectual realm. Eighteenth-century Americans, while no longer influenced as profoundly by the God of the Puritans, nevertheless continued to uphold their belief in rights and duties that were derived from a divine source. Indeed, the natural rights argument was a primary issue in the events that led to the American Revolution and ultimately to the establishment of a new nation that would be free to live according to its own ideals and to realize its own destiny. Finally, Americans during the first half of the nineteenth century tended to identify religion and progress, and their efforts to built a better society often were motivated by a mixture of spiritual zeal and social consciousness—this was particularly true in the abolitionist campaign against slavery. Thus whatever the problems and difficulties they faced, Americans for the first two centuries of their existence looked hopefully toward a better and more humane world. It is this sense of optimism and destiny that helps to explain many of the intellectual patterns of the United States during this period.

After the Civil War, as technological developments swiftly transformed the United States from an agrarian and rural nation into an urban and industrial world power, new issues arose to challenge the American people. But since the traditional premises of the older Protestant individualistic ethics seemed less and less relevant to the changing times, a search began for a new rationale that would replace the older one and enable men to cope with the new and unfamiliar problems of a complex world. In formulating a new synthesis Americans turned to contemporary advances in science, especially to evolutionary theory, in the hope of erecting a scientific ethical system. In so doing, however, they brought into question the whole religious basis of their society, creating an intellectual crisis of the first magnitude. Since the middle of the nineteenth century, therefore, Americans have continued to seek an adequate philosophical justification upon which their society could rest. After the Civil War there developed such intellectual systems as conservative Darwinism, reform Darwinism, pragmatism, and naturalism. In recent times the search for national meaning and purpose continues amidst the troubles and dilemmas that confront all mankind. That Americans, despite the formal orthodoxy of a cold war era, still seek a faith for living is proven by the persistence of numerous and opposing intellectual movements, such as Protestant neo-orthodoxy and evangelical fundamentalism, Catholic neo-Thomism, the New Conservatism, and a modified version of the liberal-progressive ethic of the early twentieth century. Where the search will lead, however, few are willing to predict with any degree of authority. Perhaps this volume can contribute to the quest by providing Americans with a knowledge of their intellectual heritage that will enable them to understand better the paradoxes and difficulties of the present.

We should like at this point to add a word of explanation. Any volume such as this must by its very nature be selective. In choosing the materials in this text, we have attempted not only to present a cross section of major figures but also to arrange their thoughts in such a way as to provide a meaningful interpretation of the course of American thought. This being the case, we have included figures that seemed to best exemplify the climate of opinion, predominant interests, and modes of thought of different generations. Because our selections are relatively long, the number of individuals that we have included has been necessarily limited; however, we feel that fewer but longer excerpts may provide the reader with deeper insights into the development of the American mind.

We have also attempted in all cases to reproduce accurately the texts in their original version. In some cases, however, spelling and punctuation have been slightly modified to conform with more modern usage.

Last, but not least, we should like to thank our friend and colleague, Professor George A. Billias, for his comments and suggestions, which have saved us from many errors. Our wives also provided that atmosphere which is so necessary for work of this kind.

G. N. G.
R. N. B.

Acknowledgments

THE EDITORS gratefully acknowledge the kind permission of the following publishers, individuals, and organizations to reprint copyrighted material in this book.

The American Academy of Political and Social Science: for selections from Lawrence Dennis, "Fascism for America," *Annals of the American Academy of Political and Social Science,* 180 (1935).

American Antiquarian Society: for selections from Cotton Mather, "The Angel of Bethesda," in Otho T. Beall, Jr., and Richard H. Shryock, eds., "Cotton Mather: First Significant Figure in American Medicine," American Antiquarian Society, *Proceedings,* 63 (April, 1953).

American Historical Review: for Charles A. Beard, "Written History as an Act of Faith," *American Historical Review,* 39 (January, 1934).

The American Scholar: for selections from Richard Hofstadter, "The Pseudo-Conservative Revolt," *The American Scholar,* 24 (Winter, 1954–1955). Copyright 1954 by the United Chapters of Phi Beta Kappa.

American Unitarian Association: for selections from Theodore Parker, *The World of Matter and the Spirit of Man* (1907), George Willis Cooke, ed.

Archives of the Diocese of Baltimore: for a manuscript letter of Bishop John Carroll to [?] Thorpe, February 17, 1785.

Beacon Press: for selections from Morton G. White, "Original Sin, Natural Law, and Politics," *Partisan Review,* 23 (Spring, 1956). This article is a shortened version of the "Epilogue for 1957" in Morton G. White, *Social Thought in America,* Beacon Press (1957).

Earl Browder: for selections from *The People's Front* (1938).

Columbia Law Review: for selections from Karl N. Llewellyn, "On Reading and Using the Newer Jurisprudence," *Columbia Law Review,* 40 (April, 1940); and Roscoe Pound, "Mechanical Jurisprudence," *ibid.,* 8 (December, 1908).

Columbia University Press: for selections from John Dewey, *Ethics* (1908); and Sidney Hook, "Naturalism and Democracy," in Yervant H. Krikorian, ed., *Naturalism and the Human Spirit* (1944).

Charles Coughlin: for selections from *Father Coughlin's Radio Discourses, 1931–1932* (1932).

John Wells Davidson: for selections from John Wells Davidson, ed., *A Crossroads of Liberalism: The 1912 Campaign Speeches of Woodrow Wilson* (1956).

John Dos Passos: for selections from *U.S.A.,* volume III (1936).

Doubleday & Company, Inc., and The World's Work (1913) Ltd.: for selections from Billy Graham, *Peace With God* (1953).

The Free Press of Glencoe, Inc.: for selections from Daniel Bell, *The End of Ideology: On the Exhaustion of Political Ideas in the Fifties* (1960).

Harper & Brothers: for selections from Twelve Southerners, *I'll Take My Stand: The South and the Agrarian Tradition* (1930).

Holt, Rinehart and Winston, Inc.: for selections from John Dewey, *The Influence of Darwin on Philosophy and Other Essays in Contemporary Thought* (1910).

Houghton Mifflin Company: for selections from Arthur M. Schlesinger, Jr., *The Vital Center: The Politics of Freedom* (1949). By permission of and arrangement with Houghton Mifflin Company, the authorized publishers.

Walter Kaufmann: for selections from Walter Kaufmann, "The Faith of a Heretic," *Harper's Magazine,* 218 (February, 1959).

William J. Kenealy, S.J.: for selections from "The Majesty of the Law," *Loyola* (New Orleans) *Law Review,* 5 (1950).

Little, Brown & Co.–Atlantic Monthly Press: for selections from Walter Lippmann, *The Public Philosophy* (1955); and Clarence B. Randall, *A Creed for Free Enterprise* (1953).

The Macmillan Company: for selections from Henry Adams, *The Degradation of the Democratic Dogma* (1919); Herbert Croly, *The Promise of American Life* (1909); Walter Rauschenbusch, *A Theology for the Social Gospel* (1917); and Walter Weyl, *The New Democracy* (1912).

Marshall Jones Company: for selections from Ralph Adams Cram, *The Nemesis of Mediocrity* (1917).

Massachusetts Historical Society: for selections from John Winthrop, "A Modell of Christian Charity," *Winthrop Papers,* II (1931).

The Nation and Reinhold Niebuhr: for selections from Reinhold Niebuhr, "The Dilemma of Modern Man," *The Nation,* 164 (February 22, 1947).

National Review: for Russell Kirk "What is the Republic," *National Review,* 3 (February 2, 1957).

The New Republic: for selections from Lewis Mumford, "The Corruption of Liberalism," *The New Republic,* 102 (April 29, 1940).

New-York Historical Society: for selections from the manuscript by Cadwallader Colden in the Colden Papers, "An Introduction to the Study of Phylosophy wrote in America for the Use of a young Gentleman."

Princeton University Press: for selections from Elihu Root, *Experiments in Government and the Essentials of the Constitution* (1913).

Random House, Inc.: for selections from Franklin Delano Roosevelt, *The Public Papers and Addresses of Franklin D. Roosevelt,* volume I (1938).

Paul R. Reynolds & Son and John Farquharson Ltd.: for selections from William James, *Pragmatism* (1907).

Theodore Roosevelt Association: for selections from *The Works of Theodore Roosevelt,* Herman Hagedorn, ed., volume 19 (1925).

Harry N. Rosenfield: for selections from Morris Raphael Cohen, *The Faith of a Liberal* (1946).

Charles Scribner's Sons and James Nisbet & Company Ltd.: for selections from Reinhold Niebuhr, *The Children of Light and the Children of Darkness* (1944).

B. F. Skinner: for selections from B. F. Skinner, "Freedom and the Control of Men," *The American Scholar,* 25 (Winter, 1955–1956).

D. G. Brinton Thompson and the trustees of the estate of Madison Grant: for selections from Madison Grant, *The Passing of the Great Race* (1916).

University of Chicago Press, Routledge & Kegan Paul Ltd., and Friedrich A. von Hayek: for selections from Friedrich A. von Hayek, *The Constitution of Liberty* (1960).

University of Chicago Press: for selections from Edward Scribner Ames, *The New Orthodoxy* (1918).

University of Notre Dame Press: for selections from Will Herberg, "Religion and Culture in Present-Day America," in Thomas T. McAvoy, ed., *Roman Catholicism and the American Way of Life* (1960).

Peter Viereck: for selections from Peter Viereck, *Shame and Glory of the Intellectuals* (1953).

Yale University Press: for selections from Thurman Arnold, *The Folklore of Capitalism* (1937); Carl Becker, *Modern Democracy* (1941); and David Riesman and others, *The Lonely Crowd* (1950).

Contents: *Volume I*

Contents: *Volume II*

Part One
THE PURITAN MIND

*P*uritanism, which dominated the intellectual life of colonial New England for nearly a century after its founding, has been a major force in shaping the development of the American mind. Not only did it influence the New England colonies, leaving a complex heritage of customs and ideas, but it also advanced with those pioneers who left New England to blaze a frontier to the West. Thus it became incorporated into the mainstream of American thought. As one authority has remarked, Puritanism "was firmly rooted in the American experience and in the emerging American mind of the eighteenth century, and from New England as a center it has radiated its influence in American civilization, for good or ill, from that day to this; and the end is not yet."[1] Indeed, it is probably safe to assert that without an understanding of Puritanism there can be no understanding of America.

Yet there is much less agreement on the precise manner in which Puritanism influenced that vague and shadowy complex often referred to as the "American character." To one group Puritanism stands for narrow-mindedness and intolerance, intellectual atrophy, a prohibition upon the enjoyment of life, a restricted and perhaps bigoted sectarianism coupled with a crippling and inhibiting sense of guilt, and an individualism that, by interpreting religion in terms of thrift and worldly success, has led to social selfishness and irresponsibility. On the other hand, there are those who credit the Puritans with planting the seeds of democracy in the New World, with founding the first college and public school system, and with preserving the intellectual and cultural heritage of Western civilization in a harsh frontier environment that in other areas led to cultural regression.

Any study of the cluster of ideas and beliefs that is loosely termed the

---

1. Max Savelle, *Seeds of Liberty: The Genesis of the American Mind* (New York, 1948), p. 27.

"American mind" must, therefore, begin with an understanding of Puritanism and its influence during the formative years of seventeenth-century New England. In undertaking such a venture, however, we must not interpret Puritanism through the mood of revolt that marks much of twentieth-century intellectual history. During the 1920's, for example, it was fashionable for the opponents of the Eighteenth Amendment to characterize those in favor of Prohibition as "Puritans." Yet the Puritans of the seventeenth century never condemned the imbibing of alcoholic beverages; indeed, they consumed large amounts of spirits in their daily lives. What they did condemn was excessive rather than moderate drinking. Similarly, we must not only avoid defining Puritanism in modern terms, but we also must be careful to distinguish between the elements in original Puritanism and the beliefs that evolved from them in later years. Puritanism, after all, was a many-sided and complex force and, like many other philosophies, included elements of contradiction as well as unity. From its trunk, to illustrate again, could grow such different branches as Unitarianism, religious revivalism, and fundamentalism. Finally, we must recognize that Puritanism can be understood only when placed in its seventeenth-century English environment. While the Puritans came into conflict with some aspects of their native culture, most of their beliefs did not appreciably differ from those of the typical Englishman of that day.

Initially, Puritanism arose as an English movement of the late sixteenth and early seventeenth centuries. It sought to reform the Anglican Church by ridding it of all "popish" elements and restoring to it the simplicity of the early Christian Church. As such, it was intimately associated with the Protestant Reformation and all that movement implied. The English Puritans, although always maintaining that they were part of the Anglican Church, were nevertheless insistent in their belief that the English Reformation had not proceeded far enough, and they struggled to enforce their views upon the established Church. In an age when religion was perhaps the major force in human society, the conflict between the dissident sects and the Anglican Church had momentous repercussions, not only for religious life, but also for social, economic, political, and intellectual life. Thus, for well over a century, from the time of Henry VIII until the reign of William and Mary, religious struggles were to play a decisive role in English history.

The Puritans who migrated to New England in the 1630's and afterward were among the more radical, although not the most radical, of the Protestant sects. Unable to force their views upon the established Church in England, the Puritans chose to leave for the New World where they would be free to translate their beliefs into practice and establish their much cherished "Bible Commonwealth." In turn, the descendents of the Puritans, though no longer accepting the creed of their ancestors, nevertheless perpetuated many traits of Puritanism and preserved them within the framework of American culture.

At the heart of the Puritan creed lay the twofold assumption of the inherent sinfulness of man and the omnipotence of God. Man, according to Puritan theology, had fallen into a state of sin and could be saved only through the grace of God. Since God, however, has granted this grace to some and not to others, certain individuals were predestined to be saved while others were predestined to be damned. Yet the Puritans were not fatalists; and their emphasis upon predestination was more theoretical than real. They accepted the challenge of sin with enthusiasm, even though they recognized their inability to achieve perfection in this world. They insisted that God, in His infinite wisdom, was not a capricious deity, despite the fact that man did not always perceive His reason and logic. Mortal reason, after all, was not God's reason, and the Puritans never attempted to gloss over their shortcomings. To the typical Puritan, the sinfulness of man was a fact that could easily be verified through experience. Recognizing mankind's imperfections, the Puritans, as Perry Miller has so ably pointed out, "held on the one hand that men must act by reason and abide by justice, and strive for an inward communication with the force that controls the world, but on the other hand . . . they must not expect that force always to be cribbed and confined by their conceptions of what is reasonable and just."[2] Puritanism was a tough-minded philosophy, and the Puritan, because of his unquestioned faith in the grandeur and glory of God, could never be disillusioned by the transitory world in which he lived. Reconciling fate and freedom and accepting the omnipotence of God, the Puritans held that human life had value only insofar as man had the freedom to choose between good and evil.

Perhaps the feature that most distinguished Puritanism from other Protestant sects was its belief that the Bible, as the revealed truth of God, was an absolute code of action that provided man with an infallible guide to life, not only in matters of religion and theology, but also in such diverse areas as politics, economics, ethics, and matters of art. The typical seventeenth-century Puritan never for a moment doubted that the universe was centered in God, and that religion constituted the very essence of life and could not be separated from it. Those who migrated to Massachusetts in the third and fourth decades of the seventeenth century, therefore, attempted to organize society along lines laid down in the Bible. Religious ideals played a dominant role in shaping the social and political institutions of the young colony. Only church members were permitted to vote; and since formal church membership was kept at a minimum, Massachusetts quickly became an oligarchy ruled by a small minority of ministers and elders. Regarding themselves as a chosen people, the Puritans vigorously worked to root out what they regarded as error, and they freely proclaimed themselves enemies of toleration. Any individuals or groups brave enough to dissent from the dictates of the ruling group—such as Roger Williams, Anne Hutchinson, or the Quakers—quickly found themselves in difficult and even dangerous positions.

In time, however, the theocracy established by the Puritans began to crumble, partly as a result of internal tensions and partly because of environmental factors. The English tradition of self-government slowly made its

---

2. Perry Miller and Thomas H. Johnson, *The Puritans* (New York, 1938), p. 57.

presence felt, and with the passage of time the power of the ministers was undermined. The breakdown of the compact Puritan village also weakened conformity. Internal discontent with the existing situation led to the migration of several groups to other areas, while the persecution of such minorities as the Quakers met with increasing opposition from within the colony. In addition, the authority of the English government was gradually reimposed upon Massachusetts, with a consequent reduction in the authority of the oligarchy. Finally, the rational and more liberal ideas of the Enlightenment, as well as the growth of a commercially oriented middle class, weakened the religious inclination of the Puritans in favor of a more secular outlook on life.

Puritanism, however, was more than simply an unsuccessful effort to organize society along Biblical lines. It was also an articulate philosophy growing out of the intellectual climate of opinion of its times. As such, Puritanism inherited not only the ideals and traditions of the Reformation and Renaissance but also those of medieval Christianity. Always adopting an intellectual rather than an intuitive or emotional approach to problems, the Puritans maintained that reason and faith were valuable allies, each reinforcing the other. Furthermore, no conflict existed between the natural world and the revealed word of God. On the contrary, since each strengthened the other, the Puritan could easily accept scientific knowledge as an adjunct to religion. Though man might be an inherently evil being, he was also a rational creature and thus was capable of understanding his actions and accepting responsibility for them. The Puritans therefore labored to unify religion and knowledge into a compatible system of thought, and they succeeded, according to their own standards, in formulating a unified and coherent philosophy of life.

The Puritan emphasis on the harmony of faith and reason, moreover, was to have a profound influence on the intellectual development of colonial New England. It is undoubtedly true that in certain areas—notably the drama, religious music, religious painting, religious sculpture, and poetry—Puritanism acted as an inhibiting force by its insistence that anything that prevented man from coming into direct communion with God was a distraction and constituted a serious danger. Yet when the intellectual level of colonial New England is compared with that of either the middle or southern colonies, the unquestioned superiority of the former is immediately noted. The establishment of a school system, a college, and a printing press within a short time after the founding of the Massachusetts Bay Colony, for example, bears witness to this fact. In other areas, including literature, verse, science, and theology, the leadership of the Puritans is equally clear. The Puritans were adamant in their opposition to ignorance, and their emphasis upon learning and education constitutes one of their most important contributions to posterity. While the harsh frontier environment in other areas led to a loss of cultural values, the Puritans managed to keep a respect for learning and ideas alive in hostile surroundings. Perhaps intellectual Puritanism was, as Samuel Eliot Morison has commented, the only alternative to the overwhelming materialism that marked the other newly settled regions, whether English, French, Dutch, or Spanish.[3]

Activistic, moralistic, even rationalistic, Puritanism began to develop in different directions on the American shores. One of its paths led to political intolerance and the suppression of dissent; another led to a comparatively high intellectual and literary level. Still another was to lead toward the relatively secular position of the next century, known as the American Enlightenment. Regardless of the distaste we might feel for certain aspects of Puritanism that may today be characterized as hypocritical, can we deny the strength of the Puritan ideal that character and nobility are values that man can achieve only by a personal struggle whereby he transcends his physical surroundings? In assessing the enduring influence of the Puritans, all of these conflicting elements must be taken into account.

The best way to study the mind of the Puritans and its influence on succeeding generations is to begin with their own writings. Fortunately, the Puritans were both articulate and prolific in putting their thoughts on paper, and they did not hesitate to express their opinions. The following pages contain a cross section of leading Puritan pronouncements on a variety of seemingly unrelated topics. Taken together, however, they do suggest a picture of a people and an attitude whose influence and importance, whether good or bad, can scarcely be disputed.

---

3. Samuel Eliot Morison, *The Intellectual Life of Colonial New England* (New York, 1956), pp. 16–17.

I

The Puritan as a Religious Type

THOUGH IT HAD many different facets, Puritanism was primarily a religious movement that sprang from the medieval conception that the meaning and purpose of human existence can be found only when men are related to God. Like their contemporaries of the Protestant Reformation, however, the Puritans rejected the doctrine that salvation could be achieved through man's efforts, and they resolutely maintained that it could be attained only through the grace of God, who freely granted it as a gift despite man's inherent sinfulness.

For the Puritan, therefore, salvation (often referred to as "regeneration") was the central element in human experience, one that far transcended all others in importance. Yet his conception of original sin and human depravity was by no means as categorical as some scholars have held. Though man might be a sinful creature, he was also a rational and responsible being, and in their theology the Puritans managed to reconcile these apparently conflicting views. Influenced by the teachings of the great French Protestant philosopher Petrus Ramus (1515–1572), they held that truth could be tested by the innate rationality of the human mind, within which dwelt a small measure of divine truth. Puritanism thus managed to combine the rising humanist tradition and a system of Christian thought in an all-embracing religious conception of the world.

Central to Puritan theology, furthermore, was the belief that the regenerate individual had undergone a concrete physical experience that was proof of his salvation. In turn, this religious experience manifested itself in the outward conduct of his life. The regenerate individual, although aware of his own shortcomings, was compelled to obey to the best of his imperfect abilities the moral ordinances of God. These ordinances served two important purposes: they provided a measure whereby man could judge the enormity of his sinfulness, and they also helped the regenerate to grow in sanctity. Thus the covenant of works, although having been invalidated by original sin, was to be construed as a practical guide, thereby applying religious values insofar as the natural world was concerned. The covenant of grace, on the other hand, introduced the individual to the mysteries of life and the unknown. So long as constituted authority, as exercised by the ministers and elders, had the power to unite religion as a way of life and as an emotional experience, the Puritan creed could remain pure and undiluted. But with the decline in the powers of the oligarchy, this restraint no longer operated, and Puritanism began to develop along divergent paths. One path led to Unitarianism, while the other led to a more emotional and revivalistic religion, both of which were to have important influences on America's intellectual and religious history.

Paradoxically, the Puritan emphasis on the covenant of grace did not lead to either a passive or a carefree conception of life, but rather to a highly activistic philosophy that was well suited to the rigors of a frontier environment. Blending together in a subtle and sophisticated manner the opposing ideas contained in the covenant of works and the covenant of grace, the typical Puritan emphatically opposed any form of monasticism or moral asceticism. Since man existed to glorify God, it followed logically that life was not tragic, despite all its difficulties and hardships. The Puritans looked at the world with a feeling of optimism rather than pessimism, with a sense of adventure rather than foreboding. They did not demand the elimination of all worldly pleasures and pursuits; they simply emphasized moderate rather than excessive indulgence, since the enjoyment of these pleasures would contribute toward the creation of a well-rounded and complete individual who would stand as living proof of the glory and omnipotence of God.

(1)

Samuel Willard

1640-1707

Born at Concord, Massachusetts, Samuel Willard graduated from Harvard in 1659. In 1678 he was called to the Old South Church in Boston, where he remained until his death. His fame also brought him the vice-presidency of Harvard in 1700, and between 1701 and 1707 he headed that institution in the absence of its president, Increase Mather. Refusing to gloss over the implications of Puritan theology, Willard argued against toleration even though he himself was moving toward a more liberal position in the practice of religion. A master of learning and logic, he delivered over the years a series of sermons outlining orthodox theology. These were published after his death in the largest volume ever to come from a colonial press.

The selection reprinted here is from Willard's sermons of April 24 and May 22, 1688, in which he attempted to show the essential difference between the covenant of grace and the covenant of works. The text is from *A Compleat Body of Divinity in Two Hundred and Fifty Expository Lectures on the Assembly's Shorter Catechism* (Boston, 1726).

Question II

WHAT RULE *hath God given to direct us, how we may glorify and enjoy Him?*

Answer

The WORD of God (which is contained in the Scriptures of the *Old & New Testament*) is the ONLY Rule to direct us, how we may glorify and enjoy Him. . . .

FOR a right Understanding, and full Explication of this Question and Answer; there are these things will call for our distinct Consideration. (1) That Man *must* have a *Rule* to direct him, or else he can never attain to his chief end. (2) That this Rule can be but *one*. (3) That the *Word of God* is the *only* Rule. (4) That this word, which is the Rule, is contained in the *Scriptures* of the *Old* and *New Testament*. . . .

Prop. III THAT *the* WORD *of* GOD *is this only Rule*. . . .

Q. 2. How *does it appear to be the only Rule?*

A. WE may here (to expedite this matter) call to mind, that there have been *two Covenants*, in which God hath traded with men about their happiness, *viz*. that of *Works*, and that of *Grace*. As to the *former*, or that of works, there needs no applying of this Consideration to it, because man is no longer to expect felicity by it. If fallen man could have attained his end according to the tenour of that, the second had been *superfluous*. Gal. 3. 21. *Is the law then against the promises of God? God forbid: for if there had been a law given which could have given life, verily Righteousness should have been by the law*. That Covenant stands armed with *Curses*, and all that are under it can expect nothing else: Ver. 10. *For as many are are of the works of the law, are under the curse: for it is written, Cursed is every one that continueth not in all things which are written in the book of the law to do them*. And yet if there were need, it might be evidenced that God's *Word* was Man's only Rule there: but because *Adam*'s apostate Children can expect Life & Salvation only according to the tenour of the Covenant of *Grace*, it will suffice to make it appear, that the Word of God is the only Rule, to direct us to glorify and enjoy him, in the ways of *this* Covenant. And this will be manifest by these Propositions.

1. THAT Man by his fall mis[sed] of the happiness offered in the first Covenant, & brought himself under a condition of *misery*. Man's happiness

consists in the *glorifying* of God, & *enjoying* him: and the fall cut him off from both. From the former, Rom. 3. 23. *For all have sinned, and come short of the glory of God:* From the latter. Isa. 59. 2. *Your iniquities have separated between you and your God. A*nd hence he fell from Life into a state of Death: for therein did the Curse consist. Gen. 2. 17. *In the day that thou eatest thereof, thou shalt surely die.* So that all the Children of men are not only born *capable* of Misery: But they are born *actually* miserable. Hence this *Death* is said to be *past upon all men,* Rom. 5. 12.

2. THAT fallen man is *no longer capable* of being made *happy* by *that* Covenant. For, though his happiness be still in attaining his end, and his end be still the same that ever it was, yet it is not to be advanced by him *in that way* wherein it was at *first* prescribed: and this, not by reason of any default in the Law or Covenant, (that is holy, & just and good) but by reason of *his own Impotency. . . .* So that this Covenant speaks nothing but *terrour* and *despair* to all those that are held under the Conditions of it.

3. THAT hence, if ever the undone Creature be *restored* to happiness, by attaining his end, there must be *another way* found out for it. If blessedness can be no longer *by the law,* then either man must *never* be blessed; Or, there must be a *new law* of blessedness provided for him; Or he must be made blessed *without any,* which cannot be; for, if he could not be happy when he was *innocent,* but by closing with his Rule, and reaching his End, much less can he be so now he is *miserable,* unless there be a way to rid him of his misery, and bring him back to felicity. If therefore the law of *works* cannot, something *else* must, or otherwise he must needs perish. And if there be another *way,* there must of necessity be another *Rule. . . .*

4. THAT the *Recovery* of fallen man from this Misery, is an act of *God's sovereign Pleasure.* It derives from hence, and hath its dependence here. If, when man had come short of his end, and lost his happiness, he had left him there without hopes forever, he could not have done him any *injury;* it had been but an Hell of *his own* procuring. Hence the Original of man's Recovery is referred to *God's Will.* Eph. 1. 5. *Having predestinated us to the adoption of children by Jesus Christ to himself, according to the good pleasure of his will.* God had once brought himself under an Obligation to give him life in case of Obedience; but he had not obliged himself to deliver him, if he should cast himself away.

5. THAT hence *the Way,* in which this recovery is to be obtained, *depends upon* that Pleasure of His. He that might have chosen, whether *ever* he would have saved us, hath the liberty of prescribing (as he sees meet) *how* he will bring it about, and upon what *Terms* we may expect it. If *he* do not restore us, none can: and if he do, it is *free Grace.* Who then shall prescribe to him? Or who shall make his terms for him? And for this reason it is, that *Salvation* is said to *belong to God.*

6. THAT as God *purposed* from Eternity to bring back a number of fallen Men, so he provided a *new Covenant-way* to accomplish it in. God hath a company of Elect or chosen ones among the ruins of the fall, whom he

appointed to felicity in the days of Eternity, before the World was, (*Eph. 1. 6.*) And when he appointed them to the *End,* he also allotted the *Means,* by which they should reach it. Eph. 1. 4. *According as he hath chosen us in him before the foundation of the world, that we should be holy, and without blame before him in love.* The new and living way was then fixed, & peremptorily resolved upon; and it was but *one* way that was then determined, unto the which the terms of the new Covenant are in the publication of it restrained. Mark 16. 16. *He that believeth and is baptized shall be saved; but he that believeth not, shall be damned.*

7. THAT *except God had revealed* this Way and Rule, it could *never* have been *known* in the World. Men nor Angels could not have so much as *published* that good news, *that there is such a thing,* unless he had first declared it: much less could they have given a *draught* of it. . . .

8. THAT *in what way soever* God reveals this will of his, *that* is to be accounted *his Word.* For Gods word is nothing else but his *making his mind known* to his Creature. . . .

9. THAT *nothing but what* GOD hath thus *revealed* to his People, doth or can belong to the *Rule.* That there *needs* no more, will be afterwards considered, when we come to observe the Perfection of Scripture: But here we observe, that there *can* be no more. We are therefore severely *forbidden* to add. . . . For any therefore of their own head to make any addition to this Rule, is a bold Intrusion upon the Divine Prerogative; an imposing upon God, which he will never admit of. . . .

(2)

John Cotton

1584-1652

Educated at Cambridge, John Cotton became a leading Anglican minister but was finally forced to resign because of his nonconformist views. In 1633 he migrated to New England. Upon his arrival in Boston, he was immediately chosen teacher of the local church, and for the next twenty years he played a leading role in the religious and political affairs of the colony. In 1636 Cotton prepared a body of laws, which was rejected by the General Court in favor of a somewhat more practical and slightly less Mosaic code. He also soon was engaged in a running controversy with Roger Williams, in which he argued against Williams' stand that only persons who had explicitly rejected the Church of England could be admitted to church membership. The two men also quarreled over the proper role of the civil authority in religious matters, with Cotton defending the orthodox position of the

Puritan theocracy while Williams argued in favor of a complete separation of religious and secular affairs. Cotton was also a prolific writer, presenting in a forceful manner the major tenets of the Puritan creed.

The selection that follows is from *The Covenant of Grace Discovering the Great Work of a Sinners Reconsiliation to God* (London, 1655), in which Cotton attempted to reconcile predestination with obedience to the laws of God.

If the Lord do give himself first in the Covenant of his grace, this may then be a doubt and a question in a Christian soul, If God give himself before any blessing, before any promise in order of nature (though he giveth himself always in a promise) if we cannot claim any blessing from God at the first in any conditional promise, therefore not by any condition in our selves, but as we received all things from God, so we claim all things from him in Jesus Christ, and so do first seek for him, and for all things in him: If thus, to what use then serveth the Law of God, which requireth such and such conditions in us, do we not abrogate the Law, & make it of none effect, and root it out from having any power over Christians? And truly some, under pretence of the Covenant of grace, have thought it altogether bootless to bind Christians unto the Law of God, and to look at it as any part of the direction of their Course. Now because this is an imputation usually reflected upon the Covenant of Grace, let us Consider therefore and enquire to what use serveth the Law of God, if God gave himself first unto his people in the Covenant of his grace.

Answ. Though the Lord giveth himself freely to the soul, and his Son, and all the blessings of the Covenant of grace, without respect unto any work of the Law; yet the Law is of special and notable use unto all the sons of men, both unto them that are not yet brought home unto God by converting grace, and also to those that are regenerate in Jesus Christ. The Apostle *Paul* did observe that the question would arise upon the doctrine of the Covenant of grace, *Gal.* 3. 16, 17, 18. *For if the blessing of Abraham came upon the people of God by Jesus Christ, to what end then serveth the Law, which came 430 years after?* It cannot disannul grace, to make the promise of God of none effect? *to what end then serveth it?* Some say it is of no use, others say that it is of such use that they had rather renounce the Covenant of grace than it: but the Answer is, it is of especial use both unto spiritual and carnal men.

First, unto carnal men, and they are of two sorts, some belong unto the election of grace, though they be not yet called; others are not written in the Lambs book of life, but will in the end finally perish, and the Law is yet of use unto both sorts of them.

For the Elect, it is of use unto them; to aggravate their sin, and to multiply it unto them as it were, that is to say, to aggravate the apprehension of the heinousness of sin upon their Consciences, and to set home the burden of sin unto their souls, thereby to drive them to feel their great need of the Lord Jesus Christ, whom otherwise they should for ever have despised. Thus the Apostle answereth in the place aforenamed, *The Law was added, because of transgressions;* that they might clearly appear, and be aggravated thereby, that a man might plainly discern how he hath made himself liable to the wrath of God, by so manifold breaches of so many Commandments in one kind or other: the Law giveth clear knowledge of sin, and so much the more doth it set on the weight of it upon the Conscience, working fear in the heart, *Rom.* 8. 15. And hence it is, that the Apostle telleth us, *Gal.* 3. 24. *The Law was our School-Master to Christ;* As a School-Master driveth his Scholar through fear unto this or that duty, either to do it himself, or (if he cannot) to get others to do it for him; so the Law of God driveth the soul through fear unto Jesus Christ; not that it doth reveal Christ a Saviour of free-grace, but the soul being once more brought down under sense of sin by the terrors of the Law, will readily & willingly hearken unto the news of *Christ a Saviour;* for being once made sensible of his own inability to redeem himself, and unworthiness to be redeemed from the wrath of God; now is the soul fitted to hear the voice of the Gospel, now is the news of Christ beautiful and glad tidings: And of this use is the Law unto the Elect of God, before they come under the Covenant of the grace of God.

2. But of what use is the Law unto other men?

First, the Disobedience of it is of use. Secondly, the Obedience of it.

1. The *Disobedience;* for if men had not known sin, it had been some pretence, though they had committed sin, but when men have the knowledge of the Law, and yet commit sin willingly, now they have no cloak for their sin. . . . Thus there is use of the Law unto disobedient persons, their disobedience will leave them without excuse, when they sin against their consciences, & against the means which the Lord hath administered unto them: for though the Lord never gave them such grace as did accompany salvation, yet such Illumination he did give them, that they needed not to have broken his Law so many ways with such wicked hands as they have done: therefore when they have been enlarged to perform many duties, & might avoid much sin, & yet will sin against their consciences, and tread under foot those means of grace that were committed unto them, It is then most righteous with God, that they should be condemned.

2. Of what use is the Obedience of the Law unto such, whom Gods soul takes no pleasure in? Truly it is of sad and dreadful use unto them, for it serveth to harden them in their sins, (though that be but an accidental use thereof) their sins are thereby made out of measure sinful, *Rom.* 7. 13. They harden their hearts marvelously.

1. By their Obedience to the Law.
2. By the Comfort they find in that Obedience.

For the first of these; the Apostle *Paul, Acts* 23. 1. had kept so good a Conscience, that he knew not any sin against the Law that he had lived in, but though he was unrebukeable, he did count it all loss afterward, *Phil.* 3. 7, 8. *Those things that before he thought had been his gain, now he counteth them but dung that he may win Christ:* when a man attaineth unto outward conformity to the Law, he is then indeed ready to justify himself, and to think that it is indeed good for poor sinful men to look for salvation by Jesus Christ: but for himself he hopeth in his self-devotion, and that he is able to save himself; these are such as justify themselves before men, to whom our Saviour speaketh, *Luke* 16. 15. And of whom he saith, that *Publicans and harlots shall go into the kingdom of heaven before them. Mat.* 21. 31, 32. For many times you shall have the most debauched and prophane more humbled and readier to hearken to the voice of Christ, and sooner convinced of the necessity of the Covenant of grace, than those that are morally righteous by the law, *Rom.* 9. 30, 31, 32 & Chap. 10. 21. Thus the Law becometh a snare unto them, and that which is of singular and wholesome use unto the children of God, is made death unto them; So, secondly, the delight and comfort which they take in their obedience, is a greater snare than the other. . . . So long as a man findeth life and comfort in his own performances, what need can he see to be grieved for the want of *Jesus Christ?* or at best, if he do grieve and find his heart comforted in grieving, and delighting in the Course of humiliation, he then thinketh he hath no need of being further solicitous about his spiritual estate. Thus we see that the Law of God is of marvelous use in the days of the Gospel; of great use unto those that belong unto God, to break their hearts for sin, and to drive them to *Jesus Christ;* and for others, the disobedience of the Law leaves them without excuse, that so disobey it. Again, the obedience of it and comfort in that obedience doth harden the hearts of others from Christ.

2. But what say you then unto men that are under a Covenant of grace, and brought unto fellowship with Christ therein? of what use is the Law of God unto such? is it utterly antiquated? or is there any more to be done about it?

Answ. The Apostle answereth this question, when he saith, *I am not without the Law to God, but under the Law to Christ,* 1 *Cor.* 9. 21. So that (mind you) the Law is of use unto the Apostle *Paul,* but how? As the Law cometh under Christ, so *Paul* cometh under the Law; this is the sum of the Answer, but that would be further explained. What meaneth he, when he sayeth, *I am under the Law to Christ?* In some sense a Christian is freed from the Law, in some sense he is under the Law; so far as the Law is any way besides or out of Christ, so far the Apostle is without the Law; so far as the Law is under Christ, so far he is under the Law; keep close to these two principles, and you shall safely avoid rocks on every hand, thus by the use of the Law shall you not go aside to a Covenant of works, nor by attendance unto grace, shall you neglect the Law. How far is the Law under Christ? When it hath brought the soul nearer unto Christ, and in a remote manner prepared him: the law is in Christ, and you subject to it in him. . . . Our Saviour Christ expoundeth the Law more spiritually, showing that *Anger* against a man's brother is a breach of the sixth Commandment, and *whosoever shall look on a woman to lust after her, hath committed Adultery with her already in his heart,* and broken the seventh Commandment. . . . Thus we see the Apostles of Jesus Christ put it upon Christians to keep the Law of God; and Christ himself beareth witness to the Law, *for God will never justify sin to be no sin, though he will justify the person of a sinner.*

Now as the Lord Jesus giveth the Law, and as it were reneweth it, so he doth also give his Spirit unto his servants, enabling them to keep it. . . . Now this Law would he not write in the hearts of his people, nor give unto them his holy Spirit, enabling them to keep it, were it not his will in *Jesus Christ,* that the Law should be the Rule of holiness and righteousness unto his people; hence it is that the children of God, though they be not under the Covenant of the Law, yet take themselves to be bound to the obedience of it, for if *Christ* have given the Law as well as *Moses,* and if he have ratified it by giving them his Spirit to teach and strengthen them to keep it, though not perfectly, yet sincerely, then they take themselves bound to obey the Law, though they be under the Covenant of grace; for *do we make void the Law through faith? God forbid; yea, we establish the Law;* for what need have Christians of free justification by Christ, if they were not bound unto the obedience of the Law by the Commandment of the Law? therefore the free justification of men under a free Covenant of grace doth establish the obedience of the Law; otherwise what need they run to Christ for the continuance of our Justification, but that we find our selves ungodly Creatures against the righteous and holy Law of God? Therefore if God have given men the Law, & his Holy Spirit to strengthen them in the obedience of it, and his grace to save them from the curse of it, then Christians are to know, that they are bound to keep the Law, they lie under the authority of it, and dare not pluck their necks from under that yoke. . . . It is manifest, because a Christian man neither looketh for justification and salvation from his obedience to the Law, nor feareth condemnation, though he fail in his obedience; and this is a fruit of his exemption from under the Covenant of the Law; for if a man should look for life by his obedience to the Law, and fear condemnation by the breach of it, this would bring a man under the Covenant of the Law; for the sanction of the Covenant of the Law is *Life* to them that obey, and to them that disobey *death and the curse;* but a Christian looketh not for life by his obedience, and that is plain, *Psal.* 143. 2. *Rom.* 3. 20. Therefore no hope of salvation from our obedience to the Law.

But methinks (you will say) *a Christian may fear his condemnation, because of his disobedience to the Law?*

Truly this is a great snare, and this doctrine will be scandalous to many a poor soul, but without cause; indeed if God give a man to be under the Covenant of grace, and not to see it, then he may fear; but if a man know himself to be under the Covenant of grace, then he doth not fear condemnation from his disobedience. . . .

But will not this make a Christian wanton against God, and cause him to abuse his liberty to hardness of heart?

No, no, this is the kindly melting of a godly heart, to consider a Redeemers love, drawing him from the power of the grave, and that he should by his sins pierce the Lord Jesus Christ, this melteth him more than all his other sins, especially considering the abounding grace of God, *which where sin hath abounded, aboundeth much more.* Thus when a man doth not look for life by his own righteousness, but knoweth the Redemption of souls to be more precious than so, this showeth a man not to be under a Covenant of works, and then his very *iniquity* shall not make him afraid, there is such a state in Christianity, and let all men know it.

But will not all men think the worse of Christian profession?

No, *David* will have all men know it, that they may see the difference between all worldly confidences, and the confidence of Christians; all the glory of worldly men will leave them to be like the Beasts that perish, and cannot redeem their souls, that the Lord only might be exalted in his Redeemed.

2   As a Christian looketh not for salvation by his obedience to the Law, nor feareth condemnation by his disobedience: So neither doth he seek for any blessing from his obedience, nor fear any curse from his disobedience. . . .

3   This also is a third effect of the freedom from the Covenant of works, that a Christian doth not look for conjugal comfort from his obedience, nor fear conjugal divorce, from his disobedience. . . . he that is freed from the Covenant of works, is freed also from expecting salvation, or fearing damnation for what he doth: He knoweth the Lord will hide his face from him, if he do evil, but he knoweth the Lord will not cast him off for ever, yet he dares not commit sin, but being under grace, he is the more affected if he shall at any time displease God, and procure chastisement to himself, and by this means the Lord doth mortify his distempers. . . .

4   And finally, the soul doth not claim his right unto any Conditional Promise by his performance of the condition, nor doth he deny himself the blessing that the Promise may reach forth unto him, though he be wanting in obedience to this or that Commandment. . . . But this is not the manner of Gods people, and yet if they look for any mercy, it is in the way of God, but not for their own goodness, their hope is in the faithfulness and free grace of God; they may make mention to the praise of God, how he hath guided them, and carried them an end in his own ways, yet they challenge nothing for any thing that they have done, but put the Lord in mind of his free Promise; that as of his free grace he hath freely promised, so from the same grace he may make good what he hath promised.

Use 1. If any therefore shall accuse the Doctrine of the Covenant of free grace, of *Antinomianism,* and say it teacheth men freedom from the Law of *Moses,* and if they commit any sin, they plead they are not bound unto the Law; we see how false such an aspersion would be, for all the people of God know that *the Lord is an avenger of every such wickedness;* There is none under a Covenant of Grace that dare allow himself in any sin, for if a man should negligently commit any sin, the Lord will school him thoroughly, and make him sadly to apprehend how unworthily he hath made bold to abuse & embezzle the treasures of the grace of God. . . .

So that the children of the Covenant of grace will only tell you, that they are free from the Covenant of the Law, but not from the Commandment of it: for as it is given by *Jesus Christ,* and ratified in the Gospel, and as Christ hath given us his Spirit, enabling us to keep it, we are under it, so far as to take our selves bound by the Authority of it: and if we do transgress against it, we know it is sin in the sight of God, & therefore it is, that the soul in such a case is sensible of the wrath and displeasure of God, whether it be his own sin, or the sin of his brethren; therefore he runneth unto God for mercy, which he would not do, if he did not know that his desert according to the Law did utterly cut him off from mercy; else would he never pray for pardon of sin, nor rejoice when the Lord helpeth him to do that which is right and just in his sight, nor bless the Lord for strengthening him unto obedience, unless he thought it to be his duty. . . .

(3)

Jonathan Edwards

1703-1758

One of America's most important minds, Jonathan Edwards defies easy classification. He is often linked with the Puritans, and he was a staunch defender of such Calvinistic doctrines as God's sovereignty and man's utter dependence on Him. But Edwards was not simply a Calvinist, for he developed a philosophical idealism and a supernaturalistic empiricism of marked originality and depth.

Edwards was born in East Windsor, Connecticut, and was educated at Yale College. After his graduation he settled in Northampton, Massachusetts, as assistant to his grandfather, Reverend Solomon Stoddard, minister of the local Congregational Church. Edwards became the regular minister in 1729. A powerful preacher, he was instrumental in helping to set in motion the Great Awakening of the 1730's and 1740's, a religious revival of a type to be repeated many times in subsequent years. However, in 1750 a rupture occurred between Edwards and his congregation, and he was dismissed. He then settled as missionary to the Indians in Stockbridge, Massachusetts, where he wrote many of his important works. In 1757 he was called to the presidency of the College of New Jersey (now Princeton), but he died shortly after his move to Princeton.

The philosophical idealism developed by Edwards held that all reality is mental; that is, that the world is an ideal order of mental reality. This is a common assertion in idealistic systems, although Edwards' argument is closest to—though developed independently of—the English divine and philosopher Bishop George Berkeley. Edwards' supernatural empiricism taught that the Spirit of God acts on the mind of a believer as an indwelling principle, and what today might be considered emotionalism was for Edwards really an experiential response to the divine. These guiding ideas, together with his Calvinist theology, were developed by Edwards in his many books and sermons, of which the following selections are but a small sample.

Following Edwards' life, a strong stream of philosophical idealism persisted through American history down to the beginning of the twentieth century. German thought was especially influential in America; less than a century after Edwards' death, such Americans as George Bancroft were studying in Germany and absorbing some of the ideals of European scholarship. Transcendentalism also had deep roots in idealism and in Plato's thought; and the famous St. Louis school of William T. Harris in the late nineteenth century continued the study of German thought. The last idealist of the tradition was Josiah Royce, who, with such students as William Ernest Hocking and Mary Whiton Calkins, gave idealism another major restatement. But for most Americans it was a final restatement: under the onslaughts of naturalism and realism the citadel of idealism toppled at the beginning of the twentieth century.

The first selection that follows is entitled "Notes on the Mind," and the second is a sermon preached in 1741 called "Sinners in the Hand of an Angry God." Both are contained in S. E. Dwight, ed., *The Works of President Edwards,* 10 vols. (New York, 1830), vol. I.

TRUTH is *The perception of the relations there are between ideas.* Falsehood is *The supposition of relations between ideas that are inconsistent with those ideas themselves; not their disagreement with things without.* All truth is in the mind, and only there. It is ideas, or what is in the mind, alone, that can be the object of the mind; and what we call Truth, is a consistent supposition of relations, between what is the object of the mind. Falsehood is an inconsistent supposition of relations. The Truth, that is in a mind, must be in that mind as to its object, and every thing pertaining to it. The only foundation of Error is inadequateness and imperfection of ideas; for, if the idea were perfect, it would be impossible but that all its relations should be perfectly perceived.

BEING. It seems strange sometimes to me, that there should be Being from all Eternity; and I am ready to say, What need was there that any thing should be? I should then ask myself, Whether it seems strange that there should be either Something, or Nothing? If so, it is not strange that there should BE; for that necessity of there being Something, or Nothing, implies it.

EXISTENCE. If we had only the sense of Seeing, we should not be as ready to conclude the visible world to have been an existence independent of perception, as we do; because the ideas we have by the sense of Feeling, are as much mere ideas, as those we have by the sense of Seeing. But we know, that the things that are objects of this sense, all that the mind views by Seeing, are merely mental Existences; because all these things, with all their modes, do exist in a looking-glass, where all will acknowledge, they exist only mentally.

Things, as to God, exist from all Eternity, alike; that is, the idea is always the same, and after the same mode. The existence of things, therefore, that are not actually in created minds, consists only in Power, or in the Determination of God, that such and such ideas shall be raised in created minds, upon such conditions.

Since all material existence is only idea, this question may be asked, In what sense may those things be said to exist, which are supposed, and ye[t] are in no actual idea of any Created minds? I answer, they exist only in Uncreated idea. But how do they exist, otherwise than they did from all Eternity, for they always were in Uncreated idea and Divine appointment. I answer, They did exist from all Eternity in Uncreated idea, as did every thing else, and as they do at present, but not in Created idea. But it may be asked, How do those things exist, which have an actual existence, but of which no created mind is conscious?—For instance, the Furniture of this room, when we are absent, and the room is shut up, and no created mind perceives it; How do these things exist?—I answer, There has been in times past such a course and succession of existences, that these things must be supposed to make the series complete, according to Divine appointment, of the order of things. And there will be innumerable things consequential, which will be out of joint, out of their constituted series, without the supposition of these. For, upon supposition of these things, are infinite numbers of things otherwise than they would be, if these were not by God thus supposed. Yea, the whole Universe would be otherwise; such an influence have these things, by their attraction and otherwise. Yea, there must be an universal attraction, in the whole system of things, from the beginning of the world to the end; and, to speak more strictly and metaphysically, we must say, in the whole system and series of ideas in all Created minds; so that these things must necessarily be put in, to make complete the system of the ideal world. That is, they must be supposed, if the train of ideas be, in the order and course, settled by the Supreme mind. So that we may answer in short, That the existence of these things is in God's supposing of them, in order to the rendering complete the series of things, (to speak more strictly, *the series of ideas,*) according to his own settled order, and that harmony of things, which he has appointed.—The supposition of God, which we speak of, is nothing else but God's acting, in the course and series of his exciting ideas, as if they, (the things supposed,) were in actual idea. . . .

Coroll. By this we may answer a more difficult question, viz. If material existence be only mental, then our bodies and organs are ideas only; and then in what sense is it true, that the Mind receives ideas by the Organs of

Sense; seeing that the Organs of Sense, themselves, exist no where but in the Mind?—*Answer.* Seeing our Organs, themselves, are ideas; the connection, that our ideas have with such and such a mode of our Organs, is no other than God's constitution, that some of our ideas shall be connected with others, according to such a settled Law and Order, so that some ideas shall follow from others as their cause.—But how can this be, seeing that ideas most commonly arise from Organs, when we have no idea of the mode of our Organs, or the manner of external objects being applied to them? I answer, Our Organs, and the motions in them and to them, exist in the manner explained above.

TRUTH, in the general, may be defined, after the most strict and metaphysical manner, *The consistency and agreement of our ideas, with the ideas of God.* I confess this, in ordinary conversation, would not half so much tend to enlighten one in the meaning of the word, as to say, *The agreement of our ideas with the things as they are.* But it should be enquired, What is it for our ideas to agree with things as they are? seeing that corporeal things exist no otherwise than mentally; and as for most other things, they are only abstract ideas. Truth, as to external things, is the consistency of our ideas with those ideas, or that train and series of ideas, that are raised in our minds, according to God's stated order and law.

Truth, as to abstract ideas, is the consistency of our ideas with themselves. As when our idea of a circle, or a triangle, or any of their parts, is agreeable to the idea we have stated and agreed to call by the name of a circle, or a triangle. And it may still be said, that Truth is, *the consistency of our ideas with themselves.* Those ideas are false, that are not consistent with the series of ideas, that are raised in our minds, by according to the order of nature.

TRUTH. After all that has been said and done, the only adequate definition of Truth is, The agreement of our ideas with existence. To explain what this existence is, is another thing. In abstract ideas, it is nothing but the ideas themselves; so their truth is their consistency with themselves. In things that are supposed to be without us, it is the determination and fixed mode of God's exciting ideas in us. So that Truth, in these things, is an agreement of our ideas with that series in God. It is existence; and that is all that we can say. It is impossible that we should explain a perfectly abstract and mere idea of existence; only we always find this, by running of it up, that God and Real Existence are the same.

Coroll. Hence we learn how properly it may be said, that God is, and that there is none else; and how proper are these names of the Deity, JEHOVAH, and I AM THAT I AM.

SPACE. Space, as has been already observed, is a necessary being if it may be called a being; and yet we have also shown, that all existence is mental, that the existence of all exterior things is ideal. Therefore it is a necessary being, only as it is a necessary idea, so far as it is a simple idea, that is necessarily connected with other simple exterior ideas, and is, as it were, their common substance or subject. It is in the same manner a necessary being, as any thing external is a being.

The real and necessary existence of Space, and its Infinity, even beyond the Universe, depend upon a like reasoning as the Extension of Spirits, and to the supposition of the reality of the existence of a Successive Duration, before the Universe: even the impossibility of removing the idea out of the mind. If it be asked, If there be Limits of the Creation, whether or no it be not possible that an Intelligent being shall be removed beyond the limits; and then whether or no there would not be distance between that Intelligent being and the limits of the Universe, in the same manner, and as properly as there is between Intelligent beings and the parts of the Universe, within its limits; I answer, I cannot tell what the Law of Nature, or the Constitution of God, would be in this case.

Coroll. There is, therefore, no difficulty in answering such questions as these. What cause was there why the Universe was placed in such a part of Space? and, Why was the Universe created at such a Time? for, if there be no Space beyond the Universe, it was impossible that it should be created in another place; and if there was no Time before, it was impossible it should be created at another time. . . .

And, indeed the secret lies here: That, which truly is the Substance of all Bodies, is *the infinitely exact, and precise, and perfectly stable idea, in God's mind, together with his stable Will, that the same shall gradually be communicated to us, and to other minds, according to certain fixed and exact established Methods and Laws:* or in somewhat different language, *the infinitely exact and precise Divine Idea, together with an answerable, perfectly exact, precise and stable Will, with respect to correspondent communications to Created Minds, and effects on their minds.*

THE WILL. It is not that, which appears the greatest good, or the greatest apparent good, that determines the Will. It is not the greatest good apprehended, or that which is apprehended to be the greatest good; but the Greatest Apprehension of Good. It is not merely by judging that any thing is a great good, that good is apprehended, or appears. There are other ways of apprehending good. The having a clear and sensible idea of any good, is one way of good's appearing, as well as judging that there is good. Therefore, all those things are to be considered—the degree of the judgment, by which a thing is judged to be good, and the contrary evil; the degree of goodness under which it appears, and the evil of the contrary; and the clearness of the idea and strength of the conception of the goodness and of the evil. And that Good, of which there is the greatest apprehension or sense, all those things being taken together, is chosen by the Will. And if there be a greater apprehension of good to be obtained, or evil escaped, by doing a thing, than in letting it alone, the Will determines to the doing it. The mind will be for the present most uneasy in neglecting it, and the mind always avoids that, in which it would be for the present most uneasy. The degree of apprehension of good, which I suppose to determine the Will, is composed of the degree of good apprehended, and the degree of apprehension. The degree of apprehension, again, is composed of the strength of the conception, and the judgment.

EXCELLENCE. 1. When we spake of Excellence in Bodies, we were obliged to borrow the word, *Consent,* from Spiritual things; but Excellence in and among Spirits is in its prime and proper sense, Being's consent to Being. There is no other proper consent but that of *Minds,* even of their Will; which, when it is of Minds towards Minds, it is *Love,* and when of Minds towards other things, it is *Choice.* Wherefore all the Primary and Original beauty or excellence, that is among Minds, is Love; and into this may all be resolved that is found among them.

2. When we spake of External excellency, we said, that *Being's consent to Being,* must needs be agreeable to *Perceiving Being.* But now we are speaking of Spiritual things, we may change the phrase, and say, that *Mind's love to Mind* must needs be lovely to *Beholding Mind;* and Being's love to Being, in general must needs be agreeable to Being that perceives it, because itself is a participation of Being, in general.

3. As to the proportion of this Love;—to greater Spirits, more, and to less, less;—it is beautiful, as it is a manifestation of love to Spirit or Being in general. And the want of this proportion is a deformity, because it is a manifestation of a defect of such a love. It shows that it is not Being, in general, but something else, that is loved, when love is not in proportion to the Extensiveness and Excellence of Being.

4. Seeing God has so plainly revealed himself to us; and other minds are made in his image, and are emanations from him; we may judge what is the Excellence of other minds, by what is his, which we have shown is Love. His Infinite Beauty, is His Infinite mutual Love of Himself. Now God is the Prime and Original Being, the First and Last, and the Pattern of all, and has the sum of all perfection. We may therefore, doubtless, conclude, that all that is the perfection of Spirits may be resolved into that which is God's perfection, which is Love.

5. There are several degrees of deformity or disagreeableness of dissent from Being. One is, when there is only merely a dissent from Being. This is disagreeable to Being (for Perceiving Being only is properly Being.) Still more disagreeable is a dissent to very excellent Being, or, as we have explained, to a Being that consents in a high degree to Being, because such a Being by such a consent becomes bigger; and a dissenting from such a Being includes, also, a dissenting from what he consents with, which is other Beings, or Being in general. Another deformity, that is more odious than mere dissent from Being, is, for a Being to dissent from, or not to consent with, a Being who consents with his Being. It is a manifestation of a greater dissent from Being than ordinary; for the Being perceiving, knows that it is natural to Being, to consent with what consents with it, as we have shown. It therefore manifests an extraordinary dissent, that consent to itself will not draw its consent. The deformity, for the same reason, is greater still, if there be

dissent from consenting Being. There are such contrarieties and jars in Being, as must necessarily produce jarring and horror in perceiving Being.

6. Dissent from such Beings, if that be their fixed nature, is a manifestation of Consent to Being in general; for consent to Being is dissent from that, which dissents from Being.

7. Wherefore all Virtue, which is the Excellency of minds, is resolved into *Love to Being;* and nothing is virtuous or beautiful in Spirits, any otherwise than as it is an exercise, or fruit, or manifestation, of this love; and nothing is sinful or deformed in Spirits, but as it is the defect of, or contrary to, these.

8. When we speak of Being in general, we may be understood of the Divine Being, for he is an Infinite Being: therefore all others must necessarily be considered as nothing. As to *Bodies,* we have shown in another place, that they have no proper Being of their own. And as to *Spirits,* they are the communications of the Great Original Spirit; and doubtless, in metaphysical strictness and propriety, He is, as there is none else. He is likewise Infinitely Excellent, and all Excellence and Beauty is derived from him, in the same manner as all Being. And all other Excellence, is, in strictness only, a shadow of his.

☆ ☆ ☆ ☆

In this verse [from Deuteronomy] is threatened the vengeance of God on the wicked unbelieving Israelites, who were God's visible people, and who lived under the means of grace; but who, notwithstanding all God's wonderful works towards them, remained (as ver. 28.) void of counsel, having no understanding in them. Under all the cultivations of heaven, they brought forth bitter and poisonous fruit; as in the two verses next preceding the text.—The expression I have chosen for my text, *Their foot shall slide in due time* [Deut. 32:35], seems to imply the following things, relating to the punishment and destruction to which these wicked Israelites were exposed.

1. That they were always exposed to *destruction;* as one that stands or walks in slippery places is always exposed to fall. This is implied in the manner of their destruction coming upon them, being represented by their foot sliding. The same is expressed, Psalm lxxiii. 18. "Surely thou didst set them in slippery places; thou castedst them down into destruction."

2. It implies, that they were always exposed to sudden unexpected destruction. As he that walks in slippery places is every moment liable to fall, he cannot foresee one moment whether he shall stand or fall the next; and when he does fall, he falls at once without warning: Which is also expressed in Psalm lxxiii. 18, 19. "Surely thou didst set them in slippery places; thou castedst them down into destruction: How are they brought into desolation as in a moment!"

3. Another thing implied is, that they are liable to fall *of themselves,*

without being thrown down by the hand of another; as he that stands or walks on slippery ground needs nothing but his own weight to throw him down.

4. That the reason why they are not fallen already, and do not fall now, is only that God's appointed time is not come. For it is said, that when that due time, or appointed time comes *their foot shall slide.* Then they shall be left to fall, as they are inclined by their own weight. God will not hold them up in these slippery places any longer, but will let them go; and then, at that very instant, they shall fall into destruction; as he that stands on such slippery declining ground, on the edge of a pit, he cannot stand alone, when he is let go he immediately falls and is lost.

The observation from the words that I would now insist upon is this. "There is nothing that keeps wicked men at any one moment out of hell, but the mere pleasure of God"—By the *mere* pleasure of God, I mean his *sovereign* pleasure, his arbitrary will, restrained by no obligation, hindered by no manner of difficulty, any more than if nothing else but God's mere will had in the least degree, or in any respect whatsoever, any hand in the preservation of wicked men one moment.—The truth of this observation may appear by the following considerations.

1. There is no want of *power* in God to cast wicked men into hell at any moment. Men's hands cannot be strong when God rises up. The strongest have no power to resist him, nor can any deliver out of his hands.—He is not only able to cast wicked men into hell, but he can most easily do it. Sometimes an earthly prince meets with a great deal of difficulty to subdue a rebel, who has found means to fortify himself, and has made himself strong by the numbers of his followers. But it is not so with God. There is no fortress that is any defence from the power of God. Though hand join in hand, and vast multitudes of God's enemies combine and associate themselves, they are easily broken in pieces. They are as great heaps of light chaff before the whirlwind; or large quantities of dry stubble before devouring flames. We find it easy to tread on and crush a worm that we see crawling on the earth; so it is easy for us to cut or singe a slender thread that any thing hangs by: thus easy is it for God, when he pleases, to cast his enemies down to hell. What are we, that we should think to stand before him, at whose rebuke the earth trembles, and before whom the rocks are thrown down?

2. They *deserve* to be cast into hell; so that divine justice never stands in the way, it makes no objection against God's using his power at any moment to destroy them. Yea, on the contrary, justice calls aloud for an infinite punishment of their sins. Divine justice says of the tree that brings forth such grapes of Sodom, "Cut it down, why cumbereth it the ground?" Luke xiii. 7. The sword of divine justice is every moment brandished over their heads, and it is nothing but the hand of arbitrary mercy, and God's mere will, that holds it back.

3. They are already under a sentence of *condemnation* to hell. They do not only justly deserve to be cast down thither, but the sentence of the law of God, that eternal and immutable rule of righteousness that God has fixed

between him and mankind, is gone out against them, and stands against them; so that they are bound over already to hell. John iii. 18. "He that believeth not is condemned already." So that every unconverted man properly belongs to hell; that is his place; from thence he is, John viii. 23. "Ye are from beneath:" And thither he is bound; it is the place that justice, and God's word, and the sentence of his unchangeable law assign to him.

4. They are now the objects of that very same *anger* and wrath of God, that is expressed in the torments of hell. And the reason why they do not go down to hell at each moment, is not because God, in whose power they are, is not then very angry with them; as he is with many miserable creatures now tormented in hell, who there feel and bear the fierceness of his wrath. Yea, God is a great deal more angry with great numbers that are now on earth; yea, doubtless, with many that are now in this congregation, who it may be are at ease, than he is with many of those who are now in the flames of hell.

So that it is not because God is unmindful of their wickedness, and does not resent it, that he does not let loose his hand and cut them off. God is not altogether such an one as themselves, though they may imagine him to be so. The wrath of God burns against them, their damnation does not slumber; the pit is prepared, the fire is made ready, the furnace is now hot, ready to receive them; the flames do now rage and glow. The glittering sword is whet, and held over them, and the pit hath opened its mouth under them.

5. The *devil* stands ready to fall upon them, and seize them as his own, at what moment God shall permit him. They belong to him; he has their souls in his possession, and under his dominion. The scripture represents them as his goods, Luke xi. 12. The devils watch them; they are ever by them at their right hand; they stand waiting for them, like greedy hungry lions that see their prey, and expect to have it, but are for the present kept back. If God should withdraw his hand, by which they are restrained, they would in one moment fly upon their poor souls. The old serpent is gaping for them; hell opens its mouth wide to receive them; and if God should permit it, they would be hastily swallowed up and lost.

6. There are in the souls of wicked men those hellish *principles* reigning, that would presently kindle and flame out into hell fire, if it were not for God's restraints. There is laid in the very nature of carnal men, a foundation for the torments of hell. There are those corrupt principles, in reigning power in them, and in full possession of them, that are seeds of hell fire. These principles are active and powerful, exceeding violent in their nature, and if it were not for the restraining hand of God upon them, they would soon break out, they would flame out after the same manner as the same corruptions, the same enmity does in the hearts of damned souls, and would beget the same torments as they do in them. The souls of the wicked are in scripture compared to the troubled sea. Isa. lvii. 20. For the present, God restrains their wickedness by his mighty power, as he does the raging waves of the troubled sea, saying, "Hitherto shalt thou come, but no further;" but if God

should withdraw that restraining power, it would soon carry all before it. Sin is the ruin and misery of the soul; it is destructive in its nature; and if God should leave it without restraint, there would need nothing else to make the soul perfectly miserable. The corruption of the heart of man is immoderate and boundless in its fury; and while wicked men live here, it is like fire pent up by God's restraints, whereas if it were let loose, it would set on fire the course of nature; and as the heart is now a sink of sin, so if sin was not restrained, it would immediately turn the soul into a fiery oven, or a furnace of fire and brimstone.

7. It is no security to wicked men for one moment, that there are no visible means of death at hand. It is no security to a natural man, that he is now in health, and that he does not see which way he should now immediately go out of the world by any accident, and that there is no visible danger in any respect in his circumstances. The manifold and continual experience of the world in all ages, shows this is no evidence, that a man is not on the very brink of eternity, and that the next step will not be into another world. The unseen, unthought-of ways and means of persons going suddenly out of the world are innumerable and inconceivable. Unconverted men walk over the pit of hell on a rotten covering, and there are innumerable places in this covering so weak that they will not bear their weight, and these places are not seen. The arrows of death fly unseen at noon-day; the sharpest sight cannot discern them. God has so many different unsearchable ways of taking wicked men out of the world and sending them to hell, that there is nothing to make it appear, that God had need to be at the expence of a miracle, or go out of the ordinary course of his providence, to destroy any wicked man, at any moment. All the means that there are of sinners going out of the world, are so in God's hands, and so universally and absolutely subject to his power and determination, that it does not depend at all the less on the mere will of God, whether sinners shall at any moment go to hell, than if means were never made use of, or at all concerned in the case.

8. Natural men's prudence and care to preserve their own lives, or the care of others to preserve them, do not secure them a moment. To this, divine providence and universal experience do also bear testimony. There is this clear evidence that men's own wisdom is no security to them from death; that if it were otherwise we should see some difference between the wise and politic men of the world, and others, with regard to their liableness to early and unexpected death: but how is it in fact? Eccles. ii. 16. "How dieth the wise man? even as the fool."

9. All wicked men's pains and *contrivance* which they use to escape hell, while they continue to reject Christ, and so remain wicked men, do not secure them from hell one moment. Almost every natural man that hears of hell, flatters himself that he shall escape it; he depends upon himself for his own security; he flatters himself in what he has done, in what he is now doing, or what he intends to do. Every one lays out matters in his own mind how he shall avoid damnation, and flatters himself that he contrives well for

himself, and that his schemes will not fail. They hear indeed that there are but few saved, and that the greater part of men that have died heretofore are gone to hell; but each one imagines that he lays out matters better for his own escape than others have done. He does not intend to come to that place of torment; he says within himself, that he intends to take effectual care, and to order matters so for himself as not to fail.

But the foolish children of men miserably delude themselves in their own schemes, and in confidence in their own strength and wisdom; they trust to nothing but a shadow. The greater part of those who heretofore have lived under the same means of grace, and are now dead, are undoubtedly gone to hell; and it was not because they were not as wise as those who are now alive: it was not because they did not lay out matters as well for themselves to secure their own escape. If we could speak with them, and inquire of them, one by one, whether they expected, when alive, and when they used to hear about hell, ever to be the subjects of that misery: we doubtless, should hear one and another reply. "No, I never intended to come here: I had laid out matters otherwise in my mind; I thought I should contrive well for myself: I thought my scheme good. I intended to take effectual care; but it came upon me unexpected; I did not look for it at that time, and in that manner; it came as a thief: Death outwitted me: God's wrath was too quick for me. Oh, my cursed foolishness! I was flattering myself, and pleasing myself with vain dreams of what I would do hereafter; and when I was saying, Peace and safety, then suddenly destruction came upon me."

10. God has laid himself under *no obligation,* by any promise to keep any natural man out of hell one moment. God certainly has made no promises either of eternal life, or of any deliverance or preservation from eternal death, but what are contained in the covenant of grace, the promises that are given in Christ, in whom all the promises are yea and amen. But surely they have no interest in the promises of the covenant of grace who are not the children of the covenant, who do not believe in any of the promises, and have no interest in the Mediator of the covenant.

So that, whatever some have imagined and pretended about promises made to natural men's earnest seeking and knocking, it is plain and manifest, that whatever pains a natural man takes in religion, whatever prayers he makes, till he believes in Christ, God is under no manner of obligation to keep him a moment from eternal destruction.

So that, thus it is that natural men are held in the hand of God, over the pit of hell; they have deserved the fiery pit, and are already sentenced to it; and God is dreadfully provoked, his anger is as great towards them as to those that are actually suffering the executions of the fierceness of his wrath in hell, and they have done nothing in the least to appease or abate that anger, neither is God in the least bound by any promise to hold them up one moment; the devil is waiting for them, hell is gaping for them, the flames gather and flash about them, and would fain lay hold on them, and swallow them up; the fire bent up in their own hearts is struggling to break out: and they have no interest in any Mediator, there are no means within reach that can be any security to them. In short, they have no refuge, nothing to take hold of; all that preserves them every moment is the mere arbitrary will, and uncovenanted, unobliged forbearance of an incensed God.

APPLICATION

The use of this awful subject may be for awakening unconverted persons in this congregation. This that you have heard is the case of every one of you that are out of Christ.—That world of misery, that lake of burning brimstone, is extended abroad under you. There is the dreadful pit of the glowing flames of the wrath of God; there is hell's wide gaping mouth open; and you have nothing to stand upon, nor any thing to take hold of; there is nothing between you and hell but the air; it is only the power and mere pleasure of God that holds you up.

You probably are not sensible of this; you find you are kept out of hell, but do not see the hand of God in it; but look at other things, as the good state of your bodily constitution, your care of your own life, and the means you use for your own preservation. But indeed these things are nothing; if God should withdraw his hand, they would avail no more to keep you from falling, than the thin air to hold up a person that is suspended in it.

Your wickedness makes you as it were heavy as lead, and to tend downwards with great weight and pressure towards hell; and if God should let you go, you would immediately sink and swiftly descend and plunge into the bottomless gulf, and your healthy constitution, and your own care and prudence, and best contrivance, and all your righteousness, would have no more influence to uphold you and keep you out of hell, than a spider's web would have to stop a fallen rock. Were it not for the sovereign pleasure of God, the earth would not bear you one moment; for you are a burden to it; the creation groans with you; the creature is made subject to the bondage of your corruption, not willingly; the sun does not willingly shine upon you to give you light to serve sin and Satan; the earth does not willingly yield her increase to satisfy your lusts; nor is it willingly a stage for your wickedness to be acted upon; the air does not willingly serve you for breath to maintain the flame of life in your vitals, while you spend your life in the service of God's enemies. God's creatures are good, and were made for men to serve God with, and do not willingly subserve to any other purpose, and groan when they are abused to purposes so directly contrary to their nature and end. And the world would spew you out, were it not for the sovereign hand of him who hath subjected it in hope. There are black clouds of God's wrath now hanging directly over your heads, full of the dreadful storm, and big with thunder; and were it not for the restraining hand of God, it would immediately burst forth upon you. The sovereign pleasure of God, for the present, stays his rough wind; otherwise it would come with fury, and your destruction would come like a whirlwind, and you would be like the chaff of the summer threshing floor.

The wrath of God is like great waters that are dammed for the present; they increase more and more, and rise higher and higher, till an outlet is given; and the longer the stream is stopped, the more rapid and mighty is its course, when once it is let loose. It is true, that judgment against your evil works has not been executed hitherto; the floods of God's vengeance have been withheld; but your guilt in the mean time is constantly increasing, and you are every day treasuring up more wrath; the waters are constantly rising, and waxing more and more mighty; and there is nothing but the mere pleasure of God, that holds the waters back, that are unwilling to be stopped, and press hard to go forward. If God should only withdraw his hand from the flood-gate, it would immediately fly open, and the fiery floods of the fierceness and wrath of God, would rush forth with inconceivable fury, and would come upon you with omnipotent power; and if your strength were ten thousand times greater than it is, yea, ten thousand times greater than the strength of the stoutest, sturdiest devil in hell, it would be nothing to withstand or endure it.

The bow of God's wrath is bent, and the arrow made ready on the string, and justice bends the arrow at your heart, and strains the bow, and it is nothing but the mere pleasure of God, and that of an angry God, without any promise or obligation at all, that keeps the arrow one moment from being made drunk with your blood. Thus all you that never passed under a great change of heart, by the mighty power of the Spirit of God upon your souls; all you that were never born again, and made new creatures, and raised from being dead in sin, to a state of new, and before altogether unexperienced light and life, are in the hands of an angry God. However you may have reformed your life in many things, and may have had religious affections, and may keep up a form of religion in your families and closets, and in the house of God, it is nothing but his mere pleasure that keeps you from being this moment swallowed up in everlasting destruction. However unconvinced you may now be of the truth of what you hear, by and by you will be fully convinced of it. Those that are gone from being in the like circumstances with you, see that it was so with them; for destruction came suddenly upon most of them; when they expected nothing of it, and while they were saying, Peace and safety: now they see, that those things on which they depended for peace and safety, were nothing but thin air and empty shadows.

The God that holds you over the pit of hell, much as one holds a spider, or some loathsome insect over the fire, abhors you, and is dreadfully provoked: his wrath towards you burns like fire; he looks upon you as worthy of nothing else, but to be cast into the fire; he is of purer eyes than to bear to have you in his sight; you are ten thousand times more abominable in his eyes, than the most hateful venomous serpent is in ours. You have offended him infinitely more than ever a stubborn rebel did his prince; and yet it is nothing but his hand that holds you from falling into the fire every moment. It is to be ascribed to nothing else, that you did not go to hell the last night; that you was suffered to awake again in this world, after you closed your eyes to sleep. And there is no other reason to be given, why you have not dropped into hell since you arose in the morning, but that God's hand has held you up. There is no other reason to be given why you have not gone to hell, since you have sat here in the house of God, provoking his pure eyes by your sinful wicked manner of attending his solemn worship. Yea, there is nothing else that is to be given as a reason why you do not this very moment drop down into hell.

O sinner! Consider the fearful danger you are in: it is a great furnace of wrath, a wide and bottomless pit, full of the fire of wrath, that you are held over in the hand of that God, whose wrath is provoked and incensed as much against you, as against many of the damned in hell. You hang by a slender thread, with the flames of divine wrath flashing about it, and ready every moment to singe it, and burn it asunder; and you have no interest in any Mediator, and nothing to lay hold of to save yourself, nothing to keep off the flames of wrath, nothing of your own, nothing that you ever have done, nothing that you can do, to induce God to spare you one moment.— And consider here more particularly,

1. *Whose* wrath it is: it is the wrath of the infinite God. If it were only the wrath of man, though it were of the most potent prince, it would be comparatively little to be regarded. The wrath of kings is very much dreaded, especially of absolute monarchs, who have the possessions and lives of their subjects wholly in their power, to be disposed of at their mere will. Prov. xx. 2. "The fear of a king is as the roaring of a lion: Whoso provoketh him to anger, sinneth against his own soul." The subject that very much enrages an arbitrary prince, is liable to suffer the most extreme torments that human art can invent, or human power can inflict. But the greatest earthly potentates in their greatest majesty and strength, and when clothed in their greatest terrors, are but feeble, despicable worms of the dust, in comparison of the great and almighty Creator and King of heaven and earth. It is but little that they can do, when most enraged, and when they have exerted the utmost of their fury. All the kings of the earth, before God, are as grasshoppers; they are nothing, and less than nothing: both their love and their hatred is to be despised. The wrath of the great King of kings, is as much more terrible than theirs, as his majesty is greater. Luke xii. 4, 5. "And I say unto you, my friends, Be not afraid of them that kill the body, and after that, have no more that they can do. But I will forewarn you whom you shall fear: fear him, which after he hath killed, hath power to cast into hell; yea, I say unto you, Fear him."

2. It is the *fierceness* of his wrath that you are exposed to. We often read of the fury of God; as in Isaiah lix. 18. "According to their deeds, accordingly he will repay fury to his adversaries." So Isaiah lxvi. 15. "For behold, the Lord will come with fire, and with his chariots like a whirlwind,

to render his anger with fury, and his rebuke with flames of fire." And in many other places. So, Rev. xix. 15. we read of "the wine press of the fierceness and wrath of Almighty God." The words are exceeding terrible. If it had only been said, "the wrath of God," the words would have implied that which is infinitely dreadful: but it is "the fierceness and wrath of God." The fury of God! the fierceness of Jehovah! Oh, how dreadful must that be! Who can utter what such expressions carry in them! But it is also "the fierceness and wrath of *Almighty* God." As though there would be a very great manifestation of his almighty power in what the fierceness of his wrath should inflict, as though omnipotence should be as it were enraged, and exerted, as men are wont to exert their strength in the fierceness of their wrath. Oh! then, what will be the consequence! What will become of the poor worms that shall suffer it! Whose hands can be strong? And whose heart can endure? To what a dreadful, inexpressible, inconceivable depth of misery must the poor creature be sunk who shall be the subject of this! . . .

3. The *misery* you are exposed to is that which God will inflict to that end, that he might show what that wrath of Jehovah is. God hath had it on his heart to show to angels and men, both how excellent his love is, and also how terrible his wrath is. Sometimes earthly kings have in mind to show how terrible their wrath is, by the extreme punishments they would execute on those that would provoke them. Nebuchadnezzar, that mighty and haughty monarch of the Chaldean empire, was willing to show his wrath when enraged with Shadrach, Meshech, and Abednego; and accordingly gave orders that the burning fiery furnace should be heated seven times hotter than it was before; doubtless, it was raised to the utmost degree of fierceness that human art could raise it. But the great God is also willing to show his wrath, and magnify his awful majesty and mighty power in the extreme sufferings of his enemies. Rom. ix. 22. "What if God, willing to show his wrath, and to make his power known, endure with much long-suffering the vessels of wrath fitted to destruction?" And seeing this is his design, and what he has determined, even to show how terrible the unrestrained wrath, the fury and fierceness of Jehovah is, he will do it to effect. There will be something accomplished and brought to pass that will be dreadful with a witness. When the great and angry God hath risen up and executed his awful vengeance on the poor sinner, and the wretch is actually suffering the infinite weight and power of his indignation, then will God call upon the whole universe to behold that awful majesty and mighty power that is to be seen in it. Isa. xxxiii. 12–14. "And the people shall be as the burnings of lime, as thorns cut up shall they be burnt in the fire. Hear ye that are far off, what I have done; and ye that are near, acknowledge my might. The sinners in Zion are afraid; fearfulness hath surprised the hypocrites," &c.

Thus it will be with you that are in an unconverted state, if you continue in it; the infinite might, and majesty, and terribleness of the omnipotent God shall be magnified upon you, in the ineffable strength of your torments. You shall be tormented in the presence of the holy angels, and in the presence of the Lamb; and when you shall be in this state of suffering, the glorious inhabitants of heaven shall go forth and look on the awful spectacle, that they may see what the wrath and fierceness of the Almighty is; and when they have seen it, they will fall down and adore that great power and majesty. Isa. lxvi. 23, 24. "And it shall come to pass, that from one new moon to another, and from one sabbath to another, shall all flesh come to worship before me, saith the Lord. And they shall go forth and look upon the carcasses of the men that have transgressed against me; for their worm shall not die, neither shall their fire be quenched, and they shall be an abhorring unto all flesh."

4. It is *everlasting* wrath. It would be dreadful to suffer this fierceness and wrath of Almighty God one moment; but you must suffer it to all eternity. There will be no end to this exquisite horrible misery. When you look forward, you shall see a long for ever, a boundless duration before you, which will swallow up your thoughts, and amaze your soul; and you will absolutely despair of ever having any deliverance, any end, any mitigation, any rest at all. You will know certainly that you must wear out long ages, millions of millions of ages, in wrestling and conflicting with this almighty merciless vengeance; and then when you have so done, when so many ages have actually been spent by you in this manner, you will know that all is but a point to what remains. So that your punishment will indeed be infinite. Oh, who can express what the state of a soul in such circumstances is! All that we can possibly say about it, gives but a very feeble, faint representation of it; it is inexpressible and inconceivable: For "who knows the power of God's anger?"

How dreadful is the state of those that are daily and hourly in the danger of this great wrath and infinite misery! But this is the dismal case of every soul in this congregation that has not been born again, however moral and strict, sober and religious, they may otherwise be. Oh that you would consider it, whether you be young or old! There is reason to think, that there are many in this congregation now hearing this discourse, that will actually be the subjects of this very misery to all eternity. We know not who they are, or in what seats they sit, or what thoughts they now have. It may be they are now at ease, and hear all these things without much disturbance, and are now flattering themselves that they are not the persons, promising themselves that they shall escape. If we knew that there was one person, and but one, in the whole congregation, that was to be the subject of this misery, what an awful thing would it be to think of! If we knew who it was, what an awful sight would it be to see such a person! How might all the rest of the congregation lift up a lamentable and bitter cry over him! But, alas! instead of one, how many is it likely will remember this discourse in hell? And it would be a wonder, if some that are now present should not be in hell in a very short time, even before this year is out. And it would be no wonder if some persons, that now sit here, in some seats of this meeting-house, in health, quiet and secure, should be there before to-morrow morning. Those of you that finally continue in a natural condition, that shall keep out of hell longest will be there in a little time! your damnation does not slumber; it will come swiftly, and, in all probability, very suddenly upon many of you. You have reason to wonder that you are not already in hell. It is doubtless the case of some whom you have seen and known, that never deserved hell more than you, and that heretofore appeared as likely to have been now alive as you. Their case is past all hope; they are crying in extreme misery and perfect despair; but here you are in the land of the living and in the house of God, and have an opportunity to obtain salvation. What would not those poor damned hopeless souls give for one day's opportunity such as you now enjoy! . . .

And let every one that is yet of Christ, and hanging over the pit of hell, whether they be old men and women, or middle aged, or young people, or little children, now hearken to the loud calls of God's word and providence. This acceptable year of the Lord, a day of such great favours to some, will doubtless be a day of as remarkable vengeance to others. Men's hearts harden, and their guilt increases apace at such a day as this, if they neglect their souls; and never was there so great danger of such persons being given up to hardness of heart and blindness of mind. God seems now to be hastily gathering in his elect in all parts of the land; and probably the greater part of adult persons that ever shall be saved, will be brought in now in a little time, and that it will be as it was on the great out-pouring of the Spirit upon the Jews in the apostles' days; the election will obtain, and the rest will be blinded. If this should be the case with you, you will eternally curse this day, and will curse the day that ever you was born, to see such a season of the pouring out of God's Spirit, and will wish that you had died and gone to hell before you had seen it. Now undoubtedly it is, as it was in the days of John the Baptist, the axe is in an extraordinary manner laid at the root of the trees, that every tree which brings not forth good fruit, may be hewn down and cast into the fire.

Therefore, let every one that is out of Christ, now awake and fly from the wrath to come. The wrath of Almighty God is now undoubtedly hanging over a great part of this congregation: Let every one fly out of Sodom: "Haste and escape for your lives, look not behind you, escape to the mountain, lest you be consumed."

II

The Beginnings of
American Political Theory

ALTHOUGH LARGELY A RELIGIOUS MOVEMENT, Puritanism also had political implications that played an important role not only in shaping the development of seventeenth-century New England but also in preparing the ground for the revolutionary ideas of the 1760's and 1770's. This is not to imply that democracy was an outgrowth of Puritanism, for the Puritans always proclaimed themselves indefatigable foes of any form of democratic or popular government. Nevertheless, there is an unbroken line of thought from Puritan political theories to those of the eighteenth-century rationalist thinkers.

The Puritans, unlike their descendants, were never able to separate religion and politics, and they always treated the two as different sides of the same coin. Their political ideology rested on the assumption that government was necessary because of original sin. Had man been good, they argued, such an instrument of restraint and regulation would have been superfluous. But since man was inherently evil, God placed over him a government designed to check his evil and selfish impulses. Although the Puritans held that each person would eventually face his Maker alone, they did not extend this individualistic theory to society. Instead, they maintained that society was a unit that existed to further certain divinely inspired ideals.

This being the case, the Puritans then logically reasoned that their system left no room for toleration of other ideas, and that the function of government was to enforce conformity according to God's laws. They therefore defined liberty as the freedom to do what was just and right, which in turn was determined by God and interpreted by the ministers and regenerate of the colony. Hence, the government of Massachusetts was in effect a dictatorship by a small minority. Lest we be too critical of Puritan religious and political intolerance, however, we should remember that their ideals did not materially differ from those of the Western world of that time.

The Puritans who came to New England, furthermore, brought with them some other basic assumptions concerning government. They accepted the existence of a fundamental law that far transcended the importance of any human law or edict of divine right monarchs. All men, regardless of their position, were subject to this law. In Puritanism the fundamental law was to be found in the Scriptures; later Americans were to find it elsewhere. But, wherever found, the concept of a higher law was destined to occupy an important place in American thought, for from it proceeded the corollary of a limited government.

Equally important was the Puritan belief that their government was based on the consent of the governed. This did not mean, however, that all people had a share in the workings of government. The eminent Puritan leader, John Winthrop, for example, argued that mankind had two forms of liberty, natural and civil. Natural liberty included the freedom to sin, and it placed man in the same category as animals. Civil liberty, on the other hand, meant the coming together of the regenerate souls, who voluntarily submitted their will to God through a government that they themselves had formed. The Puritans always stressed the voluntary character of the social compact, for, although it included only the regenerate, others who were excluded had only their own sinfulness to blame.

In effect, the Puritans were basing their government on a religious and a civil foundation, using two forms of covenant theory to buttress their logic. One covenant had been made between man and God, the other among individual men. Since the two covenants together had committed human beings to the rule of law and the control of authority, it followed that the church and state existed on a reciprocal basis, each supporting and strengthening the other.

It cannot be denied that many of the basic ideas of seventeenth-century Puritanism were not peculiar to that group alone but were common to the age as a whole. Yet the Puritans took these ideas and combined them into a coherent system of thought, which they attempted to translate into reality when they established their "Bible Commonwealth." For various reasons this experiment failed, but the political theories that had inspired this undertaking, when divorced from a religious background, did not die or disappear; a century later, many of them were being reiterated in a secular form by the revolutionary generation.

(4)

John Winthrop

1588-1649

A prominent English Puritan, Winthrop became dissatisfied with the restrictions placed upon the nonconformist sects in England. He was one of the twelve signatories to the Cambridge Agreement of 1629, in which prominent Puritans pledged themselves to migrate to America provided the charter and government of the Massachusetts Bay Company could be transferred there. Elected the first governor of Massachusetts, he served in this position or as deputy governor for the remainder of his life.

Both of the following excerpts illustrate the Puritan interpretation of the religious and civil basis of the state.

The first selection is from Winthrop's sermon "A Modell of Christian Charity" delivered aboard the *Arbella* in 1630 during the voyage to New England; the text is from the *Winthrop Papers* (Boston: Massachusetts Historical Society, 1931), vol. II. In the second selection, written in 1645, Winthrop was defending himself against the charge of having exceeded his powers. The text is from Winthrop's *The History of New England from 1630 to 1649,* James Savage, ed. (Boston, 1853), vol. II.

1. . . . We are a Company professing ourselves fellow members of Christ, in which respect only though we were absent from each other many miles, and had our employments as far distant, yet we ought to account ourselves knit together by this bond of love, and live in the exercise of it, if we would have comfort of our being in Christ, this was notorious in the practice of the Christians in former times, as is testified of the Waldenses from the mouth of one of the adversaries Aeneas Sylvius *mutuo* [*solent amare*] *penè antequam norint* [that is,] they use to love any of their own religion even before they were acquainted with them.

2. For the work we have in hand, it is by a mutual consent through a special overruling providence, and a more than an ordinary approbation of the Churches of Christ to seek out a place of Cohabitation and Consortship under a due form of Government both civil and ecclesiastical. In such cases as this the care of the public must oversway all private respects, by which not only conscience, but mere Civil policy doth bind us; for it is a true rule that particular estates cannot subsist in the ruin of the public.

3. The end is to improve our lives to do more service to the Lord the comfort and increase of the body of Christ whereof we are members that ourselves and posterity may be the better preserved from the common corruptions of this evil world to serve the Lord and work out our Salvation under the power and purity of his holy Ordinances.

4. For the means whereby this must be effected, they are twofold, a Conformity with the work and end we aim at, these we see are extraordinary, therefore we must not content ourselves with usual ordinary means whatsoever we did or ought to have done when we lived in England, the same must we do and more also where we go: That which the most in their Churches maintain as a truth in profession only, we must bring into familiar and constant practice, as in this duty of love we must love brotherly without dissimulation, we must love one another with a pure heart fervently we must bear one anothers burdens, we must not look only on our own things, but

also on the things of our brethren, neither must we think that the Lord will bear with such failings at our hands as he doth from those among whom we have lived, and that for three reasons.

1. In regard of the more near bond of marriage, between him and us, wherein he hath taken us to be his after a most strict and peculiar manner which will make him the more Jealous of our love and obedience so he tells the people of Israel, you only have I known of all the families of the Earth therefore will I punish you for your Transgressions.

2. Because the Lord will be sanctified in them that come near him. We know that there were many that corrupted the service of the Lord, some setting up Altars before his own, others offering both strange fire and strange Sacrifices also; yet there come no fire from heaven, or other sudden Judgment upon them as did upon Nadab and Abihu who yet we may think did not sin presumptuously.

3. When God gives a special Commission he looks to have it strictly observed in every Article, when he gave Saul a Commission to destroy Amaleck he indented with him upon certain Articles and because he failed in one of the least, and that upon a fair pretence, it lost him the kingdom, which should have been his reward, if he had observed his Commission: Thus stands the cause between God and us, we are entered into Covenant with him for this work, we have taken out a Commission, the Lord hath given us leave to draw our own Articles we have professed to enterprise these Actions upon these ends, we have hereupon besought him of favor and blessing: Now if the Lord shall please to hear us, and bring us in peace to the place we desire, then hath he ratified this Covenant and sealed our Commission, [and] will expect a strict performance of the Articles contained in it, but if we shall neglect the observation of these Articles which are the ends we have propounded, and dissembling with our God, shall fall to embrace this present world and prosecute our carnal intentions, seeking great things for ourselves and our posterity, the Lord will surely break out in wrath against us be revenged of such a perjured people and make us known the price of the breach of such a Covenant.

Now the only way to avoid this shipwreck and to provide for our posterity is to follow the Counsel of Micah, to do justly, to love mercy, to walk humbly with our God, for this end, we must be knit together in this work as one man, we must entertain each other in brotherly Affection, we must be willing to abridge ourselves of our superfluities, for the supply of others necessities, we must uphold a familiar Commerce together in all meekness, gentleness, patience and liberality, we must delight in each other, make others' Conditions our own, rejoice together, mourn together, labor, and suffer together, always having before our eyes our Commission and Community in the work, our Community as members of the same body, so shall we keep the unity of the spirit in the bond of peace, the Lord will be our God and delight to dwell among us, as his own people and will command a blessing upon us in all our ways, so that we shall see much more of his wisdom power goodness and truth than formerly we have been acquainted with, we shall find that the God of Israel is among us, when ten of us shall be able to resist a thousand of our enemies, when he shall make us a praise and glory, that men shall say of succeeding plantations: the Lord make it like that of New England: for we must Consider that we shall be as a City upon a Hill, the eyes of all people are upon us; so that if we shall deal falsely with our God in this work we have undertaken and so cause him to withdraw his present help from us, we shall be made a story and a by-word through the world, we shall open the mouths of enemies to speak evil of the ways of God and all professors for Gods sake; we shall shame the faces of many of Gods worthy servants, and cause their prayers to be turned into Curses upon us till we be consumed out of the good land whither we are going: And to shut up this discourse with that exhortation of Moses, that faithful servant of the Lord, in his last farewell to Israel. *Deut.* 30. Beloved there is now set before us life, and good, death and evil in that we are Commanded this day to love the Lord our God, and to love one another to walk in his ways and to keep his Commandments and his Ordinance, and his laws, and the Articles of our Covenant with him that we may live and be multiplied, and that the Lord our God may bless us in the land whither we go to possess it: But if our hearts shall turn away so that we will not obey, but shall be seduced and worship other Gods our pleasures, and profits, and serve them; it is propounded unto us this day, we shall surely perish out of the good Land whether we pass over this vast Sea to possess it;

> Therefore let us choose life,
> that we, and our Seed,
> may live; by obeying his
> voice, and cleaveing to him,
> for he is our life, and
> our prosperity.

For the other point concerning liberty, I observe a great mistake in the country about that. There is a twofold liberty, natural (I mean as our nature is now corrupt) and civil or federal. The first is common to man with beasts and other creatures. By this, man, as he stands in relation to man simply, hath liberty to do what he lists; it is a liberty to evil as well as to good. This liberty is incompatible and inconsistent with authority, and cannot endure the least restraint of the most just authority. The exercise and maintaining of this liberty makes men grow more evil, and in time to be worse than brute beasts: *omnes summus licentia deteriores* [we are all worse in liberty]. This is that great enemy of truth and peace, that wild beast, which all the ordinances of God are bent against, to restrain and subdue it. The other kind of liberty I call civil or federal, it may also be termed moral, in reference to the covenant between God and man, in the moral law, and the politic covenants and constitutions, amongst men themselves. This liberty is the proper end and object of authority, and cannot subsist without it; and it is a liberty to that only which is good, just, and honest. This liberty you are to stand for, with the hazard (not only of your goods, but) of your lives, if need be. Whatsoever crosseth this, is not authority, but a distemper thereof. This liberty is maintained and exercised in a way of subjection to authority; it is of the same kind of liberty wherewith Christ hath made us free. The woman's own choice makes such a man her husband; yet being so chosen, he is her lord, and she is to be subject to him, yet in a way of liberty, not of bondage; and a true wife accounts her subjection her honor and freedom, and would not think her condition safe and free, but in her subjection to her husband's authority. Such is the liberty of the church under the authority of Christ, her king and husband; his yoke is so easy and sweet to her as a bride's ornaments; and if through frowardness or wantonness, etc., she shake it off, at any time, she is at no rest in her spirit, until she takes it up again; and whether her Lord smiles upon her, and embraces her in his arms, or whether he frowns, or rebukes, or smites her, she apprehends the sweetness of his love in all, and is refreshed, supported, and instructed by every such dispensation of his authority over her. On the other side, ye know who they are that complain of this yoke and say, let us break their bands, etc., we will not have this man to rule over us. Even so, brethren, it will be between you and your magistrates. If you stand for your natural corrupt liberties, and will do what is good in your own eyes, you will not endure the least weight of authority; but will murmur, and oppose, and be always striving to shake off that yoke; but if you will be satisfied to enjoy such civil and lawful liberties, such as Christ allows you, then will you quietly and cheerfully submit unto that authority which is set over you, in all the administrations of it, for your good. Wherein, if we fail at any time, we hope we shall be willing (by God's assistance) to hearken to good advice from any of you, or in any other way of God; so shall your liberties be preserved, in upholding the honor and power of authority amongst you.

(5)

John Cotton

1584-1652

Cotton's writings illustrate the Puritan interpretation of the religious basis of the state. Although arguing in favor of fundamental law and inalienable rights, he could do this only by accepting Winthrop's definition of liberty, which distinguished natural from civil liberty.

The first selection is from Cotton's *A Discourse about Civil Government in a New Plantation Whose Design Is Religion* (Cambridge, 1663), and the second is a letter from Cotton to Lord Saye and Sele in 1636 defending the franchise requirements in Massachusetts, reprinted in Thomas Hutchinson, *The History of the Colony of Massachusetts-Bay, From the First Settlement Thereof in 1628, Until . . . 1691* (Boston, 1764). [For Cotton's career see pp. 11–12.]

QUESTION. Whether a new Plantation, where all or the most considerable part of free Planters profess their purpose and desire of securing to themselves and to their posterity, the pure and peaceable enjoyment of Christ's Ordinances; Whether, I say, such Planters are bound in Laying the Foundations of Church and Civil State, to take order, that all the free Burgesses be such as are in fellowship of the Church or Churches which are, or may be gathered according to Christ; and that those free Burgesses have the only power of choosing from among themselves Civil Magistrates, and men to be entrusted with transacting all public Affairs of Importance, according to the rules and directions of Scriptures?

I hold the Affirmative part of this Question upon this ground, that this course will most conduce to the good of both States; and by consequence to the common welfare of all, whereunto all men are bound principally to attend in laying the Foundation of a Commonwealth; lest Posterity rue the first Miscarriages, when it will be too late to redress them. They that are skillful in Architecture observe, that the breaking or yielding of a stone in the groundwork of a Building but the breadth of the back of a knife, will make a cleft of more than half a foot in the Fabric aloft: So important (saith mine Author) are fundamental Errors. The Lord awaken us to look to it in time, and send us his Light and Truth to lead us into the safest ways in these beginnings.

The Question being thus stated, I now proceed with Gods help to prove the Affirmative part: and thus I argue, to prove that the Form of Government which is described in the true stating of the Question is the best, and by consequence, that men that are free to choose (as in new Plantations they are) ought to establish it in a Christian Commonwealth.

ARGUMENT 1. Theocracy, or to make the Lord God our Governour is the best Form of Government in a Christian Commonwealth, and which men that are free to choose (as in new Plantations they are) ought to establish. The Form of Government described in the true stating of the Question is Theocracy, or that wherein we make the Lord God our Governour. Therefore that Form of Government which is described in the true stating of the Question, is the best Form of Government in a Christian Commonwealth, and which men that are free to choose (as in new Plantations they are) ought to establish. The Proposition is clear of itself. The Assumption I prove thus:

That Form of Government where (1) The people that have the power of choosing their Governors are in Covenant with God (2) Wherein the men chosen by them are godly men, and fitted with a spirit of Government (3) In which the Laws they rule by are the Laws of God (4) Wherein Laws are executed, inheritances allotted, and civil differences are composed, according to Gods appointment (5) In which men of God are consulted with in all hard cases, and in matters of Religion, is the Form which was received and established among the people of Israel whil'st the Lord God was their Governour, as the places of Scripture alledged show; and is the very same with that which we plead for, as will appear to him that shall examine the true stating of the Question. The Conclusion follows necessarily.

ARGUMENT 2. That Form of Government which giveth unto Christ his due preeminence, is the best Form of Government in a Christian Commonwealth, and which men that are free to choose (as in new Plantations they are) ought to establish. The Form of Government described in the true stating of the Question, is that which giveth unto Christ his due preeminence. Therefore the Form of Government which is described in the true stating of the Question, is the best Form of Government in a Christian Commonwealth, and which men that are free to choose (as in new Plantations they are) ought to establish.

The Proposition is proved out of two places of Scripture, *Col.* 1. 15 to 19. with *Eph.* 1. 21, 22. From which Texts it doth appear, that it is a preeminence due to Christ, that all things, and all Governments in the world, should serve to Christs ends, for the welfare of the Church whereof he is the Head. For (1) In relation to God, he hath this by Right of Primogeniture, as he is the first-born, and so Heir of all things, higher then the Kings of the earth. (2) In relation to the World it is said, All things were made by him, and for him, and do consist in him, and therefore it is a preeminence due to him, that they all serve him. (3) In relation to the Church, it is said, He hath made all things subject under his feet, and hath given him over all things to be Head of the Church, that in all things he might have the preeminence. And indeed that he upholdeth the Creatures, and the Order that is in them, it is for his Churches sake; when that is once complete, the world shall soon be at an end. And if you read the stories of the great Monarchies that have been, and judge of them by Scripture-light, you will find they stood or fell, according as God purposed to make use of them about some service to be done about his Church. So that the only considerable part for which the world standeth at this day, is the Church: and therefore it is a Preeminence due to Christ, that his Headship over the Church should be exalted and acknowledged, and served by all. In which respect also the Title of The first-born is given to the Members of the Church, and they are called The first-fruits of his Creatures, to show both their preeminence above others, and that they are fittest to serve to Gods ends.

The Assumption (That the Form of Government described in the true stating of the Question, doth give unto Christ his due preeminence) will easily be granted by those that shall consider what Civil Magistrates and Rulers in the Commonwealth those are, who are fittest to serve to Christ's ends for the good and welfare of his Church; which will be evident from two places of Scripture: First, in *Psa.* 2. 10, 11, 12, you have a description of those that are fitted to order Civil Affairs in their Magistracy to Christ's ends; they are such as are not only wise and learned in matters of Religion but also do reduce their knowledge into practice: they Worship the Lord in fear; and not only so, but Kiss the Son, which was a solemn & outward Profession of love, and of Subjection, and of Religious Worship, and so fitly serveth to express their joining themselves to the Church of Christ. Secondly, in *Isa.* 49. 23. it is promised to the Church, that Kings and Queens shall be their nursing-fathers and nursing-mothers, and therefore it is added, They shall worship with their faces to the earth, and lick up the dust of thy feet; which is a proverbial expression of their voluntary humbling of themselves to Christ in his Ordinances, taken from the manner of the Persians in declaring their Subjection to their Emperor, which the Apostle calls a voluntary submission to the Gospel, which is the spirit of the Members of the Churches of Christ. And for this Reason it is, that the Lord, when he molded a Communion among his own People, wherein all Civil Administrations should serve to holy ends, he described the men to whom that Trust should be committed, by certain Properties, which also qualified them for fellowship in Church-Ordinances, as Men of ability and power over their own affections; secondly, fearing God, Truly Religious, Men of Courage, hating Covetousness, men of Wisdom, men of understanding, and men known or approved of among the people of God; & chosen by the Lord from among their Brethren, & not a stranger, which is no Brother: the most of which concur to describe Church members in a Church rightly gathered and ordered, who are also in respect of their union with Christ and fellowship together, called brethren frequently in the New Testament, wherein the equity of that Rule is established to us. OBJECT. Christ will have his due Preeminence, though the Civil Rulers oppose him, and persecute the Churches, as in Rome: Therefore it is not necessary that this course be taken in Civil Affairs to establish Christs Preeminence. ANSWER. The Question is of a Christian Commonwealth that should willingly subject themselves to Christ, not of a Heathen State that shall perforce be subdued unto Christ. It is concerning what Gods people being free should choose, not what his enemies are compell'd unto.

ARGUMENT 3. That Form of Government wherein the best provision is made for the good both of the Church and of the Civil State, is the best Form of Government in a Christian Communion, and which men that are free to choose (as in new Plantations they are) ought to establish. The Form of Government described in the true stating of the Question, is that wherein the best provision is made for the good both of the Church and Civil State. Therefore the Form of Government described in the true stating of the Question, is the best Form of Government in a Christian Communion, and which men that are free to choose (as in new Plantations they are) ought to establish. The Proposition (if need be) may be confirmed from the end of all Civil Government & Administrations which is the public and common Good, whether Natural, as in the preservation of Life and Safety; or Moral, as Justice and Honesty in Human Societies; or Civil, as Peace, Liberty of Commerce; or Spiritual as to protect the Church in Spiritual, though outward, Order and Administrations in peace & purity. And this last is principally to be attended unto, and therefore such as are entrusted with this care are called The Ministers of God, to note the principal end whereunto they serve, viz. The things wherein God is most directly and immediately honored, which is in promoting man's Spiritual good, so far as they are enabled by their Civil Power.

The Assumption (That the Form of Government in the Commonwealth which we plead for, is that wherein the best provision is made for the good both of the Church and of the Civil State) may appear by the blessing of God which usually is upon the Communion, where the securing of the Spiritual good of men, in the peace and purity of Gods Ordinances, is principally attended unto by all sorts as may be proved by the state of things in the Communion of Israel, whil'st the service of the Lord was with due care attended to all the days of Joshua, and all the days of the Elders that ever-lived Joshua, which had known all the works of the Lord which he had done for Israel. Many more places of Scripture might be alleged; but I will only note *Psal.* 72. wherein all sorts of goods are assured to the Commonwealth, wherein the fear of God, that is. Matters of Religion are so regarded, as the preservation thereof to after ages is duly provided for: which how can it be done, if the course described in the true stating of the Question be neglected by those that are free to cast the Commonwealth into what Mould they please?

It is very suitable to Gods all-sufficient wisdom, and to the fullness and perfection of Holy Scriptures, not only to prescribe perfect rules for the right ordering of a private mans soul to everlasting blessedness with himself, but also for the right ordering of a mans family, yea, of the commonwealth too, so far as both of them are subordinate to spiritual ends, and yet avoid both the churches usurpation upon civil jurisdictions, *in ordine ad spiritualia,* and the commonwealths invasion upon ecclesiastical administrations, *in ordine* to civil peace, and conformity to the civil state. Gods institutions (such as the government of church and of commonwealth be) may be close and compact, and co-ordinate one to another, and yet not confounded. God hath so framed the state of church government and ordinances, that they may be compatible to any commonwealth, though never so much disordered in his frame. But yet when a commonwealth hath liberty to mold his own frame (*scriptura plenitudinem adoro*) I conceive the Scripture hath given full direction for the right ordering of the same, and that, in such sort as may best maintain the *euexia* of the church. Mr. Hooker doth often quote a saying out of Mr. Cartwright (though I have not read it in him) that no man fashioneth his house to his hangings, but his hangings to his house. It is better that the commonwealth be fashioned to the setting forth of Gods house, which is his church: than to accommodate the church frame to the civil state. Democracy, I do not conceive that ever God did ordain as a fit government either for church or commonwealth. If the people be governors, who shall be governed? As for monarchy, and aristocracy, they are both of them clearly approved, and directed in Scripture, yet so as referreth the sovereignty to himself, and setteth up Theocracy in both, as the best form of government in the commonwealth, as well as in the church.

The law, which your Lordship instanceth in [that none shall be chosen to magistracy among us, but a church member] was made and enacted before I came into the country; but I have hitherto wanted sufficient light to plead against it. The rule that directeth the choice of supreme governors, is of like equity and weight in all magistrates, that one of their brethren (not a stranger) should be set over them. Deut. 17. 15. and Jethro's counsel to Moses was approved of God, that the judges, and officers to be set over the people, should be men fearing God. Exod. 18. 21. and Solomon maketh it the joy of a commonwealth, when the righteous are in authority, and their mourning when the wicked rule, Prov. 29. 21. Job 34. 30. Your Lordship's fear, that this will bring in papal excommunication, is just, and pious: but let your Lordship be pleased again to consider whether the consequence be necessary. *Turpius ejictur quam non admittitur:* nonmembership may be a just cause of nonadmission to the place of magistracy, but yet, ejection out of his membership will not be a just cause of ejecting him out of his magistracy. A godly woman, being to make choice of an husband, may justly refuse a man that is either cast out of church fellowship, or is not yet received into it, but yet, when she is once given to him, she may not reject him then, for such defect. Mr. Humfrey was chosen for an assistant (as I hear) before the colony came over hither: and, though he be not as yet joined into church fellowship (by reason of the unsettledness of the congregation where he liveth) yet the commonwealth do still continue his magistracy to him, as knowing he waiteth for opportunity of enjoying church-fellowship shortly.

When your Lordship doubteth, that this course will draw all things under the determination of the church, *in ordine ad spiritualia* (seeing the church is to determine who shall be members, and none but a member may have to do in the government of a commonwealth) be pleased (I pray you) to conceive, that magistrates are neither chosen to office in the church, nor do govern by directions from the church, but by civil laws, and those enacted in general courts, and executed in courts of justice, by the governors and assistants. In all which, the church (as the church) hath nothing to do: only, it prepareth fit instruments both to rule, and to choose rulers, which is no ambition in the church, nor dishonor to the commonwealth, the apostle, on the contrary, thought it a great dishonor and reproach to the church of Christ, if it were not able to yield able judges to hear and determine all causes amongst their brethren. *i, Cor.* 6. i. to 5. which place alone seemeth to me fully to decide this question: for it plainly holdeth forth this argument: It is a shame to the church to want able judges of civil matters (as v. 5.) and an audacious act in any church member voluntarily to go for judgment, other where than before the saints (as v. 1.) then it will be no arrogance nor folly in church members, nor prejudice to the commonwealth, if voluntarily they never choose any civil judges but from amongst the saints, such as church members are called to be. But the former is clear: and how then can the latter be avoided. If this therefore be (as your Lordship rightly conceiveth one of the main objections if not the only one) which hindereth this commonwealth from the entertainment of the propositions of those worthy gentlemen, we entreat them, in the name of the Lord Jesus, to consider, in meekness of wisdom, it is not any conceit, or will of ours, but the holy counsel and will of the Lord Jesus (whom they seek to serve as well as we) that overruleth us in this case: and we trust will overrule them also, that the Lord only may be exalted amongst all his servants. What pity and grief were it, that the observance of the will of Christ should hinder good things from us!

But your Lordship doubteth, that if such a rule were necessary, then the church estate and the best ordered commonwealth in the world were not compatible. But let not your Lordship so conceive. For, the church submitteth itself to all the laws and ordinances of men, in what commonwealth soever they come to dwell. But it is one thing, to submit unto what they have no calling to reform: another thing, voluntarily to ordain a form of government, which to the best discerning of many of us (for I speak not of myself) is expressly contrary to rule. Nor need your Lordship fear (which yet I speak with submission to your Lordships better judgment) that this course will lay such a foundation, as nothing but a mere democracy can be built upon it. Bodine confesseth, that though it be *status popularis,* where a people choose their own governors; yet the government is not a democracy, if it be administered, not by the people, but by the governors, whether one (for then it is a monarchy, though elective) or by many, for then (as you know) it is aristocracy. In which respect it is, that church government is justly denied (even by Mr. Robinson) to be democratical, though the people choose their own officers and rulers.

Nor need we fear, that this course will, in time, cast the commonwealth into distractions, and popular confusions. For (under correction) these three things do not undermine, but do mutually and strongly maintain one another (even those three which we principally aim at) authority in magistrates, liberty in people, purity in the church. Purity, preserved in the church, will preserve well-ordered liberty in the people, and both of them establish well-balanced authority in the magistrates. God is the author of all these three, and neither is himself the God of confusion, nor are the ways the ways of confusion, but of peace.

What our brethren (magistrates or ministers, or leading freeholders) will answer to the rest of the propositions, I shall better understand before the gentlemans return from Connecticut, who brought them over. Mean while, two of the principal of them, the general court hath already condescended unto. (1) In establishing a standing council, who, during their lives, should assist the governor in managing the chiefest affairs of this little state. They have chosen, for the present, only two (Mr. Winthrop and Mr. Dudley) not willing to choose more, till they see what further better choice the Lord will send over to them, that so they may keep an open door, for such desirable gentlemen as your Lordship mentioneth. (2) They have granted the governor and assistants a negative voice, and reserved to the freemen the like liberty also. Touching other things, I hope to give your Lordship further account, when the gentleman returneth.

He being now returned, I have delivered to him an answer to the rest of your demands, according to the minds of such leading men amongst us, as I thought meet to consult withal, concealing your name from any, except two or three, who alike do concur in a joint desire of yielding to any such propositions as your Lordship demandeth, so far as with allowance from the word they may, beyond which I know your Lordship would not require any thing.

Now the Lord Jesus Christ (the prince of peace) keep and bless your Lordship, and dispose of all your times and talents to his best advantage: and let the covenant of his grace and peace rest upon your honourable family and posterity, throughout all generations.

Thus, humbly craving pardon for my boldness and length, I take leave and rest,

Your Honours to serve in Christ Jesus,
J. C.

(6)

Nathaniel Ward

1578(?)-1652

Educated at Emanuel College, Cambridge, Ward migrated to Massachusetts in 1634 and became a minister of the church in Aggawam (Ipswich). In 1638 he was appointed by the General Court to assist in drawing up a legal code, which was adopted in 1641. According to

John Winthrop, Ward himself composed these laws, known as "The Body of Liberties."

In 1645 Ward completed his most famous political work, *The Simple Cobler of Aggawam in America,* first published in England in 1647 under the pseudonym of Theodore de la Guard. Supposedly the reflections of a self-exiled cobbler upon the political and religious dissensions of the times, the tract was really a protest against the idea of toleration. Written in a simple and homely style, it remains a landmark in the history of American letters.

The text reprinted here is taken from the fifth edition, printed in London in 1713, and reproduced in Peter Force, ed., *Tracts and Other Papers, Relating Principally to the Origin, Settlement, and Progress of the Colonies in North America, from the Discovery of the Country to the Year 1776,* 4 vols. (Washington, D.C., 1836–1846), vol. III, No. 8.

If the Devil might have his free option, I believe he would ask nothing else, but liberty to enfranchise all false Religions, and to embondage the true; nor should he need: It is much to be feared that lax Tolerations upon State-pretences and planting necessities, will be the next subtle Stratagem he will spread to distate the Truth of God, and supplant the Peace of the Churches. Tolerations in things tolerable, exquisitely drawn out by the lines of the Scripture, and pencil of the Spirit, are the sacred favours of Truth, the due latitudes of Love, the fair Compartments of Christian fraternity: but irregular dispensations, dealt forth by the facilities of men, are the frontiers of error, the redoubts of Schism, the perilous irritaments of carnal and spiritual enmity.

My heart hath naturally detested four things: The standing of the Apocrypha in the Bible; Foreigners dwelling in my Country, to crowd out Native Subjects into the corners of the Earth; Alchemized Coins; Tolerations of diverse Religions, or of one Religion in segregant shapes: He that willingly assents to the last, if he examines his heart by day-light, his Conscience will tell him, he is either an Atheist, or an Heretic, or an Hypocrite, or at best a captive to some Lust: Poly-piety is the greatest impiety in the World. True Religion is *Ignis probationis,* which doth *congregare homogenea & segregare heterogenea.*

Not to tolerate things merely indifferent to weak Consciences, argues a Conscience too strong: pressed uniformity in these, causes much disunity: To tolerate more than indifferents, is not to deal indifferently with God: He that doth it, takes his Scepter out of his hand, and bids him stand by. Who hath to do to institute Religion but God. The power of all Religion and Ordinances, lies in their Purity: their Purity in their Simplicity: then are mixtures pernicious. I lived in a City, where a Papist Preached in one Church, a Lutheran in another, a Calvinist in a third; a Lutheran one part of the day, a Calvinist the other, in the same Pulpit: the Religion of that Place was but motly and meagre, their affections Leopard-like.

If the whole Creature should conspire to do the Creator a mischief, or offer him an insolency, it would be in nothing more, than in erecting untruths against his Truth, or by sophisticating his Truths with human medleys: the removing of some one iota in Scripture, may draw out all the life, and traverse all the Truth of the whole Bible: but to authorize an untruth, by a Toleration of State, is to build a sconce against the walls of Heaven, to batter God out of his Chair: To tell a practical lie, is a great Sin, but yet transient; but to set up a Theoretical untruth, is to warrant every lie that lies from its root to the top of every branch it hath, which are not a few. . . .

That State is wise, that will improve all pains and patience rather to compose, than tolerate differences in Religion. There is no divine Truth, but hath much Celestial fire in it from the Spirit of Truth: nor no irreligious untruth, without its proportion of Antifire from the spirit of Error to contradict it: the zeal of the one, the virulency of the other, must necessarily kindle Combustions. Fiery diseases seated in the Spirit, embroil the whole frame of the body: others more external and cool, are less dangerous. They which divide in Religion, divide in God; they who divide in him, divide beyond *Genus Generalissimum,* where there is no reconciliation, without atonement; that is, without uniting in him, who is One, and in his Truth, which is also one.

Wise are those men who will be persuaded rather to live within the pale of Truth, where they may be quiet, than in the purlieues, where they are sure to be hunted ever and anon, do Authority what it can. Every singular Opinion, hath a singular opinion of it self, and he that holds it a singular opinion of himself, and a simple opinion of all contra-sentients: he that confutes them, must confute all three at once, or else he does nothing; which will not be done without more stir than the Peace of the State or Church can endure.

And prudent are those Christians, that will rather give what may be given, than hazard all by yielding nothing. To sell all Peace of Country, to buy some Peace of Conscience unseasonably, is more avarice than thrift, imprudence than patience: they deal not equally, that set any Truth of God at such a rate; but they deal wisely that will stay till the Market is fallen.

My Prognostics deceive me not a little, if once within three seven years, Peace prove not such a Penny-worth at most Marts in Christendom, that he that would not lay down his Money, his Lust, his Opinion, his Will, I had almost said the best flower of his Crown for it, while he might have had it; will tell his own heart, he played the very ill husband.

Concerning Tolerations, I may further assert.

That Persecution of true Religion, and Toleration of false, are the *Jannes* and *Jambres* to the Kingdom of Christ, whereof the last is far the worst. *Augustines* Tongue had not owed his Mouth one Penny-rent though he had never spake word more in it, but this, *Nillum malum pejus libertate errandi* [nothing is more evil than the liberty of error].

Frederick, Duke of *Saxon,* spake not one foot beyond the mark when he said, He had rather the Earth should swallow him up quick, than he should give a toleration to any Opinion against any Truth of God.

He that is willing to tolerate any Religion, or discrepant way of Religion, besides his own, unless it be in matters merely indifferent, either doubts of his own, or is not sincere in it.

He that is willing to tolerate any unsound Opinion, that his own may also be tolerated, though never so sound, will for a need hang God's Bible at the Devils girdle.

Every toleration of false Religions, or Opinions hath as many Errors and Sins in it, as all the false Religions and Opinions it tolerates, and one sound one more.

That State that will give Liberty of Conscience in matters of Religion, must give Liberty of Conscience and Conversation in their Moral Laws, or else the Fiddle will be out of Tune, and some of the strings crack.

He that will rather make an irreligious quarrel with other Religions than try the Truth of his own by valuable Arguments, and peaceable Sufferings; either his Religion, or himself is irreligious.

Experience will teach Churches and Christians, that it is far better to live in a State united, though a little Corrupt, than in a State, whereof some Part is uncorrupt, and all the rest divided. . . .

I take Liberty of Conscience to be nothing but a freedom from Sin, and Error. *Conscientia in tantum libera, inquantum ab errore liberata* [conscience is so free insofar as it is free from error]. And Liberty of Error nothing but a Prison for Conscience. Then small will be the kindness of a State to build such Prisons for their Subjects.

The Scripture saith, there is nothing makes free but Truth, and Truth saith, there is no Truth but one: If the States of the World would make it their sum-operous Care to preserve this One Truth in its purity and Authority, it would ease you of all other Political cares. I am sure Satan makes it his grand, if not only task, to adulterate Truth; Falsehood is his sole Scepter, whereby he first ruffled, and ever since ruined the World. . . .

It is said, That Men ought to have Liberty of their Conscience, and that it is Persecution to debar them of it: I can rather stand amazed than reply to this: it is an astonishment to think that the brains of men should be parboil'd in such impious ignorance; Let all the wits under the Heavens lay their heads together and find an Assertion worse than this (one excepted) I will Petition to be chosen the universal Idiot of the World.

It is said, That Civil Magistrates ought not to meddle with Ecclesiastical matters.

I would answer to this so well as I could, did I not know that some Papers lately brought out of *New England,* are going to the Press, wherein the Opinions of the Elders there in a late Synod, concerning this point are manifested, which I suppose will give clearer satisfaction than I can.

(7)

Roger Williams

1603(?)-1683

After he graduated from Pembroke College, Cambridge, in 1627, Roger Williams came to New England in 1631, professing to be an orthodox Puritan. From the outset, however, he came into conflict with the ruling authorities in Massachusetts because of his unorthodox views. He was finally banished from that colony in 1635, and the following year he founded Providence, Rhode Island. He ended his life as a "seeker," maintaining that no earthly church could represent true religion.

Roger Williams frequently has been considered a forerunner or champion of democracy and religious liberty. Actually, his career cannot be understood from such a secular point of view. A religious purist, Williams did not want to contaminate religion with earthly considerations; he therefore argued for the total separation of the two, since it was the world that had corrupted the church.

The first selection is from Williams' most famous work, *The Bloudy Tenent, of Persecution, for Cause of Conscience, Discussed, in a Conference betweene Truth and Peace,* which was written in answer to John Cotton's orthodox views on persecution; the text is from the edition of 1644, Samuel L. Caldwell, ed., printed in the *Publications of the Narragansett Club* (Providence, Rhode Island, 1867), First Series, vol. III. The second selection is a letter from Williams to the town of Providence, written in January, 1655; the text is from John R. Bartlett, ed., "Letters of Roger Williams, 1632-1682," in *Publications of the Narragansett Club* (Providence, Rhode Island, 1874), First Series, vol. VI.

First, That the blood of so many hundred thousand souls of Protestants and Papists, spilt in the Wars of present and former Ages, for their respective Consciences, is not required nor accepted by Jesus Christ the Prince of Peace.

Secondly, Pregnant Scriptures and Arguments are throughout the Work proposed against the Doctrine of persecution for cause of Conscience.

Thirdly, Satisfactory Answers are given to Scriptures, and objections produced by Mr. Calvin, [Mr.] Beza, Mr. Cotton, and the Ministers of the New English Churches and others former and later, tending to prove the Doctrine of persecution for cause of Conscience.

Fourthly, The Doctrine of persecution for cause of Conscience, is proved guilty of all the blood of the Souls crying for vengeance under the Altar.

Fifthly, All Civil States with their Officers of justice in their respective constitutions and administrations are proved essentially Civil, and therefore not Judges, Governors or Defenders of the Spiritual or Christian state and Worship.

Sixthly, It is the will and command of God, that (since the coming of his Son the Lord Jesus) a permission of the most Paganish, Jewish, Turkish, or Anti-Christian consciences and worships, be granted to all men in all Nations and Countries: and they are only to be fought against with that Sword which is only (in Soul matters) able to conquer, to wit, the Sword of Gods Spirit, the Word of God.

Seventhly, The state of the Land of Israel, the Kings and people thereof in Peace & War, is proved figurative and ceremonial, and no pattern nor precedent for any Kingdom or civil state in the world to follow.

Eighthly, God requireth not an uniformity of Religion to be enacted and enforced in any civil state; which enforced uniformity (sooner or later) is the greatest occasion of civil War, ravishing of conscience, persecution of Christ Jesus in his servants, and of the hypocrisy and destruction of millions of souls.

Ninthly, In holding an enforced uniformity of Religion in a civil state, we must necessarily disclaim our desires and hopes of the Jews conversion to Christ.

Tenthly, An enforced uniformity of Religion throughout a Nation or civil state, confounds the Civil and Religious, denies the principles of Christianity and civility, and that Jesus Christ is come in the Flesh.

Eleventhly, The permission of other consciences and worships than a state professeth, only can (according to God) procure a firm and lasting peace (good assurance being taken according to the wisdom of the civil state for uniformity of civil obedience from all sorts).

Twelfthly, lastly, true civility and Christianity may both flourish in a state or Kingdom, notwithstanding the permission of diverse and contrary consciences, either of Jew or Gentile.

CHAPTER VI

Peace. The next distinction concerning the manner of persons holding forth the aforesaid practices (not only the weightier duties of the Law, but points of doctrine and worship less principal).

"Some (saith he) hold them forth in a meek and peaceable way: some with such arrogance and impetuousness, as of it self tendeth to the disturbance of civil peace.["]

Truth. In the examination of this distinction we shall discuss,

First, what is civil Peace (wherein we shall vindicate thy name the better).

Secondly, what it is to hold forth a Doctrine or Practice in this impetuousness or arrogancy.

First, for civil peace, what is it but *pax civitatis,* the peace of the City, whether an English City, Scotch, or Irish City, or further abroad, French, Spanish, Turkish City, etc.

Thus it pleased the Father of Lights to define it, *Jerem.* 29. 7. Pray for the peace of the City; which peace of the City, or Citizens, so compacted in a civil way of union, may be entire, unbroken, safe, etc. notwithstanding so many thousands of Gods people the Jews, were there in bondage, and would neither be constrained to the worship of the City Babel, nor restrained from so much of the worship of the true God, as they then could practice, as is plain in the practice of the Three Worthies, Shadrach, Misach, and Abednego, as also of Daniel, *Dan.* 3 & *Dan.* 6. (the peace of the City or Kingdom, being a far different Peace from the Peace of the Religion or Spiritual Worship, maintained & professed of the Citizens. This Peace of their Worship (which worship also in some Cities being various) being a false Peace, Gods people were and ought to be Nonconformitants, not daring either to be restrained from the true, or constrained to false Worship, and yet without breach of the Civil or City-peace, properly so called.

Peace. Hence it is that so many glorious and flourishing Cities of the World maintain their Civil peace, yea the very Americans & wildest Pagans keep the peace of their Towns or Cities; though neither in one nor the other can any man prove a true Church of God in those places, and consequently no spiritual and heavenly peace: The Peace spiritual (whether true or false) being of a higher and far different nature from the Peace of the place or people, being merely and essentially civil and humane.

Truth. O how lost are the sons of men in this point? To illustrate this: The Church or company of worshippers (whether true or false) is like unto a Body or College of Physicians in a City; like unto a Corporation, Society, or Company of East-India or Turkey-Merchants, or any other Society or Company in London: which Companies may hold their Courts, keep their Records, hold disputations; and in matters concerning their Society, may dissent, divide, break into Schisms and Factions, sue and implead each other at the Law, yea wholly break up and dissolve into pieces and nothing, and yet the peace of the City not be in the least measure impaired or disturbed; because the essence or being of the City, and so the well-being and peace thereof is essentially distinct from those particular Societies; the City-Courts, City-Laws, City-punishments distinct from theirs. The City was before them, and stands absolute and entire, when such a Corporation or Society is taken down. For instance further, The City or Civil state of Ephesus was essentially distinct from the worship of Diana in the City, or of the whole city. Again, the Church of Christ in Ephesus (which were Gods people, converted and call'd out from the worship of that City unto Christianity or worship of God in Christ) was distinct from both.

Now suppose that God remove the Candlestick from Ephesus, yea though the whole Worship of the City of Ephesus should be altered: yet (if men be true and honestly ingenuous to City-covenants, Combinations and Principles) all this might be without the least impeachment or infringement of the Peace of the City of Ephesus.

Thus in the City of Smyrna was the City itself or Civil estate one thing; The Spiritual or Religious state of Smyrna, another; The Church of Christ in Smyrna, distinct from them both; and the Synagogue of the Jews, whether literally Jews (as some think) or mystically, false Christians (as others) called the Synagogue of Satan, *Revel.* 2. distinct from all these. And notwithstanding these spiritual oppositions in point of Worship and Religion, yet hear we not the least noise (nor need we, if Men keep but the Bond of Civility) of any Civil *breach,* or *breach* of *Civil peace* amongst them: and to persecute Gods people there for Religion, that only was a breach of Civility itself.

TO THE TOWN OF PROVIDENCE

That ever I should speak or write a tittle, that tends to such an infinite liberty of conscience, is a mistake, and one which I have ever disclaimed and abhorred. To prevent such mistakes, I shall at present only propose this case: There goes many a ship to sea, with many hundred souls in one ship, whose weal and woe is common, and is a true picture of a commonwealth, or a human combination or society. It hath fallen out sometimes, that both papists and protestants, Jews and Turks, may be embarked in one ship; upon which supposal I affirm, that all the liberty of conscience, that ever I pleaded for, turns upon these two hinges—that none of the papists, protestants, Jews, or Turks, be forced to come to the ship's prayers or worship, nor compelled from their own particular prayers or worship, if they practice any. I further add, that I never denied, that notwithstanding this liberty, the commander of this ship ought to command the ship's course, yea, and also command that justice, peace and sobriety, be kept and practiced, both among the seamen and all the passengers. If any of the seamen refuse to perform their services, or passengers to pay their freight; if any refuse to help, in person or purse, towards the common charges or defence; if any refuse to obey the common laws and orders of the ship, concerning their common peace or preservation; if any shall mutiny and rise up against their commanders and officers; if any should preach or write that there ought to be no commanders or officers, because all are equal in Christ, therefore no masters nor officers, no laws nor orders, nor corrections nor punishments;—I say, I never denied, but in such cases, whatever is pretended, the commander or commanders may judge, resist, compel and punish such transgressors, according to their deserts and merits. This if seriously and honestly minded, may, if it so please the Father of lights, let in some light to such as willingly shut not their eyes.

I remain studious of your common peace and liberty.

Roger Williams

(8)

John Wise

1652-1725

A Congregational clergyman born in Roxbury, Massachusetts, Wise graduated from Harvard in 1673 and spent most of his life as a minister in Ipswich. A frequent participant in public controversies, Wise protested against the witchcraft trials in the 1690's and argued in favor of inoculation against smallpox (which was opposed by most ministers).

Wise's historical importance, however, lies in the realm of political thought. His writings here were occasioned by a proposal to transfer control of the churches from the members to the clergy and end the independence of the several churches. In attacking this proposal, Wise also critically reviewed the fundamentals of all government, separating the Biblical and rational arguments. His system of democratic church government was based on reason and nature rather than on a theological foundation. Although Wise's work was primarily concerned with church government, his ideas were extended by a later generation to apply to all government.

The text is from Wise's comprehensive and important defense of democratic Congregationalism, *A Vindication of the Government of New-England Churches* (Boston, 1717).

CHAPTER II

I shall disclose several Principles of Natural Knowledge; plainly discovering the Law of Nature; or the true sentiments of Natural Reason, with Respect to Mans Being and Government. And in this Essay I shall peculiarly confine the discourse to two heads, *viz.*

1. Of the Natural [in distinction to the Civil] and then,
2. Of the Civil Being of Man. . . .

1. I shall consider Man in a state of Natural Being, as a Free-Born Subject under the Crown of Heaven, and owing Homage to none but God him-

self. It is certain Civil Government in General, is a very Admirable Result of Providence, and an Incomparable Benefit to Mankind, yet must needs be acknowledged to be the Effect of Human Free-Compacts and not of Divine Institution; it is the Produce of Mans Reason, of Human and Rational Combinations, and not from any direct Orders of Infinite Wisdom, in any positive Law wherein is drawn up this or that Scheme of Civil Government. Government [says the Lord *Warrington*] is necessary—in that no Society of Men can subsist without it; and that Particular Form of Government is necessary which best suits the Temper and Inclination of a People. Nothing can be Gods Ordinance, but what he has particularly Declared to be such; there is no particular Form of Civil Government described in Gods Word, neither does Nature prompt it. The Government of the *Jews* was changed five Times. Government is not formed by Nature, as other Births or Productions; If it were, it would be the same in all Countries; because Nature keeps the same Method, in the same thing, in all Climates. If a Commonwealth be changed into a Monarchy, is it Nature that forms, and brings forth the Monarch? Or if a Royal Family be wholly Extinct [as in *Noah's* Case, being not Heir Apparent from Descent from *Adam*] is it Nature that must go to work [with the King Bees, who themselves alone preserve the Royal Race in that Empire] to Breed a Monarch before the People can have a King, or a Government sent over them? And thus we must leave Kings to Resolve which is their best Title to their Crowns, whether Natural Right, or the Constitution of Government settled by Human Compacts, under the Direction and Conduct of Reason. But to proceed under the head of a State of Natural Being, I shall more distinctly Explain the State of Human Nature in its Original Capacity, as Man is placed on Earth by his Maker, and Clothed with many Investitures, and Immunities which properly belong to Man separately considered. As,

1. The Prime Immunity in Mans State, is that he is most properly the Subject of the Law of Nature. He is the Favourite Animal on Earth; in that this Part of Gods Image, *viz.* Reason is Congenial with his Nature, wherein by a Law Immutable, Instamped upon his Frame, God has provided a Rule for Men in all their Actions, obliging each one to the performance of that which is Right, not only as to Justice, but likewise as to all other Moral Virtues, the which is nothing but the Dictate of Right Reason founded in the Soul of Man. . . . That which is to be drawn from Mans Reason, flowing from the true Current of that Faculty, when unperverted, may be said to be the Law of Nature; on which account, the Holy Scriptures declare it written on Mens hearts. For being endowed with a Soul, you may know from your self, how, and what you ought to act, Rom. 2. 14. *These having not a Law, are a Law to themselves.* So that the meaning is, when we acknowledge the Law of Nature to be the dictate of Right Reason, we must mean that the Understanding of Man is endowed with such a power, as to be able, from the Contemplation of human Condition to discover a necessity of Living agreeably with this Law: And likewise to find out some Principle, by which

the Precepts of it, may be clearly and solidly Demonstrated. The way to discover the Law of Nature in our own state, is by a narrow Watch, and accurate Contemplation of our Natural Condition, and propensions. Others say this is the way to find out the Law of Nature. If a Man any ways doubts, whether what he is going to do to another Man be agreeable to the Law of Nature, then let him suppose himself to be in that other Mans Room; And by this Rule effectually Executed. A Man must be a very dull Scholar to Nature not to make Proficiency in the Knowledge of her Laws. But more particularly in pursuing our Condition for the discovery of the Law of Nature, this is very obvious to view, *viz.*

1. A Principle of Self-Love, & Self-Preservation, is very predominant in every Mans Being.

2. A Sociable Disposition.

3. An Affection or Love to Mankind in General. And to give such Sentiments the force of a Law, we must suppose a God who takes care of all Mankind, and has thus obliged each one, as a Subject of higher Principles of Being, than mere Instincts. For that all Law properly considered, supposes a capable Subject, and a Superior Power; And the Law of God which is Binding, is published by the Dictates of Right Reason as other ways: Therefore says *Plutarch, To follow God and obey Reason is the same thing.* But moreover that God has Established the Law of Nature, as the General Rule of Government, is further Illustrable from the many Sanctions in Providence, and from the Peace and Guilt of Conscience in them that either obey, or violate the Law of Nature. But moreover, the foundation of the Law of Nature with relation to Government, may be thus Discovered. Man is a Creature extremely desirous of his own Preservation; of himself he is plainly Exposed to many Wants, unable to secure his own safety, and Maintenance without the Assistance of his fellows; and he is also able of returning Kindness by the furtherance of mutual Good; But yet Man is often found to be Malicious, Insolent, and easily Provoked, and as powerful in Effecting mischief, as he is ready in designing it. Now that such a Creature may be Preserved, it is necessary that he be Sociable; that is, that he be capable and disposed to unite himself to those of his own species, and to Regulate himself towards them, that they may have no fair Reason to do him harm; but rather incline to promote his Interests, and secure his Rights and Concerns. This then is a Fundamental Law of Nature, that every Man as far as in him lies, do maintain a Sociableness with others, agreeable with the main end and disposition of human Nature in general. For this is very apparent, that Reason and Society render Man the most potent of all Creatures. And Finally, from the Principles of Sociableness it follows as a fundamental Law of Nature, that Man is not so Wedded to his own Interest, but that he can make the Common good the mark of his Aim: And hence he becomes Capacitated to enter into a Civil State by the Law of Nature; for without this property in Nature, *viz.* Sociableness, which is for Cementing of parts, every Government would soon molder and dissolve.

2. The Second Great Immunity of Man is an Original Liberty Instampt upon his Rational Nature. He that intrudes upon this Liberty, Violates the Law of Nature. In this Discourse I shall waive the Consideration of Mans Moral Turpitude, but shall view him Physically as a Creature which God has made and furnished essentially with many Ennobling Immunities, which render him the most August Animal in the World, and still, whatever has happened since his Creation, he remains at the upper-end of Nature, and as such is a Creature of a very Noble Character. For as to his Dominion, the whole frame of the Lower Part of the Universe is devoted to his use, and at his Command; and his Liberty under the Conduct of Right Reason, is equal with his trust. Which Liberty may be briefly Considered, Internally as to his Mind, and Externally as to his Person.

1. The Internal Native Liberty of Mans Nature in general implies, a faculty of Doing or Omitting things according to the Direction of his Judgment. But in a more special meaning, this Liberty does not consist in a loose and ungovernable Freedom, or in an unbounded Licence of Acting. Such Licence is disagreeing with the condition and dignity of Man, and would make Man of a lower and meaner Constitution than Brute Creatures; who will in all their Liberties are kept under a better and more Rational Government, by their Instincts. Therefore as *Plutarch* says, *Those Persons only who live in Obedience to Reason, are worthy to be accounted free: They alone live as they Will, who have Learnt what they ought to Will.* So that the true Natural Liberty of Man, such as really and truly agrees to him, must be understood, as he is Guided and Restrained by the Ties of Reason, and Laws of Nature; all the rest is Brutal, if not worse.

2. Mans External Personal, Natural Liberty, Antecedent to all Human parts, or Alliances must also be considered. And so every Man must be conceived to be perfectly in his own Power and disposal, and not to be controlled by the Authority of any other. And thus every Man, must be acknowledged equal to every Man, since all Subjection and all Command are equally banished on both sides; and considering all Men thus at Liberty, every Man has a Prerogative to Judge for himself, *viz.* What shall be most for his Behoof, Happiness and Well-being.

3. The Third Capital Immunity belonging to Mans Nature, is an equality amongst Men; Which is not to be denied by the Law of Nature, till Man has Resigned himself with all his Rights for the sake of a Civil State; and then his Personal Liberty and Equality is to be cherished, and preserved to the highest degree, as will consist with all just distinctions amongst Men of Honour, and shall be agreeable with the public Good. For Man has a high valuation of himself, and the passion seems to lay its first foundation [not in Pride, but] really in the high and admirable Frame and Constitution of Human Nature. The Word Man, says my Author, is thought to carry somewhat of Dignity in its sound; and we commonly make use of this as the most proper and prevailing Argument against a rude Insulter, *viz. I am not a Beast or a Dog, but am a Man as well as your self.* Since then Human Nature agrees equally

with all persons; and since no one can live a Sociable Life with another that does not own or Respect him as a Man; It follows as a Command of the Law of Nature, that every Man Esteem and treat another as one who is naturally his Equal, or who is a Man as well as he. There be many popular, or plausible Reasons that greatly Illustrate this Equality, *viz.* that we all Derive our Being from one stock, the same Common Father of the human Race. On this Consideration *Boethius* checks the pride of the Insulting Nobility. . . .

And also that our Bodies are Composed of matter, frail, brittle, and liable to be destroyed by thousand Accidents; we all owe our Existence to the same Method of propagation. The Noblest Mortal in his Entrance on to the Stage of Life, is not distinguished by any pomp or of passage from the lowest of Mankind; and our Life hastens to the same General Mark: Death observes no Ceremony, but Knocks as loud at the Barriers of the Court, as at the Door of the Cottage. This Equality being admitted, bears a very great force in maintaining Peace and Friendship amongst Men. For that he who would use the Assistance of others, in promoting his own Advantage, ought as freely to be at their service, when they want his help on the like Occasions. . . . That it would be the greatest absurdity to believe, that Nature actually Invests the Wise with a Sovereignty over the weak; or with a Right of forcing them against their Wills; for that no Sovereignty can be Established, unless some Human Deed, or Covenant Precede: Nor does Natural fitness for Government make a Man presently Governor over another; for that as *Ulpian* says, *by a Natural Right all Men are born free;* and Nature having set all Men upon a Level and made them Equals, no Servitude or Subjection can be conceived without Inequality; and this cannot be made without Usurpation or Force in others, or Voluntary Compliance in those who Resign their freedom, and give away their degree of Natural Being. And thus we come,

2. To consider Man in a Civil State of Being; wherein we shall observe the great difference between a Natural, and Political State, for in the Latter State many Great disproportions appear, or at least many obvious distinctions are soon made amongst Men; which Doctrine is to be laid open under a few heads.

1. Every Man considered in a Natural State, must be allowed to be Free, and at his own dispose; yet to suit Mans Inclinations to Society; And in a peculiar manner to gratify the necessity he is in of public Rule and Order, he is Impelled to enter into a Civil Community; and divests himself of his Natural Freedom, and puts himself under Government; which amongst other things Comprehends the Power of Life and Death over Him; together with Authority to Enjoin him some things to which he has an utter Aversion, and to prohibit him other things, for which he may have as strong an Inclination; so that he may be often under this Authority, obliged to Sacrifice his Private, for the Public Good. So that though Man is inclined to Society, yet he is driven to a Combination by great necessity. For that the true and leading Cause of forming Governments, and yielding up Natural Liberty, and throwing Mans Equality into a Common Pile to be new Cast by the Rules of

fellowship; was really and truly to guard themselves against the Injuries Men were liable to Interchangeably; for none so Good to Man, as Man, and yet none a greater Enemy. So that,

2. The first Human Subject and Original of Civil Power is the People. For as they have a Power every Man over himself in a Natural State, so upon a Combination they can and do bequeath this Power unto others; and settle it according as their united discretion shall Determine. For that this is very plain, that when the Subject of Sovereign Power is quite Extinct, that Power returns to the People again. And when they are free, they may set up what species of Government they please; or if they rather incline to it, they may subside into a State of Natural Being, if it be plainly for the best. . . .

3. The formal Reason of Government is the Will of a Community, yielded up and surrendered to some other Subject, either of one particular Person, or more. . . .

1. The Forms of a Regular State are three only, which Forms arise from the proper and particular Subject, in which the Supreme Power Resides. As,

1. A Democracy, which is when the Sovereign Power is Lodged in a Council consisting of all the Members, and where every Member has the Privilege of a Vote. This Form of Government, appears in the greatest part of the World to have been the most Ancient. For that Reason seems to show it to be most probable, that when Men [being Originally in a condition of Natural Freedom and Equality] had thoughts of joining in a Civil Body, would without question be inclined to Administer their common Affairs, by their common Judgment, and so must necessarily to gratify that Inclination establish a Democracy; neither can it be rationally imagined, that Fathers of Families being yet Free and Independent, should in a moment, or little time take off their long delight in governing their own Affairs, & Devolve all upon some single Sovereign Commander; for that it seems to have been thought more Equitable, that what belonged to all, should be managed by all, when all had entered by Compact into one Community. . . .

A democracy is then Erected, when a Number of Free Persons, do Assemble together, in Order to enter into a Covenant for Uniting themselves in a Body: And such a Preparative Assembly hath some appearance already of a Democracy; it is a Democracy in *Embryo* properly in this Respect, that every Man hath the Privilege freely to deliver his Opinion concerning the Common Affairs. Yet he who dissents from the Vote of the Majority, is not in the least obliged by what they determine, till by a second Covenant, a Popular Form be actually Established; for not before then can we call it a Democratical Government, *viz*. Till the Right of Determining all matters relating to the public Safety, is actually placed in a General Assembly of the whole People; or by their own Compact and Mutual Agreement, Determine themselves the proper Subject for the Exercise of Sovereign Power. And to complete this State, and render it capable to Exert its Power to answer the End of a Civil State: These Conditions are necessary.

1. That a certain Time and Place be Assigned for Assembling.

2. That when the Assembly be Orderly met, as to Time and Place, that then the Vote of the Majority must pass for the Vote of the whole Body.

3. That Magistrates be appointed to Exercise the Authority of the whole for the better dispatch of Business, of every days Occurrence; who also may with more Mature Diligence, search into more important Affairs; and if in case any thing happens of greater Consequence, may report it to the Assembly; and be peculiarly Serviceable in putting all Public Decrees into Execution. Because a large Body of People is almost useless in Respect of the last Service, and of many others, as to the more Particular Application and Exercise of Power. Therefore it is most agreeable with the Law of Nature, that they Institute their Officers to act in their Name, and Stead

2. The Second Species of Regular Government, is an Aristocracy; and this is said then to be Constituted when the People, or Assembly United by a first Covenant, and having thereby cast themselves into the first Rudiments of a State; do then by Common Decree, Devolve the Sovereign Power, on a Council consisting of some Select Members; and these having accepted of the Designation, are then properly invested with Sovereign Command; and then an Aristocracy is formed.

3. The Third Species of a Regular Government, is a Monarchy which is settled when the Sovereign Power is confered on some one worthy Person. It differs from the former, because a Monarch who is but one Person in Natural, as well as in Moral account, & so is furnished with an Immediate Power of Exercising Sovereign Command in all Instances of Government; but the fore named must needs have Particular Time and Place assigned; but the Power and Authority is Equal in each. . . .

3. A Democracy. This is a form of Government, which the Light of Nature does highly value, & often directs to as most agreeable to the Just and Natural Prerogatives of Human Beings. This was of great account, in the early times of the World. And not only so, but upon the Experience of several Thousand years, after the World had been tumbled, and tossed from one Species of Government to another, at a great Expense of Blood and Treasure, many of the wise Nations of the World have sheltered themselves under it again; or at least have blandished, and balanced their Governments with it.

It is certainly a great Truth, That Mans Original Liberty after it is Resigned, [yet under due Restrictions] ought to be Cherished in all wise Governments; or otherwise a man in making himself a Subject, he alters himself from a Freeman, into a Slave, which to do is Repugnant to the Law of Nature. Also the Natural Equality of Men amongst Men must be duly favoured; in that Government was never Established by God or Nature, to give one Man a Prerogative to insult over another; therefore in a Civil, as well as in a Natural State of Being, a just Equality is to be indulged so far as that every Man is bound to Honour every Man, which is agreeable both with Nature and Religion, 1 Pet. 2. 17. *Honour all Men.*—The End of all good Government is to Cultivate Humanity, and Promote the happiness of all, and the good of every Man in all his Rights, his Life, Liberty, Estate, Honour, &c. without injury or abuse done to any. Then certainly it cannot easily be thought, that a company of Men, that shall enter into a voluntary Compact, to hold all Power in their own hands, thereby to use and improve their united force, wisdom, riches and strength for the Common and Particular good of every Member, as is the Nature of a Democracy; I say it cannot be that this sort of Constitution, will so readily furnish those in Government with an appetite, or disposition to prey upon each other, or embezzle the common Stock; as some Particular Persons may be apt to do when set off, and Entrusted with the same Power. And moreover this appears very Natural, that when the aforesaid Government or Power, settled in all, when they have Elected certain capable Persons to Minister in their affairs, and the said Ministers remain accountable to the Assembly; these Officers must needs be under the influence of many wise cautions from their own thoughts [as well as under confinement by their Commission] in their whole Administration: And from thence it must needs follow that they will be more apt, and inclined to steer Right for the main Point, *viz.* The peculiar good, and benefit of the whole, and every particular Member fairly and sincerely. And why may not these stand for very Rational Pleas in Church Order?

For certainly if Christ has settled any form of Power in his Church he has done it for his Churches safety, and for the Benefit of every Member: Then he must needs be presumed to have made choice of that Government as should least Expose his People to Hazard, either from the fraud, or Arbitrary measures of particular Men. And it is as plain as day light, there is no Species of Government like a Democracy to attain this End. There is but about two steps from an Aristocracy, to a Monarchy, and from thence but one to a Tyranny; an able standing force, and an Ill-Nature, *Ipso facto,* turns an absolute Monarch into a Tyrant; this is obvious among the Roman *Caesars,* and through the World. And all these direful Transmutations are easier in Church affairs [from the different Qualities of things] than in Civil States. For what is it that cunning and learned Men can't make the World swallow as an Article of their Creed, if they are once invested with an Uncontrollable Power, and are to be the standing Orators to Mankind in matters of Faith and Obedience?

III

Puritanism and Capitalism

PURITANISM was largely a middle-class movement that had economic as well as political implications. In fact, some students—such as Max Weber and Ernst Troeltsch—have implied that Puritanism stimulated the growth of capitalism by breaking down certain medieval economic ideals, such as the limitation on usury. It is clear that the monastic and ascetic objectives of the medieval church were incompatible with the rise of the middle class and the gradual disintegration of feudalism, and hence the new class turned to Puritanism, which was much better suited to meet its needs.

There is little doubt that Puritanism was closer than medieval theory to the material goals and values of a growing middle class that was becoming prominent in England and Western Europe after the fifteenth century. While the Puritan never thought of his religion in economic terms, he did emphasize the fact that man could serve God not by withdrawing from the world, but rather by following an occupation or calling that served the world. The Puritan emphasis on industry and enterprise appealed to the middle class in a way that could not appeal to the peasantry or nobility. Although it is difficult to show a causal relationship between capitalism and Puritanism, it is probably safe to assert that both movements tended to move closer together because of the affinity and attraction of each toward the other. Undoubtedly Puritan and capitalist ideas went into the formation of the American doctrine of laissez-faire individualism a theory that was destined to have momentous repercussions for subsequent economic and social development.

In spite of the proximity of certain Puritan values to the rising capitalistic ethic, Puritanism was more medieval than modern in its economic theory and practice. The idea of unrestrained economic individualism would have seemed a dangerous notion to any self-respecting Puritan. The statute books and court records of seventeenth-century Massachusetts abound in examples of price and wage controls instituted by the government of the colony. The Puritans, furthermore, always looked upon wealth as a gift from God given in the form of a trust; and they emphasized not only the benefits that accrued from work and wealth, but also their duties and responsibilities. In 1639, for example, one of the richest merchants in the colony was fined by the General Court (the highest legislative body) for excessive profiteering, despite the fact that there was no statute against this practice. The Puritans could never separate religion and business, and they often reiterated the medieval conception of the "just price."

In the long run, however, the Puritan ethic, when divorced from its religious background, did serve to quicken and stimulate the spirit of capitalism. The limitations placed by the Puritans on the individual and the freedom of movement within society were subordinated as time went on in favor of the enterprising and driving individual who possessed the ability and ambition to rise through his own exertions. Thus it is paradoxical that seventeenth-century Puritanism, which was diametrically opposed to economic individualism, should have played a major part in the emergence of a laissez-faire capitalistic ethic.

(9)

John Winthrop

1588-1649

The following selection is taken from Winthrop's lay sermon, "A Modell of Christian Charity," delivered aboard the *Arbella* on the trip to New England in 1630. It illustrates the medieval nature of Puritan economic ideals. The text is from the *Winthrop Papers* (Boston: Massachusetts Historical Society, 1931), vol. II. [For Winthrop's career see pp. 35–36.]

God Almighty in his most holy and wise providence hath so disposed of the Condition of mankind, as in all times some must be rich some poor, some high and eminent in power and dignity; others mean and in subjection.

THE REASON HEREOF

1. Reas: *First,* to hold conformity with the rest of his works, being delighted to show forth the glory of his wisdom in the variety and difference of the Creatures and the glory of his power, in ordering all these differences for the preservation and good of the whole, and the glory of his greatness that

as it is the glory of princes to have many officers, so this great King will have many Stewards counting himself more honoured in dispensing his gifts to man by man, than if he did it by his own immediate hand.

2. Reas: *Secondly,* That he might have the more occasion to manifest the work of his Spirit: first, upon the wicked in moderating and restraining them: so that the rich and mighty should not eat up the poor, nor the poor, and despised rise up against their superiors, and shake off their yoke; secondly, in the regenerate in exercising his graces in them, as in the great ones, their love, mercy, gentleness, temperance etc., in the poor and inferiour sort, their faith, patience, obedience, etc:

3. Reas: *Thirdly,* That every man might have need of other, and from hence they might be all knit more nearly together in the Bond of brotherly affection: from hence it appears plainly that no man is made more honourable than another or more wealthy etc., out of any particular and singular respect to himself but for the glory of his Creator and the Common good of the Creature, Man; Therefore God still reserves the property of these gifts to himself as Ezek: 16. 17. he there calls wealth his gold and his silver etc. Prov: 3. 9. he claims their service as his due honour the Lord with thy riches etc. All men being thus (by divine providence) ranked into two sorts, rich and poor; under the first, are comprehended all such as are able to live comfortably by their own means duly improved; and all others are poor according to the former distribution. There are two rules whereby we are to walk one towards another: JUSTICE and MERCY. These are always distinguished in their Act and in their object, yet may they both concur in the same Subject in each respect; as sometimes there may be an occasion of showing mercy to a rich man, in some sudden danger of distress, and also doing of mere Justice to a poor man in regard of some particular contract etc. . . .

This Law of the Gospel propounds . . . a difference of seasons and occasions there is a time when a Christian must sell all and give to the poor as they did in the Apostles times. There is a time also when a Christian (though they give not all yet) must give beyond their ability, as they of Macedonia. Cor: 2. 6. likewise community of perils calls for extraordinary liberality and so doth Community in some special service for the Church. Lastly, when there is no other means whereby our Christian brother may be relieved in this distress, we must help him beyond our ability, rather then tempt God, in putting him upon help by miraculous or extraordinary means.

This duty of mercy is exercised in the kinds, Giving, lending, and forgiving.

Quest. What rule shall a man observe in giving in respect of the measure?

Ans. If the time and occasion be ordinary he is to give out of his abundance—let him lay aside, as God hath blessed him. If the time and occasion be extraordinary he must be ruled by them; taking this withall, that then a man cannot likely do too much especially, if he may leave himself and his family under probable means of comfortable subsistence.

Objection. A man must lay up for posterity, the fathers lay up for posterity and children and he is worse than an Infidel that provideth not for his own.

Ans. For the first, it is plain, that it being spoken by way of Comparison it must be meant of the ordinary and usual course of fathers and cannot extend to times and occasions extraordinary; for the other place the Apostle speaks against such as walked inordinately, and it is without question, that he is worse than an Infidel who through his own Sloth and voluptuousness shall neglect to provide for his family.

Objection. The wise mans Eyes are in his head (saith Solomon) and foreseeth the plague, therefore we must forecast and lay up against evil times when he or his may stand in need of all he can gather.

Ans. This very Argument Solomon useth to persuade to liberality. Eccle: [11. 1.] cast thy bread upon the waters etc.: for thou knowest not what evil may come upon the land Luke 16. make you friends of the riches of Iniquity; you will ask how this shall be? very well. for first he that gives to the poor lends to the lord, and he will repay him even in this life an hundred fold to him or his. The righteous is ever merciful and lendeth and his seed enjoyeth the blessing; and besides we know what advantage it will be to us in the day of account, when many such Witnesses shall stand forth for us to witness the improvement of our Talent. And I would know of those who plead so much for laying up for time to come, whether they hold that to be Gospel Math: 16. 19. Lay not up for yourselves Treasures upon Earth etc. if they acknowledge it what extent will they allow it; if only to those primitive times let them consider the reason whereupon our Saviour grounds it, the first is that they are subject to the moth, the rust, the Thief. Secondly, They will steal away the heart, where the treasure is there will the heart be also. The reasons are of like force at all times therefore the exhortation must be general and perpetual which [applies] always in respect of the love and affection to riches and in regard of the things themselves when any special service for the church or particular distress of our brother do call for the use of them; otherwise it is not only lawful but necessary to lay up as Joseph did to have ready upon such occasions, as the Lord (whose stewards we are of them) shall call for them from us: Christ gives us an Instance of the first, when he sent his disciples for the Ass, and bids them answer the owner thus, the Lord hath need of him; so when the Tabernacle was to be built his [servant] sends to his people to call for their silver and gold etc.; and yields them no other reason but that it was for his work, when Elisha comes to the widow of Sareptah and finds her preparing to make ready her pittance for herself and family, he bids her first provide for him, he challengeth first Gods part which she must first give before she must serve her own family, all these teach us that the Lord looks that when he is pleased to call for his right in any thing we have, our own Interest we have must stand aside, till his turn be served, for the other we need look no further than to that of John I. he who hath this worlds goods and seeth his brother to need, and shut up his

Compassion from him, how dwelleth the love of god in him, which comes punctually to this Conclusion: if thy brother be in want and thou canst help him, thou needst not make doubt, what thou shouldst do, if thou lovest God thou must help him.

Quest. What rule must we observe in lending?

Ans. Thou must observe whether thy brother hath present or probable, or possible means of repaying thee, if there be none of these, thou must give him according to his necessity, rather than lend him as he requires; if he hath present means of repaying thee, thou art to look at him, not as an Act of mercy, but by way of Commerce, wherein thou art to walk by the rule of Justice, but, if his means of repaying thee be only probable or possible then is he an object of thy mercy thou must lend him, though there be danger of losing it Deut: 15. 7. If any of thy brethren be poor etc. thou shalt lend him sufficient that men might not shift off this duty by the apparent hazard, he tells them that though the Year of Jubilee were at hand (when he must remit it, if he were not able to repay it before) yet he must lend him and that cheerfully: it may not grieve thee to give him (saith he) and because some might object, why so I should soon impoverish myself and my family, he adds with all thy Work etc. for our Saviour Math: 5. 42. From him that would borrow of thee turn not away.

Quest. What rule must we observe in forgiving?

Ans. Whether thou didst lend by way of Commerce or in mercy, if he have nothing to pay thee [thou] must forgive him (except in cause where thou hast a surety or a lawful pledge) Deut. 15. 2. Every seventh year the Creditor was to quit that which he lent to his brother if he were poor as appears ver: 8 [4]: save when there shall be no poor with thee. In all these and like Cases Christ was a general rule Math: 7. 22. Whatsoever ye would that men should do to you do ye the same to them also.

Quest. What rule must we observe and walk by in cause of Community of peril?

Ans. The same as before, but with more enlargement towards others and less respect towards our selves, and our own right hence it was that in the primitive Church they sold all had all things in Common, neither did any man say that that which he possessed was his own likewise in their return out of the Captivity, because the work was great for the restoring of the church and the danger of enemies was Common to all Nehemiah exhorts the Jews to liberality and readiness in remitting their debts to their brethren, and disposeth liberally of his own to such as wanted and stands not upon his own due, which he might have demanded of them, thus did some of our forefathers in times of persecution here in England, and so did many of the faithful in other Churches whereof we keep an honourable remembrance of them, and it is to be observed that both in Scriptures and latter stories of the Churches that such as have been most bountiful to the poor Saints especially in these extraordinary times and occasions God hath left them highly Commended to posterity. . . ,

(10)

Cotton Mather

1663-1728

The eldest son of Increase Mather and the grandson of Richard Mather and John Cotton—three of the most eminent ministers of Massachusetts—Cotton Mather, after his graduation from Harvard, became a leading exponent of Puritan orthodoxy at a time when the ideals of the original founders had entered a period of decline. While taking a leading role in the affairs of the community, he was also a prodigious writer, the author of more than 450 volumes during his lifetime. Although generally conservative and orthodox in his views, he was always torn between the demands of a new age and the ideals of an older one. Most of his time was spent in an effort to reassert and strengthen the religious foundations of Puritanism in the New World.

The following selections illustrate the religious basis of Puritan economic thought and its affinity to medieval ideas. They are taken from *Durable Riches* (Boston, 1695); the first is from "The True Cause of Loosing" and the second from "The True Way of Thriving."

1. The first Counsel proper for them that have met with Losses, is that which we have, Repeated in our Context here. Thus saith the Lord of Hosts, Consider your Ways. Consideration under our Losses, is as needful as ready a way, to the Sanctification of those Losses. And there are especially two things to be thereupon Considered.

First, When we have met with Losses, we are to Consider the Hand from whence those Losses come upon us. Briefly, We are to Consider the Hand of God in all our Losses. It was well Considered and Confessed, by the Holy Job, when he had Lost a fair Estate. . . . It is the Lord that has taken away. We shall be very Fretful under our Losses, if we are not very Thoughtful under them. . . . This is the First Rule for us under our Losses; Let us acknowledge a Wise, and a just God as the First Cause of all. It has been sometimes the Good Speech of a Good Man, I can take any thing well at the Hand of God. As for our Losses, they will all Prove well if we can Take them well. . . . Let us Consider, That when we Loose Wealth, we must Remember the Lord our God; for 'tis he who denies us the power of keeping our Wealth. Perhaps our Losses may rise from the Fraud or Force of our Enemies; but let us Consider, It was our God that let Loose those Devourers upon us. . . . 'Tis the Lord Almighty that Empties us, by all the Losses that come upon us. Mark what I say; A man will never be a Looser by any

67

of his Losses, except he be Impatient under them. Now, the best Antidote against Impatience is, to Consider, 'Tis the Will of God, that I should meet with such Losses as I do.

Secondly, When we have met with Losses, we are to Consider the Ground for which those Losses come. The God of Heaven sent one Wasting Plague after another upon the poor Jews, till at last they Lost all they had in the World; but then said He, in Ezek. 14. 23. Ye shall know that I have not without a Cause, done all that I have done in it, saith the Lord. Our Losses are usually the fruit and sign of Gods Quarrels. Ordinarily our God is managing of some Controversy with us, when He causes us to Loose those things that were Comfortable to us. . . . It would be a Profitable thing for us to Loose what is Comfortable, if we might be brought thereby to Mourn for, and to Turn from our Sins, and to Humble our selves before God, with a deep Repentance. . . .

Thirdly, Under our Losses we may do well to Consider, Whether our Unthankfulness and Unfruitfulness under our Enjoyments, have not given much of Reasonableness unto our Losses. All that we have, is but a Loan from the Great God unto us. Now, if we be so Unthankful, that we will not particularly and affectionately Recognize the Kindness of God unto us in such a Loan, it is not very Reasonable that we should come to have a Loss instead of a Loan? Is it famous Threatning of God, in Deut. 28, 47, 48. Because thou servest not the Lord thy God, with Joyfulness, and Gladness of Heart, for the Abundance of all things; therefore thou shalt Serve thine Enemies in Hunger and in Thirst, and in Nakedness, and in the want of all things. It seems, we come to the Want, and the Loss of our Former Abundance; Why? Because we do not Serve God with a due Thankfulness of Heart, in and for that Abundance. . . . Don't we know that as what we have, is the Gift of God, so it must be used for the Praise of God? Know we not, that our Corn, and Wine, and Oil, and Silver, and Gold, is to be Laid out only so as may be for the glory of God? If we don't know this, we shall know that He will Take it, and we must Loose it all. . . .

Fourthly, Under our Losses we may do well to Consider, How we Got what we have Lost. . . . Many a man has been such a Fool, as to augment his Riches in some ways of Dishonesty; he has either by Fraud or Force made himself a Master of Gold, whereto he had no Right, by that Golden Rule, Do as thou wouldest be done unto. . . . It is a Righteous Thing with God, That One Loss after another should snatch away from us, those Riches, whereat we have snatched more Greedily than Honestly. . . . Yea, There is many a Godly man, who through Ignorance, or Carelessness, never made a possible Restitution of Things unlawfully Obtained, if not by himself, yet by those that Left him what he has; and so a long Series of Losses is Entail'd upon him. Thus also, such as have once Broken, by their own Extravagancies, rather than by the Unavoidable Frowns of God upon them; and have after all, had more Fraudulence, than Fair-dealing, in their Compositions with their Creditors, do ordinarily so plunge themselves into further Losses, that (as we say) no Butter will ever stick upon their Bread afterwards. Yea, If any Thing have been Gotten by any Trade, offensive unto God; such a Trade, suppose, as that wherein by Strong Drink Sold unto our Indians, the Savages have been hastened unto Hell before their Time; 'tis well if it been't Lost, all in as little a while as it was Got; and it may be, that some Good men have made the Unwary and Unhappy Trial of it. . . .

Behold, a Duty of our Christian Conversation, which according to the Divine Heraldry of the Scripture, has a very High Place in Christianity belonging to it; a Duty than which there are not many, more Acceptable to God, more Profitable to Us, more Honourable to our Profession, or more Neglected and Omitted by multitudes, that will yet wear the Name which was begun at Antioch. And it is Remarkable to see, what a broad Contradiction is herein given to the Dictates of that Common and Carnal Reason, which mankind is generally misguided by. The Ordinary Notion of the World is, If I have Bread, my own Cupboard is the fittest place to keep it in. But the Holy Spirit of God will teach us otherwise, Cast thy Bread upon the Waters. The Customary Dialect of the World is, I'll keep what I have, because I know not what Evil I may Live to see, I may Live to want it all. But we are otherwise Advised by the Holy Spirit of God; Give a Portion, because thou knowest not what Evil may be upon the Earth. 'Tis the God of Heaven, to whom we are beholden, for our Estates; our Possessions and Enjoyments, by which we are furnished against the Natural Inconveniencies of Human Life, are all bestowed upon us, by that God, whose Providence disposeth of all our Affairs. . . . The Same Covenant in which we are to make a Surrender of our Spirits and our Bodies unto God, must by a parity of Reason also Devote our Estates unto Him; and All that we Have, as well as All that we Are, must come under a Dedication to the Lord. . . . It is therefore most highly Reasonable, That we should be at the Direction of the Eternal God, as to what we do with our Estates; esteeming our selves but Stewards of those Things, whereof our Neighbours call us the Owners, and preparing our selves for the Account which we must give of our Stewardship unto Him that is, The Lord of All. Now the Orders which our Lord has given us, about our Estates, are principally Two. The First, is in 1 Tim. 5. 8. If any provide not for his own, especially those of his own House, he hath Denied the Faith. Our Estates are in the first place, to Feed and Clothe and Cherish our own Families; and we may even Lay up for our Children a part thereof, if that may be done without the Defrauding of such other Objects as God has required us, as long as we live, to be helpful unto. But then there is Another part of our Estates, that must be Consecrated unto more Pious Uses. . . .

What are those Pious Uses, that a Proportion of our Estates must be

Devoted unto? And under these Four Heads may they be Enumerated, Paying, Lending, Giving, and Forgiving.

First, then, The Paying of our Duties, to the Public Charges of the Place in which we Live, is one of those Pious Uses, which our Estates are to be put unto. Something must be paid by us, for the support of the Government, and of the Ministry. . . .

But, Secondly, The Ready Lending of what may Assist those that want Means and Helps for their Trades, is likewise one of the Pious Uses which our Estates are to be placed in. . . .

And Thirdly, The Giving of what may supply the Necessities, and Relieve the Calamities of the Indigent, is among the Pious Uses of our Estates. It was the Speech of the Apostle, in 1 John 3. 17. Whoso has this Worlds Goods, and see his Brother has Need, and shutteth up his Bowels of Compassion from him, how dwelleth the Love of God in him? We must Give of our Goods to our Brethren, when they have a manifest Need thereof. . . .

But, Fourthly, 'Tis among the Pious Uses of our Estates for us, to Forgive a Debt, when the Hand of God has made the Borrower unable to Discharge it.

(11)

Jonathan Mitchell

1624-1668

A Harvard graduate, Mitchell was selected for the important and influential post of minister of the church at Cambridge. He played a leading role in the adoption of the "Half-Way Covenant" (1662), which was an attempt to meet the problems arising from the declining religious enthusiasm of the second generation. Among the first generation the prerequisite for church membership had been a personal religious experience, a test that their children often could not pass. But under the new covenant children of the adults who were not communicants could be baptized if their parents did not dissent from the doctrines of the church. The result, therefore, was that church membership was made easier.

The selection that follows is from an election sermon preached in 1667, and it demonstrates the broad welfare functions that the Puritans assigned to government. The text is from *Nehemiah on the Wall in Troublesom Times* (Cambridge, 1671).

Quest. 1. *What is that good, or welfare of the people, which Rulers ought to seek? or Wherein doth it consist?*

Answ. Take it in the Example of *Nehemiah,* the improvement whereof the Text leads us unto. . . .

1. Consisting in their *Safety;* that *Nehemiah* taketh care for in the first place (the preservation and safety of their persons and enjoyments, both Public and Personal, Religious and Civil). To that end he builds the Wall of *Jerusalem,* for their safety, that they might not be a prey unto, or reproach amongst their Adversaries, *Nehem.* 2. 17. This is fundamentally necessary to the welfare, or well-being of a people, they cannot possibly have *well-being,* without the *preservation* of their *Being,* both Personal and Political. When *Nehemiah* came to seek the welfare of the children of *Israel,* his great business was to build the Wall of *Jerusalem,* in which place their principal Concernments, both of Religion and Government, were laid up, *Psal.* 122. 3, 4, 5. That *Jerusalem* have a Wall for the safety and preservation of it, (and of what is contained in it) is requisite to the welfare of *Israel.*

2. Their *Honesty:* Rulers are to seek to maintain, cherish and preserve *Civil Honesty* amongst a people, by restraining and redressing Injuries between man and man, and other Crimes and Misdemeanours, by the Administration and Execution of Justice; by the free passage of *Righteousness,* which assigneth to every one his own; and of *Equity* also, abating the rigour and extremity of strict Justice, where need is. *Nehemiah* left an eminent Example of this, *Neh.* 5. 7–13. causing them to deal honestly, yea mercifully with their poor brethren, according as the distress of the time required, suppressing the biting *Usury* that was among them; he frees the oppressed from their oppressions, and taketh care that *Righteousness* and *Equity* may obtain amongst the people; this also is a part of his care for the good of *Israel.* That people may live together in *all honesty* as well as *godliness,* is the care and the benefit of good Rulers, 1 *Tim.* 2. 1, 2. and so that *Judgment* and *Justice* may be faithfully administered, which is a main *Basis* of the welfare of a people, and a main part of the work of Rulers, 1 *Kings* 10. 9. *Jer.* 22. 3, 15, 16. *Amos* 5. 24. 1 *Pet.* 2. 14.

3. Their *Prosperity,* in matters of outward Estate and Livelihood, by such help as the care of Government may contribute to that end. That we commonly call (*Wealth*) is a part of the wealth or welfare of a people, though not the greatest part, as the world is apt to esteem it. Good Rulers will gladly be a furtherance thereunto, what in them lies, that the *Commonwealth* may flourish and prosper in that respect, but especially in reference to necessary livelihood, when it is a time of distress and poverty, or special scarcity in this or that, of food or clothing: when the people are in a low condition (or many of them at least) wrestling with many and great difficulties, or in a dearth, *Chap.* 5. 3. how careful is *tender-hearted Nehemiah* of the people at such a time, *Nehem.* 5. he took great care that things might be so carried on, that *poor people* might be provided of *necessaries,* and be able to sustain their Families, that they might not perish in a time of dearth and scarcity, *vers.* 2, 3, &c. this was part of the good he did for the people. . . .

4. Let people be friends and *Helpers* to their own welfare; or every one

in your several places seek the common good of the whole. If Rulers are to *seek* the welfare of the people, then surely people themselves are not to *prejudice* or neglect their own welfare. The *Patient* must contribute Endeavours towards his own health, as well as the *Physician,* else there will be but little good done. It is the Rulers work eminently, as his Place is more eminent; but it is also the work of every one, according to the compass of his capacity and opportunity, to seek the welfare of the place and people, where & among whom he lives, *Jer.* 29. 7. So the Lord speaks to Captives in *Babylon,* during the time of Gods patience with it; much more doth that duty lie on those that dwell in *Zion,* to seek the good and the peace of the place, both by Prayer to God, and by all other due means within their power. Love thy Neighbour, much more a whole *Community,* a multitude of thy Neighbours, is the Lords charge to every one. A little more particularly.

1. Be sure (every particular person, I now speak to even them that are in private capacity) to do no *hurt* to *Israel,* (to the Lords people among whom you live) either *directly,* or *indirectly;* either wilfully or carelessly: that is just contrary to seeking the welfare of the place and people where you live; which is a Moral and great duty lying upon every Soul. Woe to that person, whosoever he be, that shall be a willing or blameable cause of hurt or harm to the *Lords people* here, whom he that toucheth will be found to touch the *Apple of his Eye, Psal.* 34. 21. When God called *Abraham* forth to follow him in a way of Reformation, he gave that word along with him, *Gen.* 12. 3. and so to *Jacob* or *Israel, Gen.* 27. 29. and he did and will make it good. If you love your Souls, take heed of touching *Israel* to their hurt: yea even words that tend to the reproach or prejudice of the people of God, or Builders in *Jerusalem,* is not a small matter, *Neh.* 4. 2, 3, 4, 5. (such *Imprecations* tell us, what will be the portion of such except they repent, though not that ordinary and private Spirits should be forward to with that it might be so to particular persons) *They have provoked anger* (*Thee* is not in the Hebrew) irritated and raised spirits (by their Scoffs and Reproaches) *before,* or in respect of *the Builders.* The words may carry that meaning.

2. Think it not enough to do *no hurt,* but according to your place and opportunity do *good* to *Israel,* to that part of it in special in which the Lord hath cast you. Be willing to put forth thy self for the public good according to thy *Talent.* Hast thou Estate which the Lord hath blessed thee with, (and gotten, it may be, here under the shadow of the Government?) let not the Public suffer for want, when as thou hast it by thee. Hast thou Ability to serve the Country any other way? be ready thereunto: Do not only *pray,* but put forth *endeavours* according to capacity and opportunity for the peace and good of *Jerusalem;* else you do but dally in praying, if you will do nothing for it, *Psal.* 122. 9. Seek it in the use of all due means. A *public* Spirit even in a *private* person is a precious thing; *i.e.* according to the compass of his place to be ready to do for the common good. Could the Heathen (the *Romans* and others) produce such Sayings as these; *That man was not born for himself, but for his Country; That even to die for it is sweet: Dulce &*

decorum pro Patria mori; and boast of those among them that practised accordingly: and shall Christians be strangers to such a Public Spirit, or be backward to act for the common welfare. Here in *Nehemiahs* time every one set his hand to, to build up the Wall of *Jerusalem,* and the *particular* persons and companies that did their parts therein, are to their honour *recorded* in the holy story, *Neh.* 3. Oh that is a pleasant sight, to see all sorts contributing to the Safety, Peace, Welfare of *Jerusalem,* and joining *Hearts* and *Hands* therein, *Neh.* 4. 6. Oh! have you a mind to *build* or to save the Wall and Welfare of *Jerusalem?* Are you *cheerful, cordial, forward, industrious* therein? not a man to *talk* only, but to *work* when the case requires it. . . .

IV

Reason and Science
in Puritan Thought

THE POPULAR IMAGE of the Puritan is often that of a narrow-minded individual whose preoccupation with religion served to limit his intellectual
horizons and make him an enemy of any form of liberalism in learning. Yet
in studying the Puritan attitude toward two intellectual disciplines, education
and science, a paradox emerges—namely, that Puritanism resulted in
the raising of the intellectual level of New England to much greater heights
than existed in the middle or southern colonies. In the midst of a primitive
environment, the hardy pioneers of Massachusetts had by 1636 provided for
the establishment of a college and a short time later passed the first public
compulsory educational law in American history. Nor were the Puritans in
any way opposed to the new scientific discoveries that were slowly bringing
about a revolution in European thought. On the contrary, they were highly
receptive to and interested in the new scientific theories of their day.

In the case of the Puritans, religion undoubtedly worked as a stimulant
to intellectual ferment. Although emotion played a role in their theology, the
Puritans emphasized above all that man, though he might be an evil creature,
was also a rational and intelligent one. Since God was intelligible (up to a
point), true knowledge would help rather than hinder man's understanding
of His works and purposes. Ignorance was something to be feared, and thus
the Puritans not only demanded an educated and literate clergy, but they
also made provision for the general uplifting of the mass of the people. The
famous law of 1647, for example, required that every town in the colony
containing fifty families appoint a schoolmaster to teach the children to read
and write, and that every town of 100 or more was to make provision for
a grammar school to prepare youths for the college. In their curriculum,
furthermore, the emphasis was not solely on religion, for the classical and
humanistic standards of the English universities were taken as model examples.

Similarly, Puritanism acted as a stimulus rather than a barrier to the

74

acceptance of new scientific discoveries. No less then eleven New Englanders were elected to membership by the Royal Society of London, the greatest English scientific body, as compared with only one from South Carolina and three each from Virginia and Pennsylvania. To the Puritans the natural world was God's creation in operation, and they felt that an understanding of this world would serve as an invaluable aid in discerning divine intentions. In general, their attitude toward science was typical of European thought. When the Puritans looked upon comets as portents of things to come, they were simply echoing a belief dating from antiquity, and when they held that comets operated according to natural law, they were expressing their belief in the new astronomical theories. Similarly, the Puritans were interested in witchcraft from a scientific point of view, for this phenomenon, in their eyes —and in the eyes of most Englishmen and Europeans—was a fact that could be empirically verified. The tragic Salem witchcraft trials in 1692 were simply a feature of the age and cannot be attributed to Puritan theology or practice. Finally, such an eminent Puritan divine as Cotton Mather could champion inoculation for smallpox; the clinical treatise on inoculation communicated in 1721 to the Royal Society of London (and published in their transactions)— a landmark in medical history—was, in fact, based on Boston's experience in inoculation against smallpox.

The record left by the Puritans in their educational and scientific strivings thus established a significant precedent for later generations. Although their individual contributions were relatively insignificant, they did provide for an institutional and intellectual framework that proved vital to scholarship in the New World.

(12)

Charles Chauncy
1592(?)-1671/2

A leading Puritan intellectual, Charles Chauncy migrated to New England in 1638, after having been involved in difficulties arising from his opposition to some of Archbishop Laud's regulations in England. His ideas on baptism made him somewhat unwelcome to the more orthodox; and, although he accepted the presidency of Harvard College in 1654, it was with the stipulation that he refrain from disseminating his views on this subject. Continuing in that position until his death, he seems to have been eminently successful in his career as a college president because of his acknowledged erudition.

The following selection is from *Gods Mercy, Shewed to His People*

*in Giving Them a Faithful Ministry and Schooles of Learning for the
Continual Supplyes Thereof* (Cambridge, 1655), a commencement sermon defending a liberal education.

. . . Schools of learning are approved and appointed of God, and
of great importance for the benefit of Gods people: Seeing that the Lord
works with, & blesseth this means, for the laying up of provision, & making
of supplies for the work of the ministry; and the Lord here reckons it up
as the chiefest of all the blessings mentioned: and this was always one way
(even when there were extraordinary Prophets) of raising up of Prophets
&c: And there is much more need of schools now, when those extraordinary
Prophets are wanting.

Quest: What ground is there in the Scriptures, for Schools of learning?

Answ: Give me leave to show this as a matter called by many into question
in these days. Now the Text, and the explication thereof before shows that the
Lord did approve of them in the days of the old Testament, that is the intent of
the frequent mentioning of the sons of the Prophets, that is their scholars that
were trained up under them: besides 2 *Kings* 22. 14. There is mention of a
College (where *Huldah* the Prophetess, and no doubt many others nurtured
in a way of learning lived,) and the Hebrews have an usual word where by
they call their schools (*yeshibah*) a company of scholars that sit together
to be taught. . . . But the example of our Saviour Christ is above all, that
kept a school, first of his twelve disciples, then of the seventy disciples *Luke*
10 that he also sent forth to preach the Gospel. Yea there is a most clear and
express Commandment, that Paul gives to Timothy 2 *Tim:* 2. 2. he saith *the
things that thou hast heard of me before many witnesses, the same commit to
faithful men, who shall be able to teach others also.* Where we see that
Timothy had many school fellows that are called witnesses, and also that
Timothy is commanded to teach others, so it concerns such as God enables
to teach them that may be teachers of others, to instruct them in the things
of God.

But now it will be very needful upon this occasion for us to consider what
weight there is in the objections that diverse in these days have printed
against them.

Object. 1. Mr. Dell in his answer to *Mr. S. Simpson* allows schools of
the prophets wherein Christian religion is taught, *but against schools of
humane learning this is that that makes them Antichrists, seeing they are
contrary to, and do oppose Christ, this makes the universities stews of Antichrist, houses of lies, and to stink before God with most loathsome abomination &c:* with a multitude of other reproachful terms which Luther & others
have loaded Popish Universities withall.

Answ. 1. I do much desire that the opposers of schools & universities would speak plainly what they mean by humane learning, then we should easily come to some conclusion. Therefore let this distinction be premised, that humane learning may either be taken for all that learning that the heathen Authors or philosophers have delivered in their writings: or else all other Arts besides Theology, as they call *physics, ethics, politics &c:* take in also the grounds of language, *Latin Greek & Hebrew.* Now in the former sense, if *Mr. D.* do mean by humane learning, all that learning that the heathen men have uttered out of the light of nature: It will be a great oversight to pass such a sentence upon it. 1. Because we find in Scriptures, some testimonies out of humane writers, as *Tit:* 1. 12. *Acts* 17. 28. 1 *Cor:* 15. 33. &c: which the Spirit of God would not have alleged, if their writings had been utterly unlawful to read. 2. There are certain principles of truth written, even in corrupt nature, which heathen authors have delivered unto us, that do not cross the holy writ, 1 *Cor:* 11. 14. *doth not nature it self teach you &c:* and it cannot be denied that all truth, whosoever it be that speaks it, comes from the God of truth, as he is called several times. And who can deny but that there are found many excellent & divine moral truths in *Plato, Aristotle, Plutarch, Seneca &c:* and to condemn all pell-mell, will be an hard censure, especially to call universities Antichrists for reading of them. Besides they have treated of the works of God, most excellently in many places, and the works of God ought to be *declared by parents to their children, Psal.* 78. 2–6. Besides they have delivered many excellent sayings of God, and have attested many Scripture histories, as might be showed by several instances, out of *Justine, Tacitus &c:* and *Mr. D.* is not ignorant of them, shall all these be thrown away as antiChristian, or as lies?

Object. But they have much profaneness and filthiness in them, and besides they are made idols of in our universities, when as *ipse dixit,* and their authority goeth for current, as Scripture it self amongst them.

Answ. But 1. All heathenish writers, have not such profaneness in them. 2. Those that have, let them be condemned & abhorred, & let not youth be poisoned by them. 3. Let God be true & every man a liar, and let not man, especially any heathen be deified, or his authority be accounted on, or go cheek by jowl with the speaking in the Scriptures: this is indeed to be abhored wheresoever it is received, but *abusus non tollit usum.*

II. But now if humane learning be taken in the second sense, for all those Arts that are commonly taught in Universities, as *Physics, Ethics, Politics, Oeconomics, Rhetoric, Astronomy &c:* or also for learned tongues of *Latin, Greek, and Hebrew &c:*

1. I will be bold to affirm, that these in the true sense and right meaning thereof are Theological & Scripture learning, and are not to be accounted of as humane learning. For who can deny, that the first and second chapters of *Genesis,* and many chapters in *Job,* and the *Psalms,* and diverse other places of holy Scripture, do afford excellent and sure grounds for natural Philosophy, and a just system thereof: which *Mr. Zanchy, Daneus,* and diverse other eminent Divines have opened & declared unto us? And where are there to be

found such *Ethical, Political,* or *Moral* precepts, as are to be found in holy Scriptures? or such principles for the ordering of our lives, families, or common weals? let any man declare it unto us. And where are there such high strains of all sorts of *Rhetorical Tropes, & figures,* to be found in any Author, as there are in the writings of the *Prophets & Apostles?* and who can imagine, but that the best & surest Chronology in the world, is to be found in holy Scriptures, upon which all the computation of times in all ages in the world depends? . . .

Object: But there is no necessity of Schools or Universities, or any humane learning to teach men Divinity, or to make able preachers of the Gospel: the teaching of the Spirit of God alone is sufficient: which Mr. Dell proves by the examples of our Saviour Christ & his Apostles, seeing Christ himself had only the unction of the Spirit. Isay 61. 1–4. Luke 4. Mat: 13. 54, 55. *Besides when he would send forth preachers into all the world, he chose Fishermen, Publican, Tent makers, plain men, and of ordinary employment in the world, and only put his Spirit upon them* Acts 2. 17. *This argument is much stood upon* by Mr. Horne, & Mr. Crandon *against* M. Baxter.

Answ. 1. It is a marvelous mistake to reason from our Saviour Christ & his Apostles to these times: For our Saviour received the Spirit not by measure *John* 3. 24. and the Apostles had the miraculous & visible extraordinary gifts of the Spirit bestowed on them *Acts* 2. So the reason will stand thus. If our Saviour Christ and his Apostles, without other learning, by the miraculous and extraordinary gifts of the Spirit, were enabled and furnished sufficiently for the ministry; Then other ministers in after times (that have no such extraordinary gifts) need no other learning, but the unction of the Spirit, as if he should say, if Aholiab & Bezaleel were filled with the Spirit of God in wisdom, and in knowledge, and all manner of workmanship, to devise cunning works, (as they were *Exod.* 31. 3, 4.) then no man need to be an apprentice to learn any Mechanical trade, seeing the teaching of the Spirit is sufficient for any cunning work, who is there that would not account this reasoning ridiculous? Surely if Mr. D. had not excluded Logic & reason out of Divinity he would never have made such collections: It is much like his reasoning in an other Sermon of his, the Scripture saith that Christ shall Baptise with the holy Ghost, & with fire, therefore there is no baptism with water to be used, or to be in force. But forsooth what ever he saith, ye must expect no reason from him, ye must take all from him as dictates of the Spirit, and so all Ordinances in the Church that the Spirit hath appointed, the Spirit shall also overthrow, yea I know no reason why Mr. Dell, or any other believer, upon this ground, may not make an other Scripture, for if the same Spirit that indighted or penned the Scripture, be in the same or the like measure in Mr. Dell or other believers, as it was in the holy men of God and penmen of the Scripture, then what Mr. D. and any other believers write or say, is of equal authority with the Canonical Scriptures. So Mr. Dell and every believer is made a Pope, that can not err &c: but here I will stop & spare.

(13)

New Englands
First Fruits

> *New Englands First Fruits,* published initially in London in 1643, described conditions in New England in an attempt to raise additional funds. It provides a clear indication that the Puritans were not interested in learning simply as an adjunct to religion, but also viewed it as a means of perpetuating and advancing all knowledge. The second part, reprinted below, "In Respect of the College, and the Proceedings of Learning Therein," was probably written by Henry Dunster, the president of Harvard for fourteen years. The text is from *New Englands First Fruits* (London, 1643).

NEW ENGLANDS FIRST FRUITS

I. In Respect of the College, and the Proceedings of
Learning *Therein*

After God had carried us safe to New England, and we had builded our houses, provided necessaries for our livelihood, rear'd convenient places for Gods worship, and settled the Civil Government: One of the next things we longed for, and looked after was to advance Learning and perpetuate it to Posterity; dreading to leave an illiterate Ministry to the Churches, when our present Ministers shall lie in the Dust. And as we were thinking and consulting how to effect this great Work; it pleased God to stir up the heart of one Mr. Harvard (a godly Gentleman, and a lover of Learning, there living amongst us) to give the one half of his Estate (it being in all about 1700£ towards the erecting of a College: and all his Library: after him another gave 300£, others after them cast in more, and the public hand of the State added the rest: the College was, by common consent, appointed to be at Cambridge (a place very pleasant and accomodate) and is called (according to the name of the first founder) Harvard College.

The Edifice is very fair and comely within and without, having in it a spacious Hall; (where they daily meet at Common Lectures) Exercises, and a large Library with some Books to it, the gift of diverse of our friends, their Chambers and studies also fitted for, and possessed by the Students, and all other rooms of Office necessary and convenient, with all needful Offices thereto belonging: And by the side of the College a fair Grammar School, for

the training up of young Scholars, and fitting of them for Academical Learning, that still as they are judged ripe, they may be received into the College
of this School: Master Corlet is the Mr., who hath very well approved himself
for his abilities, dexterity and painfulness in teaching and education of the
youth under him.

Over the College is master Dunster placed, as President, a learned
conscionable and industrious man, who hath so trained up, his Pupils in the
tongues and Arts, and so seasoned them with the principles of Divinity and
Christianity, that we have to our great comfort, (and in truth) beyond our
hopes, beheld their progress in Learning and godliness also; the former of
these hath appeared in their public declamations in Latin and Greek, and
Disputations Logical and Philosophical, which they have been wonted (besides
their ordinary Exercises in the College-Hall) in the audience of the Magistrates, Ministers, and other Scholars, for the probation of their growth in
Learning, upon set days, constantly once every month to make and uphold:
The latter hath been manifested in sundry of them, by the savory breathings
of their Spirits in their godly conversation. Insomuch that we are confident,
if these early blossoms may be cherished and warmed with the influence of
the friends of Learning, and lovers of this pious work, they will by the help
of God, come to happy maturity in a short time.

Over the College are twelve Overseers chosen by the general Court, six
of them are of the Magistrates, the other six of the Ministers, who are to
promote the best good of it and (having a power of influence into all persons
in it) are to see that every one be diligent and proficient in his proper place.

2. Rules, and Precepts That Are Observed in the College

1. When any Scholar is able to understand Tully, or such like classical
Latin Author *extempore,* and make and speak true Latin in Verse and Prose,
suo ut aiunt Marte; And decline perfectly the Paradigm's of Nouns and Verbs
in the Greek tongue: Let him then and not before be capable of admission
into the College.

2. Let every Student be plainly instructed, and earnestly pressed to
consider well, the main end of his life and studies is, to know God and
Jesus Christ which is eternal life, Joh. 17. 3. and therefore to lay Christ in
the bottom, as the only foundation of all sound knowledge and Learning.

And seeing the Lord only giveth wisdom, Let every one seriously set
himself by prayer in secret to seek it of him Prov. 2. 3.

3. Every one shall so exercise himself in reading the Scriptures twice a
day, that he shall be ready to give such an account of his proficiency therein,
both in Theoretical observations of the Language, and Logic, and in Practical
and spiritual truths, as his Tutor shall require, according to his ability; seeing
the entrance of the word giveth light, it giveth understanding to the simple,
Psalm. 119. 130.

4. That they eschewing all profanation of Gods Name, Attributes, Word,

Ordinances, and times of Worship, do study with good conscience, carefully to retain God, and the love of his truth in their minds, else let them know, that (notwithstanding their Learning) God may give them up to strong delusions, and in the end to a reprobate mind, 2 Thes. 2. 11, 12. Rom. 1. 28.

5. That they studiously redeem the time; observe the general hours appointed for all the Students, and the special hours for their own Classes: and then diligently attend the Lectures, without any disturbance by word or gesture. And if in any thing they doubt, they shall inquire, as of their fellows, so, (in case of Non satisfaction) modestly of their Tutors.

6. None shall under any pretence whatsoever, frequent the company and society of such men as lead an unfit, and dissolute life.

· Nor shall any without his Tutors leave, or (in his absence) the call of Parents or Guardians, go abroad to other Towns.

7. Every Scholar shall be present in his Tutors chamber at the 7th hour in the morning, immediately after the sound of the Bell at his opening the Scripture and prayer, so also at the 5th hour at night, and then give account of his own private reading, as aforesaid in Particular the third, and constantly attend Lectures in the Hall at the hours appointed? But if any (without necessary impediment) shall absent himself from prayer or Lectures, he shall be liable to Admonition, if he offend above once a week.

8. If any Scholar shall be found to transgress any of the Laws of God, or the School, after twice Admonition, he shall be liable, if not *adultus,* to correction, if *adultus,* his name shall be given up to the Overseers of the College, that he may be admonished at the public monthly Act.

3. The Times and Order of Their Studies, Unless Experience Shall Show Cause to Alter

The second and third day of the week, read Lectures, as followeth.

To the first year at 8th of the clock in the morning Logic, the first three quarters, Physics the last quarter.

To the second year, at the 9th hour, Ethics and Politics, at convenient distances of time.

To the third year at the 10th Arithmetic and Geometry, the three first quarters, Astronomy the last.

Afternoon

The first year dispute at the second hour.
The 2d year at the 3d hour.
The 3d year at the 4th every one in his Art.

The 4th day reads Greek.

To the first year the Etymology and Syntax at the eighth hour.
To the 2d at the 9th hour, Prosodia and Dialects.

Afternoon

The first year at 2d hour practice the precepts of Grammar in such Authors as have variety of words.

The 2d year at 3d hour practice in Poësy, Nonnus, Duport, or the like.

The 3d year perfect their Theory before noon, and exercise Style, Composition, Imitation, Epitome, both in Prose and Verse, afternoon.

The fifth day reads Hebrew, and the Eastern Tongues.

Grammar to the first year hour the 8th.

To the 2d Chaldee at the 9th hour.

To the 3d Syriack at the 10th hour.

Afternoon

The first year practice in the Bible at the 2d hour.

The 2d in Ezra and Danel at the 3d hour.

The 3d at the 4th hour in Trostius New Testament.

The 6th day reads Rhetorick to all at the 8th hour.

Declamations at the 9th. So ordered that every Scholar may declaim once a month. The rest of the day *vacat Rhetoricis studiis.* The 7th day reads Divinity Catechetical at the 8th hour, Common places at the 9th hour.

Afternoon

The first hour reads history in the Winter,

The nature of plants in the Summer

The sum of every Lecture shall be examined, before the new Lecture be read.

Every Scholar, that on proof is found able to read the Originals of the Old and New Testament into the Latin tongue, and to resolve them Logically; withall being of godly life and conversation; And at any public Act hath the Approbation of the Overseers and Master of the College, is fit to be dignified with his first Degree.

Every Scholar that giveth up in writing a System, or Synopsis, or sum of Logic, Natural and Moral Philosophy, Arithmetic, Geometry and Astronomy: and is ready to defend his Theses or positions: withall skilled in the Originals as abovesaid: and of godly life & conversation: and so approved by the Overseers and Master of the College, at any public Act, is fit to be dignified with his 2d Degree.

4. *The Manner of the Late Commencement, Expressed in a Letter Sent Over from the Governour, and Diverse of the Ministers, Their Own Words These*

The Students of the first Classes that have been these four years trained up in University-Learning (for their ripening in the knowledge of the Tongues, and Arts) and are approved for their manner—as they have kept their public Acts in former years, ourselves being present, at them; so have they lately kept two solemn Acts for their Commencement, when the Governour, Magistrates, and the Ministers from all parts, with all sorts of Scholars, and others in great numbers were present, and did bear their Exercises; which were Latin and Greek Orations, and Declamations, and Hebrew Analysis, Gramatical, Logical & Rhetorical of the Psalms: And their Answers and Disputations in Logical, Ethical, Physical and Metaphysical Questions; and so were found worthy of the first degree, (commonly called Bachelor) *pro more Academiarum in Anglia:* Being first presented by the President to the Magistrates and Ministers, and by him, upon their Approbation, solemnly admitted unto the same degree, and by a Book of Arts delivered into each of their hands, and power given them to read Lectures in the Hall upon any of the Arts, when they shall be thereunto called, and a liberty of studying in the Library.

All things in the College are at present, like to proceed even as we can wish, may it but please the Lord to go on with his blessing in Christ, and stir up the hearts of his faithful, and able Servants in our own Native Country, and here, (as he hath graciously begun) to advance this Honourable and most hopeful work. The beginnings whereof and progress hitherto (generally) do fill our hearts with comfort, and raise them up to much more expectation, of the Lords goodness for hereafter, for the good of posterity, and the Churches of Christ Jesus.

> BOSTON in New-England,
> September the 26.
> 1642

Your very loving
friends, &c.

(14)

Cotton Mather

1663-1728

Both of the following selections illustrate the modern as well as the medieval elements in Puritan scientific thought. The first is from *The Christian Philosopher: A Collection of the Best Discoveries in Nature, With Religious Improvements* (London, 1721), and the second from "The Angel of Bethesda," written in the early 1720's but never published. The text of the latter is taken from Otho T. Beall, Jr., and

Richard H. Shryock, "Cotton Mather: First Significant Figure in American Medicine," American Antiquarian Society, *Proceedings,* vol. 63 (April, 1953). [For Mather's career see p. 67.]

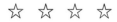

ESSAY XVI
Of the Thunder *and* Lightning

HIS *powerful Thunder, who can understand?* Yet our Philosophy will a little try to see and say something of it.

The Account of *Thunder,* given by Dr. *Hook,* is this. The Atmosphere of the Earth abounds with *nitrous Particles* of a spirituous nature, which are every where carried along with it. Besides which sort of Particles, there are also others raised up into the *Air,* which may be somewhat of the Nature of *sulphurous,* and *unctious,* and other combustible Bodies. We see Spirit of *Wine,* of *Turpentine,* of *Camphor,* and almost all other combustible Bodies, will by *Heat* be rarified into the Form of *Air,* or *Smoke,* and be raised up into the Air. All these, if they have a sufficient Degree of *Heat,* will catch *Fire,* and be turned into *Flame,* from the nitrous Parts of the Air mixing with them; as it has been proved by Thousands of Experiments. There are also other sorts of such Steams, that arise from *subterraneous* and *mineral* Bodies; which only by their coming to mix with the *Nitre* of the Air, though they have no sensible *Heat* in them, will so ferment and act upon one another, as to produce an actual *Flame.* Of this, the *Mines* are too frequent Witnesses and Sufferers. The *Lightning* seems to be very much of such an Original.

Dr. *Wallis* observes, That *Thunder* and *Lightning* have so much resemblance to *fired Gunpowder* in their *Effects,* that we may very well suppose much of the same *Causes.* The principal Ingredients in *Gunpowder,* are *Nitre* and *Sulphur.* Suppose in the Air, a convenient Mixture of *nitrous* and *sulphurous* Vapors, and those to take *fire* by accident, such an *Explosion,* and with such *Noise* and *Light* as that in the firing of *Gunpowder,* may well follow upon it; and being once kindled, it will run from place to place, as the Vapor leads it, like as in a Train of *Gunpowder.* This Explosion, high in the Air, and far from us, will do no considerable mischief. But, if it be very near us, it has terrible Consequences. The Distance of its *Place* may be estimated by the Distance of the *Time,* which there is between seeing the *Flash,* and hearing the *Clap:* For though in their Generation they be simultaneous, yet *Light* moving faster than *Sound,* they come successively to us. That there is a *nitrous* Vapor in it, we may reasonably judge, because we know of no other Body so liable to so sudden and furious Explosion. That there is a *sulphurous* one, is manifest from the Smell that attends it, and the sultry Heat, that is commonly a Forerunner of it.

The *natural Causes* of the *Thunder* do not at all release me from considering the *Interest* and *Providence* of the Glorious GOD, concerned in it.

It is a Note prepared for the Songs of the Faithful, *The* GOD *of Glory thundereth.* It is He, who

Fulmina molitur dextra, quo maxima motu
Terra tremit, fugere Ferae, & mortalia Corda
Per Gentes humilis stravit Pavor.[1]

And indeed, as the *Thunder* has in it the *Voice of* God, . . . thus there are several Points of *Piety,* wherein I am, as with a *Bath Kol,* instructed from it.

There is this *Voice* most sensibly to be heard in the *Thunder, Power belongeth unto God.* There is nothing able to stand before those *Lightnings,* which are styled the *Arrows of God.* We see Castles fall, Metal melt, Bricks themselves vitrify; all flies, when *hot Thunderbolts* are scattered upon them. The very *Mountains* are torn to pieces, when—*Feriunt summos sua Fulmina Montes* [His lightning bolts strike the tops of the mountains]. It becomes me now to say, *The Thunder of his Power who can understand?* An haughty Emperor shrinks, and shakes, and hides his guilty Head, before the powerful *Thunder* of God.

How can I hear the *Voice* of the *Almighty Thunderer,* without such Thoughts as these? *Glorious God, let me, through the Blood of a sacrificed Saviour, be in good Terms with One so able to destroy me in a moment!* And, let me be afraid of offending Him, who is possessed of such an *irresistible Artillery!*

At the same time, do I not see the *Mercy* and *Patience* of a Good God to a sinful World? The Desolations of the World, how wonderfully would they be,

Si quoties peccant Homines sua Fulmina mittat [If whenever men sin, He were to send his lightnings]! It is no rare thing for the Children of Men to die by a *Thunderbolt;* A *King* has been so slain in the midst of his Army. There was a Punishment of old used upon Criminals, by pouring hot Lead into their Mouths, which was called *Combustio Animae* [burning of the soul], and used in imitation of God's destroying Men with *Lightning;* whereby the *inward* Parts are burnt without any visible Touch upon the *outward.* This *Combustio Animae,* a Death by *Lightning,* has been frequently inflicted. Their being *asleep* at the time has not preserved them, though there be a Fancy in *Plutarch* that it would; nor would a Tent of *Seal-Skin* have done it, though some great ones have repaired unto such an *Amulet* for their Protection. *My God, I adore thy Sovereign Grace, that such a Sinner as I have not yet been by Lightning turned into Dust and Ashes before thee!*

I take notice of one thing, That as Guilt lying on the Minds of Men, makes them startle at a *Thunder-Clap.* . . . So the Miscarriages about which our Hearts do first and most of all misgive us in a *Thunder-Storm,* are those which most of all call for a *thorough Repentance* with us. There are some

---

1. [He wields the thunderbolts in his right hand, by which motion the mighty earth trembles, while beasts run away, and lowly trembling has laid low mortal hearts among the nations in the world.]

Writings which I cannot read, except I hold them against the Fire; by having my Heart held up against the *Lightning,* I may quickly read *my own Iniquity.*

Impious People are *deaf to Thunder!*

Herlicius, in his *Tractatus de Fulmine,* reckons up a considerable number of those, which might be called *Faelicia Fulmina.* Such will they be that make these Impressions upon us.

There has been a wonderful Practice lately used in several Parts of the World, which indeed is not yet become common in our Nation.

I was first instructed in it, by a Guarantee-servant of my own, long before I knew that any Europeans or Asiatics had the least Acquaintance with it, and some Years before I was enriched with the Communications of the learned Foreigners, whose Accounts I found agreeing with what I received of my Servant, when he showed me the Scar of the Wound made for the Operation; and said, that no Person ever died of the Small-Pox, in their Country that had the Courage to use it.

I have since met with a considerable Number of these Africans, who all agree in one Story; that in their Country grandy—many die of the Small-Pox; but now they learn this Way: People take Juice of Small-Pox, and Cutty-Skin, and put in a Drop; then bye'nd bye a little sicky, sicky; then very few little Things like Small-Pox; and no body die of it; and no body have Small-Pox any more. Thus in Africa, where the poor Creatures die of the Small-Pox like rotten Sheep, a Merciful God has taught them an infallible Preservative. 'Tis a common Practice, and is attended with a constant Success.

But our Advice of this Matter, as it comes from Superior Persons in the Levant, is what may have most Attention given to it.

Our first Communication comes from Dr. Emanuel Timonius R.S.S. who writes from Constantinople, in December, 1713. To this Effect.

The Practice of procuring the Small-Pox, by a Sort of Inoculation, has been introduced among the Constantinopolitans, by the Circassions and Georgians, and other Asiatics; for about forty Years.

At the first, People were cautious and afraid. But the happy Success on thousands of Persons for eight years now past, has put it out of all Suspicion. The Operation has been performed on Persons of all Ages, both Sexes, differing Temperaments, and even in the worst Constitution of the Air; and none that have used it ever died of the Small-Pox; tho' at the same Time, it were so malignant, that at least half the People died, that were affected with it in the common Way.

They that have this Inoculation practiced on them (he says) are subject unto very slight Symptoms, and hardly sensible of any Sickness; nor do what Small-Pox they have, ever leave any Scars or Pits behind them.

They make Choice of as healthy a young Person as they can find, that has the Small-Pox of the best Sort upon him; on the twelfth or thirteenth Day of his Decumibiture. With a Needle they prick some of the larger Pustules and press out the Matter coming from them into some convenient Vessel of Glass (or the like) to receive it; which ought first of all to be washed very clean with warm Water. A convenient Quantity of this Matter being thus collected, is to be stop'd close, and kept warm, in the Bosom of the Person that carries it (who ought rather to be some other Person than what visited the sick Chamber for it, lest the Infection of the Small-Pox be convey'd in the Garment as well as in the Bottle, and the intended Operation be hurt by the Infection being first convey'd another Way,) and so it should be convey'd as soon as may be, to the Person that is waiting to be the Patient.

The Patient being in a warm Chamber, is to have several small Wounds made with a Surgeons three-edged Needle, or with a Lancet, in two or more Places of the Skin; (the best Places are in the Muscles of the Arm:) till some Drops of Blood follow: and immediately let there be dropt out a Drop of the Matter in the Glass, on each of the Places; and mixed well with the Blood that is issuing out. The Wound should be covered with half a Walnut-Shell, or any such concave Vessel, and bound over, that the Matter may not be rubbed off by the Garments, for a few Hours. And now, let the Patient (having Fillets on the Wounds) keep House, and keep warm, and be careful of his Diet. The Custom at Constantinople is to abstain from Flesh and Broth, for twenty Days or more.

They choose to perform the Operation, either in the Beginning of the Winter, or the Spring.

The Small-Pox begins to appear sooner in some than in others, and with lesser Symptoms in some than in others: but, with happy Success in all. Commonly ten or twenty Pustules break out: here and there one has no more than two or three; few have an Hundred. There are some in whom no Pustule rises, but in the Places where the Incision was made, and here the Tubercles will be purulent. Yet even these, have never had the Small-Pox afterwards, tho' they have cohabited with Persons having of it. No small Quantity of Matter will run out for several Days, from the Places of the Incision. The Pocks arising from this Operation, are dried up in a short Time, and fall off; partly in thin skins, and partly vanishing by an insensible Wasting.

The Matter is hardly so thick a Pus, as in the common Small-Pox; but a thinner Kind of Sanies; whence it rarely Pits; except at the Place of the Incision, where the Cicatrices are never worn out, and where the Matter is more of the common Sort.

If an Apostem should break out in any, (which is more frequent in Infants,) yet there is no Fear, for tis heal'd safely by Suppuration. . . .

Hitherto you have Nothing but History. But a little Philosophy and Speculation may be now asked for; and an Inquiry into Causes a little endeavoured. No Doubt, among the wise Men of Inquiry, three may be found, so many Men so many Minds. Every Gentleman may form his own Hypothesis; and some of the later and more modern Curiosity will try how far the vermicular Scheme will carry them thro' a Solution of these and all Appearances in this Distemper.

I have seen the Point after this pothecary Manner talk'd about. The venomous Miasms (Let that Word serve at the present) of the Small-Pox, entering into the Body, in the Way of Inspiration, are immediately taken into the Blood of the Lungs: And, I pray, how many Pulses pass before the very Heart is pierced with them? And within how many more they are convey'd into all the Bowels, is easily apprehended by all that know Anything how the Circulation of the Blood is carried on. At the same Time, the Bowels themselves are enfeebled, and their Tone impaired, by the Venom that is thus insinuated. Behold, the Enemy at once got into the very Center of the Citadel. And the invaded Party must be very strong indeed, if it can struggle with him, and after all entirely expel and conquer him. Whereas, the Miasms of the Small-Pox being admitted in the Way of Inoculation, their Approaches are made only by the Outworks of the Citadel, and at a considerable Distance from the Center of it. The Enemy, 'tis true, gets in so far as to make some Spoil, yea, so much as to satisfy him, and leave no Prey in the Body of the Patient for him ever afterwards to seize upon. But the vital Powers are kept so clear from his Assaults, that they can manage the Combats bravely and, tho' not without a Surrender of those Humours in the Blood which the Invader makes a Seizure on, they oblige him to march out the same Way he came in, and are sure of never being troubled with him any more. But perhaps the few Words that I wrote in my introducing of the Story, may be as much to the Purpose as all of this Jargon. I'll have done with it.

I durst not engage that the Success of the Trial here will be the same that has been in all the other Countrys where it has been tried hitherto, tho' we have seen it succeed well in very different climates. Nor am I sure that if it should be made upon a Body, where the Blood is already nigh upon the Point of some unhappy Fever, this may not help to set Fire to such a Thing. But I am very confident no Person would miscarry in it, but what would most certainly have miscarried upon taking the Contagion in the common Way. Wherefore, if it be made at all, (and all the Scruples that some have about the Tempting of Providence be also got over) I advise, that it be never made but under the Management of a Physician, whose Conduct may be much relied upon, and who will wisely prepare the Body for it before he perform the Operation. I have done.

I am now able, as an Eyewitness (and more than so) to give a more full Account of the Practice, which until now I could only propose as a Matter at a greater Distance.

About the Month of May, 1721, the Small-Pox being admitted into the City of Boston, I proposed unto the Physicians of the Town, the unfailing Method of preventing Death, and many other grievous Miseries, from a tremendous Distemper, by receiving and managing the Small-Pox, in the Way of

Inoculation. One of the Physicians had the Courage to begin the Practice upon his own Children and Servants; and another expressed his Good Will unto it. But the Rest of the Practitioners treated the Proposal with an Incivility and an Inhumanity not well to be accounted for. Fresh Occasion I saw for the Complaint of a great Physician, "*Heus, quanto Dolore auger, dum video Naturae ministrum medicum, hostem ejus devenisse* [Alas, how my grief is increased when I see a physician, a minister of nature, has become an enemy]." The vilest Arts were used, and with such an Efficacy, that not only the Physician, but also the Patients under the Small-Pox inoculated were in Hazard of their very Lives from an infuriated People. But I myself had thrown into my House in the dead of the Night, a fired Granado, charged with combustible Matter, and in such a Manner, that upon its going off, it must probably have killed them that were near it, and would have certainly fired the Chamber and speedily have laid the House in Ashes. But the merciful Providence of God our Saviour so ordered it, that the Granado passing thro' the Window, had by the Iron in the Middle of the Casement such a Turn given to it, that in falling on the Floor, the fired Wild-fire in the Fuse, was violently shaken out some Distance from the Shell, and burnt out upon the Floor, without firing off the Granado.

The Opposition was carried on with a Folly, and Falsehood, and Malice, hardly ever known to be paralled'd on any Occasion. And in the Progress of the Distemper many hundreds of Lives were lost, which might have been saved, if the People had not been Satanically filled with Prejudices against this *Method of Safety*. However, the Practice went on, and tho' the Physician was under extreme Disadvantages on more Accounts than one, yet he was attended with vast Success. The Experiment has now been made on several hundreds of Persons; and upon both Male and Female, both old and young, both strong and weak, both white and black, at all Seasons, of Summer and Autumn and Winter: And they have generally professed, *they had rather undergo the Small-Pox inoculated once every Year, than undergo the Small-Pox once in their Lives after the common Way, tho' sure to live. . . .*

It has been unhappily given to some few, that have already newly received the Infection in the common Way. The Eruption has then been presently made in two or three Days after the Incision, and they have undergone the Small-Pox in the common Way; hardly escaping with their Lives; tho' some have thought, the Running of the Sores in these has been some Advantage to them.

Two or three have died under or soon after the Inoculation, from a Complication of other mortal Distempers. [An Indian Servant getting a violent Cold, fell into a pleuretic Fever, that killed her. Another Person that had long been under a crazy Melancholy and Consumption, utterly refused all Sustenance and starved herself to Death.]

But of all the Hundreds that have been under a regular Management, we know not of one but what rejoices in their having undergone the Operation.

(15)

John Winthrop, Jr.
1605/6-1676

The eldest son of Governor Winthrop of Massachusetts, young Winthrop was noted for his versatility. Educated at Trinity College in Dublin, he came to New England in 1631. Winthrop was responsible for the founding of Ipswich and New London, and also served as governor of Connecticut. He has been highly acclaimed for his scientific achievements and has sometimes been called the first American scientist.

The selection below, which illustrates Winthrop's broad scientific interests, is from a letter written by him to Sir Robert Moray, January 27, 1664, reprinted in the *Proceedings of the Massachusetts Historical Society,* Vol. 16 (1878).

HARTFORD, Jan. 27, 1664

HONORABLE SIR—

In my former I gave your honor an account of the favor I had of your letter by the Honorable Colonel Richard Nicolls. I then omitted to acquaint your honor what now I will be bold to add: that having looked upon Jupiter with a Telescope, upon the 6th of August last, I saw 5 [?] Satellites very distinctly about that Planet: I observed it with the best curiousity I could, taking very distinct notice of the number of them, by several aspects with some convenient time of intermission; & though I was not without some consideration whether that fifth might not be some fixt star with which Jupiter might at that time be in near conjunction, yet that consideration made me the more carefully to take notice whether I could discern any such difference of one of them from the other four, yet might by the more twinkling light of it or any other appearance give ground to believe that it might be a fixed star, but I could discern nothing of that nature: & I consider that the tube with which I looked upon them, though so good as to show very clearly the Satellites, yet was but of three foot & half with a concave eye-glass; & I question whether by a far better tube a fixt star can be discerned so near the body of that planet when in the ever bright activity of its light, for, if so, why are there not often if not always seen with the best tubes the like or more. Is not Jupiter often in near conjunction with them, especially *in via lactea?* I have been in much doubt whether I should mention this, which would possibly be taken from a single affirmation but a mistaken novelty: but I thought I would rather bear such censure than omit the notice of it to such worthy friends as might from the hint of it take occasion to cause more frequent observations to be made upon that planet, & at least this will at length be cleared, whether the light of Jupiter doth not take away the appearance of fixed stars so near in conjunction with it, as that they should appear within the periphery of that single *intuitus* by a tube which taketh in the body of Jupiter & that at the same unmoved aspect: & I am bold the rather to mention this as an inquiry whether any such number of Satellites or moons hath been seen by your honor or Mr. Rooke or any mathematicians or other gentlemen that have good tubes & often have the curiosity to view that planet, for possibly it may be new to me which hath been more usually known by others, though the notion of such a thing is not new to myself, for I remember I met with the like narration many years since in a little book entitled *Philosophia Naturalis* by Joh. Phociliden, though then I thought that was but a mistake of some fixed stars. An other thing I make bold to mention, upon occasion of a relation which I had lately from an understanding Seaman, that hath been Master of some vessels & often been in the West Indies (Mr. John Blackleech), he affirmed confidently that being in the Gulf of Florida he saw a great Pillar of Water (such as Commonly called Spouts) rise up from the Sea & rise higher till it joined itself to a White cloud over it. I urged it to him to be a mistake, & that it was one of those spouts (usual in the Indies & other parts) that fall from the clouds above: he confidently affirmeth it could be no mistake, his ship was near & that both himself & all in the ship with one consent judged it to rise out of the Sea. I mention not this out of any credence that it was any other than a mistake, supposing it to have been an ordinary spout falling down; yet because of his confidence in the affirmation as before upon the occasion thereof, I thought fit to commend it to your honors consideration, & the Royal Society (if you think fit), that, if they please, inquiry may be made of several Captains or Masters of Ships or other understanding Seamen that have often visited the West Indies, what the true original & manner of those Spouts are, for, however, they are of a strange nature & wonderful, & possibly there will be something reported about them & the effects of them that will be worth the knowing. Since my former I have been again at New York to give the Honorable Governor Colonel Nicolls a visit there, & left him with all there in good health & peace, & have not long since received a letter from him which signified the continuance of the same. Not far from thence upon Long Island there was last summer, at an English Plantation called Gravesend, eighteen oxen killed at once all together with lightning: & at a plantation called Stratford, as I was going last to New York, I saw a great tall oak that was stripped of so much of the bark as the breadth of four fingers from the very uppermost small top of one of the highest bows to the very bottom of the tree at the ground—that breadth I measured by my hand as high as I could reach, but by the judgment of the eye it might be narrower upward according to the proportion of the body &

bows upward, but no part of the other bark, nor the body of the tree hurt by it, & all that breadth that was taken off, it was in a kind of spiral line running at least six or eight times about the tree & bows from the top bow to the root of the tree.

But I have been too prolix in these discourses, for which I presume I may have your honors excuse, & shall not add further.

J. W.

V

Foundations of
a Literary Tradition

NOT THE LEAST PART of the intellectual and cultural legacy of the Puritans was the literary tradition that they founded in seventeenth-century New England. Like others oriented toward a religious conception of human life, the Puritans were under the compulsion of justifying their beliefs and actions. To accomplish this important task, they employed various literary means, including the sermon, poetry, and history, and they also developed a mode of expression peculiar to themselves. It is true that their efforts, which resulted in a considerable body of writing, cannot in any way match the productions of their English contemporaries. But to judge the literary output of the New England Puritans by the same standards one might apply to John Donne or George Herbert is, of course, an unfair comparison, considering the differing environments. Viewed in its own setting, the literature of the Puritans still stands as an enduring monument to their intellectual and moral strength.

As in other areas, Puritan literature was closely entwined with religion. Broadly defining the function of literature, the Puritans maintained that it was not only a means of communication, but that it would also serve to teach and convince others of the true purposes of life. Literature, therefore, had to be written in a clear and concise manner, to enable all men to understand it. Such an attitude generally made for realism and simplicity, and this facet of the literary tradition of New England was to be perpetuated by such nineteenth-century writers as Henry David Thoreau, Ralph Waldo Emerson, Francis Parkman, and Henry Adams.

Being children of the Renaissance as well as of the Reformation, the Puritans inherited the poetic traditions of their mother country. Although they objected to certain forms of poetry that they considered blasphemous or impious, the Puritans never objected to poetry as such; they read and rejoiced in the religious poetry of the English language. While most critics agree that the quality of the Puritans' own poetry was not particularly high because their creed did not emphasize the poetic mode of expression, and certain of its tenets actually placed barriers in the way of writing verse, there are still passages in the poems of figures like Edward Taylor, Anne Bradstreet, and Michael Wigglesworth that show considerable merit.

It was in their historical writing, however, that the Puritans excelled. More than any other form of expression, history fulfilled the needs of religion. In the first place, history provided a defense against the claims of the Roman Catholic Church by establishing a case for Protestantism. Secondly, history would reawaken religious interest among the second and third generations by portraying the special interest that God had shown in the Bible Commonwealth. Thirdly, if the Puritans did not write their own history, it was probable that others less sympathetic to their cause would undertake this task. Finally, and undoubtedly most important, history provided man with a record of God's workings and intentions. The function of the historian, therefore, was not only to present all the facts but also to interpret them in the light of divine purpose. The Puritan faith in God was so complete, moreover, that they did not gloss over unfavorable events, for in such events important lessons could also be found.

Conceiving of this world in epic and heroic terms, the Puritans dramatized their own history. They were not simply a people who had migrated to a new home, but rather an army fighting on behalf of their God. The historiography of seventeenth-century New England thus effectively mirrored the Puritan attitude toward literature in general—namely, that literature was an art that could be put to work for a righteous cause. To the modern student such an attitude might appear to be archaic, but the historical and literary works of the Puritans hold up surprisingly well. In his own way the Puritan, too, was an artist who was depicting a heroic age when men "fought and suffered and died courageously, because they were committed, emotionally and intellectually, to a life of faith."[1]

(16)

John Winthrop

1588-1649

During the trip to the New World Winthrop began to keep a journal, to which he added intermittently until his death. Our text is from *The History of New England From 1630 to 1649,* James Savage, ed., new

1. Kenneth B. Murdock, *Literature & Theology in Colonial New England* (Cambridge, Massachusetts, 1949), p. 97.

edition, 2 vols. (Boston, 1853), vol. I. The selection reprinted below was written in 1636. [For Winthrop's career see pp. 35–36.]

Two ships arrived here from London, and one a week before. They were full of passengers,—men, women, and children. One of them had been from London twenty-six weeks, and between land and land eighteen weeks; (the other two something less time;) their beer all spent and leaked out a month before their arrival, so as they were forced to stinking water (and that very little) mixed with sack or vinegar, and their other provisions very short and bad. Yet, through the great providence of the Lord, they came all safe on shore, and most of them sound and well liking. They had continual tempests, and when they were near the shore (being brought two or three days with a strong east wind) the weather was so thick all that time as they could not make land, and the seamen were in great perplexity, when on the sudden the fog cleared, so as they saw Cape Ann fair on their starboard bow, and presently grew thick again; yet by their compass they made their harbor. There were aboard that ship two godly ministers, Mr. Nathaniel Rogers, and Mr. Partridge, and many good people in that and the other ships; and we had prayed earnestly for them (for a small pinnace of thirty tons, which came out with them, and was come in three weeks before, brought us news of their coming). In one of the other ships, the passengers had but half a pint of drink for a day, fourteen days together; yet, through the Lord's mercy, did all well. One of the ships was overset in the night by a sudden gust, and lay so half an hour, yet righted of herself.

Cattle were grown to high rates; a good cow, £25 or £30; a pair of bulls or oxen, £40. Corn was now at 5s. the bushel, and much rye was sown with the plough this year, for about thirty ploughs were at work. Bread was at 9 and 10s. the C.; carpenters at 3s. the day, and other workmen accordingly.

Things went not well at Connecticut. Their cattle did, many of them, cast their young, as they had done the year before.

Mons. D'Aulney, captain of Penobscott or Pentagonsett, returned answer to the governour's letter, wherein he professed, that they claimed no further than to Pemaquid, nor would unless he had further order; and that he supposed, that the cause why he had no order, etc., was, that the English ambassador had dealt effectually with the cardinal of France for settling the limits for our peace, etc.

The governour, Mr. Vane, a wise and godly gentleman, held, with Mr. Cotton and many others, the indwelling of the person of the Holy Ghost in a believer, and went so far beyond the rest, as to maintain a personal union with the Holy Ghost; but the deputy, with the pastor and diverse others, denied both; and the question proceeded so far by disputation (in writing, for the peace sake of the church, which all were tender of), as at length they could not find the person of the Holy Ghost in scripture, nor in the primitive churches three hundred years after Christ. So that, all agreeing in the chief matter of substance, viz. that the Holy Ghost is God, and that he doth dwell in the believers (as the Father and Son both are said also to do), but whether by his gifts and power only, or by any other manner of presence, seeing the scripture doth not declare it,—it was earnestly desired, that the word person might be foreborn, being a term of human invention, and tending to doubtful disputation in this case.

The governour, receiving letters from his friends in England, which necessarily required his presence there, imparted the same to the council and some others; and, being thereupon resolved of his return into England, called a court of deputies, to the end he might have free leave of the country, etc. They, being assembled in court, and himself declaring the necessity of his departure, and those of the council affirming the reasons to be very urgent, though not fit to be imparted to the whole court, they desired respite to consider thereof till the morning; when one of the assistants using some pathetical passages of the loss of such a governour in a time of such danger as did hang over us, from the Indians and French, the governour broke forth into tears, and professed, that howsoever the causes propounded for his departure were such as did concern the utter ruin of his outward estate, yet he would rather have hazarded all, than have gone from them at this time, if something else had not pressed him more, viz. the inevitable danger he saw of God's judgments to come upon us for these differences and dissensions, which he saw amongst us, and the scandalous imputations brought upon himself, as if he should be the cause of all; and therefore he thought it best for him to give place for a time, etc. Upon this the court concluded that it would not be fit to give way to his departure upon these grounds. Whereupon he recalled himself, and professed, that the reasons concerning his own estate were sufficient to his own satisfaction for his departure, and therefore desired the court he might have leave to go; as for the other passage, it slipped him out of his passion, and not out of judgment. Upon this the court consented, silently, to his departure. Then the question was about supply of his place. Some were of opinion, that it should be executed by the deputy; but this scruple being cast in, that if the deputy should die, then the government would be vacant, and none have power to call any court, or to preside therein, etc., it was agreed to call a court of elections, for a new governour and deputy, in case the present deputy should be chose governour; and an order was made (in regard of the season) that such as would might send their votes by proxy, in papers sealed up and delivered to the deputies. And so this court was adjourned four days, and two days after the court of elections was to assemble. These things thus passed, diverse of the congregation of Boston met together, and agreed that they did not apprehend the necessity of the governour's departure upon the reasons alleged, and sent some of them to declare the same to the court; whereupon the governour expressed himself to be an obedient child to the church, and therefore, notwithstanding the license of the court, yet, without the leave of the church, he durst not go away.

Whereupon a great part of the court and country, who understood hereof, declared their purpose to continue him still in his place, and therefore, so soon as the day of election came, and the country were assembled, it was thought the best way for avoiding trouble, etc., not to proceed to election, but to adjourn the court to the great general court in May. And so the court of deputies, etc., continued still (for the other court was not called).

At this court the elders of the churches were called, to advise with them about discovering and pacifying the differences among the churches in point of opinion. The governour having declared the occasion to them, Mr. Dudley desired, that men would be free and open, etc. Another of the magistrates spake, that it would much further the end they came for, if men would freely declare what they held different from others, as himself would freely do, in what point soever he should be opposed. The governour said, that he would be content to do the like, but that he understood the ministers were about it in a church way, etc., which he spake upon this occasion: the ministers had met, a little before, and had drawn into heads all the points, wherein they suspected Mr. Cotton did differ from them, and had propounded them to him, and pressed him to a direct answer, affirmative or negative, to every one; which he had promised, and taken time for. The meeting being spoke of in the court the day before, the governour took great offence at it, as being without his privity, etc., which this day Mr. Peter told him as plainly of (with all due reverence), and how it had sadded the ministers' spirits, that he should be jealous of their meetings, or seem to restrain their liberty, etc. The governour excused his speech, as sudden and upon a mistake. Mr. Peter told him also, that before he came, within less than two years since, the churches were in peace, etc. The governour answered, that the light of the gospel brings a sword, and the children of the bondswoman would persecute those of the freewoman. Mr. Peter also besought him humbly to consider his youth and short experience in the things of God, and to beware of peremptory conclusions, which he perceived him to be very apt unto. He declared further, that he had observed, both in the Low Countries and here, three principal causes of new opinions and divisions thereupon: 1. Pride, new notions lift up the mind, etc. 2. Idleness. 3. [Blank.]

Mr. Wilson made a very sad speech of the condition of our churches, and the inevitable danger of separation, if these differences and alienations among brethren were not speedily remedied; and laid the blame upon these new opinions risen up amongst us, which all the magistrates, except the governour and two others, did confirm, and all the ministers but two.

In this discourse one question arose about sanctification. Mr. Cotton, in his sermon that day, had laid down this ground, that evident sanctification was an evidence of justification, and thereupon had taught, that in cases of

spiritual desertion, true desires of sanctification were found to be sanctification; and further, if a man were laid so flat upon the ground, as he could
see no desires, etc., but only, as a bruised reed, did wait at the feet of Christ,
yet here was matter of comfort for this, as found to be true.

The question here grew, whether any of these, or evident sanctification,
could be evidence to a man without a concurrent sight of his justification. The
governour and Mr. Cotton denied it.

The speech of Mr. Wilson was taken very ill by Mr. Cotton and others of
the same church, so as he and diverse of them went to admonish him. But
Mr. Wilson and some others could see no breach of rule, seeing he was
called by the court about the same matter with the rest of the olders, and
exhorted to deliver their minds freely and faithfully, both for discovering
the danger, and the means to help; and the things he spake of were only in
general, and such as were under a common fame. And being questioned
about his intent, he professed he did not mean Boston church, nor the members thereof, more than others. But this would not satisfy, but they called
him to answer publicly; and there the governour pressed it violently against
him, and all the congregation, except the deputy and one or two more, and
many of them with much bitterness and reproaches; but he answered them
all with words of truth and soberness, and with marvellous wisdom. It was
strange to see, how the common people were led, by example, to condemn
him in that, which (it was very probable) diverse of them did not understand, nor the rule which he was supposed to have broken; and that such as
had known him so long, and what good he had done for that church, should
fall upon him with such bitterness for justifying himself in a good cause; for
he was a very holy, upright man, and for faith and love inferior to none in the
country, and most dear to all men. The teacher joined with the church in
their judgment of him (not without some appearance of prejudice) yet with
much wisdom and moderation. They were eager to proceed to present censure,
but the teacher stayed them from that, telling them he might not do it, because some opposed it, but gave him a grave exhortation. The next day Mr.
Wilson preached, notwithstanding, and the Lord so assisted him, as gave great
satisfaction, and the governour himself gave public witness to him.

One of the brethren wrote to Mr. Cotton about it, and laid before him
diverse failings (as he supposed) and some reasons to justify Mr. Wilson,
and dealt very plainly with him. Mr. Cotton made a very loving and gentle
answer, clearing his intentions, and persisting in his judgment of Mr. Wilson's offence, laying down diverse arguments for it. The said brother replied
to him in like loving manner, and desired leave to show his letter to Mr. Wilson, which he readily assented unto. But for answer to his arguments, he fore-
bore to reply to Mr. Cotton, (because he was overburdened with business,)
but wrote to the two ruling elders (whom the matter most concerned) and,
by way of defence of Mr. Wilson, answered all Mr. Cotton's arguments.

Upon these public occasions, other opinions broke out publicly in the church of Boston—as that the Holy Ghost dwelt in a believer as he is in heaven; that a man is justified before he believes; and that faith is no cause of justification. And others spread more secretly—as that the letter of the scripture holds forth nothing but a covenant of works; and that the covenant of grace was the spirit of the scripture, which was known only to believers; and that this covenant of works was given by Moses in the ten command- ments; that there was a seed (viz., Abraham's carnal seed) went along in this, and there was a spirit and life in it, by virtue whereof a man might attain to any sanctification in gifts and graces, and might have spiritual and *con- tinual* communion with Jesus Christ, and yet be damned. After, it was granted, that faith was before justification, but it was only passive, an empty vessel, etc.; but in conclusion, the ground of all was found to be assurance by im- mediate revelation.

All the congregation of Boston, except four or five, closed with these opinions, or the most of them; but one of the brethren wrote against them, and bore witness to the truth; together with the pastor, and very few others joined with them.

About this time the rest of the ministers, taking offence at some doctrines delivered by Mr. Cotton, and especially at some opinions, which some of his church did broach, and for he seemed to have too good an opinion of, and too much familiarity with those persons, drew out sixteen points, and gave them to him, entreating him to deliver his judgment directly in them, which accordingly he did, and many copies thereof were dispersed about. Some doubts he well cleared, but in some things he gave not satisfaction. The rest of the ministers replied to these answers, and at large showed their dissent, and the grounds thereof; and, at the next general court, held 9th of the 1st, they all assembled at Boston, and agreed to put off all lectures for three weeks, that they might bring things to some issue. . . .

The differences in the said points of religion increased more and more, and the ministers of both sides (there being only Mr. Cotton of one party) did publicly declare their judgments in some of them, so as all men's mouths were full of them. And there being, 12 mo. 3, a ship ready to go for England, and many passengers in it, Mr. Cotton took occasion to speak to them about the differences, etc., and willed them to tell our countrymen, that all the strife amongst us was about magnifying the grace of God; one party seeking to advance the grace of God within us, and the other to advance the grace of God towards us (meaning by the one justification, and by the other sanctifica- tion); and so bade them tell them, that, if there were any among them that would strive for grace, they should come hither; and so declared some particu- lars. Mr. Wilson spake after him, and declared, that he knew none of the elders or brethren of the churches, but did labor to advance the free grace of God in justification, so far as the word of God required; and spake also about the doctrine of sanctification, and the use and necessity, etc., of it; by occasion whereof no man could tell (except some few, who knew the bottom of the matter) where any difference was: which speech, though it offended those of Mr. Cotton's party, yet it was very seasonable to clear the rest, who otherwise should have been reputed to have opposed free grace. Thus every occasion increased the contention, and caused great alienation of minds; and the members of Boston (frequenting the lectures of other ministers) did make much disturbance by public questions, and objections to their doctrines, which did any way disagree from their opinions; and it began to be as common here to distinguish between men, by being under a covenant of grace or a covenant of works, as in other countries between Protestants and Papists.

(17)

Edward Johnson
1598-1672

Having migrated to New England in 1630, Johnson helped to found the town of Woburn. A staunch defender of Puritan orthodoxy, he was also a member of the Massachusetts legislature for much of his life. His major claim to fame, however, rests on his history, which he began writing in 1650. Written primarily as a defense of Massachusetts against its detractors, Johnson's history attempted to demonstrate the many ways in which the colony had been favored by divine providence. Although not completely accurate or unbiased, the book is an important landmark in Puritan literature.

The selection is from *The Wonder-working Providence of Sion's Saviour in New England* (London, 1654).

CHAPTER I
The Sad Condition of England, When This People Removed

When England began to decline in Religion, like lukewarm Laodicea, and instead of purging out Popery, a farther compliance was sought not only in vain Idolatrous Ceremonies, but also in profaning the Sabbath, and by Proclamation throughout their Parish churches, exasperating lewd and profane persons to celebrate a Sabbath like the Heathen to Venus, Bacchus and Ceres; in so much that the multitude of irreligious lascivious and popish affected persons spread the whole land like Grasshoppers, in this very time Christ the glorious King of his Churches, raises an Army out of our English Nation, for freeing his people from their long servitude under usurping Prelacy; and because every corner of England was filled with the fury of malignant adversaries, Christ creates a New England to muster up the first of his Forces in; Whose low condition, little number, and remoteness of place made these adversaries triumph, despising this day of small things, but in this height of their pride the Lord Christ brought sudden, and unexpected destruction upon them. Thus have you a touch of the time when this work began.

Christ Jesus intending to manifest his Kingly Office toward his Churches more fully than ever yet the Sons of men saw, even to the uniting of Jew and Gentile Churches in one Faith, begins with our English Nation (whose former reformation being were imperfect) doth now resolve to cast down their false foundation of Prelacy, even in the height of their domineering dignity. And therefore in the year 1628, he stirs up his servants as the Heralds of a King to make this proclamation for Volunteers, as followeth.

"Oh yes! oh yes! oh yes! All you the people of Christ that are here Oppressed, Imprisoned and scurrilously derided, gather yourselves together, your Wives and little ones, and answer to your several Names as you shall be shipped for his service, in the Western World, and more especially for planting the united Colonies of new England; Where you are to attend the service of the King of Kings."

Upon the divulging of this Proclamation by his Heralds at Arms, many (although otherwise willing for this service) began to object as followeth:

"Can it possible be the mind of Christ (who formerly enabled so many Soldiers of his to keep their station unto the death here) that now so many brave Soldiers disciplined by Christ himself the Captain of our salvation, should turn their backs to the disheartening of their Fellow-Soldiers, and loss of further opportunity in gaining a greater number of Subjects to Christs Kingdom?"

Notwithstanding this Objection, It was further proclaimed as followeth: "What, Creature, wilt not know that Christ thy King crusheth with a rod of Iron, the Pomp and Pride of man, and must he like man cast and contrive to take his enemies at advantage? No, of purpose he causeth such instruments to retreat as he hath made strong for himself: that so his adversaries glorying in the pride of their power, insulting over the little remnant remaining, Christ causeth them to be cast down suddenly forever, and we find in stories reported, Earths Princes have passed their Armies at need over Seas and deep Torrents. Could Caesar so suddenly fetch over fresh forces from Europe to Asia, Pompey to foil? How much more shall Christ who createth all power, call over this 900 league Ocean at his pleasure, such instruments as he thinks meet to make use of in this place, from whence you are now to depart, but further that you may not delay the Voyage intended, for your full satisfaction, know this is the place where the Lord will create a new Heaven, and a new Earth in, new Churches, and a new Common-wealth together. . . .

CHAPTER VIII
Of the Wonderful Preparation the Lord Christ by His Providence,
Wrought for His Peoples Abode in This Western World

Now let all men know the admirable Acts of Christ for his Churches and
chosen, are universally over the whole Earth at one and the same time, but
sorry man cannot so discourse of them; And therefore let us leave our
English Nation in way of preparation for this Voyage intended, and tell of
the marvelous doings of Christ preparing for his peoples arrival in the
Western World, whereas the Indians report they beheld to their great wonder-
ment that perspicuous bright blazing Comet (which was so famously noted
in Europe); anon after Sun set it appeared as they say in the South-west,
about three hours, continuing in their Horizon for the space of thirty sleeps
(for so they reckon their days) after which uncouth sight they expected some
strange things to follow, and the rather, because not long before the whole
Nation of the Mattachusets were so affrighted with a Ship that arrived in
their Bay, having never seen any before, thus they report some persons among
them discerning a great thing to move toward them upon the Waters, wondering what Creature it should be, they run with their light canoes, (which are
a kind of Boats made of Birch Rinds, and sowed together with the roots of
white Cedar-Trees) from place to place, stirring up all their Countrymen
to come forth, and behold this monstrous thing; at this sudden news the
shores for many miles were filled with this naked Nation, gazing at this
wonder, till some of the stoutest among them manned out these Canoes.
Being armed with Bow and Arrows, they approached within shot of the
Ship, being becalmed, they let fly their long shafts at her, which being headed
with bone some stuck fast, and others dropped into the water, they wondering
it did not cry, but kept quietly on toward them, till all of a sudden the Master
caused a piece of Ordnance to be fired, which stroke such fear into the poor
Indians, that they hasted to shore, having their wonders exceedingly increased; but being gotten among their great multitude, they waited to see
the sequel with much amazement, till the Seamen furling up their sails came
to an Anchor, manned out their long boat, and went on shore, at those
approach, the Indians fled, although now they saw they were men, who made
signs to stay their flight, that they may have Trade with them, and to that
end they brought certain Copper-Kettles; the Indians by degrees made their
approach nearer and nearer till they came to them, when beholding their
Vessels, which they had set forth before them, the Indian knocking them
were much delighted with the sound, and much more astonished to see they
would not break, being so thin, for attaining those Vessels they brought them
much Beaver, freighting them richly away according to their desires. This was
the first working providence of Christ to stir up our English Nation, to plant
these parts in hopes of a rich Trade for Beaver-skins, and this made some

of our Countrymen make their abode in these parts, whom this Army of Christ at their comming over found as fit helps to further their design in planting the Churches of Christ; Why by a more admirable act of his Providence not long after prepared for his peoples arrival as followeth.

The Summer after the blazing Star (whose motion in the Heavens was from East to West, pointing out to the sons of men the progress of the glorious Gospel of Christ, the glorious King of his Churches) even about the year 1618. a little before the removal of that Church of Christ from Holland to Plymouth in New England, as the ancient Indians report, there befell a great mortality among them, the greatest that ever the memory of Father to Son took notice of, chiefly desolating those places, where the English afterward planted. The Country of Pockanoky, Agissawamg, it was almost wholly deserted, insomuch that the Neighbour Indians did abandon those places for fear of death, fleeing more West and by South, observing the East and by Northern parts were most smitten with this contagion. The Abarginny-men consisting of Mattachusets, Wippanaps and Tarratines were greatly weakened, and more especially the three Kingdomes of Saggamore ships of the Mattachusets, who were before this mortality most populous, having under them seven Dukedoms or petty Saggamores, and the Nianticks and Narrowganssits, who before this came were but of little note, yet were they now not much increased by such as fled thither for fear of death. The Pecods (who retained the Name of a war-like people, till afterwards conquered by the English) were also smitten at this time. Their Disease being a sore Consumption, sweeping away whole Families, but chiefly young Men and Children, the very seeds of increase. Their Powwowes, which are their Doctors, working partly by Charms, and partly by Medicine, were much amazed to see their Wigwams lie full of dead Corpes, and that now neither Squantam nor Abbamocho could help, which are their good and bad God and also their Powwows themselves were oft smitten with deaths stroke. Howling and much lamentation was heard among the living, who being possessed with great fear, oftimes left their dead unburied, their manner being such, that they remove their habitations at death of any. This great mortality being an unwonted thing, feare[d] them the more, because naturally the Country is very healthy. But by this means Christ (whose great and glorious works the Earth throughout are altogether for the benefit of his Churches and chosen) not only made room for his people to plant; but also tamed the hard and cruel hearts of these barbarous Indians, insomuch that half a handful of his people landing not long after in Plymoth-Plantation, found little resistance, of whom the Author purposes not to speak particularly, being prevented by the honored Mr. Winslow, who was an eye-witness of the work: only thus much by the way, they were sent to keep possession for their Brethren and fellow Soldiers, who arrived eight years after them, as in process of this story will God-willing appear: and verily herein they quit themselves like men, or rather Christ for and by them, maintaining the place notwithstanding the multitude of difficulties they met withall at their first landing, being in doubtful suspense what entertainment these Barbarians would give them, having with prayer supplicated the Lord in the Name of Christ their King and guide in this their undertaking, they manned out a Boat to discover what store of the Inhabitants were there. Now these men, whose courage exceeded the number, being guided by the provident hand of the most high, landed in some several places; and by making fires gave signs of their approach. Now the Indians, whose dwellings are most neer the water-side, appeared with their Bows bent and Arrows one [on] the string, let fly their long shafts among this little company, whom they might soon have enclosed, but the Lord otherwise disposed of it, for one Captain Miles Standish having his fowling-piece in a readiness, presented full at them, his shot being directed by the provident Hand of the most high God, struck the stoutest *Sachem* among them one [on] the right Arm, it being bent over his shoulder to reach an Arrow forth his Quiver, as their manner is to draw them forth in fight. At this stroke they all fled with great swiftness through the Woods and Thickets, then the English, who more thirsted after their conversion than destruction, returned to their Boat without receiving any damage, and soon after arrived where they left their Brethren, to whom they declared the good hand of God toward them, with thankful acknowledgment of this great work of his in preserving them; Yet did they all remain full of incumbred thoughts, the Indians, of whose multitudes they had now some intelligence, together with experience of spirits, and also knew well without commerce with them they were not like long to subsist.

But he, whose work they went about, wrought so rare a Providence for them, which cannot but be admired of all that hear it. Thus it fell as they were discoursing in the Boat they had built for shelter, all of a sudden, an Indian came in among them, at whose speech they were all aghast, he speaking in the English Language, *Much welcome Englishmen,* their wonder was the greater, because upon those Coasts they supposed no English had so much as set foot, and verily Christ had prepared him on purpose to give his people entertainment, the Indian having lived in England two year or thereabout, after which he returned home, and at this time had wandered into those parts in company of other Indians. All this, and the condition of the near adjoining Indians, he soon discovered unto them, at which they were transported beyond themselves very much, with what joy and the mixture of their former fear and affection intervening with the other, surprised all their senses of a sudden, that long it was ere each party could take its proper place, yea, and beyond all this Christ Jesus, by the power of his blessed Spirit, did now work upon all their faculties both of Soul and Body, [that] the great impression of his present Providence might not soon be washed off with the following incumbered cares of a Desert Wilderness; but to contract, they made use of the present opportunity, and by the instrumental means of this Indian, became acquainted and reconciled with most of the Neighbouring Indians. And afterward planted a Church of Christ there, and set up civil Government, calling the Name of the place Plymoth: under this jurisdiction there are ten Churches at this very day, this being the first place any English resorted unto for the advancement of the Kingly Government of Christ in this Western World.

(18)

Cotton Mather

1663-1728

The text of the following selection is from *Magnalia Christi Americana: or, the Ecclesiastical History of New-England, From Its First Planting in the Year 1620, Unto the Year of Our Lord, 1698,* first American edition, from the London edition of 1702, 2 vols. (Hartford, Connecticut, 1820), vol I. [For Mather's career see p. 67.]

☆ ☆ ☆ ☆

A GENERAL INTRODUCTION

§1. I write the Wonders of the CHRISTIAN RELIGION, flying from the depravations of Europe, to the American Strand: and, assisted by the Holy Author of that Religion, I do, with all conscience of Truth, required therein by Him, who is the Truth itself, report the wonderful displays of His infinite Power, Wisdom, Goodness, and Faithfulness, wherewith His Divine Providence hath irradiated an Indian Wilderness.

I relate the Considerable Matters, that produced and attended the First Settlement of COLONIES, which have been renowned for the degree of REFORMATION, professed and attained by Evangelical Churches, erected in those ends of the earth: and a Field being thus prepared, I proceed unto a relation of the Considerable Matters which have been acted thereupon.

I first introduce the Actors, that have, in a more exemplary manner served those Colonies; and give Remarkable Occurrences, in the exemplary LIVES of many Magistrates, and of more Ministers, who so lived, as to leave unto Posterity, examples worthy of everlasting remembrance.

I add hereunto, the Notables of the only Protestant University, that ever shone in that hemisphere of the New World; with particular instances of

Criolians, in our Biography, provoking the whole world, with virtuous objects of emulation.

I introduce then, the Actions of a more eminent importance, that have signalized those Colonies: whether the Establishments, directed by their Synods; with a rich variety of Synodical and Ecclesiastical Determinations; or, the Disturbances, with which they have been from all sorts of temptations and enemies tempestuated; and the Methods by which they have still weathered out each horrible tempest.

And into the midst of these Actions, I interpose an entire Book, wherein there is, with all possible veracity, a Collection made, of Memorable Occurrences; and amazing Judgments and Mercies, befalling many particular persons among the people of New England.

Let my readers expect all that I have promised them, in this Bill of Fare; and it may be they will find themselves entertained with yet many other passages, above and beyond their expectation, deserving likewise a room in History: in all which, there will be nothing, but the Author's too mean way of preparing so great entertainments, to reproach the Invitation.

§2. The reader will doubtless desire to know, what it was that

. . . tot Volvere casus
Insignes Pietate Viros, tot adire Labores,
Impulerit [impelled men noted for their piety to handle so many cases
                                    and endure so many labors].

And our History shall, on many fit occasions which will be therein offered, endeavor, with all historical fidelity and simplicity, and with as little offence as may be, to satisfy him. The sum of the matter is, that from the very beginning of the REFORMATION in the English Nation, there hath always been a generation of Godly Men, desirous to pursue the Reformation of Religion, according to the Word of God, and the Example of the best Reformed Churches; . . . And there hath been another generation of men, who have still employed the power which they have generally still had in their hands, not only to stop the progress of the desired Reformation, but also, with innumerable vexations, to persecute those that most heartily wished well unto it. There were many of the Reformers, who joined with the Reverend JOHN FOX, in the complaints which he then entered in his Martyrology, about the baits of Popery yet left in the Church; and in his wishes, God take them away, or ease us from them, for God knows they be the cause of much blindness and strife amongst men! They zealously decreed the policy of complying always with the ignorance and vanity of the People; and cried out earnestly for purer Administration in the house of God, and more conformity to the Law of Christ, and primitive Christianity: while others would not hear of going any further than the first Essay of Reformation. 'Tis very certain, that the first Reformers never intended, that what they did, should be the absolute boundary of Reformation, so that it should be a sin to proceed any further; as, by their own going beyond Wicklife, and changing and growing in their own Models also, and the confessions of Cranmer, with the Scripta Anglicana of Bucer, and a thousand other things, was abundantly demonstrated. But after a fruitless expectation, wherein the truest friends of the Reformation long waited, for to have that which Heylin himself owns to have been the design of the first Reformers, followed as it should have been, a party very unjustly arrogating to themselves, the venerable name of, The Church of England, by numberless oppressions, grievously smote those their Fellow-Servants. Then 'twas that, as our great OWEN hath expressed it, "Multitudes of pious, peaceable Protestants, were driven, by their severities, to leave their native country, and seek a refuge for their lives and liberties, with freedom, for the worship of God, in a wilderness, in the ends of the earth."

§3. It is the History of these PROTESTANTS, that is here attempted: PROTESTANTS that highly honoured and affected the Church of ENGLAND, and humbly petition to be a part of it: but by the mistake of a few powerful brethren, driven to seek a place for the exercise of the Protestant Religion, according to the light of their consciences, in the deserts of America. And in this attempt I have proposed, not only to preserve and secure the interest of Religion, in the Churches of that little country NEW ENGLAND, so far as the Lord Jesus Christ may please to bless it for that end, but also to offer unto the Churches of the Reformation, abroad in the world, some small Memorials, that may be serviceable unto the designs of Reformation, whereto, I believe, they are quickly to be awakened. . . . I do not say, that the Churches of New England are the most regular that can be; yet I do say, and am sure, that they are very like unto those that were in the first ages of Christianity. . . . In short, the first Age was the golden Age: to return unto that, will make a man a Protestant, and I may add, a Puritan. 'Tis possible, that our Lord Jesus Christ carried some thousands of Reformers into the retirements of an American desert, on purpose, that, with an opportunity granted unto many of his faithful servants, to enjoy the precious liberty of their Ministry, though in the midst of many temptations all their days, He might there, to them first, and then by them, give a specimen of many good things, which He would have His Churches elsewhere aspire and arise unto: and this being done, he knows not whether there be not all done, that New England was planted for; and whether the Plantation may not, soon after this, come to nothing. . . . But behold, ye European Churches, there are golden Candlesticks [more than twice seven times seven!] in the midst of this outer darkness: unto the upright children of Abraham, here hath arisen light in darkness. And let us humbly speak it, it shall be profitable for you to consider the light, which from the midst of this outer darkness, is now to be darted over unto the other side of the Atlantic Ocean. But we must therewithal ask your Prayers, that these golden Candlesticks may not quickly be removed out of their place! . . .

REMARKS: *ESPECIALLY UPON THE* FIRST CLASS, *IN OUR* CATALOGUE OF MINISTERS

I. All, or most, of the ministers that make up our two first classes, came over from England within the two first lustres of years, after the first settlement of the country. After the year 1640, that part of the Church of England, which took up arms in the old cause of the long Parliament, and which among all its parliament-men, commanders, lord-lieutenants, major-generals, and sea-captains, had scarce any but conformists; I say, that part of the Church of England, knowing the Puritans to be generally inclinable unto those principles of such writers as Bilson and Hooker, whereupon the Parliament then acted; and seeing them to be generally of the truest English spirit, for the preservation of the English liberties and properties, for which the Parliament then declared (although there were some non-conformists in the King's army also) it was found necessary to have the assistance of that considerable people. Whereupon ensued such a change of times, that instead of Old England's driving its best people into New, it was it self turned into New. The body of the Parliament and its friends, which were conformists in the beginning of that miserable war, before the war was ended, became such as those old non-conformists, whose union with them in political interests produced an union in religious. The Romanizing Laudians miscarried in their enterprise; the Anglican church could not be carried over to the Gallican. This was not the first instance of a shipwreck befalling a vessel bound for Rome; nor will it be the last: a vessel bound such a voyage, must be shipwrecked, though St. Paul himself were aboard.

II. The occasion upon which these excellent ministers retired into an horrid wilderness of America, and encountered the dismal hardships of such a wilderness, was the violent persecution, wherewith a prevailing party in the Church of England harassed them. In their own land they were hereby deprived, not only of their livings, but also of their liberty to exercise their ministry, which was dearer to them than their livings, yea, than their very lives: and they were exposed unto extreme sufferings, because they conscientiously dissented from the use of some things in the worship of God, which they accounted sins. But I leave it unto the consideration of mankind, whether this forbidding of such men to do their duty, were no ingredient of that iniquity, which immediately upon the departure of these good men brought upon Great Britain, and especially upon the greatest authors of this persecution, a wrath unto the uttermost, in the ensuing desolations. . . .

III. These ministers of the gospel, which were (without any odious comparison) as faithful, painful, useful ministers, as most in the nation, being thus exiled from a sinful nation, there were not known to be left so many nonconformist ministers, as there were counties in England: and yet they were quickly so multiplied, that a matter of twenty years after, there could be found far more than twenty hundred, that were so grounded in their nonconformity, as to undergo the loss of all things, rather than make shipwreck of it. . . .

IV. Most, if not all, of the ministers, who then visited these regions, were either attended or followed, with a number of pious people, who had lived within the reach of their ministry in England. These, who were now also become generally nonconformist, having found the powerful impressions of those good men's ministry upon their souls, continued there sincere affections unto that ministry, and were willing to accompany it unto those utmost ends of the earth. Indeed, the ministers of New England have this always to recommend them unto a good regard with the Crown of England, that the most flourishing plantation in all the American dominions of that crown, is more owing to them, than to any sort of men whatsoever.

V. Some of the ministers, and many of the gentlemen, that came over with the ministers, were persons of considerable estates; who therewith charitably brought over many poor families of godly people, that were not of themselves able to bear the charges of their transportation; and they were generally careful also to bring over none but godly servants in their own families, who, afterwards by God's blessing on their industry have arrived, many of them, unto such plentiful estates, that they have had occasion to think of the advice, which a famous person, gave in a public sermon, at their first coming over; You (said he) that are servants, mark what I say; I desire and exhort you to be kind a while hence, unto your master's children. It won't be long before, you that came with nothing into the country, will be rich men, when your masters, having buried their rich estates in the country, will go near to leave their families in a mean condition; wherefore, when it shall be well with you, I charge you to remember them.

VI. The ministers and christians, by whom New England was first planted, were a chosen company of men; picked out of, perhaps, all the counties in England, and this by no human contrivance, but by a strange work of God upon the spirits of men that were, no ways, acquainted with one another, inspiring them, as one man, to secede into a wilderness, they knew not where, and suffer in that wilderness they know not what. It was a reasonable expression once used by that eminent person, the present lieutenant-governor of New England in a very great assembly, God sifted three nations, that he might bring choice grain into this wilderness.

VII. The design of these refugees, thus carried into the wilderness, was, that they might there, sacrifice unto the Lord their God: it was, that they might maintain the power of godliness and practise the evangelical worship of our Lord Jesus Christ, in all the parts of it, without any human innovations and impositions: defended by charters, which at once gave them so far the protection of their King, and the election of so many of their own subordinate rulers under him, as might secure them the undisturbed enjoyment of the church-order established amongst them. I shall but repeat the words once used in a sermon preached unto the general court of the Massachusett-colony, at one of their anniversary elections. "The question was often put unto our predecessors, What went ye out into the wilderness to see? And the answer to it, is not only too excellent, but also too notorious, to be dissembled. Let all mankind know, that we came into the wilderness, because we would worship God without that Episcopacy, that common-prayer, and those unwarrantable ceremonies, with which the land of our fore fathers' sepulchres has been defiled; we came hither because we would have our posterity settled under the pure and full dispensations of the gospel; defended by rulers that should be of our selves."

VIII. None of the least concerns, that lay upon the spirits of these reformers, was the condition of their posterity: for which cause in the first constitution of their churches, they did more generally with more or less expressiveness take in their children, as under the churchwatch with themselves. They also did betimes endeavour the erection of a College, for the training up of a successive ministry in the country; but because it was likely to be some while before a considerable supply could be expected from the college, therefore they took notice of the younger, hopeful scholars, who came over with their friends from England, and assisted their liberal education; whereby being fitted for the service of the churches, they were in an orderly manner called forth to that service. Of these we have given you a number; whereof, I think, all but one or two are now gone unto their fathers.

IX. Of these ministers, there were some few, suppose ten or a dozen, that after divers years, returned into England, where they were eminently serviceable unto their generation; but, by far, the biggest part of them, continued in this country, serving their generation by the will of God. Moreover, I find near half of them signally blessed with sons, who did work for our Lord Jesus Christ, in the ministry of the gospel. . . .

X. In the beginning of the country, the ministers had their frequent meetings, which were most usually after their public and weekly or monthly lectures, wherein they consulted for the welfare of their churches; nor had they ordinarily any difficulty in their churches, which were not in these meetings offered unto consideration; for their mutual direction and assistance: and these meetings are maintained unto this day. The private Christians also had their private meetings, wherein they would seek the face, and sing the praise of God; and confer upon some questions of practical religion, for their mutual edification. And the country still is full of those little meetings; . . . Our private meetings of good people to pray and praise God, and hear sermons, either preached perhaps by the younger candidates for the ministry, (who here use to form themselves, at their entrance into their work,) or else repeated by exact writers of short-hand after their pastors; and sometimes to spend whole days in fasting and prayer, especially when any of the neighbourhood are in affliction, or when the communion of the Lord's table is approaching; those do still abound among us; but the meals that made meatings of them, are generally laid aside. I suppose, 'twas with some eye to what he had seen in this country, that Mr. Firmin has given this report, in a book printed 1681. "Plain mechanics have I known, well catechised, and humble Christians, excellent in practical piety: they kept their station, did not aspire to be preachers, but for gifts of prayer, few clergy-men must come near them. I have known some of them, when they did keep their fasts, (as they did often) they divided the work of prayer; the first begun with confession; the second went on with petition for themselves; the third with petition for church and kingdom; the fourth with thanksgiving: every one kept his own part, and did not meddle with another part. Such excellent matter, so compacted without tautologies; each of them for a good time, about an hour, if not more, apiece; to the wondering of those which joined with them. Here was no reading of liturgies: these were old Jacob's sons, they could wrestle and prevail with God."

(19)

Michael Wigglesworth

1631-1705

A graduate of Harvard, Wigglesworth, a physician, minister, and writer, spent most of his life in an attempt to perfect himself in holiness. He conceived of verse as a vehicle of serving God and educating the people. *The Day of Doom,* first published in 1662, was extraordinarily popular; eighteen hundred copies were sold the first year—a huge sale for that day, considering the colony's small population.

This selection illustrates the religious and didactic nature of Puritan poetry. The text is from *The Day of Doom,* fifth edition (Boston, 1701).

(38)
All silence keep both Goats and Sheep
   before the Judge's Throne:
With mild aspect to his Elect
   then spake the Holy One;
My Sheep draw near, your Sentence hear,
   which is to you no dread,
Who clearly now discern, and know
   your sins are pardoned.

(43)

My grace to one is wrong to none:
    none can Election claim
Amongst all those their souls that lose,
    none can Rejection blame.
He that may chuse, or else refuse,
    all men to save or spill,
May this Man chuse, and that refuse,
    redeeming whom he will.

(44)

But as for those whom I have chose
    Salvations heirs to be,
I underwent their punishment,
    and therefore set them free,
I bore their grief, and their relief
    by suffering procur'd,
That they of bliss and happiness
    might firmly be assur'd.

(147)

Christ readily makes This Reply,
    I damn you not because
You are rejected, or not elected,
    but you have broke my Laws:
It is but vain your wits to strain,
    the end and means to sever:
Men fondly seek to part or break
    what God hath link'd together.

(148)

Whom God will save, such he will have,
    the means of life to use:
Whom he'll pass by, shall chuse to dy,
    and ways of life refuse.
He that fore-sees, and fore decrees,
    in wisdom order'd has,
That man's free will electing ill,
    shall bring his will to pass.

(149)

High God's Decree, as it is free,
    so doth it none compel
Against their will to good or ill,
    it forceth none to Hell.

They have their wish whose Souls perish
    with Torments in Hell-fire,
Who rather chose their Souls to lose,
    than leave a loose desire.

(203)

What? to be sent to *Punishment,*
    and flames of *Burning Fire,*
To be surrounded, and eke confounded
    with Gods *Revengful ire.*
What? to abide, not for a tide
    these Torments, but for *Ever:*
To be released, or to be eased.
    not after years, but *Never.*

(204)

Oh, *fearful Doom!* now there's no room
    for hope or help at all:
Sentence is past which aye shall last,
    Christ will not it recall.
There might you hear them rent and tear
    the Air with their out-cries:
The hideous noise of their sad voice
    ascendeth to the Skies.

(205)

They wring their hands, their caitiff-hands
    and gnash their teeth for terrour;
They cry, they roar for anguish sore,
    and gnaw their tongues for horrour.
But get away without delay,
    Christ pities not your cry:
Depart to Hell, there may you yell,
    and roar Eternally.

(219)

The Saints behold with courage bold,
    and thankful wonderment,
To see all those that were their foes
    thus sent to punishment:
Then do they sing unto their King
    a Song of endless Praise:
They praise his Name, and do proclaim
    that just are all his ways.

Anne Bradstreet

1612-1672

The daughter of Governor Thomas Dudley, Anne Bradstreet migrated to New England in 1630. She is the author of the first important book of poems to be written in America. Although religion was the motive force behind her writing, she wrote her poetry not to instruct others but rather to express her own emotions. The following selections are from her collection *Several Poems,* second edition (Boston, 1678).

TO MY DEAR AND LOVING HUSBAND

If ever two were one, then surely we.
If ever man were lov'd by wife, then thee;
If ever wife was happy in a man,
Compare with me ye women if you can.
I prise thy love more then whole Mines of gold,
Or all the riches that the East doth hold.
My love is such that Rivers cannot quench,
Nor ought but love from thee, give recompence.
Thy love is such I can no way repay,
The heavens reward thee manifold I pray.
Then while we live, in love lets so persever,
That when we live no more, we may live ever.

A LETTER TO HER HUSBAND, ABSENT UPON PUBLIC EMPLOYMENT

My head, my heart, mine Eyes, my life, nay more,
My joy, my Magazine of earthly store,
If two be one, as surely thou and I,
How stayest thou there, whilst I at *Ipswich* lie?
So many steps, head from the heart to sever
If but a neck, soon should we be together:
I like the earth this season, mourn in black,

My Sun is gone so far in's Zodiack,
Whom whilst I 'joy'd, nor storms, nor frosts I felt,
His warmth such frigid colds did cause to melt.
My chilled limbs now numbed lie forlorn;
Return, return sweet *Sol* from *Capricorn,*
In this dead time, alas, what can I more
Then view those fruits which through thy heat I bore?
Which sweet contentment yield me for a space,
True living Pictures of their Fathers face.
O strange effect! now thou art *Southward* gone,
I weary grow, the tedious day so long;
But when thou *Northward* to me shalt return,
I wish my Sun may never set, but burn
Within the Cancer of my glowing breast,
The welcome house of him my dearest guest.
Where ever, ever stay, and go not thence,
Till natures sad decree shall call thee hence;
Flesh of thy flesh, bone of thy bone,
I here, thou there, yet both but one.

ANOTHER

Phoebus make haste, the day's too long, be gone,
The silent night's the fittest time for moan;
But stay this once, unto my suit give ear,
And tell my griefs in either Hemisphere:
(And if the whirling of thy wheels don't drown'd)
The woful accents of my doleful sound,
If in thy swift Carrier thou canst make stay,
I crave this boon, this Errand by the way,
Commend me to the man more lov'd then life,
Shew him the sorrows of his widdowed wife;
My dumpish thoughts, my groans, my brakish tears
My sobs, my longing hopes, my doubting fears,
And if he love, how can he there abide?
My interest's more than all the world beside.
He that can tell the starrs or Ocean sand,
Or all the grass that in the Meads do stand,
The leaves in th' woods the hail or drops of rain,
Or in a corn-field number every grain,
Or every mote that in the sun-shine hops,
May count my sighs, and number all my drops:
Tell him, the countless steps that thou dost trace,

That once a day, thy Spouse thou mayst embrace;
And when thou canst not treat by loving mouth,
Thy rays afar, salute her from the south.
But for one moneth I see no day (poor soul)
Like those far scituate under the pole,
Which day by day long wait for thy arise,
O how they joy when thou dost light the skyes
O *Phoebus,* hadst thou but thus long from—Thine
Restrain'd the beams of thy beloved shine,
At thy return, if so thou could'st or durst
Behold a Chaos blacker then the first.
Tell him here's worse then a confused matter,
His little world's a fathom under water,
Nought but the fervor of his ardent beams
Hath power to dry the torrent of these streams.
Tell him I would say more, but cannot well,
Oppressed minds, abruptest tales do tell.
Now post with double speed, mark what I say,
By all our loves conjure him not to stay.

Part Two

THE MIND OF THE ENLIGHTENMENT

*F*rom the viewpoint of American intellectual history, the Revolutionary period begins with Britain's defeat of France in the Seven Years' War and ends with the adoption of the Constitution. These two and a half decades witnessed the crystallization of the American Revolutionary mind, the waging of the Revolution itself, and the formation of the Union. Such momentous events provide inexhaustible and exciting materials for those studying intellectual history. For it is in these years that the American mind formulated and articulated its presuppositions and, in turn, utilized them in the destruction of one political tie and the creation of another. Never before in American history, and perhaps never since—as Professor Herbert W. Schneider observes—have public interests been so intimately linked to philosophic issues.[1]

The signing of the peace treaty between Britain and France in 1763 was a welcome event in the American colonies. The threat of French competition in the rich western fur trade was ended and a vast continent seemed ready for the colonists. But colonial rejoicing was to be short lived. Saddled with debt and facing new colonial responsibilities, Britain was already designing a new policy toward the colonies. Before a decade was over, that policy was to bring disillusionment, bitterness, discontent, and revolution to the American shores.

The changed British imperial policy began with the Sugar Act of 1764 and Stamp Act of 1765, both directed at increasing the royal treasury in London. The reaction of the colonies was immediate and bitter. They rejected the idea of direct taxes being levied by Parliament and proclaimed their opposition to such taxation in a series of resolutions and declarations of

---

1. Herbert W. Schneider, *A History of American Philosophy* (New York, 1946), p. 35.

rights. As a result Parliament repealed the Stamp Act but substituted a series of revenue measures known as the Townshend Acts of 1767, which further incensed the colonies. Parliament finally repealed the Townshend Act in 1770, but at the same time it maintained the duty on tea, and thus provoked continued colonial resentment.

Few if any colonists thought in terms of ultimate independence during the early years of grievance. Yet, in retrospect, the entire period was one of inexorable movement toward separation from Britain. Indeed, the Revolution was accomplished in the years prior to 1776. In the words of John Adams, "The Revolution was effected before the war commenced. The Revolution was in the hearts and minds of the people. . . . This radical change in the principles, opinions, sentiments, and affections of the people was the real American Revolution."

To achieve "radical change" in the public opinion of America required the continual use of all available means of communication and propaganda. And the patriots successfully employed all these means—including newspapers, pamphlets, verse and songs, speeches, and even to a small extent the theater. Nor were they above the use of directed violence (aimed primarily at property, not life); and at various commemorations, such as the fifth of March addresses in remembrance of the Boston massacre, they made effective use of all the methods of persuasion. The March addresses not only were heard by many, but also were widely read in pamphlet form. Adams wrote of them that they "were read, I had almost said, by every-body that can read, and scarcely ever with dry eyes." Many orators rose to the occasion of the day, and some of them, such as Patrick Henry and Richard Henry Lee, won renown throughout the colonies.

Many of the spokesmen of the rising revolutionary consciousness were members of the professions, a fact that tended early to give a middle-class direction to American society. The legal profession contributed many leaders to the cause. As they analyzed and stated the issues of the day, lawyers like John Adams, John Dickinson, Thomas Jefferson, and James Otis provided both active political leadership and the philosophical justification needed by the revolutionary movement. The clergy, too, particularly the New England Congregationalists, gave support to political home rule as well as to church home rule as they learned to practice politics from the pulpit. Artists and writers contributed to the movement in their own ways, and wrote patriotic songs and verses that were well received throughout the colonies, though both were more stirring than aesthetically satisfying. (Only Philip Freneau and John Trumbull were poets worthy of remembrance for their poetry.) Paul Revere is best known among the artists-craftsmen who gave expression to the ideas of the day. And patriotic writers turned out a series of almanacs, newspapers, pamphlets, and books that were important in molding public opinion. The volume, the scope, and the unanimity of thought in all this material was truly impressive.

What were the ideas and sentiments that found crystallization in this material? The answer to this question may be summed up in the phrase "the American Enlightenment." The American Enlightenment refers to a cluster of ideas, and the mentality that produced them, that became more and more dominant as the colonies moved toward nationhood and that found their consummate political expression in the Declaration of Independence and—perhaps to a lesser extent—in the Constitution.

The spirit of Enlightenment was in many ways a continuous outgrowth of Puritanism, even though it was essentially a rejection of the Puritan mind. For Puritanism had emphasized, together with its theocentrism, a form of rationalism in its ethics, politics, and theology. Nature is God's *techné,* and the ways of God (or some of them) are open to rational beings. The Enlightenment, while always acknowledging the existence of God, was to move from election to Arminianism and deism; from theocracy to Nature, rights, happiness, and tolerance; and from religious to more secular virtues. It was also to become even more worldly than Puritanism in its emphasis on progress, mission, and social justice (though Puritanism, too, unlike medieval piety, had come to grips with the world). Despite these differences, a basic continuity with the Puritans remained.

But the more direct source of the spirit of Enlightenment was the scientific writing of Sir Isaac Newton and the political philosophy of John Locke. Newton had proceeded by a rational, mathematical method to demonstrate truths, or "laws," about the physical universe. Both aspects of his work became widely influential, and in fact formed the basis of much of eighteenth-century thought on both sides of the Atlantic.

The mathematical systematization of scientific thought had been the means for Newton's synthesis, which offered a picture of nature as thoroughly orderly, lawful, and rational. The Enlightenment understandably drew the implication—with hints from Newton himself—that the mathematical-scientific method could and should be used to reach secure conclusions or laws in all fields of human concern. "The great object of human endeavor," writes Professor J. H. Randall, Jr., "was to discover what in every field was natural and reasonable, and to brush aside the accretions of irrational tradition that Reason and Nature might the more easily be free to display its harmonious order."[2]

The search for the reasonable and the natural led to a scientific study of man, including his history, his religion, his ethics, and his politics. Here, too, regularities and certainties seemed available to the rational mind. The rational was taken as the natural, and the natural was the lawful. In the field of politics—most immediately important to the American colonies—the search ended in the theory of natural law.

It was at this point that the American Enlightenment learned so much from Locke. Locke's importance for the history of ideas lies in the fact that he was one of the first philosophers to develop the philosophical conse-

---

2. John Herman Randall, Jr., *The Making of the Modern Mind* (Boston, 1940), p. 276.

quences of modern science and to show its implications for morality, religion, and politics. So pervasive was his influence that John Adams was led to remark that the Declaration of Independence was simply a recapitulation of Locke's *Second Treatise on Government.* While today we cannot be as sure as Adams was of Locke's own meaning in his political writings, or of their relation to democratic theory, or even of the precise nature of his influence on the framers of revolutionary thought, he nevertheless remains a critical figure for an understanding of the American Enlightenment.

In developing a theory of the state in harmony with Enlightenment sympathies, Locke argued that man's life in society must be governed by those regularities called the "natural law." The natural law required that men abandon outworn traditional institutions and replace them with the rational institutions of the enlightened state. Locke went even further in applying the "law of reason" to society. He argued that since there is no natural positional relation among human beings (as, for example, there is a natural spatial relation among physical substances) "hierarchies" or political aristocracies are neither natural nor inevitable. All social and political relations, including those formalized by a framework of law, are conventions men have agreed to, and so they obtain their authority solely by the consent of the individual. Likewise, religion is properly the concern of the individual himself, hence toleration not theocracy, democracy not divine right, should be the rule in human society.

As we turn to the writings of the Revolutionary period, we find these philosophical ideas of the American Enlightenment forming the background of Revolutionary thought. Even the earliest protests against British policy contained references to the natural rights of men, and such rights continued to be the basis of protest up to the Declaration of Independence itself. Perhaps even more useful historically was the derivation from natural-law theory of the right of revolution, the right to reject a political order and establish a new government. This derivation was primarily the work of Jonathan Mayhew and Thomas Paine. John Adams called Mayhew's *Discourse on Unlimited Submission and Passive Obedience* the "opening gun of the Revolution." In this work, Mayhew argued against political absolutism and the theory of divine right supporting it; as his own contribution he justified the right of revolution against any king who set himself above the law. Then Paine, the supreme pamphleteer, took over as the spokesman of revolution during the decisive events of 1776. The colonies had chosen, in their appeal to mankind's common sense, to bring all institutions, including government, before the bar of reason. Should reason demonstrate the threat of such institutions to the individual, they must be altered or overturned. The themes of the Enlightenment —reason, natural rights, progress, nature, social contract, consent, individualism, liberty and equality, rational virtue—were constantly invoked in the shaping of revolutionary opinion and revolutionary action.

And yet these ideas were not without their difficulties and ambiguities. This becomes apparent as we review the events between 1776 and the inauguration of Washington in 1789. Government during these years was centered in the Continental Congress. This group proposed and adopted the Declaration of Independence, undertook the duties of a legislative and executive body charged with conducting the war, and, in 1777, drew up the Articles of Confederation which formed the basis of government until 1789.

The achievements of the Continental Congress were impressive, but once Independence had been won many leaders of the day began to see the need for "a more perfect union." The final issue of this need was the Constitution. Once again, during the debates and the well-known compromises of the Constitutional Convention, the fundamental ideas of the Enlightenment were invoked to solve the problems of historical circumstance. Truly, the very idea that men could come together to create justice, almost to begin history anew, was itself a concept of the Enlightenment.

But did the Constitutional debates—and the Constitution—hold to the ideas of the Declaration? This continues to be a much disputed point, and even the contemporaries of the Founding Fathers were divided on their views of the Constitution. Conservatives were generally satisfied that the Constitution expressed the best political thought of the day. Other observers, such as Jefferson, were disturbed that it did not limit the tenure of office of the President or contain a bill of rights. More extreme dissent was expressed by men like George Mason, who believed it was setting up at best "a moderate aristocracy" that might devolve into monarchy or "corrupt, tyrannical aristocracy."

The Bill of Rights was soon appended to the Constitution, and before a generation had passed, most Americans had come to accept the document as a wise and effective instrument of government. The problem of relating the Constitution to the philosophy of the Enlightenment became in some ways almost an academic one—partly because that philosophy, as a philosophy, was never systematically developed, and partly because, whatever its philosophical justification, the Constitution was serving the nation effectively—and the emerging pragmatism of the American mind that was to become a dominant national characteristic soon found this sufficient justification. Yet the struggles of the day—political, economic, military, legal, even moral and religious—had produced a document truly worthy of the effort, and one that continues to serve the nation not only as a basis of law and unity but also as a national symbol.

VI

Reason and Benevolence

THE ENLIGHTENMENT not only used the methods of the rising sciences for the study of nature but also, as we have seen, extended those methods to the areas of ethics, law, politics, and religion. Certainties were available in all these areas, and starting with sure premises, the enlightened mind could arrive at moral as well as scientific truths. Science had given man a new method: it only remained to apply it generally. "I am bold enough to think," wrote Locke, "that morality is capable of demonstration, as well as mathematics."

The promise of science, then, was one motivation for reconsidering the problems of ethics. A second motive was the search for an ethics (and, in turn, a politics) that would be independent of the theoretical sanctions of church and state. As a prominent political theorist has observed, "Morality associated with either Catholicism or Protestantism was vitiated by that dependence. . . . As soon as Toleration prevailed, orthodoxy faded. That followed—if persecution, sorcery, etc., were wrong, then the religions that promoted them were not to be trusted. Conscience must look elsewhere."[1] And conscience did look elsewhere. During the eighteenth century Europeans were reviving the ancient philosophies of Stoicism and Epicureanism—ethical systems requiring no sanction of church or state—as well as developing such autonomous systems as Francis Hutcheson's theory of moral sense and the utilitarianism of Jeremy Bentham. The separation of religion and ethics was accomplished by the early leaders of the Enlightenment. And with the rising spirit of autonomous ethical values went toleration, an ideal that found its classic expression in Locke's *Essay on Toleration*.

The ethical thought of the Enlightenment was primarily derived from the Greeks, but not wholly so. It also worked within the Judaic-Christian tradition. Consequently, its philosophical heritage included the ideal of love or benevolence as well as the Greek virtues of courage, temperance, justice, and wisdom. The Enlightenment, inspired by the rationalism of science, adopted both the method of Greek ethics and the content of Christian morality, and its ethical thinking was aimed at harmonizing these two traditions.

The philosophy of the American Enlightenment was not that of traditional

---

1. G. E. Fasnacht, *Acton's Political Philosophy* (London, 1952), p. 202.

Christianity. There was, to be sure, continuity between Puritan and Enlightenment virtues—a continuity supported in part by the Puritan's insistence on the intelligibility of God in terms of art and contract. But Puritan virtues were in any case not entirely orthodox, and the secularism of the day made explicit the divorce from some of the major Christian moral traditions. Professor Schneider takes this divorce to be at the heart of the American Enlightenment in general.[2]

In the selections that follow, we find these motifs of the Enlightenment. Franklin's well-known autobiography expounds a secular humanitarianism quite true to Enlightenment ideals. President Witherspoon's lectures on moral philosophy are those of an eminent Presbyterian clergyman, yet they reflect Enlightenment influence. However, it is well to remember that the American Enlightenment, unlike the French Enlightenment, never became atheistic, though in some cases its deism bore little resemblance to traditional Christianity. In Jefferson's thought we find a lifelong struggle to formulate an ethical position that would be true to the spirit of the Enlightenment yet include the "ethics of Jesus." And in the writings of Palmer we find Enlightenment sentiments at their extreme.

(21)

Benjamin Franklin

1706-1790

> The youngest boy in a family of ten, Franklin matured early and lived to become America's first world-renowned citizen. A true symbol of the Enlightenment, he was successful in many fields, ranging from business and public affairs to theoretical science. What also distinguishes him is the relative secularization of his mind. He sought to maintain the chief Puritan virtues but to drop their theological sanctions.
>
> The selection reprinted here is from his discussion of his own moral discipline in his widely read *Autobiography,* taken from the *Memoirs of the Life and Writings of Benjamin Franklin,* 6 vols. (Philadelphia, 1808–1817), vol. I.

It was about this time I conceiv'd the bold and arduous project of arriving at moral perfection. I wish'd to live without committing any fault at

2. Schneider, *op. cit.,* p. 42.

any time; I would conquer all that either natural inclination, custom, or company might lead me into. As I knew, or thought I knew, what was right and wrong, I did not see why I might not always do the one and avoid the other. But I soon found I had undertaken a task of more difficulty than I had imagined. While my care was employ'd in guarding against one fault, I was often surprised by another; habit took the advantage of inattention; inclination was sometimes too strong for reason. I concluded, at length, that the mere speculative conviction that it was our interest to be completely virtuous, was not sufficient to prevent our slipping; and that the contrary habits must be broken, and good ones acquired and established, before we can have any dependence on a steady, uniform rectitude of conduct. For this purpose I therefore contrived the following method.

In the various enumerations of the moral virtues I had met with in my reading, I found the catalogue more or less numerous, as different writers included more or fewer ideas under the same name. Temperance, for example, was by some confined to eating and drinking, while by others it was extended to mean the moderating every other pleasure, appetite, inclination, or passion, bodily or mental, even to our avarice and ambition. I propos'd to myself, for the sake of clearness, to use rather more names, with fewer ideas annex'd to each, than a few names with more ideas; and I included under thirteen names of virtues all that at that time occurr'd to me as necesary or desirable, and annexed to each a short precept, which fully express'd the extent I gave to its meaning.

These names of virtues, with their precepts, were: (1) TEMPERANCE. Eat not to dulness; drink not to elevation. (2) SILENCE. Speak not but what may benefit others or yourself; avoid trifling conversation. (3) ORDER. Let all your things have their places; let each part of your business have its time. (4) RESOLUTION. Resolve to perform what you ought; perform without fail what you resolve. (5) FRUGALITY. Make no expense but to do good to others or yourself: *i.e.,* waste nothing. (6) INDUSTRY. Lose no time; be always employ'd in something useful; cut off all unnecessary actions. (7) SINCERITY. Use no hurtful deceit; think innocently and justly, and, if you speak, speak accordingly. (8) JUSTICE. Wrong none by doing injuries, or omitting the benefits that are your duty. (9) MODERATION. Avoid extreams; forbear resenting injuries as much as you think they deserve. (10) CLEANLINESS. Tolerate no uncleanliness in body, cloaths, or habitation. (11) TRANQUILLITY. Be not disturbed at trifles, or at accidents common or unavoidable. (12) CHASTITY. Rarely use venery but for health or offspring, never to dulness, weakness, or the injury of your own or another's peace or reputation. (13) HUMILITY. Imitate Jesus and Socrates.

My intention being to acquire the *habitude* of all these virtues, I judg'd it would be well not to distract my attention by attempting the whole at once, but to fix it on one of them at a time; and, when I should be master of that, then to proceed to another, and so on, till I should have gone thro' the thirteen; and, as the previous acquisition of some might facilitate the acquisition of certain others, I arrang'd them with that view, as they stand above. Temperance first, as it tends to procure that coolness and clearness of head, which is so necessary where constant vigilance was to be kept up, and guard maintained against the unremitting attraction of ancient habits, and the force of perpetual temptations. This being acquir'd and establish'd, Silence would be more easy; and my desire being to gain knowledge at the same time that I improv'd in virtue, and considering that in conversation it was obtain'd rather by the use of the ears than of the tongue, and therefore wishing to break a habit I was getting into of prattling, punning, and joking, which only made acceptable to trifling company, I gave *Silence* the second place. This and the next, *Order,* I expected would allow me more time for attending to my project and my studies. *Resolution,* once become habitual, would keep me firm in my endeavors to obtain all the subsequent virtues; *Frugality* and *Industry* freeing me from my remaining debt, and producing affluence and independence, would make more easy the practice of *Sincerity* and *Justice,* etc., etc. Conceiving then, that, agreeably to the advice of Pythagoras in his *Golden Verses,* daily examination would be necessary, I contrived the following method for conducting that examination.

I made a little book, in which I allotted a page for each of the virtues. I rul'd each page with red ink, so as to have seven columns, one for each day of the week, marking each column with a letter for the day. I cross'd these columns with thirteen red lines, marking the beginning of each line with the first letter of one of the virtues, on which line, and in its proper column, I might mark, by a little black spot, every fault I found upon examination to have been committed respecting that virtue upon that day.

I determined to give a week's strict attention to each of the virtues successively. Thus, in the first week, my great guard was to avoid even the least offence against *Temperance,* leaving the other virtues to their ordinary chance, only marking every evening the faults of the day. Thus, if in the first week I could keep my first line, marked *T,* clear of spots, I suppos'd the habit of that virtue so much strengthen'd, and its opposite weaken'd, that I might venture extending my attention to include the next, and for the following week keep both lines clear of spots. Proceeding thus to the last, I could go thro' a course compleat in thirteen weeks, and four courses in a year. And like him who, having a garden to weed, does not attempt to eradicate all the bad herbs at once, which would exceed his reach and his strength, but works on one of the beds at a time, and, having accomplish'd the first, proceeds to a second, so I should have, I hoped, the encouraging pleasure of seeing on my pages the progress I made in virtue, by clearing successively my lines of their spots, till in the end, by a number of courses, I should be happy in viewing a clean book, after a thirteen week's daily examination. . . .

It may be well my posterity should be informed that to this little artifice, with the blessing of God, their ancestor ow'd the constant felicity of his life, down to his 79th year in which this is written. What reverses may attend the remainder is in the hand of Providence; but, if they arrive, the reflection on past happiness enjoy'd ought to help his bearing them with more resignation. To Temperance he ascribes his long-continued health, and what is still left to him of a good constitution; to Industry and Frugality, the early easiness of his circumstances and acquisition of his fortune, with all that knowledge that enabled him to be a useful citizen, and obtained for him some degree of reputation among the learned; to Sincerity and Justice, the confidence of his country, and the honorable employs it conferred upon him; and to the joint influence of the whole mass of the virtues, even in the imperfect state he was able to acquire them, all that evenness of temper, and that cheerfulness in conversation, which makes his company still sought for, and agreeable even to his younger acquaintance. I hope, therefore, that some of my descendants may follow the example and reap the benefit.

It will be remark'd that, tho' my scheme was not wholly without religion, there was in it no mark of any of the distinguishing tenets of any particular sect. I had purposely avoided them; for, being fully persuaded of the utility and excellency of my method, and that it might be serviceable to people in all religions, and intending some time or other to publish it, I would not have any thing in it that should prejudice any one, of any sect, against it. I purposed writing a little comment on each virtue, in which I would have shown the advantages of possessing it, and the mischief attending its opposite vice; and I should have called my book THE ART OF VIRTUE,[1] because it would have shown the means and manner of obtaining virtue, which would have distinguished it from the mere exhortation to be good, that does not instruct and indicate the means, but is like the apostle's man of verbal charity, who only, without showing to the naked and hungry how or where they might get clothes or victuals, exhorted them to be fed and clothed.—James ii, 15, 16.

But it so happened that my intention of writing and publishing this comment was never fulfilled. I did, indeed, from time to time, put down short hints of the sentiments, reasonings, etc., to be made use of in it, some of which I have still by me; but the necessary close attention to private business in the earlier part of my life, and public business since, have occasioned my postponing it; for, it being connected in my mind with *a great and extensive project,* that required the whole man to execute and which an unforeseen succession of employs prevented my attending to, it has hitherto remain'd unfinish'd.

In this piece it was my design to explain and enforce this doctrine, that vicious actions are not hurtful because they are forbidden, but forbidden because they are hurtful, the nature of man alone considered; that it was, therefore, every one's interest to be virtuous who wish'd to be happy even in this world; and I should, from this circumstance (there being always in the world

---

1. Nothing so likely to make a man's fortune as virtue.

a number of rich merchants, nobility, states, and princes, who have need of honest instruments for the management of their affairs, and such being so rare), have endeavoured to convince young persons that no qualities were so likely to make a poor man's fortune as those of probity and integrity.

My list of virtues contain'd at first but twelve; but a Quaker friend having kindly informed me that I was generally thought proud; that my pride show'd itself frequently in conversation, that I was not content with being in the right when discussing any point, but was overbearing, and rather insolent, of which he convinc'd me by mentioning several instances; I determined endeavouring to cure myself, if I could, of this vice or folly among the rest, and I added Humility to my list, giving an extensive meaning to the word.

I cannot boast of much success in acquiring the *reality* of this virtue, but I had a good deal with regard to the *appearance* of it. I made it a rule to forbear all direct contradiction to the sentiments of others, and all positive assertion of my own. I even forbid myself, agreeably to the old laws of our Junto, the use of every word or expression in the language that imported a fix'd opinion, such as *certainly, undoubtedly,* etc., and I adopted, instead of them, *I conceive, I apprehend,* or *I imagine* a thing to be so or so; or it *so appears to me at present.* When another asserted something that I thought an error, I deny'd myself the pleasure of contradicting him abruptly, and of showing immediately some absurdity in his proposition; and in answering I began by observing that in certain cases or circumstances his opinion would be right, but in the present case there *appear'd* or *seem'd* to me some difference, etc. I soon found the advantage of this change in my manner; the conversations I engag'd in went on more pleasantly. The modest way in which I propos'd my opinions procur'd them a readier reception and less contradiction; I had less mortification when I was found to be in the wrong, and I more easily prevail'd with others to give up their mistakes and join with me when I happened to be in the right.

And this mode, which I at first put on with some violence to natural inclination, became at length so easy, and so habitual to me, that perhaps for these fifty years past no one has ever heard a dogmatical expression escape me. And to this habit (after my character of integrity) I think it principally owing that I had early so much weight with my fellow-citizens when I proposed new institutions, or alterations in the old, and so much influence in public councils when I became a member; for I was but a bad speaker, never eloquent, subject to much hesitation in my choice of words, hardly correct in language, and yet I generally carried my points.

In reality, there is, perhaps, no one of our natural passions so hard to subdue as *pride.* Disguise it, struggle with it, beat it down, stifle it, mortify it as much as one pleases, it is still alive, and will every now and then peep out and show itself; you will see it, perhaps, often in this history, for, even if I could conceive that I had compleatly overcome it, I should probably be proud of my humility.

John Witherspoon
1723-1794

The only clergyman to sign the Declaration of Independence, Wither-spoon received the M.A. degree from the University of Edinburgh. After he had emigrated to America, his militant tendencies made him a prominent figure in the Revolutionary period. He became president of the College of New Jersey (Princeton) in 1768 and did much to give the college a sense of its potentialities as a cultural center. His lectures on moral philosophy present an interesting union of Enlightenment and Biblical sympathies, centering on the principles of benevolence, justice, and natural rights. The latter, Witherspoon asserts in justification of the right of revolution, is to be achieved or maintained by force if neces-sary. Witherspoon's lectures soon became known throughout the colonies.

The selection is from the third volume of Witherspoon's *Works,* 4 vols. (Philadelphia, 1800).

LECTURE VIII

We come now to our duty to man. This may be reduced to a short sum, by ascending to its principle. Love to others, sincere and active, is the sum of our duty.

Benevolence, I formerly observed, ought not to be considered as the whole of virtue, but it certainly is the principle and sum of that branch of duty which regards others.

We may distinguish between (1) particular kind affection, and (2) a calm and deliberate good-will to all. The particular kind affections; as to family, friends, country, seem to be implanted by nature, to strengthen the general principle, for it is only or chiefly by doing good to those we are particularly related to, that we can promote the general happiness.

Particular kind affections should be restrained and directed by a calm good-will to all. Wherever our attachments to private persons prevents a greater good, they become irregular and excessive.

Some think that a calm and settled good-will to others, is an improvement of the particular affections, and arises from the more narrow to the more ex-tensive; from family, friends, country, to all our fellow creatures. But it seems more reasonable to say, that the general affection is a dictate of our conscience of a superior kind. If it were only an increase and extension of the private affection it would grow more weak, as the distance from ourselves increased, whereas in fact the more enlarged affections are intended to be more powerful than the confined.

When we are speaking of kind affections, it will not be improper to observe that some unbelievers have objected against the gospel, that it does not recommend private friendship and the love of our country. But if fairly considered, as the Scripture, both by example and precept, recommends all particular affections, so it is to its honor that it sets the love of mankind above them every one, and by so much insisting on the forgiveness of injuries and the love of enemies, it has carried benevolence to its greatest perfection. The parable of the Samaritan in answer to the question, who is my neighbor? is one of the greatest beauties in moral painting any where to be seen.

The love of our country to be sure, is a noble and enlarged affection, and those who have sacrificed private ease and family relations to it, have become illustrious, yet the love of mankind is still greatly superior. Sometimes attachment to country appears in a littleness of mind, thinking all other nations inferior, and foolishly believing that knowledge, virtue, and valor are all confined to themselves. As the Romans long ago made the *Punica fides* to mean deceit, so there are not wanting among us those who think that all the French are interested, treacherous and cowardly.

On the great law of love to others, I shall only say further that it ought to have for its object their greatest and best interest, and therefore implies wishing and doing them good in soul and body.

It is necessary now to descend to the application of this principle to particular duties, and to examine what are the rights or claims that one man has upon another. Rights and obligations are correlative terms. Whatever others have a just right or title to claim from me, that is my duty, or what I am obliged to do to them.

Right in general may be reduced, as to its source, to the supreme law of moral duty; for whatever men are in duty obliged to do, that they have a claim to, and other men are considered as under an obligation to permit them. Again, as our own happiness is a lawful object or end, we are supposed to have each a right to prosecute this; but as our prosecutions may interfere we limit each others rights, and a man is said to have a right or power to promote his own happiness by those means which are not in themselves criminal or injurious to others.

Rights may be divided or classed in several different ways; an attention to all of which is of use on this subject. Rights may be (1) natural or acquired. Natural rights are such as are essential to man, and universal—acquired are those that are the fruits of industry, the effects of accident or conquest. A man has a natural right to act for his own preservation and to defend himself from injury, but not a natural right to domineer, to riches (comparatively speaking) or to any particular office in a constituted state.

(2) Rights are considered as perfect and imperfect. Those are called perfect rights which can be clearly ascertained in their circumstances, and which we may make use of force to obtain when they are denied us. Imperfect rights are such as we may demand, and others ought to give us, yet we have no title to compel them. Self-preservation is a perfect right, but to have a grateful return for a favor is not a perfect right.

All the duties of justice are founded on the perfect rights; those of mercy generally on the imperfect rights.

The violation of an imperfect right is often as great an act of immorality as that of a perfect right. It is often as immoral, or more so, to refuse to supply the necessitous, or to do it too sparingly, as to commit a small injury against a man's person or fortune. Yet the last is the breach of a perfect right, and the other of an imperfect.

Human laws reach only, in ordinary cases, to the perfect rights. Sometimes imperfect rights by being carried far become perfect, as humanity and gentleness in a parent to a child may be so grossly violated as to warrant the interposition of human authority.

(3) Rights are alienable and unalienable. The first we may, according to justice and prudence, surrender or give up by our own act; the others we may not. A man may give away his own goods, lands, money. There are several things which he cannot give away, as a right over his own knowledge, thoughts, &c. Others which he ought not, as a right to judge for himself in all matters of religion, his right to self-preservation, provision, &c. Some say that liberty is unalienable, and that those who have even given it away may lawfully resume it.

The distinction between rights as alienable and unalienable is very different from that of natural and acquired. Many of the rights which are strictly natural and universal may be alienated in a state of society for the good of the whole as well as of private persons; as for example, the right of self-defence; this is in a great measure given up in a state of civil government into the hands of the public—and the right of doing justice to ourselves or to others in matters of property, is wholly given up.

(4) Rights may be considered as they differ with regard to their object. 1. Rights we have over our own persons and actions. This class is called liberty. 2. Rights over things or goods which belong to us. This is called property. 3. Rights over the persons and actions of other men. This is called authority. 4. Rights in the things which are the property of others, which are of several sorts.

When we come to the second great division of moral philosophy, politics, the above distinctions will be more fully explained—at present it is sufficient to point at them in order to show what are the great lines of duty from man to man.

Our duty to others, therefore, may be all comprehended in these two particulars, justice and mercy.

Justice consists in giving or permitting others to enjoy whatever they have a perfect right to—and making such an use of our own rights as not to encroach upon the rights of others. There is one writer, David Hume, who has derided the duty of justice, resolving it wholly into power and conveniency, and has affirmed that property is common, than which nothing can be more contrary to reason; for if there is any thing clear as a dictate of reason, it is, that there are many rights which men severally possess, which others ought not to violate. The foundation of property in goods, I will afterwards show you is plainly laid in the social state.

Another virtue which this author ridicules is chastity. This however will be found to be included in justice, and to be found in the sentiments of all nations, and to have the clearest foundation both in nature and public utility.

Mercy is the other great branch of our duty to man, and is the exercise of the benevolent principle in general, and of the several particular kind affections. Its acts, generally speaking, belong to the class of imperfect rights, which are strongly binding upon the conscience, and absolutely necessary to the subsistence of human society; yet such as cannot be enforced with rigor and precision by human laws.

Mercy may be generally explained by a readiness to do all the good offices to others that they stand in need of, and are in our power, unless they are opposed to some perfect right, or an imperfect one of greater moment.

(23)

Thomas Jefferson

1743-1826

Educated at William and Mary, Jefferson remained a man of scholarly habits and interests throughout his life. Elected a member of the Virginia House of Burgesses in 1769, he rose to fame as a champion of the Revolution and as the author of the Declaration of Independence. He later served as third President of the United States. His accomplishments, like Franklin's, ranged over the whole of human learning, and his mind was an almost complete embodiment of Enlightenment sympathies. His epitaph indicates the activities most dear to him: "Author of the Declaration of Independence; of the Statute for Religious Liberty in Virginia, and Founder of the University of Virginia."

Jefferson never achieved a truly systematic ethical position, though he spent his life in reflection on ethical problems. Influenced early by European thought, he sought to combine utilitarianism, the moral sense theory, and the ethics of Jesus in a coherent world view. The following selections from his letters show various aspects of his thought. The letters reprinted here are from Thomas Jefferson Randolph, ed., *The Writings of Thomas Jefferson*, 4 vols. (Boston, 1830), vol. III.

TO DOCTOR BENJAMIN RUSH

WASHINGTON, April 21, 1803

DEAR SIR,

In some of the delightful conversations with you, in the evenings of 1798–99, and which served as an anodyne to the afflictions of the crisis through which our country was then laboring, the Christian religion was sometimes our topic: and I then promised you, that, one day or other, I would give you my views of it. They are the result of a life of inquiry and reflection, and very different from that anti-Christian system imputed to me by those who know nothing of my opinions. To the corruptions of Christianity I am indeed opposed; but not to the genuine precepts of Jesus himself. I am a Christian, in the only sense in which he wished any one to be; sincerely attached to his doctrines, in preference to all others; ascribing to himself every *human* excellence; and believing he never claimed any other. At the short intervals since these conversations, when I could justifiably abstract my mind from public affairs, the subject has been under my contemplation. But the more I considered it, the more it expanded beyond the measure of either my time or information. In the moment of my late departure from Monticello, I received from Doctor Priestley his little treatise of "Socrates and Jesus Compared." This being a section of the general view I had taken of the field, it became a subject of reflection while on the road, and unoccupied otherwise. The result was, to arrange in my mind a syllabus, or outline of such an estimate of the comparative merits of Christianity, as I wished to see executed by some one of more leisure and information for the task, than myself. This I now send you, as the only discharge of my promise I can probably ever execute. And in confiding it to you, I know it will not be exposed to the malignant perversions of those who make every word from me a text for new misrepresentations and calumnies. I am moreover averse to the communication of my religious tenets to the public; because it would countenance the presumption of those who have endeavored to draw them before that tribunal, and to seduce public opinion to erect itself into that inquisition over the rights of conscience, which the laws have so justly proscribed. It behoves every man who values liberty of conscience for himself, to resist invasions of it in the case of others; or their case may, by change of circumstances, become his own. It behoves him, too, in his own case, to give no example of concession, betraying the common right of independent opinion, by answering questions of faith, which the laws have left between God and himself. Accept my affectionate salutations.

Th: Jefferson

Syllabus of an Estimate of the Merit of the Doctrines of Jesus, Compared with Those of Others.

In a comparative view of the Ethics of the enlightened nations of antiquity, of the Jews, and of Jesus, no notice should be taken of the corruptions of reason among the ancients, to wit, the idolatry and superstition of the vulgar, nor of the corruptions of Christianity by the learned among its professors.

Let a just view be taken of the moral principles inculcated by the most esteemed of the sects of ancient philosophy, or of their individuals; particularly Pythagoras, Socrates, Epicurus, Cicero, Epictetus, Seneca, Antoninus.

I. Philosophers. 1. Their precepts related chiefly to ourselves, and the government of those passions which, unrestrained, would disturb our tranquillity of mind. In this branch of philosophy they were really great.

2. In developing our duties to others, they were short and defective. They embraced, indeed, the circles of kindred and friends, and inculcated patriotism, or the love of our country in the aggregate, as a primary obligation: towards our neighbors and countrymen they taught justice, but scarcely viewed them as within the circle of benevolence. Still less have they inculcated peace, charity, and love to our fellow-men, or embraced with benevolence the whole family of mankind.

II. Jews. 1. Their system was Deism; that is, the belief in one only God. But their ideas of him and of his attributes were degrading and injurious.

2. Their Ethics were not only imperfect, but often irreconcilable with the sound dictates of reason and morality, as they respect intercourse with those around us; and repulsive and anti-social, as respecting other nations. They needed reformation, therefore, in an eminent degree.

III. Jesus. In this state of things among the Jews, Jesus appeared. His parentage was obscure; his condition poor; his education null; his natural endowments great; his life correct and innocent: he was meek, benevolent, patient, firm, disinterested, and of the sublimest eloquence.

The disadvantages under which his doctrines appear are remarkable.

1. Like Socrates and Epictetus, he wrote nothing himself.

2. But he had not, like them, a Xenophon or an Arrian to write for him. I name not Plato, who only used the name of Socrates to cover the whimsies of his own brain. On the contrary, all the learned of his country, entrenched in its power and riches, were opposed to him, lest his labors should undermine their advantages; and the committing to writing his life and doctrines

fell on unlettered and ignorant men; who wrote, too, from memory, and not till long after the transactions had passed.

3. According to the ordinary fate of those who attempt to enlighten and reform mankind, he fell an early victim to the jealousy and combination of the altar and the throne, at about thirty-three years of age, his reason having not yet attained the *maximum* of its energy, nor the course of his preaching, which was but of three years at most, presented occasions for developing a complete system of morals.

4. Hence the doctrines which he really delivered were defective as a whole, and fragments only of what he did deliver have come to us, mutilated, misstated, and often unintelligible.

5. They have been still more disfigured by the corruptions of schismatizing followers, who have found an interest in sophisticating and perverting the simple doctrines he taught, by engrafting on them the mysticisms of a Grecian sophist, frittering them into subtleties, and obscuring them with jargon, until they have caused good men to reject the whole in disgust, and to view Jesus himself as an impostor.

Notwithstanding these disadvantages, a system of morals is presented to us, which, if filled up in the style and spirit of the rich fragments he left us, would be the most perfect and sublime that has ever been taught by man.

The question of his being a member of the Godhead, or in direct communication with it, claimed for him by some of his followers, and denied by others, is foreign to the present view, which is merely an estimate of the intrinsic merit of his doctrines.

1. He corrected the Deism of the Jews, confirming them in their belief of one only God, and giving them juster notions of his attributes and government.

2. His moral doctrines, relating to kindred and friends, were more pure and perfect than those of the most correct of the philosophers, and greatly more so than those of the Jews; and they went far beyond both in inculcating universal philanthropy, not only to kindred and friends, to neighbors and countrymen, but to all mankind, gathering all into one family, under the bonds of love, charity, peace, common wants, and common aids. A development of this head will evince the peculiar superiority of the system of Jesus over all others.

3. The precepts of philosophy, and of the Hebrew code, laid hold of actions only. He pushed his scrutinies into the heart of man; erected his tribunal in the region of his thoughts, and purified the waters at the fountain head.

4. He taught, emphatically, the doctrine of a future state, which was either doubted, or disbelieved by the Jews; and wielded it with efficacy, as an important incentive, supplementary to the other motives to moral conduct.

☆　☆　☆　☆

TO JOHN ADAMS

MONTICELLO, October 13, 1813

DEAR SIR,

. . . To compare the morals of the Old, with those of the New Testament, would require an attentive study of the former, a search through all its books for its precepts, and through all its history for its practices, and the principles they prove. As commentaries, too, on these, the philosophy of the Hebrews must be inquired into, their Mishna, their Gemara, Cabbala, Jezirah, Sohar, Cosri, and their Talmud, must be examined and understood, in order to do them full justice. Brucker, it would seem, has gone deeply into these repositories of their ethics, and Enfield his epitomizer, concludes in these words. "Ethics were so little understood among the Jews, that, in their whole compilation called the Talmud, there is only one treatise on moral subjects. Their books of moral chiefly consisted in a minute enumeration of duties. From the law of Moses were deduced six hundred and thirteen precepts, which were divided into two classes, affirmative and negative, two hundred and forty-eight in the former, and three hundred and sixty-five in the latter. It may serve to give the reader some idea of the low state of moral philosophy among the Jews in the middle age, to add, that of the two hundred and forty-eight affirmative precepts, only three were considered as obligatory upon women; and that, in order to obtain salvation, it was judged sufficient to fulfil any one single law in the hour of death; the observance of the rest being deemed necessary, only to increase the felicity of the future life. What a wretched depravity of sentiment and manners must have prevailed, before such corrupt maxims could have obtained credit! It is impossible to collect from these writings a consistent series of moral doctrine." (Enfield, B. 4, chap. 3.) It was the reformation of this "wretched depravity" of morals which Jesus undertook. In extracting the pure principles which he taught, we should have to strip off the artificial vestments in which they have been muffled by priests, who have travestied them into various forms, as instruments of riches and power to themselves. We must dismiss the Platonists and Plotinists, the Stagyrites and Gamalielites, the Eclectics, the Gnostics and Scholastics, their essences and emanations, their Logos and Demiurgos, Æons, and Dæmons, male and female, with a long train of &c. &c. &c. or, shall I say at once, of nonsense. We must reduce our volume to the simple evangelists, select, even from them, the very words only of Jesus, paring off the amphiboligisms into which they have been led, by forgetting often, or not understanding, what had fallen from him, by giving their own misconceptions as his dicta, and expressing unintelligibly for others what they had not understood themselves. There will be found remaining the most sublime and benevolent code of morals which has ever been offered to man. I have performed this operation for my own use, by cutting verse by verse out of the printed book, and arranging the matter which is evidently his, and which is as easily distinguishable as diamonds in a dunghill. The result is an octavo of forty-six pages, of pure and unsophisticated doctrines, such as were professed and acted on by the *unlettered* Apostles, the Apostolic Fathers, and the Christians of the first century. Their Platonizing successors, indeed, in after times, in order to legitimate the corruptions which they had incorporated into the doctrines of Jesus, found it necessary to disavow the primitive Christians, who had taken their principles from the mouth of Jesus himself, of his Apostles, and the Fathers contemporary with them. They excommunicated their followers as heretics, branding them with the opprobrious name of Ebionites and Beggars.

For a comparison of the Grecian philosophy with that of Jesus, materials might be largely drawn from the same source. Enfield gives a history and detailed account of the opinions and principles of the different sects. These relate to the Gods, their natures, grades, places, and powers; the demi-Gods, and Dæmons, and their agency with man; the universe, its structure, extent, and duration; the origin of things from the elements of fire, water, air, and earth; the human soul, its essence and derivation; the *summum bonum,* and *finis bonorum;* with a thousand idle dreams and fancies on these and other subjects, the knowledge of which is withheld from man; leaving but a short chapter for his moral duties, and the principal section of that given to what he owes himself, to precepts for rendering him impassible, and unassailable by the evils of life, and for preserving his mind in a state of constant serenity.

Such a canvas is too broad for the age of seventy, and especially of one whose chief occupations have been in the practical business of life. We must leave, therefore, to others, younger and more learned than we are, to prepare this euthanasia for Platonic Christianity, and its restoration to the primitive simplicity of its founder. I think you give a just outline of the theism of the three religions when you say that the principle of the Hebrew was the fear, of the Gentile the honor, and of the Christian the love of God.

TO JOHN ADAMS

MONTICELLO, October 14, 1816

. . . This work [by Destutt-Tracy], which is on Ethics, I have not seen, but suspect I shall differ from it in its foundation, although not in its deductions. I gather from his other works that he adopts the principle of Hobbes, that justice is founded in contract solely, and does not result from the constitution of man. I believe, on the contrary, that it is instinct and innate, that the moral sense is as much a part of our constitution as that of feeling, seeing, or hearing; as a wise creator must have seen to be necessary in an animal destined to live in society: that every human mind feels pleasure in doing good to another: that the non-existence of justice is not to be inferred from the fact that the same act is deemed virtuous and right in one society which is held vicious and wrong in another; because, as the circumstances and opinions of different societies vary, so the acts which may do them right or wrong must vary also; for virtue does not consist in the act we do, but in the end it is to effect. If it is to effect the happiness of him to whom it is directed, it is virtuous, while, in a society under different circumstances and opinions, the same act might produce pain, and would be vicious. The essence of virtue is in doing good to others, while what is good may be one thing in one society, and its contrary in another. Yet, however we may differ as to the foundation of morals (and as many foundations have been assumed as there are writers on the subject nearly), so correct a thinker as Tracy will give us a sound system of morals. And, indeed, it is remarkable, that so many writers, setting out from so many different premises, yet meet all in the same conclusions. This looks as if they were guided unconsciously, by the unerring hand of instinct.

(24)

Elihu Palmer

1764-1806

A brilliant student, Palmer graduated from Dartmouth in 1787. He was a militant deist, and his extreme religious liberalism made it difficult for him to procure a position. He finally became a deistic preacher as well as founder of a deistic society in New York. Palmer also was a political liberal and he hailed the Revolution as the beginning of an age of reason. He lost his sight during a yellow fever epidemic and died a short time later, exhausted from opposing the religious opinion of his day, which found his deism too extreme even for its own liberal tendencies.

The selection here is from his *Principles of Nature; or a Development of the Moral Causes of Happiness and Misery among the Human Species* (New York, 1801).

PREFACE

The following pages have been written with a view to aid the cause of moral virtue, and extend in some small degree, the empire of human felicity. The establishment of theological systems claiming a divine origin, it is conceived, has been among the most destructive causes by which the life of man has been afflicted. History furnishes an awful picture of the fatal effects of fanaticism among the nations of the earth; but history furnishes only the exterior; there is a deeper internal wound which superstition has inflicted in the bosom of society, subversive of all moral sympathy, and of the fairest traits in the character of man. The sincerity with which many upright minds are attached to the Christian religion, can force no substantial objection against an unqualified investigation into its truth or falsehood. If it be founded in truth, it will stand the test of every examination—it will stand the test of all future ages, and become immortal. It is a point of justice to observe, that this work has been written under the misfortune and embarrassment of a total loss of sight—this, in the estimation of candid minds, will form at least a partial apology for verbal incorrectness, or the want of better arrangement in the construction of sentences; but it is not offered as constituting any kind of apology for errors of opinion or principle. On this head, the fullest examination is invited, and if any one can point out in what respect the principles herein advanced are inconsistent and erroneous, the author will be amongst the first to reject and condemn them.

But this must be done upon the ground of evidence, and not of authority, as the latter bears no relation to truth. The great moral and political questions which now agitate the world, cannot be settled by an appeal to the authority of law books, theological books, or the decisions of ecclesiastical councils—they rest upon the broad basis of evidence, and by this principle alone they must be determined. The circumstance that the author was once a public speaker in the cause of Christianity, which is here opposed, so far from forming a reasonable objection against the perusal of this work, ought to become an additional motive of attention; for it was by a candid and attentive investigation into the character of revealed religion, that he became convinced that it was neither true nor divine. It was therefore a duty which he owed to the integrity of his own mind, and what was deemed the best interests of human society to abandon that system, and assume a higher and better ground, that of Nature, and the immutability of her laws. If any one should be disposed to censure on this account, let him remember that there is more honor, and much more utility in the relinquishment, than in the retention of errors.

The AUTHOR

NEW YORK, May 1st. 25th Year of
American Independence.

Chapter I. *The Power of Intellect, Its Duty and the Obstacles That Oppose Its Progress*

The sources of hope and consolation to the human race are to be sought for in the energy of intellectual powers. To these, every specific amelioration must bear a constant and invariable reference, and whatever opposes the progress of such a power, is unquestionable in most pointed opposition to the best and most important interests of our species. The organic construction of man, induces a strong conclusion that no limits can possibly be assigned to his moral and scientific improvements. The question relative to the nature and substance of the human mind is, of much less consequence than that which relates to the extent of force and capacity, and the diversified modes of beneficial application. The strength of the human understanding is incalculable, its keenness of discernment would ultimately penetrate into every part of nature, were it permitted to operate with uncontrouled and unqualified freedom. It is because this sublime principle of man, has been constantly the object of the most scurilous abuse, and the most detestable invective from superstition, that his moral existence has been buried in the gulph of ignorance, and his intellectual powers tarnished by the ferocious and impure hand of fanaticism. Although we are made capable of sublime reflections, it has hitherto been deemed a crime to think, and a still greater crime to speak our thoughts after they have been conceived. The despotism of the universe had waged war against the power of the human understanding, and for many ages successfully combated its efforts; but the natural energy of this immortal property of human existence was incapable of being controuled by such extraneous and degrading restraints. It burst the walls of its prison; explored the earth; discovered the properties of its component parts; analyzed their natures and gave to them specific clasification and arrangement. Not content with terestrial researches, intellect abandoned the earth and travelled in quest of science through the celestial regions. The heavens were explored, the stars were counted and the revolution of the planets subjected to mathematical calculation. All nature became the theatre of human action, and man in his unbounded and ardent desire attempted to embrace the universe. Such was the nature of his powers, such their strength and fervor, that hopes and anticipations were unqualified and unlimited. The subordinate objects in the great mass of existence were decompounded, and the essential peculiarieties of their different natures deliniated with astonishing accuracy and wonderful precision. Situated in the midst of a world of physical wonders, and having made some progress in the analytical decomposition of material substances, and the relative position of revolving orbs, man began to turn his powers to the nice disquisitions of the subtle properties of his mental existence. Here the force of his faculties was opposed by the darkness and difficulties of the subject, and superstition ever ready to arrest and destroy moral improvement, cast innumerable difficulties in the way, and the bewildered mind found this part of the system of nature less accessible than the physical universe whose prominent disparities struck the understanding and presented clear discrimination. The ignorance and barbarism of former ages, it is said, furnish an awful intimation of the imbecility of our mental powers and the hopeless condition of the human race. If thought be reflected back for the purpose of recognizing through a long night of time, the miseries and ignorance of the species, there will be found, no doubt, powerful causes of lamentation; but courage will be resuscitated when the energy of intellect is displayed, and the improvement of the world which has already been made, shall be clearly exhibited to view. It is not sufficient that man acknowledge the possession of his intellectual powers, it is also necessary that these powers should be developed and their force directed to the discovery of correct principle, and the useful application of it to social life; errors, evils and vices, every where exist, and by these the world has been rendered continually wretched, and the history of mankind furnishes the most dreadful lessons, and shocks the sensibility of every human being. The savage ferocity of despotism has destroyed the harmony of society; the unrelenting cruelty of superstition has cut asunder the finest fibres that ever concreted the hearts of intelligent beings. It has buried beneath its gloomy vale all the moral properties of our existence, and entombed in the grave of ignorance and terror, the most sublime energies and the purest affections of the human mind. An important duty is therefore imposed upon intellect, and a departure from its faithful performance should be ranked among the crimes which have most disgraced and injured the felicity of the world. If the few philanthrophists who have embarked in the cause of humanity, have not been adequately rewarded, it is nevertheless true that the principle and force of duty remain the same, unbroken and incapable of being abrogated. It is the discovery and propagation of truth which ought to engage the attention of man, and call forth the powerful activity of his mind.

The nature of ancient institutions, instead of forming a reason against the activity of mind, should be considered as constituting a double stimulus; these institutions are such a complete abandonment of every just and correct principle; they have been so destructive in their operation and effects, that nothing but the strong and energetic movement of the human understanding will be capable of subverting them. The whole earth has been made the wretched abode of ignorance and misery—and to priests and tyrants these dreadful effects are to be attributed. These are the privileged monsters who have subjugated the earth, destroyed the peace and industry of society, and committed the most atrocious of all robberies—that which has robbed human nature of its intellectual property leaving all in a state of waste and barrenness. Moses, Zoroaster, Jesus, and Mahomet, are names celebrated in history; but what are they celebrated for? Have their institutions softened the savage ferocity of man? have they developed a clear system of principles either moral, scientific, or philosophical? Have they encouraged the free and unqualified operation of intellect, or rather by their institutions, has not a gloom been thrown over the clearest subjects and their examination prohibited under the severest penalties? The successors and followers of these men have adhered to the destructive lessons of their masters with undeviating tenacity. This has formed one of the most powerful obstacles to the progress of improvement, and still threatens with eternal *Damnation,* that man who shall call in question the truth of their dogmas, or the divinity of their systems.

The political tyranny of the earth, coalesced with this phalanx of religious despots, and the love of science and of virtue was nearly banished from the world. Twelve centuries of moral and political darkness in which Europe was involved, had nearly completed the destruction of human dignity, and every thing valuable or ornamental in the character of man. During this long and doleful night of ignorance, slavery and superstition, Christianity reigned triumphant—its doctrines and divinity were not called in question. The power of the Pope, the Clergy and the Church was omnipotent, nothing could restrain their frenzy, nothing could controul the cruelty of their fanaticism; with mad enthusiasm they set on foot the most bloody and terrific crusades, the object of which was to recover from infidels the *Holy Land*. Seven hundred thousand men are said to have perished in the two first expeditions which had been thus commenced and carried on by the pious zeal of the Christian church, and in the total amount, several millions were found numbered with the dead—the awful effects of religious fanaticism presuming upon the aid of Heaven. It was then that man lost all his dignity, and sunk to the condition of a brute; it was then that intellect received a deadly blow from which it did not recover till the fifteenth century. From that time to the present, the progress of knowledge has been constantly accelerated; the independence of mind has been ascerted and opposing obstacles have been gradually diminished. The Church has resigned a part of her power, the better to retain the remainder; civil tyranny has been shaken to its centre in both hemispheres; the malignity of superstition is abating and every species of *quackery,* imposture and imposition are yielding to the light and power of science. An awful contest has commenced which must terminate in the destruction of thrones and civil despotism; in the annihilation of ecclesiastical pride and domination; or on the other hand, intellect, science and manly virtue, will be crushed in one general ruin, and the world will retrograde towards a state of ignorance, barbarism and misery. The latter however is an event rendered almost impossible by the discovery of the art of printing, by the expansion of mind, and the general augmentation of knowledge. Church and State may unite to form an insurmountable barrier against the extension of thought, the moral progress of nations and the felicity of nature; but let it be recollected that the guarantee for moral and political emancipation is already deposited in the archives of every school and college, and in the mind of every cultivated and enlightened man of all countries. It will henceforth be a vain and fruitless attempt to reduce the earth to that state of slavery of which the history of former ages has furnished such an awful picture. The crimes of ecclesiastical despots are still corroding upon the very vitals of human society; the severities of civil power will never be forgotten. The destructive influence of ancient institutions will teach us to seek in nature and the knowledge of her laws for the discovery of those principles whose operation alone can emancipate the world from dreadful bondage. If in the succeeding chapters we shall be able to destroy any considerable portion of human errors, and establish some solid truths, our labours will bear a relation to the progressive improvement of the human race, which to intelligent minds, is of all considerations the most beneficial and important.

Chapter XXII. Conclusion: *Reason, Science, Virtue and Happiness*

In surveying the history of man, it is clearly discovered that the miseries and misfortunes of his existence, are, in a high degree the result of his ignorance, and his vices. Ignorance renders him savage and ferocious: while science pours into his mind the benign sentiments of humanity, and gives a new colouring to his moral existence. Reason, which every kind of supernatural Theology abhors—Reason, which is the glory of our nature, is destined eventually in the progress of future ages, to overturn the empire of superstition, and erect upon its ruins, a fabric, against which, the storms of despotism may beat in vain—against which, superstition may reek her vengeance without effect, from which she will be obliged to retire in agonizing tortures. It has been the opinion of some honest and intelligent minds, that the power of intellect is inadequate to the moral and political emancipation of man. This opinion, though sometimes it is found to be operative upon benevolent hearts, seems, however, to be at war with the intellectual structure of our existence, and the facts furnished by modern history. In the great question which relates to human improvement, the cause which is productive of thought, cannot, in any high degree, be included as influencing the final decision. It is probable, however, that the opinion which refers intellect to organic material combination, would favour most, an unlimited improvement of the human species. If thought be an effect of matter finely organized, and delicately constructed, the best method of augmenting its power, would be, to preserve the whole human system in the most pure, regular, and natural mode of operation. Parents and instructors, in this respect, are capable of doing great injury, or of producing most important benefits to future ages.

The Science of the world has been, in some measure, diminished by the propagation of an opinion, that there are only a few human beings who are possessed of what is called genius, to the exclusion of all the rest. This looks too much like mystery, and seems to include in it the idea that mind is sent from heaven, to occupy for a short time, a miserable and material tenement, and then return to its native home. It ought to be recollected that earth is the abode of man, and that of this the materials of his existence are composed. His energies, his powers, his existence—all are confined to this place of residence, and to the amelioration of sensitive and intelligent life, all his labours ought to be directed. He should learn to respect, and not despise his reason. He should learn to consider moral virtue, as the greatest good, as the most substantial joy of his existence. In order, however, to be eminently good, a full scope must be given to the operation of intellectual powers, and man must feel an unqualified confidence in his own energies. The double despotism of Church and State, has borne so hard upon human existence, that man is sunk beneath its dreadful weight; but resucitated nations are about to teach kings and tyrants, a lesson awfully impressive, in regard to the destiny which awaits the aggregate injustice of the world. The period is at hand, in which kings and thrones, and priests and hierarchies, and the long catalogue of mischiefs which they have produced, shall be swept away from the face of the earth, and burried in the grave of everlasting destruction. Then will arrive the era of human felicity, in which the heart of unfortunate man shall be consoled—then will appear the moment of national consolation, and universal freedom—then the empire of reason, of science, and of virtue, will extend over the whole earth, and man, emancipated from the barbarous despotism of antiquity, will assume to himself, his true predicament in nature, and become a standing evidence of the divinity of thought, and the unlimited power of human reason.

VII

Liberal Religion and
the Theory of Freedom

Professor Morris R. Cohen has observed that the Enlightenment's appeal to reason or nature was "simply the effort of liberal thought to examine all traditional institutions; to bring them before the bar of reason to justify themselves."[1] The men of the Enlightenment re-examined not only the principles of ethics but also those of religion and—as we have seen in Palmer's writings—the relationship between religion and the state. The results of this re-examination were twofold: the development of deism and the secular or nondenominational theory of freedom.

The writings of Locke were here, as in so much of Enlightenment thinking, the platform from which subsequent developments began. In many ways, Locke's statements on religion were in the Christian tradition: he accepted the existence of God and believed in special revelation. It was rather his basic definitions of religion and the church that departed from tradition. A church, he wrote, is "a voluntary society of men, joining themselves together of their own accord, in order to the public worshipping of God, in such a manner as they may judge acceptable to him, and effectual to the salvation of their souls." From this Locke inferred that the "care of souls is not committed to the civil magistrate, any more than to other men"; and, further, that "the care of souls cannot belong to the civil magistrate, because his power consists only in outward force: but true and saving religion is the inward persuasion of the mind, without which nothing can be acceptable to God."

In bringing religion before the "bar of reason," the American Enlightenment was aware not only of European developments but also of certain concurrent tendencies in colonial thought. John Wise and Roger Williams had already argued against theocracy, and, although their general positions were much too theological for most of the Enlightenment, their conclusions were largely acceptable. There was also some continuity between the Puritan emphasis on reason, science, and God's intelligibility and the deism of the

---

1. Morris R. Cohen, *American Thought* (New York, The Free Press of Glencoe, 1954), p. 124.

Enlightenment. But the emphasis here should be on continuity, not identity. Deism, as it evolved, was to reject most of the specifically theological doctrines of traditional Christian teaching and to base itself on natural reason as the source of religious truth. All denominations felt the liberalizing spirit of the day, even when they rejected an explicit deism. In its extreme forms, as in the belief of men like Ethan Allen, however, deism had little in common with traditional Christianity.

Deism developed partly as an outgrowth of the Enlightenment, partly as a reaction to the excessive enthusiasm of the religious revival (the so-called Great Awakening) of the 1730's and 1740's, and partly as a response to the political needs of the day. Deism began to have significant influence in America about 1760—although it did not attain its full stature until the 1780's. Its institutional development occurred within Unitarianism; King's Chapel, Boston, in 1782 became the first church officially to preach the Unitarian faith. However, the influence of deism had appeared earlier in the realm of political thought. The establishment of the new nation, in particular, gave substance to advanced political concepts, and these, in turn, reinforced the trend toward religious freedom and toleration. This trend is reflected in the Virginia Statute of Religious Liberty, Madison's *Memorial and Remonstrance,* the First Amendment, and Jefferson's many pronouncements on religious toleration. The Enlightenment thus hoped to establish political unity without religious conformity. Though some traditional Churchmen decried it, deism not only provided a rationalistic source of religion and values but also became a political theory and a defense of religious freedom.

(25)

Jonathan Mayhew
1720-1766

Educated at Harvard, Mayhew served as pastor of West Church in Boston all his life. A liberal theologian, he was noted for his learning and industry, his political liberalism, and his support of great causes. His *Discourse* seeks to justify the right of revolution by an appeal to, and reconsideration of, Scripture. It is based on the thought of Locke, Milton, Sydney, Cudworth, Clarke, and Hutcheson.

The text is from *A Discourse Concerning Unlimited Submission and Non-Resistance to the Higher Powers* (Boston, 1750).

☆　☆　☆　☆

TEXT: ROMANS 13, 1–8.

The apostle's doctrine, in the passage thus explained, concerning the office of civil rulers, and the duty of subjects, may be summed up in the following observations;[1] *viz.,*

That the end of magistracy is the good of civil society, *as such:*

That civil rulers, *as such,* are the ordinance and ministers of God; it being by his permission and providence that any bear rule; and agreeable to his will, that there should be *some persons* vested with authority in society, for the well-being of it:

That which is here said concerning civil rulers, extends to all of them in common: it relates indifferently to monarchical, republican and aristocratical government; and to all other forms which truly answer the sole end of government, the happiness of society; and to all the different degrees of authority in any particular state; to inferior officers no less than to the supreme:

That disobedience to civil rulers in the due exercise of their authority, is not merely a *political sin,* but an heinous *offence against God* and *religion:*

That the true ground and reason[2] of our obligation to be subject to the *higher powers,* is the usefulness of magistracy (when properly exercised) to human society, and its subserviency to the general welfare:

That obedience to civil rulers is here equally required under all forms of government, which answer the sole end of all government, the good of society; and to every degree of authority in any state, whether supreme or subordinate:

(From whence it follows,

That if unlimited obedience and non-resistance, be here required as a duty under any one form of government, it is also required as a duty under all other forms; and as a duty to subordinate rulers as well as to the supreme.)

---

1. The several observations here only mentioned, were handled at large in two preceding discourses upon this subject.

2. Some suppose the apostle in this passage inforces the duty of submission, with *two* arguments quite distinct from each other; one taken from this consideration, that rulers are the ordinance, and the ministers of God (ver 1, 2, and 4) and the other, from the benefits that accrue to society, from civil government (ver. 3, 4, and 6). And indeed these may be distinct motives and arguments for submission, as they may be separately viewed and contemplated. But when we consider that rulers are not the ordinance and the ministers of God, but only so far forth as they perform God's will, by acting up to their office and character, and so by being benefactors to society, this makes these arguments coincide, and run up into *one* at last: At least so far, that the former of them cannot hold good for submission where the latter fails. Put the supposition, that any man bearing the title of a magistrate, should exercise his power in such a manner as to have no claim to obedience by virtue of that argument which is founded upon the usefulness of magistracy; and you equally take off the force of the other argument also, which is founded upon his being the ordinance and minister of God. For he is no longer God's ordinance and minister than he acts up to his office and character, by exercising his power for the good of society. This is, in brief, the reason why it is said above, in the *singular* number, *that the true ground and reason,* &c. The use and propriety of this remark may possibly be more apparent in the progress of the argument concerning resistance.

And lastly, that those civil rulers to whom the apostle injoins subjection, are the persons *in possession; the powers that be;* those who are *actually* vested with authority. . . .

I now add, farther, that the apostle's argument is so far from proving it to be the duty of people to obey, and submit to, such rulers as act in contradiction to the public good,[3] and so to the design of their office, that it proves *the direct contrary.* For, please to observe, that if the end of all civil government, be the good of society; if this be the thing that is aimed at in constituting civil rulers; and if the motive and argument for submission to government, be taken from the apparent usefulness of civil authority, it follows, that when no such good end can be answered by submission, there remains an argument or motive to enforce it; if instead of this good end's being brought about by submission, a *contrary end* is brought about, and the ruin and misery of society effected by it, here is a plain and positive reason against submission in all such cases, should they ever happen. And therefore, in such cases, a regard to the public welfare, ought to make us with-hold from our rulers, that obedience and subjection which it would, otherwise, be our duty to render to them. If it be our duty, for example, to obey our king, merely for this reason, that he rules for the public welfare (which is the only argument the apostle makes use of) it follows, by a parity of reason, that when he turns tyrant, and makes his subjects his prey to devour and to destroy, instead of his charge to defend and cherish, we are bound to throw off our allegiance to him, and to resist; and that according to the tenor of the apostle's argument in this passage. Not to discontinue our allegiance, in this case, would be to join with the sovereign in promoting the slavery and misery of that society, the welfare of which, we ourselves, as well as our sovereign, are indispensably obliged to secure and promote, as far as in us lies. It is true the apostle puts no case of such a tyrannical prince; but by his grounding his argument for submission wholly upon the good of civil society; it is plain he implicitly authorises, and even requires us to make resistance, whenever this shall be necessary to the public safety and happiness. Let me make use of this easy and familiar *similitude* to illustrate the point in hand—Suppose God requires a family of children, to obey their father and not to resist him; and enforces his command with this argument; that the superintendence and care and authority of a just and kind parent, will contribute to the happiness of the whole family; so that they ought to obey him for their own sakes more than for his: Suppose this parent at length runs distracted, and attempts, in his mad fit, to cut all his children's throats: Now, in this case, is not the reason before assigned, why these children should obey their parent while he continued of a sound mind, namely, their *common good,* a reason equally conclusive for disobeying and

---

3. This does not intend, their acting so in *a few particular* instances, which the best of rulers may do through mistake, &c., but their acting so *habitually;* and in a manner which plainly shows, that they aim at making themselves great, by the ruin of their subjects.

resisting him, since he is become delirious, and attempts their ruin? It makes no alteration in the argument, whether this parent, properly speaking, loses his reason; or does, while he retains his understanding, that which is as fatal in its consequences, as any thing he could do, were he really deprived of it. This similitude needs no formal application—

But it ought to be remembered, that if the duty of universal obedience and non-resistance to our king or prince, can be argued from this passage, the same unlimited submission under a republican, or any other form of government; and even to all the subordinate powers in any particular state, can be found by it as well: which is more than those who allege it for the mentioned purpose, would be willing should be inferred from it. So that this passage does not answer their purpose; but really overthrows and confutes it. This matter deserves to be more particularly considered. The advocates for unlimited submission and passive obedience, do, if I mistake not, always speak with reference to kingly or monarchical government, as distinguished from all other forms, and, with reference to submitting to the will of the king, in distinction from all subordinate offices, acting beyond their commission, and the authority which they have received from the crown. It is not pretended that any person besides kings, have a divine right to do what they please, so that no one may resist them, without incurring the guilt of factiousness and rebellion. If any other supreme powers oppress the people, it is generally allowed, that the people may get redress, by resistance, if other methods prove ineffectual. And if any officers in a kingly government, go beyond the limits of that power which they have derived from the crown, (the supposed original source of all power and authority in the state) and attempt, illegally, to take away the properties and lives of their fellow subjects, they may be *forcibly resisted,* at least till application can be made to the crown. But as to the sovereign himself, he may not be resisted in any case; nor any of his officers, while they confine themselves within the bounds which he has prescribed to them.

This is, I think a true sketch of the principles of those who defend the doctrine of passive obedience and non-resistance. Now there is nothing in scripture which supports this scheme of political principles. As to the passage under consideration, the apostle here speaks of civil rulers in *general;* of all persons in *common,* vested with authority for the good of society, without any particular reference to one form of government, more than to another; or to the supreme power in any particular state, more than to subordinate powers. The apostle does not concern himself with the different forms of government.[4] This he supposes left entirely to human prudence and

---

4. The essence of government (I mean *good* government; and this is the *only* government which the apostle treats of in this passage) consists in the *making* and *executing of good laws*—laws attempered to the common felicity of the *governed*. And if this be, *in fact*, done, it is evidently, in itself, a thing of no consequence at all, what the *particular* form of government is; whether the legislative and executive power be lodged in *one and the same* person, or in *different* persons; whether in *one* person, whom we call an *absolute monarch*; whether in a *few*, so as to constitute an *aristocracy*; whether

discretion. Now the consequence of this is, that unlimited and passive obedience, is no more enjoined in this passage, under monarchical government, or to the supreme power in any state, than under all other species of government, which answer the end of government, or, to all the subordinate degrees of civil authority, from the highest to the lowest. Those, therefore, who would from this passage infer the guilt of resisting kings, in all cases whatever, though acting ever so contrary to the design of their office, must, if they will be consistent, go much farther, and infer from the guilt of resistance under all other forms of government; and of resisting *any petty officer* in the state, tho' acting beyond his commission, in the most arbitrary, illegal manner possible. The argument holds equally strong in both cases. All civil rulers, as such, are the *ordinance* and *ministers of God;* and they are all, by the nature of their office, and in their respective spheres and stations bound to consult the public welfare. With the same reason therefore, that any deny unlimited and passive obedience to be here injoined under a republic or aristocrasy, or any other established form of civil government; or to subordinate powers, acting in an illegal and oppressive manner; (with the same reason) others may deny, that such obedience is enjoined to a king or monarch, or any civil power whatever. For the apostle says nothing that is *peculiar to kings;* what he says, extends equally to *all* other persons whatever, vested with any civil office. They are all, in exactly the same sense, the *ordinance of God;* and the *ministers of God;* and obedience is equally injoined to be paid to them all. For, as the apostle expresses it, *there* is NO POWER *but of God:* And we are required to *render to* ALL *their* DUES; and not MORE than that DUES. And what these *dues* are, and to *whom* they are to be *rendered,* the apostle *sayeth not;* but leaves to the reason and conscience of men to determine.

Thus it appears that the common argument, grounded upon this passage, in favor of universal, and passive obedience, really overthrows itself, by proving too much, if it proves any thing at all; namely, that no civil officer is, in any case whatever, to be resisted, though acting in express contradiction to the design of his office; which no man, in his senses, ever did, or can assert.

in *many,* so as to constitute a *republic;* or whether in *three co-ordinate branches,* in such manner as to make the government *partake* something of *each* of these forms; and to be, at the same time, *essentially different* from them *all.* If the *end* be attained, it is enough. But no form of government seems to be so unlikely to accomplish this *end,* as *absolute monarchy.* Nor is there any one that has so little pretence to a *divine original,* unless it be in this sense, that God *first* introduced it into, and thereby overturned, the common wealth of *Israel,* as the curse upon that people for their *folly* and *wickedness,* particularly in desiring such a government. (See I Sam. viii. chap.) Just so God, before, sent *Quails* amongst them, as a *plague,* and a *curse,* and not as a *blessing. Numb.* chap. xi.

(26)

Thomas Paine

1737-1809

The son of a Quaker staymaker, Paine came to America in 1774, largely at the encouragement of Franklin. In 1776 he published *Common Sense,* a republican document that met with instant success and was a decisive event in the Revolutionary cause. His other political works include *The Crisis* and *The Rights of Man.* Paine served the patriot cause during the American Revolution; then in 1787 he went to France where his ideas were soon to play a prominent part in the French Revolution. In 1802, he returned to America, only to find his popularity greatly diminished because of his savage indictment of religion in *The Age of Reason.*

The following selection gives his view of the relation of religion and the state. (A subsequent selection will give his general political views.) The excerpt here is from *Common Sense* (Philadelphia, 1776).

As to religion, I hold it to be the indispensable duty of government, to protect all conscientious professors thereof, and I know of no other business which government hath to do therewith: let a man throw aside that narrowness of soul, that selfishness of principle, which the niggards of all professions are so unwilling to part with, and he will be delivered of his fears on that head. Suspicion is the companion of mean souls and the bane of all good society. For myself I fully and conscientiously believe, that it is the will of the Almighty, that there should be diversity of religious opinions among us. It affords a larger field for our Christian kindness: were we all of one way of thinking, our religious dispositions would want matter for probation: and on this liberal principle I look on the various denominations among us, to be like children of the same family differing only in what is called their Christian names.

Ethan Allen

1738-1789

Revolutionary soldier, author, colonel commander of the Green Mountain Boys, Allen is Vermont's favorite son and patriot. His *Oracle* has been referred to as the "Vermont Bible." It represents a deistic position (although Allen professed ignorance of the creed) very similar to Paine's—so similar indeed that Allen was charged with plagiarism. This book is particularly noteworthy, since it was one of the first works published in America to oppose the Christian religion.

This selection is from that book, *Reason, The Only Oracle of Man, or a Compendious System of Natural Religion* (Bennington, Vermont, 1784).

Argumentative Reflections on SUPERNATURAL *and Mysterious* REVELATION *in General*

There is not any thing, which has contributed so much to delude mankind in religious matters, as mistaken apprehensions concerning supernatural inspiration or revelation; not considering, that all true religion originates from reason, and can no otherwise be understood, but by the exercise and improvement of it; therefore they are apt to confuse their minds with such inconsistencies. In the subsequent reasonings on this subject, we shall argue against supernatural revelation in general, which will comprehend the doctrine of inspiration or immediate illumination of the mind. And first; we will premise, that a revelation consists of an assemblage of rational ideas, intelligibly arranged and understood by those to whom it may be supposed to be revealed; for otherwise, it could not exist in their minds as such. To suppose a revelation, void of rationality or understanding, or of communicating rational intelligence to those, to whom it may be supposed to be given, would be a contradiction; for that it would contain nothing except it were unintelligibleness which would be the same as to reveal and not to reveal; therefore, a revelation must consist of an assemblage of rational ideas, intelligibly communicated to those who are supposed to have been the partakers or receivers of it; from the first supposed inspiration, down to this or any other period of time. But such a revelation as this, could be nothing more or less than a transcript of the law of nature, predicated on reason, and would be no more supernatural, than the reason of man may be supposed to be. The simple definition of supernatural is, that which is "Beyond or above the powers of nature," which never was or can be understood by mankind; the first promulgators of revelation not excepted; for such revelation, doctrine, precept or instruction only, as comes within the powers of our nature, is capable of being apprehended, contemplated or understood by us, and such, as does not, is to us incomprehensible and unknown, and consequently cannot for us compose any part of revelation.

The author of human nature impressed it with certain sensitive aptitudes and mental powers, so that apprehension, reflection or understanding could no other wise be exerted or produced in the compound nature of man, but in the order prescribed by the creator. It would therefore be a contradiction in nature, and consequently impossible for God to inspire, infuse, or communicate the apprehension, reflection or understanding of any thing whatever into human nature, out of, above, or beyond the natural aptitudes, and mental powers of that nature, which was of his own production and constitution; for it would be the same as to inspire, infuse, or reveal apprehension, reflection or understanding, to that which is not; inasmuch as out of, beyond, or above the powers of nature, there could be nothing to operate upon, as a prerequisite principle to receive the inspiration or infusion of the revelation, which might therefore as well be inspired into, or revealed to nonentity, as to man. For the essence of man is that, which we denominate to be his nature, out of or above which he is as void of sensation, apprehension, reflection or understanding, as nonentity may be supposed to be; therefore such revelation as is adapted to the nature and capacity of man, and comes within his powers of perception and understanding, is the only revelation, which he is able to receive from God or man. Supernatural revelation, is as applicable to beasts, birds and fishes, as it is to us; for neither we, nor they are capable of being acted upon supernaturally, as all the possible exertions and operations of nature, which respect the natural or moral world, are truly natural. Nor does God deviate from his rectitude of nature in matters of inspiration, revelation or instruction to the moral world, any more than in that of his government of the natural. Man is a species of being who belongs in part to both worlds, therefore, was God to reveal any particular thing to us, he must of course adapt his revelation to our bodies, as well as to our souls; or to our senses as well as to our reason: but a revelation so adapted would be natural instead of supernatural. Which truly is the case respecting all our sensations, reflections and understandings. We will premise that at a future time God should superadd a sixth sense to our sensorium, and that inconceivably diverse from our present five senses, and as mysterious to us at present, as the idea of colours are to persons born blind, by which, when superadded to the other senses, we might perceive and understand such things, as at present are mysterious or supernatural to us, and which without the beforementioned sixth sense would have eternally remained so, but that sense being once added to the sensorium, would become as natural as the other senses, and the premised additional knowledge acquired by it, would be as natural as that which is produced by the instrumentality of the other five senses; so that superaddition to nature, was it possible, and a fact, would not at all contribute to evince the possibility of a supernatural revelation: so likewise admitting that God should superadd mental ability to the principle of the human soul, by which, with the five senses only, it could form simple ideas, and extend its reasonings to a far greater progression than previous to or without such additional mental ability it could have done; still the extensiveness of such supposed reasonings would be as natural, as that which may be supposed to be acquired by the previous mental powers, or that which was supposed to be acquired by the instrumentality of the sixth sense before mentioned. For if it be supposed, that either sensation or reason, or both, be ever so much enlarged by a superaddition, or the mind ever so much improved and enlarged by any and all possible methods, still progression in knowledge would not be supernatural, whether in consequence of a supposed super-addition to nature, or by the improvement of our present compounded natural powers, of sensation or reason or both. Should the perception or knowledge of colours or of sound be communicated to those who are born blind or deaf, or both, and who ever after continue to be so, such discoveries would be supernatural: as, on this position, there could have been no pre-requisite sensitive power or aptitude, which the minds of those who were supposed to be born blind or deaf, could have made use of, in acquiring the premised knowledge of colours or of sound. Therefore, when such discoveries as these are made, we must admit them to be "beyond or above the powers of nature," which is the same as supernatural; so likewise should we extend our knowledge beyond the limits of our mental capacity, or, which is the same, to understand more than we do or can understand, it would be supernatural: and when such facts as these take place in the world, it will be time enough to credit supernatural revelation. The infinitude of the wisdom of God's creation, providence and moral government will eternally remain super-natural to all finite capacities, and for that very reason we can never arrive to the comprehension of it, in any state of being and improvement whatever: inasmuch as progression can never attain to that which is infinite, so that an eternal proficiency in knowledge could not be supernatural, but on the other hand would come within the limits and powers of our nature, for otherwise such proficiency would be impossible to us; nor is the infinite knowledge of God supernatural to him, for that his perfection is also infinite. But if we break over the limits of our capacity, so as to understand any one super-natural thing, which is above or beyond the power of our natures, we might by that rule as well understand all things, and thus by breaking over the confines of finite nature and the rank of being which we hold in the universe, comprehend the knowledge of infinity. From hence we infer, that every kind and degree of apprehension, reflection and understanding, which we can attain to in any state of improvement whatever, is no more supernatural than the nature of man, from whence perception and understanding is produced, may be supposed to be so: nor has or could God Almighty ever have revealed himself to mankind in any other way or manner, but what is truly natural.

All manner of inspiration, revelation, instruction or understanding must unavoidably be denominated to be natural or supernatural, as there is no third way or medium between these two; so that if instead of the word supernatural, we adopt the word immediate, special, instantaneous, or any other phrases, yet we must be careful to affix the same definition or ideas to those several words or phraseology, as we do to the word supernatural, when applied to revelation, viz. "that which is beyond or above the powers of nature." So that when we make use of any terms whatever to define revelation, we must be sure to mean supernatural, for otherwise we should define revelation to be no more than natural, which in the opinion of some people would spoil it, and divest it of all its charms, as most believers are fond of a revelation, which they unintelligibly imagine to be supernatural, though neither they nor any body else know any thing what it is. The word *mystery,* as applied to revelation, has the same impropriety as the word supernatural. To reveal, is to make known, but for a mystery to compose any part of a revelation, is abuse; for it is the same as to reveal and not reveal at the same time; for was it revealed, it would cease to be mysterious or supernatural, but together with other parts of our knowledge would become natural. Was a revelation, like other writings, adapted to our capacity, it might like them be instructive to us; but a mysterious or supernatural one would not. For such doctrine, precept or injunction, which is unintelligible to us, the terms, positions and inferences whereof exceed our comprehension, or "concerning which our ideas are inadequate" (which is the very definition of a mystery) cannot be so much as examined into, or contemplated upon by us, nor could a state of improvement unfold those mysterious things, for which our ideas are altogether inadequate. Such knowledge as we acquire by improvement, is that to which our capacity is adequate, or we could not attain it. But admitting that the knowledge of a mysterious revelation may be arrived at merely by improvement, still such a revelation (though it is improper to call it so) could not be instructive, which must be the end and design of a supposed revelation, for such a premised improvement would have comprehended it as well without it as with it. For if reason has to advance its progression of knowledge, independent of any assistance from the supposed mysterious revelation, untill it is supposed to comprehend it, it would render it altogether uninstructive and useless; inasmuch as the comprehension or understanding of it is supposed to be obtained by the exercise and improvement of reason, without any assistance from the hidden mystery itself, which could not be revealed until reason, by natural improvement, came upsides with it, and by thus exploring the knowledge of a mysterious revelation, would at the same time nullify the usefulness of it. And as reason is naturally progressive in its operations, having once rivaled such revelation, would still advance its improvement beyond it, which, when reason had once surpassed, could gain no instruction therefrom, any more than it did in its previous progression in rivalling it.

(28)

James Madison

1751-1836

Madison was a prominent participant in the major events of the Revolution, one of the most important authors of the Constitution, and later served as the fourth President of the United States.

Madison also played a leading role in the government of Virginia and introduced much legislation, including Jefferson's bill for establishing religious freedom. His *Memorial and Remonstrance* was very influential in defeating an earlier bill to give support to established churches, and thus indirectly helped in securing the passage of Jefferson's bill. This selection is from *A Memorial and Remonstrance Against the General Assessment: Presented to the General Assembly of Virginia, at the session for the year of our Lord one thousand seven hundred and eighty-five* (Bennington, Vermont, 1811).

☆　☆　☆　☆

To the Honorable the General Assembly of the Commonwealth of Virginia

We the subscribers, citizens of the said commonwealth, having taken into serious consideration a bill, printed by order of the last session of general assembly, entitled "A bill establishing a provision for teachers of the christian religion;" & conceiving that the same, if finally armed with the sanctions of a law, will be a dangerous abuse of power; are bound as faithful members of a free state, to remonstrate against it, and declare the reasons by which we are determined. We remonstrate against the said bill:

Because we hold it for a fundamental and unalienable truth, "that religion, or the duty which we owe to the Creator, and the manner of discharging it, can be directed only by reason and conviction, not by force or violence."[1]

The religion, then, of every man, must be left to the conviction and conscience of every man; and it is the right of every man to exercise it, as these may dictate. This right is, in its nature, an unalienable right. It is

---

1. *Declaration of Rights,* Article 16.

unalienable; because the opinions of men depending only on the evidence contemplated by their own minds, cannot follow the dictates of other men. It is unalienable, also, because what is here a right towards other men, is a duty towards the Creator. It is the duty of every man to render to the Creator such homage, and such only, as he believes to be acceptable to him. This duty is precedent, both in order of time, and in degree of obligation, to the claims of civil society. Before any man can be considered as a member of civil society, he must be considered as a subject of the Governor of the universe. And if a member of civil society, who enters into any subordinate association, must always do it with a reservation of his duty to the general authority; much more must every man who becomes a member of any particular civil society, do it with a saving of his allegiance to the universal Sovereign. We maintain, therefore, that, in matters of religion, no man's right is abridged by the institution of civil society; and that religion is wholly exempted from its cognizance. True it is, that no other rule exists, by which any question which may divide a society can be ultimately determined, but by the will of the majority. But it is also true that the majority may trespass on the rights of the minority.

Because if religion be exempt from the authority of the society at large, still less can it be subject to that of the legislative body. The latter are but the creatures & vicegerents of the former. Their jurisdiction is both derivative and limited. It is limited with regard to the co-ordinate departments: more necessarily, it is limited with regard to the constituents. The preservation of a free government requires, not merely that the metes and bounds which separate each department of power, be invariably maintained; but more especially, that neither of them be suffered to overleap the great barrier which defends the rights of the people. The rulers who are guilty of such an encroachment, exceed the commission from which they receive their authority, and are tyrants. The people who submit to it, are governed by laws made neither by themselves, nor any authority derived from them, and are slaves.

Because it is proper to take alarm, at the first experiment on our liberties. We hold this prudent jealousy, to be the first duty of citizens, and one of the noblest characteristics of the late revolution. The freemen of America did not wait until usurped power had strengthened itself by exercise, and entangled the question in precedents. They saw all the consequences in the principle, and they avoided the consequences by denying the principle. We revere this lesson too much, soon to forget it. Who does not see that the same authority which can establish christianity in exclusion of all other religions, may establish, with the same ease, any particular sect of christians, in exclusion of all other sects: That the same authority which can force a citizen to contribute three pence only of his property, for the support of any one establishment, may force him to conform to any other establishment, in all cases whatsoever.

Because the bill violates that equality which ought to be the basis of every law; and which is more indispensable, in proportion as the validity or expediency of any law is more liable to be impeached. "If all men are, by nature, equally free and independent,"[2] all men are to be considered as entering into society on equal conditions, or relinquishing no more, and therefore retaining no less, one than another, of their natural rights: above all, are they to be considered as retaining an "*equal* title to the free exercises of religion, according to the dictates of conscience."[3] Whilst we assert for ourselves a freedom to embrace, to profess, and observe the religion which we believe to be of divine origin; we cannot deny an equal freedom to those whose minds have not yet yielded to the evidence which has convined us. If this freedom be abused, it is an offence against God, not against man. To God, therefore, and not to man, must an account of it be rendered.

As the bill violates equality, by subjecting some to peculiar burdens; so it violates the same principle by granting to others, peculiar exemptions. Are the Quakers and Mennonists the only sects who think a compulsive support of their religions unnecessary and unwarrantable? Can their piety alone be entrusted with the care of public worship? Ought their religions to be endowed, above all others, with extraordinary privileges, by which proselytes may be enticed from all others? We think too favorably of the justice and good sense of those denominations, to believe, that they covet pre-eminence over their fellow citizens, or that they will be seduced by them from the common opposition to the measure.

Because the bill implies, either that the civil magistrate is a judge of religious truths, or that he may employ religion as an engine of civil polity. The first is an arrogant pretension, falsified by the extraordinary opinion of rulers, in all ages, & throughout the world; the second, an unhallowed perversion of the means of salvation.

Because the establishment proposed by the bill is not requisite for the support of the christian religion. To say that it is, is a contradiction to the christian religion itself; for every page of it disavows a dependence on the power of this world; it is a contradiction to fact, for it is known that religion both existed and flourished, not only without the support of human laws, but in spite of every opposition from them; and not only during the period of miraculous aid, but long after it had been left to its own evidence and the ordinary care of providence; nay, it is a contradiction in terms; for a religion not invented by human policy, must have pre-existed and been supported, before it was established by human policy; it is moreover to weaken in those who profess this religion a pious confidence in its innate excellence and the patronage of its author; and to foster in those who still reject it, a suspicion that its friends are too conscious of its fallacies, to trust to its own merits.

Because experience witnesses that ecclesiastical establishments, instead of maintaining the purity and efficacy of religion, have had a contrary operation. During almost fifteen centuries has legal establishment to christianity

2. *Declaration of Rights,* Article 1.
3. *Declaration of Rights,* Article 16.

been on trial. What have been its fruits? More or less in all places, pride and indolence in the clergy; ignorance and servility in the laity; in both, superstition, bigotry, and persecution. Enquire of the teachers of christianity for the ages in which it appeared in its greatest lustre? those of every sect point to the ages prior to its incorporation with civil polity. Propose a restoration of this primitive state, in which its teachers depend on the voluntary rewards of their flocks, many predict its downfall. On which side ought their testimony to have greatest weight, when for, or when against their interest?

Because the establishment in question is not necessary for the support of civil government. If it be urged for the support of civil government, only as it is a means of supporting religion, and it be not necessary for the latter purpose, it cannot be necessary for the former. If religion be not within the cognizance of civil government, how can its legal establishment be said to be necessary to civil government? What influence in fact have ecclesiastical establishments had on civil society? In some instances they have been seen to erect a spiritual tyranny on the ruins of the civil authority; in more instances have they been seen the guardians of the liberties of the people. Rulers who wish to subvert the public liberty, may have found an established clergy convenient auxiliaries. A just government instituted to secure and perpetuate it, needs them not. Such a government will be best supported, by protecting every citizen in the enjoyment of his religion, with the same equal hand which protects his person and his property; by neither invading the equal rights of any sect, nor suffering any sect to invade those of another.

Because the professed establishment is a departure from that generous policy, which, offering an asylum to the persecuted and oppressed of every nation and religion, promised a lustre to our country, and an accession to the number of citizens. What a melancholy mark is the bill of sudden degeneracy! Instead of holding out an asylum to the persecuted, it is itself a signal of persecution. It degrades from the equal rank of citizens all those whose opinions in religion do not bend to those of the Legislative authority. Distant as it may be, in its present form, from the inquisition, it differs from it only in degree: the one is the first step, the other the last in the careers of intolerance. The magnanimous sufferer under the cruel scourge in foreign regions, must view the bill as a beacon on our coast, warning him to seek some other haven, where liberty and philanthropy in their due extent may offer a more certain repate from his troubles.

(29)

John Carroll

1735-1815

The first Roman Catholic bishop in the United States, John Carroll was a scholarly and able leader of the young church in America. Untouched by deism, Catholicism was nevertheless in a new environment, and Bishop Carroll recognized that the Church must adapt itself to these new conditions. In the following letter, taken from the original in the Archives of the Diocese of Baltimore, Maryland, Bishop Carroll states his objections to the ordering of American Catholic ecclesiastical affairs from Rome.

[TO FATHER THORPE]

MARYLAND,
NEAR GEORGETOWN
Feb. 17, 1785

The official information of the advices sent by you June 9th, 1784, was only received Nov. 26th. I did myself the honour of writing to you on the subject, immediately after receiving your letter, which was about the 20th of August, and of thanking you most cordially for your active and successful endeavours to render service to this country. I say successful, not because your partiality, as I presume, joined to that of my old and cheerful friend Dr. Franklin suggested me to the consideration of his Holiness; but because you have obtained some form of spiritual government to be adopted for us. It is not indeed quite such as we wish; and it cannot continue long in its present form. You well know, that in our free and jealous government, where Catholics are admitted into all public councils equally with the professors of any other Religion, it will never be suffered that their ecclesiastical Superior (be he Bishop or Prefect-Apostolic), receive his appointment from a foreign state, and only hold it at the discretion of a foreign tribunal or congregation. If even the present temper, or inattention of our Executive and legislative bodies were to overlook it for this and perhaps a few more instances, still ought we not to acquiesce and rest quiet in actual enjoyment; for the consequence, sooner or later, would certainly be, that some malicious or jealous-minded person would raise a spirit against us, and under pretence of rescuing the State from foreign influence and dependence, strip us perhaps of our common civil rights. For these reasons, every thinking man amongst us is convinced, that we neither must request or admit any other foreign interference than such, as being essential to our religion, is implied in the acknowledgment of the Bishop of Rome, by divine appointment, head of the universal Church; and the See of St. Peter being the centre of ecclesiastical unity.

I am well aware that these suggestions will sound ungrateful at Rome, and that the mention of them from us will be perhaps imputed by some of the officers of the propaganda to a remaining spirit of Jesuitism; but I own to you, that tho' I wish to treat with them upon terms of sincere unanimity and cordial concurrence in all matters tending to the service of Religion, yet I do not feel myself disposed to sacrifice to the fear of giving offence the permanent interests of Religion. I mean candidly and respectfully to state our present situation; the spirit of our people; and the sentiments of the R. Catholics, the principal of whom are ready and desirous to transmit to Rome their opinion on the probable consequences of such a spiritual government, as is laid down in my dispatches from your city. Whether I shall transmit their opinion under their own signature, I am yet uncertain; I would wish to avoid giving the Congregation, or any other person the smallest reason to suspect a cabal to defeat their measures; and if plain and honest representation will not succeed with them, I should fear the effects of intemperate obstinacy. . . .

Our objections to it [ordering American Catholic ecclesiastical affairs from Rome] are—First. We conceive our situation no longer as that of missioners; and the Ecclesiastical constitution here no longer as that of a mission. By acquiring civil and religious rights in common with other Christians, we are become a national Catholic Clergy; Colleges are now erecting for giving general and liberal education; these Colleges are open, both to masters and scholars of every religious denomination; and as we have every reason to believe, that amongst the youth trained in these different colleges, there will be frequently some inclined to the Ecclesiastical State, we Catholics propose instituting a Seminary to form them to the virtues of their future state, and to instruct them in Divinity. Thus we shall in a few years, with the blessing of providence, be able to supply this country with labourers in the Lord's vineyard, and keep up a succession, if we are indulged in a Bishop. We are not in immediate want of one, and it will be more agreeable to many of my brethren not to have any yet appointed; but whenever the time for it comes, we conceive that it will be more advantageous to Religion and less liable to give offence that he be an ordinary Bishop, and not a Vicar-Apostolic, and be chosen and presented to his Holiness by the American Cath. Clergy.

Secondly. For two reasons we think it improper to be subject in our

Ecclesiastical government to the Propaganda: the first is, that not being missioners, we conceive ourselves, not a proper object of their institutions; and the second is, that tho' our free and tolerant forms of Government (in Virginia, Maryland, and Pennsylvania) admit us to equal civil rights with other Christians, yet the leading men in our respective States often express a jealousy of any foreign jurisdiction; and surely will be more offended about submitting to it in matters not essential to our faith. I hope they will never object to our depending on the Pope in things purely spiritual; but I am sure there are men, at least in this State, who would blow up a flame of animosity against us, if they suspected that we were to be so much under the government of any Cong[regatio]n at Rome, as to receive our Superior from it, commissioned only during their good will; and that this Superior was restricted from employing any Clergyman here, but such as that Congregation should direct. I dread so much the consequences of its being known that this last direction was ever given, that I have not thought it proper to mention it to several of my Brethren.

(30)

Virginia Statute
of Religious Liberty
January 16, 1786

Jefferson characterized the struggle for religious freedom as "the severest contest in which I have ever been engaged." He regarded this statute as one of his three contributions to history. It is a powerful and moving statement, arguing that forced support of religion—even one's own—is a deprivation of liberty. Civil rights in no way depend on religious convictions, nor should anyone be compelled to profess religious beliefs.

The text is from W. W. Hening, ed., *Statutes at Large of Viriginia* (Richmond, 1820), vol. XII.

An Act for Establishing Religious Freedom

I. WHEREAS Almighty God hath created the mind free; that all attempts to influence it by temporal punishments or burthens, or by civil incapacitations, tend only to beget habits of hypocrisy and meanness, and are a departure from the plan of the Holy author of our religion, who being Lord both of body and mind, yet chose not to propagate it by coercions on either, as was in his Almighty power to do; that the impious presumption of legislators and rulers, civil as well as ecclesiastical, who being themselves but fallible and uninspired men, have assumed dominion over the faith of others, setting up their own opinions and modes of thinking as the only true and infallible, and as such endeavouring to impose them on others, hath established and maintained false religions over the greatest part of the world, and through all time; that to compel a man to furnish contributions of money for the propagation of opinions which he disbelieves, is sinful and tyrannical; that even the forcing him to support this or that teacher of his own religious persuasion, is depriving him of the comfortable liberty of giving his contributions to the particular pastor whose morals he would make his pattern, and whose powers he feels most persuasive to righteousness, and is withdrawing from the ministry those temporary rewards, which proceeding from an approbation of their personal conduct, are an additional incitement to earnest and unremitting labours for the instruction of mankind; that our civil rights have no dependence on our religious opinions, any more than our opinions in physics or geometry; that therefore the proscribing any citizen as unworthy the public confidence by laying upon him an incapacity of being called to offices of trust and emolument, unless he profess or renounce this or that religious opinion, is depriving him injuriously of those privileges and advantages to which in common with his fellow-citizens he has a natural right; that it tends only to corrupt the principles of that religion it is meant to encourage, by bribing with a monoply of worldly honours and emoluments, those who will externally profess and conform to it; that though indeed these are criminal who do not withstand such temptation, yet neither are those innocent who lay the bait in their way; that to suffer the civil magistrate to intrude his powers into the field of opinion, and to restrain the profession or propagation of principles on supposition of their ill tendency, is a dangerous fallacy, which at once destroys all religious liberty, because he being of course judge of that tendency will make his opinions the rule of judgment, and approve or condemn the sentiments of others only as they shall square with or differ from his own; that it is time enough for the rightful purposes of civil government, for its officers to interfere when principles break out into overt acts against peace and good order; and finally, that truth is great and will prevail if left to herself, that she is the proper and sufficient antagonist to error, and has nothing to fear from the conflict, unless by human interposition disarmed of her natural weapons, free argument and debate, errors ceasing to be dangerous when it is permitted freely to contradict them.

II. *Be it enacted by the General Assembly,* that no man shall be compelled to frequent or support any religious worship, place or ministry whatsoever, nor shall be enforced, restrained, molested, or burthened in his body or goods, nor shall otherwise suffer on account of his religious opinions or belief; but that all men shall be free to profess, and by argument to maintain, their opinion in matters of religion, and that the same shall in no wise diminish, enlarge or affect their civil capacities.

III. And though we well know that this assembly, elected by the people for the ordinary purposes of legislation only, have no power to restrain the acts of succeeding assemblies, constituted with powers equal to our own, and that therefore to declare this act to be irrevocable would be of no effect in law; yet as we are free to declare, and do declare, that the rights hereby asserted are of the natural rights of mankind, and that if any act shall hereafter be passed to repeal the present, or to narrow its operation, such act will be an infringement of natural right.

(31)

Benjamin Franklin

1706-1790

A belief in deism and a dedication to religious freedom characterized Franklin throughout his life. His *Autobiography* and some of his letters, including the following, discuss these beliefs. With many of the leaders of the Enlightenment, Franklin accepted the existence of God and believed in His providential concern for the world. He doubted the divinity of Jesus, however, and interpreted Christianity in terms of its high moral content.

The selection is from *Memoirs of the Life and Writings of Benjamin Franklin,* 6 vols. (Philadelphia, 1808–1817), vol. VI. [For Franklin's career, see p. 124.]

☆　☆　☆　☆

TO EZRA STILES

PHILADELPHIA,
March 9, 1790

REVEREND AND DEAR SIR:

I received your kind letter of January 28, and am glad you have at length received the portrait of Governor Yale from his family, and deposited it in the College Library. He was a great and good man, and had the merit of doing infinite service to your county by his munificence to that institution. The honour you propose doing me by placing mine in the same room with his, is much too great for my deserts; but you always had a partiality for me, and to that it must be ascribed. I am, however, too much obliged to Yale College, the first learned society that took notice of me and adorned me with its honors, to refuse a request that comes from it thro' so esteemed a friend. But I do not think any one of the portraits you mention, as in my possession, worthy of the place and company you propose to place it in. You have an excellent artist lately arrived. If he will undertake to make one for you, I shall cheerfully pay the expence, but he must not delay setting about, or I may slip thro' his fingers, for I am now in my eighty-fifth year, and very infirm. . . .

You desire to know something of my religion. It is the first time I have been questioned upon it. But I cannot take your curiosity amiss, and shall endeavor in a few words to gratify it. Here is my creed.

I believe in one God, creator of the universe. That he governs it by his Providence. That he ought to be worshipped. That the most acceptable service we render to him is doing good to his other children. That the soul of man is immortal, and will be treated with justice in another life respecting its conduct in this. These I take to be the fundamental principles of all sound religion, and I regard them as you do in whatever sect I meet with them.

As to Jesus of Nazareth, my opinion of whom you particularly desire, I think the system of morals, and his religion, as he left them to us, the best the world ever saw or is likely to see; but I apprehend it has received various corrupting changes, and I have, with most of the present dissenters in England, some doubts as to his divinity; tho' it is a question I do not dogmatize upon, having never studied it, and think it needless to busy myself with it now, when I expect soon an opportunity of knowing the truth with less trouble. I see no harm, however, in its being believed, if that belief has the good consequence, as it probably has, of making his doctrines more respected and better observed; especially as I do not perceive that the Supreme takes it amiss, by distinguishing the unbelievers in his government of the world with any peculiar marks of his displeasure.

I shall only add, respecting myself, that, having experienced the goodness of that being in conducting me prosperously thro' a long life, I have no doubt of its continuance in the next, though without the smallest conceit of meriting such goodness. My sentiments on this head you will see in the copy of an old letter enclosed, which I wrote in answer to one from a zealous religionist, whom I had relieved in a paralytic case by electricity, and who, being afraid I should grow proud upon it, sent me his serious though rather impertinent caution. I send you also the copy of another letter, which will shew something of my disposition relating to religion. With great and sincere esteem and affection, I am,

Your obliged old friend and most obedient humble servant,

B. Franklin

P.S. . . . I confide that you will not expose me to criticism and censure by publishing any part of this communication to you. I have ever let others enjoy their religious sentiments, without reflecting on them for those that appeared to me unsupportable and even absurd. All sects here, and we have a great variety, have experienced my good will in assisting them with subscriptions for building their new places of worship; and as I have never opposed any of their doctrines, I hope to go out of the world in peace with them all.

VIII

Of Men
and Government

To ESTABLISH a new nation, conceived in liberty, became the dominant motive of the American Enlightenment by the mid 1770's. By then the Stamp Act and its successors had caused widespread dissent and occasioned declarations of natural rights like the Virginia Stamp Act Resolutions and the Reverend Jonas Clarke's "Instructions of the Town of Lexington in Relation to the Stamp Act." At the same time the volume of protest literature grew and continued to spread the seeds of rebellion and the philosophy of independence.

The thought of the Enlightenment is in many ways stated most clearly in political documents of the period. The men of reason demanded political reforms, but they invoked reason and natural law to justify such action. At hand was the philosophy of Locke, with its theory of natural rights, its social contract, and its espousal of representative government. The result was that, modified and adapted to American uses, Locke provided the basic philosophy for the new nation.

Locke's thoughts on government belong to the moralistic tradition to which later thinkers like Rousseau, Marx, and, in our own time, John Dewey also belong, namely, that political doctrines reflect a moral position and are in fact designed to promote it. Thus, for Locke, the state of nature provides a norm for man's life in society, natural rights are specifications of that norm, and the social contract is a general *moral* agreement to establish a government that will have limited functions and seek to protect natural rights. Indeed, the contract is itself largely an expression of Enlightenment values.

America's actual political experience seemed to suggest and support these values. In many of the colonies, government had been based on royal charters, which seemed to confirm the social contract doctrine. The Virginians, with their quasi-aristocratic society, had practiced a kind of limited government akin to Locke's model. And the activities of pioneers, hunters, and trappers seemed to verify the individualism of Locke's state of nature. Finding Locke confirmed in experience, the Enlightenment believed he had divined political truth. The master assumption of American political thought, the reality of atomistic social freedom, soon ceased to be an assumption and became an absolute.[1]

Lord Bryce observed that American government "is the work of men who believed in original sin and were resolved to leave open for transgressors no door which they could possibly shut. . . . The aim of the constitution seems to be not so much to attain great common ends by securing a good government as to avert the evils which will flow not merely from a bad government but from any government strong enough to threaten the pre-existing communities and individual citizens."[2] Though they might seldom use the term "original sin," the Founding Fathers, unlike some of their European contemporaries, had not basically changed their view of human nature. Government was, after all, the work of men and men cannot fully be trusted. But even this hearty Puritanism was turned to republican uses; for if men need government to curb their unruly passions, men in government cannot be trusted too much because they also have the passions of men.

More like a lawyer's brief than the Declaration, and in the opinion of some authorities, representing a conservative trend away from the spirit of the Declaration, the Constitution was constructed in response to the problems of the day as much as to the demands of a philosophy. An implicit pragmatism in the American mind is evident in the Constitutional debates and compromises. Yet its doctrines of federalism and the separation of powers nevertheless reflect Enlightenment sentiments as directly as does the Declaration itself.

(32)

James Otis

1725-1783

Graduated from Harvard in 1743, Otis became a member of the bar in Boston and held many political offices. A scholar in the law and a student of the classics, he had a quick mind and was an able pleader. His *Vindication* brought him much abuse, yet he struck a high note of patriotism in it. His *Rights of the British Colonies Asserted and Proved* (1764) has been called "one of the earliest and ablest pamphlets written from the natural law point of view." Indeed, in the years before the Revolution his pamphlets had more influence than those of any

---

1. See further Louis Hartz, *The Liberal Tradition in America* (New York, 1955).
2. James Bryce, *The American Commonwealth,* 2 vols. (New York, 1889), vol. I, p. 306.

other American except John Dickinson, and they were of unique importance in the formation of the revolutionary mind.

The selection given here is from *A Vindication of the Conduct of the House of the Province of Massachusetts-Bay* (Boston, 1762).

The Journal stand thus, "Read and Ordered, that Mr. Otis, Mr. Tyler, Captain Cheever, Col. Clap and Mr. Witt, take said message under consideration, and report an answer thereto."

Sept. the 15th, The committee reported the following answer and Remonstrance, Viz.

May it please your Excellency,

The House have duly attended to your Excellency's message of the 11th, Instant, relating to the Massachusetts *Sloop,* and are humbly of opinion that there is not the least *necessity* for keeping up her present complement of men, and therefore desire that your Excellency would be pleased to reduce them to six, the old establishment made for said Sloop by the General Court.

Justice to our selves, and to our constituents oblige us to remonstrate against the method of making or increasing establishments by the Governor and council.

It is in effect taking from the house their most darling privilege, the right of originating all Taxes.

It is in short annihilating one branch of the legislature. And when once the Representatives of a people give up this Privilege, the Government will very soon become arbitrary.

No Necessity therefore can be sufficient to justify a house of Representatives in giving up such a Privilege; *for it would be of little consequence to the people whether they were subject to George or Lewis, the King of Great Britain or the French King, if both were arbitrary, as both would be if both could levy Taxes without Parliament.*

Had this been the first instance of the kind, we might not have troubled your Excellency about it; but lest the matter should grow into precedent; we earnestly beseech your Excellency, as you regard the peace and welfare of the Province, that no measures of this nature be taken for the future, let the advice of the council be what it may.

Which being read, was accepted by a large majority, and soon after sent up and presented to his Excellency by Captain Goldthwait, Mr. Otis, Captain Taylor, Mr. Cushing and Mr. Bordman.

The same day the above remonstrance was delivered, the Town was alarmed with a report that the House had sent a message to his Excellency reflecting upon his Majesty's person and government, and highly derogatory from his crown and dignity, and therein desired that his Excellency would in no case take the advice of his majesty's council. About five of the clock P.M. the same day Mr. *Speaker* communicated to the house a Letter from the Governor of the following purport.

SIR,

I have this morning received a message from the house, which I here inclose, in which the King's name, dignity, and cause, are so improperly treated, that I am obliged to desire you to recommend earnestly to the house, that it may not be entered upon the Minutes in the terms it now stands. For if it should, I am satisfied that you will again and again wish some parts of it were expunged; especially if it should appear, as I doubt not but it will, when I enter upon my vindication, that there is not the least ground for the insinuation under colour of which that sacred and well-beloved name is so disrespectfully brought into Question.

Your's, &c.

Fra: Bernard

September 15th. To the Honourable Speaker of the House of Representatives

Upon the reading of this letter, it was moved to insert these words, to wit, "with all due reverence to Majesty's sacred Person and Government, to both which we profess the sincerest attachment and loyalty be it spoken" "it would be of little importance," &c. But a certain member crying "*Rase them,*" "*Rase them,*"[1] the proposed amendment was dropped, it being obvious, that the remonstrance would be the same in effect, with or without the words excepted against. These dreadful words, under which his Excellency had placed a black mark, were accordingly erased and expunged, and the Message returned to the Speaker.

In the course of the debate a new and surprizing doctrine was advanced. We have seen the times when the majority of a council by their words and actions have seemed to think themselves obliged to comply with every Thing proposed by the Chair, and to have no rule of conduct but a Governor's will and pleasure. But now for the first time, it was asserted that the Governor in all cases was obliged to act according to the advice of the council, and consequently would be deemed to have no Judgment of his own.

In order to excuse if not altogether justify the offensive Passage, and clear it from ambiguity, I beg leave to premise two or three *data.*[2] (1) God made

---

1. Meaning that part of the remonstrance which is in Italic.
2. The natural liberty of man is to be free from any superior power on earth, and not to be under the will or legislative authority of man; but to have only the law of nature for his rule. The liberty of man in society, is to be under no other legislative power, but that established by consent in the common wealth; nor under the dominion of any will, or restraint of any law, but what that legislature shall enact according to the trust put in it. Freedom is not what Sir *Robert Filmer* tells us, O. A. 55. A liberty for every one to do what he lists, to live as he pleases, and not to be tied by any laws. But freedom of men under government, is to have a standing rule to live by, common to every one of that society, and made by the legislative power erected in it; a liberty to follow my own will in all things where that rule prescribes not, and not to be subject to the unknown, unconstant, uncertain, arbitrary will of another man; a freedom of nature is to be under no restraint but the law of nature. This freedom from absolute arbitrary power, is so necessary to, and closely joined with a man's preservation, that he cannot part with it but by what forfeits his preservation & life together. For a man not having power over his own life, cannot by compact or his own consent enslave himself to any one, nor put himself under the absolute, arbitrary power of another, to take away his life when he pleases: no body can give more power than he has himself. He that cannot

all men naturally equal. (2) The ideas of earthly superiority, pre-eminence and grandeur are educational, at least acquired, not innate. (3) Kings were (and plantation Governor's should be) made for the good of the people, and not the people for them. (4) No government has a right to make hobby horses, asses and slaves of the subject, nature having made sufficient of the two former, for all the lawful purposes of man, from the harmless peasant in the field, to the most refined politician in the cabinet; but none of the last, which infallibly proves they are unnecessary. (5) Tho' most governments are *de facto* arbitrary, and consequently the curse and scandal of human nature; yet none are *de jure* arbitrary. (6) The British constitution of government as now established in his Majesty's person and family, is the wisest and best in the world. (7) The King of Great Britain is the best as well as most glorious

---

take away his own life, cannot give another power over it. Locke's *Discourse on Govern't*. Part II. Ch. IV.

The legislative, whether placed in one or more, whether it be always in being, or only by intervals, though it be the supreme power in every common-wealth, yet in the utmost bounds of it, it is limited to the public good of the society, it is a power that hath no end but preservation; and those can never have a right to destroy, enslave or designedly to impoverish the subjects.

These are the bounds to which the trust that is put in them, by the Society, and the laws of God and nature, have set to the legislative power of every common wealth, in all forms of government.

First, They are to govern by established promulgated laws, not to be varied in particular cases; but to have one rule for rich and poor, and for the favourite at court, and the countryman at plough.

Secondly, These laws ought to be designed for no other end ultimately, but the good of the people.

Thirdly, They must not raise taxes on the property of the people, without the consent of the people, given by themselves or deputies.

Fourthly, The legislature neither must nor can transfer the power of making laws to any body else, nor place it any where but where the people have. *Id*. Ch. XI.

Where the legislative and executive power are in distinct hands, as they are in all moderated monarchies and well formed governments, there the good of the society requires that several things should be left to the discretion of him that has the supreme executive power. This power to act according to discretion for the public good, without the prescription of Law, and sometimes even against it, is that which is called PREROGATIVE.

This power, while employed for the benefit of the community, and suitably to the trust and ends of government, is undoubted Prerogative, and never is questioned. For the people are very seldom or never scrupulous or nice in the point, they are far from examining Prerogative whilst it is in any tolerable degree employed for the use it was meant, that is, for the good of the people, and not manifestly against it. But if there comes to be a question between the executive power and the people, about a thing claimed as a prerogative, the tendency of the exercise of such prerogative to the good or hurt of the people, will easily decide the question. Prerogative is nothing but the power of doing public good without a rule. The old question will be asked in this matter of Prerogative, but who shall be judge when this power is made a right use of? I answer, between an executive power in being with such prerogative, and a legislative, that depends upon his will, for their convening, there can be no judge on earth, as there can be none between the legislative and the people. Should either the executive or legislative, when they have got this power in their hands, design or go about to destroy them, the people have no other remedy in this, as in other cases, when they have no judge upon earth, but to appeal to heaven. Nor let any one think that this lays a perpetual foundation for disorder, for this operates not 'till the inconveniency is so great that the majority feel it, and are weary of it, and find a necessity to have it

Monarch upon the Globe, and his subjects the happiest in the universe. (8) It is most humbly presumed the King would have all his plantation Governors follow his royal example, in a wise and strict adherence to the principles of the British constitution, by which in conjunction with his other royal virtues, he is enabled to reign in the hearts of a brave and generous, free and loyal people. (9) This is the summit, the *ne plus ultra* of human glory and felicity. (10) The French King is a despotic arbitrary prince, and consequently his subjects are very miserable.

Let us now take a more careful review of this passage, which by some out of doors has been represented as seditious, rebellious and traiterous. I hope none however will be so wanting to the interests of their country, as to represent the matter in this light on the east side of the Atlantic, tho' recent

---

amended. But this the executive power or wise Princes never need come in the danger of; and it is the thing of all others, they have most need to avoid; as of all others the most perilous. *Id.* Ch. XIV.

"Fatherly authority, or a right of fatherhood in our Author's sense (i.e. Sir *Robert Filmer*) is a divine unalterable right of sovereignty, whereby a Father, or a Prince, (and a Governor might have been added) hath an absolute, arbitrary, unlimited, & unlimitable power over the lives, liberties and estates of his children and subjects: so that he may take or alienate their estates, sell, castrate or use their persons as he pleases, they being all his slaves, and he Lord Proprietor of every thing, and his unbounded will their law." *Locke on Govt.* B. I. Ch. II.

"He that will not give just occasion to think that all government in the world is the product only of force and violence, and that men live together by no other rules but that of beasts, where the strongest carries it, and so lay a foundation for perpetual disorder, mischief, tumult, sedition and rebellion, (things that the followers of that hypothesis, i.e. *Filmer,* and the advocates for passive obedience, so loudly cry out against) must of necessity find out another rise of government, another original of political power, and another way of designing and knowing the persons that have it, than what Sir *R. Filmer* hath taught us." *Locke on Govt.* B. II. Ch. II.

This other original Mr. *Locke* has demonstrated to be the consent of a free people. It is possible there are a few, and I desire to thank God there is no reason to think there are many among us, that can't bear the names of LIBERTY and PROPERTY, much less that the things signified by those terms, should be enjoyed by the vulgar. These may be inclined to brand some of the principles advanced in the vindication of the house, with the odious epithets *seditious* and *levelling.* Had any thing to justify them been quoted from Col. *Algernon, Sidney,* or other British Martyrs, to the liberty of their country, an outcry of rebellion would not be surprising. The authority of Mr. *Locke* has therefore been preferred to all others, for these further reasons, (1) He was not only one of the most wise, as well as most honest, but the most impartial man that ever lived. (2) He professedly wrote his discourses on Government, as he himself expresses it, "To establish the throne of the great restorer king *William,* to make good his title in the consent of the people, which being the only one of all lawful governments, he had more fully and clearly, than any Prince in christendom, and to justify to the world, the people of England whose love of liberty, their just and natural rights, with their resolution to preserve them, saved the nation when it was on the brink of slavery and ruin." By this title, our Illustrious Sovereign GEORGE the III. (whom GOD long preserve) now holds. (3) Mr. *Locke* was as great an ornament, under a crown'd head, as the church of England ever had to boast off. Had all her sons been of his wise, moderate, tolerant principles, we should probably never have heard of those civil dissensions that have so often brought the nation to the borders of perdition. Upon the score of his being a Churchman however, his sentiments are less liable to the invidious reflections and insinuations that High flyers, Jacobites, and other stupid Bigots, are apt too liberally to bestow, not only upon Dissenters of all denominations, but upon the moderate; and therefore infinitely the most valuable part of the Church of England itself.

instances of such a conduct might be quoted, wherein the province has after its most strenuous efforts, during this and other wars, been painted in all the odious colours that avarice, malice and the worst passions could suggest.

The house assert, that "it would be of little consequence to the people, whether they were subject to George or Lewis, the King of Great Britain or the French King, if both were arbitrary, as both would be, if both could levy taxes without parliament." Or in the same words transposed without the least alteration of the sense.

It would be of little consequence to the people whether they were subject to George the King of Great Britain, or Lewis the French King, if both were arbitrary, as both would be, if both could levy taxes without parliament.

The first question that would occur to a philosopher, if any question could be made about it, would be whether the position were true. But truth being of little importance with most modern politicians, we shall touch lightly upon that topic, and proceed to inquires of a more interesting nature.

That arbitrary government implies the worst of temporal evils, or at least the continual danger of them is certain. That a man would be pretty equally subjected to these evils under every arbitrary government, is clear. That I should die very soon after my head should be cut off, whether by a sabre or a broad sword, whether chopped off to gratify a tyrant by the christian name of *Tom, Dick* or *Harry* is evident. That the name of the tyrant would be of no more avail to save my life than the name of the executioner, needs no Proof. It is therefore manifestly of no importance what a prince's christian name is, if he be arbitrary, any more, indeed, than if he were not arbitrary. So the whole amount of this dangerous proposition may at least in one view be reduced to this, viz. *It is of little importance what a King's christian name is.* It is indeed of importance that a King, a Governor, and all other good christians should have a christian name, but whether Edward, Francis or William, is of none, that I can discern. It being a rule to put the most mild and favourable construction upon words that they can possibly bear, it will follow that this proposition is a very harmless one, that cannot by any means tend to prejudice his Majesty's Person, Crown, Dignity or Cause, all which I deem equally sacred with his Excellency.

If this proposition will bear an hundred different constructions, they must all be admitted before any that imports any bad meaning, much more a treasonable one.

It is conceived the house intended nothing disrespectful of His Majesty, his Government or Governor, in those words. It would be very injurious to insinuate this of a house that upon all occasions has distinguished itself by a truly loyal spirit, and which spirit possesses at least nine hundred and ninety-nine in a thousand of their constituents throughout the province. One good natured construction at least seems to be implied in the assertion, and that pretty strongly, viz. that in the present situation of Great Britain and France, it is of vast importance to be a Briton, rather than a Frenchman; as the French King is an arbitrary despotic Prince; but the King of Great Britain is not so *de jure, de facto,* nor by *inclination;* a greater difference on this side the *Grave* cannot be found, than that which subsists between British subjects, and the slaves of tyranny.

Perhaps it may be objected that there is some difference even between arbitrary Princes in this respect at least, that some are more rigorous than others. It is granted, but then let it be remembered, that the life of man is as a vapour that soon vanisheth away, and we know not who may come after him, a wise man or a fool; tho' the chances before and since Solomon, have ever been in favour of the latter. Therefore it is said of little consequence. Had it been *No* instead of *little,* the clause upon the most rigid stricture might have been found barely exceptionable.

Some fine Gentlemen have charged the expression as indelicate. This is a capital impeachment in politics, and therefore demands our most serious attention. The idea of delicacy in the creed of some politicians, implies that an inferior should at the peril of all that is near and dear to him (i.e. his interest) avoid every the least trifle that can offend his superior. Does my superior want my estate? I must give it him, and that with a good grace, which is appearing, and if possible being really obliged to him that he will condesend to take it. The reason is evident; it might give him some little pain or uneasiness to see me whimpering, much more openly complaining at the loss of a little glittering dirt. I must according to this system not only endeavour to acquire my self, but impress upon all around me a reverence and *passive obedience* to the sentiments of my superior, little short of adoration. Is the superior in contemplation a king, I must consider him as God's vicegerent, cloathed with unlimited power, his will the supreme law, and not accountable for his actions, let them be what they may, to any tribunal upon earth. Is the superior a plantation governor? he must be viewed not only as the most excellent representation of majesty, but as a viceroy in his department, and *quoad* provincial administration, to all intents and purposes vested with all the prerogatives that were ever exercised by the most absolute prince in Great Britain.

The votaries of this sect are all Monopolizers of offices, Peculators, Informers, and generally the Seekers of all kinds. It is better, say they, "to give up any thing, and every thing quietly, than contend with a superior, who by his prerogative can do, and (as the vulgar express it) right or wrong, will have whatever he pleases." For you must know, that according to some of the most refined and fashionable systems of modern politics, the ideas of right and wrong, and all the moral virtues, are to be considered only as the vagaries of a weak or distempered imagination in the possessor, and of no use in the world, but for the skilful politician to convert to his own purposes of power and profit.

With these,

The Love of Country is an empty Name,
For Gold they hunger: but n'er thirst for Fame.

It is well known that the least "patriotic spark" unawares "catched," and discovered, disqualifies a candidate from all further preferment in this famous and flourishing order of knights errant. It must however be confessed they are so catholic as to admit all sorts from the knights of the post to a garter and Star; provided they are thoroughly divested of the fear of God, and the love of mankind, and have concentrated all their views in *dear self,* with them the only "sacred and well-beloved name," or thing in the universe. See Cardinal Richlieu's *Political Testament,* and the greater Bible of the Sect, Mandeville's *Fable of the Bees.* Richlieu expressly in solemn earnest, without any sarcasm or irony, advises the discarding all honest men from the presence of a prince, and from even the purlious of a court. According to Mandeville, "*The* moral virtues are the political offspring which flattery begot upon pride." The most darling principle of the great Apostle of the order, who has done more than any mortal towards diffusing corruption, not only thro' the three kingdoms, but thro' the remotest dominions, is, "that every man has his price, and that if you bid high enough, you are sure of him."

To those who have been taught to bow at the name of a King, with as much ardor and devotion as a papist at the sight of a crucifix, the assertion under examination may appear harsh; but there is an immense difference between the sentiments of a British house of commons remonstrating, and those of a courtier cringing for a favour. A house of Representatives here at least, bears an equal proportion to a Governor, with that of a house of Commons to the King. There is indeed one difference in favour of a house of Representatives; when a house of Commons address the King they speak to their Sovereign, who is truly the most august Personage upon earth: When a house of Representatives remonstrate to a Governor, they speak to a fellow subject; tho' a superior, who is undoubtedly entitled to decency and respect; but I hardly think to quite so much Reverence as his master.

It may not be amiss to observe, that a form of speech may be, in so sort improper, when used *arguendo,* or for illustration, speaking of the King, which same form might be very harsh, indecent and even ridiculous, if spoken to the King.

The expression under censure has had the approbation of diverse Gentlemen of sense, who are quite unprejudiced by any party. They have taken it to imply a compliment rather than any indecent reflection, upon his Majesty's wise and gracious administration. It seems strange therefore that the house should be so suddenly charged by his Excellency with *Impropriety, groundless Insinuations,* &c.

What cause of so bitter Repentance, *again* and *again,* could possibly have taken place, if this clause had been printed in the Journal, I can't imagine. If the case be fairly represented, I guess the province can be in no danger from a house of Representatives daring to speak plain English, when they are complaining of a grievance. I sincerely believe the house had no disposition to enter into any contest with the Governor or Council. Sure I am that the promoters of this address had no such view. On the contrary, there is the highest reason to presume that the house of Representatives will at all times rejoice in the prosperity of the Governor and Council, and contribute their utmost assistance, in supporting those two branches of the legislature, in all their just rights and preheminence. But the house is and ought to be jealous and tenacious of its own priviledges; these are a sacred deposit intrusted by the people, and the jealousy of them is a godly jealousy.

(33)

Samuel Adams

1722-1803

> Revolutionary statesman and author, Sam Adams was said to have had but one occupation, public business. A graduate of Harvard, he soon became a leading figure in Massachusetts politics, and represented that colony as a delegate to the Continental Congress. He was a skillful polemic writer and continued the natural law philosophy that began in America with John Wise and found consummate expression in the Declaration of Independence. He has been called "the Father of the American Revolution."
>
> This selection is from *The Rights of the Colonists* (Old South Leaflets: n. p., n. d.), vol. VII.

REPORT OF THE COMMITTEE OF CORRESPONDENCE TO THE BOSTON TOWN MEETING, NOV. 20, 1772

I. Natural Rights of the Colonists as Men

Among the natural rights of the Colonists are these: *First, a right to life; Secondly,* to liberty; *Thirdly,* to property; together with the right to support and defend them in the best manner they can. These are evident branches of, rather than deductions from, the duty of self-preservation, commonly called the first law of nature.

All men have a right to remain in a state of nature as long as they please;

and in case of intolerable oppression, civil or religious, to leave the society they belong to, and enter into another.

When men enter into society, it is by voluntary consent; and they have a right to demand and insist upon the performance of such conditions and previous limitations as form an equitable *original compact.*

Every natural right not expressly given up, or, from the nature of a social compact, necessarily ceded, remains.

All positive and civil laws should conform, as far as possible, to the law of natural reason and equity.

As neither reason requires nor religion permits the contrary, every man living in or out of a state of civil society has a right peaceably and quietly to worship God according to the dictates of his conscience.

"Just and true liberty, equal and impartial liberty," in matters spiritual and temporal, is a thing that all men are clearly entitled to by the eternal and immutable laws of God and nature, as well as by the law of nations and all well-grounded municipal laws, which must have their foundation in the former.

In regard to religion, mutual toleration in the different professions thereof is what all good and candid minds in all ages have ever practised, and, both by precept and example, inculcated on mankind. And it is now generally agreed among Christians that this spirit of toleration, in the fullest extent consistent with the being of civil society, is the chief characteristic mark of the Church.[1] Insomuch that Mr. Locke has asserted and proved, beyond the possibility of contradiction on any solid ground, that such toleration ought to be extended to all whose doctrines are not subversive of society. The only sects which he thinks ought to be, and which by all wise laws are excluded from such toleration, are those who teach doctrines subversive of the civil government under which they live. The Roman Catholics or Papists are excluded by reason of such doctrines as these, that princes excommunicated may be deposed, and those that they call heretics may be destroyed without mercy; besides their recognizing the Pope in so absolute a manner, in subversion of government, by introducing, as far as possible into the states under whose protection they enjoy life, liberty, and property, that solecism in politics, *imperium in imperio,* leading directly to the worst anarchy and confusion, civil discord, war, and bloodshed.

The natural liberty of man, by entering into society, is abridged or restrained, so far only as is necessary for the great end of society, the best good of the whole.

In the state of nature every man is, under God, judge and sole judge of his own rights and of the injuries done him. By entering into society he agrees to an arbiter or indifferent judge between him and his neighbors; but he no more renounces his original right than by taking a cause out of the ordinary court of law, and leaving the decision to referees or indifferent arbitrators. In

---

1. See Locke's Letters on Toleration.

the last case, he must pay the referees for time and trouble. He should also be willing to pay his just quota for the support of government, the law, and the constitution; the end of which is to furnish indifferent and impartial judges in all cases that may happen, whether civil, ecclesiastical, marine, or military.

The *natural* liberty of man is to be free from any superior power on earth, and not to be under the will or legislative authority of man, but only to have the law of nature for his rule.[2]

In the state of nature men may, as the patriarchs did, employ hired servants for the defence of their lives, liberties, and property; and they should pay them reasonable wages. Government was instituted for the purpose of common defence, and those who hold the reins of government have an equitable, natural right to an honorable support from the same principle that "the laborer is worthy of his hire." But then the same community which they serve ought to be the assessors of their pay. Governors have no right to seek and take what they please; by this, instead of being content with the station assigned them, that of honorable servants of the society, they would soon become absolute masters, despots, and tyrants. Hence, as a private man has a right to say what wages he will give in his private affairs, so has a community to determine what *they* will give and grant of their substance for the administration of public affairs. And, in both cases, more are ready to offer their service at the proposed and stipulated price than are able and willing to perform their duty.

In short, it is the greatest absurdity to suppose it in the power of one, or any number of men, at the entering into society, to renounce their essential natural rights, or the means of preserving those rights; when the grand end of civil government, from the very nature of its institution, is for the support, protection, and defence of those very rights; the principal of which, as is observed, are Life, Liberty, and Property. If men, through fear, fraud, or mistake, should in terms renounce or give up any essential natural right, the eternal law of reason and the grand end of society would absolutely vacate such renunciation. The right to freedom being the gift of God Almighty, it is not in the power of man to alienate this gift and voluntarily become a slave.

II. The Rights of the Colonists as Christians

These may be best understood by reading and carefully studying the institutes of the great Law Giver and Head of the Christian Church, which are to be found clearly written and promulgated in the New Testament.

By the act of the British Parliament, commonly called the Toleration Act, every subject in England, except Papists, &c., was restored to, and re-established in, his natural right to worship God according to the dictates of his own conscience. And, by the charter of this Province, it is granted, ordained, and established (that is, declared as an original right) that there shall be liberty of conscience allowed in the worship of God to all Christians, except

2. Locke on Government.

Papists, inhabiting, or which shall inhabit or be resident within, such Province or Territory.[3] Magna Charta itself is in substance but a constrained declaration or proclamation and promulgation in the name of the King, Lords, and Commons, of the sense the latter had of their original, inherent, indefeasible natural rights,[4] as also those of free citizens equally perdurable with the other. That great author, that great jurist, and even that court writer, Mr. Justice Blackstone, holds that this recognition was justly obtained of King John, sword in hand. And peradventure it must be one day, sword in hand, again rescued and preserved from total destruction and oblivion.

III. The Rights of the Colonists as Subjects

A commonwealth or state is a body politic, or civil society of men, united together to promote their mutual safety and prosperity by means of their union.[5]

The absolute rights of Englishmen and all freemen, in or out of civil society, are principally personal security, personal liberty, and private property.

All persons born in the British American Colonies are, by the laws of God and nature and by the common law of England, exclusive of all charters from the Crown, well entitled, and by acts of the British Parliament are declared to be entitled, to all the natural, essential, inherent, and inseparable rights, liberties, and privileges of subjects born in Great Britain or within the realm. Among those rights are the following, which no man, or body of men, consistently with their own rights as men and citizens, or members of a society, can for themselves give up or take away from others.

First, "The first fundamental, positive law of all commonwealths or states is the establishing the legislative power. As the first fundamental *natural* law, also, which is to govern even the legislative power itself, is the preservation of the society."[6]

Secondly, The Legislative has no right to absolute, arbitrary power over the lives and fortunes of the people; nor can mortals assume a prerogative not only too high for men, but for angels, and therefore reserved for the exercise of the Deity alone.

"The Legislative cannot justly assume to itself a power to rule by extempore arbitrary decrees; but it is bound to see that justice is dispensed, and that the rights of the subjects be decided by promulgated, standing, and known laws, and authorized *independent judges*"; that is, independent, as far as possible, of Prince and people. "There should be one rule of justice for rich and poor, for the favorite at court, and the countryman at the plough."[7]

---

3. See 1 Wm. and Mary, St. a, c. 18, and Massachusetts Charter.

4. Lord Coke's inst. Blackstone's Commentaries, VI. p. 122. The Bill of Rights and the Act of Settlement.

5. See Locke and Vattel.

6. Locke on Government. *Salus populi suprema lex esto.* [Let the welfare of the people be the supreme law.]

7. Locke.

Thirdly, The supreme power cannot justly take from any man any part of his property, without his consent in person or by his representative.

These are some of the first principles of natural law and justice, and the great barriers of all free states and of the British Constitution in particular. It is utterly irreconcilable to these principles and to many other fundamental maxims of the common law, common sense, and reason that a British House of Commons should have a right at pleasure to give and grant the property of the Colonists. (That the Colonists are well entitled to all the essential rights, liberties, and privileges of men and freemen born in Britain is manifest not only from the Colony charters in general, but acts of the British Parliament.) The statute of the 13th of Geo. 2, c. 7, naturalizes even foreigners after seven years' residence. The words of the Massachusetts charter are these: "And further, our will and pleasure is, and we do hereby for us, our heirs, and successors, grant, establish, and ordain, that all and every of the subjects of us, our heirs, and successors, which shall go to, and inhabit within our said Province or Territory, and every of their children, which shall happen to be born there or on the seas in going thither or returning from thence, shall have and enjoy all liberties and immunities of free and natural subjects within any of the dominions of us, our heirs, and successors, to all intents, constructions, and purposes whatsoever, as if they and every one of them were born within this our realm of England."

Now what liberty can there be where property is taken away without consent? Can it be said with any color of truth and justice, that this continent of three thousand miles in length, and of a breadth as yet unexplored, in which, however, it is supposed there are five millions of people, has the least voice, vote, or influence in the British Parliament? Have they all together any more weight or power to return a single member to that House of Commons who have not inadvertently, but deliberately, assumed a power to dispose of their lives, liberties, and properties, than to choose an Emperor of China? Had the Colonists a right to return members to the British Parliament, it would only be hurtful; as, from their local situation and circumstances, it is impossible they should ever be truly and properly represented there. The inhabitants of this country, in all probability, in a few years, will be more numerous than those of Great Britain and Ireland together; yet it is absurdly expected by the promoters of the present measures that these, with their posterity to all generations, should be easy, while their property shall be disposed of by a House of Commons at three thousand miles' distance from them, and who cannot be supposed to have the least care or concern for their real interest; who have not only no natural care for their interest, but must be *in effect* bribed against it, as every burden they lay on the Colonists is so much saved or gained to themselves. Hitherto, many of the Colonists have been free from quit rents; but if the breath of a British House of Commons can originate an act for taking away all our money, our lands will go next, or be subject to rack rents from haughty and relentless landlords, who will ride at ease, while we are trodden in the dirt. The Colonists have been branded with the odious names of traitors and rebels only for complaining of their grievances. How long such treatment will or ought to be borne, is submitted.

(34)

Massachusettensis

December 12, 1774

Opposition to the revolutionary movement was forceful and at times articulate. Even many of those who thought the colonies had been unjustly treated hoped for reconciliation rather than rebellion. One of the more influential debates between Revolutionary and Loyalist was that between John Adams and Daniel Leonard. (At the time Adams thought his unnamed opponent was Jonathan Sewall.)

Our selection gives one of Leonard's statements favoring the Loyalist cause. Arguing that revolutionary acts are treason and that treason is in no way justifiable, Leonard appeals both to principle and to practical considerations such as the military power of Britain as he tries to show the folly of the revolutionary attitude toward the Crown.

The text used here is from John Adams and Jonathan Sewall (Daniel Leonard), *Novanglus, and Massachusettensis* (Boston, 1819).

MY DEAR COUNTRYMEN,

When a people, by what means soever, are reduced to such a situation that everything they hold dear, as men and citizens, is at stake, it is not only excusable, but even praiseworthy for an individual to offer to the public any thing, that he may think has a tendency to ward off the impending danger; nor should he be restrained from an apprehension that what he may offer will be unpopular, any more than a physician should be restrained from prescribing a salutary medicine, through fear it might be unpalatable to his patient. . . .

My dear countrymen, let us divest ourselves of prejudice, take a view of our present wretched situation, contrast it with our former happy one, carefully investigate the cause, and industriously seek some means to escape the evils we now feel, and prevent those that we have reason to expect.

We have been so long advancing to our present state, and by such gradations, that perhaps many of us are insensible of our true state and real danger. Should you be told that acts of high treason are flagrant through the country, that a great part of the province is in actual rebellion, would you believe it true? Should you not deem the person asserting it, an enemy to the province? Nay, should you not spurn him from you with indignation? Be calm, my friends; it is necessary to know the worst of a disease, to enable us to provide an effectual remedy. Are not the bands of society cut asunder, and the sanctions that held man to man, trampled upon? Can any of us recover a debt, or obtain compensation for an injury, by law? Are not many persons, whom once we respected and revered, driven from their homes and families, and forced to fly to the army for protection, for no other reason but their having accepted commissions under our king? Is not civil government dissolved? Some have been made to believe that nothing short of attempting the life of the king, or fighting his troops, can amount to high treason or rebellion. If, reader, you are one of those, apply to an honest lawyer, (if such an one can be found) and enquire what kind of offence it is for a number of men to assemble armed, and forcibly to obstruct the course of justice, even to prevent the king's courts from being held at their stated terms; for a body of people to seize upon the king's provincial revenue; I mean the monies collected by virtue of grants made by the general court to his majesty for the support of his government, within this province; for a body of men to assemble without being called by authority, and to pass governmental acts; or for a number of people to take the militia out of the hands of the king's representative, or to form a new militia, or to raise men and appoint officers for a public purpose, without the order or permission of the king, or his representative; or for a number of men to take to their arms, and march with a professed design of opposing the king's troops; ask, reader, of such a lawyer, what is the crime, and what the punishment; and if, perchance, thou art one that hast been active in these things, and art not insensibility itself, his answer will harrow up thy soul.

I assure you, my friends, I would not that this conduct should be told beyond the borders of this province; I wish it were consigned to perpetual oblivion; but alas, it is too notorious to be concealed; our news-papers have already published it to the world; we can neither prevent nor conceal it. The shaft is already sped, and the utmost exertion is necessary to prevent the blow. We already feel the effects of anarchy; mutual confidence, affection, and tranquility, those sweetners of human life, are succeeded by distrust, hatred, and wild uproar; the useful arts of agriculture and commerce are neglected for caballing, mobbing this or the other man, because he acts, speaks, or is suspected of thinking different from the prevailing sentiment of the times, in purchasing arms, and forming a militia; O height of madness! with a professed design of opposing Great Britain. I suspect many of us have been induced to join in these measures, or but faintly to oppose them, from an apprehension that Great Britain would not, or could not exert herself sufficiently to subdue America. Let us consider this matter. However closely we may hug ourselves in the opinion, that the parliament has no right to tax or legislate for us, the people of England hold the contrary opinion as firmly.

They tell us we are a part of the British empire; that every state, from the nature of government, must have a supreme, uncontrolable power, co-extensive with the empire itself; and that that power is vested in parliament. It is as unpopular to deny this doctrine in Great Britain, as it is to assert it in the colonies; so there is but little probability of serving ourselves at this day by our ingenious distinctions between a right of legislation for one purpose, and not for another. We have bid them defiance; and the longest sword must carry it, unless we change our measures. Mankind are the same, in all parts of the world. The same fondness for dominion that presides in the breast of an American, actuates the breast of an European. If the colonies are not a part of the British empire already, and subject to the supreme authority of the state, Great Britain will make them so. Had we been prudent enough to con-fine our opposition within certain limits, we might have stood some chance of succeeding once more; but alas, we have passed the Rubicon. It is now uni-versally said and believed, in England, that if this opportunity of reclaim-ing the colonies, and reducing them to a sense of their duty is lost, they, in truth, will be dismembered from the empire, and become as distinct a state from Great Britain, as Hanover; that is, although they may continue their allegiance to the person of the king, they will own none to the imperial crown of Great Britain, nor yield obedience to any of her laws, but such as they shall think proper to adopt. Can you indulge the thought one moment, that Great Britain will consent to this? For what has she protected and defended the colonies against the maritime powers of Europe, from their first British settle-ment to this day? For what did she purchase New York of the Dutch? For what was she so lavish of her best blood and treasure in the conquest of Canada, and other territories in America? Was it to raise up a rival state, or to enlarge her own empire? Or if the consideration of empire was out of the question, what security can she have of our trade, when once she has lost our obedience? I mention these things, my friends, that you may know how people reason upon the subject in England; and to convince you that you are much deceived, if you imagine that Great Britain will accede to the claims of the colonies, she will as soon conquer New England as Ireland or Canada, if either of them revolted; and by arms, if the milder influences of govern-ment prove ineffectual. . . .

I have as yet said nothing of the difference in sentiment among ourselves. Upon a superficial view we might imagine that this province was nearly unanimous; but the case is far different. A very considerable part of the men of property in this province, are at this day firmly attached to the cause of government; bodies of men, compelling persons to disavow their sentiments, to resign commissions, or to subscribe leagues and covenants, has wrought no change in their sentiments; it has only attached them more closely to govern-ment, and caused them to wish more fervently, and to pray more devoutly, for its restoration. These, and thousands beside, if they fight at all, will fight under the banners of loyalty. I can assure you that associations are now forming in several parts of this province, for the support of his majesty's government and mutual defense; and let me tell you, whenever the royal standard shall be set up, there will be such a flocking to it, as will astonish the most obdurate. And now, in God's name, what is it that has brought us to this brink of destruction? Has not the government of Great Britain been as mild and equitable in the colonies, as in any part of her extensive dominions? Has not she been a nursing mother to us, from the days of our infancy to this time? Has she not been indulgent almost to a fault? Might not each one of us at this day have sat quietly under his own vine and fig-tree, and there have been none to make us afraid, were it not for our own folly? Will not posterity be amazed, when they are told that the present distruction took its rise from a three penny duty on tea, and call it a more unaccountable frenzy, and more disgraceful to the annals of America, than that of the witchcraft?

I will attempt in the next paper to retrace the steps and mark the progressions that led us to this state. I promise to do it with fidelity; and if any thing should look like reflecting on individuals or bodies of men, it must be set down to my impartiality, and not to a fondness for censuring.

MASSACHUSETTENSIS

(35)

The Virginia Bill
of Rights
June 12, 1776

Drawn up by George Mason, the Virginia Bill of Rights was the first such statement of rights to be adopted after the outbreak of war. It was designed to accompany the Virginia constitution. The Bill was used by Jefferson in phrasing the first part of the Declaration. It also was widely copied by the other colonies, as they drafted state constitutions, and it became the basis of the first ten Amendments to the Constitution.

The text of this selection is from *The Constitutions of the United States* (Winchester, Virginia, 1811). [For Mason's career, see below, p. 208.]

A declaration of rights made by the representatives of the good people of Virginia, assembled in full and free convention; which rights do pertain to them and their posterity, as the basis and foundation of government.

1. That all men are by nature equally free and independent, and have

certain inherent rights, of which, when they enter into a state of society, they cannot by any compact deprive or divest their posterity; namely, the enjoyment of life and liberty, with the means of acquiring and possessing property, and pursuing and obtaining happiness and safety.

2. That all power is vested in, and consequently derived from, the people; that magistrates are their trustees and servants, and at all times amenable to them.

3. That government is, or ought to be instituted for the common benefit, protection, and security of the people, nation, or community; of all the various modes and forms of government, that is best which is capable of producing the greatest degree of happiness and safety, and is most effectually secured against the danger of maladministration; and that when any government shall be found inadequate or contrary to these purposes, a majority of the community hath an indubitable, unalienable and indefeasible right to reform, alter or abolish it, in such manner as shall be judged most conducive to the public weal.

4. That no man, or set of men, are entitled to exclusive or separate emoluments or privileges from the community, but in consideration of public services; which, not being descendible, neither ought the offices of magistrate, legislator or judge to be hereditary.

5. That the legislative and executive powers of the state should be separate and distinct from the judiciary; and that the members of the two first may be restrained from oppression, by feeling and participating the burthens of the people, they should, at fixed periods, be reduced to a private station, return into that body from which they were originally taken, and the vacancies be supplied by frequent, certain, and regular elections, in which all, or any part of the former members to be again eligible or ineligible, as the laws shall direct.

6. That elections of members to serve as representatives of the people in assembly, ought to be free; and that all men having sufficient evidence of permanent common interest with, and attachment to the community, have the right of suffrage, and cannot be taxed or deprived of their property for public uses, without their own consent, or that of their representatives so elected, nor bound by any law to which they have not, in like manner, assented for the public good.

7. That all power of suspending laws, or the execution of laws, by any authority without consent of the representatives of the people, is injurious to their rights, and ought not to be exercised.

8. That in all capital or criminal prosecutions a man hath a right to demand the cause and nature of his accusation, to be confronted with the accusers and witnesses, to call for evidence in his favour, and to a speedy trial by an impartial jury of his vicinage, without whose unanimous consent he cannot be found guilty; nor can he be compelled to give evidence against himself; that no man be deprived of his liberty, except by the law of the land or the judgment of his peers.

9. That excessive bail ought not to be required, nor excessive fines imposed, nor cruel and unusual punishments inflicted.

10. That general warrants, whereby an officer or messenger may be commanded to search suspected places without evidence of a fact committed, or to seize any person or persons not named, or whose offence is not particularly described and supported by evidence, are grievous and oppressive, and ought not to be granted.

11. That in controversies respecting property, and in suits between man and man, the ancient trial by jury is preferable to any other, and ought to be held sacred.

12. That the freedom of the press is one of the great bulwarks of liberty, and can never be restrained but by despotic governments.

13. That a well-regulated militia, composed of the body of the people trained to arms, is the proper, natural and safe defence of a free state; that standing armies in time of peace should be avoided as dangerous to liberty; and that in all cases the military should be under strict subordination to, and governed by, the civil power.

14. That the people have a right to uniform government; and, therefore, that no government separate from, or independent of the government of Virginia, ought to be erected or established within the limits thereof.

15. That no free government, or the blessings of liberty, can be preserved to any people, but by a firm adherence to justice, moderation, temperance, frugality and virtue, and by frequent recurrence to fundamental principles.

16. That religion, or the duty which we owe to our Creator, and the manner of discharging it, can be directed only by reason and conviction, not by force, or violence; and therefore all men are equally entitled to the free exercise of religion, according to the dictates of conscience; and that it is the natural duty of all to practise Christian forbearance, love, and charity towards each other.

(36)

The Declaration of Independence
July 4, 1776

Largely the product of Jefferson's pen, this document provides a brief but forceful summary of the political thought of the day. Though later generations of Americans were to question the Enlightenment premises it reflects, it nevertheless can be called the major political expression of the American mind.

The text is from *The Constitutions of the United States* (Winchester, Virginia, 1811).

In Congress, July 4, 1776, The Unanimous Declaration Of The Thirteen United States of America

When in the Course of human events, it becomes necessary for one people to dissolve the political bands which have connected them with another, and to assume among the Powers of the earth the separate and equal station to which the Laws of Nature and of Nature's God entitle them, a decent respect to the opinions of mankind requires that they should declare the causes which impel them to the separation.

We hold these truths to be self-evident, that all men are created equal, that they are endowed by their Creator with certain unalienable Rights, that among these are Life, Liberty and the pursuit of Happiness. That to secure these rights, governments are instituted among Men, deriving their just powers from the consent of the governed. That whenever any Form of Government becomes destructive of these ends, it is the Right of the People to alter or to abolish it, and to institute new Government, laying its foundation on such principles and organizing its powers in such form, as to them shall seem most likely to effect their Safety and Happiness. Prudence, indeed, will dictate that Governments long established should not be changed for light and transient causes; and accordingly all experience hath shown, that mankind are more disposed to suffer, while evils are sufferable, than to right themselves by abolishing the forms to which they are accustomed. But when a long train of abuses and usurpations, pursuing invariably the same Object evinces a design to reduce them under absolute Despotism, it is their right, it is their duty, to throw off such Government, and to provide new Guards for their future security. Such has been the patient sufferance of these Colonies; and such is now the necessity which constrains them to alter their former Systems of Government. The history of the present King of Great Britain is a history of repeated injuries and usurpations, all having in direct object the establishment of an absolute Tyranny over these States. To prove this, let Facts be submitted to a candid world.

He has refused his Assent to Laws, the most wholesome and necessary for the public good.

He has forbidden his Governors to pass Laws of immediate and pressing importance, unless suspended in their operation till his Assent should be obtained; and when so suspended, he has utterly neglected to attend to them.

He has refused to pass other Laws for the accommodation of large districts of people, unless those people would relinquish the right of Representation in the Legislature, a right inestimable to them and formidable to tyrants only.

He has called together legislative bodies at places unusual, uncomfortable, and distant from the depository of their Public Records, for the sole purpose of fatiguing them into compliance with his measures.

He has dissolved Representative Houses repeatedly, for opposing with manly firmness his invasions on the rights of the people.

He has refused for a long time, after such dissolutions, to cause others to be elected; whereby the Legislative Powers, incapable of Annihilation, have returned to the People at large for their exercise; the State remaining in the mean time exposed to all the dangers of invasion from without, and convulsions within.

He has endeavoured to prevent the population of these States; for that purpose obstructing the Laws of Naturalization of Foreigners; refusing to pass others to encourage their migration hither, and raising the conditions of new Appropriations of Lands.

He has obstructed the Administration of Justice, by refusing his Assent to Laws for establishing Judiciary Powers.

He has made Judges dependent on his Will alone, for the tenure of their offices, and the amount and payment of their salaries.

He has erected a multitude of New Offices, and sent hither swarms of Officers to harass our People, and eat out their substance.

He has kept among us, in times of peace, Standing Armies without the Consent of our Legislature.

He has affected to render the Military independent of and superior to the Civil Power.

He has combined with others to subject us to a jurisdiction foreign to our constitution, and unacknowledged by our laws; giving his Assent to their acts of pretended legislation:

For quartering large bodies of armed troops among us:

For protecting them, by a mock Trial, from Punishment for any Murders which they should commit on the Inhabitants of these States:

For cutting off our Trade with all parts of the world:

For imposing taxes on us without our Consent:

For depriving us in many cases, of the benefits of Trial by Jury:

For transporting us beyond Seas to be tried for pretended offenses:

For abolishing the free System of English Laws in a neighbouring Province, establishing therein an Arbitrary government, and enlarging its Boundaries so as to render it at once an example and fit instrument for introducing the same absolute rule into these Colonies:

For taking away our Charters, abolishing our most valuable Laws, and altering fundamentally the Forms of our Governments:

For suspending our own Legislature, and declaring themselves invested with Power to legislate for us in all cases whatsoever.

He has abdicated Government here, by declaring us out of his Protection and waging War against us.

He has plundered our seas, ravaged our Coasts, burnt our towns, and destroyed the lives of our people.

He is at this time transporting large armies of foreign mercenaries to compleat the works of death, desolation and tyranny, already begun with circumstances of Cruelty & perfidy scarcely paralleled in the most barbarous ages, and totally unworthy the Head of a civilized nation.

He has constrained our fellow Citizens taken Captive on the high Seas to bear Arms against their Country, to become the executioners of their friends and Brethren, or to fall themselves by their Hands.

He has excited domestic insurrections amongst us, and has endeavoured to bring on the inhabitants of our frontiers, the merciless Indian Savages, whose known rule of warfare, is an undistinguished destruction of all ages, sexes and conditions.

In every stage of these Oppressions We have Petitioned for Redress in the most humble terms: Our repeated Petitions have been answered only by repeated injury. A Prince, whose character is thus marked by every act which may define a Tyrant, is unfit to be the ruler of a free People.

Nor have We been wanting in attention to our British brethren. We have warned them from time to time of attempts by their legislature to extend an unwarrantable jurisdiction over us. We have reminded them of the circumstances of our emigration and settlement here. We have appealed to their native justice and magnanimity, and we have conjured them by the ties of our common kindred to disavow these usurpations, which, would inevitably interrupt our connections and correspondence. They too have been deaf to the voice of justice and of consanguinity. We must, therefore, acquiesce in the necessity, which denounces our Separation, and hold them, as we hold the rest of mankind, Enemies in War, in Peace Friends.

We, therefore, the Representatives of the united States of America, in General Congress, Assembled, appealing to the Supreme Judge of the World for the rectitude of our intentions, do, in the Name, and by Authority of the good People of these Colonies, solemnly Publish and declare, That these United Colonies are, and of right ought to be Free and Independent States; that they are Absolved from all Allegiance to the British Crown, and that all political connection between them and the State of Great Britain, is and ought to be totally dissolved; and that as Free and Independent States, they have full Power to levy War, conclude Peace, contract Alliances, establish Commerce, and to do all other Acts and Things which Independent States may of right do: And for the support of this Declaration, with a firm reliance on the Protection of Divine Providence, we mutually pledge to each other our Lives, our Fortunes and our sacred Honor.

(37)

Thomas Paine

1737-1809

The popular influence of Paine's *Common Sense* can hardly be over-estimated. It presented the revolutionary arguments with moving force and brought the young nation some unanimity of opinion. Arguing that society is a good but government a necessary evil, Paine moves to the Enlightenment ideals of consent of the governed and natural rights. He seeks also to show the impossibility of the colonies remaining under the rule of the British monarch.

The text of the selection is from *Common Sense* (Philadelphia, 1776). [For Paine's career, see above, p. 151.]

Of the Origin and Design of GOVERNMENT *in General, with* Concise Remarks on the ENGLISH CONSTITUTION

Some writers have so confounded society with government, as to leave little or no distinction between them; whereas, they are not only different, but have different origins. Society is produced by our wants, and government by our wickedness; the former promotes our happiness *possitively* by uniting our affections, the latter *negatively* by restraining our vices. The one encourages intercourse, the other creates distinctions. The first is a patron, the last a punisher.

Society in every state is a blessing, but Government even in its best state is but a necessary evil; in its worst state an intolerable one: for when we suffer, or are exposed to the same miseries by *a Government,* which we might expect in a country *without Government,* our calamity is heightened by reflecting that we furnish the means by which we suffer. Government like dress is the badge of lost innocence, the palaces of kings are built on the ruins of the bowers of paradise. For were the impulses of conscience clear, uniform, and irresistibly obeyed, man would need no other lawgiver; but that not being the case, he finds it necessary to surrender up a part of his property to furnish means for the protection of the rest; and this he is induced to do, by the same prudence which in every other case advises him, out of two evils to choose the least. *Wherefore,* security being the true design and end of government, it unanswerably follows, that whatever *form* thereof appears most likely to ensure it to us, with the least expence and greatest benefit, is preferable to all others.

In order to gain a clear and just idea of the design and end of government, let us suppose a small number of persons settled in some sequestered part of the earth, unconnected with the rest; they will then represent the first peopling of any country, or of the world. In this state of natural liberty, society will be their first thought. A thousand motives will excite them thereto, the strength of one man is so unequal to his wants, and his mind so unfitted for perpetual solitude, that he is soon obliged to seek assistance and relief of another, who in his turn requires the same. Four or five united would be able to raise a tolerable dwelling in the midst of a wilderness, but *one* man might labour out the common period of life without accomplishing any thing; when he had felled his timber he could not remove it, nor erect it after it was removed; hunger in the mean time would urge him from his work, and every different want call him a different way. Disease, nay even misfortune would be death; for tho' neither might be mortal, yet either would disable him from living, and reduce him to a state in which he might rather be said to perish, than to die.

Thus necessity like a gravitating power would soon form out newly arrived emigrants into society, the reciprocal blessings of which, would supersede, and render the obligations of law and government unnecessary while they remained perfectly just to each other; but as nothing but Heaven is impregnable to vice, it will unavoidably happen that in proportion as they surmount the first difficulties of emigration, which bound them together in a common cause, they will begin to relax in their duty and attachment to each other: and this remissness will point out the necessity of establishing some form of government to supply the defect of moral virtue.

Some convenient Tree will afford them a State-House, under the branches of which the whole Colony may assemble to deliberate on public matters. It is more than probable that their first laws will have the title only of REGULA-TIONS and be enforced by no other penalty than public disesteem. In this first parliament every man by natural right will have a seat.

But as the colony increases, the public concerns will increase likewise, and the distance at which the members may be separated, will render it too inconvenient for all of them to meet on every occasion as at first, when their number was small, their habitations near, and the public concerns few and trifling. This will point out the convenience of their consenting to leave the legislative part to be managed by a select number chosen from the whole body, who are supposed to have the same concerns at stake which those have who appointed them, and who will act in the same manner as the whole body would act were they present. If the colony continues increasing, it will become necessary to augment the number of the representatives, and that the interest of every part of the colony may be attended to, it will be found best to divide the whole into convenient parts, each part sending its proper number: and that the *elected* might never form to themselves an interest separate from the electors, prudence will point out the propriety of having elections often: be-cause as the elected might by that means return and mix again with the general body of the electors in a few months, their fidelity to the public will be secured by the prudent reflexion of not making a rod for themselves. And as this frequent interchange will establish a common interest with every part of the community, they will mutually and naturally support each other, and on this (not on the unmeaning name of king), depends the *strength of government; and the happiness of the governed.*

Here then is the origin and rise of government; namely, a mode rendered necessary by the inability of moral virtue to govern the world; here too is the design and end of government, viz. Freedom and security. And however our eyes may be dazzled with show, or our ears deceived by sound; however prejudice may warp our wills, or interest darken our understanding, the simple voice of nature and of reason will say, 'tis right.

I draw my idea of the form of government from a principle in nature which no art can overturn, viz. That the more simple any thing is, the less liable it is to be disordered, and the easier repaired when disordered; and with this maxim in view I offer a few remarks on the so much boasted constitution of England. That it was noble for the dark and slavish times in which it was erected, is granted. When the world was over-run with tyranny the least remove therefrom was a glorious rescue. But that it is imperfect, subject to convulsions, and incapable of producing what it seems to promise is easily demonstrated.

Absolute governments, (tho' the disgrace of human nature) have this advantage with them, that they are simple; if the people suffer, they know the head from which their suffering springs; know likewise the remedy; and are not bewildered by a variety of causes and cures. But the constitution of England is so exceedingly complex, that the nation may suffer for years together without being able to discover in which part the fault lies, some will say in one and some in another, and every political physician will advise a different medicine.

I know it is difficult to get over local or long standing prejudices, yet if we will suffer ourselves to examine the component parts of the English constitution, we shall find them to be the base remains of two ancient tyrannies, compounded with some new Republican materials.

First. The remains of Monarchical tyranny in the person of the King.

Secondly. The remains of Aristocratical tyranny in the persons of the Peers.

Thirdly. The new Republican materials, in the persons of the Commons, on whose virtue depends the freedom of England.

The two first by being hereditary are independent of the People; wherefore in a *constitutional sense* they contribute nothing towards the freedom of the State.

To say that the constitution of England is an *union* of three powers reciprocally *checking* each other, is farcical, either the words have no meaning or they are flat contradictions.

To say that the Commons are a check upon the King, presupposes two things.

First. That the King is not to be trusted without being looked after; or in other words, that a thirst for absolute power is the natural disease of Monarchy.

Secondly. That the Commons by being appointed for that purpose, are either wiser or more worthy of confidence than the Crown.

But as the same constitution which gives the Commons a power to check the King by with-holding the supplies, gives afterwards the King a power to check the Commons by empowering him to reject their other bills; it again supposes that the King is wiser than those, whom it has already supposed to be wiser than him. A mere absurdity!

There is something exceedingly ridiculous in the composition of Monarchy; it first excludes a man from the means of information, yet empowers him to act in cases where the highest judgment is required. The state of a king shuts him from the World, yet the business of a King requires him to know it thoroughly: wherefore, the different parts by unnaturally opposing and destroying each other, prove the whole character to be absurd and useless.

Some writers have explained the English constitution thus; the King say they is one, the People another; the Peers are an house in behalf of the King; the Commons in behalf of the People; But this hath all the distinctions of an house divided against itself; and tho' the expressions be pleasantly arranged, yet when examined they appear idle and ambiguous: and it will always happen, that the nicest construction that words are capable of, when applied to the description of some thing which either cannot exist, or is too incomprehensible to be within the compass of description, will be words of sound only, and tho' they may amuse the ear, they cannot inform the mind: for this explanation includes a previous question, viz. *how came the King by a power which the People are afraid to trust and always obliged to check?* Such a power could not be the gift of a wise People, neither can any power *which needs checking* be from God: yet the provision which the constitution makes, supposes such a power to exist.

But the provision is unequal to the task, the means either cannot, or will not accomplish the end, and the whole affair is a *Felo de se:* for as the greater weight will always carry up the less, and as all the wheels of a machine are put in motion by one, it only remains to know which power in the constitution has the most weight, for that will govern: and tho' the others, or a part of them, may clog, or check the rapidity of its motion, yet so long as they cannot stop it, their endeavours will be ineffectual: the first moving power will at last have its way, and what it wants in speed will be supplied by time.

That the crown is this overbearing part in the English constitution needs not be mentioned, and that it derives its whole consequences merely from being the giver of places and pensions is self-evident, wherefore, tho' we have been wise enough to lock the door against absolute Monarchy, we at the same time have been foolish enough to put the Crown in possession of the key.

The prejudice of Englishmen in favour of their own government by King, Lords and Commons, arises as much or more from national pride than reason. Individuals are undoubtedly safer in England than in some other Countries: but the *will* of the King is as much the *law* of the land in Britain as in France, with this difference, that instead of proceeding directly from his mouth, it is handed to the People under the more formidable shape of an act of Parliament. For the fate of Charles the first, hath only made Kings more subtle—not more just.

Wherefore laying aside all national pride and prejudice in favour of modes and forms, the plain truth is, that *it is wholly owing to the constitution of the People, and not to the constitution of the Government* that the Crown is not as oppressive in England as in Turkey.

An inquiry into the *constitutional errors* in the English form of government, is at this time highly necessary; for as we are never in a proper condition of doing justice to others, while we continue under the influence of some leading partiality, so neither are we capable of doing it to ourselves while we remain fettered by any obstinate prejudice. And as a man who is attached to a prostitute is unfitted to choose or judge of a wife, so any prepossession in favour of a rotten constitution of government will disable us from discerning a good one.

OF MONARCHY AND HEREDITARY SUCCESSION

Mankind being originally equals in the order of creation, the equality could only be destroyed by some subsequent circumstance: the distinctions of rich and poor may in a great measure be accounted for, and that without having recourse to the harsh ill-sounding names of oppression and avarice. Oppression is often the *consequence,* but seldom or never the *means* of riches: and tho' avarice will preserve a man from being necessitously poor, it generally makes him too timorous to be wealthy.

But there is another and greater distinction for which no truly natural or religious reason can be assigned, and that is, the distinction of Men into KINGS and SUBJECTS. Male and female are the distinctions of nature, good and bad the distinctions of Heaven; but how a race of Men came into the World so exalted above the rest, and distinguished like some new species, is worth enquiring into, and whether they are the means of happiness or of misery to mankind.

In the early ages of the World according to the Scripture chronology there were no Kings; the consequence of which was there were no wars; it is the pride of Kings which throws mankind into confusion. Holland without a

King hath enjoyed more peace for this last century, than any of the Monarchical governments in Europe. Antiquity favours the same remark; for the quiet and rural lives of the first Patriarchs hath a happy something in them, which vanishes away when we come to the history of Jewish royalty.

Government by Kings was first introduced into the World by the Heathens, from whom the children of Israel copied the custom. It was the most prosperous invention the Devil ever set on foot for the promotion of idolatry. The Heathens paid divine honors to their deceased Kings, and the Christian World hath improved on the plan by doing the same to their living ones. How impious is the title of sacred Majesty applied to a worm, who in the midst of his splendor is crumbling into dust!

As the exalting one man so greatly above the rest cannot be justified on the equal rights of nature, so neither can it be defended on the authority of scripture; for the will of the Almighty as declared by Gideon and the prophet Samuel, expressly disapproves of Government by Kings. All anti-monarchical parts of scripture have been very smoothly glossed over in monarchical governments, but they undoubtedly merit the attention of Countries which have their governments yet to form. *"Render unto Caesar the things which are Caesar's"* is the scripture doctrine of Courts, yet it is no support of monarchical government, for the Jews at that time were without a King and in a state of vassalage to the Romans.

(38)

John Adams

1736-1826

Adams graduated from Harvard in 1755 and began his career as a lawyer. He became a leading patriot during the Revolution and later served as second President of the United States. He had few of the qualities of personal leadership that marked his cousin, Sam Adams; it was rather through his skills as a constitutional lawyer that he influenced American events. He held many political offices and was the author of scores of important political papers and documents.

The following selection, advancing the republican theory of separation of powers in government, clearly represents the climate of opinion of the day. It is taken from *Thoughts on Government, in a Letter from a Gentleman to his Friend* (Boston, 1776).

MY DEAR SIR:

If I was equal to the task of forming a plan for the government of a colony, I should be flattered with your request and very happy to comply with it because, as the divine science of politics is the science of social happiness, and the blessings of society depend entirely on the constitutions of government, which are generally institutions that last for many generations, there can be no employment more agreeable to a benevolent mind than a research after the best.

Pope flattered tyrants too much when he said,

> For forms of government let fools contest,
> That which is best administered is best.

Nothing can be more fallacious than this. But poets read history to collect flowers, not fruits; they attend to fanciful images, not the effects of social institutions. Nothing is more certain from the history of nations and nature of man than that some forms of government are better fitted for being well administered than others.

We ought to consider what is the end of government before we determine which is the best form. Upon this point all speculative politicians will agree that the happiness of society is the end of government, as all divines and moral philosophers will agree that the happiness of the individual is the end of man. From this principle it will follow that the form of government which communicates ease, comfort, security, or, in one word, happiness to the greatest number of persons and in the greatest degree is the best.

All sober inquiries after truth, ancient and modern, pagan and Christian, have declared that the happiness of man, as well as his dignity, consists in virtue. Confucius, Zoroaster, Socrates, Mahomet, not to mention authorities really sacred, have agreed in this.

If there is a form of government, then, whose principle and foundation is virtue, will not every sober man acknowledge it better calculated to promote the general happiness than any other form?

Fear is the foundation of most governments; but it is so sordid and brutal a passion and renders men in whose breasts it predominates so stupid and miserable that Americans will not be likely to approve of any political institution which is founded on it.

Honor is truly sacred but holds a lower rank in the scale of moral excellence than virtue. Indeed, the former is but a part of the latter and consequently has not equal pretensions to support a frame of government productive of human happiness.

The foundation of every government is some principle or passion in the minds of the people. The noblest principles and most generous affections in our nature, then, have the fairest chance to support the noblest and most generous models of government.

A man must be indifferent to the sneers of modern Englishmen to mention in their company the names of Sidney, Harrington, Locke, Milton, Nedham, Neville, Burnet, and Hoadly. No small fortitude is necessary to confess that one has read them. The wretched condition of this country, however, for ten or fifteen years past has frequently reminded me of their principles and reasonings. They will convince any candid mind that there is no good government but what is republican. That the only valuable part of the British constitution is so because the very definition of a republic is "an empire of laws, and not of men." That, as a republic is the best of governments, so that particular arrangement of the powers of society or, in other words, that form of government which is best contrived to secure an impartial and exact execution of the laws is the best of republics.

Of republics there is an inexhaustible variety because the possible combinations of the powers of society are capable of innumerable variations.

As good government is an empire of laws, how shall your laws be made? In a large society inhabiting an extensive country, it is impossible that the whole should assemble to make laws. The first necessary step, then, is to depute power from the many to a few of the most wise and good. But by what rules shall you choose your representatives? Agree upon the number and qualifications of persons who shall have the benefit of choosing or annex this privilege to the inhabitants of a certain extent of ground.

The principal difficulty lies, and the greatest care should be employed, in constituting this representative assembly. It should be in miniature an exact portrait of the people at large. It should think, feel, reason, and act like them.

That it may be the interest of this assembly to do strict justice at all times, it should be an equal representation, or, in other words, equal interests among the people should have equal interests in it. Great care should be taken to effect this and to prevent unfair, partial, and corrupt elections. Such regulations, however, may be better made in times of greater tranquility than the present; and they will spring up themselves naturally when all the powers of government come to be in the hands of the people's friends. At present, it will be safest to proceed in all established modes to which the people have been familiarized by habit.

A representation of the people in one assembly being obtained, a question arises whether all the powers of government—legislative, executive, and judicial—shall be left in this body? I think a people cannot be long free, nor ever happy, whose government is in one assembly. . . .

But shall the whole power of legislation rest in one assembly? Most of the foregoing reasons apply equally to prove that the legislative power ought to be more complex, to which we may add that if the legislative power is wholly in one assembly and the executive in another or in a single person, these two powers will oppose and encroach upon each other until the contest shall end in war, and the whole power, legislative and executive, be usurped by the strongest.

The judicial power, in such case, could not mediate or hold the balance between the two contending powers because the legislative would undermine it. And this shows the necessity, too, of giving the executive power a negative upon the legislative; otherwise this will be continually encroaching upon that.

To avoid these dangers, let a distinct assembly be constituted as a mediator between the two extreme branches of the legislature, that which represents the people and that which is vested with the executive power.

Let the representative assembly then elect by ballot, from among themselves or their constituents or both, a distinct assembly which, for the sake of perspicuity, we will call a council. It may consist of any number you please, say twenty or thirty, and should have a free and independent exercise of its judgment and consequently a negative voice in the legislature. . . .

The dignity and stability of government in all its branches, the morals of the people, and every blessing of society depend so much upon an upright and skillful administration of justice that the judicial power ought to be distinct from both the legislative and executive, and independent upon both, that so it may be a check upon both, as both should be checks upon that. The judges, therefore, should be always men of learning and experience in the laws, of exemplary morals, great patience, calmness, coolness, and attention. Their minds should not be distracted with jarring interests; they should not be dependent upon any man, or body of men. To these ends, they should hold estates for life in their offices; or, in other words, their commissions should be during good behavior and their salaries ascertained and established by law. For misbehavior the grand inquest of the colony, the house of representatives, should impeach them before the governor and council, where they should have time and opportunity to make their defense; but, if convicted, should be removed from their offices and subjected to such other punishment as shall be thought proper. . . .

A constitution founded on these principles introduces knowledge among the people and inspires them with a conscious dignity becoming freemen; a general emulation takes place which causes good humor, sociability, good manners, and good morals to be general. That elevation of sentiment inspired by such a government makes the common people brave and enterprising. That ambition which is inspired by it makes them sober, industrious, and frugal. You will find among them some elegance, perhaps, but more solidity; a little pleasure, but a great deal of business; some politeness, but more civility. If you compare such a country with the regions of domination, whether monarchical or aristocratical, you will fancy yourself in Arcadia or Elysium. . . .

You and I, my dear friend, have been sent into life at a time when the greatest lawgivers of antiquity would have wished to live. How few of the human race have ever enjoyed an opportunity of making an election of government—more than of air, soil, or climate—for themselves or their children! When, before the present epoch, had three millions of people full power and a fair opportunity to form and establish the wisest and happiest government that human wisdom can contrive? I hope you will avail yourself and your country of that extensive learning and indefatigable industry which you possess to assist her in the formation of the happiest governments and the best character of a great people. For myself, I must beg you to keep my name out of sight; for this feeble attempt, if it should be known to be mine, would oblige me to apply to myself those lines of the immortal John Milton in one of his sonnets:

> I did but prompt the age to quit their clogs
> By the known rules of ancient liberty,
> When straight a barbarous noise environs me
> Of owls and cuckoos, asses, apes, and dogs.

(39)

Thomas Jefferson

1743-1826

In addition to separation of powers, democratic theory placed great emphasis on the doctrine of the "consent of the governed." A just government, the men of the Enlightenment believed, can have its only legitimate foundation in the will of the people. In the following selections, Jefferson states his convictions on consent as the true sanction of all good government. To some of his contemporaries, these beliefs seemed somewhat extreme; yet the basic principle they reflect was accepted by the Enlightenment as essential to republican government.

The selections reprinted here are taken from the third and fourth volumes of *Memoir, Correspondence, and Miscellanies from the Papers of Thomas Jefferson,* T. J. Randolph, ed., 4 vols. (Boston, 1830). [For Jefferson's career, see above, pp. 132–133.]

TO GOUVERNEUR MORRIS

PHILADELPHIA,
November 7, 1792

. . . It accords with our principles to acknowledge any government to be rightful which is formed by the will of the nation substantially declared. The late government was of this kind and was accordingly acknowledged by all the branches of ours. So any alteration of it, which shall be made by the will of the nation substantially declared, will doubtless be acknowledged in like manner.

TO JOHN W. EPPES

MONTICELLO,
June 24, 1813

. . . But what limits, it will be asked, does this prescribe to their powers? What is to hinder them from creating a perpetual debt? The laws of nature, I answer. The earth belongs to the living, not to the dead. The will and the power of man expire with his life, by nature's law. Some societies give it an artificial continuance, for the encouragement of industry; some refuse it, as our aboriginal neighbors, whom we call barbarians. The generations of men may be considered as bodies or corporations. Each generation has the usufruct of the earth during the period of its continuance. When it ceases to exist, the usufruct passes on to the succeeding generation, free and unincumbered, and so on, successively, from one generation to another for ever. We may consider each generation as a distinct nation, with a right, by the will of its majority, to bind themselves, but none to bind the succeeding generation, more than the inhabitants of another country.

☆ ☆ ☆ ☆

TO JOHN ADAMS

MONTICELLO,
October 28, 1813

. . . I agree with you that there is a natural aristocracy among men. The grounds of this are virtue and talents. Formerly, bodily powers gave place among the *aristoi*. But since the invention of gun powder has armed the weak as well as the strong with missle death, bodily strength, like beauty, good humor, politeness, and other accomplishments, has become but an auxiliary ground of distinction. There is also an artificial aristocracy, founded on wealth and birth, without either virtue or talents; for with these it would belong to the first class. The natural aristocracy I consider as the most precious gift of nature for the instruction, the trusts, and government of society. And, indeed, it would have been inconsistent in creation to have formed man for the social state and not to have provided virtue and wisdom enough to manage the concerns of the society. May we not even say that that form of government is the best which provides the most effectually for a pure selection of these natural *aristoi* into the offices of government? The artificial aristocracy is a mischievous ingredient in government, and provision should be made to prevent its ascendency. On the question what is the best provision, you and I differ, but we differ as rational friends, using the free exercise of our own reason and mutually indulging its errors. You think it best to put the pseudo-*aristoi* into a separate chamber of legislation, where they may be hindered from doing mischief by their co-ordinate branches and where, also, they may be a protection to wealth against the agrarian and plundering enterprises of the majority of the people. I think that to give them power in order to prevent them from doing mischief is arming them for it and increasing instead of remedying the evil.

TO JOHN TAYLOR

MONTICELLO,
May 28, 1816

. . . If, then, the control of the people over the organs of their government be the measure of its republicanism (and I confess I know no other measure), it must be agreed that our governments have much less of republicanism than ought to have been expected; in other words, that the people have less regular control over their agents, than their rights and their interest require. And this I ascribe, not to any want of republican dispositions in those who formed these constitutions, but to a submission of true principle to

European authorities, to speculators on government, whose fears of the people have been inspired by the populace of their own great cities, and were unjustly entertained against the independent, the happy, and therefore orderly citizens of the United States. . . .

On this view of the import of the term *republic*, instead of saying, as has been said, "that it may mean any thing or nothing," we may say with truth and meaning, that governments are more or less republican, as they have more or less of the element of popular election and control in their composition: and believing, as I do, that the mass of the citizens is the safest depository of their own rights, and especially, that the evils flowing from the duperies of the people, are less injurious than those from the egoism of their agents, I am a friend to that composition of government which has in it the most of this ingredient. And I sincerely believe, with you, that banking establishments are more dangerous than standing armies; and that the principle of spending money to be paid by posterity, under the name of funding, is but swindling futurity on a large scale.

(40)

James Madison

1751-1836

Unlike their European counterparts, the men of the American Enlightenment did not adopt a facile optimism about human nature. But even their "realism" was turned to republican purposes. Madison is an instructive example, for though his analysis of behavior in terms of self-interest and faction is within the tradition that sees government as a necessary evil, he himself was totally committed to federal republicanism.

The selection here is from the famous *Federalist* No. 10, first printed in the *New York Packet,* Friday, November 23, 1787. [For Madison's career, see above, p. 156.]

TO THE PEOPLE OF THE STATE OF NEW YORK:

Among the numerous advantages promised by a well-constructed Union, none deserves to be more accurately developed than its tendency to break and control the violence of faction. The friend of popular governments never finds himself so much alarmed for their character and fate, as when he contemplates their propensity to this dangerous vice. He will not fail, therefore, to set a due value on any plan which, without violating the principles to which he is attached, provides a proper cure for it. The instability, injustice, and confusion introduced into the public councils, have, in truth, been the mortal diseases under which popular governments have everywhere perished; as they continue to be the favorite and fruitful topics from which the adversaries to liberty derive their most specious declamations. The valuable improvements made by the American constitutions on the popular models, both ancient and modern, cannot certainly be too much admired; but it would be an unwarrantable partiality, to contend that they have as effectually obviated the danger on this side, as was wished and expected. Complaints are everywhere heard from our most considerate and virtuous citizens, equally the friends of public and private faith, and of public and personal liberty, that our governments are too unstable, that the public good is disregarded in the conflicts of rival parties, and that measures are too often decided, not according to the rules of justice and the rights of the minor party, but by the superior force of an interested and overbearing majority. However anxiously we may wish that these complaints had no foundation, the evidence of known facts will not permit us to deny that they are in some degree true. It will be found, indeed, on a candid review of our situation, that some of the distresses under which we labor have been erroneously charged on the operation of our governments; but it will be found, at the same time, that other causes will not alone account for many of our heaviest misfortunes; and, particularly, for that prevailing and increasing distrust of public engagements, and alarm for private rights, which are echoed from one end of the continent to the other. These must be chiefly, if not wholly, effects of the unsteadiness and injustice with which a factious spirit has tainted our public administrations.

By a faction, I understand a number of citizens, whether amounting to a majority or minority of the whole, who are united and actuated by some common impulse of passion, or of interest, adverse to the rights of other citizens, or to the permanent and aggregate interests of the community.

There are two methods of curing the mischiefs of faction: the one, by removing its causes: the other, by controlling its effects.

There are again two methods of removing the causes of faction: the one by destroying the liberty which is essential to its existence: the other, by giving to every citizen the same opinions, the same passions, and the same interests.

It could never be more truly said than of the first remedy, that it was worse than the disease. Liberty is to faction what air is to fire, an element without which it instantly expires. But it could not be less folly to abolish liberty, which is essential to political life, because it nourishes faction, than it would be to wish the annihilation of air, which is essential to animal life, because it imparts to fire destructive agency.

The second expedient is as impracticable as the first would be unwise. As long as the reason of man continues fallible, and he is at liberty to exercise it, different opinions will be formed. As long as the connection subsists between his reason and his self-love, his opinions and his passions will have a reciprocal influence on each other; and the former will be objects to which the latter will attach themselves. The diversity in the faculties of man, from which the rights of property originate, is not less an insuperable obstacle to a uniformity of interests. The protection of these faculties is the first object of government. From the protection of different and unequal faculties of acquiring property, the possession of different degrees and kinds of property immediately results; and from the influence of these on the sentiments and views of the respective proprietors, ensues a division of the society into different interests and parties.

The latent causes of faction are thus sown in the nature of man; and we see them everywhere brought into different degrees of activity, according to the different circumstances of civil society. A zeal for different opinions concerning religion, concerning government, and many other points, as well of speculation as of practice; an attachment of different leaders ambitiously contending for pre-eminence and power; or to persons of other descriptions whose fortunes have been interesting to the human passions, have, in turn, divided mankind into parties, inflamed them with mutual animosity, and rendered them much more disposed to vex and oppress each other than to co-operate for their common good. So strong is this propensity of mankind to fall into mutual animosities, that where no substantial occasion presents itself, the most frivolous and fanciful distinctions have been sufficient to kindle their unfriendly passions and excite their most violent conflicts. But the most common and durable source of factions has been the various and unequal distribution of property. Those who hold and those who are without property have even formed distinct interests in society. Those who are creditors, and those who are debtors, fall under a like discrimination. A landed interest, a manufacturing interest, a mercantile interest, a moneyed interest, with many lesser interests, grow up of necessity in civilized nations, and divide them into different classes, actuated by different sentiments and views. The regulation of these various and interfering interests forms the principal task of modern legislation, and involves the spirit of party and faction in the necessary and ordinary operations of the government.

No man is allowed to be a judge in his own cause, because his interest would certainly bias his judgment, and, not improbably, corrupt his integrity. With equal, nay with greater reason, a body of men are unfit to be both judges and parties at the same time; yet what are many of the most important acts of legislation, but so many judicial determinations, not indeed concerning the rights of single persons, but concerning the rights of large bodies of citizens? And what are the different classes of legislators but advocates and parties to the causes which they determine? Is a law proposed concerning private debts? It is a question to which the creditors are parties on one side and the debtors on the other. Justice ought to hold the balance between them. Yet the parties are, and must be, themselves the judges; and the most numerous party, or, in other words, the most powerful faction must be expected to prevail. Shall domestic manufactures be encouraged, and in what degree, by restrictions on foreign manufactures? are questions which would be differently decided by the landed and the manufacturing classes, and probably by neither with a sole regard to justice and the public good. The apportionment of taxes on the various descriptions of property is an act which seems to require the most exact impartiality; yet there is, perhaps, no legislative act in which greater opportunity and temptation are given to a predominant party to trample on the rules of justice. Every shilling with which they overburden the inferior number, is a shilling saved to their own pockets.

It is in vain to say that enlightened statesmen will be able to adjust these clashing interests, and render them all subservient to the public good. Enlightened statesmen will not always be at the helm. Nor, in many cases, can such an adjustment be made at all without taking into view indirect and remote considerations, which will rarely prevail over the immediate interest which one party may find in disregarding the rights of another or the good of the whole.

The inference to which we are brought is, that the *causes* of faction cannot be removed, and that relief is only to be sought in the means of controlling its *effects*.

If a faction consists of less than a majority, relief is supplied by the republican principle, which enables the majority to defeat its sinister views by regular vote. It may clog the administration, it may convulse the society; but it will be unable to execute and mask its violence under the forms of the Constitution. When a majority is included in a faction, the form of popular government, on the other hand, enables it to sacrifice to its ruling passion or interest both the public good and the rights of other citizens. To secure the public good and private rights against the danger of such a faction, and at the same time to preserve the spirit and the form of popular government, is then the great object to which our inquiries are directed. Let me add that it is the great desideratum by which this form of government can be rescued from the opprobrium under which it has so long labored, and be recommended to the esteem and adoption of mankind.

By what means is this object attainable? Evidently by one of two only. Either the existence of the same passion or interest in a majority at the same time must be prevented, or the majority having such coexistent passion or interest, must be rendered, by their number and local situation, unable to concert and carry into effect schemes of oppression. If the impulse and the opportunity be suffered to coincide, we well know that neither moral nor religious motives can be relied on as an adequate control. They are not found to be such on the injustice and violence of individuals, and lose their efficacy in proportion to the number combined together, that is, in proportion as their efficacy becomes needful.

From this view of the subject it may be concluded that a pure democracy, by which I mean a society consisting of a small number of citizens, who assemble and administer the government in person, can admit of no cure for the mischiefs of faction. A common passion or interest will, in almost every case, be felt by a majority of the whole; a communication and concert result from the form of government itself; and there is nothing to check the inducements to sacrifice the weaker party or an obnoxious individual. Hence it is that such democracies have ever been spectacles of turbulence and contention; have ever been found incompatible with personal security or the rights of property; and have in general been as short in their lives as they have been violent in their deaths. Theoretic politicians, who have patronized this species of government, have erroneously supposed that by reducing mankind to a perfect equality in their political rights, they would, at the same time, be perfectly equalized and assimilated in their possessions, their opinions, and their passions.

A republic, by which I mean a government in which the scheme of representation takes place, opens a different prospect, and promises the cure for which we are seeking. Let us examine the points in which it varies from pure democracy, and we shall comprehend both the nature of the cure and the efficacy which it must derive from the Union.

The two great points of difference between a democracy and a republic are: first, the delegation of the government, in the latter, to a small number of citizens elected by the rest; secondly, the greater number of citizens, and greater sphere of country, over which the latter may be extended.

The effect of the first difference is, on the one hand, to refine and enlarge the public views, by passing them through the medium of a chosen body of citizens, whose wisdom may best discern the true interest of their country, and whose patriotism and love of justice will be least likely to sacrifice it to temporary or partial considerations. Under such a regulation, it may well happen that the public voice, pronounced by the representatives of the people, will be more consonant to be public good than if pronounced by the people themselves, convened for the purpose. On the other hand, the effect may be inverted. Men of factious tempers, of local prejudices, or of sinister designs, may, by intrigue, by corruption, or by other means, first obtain the suffrages, and then betray the interests, of the people. The question resulting is, whether small or extensive republics are more favorable to the election of proper guardians of the public weal; and it is clearly decided in favor of the latter by two obvious considerations:

In the first place, it is to be remarked that, however small the republic may be, the representatives must be raised to a certain number, in order to guard against the cabals of a few; and that, however large it may be, they must be limited to a certain number, in order to guard against the confusion of a multitude. Hence, the number of representatives in the two cases not being in proportion to that of the two constituents, and being proportionally greater in the small republic, it follows that, if the proportion of fit characters be not less in the large than in the small republic, the former will present a greater option, and consequently a greater probability of a fit choice.

In the next place, as each representative will be chosen by a greater number of citizens in the large than in the small republic, it will be more difficult for unworthy candidates to practise with success the vicious arts by which elections are too often carried; and the suffrages of the people being more free, will be more likely to centre in men who possess the most attractive merit and the most diffusive and established characters.

It must be confessed that in this, as in most other cases, there is a mean, on both sides of which inconveniences will be found to lie. By enlarging too much the number of electors, you render the representative too little acquainted with all their local circumstances and lesser interests; as by reducing it too much, you render him unduly attached to these, and too little fit to comprehend and pursue great and national objects. The federal Constitution forms a happy combination in this respect; the great and aggregate interests being referred to the national, the local and particular to the State legislatures.

The other point of difference is, the greater number of citizens and extent of territory which may be brought within the compass of republican than of democratic government; and it is this circumstance principally which renders factious combinations less to be dreaded in the former than in the latter. The smaller the society, the fewer probably will be the distinct parties and interests composing it; the fewer the distinct parties and interests, the more frequently will a majority be found of the same party; and the smaller the number of individuals composing a majority, and the smaller the compass within which they are placed, the more easily will they concert and execute their plans of oppression. Extend the sphere and you take in a greater variety of parties and interests; you make it less probable that a majority of the whole will have a common motive to invade the rights of other citizens; or if such a common motive exists, it will be more difficult for all who feel it to discover their own strength, and to act in unison with each other. Besides other impediments, it may be remarked that, where there is a consciousness of unjust or dishonorable purposes, communication is always checked by distrust in proportion to the number whose concurrence is necessary.

Hence, it clearly appears, that the same advantage which a republic has over a democracy, in controlling the effects of faction, is enjoyed by a large over a small republic—is enjoyed by the Union over the States composing it. Does the advantage consist in the substitution of representatives whose enlightened views and virtuous sentiments render them superior to local prejudices and to schemes of injustice? It will not be denied that the representation of the Union will be most likely to possess these requisite endowments. Does it consist in the greater security afforded by a greater variety of parties, against the event of any one party being able to outnumber and oppress the rest? In an equal degree does the increased variety of parties comprised within the Union, increase this security. Does it, in fine, consist in the greater obstacles opposed to the concert and accomplishment of the secret wishes of an unjust and interested majority? Here, again, the extent of the Union gives it the most palpable advantage.

The influence of factious leaders may kindle a flame within their particular States, but will be unable to spread a general conflagration through the other States. A religious sect may degenerate into a political faction in a part of the Confederacy; but the variety of sects dispersed over the entire face of it must secure the national councils against any danger from that source. A rage for paper money, for an abolition of debts, for an equal division of property, or for any other improper or wicked project, will be less apt to pervade the whole body of the Union than a particular member of it; in the same proportion as such a malady is more likely to taint a particular county or district, than an entire State.

In the extent and proper structure of the Union, therefore, we behold a republican remedy for the diseases most incident to republican government. And according to the degree of pleasure and pride we feel in being republicans, ought to be our zeal in cherishing the spirit and supporting the character of Federalists.

PUBLIUS

(41)

George Mason 1725-1792
James Iredell 1751-1799

The Constitution as presented to the nation by the Convention met with general though not unanimous approval. The lack of a bill of rights, and the relatively strong central government established by the powers assigned to the three branches were the major points of disagreement. Among those who campaigned actively against the adoption of the Constitution was George Mason. Mason, a leading Virginia statesman, had been a firm, though somewhat off-stage, supporter of the Revolution. An important reason for his opposition to the Constitution was his personal disapproval of slavery, which was given official recognition in the provision dealing with apportioning membership in Congress.

One of the more influential replies to Mason's *Objections* was written by James Iredell, a North Carolina lawyer and patriot. Iredell was an ardent supporter of the Constitution; his reply to Mason probably persuaded Washington later to appoint him to the Supreme Court.

The selections are from George Mason, "The Objections of the

Hon. George Mason to the Proposed Foederal Constitution," and James Iredell, "Answers to Mr. Mason's objections to the new Constitution," both in Paul Leicester Ford, ed., *Pamphlets on the Constitution of the United States* (Brooklyn, 1888).

There is no declaration of rights: and the laws of the general government being paramount to the laws and constitutions of the several states, the declarations of rights, in the separate states, are no security. Nor are the people secured even in the enjoyment of the benefit of the common law, which stands here upon no other foundation than its having been adopted by the respective acts forming the constitutions of the several states.

In the House of Representatives there is not the substance, but the shadow only of representation; which can never produce proper information in the legislature, or inspire confidence in the people. The laws will, therefore, be generally made by men little concerned in, and unacquainted with their effects and consequences.[1]

The Senate have the power of altering all money-bills, and of originating appropriations of money, and the salaries of the officers of their appointment, in conjunction with the President of the United States—although they are not the representatives of the people, or amenable to them. These, with their other great powers, (viz. their powers in the appointment of ambassadors, and all public officers, in making treaties, and in trying all impeachments) their influence upon, and connection with, the supreme executive from these causes, their duration of office, and their being a constant existing body, almost continually sitting, joined with their being one complete branch of the legislature, will destroy any balance in the government, and enable them to accomplish what usurpations they please, upon the rights and liberties of the people.

The judiciary of the United States is so constructed and extended, as to absorb and destroy the judiciaries of the several states; thereby rendering laws as tedious, intricate, and expensive, and justice as unattainable by a great part of the community, as in England; and enabling the rich to oppress and ruin the poor.

The President of the United States has no constitutional council (a thing unknown in any safe and regular government). He will therefore be unsupported by proper information and advice; and will generally be directed by minions and favorites—or he will become a tool to the Senate—or a council of state will grow out of the principal officers of the great departments—the worst and most dangerous of all ingredients for such a council, in a free

---

1. This objection has been in some degree lessened, by an amendment, often before refused, and at last made by an erasure, after the engrossment upon parchment, of the word forty, and inserting thirty, in the third clause of the second section of the first article.

country; for they may be induced to join in any dangerous or oppressive measures, to shelter themselves, and prevent an inquiry into their own misconduct in office. Whereas, had a constitutional council been formed (as was proposed) of six members, viz., two from the eastern, two from the middle, and two from the southern states, to be appointed by vote of the states in the House of Representatives, with the same duration and rotation of office as the Senate, the executive would always have had safe and proper information and advice; the president of such a council might have acted as Vice-President of the United States, *pro tempore,* upon any vacancy or disability of the chief magistrate; and long continued sessions of the Senate, would in a great measure have been prevented. From this fatal defect of a constitutional council, has arisen the improper power of the Senate, in the appointment of the public officers, and the alarming dependence and connection between that branch of the legislature and the supreme executive. Hence, also, sprung that unnecessary officer, the Vice-President, who, for want of other employment, is made President of the Senate; thereby dangerously blending the executive and legislative powers; besides always giving to some one of the states an unnecessary and unjust pre-eminence over the others.

The President of the United States has the unrestrained power of granting pardon for treason; which may be sometimes exercised to screen from punishment those whom he had secretly instigated to commit the crime, and thereby prevent a discovery of his own guilt. By declaring all treaties supreme laws of the land, the executive and the Senate have, in many cases, an exclusive power of legislation, which might have been avoided, by proper distinctions with respect to treaties, and requiring the assent of the House of Representatives, where it could be done with safety.

By requiring only a majority to make all commercial and navigation laws, the five southern states (whose produce and circumstances are totally different from those of the eight northern and eastern states) will be ruined: for such rigid and premature regulations may be made, as will enable the merchants of the northern and eastern states not only to demand an exorbitant freight, but to monopolize the purchase of the commodities, at their own price, for many years, to the great injury of the landed interest, and impoverishment of the people: and the danger is the greater, as the gain on one side will be in proportion to the loss on the other, Whereas, requiring two-thirds of the members present in both houses, would have produced mutual moderation, promoted the general interest, and removed an insuperable objection to the adoption of the government.

Under their own construction of the general clause at the end of the enumerated powers, the Congress may grant monopolies in trade and commerce, constitute new crimes, inflict unusual and severe punishments, and extend their power as far as they shall think proper; so that the state legislatures have no security for the powers now presumed to remain to them; or the people for their rights. There is no declaration of any kind for preserving the liberty of the press, the trial by jury in civil cases, nor against the danger of standing armies in time of peace.

The state legislatures are restrained from laying export duties on their own produce—the general legislature is restrained from prohibiting the further importation of slaves for twenty odd years, though such importations render the United States weaker, more vulnerable, and less capable of defence. Both the general legislature, and the state legislatures are expressly prohibited making *ex post facto* laws, though there never was, nor can be, a legislature, but must and will make such laws, when necessity and the public safety require them, which will hereafter be a breach of all the constitutions in the union, and afford precedents for other innovations.

This government will commence in a moderate aristocracy; it is at present impossible to foresee whether it will, in its operation, produce a monarchy, or a corrupt oppressive aristocracy; it will most probably vibrate some years between the two, and then terminate in the one or the other.

GEO. MASON

I. Objection

"There is no declaration of rights, and the laws of the general government being paramount to the laws and constitutions of the several States, the declarations of rights in the separate States are no security. Nor are the people secured even in the enjoyment of the benefit of the common law, which stands here upon no other foundation than its having been adopted by the respective acts forming the Constitutions of the several States."

Answer

1. As to the want of a declaration of rights. The introduction of these in England, from which the idea was originally taken, was in consequence of usurpations of the Crown, contrary, as was conceived, to the principles of their government. But there no original constitution is to be found, and the only meaning of a declaration of rights in that country is, that in certain particulars specified, the Crown had no authority to act. Could this have been necessary had there been a constitution in being by which it could have been clearly discerned whether the Crown had such authority or not? Had the people, by a solemn instrument, delegated particular powers to the Crown at the formation of their government, surely the Crown, which in that case could claim under that instrument only, could not have contended for more power than was conveyed by it. So it is in regard to the new Constitution here: the future government which may be formed under that authority certainly cannot act beyond the warrant of that authority. As well might they attempt

to impose a King upon America, as go one step in any other respect beyond the terms of their institution. The question then only is, whether more power will be vested in the future government than is necessary for the general purposes of the union. This may occasion a ground of dispute—but after expressly defining the powers that are to be exercised, to say that they shall exercise no other powers (either by a general or particular enumeration) would seem to me both nugatory and ridiculous. As well might a Judge when he condemns a man to be hanged, give strong injunctions to the Sheriff that he should not be beheaded.

2. As to the common law, it is difficult to know what is meant by that part of the objection. So far as the people are now entitled to the benefit of the common law, they certainly will have a right to enjoy it under the new Constitution until altered by the general legislature, which even in this point has some cardinal limits assigned to it. What are most acts of Assembly but a deviation in some degree from the principles of the common law? The people are expressly secured (contrary to Mr. Mason's wishes) against *ex post facto* laws; so that the tenure of any property at any time held under the principles of the common law, cannot be altered by any future act of the general legislature. The principles of the common law, as they now apply, must surely always hereafter apply, except in those particulars in which express authority is given by this constitution; in no other particulars can the Congress have authority to change it, and I believe it cannot be shown that any one power of this kind given is unnecessarily given, or that the power would answer its proper purpose if the legislature was restricted from any innovations on the principles of the common law, which would not in all cases suit the vast variety of incidents that might arise out it.

Progress and the Trust in Science

THE EARLIEST SPOKESMEN of the scientific revolution were quick to argue that science provided the clue and the tool for improving the human species. Francis Bacon defined knowledge as power, and his campaign for science was really one to make the satisfaction of human needs a principal criterion in the field of knowledge. Others made even more explicit the optimistic views of the first apologists of science. Although they were more realistic than present-day critics of the age of reason would admit, they nevertheless did believe, in the words of Priestley, that "the human powers will, in fact, be enlarged . . . men will make their situation in this world more easy and comfortable . . . [and] communicate happiness to others. Thus, whatever was the beginning of this world, the end will be glorious and paradisaical, beyond what our imaginations can now conceive."[1] Happiness was the norm of Enlightenment ethics, and the methods and conclusions of science were the primary means to that end.

In America, the Puritans helped prepare the way for the acceptance of science. Calvinists in theory but practical Arminians in fact, the Puritans had rejected otherworldliness for activity in this world. (Thus Yankee ingenuity and American technology, too, have roots in Puritanism.) And the men of the Enlightenment furthered the acceptance of science, and indeed purified the scientific impulse by removing the Puritan's theological concern. At any rate, during the Enlightenment science and invention became dominant interests. The list of contemporary American scientists was impressive, and although a utilitarian interest sometimes dampened the pursuit of pure science, the age was generally a scientifically productive one.

The Revolutionary War also gave the Enlightenment's sanction of science a special emphasis and a sense of urgency. The prophets of science as well as the men of science—the latter perhaps less optimistically than the former, however—believed that the causes of science and liberty were inseparable

---

1. Joseph Priestley, *An Essay on the First Principles of Government, and on the Nature of Political, Civil, and Religious Liberty* (2nd ed., London, 1771), pp. 4–5.

and that one depended upon the other. As Jeremy Belknap was to express it, the basic desire of the Enlightenment was to make America the "Mistress of the Sciences as well as the Asylum of Liberty." This desire led in fact to proposals to organize science on a federal basis, similar to America's political structure. One must conclude with Brooke Hindle that "science was so central to the thought of the Enlightenment and it lay so directly behind the Revolutionary argument, that the men who made the American Revolution were thoroughly committed to the pursuit of science. . . . The unprecedented richness of modern America is a monument to the faith of the Revolutionary generation in the power and beneficence of science, just as its form of government is a monument to their faith in man's capacity to govern himself."[2]

Yet, despite its emphasis on progress and science, the American Enlightenment did maintain a sense of realism about human nature, primarily because it viewed human nature as a constant. Progress was essentially a teleological process aiming toward a rather fixed pattern of relations insuring happiness and was to be achieved by scientific reason in its study of nature, man, and human behavior. Perhaps the words of Jefferson—among the more optimistic believers in the perfectibility of man—can be taken as a summary of the Enlightenment's tempered belief in science and progress. He wrote: "Although I do not, with some enthusiasts, believe that the human condition will ever advance to such a state of perfection as that there shall no longer be pain or vice in the world, yet I believe it susceptible of much improvement, and most of all, in matters of government and religion; and that the diffusion of knowledge among the people is to be the instrument by which it is to be effected."[3]

(42)

Cadwallader Colden

1688-1776

Educated in medicine at the University of Edinburgh, Colden emigrated to America in 1710. He held a number of positions in the Province of New York, including that of lieutenant governor. He became the most competent Newtonian of his day and elaborated Newton's views in a number of treatises. About 1760 he wrote an introductory statement of his natural philosophy for one Peter Delancy and sent a copy to his own son Alexander.

2. Brooke Hindle, *The Pursuit of Science in Revolutionary America* (Chapel Hill, 1956), p. 385
3. To Pierre Samuel Dupont de Nemours, April 24, 1816.

The selection here is from this work, entitled "An Introduction to the Study of Phylosophy wrote in America for the Use of a young Gentleman," a manuscript in the Colden papers, New-York Historical Society.

SECT: I

You are now, my ———, going to the college, in order to learn those principles, which may be of use to you in all your future inquiries; and to acquire that knowledge, by which you may be enabled to distinguish yourself in every part of your life, either in public employments, or in private life, or that you may become an useful member of the commonwealth and of a private family. But the common methods of teaching, hitherto generally in use in the public Schools, is so far from answering these good purposes, that it serves only to fill young people's heads with useless notions and prejudices, which unfit them for the acquiring of real and useful knowledge. The design of my present writing is to guard you against these common errors, and to instruct you how to avoid them. In doing this I have supposed that you have a general notion of the sciences, which are usually taught. I could not do otherwise, within the limits I have set to myself, and therefore be not discouraged, if at present you do not comprehend the full scope and view of what I write. When you come to read in any of the sciences I hope you will then find it of use to you.

History informs us, that the Egyptian priests, the Chaldeans and Persian magi had acquired great knowledge in physics, before the Christian era, such as exceeds the knowledge of the most learned of the moderns. It is certain that they had carried Geometry, Astronomy and Mechanics, to a great perfection. The Greeks were only mere Scholars of the Egyptians. It may be questioned whether they made any discovery absolutely their own: and it is not improbable, that, like mere Scholars, they did not perfectly understand the principles of the Egyptian philosophy; and yet it is from the Greeks only that we have any knowledge of the learning of these ancients. Pythagoras was the best instructed of any of the Greeks in the Egyptian learning. It appears from the little which remains of his doctrine, that the Egyptians knew what of late times has been called the Copernican System, and that he knew the general apparent attraction between bodies, which has been rediscovered in the last century by Sir Isaac Newton. But as we have nothing remaining of the Pythagorean philosophy, except what is found in a few abstracts in much later writers, we know very little of what were the true principles of that philosophy. It may be that we are now regaining the Principles of Physics, which were known many ages before the beginning of the Christian era.

Wars, and the erruption of barbarous nations into the countries where learning flourished, have been the destruction of knowledge in those countries. But nothing so much prevented the propagation of knowledge as the Craft of the pagan priests, who, in order to secure their influence over the people, confined learning to their own order, and communicated their knowledge only to the *Initiated,* to such only of whose taciturnity and fidelity, after a severe trial, they were well assured. Whoever attempted to put mankind on a free inquiry into the truth of popularly received opinions, certainly suffered under a cruel persecution of the heathen priests. Socrates was persecuted and condemned to death, as a corrupter of youth, as an enemy to the Gods, and of the orthodox religion of his country; and yet Socrates, in all after ages, has been deemed the wisest man, and the man of the greatest probity that ever appeared among the pagans.

Nothing, in later ages, so much obstructed the advancement of knowledge as the craft of the popish priests, when they, in imitation of the pagan priests, founded the power of their dominion on the ignorance and credulity of the laity: by which they established a Tyranny in the Pope and the Clergy over Kings and Princes as well as over private persons, under pretence of their being intrusted with the keys of heaven and hell, and exerted their power more absolutely than ever had been done by any potentate before that time. To serve these purposes, all books, which might propagate real and useful knowledge, and thereby detect this priestcraft, were proscribed: they were, under the severest penalties, ordered to be brought in and burnt, and it became an unpardonable sin to read them. For the same purposes, the clergy assumed the sole power of licensing books; that is, without their consent no book could be published or was permitted to be read. By these means the best books of antiquity are lost, or curtailed, while the lascivious poets are transmitted to us entire. Copernicus durst not publish his system, till he was near his death, when he thought himself out of the reach of their persecution. He lived to see only one printed copy of it. Galileo was the first who applied the telescope to astronomical observations, and thereby absolutely confirmed the Copernican system. The nobility of Italy flocked to his house to view the planets. They saw clearly that the planets are really globular bodies, similar to our earth: and they saw the satellites of Jupiter, like so many moons, moving round the body of that planet. The priests could not bear that they should be convicted of teaching errors in philosophy, or that any knowledge can be obtained otherwise than from them. Galileo was clapt into the inquisition, and to free himself from the rack and a cruel death, he was forced to recant, and to give himself the lie publicly, he was forced to deny the truth of what he and many others had seen distinctly. Had not the reformation in religion taken place about that time, and several nations thrown off the authority of the Pope, the learning and knowledge of the present age had been nipt in the bud, and we should at this day have been in barbarous ignorance.

Nothing was so effectual in establishing the dominion of the priests as the Education of youth, which they assumed solely to themselves. All the professors and teachers in the public Schools and universities were priests, none others were allowed to teach, nor are any others allowed at this day in popish countries. They know well how easy it is to instill strong prejudices into young minds, and of what force these prejudices are in the whole course of life. . . .

SECT: IV

Matter or body (which is some certain quantity of matter) in some degree or other resists our touch, and thereby excites the sense of feeling. This is so general an observation that if we can feel nothing in any place we conclude there is no body there.

When a body is at rest it requires some force to move it. If it require a certain degree of force to make a body move one foot in a second, it requires double that force to make it move two feet in a second, and thrice the force to make it move three feet in the same time. Again if it require a certain force to move a certain quantity of matter one foot in a second, it requires a double force to move a double quantity of the same matter the same distance in the same time, and thrice the force to move a treble quantity of matter. From these observations, which may be made every day, it is evident, that there is some power or force in matter, by which it persists, in its present state, and resists any change of its state. It cannot be by mere inactivity, or by doing nothing: because one absolute want of any thing cannot be greater or less than any other absolute want. It is nonsense to say, one thing does nothing, and another thing does twice as much nothing.

If a body swimming in water, receive any degree of motion, it from time to time loses its motion gradually, till at last it rests. If the same body receive the same degree of motion in the air, it loses its motion at last, but continues it to a greater distance and longer time. If the same body be put in motion in a place void of air, it continues its motion longer than it did in air. From these observations it is concluded, that a body once put in motion, would continue to move with the same degree of velocity, if it meet with no resistance from some other body, or from the medium in which it moves. And if any quantity of matter, moving with a certain velocity, require a certain degree of force to stop it, double the quantity of matter, moving with the same velocity, requires double the force to stop it, and so on. From these observations equally true, at all times and in all places, it is concluded, that there is a power or force in matter, by which it persists in its present state, whether it be in motion or at rest. When two bodies move with the same degree of motion, and have different force, and this difference is constantly observed to be in proportion to the quantity of matter in each, it cannot arise from the motion; for it is equal in both; and therefore can only arise from the quantity of matter, to which it is allwise in proportion.

When you take a ball in your hand, and put your hand and the ball in motion, and then suddenly withdraw your hand from the ball, the ball continues to move after your hand, which gave it motion, is withdrawn from it. So likewise when a ball receives motion, from the explosion of gunpowder within a gun barrel, the ball continues its motion with great velocity to a great distance, after the gunpowder has entirely ceased to act upon it. What is it, which continues this motion in the ball, after your hand is withdrawn and the gunpowder ceases to act? Not your hand, nor the gunpowder; for nothing can act where it is not, nor after it has ceased to act. If you attend to the proper conception of cause and effect, any thing can as little act at the distance of one hair's breadth, as it can at the distance of one thousand miles, without something passing from it to the other thing on which it acts, or without some middle thing or medium, by which the action is continued from the one to the other: for nothing can act where it is not, or produce any effect after it has ceased to act, more than it can after it has ceased to be or to exist. Therefore the continuance of motion in the ball is by some power in the ball itself, that is, by that power by which matter resists all change in its present state, whether it be in motion or at rest.

You have my ——— thrown many a stone, without imagining that there was any difficulty in conceiving how the stone moved of itself, after it was gone from your hand. You may hence learn, how the powers of things may be discovered, from the most common and trivial effects, when properly and attentively considered: and that a truly philosophic turn of mind can never want opportunities of improving in knowledge, without the expense of any apparatus for experiments.

Sir Isaac was the first who observed this power in matter, that it is essential to it and distinguishes it from all other Beings. Is it not wonderful, that where the means of discovery are so easy and obvious, that the discovery was not made before his time: Tho' it be a power every where to be observed, from its effects, and without which none of the phenomena of matter can be explained, and the understanding of it be of the greatest use in the arts and Sciences? Can any other reason be given, than that the inquisitive mind was diverted by the vain subtleties of the schools, and the prejudices early received there?

Sir Isaac Newton called this power in matter *Vis inertia.* It is difficult to find an English word to convey a proper idea of this power. It has been commonly turned into the word *Inactivity,* and this was done, I suppose, in favour of the prevailing opinion, that matter is absolutely passive and unactive. But this can never express Sir Isaac Newton's meaning: for to talk of a power or force which does nothing, can only serve to make people laugh. It is as plain a contradiction to say force without action as to say force without force. Power without force, and force without action, or which does nothing is as unintelligible as any absurdity can be. This power is more properly called the power of resisting any change in its present state, whether it be in motion or at rest, as Sir Isaac defines it; for resistance carries the idea of force and of action with it, or of doing something.

Some cannot conceive any action without motion. This arises from a faulty connection of ideas, by joining motion to all kind of action: for which no kind of reason can be given. Thinking is certainly doing something, or is a kind of action; but we conceive no kind of motion in thinking. Some likewise expect that we shall tell them in what manner the resisting power acts. To this it is answered, that we cannot explain the manner of acting of any simple power otherwise than by its effects. Motion can no otherwise be explained than by change of place; but change of place is only the effect of motion: and the effects of the resisting power can be as clearly shewn, as the effects of motion can be.

I told you before that the school learning is really a misapplication of time, in learning of things which exist nowhere, but in the imaginations of idle, monkish, useless men, and serves no good purpose in life. It is otherwise in acquiring knowledge of the powers and force of those things on which our well being depends. Our life and health, our pleasures and pain all depend on the powers of those beings, which constitute the human system, and on the powers of other beings, which are continually acting upon it. Not only the speculative Sciences, the explaining of all the phenomena which strike our senses, depend on the knowledge of these powers; but likewise all the practical arts depend on them. This knowledge is useful to us in every circumstance of life, whether as individuals and private persons, or as members of Society, as will very evidently appear to you, when you shall apply your thoughts to any particular art or Science.

From the resisting power of matter we form a clear conception of its impenetrability, or that no quantity of matter can occupy the same space, which any other quantity of matter does: for if it could, we lose the idea of its resisting power, this power must be supposed to be destroyed, and with it we lose every conception we have of matter. We cannot conceive two quantities of matter in the same space, without losing any idea we have at least of one of them: all ideas which distinguish them are lost. In short, take away the idea of resistance from matter and we have no idea of matter remaining. Its essence, therefore, consists in its power of resisting all change of its present state, from which all the phenomena or properties of matter are deduced, as the effects of this power, and without it none of them can be understood. . . .

SECT: VI

The occult qualities have been long exploded and excluded from the republic of learning, as only artful coverings of ignorance, by which pretenders to knowledge would make others believe that they know things of which they are absolutely ignorant. This they do by imposing words, which have no meaning, in place of real knowledge. When you ask one of these learned Doctors, who is unwilling to be thought ignorant of any thing, by what means amber draws a straw, or a feather to it. They gravely tell you it is by an occult quality in the amber. Why a stone falls to the earth. It is by an occult quality in the stone, by which it allwise tends to the center of the earth. Put these answers into plain English and they are no other than this. Amber attracts a feather or a straw; but I know not how. A stone allwise falls to the ground; but I know not why. Such plain and direct answers are inconsistent with the pretensions of the learned professor: and, which is worse, would not please the Scholar. Mankind in general are better pleased to be duped, with the unmeaning appearance of knowledge; than to allow that their teachers are ignorant or deceitful.

Notwithstanding that in this enlightened age, no maxims in philosophy are admitted, but what are self evident, and which the unlearned as well as the learned clearly perceive to be true: and no theorem or conclusions are received, but what are demonstratively deduced from these maxims; yet we find many, of great reputation for their knowledge in physics, asserting, that all bodies attract each other, while at a distance from each other, without supposing any thing between these bodies, or passing from the one to the other, by which any kind of action can pass from the one to the other; but by some inherent quality or power in the bodies themselves. Can anything in the occult qualities of the Schools be more absurd than this? If it be supposed, that a body can act on another at the least distance from where it is, without something passing or some medium between them, by which the action is continued, it may in the like manner act at the greatest distance with equal force: for where nothing passes and nothing is between the bodies, no reason can be given for its acting with less force at any distance. It supposes, that bodies act where they are not, and with equal reason they may be supposed to act after they have ceased to be. I can see no reason why a man, who admits of this mutual attraction in bodies, should be shocked at Transubstantiation, or at any other fashionable absurdity.

Innumerable phenomena shew that all bodies tend to each other, by some force or other; but no phenomenon can shew that it is done by an attractive quality in themselves: nor can it be done by any of emission from themselves, for no motion from a body can give motion to the same body. It seems then necessary to conclude, that this mutual tendency and motion of bodies to each other is by the action of some medium, surrounding all bodies, or in which all bodies are placed. The knowledge of the nature or power of this medium can only be obtained, as the knowledge of all other powers is, by an accurate observation of the effects or phenomena produced by it. I suppose none will affirm, that nothing exists, but what we either feel, see, hear, smell or taste. The existence of some things may be as evident by reflection on the phenomena, or on the effects produced by them, or by reasoning, as the existence of others is by immediate perception. Where effects are evidently perceived, it is with the greatest certainty concluded, that something exists which has sufficient power to produce these effects. In truth we have no other method to discover the existence of any thing, but by its effects either mediately, or immediately on the senses. Neither can I conceive any necessity to think that this medium consists either of resisting matter or of light, or of both united. Its effects shew it to be something different from either of them. Some being which has a power peculiar to itself, the nature of which is to be discovered by its effects, as the powers of matter and light are, by an accurate observation of the effects produced by them.

From an accurate observation of the effects between bodies at a distance from each other, I conclude, that the parts of the medium in which they are placed are all, in every respect, contiguous; and therefore it cannot be conceived as consisting of particles, of any shape or dimensions. Never the less, it may be conceived as of different quantities, or as occupying a smaller or larger quantity of space, in the same manner as space is considered as of different quantities. From the same observation I conclude that this medium receives equally the action of resisting from any contiguous body, or of motion from light which passes through it: and that the parts or quantity of the medium contiguous to the body receives the action immediately from the body and communicates the same to the next contiguous parts of quantity and so on to a great distance. This communication to the greatest distance is done in one instant, because there is no distance between the parts of the medium, in the same manner as any motion is communicated from one end of a rod, however long it be, in the same instant to the other end. Immediately after any quantity of this medium has received the action, either of resisting or of moving, it reacts the same with the same force which it received. This alternate action and reaction is made evident in Sir Isaac Newton's optics, by the alternate transmission and stopping of light on passing through pellucid bodies. You may imagine this reaction as something similar to what you feel, when taking one end of a rod in your hand, you push the other end against a wall, you feel the wall react or push the rod against your hand, with the same force with which you pushed the rod. In the next place it is constantly observed, that the resisting power in matter, is opposite, or a negative power to motion: it allwise either destroys, or stops, or lessens the action of motion.

These observations being premised, Call this medium Ether, for it is proper to give it a name, suppose the Ether, surrounding any spherical body of resisting matter, be divided into equidistant concentric spherical surfaces, it is evident that these spherical surfaces increase the farther they are from the center of the spherical body. Geometers demonstrate that this increase is in the ratio of the squares of their diameters or of the distance of the surface from the common center. Again it is observed that if any certain force communicate a degree of force to any certain quantity, it communicates half the degree of force to double the quantity, or that the degree of action communicated is reciprocal to the quantity of the thing which receives the action. Then it follows that the quantity of the action of resisting, which is communicated to the several parts of Ether surrounding a spherical body, decreases continually from the body, in a ratio reciprocal to the square of their distance from the body. Since the action of resistance is negative to motion, if motion be communicated by light to the Ether the reaction of motion will be more lessened the nearer the parts of the Ether are to the body: consequently the reaction will be allwise stronger on the side of any small body farther distant from the other large spherical body than on the side nearest to it and the little body will be moved toward the great body. Thus I have endeavoured to give you some conception how one body may appear to be attracted by an other at a distance from it, tho' the effect be really that of a third thing acting upon it. . . .

No doubt, the method of geometrical demonstration, and algebraical investigation is the best Logic: and may be of the greatest use, in accustoming young people to a regular method of reasoning. But to be perpetually poring on lines and figures, and jumbling together algebraic characters, cramps the imagination; they become like the dog in a wheel, perpetually running the same round, and is good for nothing else. You will find some of these high mathematicians, as ignorant of the true principles of knowledge, as any pretenders whatsoever, and as little fitted for the most useful parts of life, or for common conversation.

The gentleman, who proposes to be generally useful in society, ought not to fix his thoughts singly on any one branch of science, but to have a competent knowledge of the principles of every branch, which he may obtain without fatiguing his imagination, by too continued an application. While he reads and thinks by turns, he should, in the intervals, cultivate his intellectual faculties by general conversation, where he may obtain more useful knowledge, than can be learned from books. The mere Scholar, the mere Physician, the mere Lawyer, Musician or painter, take them out of their own way, and they are often more insipid, than the mere plowman.

(43)

David Ramsey

1749-1815

Physician, historian, and patriot, Ramsey graduated from the College of New Jersey (Princeton) in 1765 and received his medical degree from the College (University) of Pennsylvania in 1772. He developed a successful practice but was also absorbed in politics, an interest that culminated in his service as a delegate to the Continental Congress from South Carolina. He made significant contributions to medicine but became even more famous as a historian.

The following selection is an expression of the Enlightenment's hope in science and democracy. It is from "An Oration on the advantages of American Independence," *The United States Magazine,* vol. I (1779).

FRIENDS AND FELLOW CITIZENS,

Impressed with the deepest sense of my insufficiency, I rise to address you, with peculiar diffidence. When I consider the knowledge and eloquence necessary to display the glorious prospects which Independence opens to this continent, I am stung with a degree of self-reproach for undertaking the important task. But your known attachment to the cause of America encourages me to hope, that you will receive with indulgence, a well intended exertion to promote her welfare; and emboldens me to cast myself on that candour, which looks with kindness on the feeblest efforts of an honest mind.

We are now celebrating the anniversary of our emancipation from British tyranny; an event that will constitute an illustrious era in the history of the world, and which promises an extension of all those blessings to our country, for which we would choose to live, or dare to die.

Our present form of government is every way preferable to the royal one we have lately renounced. It is much more favourable to purity of morals, and better calculated to promote all our important interests. Honesty, plain-dealing, and simple manners, were never made the patterns of courtly behaviour. Artificial manners always prevail in kingly governments; and royal courts are reservoirs, from whence insincerity, hypocrisy, dissimulation, pride, luxury, and extravagance, deluge and overwhelm the body of the people. On the other hand, republics are favourable to truth, sincerity, frugality, industry, and simplicity of manners. Equality, the life and soul of Commonwealths, cuts off all pretensions to preferment, but those which arise from extraordinary merit: Whereas in royal governments, he that can best please his superiors, by the low arts of fawning and adulation, is most likely to obtain favour.

It was the interest of Great Britain to encourage our dissipation and extravagance, for the two-fold purpose of *increasing the sale of her manufactures,* and of *perpetuating our subordination.* In vain we sought to check the growth of luxury, by sumptuary laws; every wholesome restraint of this kind was sure to meet with the royal negative: While the whole force of example was employed to induce us to copy the dissipated manners of the country from which we sprung. If therefore, we had continued dependent, our frugality, industry, and simplicity of manners, would have been lost in an imitation of British extravagance, idleness, and false refinements.

How much more happy is our present situation, when necessity co-operating with the love of our country, compels us to adopt both public and private economy? Many are now industriously clothing themselves and their families in sober home-spun, who, had we remained dependent, would have been spending their time in idleness, and strutting in the costly robes of British gaiety.

The arts and sciences, which languished under the low prospects of subjection, will now raise their drooping heads, and spread far and wide, till they have reached the remotest parts of this untutored continent. It is the happiness of our present constitution, that all offices be open to men of merit, of whatever rank or condition; and the reins of state may be held by the son of the poorest man, if possessed of abilities equal to the important station. We are no more to look up for the blessings of government to hungry courtiers, or the needy dependents of British nobility; but must educate our own children for these exalted purposes. When subjects, we had scarce any other share in government, but to obey the arbitrary mandates of a British Parliament: But Honor with her dazzling pomp, interest with her golden lure, and patriotism with her heart-felt satisfaction, jointly call upon us now to qualify ourselves and posterity for the bench, the army, the navy, the learned professions, and all the departments of civil government. The independence of our country holds forth such generous encouragement to youth, as cannot fail of making many of them despise the syren calls of luxury and mirth, and pursue heaven-born wisdom with unwearied application. A few years will now produce a much greater number of men of learning and abilities, than we could have expected for ages in our boyish state of minority, guided by the leading-strings of a parent country.

How trifling the objects of deliberation that came before our former legislative assemblies, compared with the great and important matters, on which they must now decide! They might then, *with the leave of the King,* his governours and councils, make laws about *yoking hogs, branding cattle,* or *marking rice;* but they are now called upon to determine on peace and war, treaties and negociations with foreign states, and other subjects interesting to the peace, liberty, sovereignty, and independence of a wide extended empire. No wonder, that so little attention has been paid to learning; for ignorance was better than knowledge, while our abject and humiliating condition so effectually tended to crush the exertions of the human mind, and to extinguish a generous ardor for literary pre-eminence.

The times in which we live, and the governments we have lately adopted, all conspire to fan the sparks of genius in every breast, and kindle them into flame. When like children, we were under the guardianship of a foreign power, our limited attention was naturally engrossed by agriculture, or directed to the low pursuit of wealth. In this state, the powers of the soul, benumbed with ease and indolence, sunk us into sloth and effeminacy. Hardships, dangers, and proper opportunities, give scope to active virtues, and rouse the mind to such vigorous exertions, as command the admiration of an applauding world. Rome, when she filled the earth with the terror of her arms, sometimes called her Generals from the plough: In like manner, the great want of proper persons to fill high stations, has drawn from obscurity many illustrious characters, which will dazzle the world with the splendor of their names. The necessities of our country require the utmost exertions of all our powers; from which vigorous united efforts, much more improvement of the human mind is to be expected, than if we had remained in a torpid state of dependence. . . .

Thus might I go through the whole circle of the arts and sciences, and shew, that while we remained British subjects, cramped and restrained by the limited view of dependence, each one of them would dwindle and decay, compared with the perfection and glory in which they will bloom and flourish, under the enlivening sun-shine of Freedom and Independence.

I appeal to the experience of all, whether they do not feel an elevation of soul growing out of the emancipation of their country, while they recollect that they are no longer subject to lawless will, but possess the powers of self-government, and are called upon to bear an active part in supporting and perpetuating the sovereignty of the United States; and in organizing them in such a manner, as will produce the greatest portion of political happiness to the present and future generations. In this elevation of soul, consists true genius; which is cramped by kingly government, and can only flourish in free states.

The attention of thousands is now called forth from their ordinary employments to subjects connected with the sovereignty and happiness of a great continent. As no one can tell to what extent, the human mind may be cultivated; so no one can foresee what great events may be brought into existence, by the exertions of so many minds expanded by close attention to subjects of such vast importance.

The Royal Society was founded immediately after the termination of the civil wars in England. In like manner, may we not hope, as soon as this contest is ended, that the exalted spirits of our politicians and warriors will engage in the enlargement of public happiness, by cultivating the arts of peace, promoting usefull knowledge, with an ardor equal to that which first roused them to bleed in the cause of liberty and their country? Their genius sharpened by their present glorious exertions, will naturally seek for a continuance of suitable employment. Having, with well-tried swords and prudent counsels, secured liberty and independence for themselves and posterity, their great souls will stoop to nothing less than concerting wise schemes of civil policy and happiness—instructing the world in useful arts —and extending the empire of science. I fore-see societies formed of our heroes and statesmen, released from their present cares; some of which will teach mankind to plough, sow, plant, build, and improve the rough face of Nature; while others critically examine the various productions of the animal, vegetable, and mineral kingdoms, and teach their countrymen to "look through Nature up to Nature's God." Little has been hitherto done towards completing the natural history of America, or for the improvement of agriculture, and the peaceful arts of civil life; but who will be surprised at this, who considers, that during the long past night of 150 years, our minds were depressed, and our activity benumbed by the low prospects of subjection? Future diligence will convince the world, that past inattention was the effect of our dependent form of government. . . .

A zeal for promoting learning, unknown in the days of our subjection, has already begun to overspread these United States. In the last session of our Assembly, three societies were incorporated for the laudable purpose of erecting seminaries of education. Nor is the noble spirit confined to us alone: Even now, amidst the tumults of war, literary institutions are forming all over the continent, which must light up such a blaze of knowledge, as cannot fail to burn, and catch, and spread, until it has finally illuminated, with the rays of science, the most distant retreats of ignorance and barbarity. . . .

The tyrants and landlords of the Old World, who hold a great part of their fellow men in bondage because of their dependence for land, will be obliged to relax of their arbitrary treatment, when they find that America is an asylum for freemen from all quarters of the globe. They will be cautious of adding to the oppressions of their poor subjects and tenants, lest they should force them to abandon their country for the enjoyment of the sweets of American Liberty. In this view of the matter, I am confident that the cause of America is the cause of Human Nature, and that it will extend its influence to thousands who will never see it, and procure them a mitigation of the cruelties and oppressions imposed by their arbitrary task-masters. . . .

When I anticipate in imagination the future glory of my country, and the illustrious figure it will soon make on the theatre of the world, my heart distends with generous pride for being an American. What a substratum for an empire! compared with which, the foundation of the Macedonian, the Roman, and the British, sink into insignificance. Some of our large States have territory superior to the island of Great Britain; whilst the whole together, are little inferior to Europe itself. Our Independence will people this extent of country with freemen, and will stimulate the innumerable inhabitants thereof, by every motive, to perfect the acts of government, and to extend human happiness.

I congratulate you on our glorious prospects. Having for three long years weathered the storms of adversity, we are at length arrived in view of the calm haven of peace and security. We have laid the foundations of a new empire, which promises to enlarge itself to vast dimensions, and to give happiness to a great continent. It is now our turn to figure on the face of the earth, and in the annals of the world. The arts and sciences are planted among us, and, fostered by the auspicious influence of equal governments, are growing up to maturity; while truth and freedom flourish by their sides. Liberty, both civil and religious, in her noon-tide blaze, shines forth with unclouded lustre on all ranks and denominations of men.

Ever since the flood, true religion, literature, arts, empire, and riches, have taken a slow and gradual course from east to west, and are now about fixing their long and favourite abode in this new western world. Our sun of political happiness is already risen, and hath lifted his head over the mountains, illuminating our hemisphere with liberty, light, and polished life. Our Independence will redeem one quarter of the globe from tyranny and oppression, and consecrate it the chosen seat of truth, justice, freedom, learning and religion. We are laying the foundation of happiness for countless millions. Generations yet unborn will bless us for the blood-bought inheritance we are about to bequeath them. Oh happy times! Oh glorious days! Oh kind, indulgent, bountiful Providence, that we live in this highly favoured period, and have the honour of helping forward these great events, and of suffering in a cause of such infinite importance!

X

The Enlightenment

"THE PRESENT AGE is an enlightened one," observed the Rev. Charles Backus in 1788.[1] Self-consciously enlightened it was, and little wonder that it bequeathed to America a sense of mission and national greatness. "It is impossible not to be sensible that we are acting for all mankind," Jefferson wrote Joseph Priestley in 1802. This belief in America stemmed from the Enlightenment's view of the drama of history—a sense that history was starting anew and that the future would fulfill mankind's dream of freedom and happiness. The introduction of the new principle of representative democracy, wrote Jefferson to J. H. Tiffany in 1816, "has rendered useless almost everything written before on the structure of government," and, we might add, on civilization. It was to remain for the next generation of Americans to create the past and mold the tradition necessary to hold the nation together.

Benevolence, natural rights, happiness, reason, deism, freedom, individualism, utilitarianism, progress, science, republicanism—these were the major ideas of the Enlightenment. The following selections—one a sermon, the other a poem—are summary statements of the *Weltanschauung* and values of the Enlightenment. It is hoped they will bring together for the reader the many themes of the preceding pages.

The Enlightenment had produced a nation, yet its creative force seemed to decline with this very achievement. Nor did it produce any major philosophers to act as its spokesmen. Perhaps such men as Jefferson or Madison could have risen to the task, but they were too engaged in the political affairs of the day. Perhaps, as Professor Joseph Blau has written, the Enlightenment's failure to develop a theory of human nature spelled its doom. Perhaps it was inevitable that the expanding nation would find Enlightenment ideas partial and inadequate. Indeed, the infant pragmatism of the American mind may have found philosophical justifications unnecessary. Whatever the reasons, the Enlightenment gave the nation a vision of greatness but failed to hold the hearts of men.

---

1. See the selection below, p. 231.

44

Charles Backus

1749-1803

Born in Norwich, Connecticut, Backus graduated from Yale in 1769, where he showed special proficiency in science. He studied theology there under the Rev. Dr. Hart, and after his ordination in 1773 he became pastor of the Congregational church in Somers. He developed a reputation both as a preacher and theologian and was given an honorary Doctor of Divinity degree from Williams College in 1801.

Just as Backus' education reflected his scientific and religious interests, the following selection is an expression of Enlightenment sympathies, together with a pervasive "sense of sin." It is from *A Sermon Preached in Long-Meadow at the Publick Fast, April 17, 1788* (Springfield, 1788).

ECCLESIASTES VII. 10

Say not thou, what is the cause that the former days were better than these? for thou dost not enquire wisely concerning this.

Complaints under those sufferings, which are inseparable from the present state of man, evidence a bad temper of mind. Invectives against the wickedness of the times, are apparently designed in some instances, as an apology, to quiet the conscience of the exclaimer in sin, and to keep off the home enquiry *what have I done.* Corrupt as the world may be, we are not driven by any fatal necessity, to follow bad examples: *Lot* kept his garments undefiled even in *Sodom.*

It is not so easy, as it may seem to a superficial observer, to determine what particular ages are most corrupt. It hurts our feelings, and endangers our reputation, to speak evil of the dead, who were held but in moderate esteem, while they were living: As a natural consequence, we magnify their virtues, and draw a veil over their faults. Besides, those impressions which we receive in early life, are commonly the strongest. When discernment is small, and the passions are warm, we are liable to think too highly of the characters then in repute. Hence, we find that old people in general, give the preference to the manners of the times, which they saw when they were young. Add to this, we are more shock'd with vice in new than in ancient forms. Mode and fashion will have influence on vicious conduct: wickedness will vary it's manner of expression. These new appearances alone, are sometimes taken for a worse heart; whereas, human nature is always essentially the same. *As in water face answereth to face; so the heart of man to man.*

Preferring former days to the present, is a very ancient practice. *Solomon* takes notice of the custom in his time, and declares, that the *cause* of the supposed degeneracy was not wisely sought. It cannot be his design, to forbid all comparisons betwixt the faith and the manners of different ages. The inspired writers abound with such comparisons, and found many of their reproofs and warnings upon them. The reproof in the text, is pointed against a murmuring temper, under those calamities which the present generation feel: And against all those, who while they smart under the rod, never search after the apparent *moral causes* of their punishment. If we are governed by such a spirit of blindness, when enquiring *why the former days were better than these,* our decisions will be rash and ill-founded, and the charge of folly will be patient under the frowns of Providence, in the worst times; to practice self-examination, and to be humbled under the mighty hand of God.

That the present times are bad, needs no formal proof to any one, whose senses are exercised to discern good and evil. The badness of the times, will certainly be acknowledged by every religious assembly, which can be collected within the United States of America. My present design, is, to advert to some of the obvious causes which render the present days evil.

In the first place, we have had too high expectations from the world. This temper has been in man's heart ever since the fall; but it rises to a higher pitch, and shows itself more, on some occasions than on others. We were lately placed in a situation, which gave unusual scope to all our wishes. The ardour, which glow'd in almost every breast, in the beginning of the war with Britain, we may remember, but we can never describe. In effecting the late memorable Revolution, the generality of all ranks vied with each other, in their zeal and exertions. Their motives indeed were very different; but happening to fix upon the same general object, a very great apparent union existed. In the day when our hopes were brightest, the imagination of the Poet knew no bounds, in describing what America *would* be. The Philosopher became a Rhapsodist, in contemplating the importance of the American Revolution. After a perilous and bloody conflict, we have obtained our Independence. A vast and fertile country, comprising a great variety of soils and climates, has been ceded to us by the late treaty of peace. We have had the very rare privilege, of deliberately forming a plan of government for ourselves. Fortunate Usurpers have given law to most other nations. The few who have escaped so hard a lot, have obtained a partial security of their nobles or kings. But in America; *the People* have had an opportunity of forming a compact *betwixt themselves;* from which alone, their rulers derive all their authority to govern.

In looking forward to those events, which enraptured our minds in prospect, we raised our expectations of happiness from the world, beyond what it can afford. In the most eligible and promising state of human society, man is still born to trouble. Disappointments will increase, in proportion as we calculate too highly for enjoyment, on this side the grave. Human depravity will show itself in a thousand forms. The greatest outward blessings may be awfully abused; and a country, the first for privileges since the deluge, may become the most wretched spot on the globe—which Heaven avert! Where-ever our lot is cast, we must be joined in society with those, who are char-acterized in the Book of God, as *hateful, and hating one another*. As though the necessary evils of life, were not enough to embitter our days, mankind rack their inventions, and exert their malice, to add to each other's misery. It should seem, that companions in danger, would maintain the closer friendship, when the danger is past; but it is too often the case, that with the return of prosperity, all fraternal love is done away. Contentions with a foreign enemy, are frequently followed with domestic broils. How vain is it for us in a world like this, to look for a paradise? Man has seen none upon the earth, since he was banished from the Garden of *Eden*. He will never see another, except in the New Jerusalem. Pride, or ignorance, will prevent an acknowl-edgment from most persons, that they ever expected to be made completely happy by any situation in life. But from comparing our present temper with our past high professions, it becomes very evident, that we once felt, that to be an *American,* was but another name for *a happy man.*

Countries, like individuals, commonly enjoy most quiet when they are young. Their public expences are small; and less personal liberty need be sacrificed, to secure the public good. Before they are brought into notice, ambition and intrigue can have but small scope, in hurrying them on to dangerous enterprises, or in fomenting divisions. We are grown numerous; our colonial relation has come to an end;—it can never return. Our youth is over. We are called in Providence, to take rank with the kingdoms of the world. We have a national character to support, and national dangers to encounter. The present era is highly critical and important. It must extend vast influence, to the happiness or misery of unborn millions. . . .

The present age is an enlightened one. Theories capable of being cor-rected and improved by experiment, have been greatly elucidated. Principles, venerable for their antiquity, have been freely examined, and absurdities ex-posed. Few, if any, can be found, who will seriously maintain, that the first discovery of a Pagan country, by a Christian prince or state, gives the latter a right to the soil; and to crush or expel the natives, in case of opposition to their usurped claim. The principles of civil liberty were never better under-stood. Conviction has generally obtained, that all mankind, of whatever colour or descent, are by nature, equally entitled to freedom: That voluntary as-sociations are the only equitable origin of civil government; and that rulers as well as subjects are limited by the constitution. The rights of conscience, have been set in a clear and convincing light.[1] The idea of attempting an uniformity of faith and worship by *coercion,* is generally acknowledged, to have a much more direct tendency, to make martyrs or hypocrites, than to convince the world that Christianity is from God.

Reason is to be reckoned amongst the choicest gifts of the beneficent Creator. We cannot be sufficiently thankful to the God of Providence, for granting us opportunity to cultivate and improve our rational powers. But this kind of liberty is often used for *an occasion to the flesh.* Self-evident moral principles are treated as great uncertainties: Attempts are made to take off the restraints of the self-denying lessons of Christianity; and infidelity lifts up it's head. . . .

IMPROVEMENT

Having pointed out the leading causes of the present bad times, we are admonished, on a review of our subject,

---

1. The religious toleration in the United States, is without a precedent, in the history of mankind. It will probably never be abridged, whatever changes may take place in our political system. It must be followed with great consequences. Had it happened a few centuries ago, in any single place, of much importance, it would, in all probability, have paved the way for some unfeeling, merciless establishment. The endless variety of opinionists, may enjoy their respective modes of worship, in this land, without the least controul from the ruling powers. Ignorance joined with wildness, is much emboldened to vent itself in it's usual tremendous vociferation. Teachers of this stamp may flourish for a time, in their proper soil. But their influence cannot be lasting, in any great extent, in a country of such religious freedom, and where science is making such rapid advances. It will be nothing new or strange, should indifference to all religion, follow in those places, where the enthusiastic tribes have gained many adherents. Superstition paves the way for infidelity. The raving fanaticism in *Cromwel's* time, fitted the English nation for the licentiousness which came like a flood, in the reign of *Charles* the second. Infidelity threatens to take a wide spread in our young empire. But gloomy as the prospect is, we may derive consolation from the assurance, that *the wrath of man praises God,* and that *the remainder of wrath he will restrain.* God may improve infidelity to destroy all remaining superstition. The general course of events in *Christendom,* for the last hundred years, leads us to this conclusion.

All the friends of the REDEEMER, especially his Ministers, are loudly called upon, to see that their faith *does not stand in the wisdom of men, but in the power of God.* The public teachers of the church will do much to support religion, or to bring it into contempt. It becomes them to act with great caution, in introducing persons into the Ministry. Let dullness, ignorance, and characters whose piety is doubtful, receive no encouragement of entering into the sacred employment. A well-grounded union amongst Ministers, would add much to the reputation and influence of their order. It is ardently to be desired, that such as are agreed in the great essentials of Christianity, and have it's real glory at heart, might be more closely united together. To promote so benevolent a design, it will be necessary, to discriminate betwixt blind zealots on the one hand, and time-serving latitudinarians on the other; to encourage a spirit of free enquiry; and above all, to put on much more of that *charity, which is the bond of perfectness.* Should we behold infidelity, evangelical, enlightened, pious teachers, firmly knit together in love, we might indulge the pleasing hope, that the day was dawning, when the prediction of Isaiah, shall receive it's full accomplishment. *Thy watchmen shall lift up the voice, with the voice together shall they sing; for they shall see eye to eye, when the Lord shall bring again Zion.*

I. To put our trust in the living God. In Him *there is everlasting strength.* He will never disappoint the hope of those, who submit to his government, and rest upon his promises. The higher our expectations are raised by earthly prospects, the more poignant sorrow shall we feel, by the unavoidable disappointments of human life. Happy are they, who have learned to treat all objects according to their worth. Such alone are living to good purpose, and shall finally triumph over all the evils of time. If our minds are stayed on God, he will keep them in peace. We shall, under all our trials, maintain the fortitude of the Psalmist, *God is our refuge and strength, a very present help in trouble. Therefore we will not fear, though the earth be removed, and though the mountains be carried into the midst of the sea; though the waters thereof roar and be troubled, though the mountains shake with the swelling thereof.*

II. WE may see the necessity of great circumspection in our conduct, at the present time. We are surrounded with temptations. There are some, whose selfish interest prompts them, to use every artifice to deceive. Such may be known, by their addressing the passions rather than the reason of their fellowmen. Let us *judge not according to the appearance, but judge righteous judgment.* A candid, impartial temper, is the only proper frame of mind for interesting decisions. Should we throw this aside, we shall be towed upon those rocks of perdition, which prove the ruin of the presumptuous.

If *America* should lose sight of the principles of the late Revolution, she will become wretched in the extreme. In that case, dire necessity would control all the enlightened speculations of the closet, on the rights and liberties of mankind. The sage and the patriot, would give way to established absurdities, from motives similar to those which have shut their mouths, in other countries and ages. Should we crumble in pieces, despotism will follow; and those who had been the first, to detest any former usurpation, will be the last to alarm the fears of the multitude. To guard against such evils, let our temper and conduct correspond, with the present important stage of our national existence. Let us, in our respective spheres of action and influence, countenance and support such measures, as shall tend to give union and prosperity to our infant empire.

While the good man is anxious for the political salvation of his country, his heart trembles yet more for the ARK OF GOD. Should the means of grace be taken away, *the glory will depart from our Israel.* No miracle is necessary, to remove our candlestick out of it's place. Let Christianity be treated with general neglect and contempt, it will soon cease to enlighten any people.

That Divine religion which we enjoy, is not now opposed by the secular arm, as it was in former ages. But the feelings of the heart towards it, are not altered; it's native enmity remains. The indifference which prevails, and the skepticism and ridicule, which are at present employed against the cause of the REDEEMER, are doing the work of the bloody persecutors of former times. Mankind are, at least, in as great danger of being laughed out of religion, as of being deterred from it, by fire and faggots. What holy zeal and vigilance become us, that we be not carried down the torrent of licentiousness and infidelity. Let us *receive a kingdom which cannot be moved; and watch and pray, that we enter not into temptation.*

Lastly, let us all be awakened to unfeigned repentance, and a thorough amendment of life. When God's hand is lifted up in wrath, we are solemnly warned, to search and try our ways, and turn unto him. If we forget the mighty works of our great REDEEMER, we provoke him to cast us out of his holy protection. Nothing will make real good times but reformation. Let us reverence the name and attributes of God. If we have any regard for sacred things, or any desire that Christian ordinances might be continued to us, we must *call the Sabbath a delight, the holy of the Lord, honourable.*

Let us resolve, that as for us and our houses, *we will serve the Lord.* Our holy religion requires us to make a dedication of our all unto God. If public religious bonds be omitted, or degenerate into *mere ceremony,* we may justly fear, that the rising generation will be ignorant of God. Let us not forget any of the duties belonging either to the first or the second table of the Law. While we are pious towards God, let us be just, beneficent and merciful towards men. *Thus speaketh the* LORD OF HOSTS, *saying, execute true judgment, and shew mercy and compassion, every man to his brother: and oppress not the widow, nor the fatherless, the stranger nor the poor; and let none of you imagine evil against his brother in your heart.*[2]

Every man may promote the good of society. Every member has it's office in the body politic, as in the natural body. A truly benevolent mind will be as willing to hold a lower as a higher station, when it appears necessary to promote the general good. Let us imitate the meekness of the great Founder of our religion; and prove by our behaviour, that we are more zealous to be found citizens of the heavenly Zion, than to obtain the plaudit of capricious mortals. We have here no continuing city. May we look for one, which cannot be shaken by the broils and tumults of this world.

With holy happiness in view, how ardently shall we desire, that the spirit of the gospel might spread throughout our land, and the whole habitable globe? If we are true Christians, we are sincere friends to mankind. We are unworthy of the name, if we do not fervently pray, that wars might cease, and that all the nations and tribes of men, might be united together in the bonds of love. May the period soon commence, when *the kingdoms of this world, shall become the kingdoms of our Lord, and of his Christ.*

To God only wise, be glory through Jesus Christ forever. AMEN.

---

2. *Zecha.* vii, 9, 10.

45

Joel Barlow

1754-1812

Joel Barlow was a poet, statesman, and one of the most liberal thinkers of his age. After he received his B.A. from Yale in 1778, he led a
varied career that included the study of philosophy, the practice of
law, and participation in French politics.

Barlow penned many political pieces in addition to his more formal
literary efforts. His best-known poem, *Columbiad,* was envisioned by
Barlow as early as 1779. Its purpose was clearly stated in its preface:
"My object is altogether of a moral and political nature. I wish to encourage and strengthen, in the rising generation, a sense of the importance of republican institutions; as being the great foundation of
public and private happiness, the necessary aliment of future and permanent ameliorations in the condition of human nature." The poem
made Barlow one of the new nation's leading literary figures. The following selection is from *Columbiad* (Philadelphia, 1808).

Thro Europe's wilds when feudal nations spread,
The pride of conquest every legion led.
Each fur-clad chief, by servile crowds adored,
O'er conquer'd realms assumed the name of lord,
Built the proud castle, ranged the savage wood,
Fired his grim host to frequent fields of blood,
With new made honors lured his subject bands,
Price of their lives, and purchase of their lands;
For names and titles bade the world resign
Their faith, their freedom and their rights divine.
    Contending baronies their terrors spread,
And slavery follow'd where the standard led;
Till, little tyrants by the great o'erthrown,
The spoils of nobles build the regal crown;
Wealth, wisdom, virtue, every claim of man
Unguarded fall to consummate the plan.
Ambitious cares, that nature never gave,
Torment alike the monarch and the slave,
Thro all degrees in gradual pomp ascend,
Honor, the name, but tyranny the end.

Far different honors here the heart shall claim,
Sublimer objects, deeds of happier fame;
A new creation waits the western shore,
And moral triumphs o'er monarchic power.
Thy freeborn sons, with genius unconfined,
Nor sloth can slacken nor a tyrant bind;
With self-wrought fame and worth internal blest,
No venal star shall brighten on their breast,
Nor king-created name nor courtly art
Damp the bold thought or desiccate the heart.
Above all fraud, beyond all titles great,
Truth in their voice and sceptres at their feet,
Like sires of unborn states they move sublime,
Look empires thro and span the breadth of time,
Hold o'er the world, that men may choose from far
The palm of peace, or scourge of barbarous war;
Till their example every nation charms,
Commands its friendship and its rage disarms.

Here social man a second birth shall find,
And a new range of reason lift his mind,
Feed his strong intellect with purer light,
A nobler sense of duty and of right,
The sense of liberty; whose holy fire
His life shall temper and his laws inspire,
Purge from all shades the world-embracing scope
That prompts his genius and expands his hope.

When first his form arose erect on earth,
Parturient nature hail'd the wondrous birth,
With fairest limbs and finest fibres wrought,
And framed for vast and various toils of thought.
To aid his promised powers with loftier flight,
And stretch his views beyond corporeal sight,
Prometheus came, and from the floods of day
Sunn'd his clear soul with heaven's internal ray,
The expanding spark divine; that round him springs,
And leads and lights him thro the immense of things,
Probes the dense earth, explores the soundless main,
Remoulds their mass thro all its threefold reign,
O'er great, o'er small extends his physic laws,
Empalms the empyrean or dissects a gaz,
Weighs the vast orbs of heaven, bestrides the sky,
Walks on the windows of an insect's eye;
Turns then to self, more curious still to trace
The whirls of passion that involve the race,
That cloud with mist the visual lamp of God,

And plunge the poignard in fraternal blood.
Here fails his light. The proud Titanian ray
O'er physic nature sheds indeed its day;
Yet leaves the moral in chaotic jars,
The spoil of violence, the sport of wars,
Presents contrasted parts of one great plan,
Earth, heaven subdued, but man at swords with man;
His wars, his errors into science grown,
And the great cause of all his ills unknown.

     But when he steps on these regenerate shores,
His mind unfolding for superior powers,
FREEDOM, his new Prometheus, here shall rise,
Light her new torch in my refulgent skies,
Touch with a stronger life his opening soul,
Of moral systems fix the central goal,
Her own resplendent essence. Thence expand
The rays of reason that illume the land;
Thence equal rights proceed, and equal laws,
Thence holy Justice all her reverence draws;
Truth with untarnish'd beam descending thence,
Strikes every eye, and quickens every sense,
Bids bright Instruction spread her ample page,
To drive dark dogmas from the inquiring age,
Ope the true treasures of the earth and skies,
And teach the student where his object lies.

     Sun of the moral world! effulgent source
Of man's best wisdom and his steadiest force,
Soul-searching Freedom! here assume thy stand,
And radiate hence to every distant land;
Point out and prove how all the scenes of strife,
The shock of states, the impassion'd broils of life,
Spring from unequal sway; and how they fly
Before the splendor of thy peaceful eye;
Unfold at last the genuine social plan,
The mind's full scope, the dignity of man,
Bold nature bursting thro her long disguise,
And nations daring to be just and wise.

     Yes! righteous Freedom, heaven and earth and sea
Yield or withhold their various gifts for thee;
Protected Industry beneath thy reign
Leads all the virtues in her filial train;
Courageous Probity with brow serene,
And Temperance calm presents her placid mien;
Contentment, Moderation, Labor, Art,
Mould the new man and humanize his heart;

To public plenty private ease dilates,
Domestic peace to harmony of states.
Protected Industry, careering far,
Detects the cause and cures the rage of war,
And sweeps, with forceful arm, to their last graves,
Kings from the earth and pirates from the waves. . . .
Equality of Right is nature's plan;
And following nature is the march of man.
Whene'er he deviates in the least degree,
When, free himself, he would be more than free,
The baseless column, rear'd to bear his bust,
Falls as he mounts, and whelms him in the dust.

    See Rome's rude sires, with autocratic gait,
Tread down their tyrant and erect their state;
Their state secured, they deem it wise and brave
That every freeman should command a slave,
And, flusht with franchise of his camp and town,
Rove thro the world and hunt the nations down;
Master and man the same vile spirit gains,
Rome chains the world, and wears herself the chains.

    Mark modern Europe with her feudal codes,
Serfs, villains, vassals, nobles, kings and gods,
All slaves of different grades, corrupt and curst
With high and low, for senseless rank athirst,
Wage endless wars; not fighting to be free,
But *cujum pecus,* whose base herd they'll be.

    Too much of Europe, here transplanted o'er,
Nursed feudal feelings on your tented shore,
Brought sable serfs from Afric, call'd it gain,
And urged your sires to forge the fatal chain.
But now, the tents o'erturn'd, the war dogs fled,
Now fearless Freedom rears at last her head
Matcht with celestial Peace—my friends, beware
To shade the splendors of so bright a pair;
Complete their triumph, fix their firm abode,
Purge all privations from your liberal code,
Restore their souls to men, give earth repose,
And save your sons from slavery, wars and woes.

    Based on its rock of Right your empire lies,
On walls of wisdom let the fabric rise;
Preserve your principles, their force unfold,
Let nations prove them and let kings behold.
EQUALITY, your first firm-grounded stand;
Then FREE ELECTION; then your FEDERAL BAND;
This holy Triad should forever shine

The great compendium of all rights divine,
Creed of all schools, whence youths by millions draw
Their themes of right, their decalogues of law;
Till men shall wonder (in these codes inured)
How wars were made, how tyrants were endured.

Then shall your works of art superior rise,
Your fruits perfume a larger length of skies,
Canals careering climb your sunbright hills,
Vein the green slopes and strow their nurturing rills,
Thro tunnel'd heights and sundering ridges glide,
Rob the rich west of half Kenhawa's tide,
Mix your wide climates, all their stores confound,
And plant new ports in every midland mound.
Your lawless Mississippi, now who slimes
And drowns and desolates his waste of climes,
Ribb'd with your dikes, his torrent shall restrain,
And ask your leave to travel to the main;
Won from his wave while rising cantons smile,
Rear their glad nations and reward their toil.

Thus Nile's proud flood to human hands of yore
Raised and resign'd his tide-created shore,
Call'd from his Ethiop hills their hardy swains,
And waved their harvests o'er his newborn plains;
Earth's richest realm from his tamed current sprung;
There nascent science toned her infant tongue,
Taught the young arts their tender force to try,
To state the seasons and unfold the sky;
Till o'er the world extended and refined,
They rule the destinies of humankind. . . .
Great without pomp their modest walls expand,
Harvard and Yale and Princeton grace the land,
Penn's student halls his youths with gladness greet,
On James's bank Virginian Muses meet,
Manhattan's mart collegiate domes command,
Bosom'd in groves, see growing Dartmouth stand;
Bright o'er its realm reflecting solar fires,
On yon tall hill Rhode Island's seat aspires.

Thousands of humbler name around them rise,
Where homebred freemen seize the solid prize;
Fixt in small spheres, with safer beams to shine,
They reach the useful and refuse the fine,
Found, on its proper base, the social plan,
The broad plain truths, the common sense of man,
His obvious wants, his mutual aids discern,
His rights familiarize, his duties learn,

Feel moral fitness all its force dilate,
Embrace the village and comprise the state.
Each rustic here who turns the furrow'd soil,
The maid, the youth that ply mechanic toil,
In equal rights, in useful arts inured,
Know their just claims, and see their claims secured;
They watch their delegates, each law revise,
Its faults designate and its merits prize,
Obey, but scrutinize; and let the test
Of sage experience prove and fix the best.

     Here, fired by virtue's animating flame,
The preacher's task persuasive sages claim,
To mould religion to the moral mind,
In bands of peace to harmonize mankind,
To life, to light, to promised joys above
The soften'd soul with ardent hope to move.
No dark intolerance blinds the zealous throng,
No arm of power attendant on their tongue;
Vext Inquisition, with her flaming brand,
Shuns their mild march, nor dares approach the land.
Tho different creeds their priestly robes denote,
Their orders various and their rites remote,
Yet one their voice, their labors all combined,
Lights of the world and friends of humankind.
So the bright galaxy o'er heaven displays
Of various stars the same unbounded blaze;
Where great and small their mingling rays unite,
And earth and skies exchange the friendly light.

     And lo, my son, that other sapient band,
The torch of science flaming in their hand!
Thro nature's range their searching souls aspire,
Or wake to life the canvass and the lyre.
Fixt in sublimest thought, behold them rise
World after world unfolding to their eyes,
Lead, light, allure them thro the total plan,
And give new guidance to the paths of man.

     Yon meteor-mantled hill see Franklin tread,
Heaven's awful thunders rolling o'er his head;
Convolving clouds the billowy skies deform,
And forky flames emblaze the blackening storm.
See the descending streams around him burn,
Glance on his rod and with his finger turn;
He bids conflicting fulminants expire
The guided blast, and holds the imprison'd fire.
No more, when doubling storms the vault o'erspread,

The livid glare shall strike thy race with dread,
Nor towers nor temples, shuddering with the sound,
Sink in the flames and shake the sheeted ground.
His well tried wires, that every tempest wait,
Shall teach mankind to ward the bolts of fate,
With pointed steel o'ertop the trembling spire,
And lead from untouch'd walls the harmless fire;
Fill'd with his fame while distant climes rejoice,
Wherever lightning shines or thunder rears its voice.

    And see sage Rittenhouse, with ardent eye,
Lift the long tube and pierce the starry sky;
Clear in his view the circling planets roll,
And suns and satellites their course control.
He marks what laws the widest wanderers bind,
Copies creation in his forming mind,
Sees in his hall the total semblance rise,
And mimics there the labors of the skies.
There student youths without their tubes behold
The spangled heavens their mystic maze unfold,
And crowded schools their cheerful chambers grace
With all the spheres that cleave the vast of space.

    To guide the sailor in his wandering way,
See Godfrey's glass reverse the beams of day.
His lifted quadrant to the eye displays
From adverse skies the counteracting rays;
And marks, as devious sails bewilder'd roll,
Each nice gradation from the stedfast pole. . . .
Tis thus Society's small sources rise;
Thro passions wild her infant progress lies;
Fear, with its host of follies, errors, woes,
Creates her obstacles and forms her foes;
Misguided interest, local pride withstand,
Till long tried ills her growing views expand,
Till tribes and states and empires find their place,
Whose mutual wants her widest walks embrace;
Enlighten'd interest, moral sense at length,
Combine their aids to elevate her strength,
Lead o'er the world her peace-commanding sway,
And light her steps with everlasting day.

    From that mark'd stage of man we now behold,
More rapid strides his coming paths unfold;
His continents are traced, his islands found,
His well taught sails on all his billows bound,
His varying wants their new discoveries ply,
And seek in earth's whole range their sure supply.

First of his future stages, thou shalt see
His trade unfetter'd and his ocean free.
From thy young states the code consoling springs,
To strip from vulture War his naval wings;
In views so just all Europe's powers combine,
And earth's full voice approves the vast design.
Tho still her inland realms the combat wage,
And hold in lingering broils the unsettled age,
Yet no rude shocks that shake the crimson plain
Shall more disturb the labors of the main;
The main that spread so wide his travell'd way,
Liberal as air, impartial as the day,
That all thy race the common wealth might share,
Exchange their fruits and fill their treasures there,
Their speech assimilate, their counsels blend,
Till mutual interest fix the mutual friend.
Now see, my son, the destined hour advance;
Safe in their leagues commercial navies dance,
Leave their curst cannon on the quay-built strand,
And like the stars of heaven a fearless course command.

Part Three

THE MIND OF A NATION

$\mathcal{A}$ T the beginning of the nineteenth century America faced the task of creating a nation. The events of 1776 and 1787 had produced a body of principles that—however much historical experience would change —were to set the fundamental cast of the American mind. But a nation with a central sovereignty, a common past and traditions, and common cultural aspirations still had to be brought into being. Three factors—events, ideas, and environment—were involved in the making of the American nation; and, though most of the ideas were part of Western tradition, as Professor Gabriel observes, "the configuration of the cluster was unique."[1]

The new nation was soon confronted by events that threatened its survival. Just before 1800, two of them posed the problem of national union in a particularly striking way. In 1793 an alliance with France dating from 1778 nearly drew the United States into war with Britain. The alliance was ended in 1800, but not before Americans had received many warnings about the evils of "entangling alliances." In 1794 the Whiskey Rebellion, though unsuccessful, was a serious challenge to the authority of the new central government. The years following 1800 also saw many important and challenging events, but perhaps the most crucial was the War of 1812. This engagement produced, it is true, internal dissensions that threatened the nation's very existence. But what is more important, it also produced new national heroes and a sense of unity and national purpose. At the conclusion of this war, America turned its back on Europe, and set its face westward. As the frontier expanded, the nation seemed to achieve a clearer sense of its own identity. In 1823 the Monroe Doctrine formalized America's isolation from Europe into a foreign policy. From this date onward, America still faced crucial problems—even that supreme test of democratic principles, the Civil War

1. Ralph H. Gabriel, *The Course of American Democratic Thought,* 2nd ed. (New York, 1956), p. 14.

—but these were problems of an expanding, industrializing country rather than those of a nation at birth.

By 1815 Americans had restated their republican heritage in terms of three beliefs: individualism, the higher law, and the humane ends of government. To be sure, there were Federalists who still tried to interpret these ideas in terms of an older, more aristocratic persuasion (as late as 1837 Noah Webster wanted to eliminate the popular election of presidents), yet they were heard more out of respect for their past contributions than for their present ideas. But within a few more years Federalism was dead, and in the center of the stage stood the American democrat and "the common man." The presidency of Andrew Jackson, with its "equal rights for all, special privilege for none," marked the culmination of the hopes and fears, aspirations and, sometimes, disappointments, of a nation of democrats.

The democratic interpretation of the heritage of the golden past, which for Americans now meant the era of the Revolution, was an idealized one. As Vernon Parrington[2] interpreted the Romantic period, Americans glorified the ideal of individualism in every area of human concern—political, economic, and cultural. From this ideal, in turn, came a number of important implications. The first and most immediate concerned independence and its corollary, self-reliance. Born an individual, the American was born free, and in fact his freedom seemed to him less a consequence of political theory than a political fact. Self-reliance, understood in a Puritan sense even after Emerson gave it a Transcendentalist context, was the moral ideal for the freedom the American had. Secondly, Americans felt themselves duty-bound to explore the providential theme of equality. Again, it was the Jacksonians who waged battle for this ideal; and they contributed a special meaning to it—namely, equality of opportunity. Walt Whitman was to sing the praises of equality and individualism even after the end of the Romantic era. Thirdly, such equality, combined with Puritan virtues and a republican order, helped to create a feeling of optimism, a sense of a nation being called to greatness. "Perhaps no theme," writes Professor Burns in his study of the idea of mission, "has ever dominated the minds of the leaders of this nation to the same extent as the idea that America occupies a unique place and has a special destiny among the nations of the earth."[3] Longfellow's verse, "Humanity with all its fears/ With all its hopes of future years/ Is hanging breathless on thy fate," expressed the thought in a way that, if it displeased critics, yet brought the sense of America's mission even to the child. The idea of mission, concludes Professor Gabriel, is "the culminating doctrine of the American democratic faith,"[4] and—as the circle completes itself—this same idea reinforced that of nationalism.

---

2. See volume II of his *Main Currents in American Thought* (New York, 1927), *passim*.

3. Edward McNall Burns, *The American Idea of Mission* (New Brunswick, N.J., 1957), p. 5.

4. Gabriel, *op. cit.*, p. 80.

Another formative factor in the American experience has been the American environment, with its sense of spaciousness, its isolation from Europe, and its developing frontier. All three of these features tended to reinforce individualism and to provide an experiential basis for the American dream. Professor Louis Hartz has commented extensively on this reinforcement, attempting to show that the American environment tended to confirm John Locke's analysis to such a degree that Locke seemed less to be proposing a political theory than to be describing political actuality.[5] Professor Richard Hofstadter has also quipped that "it is our fate as a nation, not to have ideologies but to be one." America's isolation from Europe allowed her to pursue internal development in a way impossible for other Western nations, and the rich resources of a virgin continent provided the materials for individuals to practice their individualism in an unprecedented way. "It was not, in short," writes Professor Commager, "particular environments that determined the American character or created the American type but the whole of the American environment—the sense of spaciousness, the invitation to mobility, the atmosphere of independence, the encouragement to enterprise and to optimism."[6]

But in many ways it was the frontier that provided Americans with their unique confirmation of individualism. Lord Bryce wrote that "the West may be called the most distinctively American part of America because the points in which it differs from the East are the points in which America as a whole differs from Europe."[7] The frontier, as Tocqueville observed more than a century ago, placed men, at least initially, in a condition of equality. The actions of the hunter, trapper, trader, and frontier farmer were those of individualists of the mold of the rural farmer that many of the Founding Fathers—particularly, Jefferson—had in mind when they dreamed of an agrarian society.

The famous American historian Frederick J. Turner viewed the frontier as the fundamental cause of America's unique historical development. Lord Bryce, too, believed that the American environment, with its free land and advance of settlement westward, was the feature that most distinguished American from European civilization. Of special importance was the "safety-valve" function of the frontier in relieving pressures of discontent in the East. Turner and his followers also related the frontier to a number of emerging American characteristics: nationalism, individualism, inventiveness, and materialism. More recent historical judgment has modified Turner's thesis, and holds that the frontier did not originate these characteristics but rather helped to strengthen them once they began to crystallize as important features of the American mind. Along the same line, Professor Billington has stated, "most

5. Louis Hartz, *The Liberal Tradition in America* (New York, 1955), *passim.*
6. Henry Steele Commager, *The American Mind* (New Haven, 1952), pp. 4–5.
7. James Bryce, *The American Commonwealth*, 2 vols. (New York, 1888), vol. II, p. 311.

historians today would agree that political institutions have been altered but not completely transformed by the frontier process."[8]

But, while the actual frontier was not as formative a feature in America's development as Turner believed, the imagined frontier—the frontier of story, saga, and song—cast its spell over the American mind. Thus, a "frontier mentality" became a further characteristic of the American. And with this mentality went a frontier faith, a faith in common humanity that was rooted and expressed in the spontaneous and autonomous strivings of the individual. Recognizing man as a creative agent, this mentality sensed the ultimate value of man as an individual member of society; and in fact this insight into individualism often compensated for the cultural sterility that sometimes accompanied pioneering life. Thus the frontiersman found in action what Locke and the Founding Fathers had divined in theory.

In two areas especially, politics and economics, the individualistic dreams of the American democrat were especially sympathetic to the Romantic mind. The hopes of political individualism centered on the ideas of equal rights and universal suffrage—the former to be achieved, of course, by the latter. By the early nineteenth century most property qualifications for voting had been dropped, though suffrage was not extended without controversy. Fisher Ames spoke of democracy as "an illuminated Hell," Noah Webster declared that a pending bill to democratize Massachusetts suffrage would prostrate the wealth of individuals "to the rapaciousness of a merciless gang who had nothing to lose," and Chancellor James Kent used his every talent to prevent the extension of suffrage in New York. But the efforts of these Federalists were futile, and by the time of Jackson male suffrage was almost universal. The real issue in the struggle, as Federalists saw it, had been the conflict between the rich and poor, though in a broader sense it was also a question of democracy versus aristocracy. But the Federalists failed to perceive that in a nation of individualists the poor would strive to achieve riches themselves rather than to oppose the accumulation of wealth. This shared individualistic view helped Americans solve the classic problem of democracy, majority rule and minority rights, for when a nation is united in an individualistic vision, the majority will not destroy it for a minority. Americans willingly came to accept the principle of majority rule, and it was to fail them only once— during the Civil War.

In the economic sphere, also, individualism found unique expression. The economic ideal of both Jefferson and the Jacksonians was an agrarian republic, but this dream was becoming dated even during Jefferson's day. Actually, the American economy was undergoing profound changes during the first half of the century, as the Industrial Revolution brought the factory system and the rise of industrial towns to the New World. These changes caused a virtual revolution in American economic life. This economic growth occurred, of course, in a democratic society—in fact, as Jackson's war against

---

8. Ray A. Billington, *The American Frontier* (Washington, D.C., 1958), p. 18.

the Bank and special privilege indicates, in a society dedicated to the premise of equal opportunity.

The result of these political ideals and economic changes was a laissez-faire capitalism. Economic democracy in America came to mean that individuals should participate in economic processes as they participate in political affairs (though later generations of Americans were to wonder about the reality of this participation). Add to this the Puritan virtues of work, thrift, inconspicuous consumption, simplicity, order, and the belief that property is an outward and visible sign of an inner and invisible state, and the basis for America's mobile, acquisitive, and productive economic order was complete. "During the thirty-odd years between the Peace of Paris and the end of the War of 1812," Parrington writes of these economic changes, "that older America was dying. The America that succeeded was a shifting, restless world, youthfully optimistic, eager to better itself."[9]

What were the characteristics of the nineteenth-century American? No listing can be fully adequate, but some generalization can be made. The American's optimism grew out of his fortitude, his energy, and his confidence in a future that seemed limitless in its promise. "Go west, young man," referred both to the frontier, as a safety valve that solved some of the problems of life, and to the future promise of America in which, it was sanguinely believed, solutions would be found to all problems. The American's "common sense" led him to a practical ethics, to a conduct based on religion but not always devout. His quantitative cast made him practical and material: even his culture was built on and out of material, not necessarily because his reality was material but because his interests were practical. His individualism led him to experiment and innovate, to distrust and sometimes to disregard authority, and to be tolerant. Lest he be seen as a man of only virtues, mention should also be made of the American's romantic view of sex, his sentimentalism, and his provincialism.

A romanticized Lockianism—if such it may be called—remained the dominant cast of the American mind through mid-century. It is Professor Hartz's ably argued thesis[10] that the Lockian view constituted the basic problem of American society. The chief danger to that society was not the tyranny of the majority but the pressure of unanimity. The European world of the Enlightenment, Hartz writes, had shaped the political and philosophic thought of the founders of the Republic. America did not have to throw off the shackles of feudalism or wage the social revolutions of Europe, and consequently Locke's theories often were regarded less as premises of political behavior than as absolutes. Hence, as de Tocqueville pointed out, the danger to America was that, lacking a feudal past, equality here would lead to a tyranny of the majority. America, it seemed, had begun its existence as Locke had indicated, in a state of nature, and by contractual arrangements

---

9. Parrington, *op. cit.,* II, viii.
10. Hartz, *op. cit., passim.*

instituted government. This pattern in turn shaped the American mind in all its expressions (here the mind of the South may be the exception). America in the nineteenth century retained its liberal—that is, Lockian—inheritance, responded to an expanding frontier and changing economic conditions, and established a political, economic, and to some extent cultural nationalism. The accomplishments of this half-century were substantial though less dramatic than the splendor of the preceding era.

XI

An American Nationalism

A NUMBER of emerging characteristics of the American mind have been noted in earlier sections, but for the first half of the nineteenth century none is more important or central than those of nationalism and its corollary, national mission. When Washington assumed office, the American people faced the crucial task of giving reality to the hopes for national greatness expressed in the Constitution. The task was not an easy one, for Americans were still divided over the kind of nation they wanted to create—a division that reached its climax in the presidential campaign of 1800. Yet a sense of national identity and national pride were gradually developing among the people. Nationalism soon passed beyond patriotism and became America's abiding ideal.

Conscious efforts to awaken the nationalistic spirit were undertaken in all the major areas of national endeavor. Under Washington attempts to develop a national economy were begun by Alexander Hamilton, and an avowed economic nationalism was later promoted by such men as Mathew Carey and Henry Clay. The decisions of Chief Justice John Marshall, often criticized and sometimes bitterly attacked by the Jeffersonians, not only strengthened federal authority but also helped to write nationalism into the law. Achievements of the federal government also helped to strengthen national pride; the Louisiana Purchase, the War of 1812, and the Monroe Doctrine marked major steps in this direction.

Among the most important efforts in creating American nationalism, however, were those of writers and artists. Even as these groups had contributed greatly to the Revolutionary cause, so they now turned to the problems of the nation. Noah Webster wrote of the necessity of a national language as a bond of union, and he called on writers and Americans generally to create a national instrument of expression and communication. Literary artists in particular accepted Webster's challenge—especially those in New York and New England, such as Washington Irving, William Cullen Bryant, and Henry Wadsworth Longfellow. These writers produced a "literary nationalism." So important was their work that they may be ranked among the founding fathers of American nationalism. They posed the question of a national literature (see the selection on page 269 from Longfellow's novel *Kavanagh*), and then endeavored to create it. But before the young republic could become a nation in fact as well as name, Americans had to gain a sense of a common past, and a common body of experiences and ideals. From Joel Barlow at the beginning of the period to Herman Melville and Walt Whitman at its end, American writers were concerned with this national problem.

Nationalism, of course, was not peculiar to America; pride of country is experienced by all peoples. Yet American nationalism was unique in that it was part of the larger national mystique of America's mission to embody freedom for all mankind. The eyes of the world were on the American experiment in democracy. But could men be trusted to govern themselves? Were the republican principles that Jefferson hoped would be eternal adequate for the government of men? Americans voiced clear, affirmative answers to all such questions, for themselves and for mankind. For was not America's mission to be the repository of political truths and the political hope of the world? An abiding faith in this mission and destiny has marked the American mind from its inception to the present day.

(46)

Thomas Jefferson
1743-1826

Elected President in 1800 after a bitter campaign that left the American people deeply divided, Jefferson faced problems of enormous complexity as he assumed the presidential office. In his First Inaugural Address, therefore, he set himself the task of rekindling the flame of democratic hopes. Brief, eloquent, and reflecting the best elements of eighteenth-century style, his Address harks back to the principles of the Declaration of Independence and anticipates the glories of America's future, "destinies beyond the reach of mortal eye." It is an ode to liberty, and to toleration, even of those who would dissolve the Union or change its republican form. It rejoices in the principles of republican government that, uniting all, assures prosperity, progress, and the pursuit of happiness.

The text reprinted here is from *The Inaugural Speeches of Washington, Adams and Jefferson* (Boston, 1802). [For Jefferson's career, see above, pp. 132–133.]

FRIENDS AND FELLOW-CITIZENS:

Called upon to undertake the duties of the first executive office of our country, I avail myself of the presence of that portion of my fellow-citizens which is here assembled to express my grateful thanks for the favor with which they have been pleased to look toward me, to declare a sincere consciousness that the task is above my talents, and that I approach it with those anxious and awful presentiments which the greatness of the charge and the weakness of my powers so justly inspire. A rising nation, spread over a wide and fruitful land, traversing all the seas with the rich productions of their industry, engaged in commerce with nations who feel power and forget right, advancing rapidly to destinies beyond the reach of mortal eye—when I contemplate these transcendent objects, and see the honor, the happiness, and the hopes of this beloved country committed to the issue and the auspices of this day, I shrink from the contemplation, and humble myself before the magnitude of the undertaking. Utterly, indeed, should I despair did not the presence of many whom I here see remind me that in the other high authorities provided by our Constitution I shall find resources of wisdom, of virtue, and of zeal on which to rely under all difficulties. To you, then, gentlemen, who are charged with the sovereign functions of legislation, and to those associated with you, I look with encouragement for that guidance and support which may enable us to steer with safety the vessel in which we are all embarked amidst the conflicting elements of a troubled world.

During the contest of opinion through which we have passed the animation of discussions and of exertions has sometimes worn an aspect which might impose on strangers unused to think freely and to speak and to write what they think; but this being now decided by the voice of the nation, announced according to the rules of the Constitution, all will, of course, arrange themselves under the will of the law, and unite in common efforts for the common good. All, too, will bear in mind this sacred principle, that though the will of the majority is in all cases to prevail, that will to be rightful must be reasonable; that the minority possess their equal rights, which equal law must protect, and to violate would be oppression. Let us, then, fellow-citizens, unite with one heart and one mind. Let us restore to social intercourse that harmony and affection without which liberty and even life itself are but dreary things. And let us reflect that, having banished from our land that religious intolerance under which mankind so long bled and suffered, we have yet gained little if we countenance a political intolerance as despotic, as wicked, and capable of as bitter and bloody persecutions. During the throes and convulsions of the ancient world, during the agonizing spasms of infuriated man, seeking through blood and slaughter his long-lost liberty, it was not wonderful that the agitation of the billows should reach even this distant and peaceful shore; that this should be more felt and feared by some and less by others, and should divide opinions as to measures of safety. But every difference of opinion is not a difference of principle. We have called by different names brethren of the same principle. We are all Republicans, we are all Federalists. If there be any among us who would wish to dissolve this Union or to change its republican form, let them stand undisturbed as monuments of the safety with which error of opinion may be tolerated where reason is left free to combat it. I know, indeed, that some honest men fear that a republican government can not be strong, that this Government is not strong enough; but would the honest patriot, in the full tide of successful experiment, abandon a government which has so far kept us free and firm on the theoretic and visionary fear that this Government, the world's best hope, may by possibility want energy to preserve itself? I trust not. I believe this, on the contrary, the strongest Government on earth. I believe it the only one where every man, at the call of the law, would fly to the standard of the law, and would meet invasions of the public order as his own personal concern. Sometimes it is said that man can not be trusted with the government of himself. Can he, then, be trusted with the government of others? Or have we found angels in the forms of kings to govern him? Let history answer this question.

Let us, then, with courage and confidence pursue our own Federal and Republican principles, our attachment to union and representative government. Kindly separated by nature and a wide ocean from the exterminating havoc of one quarter of the globe; too high-minded to endure the degradations of the others; possessing a chosen country, with room enough for our descendants to the thousandth and thousandth generation; entertaining a due sense of our equal right to the use of our own faculties, to the acquisitions of our own industry, to honor and confidence from our fellow-citizens, resulting not from birth, but from our actions and their sense of them; enlightened by a benign religion, professed, indeed, and practiced in various forms, yet all of them inculcating honesty, truth, temperance, gratitude, and the love of man; acknowledging and adoring an overruling Providence, which by all its dispensations proves that it delights in the happiness of man here and his greater happiness hereafter—with all these blessings, what more is necessary to make us a happy and a prosperous people? Still one thing more, fellow-citizens—a wise and frugal Government, which shall restrain men from injuring one another, shall leave them otherwise free to regulate their own pursuits of industry and improvement, and shall not take from the mouth of labor the bread it has earned. This is the sum of good government, and this is necessary to close the circle of our felicities.

About to enter, fellow-citizens, on the exercise of duties which comprehend everything dear and valuable to you, it is proper you should understand what I deem the essential principles of our Government, and consequently those which ought to shape its Administration. I will compress them within the narrowest compass they will bear, stating the general principle, but not all its limitations. Equal and exact justice to all men, of whatever state or persuasion, religious or political; peace, commerce, and honest friendship with all nations, entangling alliances with none; the support of the State governments in all their rights, as the most competent administrations for our domestic concerns and the surest bulwarks against antirepublican tendencies; the preservation of the General Government in its whole constitutional vigor, as the sheet anchor of our peace at home and safety abroad; a jealous care of the right of election by the people—a mild and safe corrective of abuses which are lopped by the sword of revolution where peaceable remedies are unprovided; absolute acquiescence in the decisions of the majority, the vital principle of republics, from which is no appeal but to force, the vital principle and immediate parent of despotism; a well-disciplined militia, our best reliance in peace and for the first moments of war, till regulars may relieve them; the supremacy of the civil over the military authority; economy in the public expense, that labor may be lightly burthened; the honest payment of our debts and sacred preservation of the public faith; encouragement of agriculture, and of commerce as its handmaid; the diffusion of information and arraignment of all abuses at the bar of the public reason; freedom of religion; freedom of the press, and freedom of person under the protection of the habeas corpus, and trial by juries impartially selected. These principles form the bright constellation which has gone before us and guided our steps through an age of revolution and reformation. The wisdom of our sages and blood of our heroes have been devoted to their attainment. They should be the creed of our political faith, the text of civic instruction, the touchstone by which to try the services of those we trust; and should we wander from them in moments of error or of alarm, let us hasten to retrace our steps and to regain the road which alone leads to peace, liberty, and safety.

I repair, then, fellow-citizens, to the post you have assigned me. With experience enough in subordinate offices to have seen the difficulties of this the greatest of all, I have learnt to expect that it will rarely fall to the lot of imperfect man to retire from this station with the reputation and the favor which bring him into it. Without pretensions to that high confidence you reposed in our first and greatest revolutionary character, whose preeminent services had entitled him to the first place in his country's love and destined for him the fairest page in the volume of faithful history, I ask so much confidence only as may give firmness and effect to the legal administration of your affairs. I shall often go wrong through defect of judgment. When right, I shall often be thought wrong by those whose positions will not command a view of the whole ground. I ask your indulgence for my own errors, which will never be intentional, and your support against the errors of others, who may condemn what they would not if seen in all its parts. The approbation implied by your suffrage is a great consolation to me for the past, and my future solicitude will be to retain the good opinion of those who have bestowed it in advance, to conciliate that of others by doing them all the good in my power, and to be instrumental to the happiness and freedom of all.

Relying, then, on the patronage of your good will, I advance with obedience to the work, ready to retire from it whenever you become sensible how much better choice it is in your power to make. And may that Infinite Power which rules the destinies of the universe lead our councils to what is best, and give them a favorable issue for your peace and prosperity.

(47)

Noah Webster

1758-1843

> Graduating from Yale after a short period of military service, Noah Webster began a career as a writer and lecturer that was to earn him the title "Schoolmaster to America." In a series of lectures and books he emphasized the necessity of an American language and an American system of education, both for national unity and national character. America, he believed, "must be as independent in *literature* as she is in *politics,* as famous for *arts* as for *arms.*" His zeal on behalf of the Constitution, his long humanitarian career, and his concern with America's cultural development earned him a place among the major figures of his day.
>
> This selection, one of Webster's many pleas for a national language, is from his *Dissertations on the English Language* (Boston, 1789).

A regular study of language has, in all civilized countries, formed a part of a liberal education. The Greeks, Romans, Italians and French successively improved their native tongues, taught them in Academies at home, and rendered them entertaining and useful to the foreign student.

The English tongue, tho' later in its progress towards perfection, has attained to a considerable degree of purity, strength and elegance, and been employed by an active and scientific nation to record almost all the events and discoveries of ancient and modern times.

This language is the inheritance which the Americans have received from their British parents. To cultivate and adorn it, is a task reserved for men who shall understand the connection between language and logic, and form an adequate idea of the influence which a uniformity of speech may have on national attachments.

It will be readily admitted that the pleasures of reading and conversing, the advantage of accuracy in business, the necessity of clearness and precision in communicating ideas, require us to be able to speak and write our own tongue with ease and correctness. But there are more important reasons why the language of this country should be reduced to such fixed principles as may give its pronunciation and construction all the certainty and uniformity which any living tongue is capable of receiving.

The United States were settled by emigrants from different parts of Europe. But their descendants mostly speak the same tongue; and the intercourse among the learned of the different States, which the revolution has begun and an American Court will perpetuate, must gradually destroy the differences of dialect which our ancestors brought from their native countries. This approximation of dialects will be certain; but without the operation of other causes than an intercourse at Court, it will be slow and partial. The body of the people, governed by habit, will still retain their respective peculiarities of speaking; and for want of schools and proper books, fall into many inaccuracies, which, incorporating with the language of the state where they live, may imperceptibly corrupt the national language. Nothing but the establishment of schools and some uniformity in the use of books, can annihilate differences in speaking and preserve the purity of the American tongue. A sameness of pronunciation is of considerable consequence in a political view, for provincial accents are disagreeable to strangers and sometimes have an unhappy effect upon the social affections. All men have local attachments, which lead them to believe their own practice to be the least exceptionable. Pride and prejudice incline men to treat the practice of their neighbors with some degree of contempt. Thus small differences in pronunciation at first excite ridicule—a habit of laughing at the singularities of strangers is followed by disrespect—and without respect friendship is a name, and social intercourse a mere ceremony.

These remarks hold equally true with respect to individuals, to small societies, and to large communities. Small causes, such as a nick-name or a vulgar tone in speaking, have actually created a dissocial spirit between the inhabitants of the different states, which is often discoverable in private business and public deliberations. Our political harmony is therefore concerned in a uniformity of language.

As an independent nation, our honor requires us to have a system of our own, in language as well as government. Great Britain, whose children we are and whose language we speak, should no longer be *our* standard, for the taste of her writers is already corrupted and her language on the decline. But if it were not so, she is at too great a distance to be our model and to instruct us in the principles of our own tongue.

It must be considered further that the English is the common root or stock from which our national language will be derived. All others will gradually waste away—and within a century and a half North America will be peopled with a hundred millions of men, *all speaking the same language.* Place this idea in comparison with the present and possible future bounds of the language in Europe—consider the Eastern (that is, European) Continent as inhabited by nations, whose knowledge and intercourse are embarrassed by differences of language; then anticipate the period when the people of one quarter of the world will be able to associate and converse together like children of the same family. Compare this prospect, which is not visionary, with the state of the English language in Europe, almost confined to an island and to a few millions of people; then let reason and reputation decide how far America should be dependent on a transatlantic nation for her standard and improvements in language.

Let me add, that whatever predilection the Americans may have for their native European tongues, and particularly the British descendants for the English, yet several circumstances render a future separation of the American tongue from the English necessary and unavoidable. The vicinity of the European nations, with the uninterrupted communication in peace and the changes of domination in war, are gradually assimilating their respective languages. The English with others is suffering continual alterations. America, placed at a distance from those nations, will feel, in a much less degree, the influence of the assimilating causes; at the same time numerous local causes, such as a new country, new associations of people, new combinations of ideas in arts and science, and some intercourse with tribes wholly unknown in Europe, will introduce new words into the American tongue. These causes will produce in a course of time a language in North America as different from the future language of England as the modern Dutch, Danish, and Swedish are from the German or from one another: Like remote branches of a tree springing from the same stock; or rays of light, shot from the same center, and diverging from each other in proportion to their distance from the point of separation.

Whether the inhabitants of America can be brought to a perfect uniformity in the pronunciation of words, it is not easy to predict; but it is certain that no attempt of the kind has been made, and an experiment, begun and pursued on the right principles, is the only way to decide the question. Schools in Great Britain have gone far towards demolishing local dialects—commerce has also had its influence—and in America these causes, operating more generally, must have a proportional effect. . . .

Rapid changes in language proceed from violent causes, but these causes cannot be supposed to exist in North America. It is contrary to all rational calculation that the United States will ever be conquered by any one nation, speaking a different language from that of the country. Removed from the danger of corruption by conquest, our language can change only with the slow operation of the cause before-mentioned and the progress of the arts and sciences, unless the folly of imitating our parent country should continue to govern us and lead us into endless innovation. This folly however will lose its influence gradually, as our particular habits of respect for that country shall wear away and our *amor patriæ* acquire strength and inspire us with a suitable respect for our own national character.

We have therefore the fairest opportunity of establishing a national language and of giving it uniformity and perspicuity in North America that ever presented itself to mankind. Now is the time to begin the plan. The minds of the Americans are roused by the events of a revolution; the necessity of organizing the political body and of forming constitutions of government that shall secure freedom and property, has called all the faculties of the mind into exertion; and the danger of losing the benefits of independence has disposed every man to embrace any scheme that shall tend, in its future operation, to reconcile the people of America to each other and weaken the prejudices which oppose a cordial union. . . .

A *national language* is a bond of *national union.* Every engine should be employed to render the people of this country *national,* to call their attachments home to their own country, and to inspire them with the pride of national character. However they may boast of Independence and the freedom of their government, yet their *opinions* are not sufficiently independent; an astonishing respect for the arts and literature of their parent country and a blind imitation of its manners are still prevalent among the Americans. Thus an habitual respect for another country, deserved indeed and once laudable, turns their attention from their own interests and prevents their respecting themselves. . . .

Now is the time, and *this* the country, in which we may expect success in attempting changes favorable to language, science, and government. Delay, in the plan here proposed, may be fatal; under a tranquil general government, the minds of men may again sink into indolence; a national acquiescence in error will follow; and posterity be doomed to struggle with difficulties which time and accident will perpetually multiply.

Let us then seize the present moment and establish a *national language* as well as a national government. Let us remember that there is a certain respect due to the opinions of other nations. As an independent people our reputation abroad demands that in all things we should be federal, be *national;* for if we do not respect *ourselves,* we may be assured that *other nations* will not respect us. In short, let it be impressed upon the mind of every American, that to neglect the means of commanding respect abroad is treason against the character and dignity of a brave independent people.

(48)

James Monroe

1758-1831

Monroe was educated at the College of William and Mary but interrupted his education to serve in the Revolution. He held several important diplomatic posts aboard and was Secretary of State under Madison. Elected President in 1816, Monroe's major achievement was the formulation of a new American foreign policy, the "Monroe Doctrine," in his message to Congress in December, 1823. Monroe's Secretary of State, John Quincy Adams, took an active part in formulating the principles of this policy, and actually wrote the passage on non-colonialization at the conclusion of the first paragraph. But the rest of the document is Monroe's. The Monroe Doctrine sets forth four major principles: (1) the American continent was to be considered closed to further colonialization by European powers, (2) the United States would regard any intervention by European powers in the Americas as a threat to its safety, (3) the United States would not interfere with existing European colonies and (4) the United States would not intervene in European affairs. Thus the Monroe Doctrine enabled the American nation to concentrate its energies on its own internal development.

The text used here is "Monroe's Message to Congress of December 2, 1823," from J. D. Richardson, ed., *A Compilation of the Messages and Papers of the Presidents, 1789–1902,* 10 vols. (Washington, D.C., 1903), vol. II.

At the proposal of the Russian Imperial Government, made through the minister of the Emperor residing here, a full power and instructions have been transmitted to the minister of the United States at St. Petersburg to arrange by amicable negotiations the respective rights and interests of the two nations on the northwest coast of this continent. A similar proposal had been made by His Imperial Majesty to the Government of Great Britain, which has likewise been acceded to. The Government of the United States has been desirous by this friendly proceeding of manifesting the great value which they have invariably attached to the friendship of the Emperor and their solicitude to cultivate the best understanding with his Government. In the discussions to which this interest has given rise and in the arrangements by which they may terminate the occasion has been judged proper for asserting, as a principle in which the rights and interests of the United States are involved, that the American continents, by the free and independent condition which they have assumed and maintain, are henceforth not to be considered as subjects for future colonization by any European powers. . . .

It was stated at the commencement of the last session [of Congress] that a great effort was then making in Spain and Portugal to improve the condition of the people of those countries, and that it appeared to be conducted with extraordinary moderation. It need scarcely be remarked that the result has been so far very different from what was then anticipated. Of events in that quarter of the globe, with which we have so much intercourse and from which we derive our origin, we have always been anxious and interested spectators. The citizens of the United States cherish sentiments the most friendly in favor of the liberty and happiness of their fellow-men on that side of the Atlantic. In the wars of the European powers in matters relating to themselves we have never taken any part, nor does it comport with our policy so to do. It is only when our rights are invaded or seriously menaced that we resent injuries or make preparation for our defense. With the movements in this hemisphere we are of necessity more immediately connected, and by causes which must be obvious to all enlightened and impartial observers. The political system of the allied powers is essentially different in this respect from that of America. This difference proceeds from that which exists in their respective Governments; and to the defense of our own, which has been achieved by the loss of so much blood and treasure, and matured by the wisdom of their most enlightened citizens, and under which we have enjoyed unexampled felicity, this whole nation is devoted. We owe it, therefore, to candor and to the amicable relations existing between the United States and those powers to declare that we should consider any attempt on their part to extend their system to any portion of this hemisphere as dangerous to our peace and safety. With the existing colonies or dependencies of any European power we have not interfered and shall not interfere. But with the Governments who have declared their independence and maintained it, and whose independence we have, on great consideration and on just principles, acknowledged, we could not view any interposition for the purpose of oppressing them, or controlling in any other manner their destiny, by any European power in any other light than as the manifestation of an unfriendly disposition toward the United States. In the war between those new Governments and Spain we declared our neutrality at the time of their recognition, and to this we have adhered, and shall continue to adhere, provided no change shall occur which, in the judgment of the competent authorities of this Government, shall make a corresponding change on the part of the United States indispensable to their security.

The late events in Spain and Portugal show that Europe is still unsettled. Of this important fact no stronger proof can be adduced than that the allied powers should have thought it proper, on any principle satisfactory to themselves, to have interposed by force in the internal concerns of Spain. To what extent such interposition may be carried, on the same principle, is a question in which all independent powers whose governments differ from theirs are interested, even those most remote, and surely none more so than the United States. Our policy in regard to Europe, which was adopted at an early stage of the wars which have so long agitated that quarter of the globe, nevertheless remains the same, which is, not to interfere in the internal concerns of any of its powers; to consider the government *de facto* as the legitimate government for us; to cultivate friendly relations with it, and to preserve those relations by a frank, firm, and manly policy, meeting in all instances the just claims of every power, submitting to injuries from none. But in regard to those continents circumstances are eminently and conspicuously different. It is impossible that the allied powers should extend their political system to any portion of either continent without endangering our peace and happiness; nor can anyone believe that our southern brethren, if left to themselves, would adopt it of their own accord. It is equally impossible, therefore, that we should behold such interposition in any form with indifference. If we look to the comparative strength and resources of Spain and those new Governments, and their distance from each other, it must be obvious that she can never subdue them. It is still the true policy of the United States to leave the parties to themselves, in the hope that other powers will pursue the same course.

(49)

James Fenimore Cooper

1789-1851

Cooper was born in Burlington, New Jersey in 1851; soon thereafter his family moved to the frontier settlement founded by his father at Cooperstown, New York. Expelled from Yale in his junior year, he joined the merchant marine and later the navy. In 1811 he married and settled down to the aristocratic life of a country gentleman. Then followed a literary career that produced thirty-two novels, several voluminous histories, and many essays.

During a trip to Europe in 1826, Cooper became interested in social criticism. Vexed by the European ignorance of America that he discovered, he wrote three novels and his informative *Notions of the Americans* to show the superiority of American republicanism over European aristocracy. But on his return to America in 1833, he became disillusioned with the republican virtues he had once extolled. Subsequently, Cooper became a severe and none-too-popular critic of American crudeness. Despite the controversies his criticism provoked and the frequent legal actions he was involved in, Cooper continued to write and enjoy his reputation as one of America's greatest novelists.

The *Notions* is by no means Cooper's later view of America, but when written it represented a forceful, if somewhat idealized, statement of the American experience. The text is selected from Letter xxxviii of *Notions of the Americans* (Philadelphia, 1828).

☆ ☆ ☆ ☆

TO SIR EDWARD WALLTER, BART. &c. &c.

WASHINGTON, ——

Having given so much of our attention to the subject of the sources of the national importance possessed by the Americans, it may not be without its use to devote an hour to the consideration of the manner in which they will probably be used. The points of main interest are, whether the present republican institutions of the country will endure, and whether the States will long continue to act as one people, or will submit to be divided into two or more confederacies.

The first fact that strikes an intelligent man, in considering the structure of this government, and the state of society that exists under it, is its perfectly natural formation. It is scarcely possible, I am not sure that it is possible, to conceive of a community which has attained the advantages of high civilization, that is less artificial.

In order that individual efforts should be excited (without which nations must inevitably become sluggish, and finally barbarous, though dwelling in any abundance,) the rights of property are respected. Beyond this the law leaves every man (the slaves in the southern States excepted) on grounds of perfect equality. This equality is, however, an equality of rights only; since talents, money, and enterprise, being left to their natural influences, produce their natural effects, and no more.

In respect to the continuation of the present republican institutions of this country, every fact, every symptom, and all reasoning, is, I think, in their favour. In the first place, they have, in substance, continued for nearly, and in some instances for quite, two centuries. The habits of the people, their education, their feelings, and their interests, unite to preserve them. It is true, there are not many instances in the world, of governments on an extended scale, existing for any great length of time, in forms nearly resembling those of the United States; but there are examples enough to prove that governments have endured for centuries on *principles* that will make this endure, though policy were less active than it is in contributing to its preservation. We will endeavour to find some of them. The government of England is representative, and to a great degree it is free; that is to say, it is a government of laws, instead of being a government of will, which I take it constitutes the essential difference between liberty and despotism. Now, the main point of difference between the government of England, and that of the United States, is in the bodies that are the respective repositories of power. In the former country, the power is in the aristocracy; in the latter country, it is in the people. That the latter is more natural, is sufficiently evident, from the fact that England itself has been quietly tending towards the same result, during two centuries, under circumstances that have been calculated to bring natural influences into play. It is true, that the power still rests in the aristocracy, but it is not an aristocracy that is exclusive. To speak of the *governing* aristocracy of England, as a class of nobles, is absurd; it is the aristocracy of wealth, of talents, and of enterprise, that rules Great Britain. Were the avenues to political power closed against the approach of new aspirants, the government of Great Britain would be overturned in a dozen years. It is not in the power of art to repress the energy of natural influences, when they have once gathered head. The effect of vast commerce, of intelligence diffused to a certain degree, and of individual enterprise, has been to wrest the power from the crown, to curtail its influence in the lords, and to repose most of its exercise in the commons. Now, all that democracy can do without recourse to violence in England, is here done, because it is obeying a natural law. But the very difficulty which is found in effecting a final triumph (as by compelling the lords to acquiesce at all times in the wishes of the commons) proves the difficulty of completely wresting power from those who hold it, though they may happen to be the few. So far it is an argument in favour of the perpetuity of the American democracies, for they, too, are used to the authority of the people. Still, public opinion, which is no more than popular law, is so triumphant, that it is difficult to conceive a question on which a clear majority of the people of England should be decidedly united, that the three estates would incur the risk of opposing. Let us turn the picture to the side of America.

Here we have a government in which the people are the sources of power. The state of society is precisely that (though in a still higher degree) which in England has wrought a change from absolute monarchy to a species of qualified aristocracy. Instead of waiting for the march of natural events, circumstances permitted that they should be anticipated. They have been anticipated, and so far from a reaction being the result, greater harmony is daily occurring between causes and effects, as the government gets more adapted to practical objects.

I see but one possible manner in which the people of the United States can ever lose any of their liberty. They may enact laws of a more rigid character as the advancement or corruption of society shall require them, and they may possibly be driven to some slight curtailments of the franchise for the same reason: but this will, in no degree, change the principle of their government. By losing their intelligence, the people of the United States may lose the consciousness of their rights, and with it their enjoyment. But all experience goes to show how difficult it is to wrest vested rights from communities.

But the vulgar argument against the perpetuity of the American government, is the impossibility that the rich should not govern the poor, and the intellectual the weak of mind. The continuation of property in families, and its consequent accumulation in individuals, by entails, is a provision of aristocracy in order to secure its power. The very provision itself argues a consciousness of natural weakness. It is evident, that it is as unjust as it is opposed to our common affections, to make one child affluent at the expense of half a dozen others. No man, left to the operation of natural feeling, would do so cruel an act. This fact is sufficiently proved by the example of the Americans themselves, who have a perfect right to do this injustice if they please, by simply making those in existence, and who have a natural hold on their affections, the subjects of the wrong. Still no man does it. It is true that the father of an only son might create a sort of short entail, that should work injustice to descendants he could not know; or a father who was educated under an artificial system, where advantages are actually established from the practice, might do the same thing; but we have proof in the United States, that the father will not do it, under the operation of natural causes. Now, the Americans have taken care that this artificial state of things shall not occur, for strict entails cannot be made; and if one father should be so obdurate and unnatural as to do a wrong, in order to rob parties who were strangers to him, of their natural rights to his estate, he has no pledge that his son will be as absurd as himself. There is no truth more certain, than that property will regulate itself when left to itself. It will change hands often, and become the reward of industry, talent, and enterprise. But we have no need of speculating in order to know what effect money will produce on the institutions of America. There are thousands of rich men here, and of very rich men too, and there is not a class of the community that has less political power. There are many reasons why it should be so.

Wealth gives no direct influence in politics. Seats in Congress are not bought and sold. Then the owners of great wealth are two-thirds of the time more agreeably employed in its increase, than in courting popularity, without which, nothing political can be done; and there is also a reluctance to give men, who have much money, places of much profit at all. But it is plain, that wealth, even supposing it could be brought to act in concert throughout a country like this, can never work a change in its institutions, until it can be accumulated for generations; and that is a result the institutions themselves forbid. Indeed, so little do I think a danger that is so often named is to be dreaded, that I think there would be vastly more danger, that the people of a nation like this would find means to strip any given set of men of exorbitant wealth, than the set of men themselves would find means to strip the nation of its liberties. Neither case is likely to occur, however, since the danger is scarcely within the bounds of a reasonable probability.

Talents may unite to destroy the rights of the people. I take it, that talents are just as likely to regulate themselves, and to produce an equality, as money. It is not in nature, that any great number of talented men should conspire to overturn the government, since, in the first place, it would require an improbable unanimity of talent, and, in the second place, a majority of the conspirators would be literally selling their birthrights for messes of pottage. If there be a country in the world where talent has already a certain and manly road to preferment, it is in this. Under the present system, each man can work for himself, whereas, by changing it to a monarchy, the many would have to toil for the advantage of the few. As to those inducements which are known to influence men in Europe, such as titles, and decorations, they are entirely artificial; and I know, from observation, that it would be a difficult matter to get, even now, a vast proportion of the Americans to consent to use them. We are completely the creatures of habit in all these matters, and it is the habit of the American to look on distinctions of this nature with a cold eye. This peculiarity of opinion is gaining ground daily, for there was, for a time, on precisely the same principle of habit, a lingering of the ancient prejudices. We should never forget that the moral influence of this nation is beginning to manifest itself in stronger colours every hour. The time, I think, is near, when the American gentleman will pride himself as much on his peculiar simplicity, as gentlemen of our nations take pride in their quarterings and titles. The strength of this feeling will keep even pace with the power of the nation, until it will become difficult indeed, to persuade a man that glories in having no worldly superior, to submit to a division of society, that, by an artificial arrangement, shall place him beneath so many others. You will remember, that the great difference between this government and most others, is the important fact, that the Americans began at the bottom to raise their superstructure, whereas we have, in nearly every instance, begun at the top to work downwards. Men have been elevated towards the throne in our systems; but in what manner are you to elevate a man who finds himself already at the summit? It is true, that if a hundred, or a thousand Americans could monopolize the honors and emoluments of a change of government, that number might conspire to keep their present elevation, and force the rest of the nation below them. But a thousand, nor ten thousand men of the highest talent, could not persuade a million to give up rights that they are educated to believe inherent, even if these ten thousand could agree among themselves as to the gradations of their own rewards. A nobleman of France, or of England, cannot understand the sort of veneration that a vizier feels for the Grand Turk; and any attempt on the part of the sovereigns of these two countries, to bring the peers into the abject submission that is practised in the seraglio, would induce a singular commotion. Now, to the American it is just as inconceivable how one man can yield precedency, or respect, or submission to another, merely because he happens to be born an eldest son. You see all this is artificial, and the fact of its long existence in the world establishes nothing, but the opinions of the world. Opinions that are the nearest to nature, are the least liable to change. The world thought that the sun moved round the earth until quite lately, and yet the fact, I believe, is not so. We will sum up this argument in a very few words. Ten centuries ago, one century since, nay, twenty years since, very different opinions existed in Europe on the subject of governments from those that are now getting into fashion. The tendency is to natural rights, at the expense of artificial institutions. In some few instances, change has been attempted by revolution; but revolution is a dangerous remedy. The Americans had no revolution, strictly speaking; they have only preceded the rest of Christendom in their reforms, because circumstances permitted it. If they have gone farther than it may be wise for other nations to follow, it is no reason that they are not safe themselves. So has England gone farther than France, and France farther than Sweden, and Sweden farther than Russia. There is no danger of reaction in America, for there has been no blow to produce the rebound. The progress has been steady and natural; and there must be a gradual return to the ignorance of the thirteenth and fourteenth centuries, to effect any material change. It is odd enough, that in an age when even despotism is fettered by public opinion, men should affect to believe that a people who feel its influence more than any other, who have fortified their institutions by law, by habit, and by common sense, are liable to be affected by causes that are hourly losing their ascendancy in every other country.

I shall state one more simple fact, leaving you to reason on it for yourself. So far from increasing familiarity and intercourse with the system of Europe producing any desire for imitation on the part of those Americans who are brought in contact with our privileged orders, it is notorious, that it produces quite a contrary effect.

But the question of infinitely the most interest is that which touches the durability of the confederation. It is the only one of the two that is worthy of grave comment. . . .

The confederated government of the United States has not power enough to make itself dangerous to the rights of the States. In the first place, it is no more than a representation of the people in another form; and there is little probability that any decidedly unpopular policy can long continue, if, indeed, it could be adopted at all. Each hour lessens the danger of particular States receding from the Union, by lessening their relative importance. Even New York, with ten millions of inhabitants, would be embarrassed, surrounded by a powerful rival of fifty or sixty millions. The great communities would be safer, and more important, by exercising their natural influence in the confederation, and the smaller could not exist separately. But it may be thought that the separation will take place in such a manner as to divide the present Union into two great nations. That these expectations are vague, and founded on a general reasoning that may be false when applied to a particular case, is evident by the fact that men are divided on the grounds of this separation. Some say that the slave holders will separate from their northern brethren; and some think that the line will be drawn north and south. Now, in point of fact, there is no solid reason in either of these opinions, except as they have a general reference to the difficulty of keeping such masses of men together. My own opinion is, that the United States are now passing, or, in fact, have in a great measure passed, the ordeal of the durability of the Union. . . .

Now, where are we to seek a rational argument for believing that this confederation will dissolve? Its plan of government leaves as few matters of contention as possible; while the interests, the habits, the feelings, and the history, of the people, are the same. Moral and physical causes unite to keep them together, while nothing indicates that they must divide, but sage and incredulous shakings of the head! I make no doubt, that if Cœur de Lion had been told his brother would be forced to grant a charter to his barons, his head would have been shaken too; and that Queen Elizabeth would not have believed that the royal *veto* could ever slumber for a century; or that

Isabel might have entertained rational doubts of her American provinces becoming more important dominions than her own Aragon—and yet all these things have come to pass! Are we to believe for ever only what we wish? We are told that China contains a hundred and fifty millions of people, in one empire; and why are we to believe that semi-barbarians have more wisdom than a nation that has shown itself as shrewd, as firm, and as constant as the Americans?

Let us give one moment's attention to the political history of the republic since its establishment.

Between the years 1775 and 1789, a confederation existed, which, though it imperfectly answered the objects of the war, partook of that flimsiness of texture which has proved the bane and weakness of so many previous political unions. The Americans, instead of becoming impatient and restive under acknowledged difficulties, deliberately went to work to remedy the evil. The present constitution was formed. Its chief merit consists in its yielding to unavoidable evils, its consulting natural objects, and its profiting by those advantages which had endured the test of time. This is a broad foundation on which to repose the fabric of government.

Until near the end of Washington's administration, the Americans were scarcely treated with the courtesy that was due to a nation. The character of that illustrious man lent a dignity to his government, which adventitious circumstances would have refused. England boldly held military posts within the undeniable limits of the country, and a thousand indignities, and numberless acts of injustice, disgraced the history of that period. Commanders of vessels of war exercised a lawless authority on the coasts of the republic; and there is an instance on record of a captain of a sloop of war, openly and insolently refusing to obey the civil authorities of the country, because he knew that he commanded a greater nautical force than that of the whole republic united. At that day, Europeans generally believed these people black and barbarous; and they listened to accounts of their proceedings, as we listen to the events of farther India.

Then followed the general war, with its abuses. The vast commerce of America grew, but it became a prey to all the belligerents. Acts, that would disgrace any man of the smallest pretension to character, were committed by boastful nations, under the pitiful plea of power; and the complaints of a remote people, were despised and ridiculed, for no other reason than that they were a nation weak and dispersed. But a mighty spirit was in the land. The statesmen were wary, firm in their principles, yielding to events while they protested against injustice, and watchful to let no opportunity of regaining their rights pass without improvement. At this period, an immense region, which possessed countless positive advantages, which offered a foothold to rivals, and which was a constant temptation to division among themselves, was peaceably acquired. The purchase of Louisiana was the greatest masterstroke of policy that has been done in our times. All the wars, and conquests, and cessions of Europe, for the last hundred years, sink into insignificance, compared with the political consequences that are dependent on this increase of territory. Spain had been accessory to the wrongs, and Spain too was quietly made to contribute to the peace and security of the republic, by a cession of the Floridas.

A new era is now about to dawn on this nation. It has ceased to creep; it begins to walk erect among the powers of the earth. All these things have occurred within the life of man. Europeans may be reluctant to admit the claims of a competitor, that they knew so lately a pillaged, a wronged, and a feeble people; but Nature will have her laws obeyed, and the fulfillment of things must come. The spirit of greatness is in this nation: its means are within their grasp; and it is as vain as it is weak to attempt to deny results that every year is rendering more plain, more important, and more irresistible.

(50)

Henry Wadsworth Longfellow

1807-1882

Educated at Bowdoin College, Longfellow became one of the most popular poets of the nineteenth century. His writing ranged from the overfluent "Hymn to the Night" and "A Psalm of Life" to his fine sonnets, which are deepened by the scholarship also revealed in his translations of Dante. Longfellow was one of the major literary spokesmen of America's growing sense of national greatness. This selection, a discussion of national literature, is from Chapter XX of his novel *Kavanag*h (Boston, 1849).

Meanwhile, things had gone on very quietly and monotonously in Mr. Churchill's family. Only one event, and that a mysterious one, had disturbed its serenity. It was the sudden disappearance of Lucy, the pretty orphan girl; and, as the booted centipede, who had so much excited Mr. Churchill's curiosity, disappeared at the same time, there was little doubt that they had gone away together. But whither gone, and wherefore, remained a mystery.

Mr. Churchill, also, had had his profile, and those of his wife and children, taken, in a very humble style, by Mr. Bantam, whose advertisement he had noticed on his way to school nearly a year before. His own was considered the best, as a work of art. The face was cut out entirely; the collar of the coat velvet; the shirt collar very high and white; and the top of his head ornamented with a crest of hair turning up in front, though his own turned down,—which slight deviation from nature was explained and justified by the painter as a license allowable in art.

One evening, as he was sitting down to begin, for at least the hundredth time, the great Romance,—subject of so many resolves and so much remorse, so often determined upon but never begun,—a loud knock at the street door, which stood wide open, announced a visitor. Unluckily, the study door was likewise open; and consequently, being in full view, he found it impossible to refuse himself; nor, in fact, would he have done so, had all the doors been shut and bolted,—the art of refusing one's self being at that time but imperfectly understood in Fairmeadow. Accordingly, the visitor was shown in.

He announced himself as Mr. Hathaway. Passing through the village, he could not deny himself the pleasure of calling on Mr. Churchill, whom he knew by his writings in the periodicals, though not personally. He wished, moreover, to secure the coöperation of one, already so favorably known to the literary world, in a new Magazine he was about to establish, in order to raise the character of American literature, which, in his opinion, the existing reviews and magazines had entirely failed to accomplish. A daily increasing want of something better was felt by the public, and the time had come for the establishment of such a periodical as he proposed. After explaining, in rather a florid and exuberant manner, his plan and prospects, he entered more at large into the subject of American literature, which it was his design to foster and patronize.

"I think, Mr. Churchill," said he, "that we want a national literature commensurate with our mountains and rivers,—commensurate with Niagara, and the Alleghanies, and the Great Lakes!"

"Oh!"

"We want a national epic that shall correspond to the size of the country; that shall be to all other epics what Banvard's Panorama of the Mississippi is to all other paintings,—the largest in the world!"

"Ah!"

"We want a national drama in which scope enough shall be given to our gigantic ideas, and to the unparalleled activity and progress of our people!"

"Of course."

"In a word, we want a national literature altogether shaggy and unshorn, that shall shake the earth, like a herd of buffaloes thundering over the prairies!"

"Precisely," interrupted Mr. Churchill; "but excuse me!—are you not confounding things that have no analogy? Great has a very different meaning when applied to a river, and when applied to a literature. Large and shallow may perhaps be applied to both. Literature is rather an image of the spiritual world, than of the physical, is it not?—of the internal, rather than the external. Mountains, lakes, and rivers are, after all, only its scenery and decorations, not its substance and essence. A man will not necessarily be a great poet because he lives near a great mountain. Nor, being a poet, will he necessarily write better poems than another, because he lives nearer Niagara."

"But, Mr. Churchill, you do not certainly mean to deny the influence of scenery on the mind?"

"No, only to deny that it can create genius. At best, it can only develop it. Switzerland has produced no extraordinary poet; nor, as far as I know, have the Andes, or the Himalaya mountains, or the Mountains of the Moon in Africa."

"But, at all events," urged Mr. Hathaway, "let us have our literature national. If it is not national, it is nothing."

"On the contrary, it may be a great deal. Nationality is a good thing to a certain extent, but universality is better. All that is best in the great poets of all countries is not what is national in them, but what is universal. Their roots are in their native soil; but their branches wave in the unpatriotic air, that speaks the same language unto all men, and their leaves shine with the illimitable light that pervades all lands. Let us throw all the windows open; let us admit the light and air on all sides; that we may look towards the four corners of the heavens, and not always in the same direction."

"But you admit nationality to be a good thing?"

"Yes, if not carried too far; still, I confess, it rather limits one's views of truth. I prefer what is natural. Mere nationality is often ridiculous. Every one smiles when he hears the Icelandic proverb. 'Iceland is the best land the sun shines upon.' Let us be natural, and we shall be national enough. Besides, our literature can be strictly national only so far as our character and modes of thought differ from those of other nations. Now, as we are very like the English,—are, in fact, English under a different sky,—I do not see how our literature can be very different from theirs. Westward from hand to hand we pass the lighted torch, but it was lighted at the old domestic fireside of England."

"Then you think our literature is never to be anything but an imitation of the English?"

"Not at all. It is not an imitation, but, as some one has said, a continuation."

"It seems to me that you take a very narrow view of the subject."

"On the contrary, a very broad one. No literature is complete until the language in which it is written is dead. We may well be proud of our task and of our position. Let us see if we can build in any way worthy of our forefathers."

"But I insist upon originality."

"Yes; but without spasms and convulsions. Authors must not, like Chinese soldiers, expect to win victories by turning somersets in the air."

"Well, really, the prospect from your point of view is not very brilliant. Pray, what do you think of our national literature?"

"Simply, that a national literature, is not the growth of a day. Centuries must contribute their dew and sunshine to it. Our own is growing slowly but surely, striking its roots downward, and its branches upward, as is natural; and I do not wish, for the sake of what some people call originality, to invert it, and try to make it grow with its roots in the air. And as for having it so savage and wild as you want it, I have only to say, that all literature, as well as all art, is the result of culture and intellectual refinement."

"Ah! we do not want art and refinement; we want genius,—untutored, wild, original, free."

"But, if this genius is to find any expression, it must employ art, for art is the external expression of our thoughts. Many have genius, but, wanting art, are forever dumb. The two must go together to form the great poet, painter, or sculptor."

"In that sense, very well."

"I was about to say also that I thought our literature would finally not be wanting in a kind of universality. As the blood of all nations is mingling with our own, so will their thoughts and feelings finally mingle in our literature. We shall draw from the Germans, tenderness; from the Spaniards, passion; from the French, vivacity,—to mingle more and more with our English solid sense. And this will give us universality, so much to be desired."

(51)

Joseph Story

1779-1845

Joseph Story attended the academy at Marblehead, Massachusetts, shortly after its founding and later studied at Harvard. He then practiced law in Marblehead and became active in Massachusetts affairs, where he served in the legislature and held other political posts. When in 1811 he was appointed associate justice of the United States Supreme Court, he was the youngest appointee in the history of the Court. During his years on the high bench his opinions showed great breadth of learning. He became particularly well known for his dissent in *Charles River Bridge* v. *Warren Bridge,* in which he opposed the majority's emphasis on the social responsibility of private property. In 1842 he drew up the rules of equity practice for the Court.

Of Story's many writings, his *Commentaries* (1833) were the most immediately successful, and they earned him an international reputation. His praise of republican principles and his hopes for America's future are expressed in the following selection, which is from the "Concluding Remarks" of his *Commentaries on the Constitution of the United States,* 2 vols. (Boston, 1891), vol. II.

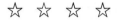

§ 1910. We have now reviewed all the provisions of the original constitution of the United States, and all the amendments which have been incorporated into it. And here the task originally proposed in these Commentaries is brought to a close. Many reflections naturally crowd upon the mind at such a moment,—many grateful recollections of the past, and many anxious thoughts of the future. The past is secure. It is unalterable. The seal of eternity is upon it. The wisdom which it has displayed and the blessings which it has bestowed, cannot be obscured; neither can they be debased by human folly or human infirmity. The future is that which may well awaken the most earnest solicitude, both for the virtue and the permanence of our republic. The fate of other republics—their rise, their progress, their decline, and their fall—are written but too legibly on the pages of history, if indeed they were not continually before us in the startling fragments of their ruins. They have perished, and perished by their own hands. Prosperity has enervated them, corruption has debased them, and a venal populace has consummated their destruction. Alternately the prey of military chieftains at home, and of ambitious invaders from abroad, they have been sometimes cheated out of their liberties by servile demagogues; sometimes betrayed into a surrender of them by false patriots; and sometimes they have willingly sold them for a price to the despot who has bidden highest for his victims. They have disregarded the warning voice of their best statesmen; and have persecuted and driven from office their truest friends. They have listened to the fawning sycophant, and the base calumniator of the wise and the good. They have reverenced power more in its high abuses and summary movements than in its calm and constitutional energy, when it dispensed blessings with an unseen but liberal hand. They have surrendered to faction what belonged to the country. Patronage and party, the triumph of a leader, and the discontents of a day, have outweighed all solid principles and institutions of government. Such are the melancholy lessons of the past history of republics down to our own.

§ 1911. It is not my design to detain the reader by any elaborate reflections addressed to his judgment, either by way of admonition or of encouragement. But it may not be wholly without use to glance at one or two considerations, upon which our meditations cannot be too frequently indulged.

§ 1912. In the first place, it cannot escape our notice, how exceedingly difficult it is to settle the foundations of any government upon principles which do not admit of controversy or question. The very elements out of which it is to be built are susceptible of infinite modifications; and theory too often deludes us by the attractive simplicity of its plans, and imagination by the visionary perfection of its speculations. In theory, a government may promise the most perfect harmony of operations in all its various combinations. In practice, the whole machinery may be perpetually retarded, or thrown out of order by accidental mal-adjustments. In theory, a government may seem deficient in unity of design and symmetry of parts, and yet in practice it may work with astonishing accuracy and force for the general welfare. Whatever, then, has been found to work well in experience should be rarely hazarded upon conjectural improvements. Time and long and steady operation are indispensable to the perfection of all social institutions. To be of any value they must become cemented with the habits, the feelings, and the pursuits of the people. Every change discomposes for a while the whole arrangements of the system. What is safe is not always expedient; what is new is often pregnant with unforeseen evils and imaginary good.

§ 1913. In the next place, the slightest attention to the history of the national constitution must satisfy every reflecting mind how many difficulties attended its formation and adoption, from real or imaginary differences of interest, sectional feelings, and local institutions. It is an attempt to create a national sovereignty, and yet to preserve the State sovereignties; though it is impossible to assign definite boundaries in every case to the powers of each. The influence of the disturbing causes which, more than once in the convention, were on the point of breaking up the Union, have since immeasurably increased in concentration and vigor. The very inequalities of a government confessedly founded in a compromise were then felt with a strong sensibility; and every new source of discontent, whether accidental or permanent, has since added increased activity to the painful sense of these inequalities. The North cannot but perceive that it has yielded to the South a superiority of representatives, already amounting to twenty-five, beyond its due proportion; and the South imagines that with all this preponderance in representation, the other parts of the Union enjoy a more perfect protection of their interests than her own. The West feels her growing power and weight in the Union; and the Atlantic States begin to learn that the sceptre must one day depart from them. If, under these circumstances, the Union should once be broken up, it is impossible that a new constitution should ever be formed embracing the whole territory. We shall be divided into several nations or confederacies, rivals in power and interest, too proud to brook injury, and too close to make retaliation distant or ineffectual. Our very animosities will, like those of all other kindred nations, become more deadly, because our lineage, laws, and language are the same. Let the history of the Grecian and Italian republics warn us of our dangers. The national constitution is our last and our only security. United we stand, divided we fall.

§ 1914. If these Commentaries shall but inspire in the rising generation a more ardent love of their country, an unquenchable thirst for liberty, and a profound reverence for the Constitution and the Union, then they will have accomplished all that their author ought to desire. Let the American youth never forget that they possess a noble inheritance, bought by the toils and sufferings and blood of their ancestors, and capable, if wisely improved and faithfully guarded, of transmitting to their latest posterity all the substantial blessings of life, the peaceful enjoyment of liberty, property, religion, and independence. The structure has been erected by architects of consummate skill and fidelity; its foundations are solid; its compartments are beautiful as well as useful; its arrangements are full of wisdom and order; and its defences are impregnable from without. It has been reared for immortality, if the work of man may justly aspire to such a title. It may, nevertheless, perish in an hour by the folly or corruption or negligence of its only keepers—THE PEOPLE. Republics are created by the virtue, public spirit, and intelligence of the citizens. They fall when the wise are banished from the public councils, because they dare to be honest; and the profligate are rewarded, because they flatter the people in order to betray them.

XII

The Rise of
the Common Man

ONE of the most serious problems confronting the new nation had been the conflict between aristocracy and democracy. Generally, the struggle had been waged between the Federalists, who supported the aristocratic view, and the Jeffersonians, who favored an appeal to the people. By 1828 the republican philosophy of Jefferson had won the victory. By then the suffrage had been extended so that nearly all male citizens had gained the right to vote.

The election of Andrew Jackson in 1828 symbolized the final defeat of Federalist values and institutionalized America's democratic premises. The "common man" had come into his own even before 1828, but the election of Jackson was symbolic of his triumph. That election made many conservative Americans question whether the republic could survive the rule of the people. "The reign of 'King Mob' seemed triumphant," as one Federalist put it. And Jackson's two terms did bring with them republican rule. The spoils system, though decried by conservatives, served the immediate purpose of ridding government of an entrenched aristocracy of civil servants and of bringing government closer to the people. In this respect, the crucial importance of Jackson's war against the Second Bank of the United States cannot be overestimated. The Bank, headed by Nicholas Biddle, had come to exert tremendous power over the American economy, and symbolized all the older aristocratic values of power, privilege, and inequality. In Jackson's eyes, the Bank was a "money power," a monopoly which wealthy eastern aristocrats used to advance their own fortunes. The Bank was for him a veritable "monster,"[1] threatening the independence of republican government, creating a monied elite, and destroying equality of opportunity for the masses. Jackson saw (though not always too clearly) the Bank as a portent of a changing economic order, in which credit and finance capital would play a leading role in economic change and development. His own appeal to hard money, enterprise, and the simple republican virtues reflected the older,

---

1. See Marvin Meyers, *The Jacksonian Persuasion* (Stanford, California, 1957), Chapter 5.

Puritan values of thrift, hard work, and self-reliance. Thus Jackson was caught in the dilemma of seeking to conserve the old republican order without impeding the development of emerging capitalism.

Historians, reflecting the period's turmoils, interpret the crosscurrents and complexities in a variety of ways. Charles M. Wiltse denies that Jackson was a liberal democrat at all, and regards him, rather, as a president bent on consolidating personal and political power. Bray Hammond sees business —especially the independent entrepreneurs—as the driving force behind Jacksonianism; Richard Hofstadter, too, interprets it as a nation-wide movement favoring the middle class. Arthur M. Schlesinger, Jr., sees a class struggle rather than sectional differences underlying Jacksonianism, and views its mainsprings as an eastern working-class movement that foreshadowed the New and Fair Deals. Finally, Marvin Meyers finds the basic impulse of Jacksonianism to be an effort to restore the old republican virtues that were being lost in the changing social and economic conditions of the day.

However much historians disagree about Jackson, there is little question that his presidency climaxed a revolution in political values. As Schlesinger puts it, "It destroyed neo-Federalism as a public social philosophy and restated fundamentally the presuppositions of American political life. No one ever again could talk with hope of success in the language of Fisher Ames, of Chancellor Kent, of Jeremiah Mason."[2] Thus, ironically enough, what began as an attempt to restore the virtues of republicanism, in the end produced a profound social transformation in American life. Few periods indeed are as appealing to the student of American history as Jacksonian democracy.

(52)

Kent-Sanford Debates

1821

From 1800 to the election of Jackson, the franchise was gradually extended to include most male citizens. However, in every state there were those who opposed this trend. New York provides a good example. In 1821 a Constitutional Convention dropped substantially all property qualifications for voting. The leader of the opposition in New York was Chancellor James Kent (1763–1847).

Kent graduated from Yale in 1781 and was elected three times on the Federalist ticket to the New York State Assembly. He was appointed Chief Justice of the New York Supreme Court and Chancellor

---

2. Arthur M. Schlesinger, Jr., *The Age of Jackson* (Boston, 1945), p. 267.

of the New York Court of Chancery. Throughout his career he remained a steadfast conservative.

One of the chief supporters of the measure to drop property qualifications for voting in New York was Nathan Sanford (1777–1838), a legislator and jurist who succeeded Kent as Chancellor. Sanford later served as United States Senator, and was an unsuccessful candidate for Vice-President.

Part of the Kent-Sanford debates is given in the following selection. The text used here is from *Reports of the Proceedings and Debates of the Convention of 1821 Assembled for the Purpose of Amending the Constitution of the State of New York* (Albany, 1821).

[CHANCELLOR KENT]: By the report before us, we propose to annihilate, at one stroke, all those property distinctions and to bow before the idol of universal suffrage. That extreme democratic principle, when applied to the legislative and executive departments of government, has been regarded with terror by the wise men of every age because, in every European republic, ancient and modern, in which it has been tried, it has terminated disastrously and been productive of corruption, injustice, violence, and tyranny. And dare we flatter ourselves that we are a peculiar people who can run the career of history, exempted from the passions which have disturbed and corrupted the rest of mankind? If we are like other races of men, with similar follies and vices, then I greatly fear that our posterity will have reason to deplore, in sackcloth and ashes, the delusion of the day. . . .

Now, sir, I wish to preserve our senate as the representative of the landed interest. I wish those who have an interest in the soil to retain the exclusive possession of a branch in the legislature as a stronghold in which they may find safety through all the vicissitudes which the state may be destined, in the course of Providence, to experience. I wish them to be always enabled to say that their freeholds cannot be taxed without their consent. The men of no property, together with the crowds of dependents connected with great manufacturing and commercial establishments, and the motley and undefinable population of crowded ports, may, perhaps, at some future day, under skilful management, predominate in the assembly, and yet we should be perfectly safe if no laws could pass without the free consent of the owners of the soil. That security we at present enjoy; and it is that security which I wish to retain.

The apprehended danger from the experiment of universal suffrage applied to the whole legislative department is no dream of the imagination. It is too mighty an excitement for the moral constitution of men to endure. The tendency of universal suffrage is to jeopardize the rights of property and the principles of liberty. There is a constant tendency in human society, and the history of every age proves it; there is a tendency in the poor to covet and to share the plunder of the rich; in the debtor to relax or avoid the obligation of contracts; in the majority to tyrannize over the minority and trample down their rights; in the indolent and the profligate to cast the whole burdens of society upon the industrious and the virtuous; and *there is a tendency in ambitious and wicked men to inflame these combustible materials.* It requires a vigilant government, and a firm administration of justice, to counteract that tendency. Thou shalt not covet; Thou shalt not steal, are divine injunctions induced by this miserable depravity of our nature. Who can undertake to calculate with any precision how many millions of people this great state will contain in the course of this and the next century, and who can estimate the future extent and magnitude of our commercial ports? The disproportion between the men of property and the men of no property will be in every society in a ratio to its commerce, wealth, and population. We are no longer to remain plain and simple republics of farmers like the New England colonists or the Dutch settlements on the Hudson. We are fast becoming a great nation, with great commerce, manufactures, population, wealth, luxuries, and with the vices and miseries that they engender. One-seventh of the population of the city of Paris at this day subsists on charity, and one-third of the inhabitants of that city die in the hospitals; what would become of such a city with universal suffrage? France has upward of four, and England upward of five millions of manufacturing and commercial laborers without property. Could these kingdoms sustain the weight of universal suffrage? The radicals in England, with the force of that mighty engine, would at once sweep away the property, the laws, and the liberties of that island like a deluge. . . .

Liberty, rightly understood, is an inestimable blessing, but liberty without wisdom, and without justice, is no better than wild and savage licentiousness. The danger which we have hereafter to apprehend is not the want, but the abuse, of liberty. We have to apprehend the oppression of minorities and· a disposition to encroach on private right—to disturb chartered privileges—and to weaken, degrade, and overawe the administration of justice; we have to apprehend the establishment of unequal and, consequently, unjust systems of taxation and all the mischiefs of a crude and mutable legislation. A stable senate, exempted from the influence of universal suffrage, will powerfully check these dangerous propensities, and such a check becomes the more necessary, since this Convention has already determined to withdraw the watchful eye of the judicial department from the passage of laws. . . .

Mr. N. SANFORD took the floor. The question before us is the right of suffrage—who shall, or who shall not, have the right to vote. The committee have presented the scheme they thought best; to abolish all existing distinctions and make the right of voting uniform. Is this not right? Where did these distinctions arise? They arose from British precedents. In England they have their three estates, which must always have their separate interests represented. Here there is but one estate—the people. To me the only qualifications seem to be the virtue and morality of the people; and if they may be safely intrusted to vote for one class of our rulers, why not for all? In my opinion, these distinctions are fallacious. We have the experience of almost all the other states against them. The principle of the scheme now proposed is that those who bear the burdens of the state should choose those that rule it. There is no privilege given to property as such; but those who contribute to the public support we consider as entitled to a share in the election of rulers. The burdens are annual, and the elections are annual, and this appears proper. To me, and the majority of the committee, it appeared the only reasonable scheme that those who are to be affected by the acts of the government should be annually entitled to vote for those who administer it. Our taxes are of two sorts, on real and personal property. The payment of a tax on either, we thought, equally entitled a man to a vote, and thus we intended to destroy the odious distinctions of property which now exist. But we have considered personal service, in some cases, equivalent to a tax on personal property, as in work on the high roads. This is a burden and should entitle those subject to it to equivalent privileges. The road duty is equal to a poll tax on every male citizen, of twenty-one years, of 62½ cents per annum, which is about the value of each individual's work on the road. This work is a burden imposed by the legislature—a duty required by rulers, and which should entitle those subject to it to a choice of those rulers. Then, sir, the militia next presents itself; the idea of personal service, as applicable to the road duty, is, in like manner, applicable here; and this criterion has been adopted in other states. In Mississippi mere enrolment gives a vote. In Connecticut, as is proposed here, actual service, and that without the right of commutation, is required. The duty in the militia is obligatory and onerous. The militia man must find his arms and accoutrements and lose his time. But, after admitting all these persons, what restrictions, it will be said, are left on the right of suffrage? 1st. The voter must be a citizen. 2d. The service required must be performed within the year, on the principle that taxation is annual, and election annual; so that when the person ceases to contribute or serve, he ceases to vote.

A residence is also required. We propose the term of six months, because we find it already in the constitution; but we propose this residence in the state and not in the county or town, so that, wherever a voter may be at the time of election, he may vote there, if he has been a resident of the state for six months. The object of this was to enable those who move, as very many do, in the six months preceding an election, out of the town or ward in which they have resided, to retain the right of voting in their new habitations. The term of six months is deemed long enough to qualify those who come into our state from abroad to understand and exercise the privileges of a citizen here. Now, sir, this scheme will embrace almost the whole male population of the state. There is perhaps no subject so purely matter of opinion as the question how far the right of suffrage may be safely carried. We propose to carry it almost as far as the male population of the state. The Convention may perhaps think this too broad. On this subject we have much experience; yet there are respectable citizens who think this extension of suffrage unfavorable to the rights of property. Certainly this would be a fatal objection, if well founded;

for any government, however constituted, which does not secure property to its rightful owners is a bad government. But how is the extension of the right of suffrage unfavorable to property? Will not our laws continue the same? Will not the administration of justice continue the same? And if so, how is private property to suffer? Unless these are changed, and upon them rest the rights and security of property, I am unable to perceive how property is to suffer by the extension of the right of suffrage. But we have abundant experience on this point in other states. Now, sir, in many of the states the right of suffrage has no restriction; every male inhabitant votes. Yet what harm has been done in those states? What evil has resulted to them from this cause? The course of things in this country is for the extension and not the restriction of popular rights. I do not know that in Ohio or Pennsylvania, where the right of suffrage is universal, there is not the same security for private rights and private happiness as elsewhere. Every gentleman is aware that the scheme now proposed is derived from the law calling this Convention, and in the constitution of this body we have the first fruits of the operation of the principle of extensive suffrage—and will anyone say that this example is not one evincing the discretion with which our people exercise this right? In our town meetings too, throughout the state, we have the same principle. In our town elections we have the highest proof of the virtue and intelligence of our people; they assemble in town meetings as a pure democracy and choose their officers and local legislatures, if I may so call them; and if there is any part of our public business well done, it is that done in town meetings. Is not this a strong practical lesson of the beneficial operation of this principle? This scheme has been proposed by a majority of the committee; they think it safe and beneficial, founded in just and rational principles, and in the experience of this and neighboring states. The committee have no attachment, however, to this particular scheme and are willing to see it amended or altered if it shall be judged for the interest of the people.

(53)

Andrew Jackson

1767-1845

Born in South Carolina of immigrant parents who had come to the United States from the northern part of Ireland in 1765, Jackson was orphaned at fourteen and grew up without benefit of any formal schooling. He moved westward and settled in Tennessee, where he became a prosperous planter. He represented Tennessee both in the Senate and in the House. However, he achieved his national reputation in 1815 as a result of his leadership against the British in the battle of New Orleans. In 1821, Jackson was named governor of the Florida Territory, and in 1823 he was again elected to the Senate. In 1828 he was elected President and served two eventful terms in that office.

In many ways Jackson personified the American dream. His famous war against the Second Bank of the United States, the symbol to millions of Americans of business privilege, and all special privilege, endeared him to a nation that rejected ideas and institutions that barred the way to equal rights and equality of opportunity.

This text of his veto message on the act renewing the charter of the Bank, July 10, 1832, is from J. D. Richardson, ed., *A Compilation of the Messages and Papers of the Presidents, 1789–1902,* 10 vols. (Washington, 1903), vol. II.

The present corporate body, denominated the president, directors, and company of the Bank of the United States, will have existed at the time this act is intended to take effect twenty years. It enjoys an exclusive privilege of banking under the authority of the General Government, a monopoly of its favor and support, and, as a necessary consequence, almost a monopoly of the foreign and domestic exchange. The powers, privileges, and favors bestowed upon it in the original charter, by increasing the value of the stock far above its par value, operated as a gratuity of many millions to the stockholders. . . .

The act before me proposes another gratuity to the holders of the same stock, and in many cases to the same men, of at least seven millions more. . . . It is not our own citizens only who are to receive the bounty of our Government. More than eight millions of the stock of this bank are held by foreigners. By this act the American Republic proposes virtually to make them a present of some millions of dollars. For these gratuities to foreigners and to some of our own opulent citizens the act secures no equivalent whatever. They are the certain gains of the present stockholders under the operation of this act, after making full allowance for the payment of the bonus.

Every monopoly and all exclusive privileges are granted at the expense of the public, which ought to receive a fair equivalent. The many millions which this act proposes to bestow on the stockholders of the existing bank must come directly or indirectly out of the earnings of the American people. . . .

It is not conceivable how the present stockholders can have any claim to the special favor of the Government. The present corporation has enjoyed its monopoly during the period stipulated in the original contract. If we must have such a corporation, why should not the Government sell out the whole stock and thus secure to the people the full market value of the privileges granted? Why should not Congress create and sell twenty-eight millions of stock, incorporating the purchases with all the powers and privileges secured in this act and putting the premium upon the sales into the Treasury?

But this act does not permit competition in the purchase of this monopoly. It seems to be predicated on the erroneous idea that the present stockholders have a prescriptive right not only to the favor but to the bounty of Government. It appears that more than a fourth part of the stock is held by foreigners and the residue is held by a few hundred of our own citizens, chiefly of the richest class. For their benefit does this act exclude the whole American people from competition in the purchase of this monopoly and dispose of it for many millions less than it is worth. This seems the less excusable because some of our citizens not now stockholders petitioned that the door of competition might be opened, and offered to take a charter on terms much more favorable to the Government and country.

But this proposition, although made by men whose aggregate wealth is believed to be equal to all the private stock in the existing bank, has been set aside, and the bounty of our Government is proposed to be again bestowed on the few who have been fortunate enough to secure the stock and at this moment wield the power of the existing institution. I can not perceive the justice or policy of this course. If our Government must sell monopolies, it would seem to be its duty to take nothing less than their full value, and if gratuities must be made once in fifteen or twenty years let them not be bestowed on the subjects of a foreign government nor upon a designated and favored class of men in our own country. It is but justice and good policy, as far as the nature of the case will admit, to confine our favors to our own fellow-citizens, and let each in his turn enjoy an opportunity to profit by our bounty. . . .

Is there no danger to our liberty and independence in a bank that in its nature has so little to bind it to our country? The president of the bank has told us that most of the State banks exist by its forbearance. Should its influence become concentered, as it may under the operation of such an act as this, in the hands of a self-elected directory whose interests are identified with those of the foreign stockholders, will there not be cause to tremble for the purity of our elections in peace and for the independence of our country in war? Their power would be great whenever they might choose to exert it; but if this monopoly were regularly renewed every fifteen or twenty years on terms proposed by themselves, they might seldom in peace put forth their strength to influence elections or control the affairs of the nation. But if any private citizen or public functionary should interpose to curtail its powers or prevent a renewal of its privileges, it can not be doubted that he would be made to feel its influence.

Should the stock of the bank principally pass into the hands of the subjects of a foreign country, and we should unfortunately become involved in a war with that country, what would be our condition? Of the course which would be pursued by a bank almost wholly owned by the subjects of a foreign power, and managed by those whose interests, if not affections, would run in the same direction there can be no doubt. All its operations within would be in aid of the hostile fleets and armies without. Controlling our currency, receiving our public moneys, and holding thousands of our citizens in dependence, it would be more formidable and dangerous than the naval and military power of the enemy.

If we must have a bank with private stockholders, every consideration of sound policy and every impulse of American feeling admonishes that it should be *purely American*. Its stockholders should be composed exclusively of our own citizens, who at least ought to be friendly to our Government and willing to support it in times of difficulty and danger. . . .

The bank is professedly established as an agent of the executive branch of the Government, and its constitutionality is maintained on that ground. Neither upon the propriety of present action nor upon the provisions of this act was the Executive consulted. It has had no opportunity to say that it neither needs nor wants an agent clothed with such powers and favored by such exemptions. There is nothing in its legitimate functions which makes it necessary or proper. Whatever interest or influence, whether public or private, has given birth to this act, it can not be found either in the wishes or necessities of the executive department, by which present action is deemed premature, and the powers conferred upon its agent not only unnecessary, but dangerous to the Government and country.

It is to be regretted that the rich and powerful too often bend the acts of government to their selfish purposes. Distinctions in society will always exist under every just government. Equality of talents, of education, or of wealth can not be produced by human institutions. In the full enjoyment of the gifts of Heaven and the fruits of superior industry, economy, and virtue, every man is equally entitled to protection by law; but when the laws undertake to add to these natural and just advantages artificial distinctions, to grant titles, gratuities, and exclusive privileges, to make the rich richer and the potent more powerful, the humble members of society—the farmers, mechanics, and laborers—who have neither the time nor the means of securing like favors to themselves, have a right to complain of the injustice of their Government. There are no necessary evils in government. Its evils exist only in its abuses. If it would confine itself to equal protection, and, as Heaven does its rains, shower its favors alike on the high and the low, the rich and the poor, it would be an unqualified blessing. In the act before me there seems to be a wide and unnecessary departure from these just principles.

Nor is our Government to be maintained or our Union preserved by invasions of the rights and powers of the several States. In thus attempting to make our General Government strong we make it weak. Its true strength consists in leaving individuals and States as much as possible to themselves —in making itself felt, not in its power, but in its beneficence; not in its control, but in its protection; not in binding the States more closely to the center, but leaving each to move unobstructed in its proper orbit.

Experience should teach us wisdom. Most of the difficulties our Government now encounters and most of the dangers which impend over our Union have sprung from an abandonment of the legitimate objects of Government by our national legislation, and the adoption of such principles as are embodied in this act. Many of our rich men have not been content with equal protection and equal benefits, but have besought us to make them richer by act of Congress. By attempting to gratify their desires we have in the results of our legislation arrayed section against section, interest against interest, and man against man, in a fearful commotion which threatens to shake the foundations of our Union. It is time to pause in our career to review our principles, and if possible revive that devoted patriotism and spirit of compromise which distinguished the sages of the Revolution and the fathers of our Union. If we can not at once, in justice to interests vested under improvident legislation, make our Government what it ought to be, we can at least take a stand against all new grants of monopolies and exclusive privileges, against any prostitution of our Government to the advancement of the few at the expense of the many, and in favor of compromise and gradual reform in our code of laws and system of political economy.

(54)

Timothy Flint

1780-1840

Graduated from Harvard in 1800, Flint became a preacher and writer. In 1815 he undertook, partly for reasons of health, a missionary tour of the West. Frontier life provided him with materials for his voluminous writings, which included a number of novels. Flint held a romantic and idealized notion of the frontier settler, and undoubtedly he experienced frequent disillusionment. Yet he continued to soften frontier harshness and vulgarity and to praise heroism and nobility. Eastern writers were frequent borrowers from Flint when they wrote on the West.

The selection below is from Letter XVII of Flint's *Recollections of the Last Ten Years* (Boston, 1826).

The people in the Atlantic states have not yet recovered from the horror, inspired by the term "backwoodsman." This prejudice is particularly strong in New England, and is more or less felt from Maine to Georgia. When I first visited this country, I had my full share, and my family by far too much for their comfort. In approaching the country, I heard a thousand stories of gougings, and robberies, and shooting down with the rifle. I have travelled in these regions thousands of miles under all circumstances of exposure and danger. I have travelled alone, or in company only with such as needed protection, instead of being able to impart it; and this too, in many instances, where I was not known as a minister, or where such knowledge would have had no influence in protecting me. I never have carried the slightest weapon of defense. I scarcely remember to have experienced any thing that resembled insult, or to have felt myself in danger from the people. I have often seen men that had lost an eye. Instances of murder, numerous and horrible in their circumstances, have occurred in my vicinity. But they were such lawless rencounters, as terminate in murder every where, and in which the drunkenness, brutality, and violence were mutual. They were catastrophes, in which quiet and sober men would be in no danger of being involved. When we look round these immense regions, and consider that I have been in settlements three hundred miles from any court of justice, when we look at the position of the men, and the state of things, the wonder is, that so few outrages and murders occur. The gentlemen of the towns, even here, speak often with a certain contempt and horror of the backwoodsmen. I have read, and not without feelings of pain, the bitter representations of the learned and virtuous Dr. Dwight, in speaking of them. He represents these vast regions, as a grand reservoir for the scum of the Atlantic states. He characterizes in the mass the emigrants from New England, as discontented coblers, too proud, too much in debt, too unprincipled, too much puffed up with self-conceit, too strongly impressed that their fancied talents could not find scope in their own country, to stay there. It is true there are worthless people here, and the most so, it must be confessed, are from New England. It is true there are gamblers, and gougers, and outlaws; but there are fewer of them, than from the nature of things, and the character of the age and the world, we ought to expect. But it is unworthy of the excellent man in question so to designate this people in the mass. The backwoodsman of the west, as I have seen him, is generally an amiable and virtuous man. His general motive for coming here is to be a freeholder, to have plenty of rich land, and to be able to settle his children about him. It is a most virtuous motive. And not-withstanding all that Dr. Dwight and Talleyrand have said to the contrary, I fully believe, that nine in ten of the emigrants have come here with no other motive. You find, in truth, that he has vices and barbarisms, peculiar to his situation. His manners are rough. He wears, it may be, a long beard. He has a great quantity of bear or deer skins wrought into his household establishment, his furniture, and dress. He carries a knife, or a dirk in his bosom, and when in the woods has a rifle on his back, and a pack of dogs at his heels. An Atlantic stranger, transferred directly from one of our cities to his door, would recoil from a rencounter with him. But remember, that his rifle and his dogs are among his chief means of support and profit. Remember, that all his first days here were passed in dread of the savages. Remember, that he still encounters them, still meets bears and panthers. Enter his door, and tell him you are benighted, and wish the shelter of his cabin for the night. The welcome is indeed seemingly ungracious: "I reckon you can stay," or "I suppose we must let you stay." But this apparent ungraciousness is the harbinger of every kindness that he can bestow, and every comfort that his cabin can afford. Good coffee, corn bread and butter, venison, pork, wild and tame fowls are set before you. His wife, timid, silent, reserved, but constantly attentive to your comfort, does not sit at the table with you, but like the wives of the patriarchs, stands and attends on you. You are shown to the best bed which the house can offer. When this kind of hospitality has been afforded you as long as you choose to stay, and when you depart, and speak about your bill, you are most commonly told with some slight mark of resentment, that they do not keep tavern. Even the flaxen-headed urchins will turn away from your money.

In all my extensive intercourse with these people, I do not recollect but one instance of positive rudeness and inhospitality. It was on the waters of the Cuivre of the upper Mississippi; and from a man to whom I had presented bibles, who had received the hospitalities of my house, who had invited me into his settlement to preach. I turned away indignantly from a cold and reluctant reception here, made my way from the house of this man, who was a German and comparatively rich, through deep and dark forests, and amidst the concerts of wolves howling on the neighbouring hills. Providentially, about midnight, I heard the barking of dogs at a distance, made my way to the cabin of a very poor man, who arose at midnight, took me in, provided supper, and gave me a most cordial reception.

With this single exception, I have found the backwoodsmen to be such as I have described; a hardy, adventurous, hospitable, rough, but sincere and upright race of people. I have received so many kindnesses from them, that it becomes me always to preserve a grateful and affectionate remembrance of them. If we were to try them by the standard of New England customs and opinions, that is to say, the customs of a people under entirely different circumstances, there would be many things in the picture, that would strike us offensively. They care little about ministers, and think less about paying them. They are averse to all, even the most necessary restraints. They are destitute of the forms and observances of society and religion; but they are sincere and kind without professions, and have a coarse, but substantial morality, which is often rendered more striking by the immediate contrast of the graceful bows, civility, and professions of their French Catholic neighbours, who have the observances of society and the forms of worship, with often but a scanty modicum of the blunt truth and uprightness of their unpolished neighbours.

(55)

George Bancroft

1800-1891

One of America's first accomplished historians, Bancroft was also one of the first Americans to submit himself to the rigors of German university training. After unsuccessful attempts to transplant that rigor to American education, he became a publicist and an active Jacksonian partisan. He also began work on his *History of the United States,* the first volume of which appeared in 1834. After an active life in politics and government, Bancroft retired in 1874 to spend his last years revising and completing his *History.*

A basic democratic faith underlies all Bancroft's writing; indeed, it is fashionable to remark that every line of his *History* voted for Andrew Jackson. Bancroft's discourse on the "Office of the People" is a summary statement of that faith.

The text here is from "The Office of the People in Art, Government, and Religion (An Oration Delivered Before the Adelphi Society of Williamstown College, in August, 1835)," in *Literary and Historical Miscellanies* (New York, 1855).

The material world does not change in its masses or in its powers. The stars shine with no more lustre than when they first sang together in the glory of their birth. The flowers that gemmed the fields and the forests, before America was discovered, now bloom around us in their season. The sun that shone on Homer shines on us in unchanging lustre. The bow that beamed on the patriarch still glitters in the clouds. Nature is the same. For her no new forces are generated; no new capacities are discovered. The earth turns on its axis, and perfects its revolutions, and renews its seasons, without increase or advancement.

But a like passive destiny does not attach to the inhabitants of the earth. For them the expectations of social improvement are no delusion; the hopes of philanthropy are more than a dream. The five senses do not constitute the whole inventory of our sources of knowledge. They are the organs by which thought connects itself with the external universe; but the power of thought is not merged in the exercise of its instruments. We have functions which connect us with heaven, as well as organs which set us in relation with earth. We have not merely the senses opening to us the external world, but an internal sense, which places us in connexion with the world of intelligence and the decrees of God.

There is a *spirit in man:* not in the privileged few; not in those of us only who by the favor of Providence have been nursed in public schools: *It is in man:* it is the attribute of the race. The spirit, which is the guide to truth, is the gracious gift to each member of the human family.

Reason exists within every breast. I mean not that faculty which deduces inferences from the experience of the senses, but that higher faculty, which from the infinite treasures of its own consciousness, originates truth, and assents to it by the force of intuitive evidence; that faculty which raises us beyond the control of time and space, and gives us faith in things eternal and invisible. There is not the difference between one mind and another, which the pride of philosophers might conceive. To them no faculty is conceded, which does not belong to the meanest of their countrymen. . . .

In like manner the best government rests on the people and not on the few, on persons and not on property, on the free development of public opinion and not on authority; because the munificent Author of our being has conferred the gifts of mind upon every member of the human race without distinction of outward circumstances. Whatever of other possessions may be engrossed, mind asserts its own independence. Lands, estates, the produce of mines, the prolific abundance of the seas, may be usurped by a privileged class. Avarice, assuming the form of ambitious power, may grasp realm after realm, subdue continents, compass the earth in its schemes of aggrandizement, and sigh after other worlds; but mind eludes the power of appropriation; it exists only in its own individuality; it is a property which cannot be confiscated and cannot be torn away; it laughs at chains; it bursts from imprisonment; it defies monopoly. A government of equal rights must, therefore, rest upon mind; not wealth, not brute force, the sum of the moral intelligence of the community should rule the State. Prescription can no more assume to be a valid plea for political injustice; society studies to eradicate established abuses, and to bring social institutions and laws into harmony with moral right; not dismayed by the natural and necessary imperfections of all human effort, and not giving way to despair, because every hope does not at once ripen into fruit.

The public happiness is the true object of legislation, and can be secured only by the masses of mankind themselves awakening to the knowledge and the care of their own interests. Our free institutions have reversed the false and ignoble distinctions between men; and refusing to gratify the pride of caste, have acknowledged the common mind to be the true material for a commonwealth. Every thing has hitherto been done for the happy few. It is not possible to endow an aristocracy with greater benefits than they have already enjoyed; there is no room to hope that individuals will be more highly gifted or more fully developed than the greatest sages of past times. The world can advance only through the culture of the moral and intellectual powers of the people. To accomplish this end by means of the people themselves, is the highest purpose of government. If it be the duty of the individual to strive after a perfection like the perfection of God, how much more ought a nation to be the image of Deity. The common mind is the true Parian marble, fit to be wrought into likeness to a God. The duty of America is to secure the culture and the happiness of the masses by their reliance on themselves.

The absence of the prejudices of the old world leaves us here the opportunity of consulting independent truth; and man is left to apply the instinct of freedom to every social relation and public interest. We have approached so near to nature, that we can hear her gentlest whispers; we have made Humanity our lawgiver and our oracle; and, therefore, the nation receives, vivifies and applies principles, which in Europe the wisest accept with distrust. Freedom of mind and of conscience, freedom of the seas, freedom of industry, equality of franchises, each great truth is firmly grasped, comprehended and enforced; for the multitude is neither rash nor fickle. In truth, it is less fickle than those who profess to be its guides. Its natural dialectics surpass the logic of the schools. Political action has never been so consistent and so unwavering, as when it results from a feeling or a principle, diffused through society. The people is firm and tranquil in its movements, and necessarily acts with moderation, because it becomes but slowly impregnated with new ideas; and effects no changes, except in harmony with the knowledge which it has acquired. Besides, where it is permanently possessed of power, there exists neither the occasion nor the desire for frequent change. It is not the parent of tumult; sedition is bred in the lap of luxury, and its chosen emissaries are the beggared spendthrift and the impoverished libertine. The government by the people is in very truth the strongest government in the world. Discarding the implements of terror, it dares to rule by moral force, and has its citadel in the heart.

Such is the political system which rests on reason, reflection, and the free expression of deliberate choice. There may be those who scoff at the suggestion, that the decision of the whole is to be preferred to the judgment of the enlightened few. They say in their hearts that the masses are ignorant; that farmers know nothing of legislation; that mechanics should not quit their workshops to join in forming public opinion. But true political science does indeed venerate the masses. It maintains, not as has been perversely asserted, that "the people can make right," but that the people can DISCERN right. Individuals are but shadows, too often engrossed by the pursuit of shadows; the race is immortal: individuals are of limited sagacity; the common mind is infinite in its experience: individuals are languid and blind; the many are ever wakeful: individuals are corrupt; the race has been redeemed: individuals are time-serving; the masses are fearless: individuals may be false, the masses are ingenuous and sincere: individuals claim the divine sanction of truth for the deceitful conceptions of their own fancies; the Spirit of God breathes through the combined intelligence of the people. Truth is not to be ascertained by the impulses of an individual; it emerges from the contradictions of personal opinion; it raises itself in majestic serenity above the strifes of parties and the conflict of sects; it acknowledges neither the solitary mind, nor the separate faction as its oracle; but owns as its only faithful interpreter the dictates of pure reason itself, proclaimed by the general voice of mankind. The decrees of the universal conscience are the nearest approach to the presence of God in the soul of man.

Thus the opinion which we respect is, indeed, not the opinion of one or of a few, but the sagacity of the many. It is hard for the pride of cultivated philosophy to put its ear to the ground, and listen reverently to the voice of lowly humanity; yet the people collectively are wiser than the most gifted individual, for all his wisdom constitutes but a part of theirs. When the great sculptor of Greece was endeavoring to fashion the perfect model of beauty, he did not passively imitate the form of the loveliest woman of his age; but he gleaned the several lineaments of his faultless work from the many. And so it is, that a perfect judgment is the result of comparison, when error eliminates error, and truth is established by concurring witnesses. The organ of truth is the invisible decision of the unbiased world; she pleads before no tribunal but public opinion; she owns no safe interpreter but the common mind; she knows no court of appeals but the soul of humanity. It is when the multitude give counsel, that right purposes find safety; theirs is the fixed-ness that cannot be shaken; theirs is the understanding which exceeds in wisdom; theirs is the heart, of which the largeness is as the sand on the sea-shore.

It is not by vast armies, by immense natural resources, by accumulations of treasure, that the greatest results in modern civilization have been accomplished. The traces of the career of conquest pass away, hardly leaving a scar on the national intelligence. The famous battle grounds of victory are, most of them, comparatively indifferent to the human race; barren fields of blood, the scourges of their times, but affecting the social condition as little as the raging of a pestilence. Not one benevolent institution, not one ameliorating principle in the Roman state, was a voluntary concession of the aristocracy; each useful element was borrowed from the Democracies of Greece, or was a reluctant concession to the demands of the people. The same is true in modern political life. It is the confession of an enemy to Democracy, that *"All the great and noble institutions of the world have come from popular efforts."*

It is the uniform tendency of the popular element to elevate and bless Humanity. The exact measure of the progress of civilization is the degree in which the intelligence of the common mind has prevailed over wealth and brute force; in other words, the measure of the progress of civilization is the progress of the people. Every great object, connected with the benevolent exertions of the day, has reference to the culture of those powers which are alone the common inheritance. For this the envoys of religion cross seas, and visit remotest isles; for this the press in its freedom teems with the productions of maturest thought; for this the philanthropist plans new schemes of education; for this halls in every city and village are open to the public instructor. Not that we view with indifference the glorious efforts of material industry; the increase in the facility of internal intercourse; the accumulations of thrifty labor; the varied results of concentrated action. But even there it is mind that achieves the triumph. It is the genius of the architect that gives beauty to the work of human hands, and makes the temple, the dwelling, or the public edifice, an outward representation of the spirit of propriety and order. It is science that guides the blind zeal of cupidity to the construction of the vast channels of communication, which are fast binding the world into one family. And it is as a method of moral improvement, that these swifter means of intercourse derive their greatest value. Mind becomes universal property; the poem that is published on the soil of England, finds its response on the shores of Lake Erie and the banks of the Missouri, and is admired near the sources of the Ganges. The defence of public liberty in our own halls of legislation penetrates the plains of Poland, is echoed along the mountains of Greece, and pierces the darkest night of eastern despotism.

The universality of the intellectual and moral powers, and the necessity of their development for the progress of the race, proclaim the great doctrine of the natural right of every human being to moral and intellectual culture. It is the glory of our fathers to have established in their laws the equal claims of every child to the public care of its morals and its mind. From this principle we may deduce the universal right to leisure; that is, to time not appropriated to material purposes, but reserved for the culture of the moral affections and the mind. It does not tolerate the exclusive enjoyment of leisure by a privileged class; but defending the rights of labor, would suffer none to sacrifice the higher purposes of existence in unceasing toil for that which is not life. Such is the voice of nature; such the conscious claim of the human mind. The universe opens its pages to every eye; the music of creation resounds in every ear; the glorious lessons of immortal truth, that are written in the sky and on the earth, address themselves to every mind, and claim attention from every human being. God has made man upright, that he might look before and after; and he calls upon every one not merely to labor, but to reflect; not merely to practise the revelations of divine will, but to contemplate the displays of divine power. Nature claims for every man leisure, for she claims every man as a witness to the divine glory, manifested in the created world.

(56)

Walt Whitman

1819-1892

One of America's great poets, Walt Whitman was raised on Long Island but left home at the age of eleven and spent several years wandering about the East. Self-educated, he taught school and edited a series of country newspapers. In 1846 he became editor of *The Brooklyn Daily Eagle;* later, after managing a New Orleans paper for a short time, he returned to settle permanently in Brooklyn. His first major work was *Leaves of Grass* (1855), a small volume of twelve poems and a preface. Several editions of this work were published in Whitman's lifetime. During the Civil War, Whitman served as a nurse in a Washington hospital. Stricken with paralysis in 1873, he lived in Camden, New Jersey, until his death on March 26, 1892.

Two related passions motivated Whitman's work: his dedication to democracy and his concern for the individual (his discovery of Emerson's theory of self-reliance unified his thought and related him to the Transcendentalists). To these two ideals he was almost religiously dedicated, and he often stressed this underlying sense of mission in his writings. Rejecting creeds, churches, formal philosophies, and the structures of laws, he emphasized man's infinite capacity to realize his full stature in a democratic environment. This view he called "personalism."

Published in 1871, *Democratic Vistas* expresses in prose the same values and ideals found in his poetry, and in many ways is one of the best nineteenth-century definitions and vindications of democracy. The selection is from the text in *Prose Works* (Philadelphia, n.d.).

But sternly discarding, shutting our eyes to the glow and grandeur of the general superficial effect, coming down to what is of the only real importance, Personalities, and examining minutely, we question, we ask, Are there, indeed, *men* here worthy the name? Are there athletes? Are there perfect women, to match the generous material luxuriance? Is there a pervading atmosphere of beautiful manners? Are there crops of fine youths, and majestic old persons? Are there arts worthy freedom and a rich people? Is there a great moral and religious civilization—the only justification of a great material one? Confess that to severe eyes, using the moral microscope upon humanity, a sort of dry and flat Sahara appears these cities, crowded with petty grotesques, malformations, phantoms, playing meaningless antics. Confess that everywhere, in shop, street, church, theatre, barroom, official chair, are pervading flippancy and vulgarity, low cunning, infidelity—everywhere the youth puny, impudent, foppish, prematurely ripe—everywhere an abnormal libidinousness, unhealthy forms, male, female, painted, padded, dyed, chignon'd, muddy complexions, bad blood, the capacity for good motherhood deceasing or deceas'd, shallow notions of beauty, with a range of manners, or rather lack of manners, (considering the advantages enjoy'd,) probably the meanest to be seen in the world.[1]

Of all this, and these lamentable conditions, to breathe into them the breath recuperative of sane and heroic life, I say a new founded literature, not merely to copy and reflect existing surfaces, or pander to what is called taste —not only to amuse, pass away time, celebrate the beautiful, the refined, the past, or exhibit technical, rhythmic, or grammatical dexterity—but a literature underlying life, religious, consistent with science, handling the elements and forces with competent power, teaching and training men—and, as perhaps the most precious of its results, achieving the entire redemption of woman out of these incredible holds and webs of silliness, millinery, and every kind of dyspeptic depletion—and thus insuring to the States a strong and sweet Female Race, a race of perfect Mothers—is what is needed.

And now, in the full conception of these facts and points, and all that they infer, pro and con—with yet unshaken faith in the elements of the American masses, the composites, of both sexes, and even consider'd as individuals—and ever recognizing in them the broadest bases of the best literary and esthetic appreciation—I proceed with my speculations, Vistas.

First, let us see what we can make out of a brief, general, sentimental consideration of political democracy, and whence it has arisen, with regard to some of its current features, as an aggregate, and as the basic structure of our future literature and authorship. We shall, it is true, quickly and continually find the origin-idea of the singleness of man, individualism, asserting itself, and cropping forth, even from the opposite ideas. But the mass, or lump character, for imperative reasons, is to be ever carefully weigh'd, borne in mind, and provided for. Only from it, and from its proper regulation and potency, comes the other, comes the chance of individualism. The two are contradictory, but our task is to reconcile them.[2]

---

1. Of these rapidly-sketch'd hiatuses, the two which seem to me most serious are, for one, the condition, absence, or perhaps the singular abeyance, of moral conscientious fibre all through American society; and, for another, the appalling depletion of women in their powers of sane athletic maternity, their crowning attribute, and ever making the woman, in loftiest spheres, superior to the man.

I have sometimes thought, indeed, that the sole avenue and means of a reconstructed sociology depended, primarily, on a new birth, elevation, expansion, invigoration of woman, affording, for races to come, (as the conditions that antedate birth are indispensable,) a perfect motherhood. Great, great, indeed, far greater than they know, is the sphere of women. But doubtless the question of such new sociology all goes together, includes many varied and complex influences and premises, and the man as well as the woman, and the woman as well as the man.

2. The question hinted here is one which time only can answer. Must not the virtue of modern Individualism, continually enlarging, usurping all, seriously affect, perhaps keep down entirely, in America, the like of the ancient virtue of Patriotism, the fervid and absorbing love of general country? I have no doubt myself that the two will merge,

The political history of the past may be summ'd up as having grown out of what underlies the words, order, safety, caste, and especially out of the need of some prompt deciding authority, and of cohesion at all cost. Leaping time, we come to the period within the memory of people now living, when, as from some lair where they had slumber'd long, accumulating wrath, sprang up and are yet active, (1790, and on even to the present, 1870,) those noisy eructations, destructive iconoclasms, a fierce sense of wrongs, amid which moves the form, well known in modern history, in the old world, stain'd with much blood, and mark'd by savage reactionary clamors and demands. These bear, mostly, as on one inclosing point of need.

For after the rest is said—after the many time-honor'd and really true things for subordination, experience, rights of property, etc., have been listen'd to and acquiesced in—after the valuable and well-settled statement of our duties and relations in society is thoroughly conn'd over and exhausted —it remains to bring forward and modify everything else with the idea of that Something a man is, (last precious consolation of the drudging poor,) standing apart from all else, divine in his own right, and a woman in hers, sole and untouchable by any canons of authority, or any rule derived from precedent, state-safety, the acts of legislatures, or even from what is called religion, modesty, or art. The radiation of this truth is the key of the most significant doings of our immediately preceding three centuries, and has been the political genesis and life of America. Advancing visibly, it still more advances invisibly. Underneath the fluctuations of the expressions of society, as well as the movements of the politics of the leading nations of the world, we see steadily pressing ahead and strengthening itself, even in the midst of immense tendencies toward aggregation, this image of completeness in separatism, of individual personal dignity, of a single person, either male or female, characterized in the main, not from extrinsic acquirements or position, but in the pride of himself or herself alone; and, as an eventual conclusion and summing up, (or else the entire scheme of things is aimless, a cheat, a crash,) the simple idea that the last, best dependence is to be upon humanity itself, and its own inherent, normal, full-grown qualities, without any superstitious support whatever. This idea of perfect individualism it is indeed that deepest tinges and gives character to the idea of the aggregate. For it is mainly or altogether to serve independent separatism that we favor a strong generalization, consolidation. As it is to give the best vitality and freedom to the rights of the States, (every bit as important as the right of nationality, the union,) that we insist on the identity of the Union at all hazards.

The purpose of democracy—supplanting old belief in the necessary absoluteness of establish'd dynastic rulership, temporal, ecclesiastical, and scholastic, as furnishing the only security against chaos, crime, and ignorance —is, through many transmigrations, and amid endless ridicules, arguments,

---

and will mutually profit and brace each other, and that from them a greater product, a third, will arise. But I feel that at present they and their oppositions form a serious problem and paradox in the United States.

and ostensible failures, to illustrate, at all hazards, this doctrine or theory that man, properly train'd in sanest, highest freedom, may and must become a law, and series of laws, unto himself, surrounding and providing for, not only his own personal control, but all his relations to other individuals, and to the State; and that, while other theories, as in the past histories of nations, have proved wise enough, and indispensable perhaps for their conditions, *this,* as matters now stand in our civilized world, is the only scheme worth working from, as warranting results like those of Nature's laws, reliable, when once establish'd to carry on themselves.

The argument of the matter is extensive, and, we admit, by no means all on one side. What we shall offer will be far, far from sufficient. But while leaving unsaid much that should properly even prepare the way for the treatment of this many-sided question of political liberty, equality, or republicanism—leaving the whole history and consideration of the feudal plan and its products, embodying humanity, its politics and civilization, through the retrospect of past time, (which plan and products, indeed, make up all of the past, and a large part of the present)—leaving unanswer'd, at least by any specific and local answer, many a well-wrought argument and instance, and many a conscientious declamatory cry and warning—as, very lately, from an eminent and venerable person abroad[3]—things, problems, full of doubt, dread, suspense, (not new to me, but old occupiers of many an anxious hour in city's din, or night's silence,) we still may give a page or so, whose drift is opportune. Time alone can finally answer these things. But as a substitute in passing, let us, even if fragmentarily, throw forth a short direct or indirect suggestion of the premises of that other plan, in the new spirit, under the new forms, started here in our America.

As to the political section of Democracy, which introduces and breaks ground for further and vaster sections, few probably are the minds, even in these republican States, that fully comprehend the aptness of that phrase, "THE GOVERNMENT OF THE PEOPLE, BY THE PEOPLE, FOR THE PEOPLE," which we inherit from the lips of Abraham Lincoln; a formula whose verbal shape is homely wit, but whose scope includes both the totality and all minutiæ of the lesson.

The People! Like our huge earth itself, which, to ordinary scansion, is full of vulgar contradictions and offence, man, viewed in the lump, displeases, and is a constant puzzle and affront to the merely educated classes. The rare,

---

3. "SHOOTING NIAGARA." I was at first roused to much anger and abuse by this essay from Mr. Carlyle, so insulting to the theory of America—but happening to think afterwards how I had more than once been in the like mood, during which his essay was evidently cast, and seen persons and things in the same light, (indeed some might say there are signs of the same feeling in these Vistas)—I have since read it again, not only as a study, expressing as it does certain judgments from the highest feudal point of view, but have read it with respect as coming from an earnest soul, and as contributing certain sharp-cutting metallic grains, which, if not gold or silver, may be good hard, honest iron.

cosmical, artist-mind, lit with the Infinite, alone confronts his manifold and oceanic qualities—but taste, intelligence and culture, (so-called,) have been against the masses, and remain so. There is plenty of glamour about the most damnable crimes and hoggish meannesses, special and general, of the feudal and dynastic world over there, with its *personnel* of lords and queens and courts, so well-dress'd and so handsome. But the People are ungrammatical, untidy, and their sins gaunt and ill-bred. . . .

I say the mission of government, henceforth, in civilized lands, is not repression alone, and not authority alone, not even of law, nor by that favorite standard of the eminent writer, the rule of the best men, the born heroes and captains of the race, (as if such ever, or one time out of a hundred, get into the big places, elective or dynastic)—but higher than the highest arbitrary rule, to train communities through all their grades, beginning with individuals and ending there again, to rule themselves. What Christ appear'd for in the moral-spiritual field for human-kind, namely, that in respect to the absolute soul, there is in the possession of such by each single individual, something so transcendent, so incapable of gradations, (like life,) that, to that extent, it places all beings on a common level, utterly regardless of the distinctions of intellect, virtue, station, or any height or lowliness whatever—is tallied in like manner, in this other field, by democracy's rule that men, the nation, as a common aggregate of living identities, affording in each a separate and complete subject for freedom, worldly thrift and happiness, and for a fair chance for growth, and for protection in citizenship, &c., must, to the political extent of the suffrage or vote, if no further, be placed, in each and in the whole, on one broad, primary, universal, common platform.

The purpose is not altogether direct; perhaps it is more indirect. For it is not that democracy is of exhaustive account, in itself. Perhaps, indeed, it is, (like Nature,) of no account in itself. It is that, as we see, it is the best, perhaps only, fit and full means, formulater, general caller-forth, trainer, for the million, not for grand material personalities only, but for immortal souls. To be a voter with the rest is not so much; and this, like every institute, will have its imperfections. But to become an enfranchised man, and now, impediments removed, to stand and start without humiliation, and equal with the rest; to commence, or have the road clear'd to commence, the grand experiment of development, whose end, (perhaps requiring several generations,) may be the forming of a full-grown man or woman—that *is* something. To ballast the State is also secured, and in our times is to be secured, in no other way.

We do not, (at any rate I do not,) put it either on the ground that the People, the masses, even the best of them, are, in their latent or exhibited qualities, essentially sensible and good—nor on the ground of their rights; but that good or bad, rights or no rights, the democratic formula is the only safe and preservative one for coming times. We endow the masses with the suffrage for their own sake, no doubt; then, perhaps still more, from another point of view, for community's sake. Leaving the rest to the sentimentalists, we present freedom as sufficient in its scientific aspect, cold as ice, reasoning, deductive, clear and passionless as crystal. . . .

And, topping democracy, this most alluring record, that it alone can bind, and ever seeks to bind, all nations, all men, of however various and distant lands, into a brotherhood, a family. It is the old, yet ever-modern dream of earth, out of her eldest and her youngest, her fond philosophers and poets. Not that half only, individualism, which isolates. There is another half, which is adhesiveness or love, that fuses, ties and aggregates, making the races comrades, and fraternizing all. Both are to be vitalized by religion, (sole worthiest elevator of man or State,) breathing into the proud, material tissues, the breath of life. For I say at the core of democracy, finally, is the religious element. All the religions, old and new, are there. Nor may the scheme step forth, clothed in resplendent beauty and command, till these, bearing the best, the latest fruit, the spiritual, shall fully appear. . . .

Did you, too, O friend, suppose democracy was only for elections, for politics, and for a party name? I say democracy is only of use there that it may pass on and come to its flower and fruits in manners, in the highest forms of interaction between men, and their beliefs—in religion, literature, colleges, and schools—democracy in all public and private life, and in the army and navy.[4] I have intimated that, as a paramount scheme, it has yet few or no full realizers and believers. I do not see, either, that it owes any serious thanks to noted propagandists or champions, or has been essentially help'd, though often harm'd, by them. It has been and is carried on by all the moral forces, and by trade, finance, machinery, intercommunications, and, in fact, by all the developments of history, and can no more be stopp'd than the tides, or the earth in its orbit. Doubtless, also, it resides, crude and latent, well down in the hearts of the fair average of the American-born people, mainly in the agricultural regions. But it is not yet, there or anywhere, the fully-receiv'd, the fervid, the absolute faith.

I submit, therefore, that the fruition of democracy, on aught like a grand scale, resides altogether in the future. As, under any profound and comprehensive view of the gorgeous-composite feudal world, we see in it, through the long ages and cycles of ages, the results of a deep, integral, human and divine principle, or fountain, from which issued laws, ecclesia, manners, institutes, costumes, personalities, poems, (hitherto unequall'd,) faithfully partaking of their source, and indeed only arising either to betoken it, or to furnish parts of that varied-flowing display, whose centre was one and absolute—so, long ages hence, shall the due historian or critic make at least an equal retrospect, an equal history for the democratic principle. It too must be adorn'd, credited with its results—then, when it, with imperial power,

---

4. The whole present system of the officering and personnel of the army and navy of these States, and the spirit and letter of their trebly-aristocratic rules and regulations, is a monstrous exotic, a nuisance and revolt, and belong here just as much as orders of nobility, or the Pope's council of cardinals. I say if the present theory of our army and navy is sensible and true, then the rest of America is an unmitigated fraud.

through amplest time, has dominated mankind—has been the source and test of all the moral, esthetic, social, political, and religious expressions and institutes of the civilized world—has begotten them in spirit and in form, and has carried them to its own unprecedented heights—has had, (it is possible,) monastics and ascetics, more numerous, more devout than the monks and priests of all previous creeds—has sway'd the ages with a breadth and rectitude tallying Nature's own—has fashion'd, systematized, and triumphantly finish'd and carried out, in its own interest, and with unparallel'd success, a new earth and a new man.

XIII

American
Liberal Capitalism

IN 1789 America had an agrarian and mercantile economy, rather than an industrial one. Among the controversial issues of the day was that of America's economic future. Jeffersonians held largely to the agrarian ideal, believing that a nation of farmers best insured the future of republican principles. The vision of industrial greatness for America was reserved for Alexander Hamilton, who not only labored to strengthen the authority of the federal government but also espoused an economic nationalism as the basis for American capitalism. The promotion of manufacturing, a balanced economy, a protective tariff, and a policy of internal improvements sponsored by the federal government were among the ideas proposed by Hamilton for the nation's growth.

Hamilton's views thus raised another debated issue, that of the role of the federal government in the nation's economic development. Some Americans favored individual enterprise without federal interference or aid. Others like Henry Clay and John Quincy Adams continued to favor Hamiltonian ideas, as embodied in their "American Plan" for national economic development.

The Jacksonian era, however, with its struggle over the tariff, the Bank, and chartered privilege, marked an attempt to halt governmental action in economic affairs. Yet the Jacksonians were related to emerging American capitalism in a paradoxical way. They had achieved power partly because the nation's expanding commerce, industry, and urbanization had undermined aristocratic ideas and furthered the spread of the democratic belief. The Jacksonian movement thus grew out of these changes in the economy, and out of a common desire to promote economic opportunity still further by removing restrictions and privileges. Yet many of their policies supported the cause of America's emerging capitalism even as they questioned it. Chief Justice Taney's decision in *Charles River Bridge* opened wider doors of economic opportunity. The journalist William Leggett, an ardent Jacksonian, in his concern with rights and power, demanded economic liberty within the republican framework, and thus became a spokesman of unconditional laissez faire. The conservative Federalism of Hamilton and John Adams was dead in the 1830's, but the economic development they foresaw had become reality. Herein lies the paradox of Jacksonianism. It traced its political beliefs to the earlier ideals of the republic but at the same time it helped advance economic trends that clearly prefigured future American capitalism.

Actually, the development of the American economy soon outdistanced the ideas Americans had formulated in the realm of economics. Economic activity—"materialism" some critics called it—soon changed the fate of the nation. The continent's rich resources were discovered and exploited, canals, turnpikes, and railroads were built, vast tracts of land were opened up, and immigrant labor from Europe arrived in growing numbers to man the new mills and factories that sprang up everywhere in the East. Economic expansion brought many serious problems as well: the use of child labor, the low wages and long hours in the new mines and factories, the suffering caused by depressions and unemployment, to name but a few. A few individuals like Robert Owen (1771–1858) and Albert Brisbane (1809–1890) tried unsuccessful utopian experiments to solve these problems. Most Americans, however, were confident that the wonders of the new economy would bring its own solutions. Not always fully understood, the emerging capitalism seemed almost inevitable. Indeed, to many Americans an attack on their economic system (and this system was frequently defined in terms of individual enterprise, free competition, and nationalism) was regarded as an attack on a fundamental tenet of American democracy.

(57)

Alexander Hamilton

1757-1804

Brilliant and aggressive, Hamilton reached the peak of his astonishing career as Secretary of the Treasury under Washington. Born in the West Indies, he was educated at King's College (Columbia University). He became an officer in the Revolutionary War and rose to become one of Washington's most trusted aides. Following Washington's retirement, he became President Adams' rival for the leadership of the Federalist party. Hamilton also incurred the enmity of Aaron Burr, as a result of his role in denying Burr the Presidency in 1800. And when Burr was later defeated for the governorship of New York, partly through Hamilton's efforts, he challenged Hamilton to a duel and killed him at Weehawken, New Jersey, on July 12, 1804.

As a master of economic thought, Hamilton labored ceaselessly for a strong national government and for a nationalistic basis for

American capitalism. His plans for funding the national debt, for assuming the states' war obligations, and for a national bank are familiar to all Americans.

In his *Report on the Subject of Manufactures* Hamilton abandoned the internationalism of the classical English economists, including Adam Smith, and argued for a balanced economy, the virtues of industry, and protective tariffs to stimulate manufacturing enterprises. The text for the excerpts reprinted here is *The Works of Alexander Hamilton*, J. C. Hamilton, ed., 3 vols. (New York, 1810), vol. I.

Without contending for the superior productiveness of manufacturing industry, it may conduce to a better judgment of the policy which ought to be pursued respecting its encouragement, to contemplate the subject under some additional aspects, tending not only to confirm the idea that this kind of industry has been improperly represented as unproductive in itself, but to evince, in addition, that the establishment and diffusion of manufactures have the effect of rendering the total mass of useful and productive labor, in a community, greater than it would otherwise be. In prosecuting this discussion, it may be necessary briefly to résumé and review some of the topics which have been already touched.

To affirm that the labor of the manufacturer is unproductive, because he consumes as much of the produce of land as he adds value to the raw material which he manufactures, is not better founded than it would be to affirm that the labor of the farmer, which furnishes materials to the manufacturer, is unproductive, because he consumes an equal value of manufactured articles. Each furnishes a certain portion of the produce of his labor to the other, and each destroys a corresponding portion of the produce of the labor of the other. In the meantime, the maintenance of two citizens, instead of one, is going on; the State has two members instead of one; and they, together, consume twice the value of what is produced from the land.

If, instead of a farmer and artificer, there were a farmer only, he would be under the necessity of devoting a part of his labor to the fabrication of clothing and other articles, which he would procure of the artificer, in the case of there being such a person; and of course he would be able to devote less labor to the cultivation of his farm, and would draw from it a proportionately less product. The whole quantity of production, in this state of things, in provisions, raw materials, and manufactures, would certainly not exceed in value the amount of what would be produced in provisions and raw materials only, if there were an artificer as well as a farmer.

Again, if there were both an artificer and a farmer, the latter would be left at liberty to pursue exclusively the cultivation of his farm. A greater quantity of provisions and raw materials would, of course, be produced, equal, at least, as has been already observed, to the whole amount of the provisions, raw materials, and manufactures, which would exist on a contrary supposition. The artificer, at the same time, would be going on in the production of manufactured commodities, to an amount sufficient, not only to repay the farmer, in those commodities, for the provisions and materials which were procured from him, but to furnish the artificer himself with a supply of similar commodities for his own use. Thus, then, there would be two quantities or values in existence, instead of one; and the revenue and consumption would be double, in one case, what it would be in the other.

If, in place of both of these suppositions, there were supposed to be two farmers and no artificer, each of whom applied a part of his labor to the culture of land and another part to the fabrication of manufactures; in this case, the portion of the labor of both, bestowed upon land, would produce the same quantity of provisions and raw materials only, as would be produced by the entire sum of the labor of one, applied in the same manner; and the portion of the labor of both, bestowed upon manufactures, would produce the same quantity of manufactures only, as would be produced by the entire sum of the labor of one, applied in the same manner. Hence, the produce of the labor of the two farmers would not be greater than the produce of the labor of the farmer and artificer; and hence it results, that the labor of the artificer is as positively productive as that of the farmer, and as positively augments the revenue of the society.

The labor of the artificer replaces to the farmer that portion of his labor with which he provides the materials of exchange with the artificer, and which he would otherwise have been compelled to apply to manufactures; and while the artificer thus enables the farmer to enlarge his stock of agricultural industry, a portion of which he purchases for his own use, he also supplies himself with the manufactured articles of which he stands in need. He does still more. Besides this equivalent, which he gives for the portion of agricultural labor consumed by him, and this supply of manufactured commodities for his own consumption, he furnishes still a surplus, which compensates for the use of the capital advanced, either by himself or some other person, for carrying on the business. This is the ordinary profit of the stock employed in the manufactory, and is, in every sense, as effective an addition to the income of the society as the rent of land.

The produce of the labor of the artificer, consequently, may be regarded as composed of three parts: one, by which the provisions for his subsistence and the materials for his work are purchased of the farmer; one, by which he supplies himself with manufactured necessaries; and a third, which constitutes the profit on the stock employed. The two last portions seem to have been overlooked in the system which represents manufacturing industry as barren and unproductive.

In the course of the preceding illustrations, the products of equal quantities of the labor of the farmer and artificer have been treated as if equal to each other. But this is not to be understood as intending to assert any such precise equality. It is merely a manner of expression, adopted for the sake of simplicity and perspicuity. Whether the value of the produce of the labor of the farmer be somewhat more or less than that of the artificer, is not material to the main scope of the argument, which, hitherto, has only aimed at showing that the one, as well as the other, occasions a positive augmentation of the total produce and revenue of the society.

It is now proper to proceed a step further, and to enumerate the principal circumstances from which it may be inferred that manufacturing establishments not only occasion a positive augmentation of the produce and revenue of the society, but that they contribute essentially to rendering them greater than they could possibly be without such establishments. These circumstances are:

1. The division of labor.

2. An extension of the use of machinery.

3. Additional employment to classes of the community not ordinarily engaged in the business.

4. The promoting of emigration from foreign countries.

5. The furnishing greater scope for the diversity of talents and dispositions, which discriminate men from each other.

6. The affording a more ample and various field for enterprise.

7. The creating, in some instances, a new, and securing, in all, a more certain and steady demand for the surplus produce of the soil.

Each of these circumstances has a considerable influence upon the total mass of industrious effort in a community; together, they add to it a degree of energy and effect which is not easily conceived. Some comments upon each of them, in the order in which they have been stated, may serve to explain their importance.

1. As to the Division of Labor

It has justly been observed, that there is scarcely any thing of greater moment in the economy of a nation than the proper division of labor. The separation of occupations causes each to be carried to a much greater perfection than it could possibly acquire if they were blended. This arises principally from three circumstances:

1st. The greater skill and dexterity naturally resulting from a constant and undivided application to a single object. It is evident that these properties must increase in proportion to the separation and simplification of objects, and the steadiness of the attention devoted to each; and must be less in proportion to the complication of objects, and the number among which the attention is distracted.

2d. The economy of time, by avoiding the loss of it, incident to a frequent transition from one operation to another of a different nature. This depends on various circumstances: the transition itself, the orderly disposition of the implements, machines, and materials employed in the operation to be relinquished, the preparatory steps to the commencement of a new one, the interruption of the impulse which the mind of the workman acquires from being engaged in a particular operation, the distractions, hesitations, and reluctances which attend the passage from one kind of business to another.

3d. An extension of the use of machinery. A man occupied on a single object will have it more in his power, and will be more naturally led to exert his imagination, in devising methods to facilitate and abridge labor, than if he were perplexed by a variety of independent and dissimilar operations. Besides this the fabrication of machines, in numerous instances, becoming itself a distinct trade, the artist who follows it has all the advantages which have been enumerated, for improvement in his particular art; and, in both ways, the invention and application of machinery are extended.

And from these causes united, the mere separation of the occupation of the cultivator from that of the artificer, has the effect of augmenting the productive powers of labor, and with them, the total mass of the produce or revenue of a country. In this single view of the subject, therefore, the utility of artificers or manufacturers, towards producing an increase of productive industry, is apparent.

2. As to an Extension of the Use of Machinery, a Point Which, Though Partly Anticipated, Requires to Be Placed in One or Two Additional Lights

The employment of machinery forms an item of great importance in the general mass of national industry. It is an artificial force brought in aid of the natural force of man; and, to all the purposes of labor, is an increase of hands, an accession of strength, unencumbered too by the expense of maintaining the laborer. May it not, therefore, be fairly inferred, that those occupations which give greatest scope to the use of this auxiliary, contribute most to the general stock of industrious effort, and, in consequence, to the general product of industry?

It shall be taken for granted, and the truth of the position referred to observation, that manufacturing pursuits are susceptible, in a greater degree, of the application of machinery, than those of agriculture. If so, all the difference is lost to a community which, instead of manufacturing for itself, procures the fabrics requisite to its supply from other countries. The substitution of foreign for domestic manufactures is a transfer to foreign nations of the advantages accruing from the employment of machinery, in the modes in which it is capable of being employed with most utility and to the greatest extent.

The cotton-mill, invented in England, within the last twenty years, is a signal illustration of the general proposition which has been just advanced. In consequence of it, all the different processes for spinning cotton are performed by means of machines, which are put in motion by water, and attended chiefly by women and children—and by a smaller number of persons, in the whole, than are requisite in the ordinary mode of spinning. And it is an advantage of great moment, that the operations of this mill continue with convenience during the night as well as through the day. The prodigious effect of such a machine is easily conceived. To this invention is to be attributed, essentially, the immense progress which has been so suddenly made in Great Britain, in the various fabrics of cotton.

3. As to the Additional Employment of Classes of the Community Not Originally Engaged in the Particular Business

This is not among the least valuable of the means by which manufacturing institutions contribute to augment the general stock of industry and production. In places where those institutions prevail, besides the persons regularly engaged in them, they afford occasional and extra employment to industrious individuals and families, who are willing to devote the leisure resulting from the intermissions of their ordinary pursuits to collateral labors, as a resource for multiplying their acquisitions or their enjoyments. The husbandman himself experiences a new source of profit and support from the increased industry of his wife and daughters, invited and stimulated by the demands of the neighboring manufactories.

Besides this advantage of occasional employment to classes having different occupations, there is another, of a nature allied to it, and of a similar tendency. This is the employment of persons who would otherwise be idle, and in many cases a burthen on the community, either from the bias of temper, habit, infirmity of body, or some other cause, indisposing or disqualifying them for the toils of the country. It is worthy of particular remark that, in general, women and children are rendered more useful, and the latter more early useful, by manufacturing establishments, than they would otherwise be. Of the number of persons employed in the cotton manufactories of Great Britain, it is computed that four sevenths nearly are women and children, of whom the greatest proportion are children, and many of them of a tender age.

And thus it appears to be one of the attributes of manufactures, and one of no small consequence, to give occasion to the exertion of a greater quantity of industry, even by the same number of persons, where they happen to prevail, than would exist if there were no such establishments.

4. As to the Promoting of Emigration from Foreign Countries

Men reluctantly quit one course of occupation and livelihood for another, unless invited to it by very apparent and proximate advantages. Many who would go from one country to another, if they had a prospect of continuing with more benefit the callings to which they have been educated, will often not be tempted to change their situation by the hope of doing better in some other way. Manufacturers who, listening to the powerful invitations of a better price for their fabrics or their labor, of greater cheapness of provisions and raw materials, of an exemption from the chief part of the taxes, burthens, and restraints which they endure in the Old World, of greater personal independence and consequence, under the operation of a more equal government, and of what is far more precious than mere religious toleration, a perfect equality of religious privileges, would probably flock from Europe to the United States, to pursue their own trades or professions, if they were once made sensible of the advantages they would enjoy, and were inspired with an assurance of encouragement and employment, will with difficulty, be induced to transplant themselves, with a view to becoming cultivators of land.

If it be true, then, that it is the interest of the United States to open every possible avenue to emigration from abroad, it affords a weighty argument for the encouragement of manufactures; which, for the reasons just assigned, will have the strongest tendency to multiply the inducements to it.

Here is perceived an important resource, not only for extending the population, and with it the useful and productive labor of the country, but likewise for the prosecution of manufactures, without deducting from the number of hands which might otherwise be drawn to tillage, and even for the indemnification of agriculture for such as might happen to be diverted from it. Many, whom manufacturing views would induce to emigrate, would, afterwards, yield to the temptations which the particular situation of this country holds out to agricultural pursuits. And while agriculture would, in other respects, derive many signal and unmingled advantages from the growth of manufactures, it is a problem whether it would gain or lose, as to the article of the number of persons employed in carrying it on.

5. As to the Furnishing Greater Scope for the Diversity of Talents and Dispositions, which Discriminate Men from Each Other

This is a much more powerful means of augmenting the fund of national industry, than may at first sight appear. It is a just observation, that minds of the strongest and most active powers for their proper objects, fall below mediocrity, and labor without effect, if confined to uncongenial pursuits. And it is thence to be inferred, that the results of human exertion may be immensely increased by diversifying its objects. When all the different kinds of industry obtain in a community, each individual can find his proper element, and can call into activity the whole vigor of his nature. And the community is benefited by the services of its respective members, in the manner in which each can serve it with most effect.

If there be any thing in a remark often to be met with, namely, that there is, in the genius of the people of this country, a peculiar aptitude for mechanic improvements, it would operate as a forcible reason for giving opportunities to the exercise of that species of talent, by the propagation of manufactures.

6. As to the Affording a More Ample and Various Field for Enterprise

This also is of greater consequence in the general scale of national exertion than might, perhaps, on a superficial view be supposed, and has effects not altogether dissimilar from those of the circumstance last noticed. To cherish and stimulate the activity of the human mind, by multiplying the objects of enterprise, is not among the least considerable of the expedients by which the wealth of a nation may be promoted. Even things in themselves not positively advantageous sometimes become so, by their tendency to provoke exertion. Every new scene which is opened to the busy nature of man to rouse and exert itself, is the addition of a new energy to the general stock of effort.

The spirit of enterprise, useful and prolific as it is, must necessarily be contracted or expanded, in proportion to the simplicity or variety of the occupations and productions which are to be found in a society. It must be less in a nation of mere cultivators, than in a nation of cultivators and merchants; less in a nation of cultivators and merchants, than in a nation of cultivators, artificers, and merchants.

7. As to the Creating, in Some Instances, a New, and Securing, in All, a More Certain and Steady Demand for the Surplus Produce of the Soil

This is among the most important of the circumstances which have been indicated. It is a principal means by which the establishment of manufactures contributes to an augmentation of the produce or revenue of a country, and has an immediate and direct relation to the prosperity of agriculture.

It is evident that the exertions of the husbandman will be steady or fluctuating, vigorous or feeble, in proportion to the steadiness or fluctuation, adequateness or inadequateness, of the markets on which he must depend for the vent of the surplus which may be produced by his labor; and that such surplus, in the ordinary course of things, will be greater or less in the same proportion.

For the purpose of this vent, a domestic market is greatly to be preferred to a foreign one; because it is, in the nature of things, far more to be relied upon.

It is a primary object of the policy of nations, to be able to supply themselves with subsistence from their own soils; and manufacturing nations, as far as circumstances permit, endeavor to procure from the same source the raw materials necessary for their own fabrics. This disposition, urged by the spirit of monopoly, is sometimes even carried to an injudicious extreme. It seems not always to be recollected, that nations who have neither mines nor manufactures can only obtain the manufactured articles of which they stand in need, by an exchange of the products of their soils; and that if those who can best furnish them with such articles are unwilling to give a due course to this exchange, they must, of necessity, make every possible effort to manufacture for themselves; the effect of which is, that the manufacturing nations abridge the natural advantages of their situation, through an unwillingness to permit the agricultural countries to enjoy the advantages of theirs, and sacrifice the interests of a mutually beneficial intercourse to the vain project of selling every thing and buying nothing.

But it is also a consequence of the policy which has been noted, that the foreign demand for the products of agricultural countries is, in a great degree, rather casual and occasional, than certain or constant. To what extent injurious interruptions of the demand for some of the staple commodities of the United States may have been experienced from that cause, must be referred to the judgment of those who are engaged in carrying on the commerce of the country; but it may be safely affirmed, that such interruptions are, at times, very inconveniently felt, and that cases not unfrequently occur, in which markets are so confined and restricted as to render the demand very unequal to the supply.

Independently, likewise, of the artificial impediments which are created by the policy in question, there are natural causes tending to render the external demand for the surplus of agricultural nations a precarious reliance. The differences of seasons in the countries which are the consumers, make immense differences in the produce of their own soils, in different years; and consequently in the degrees of their necessity for foreign supply. Plentiful harvests with them, especially if similar ones occur at the same time in the countries which are the furnishers, occasion, of course, a glut in the markets of the latter.

Considering how fast and how much the progress of new settlements in the United States must increase the surplus produce of the soil, and weighing seriously the tendency of the system which prevails among most of the commercial nations of Europe, whatever dependence may be placed on the force of natural circumstances to counteract the effects of an artificial policy, there appear strong reasons to regard the foreign demand for that surplus as too uncertain a reliance, and to desire a substitute for it in an extensive domestic market.

To secure such a market there is no other expedient than to promote manufacturing establishments. Manufacturers, who constitute the most numerous class, after the cultivators of land, are for that reason the principal consumers of the surplus of their labor.

This idea of an extensive domestic market for the surplus produce of the soil, is of the first consequence. It is, of all things, that which most effectually conduces to a flourishing state of agriculture. If the effect of manufactories should be to detach a portion of the hands which would otherwise be engaged in tillage, it might possibly cause a smaller quantity of lands to be under cultivation; but, by their tendency to procure a more certain demand for the surplus produce of the soil, they would, at the same time, cause the lands which were in cultivation to be better improved and more productive. And while by their influence, the condition of each individual farmer would be meliorated, the total mass of agricultural production would probably be increased. For this must evidently depend as much upon the degree of improvement, if not more, than upon the number of acres under culture.

It merits particular observation, that the multiplication of manufactories not only furnishes a market for those articles which have been accustomed to be produced in abundance in a country, but it likewise creates a demand for such as were either unknown or produced in inconsiderable quantities. The bowels as well as the surface of the earth are ransacked for articles which were before neglected. Animals, plants, and minerals acquire a utility and a value which were before unexplored.

The foregoing considerations seem sufficient to establish, as general propositions, that it is the interest of nations to diversify the industrious pursuits of the individuals who compose them; that the establishment of manufactures is calculated not only to increase the general stock of useful and productive labor, but even to improve the state of agriculture in particular,— certainly to advance the interests of those who are engaged in it.

(58)

Daniel Raymond

1786-1849(?)

Born near New Haven, Daniel Raymond was one of America's first important economists. He lived in Baltimore and practiced law for many years. In 1840 he moved to Cincinnati, where he lived for the remainder of his life. A highly original economist, he wrote his *Thoughts on Political Economy* because no systematic treatise on economics had yet appeared in the United States. In this work he opposed the classical English and French economists, arguing that national wealth is different from individual wealth and advocating protective tariffs for American industry. Raymond's work was imbued with a pervasive economic nationalism. It was a firm espousal of emerging capitalism though it also envisioned the utility of certain types of welfare legislation. In this and other ways his lively discussion anticipated many later economic developments.

This selection is from *Thoughts on Political Economy* (Baltimore, 1820).

If we would have correct and clear notions of national wealth, we must be careful to keep in mind the distinct notion of a nation itself, and not confound it with the individuals, or any portion of individuals of which that nation is composed; a thing that is often done by the best writers on political economy. It is indeed the prevailing error of every writer on the subject that I have read. While they profess to treat of national interests, they depart from the subject and treat of individual interests, or of the interests of some constituent part of the nation, which causes ambiguity and want of precision. This proceeds more from carelessness than ignorance, for it cannot be supposed that any writer is ignorant of the meaning of the word *nation*. It is however of little use to know the meaning of the word, unless that meaning is constantly attached to it.

A nation, it is true, is an artificial being, or a legal entity, composed of millions of natural beings; still it possesses all the properties and attributes of a being, which are as distinct and strongly marked, as the properties and attributes of any natural being, and these must be constantly borne in mind, if we would reason correctly on the interests or rights of this being.

A nation is a UNITY, and possesses all the properties of unity. It possesses a unity of rights; a unity of interests, and a unity of possessions; and he who professes to treat of the interests of this unity, but departs from them, and treats of the interests of some constituent part of it, will just as certainly arrive at a wrong conclusion, as the arithmetician would, who in performing an algebraic computation, should leave out one term of the equation.

The interests of a nation, and the interests of individuals composing that nation, may, it is true, and often are, in unison. They may be identical, but they are not necessarily so—so far is this from being the case, that they are often directly opposite. So national and individual wealth may be one and the same, but they are not necessarily so. It will be shown hereafter, that individual wealth is often national poverty, and I think I shall be able to show, conclusively, that the word wealth, as applied to individuals, never can, with propriety be applied to a nation. It is true, that an individual may be wealthy or possess wealth, but a nation never can possess wealth, in that sense of the word in which it is always applied to individuals.

What then, in the ordinary acceptation of the term, constitutes individual wealth?

The word property, includes lands, goods, money, and stock. Stock may, perhaps, more properly be denominated the representative of property, so that property, will then only include lands, goods, and money, or what lawyers denominate real and personal property, which includes every thing that is the subject of property. The quantity, or rather the value of these, that an individual possesses, ascertains the amount of his wealth, or riches. The word wealth, when applied to an individual, means nothing but property, according to the above definition. A man who has neither land nor goods, is never said to be wealthy or rich. He may possess talents or skill, which will enable him to procure the necessaries and comforts of life in great abundance, still we do not say of such a man that he is wealthy or rich, although his talents and his skill, may be a means by which he can acquire wealth. . . .

The term wealth, according to this definition, never can be applicable to a nation. No nation ever did, or ever will possess property, for the use of which, it can obtain the necessaries and comforts of life for a single day, much less for months and years. A nation, it is true, may possess money, which it may loan to other nations, and receive for the use of it, a quantity of the necessaries and comforts of life, or it may exchange the money for them, but this can never be done to any considerable extent. It is impossible, in the nature of things, that any nation should possess such a fund, as would enable it to purchase the necessaries and comforts of life, from other nations, in sufficient quantities to supply the nation for a single week; and if a quantity of property, money, goods, or lands, which will enable an individual to supply himself with the necessaries and comforts of life, for a week only, does not constitute him a man of wealth, with what propriety can it be said, that a nation, with less means, in proportion to its wants, possesses wealth in the same sense of the word?

My object is not to prove that there is, or can be, no such thing as national wealth; but only, that there is, or can be, no such thing as national wealth, in that sense of the word, in which it is applicable to individuals. From this, it will follow, that when the term wealth, is applied to a nation, in the same sense we apply it to individuals, it conveys an erroneous idea, and that national wealth is something totally distinct from individual wealth. . . .

A nation is, as it were, alone in the world. It is a huge unwieldy being, possessing as a nation no locomotive powers. It is situated at a vast distance from any other nation. Its lands it cannot rent, nor sell; but must cultivate them itself—its money it cannot loan—it daily consumes such a vast quantity of the necessaries of life, that if they were brought from foreign countries, it would require the shipping of all the world to bring them.

This huge artificial being, is composed of millions of natural beings, upon whom the sentence has been pronounced, "in the sweat of thy face shalt thou eat bread."

The same law that governs all the parts must also govern the whole. A nation never can, therefore, eat bread, but in the sweat of its own face. It may, it is true, plunder and rob its neighbors, and in that way obtain a little portion of subsistence without labor; but this is a thing of too small an amount, to be taken into consideration, in a system of political economy— it is a very small exception to the general rule.

It being then established that national wealth is something totally different from individual wealth, it follows, that the word *wealth,* when applied to a nation, must have a totally different meaning from the one we attach to it, when applied to individuals.

What then is this meaning? What is the true definition of national wealth? I shall define it, *a capacity for acquiring the necessaries and comforts of life.*

This definition will, I believe, include every thing that can constitute national wealth. A capacity for acquiring by labor, the necessaries and comforts of life, for all its citizens, is as high a degree of national wealth, as any nation ever did, or ever can hope to obtain; and the comparative wealth of different nations, will always depend upon the extent of this capacity. If one nation possesses a greater capacity for acquiring the necessaries and comforts of life than another, it possesses a greater share of national wealth.

This capacity never can exist independent of labor. Its extent, however, will depend upon a great variety of other circumstances. It will be materially influenced by the nature of the government. The energies of a nation, can be more fully developed, under a free, than under an arbitrary or tyrannical government.

This capacity will also depend materially upon the climate and soil of the country; on the extent of territory in proportion to the number of inhabitants; on the denseness of population; upon the equal or unequal division of property; upon the state of cultivation and improvement; on the degree of perfection to which the arts and sciences have been carried; on the nation's advantageous situation for commerce. But more than any one thing else, this capacity depends on the industrious habits of the people.

A nation may possess the most extensive and fertile country, susceptible of being made to yield, in the greatest abundance, all the most valuable products of the earth; still if the people have not industry, it will profit them nothing; they will be poor and wretched. On the contrary, let a country be ever so sterile by nature, yielding most sparingly the fruits of the earth, still, with industry, the people may possess a much greater capacity for acquiring the necessaries and comforts of life, than their idle neighbors, who are blessed with all the advantages of climate and soil.

An individual who possesses industrious habits, has a much greater capacity for acquiring the necessaries and comforts of life, than one in otherwise similar circumstances, but of idle habits. So a nation, whose people are confirmed in habits of industry, and are accustomed to labor, possesses a much greater capacity for acquiring the necessaries and comforts of life, than another nation, otherwise similarly situated, but whose people are of less industrious habits. Industrious habits, therefore, constitute a very important item, in the stock of national wealth.

Although a nation can never attain to positive wealth, in that sense of the word that we apply it to individuals, it does not follow, that there is no such thing as national wealth, or that it cannot be augmented. If one nation has a greater stock of industry than another, it has, in this particular, a greater capacity for acquiring the necessaries and comforts of life than the other, and therefore, a greater share of national wealth. So, if one nation has made greater improvement in the arts and sciences—in agriculture: if its lands are in a higher state of cultivation, if its roads, bridges, canals, mills, buildings, and improvements, are in a greater state of perfection than those of another nation, it has, for all these reasons, a greater capacity for acquiring the necessaries and comforts of life, and possesses a greater stock of national wealth. So, if it has a better government—if its territory be more extensive, in proportion to its population—if it be more advantageously situated for commerce—if its citizens enjoy exclusive privileges, in consequence of colonial monopolies, navigation laws, or any other laws, that give the nation advantages over other nations, it has, for all these reasons, a greater capacity for acquiring the necessaries and comforts of life, and therefore, possesses greater national wealth than a nation that does not enjoy these privileges and advantages.

This constitutes national wealth, according to the true and natural definition; still the nation is not wealthy, in that sense of the word in which we say an individual is wealthy. It is wealthy, or rich, in that sense of the word, in which an industrious mechanic is rich, who has a good trade, but no property; in that sense of the word in which a man is rich, who has a piece of land, sufficient to grow him all the necessaries of life, but which he is obliged, from necessity, to cultivate with his own hands; rich in that sense of the word, in which God made man rich, when he placed him in a situation where he had the power of "eating bread in the sweat of his face."

(59)

Roger Brooke Taney

1777-1864

Born in Maryland, Taney graduated from Dickinson College in 1795. He began his career as a lawyer, and then was elected to the state legislature as a Federalist. However, he soon broke with the Federalist party, and in 1824 he supported Jackson's candidacy. After Jackson's defeat, Taney became chairman of Jackson's campaign committee during the 1828 election. In 1831 he was named Attorney General, firmly supported Jackson in the war against the Bank, and also served briefly as Jackson's Secretary of the Treasury. In 1836, Jackson appointed Taney as Chief Justice of the Supreme Court.

His famous majority opinion in the case of *Charles River Bridge* v. *Warren Bridge* (1837) grew out of his experiences in the Bank controversy, and its argument that a grant of exclusive rights to property cannot be inferred from a public charter became a basic plank of American constitutional law. This selection from Taney's opinion is from Richard Peters, ed., *Reports of Cases Argued and Adjudged by the Supreme Court of the United States* (Philadelphia, 1837).

TANEY, C. J. . . . Borrowing, as we have done, our system of jurisprudence from the English law . . . it would present a singular spectacle, if, while the courts in England are restraining, within the strictest limits, the spirit of monopoly, and exclusive privileges in nature of monopolies, and confining corporations to the privileges plainly given to them in their charter, the courts of this country should be found enlarging these privileges by implication; and construing a statute more unfavorably to the public, and to the rights of the community, than would be done in a like case in an English court of justice. . . .

The case now before the Court is, in principle, precisely the same [as *Providence Bank v. Billings* (1830)]. It is a charter from a state; the act of incorporation is silent in relation to the contested power. The argument in favor of the proprietors of the Charles River bridge, is the same, almost in words, with that used by the Providence Bank; that is, that the power claimed by the state, if it exists, may be so used as to destroy the value of the franchise they have granted to the corporation. The argument must receive the same answer; and the fact that the power has been already exercised, so as to destroy the value of the franchise, cannot in any degree affect the principle. The existence of the power does not, and cannot, depend upon the circumstance of its having been exercised or not.

It may, perhaps, be said, that in the case of the Providence Bank, this Court were speaking of the taxing power; which is of vital importance to the very existence of every government. But the object and end of all government is to promote the happiness and prosperity of the community by which it is established; and it can never be assumed, that the government intended to diminish its power of accomplishing the end for which it was created. And in a country like ours, free, active and enterprising, continually advancing in numbers and wealth, new channels of communication are daily found necessary, both for travel and trade, and are essential to the comfort, convenience and prosperity of the people. A state ought never to be presumed to surrender this power, because, like the taxing power, the whole community have an interest in preserving it undiminished. And when a corporation alleges, that a state has surrendered, for seventy years, its power of improvement and public accommodation, in a great and important line of travel, along which a vast number of its citizens must daily pass, the community have a right to insist, in the language of this Court, above quoted, "that its abandonment ought not to be presumed, in a case, in which the deliberate purpose of the state to abandon it does not appear." The continued existence of a government would be of no great value, if, by implications and presumptions, it was disarmed of the powers necessary to accomplish the ends of its creation, and the functions it was designed to perform, transferred to the hands of privileged corporations. The rule of construction announced by the Court, was not confined to the taxing power, nor is it so limited, in the opinion delivered. On the contrary, it was distinctly placed on the ground, that the interests of the community were concerned in preserving, undiminished, the power then in question; and whenever any power of the state is said to be surrendered or diminished, whether it be the taxing power, or any other affecting the public interest, the same principle applies, and the rule of construction must be the same. No one will question, that the interests of the great body of the people of the state, would, in this instance, be affected by the surrender of this great line of travel to a single corporation, with the right to exact toll, and exclude competition, for seventy years. While the rights of private property are sacredly guarded, we must not forget, that the community also have rights, and that the happiness and well-being of every citizen depends on their faithful preservation.

Adopting the rule of construction above stated as the settled one, we proceed to apply it to the charter of 1785 to the proprietors of the Charles River bridge. This act of incorporation is in the usual form, and the privileges such as are commonly given to corporations of that kind. It confers on them the ordinary faculties of a corporation, for the purpose of building the bridge; and establishes certain rates of toll, which the company are authorized to take. This is the whole grant. There is no exclusive privilege given to them over the waters of Charles River, above or below their bridge; no right to erect another bridge themselves, nor to prevent other persons from erecting one, no engagement from the State, that another shall not be erected; and no undertaking not to sanction competition, nor to make improvements that may diminish the amount of its income. Upon all these subjects the charter is silent; and nothing is said in it about a line of travel, so much insisted on in the argument, in which they are to have exclusive privileges. No words are used from which an intention to grant any of these rights can be inferred. If the plaintiff is entitled to them, it must be implied, simply from the nature of the grant, and cannot be inferred from the words by which the grant is made. . . .

The inquiry then is, does the charter contain such a contract on the part of the State? Is there any such stipulation to be found in that instrument? It must be admitted on all hands, that there is none—no words that even relate to another bridge, or to the diminution of their tolls, or to the line of travel. If a contract on that subject can be gathered from the charter, it must be by implication, and cannot be found in the words used. Can such an agreement be implied? The rule of construction before stated is an answer to the question. In charters of this description, no rights are taken from the public, or given to the corporation, beyond those which the words of the charter, by their natural and proper construction, purport to convey. There are no words which import such a contract as the plaintiffs in error contend for, and none can be implied. . . . The whole community are interested in this inquiry, and they have a right to require that the power of promoting their comfort and convenience, and of advancing the public prosperity, by providing safe, convenient, and cheap ways for the transportation of produce and the purposes of travel, shall not be construed to have been surrendered or diminished by the State, unless it shall appear by plain words that it was intended to be done. . . .

Indeed, the practice and usage of almost every State in the Union old enough to have commenced the work of internal improvement, is opposed to the doctrine contended for on the part of the plaintiffs in error. Turnpike roads

have been made in succession, on the same line of travel; the later ones interfering materially with the profits of the first. These corporations have, in
some instances, been utterly ruined by the introduction of newer and better
modes of transportation and travelling. In some cases, railroads have rendered
the turnpike roads on the same line of travel so entirely useless, that the
franchise of the turnpike corporation is not worth preserving. Yet in none of
these cases have the corporations supposed that their privileges were invaded,
or any contract violated on the part of the State. . . .

And what would be the fruits of this doctrine of implied contracts on the
part of the States, and of property in a line of travel by a corporation, if it
should now be sanctioned by this Court? To what results would it lead us? If
it is to be found in the charter to this bridge, the same process of reasoning
must discover it, in the various acts which have been passed, within the last
forty years, for turnpike companies. . . . If this Court should establish the
principles now contended for, what is to become of the numerous railroads
established on the same line of travel with turnpike companies, and which
have rendered the franchises of the turnpike corporations of no value? Let it
once be understood that such charters carry with them these implied contracts,
and give this unknown and undefined property in a line of travelling, and
you will soon find the old turnpike corporations awakening from their sleep
and calling upon this Court to put down the improvements which have taken
their place. The millions of property which have been invested in railroads and
canals upon lines of travel which had been before occupied by turnpike
corporations will be put in jeopardy. We shall be thrown back to the improvements of the last century, and obliged to stand until the claims of the
old turnpike corporations shall be satisfied, and they shall consent to permit
these States to avail themselves of the lights of modern science, and to partake of the benefit of those improvements which are now adding to the
wealth and prosperity, and the convenience and comfort, of every other part of
the civilized world. Nor is this all. This Court will find itself impelled to fix,
by some arbitrary rule, the width of this new kind of property in a line of
travel. . . . This Court are not prepared to sanction the principles which must
lead to such results.

(60)

William Leggett

1801-1839

After attending Georgetown College, Leggett spent a short time in the
Navy as a midshipman. Then, under William Cullen Bryant, he became part owner and assistant editor of the New York *Evening Post.*

From 1836 until his death he was editor of the *Plaindealer*. A warm Jacksonian, he discussed the political issues of his day with vigor and insight. Fearless in his writings, he championed many liberal causes. His support of individual rights against special privilege in the economic field served as a healthy guidepost for America's rising capitalism.

The selection here is from Theodore Sedgwick, Jr., ed., *A Collection of the Political Writings of William Leggett*, 2 vols. (New York, 1840), vol I.

Since the organization of the Government of the United States the people of this country have been divided into two great parties. One of these parties has undergone various changes of name; the other has continued steadfast alike to its appellation and to its principles, and is now, as was at first, the DEMOCRACY. Both parties have ever contended for the same opposite ends which originally caused the division—whatever may have been, at different times, the particular means which furnished the immediate subject of dispute. The great object of the struggles of the Democracy has been to confine the action of the General Government within the limits marked out in the Constitution: the great object of the party opposed to the Democracy has ever been to overleap those boundaries, and give to the General Government greater powers and a wider field for their exercise. The doctrine of the one party is that all power not expressly and clearly delegated to the General Government, remains with the States and with the People: the doctrine of the other party is that the vigor and efficacy of the General Government should be strengthened by a free construction of its powers. The one party sees danger from the encroachments of the General Government; the other affects to see danger from the encroachments of the States.

This original line of separation between the two great political parties of the republic, though it existed under the old Confederation, and was distinctly marked in the controversy which preceded the formation and adoption of the present Constitution, was greatly widened and strengthened by the project of a National Bank, brought forward in 1791. This was the first great question which occurred under the new Constitution to test whether the provisions of that instrument were to be interpreted according to their strict and literal meaning; or whether they might be stretched to include objects and powers which had never been delegated to the General Government, and which consequently still resided with the states as separate sovereignties.

The proposition of the Bank was recommended by the Secretary of the Treasury on the ground that such an institution would be "of primary importance to the prosperous administration of the finances, and of the greatest utility in the operations connected with the support of public credit." This scheme, then, as now, was opposed on various grounds; but the constitutional objection constituted then, as it does at the present day, the main reason of the uncompromising and invincible hostility of the democracy to the measure. They considered it as the exercise of a very important power which had never been given by the states or the people to the General Government, and which the General Government could not therefore exercise without being guilty of usurpation. Those who contended that the Government possessed the power, effected their immediate object; but the controversy still exists. And it is of no consequence to tell the democracy that it is now established by various precedents, and by decisions of the Supreme Court, that this power is fairly incidental to certain other powers expressly granted; for this is only telling them that the advocates of free construction have, at time, had the ascendancy in the Executive and Legislative, and, at all times, in the Judiciary department of the Government. The Bank question stands now on precisely the same footing that it originally did; it is now, as it was at first, a matter of controversy between the two great parties of this country—between parties as opposite as day and night—between parties which contend, one for the consolidation and enlargement of the powers of the General Government, and the other for strictly limiting that Government to the objects for which it was instituted, and to the exercise of the means with which it was entrusted. The one party is for a popular Government; the other for an aristocracy. The one party is composed, in a great measure, of the farmers, mechanics, laborers, and other producers of the middling and lower classes (according to the common gradation by the scale of wealth), and the other of the consumers, the rich, the proud, the privileged—of those who, if our Government were converted into an aristocracy, would become our dukes, lords, marquises and baronets. The question is still disputed between these two parties—it is ever a new question—and whether the democracy or the aristocracy shall succeed in the present struggle, the fight will be renewed, whenever the defeated party shall be again able to muster strength enough to take the field. The privilege of self-government is one which the people will never be permitted to enjoy unmolested. Power and wealth are continually stealing from the many to the few. There is a class continually gaining ground in the community, who desire to monopolize the advantages of the Government, to hedge themselves round with exclusive privileges, and elevate themselves at the expense of the great body of the people. These, in our society, are emphatically the aristocracy; and these, with all such as their means of persuasion, or corruption, or intimidation, can move to act with them, constitute the party which are now struggling against the democracy, for the perpetuation of an odious and dangerous moneyed institution.

Putting out of view, for the present, all other objections to the United States Bank—that it is a monopoly, that it possesses enormous and overshadowing power, that it has been most corruptly managed, and that it is identified with political leaders to whom the people of the United States must ever be strongly opposed—the constitutional objection alone is an insurmountable objection to it.

The Government of the United States is a limited sovereignty. The powers which it may exercise are expressly enumerated in the Constitution. None not thus stated, or that are not "necessary and proper" to carry those which are stated into effect, can be allowed to be exercised by it. The power to establish a bank is not expressly given; neither is incidental; since it cannot be shown to be "necessary" to carry the powers which are given, or any of them, into effect. That power cannot therefore be exercised without transcending the Constitutional limits.

This is the democratic argument stated in its briefest form. The aristocratic argument in favour of the power is founded on the dangerous heresy that the Constitution says one thing, and means another. That *necessary* does not mean *necessary,* but simply *convenient.* By a mode of reasoning not looser than this is would be easy to prove that our Government ought to be changed into a Monarchy, Henry Clay crowned King, and the opposition members of the Senate made peers of the realm; and power, place, and prerequisites given to them and their heirs forever. . . .

But it is in relation to his course with regard to the Bank of the United States, that he [President Jackson] appears most emphatically as the champion of the Constitution and the EQUAL RIGHTS of the people. Fully aware of the great truth, that monopolies, whether of rank or privilege, whether possessed by virtue of hereditary descent or conferred by legislative folly or legislative corruption, were the most sly and dangerous enemies to equal rights ever devised by the cunning of avarice or the wiles of ambition, he saw in the vast accumulation of power in that institution, and its evident disposition to exercise, as well as perpetuate it, the elements of destruction to the freedom of the people and the independence of their government. He, therefore, with the spirit and firmness becoming his character and station as the ruler of a free people, determined to exercise his constitutional prerogative in arresting its usurpations, and preventing their being perpetuated.

The child, the champion, and the representative of the great democracy of the United States, he felt himself identified with their interests and feelings. He was one of themselves, and as such had long seen and felt the oppressions which a great concentrated money power, extending its influence, nay, its control, over the currency, and consequently the prosperity of the country throughout every nook and corner of the land, had inflicted or might inflict upon the people. He saw in the nature, and in the acts, of this enormous monopoly, an evident tendency, as well as intention, to subjugate the states and their government to its will; and like himself, and in conformity with the whole tenor of his life, he resolved to risk his place, his popularity, his repose, in behalf of the EQUAL RIGHTS of the people.

He saw, moreover, as every true democrat must see, who interprets the Constitution upon its true principles, that the creation of a Bank with the privilege of establishing its branches in every state, without their consent, was not delegated by the states to the general government; and he saw that by one of the first declaratory amendments of the Constitution, that *"The powers not delegated to the United States by the Constitution, nor prohibited to it by the states, are reserved to the states respectively, or to the people."*

But there is, unfortunately, a clause in the Constitution, which is somewhat of the consistency of India rubber, and by proper application can be stretched so as to unite the opposite extremes of irreconcilable contradictions. It is somewhat like the old gentleman's will in the Tale of a Tub, about which Lord Peter, Martin and Jack disputed so learnedly, and which at one time was a loaf of brown bread, at another a shoulder of mutton. It admits of a wonderful latitude of construction, and an ingenious man can find no great difficulty in interpreting it to suit his own particular interests. We allude to the following, which will be found among the enumeration of the powers of Congress:

"To make all laws which shall be *necessary and proper* for carrying into execution the foregoing powers, and all other powers vested in the government of the United States, or in any department or officer thereof."

The sticklers for state rights in the Convention which adopted the Constitution, and in the State Conventions to which it was referred for acceptance or rejection, did not much relish this saving clause. They imagined they saw in it a sort of Pandora's box, which if only fairly opened, would cast forth a legion of constructive powers and constructive usurpations. They thought they perceived in these two little words "NECESSARY PROPER" a degree of elasticity which might be expanded so as to comprehend almost any thing that a majority of Congress might choose to ascribe to them. They were, in our opinion, not much mistaken in their anticipations, although probably they scarcely dreamed that the constructive ingenuity of the times would find that to be indispensably "necessary" which the country was enabled for many years to dispense with, during which time it enjoyed a degree of prosperity which excited the envy and admiration of the world!

However this may be, the people of the United States will do well to bear in mind, when they hear General Jackson denounced as a tyrant and usurper for the course he has pursued in relation to the Bank, that this institution has no other legs in the Constitution to stand upon than those two, little words "necessary and proper." If it is necessary and proper, then it may be rechartered under the Constitution; but it has no right to demand a recharter. If it is not necessary and proper, then it ought never to have been chartered, and ought not to be continued one moment longer than the faith of the nation is pledged.

As this is one of those points which rests on the nice interpretation of words, it naturally depends for its decision on the general bias of the two parties in the controversy. The party attached by habit, education, interests, or prejudice to a consolidated or strong government, will interpret "necessary and proper" one way, and the party opposed to any accumulation of constructive powers in the federal government, will interpret them the other way. General Hamilton, for example, considered a Bank of the United States "necessary and proper," while Mr. Jefferson believed, and has repeatedly denounced it, to be the most dangerous infraction of the constitution ever attempted under the cloak of constructive power. Such has always been the opinion of the great leaders of the democracy of the United States, although some of them have yielded to the voice of a majority of Congress, mistaking it for that of the people.

We have premised thus much in order to show that the course pursued by General Jackson, in regard to the Bank of the United States, is in perfect consonance with the known principles of the democracy, the people of the United States. When the Democratic Party had the ascendency, they took the first opportunity that offered to put an end to the First Bank of the United States, and now they avail themselves of a similar occasion to give a like demonstration of their settled principles and policy. General Jackson would not have been re-elected by that party, against all the corruptions of the Bank, combined with the whole force of all the disjointed, incongruous elements of opposition, *after* he had placed his Veto on its re-charter, had he not acted in this instance in strict conformity with the sentiments of a great majority of the democracy of the United States. Here as in every other act of his administration, they saw in him the great opponent of monopolies, the stern, inflexible champion of EQUAL RIGHTS.

With regard to the other alleged acts of despotism charged upon this true unwavering patriot, such as the removal of Mr. Duane from office, and the appointment of one of the very ablest and purest men of this country in his stead; the subsequent removal of the deposits from the Bank of the United States, and the protest against the ex parte condemnation of the "Independent Aristocratic Body," more has already been said in his defence than such charges merited. We do not believe the Senators making them believed one word they themselves uttered on the subject, because, though tainted to the core by personal antipathies and personal ambition, they are men of too clear intellect, seriously to cherish such ideas of the constitution as they have lately put forth to the people. These speeches and denunciations, like those on the subject of universal distress and bankruptcy, were merely made for effect. They certainly could not believe that what the constitution expressly delegates was intended to be withheld; that what was expressly conceded by the charter of the Bank of the United States was intended to be denied; or that the exercise of a privilege inherent in human nature, to wit, that of self-defence, was an outrage on the privileges of the Senate. Real honest error may sometimes be combated successfully by argument; but we know of no way of convincing a man who only affects to be in the wrong in order to deceive others, and shall therefore spare ourselves and our readers any further discussion with opponents who are not in earnest, but who have so high an opinion of the sagacity of the people, that they think they can make them believe what they do not believe themselves.

It will be perceived from this brief analysis of the leading measures of General Jackson's administration, that all his "tyranny" has consisted in successfully interposing the Constitution of the United States in defence of the EQUAL RIGHTS of the people; and that all his "usurpations" have been confined to checking those of the advocates of consolidation, disunion, monopolies, and lastly a great consolidated moneyed aristocracy, equally dangerous to liberty from the point it legally possesses, and those it has usurped. Yet this is the man whom the usurpers themselves denounce as a usurper. This is the man against whom the concentrated venom of disappointed ambition and baffled avarice is vainly striving to contend in the heads and hearts of the American people, and bury under a mass of wilful calumnies. This is the very man whose whole soul is wound up to the great and glorious task of restoring the EQUAL RIGHTS of his fellow-citizens, as they are guaranteed by the letter and spirit of the constitution. May Providence send us a succession of such usurpers as Andrew Jackson, and spare the people from such champions of liberty as Henry Clay, John C. Calhoun, Daniel Webster, George Poindexter, and Nicholas Biddle! . . .

"DO NOT GOVERN TOO MUCH," is a maxim which should be placed in large letters over the speaker's chair in all legislative bodies. The old proverb "too much of a good thing is good for nothing," is most especially applicable to the present time, when it would appear, from the course of our legislation, that common sense, common experience, and the instinct of self-preservation, are utterly insufficient for the ordinary purposes of life; that the people of the United States are not only incapable of self-government, but of taking cognizance of their individual affairs; that industry requires protection, enterprise bounties, and that no man can possibly find his way in broad day light without being tied to the apron string of a legislative dry-nurse. The present system of our legislation seems founded on the total incapacity of mankind to take care of themselves or to exist without legislative enactment. Individual property must be maintained by invasions of personal rights, and the "general welfare" secured by monopolies and exclusive privileges.

The people of the United States will discover when too late that they may be enslaved by laws as well as by the arbitrary will of a despot; that unnecessary restraints are the essence of tyranny; and that there is no more effectual instrument of depriving them of their liberties, than a legislative body, which is permitted to do anything it pleases under the broad mantle of THE PUBLIC GOOD—a mantle which, like charity, covers a multitude of sins, and like charity is too often practised at the expense of other people.

XIV

American Revivalism

AMERICA'S RELIGIOUS CONCERN, noted in earlier periods of its history, continued into the nineteenth century. Unlike some of their European counterparts, Americans invoked religious premises for their thought and action. They sought to provide religious justification for their most cherished beliefs —individualism, human rights, liberty, and equal opportunity (and even, in the South, for the institution of slavery). This concern was also expressed in a number of religious trends.

The deism of the preceding generation that had so often been called upon to sanction revolutionary purposes was now a much weakened force, partly because of the excesses of the French Revolution, which had become identified with deism and even atheism, and partly because of the failure of deism to satisfy the religious and emotional needs of Americans. In its place came a revival of religious fervor known as the Second Great Awakening. Led by such men as President Timothy Dwight of Yale, it inspired a nationwide religious zeal that was reflected in renewed missionary activities among the Indians, and, more importantly, in the increased religious fervor in nearly all sects and denominations, whether rural or urban. In the East a new Unitarianism sought to liberalize Christianity and relate it to the advances of science. Roman Catholicism, organized under Bishop John Carroll, continued its growth as immigration increased after 1815. Finally, a bewildering number of new religious sects sprang up, fostered perhaps by the expanse and individualism of America.

The camp meeting, America's unique contribution to religion, also developed during this period. As the frontier moved westward, evangelical Protestantism accompanied it, especially that of the Baptists and Methodists. It was to meet the peculiar needs of the frontier, with its scattered population, its lack of established churches and clergy, and its isolated and emotionally deprived circumstances that the camp meeting arose. To the tents of the evangelical preachers, settlers came from miles around. The camp meeting often lasted for several days. Revival services stressing the themes of heaven and hell, sin and salvation, were interspersed with periods of social get-togethers where families could visit with neighbors and friends. In this way, the camp meeting provided at least a minimum of social and religious fulfillment. It brought the frontier both religious idealism and social fellowship.

By mid-century the fervor underlying renewed Christian faith permeated American life, supporting and sustaining it. Evangelical Protestantism especially seemed to support the basic American ideals of liberty, individualism, and mission: liberty, for redemption from sin freed the believer; individualism, for the call of the Gospel was to the individual believer; and mission, for evangelicalism fostered the millennial hope. Even America's emphasis on the practical found support in evangelicalism, for revival meetings served emotional needs in a direct, pragmatic way, and later were to issue in a variety of reform movements.

This chapter in the history of American religion has often been criticized. And it is true that the religion of the period sometimes led to an excessive emotionalism that developed few theological interests. It is also true that it fostered anti-intellectualism, and produced individuals who were religious but not always devout, and sometimes confused the religious mission with practical human wishes. Yet revivalism played an important, even a necessary, role in the development of the nation. American life, and especially the frontier, was, as Professor Gabriel observed, "crude, turbulent, and godless. Evangelical Protestantism, more than any other force, tamed it."[1]

(61)

Timothy Dwight

1752-1817

Entering Yale at the age of thirteen, Dwight graduated in 1769 with highest honors. He soon became a prominent member of the group of Federalist writers known as the "Hartford Wits." During the Revolutionary War he served as an instructor at West Point; afterward he settled in Massachusetts, where his fame as a writer and Congregationalist preacher quickly spread.

Dwight's mother was Mary Edwards, daughter of Jonathan Edwards, who had helped inspire the first Great Awakening in the 1730's. Theologically, Dwight belonged to the school of his grandfather. A rigid Calvinist and staunch Federalist, he warned his generation against the perils of both infidelity and democracy. As president of Yale from 1795 to 1817, Dwight was the personification of the finest qualities in Connecticut Puritanism—and also of its narrowness.

This selection is from *The Dignity and Excellence of the Gospel* (New York, 1812).

1. Ralph H. Gabriel, *The Course of American Democratic Thought,* 2nd ed. (New York, 1956), p. 33.

The Gospel, by which I intend, in this discourse, the Scriptures at large, is a *History of the Mediatorial Kingdom of the Deity;* of that kingdom, which involves all the concerns of the children of Adam. From every other history it is infinitely different in the nobleness of its subject. Kings and heroes, nations and empires, the highest subjects of other histories, have here little significance. Jehovah is the Potentate, the Messiah the Hero, his children the nation, his actions the events, and his kingdom the empire, which engross the labors of the sacred historians.

The Design of this kingdom, is the salvation of an endless multitude of immortal beings. In this design are equally included their deliverance from sin and misery, and their exaltation to virtue and happiness, which will know no end.

The Theatre, in which this design, and all the events, connected with its accomplishment, are complete, is proportionally majestic; and is formed of heaven, earth, and hell; the stage of probation, and the seats of retribution, for the righteous and the wicked.

Proportionally dignified also, are *the Actors* in this magnificent plot. Kings and nations are, here, forgotten. Moral dignity is alone regarded, where the design is salvation; and the actors, employed in accomplishing it, are prophets and apostles, the general Assembly of the first-born, principalities, and powers, in heavenly places, and the infinitely glorious persons of the Godhead.

The Duration of this kingdom is eternal.

The Laws, by which it is governed, are, like the Author of them, holy, just, and good. They are so simple, as to be comprised in two commands; yet so extensive, as to reach all the possible actions of intelligent creatures; so short, and so plain, as to be sufficiently understood, easily remembered, and obviously applied by every moral agent; so honourable to the law-giver, as if nothing beside his honour had been consulted in their formation; so beneficent to his subjects, as if devised only for their happiness.

The Ultimate End of this kingdom is the manifestation of the glory, or excellency, of God. For the accomplishment of this end, *He, who was in the form of God, and thought it no robbery to be equal with God, made himself of no reputation; took upon him the form of a servant; and was made in the likeness of men. And being found in fashion as a man, he became obedient unto death, even the death of the cross. Wherefore God hath highly exalted him, and given him a name, which is above every name, that is named in this world, and that which is to come: that of the name of Jesus every knee should bow, of things in heaven, and things in the earth, and things under the earth; and every tongue confess, that he is Lord, to the glory of God, the Father.*

The benevolence of God is the glory of his character. "*God,*" saith the apostle John, "*is love.*" This peculiarly divine attribute was illustriously displayed to the angels in heaven, in the communication of their exalted powers, in quickening their minds with unmingled virtue, and in replenishing them with pure and immortal enjoyment. But these *just* beings *need no repentance.* They have ever been obedient, and, therefore, have ever been happy. They could not be forgiven; for they had never sinned. They could not be redeemed; for they had never been cast off.

But in fallen man the benevolence of God found a new object; an object, on which its finished beauty might be exhibited in a manner, unknown even to angels. *God commendeth his love to us,* to angels, and to all beings, who are witnesses of it, *in that, while we were yet sinners, he gave his Son to die for us.* This is the consideration, on which the apostles dwell with such transport, when they descant upon *the height and the depth, the length and the breadth, of the love of Christ, which passeth knowledge.* This was the theme, which warmed the tongue of the angel, when he said to the shepherds of *Bethlehem,* "*Behold I bring you glad tidings of great joy, which shall be unto all people!*" This was the enrapturing subject, which tuned the voices of his heavenly companions when they sang, "*Glory to God in the highest, and on earth peace; good-will towards men!*"

Mankind were the lowest order of rational beings; were born of the dust; and were allied to worms. Still they had revolted from God; and with the impudence, as well as the hostility, of rebellion, had said unto him, "*Depart from us, for we desire not the knowledge of thy ways. Who is the Almighty, that we should serve him; and what profit shall we have, if we pray unto him?*" Although *His eternal power and Godhead were from the beginning, clearly seen* throughout the world, *being* every where *understood by* any mind willing to understand them; they denied his perfections; impeached his government; questioned his existence; and *said in their hearts,* "*There is no God.*" *Creatures,* and those the vilest, and most insignificant, *they worshipped, rather than the Creator.* From the east to the west, from the north to the south, temples innumerable, raised for the worship of stocks, and men, and devils, insulted the Skies: and altars, *from the rising of the sun, to the going down of the same,* smoked, not with incense and oblations only; not with victims, selected from the fold and the stall; but with human blood. Nations immolated the best, and brightest youths of their age and country. Parents *caused their* own *children to pass through the fire unto Moloch.*

Equally gross, vile, and dreadful, was their conduct to each other. Rulers wielded a sceptre of iron: and every where set up the gaol and the gibbet, the stake and the cross, as the instruments of their sway, and the symbols of their character. The hero waded through the blood, and planted his laurels amid the bones, of men. Fields were *sown with salt;* and cities rose in flames to heaven. The robber haunted the high-way; the thief prowled around the cottage; and the assassin lurked behind the curtain of night. The soul was infected with a plague; and without a physician, without a remedy, to check the malignant poison, it decayed, died, and became a loathsome mass of corruption.

Thus the world was one great scene of desolation. Nor were its miseries allayed even by hope, that *balm of Gilead* to *a wounded spirit.* Its *situation* was dreadful; its *prospects* were replete with horror. With heaven its communication was cut off. God was unknown, and forgotten. The path of life was unoccupied, and unsought. Year after year, and age after age, rolled over its melancholy regions; and saw no messenger arrive from distant, happier climes, with tidings of restoration, or deliverance. It was a world in ruins; a vast sepulchre, hung round with darkness, and replenished with decay and death; where no sound of consolation pierced the slumbering ear, and no beam of hope reillumined the eye, closed in eternal night.

On such a world it was impossible for God to look without abhorrence. That righteous law, by which he governs the universe, had declared, *"The soul, which sinneth, shall die."* But every child of *Adam* had sinned: all, therefore, were irreversibly condemned to death. Nor could the *law pass,* without the fulfilment of every *jot, and tittle,* included in it; although the fulfilment should require the destruction of *the heavens and the earth.* In this state of absolute despair, *the Father of all mercies* was pleased to say, *"Deliver the soul of man from going down to the pit; for I have found a ransom."* Heaven was startled at the declaration; and the bosoms of all its inhabitants trembled with astonishment and rapture. They had seen their own apostate companions cast out of the regions of happiness, and *"reserved in chains, under darkness, to the judgment of the great day."* No favourable destiny could be expected for man.

The ransom found, was the life of the Son of God, the brightness of his glory, and the express image of his person. The gift, on the part of the Father, was the greatest of all gifts. The self-denial on the part of the Son, was the highest possible self-denial. The sacrifice was infinite; and could not be demanded even by a suffering universe. It was conceived only by boundless wisdom; it could be executed only by boundless love.

The destiny of our race, announced by the law of God, and the reversion, proclaimed by the Gospel of his Son, will strongly illustrate the nature of this transaction. The interests of the immense and eternal kingdom of JEHOVAH demand, absolutely, the final exclusion of all those, who rebel against his government, from every future good. Sin is the die, which, cast once, is cast for ever. The career, once entered upon, is endless. None that commence it turn again; neither take they hold of the paths of life. Misery is both its concomitant, and its consequence. To sin, and suffer, through ages which cannot end, was, therefore, the certain, final allotment of every child of Adam. The sin was entire; the suffering was complete. The sinner was removed beyond the desire, and beyond the attainment, of any virtuous, or amiable quality. The sufferer was placed beyond the hope, and beyond the possibility, of any alleviation, or of any end of his woe. To such beings, how vast must be the accumulation of wretchedness, in the progress of ages! Proportional is the value of the deliverance, and the extent of the wisdom, and goodness, by which it is accomplished.

Proportionally bright and glorious, also, is the destiny, opened by the promises of the Gospel. "He, that spared not his own Son," saith the apostle, "but delivered him up for us all, how shall he not with him, also, freely give us all things?" The greatest gift He has already bestowed; it cannot be strange, that He should willingly give every thing else to those, on whom it was bestowed. A mind here, pure and perfect, united to a body immortal like itself, and refashioned like the glorious body of Christ, will begin and advance in, an eternal progress of knowledge, virtue, and enjoyment; of gratitude, adoration, and praise; of moral glory, and divine beauty; in the house of God; amid the innumerable company of angels; and united to the general assembly of the first born. Beneficence will be its business; heaven will be its home. No enemy will disturb, no fear lessen, no casualty interrupt, and no succession of ages terminate, the transports of the blessed. Before the throne of infinite mercy they will sing, with the harps of angels, "Unto Him, that loved us, and washed us from our sins in his own blood, and hath made us kings, and priests, unto God, even his Father; to him be glory, and dominion for ever. Amen."

Perfectly suited to the magnificence of this scheme are the Doctrines and Precepts of the Gospel. The doctrines are, every where, such as become the Author of them; such as *become godliness;* such as are plainly derived from the Wisdom, and fraught with the Excellence, of JEHOVAH. His character is here drawn by an unerring hand. The lines are all lines of the most perfect symmetry; the colours are the colours of heaven. United, they form the only portrait, beneath the sun, in which is seen the likeness of a God. Heathen philosophers, and modern Infidels, have only caricatured their Maker.

Equally noble and excellent are the Precepts. The heathen philosophers understood not the nature of virtue, or of vice; nor discerned the boundary, by which they are separated. Infidels have voluntarily blended them; and left them a mere mass of mixture and confusion. The distinction between them was originally begun, and has ever been continued, in the Gospel. With a discrimination, unknown to all other moral systems, it separates universally, good and evil thoughts, words, and actions; and suffers not a single transgression of the most exact, and most refined, bounds of virtuous conduct.

So comprehensive are the doctrines of the Gospel that they involve all moral truth, known by man: so extensive are the precepts, that they require every virtue, and forbid every sin. Nothing has been added to either by the labours of philosophy, or the progress of human experience.

Proportionally noble, also, are the sentiments, and even the descriptions, contained in the Gospel. Compared with them the highest efforts of Greece and Rome, celebrated as they have have been, are low, little, and childish. This was, indeed, a thing of course. The gods, whose characters and actions were the basis of their moral and religious systems, were themselves vicious, grovelling, despicable beings; greatly inferior in respectability, and worth, to such men, as Atticus, or *Titus Vespasian.* But the mind of the moral teacher will never ascend higher, than the character, which he forms of the object of his worship. In some instances, I readily acknowledge, they uttered noble and sublime thoughts concerning their deities; particularly concerning Jupiter, the chief of their dii majores[1] gentium. But, for all these thoughts they were indebted, originally, to hints, gleaned from foreigners, and derived ultimately from Revelation. Aided in this manner, their minds, which, in several instances, were of a superior mold, formed conceptions of this nature, which were honourable to their talents. But every such effort was merely the leap, not the steady flight, of imagination: much less was it the elevated course of enlightened intelligence. Accordingly the whole representation of the subject, made by any such writer, is a monstrous mass of debasement, varied, in solitary instances only, by more just and elevated conceptions. By the Scriptural writers we are uniformly presented, not with the unworthy actions of gods plural; imperfect; mutable; debased with human immoralities; unable to discern, or prevent, the course of things established by fate; dissenting from each other with mutual enmity, and mutual sufferings, endangered by the rebellion of creatures, and defended by their assistance; but with the perfect agency of JEHOVAH; by whose wisdom all things were contrived; by whose word they were created; by whose arm they are upheld; and to whose glory, with a solemn progress, they unceasingly operate; unfolded in images, and declarations, so noble and majestic, as to wear on their very face the impression of divinity.

The Catastrophe, by which all the intricacies, and wonders, of this immense plot are unravelled, is formed by the proceedings of the final day. The Son of God will then descend from heaven in clouds; surrounded by the glory of his Father, and accompanied by all his holy Angels. He will then summon the dead from the grave; and reanimate the dust, of which their bodies were formed. The innumerable nations of men will stand upon their feet in a moment; and be gathered around the tribunal of Infinite Justice. The wicked will be doomed to everlasting fire, prepared for the devil and his angels: and the righteous admitted to the kingdom, prepared for them from the foundation of the world. The visible *heavens will* then *pass* away with a great noise; the earth will be consumed with fire; the Son will deliver up the Kingdom to God, even the Father; and God will be all in all.

Thus, my brethren, have I attempted to illustrate the nature of this subject; and have exhibited, in a very imperfect and summary manner, the parts, of which it is primarily constituted. Into these things angels earnestly desire to look, and all, who, like angels, relish the beauty, greatness, and glory, of the Godhead.

---

1. Superior gods.

(62)

Charles G. Finney

1792-1875

Long associated with Oberlin College, Finney served as its president from 1851 to 1866. He began his career as a lawyer in New York, but his own reading of the Bible and certain personal experiences resulted in an emotionally intense religious conversion. In 1824 he was licensed to preach by the St. Lawrence Presbytery, and he began to conduct revival services throughout the middle and eastern states. Finney was masterful in portraying man's guilt and disobedience and he had a remarkable appeal to all classes of Americans.

Finney was the outstanding evangelist of the early nineteenth century. His theology was that of a New England Calvinist, but his emphasis on the efficacy of individual repentance was unique.

The selection reprinted here is from his *Lectures on Systematic Theology* (Oberlin, 1846), which were delivered during his tenure at Oberlin, where he was called after his revival work.

How Moral Depravity Is to be Accounted For

1. It consists, remember, in the committal of the will to the gratification or indulgence of self—in the will's following or submitting itself to be governed by the impulses and desires of the sensibility instead of submitting itself to the law of the intelligence.

2. This definition of the thing shows how it is to be accounted for namely: The sensibility acts as a powerful impulse to the will from the moment of birth, and secures the consent and activity of the will to procure its gratification, before the reason is at all developed. The will is thus committed to the gratification of feeling and appetite, when first the idea of moral obligation is developed. This committed state of the will is not moral depravity, and has no moral character until the idea of moral obligation is developed. The moment this idea is developed, this committal of the will to self-indulge must be abandoned or it becomes selfishness, or moral depravity. But as the will is already in a state of committal, and has to some extent already formed the habit of seeking to gratify feeling, and as the idea of moral obligation is at first but feebly developed, unless the Holy Spirit interferes to shed light on the soul, the will, as might be expected retains its hold on self-gratification. Here moral character does and must commence. Let it be remembered that

selfishness consists in the supreme and ultimate choice, or in the preference of self-gratification as an end, or for its own sake, over all other interests. Now, as the choice of an end implies and includes the choice of the means, selfishness of course, causes all that outward life and activity that makes up the entire history of sinners.

This selfish choice is the wicked heart—the sinful nature—the propensity to sin—the sinful appetite—the craving for sin, and all that causes what is generally termed actual transgression. This sinful choice, is properly enough called indwelling sin. It is the latent, standing, controlling preference of the mind, and the cause of all the outward and active life. It is not the choice of sin, but the choice of self-gratification, which choice is sin.

Again. It should be remembered that the physical depravity of our race has much to do with our moral depravity. A diseased physical system renders the appetites, passions, temper, and propensities more clamorous and despotic in their demands, and of course confirms and strengthens selfishness. It should be distinctly understood that physical depravity has no moral character in itself. But yet it is a source of fierce temptation to selfishness. The human sensibility is, manifestly, deeply physically depraved, and as sin or moral depravity consists in committing the will to the gratification of the sensibility, its physical depravity will mightily strengthen moral depravity. Moral depravity is then universally owing to temptation. That is, the soul is tempted to self-indulgence, and yields to the temptation, and this yielding, and not the temptation, is sin or moral depravity. This is manifestly the way in which Adam and Eve became morally depraved. They were tempted, even by un-depraved appetite, to prohibited indulgence, and were overcome. The sin did not lie in the constitutional desire of food, or of knowledge, nor in the excited state of these appetites or desires, but in the consent of the will to prohibited indulgence. . . .

The Universal Necessity of Regeneration

1. The necessity of regeneration as a condition of salvation must be coextensive with moral depravity. This has been shown to be universal among the unregenerate moral agents of our race. It surely is impossible that a world or a universe of unholy or selfish beings should be happy. It is impossible that heaven should be made up of selfish beings. It is intuitively certain that without benevolence or holiness no moral being can be ultimately happy. Without regeneration a selfish soul can by no possibility be fitted either for the employments or for the enjoyments of heaven.

2. The scriptures expressly teach the universal necessity of regeneration. "Jesus answered and said unto him, Verily, verily, I say unto thee, Except a man be born again, he cannot see the kingdom of God."—Jon. 3: 3. "For in Christ Jesus neither circumcision availeth any thing, nor uncircumcision but a new creature."—Gal. 6: 15.

Agencies Employed in Regeneration

1. The scriptures often ascribe regeneration to the Spirit of God. "Jesus answered, Verily, verily, I say unto Thee, Except a man be born of water and of the Spirit, he cannot enter into the Kingdom of God. That which is born of the flesh is flesh; and that which is born of the Spirit is spirit."— Jon. 1: 15.

2. We have seen that the subject is active in regeneration, that regeneration consists in the sinner changing his ultimate choice, intention, preference; or in changing from selfishness to love or benevolence; or in other words in turning from supreme choice of self-gratification to the supreme love of God and the equal love of his neighbor. Of course the subject of regeneration must be an agent in the work.

3. There are generally other agents, one or more human beings concerned in persuading the sinner to turn. The bible recognizes both the subject and the preacher as agents in the work. Thus Paul says: "I have begotten you through the gospel." Here the same word is used which is used in another case where regeneration is ascribed to God. . . .

Instrumentalities Employed in the Work

1. Truth. This must from the nature of regeneration be employed in effecting it, for regeneration is nothing else than the will being duly influenced by truth.

2. There may be and often are many providences concerned in enlightening the mind and in inducing regeneration. These are instrumentalities. They are means or instruments of presenting the truth. Mercies, judgments, men, measures, and in short all those things that conduce to enlightening the mind, are instrumentalities employed in affecting it.

Those who hold to physical or constitutional moral depravity must hold of course to constitutional regeneration, and of course consistency compels them to maintain that there is but one agent employed in regeneration, and that is the Holy Spirit, and that no instrument whatever is employed, because the work is according to them an act of creative power; that the very nature is changed and of course no instrument can be employed, any more than in the creation of the world. These theologians have affirmed over and over again that regeneration is a miracle; that there is no tendency whatever in the gospel however presented, and whether presented by God or man, to regenerate the heart. Dr. Griffin in his Park Street Lectures maintains that the gospel in its natural and necessary tendency creates and perpetuates only opposition to and hatred of God until the heart is changed by the Holy Spirit. He understands the carnal mind to be not a voluntary state, not a minding of the flesh, but the very nature and constitution of the mind, and that the enmity against God is a part, attribute, or appetite of the nature itself. Consequently he must deny the adaptability of the gospel to regenerate the soul. It has been proclaimed by this class of theologians times without number that there is no philosophical connection between the preaching of the gospel and the regeneration of sinners, no adaptedness in the gospel to produce that result; but on the contrary that it is adapted to produce an opposite result. The favorite illustrations of their views have been Ezekiel's prophesying over the dry bones and Christ's restoring sight to the blind man by putting clay on his eyes. Ezekiel's prophesying over the dry bones had no tendency to quicken them they say. And the clay used by the Savior was calculated rather to destroy than to restore sight. This shows how easy it is for men to adopt a pernicious and absurd philosophy and then find or think they find it supported by the bible. What must be the effect of inculcating the dogma that the gospel has nothing to do with regenerating the sinner? Instead of telling him that regeneration is nothing else than his embracing the gospel to tell him that he must wait and first have his constitution recreated before he can possibly do any thing but oppose God? This is to tell him the greatest and most abominable and ruinous of falsehoods. It is to mock his intelligence. What! call on him on pain of eternal death to believe, to embrace the gospel; to love God with all his heart and at the same time, represent him as entirely helpless and constitutionally the enemy of God and of the gospel and as being under the necessity of waiting for God to regenerate his nature before it is possible for him to do otherwise than to hate God with all his heart? O Orthodoxy, falsely so called, how absurd and false thou art! What an enemy of God; what a stumbling block to man; what a leaven of unrighteousness and of hell is such a dogma as this! But a few years have elapsed since almost the entire church were settled down in the delusion of a passive regeneration.

In regeneration the subject is both passive and active.

1. That he is active is plain from what has been said and from the nature of the change.

2. That he is at the same time passive is plain from the fact that he acts only when and as he is acted upon. That is, he is passive in the perception of the truth presented by the Holy Spirit. I know that this perception is no part of regeneration. It is the condition and the occasion of regeneration. Therefore the subject of regeneration must be a passive recipient or percipient of the truth presented by the Holy Spirit at the moment and during the act of regeneration. The Spirit acts upon him through or by the truth. Thus far he is passive. He closes with the truth. Thus far he is active. What a mistake those theologians have fallen into who represent the subject as altogether passive in regeneration! This rids the sinner at once of the conviction of any duty or responsibility about it. It is wonderful that such an absurdity should have been so long maintained in the church. But while it is maintained, it is no wonder that sinners are not converted to God. Why, while the sinner

believes this, it is impossible if he has it in mind that he should be regenerated. He stands and waits for God to do what God requires him to do, and which no one can do for him. Neither God nor any other being can regenerate him if he will not turn. If he will not change his choice, it is impossible that it should be changed. Sinners who have been taught thus and have believed what they have been taught, would never have been regenerated had not the Holy Spirit drawn off their attention from this error, and ere they were aware, induced them to close in with the offer of life.

What is Implied in Regeneration

1. The nature of the change shows that it must be instantaneous. It is a change of choice or of intention. This must be instantaneous. The preparatory work of conviction and enlightening the mind may have been gradual and progressive. But when regeneration occurs, it must be instantaneous.

2. It implies an entire present change of moral character, that is, a change from entire sinfulness to entire holiness. We have seen that it consists in a change from selfishness to benevolence. We have also seen that selfishness and benevolence cannot co-exist in the same mind; that selfishness is a state of supreme and entire consecration to self; that benevolence is a state of entire and supreme consecration to God and the good of the universe. Regeneration then surely implies an entire change of moral character.

Again: The bible represents regeneration as a dying to sin and becoming alive to God. Death in sin is total depravity. This is generally admitted. Death to sin and becoming alive to God, must imply entire present holiness.

3. The scriptures represent regeneration as the condition of salvation in such a sense that if the subject should die immediately after regeneration and without any further change, he would go immediately to heaven.

Again: The scripture requires only perseverance in the first love as the condition of salvation, in case the regenerate soul should live long in the world subsequent to regeneration.

4. When the scriptures require us to grow in grace and in the knowledge of the Lord Jesus Christ, this does not imply that there is yet sin remaining in the regenerate heart which we are required to put away only by degrees. But the spirit of the requirement must be that we should acquire as much knowledge as we can of our moral relations, and continue to conform to all truth as fast we know it. This and nothing else is implied in abiding in our first love, or abiding in Christ, living and walking in the Spirit, etc. . . .

5. The true saint is distinguished by his firm adherence to all the principles and rules of the Divine government. He is a reformer from principle, and needs not the gale of popular excitement or of popular applause to put and keep him in motion. His intellect and conscience have taken the control of his will, or the will has renounced the impulses of the sensibility as its law, and voluntarily committed itself to the demands of the reason. This fact must

appear both on the field of his consciousness, and also in most instances be very manifest to others. His zeal does not wax and wane with every breeze of excitement. He is not carried away by every change in the effervescing sensibility. The law of reason being written in his heart, he does not at one time appear reasonable and to be influenced by conscience and a regard to the law of love, and at another to be infinitely unreasonable and to have little or no regard to God or his laws. He fears and shuns popular excitements as he does all other temptations. He loathes and resists them. The excitements of politics and business and amusements are regarded by him with a jealous eye. He dreads their influence on his sensibility, and when he feels them, it causes a deep struggle and groaning of spirit, because the will, adhering to the law of conscience, steadfastly resists them. Such like excitements instead of being his element and the aliment of his life, are a grief and a vexation to him. Instead of living, and moving, and having his being as it were in the midst of them and by them, he is only annoyed by them. They are not the moving spring of his activity, but only embarrass his spiritual life. His spiritual life is founded in the law of the intelligence, and supported by the light of the Holy Spirit poured upon his intellect through the truth. He steadily resists the flood tides of mere feeling on every subject and abides truth and principle and moral law whatever may be the circumstances of worldly or religious excitement around him. Be it ever remembered, it is moral law, moral principle, the law of love, and not mere feeling, that governs him.

The sinner or deceived professor, for they are one, is right over against this. Excitement is his element and his life. He has truly no moral principle except in theory. He is never truly influenced by truth, law, reason, but always by excitement of some kind. His activity is based on this; hence he is not disturbed and embarrassed in his movements by excitements of any kind, any longer than it takes to put down one form of excitement and take on another. If when he is much interested and excited and carried away in one direction, a counter influence or excitement comes in his way, he is taken aback for the time being. He is disconcerted and embarrassed, perhaps displeased. But you will soon see him go about and fill away to the new excitement. Excitement is his life, and although like a ship at sea, he is thrown into temporary confusion by a sudden change of the winds and waves, so, like her whose life and activity are the breezes and gale and the ocean wave, he readily accommodates his sails and his course to the ever changing breeze and currents of excitement in the midst of which he loves to live, and on the foaming surface of which he is borne along. If you wish to move him, you must strongly appeal to his feelings. Reason does not, can not govern him. 'Tis not enough to say to him, Thus saith the Lord. He will admit the right, but surely will not do it. He will not go that way, unless you can first make his feelings move in that direction. He holds the truth only in theory and in unrighteousness. It is not the law of his life, his heart, his warmest affections and sympathies. Present considerations to his intelligence: unless they excite his sensibility, and arouse his hopes, or fears, or feelings in some direction, you might as well attempt to change the course of the winds by your words. His imagination must be aroused and set on fire. His sensibility must be reached, enkindled. The gales of excitement must be awaked, and the mainspring of his action must be touched and directed to impel his will, before you can quicken him into life. His feelings are his law.

The saint is justified, and he has the evidence of it in the peace of his own mind. He is conscious of obeying the law of reason and of love. Consequently he naturally has that kind and degree of peace that flows from the harmony of his will with the law of his intelligence. He sometimes has conflicts with the impulses of feeling and desire. But unless he is overcome, these conflicts, though they may cause him inwardly and perhaps audibly to groan, do not interrupt his peace. There are still the elements of peace within him. His heart and conscience are at one, and while this is so, he has thus far the evidence of justification in himself. That is, he knows that God can not condemn his present state. Conscious as he is of conformity of heart to the moral law he can not but affirm to himself that the lawgiver is pleased with his present attitude. But further, he has also within the Spirit of God witnessing with his spirit that he is a child of God, forgiven, accepted, adopted. He feels the filial spirit drawing his heart to exclaim, Father, Father. He is conscious that he pleases God and has God's smile of approbation.

He is at peace with himself because he affirms his heart to be in unison with the law of love. His conscience does not upbraid, but smile. The harmony of his own being is a witness to himself that this is the state in which he was made to exist. He is at peace with God, because he and God are pursuing precisely the same end and by the same means. There can be no collision, no controversy between them. He is at peace with the universe in the sense that he has no ill-will and no malicious feelings or wish to gratify in the injury of any one of all the creatures of God. He has no fear but to sin against God. He is not influenced on the one hand by the fear of hell, nor on the other by the hope of reward. He is not anxious about his own salvation, but prayerfully and calmly leaves that question in the hands of God and concerns himself only to promote the highest glory of God and the good of being. "Being justified by faith he has peace with God through our Lord Jesus Christ." "There is now no condemnation to them that are in Christ Jesus, who walk not after the flesh, but after the Spirit."

The sinner's experience is the opposite of this. He is under condemnation, and seldom can so far deceive himself, even in his most religious moods, as to imagine that he has a consciousness of acceptance either with his own conscience or with God. There is almost never a time in which he has not a greater or less degree of restlessness and misgiving within. Even when he is most engaged in religion as he supposes, he finds himself dissatisfied with himself. Something is wrong. There is a struggle and a pang. He may not exactly see where and what the difficulty is. He does not after all obey reason and conscience, and is not governed by the law and will of God. Not having the consciousness of this obedience, his conscience does not smile. He sometimes feels deeply, and acts as he feels, and is conscious of being sincere in the sense of feeling what he says and acting in obedience to deep feeling. But this does not satisfy conscience. He is more or less wretched after all. He has not true peace. Sometimes he has a self-righteous quiet and enjoyment. But this is neither peace of conscience nor peace with God. He after all feels uneasy and condemned, notwithstanding all his feeling and zeal and activity. They are not of the right kind. Hence they do not satisfy the conscience. . . .

God's will is not his law; but his own sensibility is his law. With him it is not enough to know the will of God; he must also have his sensibility excited in that direction before he goes. He does not mean or expect to avoid every form and degree of iniquity. His heart has not renounced sin as sin. It has not embraced the will of God from principle, and of course has not embraced the whole will of God. With him it is a small thing to commit what he calls little sins. This shows conclusively where he is. If the will of God were his law—as this is as really opposed to what he calls little as to what he calls great sins, he would not expect and intend to disobey God in one thing more than in another. He could know no little sins, since they conflict with the will of God. He goes about to pick and choose among the commandments of God, sometimes yielding an outward obedience to those that conflict least with his inclinations, and which therefore will cost him the least self-denial, but evading and disregarding those that lay the ax to the root of the tree and prohibit all selfishness. The sinner or deceived professor does not in fact seriously mean or expect wholly to obey God. He thinks that this is common to all Christians. He as much expects to sin every day against God as he expects to live, and does not think this at all inconsistent with his being a real though imperfect Christian. He is conscious of indulging in some sins, and that he has never repented of them and put them away, but he thinks that this also is common to all Christians, and therefore it does not slay his false hope. He would much sooner indulge in gluttony than in drunkenness because the latter would more seriously affect his reputation. He would not hesitate to indulge wanton thoughts and imaginations when he would not allow himself in outward licentiousness because of its bearing upon his character, and as he says, upon the cause of God. He will not hesitate to take little advantages of his neighbor, to amass a fortune in this way while he would recoil from robbing on the highway or on the high seas; for this would injure his reputation with man, and as he thinks, more surely destroy his soul. Sinners sometimes become exceedingly self-righteous and aim at what they call perfection. But unless they are very ignorant they soon become discouraged and cry out, O wretched man that I am, who shall deliver me from the body of this death? They, however, almost always satisfy themselves with a mere outward morality and that, as I have said, not descending to what they call little sins.

(63)

Peter Cartwright
1785-1872

Peter Cartwright was one of the most notable camp-meeting preachers of the Middle West. Born in Kentucky, he was converted to Methodism at the age of sixteen during a camp meeting. He then began to proselytize among his acquaintances and, although he had little schooling, he was given a license to preach in 1802. For fifty years he rode Methodist circuits in Kentucky, Tennessee, Indiana, Illinois, and Ohio. His descriptions of the circuit rider's life and experiences provide an excellent portrait of the emotional yet muscular Christianity practiced among the midwesterners.

This selection is from one of his autobiographical works, *The Backwoods Preacher* (New York, 1857).

My appointment, during 1805–6, was on the Scioto Circuit, Ohio State and District. John Sale was presiding elder, and James Quinn was senior preacher, or preacher in charge. The reader will see how greatly I was favoured the first two years of my regular itinerant life, to be placed under two such men as Benjamin Lakin and James Quinn, and more, two such presiding elders as William M'Kendree and John Sale. These four men were able ministers of Jesus Christ, lived long, did much good, witnessed a good confession, died happy, and are all now safely housed in heaven. Peace to their memory for ever!

Scioto Circuit extended from the Ohio River to Chillicothe, situated on that river; and crossed it near the mouth, at what is now called Portsmouth. It was a four-weeks' Circuit, and there were 474 members on it. Dr. Tiffin, who was governor of the State, was a local preacher; and both he and his wife were worthy members of our Church. He lived at Chillicothe, then the seat of government for the State.

There were two incidents happened while I was on the east end of this Circuit, which I will relate.

We had an appointment near Eagle Creek. Here the Shakers broke in Mr. Dunlevy, whom we have mentioned elsewhere as having been a regular Presbyterian minister, who had left that Church and joined the New Lights. His New Light increased so fast, that he lost what little sense he had, and was now a ranting Shaker. He came up here, and roared and fulminated a

while, led many astray, flourished for some time, and then his influence died away, and he left for parts unknown.

On the south-eastern part of the Circuit, we took in a new preaching place, at a Mr. Moor's. We gave them Sunday preaching. Mr. Moor had built a large hewn log-house, two stories high. There was no partition in the second story; but it was seated, and he gave it to us to preach in. Not far from this place lived a regularly educated Presbyterian preacher, who had a fine family, and was in many respects a fine man, but, unhappily, he had contracted a love for strong drink. He had preached in this neighborhood, and was much beloved, for he was withal a very good preacher.

In making my way on one occasion to Mr. Moor's, to my Sunday appointment, I got lost and was belated, and when I arrived, there was a large assembly collected, and this minister was preaching to them, and he preached well, and I was quite pleased with the sermon so far as I heard it. When he was done, he undertook to make a public apology for a drunken spree he had got into a few days before. "Well," thought I, "this is right; all right, I suppose!" But to excuse himself for his unaccountable love of whiskey, he stated that he had been informed by his mother that before he was born she longed for whiskey; and he supposed that this was the cause of his appetite for strong drink, for he had loved it from his earliest recollection. This was the substance of his apology.

I felt somewhat indignant at this; and when I rose to close after him, I stated to the congregation that I thought the preacher's apology for drunkenness was infinitely worse than the act of drunkenness itself; that I looked upon it as a lie, and a downright slander on his mother; and that I believed his love of whiskey was the result of the intemperate use of it, in which he had indulged until he formed the habit; and that I, for one, was not willing to accept or believe the truth of his apology; that I feared the preacher would live and die a drunkard, and be damned at last; and that I hoped the people there would not receive him as a preacher until he gave ample evidence that he was entirely cured of drunkenness.

After I made these statements, I felt that God was willing to bless the people there and then; and, raising my voice, gave them as warm an exhortation as I could command. Suddenly an awful power fell on the congregation, and they instantly fell right and left, and cried aloud for mercy. I suppose there were not less than thirty persons smitten down; the young, the old, the middle-aged, indiscriminately, were operated on in this way. My voice at that day was strong and clear; and I could sing, exhort, pray, and preach almost all the time, day and night. I went through the assembly, singing, exhorting, praying, and directing poor sinners to Christ. While I was thus engaged, the Presbyterian minister left.

There were a few scattered members of the Church around this place, who got happy and shouted aloud for joy, and joined in and exhorted sinners, and they helped me very much. Indeed, our meeting lasted all night, and the greater part of next day. Between twenty and thirty professed religion, and joined the Church; and fully as many more went home under strong conviction and in deep distress. Many of them afterward obtained religion, and joined the Church.

There was a very remarkable case that I will mention here. There was one lady about forty-five years old, who was a member of the Presbyterian Church, and a very rigid predestinarian. Her husband was a Methodist, and several of their children had obtained religion among the young converts. This lady got powerfully convicted, and concluded that she never had any religion. She had fallen to the floor under the mighty power of God. She prayed and agonized hard for days. At length the devil tempted her to believe that she was a reprobate, and that there was no mercy for her. She went into black despair under this temptation of the devil, and such was the desperate state of her mind, that at length she conceived that she was Jesus Christ, and took it upon her, in this assumed character, to bless and curse any and all that came to see her.

The family were, of course, greatly afflicted, and the whole neighbourhood were in great trouble at this afflictive dispensation. Her friends and all of us used every argument in our power, but all in vain. She at length utterly refused to eat, or drink, or sleep. In this condition she lingered for thirteen days and nights, and then died without ever returning to her right mind. A few persecutors and opposers of the Methodists tried to make a great fuss about this affair, but they were afraid to go far with it, for fear the Lord would send the same affliction on them.

The Hockhocking River lay immediately north of us, the Scioto River between us. John Meek and James Axley were assigned to that circuit. The Circuit reached from Scioto to Zanesville, on the Muskingum River. It was a hard and laborious Circuit. Brother Meek's health failed, and Brother Sale, our presiding elder, moved me from Scioto, and placed me on this Circuit with Brother Axley. I was sorry to leave the Brethren on the Scioto Circuit, and especially Brother Quinn, whom I dearly loved; but Brother Sale was still my presiding elder, and Brother Quinn's family lived in Hockhocking Circuit, and a precious family it was.

I got to see Brother Quinn every round. Brother Axley and myself were like Jonathan and David. There were no parsonages in those days, and Brother Quinn lived in a little cabin on his father-in-law's land. He had several children, and his cabin was small. When the preachers would come to see him, they would eat and converse with Brother Quinn and family, but would sleep at old Father Teel's, Brother Quinn's father-in-law. The first time I came round, I spent the afternoon with Brother Quinn. He made some apologies, and told me I could sleep better at Father Teel's. "But," said he, "I will tell you how you must do. You will sleep, at Father Teel's, in one part of his double cabin; he and his family will sleep in the other. His custom is to rise early. As soon as ever he dresses himself he commences giving out a hymn, sings, and then goes to prayer; he does not even wait for his family to get up. He serves the preachers the same way. He never was known to wait

a minute for any preacher except Bishop Asbury. You must rise early, dress quickly, and go right into the other room, if you want to be at morning prayer. I thought I would tell you beforehand, that you might not be taken by surprise."

I thanked him. "But," said I, "why don't the preachers cure the old man of this disorderly way?"

"O, he is old and set in his way," said Brother Quinn.

"You may rest assured I will cure him," said I.

"O, no," said he, "you cannot."

So I retired to old Father Teel's to sleep. We had family prayer, and I retired to rest. I had no fear about the matter; for I was a constant early riser, and always thought it very wrong for preachers to sleep late and keep the families waiting on them. Just as day broke I awoke, rose up, and began to dress; but had not nigh accomplished it when I distinctly heard Teel give out his hymn and commence singing, and about the time I had got dressed I heard him commence praying. He gave thanks to God that they had been spared through the night, and were all permitted to see the light of a new day, and at the same time I suppose every one of his family were fast asleep. I deliberately opened the door and walked out to the well, washed myself, and then walked back to my cabin. Just as I got to the door, the old brother opened his door, and, seeing me, said:—

"Good morning, sir. Why, I did not know you were up."

"Yes," said I; "I have been up some time."

"Well, brother," said he, "why did you not come in to prayers?"

"Because," said I, "it is wrong to pray of a morning in the family before we wash."

The old brother passed on, and no more was said at that time. That evening, just before we were about to retire to rest, the old brother set out the book and said to me:—

"Brother, hold prayers with us."

"No, sir," said I.

Said he: "Come, brother, take the book and pray with us."

"No, sir," said I; "you love to pray so well you may do it yourself."

He insisted, but I persistently refused, saying,—

"You are so fond of praying yourself, that you even thanked God this morning that He had spared you all to see the light of a new day, when your family had not yet opened their eyes, but were all fast asleep. And you have such an absurd way of holding prayers in your family, that I do not wish to have anything to do with it."

He then took up the book, read, and said prayers, but you may rely on it the next morning things were much changed. He waited for me, and had all his family up in order. He acknowledged his error, and told me it was one of the best reproofs he ever got. I then prayed with the family, and after that all went on well.

Our last quarterly-meeting was a camp-meeting. We had a great many tents, and a large turn-out for a new country, and, perhaps, there never was a greater collection of rabble and rowdies. They came drunk, and armed with dirks, clubs, knives, and horse-whips, and swore they would break up the meeting. After interrupting us very much on Saturday night, they collected early on Sunday morning, determined on a general riot. At eight o'clock I was appointed to preach. About the time I was half through my discourse, two very fine-dressed young men marched into the congregation with loaded whips, and hats on, and rose up and stood in the midst of the ladies, and began to laugh and talk. They were near the stand, and I requested them to desist and get off the seats; but they cursed me, and told me to mind my own business, and said they would not get down.

I stopped trying to preach, and called for a magistrate. There were two at hand, but I saw they were both afraid. I ordered them to take these men into custody, but they said they could not do it. I told them, as I left the stand, to command me to take them, and I would do it at the risk of my life. I advanced toward them. They ordered me to stand off, but I advanced. One of them made a pass at my head with his whip, but I closed in with him, and jerked him off the seat. A regular scuffle ensued. The congregation by this time were all in commotion. I heard the magistrates give general orders, commanding all friends of order to aid in suppressing the riot. In the scuffle I threw my prisoner down, and held him fast; he tried his best to get loose; I told him to be quiet, or I would pound his chest well. The mob rose, and rushed to the rescue of the two prisoners, for they had taken the other young man also. An old and drunken magistrate came up to me, and ordered me to let my prisoner go. I told him I should not. He swore if I did not, he would knock me down. I told him to crack away. Then one of my friends, at my request, took hold of my prisoner, and the drunken justice made a pass at me; but I parried the stroke, and seized him by the collar and the hair of the head, and, fetching him a sudden jerk forward, brought him to the ground, and jumped on him. I told him to be quiet, or I would pound him well. The mob then rushed to the scene; they knocked down seven magistrates, and several preachers and others.

I gave up my drunken prisoner to another, and threw myself in front of the friends of order. Just at this moment, the ringleader of the mob and I met; he made three passes at me, intending to knock me down. The last time he struck at me, by the force of his own effort, he threw the side of his face toward me. It seemed at that moment I had not power to resist temptation, and I struck a sudden blow in the burr of the ear and dropped him to the earth. Just at that moment the friends of order rushed by hundreds on the mob, knocking them down in every direction. In a few minutes, the place became too strait for the mob, and they wheeled and fled in every direction; but we secured about thirty prisoners, marched them off to a vacant tent, and put them under guard till Monday morning, when they were tried, and every man was fined to the utmost limits of the law. The aggregate amount of fines and costs was near three hundred dollars. They fined my old drunken magis-

trate twenty dollars, and returned him to court, and he was cashiered of his office. On Sunday, when we had vanquished the mob, the whole encampment was filled with mourning; and although there was no attempt to resume preaching till evening, yet such was our confused state, that there was not then a single preacher on the ground willing to preach, from the presiding elder, John Sale, down. Seeing we had fallen on evil times, my spirit was stirred within me. I said to the elder, "I feel a clear conscience; for under the necessity of the circumstances we have done right; and now I ask to let me preach."

"Do," said the elder; "for there is no other man on the ground can do it."

The encampment was lighted up, the trumpet blown, I rose in the stand, and required every soul to leave the tents and come into the congregation. There was a general rush to the stand. I requested the brethren, if ever they prayed in all their lives, to pray now. My voice was strong and clear, and my preaching was more of an exhortation and encouragement than anything else. My text was, "The gates of hell shall not prevail." In about thirty minutes the power of God fell on the congregation in such a manner as is seldom seen; the people fell in every direction, right and left, front and rear. It was supposed that not less than three hundred fell like dead men in mighty battle; and there was no need of calling mourners, for they were strewed all over the camp-ground; loud wailings went up to heaven from sinners for mercy, and a general shout from Christians, so that the noise was heard afar off. Our meeting lasted all night, and Monday and Monday night; and when we closed on Tuesday, there were two hundred who had professed religion, and about that number joined the Church.

XV

The Transcendentalist
Interlude

NEW ENGLAND TRANSCENDENTALISM was another characteristic expression of the American mind. Unsatisfied by the Enlightenment's rationalism or the religion of their own day, distrustful both of the new science and the emphasis on business and materialism, Transcendentalists sought a new faith. The result was a high romantic idealism mixed with a practical sense of social responsibility. Less a systematic philosophy than a "call" or an individual challenge, Transcendentalism sought to redefine the American ideal of individualism in terms of a romantic *Weltanschauung* and to promote the humanitarian ends that view entailed.

For their philosophical and theological views, Transcendentalists drew inspiration from many sources, especially Christianity (or more precisely, Unitarianism), Platonism, and Oriental mysticism. And though they expressed their convictions in highly individualistic ways, they did develop a core of central doctrines that defined their position. They accepted the Christian ethic and shared its belief that the world has a moral purpose and destiny. The moral law, wrote Emerson, "lies at the center of nature and radiates to the circumference." Every physical fact, he believed, is related to and expresses a moral fact: hence all reality must be viewed in moral terms. Secondly, the Transcendentalists accepted the Platonic doctrine that the world of nature is not the real world, but merely the appearance or phenomenon of a more basic spiritual reality. Since nature had no substantive reality of its own, it follows that nature is divine only as it expresses the divine spirit. Thirdly, the Transcendentalists, following Eastern mystics, believed that man has the ability to know "higher" truths directly or intuitively. Thus they believed that a philosophy limiting knowledge to the wisdom of the senses could only be partial and inadequate; it was their view that man could grasp moral and spiritual truths by direct insight. Finally, the Transcendentalists believed in the divinity and dignity of man, urging that man's free creative capacities give him the potential for higher development if he would but practice self-trust and self-reliance.

Transcendentalist humanitarianism was an outgrowth of this final point, the worth of the individual. Channing made the moral character and concerns of God and men basic in his philosophy of Unitarianism. Parker in his many writings and activities fought against privilege and social injustice from a theological vantage point; he has been called America's first "theological rebel," and was also the most distinguished metaphysician of the group. Thoreau, concerned for a true democracy that recognized the individual, wrestled with such social problems as individual rights, justice, and majority rule. All members of the group—even to some extent the remote Emerson—identified themselves with the major reform movements of the day, from abolition to labor law reforms. Thus the Transcendentalist creed combined an intense idealism with pragmatic involvement.

Transcendentalism produced the only major American philosophers to appear in the century and a half between Jonathan Edwards and the Pragmatists. (The men of the Enlightenment never realized their potential for philosophical achievement, perhaps because they were too narrowly interested in political affairs.) However, Transcendentalism itself did not develop into a major American philosophy, or even a widely held doctrine. Its idealism was philosophical and theoretical, whereas the idealism of most Americans was moral and practical. Its distrust of science and technology did not suit the temper of an industrializing nation, nor did it clearly enough define the relation between philosophic thought and social action.

(64)

William Ellery Channing
1780-1842

After studying at Harvard, Channing became a tutor to the children of a wealthy Virginia planter. His stay in the South left him with a strong hatred of slavery and he began to develop humanitarian interests. Returning to New England in 1803, he became Unitarian minister of the Federal Street Society, and remained in this position throughout his life. Clear in style, tolerant in manner, yet aristocratic in temper, Channing was one of the most effective speakers and writers of his generation.

Channing has been identified with both the American Enlightenment and Transcendentalism. Many of his religious conceptions are akin to those of the Enlightenment: individualism, the goodness of man, human brotherhood, the unity of God, and the centrality of moral character. Yet he also believed with the Transcendentalists that every human being has within him the greatest idea of all, the idea of God. These concepts are presented in the following sermon on "Unitarian Christianity," which has been called the best expression of the belief of the new denomination. Channing also became the leader of the liberal wing of the Christian church in America, and his attacks on Calvinism caused a modification in Calvinist tenets that had been firmly defended since the time of John Cotton.

This selection is from *A Sermon delivered at the Ordination of the Reverend Jared Sparks, Baltimore, May 5, 1819* (Baltimore, 1819).

I Thess. 5:21: *Prove all things; hold fast that which is good.*

The peculiar circumstances of this occasion not only justify but seem to demand a departure from the course generally followed by preachers at the introduction of a brother into the sacred office. It is usual to speak of the nature, design, duties, and advantages of the Christian ministry; and on these topics I should now be happy to insist, did I not remember that a minister is to be given this day to a religious society whose peculiarities of opinion have drawn upon them much remark, and, may I not add, much reproach. Many good minds, many sincere Christians, I am aware, are apprehensive that the solemnities of this day are to give a degree of influence to principles which they deem false and injurious. The fears and anxieties of such men I respect; and, believing that they are grounded in part on mistake, I have thought it my duty to lay before you, as clearly as I can, some of the distinguishing opinions of that class of Christians in our country who are known to sympathize with this religious society. I must ask your patience, for such a subject is not to be despatched in a narrow compass. I must also ask you to remember that it is impossible to exhibit, in a single discourse, our views of every doctrine of revelation, much less the differences of opinion which are known to subsist among ourselves. I shall confine myself to topics on which our sentiments have been misrepresented, or which distinguish us most widely from others. May I not hope to be heard with candor? God deliver us all from prejudice and unkindness, and fill us with the love of truth and virtue!

There are two natural divisions under which my thoughts will be arranged. I shall endeavor to unfold, 1st, The principles which we adopt in interpreting the Scriptures; and 2ndly, Some of the doctrines which the Scriptures, so interpreted, seem to us clearly to express.

I. We regard the Scriptures as the records of God's successive revelations to mankind, and particularly of the last and most perfect revelation of his will by Jesus Christ. Whatever doctrines seem to us to be clearly taught in the Scriptures, we receive without reserve or exception. We do not, however, attach equal importance to all the books in this collection. Our religion, we believe, lies chiefly in the New Testament. The dispensation of Moses, compared with that of Jesus, we consider as adapted to the childhood of the human race, a preparation for a nobler system, and chiefly useful now as serving to confirm and illustrate the Christian Scriptures. Jesus Christ is the only master of Christians, and whatever he taught, either during his personal ministry or by his inspired Apostles, we regard as of divine authority, and profess to make the rule of our lives.

Our leading principle in interpreting Scripture is this, that the Bible is a book written for men, in the language of men, and that its meaning is to be sought in the same manner as that of other books. We believe that God, when He speaks to the human race, conforms, if we may so say, to the established rules of speaking and writing. How else would the Scriptures avail us more than if communicated in an unknown tongue? . . .

We profess not to know a book which demands a more frequent exercise of reason than the Bible. In addition to the remarks now made on its infinite connections, we may observe, that its style nowhere affects the precision of science or the accuracy of definition. Its language is singularly glowing, bold, and figurative, demanding more frequent departures from the literal sense than that of our own age and country, and consequently demanding more continual exercise of judgment. We find, too, that the different portions of this book, instead of being confined to general truths, refer perpetually to the times when they were written, to states of society, to modes of thinking, to controversies in the church, to feelings and usages which have passed away, and without the knowledge of which we are constantly in danger of extending to all times and places what was of temporary and local application. We find, too, that some of these books are strongly marked by the genius and character of their respective writers, that the Holy Spirit did not so guide the Apostles as to suspend the peculiarities of their minds, and that a knowledge of their feelings, and of the influences under which they were placed, is one of the preparations for understanding their writings. With these views of the Bible, we feel it our bounden duty to exercise our reason upon it perpetually, to compare, to infer, to look beyond the letter to the spirit, to seek in the nature of the subject and the aim of the writer his true meaning; and, in general, to make use of what is known for explaining what is difficult, and for discovering new truths. . . .

We do not announce these principles as original, or peculiar to ourselves. All Christians occasionally adopt them, not excepting those who most vehemently decry them when they happen to menace some favorite article of their creed. All Christians are compelled to use them in their controversies with infidels. All sects employ them in their warfare with one another. All willingly avail themselves of reason when it can be pressed into the service of their own party, and only complain of it when its weapons wound themselves. None reason more frequently than those from whom we differ. It is astonishing what a fabric they rear from a few slight hints about the fall of our first parents; and how ingeniously they extract from detached passages mysterious doctrines about the divine nature. We do not blame them for reasoning so abundantly, but for violating the fundamental rules of reasoning, for sacrificing the plain to the obscure, and the general strain of Scripture to a scanty number of insulated texts. . . .

II. Having thus stated the principles according to which we interpret Scripture, I now proceed to the second great head of this discourse, which is, to state some of the views which we derive from that sacred book, particularly those which distinguish us from other Christians.

1. In the first place, we believe in the doctrine of God's UNITY, or that there is one God, and one only. To this truth we give infinite importance, and we feel ourselves bound to take heed lest any man spoil us of it by vain philosophy. The proposition that there is one God seems to us exceedingly plain. We understand by it that there is one being, one mind, one person, one intelligent agent, and one only, to whom underived and infinite perfection and dominion belong. We conceive that these words could have conveyed no other meaning to the simple and uncultivated people who were set apart to be the depositaries of this great truth, and who were utterly incapable of understanding those hairbreadth distinctions between being and person which the sagacity of later ages has discovered. We find no intimation that this language was to be taken in an unusual sense, or that God's unity was a quite different thing from the oneness of other intelligent beings.

We object to the doctrine of the Trinity, that whilst acknowledging in words, it subverts in effect, the unity of God. According to this doctrine, there are three infinite and equal persons, possessing supreme divinity, called the Father, Son, and Holy Ghost. Each of these persons, as described by theologians, has his own particular consciousness, will, and perceptions. They love each other, converse with each other, and delight in each other's society. They perform different parts in man's redemption, each having his appropriate office, and neither doing the work of the other. The Son is mediator, and not the Father. The Father sends the Son, and is not himself sent; nor is He conscious, like the Son, of taking flesh. Here, then, we have three intelligent agents, possessed of different consciousness, different wills, and different perceptions, performing different acts, and sustaining different relations; and if these things do not imply and constitute three minds or beings, we are utterly at a loss to know how three minds or beings are to be formed. It is difference of properties, and acts, and consciousness, which leads us to the belief of different intelligent beings, and, if this mark fails us, our whole knowledge falls; we have no proof that all the agents and persons in the universe are not one and the same mind. When we attempt to conceive of three Gods, we can do nothing more than represent to ourselves three agents, distinguished from each other by similar marks and peculiarities to those which separate the persons of the Trinity; and when common Christians hear these persons spoken of as conversing with each other, loving each other, and performing different acts, how can they help regarding them as different beings, different minds?

We do, then, with all earnestness, though without reproaching our brethren, protest against the irrational and unscriptural doctrine of the

Trinity. "To us," as to the Apostle and the primitive Christians, "there is one God, even the Father." With Jesus, we worship the Father, as the only living and true God. We are astonished that any man can read the New Testament and avoid the conviction that the Father alone is God. We hear our Saviour continually appropriating this character to the Father. We find the Father continually distinguished from Jesus by this title. "God sent his Son." "God anointed Jesus." Now, how singular and inexplicable is this phraseology, which fills the New Testament, if this title belong equally to Jesus, and if a principal object of this book is to reveal him as God, as partaking equally with the Father in supreme divinity! We challenge our opponents to adduce one passage in the New Testament where the word God means three persons, where it is not limited to one person, and where, unless turned from its usual sense by the connection, it does not mean the Father. Can stronger proof be given that the doctrine of three persons in the Godhead is not a fundamental doctrine of Christianity? . . .

2. Having thus given our views of the unity of God, I proceed, in the second place, to observe that we believe in the unity of Jesus Christ. We believe that Jesus is one mind, one soul, one being, as truly one as we are, and equally distinct from the one God. We complain of the doctrine of the Trinity, that, not satisfied with making God three beings, it makes Jesus Christ two beings, and thus introduces infinite confusion into our conceptions of his character. This corruption of Christianity, alike repugnant to common sense and to the general strain of Scripture, is a remarkable proof of the power of a false philosophy in disfiguring the simple truth of Jesus.

According to this doctrine, Jesus Christ, instead of being one mind, one conscious, intelligent principle, whom we can understand, consists of two souls, two minds; the one divine, the other human; the one weak, the other almighty; the one ignorant, the other omniscient. Now we maintain that this is to make Christ two beings. To denominate him one person, one being, and yet to suppose him made up of two minds, infinitely different from each other, is to abuse and confound language, and to throw darkness over all our conceptions of intelligent natures. According to the common doctrine, each of these two minds in Christ has its own consciousness, its own will, its own perceptions. They have, in fact, no common properties. The divine mind feels none of the wants and sorrows of the human, and the human is infinitely removed from the perfection and happiness of the divine. Can you conceive of two beings in the universe more distinct? We have always thought that one person was constituted and distinguished by one consciousness. The doctrine that one and the same person should have two consciousnesses, two wills, two souls, infinitely different from each other, this we think an enormous tax on human credulity. . . .

3. Having thus given our belief on two great points, namely that there is one God, and that Jesus Christ is a being distinct from and inferior to God, I now proceed to another point on which we lay still greater stress. We believe in the *moral perfection of God*. We consider no part of theology so im-

portant as that which treats of God's moral character; and we value our views of Christianity chiefly as they assert his amiable and venerable attributes.

It may be said that in regard to this subject all Christians agree, that all ascribe to the Supreme Being infinite justice, goodness, and holiness. We reply, that it is very possible to speak of God magnificently, and to think of him meanly; to apply to his person high-sounding epithets, and to his government principles which make him odious. The Heathens called Jupiter the greatest and the best; but his history was black with cruelty and lust. We cannot judge of men's real idea of God by their general language, for in all ages they have hoped to soothe the Deity by adulation. We must inquire into their particular views of his purposes, of the principles of his administration, and of his disposition towards his creatures.

We conceive that Christians have generally leaned towards a very injurious view of the Supreme Being. They have too often felt as if He were raised, by his greatness and sovereignty, above the principles of morality, above those eternal laws of equity and rectitude to which all other beings are subjected. We believe that in no being is the sense of right so strong, so omnipotent, as in God. We believe that his almighty power is entirely submitted to his perceptions of rectitude; and this is the ground of our piety. It is not because He is our Creator merely, but because He created us for good and holy purposes; it is not because his will is irresistible, but because his will is the perfection of virtue, that we pay him allegiance. We cannot bow before a being, however great and powerful, who governs tyrannically. We respect nothing but excellence, whether on earth or in heaven. We venerate not the loftiness of God's throne, but the equity and goodness in which it is established.

We believe that God is infinitely good, kind, benevolent, in the proper sense of these words—good in disposition as well as in act; good not to a few, but to all; good to every individual, as well as to the general system.

We believe, too, that God is just; but we never forget that his justice is the justice of a good being, dwelling in the same mind, and acting in harmony, with perfect benevolence. By this attribute we understand God's infinite regard to virtue or moral worth expressed in a moral government; that is, in giving excellent and equitable laws, and in conferring such rewards, and inflicting such punishments, as are best fitted to secure their observance. God's justice has for its end the highest virtue of the creation, and it punishes for this end alone; and thus it coincides with benevolence; for virtue and happiness, though not the same, are inseparably conjoined. . . .

4. Having thus spoken of the unity of God; of the unity of Jesus, and his inferiority to God; and of the perfections of the divine character; I now proceed to give our views of the mediation of Christ, and of the purposes of his mission. With regard to the great object which Jesus came to accomplish, there seems to be no possibility of mistake. We believe that he was sent by the Father to effect a moral or spiritual deliverance of mankind; that is, to

rescue men from sin and its consequences, and to bring them to a state of everlasting purity and happiness. We believe, too, that he accomplishes this sublime purpose by a variety of methods—by his instructions respecting God's unity, parental character, and moral government, which are admirably fitted to reclaim the world from idolatry and impiety, to the knowledge, love, and obedience of the Creator; by his promises of pardon to the penitent, and of divine assistance to those who labor for progress in moral excellence; by the light which he has thrown on the path of duty; by his own spotless example, in which the loveliness and sublimity of virtue shine forth to warm and quicken as well as guide us to perfection; by his threatenings against incorrigible guilt; by his glorious discoveries of immortality; by his sufferings and death; by that signal event, the resurrection, which powerfully bore witness to his divine mission, and brought down to men's senses a future life; by his continual intercession, which obtains for us spiritual aid and blessings; and by the power with which he is invested of raising the dead, judging the world, and conferring the everlasting rewards promised to the faithful. . . .

5. Having thus stated our views of the highest object of Christ's mission, that it is the recovery of men to virtue, or holiness, I shall now, in the last place, give our views of the nature of Christian virtue, or true holiness. We believe that all virtue has its foundation in the moral nature of man, that is, in conscience, or his sense of duty, and in the power of forming his temper and life according to conscience. We believe that these moral faculties are the grounds of responsibility, and the highest distinctions of human nature, and that no act is praiseworthy any further than it springs from their exertion. We believe that no dispositions infused into us without our own moral activity are of the nature of virtue, and therefore we reject the doctrine of irresistible divine influence on the human mind, moulding it into goodness as marble is hewn into a statue. Such goodness, if this word may be used, would not be the object of moral approbation, any more than the instinctive affections of inferior animals, or the constitutional amiableness of human beings.

By these remarks, we do not mean to deny the importance of God's aid or Spirit; but by his Spirit we mean a moral, illuminating, and persuasive influence, not physical, not compulsory, not involving a necessity of virtue. We object, strongly, to the idea of many Christians respecting man's impotence and God's irresistible agency on the heart, believing that they subvert our responsibility and the laws of our moral nature, that they make men machines, that they cast on God the blame of all evil deeds, that they discourage good minds, and inflate the fanatical with wild conceits of immediate and sensible inspiration. . . .

I have thus given the distinguishing views of those Christians in whose names I have spoken. We have embraced this system not hastily or lightly, but after much deliberation; and we hold it fast, not merely because we believe it to be true, but because we regard it as purifying truth, as a doctrine according to godliness, as able to "work mightily" and to "bring forth fruit" in them who believe. That we wish to spread it, we have no desire to conceal;

but we think that we wish its diffusion because we regard it as more friendly to practical piety and pure morals than the opposite doctrines, because it gives clearer and nobler views of duty, and stronger motives to its perform-ance, because it recommends religion at once to the understanding and the heart, because it asserts the lovely and venerable attributes of God, because it tends to restore the benevolent spirit of Jesus to his divided and afflicted church, and because it cuts off every hope of God's favor except that which springs from practical conformity to the life and precepts of Christ. We see nothing in our views to give offence save their purity, and it is their purity which makes us seek and hope their extension through the world.

(65)

Theodore Parker

1810-1860

Like Channing, Parker was a leading Unitarian clergyman. He was the son of a Lexington farmer, and his grandfather had been captain of the Minutemen who fought on Lexington Common. Too poor to attend college, he was able to earn enough by teaching school to spend two years at Harvard Divinity School. He was the most learned clergy-man of his time, a master of twenty languages who was at home among both American and European scholars. He gave Transcenden-talism its most systematic philosophical statement.

Parker was not merely a scholarly theologian, however. His ser-mons on slavery and his protests against injustice are moving exhorta-tions. Few causes of social protest failed to gain his influential sup-port. Parker was thus an interesting combination of the man of letters and the political activist.

The selection here is from *The World of Matter and the Spirit of Man* (Boston, 1907).

This is the problem of metaphysics,—to explain the facts of hu-man consciousness. In metaphysics there are and have long been two schools of philosophers. The first is the sensational school. Its most important meta-physical doctrine is this: There is nothing in the intellect which was not first in the senses. Here "intellect" means the whole intellectual, moral, affectional and religious consciousness of man. The philosophers of this school claim to have reached this conclusion legitimately by the inductive method. It was at first an hypothesis; but after analyzing the facts of consciousness, interrogating all the ideas and sentiments and sensations of man, they say the hypothesis is proved by the most careful induction. They appeal to it as a principle, as a maxim, from which other things are deduced. They say that experience by one or more of the senses is the ultimate appeal in philosophy: all that I know is of sensational origin; the senses are the windows which let in all the light I have; the senses afford a sensation. I reflect upon this, and by reflection transform a sensation into an idea. An idea, therefore, is a transformed sensation. . . .

Sensationalism must have a philosophy of religion, a theology; let us see what theology. There are two parties; one goes by philosophy, the other mistrusts philosophy.

1. The first thing in theology is to know God. The idea of God is the touchstone of a theologian. Now to know the existence of God is to be certain thereof as of my own existence. "Nothing in the intellect which was not first in the senses," says sensationalism; "all comes by sensational experience and reflection thereon." Sensationalism—does that give us the idea of God? I ask the sensationalist, "Does the sensational eye see God?" "No." "The ear hear him?" "No." "Do the organs of sense touch or taste him?" "No." "How then do you get the idea of God?" "By induction from facts of observation *a posteriori.* The senses deal with finite things; I reflect on them, put them all together I assume that they have *cause;* then by inductive method I find out the character of that cause: that is God." Then I say, "But the senses deal with only finite things, so you must infer only a finite maker, else the induction is imperfect. So you have but a finite God. Then these finite things, measured only by my experience, are imperfect things. Look at disorders in the frame of nature; the sufferings of animals, the miseries of men; here are seeming imperfections which the sensational philosopher staggers at. But to go on with this induction: from an imperfect work you must infer an imperfect author. So the God of sensationalism is not only finite, but imperfect even at that. But am I certain of the existence of the finite and imperfect God? The existence of the outward world is only an hypothesis, its laws hypothetical; all that depends on that or them is but an hypothesis—the truth of your faculties, the forms of matter only an hypothesis: so the existence of God is not a certainty; he is but our hypothetical God. But a hypothetical God is no God at all, not the living God: an imperfect God is no God at all, not the true God: a finite God is no God at all, not the absolute God. But this hypothetical, finite, imperfect God, where is he? In matter? No. In spirit? No. Does he act in matter or spirit? No, only now and then he did act by miracle; he is outside of the world of matter and spirit. Then he is a non-resident, an absentee. A non-resident God is no God at all, not the all-present God. . . ."

But another party comes out of the same school to treat of religious matters; they give their philosophy a vacation, and to prove the existence of God they go back to tradition, and say, "Once God revealed himself to the senses of men; they heard him, they saw him, they felt him; so to them the existence of God was not an induction, but a fact of observation; they told it to others, through whom it comes to us; we can say it is not a fact of observation but a fact of testimony."

"Well," I ask, "are you certain then?" "Yes." "Quite sure? Let me look. The man to whom God revealed himself may have been mistaken; it may have been a dream, or a whim of his own, perhaps a fib; at any rate, he was not philosophically certain of the existence of the outward world in general; how could he be of anything that took place in it? Next, the evidence which relates the transaction is not wholly reliable: how do I know the books which tell of it tell the truth, that they were not fabricated to deceive me? All that rests on testimony is a little uncertain if it took place one or two thousand years ago; especially if I know nothing about the persons who testify or of that whereof they testify; still more so if it be a thing, as you say, unphilosophical and even supernatural."

So, then, the men who gave a vacation to their philosophy have slurred the philosophical argument for a historical, the theological for the mythological, and have gained nothing except the tradition of God. By this process we are as far from the infinite God as before, and have only arrived at the same point where the philosophy left us. . . .

I come now to the other school. This is distinguished by its chief metaphysical doctrine, that there is in the intellect (or consciousness), something that never was in the senses, to wit, the intellect (or consciousness) itself; that man has faculties which transcend the senses; faculties which give him ideas and intuitions that transcend sensational experience; ideas whose origin is not from sensation, nor their proof from sensation. This is the transcendental school. They maintain that the mind (meaning thereby all which is not sense) is not a smooth tablet on which sensation writes its experience, but is a living principle which of itself originates ideas when the senses present the occasion; that, as there is a body with certain senses, so there is a soul or mind with certain powers which give the man sentiments and ideas. This school maintains that it is a fact of consciousness itself that there is in the intellect somewhat that was not first in the senses; and also that they have analyzed consciousness, and by the inductive method established the conclusion that there is a consciousness that never was sensation, never could be; that our knowledge is in part *a priori;* that we know, 1, certain truths of necessity; 2, certain truths of intuition, or spontaneous consciousness; 3, certain truths of demonstration, a voluntary consciousness; all of these truths not dependent on sensation for cause, origin, or proof. Facts of observation, sensational experience, it has in common with the other school. . . .

Transcendentalism admits a religious faculty, element, or nature in man, as it admits a moral, intellectual and sensational faculty—that man by nature is a religious being as well as moral, intellectual, sensational; that this religious faculty is adequate to its purposes and wants, as much so as the others, as the eye acquainting us with light; and that this faculty is the source of religious emotions, of the sentiments of adoration, worship. Through this we have consciousness of God as through the senses consciousness of matter. In connection with reason it gives us the primary ideas of religion, ideas which transcend experience.

Now the transcendental philosophy legitimates the ideas of religion by reference to human nature. Some of them it finds truths of necessity, which cannot be conceived of as false or unreal without violence to reason; some it finds are truths of consciousness—of spontaneous consciousness, or intuition; some, truths of voluntary consciousness, or demonstration, inductive or deductive. Such ideas, capable of this legitimation, transcend experience, require and admit no further proof; as true before experience as after; true before time, after time, eternally; absolutely true. On that rock transcendentalism founds religion, sees its foundation, and doubts no more of religious truths than of the truths of mathematics. All the truths of religion it finds can be verified in consciousness today, what cannot is not religion. But it does not neglect experience. In human history it finds confirmations, illustrations, of the ideas of human nature, for history represents the attempt of mankind to develop human nature. So then as transcendentalism in philosophy legitimates religion by a reference to truths of necessity, to truths of consciousness, it illustrates religion by facts of observation, facts of testimony.

By sensationalism religious faith is a belief, more or less strange, in a probability, a credibility, a possibility. By transcendentalism religious faith is the normal action of the whole spiritual nature of man, which gives him certain knowledge of a certainty not yet attainable by experience; where understanding ends faith begins, and out-travels the understanding. Religion is natural to man, is justice, piety—free justice, free piety, free thought. The form thereof should fit the individual; hence there will be a unity of substance, diversity of form. So a transcendental religion demands a transcendental theology.

The transcendental philosophy appears in its doctrine of God. The idea of God is a fact given in the consciousness of man; consciousness of the infinite is the condition of a consciousness of the finite. I learn of a finite thing by sensation, I get an idea thereof; at the same time the idea of the infinite unfolds in me. I am not conscious of my own existence except as a finite existence, that is, as a dependent existence; and the idea of the infinite, of God on whom I depend, comes at the same time as the logical correlative of a knowledge of myself. So the existence of God is a certainty; I am as certain of that as of my own existence. Indeed without that knowledge I know nothing. Of this I am certain—I am; but of this as certain—God is; for if I am, and am finite and dependent, then this presupposes the infinite and independent. So the idea of God is *a priori;* rests on facts of necessity, on facts of consciousness.

Then transcendentalism uses the other mode, the *a posteriori.* Starting with the infinite, it finds signs and proofs of him everywhere, and gains evidence of God's existence in the limits of sensational observation; the thing refers to its maker, the thought to the mind, the effect to the cause, the created to the creator, the finite to the infinite; at the end of my arms are two major prophets, ten minor prophets, each of them pointing the transcendental philosopher to the infinite God, of which he has consciousness without the logical process of induction.

Then the character of God as given in the idea of him, given in consciousness—that represents God as a being, not with the limitations of impersonality (that is to confound God with matter); not with the limitations of personality (that confounds him with man); but God with no limitations, infinite, absolute; looked at from sensation, infinite power; from thought, infinite intellect; from the moral sense, infinite conscience; from the emotional, infinite affection; from the religious, infinite soul; from all truth, the whole human nature names him Infinite Father!

God is immanent in matter, so it is; immanent in spirit, so it is. He acts also as God in matter and spirit, acts perfectly; laws of matter or of spirit are modes of God's acting, being; as God is perfect, so the mode of his action is perfect and unchangeable. Therefore, as God is ever in matter and spirit, and where God is is wholly God active, so no intervention is possible. God cannot come where he already is, so no miracle is possible. A miracle *a parte humanâ* is a violation of what is a law to man; a miracle to God—*a parte divinâ*—is a violation of what is law to God; the most extraordinary things that have been seem miracles *a parte humanâ*—laws, *a parte divinâ.* But though God is immanent in matter and in spirit, he yet transcends both matter and spirit, has no limitations. Indeed all perfection of immanence and transcendence belong to him—the perfection of existence, infinite being; the perfection of space, immensity; the perfection of time, eternity; of power, all-mightiness; of mind, all-knowingness; of affection, all-lovingness; of will, absolute freedom, absolute justice, absolute right. His providence is not merely general, but universal, so special in each thing. Hence the universe partakes of his perfection, is a perfect universe for the end he made it for. . . .

The sensational philosophy, with all its evils, has done the world a great service. It has stood up for the body, for common sense, protested against spiritual tyranny, against the spiritualism of the middle ages which thought the senses wicked and the material world profane. To sensationalism we are indebted for the great advance of mankind in physical science, in discovery, arts, mechanics, and for many improvements in government. Some of its men are great names—Bacon, Locke, Newton. Let us do them no dishonor; they saw what they could, told it; they saw not all things that are, saw some which are not. In our day no one of them would be content with the philosophy they all agreed in then. Hobbes and Hume have done us service; the Socinians, Priestley, Collins, Berkeley, Dodwell, Mandeville, Edwards. To take the good and leave the ill is our part; but the doubts which this philosophy raises, the doubt of Hume, the doubt of Hobbes, of the English Deists in general, do not get answered by this philosophy. For this we have weapons forged by other hands, tempered in another spring.

Transcendentalism has a work to do, to show that physics, politics, ethics, religion rest on facts of necessity, facts of intuition, facts of demonstration, and have their witness and confirmation in facts of observation. It is the work of transcendentalism to give us politics which represent God's thought of a state,—the whole world, each man free; to give us morals which leave the man a complete individual, no chord rent from the human harp—yet complete in his social character, no string discordant in the social choir; to give us religion worthy of God and man,—free goodness, free piety, free thought. That is not to be done by talking at random, not by idleness, not by railing at authority, calumniating the past or the present; not by idle brains with open mouth, who outrage common sense; but the diligent toil, brave discipline, patience to wait, patience to work. Nothing comes of nothing, foolishness of fools; but something from something, wise thought from thinking men; and of the wise thought comes a lovely deed, life, laws, institutions for mankind.

The problem of transcendental philosophy is no less than this, to revise the experience of mankind and try its teachings by the nature of mankind; to test ethics by conscience, science by reason; to try the creeds of the churches; the constitutions of the states by the constitution of the universe; to reverse what is wrong, supply what is wanting, and command the just. To do this in a nation like ours, blinded still by the sensational philosophy, devoted chiefly to material interests, its politics guided by the madness of party more than sober reason; to do this in a race like the Anglo-Saxon, which has an obstinate leaning to a sensational philosophy, which loves facts of experience, not ideas of consciousness, and believes not in the First-Fair, First-Perfect, First-Good, is no light work; not to be taken in hand by such as cannot bear the strife of tongues, the toil, the heat, the war of thought; not to be accomplished by a single man, however well-born and well-bred; not by a single age and race. It has little of history behind, for this philosophy is young. It looks to a future, a future to be made; a church whose creed is truth, whose worship love; a society full of industry and abundance, full of wisdom, virtue, and the poetry of life; a state with unity among all, with freedom for each; a church without tyranny, a society without ignorance, want, or crime, a state without oppression; yes, a world with no war among the nations to consume the work of their hands, and no restrictive policy to hinder the welfare of mankind. That is the human dream of the transcendental philosophy. Shall it ever become a fact? History says, No; human nature says, Yes.

Ralph Waldo Emerson

1803-1882

Emerson was the most widely read of the Transcendentalists. He graduated from Harvard in 1821, taught school for a short time, and then attended Harvard Divinity School, where he was ordained in the Unitarian ministry. In 1829 Emerson became minister of the Old North Church in Boston; but becoming dissatisfied with formal, institutionalized religion, he resigned in 1832 and settled in Concord, where he remained for the rest of his life.

A stream of essays and addresses came from Emerson's pen, all giving expression to his romantic Platonism. Behind nature, Emerson taught, lies a higher spiritual world; and the individual personality, containing a "spark of the divine" within it, realizes itself through the individualistic virtues. In its emphasis on individualism, Transcendentalism gave expression to dominant American values.

This selection is from Emerson's essays on "Self-Reliance," in *Essays, First Series* (Boston, 1883), and "Success," in *Society and Solitude* (Boston, 1898).

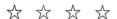

I read the other day some verses written by an eminent painter which were original and not conventional. The soul always hears an admonition in such lines, let the subject be what it may. The sentiment they instill is of more value than any thought they may contain. To believe your own thought, to believe that what is true for you in your private heart is true for all men,—that is genius. Speak your latent conviction, and it shall be the universal sense; for the inmost in due time becomes the outmost, and our first thought is rendered back to us by the trumpets of the Last Judgment. Familiar as the voice of the mind is to each, the highest merit we ascribe to Moses, Plato and Milton is that they set at naught books and traditions, and spoke not what men, but what *they* thought. A man should learn to detect and watch that gleam of light which flashes across his mind from within, more than the lustre of the firmament of bards and sages. Yet he dismisses without notice his thought, because it is his. In every work of genius we recognize our own rejected thoughts; they come back to us with a certain alienated majesty. Great works of art have no more arresting lesson for us than this. They teach us to abide by our spontaneous impression with good-humored inflexibility than most when the whole cry of voices is on the other side. Else to-morrow a stranger will say with masterly good sense precisely what we have thought and felt all the time, and we shall be forced to take with shame our own opinion from another.

There is a time in every man's education when he arrives at the conviction that envy is ignorance; that imitation is suicide; that he must take himself for better for worse as his portion; that though the wide universe is full of good, no kernel of nourishing corn can come to him but through his toil bestowed on that plot of ground which is given to him to till. The power which resides in him is new in nature, and none but he knows what that is which he can do, nor does he know until he has tried. Not for nothing one face, one character, one fact, makes much impression on him, and another none. This sculpture in the memory is not without preëstablished harmony. The eye was placed where one ray should fall, that it might testify of that particular ray. We but half express ourselves, and are ashamed of that divine idea which each of us represents. It may be safely trusted as proportionate and of good issues, so it be faithfully imparted, but God will not have his work made manifest by cowards. A man is relieved and gay when he has put his heart into his work and done his best; but what he has said or done otherwise shall give him no peace. It is a deliverance which does not deliver. In the attempt his genius deserts him; no muse befriends; no invention, no hope.

Trust thyself: every heart vibrates to that iron string. Accept the place the divine providence has found for you, the society of your contemporaries, the connection of events. Great men have always done so, and confided themselves childlike to the genius of their age, betraying their perception that the absolutely trustworthy was seated at their heart, working through their hands, predominating in all their being. And we are now men, and must accept in the highest mind the same transcendent destiny; and not minors and invalids in a protected corner, not cowards fleeing before a revolution, but guides, redeemers and benefactors, obeying the Almighty effort and advancing on Chaos and the Dark. . . .

Whoso would be a man, must be a nonconformist. He who would gather immortal palms must not be hindered by the name of goodness, but must explore if it be goodness. Nothing is at last sacred but the integrity of your own mind. Absolve you to yourself, and you shall have the suffrage of the world. I remember an answer which when quite young I was prompted to make to a valued adviser who was wont to importune me with the dear old doctrines of the church. On my saying, "What have I to do with the sacredness of traditions, if I live wholly from within?" my friend suggested,—"But these impulses may be from below, not from above." I replied, "They do not seem to me to be such; but if I am the Devil's child, I will live then from the Devil." No law can be sacred to me but that of my nature. Good and bad are but names very readily transferable to that or this; the only right is what is after my constitution; the only wrong what is against it. A man is to carry himself in the presence of all opposition as if every thing were titular and ephemeral but he. I am ashamed to think how easily we capitulate to badges and names, to large societies and dead institutions. Every decent and well-spoken individual affects and sways me more than is right. I ought to go upright and vital, and speak the rude truth in all ways. If malice and vanity wear the coat of philanthropy, shall that pass? If an angry bigot assumes this bountiful cause of Abolition, and comes to me with his last news from Barbadoes, why should I not say to him, 'Go love thy infant; love thy wood chopper; be good-natured and modest; have that grace; and never varnish your hard, un-charitable ambition with this incredible tenderness for black folk a thousand miles off. Thy love afar is spite at home.' Rough and graceless would be such greeting, but truth is handsomer than the affectation of love. Your goodness must have some edge to it,—else it is none. The doctrine of hatred must be preached, as the counteraction of the doctrine of love, when that pules and whines. I shun father and mother and wife and brother when my genius calls me. I would write on the lintels of the door-post, *Whim.* I hope it is some-what better than whim at last, but we cannot spend the day in explanation. Expect me not to show cause why I seek or why I exclude company. Then again, do not tell me, as a good man did to-day, of my obligation to put all poor men in good situations. Are they *my* poor? I tell thee thou foolish philanthropist that I grudge the dollar, the dime, the cent I give to such men as do not belong to me and to whom I do not belong. There is a class of persons to whom by all spiritual affinity I am bought and sold; for them I will go to prison if need be; but your miscellaneous popular charities: the education at college of fools; the building of meeting-houses to the vain end to which many now stand; alms to sots, and the thousand-fold Relief Societies; —though I confess with shame I sometimes succumb and give the dollar, it is a wicked dollar, which by and by I shall have the manhood to withhold.

Virtues are, in the popular estimate, rather the exception than the rule. There is the man *and* his virtues. Men do what is called a good action, as some piece of courage or charity, much as they would pay a fine in expiation of daily nonappearance on parade. Their works are done as an apology or extenuation of their living in the world,—as invalids and the insane pay a high board. Their virtues are penances. I do not wish to expiate, but to live. My life is for itself and not for a spectacle. I much prefer that it should be of a lower strain, so it be genuine and equal, than that it should be glittering and unsteady. I wish it to be sound and sweet, and not to need diet and bleeding. I ask primary evidence that you are a man, and refuse this appeal from the man to his actions. I know that for myself it makes no difference whether I do or forbear those actions which are reckoned excellent. I cannot consent to pay for a privilege where I have intrinsic right. Few and mean as my gifts may be, I actually am, and do not need for my own assurance or the assurance of my fellows any secondary testimony.

What I must do is all that concerns me, not what the people think. This rule, equally arduous in actual and in intellectual life, may serve for the whole distinction between greatness and meanness. It is the harder because you will always find those who think they know what is your duty better than you know it. It is easy in the world to live after the world's opinion; it is easy in solitude to live after our own; but the great man is he who in the midst of the crowd keeps with perfect sweetness the independence of solitude. . . .

For nonconformity the world whips you with its displeasure. And therefore a man must know how to estimate a sour face. The by-standers look askance on him in the public street or in the friend's parlor. If this aversion had its origin in contempt and resistance like his own he might well go home with a sad countenance; but the sour faces of the multitude, like their sweet faces, have no deep cause, but are put on and off as the wind blows and a newspaper directs. Yet is the discontent of the multitude more formidable than that of the senate and the college. It is easy enough for a firm man who knows the world to brook the rage of the cultivated classes. Their rage is decorous and prudent, for they are timid, as being very vulnerable themselves. But when to their feminine rage the indignation of the people is added, when the ignorant and the poor are aroused, when the unintelligent brute force that lies at the bottom of society is made to growl and mow, it needs the habit of magnanimity and religion to treat it godlike as a trifle of no concernment.

The other terror that scares us from self-trust is our consistency; a reverence for our past act or word because the eyes of others have no other data for computing our orbit than our past acts, and we are loath to disappoint them.

But why should you keep your head over your shoulder? Why drag about this corpse of your memory, lest you contradict somewhat you have stated in this or that public place? Suppose you should contradict yourself; what then? It seems to be a rule of wisdom never to rely on your memory alone, scarcely even in acts of pure memory, but to bring the past for judgment into the thousand-eyed present, and live ever in a new day. In your metaphysics you have denied personality to the Deity, yet when the devout motions of the soul come, yield to them heart and life, though they should clothe God with shape and color. Leave your theory, as Joseph his coat in the hand of the harlot, and flee.

A foolish consistency is the hobgoblin of little minds, adored by little statesmen and philosophers and divines. With consistency a great soul has simply nothing to do. He may as well concern himself with his shadow on the wall. Speak what you think now in hard words and to-morrow speak what to-morrow thinks in hard words again, though it contradict every thing you said to-day. "Ah, so you shall be sure to be misunderstood." Is it so bad then to be misunderstood? Pythagoras was misunderstood, and Socrates, and Jesus, and Luther, and Copernicus, and Galileo, and Newton, and every pure and wise spirit that ever took flesh. To be great is to be misunderstood.

I hope in these days we have heard the last of conformity and consistency. Let the words be gazetted and ridiculous henceforward. Instead of the gong for dinner, let us hear a whistle from the Spartan fife. Let us never bow and apologize more. A great man is coming to eat at my house. I do not wish to please him; I wish that he should wish to please me. I will stand here for humanity, and though I would make it kind, I would make it true. Let us affront and reprimand the smooth mediocrity and squalid contentment of the times, and hurl in the face of custom and trade and office, the fact which is the upshot of all history, that there is a great responsible Thinker and Actor working wherever a man works; that a true man belongs to no other time or place, but is the centre of things. Where he is, there is nature. He measures you and all men and all events. Ordinarily, every body in society reminds us of somewhat else, or of some other person. Character, reality, reminds you of nothing else; it takes place of the whole creation. The man must be so much that he must make all circumstances indifferent. Every true man is a cause, a country, and an age; requires infinite spaces and numbers and time fully to accomplish his design; and posterity seem to follow his steps as a train of clients. A man Cæsar is born, and for ages after we have a Roman Empire. Christ is born, and millions of minds so grow and cleave to his genius that he is confounded with virtue and the possible of man. An institution is the lengthened shadow of one man; as, Monachism, of the Hermit Antony; the Reformation, of Luther; Quakerism, of Fox; Methodism, of Wesley; Abolition, of Clarkson. Scipio, Milton called "the height of Rome;" and all history resolves itself very easily into the biography of a few stout and earnest persons. . . .

This is the ultimate fact which we so quickly reach on this, as on every topic, the resolution of all into the ever-blessed ONE. Self-existence is the attribute of the Supreme Cause, and it constitutes the measure of good by the degree in which it enters into all lower forms. All things real are so by so much virtue as they contain. Commerce, husbandry, hunting, whaling, war, eloquence, personal weight, are somewhat, and engage my respect as examples of its presence and impure action. I see the same law working in nature for conservation and growth. Power is, in nature, the essential measure of right. Nature suffers nothing to remain in her kingdoms which cannot help itself. The genesis and maturation of a planet, its poise and orbit, the bended tree recovering itself from the strong wind, the vital resources of every animal and vegetable, are demonstrations of the self-sufficing and therefore self-relying soul.

Thus all concentrates: let us not rove; let us sit at home with the cause. Let us stun and astonish the intruding rabble of men and books and institutions by a simple declaration of the divine fact. Bid the invaders take the shoes from off their feet, for God is here within. Let our simplicity judge them, and our docility to our own law demonstrate the poverty of nature and fortune beside our native riches.

But now we are a mob. Man does not stand in awe of man, nor is his genius admonished to stay at home, to put itself in communication with the internal ocean, but it goes abroad to beg a cup of water of the urns of other men. We must go alone. I like the silent church before the service begins, better than any preaching. How far off, how cool, how chaste the persons look, begirt each one with a precinct or sanctuary! So let us always sit. Why should we assume the faults of our friend, or wife, or father, or child, because they sit around our hearth, or are said to have the same blood? All men have my blood and I have all men's. Not for that will I adopt their petulance or folly, even to the extent of being ashamed of it. But your isolation must not be mechanical, but spiritual, that is, must be elevation. At times the whole world seems to be in conspiracy to importune you with emphatic trifles. Friend, client, child, sickness, fear, want, charity, all knock at once at thy closet door and say, —"Come out unto us." But keep thy state; come not into their confusion. The power men possess to annoy me I give them by a weak curiosity. No man can come near me but through my act. "What we love that we have, but by desire we bereave ourselves of the love." . . .

The populace think that your rejection of popular standards is a rejection of all standard, and mere antinomianism; and the bold sensualist will use the name of philosophy to gild his crimes. But the law of consciousness abides. There are two confessionals, in one or the other of which we must be shriven. You may fulfil your round of duties by clearing yourself in the *direct,* or in the *reflex* way. Consider whether you have satisfied your relations to father, mother, cousin, neighbor, town, cat and dog; whether any of these can upbraid you. But I may also neglect this reflex standard and absolve me to myself. I have my own stern claims and perfect circle. It denies the name of duty to many offices that are called duties. But if I can discharge its debts it enables me to dispense with the popular code. If any one imagines that this law is lax, let him keep its commandment one day.

And truly it demands something godlike in him who has cast off the common motives of humanity and has ventured to trust himself for a task-master. High be his heart, faithful his will, clear his sight, that he may in good earnest be doctrine, society, law, to himself, that a simple purpose may be to him as strong as iron necessity is to others!

Our American people cannot be taxed with slowness in performance or in praising their performance. The earth is shaken by our enginery. We are feeling our youth and nerve and bone. We have the power of territory and of sea-coast, and know the use of these. We count our census, we read our growing valuations, we survey our map, which becomes old in a year or two. Our eyes run approvingly along the lengthened lines of railroad and telegraph. We have gone nearest to the Pole. We have discovered the Antarctic continent. We interfere in Central and South America, at Canton, and in Japan; we are adding to an already enormous territory. Our political constitution is the hope of the world, and we value ourselves on all these feats.

'Tis the way of the world; 'tis the law of youth, and of unfolding strength. Men are made each with some triumphant superiority, which, through some adaptation of fingers or ear or eye or ciphering or pugilistic or musical or literary craft, enriches the community with a new art; and not only we, but all men of European stock, value these certificates. Giotto could draw a perfect circle: Erwin of Steinbach could build a minster; Olaf, king of Norway, could run round his galley on the blades of the oars of the rowers when the ship was in motion; Ojeda could run out swiftly on a plank projected from the top of a tower, turn round swiftly and come back; Evelyn writes from Rome: "Bernini, the Florentine sculptor, architect, painter and poet, a little before my coming to Rome, gave a public opera, wherein he painted the scenes, cut the statues, invented the engines, composed the music, writ the comedy and built the theatre." . . .

These feats have, to be sure, great difference of merit, and some of them involve power of a high kind. But the public values the invention more than the inventor does. The inventor knows there is much more and better where this came from. The public sees in it a lucrative secret. Men see the reward which the inventor enjoys, and they think, "How shall we win that?" Cause and effect are a little tedious; how to leap to the result by short or by false means? We are not scrupulous. What we ask is victory, without regard to the cause; after the Rob Roy rule, after the Napoleon rule, to be the strongest to-day,—the way of the Talleyrands, prudent people, whose watches go faster than their neighbors', and who detect the first moment of decline and throw themselves on the instant on the winning side. I have heard that Nelson used to say, "Never mind the justice or the impudence, only let me succeed." Lord Brougham's single duty of counsel is, "to get the prisoner clear." Fuller says 'tis a maxim of lawyers that "a crown once worn cleareth all defects of the wearer thereof." *Rien ne réussit mieux que le succès.* And we Americans are tainted with this insanity, as our bankruptcies and our reckless politics may show. We are great by exclusion, grasping, and egotism. Our success takes from all what it gives to one. 'Tis a haggard, malignant, careworn running for luck.

Egotism is a kind of buckram that gives momentary strength and concentration to men, and seems to be much used in nature for fabrics in which local and spasmodic energy is required. I could point to men in this country, of indispensable importance to the carrying on of American life, of this humor, whom we could ill spare; any one of them would be a national loss. But it spoils conversation. They will not try conclusions with you. They are ever thrusting this pampered self between you and them. It is plain they have a long education to undergo to reach simplicity and plain-dealing, which are what a wise man mainly cares for in his companion. Nature knows how to convert evil to good; Nature utilizes misers, fanatics, show-men, egotists, to accomplish her ends; but we must not think better of the foible for that. The passion for sudden success is rude and puerile, just as war, cannons, and executions are used to clear the ground of bad, lumpish, irreclaimable savages, but always to the damage of the conquerors.

I hate this shallow Americanism which hopes to get rich by credit, to get knowledge by raps on midnight tables, to learn the economy of the mind by phrenology, or skill without study, or mastery without apprenticeship, or the sale of goods through pretending that they sell, or power through making believe you are powerful, or through a packed jury or caucus, bribery and "repeating" votes, or wealth by fraud. They think they have got it, but they have got something else,—a crime which calls for another crime, and another devil behind that; these are steps to suicide, infamy, and the harming of mankind. We countenance each other in this life of show, puffing, advertisement, and manufacture of public opinion; and excellence is lost sight of in the hunger for sudden performance and praise.

There was a wise man, an Italian artist, Michel Angelo, who writes thus of himself: "Meanwhile the Cardinal Ippolito, in whom all my best hopes were placed, being dead, I began to understand that the promises of this world are for the most part vain phantoms, and that to confide in one's self, and become something of worth and value, is the best and safest course." Now, though I am by no means sure that the reader will assent to all my propositions, yet I think we shall agree in my first rule for success,—that we shall drop the brag and the advertisement, and take Michel Angelo's course, "to confide in one's self, and be something of worth and value."

Each man has an aptitude born with him. Do your work. I have to say this often, but nature says it oftener. 'Tis clownish to insist on doing all with one's own hands, as if every man should build his own clumsy house, forge his hammer, and bake his dough; but he is to dare to do what he can do best; not help others as they would direct him, but as he knows his helpful power to be. To do otherwise is to neutralize all those extraordinary special talents distributed among men. Yet whilst this self-truth is essential to the exhibition of the world and to the growth and glory of each mind, it is rare to find a man who believes his own thought or who speaks that which he was created to say. As nothing astonishes men so much as common-sense and plain dealing, so nothing is more rare in any man than an act of his own. Any work looks wonderful to him, except that which he can do. We do not believe our own thought; we must serve somebody; we must quote somebody; we dote on the old and the distant; we are tickled by great names; we import the religion of other nations; we quote their opinions; we cite their laws. The gravest and learnedest courts in this country shudder to face a new question, and will wait months and years for a case to occur that can be tortured into a precedent, and thus throw on a bolder party the *onus* of an initiative. Thus we do not carry a counsel in our breasts, or do not know it; and because we cannot shake off from our shoes this dust of Europe and Asia, the world seems to be born old, society is under a spell, every man is a borrower and a mimic, life is theatrical and literature a quotation; and hence that depression of spirits, that furrow of care, said to mark every American brow.

Self-trust is the first secret of success, the belief that if you are here the authorities of the universe put you here, and for cause, or with some task strictly appointed you in your constitution, and so long as you work at that you are well and successful. It by no means consists in rushing prematurely to a showy feat that shall catch the eye and satisfy spectators. It is enough if you work in the right direction. So far from the performance being the real success, it is clear that the success was much earlier than that, namely, when all the feats that make our civility were the thoughts of good heads. The fame of each discovery rightly attaches to the mind that made the formula which contains all the details, and not to the manufacturers who now make their gain by it; although the mob uniformly cheers the publisher, and not the inventor. It is the dullness of the multitude that they cannot see the house in the ground-plan; the working, in the model of the projector. Whilst it is a thought, though it were a new fuel, or a new food, or the creation of agriculture, it is cried down, it is a chimera; but when it is a fact, and comes in the shape of eight per cent, ten per cent, a hundred per cent, they cry, "It is the voice of God." Horatio Greenough the sculptor said to me of Robert Fulton's visit to Paris: "Fulton knocked at the door of Napoleon with steam, and was rejected; and Napoleon lived long enough to know that he had excluded a greater power than his own." . . .

My next point is that in the scale of powers it is not talent but sensibility which is best: talent confines, but the central life puts us in relation to all. How often it seems the chief good to be born with a cheerful temper and well adjusted to the tone of the human race. Such a man feels himself in harmony, and conscious by his receptivity of an infinite strength. Like Alfred, "good fortune accompanies him like a gift of God." Feel yourself, and be not daunted by things. 'Tis the fulness of man that runs over into objects, and makes his Bibles and Shaksperes and Homers so great. The joyful reader borrows of his own ideas to fill their faulty outline, and knows not that he borrows and gives. . . .

The fundamental fact in our metaphysic constitution is the correspondence of man to the world, so that every change in that, writes a record in the mind. The mind yields sympathetically to the tendencies or law which stream through things and make the order of nature; and in the perfection of this correspondence or expressiveness, the health and force of man consist. If we follow this hint into our intellectual education, we shall find that it is not propositions, not new dogmas and a logical exposition of the world that are our first need; but to watch and tenderly cherish the intellectual and moral sensibilities, those fountains of right thought, and woo them to stay and make their home with us. Whilst they abide with us we shall not think amiss. Our perception far outruns our talent. We bring a welcome to the highest lessons of religion and of poetry out of all proportion beyond our skill to teach. And, further, the great hearing and sympathy of men is more true and wise than their speaking is wont to be. A deep sympathy is what we require for any student of the mind; for the chief difference between man and man is a difference of impressionability. Aristotle or Bacon or Kant propound some maxim which is the key-note of philosophy thenceforward. But I am more interested to know that when at last they have hurled out their grand word, it is only some familiar experience of every man in the street. If it be not, it will never be heard of again.

Ah! if one could keep this sensibility, and live in the happy sufficing present, and find the day and its cheap means contenting, which only ask receptivity in you, and no strained exertion and cankering ambition, over-stimulating to be at the head of your class and the head of society, and to have distinction and laurels and consumption! We are not strong by our power to penetrate, but by our relatedness. The world is enlarged for us, not by new objects, but by finding more affinities and potencies in those we have. . . .

One more trait of true success. The good mind chooses what is positive, what is advancing—embraces the affirmative. Our system is one of poverty. 'Tis presumed, as I said, there is but one Shakspeare, one Homer, one Jesus, —not that all are or shall be inspired. But we must begin by affirming. Truth and goodness subsist forevermore. It is true there is evil and good, night and day: but these are not equal. The day is great and final. The night is for the day, but the day is not for the night. What is this immortal demand for more, which belongs to our constitution? this enormous ideal? There is no such critic and beggar as this terrible Soul. No historical person begins to content us. We know the satisfactoriness of justice, the sufficiency of truth. We know the answer that leaves nothing to ask. We know the Spirit by its victorious tone. The searching tests to apply to every new pretender are amount and quality,—what does he add? and what is the state of mind he leaves me in? Your theory is unimportant; but what new stock you can add to humanity, or how high you can carry life? A man is a man only as he makes life and nature happier to us.

I fear the popular notion of success stands in direct opposition in all points to the real and wholesome success. One adores public opinion, the other private opinion; one fame, the other desert; one feats, the other humility; one lucre, the other love; one monopoly, and the other hospitality of mind.

We may apply this affirmative law to letters, to manners, to art, to the decorations of our houses, etc. I do not find executions or tortures or lazar-houses, or grisly photographs of the field on the day after the battle, fit subjects for cabinet pictures. I think that some so-called "sacred subjects" must be treated with more genius than I have seen in the masters of Italian or Spanish art to be right pictures for houses and churches. Nature does not invite such exhibition. Nature lays the ground-plan of each creature accurately, sternly fit for all his functions; then veils it scrupulously. See how carefully she covers up the skeleton. The eye shall not see it; the sun shall not shine on it. She weaves her tissues and integuments of flesh and skin and hair and beautiful colors of the day over it, and forces death down underground, and makes haste to cover it up with leaves and vines, and wipes carefully out every trace by new creation. Who and what are you that would lay the ghastly anatomy bare?

Don't hang a dismal picture on the wall, and do not daub with sables and glooms in your conversation. Don't be a cynic and disconsolate preacher.

Don't bewail and bemoan. Omit the negative propositions. Nerve us with incessant affirmatives. Don't waste yourself in rejection, nor bark against the bad, but chant the beauty of the good. When that is spoken which has a right to be spoken, the chatter and the criticism will stop. Set down nothing that will not help somebody—

> "For every gift of noble origin
> Is breathed upon by Hope's perpetual breath."

The affirmative of affirmatives is love. As much love, so much perception. As caloric to matter, so is love to mind; so it enlarges, and so it empowers it. Good-will makes insight, as one finds his way to the sea by embarking on a river. I have seen scores of people who can silence me, but I seek one who shall make me forget or overcome the frigidities and imbecilities into which I fall. The painter Giotto, Vasari tells us, renewed art because he put more goodness into his heads. To awake in man and to raise the sense of worth, to educate his feeling and judgment so that he shall scorn himself for a bad action, that is the only aim.

'Tis cheap and easy to destroy. There is not a joyful boy or an innocent girl buoyant with fine purposes of duty, in all the street full of eager and rosy faces, but a cynic can chill and dishearten with a single word. Despondency comes readily enough to the most sanguine. The cynic has only to follow their hint with his bitter confirmation, and they check that eager courageous pace and go home with heavier step and premature age. They will themselves quickly enough give the hint he wants to the cold wretch. Which of them has not failed to please where they most wished it? or blundered where they were most ambitious of success? or found themselves awkward or tedious or incapable of study, thought, or heroism, and only hoped by good sense and fidelity to do what they could and pass unblamed? And this witty malefactor makes their little hope less with satire and skepticism, and slackens the springs of endeavor. Yes, this is easy; but to help the young soul, add energy, inspire hope and blow the coals into a useful flame; to redeem defeat by new thought, by firm action, that is not easy, that is the work of divine men.

We live on different planes or platforms. There is an external life, which is educated at school, taught to read, write, cipher, and trade; taught to grasp all the boy can get, urging him to put himself forward, to make himself useful and agreeable in the world, to ride, run, argue and contend, unfold his talents, shine, conquer and possess.

But the inner life sits at home, and does not learn to do things, nor value these feats at all. 'Tis a quiet, wise perception. It loves truth, because it is itself real; it loves right, it knows nothing else; but it makes no progress; was as wise in our first memory of it as now; is just the same now in maturity and hereafter in age, it was in youth. We have grown to manhood and woman-hood; we have powers, connection, children, reputations, professions: this makes no account of them all. It lives in the great present; it makes the present great. This tranquil, well-founded, wide-seeing soul is no express-rider, no attorney, no magistrate: it lies in the sun and broods on the world. A person of this temper once said to a man of much activity, "I will pardon you that you do so much, and you me that I do nothing." And Euripides says that "Zeus hates busybodies and those who do too much."

(67)

Henry David Thoreau

1817-1862

Born in Concord, Massachusetts, Thoreau graduated from Harvard at the age of twenty but characteristically refused his diploma. He taught school for some years, and then lived in the Emerson household as handyman. From July 4, 1845, to September 6, 1847, he carried out his famous experiment in solitude at Walden Pond near Concord. His search for the essentials of individualism, and his challenge of prevailing standards he recorded in *Walden*, his most widely read book.

Throughout his life, Thoreau struggled to maintain his independence and integrity. He never married and was something of a misanthrope. He had scant respect for society's institutions, and preferred jail to taxes. His essay on "Civil Disobedience" is a fervent protest against a nation that launched an unjust war on Mexico and that seemed to crush blindly individuality. Yet Thoreau's passionate individualism was not without its contradictions, for at various times he advocated collective action to reform social conditions.

The selection here is from "Civil Disobedience," in *The Writings of Henry David Thoreau*, 11 vols. (Boston, 1884–1900), vol. X.

I heartily accept the motto—"That government is best which governs least"; and I should like to see it acted up to more rapidly and systematically. Carried out, it finally amounts to this, which also I believe—"That government is best which governs not at all"; and when men are prepared for it, that will be the kind of government which they will have. Government is at best but an expedient; but most governments are usually, and all governments are sometimes, inexpedient. The objections which have been brought against a standing army, and they are many and weighty, and deserve to prevail, may also at last be brought against a standing government. The standing army is only an arm of the standing government. The government itself, which is only the mode which the people have chosen to execute their will, is equally liable to be abused and perverted before the people can act through it. Witness the present Mexican War, the work of comparatively a few individuals using the standing government as their tool; for, in the outset, the people would not have consented to this measure.

This American government—what is it but a tradition, though a recent one, endeavoring to transmit itself unimpaired to posterity, but each instant losing some of its integrity? It has not the vitality and force of a single living man; for a single man can bend it to his will. It is a sort of wooden gun to the people themselves. But it is not the less necessary for this; for the people must have some complicated machinery or other, and hear its din, to satisfy that idea of government which they have. Governments show thus how successfully men can be imposed on, even impose on themselves, for their own advantage. It is excellent, we must all allow. Yet this government never of itself furthered any enterprise, but by the alacrity with which it got out of its way. *It* does not keep the country free. *It* does not settle the West. *It* does not educate. The character inherent in the American people has done all that has been accomplished; and it would have done somewhat more, if the government had not sometimes got in its way. For government is an expedient by which men would fain succeed in letting one another alone; and, as has been said, when it is most expedient, the governed are most let alone by it. Trade and commerce, if they were not made of India-rubber, would never manage to bounce over the obstacles which legislators are continually putting in their way; and, if one were to judge these men wholly by the effects of their actions and not partly by their intentions, they would deserve to be classed and punished with those mischievous persons who put obstructions on the railroads.

But, to speak practically and as a citizen, unlike those who call themselves no-government men, I ask for, not at once no government, but *at once* a better government. Let every man make known what kind of government would command his respect, and that will be one step toward obtaining it.

After all, the practical reason why, when the power is once in the hands of the people, a majority are permitted, and for a long period continue, to rule is not because they are most likely to be in the right, nor because this seems fairest to the minority, but because they are physically the strongest. But a government in which the majority rule in all cases cannot be based on justice, even as far as men understand it. Can there not be a government in which majorities do not virtually decide right and wrong, but conscience?—in which majorities decide only those questions to which the rule of expediency is applicable? Must the citizen ever for a moment, or in the least degree, resign his conscience to the legislator? Why has every man a conscience, then? I think that we should be men first, and subjects afterward. It is not desirable to cultivate a respect for the law, so much as for the right. The only obligation which I have a right to assume is to do at any time what I think right. It is truly enough said, that a corporation has no conscience; but a corporation of conscientious men is a corporation *with* a conscience. Law never made men a whit more just; and, by means of their respect for it, even the well-disposed are daily made the agents of injustice. A common and natural result of an undue respect for law is, that you may see a file of soldiers, colonel, captain, corporal, privates, powder-monkeys, and all, marching in admirable order over hill and dale to the wars, against their wills, ay, against their common sense and consciences, which makes it very steep marching indeed, and produces a palpitation of the heart. They have no doubt that it is a damnable business in which they are concerned; they are all peaceably inclined. Now, what are they? Men at all? or small movable forts and magazines, at the service of some unscrupulous man in power? . . .

How does it become a man to behave toward this American government to-day? I answer, that he cannot without disgrace be associated with it. I cannot for an instant recognize that political organization as *my* government which is the *slave's* government also.

All men recognize the right of revolution; that is, the right to refuse allegiance to, and to resist, the government, when its tyranny or its inefficiency are great and unendurable. But almost all say that such is not the case now. But such was the case, they think, in the Revolution of '75. If one were to tell me that this was a bad government because it taxed certain foreign commodities brought to its ports, it is most probable that I should not make an ado about it, for I can do without them. All machines have their friction; and possibly this does enough good to counterbalance the evil. At any rate, it is a great evil to make a stir about it. But when the friction comes to have its machine, and oppression and robbery are organized, I say, let us not have such a machine any longer. In other words, when a sixth of the population of a nation which has undertaken to be the refuge of liberty are slaves, and a whole country is unjustly overrun and conquered by a foreign army, and subjected to military law, I think that it is not too soon for honest men to rebel and revolutionize. What makes this duty the more urgent is the fact that the country so overrun is not our own, but ours is the invading army. . . .

All voting is a sort of gaming, like checkers or backgammon, with a slight moral tinge to it, a playing with right and wrong, with moral questions; and betting naturally accompanies it. The character of the voters is not staked. I cast my vote, perchance, as I think right; but I am not vitally concerned that that right should prevail. I am willing to leave it to the majority. Its obligation, therefore, never exceeds that of expediency. Even voting *for the right* is *doing* nothing for it. It is only expressing to men feebly your desire that it should prevail. A wise man will not leave the right to the mercy of chance, nor wish it to prevail through the power of the majority. There is but little virtue in the action of masses of men. When the majority shall at length vote for the abolition of slavery, it will be because they are indifferent to slavery, or because there is but little slavery left to be abolished by their vote. *They* will then be the only slaves. Only *his* vote can hasten the abolition of slavery who asserts his own freedom by his vote. . . .

As for adopting the ways which the state has provided for remedying the evil, I know not of such ways. They take too much time, and a man's life will be gone. I have other affairs to attend to. I came into this world, not chiefly to make this a good place to live in, but to live in it, be it good or bad. A man has not everything to do, but something; and because he cannot do *everything,* it is not necessary that he should do *something* wrong. It is not my business to be petitioning the Governor or the Legislature any more than it is theirs to petition me; and if they should not hear my petition, what should I do then? But in this case the state has provided no way: its very Constitution is the evil. This may seem to be harsh and stubborn and unconciliatory; but it is to treat with the utmost kindness and consideration the only spirit that can appreciate or deserves it. So is all change for the better, like birth and death, which convulse the body.

I do not hesitate to say, that those who call themselves Abolitionists should at once effectually withdraw their support, both in person and property, from the government of Massachusetts, and not wait till they constitute a majority of one, before they suffer the right to prevail through them. I think that it is enough if they have God on their side, without waiting for that other one. Moreover, any man more right than his neighbors constitutes a majority of one already. . . .

Under a government which imprisons any unjustly, the true place for a just man is also a prison. The proper place to-day, the only place which Massachusetts has provided for her freer and less desponding spirits, is in her prisons, to be put out and locked out of the State by her own act, as they have already put themselves out by their principles. It is there that the fugitive slave, and the Mexican prisoner on parole, and the Indian come to plead the wrongs of his race should find them: on that separate, but more free and honorable ground, where the State places those who are not *with* her, but *against* her—the only house in a slave State in which a free man can abide with honor. If any think that their influence would be lost there, and their voices no longer afflict the ear of the State, that they would not be as an enemy within its walls, they do not know by how much truth is stronger than error, nor how much more eloquently and effectively he can combat injustice who has experienced a little in his own person. . . .

I have paid no poll-tax for six years. I was put into jail once on this account, for one night; and, as I stood considering the walls of solid stone, two or three feet thick, the door of wood and iron, a foot thick, and the iron grating which strained the light, I could not help being struck with the foolishness of that institution which treated me as if I were mere flesh and blood and bones, to be locked up. I wondered that it should have concluded at length that this was the best use it could put me to, and had never thought to avail itself of my services in some way. . . .

The authority of government, even such as I am willing to submit to—for I will cheerfully obey those who know and can do better than I, and in many things even those who neither know nor can do so well—is still an impure one: to be strictly just, it must have the sanction and consent of the governed. It can have no pure right over my person and property, but what I concede to it. The progress from an absolute to a limited monarchy to a democracy, is a progress toward a true respect for the individual. Even the Chinese philosopher was wise enough to regard the individual as the basis of the empire. Is a democracy, such as we know it, the last improvement possible in government? Is it not possible to take a step further towards recognizing and organizing the rights of man? There will never be a really free and enlightened State until the State comes to recognize the individual as a higher and independent power, from which all its own power and authority are derived, and treats him accordingly. I please myself with imagining a State at last which can afford to be just to all men, and to treat the individual with respect as a neighbor; which even would not think it inconsistent with its own repose if a few were to live aloof from it, not meddling with it, nor embraced by it, who fulfilled all the duties of neighbors and fellow men. A state which bore this kind of fruit, and suffered it to drop off as fast as it ripened, would prepare the way for a still more perfect and glorious State, which also I have imagined, but not yet anywhere seen.

XVI

Progress, Reform, and Utopia

ONE OF THE MAIN CHARACTERISTICS of the romantic-democratic mind of nineteenth-century America was its impulse toward reform. Unsystematic and sometimes inconsistent in its ideology, the American response to the pressures and problems attending rapid social and economic change was the reform movements (and sometimes utopian dreams) that extended to nearly all areas of the nation's institutional life. The slavery issue, of course, soon dominated the national scene, but it should not blind one to the larger outlines of the reform pattern.

The uniqueness of America's reformers lies in the fact that they directed their efforts not so much on a class basis—classes were poorly defined and, in any case, contrary to the political ideals of the day—as toward the correction of specific institutional evils. American reformers moved to correct the institutional restraints that prevented self-realization and the pursuit of happiness promised to every individual. Freedom from these restraints seemed to many reformers a part of America's destiny; the conquest of nature suggested the possibility of the conquest of social problems as well. Thus for a variety of reasons, America became a nation of reformers, for, as Emerson put it, "What is a man born for but to be a Reformer, a Remaker of what man has made . . . , imitating that great Nature which embosoms us all, and which sleeps no moment on an old past, but every hour repairs herself, yielding us every morning a new day, and with every pulsation a new life?" In these words, the sage of Concord expressed the spirit of the movement that inspired men and women in their efforts to uproot capital punishment, abolish slavery, end illiteracy and ignorance, and bring about an end to war. This reforming spirit also agitated for equal rights for women, preached humane treatment of the insane, and urged prison reform.

But what were the reasons for this reforming impulse? Perhaps no list can be complete, but the following reasons must certainly be mentioned. America's Enlightenment inheritance, with evangelical Christianity and Jacksonian sentiments, seemed to demand application in reform movements that freed individuals and offered them equal opportunities for full and abundant living. The idea of progress, present in the American mind and receiving support from such European reform movements as utilitarianism, held forth yet another inspiring ideal; and the social and economic tensions of an expanding nation, including the rise of the city as a factor in American culture, pressed reformers on.[1]

Beginning as informal protest, many reform movements ended with the enactment of corrective legislation—thus in fact making the state an agent of reform as well. Others, of course, were never brought to fruition. Yet whatever the outcome of its separate currents, the reform movement as a whole had a marked influence on subsequent American history.

(68)

Horace Mann

1796-1859

The name of Horace Mann is synonymous with public education in America. Unable to afford an elementary education, Mann educated himself and was admitted to Brown University, where he graduated with highest honors in 1819. Shortly thereafter, he entered the legal profession and became a successful lawyer. In 1827, he was elected to the Massachusetts House of Representatives, where he was responsible for a number of reform measures, including the establishment of the first state-supported mental hospital in Massachusetts and the creation of a state board of education.

Mann was appointed the first secretary of the Massachusetts Board of Education in 1837 and held this position until 1848. His annual reports and his many addresses in which he explored educational philosophy, as well as matters of educational practice, occupy a commanding position in American educational history. In his later years he held a seat in Congress, and, in 1853 he accepted the presidency of Antioch College. Puritan in personal outlook and a moderate Whig in politics, Mann is a representative figure of the reform movement.

This selection from Mann's lecture, "The Necessity of Education in a Republican Government," is from *Life and Works of Horace Mann*, 4 vols. (Boston, 1891), vol. II.

1. David Donald has advanced a provocative interpretation of the abolitionist reformers. He argues that most of them came from old-line Yankee Protestant families of middle-class backgrounds. Finding that their traditional position of leadership was being lost to the rising business class in the Northeast and disliking a life devoted to the pursuit of material ends, they turned to reform as a means of self-assertion as well as in the hope of regaining status. See David Donald, *Lincoln Reconsidered* (New York, 1956), pp. 19–36.

My friends, is it not manifest to us all, that no individual, unless he has some acquaintance with the lower forms of education, can superintend even the coarsest and most common interests of life, without daily error and daily shame? The general utility of knowledge, also, and the higher and more enduring satisfactions of the intellect, resulting from the discovery and contemplation of those truths with which the material and the spiritual universe are alike filled, impart to this subject a true dignity and a sublime elevation. But, in its office of attempering feelings which otherwise would blast or consume us;—in its authority to say to the clamorous propensities of our nature, "Peace, be still!"—in its auxiliary power to fit us for the endearments of domestic, for the duties of social, and for the sanctity of immortal life;—in its twofold office of enhancing the enjoyment which each one of us may feel in the virtue and happiness of all others, and of increasing the virtue and happiness of all others, to make a larger fund for common enjoyment;—in these high and sacred prerogatives, the cause of education lays claim to our mind and heart and strength, as one of the most efficient instruments prepared by the Creator for the welfare of His creatures, and the honor of Himself.

Take any individual you please, separate him from the crowd of men, and look at him, apart and alone,—like some Robinson Crusoe in a far-off island of the ocean, without any human being around him, with no prospect of leaving any human being behind him,—and, even in such a solitude, how authoritative over his actions, how decisive of his contemplations and of his condition, are the instructions he received and the habits he formed in early life! But now behold him as one of the tumultuous throng of men; observe the wide influences which he exerts upon others,—in the marts of business, in the resorts of pleasure, in the high places of official trust,—and reflect how many of all these influences, whether beneficent or malign, depend upon the education he has received, and you will have another gauge or standard whereby to estimate the importance of our theme. Look at him again, not as a being, coming, we know not whence, alighting for a brief residence upon this earth, and then making his exit through the door of the tomb, to be seen and heard of no more, and leaving no more impression upon society of his ways or works, than the sea-bird leaves upon the surface of the deep, when she stoops from the upper air, dips her breast for a moment in the wave, and then rises again to a viewless height; but look at him in his relations to posterity, as the father of a family, as a member of a generation which sows those seeds of virtue or vice, that, centuries hence, shall bear fruit or poison; —look at him as a citizen in a free government, throwing his influence and his vote into one or the other of the scales where peace and war, glory and infamy, are weighed;—look at him in these relations, and consider how a virtuous or a vicious education tends to fit or to unfit him for them all, and you will catch one more glimpse of the importance of the subject now presented to your consideration. But if we ascend to a still higher point of vision, and,—forgetting the earthly, personal career, and the wide sphere of social influences, and those acts of life which survive life,—fasten our eyes upon effects which education may throw forward into immortal destinies, it is then that we are awed, amazed, overpowered, by the thought, that we have been created and placed in a system, where the soul's eternal flight may be made higher or lower by those who plume its tender wings and direct its early course. Such is the magnitude, the transcendence of this subject. In a philosophical view, beginning at what point we will, and following the most rigid connection and dependence of cause and effect, of antecedent and consequence, we shall find that education is intimately related to every good, and to every evil, which, as mortal, or as immortal beings, we can desire or dread. . . .

I venture, my friends, at this time, to solicit your attention, while I attempt to lay before you some of the relations which we bear to the cause of Education, because we are the citizens of a Republic; and thence to deduce some of the reasons, which, under our political institutions, make the proper training of the rising generation the highest earthly duty of the risen.

It is a truism, that free institutions multiply human energies. A chained body cannot do much harm; a chained mind can do as little. In a despotic government, the human faculties are benumbed and paralyzed; in a Republic, they glow with an intense life, and burst forth with uncontrollable impetuosity. In the former, they are circumscribed and straitened in their range of action; in the latter, they have "ample room and verge enough," and may rise to glory or plunge into ruin. Amidst universal ignorance, there cannot be such wrong notions about right, as there may be in a community partially enlightened; and false conclusions which have been reasoned out are infinitely worse than blind impulses.

To demonstrate the necessity of education in our government, I shall not attempt to derive my proofs from the history of other Republics. Such arguments are becoming stale. Besides, there are so many points of difference between our own political institutions, and those of any other government calling itself free, which has ever existed, that the objector perpetually eludes or denies the force of our reasoning, by showing some want of analogy between the cases presented.

I propose, therefore, on this occasion, not to adduce, as proofs, what has been true only in past times; but what is true at the present time, and must always continue to be true. I shall rely, not on precedents, but on the nature of things; and draw my arguments less from history than from humanity.

Now it is undeniable that, with the possession of certain higher faculties, —common to all mankind,—whose proper cultivation will bear us upward to hitherto undiscovered regions of prosperity and glory, we possess, also, certain lower faculties or propensities,—equally common,—whose improper indulgence leads, inevitably, to tribulation, and anguish, and ruin. The propensities to which I refer seem indispensable to our temporal existence, and, if restricted within proper limits, they are promotive of our enjoyment; but, beyond those limits, they work dishonor and infatuation, madness and despair. As servants, they are indispensable; as masters, they torture as well as tyrannize. Now despotic and arbitrary governments have dwarfed and crippled the powers of doing evil as much as the powers of doing good; but a republican government, from the very fact of its freedom, unreins their speed, and lets loose their strength. It is justly alleged against despotisms, that they fetter, mutilate, almost extinguish the noblest powers of the human soul; but there is a *per contra* to this, for which we have not given them credit;—they circumscribe the ability to do the greatest evil, as well as to do the greatest good.

My proposition, therefore, is simply this: If republican institutions do wake up unexampled energies in the whole mass of a people, and give them implements of unexampled power wherewith to work out their will, then these same institutions ought also to confer upon that people unexampled wisdom and rectitude. If these institutions give greater scope and impulse to the lower order of faculties belonging to the human mind, then they must also give more authoritative control and more skilful guidance to the higher ones. If they multiply temptations, they must fortify against them. If they quicken the activity and enlarge the sphere of the appetites and passions, they must, at least in an equal ratio, establish the authority and extend the jurisdiction of reason and conscience. In a word, we must not add to the impulsive, without also adding to the regulating forces.

If we maintain institutions, which bring us within the action of new and unheard-of powers, without taking any corresponding measures for the government of those powers, we shall perish by the very instruments prepared for our happiness.

The truth has been so often asserted, that there is no security for a republic but in morality and intelligence, that a repetition of it seems hardly in good taste. But all permanent blessings being founded on permanent truths, a continued observance of the truth is the condition of a continued enjoyment of the blessing. I know we are often admonished that, without intelligence and virtue, as a chart and a compass, to direct us in our untried political voyage, we shall perish in the first storm; but I venture to add that, without these qualities, we shall not wait for a storm,—we cannot weather a calm. If the sea is as smooth as glass we shall founder, for we are in a stone boat. Unless these qualities pervade the general head and the general heart, not only will republican institutions vanish amongst us, but the words *prosperity* and *happiness* will become obsolete. And all this may be affirmed, not from historical examples merely, but from the very constitution of our nature. We are created and brought into life with a set of innate, organic dispositions or propensities, which a free government rouses and invigorates, and which, if not bridled and tamed, by our actually seeing the eternal laws of justice, as plainly as we can see the sun in the heavens,—and by our actually feeling the sovereign sentiment of duty, as plainly as we feel the earth beneath our feet—will hurry us forward into regions populous with every form of evil. . . .

Our propensities have no affinity with reason or conscience. Did you ever hear two persons conversing about a third, whose ruin and infamy they agreed had come from the amount of his fortune, or from his facilities for indulgence, when, in the very breath in which they spoke of the resistless power of the temptation over him, they did not add that, in their own persons, they should be willing to run the same risk? This is the language of all the propensities. They are willing to run any risk, whether it be of health or of character, of time or of eternity. This explains how it is, that some men not wholly lost to virtue,—men who acknowledge their responsibleness to God, and their obligations to conscience,—but in whom the propensities predominate and tyrannize;—I say this explains how it is that such men, when stung and maddened by the goadings of desire, wish themselves bereft of their better attributes, that they might give full career to passion, without remorse of conscience or dread of retribution. That human depravity, which, hitherto, has made the history of our race, like the roll of the prophet, a record of lamentation and mourning and woe, has worked out through these propensities; and, if the very substance and organization of human nature be not changed, by the eradication of these instincts, that depravity which is, to a greater or less degree, to make the future resemble the past, will pour out its agonies and its atrocities though the same channels!

Such, then, are our latent capabilities of evil,—all ready to be evolved, should the restraints of reason, conscience, religion, be removed. Here are millions of men, each with appetites capacious of infinity, and raging to be satisfied out of a supply of means too scanty for any one of them. Millions of coveting eyes are fastened on the same object—millions of hands thrust out to seize it. What ravening, torturing, destroying, then, must ensue, if these hounds cannot be lashed back into their kennel! They must be governed; they cannot be destroyed. Nature declares that the germs, the embryos, of these incipient monsters, shall not be annihilated. She reproduces them with every human being that comes into the world. Nor, indeed, is it desirable, even if it were practicable, that they should be wholly expunged and razed out of our constitution. He who made us, knew our circumstances and necessities, and He has implanted them in our nature too deep for eradication. Besides, within their proper sphere, they confer an innocent, though a subordinate enjoyment. Certainly, we would not make all men hermits and anchorites. Let us be just, even to the appetites. No man is the worse because he keenly relishes and enjoys the bountiful provisions which Heaven has made for his food, his raiment, and his shelter. Indeed, why were these provisions ever made, if they are not to be enjoyed? Surely they are not superfluities and supernumeraries, cumbering a creation which would have been more perfect without them. Let them then be acquired and enjoyed, though always with moderation and temperance. Let the lover of wealth seek wealth by all honest means, and with earnestness, if he will; let him surround himself with the comforts and the embellishments of life, and add the pleasures of beauty to the pleasures of utility. Let every honorable man indulge a quick and sustaining confidence in his own worthiness, whenever disparaged or maligned; and let him count upon the affections of his friends, and the benedictions of his race, as a part of the solid rewards of virtue. These, and kindred feelings, are not to be crushed, extinguished. Let them rouse themselves in presence of their objects, and rush out to seize them, and neigh, like a war-horse for the battle —only let them know that they have a rider, to whose eye no mist can dim the severe line they are never to pass, and whose arm can bend every neck of them, like the twig of an osier. . . .

Let us now turn for a moment to see what means and stimulants our institutions have provided for the use of the mighty powers and passions they have unloosed. No apparatus so skilful was ever before devised. Instead of the slow and cumbrous machinery of former times, we have provided that which is quick-working and far-reaching, and which may be used for the destruction as easily as for the welfare of its possessors. Our institutions furnish as great facilities for wicked men, in all departments of wickedness, as phosphorus and lucifer matches furnish to the incendiary. What chemistry has done, in these preparations, over the old art of rubbing two sticks together, for the wretch who would fire your dwelling, our social partnerships have done for flagitious and unprincipled men. Through the right—almost universal— of suffrage, we have established a community of power; and no proposition is more plain and self-evident, than that nothing but mere popular inclination lies between a community of power and a community in every thing else. And though, in the long-run, and when other things are equal, a righteous cause always has a decisive advantage over an evil one, yet, in the first onset between right and wrong, bad men possess one advantage over the good. They have double resources—two armories. The arts of guilt are as welcome to them as the practices of justice. They can use poisoned weapons as well as those approved by the usages of war.

Again; has it been sufficiently considered, that all which has been said— and truly said—of the excellence of our institutions, if administered by an upright people, must be reversed and read backwards, if administered by a corrupt one? I am aware that some will be ready to say, "We have been unwise and infatuated to confide all the constituents of our social and political welfare to such irresponsible keeping." But let me ask of such,—of what avail is their lamentation? The irresistible movement in the diffusion of power is still progressive, not retrograde. Every year puts more of social strength into the hands of physical strength. The arithmetic of numbers is more and more excluding all estimate of moral forces, in the administration of government. And this, whether for good or for evil, will continue to be. Human beings cannot be remanded to the dungeons of imbecility, if they are to those of ignorance. The sun can as easily be turned backwards in its course, as one particle of that power, which has been conferred upon the millions, can be again monopolized by the few. To discuss the question, therefore, whether our institutions are not too free, is, for all practical purposes, as vain as it would be to discuss the question whether, on the whole, it was a wise arrangement on the part of Divine Providence, that the American continent should ever have been created, or that Columbus should have discovered it. And let me ask, further, have those who believe our institutions to be too free, and who, therefore, would go back to less liberal ones,—have they settled the question, how far back they will go? Will they go back to the dark ages, and recall an eclipse which lasted centuries long? or will they ascend a little higher for their models, to a time when our ancestors wore undressed skins, and burrowed in holes of the earth? or will they strike at once for the institutions of Egypt, where, though the monkey was a god, there was still a sufficient distance between him and his human worshipper? But all such discussions are vain. The oak will as soon go back into the acorn, or the bird into its shell, as we return to the monarchical or aristocratic forms of by-gone ages. . . .

Again, then, I ask, with unmitigated anxiety, what institutions we now possess, that can furnish defence or barrier against the action of those propensities, which each generation brings into the world as a part of its being, and which our institutions foster and stimulate into unparalleled activity and vigor? Can any Christian man believe, that God has so constituted and so governs the human race, that it is always and necessarily to be suicidal of its earthly welfare? No! the thought is impious. The same Almighty Power which implants in our nature the germs of these terrible propensities, has endowed us also with reason and conscience and a sense of responsibility to Him; and, in his providence, he has opened a way by which these nobler faculties can be elevated into dominion and supremacy over the appetites and passions. But if this is ever done, it must be mainly done during the docile and teachable years of childhood. I repeat it, my friends, *if this is ever done, it must be mainly done during the docile and teachable years of childhood.* Wretched, incorrigible, demoniac, as any human being may ever have become, there was a time when he took the first step in error and in crime; when, for the first time, he just nodded to his fall, on the brink of ruin. Then, ere he was irrecoverably lost, ere he plunged into the abyss of infamy and guilt, he might have been recalled, as it were by the waving of the hand. Fathers, mothers, patriots, Christians! it is this very hour of peril through which our children are now passing. They know it not, but we know it; and where the knowledge is, there rests the responsibility. Society is responsible;—not society considered as an abstraction, but society as it consists of living members, which members we are. Clergymen are responsible;—all men who have enjoyed the opportunities of a higher education in colleges and universities are responsible, for they can convert their means, whether of time or of talent, into instruments for elevating the masses of the people. The conductors of the public press are responsible, for they have daily access to the public ear, and can infuse just notions of this high duty into the public mind. Legislators and rulers are responsible. In our country, and in our times, no man is worthy the honored name of a statesman, who does not include the highest practicable education of the people in all his plans of administration. He may have eloquence, he may have a knowledge of all history, diplomacy, jurisprudence; and by these he might claim, in other countries, the elevated rank of a statesman; but, unless he speaks, plans, labors, at all times and in all places, for the culture and edification of the whole people, he is not, he cannot be, an American statesman.

If this dread responsibility for the fate of our children be disregarded, how, when called upon, in the great eventful day, to give an account of the manner in which our earthly duties have been discharged, can we expect to escape the condemnation: "Inasmuch as ye have not done it to one of the least of these, ye have not done it unto me"?

(69)

William Lloyd Garrison

1805-1879

William Lloyd Garrison gained fame as the leading American abolitionist. He was born in Newburyport, Massachusetts, to a family of modest circumstances. He had little formal schooling and at fourteen he was indentured to a printer. He soon became expert in this trade and then tried his hand at writing; before long he gained recognition as an author and editor. Leaving Newburyport, he established a number of short-lived journals. Then in 1831, he founded (with his partner Isaac Knapp) the Boston *Liberator*, a journal that was destined to influence the reform movement for the next thirty-five years. Though Garrison's paper backed temperance, pacifism, and opposition to capital punishment and imprisonment for debt, it was in the abolitionist cause that the *Liberator* achieved greatest fame. Garrison was a vigorous campaigner on behalf of the radical wing of the abolitionist movement, and he spoke at antislavery rallies and demonstrations in addition to his publishing efforts. After the Civil War, Garrison's interest in reform continued, and he became president of the Free Trade League, which advocated the end of all barriers to trade between the nations of the world.

This selection is from an address given at the Park Street Church in Boston on July 4, 1829, in which Garrison, though then only twenty-four, displayed his many powers as an orator. It was printed in the *National Philanthropist and Investigator* of July 22 and 29, 1829, and is taken from the first volume of *William Lloyd Garrison; The Story of His Life Told By His Children,* 4 vols. (New York, 1885), vol. I.

☆ ☆ ☆ ☆

I speak not as a partisan or an opponent of any man or measures, when I say, that our politics are rotten to the core. *We* boast of our freedom, who go shackled to the polls, year after year, by tens, and hundreds, and thousands! We talk of free agency, who are the veriest machines—that merest automata—in the hands of unprincipled jugglers! We prate of integrity, and virtue, and independence, who sell our birthright for office, and who, nine times in ten, do not get Esau's bargain—no, not even a mess of pottage! Is it republicanism to say, that the majority can do no wrong? Then I am not a republican. Is it aristocracy to say, that the people sometimes shamefully abuse their high trust? Then I am an aristocrat. It is not the appreciation, but the abuse of liberty, to withdraw altogether from the polls, or to visit them merely as a matter of form, without carefully investigating the merits of candidates. The republic does not bear a charmed life: our prescriptions administered through the medium of the ballot-box—the mouth of the political body—may kill or cure, according to the nature of the disease and our wisdom in applying the remedy. It is possible that a people may bear the title of freemen who execute the work of slaves. To the dullest observers of the signs of the times, it must be apparent that we are rapidly approximating to this condition. . . .

But there is another evil, which, if we had to contend against nothing else, should make us quake for the issue. It is a gangrene preying upon our vitals—an earthquake rumbling under our feet—a mine accumulating materials for a national catastrophe. It should make this a day of fasting and prayer, not of boisterous merriment and idle pageantry—a day of great lamentation, not of congratulatory joy. It should spike every cannon, and haul down every banner. Our garb should be sackcloth—our heads bowed in the dust—our supplications, for the pardon and assistance of Heaven.

Last week this city was made breathless by a trial of considerable magnitude. The court chamber was inundated for hours, day after day, with a dense and living tide which swept along like the rush of a mountain torrent. Tiers of human bodies were piled up to the walls, with almost miraculous condensation and ingenuity. It seemed as if men abhorred a vacuum equally with Nature: they would suspend themselves, as it were, by a nail, and stand upon air with the aid of a peg. Although it was a barren, ineloquent subject, and the crowd immense, there was no perceptible want of interest—no evidence of impatience. The cause was important, involving the reputation of a distinguished citizen. There was a struggle for mastery between two giants—a test of strength in tossing mountains of law. The excitement was natural.[1]

I stand up here in a more solemn court, to assist in a far greater cause; not to impeach the character of one man, but of a whole people; not to recover the sum of a hundred thousand dollars, but to obtain the liberation of

---

1. The case was that of Farnum, Executor of Tuttle Hubbard, vs. Brooks, and was heard in the Mass. Supreme Court. The "two giants" in opposition were William Wirt, ex-Attorney-General of the United States, and Daniel Webster. Wirt's eloquence made a great impression. (Boston *Traveller,* June 23, 30, 1829; *Columbian Centinel,* June 27.)

two millions of wretched, degraded beings, who are pining in hopeless bondage—over whose sufferings scarcely an eye weeps, or a heart melts, or a tongue pleads either to God or man. I regret that a better advocate had not been found, to enchain your attention and to warm your blood. Whatever fallacy, however, may appear in the argument, there is no flaw in the indictment; what the speaker lacks, the cause will supply.

Sirs, I am not come to tell you that slavery is a curse, debasing in its effect, cruel in its operation, fatal in its continuance. The day and the occasion require no such revelation. I do not claim the discovery as my own, that "all men are born equal," and that among their inalienable rights are "life, liberty, and the pursuit of happiness." Were I addressing any other than a free and Christian assembly, the enforcement of this truth might be pertinent. Neither do I intend to analyze the horrors of slavery for your inspection, nor to freeze your blood with authentic recitals of savage cruelty. Nor will time allow me to explore even a furlong of that immense wilderness of suffering which remains unsubdued in our land. I take it for granted that the existence of these evils is acknowledged, if not rightly understood. My object is to define and enforce our duty, as Christians and Philanthropists.

On a subject so exhaustless, it will be impossible, in the moiety of an address, to unfold all the facts which are necessary to its full development. In view of it, my heart swells up like a living fountain, which time cannot exhaust, for it is perpetual. Let this be considered as the preface of a noble work, which your inventive sympathies must elaborate and complete.

I assume as distinct and defensible propositions,

I. That the slaves of this country, whether we consider their moral, intellectual or social condition, are preeminently entitled to the prayers, and sympathies, and charities, of the American people; and their claims for redress are as strong as those of any Americans could be in a similar condition.

II. That, as the free States—by which I mean non-slaveholding States—are constitutionally involved in the guilt of slavery, by adhering to a national compact that sanctions it; and in the danger, by liability to be called upon for aid in case of insurrection; they have the right to remonstrate against its continuance, and it is their duty to assist in its overthrow.

III. That no justification plea for the perpetuity of slavery can be found in the condition of its victims; and no barrier against our righteous interference, in the laws which authorize the buying, selling and possessing of slaves, nor in the hazard of a collision with slaveholders.

IV. That education and freedom will elevate our colored population to a rank with the white—making them useful, intelligent and peaceable citizens.

In the first place, it will be readily admitted, that it is the duty of every nation primarily to administer relief to its own necessities, to cure its own maladies, to instruct its own children, and to watch over its own interests. He is "worse than an infidel" who neglects his own household, and squanders his earnings upon strangers; and the policy of that nation is unwise which seeks to proselyte other portions of the globe at the expense of its safety and happiness. Let me not be misunderstood. My benevolence is neither contracted nor selfish. I pity that man whose heart is not larger than a whole continent. I despise the littleness of that patriotism which blusters only for its own rights, and, stretched to its utmost dimensions, scarcely covers its native territory; which adopts as its creed the right to act independently, even to the verge of licentiousness, without restraint, and to tyrannize wherever it can with impunity. This sort of patriotism is common. I suspect the reality, and deny the productiveness, of that piety which confines its operations to a particular spot—if that spot be less than the whole earth; nor scoops out, in every direction, new channels for the waters of life. Christian charity, while it "begins at home," goes abroad in search of misery. It is as copious as the sun in heaven. It does not, like the Nile, make a partial inundation, and then withdraw; but it perpetually overflows, and fertilizes every barren spot. It is restricted only by the exact number of God's suffering creatures. But I mean to say, that, while we are aiding and instructing foreigners, we ought not to forget our own degraded countrymen; that neither duty nor honesty requires us to defraud ourselves that we may enrich others.

The condition of the slaves, in a religious point of view, is deplorable, entitling them to a higher consideration, on our part, than any other race; higher than the Turks or Chinese, for they have the privileges of instruction; higher than the Pagans, for they are not dwellers in a gospel land; higher than our red men of the forest, for we do not bind them with gyves, nor treat them as chattels.

And here let me ask, What has Christianity done, by direct effort, for our slave population? Comparatively nothing. She has explored the isles of the ocean for objects of commiseration; but, amazing stupidity! she can gaze without emotion on a multitude of miserable beings at home, large enough to constitute a nation of freemen, whom tyranny has heathenized by law. In her public services they are seldom remembered, and in her private donations they are forgotten. From one end of the country to the other, her charitable societies form golden links of benevolence, and scatter their contributions like raindrops over a parched heath; but they bring no sustenance to the perishing slave. The blood of souls is upon her garments, yet she heeds not the stain. The clankings of the prisoner's chains strike upon her ear, but they cannot penetrate her heart.

I have said that the claims of the slaves for redress are as strong as those of any Americans could be, in a similar condition. Does any man deny the position? The proof, then, is found in the fact, that a very large proportion of our colored population were born on our soil, and are therefore entitled to all the privileges of American citizens. This is their country by birth, not by adoption. Their children possess the same inherent and unalienable rights as ours, and it is a crime of the blackest dye to load them with fetters.

Every Fourth of July, our Declaration of Independence is produced, with a sublime indignation, to set forth the tyranny of the mother country, and to challenge the admiration of the world. But what a pitiful detail of grievances does this document present, in comparison with the wrongs which our slaves endure! In the one case, it is hardly the plucking of a hair from the head; in the other, it is the crushing of a live body on the wheel—the stings of the wasp contrasted with the tortures of the Inquisition. Before God, I must say, that such a glaring contradiction as exists between our creed and practice the annals of six thousand years cannot parallel. In view of it, I am ashamed of my country. I am sick of our unmeaning declamation in praise of liberty and equality; of our hypocritical cant about the unalienable rights of man. I could not, for my right hand, stand up before a European assembly, and exult that I am an American citizen, and denounce the usurpations of a kingly government as wicked and unjust; or, should I make the attempt, the recollection of my country's barbarity and despotism would blister my lips, and cover my cheeks with burning blushes of shame.

Will this be termed a rhetorical flourish? Will any man coldly accuse me of intemperate zeal? I will borrow, then, a ray of humanity from one of the brightest stars in our American galaxy, whose light will gather new effulgence to the end of time. "This, sirs, is a cause that would be dishonored and betrayed if I contented myself with appealing only to the understanding. It is too cold, and its processes are too slow for the occasion. I desire to thank God that, since he has given me an intellect so fallible, he has impressed upon me an instinct that is sure. On a question of shame and honor—liberty and oppression—reasoning is sometimes useless, and worse. I feel the decision in my pulse: if it throws no light upon the brain, it kindles a fire at the heart." . . .

I come to my second proposition:—the right of the free States to remonstrate against the continuance, and to assist in the overthrow of slavery.

This, I am aware, is a delicate subject, surrounded with many formidable difficulties. But if delay only adds to its intricacy, wherefore shun an immediate investigation? I know that we, of the North, affectedly believe that we have no local interest in the removal of this great evil; that the slave States can take care of themselves, and that any proffered assistance, on our part, would be rejected as impertinent, dictatorial or meddlesome; and that we have no right to lift up even a note of remonstrance. But I believe that these opinions are crude, preposterous, dishonorable, unjust. Sirs, this is a business in which, as members of one great family, we have a common interest; but we take no responsibility, either individually or collectively. Our hearts are cold— our blood stagnates in our veins. We act, in relation to the slaves, as if they were something lower than the brutes that perish.

On this question, I ask no support from the injunction of Holy Writ, which says:—"therefore all things whatsoever ye would that men should do to you, do ye even so to them: for this is the law and the prophets." I throw aside the common dictates of humanity. I assert the right of the free States to demand a gradual abolition of slavery, because, by its continuance, they participate in the guilt thereof, and are threatened with ultimate destruction; because they are bound to watch over the interests of the whole country, without reference to territorial divisions; because their white population is nearly double that of the slave States, and the voice of this overwhelming majority should be potential; because they are now deprived of their just influence in the councils of the nation; because it is absurd and anti-republican to suffer property to be represented as men, and *vice versa*.[2] Because it gives the South an injust ascendancy over other portions of territory, and a power which may be perverted on every occasion. . . .

Now I say that, on the broad system of equal rights, this monstrous inequality should no longer be tolerated. If it cannot be speedily put down—not by force, but by fair persuasion; if we are always to remain shackled by unjust Constitutional provisions, when the emergency that imposed them has long since passed away; if we must share in the guilt and danger of destroying the bodies and souls of men, *as the price of our Union;* if the slave States will haughtily spurn our assistance, and refuse to consult the general welfare; then the fault is not ours if a separation eventually take place. . . .

It may be objected, that the laws of the slave States form insurmountable barriers to any interference on our part.

Answer. I grant that we have not the right, and I trust not the disposition, to use coercive measures. But do these laws hinder our prayers, or obstruct the flow of our sympathies? Cannot our charities alleviate the condition of the slave, and perhaps break his fetters? Can we not operate upon public sentiment, (the lever that can move the moral world,) by way of remonstrance, advice, or entreaty? Is Christianity so powerful that she can tame the red men of our forests, and abolish the Burman caste, and overthrow the gods of Paganism, and liberate lands over which the darkness of Superstition has lain for ages; and yet so weak, in her own dwelling-place, that she can make no impression upon her civil code? Can she contend successfully with cannibals, and yet be conquered by her own children?

Suppose that, by a miracle, the slaves should suddenly become white. Would you shut your eyes upon their sufferings, and calmly talk of Constitutional limitations? No; your voice would peal in the ears of the taskmasters like deep thunder; you would carry the Constitution by force, if it could not be taken by treaty; patriotic assemblies would congregate at the corners of every street; the old Cradle of Liberty would rock to a deeper tone than ever echoed therein at British aggression; the pulpit would acquire new and unusual eloquence from our holy religion. The argument, that these white slaves are degraded, would not then obtain. You would say, it is enough that they are white, and in bondage, and they ought immediately to be set free. You would multiply your schools of instruction, and your temples of worship, and rely on them for security. . . .

But the plea is prevalent, that any interference by the free States, however benevolent or cautious it might be, would only irritate and inflame the jealousies of the South, and retard the cause of emancipation. If any man

---

2. By the three-fifths representation clause of the Federal Constitution, Art. I., Sec. ii., 3.

believes that slavery can be abolished without a struggle with the worst passions of human nature, quietly, harmoniously, he cherishes a delusion. It can never be done, unless the age of miracles return. No; we must expect a collision, full of sharp asperities and bitterness. We shall have to contend with the insolence, and pride, and selfishness, of many a heartless being. But these can be easily conquered by meekness, and perseverance, and prayer.

Sirs, the prejudices of the North are stronger than those of the South;— they forge and rivet the chains of the nation. Conquer them, and the victory is won. The enemies of emancipation take courage from our criminal timidity. They have justly stigmatized us, even on the floor of Congress, with the most contemptuous epithets. We are (they say) their "white slaves,"[3] afraid of our shadows, who have been driven back to the wall again and again; who stand trembling under their whips; who turn pale, retreat, and surrender, at a talismanic threat to dissolve the Union. . . .

It is often despondingly said, that the evil of slavery is beyond our control. Dreadful conclusion, that puts the seal of death upon our country's existence! If we cannot conquer the monster in his infancy, while his cartilages are tender and his limbs powerless, how shall we escape his wrath when he goes forth a gigantic cannibal, seeking whom he may devour? If we cannot safely unloose two millions of slaves now, how shall we bind upwards of TWENTY MILLIONS at the close of the present century? But there is no cause for despair. We have seen how readily, and with what ease, that horrid gorgon, Intemperance, has been checked in his ravages. Let us take courage. Moral influence, when in vigorous exercise, is irresistible. It has an immortal essence. It can no more be trod out of existence by the iron foot of time, or by the ponderous march of iniquity, than matter can be annihilated. It may disappear for a time; but it lives in some shape or other, in some place or other, and will rise with renovated strength. Let us, then, be up and doing. In the simple and stirring language of the stout-hearted Lundy, "all the friends of the cause must go to work, keep to work, hold on, and never give up."

If it be still objected, that it would be dangerous to liberate the present race of blacks;

I answer—the emancipation of all the slaves of this generation is most assuredly out of the question. The fabric, which now towers above the Alps, must be taken away brick by brick, and foot by foot, till it is reduced so low that it may be overturned without burying the nation in its ruins. Years may elapse before the completion of the achievement; generations of blacks may go down to the grave, manacled and lacerated, without a hope for their children; the philanthropists who are now pleading in behalf of the oppressed, may not live to witness the dawn which will precede the glorious day of universal emancipation; but the work will go on—laborers in the cause will multiply— new resources will be discovered—the victory will be obtained, worth the

---

3. In Henry Adams's *Life of John Randolph* we read (p. 281): "On another occasion, he [Randolph] is reported as saying of the people of the North, 'We do not govern them by our black slaves, but by their own white slaves.'"

desperate struggle of a thousand years. Or, if defeat follow, woe to the safety of this people! The nation will be shaken as if by a mighty earthquake. A cry of horror, a cry of revenge, will go up to heaven in the darkness of midnight, and re-echo from every cloud. Blood will flow like water—the blood of guilty men, and of innocent women and children. Then will be heard lamentations and weeping, such as will blot out the remembrance of the horrors of St. Domingo. The terrible judgments of an incensed God will complete the catastrophe of republican America.

And since so much is to be done for our country; since so many prejudices are to be dispelled, obstacles vanquished, interests secured, blessings obtained; since the cause of emancipation must progress heavily, and meet with much unhallowed opposition—why delay the work? There must be a beginning, and now is a propitious time—perhaps the last opportunity that will be granted us by a long-suffering God. No temporizing, lukewarm measures will avail aught. We must put our shoulders to the wheel, and heave with our united strength. Let us not look coldly on and see our Southern brethren[4] contending single-handed against an all-powerful foe—faint, weary, borne down to the earth. We are all alike guilty. Slavery is strictly a national sin. New England money has been expended in buying human flesh; New England ships have been freighted with sable victims; New England men have assisted in forging the fetters of those who groan in bondage.

I call upon the ambassadors of Christ everywhere to make known this proclamation: "Thus saith the Lord God of the Africans, Let this people go, that they may serve me." I ask them to "proclaim liberty to the captives, and the opening of the prison to them that are bound"—to light up a flame of philanthropy that shall burn till all Africa be redeemed from the night of moral death, and the song of deliverance be heard throughout her borders.

I call upon the churches of the living God to lead in this great enterprise.[5] If the soul be immortal, priceless, save it from remediless woe. Let them combine their energies, and systematize their plans, for the rescue of suffering humanity. Let them pour out their supplications to heaven in behalf of the slave. Prayer is omnipotent: its breath can melt adamantine rocks —its touch can break the stoutest chains. Let antislavery charity-boxes stand uppermost among those for missionary, tract and educational purposes. On this subject, Christians have been asleep; let them shake off their slumbers, and arm for the holy contest.

I call upon our New England women to form charitable associations to relieve the degraded of their sex. As yet, an appeal to their sympathies was

---

4. An allusion to the few antislavery societies among the Friends in some of the Southern States.

5. So Daniel Webster, in his Plymouth oration, Dec. 22, 1820, of the African slave-trade and of New England complicity with it: "I invoke the ministers of our religion, that they proclaim its denunciation of these crimes, and add its solemn sanctions to the authority of human laws. If the pulpit be silent whenever or wherever there may be a sinner bloody with his guilt within the hearing of its voice, the pulpit is false to its trust" (*Works,* 1:46).

never made in vain. They outstrip us in every benevolent race. Females are doing much for the cause at the South; let their example be imitated, and their exertions surpassed, at the North.

I call upon our citizens to assist in establishing auxiliary colonization societies in every state, county and town. I implore their direct and liberal patronage to the parent society.

I call upon the great body of newspaper editors to keep this subject constantly before their readers; to sound the trumpet of alarm, and to plead eloquently for the rights of man. They must give the tone to public sentiment. One press may ignite twenty; a city may warm a State; a State may impart a generous heat to a whole country.

I call upon the American people to enfranchise a spot over which they hold complete sovereignty; to cleanse that worse than Augean stable, the District of Columbia, from its foul impurities. I ask them to sustain Congress in any future efforts to colonize the colored population of the States. I conjure them to select those as Representatives who are not too ignorant to know, too blind to see, nor too timid to perform their duty.

I will say, finally, that I despair of the republic while slavery exists therein. If I look up to God for success, no smile of mercy or forgiveness dispels the gloom of futurity; if to our own resources, they are daily diminishing; if to all history, our destruction is not only possible, but almost certain. Why should we slumber at this momentous crisis? If our hearts were dead to every throb of humanity; if it were lawful to oppress, where power is ample; still, if we had any regard for our safety and happiness, we should strive to crush the Vampire which is feeding upon our life-blood. All the selfishness of our nature cries aloud for a better security. Our own vices are too strong for us, and keep us in perpetual alarm; how, in addition to these, shall we be able to contend successfully with millions of armed and desperate men, as we must eventually, if slavery do not cease?

(70)

Timothy Dwight Weld

1803-1895

The slavery question became the predominant issue on the national scene in the decade before 1860. Increasingly, the spokesmen for abolition captured the imagination of large segments of the American public. One of the most important figures in the abolitionist movement was Timothy Dwight Weld, who represented a forceful but somewhat more moderate stand than Garrison. Descended from a line of New England clergymen, Weld was converted by the Presbyterian revivalist Charles G. Finney and spent two years on the preaching circuit. He next labored for the cause of temperance and was then attracted to the antislavery movement. From 1830 on, he sought to preach the evils of slavery and became one of the most effective abolitionists in the country. Among many other activities, he helped to organize the antislavery bloc in Congress. Weld was in fact one of the most important figures of his time.

The selection is from Weld's book *American Slavery As It Is* (New York, 1839), which influenced most subsequent abolitionist literature.

Reader, you are empaneled as a juror to try a plain case and bring in an honest verdict. The question at issue is not one of law, but of fact —"What is the actual condition of the slaves in the United States?" A plainer case never went to a jury. Look at it. TWENTY-SEVEN HUNDRED THOUSAND PERSONS in this country, men, women, and children, are in SLAVERY. Is slavery, as a condition for human beings, good, bad, or indifferent? We submit the question without argument. You have common sense, and conscience, and a human heart;—pronounce upon it. You have a wife, or a husband, a child, a father, a mother, a brother or a sister—make the case your own, make it theirs, and bring in your verdict. The case of Human Rights against Slavery has been adjudicated in the court of conscience times innumerable. The same verdict has always been rendered—"guilty;" the same sentence has always been pronounced, "Let it be accursed;" . . . His heart is false to human nature, who will not say "Amen." There is not a man on earth who does not believe that slavery is a curse. Human beings may be inconsistent, but human *nature* is true to herself. She has uttered her testimony against slavery with a shriek ever since the monster was begotten; and till it perishes amidst the execrations of the universe, she will traverse the world on its track, dealing her bolts upon its head, and dashing against it her condemning brand. . . .

Two millions seven hundred thousand persons in these States are in this condition. They were made slaves and are held such by force, and by being put in fear, and this for no crime! Reader, what have you to say of such treatment? Is it right, just, benevolent? Suppose I should seize you, rob you of your liberty, drive you into the field, and make you work without pay as long as you live, would that be justice and kindness, or monstrous injustice and cruelty? Now, every body knows that the slaveholders do these things to the slaves every day, and yet it is stoutly affirmed that they treat them well and kindly, and that their tender regard for their slaves restrains the masters from inflicting cruelties upon them. We shall go into no metaphysics to show the absurdity of this pretence. The man who *robs* you every day, is, forsooth, quite too tender-hearted ever to cuff or kick you! True, he can snatch your money, but he does it gently lest he should hurt you. He can empty your pockets without qualms, but if your *stomach* is empty, it cuts him to the quick. He can make you work a life time without pay, but loves you too well to let you go hungry. He fleeces you of your *rights* with a relish, but is shocked if you work bareheaded in summer, or in winter without warm stockings. He can make you go without your *liberty,* but never without a shirt. He can crush, in you, all hope of bettering your condition, by vowing that you shall die his slave, but though he can coolly torture your feelings, he is too compassionate to lacerate your back—he can break your heart, but he is very tender of your skin. He can strip you of all protection and thus expose you to all outrages, but if you are exposed to the *weather,* half clad and half sheltered, how yearn his tender bowels! What! slaveholders talk of treating men well, and yet not only rob them of all they get, and as fast as they get it, but rob them of *themselves,* also; their very hands and feet, all their muscles, and limbs, and senses, their bodies and minds, their time and liberty and earnings, their free speech and rights of conscience, their right to acquire knowledge, and property, and reputation;—and yet they, who plunder them of all these, would fain make us believe that their soft hearts ooze out so lovingly toward their slaves that they always keep them well housed and well clad, never push them too hard in the field, never make their dear backs smart, nor let their dear stomachs get empty.

But there is no end to these absurdities. Are slaveholders dunces, or do they take all the rest of the world to be, that they think to bandage our eyes with such thin gauzes? Protesting their kind regard for those whom they hourly plunder of all they have and all they get! What! when they have seized their victims, and annihilated all their *rights,* still claim to be the special guardians of their *happiness!* Plunderers of their liberty, yet the careful suppliers of their wants? Robbers of their earnings, yet watchful sentinels round their interests, and kind providers of their comforts? Filching all their time, yet granting generous donations for rest and sleep? Stealing the use of their muscles, yet thoughtful of their ease? Putting them under *drivers,* yet careful that they are not hard-pushed? Too humane forsooth to stint the stomachs of their slaves, yet force their *minds* to starve, and brandish over them pains and penalties, if they dare to reach forth for the smallest crumb of knowledge, even a letter of the alphabet!

It is no marvel that slaveholders are always talking of their *kind treatment* of their slaves. The only marvel is, that men of sense can be gulled by such professions. Despots always insist that they are merciful. . . .

As slaveholders and their apologists are volunteer witnesses in their own cause, and are flooding the world with testimony that their slaves are kindly treated; that they are well fed, well clothed, well housed, well lodged, moderately worked, and bountifully provided with all things needful for their comfort, we propose—first, to disprove their assertions by the testimony of a multitude of impartial witnesses, and then to put slaveholders themselves through a course of cross-questioning which shall draw their condemnation out of their own mouths. We will prove that the slaves in the United States are treated with barbarous inhumanity; that they are overworked, underfed, wretchedly clad and lodged, and have insufficient sleep; that they are often made to wear round their necks iron collars armed with prongs, to drag heavy chains and weights at their feet while working in the field, and to wear yokes, and bells, and iron horns; that they are often kept confined in the stocks day and night for weeks together, made to wear gags in their mouths for hours or days, have some of their front teeth torn out or broken off, that they may be easily detected when they run away; that they are frequently flogged with terrible severity, have red pepper rubbed into their lacerated flesh, and hot brine, spirits of turpentine, &c., poured over the gashes to increase the torture; that they are often stripped naked, their backs and limbs cut with knives, bruised and mangled by scores and hundreds of blows with the paddle, and terribly torn by the claws of cats, drawn over them by their tormentors; that they are often hunted with bloodhounds and shot down like beasts, or torn in pieces by dogs; that they are often suspended by the arms and whipped and beaten till they faint, and when revived by restoratives, beaten again till they faint, and sometimes till they die; that their ears are often cut off, their eyes knocked out, their bones broken, their flesh branded with red hot irons; that they are maimed, mutilated and burned to death over slow fires. All these things, and more, and worse, we shall *prove*. Reader, we know whereof we affirm, we have weighed it well; *more and worse* WE WILL PROVE. Mark these words, and read on; we will establish all these facts by the testimony of scores and hundreds of eye witnesses, by the testimony of *slaveholders* in all parts of the slave states, by slaveholding members of Congress and of state legislatures, by ambassadors to foreign courts, by judges, by doctors of divinity, and clergymen of all denominations, by merchants, mechanics, lawyers and physicians, by presidents and professors in colleges and *professional* seminaries, by planters, overseers and drivers. We shall show, not merely that such deeds are committed, but that they are frequent; not done in corners, but before the sun; not in one of the slave states, but in all of them; not perpetrated by brutal overseers and drivers merely, but by magistrates, by legislators, by professors of religion, by preachers of the gospel, by governors of states, by "gentlemen of property and standing," and by delicate females moving in the "highest circles of society." . . .

The barbarous indifference with which slaveholders regard the forcible sundering of husbands and wives, parents and children, brothers and sisters, and the unfeeling brutality indicated by the language in which they describe the efforts made by the slaves, in their yearnings after those from whom they have been torn away, reveals a "public opinion" towards them as dead to their agony as if they were cattle. It is well nigh impossible to open a southern paper without finding evidence of this. Though the truth of this assertion can hardly be called in question, we subjoin a few illustrations, and could easily give hundreds. . . .

From the "Savannah Georgian," Jan. 17, 1839.

$100 reward will be given for my two fellows, Abram and Frank. Abram has a *wife* at Colonel Stewart's, in Liberty county, and a *sister* in Savannah, at Capt. Grovenstine's. Frank has a *wife* at Mr. Le Cont's, Liberty county; a *mother* at Thunderbolt, and a *sister* in Savannah.

WM. ROBARTS.

Walhourville, 5th Jan. 1839.

From the "Lexington (Ky.) Intelligencer," July, 1838.

$160 Reward.—Ranaway from the subscribers, living in this city, on Saturday 16th inst. a negro man, named Dick, about 37 years of age. It is highly probable said boy will make for New Orleans, as *he has a wife* living in that city, and he has been heard to say frequently that *he was determined to go to New Orleans.*

DRAKE & THOMPSON.

Lexington, June 17, 1838.

From the "Southern Argus," Oct. 31, 1837.

Runaway—my negro man, Frederick, about 20 years of age. He is no doubt near the plantation of G. W. Corprew, Esq. of Noxubbee county, Mississippi, as *his wife belongs to that gentleman, and he followed her from my residence.* The above reward will be paid to any one who will confine him in jail and inform me of it at Athens, Ala.

KERKMAN LEWIS.

From the "Richmond (Va.) Compiler," Sept. 8, 1837.

Ranaway from the subscriber, Ben. He ran off without any known cause, and *I suppose he is aiming to go to his wife, who was carried from the neighborhood last winter.*

JOHN HUNT.

From the "Jackson (Tenn.) Telegraph," Sept. 14, 1838.

Committed to the jail of Madison county, a negro woman, who calls her name Fanny, and says she belongs to William Miller, of Mobile. She formerly belonged to John Givins, of this county, who now owns *several of her children.*

DAVID SHROPSHIRE, Jailor.

From the "Richmond (Va.) Enquirer," Feb. 20, 1838.

Stop the Runaway! ! !—$25 Reward. Ranaway from the Eagle Tavern, a negro fellow, named Nat. He is no doubt attempting to *follow his wife, who was lately sold to a speculator named Redmond.* The above reward will be paid by Mrs. Lucy M. Downman, of Sussex county, Va.

Multitudes of advertisements like the above appear annually in the southern papers. Reader, look at the preceding list—mark the unfeeling barbarity with which their masters and *mistresses* describe the struggles and perils of sundered husbands and wives, parents and children, in their weary midnight travels through forests and rivers, with torn limbs and breaking hearts, seeking the embraces of each other's love. In one instance, a mother torn from all her children and taken to a remote part of another state, presses her way back through the wilderness, hundreds of miles, to clasp once more her children to her heart; but, when she has arrived within a few miles of them, in the same county, is discovered, seized, dragged to jail, and her purchaser told, through an advertisement, that she awaits his order. But we need not trace out the harrowing details already before the reader.

(71)

Samuel Gridley Howe

1801-1876

Descended from an old Puritan family that had migrated to New England in the 1630's, Samuel Gridley Howe typified the mid-nineteenth-century reformer whose philosophy was based on an ardent faith in the idea of progress. He graduated from Brown University in 1821 and received his M.D. from Harvard three years later. He then set out into the world determined to help the less fortunate and oppressed peoples. First he spent nearly six years in Greece, aiding that land's struggle for independence and then helping to rebuild that devastated country. Then he returned to the United States, where he took charge of a school for the blind (the Perkins Institution) incorporated by the Massachusetts Legislature, and he achieved an international reputation for his pioneer efforts in educating the blind and the deaf-blind. Howe also worked with the mentally retarded and played an active role in general educational reform, antislavery, and other reform movements.

The following selection, "Insanity in Massachusetts," from the *North American Review,* vol. 66 (January, 1843), was written by Howe when a member of the Massachusetts Legislature. It was written as part of his fight for a bill authorizing the establishment of additional quarters at the State Lunatic Hospital at Worcester, one of the earliest and most famous state institutions for the care of the insane in the United States.

It has always been a defect of the social system, that a part of the population is dependent upon the rest for the means of subsistence. It is as true in the nineteenth, as it was in the first century, "The poor ye have always with you"; and the question, which has been asked by statesmen of all ages and of all countries, "What can best be done with them?" remains as yet without a satisfactory answer. In its early stages, society disposes of the question summarily, ridding itself of the old and the helpless by violence or exposure; but with advancing civilization better feelings are developed, and men revolt at such treatment of the unfortunate. They preserve the feeble in life, and pauperism appears.

The first efforts for the relief of the dependent, are generally the dictates of blind feeling, unenlightened by intellect, and therefore they often fail of their object. Hence we see private charity, and charitable institutions, often disappointing the hopes of the benevolent; and vast and expensive systems for the relief of the poor are entailed upon society, which are of doubtful efficacy, if they do not act as positive premiums upon pauperism. At any rate, so many difficulties surround the subject, and so manifest has been the failure of public systems for the support of the poor, that many wise and good men question their expediency; and they adduce powerful arguments to show that society, as such, should never step forth to relieve want, which could have been foreseen and provided against, or to assume responsibilities and cares, which should devolve upon individuals. It is maintained, and with much plausibility, that private charity is the natural source of comfort and support for the suffering and the needy, and that it would be sufficient for all purposes, if society, by assuming the charge of the poor, did not prevent its exercise, and thus check its development. Be this as it may, it is certain, that there are many cases of want or suffering, which in the present state of society could not have been foreseen or avoided by the victims; which private charity is not competent to relieve; and the care of which certainly devolves upon society, especially as some of them are caused by its defective organization. Hence arises the obligation of society to provide for, and instruct helpless orphans, the blind, and the deaf-mutes, and to take care of the insane. It is of this last class that we propose to say a few words in the following article.

Of all the ills which flesh is heir to, there is perhaps none so dreadful as insanity. Utter poverty, hideous deformity, mutilation of limbs, deafness, blindness, all these, sad as they are, leave alive the human affections, and admit the consolations of sympathy and love; while insanity not only makes man utterly dependent upon others for the supply of his physical wants, but it strips him of the noblest attributes of humanity. It so utterly sears his heart, that no affection for another can grow upon it, no love from others can penetrate within it; and the unhappy victim sinks into apathetic indifference to common decency, or is so excited as to crush the life out of the mother who bore him, as coolly as he would trample upon a worm.

Of insane persons and idiots, there are, in the United States, according to the census of 1840, 17,434; in New England 3,576; and in Massachusetts, 1,271. Of these last, 644 are at public charge, and 627 at private charge. But, appalling as this statement is, it is unfortunately short of the truth, for the Pauper Abstract, published by the State authority in the same year, gave 887 as the number at public charge in Massachusetts. The cause of the discrepancy is clear; the town officers, besides a personal acquaintance with all the individuals in their neighbourhood, have the means of knowing, from the town records, how many insane are at public charge; while the United States Marshals, embracing larger sections, and taking hearsay evidence, miss those cases in which persons are ashamed to own they have an insane relative. The same discrepancy has occurred in other States, whence local returns have been made; so that we are safe in putting down the insane and idiots of Massachusetts, who are at public charge, to be at least 887. There are no means of testing the accuracy of the United States census in regard to the number of those at private charge, which it states to be 627; but, the same causes for concealment operating still more strongly than in the case of the paupers, we may safely add to it in the same proportion, and compute the real number to be at least 862; which, added to that of the paupers, gives us the number of 1749 insane and idiots in this Commonwealth.

What is the duty of the State towards these its unfortunate children? With regard to the paupers it is clear and imperative; it is what should be the duty of every Christian government,—to provide the best means for the cure of the curable, and to take kind care of the incurable. This duty of society, besides being urged by every consideration of humanity, will be seen to be more imperative if we consider that insanity is in many cases the result of imperfect or vicious social institutions and observances. Most writers assert, that insanity is not known among savage nations; but, without admitting this to be strictly true, it cannot be denied that civilization, in its progress, is rife with causes which over-excite individuals, and result in the loss of mental equilibrium. We have hardly space to allude to all of these; but among them are revolutions, party strifes, unwise and capricious legislation, causing commercial speculations and disasters; false standards of worth and rank; undue encouragement of the propensities and passions; social rivalry; social intemperance; some fashions and conventional usages; religious and political excitement. These, and a variety of other causes, for which society is in fault, are productive of a large proportion of the cases of insanity which exist in its bosom. But if to these we add the still larger number, which arise from ignorance of the natural laws, which ignorance society should enlighten by providing proper public instruction, we can fairly lay at its door almost all of the cases of insanity which occur. . . .

We, of the North, are called a cold-blooded people; and it may be so; but the blood rushes with the momentum, as well as the coldness, of quicksilver, through our veins. We live upon the high-pressure principle within, and pile on additional atmospheres of caution and reserve without, in order to prevent an explosion. Men walk the streets with measured gait and solemn aim, looking as stiff as a steamboat boiler, but, like that, perhaps, are heaving with an inward force just ready to rend them. There is no creed so comprehensive, no dogma so contracted, no scheme so wild, but cold and iron men will embrace and cherish it, with

> "all the zeal,
> Which young and fiery converts feel,"

They wait not until a cloud, as big as a man's hand, shall portend that it is to cover the firmament, but the very specks on their finger nails, steadily regarded, soon grow big enough to exclude every thing else from their mental horizon. Then, the general and exciting struggle for wealth, with all its exhilarating hopes, its sudden reverses, its constant fluctuations; and the more general anxiety for the good opinion of others, which twists so many into false positions, represses so many natural impulses, and gives so much care and anxiety about appearances.

But, be the causes what they may, here, within the precincts of Massachusetts, are more than seventeen hundred human beings, our fellow-citizens, who are insane or idiotic; and of these, eight hundred and eighty-seven are entirely dependent upon the public for food and clothing, for the means of keeping out of fire and water, and for restraint from imbruing their hands in the blood of their fellows. And how does the public discharge its duty towards them? The State makes provision, in its noble establishment at Worcester, for 229 patients, but the poor do not have the sole benefit of this; and the County of Suffolk provides for 100 more, in its commodious and excellent Hospital at South Boston. The others, over 500 in number, are, for the most part, in the almshouses and the jails.

We select, for description, the establishment at South Boston, as we knew it under the excellent management of Dr. Butler, because its patients are wholly of the pauper class. The building is a commodious and pleasant one, constructed expressly for the purpose, with all the modern improvements, and pleasantly situated upon the seashore, with a garden in front. Its inmates were of the worst and most hopeless class of cases; they were the raving madmen, and the gibbering idiot, whom, in the language of the inspectors, we had formerly seen, "tearing their clothes amid severe cold, lacerating their bodies, contracting most filthy habits, without self-control, unable to restrain the worst feelings, endeavouring to injure those who approached them, giving vent to their irritation in the most passionate, profane, and filthy language; fearing and feared, hating and almost hated!" Now, they are all neatly clad by day, and comfortably lodged in separate rooms by night. They walk quietly, and with self-respect, about the spacious and airy halls, or sit in listening groups around the daily paper; or they dig in the garden, or handle edge-tools, or stroll about the neighbourhood with kind and careful attendants. They attend soberly and reverently upon religious exercises, and make glad music with their united voices. Such is the situation of the insane and idiots of the city of Boston; and although only 28 out of 171 have been cured, and the rest will probably wear out their lives in hopeless insanity, yet there is a melancholy pleasure in witnessing the great amount of animal happiness they enjoy, in seeing the kind regard paid to prostrate humanity,— the respect shown to the deserted temple of reason. It is only, as it were, twining fresh flowers on the graves of the dead; still it is a grateful sight to the humane, and a more certain indication of high civilization, than the most refined taste in literature and the arts, or the most fastidious observance of social etiquette.

But, alas! such is not the picture presented by the insane in most other parts of our Commonwealth; for, saving those at Worcester, they are incarcerated in the same prisons with criminals; they are immured in narrow and cheerless cells; they are under the charge of ignorant and sometimes of depraved persons; or they are in the almshouses, shut up in cold and cheerless rooms, sometimes chained to the walls, often confined in narrow cages, without a chair or bed, and with nothing but the straw on which they lie down like the brutes.

But such general description cannot convey an adequate idea of the utterly forlorn and degraded condition, to which scores and hundreds of our brethren are reduced; we will, therefore, give some particular cases, which we have ourselves witnessed, during the last three months, in places within thirty miles of Boston.

In one of these towns we approached a large old building, like a farm-house, and were about to inquire for the poorhouse, when our attention was attracted by a sort of cage or pen, constructed at the end of a wood-shed, facing upon the road. The thought occurred, that it might be the cage of an insane person. We dismounted and approached the place, and, looking through the bars, found it was a cage about six feet square. The floor was covered with trampled straw; and we saw only an old, ragged, and filthy coverlet, in one corner; but, as we looked more narrowly at this, a sudden motion of one side of it disclosed the head and face of a human being, which were hidden again, as soon as the glaring eyes had been fixed for an instant upon us.

The first shock was too painful to be described; to find humanity so utterly degraded, to see a human being crouching, like a wild beast in his lair, caged up by the side of the public road, exposed to the gaze of every passer by, unwashed, unshaven, unshorn, with no covering but a filthy coverlet, with not even a cup of water by his side, was revolting beyond measure.

Having found the keeper of the house, we unfastened the door of the cage and entered it. There was no article of furniture at all; nothing but the straw, with here and there a stale crust of bread. The poor inmate was crouching in a corner, and drawn up in the smallest possible space; he would not speak nor move, except when we attempted gently to uncover his head, which he would bury in the folds of his rotten coverlet, and by his motions disclose to sight his naked limbs. We made some inquiries concerning his history, and found, that he was about forty years old; that he had once been the owner of a small farm in the neighbourhood; that he had suffered, or supposed he had suffered, grievous wrong, and had become a maniac; he had been sent to a hospital, but was returned upon the town as incurable, and put into this den, probably for life. The keeper did not seem to be an in-human man, but was ignorant, and utterly unfit for the care of the insane. On being asked, how he managed him, he replied, that he had now no difficulty, and "had not *licked* him for over a year!"—that at first he "had a fight with him, and had to knock him down four times before he could master him;" and that "since then he had been obedient." He added, how-ever, that the overseers of the poor had charged him never to strike the man again.

In the next town to this, we found in a shed adjoining the almshouse, and in an inclosure twelve feet long by about eight feet wide, made with oak plank and without any window, a middle-aged man, stark mad, and in a state of entire nudity. His condition was about the same as that of the poor creature last described, except that his pen was larger, and was not exposed to the gaze of every passer-by; but he was in a state of entire privation of all the comforts, and even of the common decencies, of life. The almshouse was clean, and the keeper's family seemed worthy, humane people, who took good care of all the inmates, except the poor wretch in the shed; for him, they seemed to think they had done all, when they thrust through the narrow opening in his cage, his daily allowance of food and drink. . . .

We maintain, that, in the present state of society, the insane and idiots can-not be kept in the almshouse without physical suffering and abuse, and degradation; without becoming worse themselves, and presenting a demoral-izing picture to others; without immorality and sin. Much might be said upon the demoralizing influence, upon our children, of thus treating our fellow-creatures. The Spartans, when they made their Helots drunk in public, at least extracted from humanity, which they degraded and crushed, a moral on temperance, for their children; but we, when we show them a man made in God's image, degraded below the brutes, less cared for than the horse and the ox, exhibit our own shame, and teach them a lesson of unmitigated im-morality. Hence, it is no uncommon thing to have a crowd of boys about an almshouse cage, trying by mockery, and perhaps by throwing stones, to rouse up the unhappy insane man from temporary quiet, or sleep, into raving fury.

There are objections equally strong against confining the insane, even those who are incurable, in jails and houses of correction. In answer to a query on this subject Dr. Woodward, of the Massachusetts Lunatic Asylum at Worcester, writes to us thus; "In the jails, the insane are hardly in a better condition than in the almshouses; they are crowded together in apartments badly warmed and ventilated; or they are secluded in some solitary room, cold, dirty, ragged, without society, with bad air to breathe, and scanty and bad food to eat." Besides, the sense of justice revolts at the thought of in-carcerating innocent victims of misfortune in the receptacle of guilt; and the voice of experience tells us, that when so confined they grow more violent, or sink into *dementia,* are neglected, and ill treated. The jailers and keepers of houses of correction, may be men of humanity; but they do not know how to treat insanity any more than they know how to treat scarlet fever; nor have they the means to do so, provided they did know.

County hospitals have been proposed; but against them every one who is acquainted with the subject will protest, unless indeed they can be so large, and so well endowed as to form independent establishments, with a medical superintendent, and a corps of officers and attendants, who should be exclusively devoted to them. An establishment for the insane must be a thing by itself; must have its own peculiar organization, and not be part of, or an appendage to, another institution; else it will degenerate into a place of mere safekeeping. . . .

There are excellent hospitals recently established in Maine and in Vermont, which are not yet full; and, should they not suffice, new establishments would start up at once. It is true, there are great objections to private madhouses; the recent developments in England show what horrid abuses are there committed, even at this day; and we fear, that there are some in this country where a grand jury might find matter for presentment. It is certainly highly desirable, that the State should furnish a place, where all its lunatic subjects might be treated for a moderate compensation; but this, we repeat, is not strictly a State's legal duty, while the care of the paupers is both a legal and a moral duty. Let that then be first discharged, and let us trust, that, when the present generation of incurable cases shall have passed away, better treatment will prevent such an accumulation again; while stricter temperance, and a more general acquaintance with physiology, will diminish the proximate causes.

Let all then, who, by word or deed, can command any influence, exercise it to discharge this duty, and to confer this blessing upon those whom misfortune has made dependent upon them. Let them visit the almshouses and prisons, and see for themselves the deplorable condition of their brethren; their visits will at least have the effect of causing greater vigilance, cleanliness, and attention on the part of the keepers. There is room here for all to work, women as well as men. Come, then, ye whose bosoms heave with just indignation at the oppression of man in distant lands; here are victims of dreadful oppression at your very doors. Come, ye who lament the heathenish customs of ignorant pagans, and would fain teach them Christianity; here are worse than heathenish customs in our very towns and villages. Come, ye who are filled with sickly sentimentality, who weep over imaginary sufferings of imaginary beings, who sigh for some opportunity of doing heroic deeds, who are speculating upon human progress; here are realities to be grappled with, here is misery to be alleviated, here is degraded humanity to be lifted up.

Finally, let the State government be urged to make immediate and ample provision for *all* the indigent insane, cost what it may cost. Massachusetts is not too poor to do any thing that can be shown to be her duty.

Albert Brisbane

1809-1890

Born in Batavia, New York, of fairly well-to-do parents, Albert Brisbane was educated by private tutors. At eighteen, he went to Paris, where he studied under such outstanding French figures as Cousin and Guizot. Disappointed in the social philosophy of these French thinkers, he went to Berlin to study under Hegel—again, however, with unsatisfactory results. Shortly after the Revolution of 1830 he returned to Paris, convinced that human misery could be alleviated only through a radical and fundamental reconstruction of society. Momentarily the ideas of utopian socialist Saint-Simon caught his attention, but after reading Charles Fourier's *Traité de l'Association Domestique-Agricole* (1821–1822), he was even more impressed with the latter's idea of dignifying and rendering manual labor attractive through associative living.

After two years of study with Fourier, Brisbane returned to the United States, and in 1839 began a public campaign to win popular support for his ideas. In 1840 he published his famous *Social Destiny of Man; or, Association and Reorganization of Industry*. Brisbane received vigorous support from Horace Greeley's *New York Tribune*, and under the excitement of the idea about forty experiments in "associationism," or communal living, were started; all of them, however, failed.

The following selection is from a later statement on associationism by Brisbane entitled *Association; or A Concise Exposition of the Practical Part of Fourier's Social Science* (New York, 1843).

OBJECT OF ASSOCIATION

The Doctrine of Association can only be understood by a careful and unprejudiced examination, and this we solicit from all candid and impartial Minds who are interested in the cause of social progress and improvement, and human happiness. We urge it upon them as due at once to themselves and to a doctrine which promises confidently a solution of the great problem of Social Evil.

Those who desire a more thorough exposition of the laws and principles of Association than are presented in this practical Sketch, will find a broad and inviting field of investigation thrown open to them in the profound treatise of *Charles Fourier,* the discoverer and revealer of these laws to the world.

Although we cannot explain in a few words the Doctrine of Association, we will state at least the great end and object it has in view. It is THE ELEVATION OF MAN * * * His complete and universal DEVELOP-MENT—Moral, Intellectual, and Physical * * * His HAPPINESS on Earth.

This is our Aim * * * this is our supreme Desire * * * our Hope * * * our Faith * * * and its *realization,* the Work of our Lives.

We seek the elevation and happiness of all Classes—of the Race collectively and individually. And first of all, we seek to elevate the *Laboring Classes—Toiling Millions,* who comprise the vast majority of Mankind. Their days are spent in incessant and repugnant toil * * * amid poverty and privation * * * and instead of being MEN, possessing all the attributes of Humanity, their higher nature is smothered and degraded, and they are poor and dependent Hirelings, Serfs or Slaves—oppressed victims of a false Social Order. They must be raised from their lowly condition, and elevated to the position to which God has destined Man upon earth.

And, second, we wish to improve and exalt the condition of the *Rich* or *Higher Classes,*—of those who are the Possessors of the meagre advantages which a world of general poverty, conflict and disorder can yield. They possess Wealth or the means of satisfying their physical wants, but they are without that high order or moral or intellectual Happiness, which constitutes the charm and fullness of existence, and they pine and suffer in the midst of abundance. Devoured by ennui and lassitude, harassed often by anxiety and physical debility, the social affections and the aspirations of the soul, unsatisfied or violated, they enjoy in reality but few higher advantages than *food, clothing* and *shelter,* which are natural gifts of God to the animal creation. The slight advantages which they possess are held with uncertainty and maintained with difficulty; they are constantly exposed to reverses, and are frequently overwhelmed with unforeseen and unavoidable ruin. They are in the scale of social existence, so far below the standard to which all Mankind can be raised, that we look upon them as common sufferers of a false Social Order.

We wish to elevate all Classes then, and all Mankind.

To the Laboring Classes we wish to give abundance * * * Attractive Industry * * * pecuniary independence and knowledge. To the Rich we wish to secure health * * * pleasing activity. . . . security against reverses and freedom from care, anxiety, ennui and lassitude.

And to all the complete happiness which will result from the satisfaction of the social sympathies and affections and the higher moral and intellectual sentiments, and from the conviction of performing their Destiny upon Earth. . . . and thus realize the divine spectacle of universal prosperity. . . . universal contentment, . . . universal happiness!

We believe that this great end—*the universal elevation and universal happiness of* MAN—can be attained. And why?—First, because we have *Faith in God and the Universality of His Providence.*

Faith in Man, and his capability of good affections and Social Religious Harmony.

Faith that the Human Race are reserved a high Destiny to fulfill upon Earth.

Second, because it can be demonstrated by *Science,* that all the elements of happiness exist in and around us. . . . the *moral elements in Man*—in the Intelligence and Passion with which he is endowed. . . . the *material elements in nature*—in her infinitely rich, varied and beautiful creations—and that they require only to be properly developed, combined and employed to secure to Man his happiness and elevation.

The object of this Publication is to prove the truth of the foundation on which our faith rests, and to explain an organization of Society in which all these elements can be so combined as to secure the end in view.

Let our Doctrines be judged by the standard of enlightened Reason, which examines and analyzes carefully and impartially; and by the standard of liberal Faith and the spirit of universality which opens the Mind to the examination of new views and doctrines, and leads it to accept Truth wherever it is found.

We believe that in the present state of complicated suffering and evil which exist in the world, it is a sacred duty on the part of every true and just Mind to seek earnestly for the means of reform, and that this duty has been strictly enjoined upon the Christian world with the promise of success, if conscientious search were made, . . . *"seek and ye shall find; there is nothing covered that shall not be revealed; and hid that shall not be known,"* . . . and we believe that they also who will not seek, but declare that nothing can be found, that suffering and evil must always exist, and that no great reforms can be effected, or doubters of the goodness and providence of God, and do not fulfill their duty to Him and to the cause of Humanity.

We believe that the past and present period of poverty, suffering, discord and subversion upon the earth, has been necessarily incident to the infancy or first age in the career of the Human Race, which is a time of social ignorance and political weakness, and that we are now upon the verge of a great social Transformation from the present state of general Poverty and social Discord to a state of general Prosperity and social Harmony.

We believe that the Providence of God is *universal,* and that it extends to the spiritual or moral as well as the material world; that He has created with the same infinite wisdom the Attractions and Passions in Man, that He has the material Wonders of the Universe; and we believe that *Charles Fourier* has discovered the laws which govern the spiritual world as *Newton* and others have discovered a part of the laws which govern the material world, and that Association based upon these laws will conquer social evil and human misery, conquer false philosophy and controversial politics, and national indigence and spurious civilization.

We believe, that the time is fast coming when *Man,* the universal human Soul, that which is God upon earth and the only which is God and is Divine.

. . . who now hates the earth as a prison-house because it is full of discords, and who curses it as he toils over it in repugnant labor, will love it, and bless it, and embellish it, and fill it with material and spiritual Harmonies.

Up to the present time we have only been able to admire the wisdom of God in the *material world,* as it bursts forth in the celestial spheres, and is displayed in the beautiful creations of nature: we believe that, now, for the first time, we shall see it in the *moral world*—in the harmony of the Passions, in their complete development and perfect accord in Universal Association, and that this beautiful work alone can give us an idea of the fullness of the wisdom and glory of the Creator.

NECESSITY OF A SOCIAL REFORM

When new views and principles are put forth, they invariably meet with the opposition and condemnation of the great majority of men, no matter how good or true they may be, or how important the results which they promise to realize. Against this procedure we protest, and, in behalf of suffering Humanity, we ask that preconceived notions and prejudices as well as hasty criticism be for a time laid aside, and an impartial and conscientious investigation of the system, which we advocate, be entered into.

If we look around us, we see numerous Parties, laboring isolatedly to carry out various reforms—political, administrative, currency, abolition, temperance, moral, etc.—which proves, *First,* the depth and extent of the evil that preys upon Society, and *Second,* the necessity of a fundamental Reform, which will attack that evil at its root and eradicate it effectually, instead of lopping off a few branches. If the plan of such a reform has really been discovered, how worthy of the candid examination of every being, whose Soul burns with a desire to see poverty and misery banished from the earth, and who feels a sacred pride for the happiness and elevation of his Race!

To meet and disarm fears and suspicions which may arise in the conservative Mind, we will hasten to state that the reform we contemplate, although fundamental in its character, is not destructive, but constructive; it will not tear down, but build up; it will respect what is true and good in Society, and will change quietly and by substitution, what is false and defective; it will violate no rights, injure no class; it will not impoverish the Rich to enrich slightly the Poor; it will not change the victims of poverty and misery, but will improve and elevate the condition of all, without taking from any. It can moreover be tried on a small scale, and it will only spread, when practice has shown its superiority over the present system. Unlike political reforms, which, to effect the smallest change of policy, agitate and often convulse a whole country, and array one half of the People against the other half, it will not affect a space as large as a township and but a few hundred persons, and will not extend beyond these narrow limits unless its advantages

—*practically demonstrated*—excite a strong and general approbation in its favor.

To show the necessity of a Social Reform, we will glance at the misery which exists upon earth; its extent, depth, and intensity prove that political and other partial reforms can effect but little permanent good, and that recourse must be had to new and thorough measures.

HUMAN MISERY

If we look abroad over the earth and examine the condition of the Human Race upon it, what do we see? A spectacle at which the soul shudders. A large majority of our fellow-creatures are slaves, serfs or poor hired laborers, toiling from fear of the lash or fear of want to obtain a miserable subsistence, or to produce the means of supporting a favored few in luxury and idle ease. Discords and hatreds are rife among them, and the darkest selfishness benumbs their hearts and renders them indifferent to each other's misery. There are millions upon millions of beings, who are now suffering every variety of physical wretchedness and moral woe; there are hearts that are torn with care and anxiety—bodies that are worn out with overburdening toil; there are multitudes of miserable wretches immured in gloomy prisons and dungeons, expiating by suffering and ignominy, crimes into which they were plunged by poverty, ignorance and other circumstances over which they had no control—far less culpable in many cases than the false Society which exposed them to become outcasts and criminals; there are other multitudes of beings buried in dismal and suffocating mines, toiling in the bowels of the earth with the dim lamp, the pick-axe and the wheelbarrow for their only companions; there are members of the human family, who, at this moment, are mounting the bloody scaffold, where the soul, amidst awful horror and despair, is to be torn by violence asunder from the body, and launched into an unknown future. All these varied woes and miseries exist, and there are *living, feeling Souls that must undergo them!*

The affections and sympathies of the heart are also outraged and violated; there are parents who see their offspring exposed to privations which they cannot alleviate, or led astray by the temptations, vices and crimes of a false Society, and engulfed in ruin. There are broken friendships, disappointed loves, thwarted ambitions, and other mental sufferings which tongue cannot tell and language cannot depict.

The surface of the Earth is in as miserable a condition as the Race upon it. Vast deserts and marshes, which generate pestilential winds and miasmatic exhalations—the source of the most frightful diseases, such as the plague, the cholera, the yellow fever, &c., and wild forests, and plains, inhabited by noxious reptiles, and savage beasts cover at least three-fourths of it. The portion which has been brought under cultivation is but miserably cultivated, and parts are devoted to the worst of purposes; here we see regions exhausted in the production of noxious plants, like the poppy and tobacco, which are grown to furnish mental vacuity and idleness with the means of a momentary occupation and excitement: there districts planted with grain—not to sustain life—but to be converted into a poisonous liquid, which may afford to degraded masses a brutal exhilaration with its attendants, folly, disease and death. Besides, whole regions have been devastated by fire and sword, and remain in a neglected state—monuments of the folly and madness of nations.

Such is the spectacle which a general view of the condition of the Earth and the Race upon it, presents! Does it not call for some great Reforms? . . .

CONTRAST BETWEEN ASSOCIATION AND THE PRESENT SOCIAL ORDER

If we wish to picture to ourselves in imagination an Association established and in operation, we must imagine spreading out before us a fine Domain, covering an area of three miles square, beautifully and scientifically cultivated, diversified with gardens, fields, fruit-orchards, vineyards, meadows and woodlands; in the centre a large and elegant Edifice, with spacious and commodious outhouses, combining architectural beauty with convenience and economy; fine flocks, teams and implements greeting everywhere the eye, and an intelligent and prosperous Population engaged from Attraction in the care and cultivation of the whole. The Useful and the Beautiful would be in every way united: the loveliness of Nature would be heightened by the works of Man; and the charms of Social life and the pursuits of Art and Science and useful Industry, would be in every way combined.

Would not eighteen hundred persons, united in an Association, prosecuting with order and economy all their industrial and business operations, and dividing equitably the product of their Labor and Talent—each receiving a share according to the part which he or she has taken in creating it—live much more in accordance with the dictates of wisdom, than if they were divided into three hundred families, inhabiting as many isolated little tenements, as lonely in general as they are inconvenient, with poor farms and workshops, poor flocks, tools, implements and machinery, and without the charm of varied social relations,—without Art, Science and other intellectual enjoyments, which give to human existence its elevation, and constitute the true life of Man? We leave the reader to answer the question himself.

To furnish more data for forming an opinion, let us contrast more minutely the manner in which three hundred families now live, and the manner in which they would live in Association. The contrast will show us the immense superiority of Association, as regards Economy, and Unity of action and interests over the present System.

Three hundred families require at present three hundred separate houses, three hundred kitchens, three hundred kitchen fires, three hundred sets of cooking utensils, three hundred women to do the cooking—and if they are farming families—three hundred little farms, three hundred barns and sheds, three hundred teams, innumerable walls and fences, and every thing else equally as complicated and uselessly wasteful.

All the cares and labor attendant upon providing for the wants of a family, such as cooking, washing, marketing and keeping up fires, must be gone through with three hundred times daily by the three hundred families, and with the same detail as for an assemblage of eighteen hundred persons, except the difference of scale.

Association will avoid this monstrous complication and waste; instead of three hundred little kitchens and three hundred fires, it will have four or five large and convenient kitchens, with as many fires, by means of which, not only the cooking can be done, but the entire Edifice warmed; instead of three hundred little fireplaces and cooking stoves, and as many sets of cooking utensils, it will have its extensive kitchen ranges, its large boilers and ovens, and machinery on the largest scale and the best that can be invented for facilitating culinary operations; instead of three hundred women to do the cooking, it will have a few experienced cooks, engaged by turns every other day; instead of three hundred poor teams, half the time idle, it will have merely the requisite number, and of the best quality; instead of the immense number of walls and fences now required, it will have a few extensive hedges; and instead of making all its sales and purchases at retail, paying in profits to traders one-half of the product of its labor, it will make them at wholesale, and in the most economical manner.

To what immense Economies would Association give rise! What a source of Riches it would be! We live in an Age, the all-absorbing desire of which is wealth. If men would but add sentiments of justice and philanthropy to their greedy strife after money, they would see, that it is only in Association that their wishes can be satisfied, and that all can attain prosperity.

If people would associate, economize and apply their talents and energies in a judicious manner, they could produce wealth in abundance, and escape want and anxiety; whereas in striving to wrest from each other by fraud, over-reaching and other unjust means the little that is produced under the present false and repugnant system of Labor, ninety-nine out of a hundred live amidst cares and perplexities, and die in poverty and destitution.

If we descend to minute details, we shall be surprised at the immense saving which Association will effect—not only in time and money, but in useless and repulsive drudgery. Three hundred families require at present upon an average six hundred fires. In an Association four or five large fires only would be necessary, and one-twentieth part of the fuel, which is now consumed, would be sufficient; by means of tubes or other apparatus the public halls, saloons, reading-rooms, library, etc. could be warmed, so that a few parlor fires in the private apartments only would be required, which could also be heated by the same process, if desired. Here is an economy of nineteen-twentieths in fuel, to which is to be added the saving of a most repulsive drudgery. Three hundred poor servants must rise at present every morning, even in the depth of winter, to light the fires; in an Association, on the contrary, the large fires would not be left to go out over night, so that in the morning it would only be necessary to charge the furnaces, which could be done with little trouble from properly constructed coal receivers. The night watch would, before retiring, attend to this duty. By this means three hundred servants would be saved one of the most repugnant and dirty occupations that has now to be performed. What can be more revolting than to see a female servant, shivering with cold on a winter's morning, scraping coals and cinders with her bare hands from a grate?

With the present system of isolated households, three hundred families must devote every week or two a day to washing, which amounts in the course of the year, for the three hundred families, to ten or twelve thousand days' work. Three hundred women have to spend, in dirty kitchens and over hot fires, one day out of the seven in toiling at the wash-tub.

Association will avoid also this useless and repulsive drudgery. It will have a large wash-room, fitted up with every convenience and supplied with proper machinery, to which the clothes, collected and assorted once or twice a month, will be carried and put into different vats, where with the aid of a cleansing process used in Switzerland, or some better which may be invented, they can be washed, and with scarcely any hand-labor, far better than they are now. To do the heavier and plainer kinds of ironing, mangles or large rollers would be used; and to do the lighter kinds, some groups of women and girls, having a taste for the occupation, would devote themselves, as required, to it.

The inventive Genius of Man has never been directed to the constructing of machinery for performing kitchen and other household work upon a large and economical scale, because it has not been required, and could not be used in the isolated household. It is only in large Associations, where everything would be done upon a vast scale, that such machinery could be employed, and domestic labor with its aid immensely abridged.

Household work is now carried on in the rudest manner that can be conceived; it is as much below what it could be, as travelling in scows, pushed along by poles, is below journeying in elegant steamboats. Still the vast majority of persons cling from habit to the isolated household, when, if they would examine its mechanism with impartiality, they would see that it is the source, not only of waste and poverty, but, to a great extent, of discord and selfishness.

The system of Isolated Families is the foundation upon which all past and present Societies have been based. As the system is essentially defective, so are the Societies which have been founded upon it. We must reform the basis before we can erect a good superstructure, or a true Social Order. . . .

IMPOSSIBILITY OF ANY TYRANNY
OF CAPITAL IN ASSOCIATION

It is often asked, whether one or more capitalists will not become owners of the stock of an Association, and exercise a tyrannical control and dictation over its members and its affairs. Nothing of the kind can take place; to explain this, we will suppose an extreme case—we will suppose that one individual has become the proprietor of all the stock of an Association. This monopoly will give him, as we shall see, no arbitrary control over the Association and its affairs.

The Council of Industry—the members of which will be elected by the inhabitants of the Association—will have a general supervision of the domain, workshops and manufactories, and the regulation of its industrial affairs and interests. The person who owns the stock may be elected a member of this Council, and, as such, will have a voice in the management of its affairs, but out of the Council and as a private individual, he can exercise no control; he cannot dictate, for example, the system of cultivation which shall be pursued, the crops which shall be grown, the branches of manufactures which shall be prosecuted, where the fences or hedges shall be located, how the fields and gardens shall be laid out and cultivated, or direct any similar operations. All these details must come under the direction of the Council, which, composed of the most talented and experienced members of the Association, will of course be able to exercise a far more judicious control than can a single individual.

No individual in Association will possess the absolute ownership of the soil, manufactories and other means of production as at present, "to use and abuse them as he wishes," and to prevent the rest of the members from working upon or in them, if his caprice shall so dictate; he will own the stock, which represents them—a much more desirable form of property— but the soil and manufactories will remain under the control and direction of the Association, and the Right of working in or upon them will be secured to all its members. We see this restriction upon capitalists in operation at present in stock companies: a stockholder in a railroad cannot, for example, alter the direction or tear up a part of the track equal in value to his stock, or prevent travellers from going over the road,—and this restriction is found advantageous to all.

Capitalists will possess in Association very great advantages: their money will be safely invested; they will be exempt from the frauds, revulsions and the numerous accidents of business, which ruin upon an average three-fourths of them; they will be relieved from the anxiety and the trouble of constant supervision, and as the profits of Association will be large, they will receive a liberal interest on their money.

But Capitalists in Association will not wish to exercise any dictation or tyranny; they would disgust their fellow-men by such a course, who, being secured the Right of Labor or of constant employment, would be pecuniarily independent, and would not submit to any imposition: should capitalists, however, endeavor to exercise any tyranny, the members could move off in a body and leave their property unproductive;—and, besides, any arbitrary dictation on their part would derange the operations of Industry, decrease production, and lessen as a consequence their profits. The Tyranny of Capital, one of the last relics of tyranny, and the most repulsive, will be swept from the face of the earth by Association!

If it be feared by some persons that a few individuals in an Association will monopolize the stock, and exercise an absolute control, it is very confidently asserted by others that the selfishness of men, and their rapacity to acquire wealth, will be insurmountable obstacles to social Union and Concord. Let us answer this objection.

The reader will bear in mind that the interest upon the capital or shares will be paid out of the *total product* of the Association, so that no one can desire large profits for himself without desiring the same for all the other members.

Suppose then that there are some extremely avaricious persons in an Association, who are very desirous of accumulating wealth: what means will they have to employ to attain their end? They will have to see that all parts of the domain are cultivated in the best manner—all branches of manufactures prosecuted judiciously—that the edifices, implements, machinery, etc. are not injured, and that no waste takes place. This is the policy which they will have to pursue. They cannot, as a consequence, promote their own prosperity without promoting at the same time the prosperity of all the other members; their thirst for gain will not be satisfied, as at present, at the expense of their fellow-men, but will, on the contrary, conduce to their welfare. By this means individual selfishness will be neutralized, and made to subserve the good of the whole.

Under the present condition of things, the injury done to others by extortion or fraud, is individual gain; but in Association, where the interests of the Individual and those of the Mass are *identical,* no one can add to his own store without adding to that of the rest of the community.

If there were in an Association some of those very parsimonious persons, who are now looked upon with dislike, they would be found quite useful. They would attend to all minor details and minutiae, and see that nothing was wasted or misapplied. The great majority of persons would feel no inclination for such a careful supervision, but as they would see the importance of it, for little wastes lead to large losses, they would feel indebted to those who attend to such details and relieved them of the task. In Association *Selfishness will be rendered Social,* and be made to serve the interests of the whole; at present, it is *exclusive* or *individual,* and leads to the plundering of the Mass. . . .

GUARANTEE OF AN AMPLE SUFFICIENCY

An *Ample Sufficiency,* or the means of supplying the physical wants and of securing health, comfort and agreeable recreation, must be guarantied to every human being. This provision is termed by Fourier the *"Minimum,"* to which every being is entitled by virtue of his humanity and his existence upon the earth. It will comprise an abundant supply of food, clothing, lodging and recreation;—or more strictly defined, admission to the public tables; the possession of a good apartment; changes of comfortable and genteel clothing; the privilege of entering and using the libraries, reading-rooms, baths, etc., and the right of attending concerts, festivities, the amusements of the Association, and social unions and public assemblies.

Man without the full satisfaction of all his physical wants, without an abundant supply of the material comforts which his physical nature requires, without freedom from care and anxiety for himself and his family for the present and the future, without pecuniary independence, cannot enjoy his most precious rights, cannot possess perfect Liberty, for his time and his person are not his own, and cannot give freedom and expansion to higher sentiments and feelings of his nature.

The guarantee to every individual of a Sufficiency or *Minimum,* is consequently the first condition of a true Social Order. Without it, there is that frightful *Uncertainty of the Future* with its harassing cares and slavish dependency, which render it necessary for every being to think exclusively of himself, to practice selfishness and smother the generous feelings and affections of the soul.

The objection will be raised that if Association guaranties a Sufficiency to Man, he will abandon Industry, and pass his time in idleness: he would do so, if Industry were to remain repugnant and degrading as it now is; and hence the absolute necessity of rendering Industry Attractive, so as to induce man to devote himself with pleasure to its pursuits, and produce enough to secure to Society a reciprocal guarantee for its guarantee of a Sufficiency—that is, a return for its advances.

"There is," says Fourier, "no real liberty or independence, without the guarantee of a Sufficiency or Minimum.

"There is no Sufficiency, without Attractive Industry.

"There can be no Attractive Industry with the present isolated and individual system of Labor.

"Consequently a Sufficiency, sustained by a system of Attractive Industry, is the sole avenue to Liberty and Independence.

"To enter this avenue, we must extricate ourselves from the present false and incoherent system of Society called Civilization, and enter into the Combined or Associated Order."

This Institution of the Combined Order—the guarantee of a "Minimum" —will be the inauguration of a Social Providence in human societies, and the practical realization of the prayer of Christ, that Humanity should have its "daily bread." It will correspond to that wish as the *Sacred Legion* will correspond to the act of humble devotion and charity referred to in describing that Corporation. It could be shown that there will be in the Combined Order, institutions and practical arrangements which will correspond to or be types of all the precepts and wishes of Christ. . . .

SYSTEM OF INTERNAL GOVERNMENT IN ASSOCIATION

There can be in Association no individual control, dictation or tyranny. With the universal intelligence and independence which will exist in the Combined Order, Government—social, civil and religious—must be the result of the *collective Will,* expressed by vote, and as it concerns all alike, it must be administered alike for the interests of all.[1]

The industrial and business affairs of an Association will be confided to

---

1. We cannot enter into a scientific explanation of the Government of the Combined Order, for to do so, it would be necessary to explain the *true function* of government, which is a question of an intricate and profound character: we will state, however, in general terms that it is the securing a full and harmonious Development and right direction of the moral Powers (the passions and the sentiments) in the human soul, and that this is directly the converse of the function of Government in false and subversive Societies, which has for its object the general repression and subjection of the human passions and sentiments. We have an illustration of the nature of the function of true Government in the Clergy, whose office it is to develop, cultivate and exalt the Religious Sentiment. In the Combined Order there will be Officers whose functions in regard to the other radical spiritual elements in man—of which there are twelve—will be analogous to that of the Clergy in regard to the Religious Sentiment. Every radical Passion, as well as the Pivotal one of Religion, will have its Institution and its Officers, and the object of all will be a complete moral, intellectual and physical development of Humanity. In the subversive societies of the world, under the period of social discord and incoherence, called the "Curse," which prevails during the infancy or early ages of Humanity, and which is a time of social weakness and ignorance, the passions are in a general state of false action and disorder; they have then necessarily to be repressed, subdued and controlled, and to do this is the function of Government. The religious sentiment being the highest, and the tie of Unity between God and Humanity, has commanded respect, maintained its position, and performed to a great extent, although not fully, its true function, for it has had to take a part in the general work of repression and subjection.

The function of Government in a false social order being mainly the repression and subjection of misdirected and misdeveloped human Passions, it must have Officers whose functions shall correspond to this work. This explains the existence of the Executioner, of the Jailor, the Sheriff, the Gens-d'armes, the Bailiff, the Policeman, the Judge, and other Officers of Courts, together with Legislators who enact criminal codes, and the Heads of Government who supervise their execution.

The present system of Government offers us in its general character a reversed image of the true system of Government, and can be studied to advantage by contrasts or opposites.

We have touched upon this subject to show that the question of Government in Association is solved by the social science discovered by Fourier, and that it is based in Association upon scientific and natural Laws.

Councils elected annually by the members. There will be a Council at the head of each department of general interests, composed of members best qualified to fill the various departments. The Council first in rank and importance, which we will superficially describe, will be the *Council of Industry.* This Council will supervise the Industrial Interests of the Association. It will consist of those persons who possess the most knowledge, skill and experience in the various branches of Industry, and in the Arts and Sciences. As in Association Women will take an active part in various industrial pursuits, they will necessarily form a part of the Supreme Council of Industry.

The function of the Council of Industry will not be mandatory but advisory in its character. It will not direct and order what shall be done, but counsel and advise with the Groups and Series as regards the direction of affairs. Composed of the heads of the Series, and the members most distinguished for their practical and scientific attainments, the suggestions and advice of this Council will always be received with deference by the various Groups engaged in Industry, but its opinion will not be binding or obligatory. For example, the Council of Industry may, from various observations, inform a Series engaged in growing grain, that such or such a time is the best for reaping; the Series will receive with deference this advice, but it will not be obliged to follow it, for as the responsibility of success and the *direct* interest rest with each Series, it must, of course, have the power to consult its own wishes in regard to its own branch of Industry, but as the general interests of the Council and the Series are identical, and as Science and true Principles will always govern the enlightened Producers of Association, the Series will seldom differ in opinion with the Council, and never to the sacrifice of important interests.

This example shows how the intelligence and knowledge of the Council of Industry will be brought to bear upon every industrial pursuit, and confer advice that will be invaluable, without being dictatorial, or interfering with and superseding individual opinion and action. Thus the workmen of every Series in an Association will have at all times the advantage of the advice and counsel of a body of experienced men, without being subject to arbitrary control or dictation.

There are general interests, however, confided to the Council of Industry, in which it will have supreme control. With a complete knowledge of the qualities and capacities of the soil of the Domain, by chemical analysis and other means, it will appropriate it to different uses according to its character, and the general scenic harmony to be maintained in its distribution; it will point out, for example, where fruit orchards and vineyards, meadows and woodlands, vegetable and flower gardens shall be located; where walls and hedges shall be placed, and the principal branches of Industry which shall be prosecuted; it will ascertain the value and importance of all new inventions in the mechanical arts, in machinery and implements, new discoveries in agriculture and improvements of all kinds, and introduce them accordingly, and will take measures to procure the best races of animals and the finest varieties of fruits, grains, vegetables, flowers, shrubbery, etc.

In manufactures the same general supervision would be exercised by the Council of Industry. It will be, so to say, the *Industrial College* of the Association, and will shed the light of its science and its array of talent over all the industrial affairs of the community; and at all times the Groups and Series will find it an intelligent and faithful guide to aid and direct them in their pursuits.

As the Council of Industry governs and supervises the Domain and the Industrial affairs of the Association, other Councils will govern and regulate other Departments, and nowhere will individual Authority be exercised, or official power be oppressive.

A *Council of Industry Arrangements* would have the management of the internal affairs of the Association, such as letting the apartments, attending to the daily supplies of provisions, etc.

A *Council of Arbiters,* who will settle by arbitration all difficulties and differences that may arise between individuals of the Association, and judge all misdemeanors. When Association becomes general, and the system is fully carried out, this Council will be done away with, and any infraction of the laws of social Harmony will be judged by the Corporation or Series having the maintenance of those laws. We will cite merely one example—cruelty towards animals, which would come before and be judged by the tribunal of the Sacred Legion.

Until Association is fully established the Civil Law of the land will remain in force.

A *Commercial Council* will effect the sales and purchases of the Association, keep the Books or Accounts, and have charge of the Treasury. The members of this Council would be required to give security for the faithful performance of their trusts and the safety of the funds confided to their care.

These Councils will be elected annually by the members of the Association.

GENERAL GOVERNMENT

The General Government of the Combined Order will, like the Internal Government of single Associations, be Representative, and will embrace and supervise all social interests and departments of human activity. There will be State, National and higher Legislative Bodies, of which the system of Government of the United States, with its State and National Legislatures, gives a general idea. These Legislative Bodies will be grand Councils of Industry, Art and Science, and their mission will be to develop the resources of Nations, to supervise national improvements, and to encourage and perfect

Agriculture, Manufactures, and the Arts and Sciences, for which now almost nothing is done by government, with the exception of a few partial and indirect attempts to encourage Manufactures.

The energies of Government throughout the world are at present miserably paralyzed by party spirit, and wasted in party intrigues; the political power is unfortunately too much in the hands of selfish cliques and parties, and too much the servant of Trade, Capital, Privilege and exclusive interests. In the Government of the Combined Order there will be Unity of purpose, and the intelligence and energy centered in it will be directed to the encouragement and development of Universal interests.

(73)

Margaret Fuller

1810-1850

One of the most brilliant and scholarly of American women, Margaret Fuller was born in Cambridge, Massachusetts. Educated strictly and thoroughly by her father, she was something of a child prodigy. After a brief career as a teacher, under Emerson's sponsorship she became editor of the *Dial,* the important magazine of the Transcendentalists. She married the Italian Marquis Giovanni Angelo Ossoli, a follower of Mazzini, and was in Rome during the ill-fated republican uprising in that city in 1848–1849. Sailing for home, she and her family lost their lives in a shipwreck.

Margaret Fuller was an ardent spokesman for women's rights. Her writings contained eloquent pleas for equality between the sexes and especially for a recognition of women's intellectual needs and capacities.

The selection here is from her book, *Women in the Nineteenth Century* (Boston, 1874), which was first published in 1845.

 ☆ ☆ ☆ ☆

Not a few believe, and men themselves have expressed the opinion, that the time is come when Eurydice is to call for an Orpheus, rather than Orpheus for Eurydice; that the idea of Man, however imperfectly brought out, has been far more so than that of Woman: that she, the other half of the same thought, the other chamber of the heart of life, needs now take her turn in the full pulsation, and that improvement in the daughters will best aid in the reformation of the sons of this age.

It should be remarked that, as the principle of liberty is better understood, and more nobly interpreted, a broader protest is made in behalf of Woman. As men become aware that few men have had a fair chance, they are inclined to say that no women have had a fair chance. The French Revolution, that strangely disguised angel, bore witness in favor of Woman, but interpreted her claims no less ignorantly than those of Man. Its idea of happiness did not rise beyond outward enjoyment, unobstructed by the tyranny of others. The title it gave was "citoyen," "citoyenne;" and it is not unimportant to Woman that even this species of equality was awarded her. Before, she could be condemned to perish on the scaffold for treason, not as a citizen, but as a subject. The right with which this title then invested a human being was that of bloodshed and license. The Goddess of Liberty was impure. As we read the poem addressed to her, not long since, by Beranger, we can scarcely refrain from tears as painful as the tears of blood that flowed when "such crimes were committed in her name." Yes! Man, born to purify and animate the unintelligent and the cold, can, in his madness, degrade and pollute no less the fair and the chaste. Yet truth was prophesied in the ravings of that hideous fever, caused by long ignorance and abuse. Europe is conning a valued lesson from the blood-stained page. The same tendencies, further unfolded, will bear good fruit in this country. . . .

We will not speak of the innumerable instances in which profligate and idle men live upon the earnings of industrious wives; or if the wives leave them, and take with them the children, to perform the double duty of mother and father, follow from place to place, and threaten to rob them of the children, if deprived of the rights of a husband, as they call them, planting themselves in their poor lodgings, frightening them into paying tribute by taking from them the children, running into debt at the expense of these otherwise so overtasked helots. Such instances count up by scores within my own memory. I have seen the husband who had stained himself by a long course of low vice, till his wife was wearied from her heroic forgiveness, by finding that his treachery made it useless, and that if she would provide bread for herself and her children, she must be separate from his ill fame—I have known this man come to install himself in the chamber of a woman who loathed him, and say she should never take food without his company. I have known these men steal their children, whom they knew they had no means to maintain, take them into dissolute company, expose them to bodily danger, to frighten the poor woman, to whom, it seems, the fact that she alone had borne the pangs of their birth, and nourished their infancy, does not give an equal right to them. I do believe that this mode of kidnapping— and it is frequent enough in all classes of society—will be by the next age viewed as it is by Heaven now, and that the man who avails himself of the shelter of men's laws to steal from a mother her own children, or arrogate any superior right in them, save that of superior virtue, will bear the stigma he deserves, in common with him who steals grown men from their motherland, their hopes, and their homes.

I said, we will not speak of this now; yet I *have* spoken, for the subject makes me feel too much. I could give instances that would startle the most vulgar and callous; but I will not, for the public opinion of their own sex is already against such men, and where cases of extreme tyranny are made known, there is private action in the wife's favor. But she ought not to need this, nor, I think, can she long. Men must soon see that as, on their own ground, Woman is the weaker party, she ought to have legal protection, which would make such oppression impossible. But I would not deal with "atrocious instances," except in the way of illustration, neither demand from men a partial redress in some one matter, but go to the root of the whole. If principles could be established, particulars would adjust themselves aright. Ascertain the true destiny of Woman; give her legitimate hopes, and a standard within herself; marriage and all other relations would by degrees be harmonized with these. . . .

But if, in reply, we admit as truth that Woman seems destined by nature rather for the inner circle, we must add that the arrangements of civilized life have not been, as yet, such as to secure it to her. Her circle, if the duller, is not the quieter. If kept from "excitement," she is not from drudgery. Not only the Indian squaw carries the burdens of the camp, but the favorites of Louis XIV. accompany him in his journeys, and the washerwoman stands at her tub, and carries home her work at all seasons, and in all states of health. Those who think the physical circumstances of Woman would make a part in the affairs of national government unsuitable, are by no means those who think it impossible for negresses to endure field work, even during pregnancy, or for sempstresses to go through their killing labors.

As to the use of the pen, there was quite as much opposition to Woman's possessing herself of that help to free agency as there is now to her seizing on the rostrum or the desk; and she is likely to draw, from a permission to plead her cause that way, opposite inferences to what might be wished by those who now grant it.

As to the possibility of her filling with grace and dignity any such position, we should think those who had seen the great actresses, and heard the Quaker preachers of modern times, would not doubt that Woman can express publicly the fulness of thought and creation, without losing any of the peculiar beauty of her sex. What can pollute and tarnish is to act thus from any motive except that something needs to be said or done. Woman could take part in the processions, the songs, the dances of old religion; no one fancied her delicacy was impaired by appearing in public for such a cause.

As to her home, she is not likely to leave it more than she now does for balls, theatres, meetings for promoting missions, revival meetings, and others to which she flies, in hope of an animation for her existence commensurate with what she sees enjoyed by men. Governors of ladies' fairs are no less engrossed by such a charge, than the governor of a state by his; presidents of Washingtonian societies no less away from home than presidents of conventions. If men look straitly to it, they will find that, unless their lives are domestic, those of the women will not be. A house is no home unless it contain food and fire for the mind as well as for the body. The female Greek, of our day, is as much in the street as the male to cry, "What news?" We doubt not it was the same in Athens of old. The women, shut out from the market place, made up for it at the religious festivals. For human beings are not so constituted that they can live without expansion. If they do not get it in one way, they must in another, or perish.

As to men's representing women fairly at present, while we hear from men who owe to their wives not only all that is comfortable or graceful, but all that is wise, in the arrangement of their lives, the frequent remark, "You cannot reason with a woman,"—when from those of delicacy, nobleness, and poetic culture, falls the contemptuous phrase "women and children," and that in no light sally of the hour, but in works intended to give a permanent statement of the best experiences,—when not one man, in the million, shall I say? no, not in the hundred million, can rise above the belief that Woman was made *for Man*,—when such traits as these are daily forced upon the attention, can we feel that Man will always do justice to the interests of Woman? Can we think that he takes a sufficiently discerning and religious view of her office and destiny *ever* to do her justice, except when prompted by sentiment, —accidentally or transiently, that is, for the sentiment will vary according to the relations in which he is placed? The lover, the poet, the artist, are likely to view her nobly. The father and the philosopher have some chance of liberality; the man of the world, the legislator for expediency, none.

Under these circumstances, without attaching importance, in themselves, to the changes demanded by the champions of Woman, we hail them as signs of the times. We would have every arbitrary barrier thrown down. We would have every path laid open to Woman as freely as to Man. Were this done, and a slight temporary fermentation allowed to subside, we should see crystallizations more pure and of more various beauty. We believe the divine energy would pervade nature to a degree unknown in the history of former ages, and that no discordant collision, but a ravishing harmony of the spheres, would ensue.

Yet, then and only then will mankind be ripe for this, when inward and outward freedom for Woman as much as for Man shall be acknowledged as a *right*, not yielded as a concession. As the friend of the negro assumes that one man cannot by right hold another in bondage, so should the friend of Woman assume that Man cannot by right lay even well-meant restrictions on Woman. If the negro be a soul, if the woman be a soul, apparelled in flesh, to one Master only are they accountable. There is but one law for souls, and, if there is to be an interpreter of it, he must come not as man, or son of man, but as son of God. . . .

It is therefore that I would have Woman lay aside all thought, such as she habitually cherishes, of being taught and led by men. I would have her, like the Indian girl, dedicate herself to the Sun, the Sun of Truth, and go nowhere if his beams did not make clear the path. I would have her free from compromise, from complaisance, from helplessness, because I would have her good enough and strong enough to love one and all beings, from the fulness, not the poverty of being. . . .

Women of my country!—Exaltadas! if such there be,—women of English, old English nobleness, who understand the courage of Boadicea, the sacrifice of Godiva, the power of Queen Emma to tread the red-hot iron unharmed, —women who share the nature of Mrs. Hutchinson, Lady Russell, and the mothers of our own revolution,—have you nothing to do with this? You see the men, how they are willing to sell shamelessly the happiness of countless generations of fellow-creatures, the honor of their country, and their immortal souls, for a money market and political power. Do you not feel within you that which can reprove them, which can check, which can convince them? You would not speak in vain; whether each in her own home, or banded in unison.

Tell these men that you will not accept the glittering baubles, spacious dwellings, and plentiful service, they mean to offer you through these means. Tell them that the heart of Woman demands nobleness and honor in Man, and that, if they have not purity, have not mercy, they are no longer fathers, lovers, husbands, sons of yours.

This cause is your own, for, as I have before said, there is a reason why the foes of African Slavery seek more freedom for women; but put it not upon that ground, but on the ground of right.

If you have a power, it is a moral power. The films of interest are not so close around you as around the men. If you will but think, you cannot fail to wish to save the country from this disgrace. Let not slip the occasion, but do something to lift off the curse incurred by Eve.

You have heard the women engaged in the Abolition movement accused of boldness, because they lifted the voice in public, and lifted the latch of the stranger. But were these acts, whether performed judiciously or no, *so* bold as to dare before God and Man to partake the fruits of such offence as this?

You hear much of the modesty of your sex. Preserve it by filling the mind with noble desires that shall ward off the corruptions of vanity and idleness. A profligate woman, who left her accustomed haunts and took service in a New York boarding-house, said "she had never heard talk so vile at the Five Points, as from the ladies at the boarding-house." And why? Because they were idle; because, having nothing worthy to engage them, they dwelt, with unnatural curiosity, on the ill they dared not go to see.

It will not so much injure your modesty to have your name, by the unthinking, coupled with idle blame, as to have upon your soul the weight of not trying to save a whole race of women from the scorn that is put upon *their* modesty.

Think of this well! I entreat, I conjure you, before it is too late. It is my belief that something effectual might be done by women, if they would only consider the subject, and enter upon it in the true spirit,—a spirit gentle, but firm, and which feared the offence of none, save One who is of purer eyes than to behold iniquity.

(74)

Wendell Phillips

1811-1884

Born in Boston of a wealthy, well-established family, Phillips had the advantages of education and position. His father, in fact, achieved fame as the first mayor of Boston. Graduating from Harvard in 1831, Phillips entered law school and was subsequently admitted to the bar. Under the influence of Garrison, he soon came to take an active part in the antislavery movement. Leaving his legal practice, he quickly achieved fame as a reform agitator, principally as an abolitionist but also as a spokesman for other reforms. He became a skilled platform orator with a direct, brilliant, and controlled style; indeed, more than any other orator, he was responsible for introducing a colloquial style into American public speaking.

This selection is an address on the labor movement delivered late in Phillip's life. It reflects a life-long interest in labor reform as well as powerful oratory. The text is from "The Foundation of the Labor Movement," an address delivered at the Music Hall in Boston on October 31, 1871, printed in *Speeches, Lectures, and Letters,* Second Series (Boston, 1905).

Ladies and Gentlemen: We are sometimes so near an object that we cannot see it. I could place you so near the City Hall to-night that you would not know whether you were looking at a ton of granite or a wall of a large building. So it is with a fact. The men who stand the nearest to it are often the last to recognize either its breadth or its meaning. Perhaps the last men to appreciate a fact are the men nearest to whose eyes it passes; and it is just so in government. We are hardly aware of the changes that are taking place about us; our children will understand them distinctly.

There is a large class among our German fellow-citizens who advocate the abolition of the Presidency. The thoughtful in that class perceive, what the ordinary passer-by does not recognize, that we are daily abolishing the Presidency, and the movement of the country for fifty years has been toward the abolition of the Presidency. You see this tendency in a variety of circumstances. When we were first a nation, the greatest men among us were chosen President, and named for President; but now we don't think of putting up a first-rate man.

There is another feature we don't see—that the government is fast being monopolized by the House of Representatives. If we go on as we have done for half a century, there will be no government in this country except the House. Whatever defies the power of the great House will go down. Whether harmonious and beneficent results will follow our adoption of the system, depends upon whether the great mass of men and women, with universal suffrage as their sheet-anchor, can work out through these results one single tool like the House.

I have only gone into this statement to approach a second point; and that is, we stand on the moment when the people actually put their hands forth for power. We stand at an epoch when the nature of the government is undergoing a fundamental change. I have been speaking of machines, whether we should operate through a Senate and President, or solely through a House. I have been speaking of the spindles and wheels. Below that lies the water power. The water power of Great Britain has been the wealth of thirty thousand land-holders—thirty thousand land-holding families, perhaps seven hundred thousand or a million voters. With us, the water power is to be the ballots of ten millions of adult men and women, scattered through all classes, rich and poor, educated and ignorant, prompt and conservative, radical and timid, all modes and kinds and qualities of mind. Well, that brings me to the form which this great advance of the people takes. It is the working masses that are really about to put their hands to the work of governing.

It is no accident, no caprice of an individual, no mere shout of the political arena, that heralds today the great Labor movement of the United States.

But in the mean time, over the horizon, looming at first and now almost touching its meridian, comes up another power—I mean the power of wealth, the inordinate power of capital. Our fathers, when they prevented entail, when they provided for the distribution of estates, thought they had erected a bulwark against the money power that had killed Great Britain. They forgot that money could combine; that a moneyed corporation was like the papacy —a succession of persons with a unity of purpose; that it never died; that it never by natural proclivity became imbecile. The grandson of a king is neces-sarily one third an idiot; but the third generation of a money corporation is wiser for the experience of predecessors, and preserves the same unity of purpose.

This great money power looms over the horizon at the very moment when, to every thoughtful man, the power of the masses concentrating in the House of Representatives is to become the sole omnipotence of the State. Naturally so ominous a conjecture provokes resistance; naturally a peril so immediate prompts the wealthy class of the community to combine for de-fence.

The land of England has ruled it for six hundred years. The corporations of America mean to rule it in the same way, and unless some power more radical than that of ordinary politics is found, will rule it inevitably. I confess that the only fear I have in regard to republican institutions is whether, in our day, any adequate remedy will be found for this incoming flood of the power of incorporated wealth. No statesman, no public man yet, has dared to defy it. Every man that has met it has been crushed to powder; and the only hope of any effectual grapple with it is in rousing the actual masses, whose interests permanently lie in an opposite direction, to grapple with this great force; for you know very well that our great cities are the radiating points from which go forth the great journalism, the culture, the education, the commercial influences, that make and shape the nation. The great cities are the arsenals of great wealth, where wealth manages every thing its own way.

Now, gentlemen, to me the Labor movement means just this: It is the last noble protest of the American people against the power of incorporated wealth, seeking to do over again what the Whig aristocracy of Great Britain has successfully done for two hundred years. Thirty thousand families own Great Britain today; and if you multiply John Bright by a hundred, and double his eloquence, it seems impossible that he should save England from a violent convulsion in the great grapple between such a power and the people who have determined to have their way.

Men blame us, the representatives of the working-men of the nation, that we come into politics. The other day it was my good fortune to meet that distinguished Frenchman, Monsieur Coquerel; and he asked me what was the motto of the working-men of the United States. I said to him, "Short hours, better education, cooperation in the end, and in the mean time a political movement that will concentrate the thought of the country upon this thing."

Now, here I take issue with the best critic which the Labor movement has met: I refer to Rev. Samuel Johnson of Salem, one of the thinkers who has spread out before the people his objections to the Labor movement of this country. His first objection is, that we will hurry into politics. Well, now, our answer to him, and to the score of other scholars who have been criticizing us, is this: Gentlemen, we see the benefit of going into politics. If we had not rushed into politics, had not taken Massachusetts by the four corners and shaken her, you never would have written your criticisms. We rush into politics because politics is the safety valve. We could discuss as well as you, if you would only give us bread and houses, fair pay and leisure, and opportunities to travel. We could sit and discuss the question for the next fifty years. It's a very easy thing to discuss, for a gentleman in his study, with no anxiety about to-morrow. Why, the ladies and gentlemen of the reign of Louis XV. and Louis XVI., in France, seated in gilded saloons and on Persian carpets, surrounded with luxury, with the products of India, and the curious manufactures of ingenious Lyons and Rheims, discussed the rights of man, and balanced them in dainty phrases, and expressed them in such quaint generalizations that Jefferson borrowed the Declaration of Independence from their hands. There they sat, balancing and discussing sweetly, making out new theories, and daily erecting a splendid architecture of debate, till the angry crowd broke open the doors, and ended the discussion in blood. They waited too long, discussed about half a century too long. You see, discussion is very good when a man has bread to eat, and his children all portioned off, and his daughters married, and his house furnished and paid for, and his will made; but discussion is very bad when—

> "Ye hear the children weeping, O my brothers!
> Ere the sorrow comes with years;"

discussion is bad when a class bends under actual oppression. We want immediate action.

We would fain save this issue from an outbreak of actual violence. Therefore we go into politics.

Well, then, our critic goes on to say, "What do you call yourselves Labor party for? All men labor. Rufus Choate labors. Daniel Webster labors. Why do you confine your party to the men that work?" Well, now, we confine it because thus there is no mistake. Now, suppose you should take up a book presenting the condition of the laboring classes of Great Britain. Mr. Gladstone works harder than any other man there; Lord Brougham did more work than any other man there; Lord Palmerston, up to his eightieth year, worked hard as any man there. But if you were to take up a book on the working-men of Great Britain, do you think you would find the condition of Lord Brougham there? If you took up a book on the British laboring class, or how much they eat, what kind of houses they live in, etc., do you think you would find Gladstone's income, and the number of rooms he had in his house, and how many children he had had the last fifty years? So if an Englishman came here, and said, "I want to know something about your working-men. Please let me hear it from some of themselves. Whom shall I go to?" Would you send him to Daniel Webster or Rufus Choate? But Daniel Webster did as much work as any man of his day. Would you have him sent to Rufus Choate? But Rufus Choate was a hard-working man. John Marshall and Lemuel Shaw did as much work as any men in Massachusetts or Virginia; but if George Combe had come to this country, and said, "I want to see a specimen of the laboring class of the United States," I doubt whether any man would have sent him to Lemuel Shaw. I ask the critics of the Labor movement, whether any man ever misunderstood this? Every man who reads of the Labor Question knows that it means the movement of the men that earn their living with their hands; that are employed, and paid in wages; are gathered under roofs of factories; sent out on farms; sent out on ships; gathered on the walls. In popular acceptation, the working class means the men that work with their hands, for wages, so many hours a day, employed by great capitalists; that work for everybody else.

Why do we move for this class? "Why," says Mr. Johnson, "don't you move for all working-men?" Because, while Daniel Webster gets forty thousand dollars for arguing the Mexican claims, there is no need of anybody's moving for him. While Rufus Choate gets five thousand dollars for making one argument to a jury, there is no need of moving for him, or for the men that work with their brains,—that do highly disciplined and skilled labor, invent, and write books. The reason why the Labor movement confines itself to a single class is because that class of work does not get paid, does not get protection. Mental labor is adequately paid, and more that adequately protected. It can shift its channels; it can vary according to the supply and demand. If a man fails as a minister, why, he becomes a railway conductor. If that doesn't suit him, he turns out, and becomes the agent of an insurance office. If that doesn't suit, he goes West, and becomes governor of a Territory. And if he finds himself incapable of either of these positions, he comes home, and gets to be a city editor. He varies his occupation as he pleases, and doesn't need protection. But the great mass, chained to a trade, doomed to be ground up in the mill of supply and demand, that work so many hours a day, and must run in the great ruts of business,—they are the men whose inadequate protection, whose unfair share of the general product claims a movement in their behalf.

Well, the third charge brought by Mr. Johnson against us is, that we are cruel—we combine; we prevent this man from laboring there, and we won't let that man learn our trade; we form trades-unions. To be sure we do. We say to the Chinese, "Stay at home. Don't come here by importation; come by immigration." We say to the crowding millions who try to swamp our trade, "Stand aloof; we won't teach you." We say to the mills of Lowell, who have turned us out of doors, "We'll starve you into submission." Well, "it's a narrow contest. It's an unjust, it's a cruel, it's an avaricious method." So it is. Where did we learn it? Learned it of capital, learned it of our enemies.

I know labor is narrow; I know she is aggressive; I know she arms herself with the best weapon that a corrupt civilization furnishes,—all true. Where do we get these ideas? Borrowed them from capital, every one of them; and when you advance to us on the level of peace, unarmed, we'll meet you on the same. While you combine and plot and defend, so will we.

But Mr. Johnson says, "Come into the world with the white banner of peace." Ay, we will, when you disarm. How foolish it would have been for Grant to send home his Sharp's rifles to Springfield, and garner all his cannon in New York, and put all his monitors in the harbor of Norfolk, and go down to Virginia with eighty thousand unarmed men, to look her in the face! Labor comes up, and says, "They have shotted their cannon to the lips; they have rough-ground their swords as in battle; they have adopted every new method; they have invented every dangerous machine,—and it is all planted like a great park of artillery against us. They have incorporated wealth; they have hidden behind banks; they have concealed themselves in currency; they have sheltered themselves in taxation; they have passed rules to govern us,—and we will improve upon the lesson they have taught us. When they disarm, we will—not before."

Well, then, the fourth charge is found in the *Daily Advertiser*. We had a meeting at Framingham, and passed a set of resolutions; we adopted a platform; and the next day the *Daily Advertiser* granted us the condescension of an article, criticising our action, especially mine; and they described what we had adopted. They painted its horrible tendency. They said, "If you adopt that principle, it will lead you to that (and so on to that) till the final result will be—" I held my breath. I said to myself, "What will it probably be? Perhaps the stereotyped ghost of the French Revolution; that's what's coming." "The final result will be—" Horrible! I thought probably they would paint a millionaire hanging on every lamp-post. "The final result—" Perhaps it will be Mormonism; society dissolved into its original elements. Horrible! I began to feel a faint sensation; but I concluded to read on: "The final result will be an equalization of property." Horrible, horrible! Actually, men will be almost equal! An equalization of property! Any man that does that ought to be hanged. Well, we do mean it; we do mean just that. That's the meaning of the Labor movement,—an equalization of property. The *Advertiser* has found us out, actually discovered our plot. He's let the cat out of the bag. We didn't mean to have told you, but it is so. What we need is an equalization of property—nothing else. My ideal of a civilization is a very high one; but the approach to it is a New England town of some two thousand inhabitants, with no rich man and no poor man in it, all mingling in the same society, every child at the same school, no poorhouse, no beggar, opportunities equal, nobody too proud to stand aloof, nobody too humble to be shut out. That's New England as it was fifty years ago, the horrible creature that the *Daily Advertiser* fears. That's what Framingham proposes to bring about. But why isn't Framingham contented? Because the civilization that lingers beautifully on the hillsides of New England, nestles sweetly in the valleys of Vermont, the moment it approaches a crowd like Boston, or a million of men gathered in one place like New York—rots. It cannot force the crowd; it cannot stand the great centres of modern civilization.

Our civilization cannot stand the city. One reason is, it has got some hidden disease. Another reason is, the moment it flows out into the broad, deep activity of the nineteenth century, it betrays its weakness, and copies Europe. The moment this sweet-scented, dew-smelling Vermont flows down into the slums of New York, it becomes like London. The moment the North gathers its forces, and goes down the Mississippi Valley into New Orleans, social science stands aghast. Modern civilization shrinks back at the terrible evil which she can neither fathom nor cure, just as she does in Europe.

What is our cause? It is this: there are three hundred and fifty millions of human beings in what you call Christendom, and two hundred millions of them don't have enough to eat from January to December. I won't ask for culture, for opportunities for education, for travel, for society; but two hundred millions of men gathered under Christendom don't have even enough to eat. A hundred thousand men in the city of New York live in dwellings that a rich man wouldn't let his horse stay in a day.

But that isn't anything. You should go up to beautiful Berkshire with me, into the factories there. It shall be the day after a Presidential election. I will go with you into a counting-room—four hundred employees. The partners are sitting down, the day after a Presidential election. They take the list of workmen, and sift them out; and every man that has not voted the ticket they wanted is thrown out to starve just as if he were cattle. That's Christian civilization! that's Massachusetts! I don't like that significant fact. I leap from that town into a large mill, with five hundred employees, and say to the master, "How about the dwellings of your operatives? How many hours do they have at home?" "Well, I hope they don't have any. The best-ventilated place they are ever in is my mill. They had better stay here sixteen hours out of the twenty-four; it keeps them out of mischief better than any other place. As long as they work, they are not doing worse. I cannot attend to their houses." I say to him, "It seems to me you do the same for your ox." That's another significant fact of our civilization. I go to Lowell, and I say to a young girl, wandering in the streets, "How is this?" "Well, I worked here seven years, and I thought I would leave that mill and go to another; and the corporation won't give me my ticket. I have sued them in the Supreme Court, and I cannot get it; and here I am, penniless, in Eastern Massachusetts." That's Christian civilization. I am picking up, not individual facts, but significant rules, that were made for labor.

You say, "What does labor need in New England?" It needs justice. Mr. Stewart, in New York, has bought a whole town; and he is going to build model houses, and house there all the labor he can get to go into them. Yet the civilization which alone can look the New Testament in the face is a civilization where one man does not depend on the pity of another man's building him a model lodging-house; the civilization which alone can look the New Testament in the face is a civilization where one man could not build, and another man would not need, that sort of refuge.

No, gentlemen, what we mean is this: the labor of yesterday, your capital, is protected sacredly. Not so the labor of to-day. The labor of yesterday gets twice the protection and twice the pay that the labor of today gets. Capital gets twice the protection and twice the pay.

Now, we mean a radical change, and in the few minutes that are left me, I want to indicate our object.

We mean certain great radical changes. I am not quite of the opinion of Mr. Secretary Boutwell, when he said here the other night, that fifty years hence the idea that a man could own land, and leave it to his children, would be ridiculous. I have not quite come to that. But then, you know there is a reason for it; he is a radical, and I have always been a conservative. There is a curious thing underlies lands. We are not quite certain that we have got the best system. Secretary Boutwell may be right. Seventy years ago a man offered to a relative of mine all the land between Federal Street and Hawley

Street, between Milk Street and Franklin, for thirty-three hundred dollars. He came to him day after day, urging him to purchase; and the answer was, "I am not rich enough to have a cow-pasture at that price, and I couldn't use it for anything else,"—that tract of land which to-day, gentlemen, as you know, would sell for three million dollars. Now, labor goes about, like Socrates, asking questions. We don't assume anything. When we were little boys, and did our sums on the slate, and the answer came out wrong, we didn't break the slate. We went to the master; and he said, "Go back; there's a mistake somewhere; if you examine, you will find it." I come into a civilization in which two men out of three don't have enough to eat. I come into New York, where it is a rich man that supplies a lodging for houseless poverty. I say to myself, "That course isn't right; there's a mistake somewhere." Do unto others as you would have others do unto you. The end of things is New York. That doesn't cohere. Where is the mistake? It is somewhere, and the Labor movement is trying to find it out.

Again, gentlemen, we have another doubt to express. Are you quite certain that capital—the child of artificial laws, the product of society, the mere growth of social life—has a right to only an equal burden with labor, the living spring? We doubt it so much that we think we have invented a way to defeat Tom Scott, of the Pennsylvania Central. We think we have devised a little plan—Abraham Lincoln used to have a little story—by which we will save the Congress of the Nation from the moneyed corporations of the State. When we get into power, there is one thing we mean to do. If a man owns a single house, we will tax him one hundred dollars. If he owns ten houses of like value, we won't tax him one thousand dollars, but two thousand dollars. If he owns a hundred houses, we won't tax him ten thousand dollars, but sixty thousand dollars; and the richer a man grows, the bigger his tax, so that when he is worth forty million dollars he will not have more than twenty thousand dollars a year to live on. We'll double and treble and quintuple and sextuple and increase tenfold the taxes, till Stewart, out of his uncounted millions, and the Pennsylvania Central, out of its measureless income, shall not have anything more than a moderate lodging and an honest table. The corporations we would have are those of associated labor and capital—co-operation.

We'll crumble up wealth by making it unprofitable to be rich. The poor man shall have a larger income in proportion as he is poor. The rich man shall have a lesser income in proportion as he is rich. You will say, "Is that just?" My friends, it is safe. Man is more valuable than money. You say, "Then capital will go to Europe." Good heavens, let it go!

If other States wish to make themselves vassals to wealth, so will not we. We will save a country equal from end to end. Land, private property, all sorts of property, shall be so dearly taxed that it shall be impossible to be rich; for it is in wealth, in incorporated, combining, perpetuated wealth, that the danger of labor lies.

XVII

The Mind of the South

THE EXISTENCE of slavery in America constituted the great challenge to American ideals of democracy, equality, and opportunity. Earlier in the century, thoughtful southerners had realized—as did Jefferson himself—that slavery was an evil and should be destroyed. Yet even in Jefferson's lifetime, the invention of the cotton gin and the subsequent rapid growth of the cotton-slave economy were making slavery profitable and even necessary to the South. The last southern emancipation effort occurred in Virginia in 1832, and thereafter antislavery sentiment all but died in the South. Southerners now came to the defense of slavery, first as a necessary evil and then, as the Civil War approached, as a positive good.

The struggle over the slavery question grew more formidable each decade. From the 1820's on, a series of compromises relating to the extension of slavery into the new territories, attempted to maintain national unity by balancing political power and sectional interests. But the conflict went deeper than a battle for political power and posed fundamental economic problems and moral issues. Indeed, it was this combination of interests in both North and South that made the impending clash between the states more inevitable and catastrophic.

The arguments for slavery were based on a variety of premises: economic need, states' rights, the Biblical sanction of slavery, and the inferior status of the Negro race. Underlying all such arguments, however, was what may be called the "plantation mind"—an image of a landed, feudal aristocracy that would counterbalance the industrial North. More imaginary than real, this mind fortified itself by repeating the arguments of Europe's reactionary spokesmen. George Fitzhugh, for example, announced that "we begin a great conservative reaction. . . . We attempt to roll back the Reformation in its political phases." And John C. Calhoun invoked a sophisticated, though dated, political philosophy to maintain the integrity of the South's sectional interests. The United States, Calhoun argued, was not an organic union; and within this structure simple majority rule did not always serve the interests of justice. From this he took his famous doctrine of "concurrent majority," which in effect would have given each section of the nation a veto power over the actions of the federal authority.

The southern mind had eloquent spokesmen in such men as Fitzhugh and Calhoun, and yet it did not escape ideological difficulties. Much of this difficulty arose from the fact that slavery did not fit into any of the traditional categories of American social thought, try as the South might to make it fit. In Calhoun these difficulties are especially clear. He destroyed Locke's state of nature and then evolved a theory of minority rights that were based squarely on the doctrine of consent; he defended slavery on the basis of the "divinity of existing coercions" and then sought to defend the South from economic enslavement by the North; and he construed the Constitution, as Professor Hartz puts it, as a compact among the states that "left nothing to tradition, nothing to force, and nothing to God."[1]

Reaction to slavery in the North, while sometimes based on economic considerations, generally sprang from deep moral conviction. Slavery was an evil, thoughtful northerners believed, and abolition was the only solution. Abolitionist literature undoubtedly exaggerated the lurid features of slavery and encouraged an emotional reaction to the problem. Yet the "peculiar institution" of slavery and the mentality that supported it were outside the main current of American development and thought, and would not survive the terrible struggle about to begin. But the romanticized picture of the antebellum South (largely a creation of the imagination) continued as a living symbol for later generations of southerners.

(75)

John C. Calhoun

1782-1850

Calhoun served the nation long and ably as a Congressman from South Carolina, Secretary of War under Monroe, Vice-President under Jackson, Secretary of State under Tyler, and as Senator from South Carolina. A brilliant politician, he was also the leading political theorist of his generation.

Calhoun devoted his formidable skills to the defense of slavery as an institution essential to the survival of the South. In this effort he became the acknowledged champion of states' rights. Rejecting the principle of majority rule on the ground that majorities can be tyrannical, he developed the theory of concurrent majority as an alternative that would protect sectional interests.

---

1. On these inconsistencies and the relation of the southern mind to American liberalism, see Louis Hartz, *The Liberal Tradition in America* (New York, 1955), Part Four: The Reactionary Enlightenment.

This selection is from "A Disquisition on Government," *The Works of John C. Calhoun,* 6 vols. (New York, 1876), vol. I.

In order to have a clear and just conception of the nature and object of government, it is indispensable to understand correctly what that constitution or law of our nature is in which government originates, or to express it more fully and accurately—that law without which government would not and with which it must necessarily exist. Without this, it is as impossible to lay any solid foundation for the science of government as it would be to lay one for that of astronomy without a like understanding of that constitution or law of the material world according to which the several bodies composing the solar system mutually act on each other and by which they are kept in their respective spheres. The first question, accordingly, to be considered, What is that constitution or law of our nature without which government would not exist and with which its existence is necessary?

In considering this, I assume as an incontestable fact that man is so constituted as to be a social being. His inclinations and wants, physical and moral, irresistibly impel him to associate with his kind; and he has, accordingly, never been found, in any age or country, in any state other than the social. In no other, indeed, could he exist, and in no other—were it possible for him to exist—could he attain to a full development of his moral and intellectual faculties or raise himself, in the scale of being, much above the level of the brute creation.

I next assume also as a fact not less incontestable that, while man is so constituted as to make the social state necessary to his existence and the full development of his faculties, this state itself cannot exist without government. The assumption rests on universal experience. In no age or country has any society or community ever been found, whether enlightened or savage, without government of some description.

Having assumed these as unquestionable phenomena of our nature, I shall, without further remark, proceed to the investigation of the primary and important question, What is that constitution of our nature which, while it impels man to associate with his kind, renders it impossible for society to exist without government?

The answer will be found in the fact (not less incontestable than either of the others) that, while man is created for the social state and is accordingly so formed as to feel what affects others as well as what affects himself, he is, at the same time, so constituted as to feel more intensely what affects him directly than what affects him indirectly through others, or, to express it differently, he is so constituted that his direct or individual affections are stronger than his sympathetic or social feelings. I intentionally avoid the expression "*selfish* feelings" as applicable to the former, because, as commonly used, it implies an unusual excess of the individual over the social feelings in the person to whom it is applied and, consequently, something depraved and vicious. My object is to exclude such inference and to restrict the inquiry exclusively to facts in their bearings on the subject under consideration, viewed as mere phenomena appertaining to our nature—constituted as it is; and which are as unquestionable as is that of gravitation or any other phenomenon of the material world.

In asserting that our individual are stronger than our social feelings, it is not intended to deny that there are instances, growing out of peculiar relations —as that of a mother and her infant—or resulting from the force of education and habit over peculiar constitutions, in which the latter have overpowered the former; but these instances are few and always regarded as something extraordinary. The deep impression they make, whenever they occur, is the strongest proof that they are regarded as exceptions to some general and well-understood law of our nature, just as some of the minor powers of the material world are apparently to gravitation.

I might go farther and assert this to be a phenomenon not of our nature only, but of all animated existence throughout its entire range, so far as our knowledge extends. It would, indeed, seem to be essentially connected with the great law of self-preservation which pervades all that feels, from man down to the lowest and most insignificant reptile or insect. In none is it stronger than in man. His social feelings may, indeed, in a state of safety and abundance, combined with high intellectual and moral culture, acquire great expansion and force, but not so great as to overpower this all-pervading and essential law of animated existence.

But that constitution of our nature which makes us feel more intensely what affects us directly than what affects us indirectly through others necessarily leads to conflict between individuals. Each, in consequence, has a greater regard for his own safety or happiness than for the safety or happiness of others, and, where these come in opposition, is ready to sacrifice the interests of others to his own. And hence the tendency to a universal state of conflict between individual and individual, accompanied by the connected passions of suspicion, jealousy, anger, and revenge—followed by insolence, fraud, and cruelty—and, if not prevented by some controlling power, ending in a state of universal discord and confusion destructive of the social state and the ends for which it is ordained. This controlling power, wherever vested or by whomsoever exercised, is *Government.*

It follows, then, that man is so constituted that government is necessary to the existence of society, and society to his existence and the perfection of his faculties. It follows also that government has its origin in this twofold constitution of his nature: the sympathetic or social feelings constituting the remote, and the individual or direct the proximate, cause. . . .

But government, although intended to protect and preserve society, has itself a strong tendency to disorder and abuse of its powers, as all experience and almost every page of history testify. The cause is to be found in the same constitution of our nature which makes government indispensable. The powers which it is necessary for government to possess in order to repress violence and preserve order cannot execute themselves. They must be administered by men in whom, like others, the individual are stronger than the social feelings. And hence the powers vested in them to prevent injustice and oppression on the part of others will, if left unguarded, be by them converted into instruments to oppress the rest of the community. That by which this is prevented, by whatever name called, is what is meant by *constitution,* in its most comprehensive sense, when applied to *government.*

Having its origin in the same principle of our nature, *constitution* stands to *government* as *government* stands to *society;* and as the end for which society is ordained would be defeated without government, so that for which government is ordained would, in a great measure, be defeated without constitution. But they differ in this striking particular. There is no difficulty in forming government. It is not even a matter of choice whether there shall be one or not. Like breathing, it is not permitted to depend on our volition. Necessity will force it on all communities in some one form or another. Very different is the case as to constitution. Instead of a matter of necessity, it is one of the most difficult tasks imposed on man to form a constitution worthy of the name, while to form a perfect one—one that would completely counteract the tendency of government to oppression and abuse and hold it strictly to the great ends for which it is ordained—has thus far exceeded human wisdom, and possibly ever will. From this another striking difference results. Constitution is the contrivance of man, while government is of divine ordination. Man is left to perfect what the wisdom of the Infinite ordained as necessary to preserve the race.

With these remarks I proceed to the consideration of the important and difficult question, How is this tendency of government to be counteracted? . . .

In answering the important question under consideration it is not necessary to enter into an examination of the various contrivances adopted by these celebrated governments to counteract this tendency to disorder and abuse, nor to undertake to treat of constitution in its most comprehensive sense. What I propose is far more limited: to explain on what principles government must be formed in order to resist by its own interior structure—or to use a single term, *organism*—the tendency to abuse of power. This structure, or organism, is what is meant by constitution, in its strict and more usual sense; and it is this which distinguishes what are called "constitutional" governments from "absolute." It is in this strict and more usual sense that I propose to use the term hereafter.

How government, then, must be constructed in order to counteract, through its organism, this tendency on the part of those who make and execute the laws to oppress those subject to their operation is the next question which claims attention.

There is but one way in which this can possibly be done, and that is by such an organism as will furnish the ruled with the means of resisting successfully this tendency on the part of the rulers to oppression and abuse. Power can only be resisted by power—and tendency by tendency. Those who exercise power and those subject to its exercise—the rulers and the ruled—stand in antagonistic relations to each other. The same constitution of our nature which leads rulers to oppress the ruled—regardless of the object for which government is ordained—will, with equal strength, lead the ruled to resist when possessed of the means of making peaceable and effective resistance. Such an organism, then, as will furnish the means by which resistance may be systematically and peaceably made on the part of the ruled to oppression and abuse of power on the part of the rulers is the first and indispensable step toward *forming* a constitutional government. And as this can only be effected by or through the right of suffrage—the right on the part of the ruled to choose their rulers at proper intervals and to hold them thereby responsible for their conduct—the responsibility of the rulers to the ruled, through the right of suffrage, is the indispensable and primary principle in the *foundation* of a constitutional government. When this right is properly guarded, and the people sufficiently enlightened to understand their own rights and the interests of the community and duly to appreciate the motives and conduct of those appointed to make and execute the laws, it is all-sufficient to give to those who elect effective control over those they have elected.

I call the right of suffrage the indispensable and primary principle, for it would be a great and dangerous mistake to suppose, as many do, that it is, of itself, sufficient to form constitutional governments. To this erroneous opinion may be traced one of the causes why so few attempts to form constitutional governments have succeeded, and why of the few which have, so small a number have had durable existence. It has led not only to mistakes in the attempts to form such governments, but to their overthrow when they have, by some good fortune, been correctly formed. So far from being, of itself, sufficient—however well guarded it might be and however enlightened the people—it would, unaided by other provisions, leave the government as absolute as it would be in the hands of irresponsible rulers; and with a tendency, at least as strong, toward oppression and abuse of its powers. . . .

As, then, the right of suffrage, without some other provision, cannot counteract this tendency of government, the next question for consideration is, What is that other provision? This demands the most serious consideration, for of all the questions embraced in the science of government it involves a principle, the most important and the least understood, and when understood, the most difficult of application in practice. It is, indeed, emphatically that principle which *makes* the constitution, in its strict and limited sense.

From what has been said, it is manifest that this provision must be of a character calculated to prevent any one interest or combination of interests from using the powers of government to aggrandize itself at the expense of the others. Here lies the evil: and just in proportion as it shall prevent, or fail to prevent it, in the same degree it will effect, or fail to effect, the end intended to be accomplished. There is but one certain mode in which this result can be secured, and that is by the adoption of some restriction or limitation which shall so effectually prevent any one interest or combination of interests from obtaining the exclusive control of the government as to render hopeless all attempts directed to that end. There is, again, but one mode in which this can be effected, and that is by taking the sense of each interest or portion of the community which may be unequally and injuriously affected by the action of the government separately, through its own majority or in some other way by which its voice may be fairly expressed, and to require the consent of each interest either to put or to keep the government in action. This, too, can be accomplished only in one way, and that is by such an organism of the government—and, if necessary for the purpose, of the community also—as will, by dividing and distributing the powers of government, give to each division or interest, through its appropriate organ, either a concurrent voice in making and executing the laws or a veto on their execution. It is only by such an organism that the assent of each can be made necessary to put the government in motion, or the power made effectual to arrest its action when put in motion; and it is only by the one or the other that the different interests, orders, classes, or portions into which the community may be divided can be protected, and all conflict and struggle between them prevented—by rendering it impossible to put or to keep it in action without the concurrent consent of all.

Such an organism as this, combined with the right of suffrage, constitutes, in fact, the elements of constitutional government. The one, by rendering those who make and execute the laws responsible to those on whom they operate, prevents the rulers from oppressing the ruled; and the other, by making it impossible for any one interest or combination of interests, or class, or order, or portion of the community to obtain exclusive control, prevents any one of them from oppressing the other. It is clear that oppression and abuse of power must come, if at all, from the one or the other quarter. From no other can they come. It follows that the two, suffrage and proper organism combined, are sufficient to counteract the tendency of government to oppression and abuse of power and to restrict it to the fulfillment of the great ends for which it is ordained.

(76)

George Fitzhugh

1806-1881

A prominent Virginia lawyer and planter, Fitzhugh became a leading defender of slavery. Fitzhugh argued that the existence of slavery lent stability to society and reduced the amout of thievery and crime. Thus, for Fitzhugh slavery was not a necessary evil but rather a positive good, for it freed the South from the mounting social and economic problems of the rest of the world. His first important book, *Sociology for the South* (1854), with its arguments against laissez-faire capitalism, attracted little attention. His next work, however, was much more vigorous and carried the argument to the enemy camp. Free society, he wrote, is a failure, and the philosophy upon which it is based—social contract, natural rights, rule of law—is false. Rather, America must return to the political theories of Aristotle that are based on the social nature of man and a hierarchical view of society.

The selection here is from *Cannibals All!* (Richmond, 1857).

We are, all, North and South, engaged in the White Slave Trade, and he who succeeds best, is esteemed most respectable. It is far more cruel than the Black Slave Trade, because it exacts more of its slaves, and neither protects nor governs them. We boast, that it exacts more, when we say, "that the *profits* made from employing free labor are greater than those from slave labor." The profits, made from free labor, are the amount of the products of such labor, which the employer, by means of the command which capital or skill gives him, takes away, exacts or "exploitates" from the free laborer. The profits of slave labor are that portion of the products of such labor which the power of the master enables him to appropriate. These profits are less, because the master allows the slave to retain a larger share of the results of his own labor, than do the employers of free labor. But we not only boast that the White Slave Trade is more exacting and fraudulent (in fact, though not in intention,) than Black Slavery; but we also boast, that it is more cruel, in leaving the laborer to take care of himself and family out of the pittance which skill or capital have allowed him to retain. When the day's labor is ended, he is free, but is overburdened with the cares of family and household, which make his freedom an empty and delusive mockery. But his employer is really free, and may enjoy the profits made by others' labor, without a care, or a trouble, as to their well-being. The negro slave is free, too, when the labors of the day are over, and free in mind as well as body; for the master provides food, raiment, house, fuel, and everything else necessary to the physical well-being of himself and family. The master's labors commence just when the slave's end. No wonder men should prefer white slavery to capital, to negro slavery, since it is more profitable, and is free from all the cares and labors of black slaveholding.

Now, reader, if you wish to know yourself—to "descant on your own deformity"—read on. But if you would cherish self-conceit, self-esteem, or self-appreciation, throw down our book; for we will dispel illusions which have promoted your happiness, and show you that what you have considered and practiced as virtue, is little better than moral Cannibalism. But you will find yourself in numerous and respectable company; for all good and respectable people are "Cannibals all," who do not labor, or who are successfully trying to live without labor, on the unrequited labor of other people: whilst low, bad, and disreputable people, are those who labor to support themselves, and to support said respectable people besides. Throwing the negro slaves out of the account, and society is divided in Christendom into four classes: the rich, or independent respectable people, who live well and labor not at all; the professional and skillful respectable people, who do a little light work, for enormous wages; the poor hard-working people, who support every body, and starve themselves; and the poor thieves, swindlers and sturdy beggars, who live like gentlemen, without labor, on the labor of other people. The gentlemen exploitate, which being done on a large scale, and requiring a great many victims, is highly respectable—whilst the rogues and beggars take so little from others, that they fare little better than those who labor.

But, reader, we do not wish to fire into the flock. "Thou art the man!" You are a Cannibal! and if a successful one, pride yourself on the number of your victims, quite as much as any Feejee chieftain, who breakfasts, dines and sups on human flesh. And your conscience smites you, if you have failed to succeed, quite as much as his, when he returns from an unsuccessful foray.

Probably, you are a lawyer, or a merchant, or a doctor, who have made by your business fifty thousand dollars, and retired to live on your capital. But, mark! not to spend your capital. That would be vulgar, disreputable, criminal. That would be, to live by your own labor; for your capital is your amassed labor. That would be, to do as common working men do; for they take the pittance which their employers leave them, to live on. They live by labor; for they exchange the results of their own labor for the products of other people's labor. It is, no doubt, an honest, vulgar way of living; but not at all a respectable way. The respectable way of living is, to make other people work for you, and to pay them nothing for so doing—and to have no concern about them after their work is done. Hence, white slaveholding is much more respectable than negro slavery—for the master works nearly as hard for the negro, as he for the master. But you, my virtuous, respectable reader, exact three thousand dollars per annum from white labor, (for your income is the product of white labor,) and make not one cent of return in any form. You retain your capital, and never labor, and yet live in luxury on the labor of others. Capital commands labor, as the master does the slave. Neither pays for labor; but the master permits the slave to retain a larger allowance from the proceeds of his own labor, and hence "free labor is cheaper than slave labor." You, with the command over labor which your capital gives you, are a slave owner—a master, without the obligations of a master. They who work for you, who create your income, are slaves, without the rights of slaves. Slaves without a master! Whilst you were engaged in amassing your capital, in seeking to become independent, you were in the White Slave Trade. To become independent, is to be able to make other people support you, without being obliged to labor for *them.* Now, what man in society is not seeking to attain this situation? He who attains it, is a slave owner, in the worst sense. He who is in pursuit of it, is engaged in the slave trade. You, reader, belong to the one or other class. The men without property, in free society, are theoretically in a worse condition than slaves. Practically, their condition corresponds with this theory, as history and statistics every where demonstrate. The capitalists, in free society, live in ten times the luxury and show that Southern masters do, because the slaves to capital work harder and cost less, than negro slaves.

The negro slaves of the South are the happiest, and, in some sense, the freest people in the world. The children and the aged and infirm work not at all, and yet have all the comforts and necessaries of life provided for them. They enjoy liberty, because they are oppressed neither by care nor labor. The women do little hard work, and are protected from the despotism of their husbands by their masters. The negro men and stout boys work, on the average, in good weather, not more than nine hours a day. The balance of their time is spent in perfect abandon. Besides, they have their Sabbaths and holidays. White men, with so much of license and liberty, would die of ennui; but negroes luxuriate in corporeal and mental repose. With their faces upturned to the sun, they can sleep at any hour; and quiet sleep is the greatest of human enjoyments. "Blessed be the man who invented sleep." 'Tis happiness in itself—and results from contentment with the present, and confident assurance of the future. We do not know whether free laborers ever sleep. They are fools to do so; for, whilst they sleep, the wily and watchful capitalist is devising means to ensnare and exploitate them. The free laborer must work or starve. He is more of a slave than the negro, because he works longer and harder for less allowance than the slave, and has no holiday, because the cares of life with him begin when its labors end. He has no liberty, and not a single right. We know, 'tis often said, air and water, are common property, which all have equal right to participate and enjoy; but this is utterly false. The appropriation of the lands carries with it the appropriation of all on or above the lands, *usque ad cœlum, aut ad inferos.* A man cannot breathe the air, without a place to breathe it from, and all places are appropriated. All water is private property "to the middle of the stream," except the ocean, and that is not fit to drink.

Free laborers have not a thousandth part of the rights and liberties of negro slaves. Indeed, they have not a single right or a single liberty, unless it be the right or liberty to die. But the reader may think that he and other capitalists and employers are freer than negro slaves. Your capital would soon vanish, if you dared indulge in the liberty and abandon of negroes. You hold your wealth and position by the tenure of constant watchfulness, care and circumspection. You never labor; but you are never free.

Where a few own the soil, they have unlimited power over the balance of society, until domestic slavery comes in, to compel them to permit this balance of society to draw a sufficient and comfortable living from "terra mater." Free society, asserts the right of a few to the earth—slavery, maintains that it belongs, in different degrees, to all.

But, reader, well may you follow the slave trade. It is the only trade worth following, and slaves the only property worth owning. All other is worthless, a mere *caput mortuum,* except in so far as it vests the owner with the power to command the labors of others—to enslave them. Give you a palace, ten thousand acres of land, sumptuous clothes, equipage and every other luxury; and with your artificial wants, you are poorer than Robinson Crusoe, or the lowest working man, if you have no slaves to capital, or domestic slaves. Your capital will not bring you an income of a cent, nor supply one of your wants, without labor. Labor is indispensable to give value to property, and if you owned every thing else, and did not own labor, you would be poor. But fifty thousand dollars means, and is, fifty thousand dollars worth of slaves. You can command, without touching on that capital, three thousand dollars' worth of labor per annum. You could do no more were you to buy slaves with it, and then you would be cumbered with the cares of governing and providing for them. You are a slaveholder now, to the amount of fifty thousand dollars, with all the advantages, and none of the cares and responsibilities of a master.

"Property in man" is what all are struggling to obtain. Why should they not be obliged to take care of man, their property, as they do their horses and their hounds, their cattle and their sheep. Now, under the delusive name of liberty, you work him, "from morn to dewy eve"—from infancy to old age —then turn him out to starve. You treat your horses and hounds better. Capital is a cruel master. The free slave trade, the commonest, yet the cruelest of trades. . . .

Nothing written on the subject of slavery from the time of Aristotle, is worth reading, until the days of the modern Socialists. Nobody, treating of it, thought it worth while to enquire from history and statistics, whether the physical and moral condition of emancipated serfs or slaves had been improved or rendered worse by emancipation. None would condescend to compare the evils of domestic slavery with the evils of liberty without property. It entered no one's head to conceive a doubt as to the actual freedom of the emancipated. The relations of capital and labor, of the property-holders to the non-property-holders, were things about which no one had thought or written. It never occurred to either the enemies or the apologists for slavery, that if no one would employ the free laborer, his condition was infinitely worse than that of actual slavery—nor did it occur to them, that if his wages were less than the allowance of the slave, he was less free after emancipation than before. St. Simon, Fourier, Owen, Fanny Wright, and a few others, who discovered and proclaimed that property was not only a bad master, but an intolerable one, were treated as wicked visionaries. After the French and other revolutions in Western Europe in 1830, all men suddenly discovered that the social relations of men were false, and that social, not political, revolutions were needed. Since that period, almost the whole literature of free society is but a voice proclaiming its absolute and total failure. Hence the works of the socialists contain the true defence of slavery. . . .

In the *Liberator* of the 19th December, we observe that the editor narrows down the slavery contest to the mere question, whether "Man may rightfully hold property in man?"

We think we can dispose of this objection to domestic slavery in a very few words.

Man is a social and gregarious animal, and all such animals hold property in each other. Nature imposes upon them slavery as a law and necessity of their existence. They live together to aid each other, and are slaves under Mr. Garrison's higher law. Slavery arises under the higher law, and is, and ever must be, coeval and coextensive with human nature.

We will enumerate a few of its ten thousand modifications.

The husband has a legally recognized property in his wife's services, and may legally control, in some measure, her personal liberty. She is his property and his slave.

The wife has also a legally recognized property in the husband's services. He is her property, but not her slave.

The father has property in the services and persons of his children till they are twenty-one years of age. They are his property and his slaves.

Children have property, during infancy, in the services of each parent.

Infant negroes, sick, infirm and superannuated negroes, hold most valuable property in the services and capital of their masters. The masters hold no property in such slaves, because, for the time, they are of no value.

Owners and captains of vessels own property in the services of sailors, and may control their personal liberty. They (the sailors) are property, and slaves also.

The services and persons, lives and liberty of soldiers and of officers, belong to the Government; they are, whilst in service, both property and slaves.

Every white working man, be he clerk, carpenter, mechanic, printer, common laborer, or what else, who contracts to serve for a term of days, months, or years, is, for such term, the property of his employer. He is not a slave, like the wife, child, apprentice, sailor or soldier, because, although the employer's right to his services be equally perfect, his remedy to enforce such right is very different. In the one case, he may resort to force to compel compliance; in the other, he is driven to a suit for damages.

Again: Every capitalist holds property in his fellow men to the extent of the profits of his capital, or income. The only income possibly resulting from capital, is the result of the property which capital bestows on its owners, in the labor of other people. . . .

All civilized society recognizes, and, in some measure, performs the obligation to support and provide for all human beings, whether natives or foreigners, who are unable to provide for themselves. Hence poor-houses, etc.

Hence all men hold valuable property, actual or contingent, in the services of each other.

If, Mr. Garrison, this be the only difficulty to be adjusted between North and South, we are sure that your little pet, Disunion, "living will linger, and lingering will die."

When Mr. Andrews and you have quite "expelled human nature," dissolved and disintegrated society, and reduced mankind to separate, independent, but conflicting monads, or human atoms—then, and not till then, will you establish the "sovereignty of the individual," and destroy the property of man in man.

(77)

William Gilmore Simms

1806-1870

Born in Charleston, South Carolina, Simms began his career as a newspaper editor. He had published five volumes of poetry before his first novel appeared in 1833. Thereafter, a steady stream of novels came from his pen. Like Cooper, whom he imitated, Simms turned to social criticism in his writings, giving emphatic statement to the philosophy of the old, slave-holding, aristocratic South.

In this selection the author is accompanying a northerner through the South. Their conversations with travelers are used to define the differences that divided the two sections. The text is from the discussion of the southern economy in *Southward Ho!* (New York, 1854).

A long, and to us a comparatively interesting, conversation followed—Virginia, her resources, characteristics, scenery, and general morals, affording the principal subject. In this conversation, which occasionally ran into politics—in which some of the party showed their teeth very decidedly—the whole of our group was brought out, the ladies excepted. They had retired for the night. Most of us had rambled in Virginia at different periods; and it was in the delivery of recollections and impressions that we passed naturally into discussion. I propose to give *bits* only of this conversation, leaving out the bites—confining my report to the innocuous portions of the dialogue, and omitting certain sharp passages which occasionally followed the thoughtless or the wanton shaft. One of our "Down-East" brethren threw down the ball of provocation, dealing in a wholesale, if not wholesome, diatribe against all Southern agriculture. As his opinions are those of a somewhat numerous class, and as they are working no little mischief at the present day, it may be as well to record, with tolerable fullness, the portion of the dialogue which ensued upon their utterance.

"You pass through Virginia," said he, "as through a desert. The towns are few, and these all look old and wretched. The houses need paint, and are frequently in dilapidation. The culture is coarse and clumsy, the implements rude, and the people seem entirely ignorant of all improvements. They plough, plant, and reap precisely as their fathers did a hundred years ago, and without doing any justice to their lands. The lands have never been properly worked, and manures are but little known, and less esteemed. In favorite regions, along water-courses easily accessible, the plantations have been abandoned as entirely exhausted—sold for a song, at an average, perhaps, of a dollar an acre. The same lands, in the hands of New York farmers, have been bought up, improved, made valuable for wheat-crops, and raised to a value ranging from fifteen to seventy-five dollars per acre. Thirty bushels of wheat have been raised to the acre, on tracts which have been thrown out as barren. A like history belongs to North and South Carolina, where similar ignorance of farming, and of agricultural implements, similar coarseness and clumsiness in the cultivation of the soil, have led to similar results—the disparaged value of the lands, their abandonment, and the neglect and dilapidation of towns and houses."

"You simply know nothing about the matter," said one of the party sharply in reply—"or rather, you know just enough of the truth to involve yourself in a monstrous error. I too have travelled in the regions of which you speak, and can venture to say something on the subject, which has its bright as well as gloomy aspects. It is not all gloomy, though it is seldom that the hurrying traveller sees or suspects any other. That you see few or no towns, and that these look desolate, are the natural effects of the life of a people purely agricultural. The southern people do not live in towns if they can avoid them. The culture and command of extensive tracts of land and forest give them a distaste to city life, where they feel restrained by a sense of confinement, and by manners of artificial character—a rigid conventionalism, imposing fetters upon that ease and freedom of bearing which belongs to the forest population. Besides, public opinion in the South is unfriendly to the growth of large cities, which many of their leading minds hold to be always of the most mischievous moral tendency—as, indeed, the *North* begins also to discover. Mr. Jefferson pronounced them the *sinks* and sewers of the commonwealth, to be tolerated only as among the dirty national necessities; and the *instincts* of the great body of the agricultural population have led them rightly in the same direction. They have learned to doubt the wholesomeness of the atmosphere of city life. Regarding towns as the mere agencies of the producer, they do not desire to see them absorbing a larger population than is necessary to the actual business which they have to perform.

"You, at the North, on the contrary, look to your flourishing towns, your fine houses, great masses of brick and stone, with thousands jostling in the thoroughfares, as proofs of prosperity and civilization; though, of these thousands, thousands live by beggary, by theft, chicanery, and the constantly active exercise of a thousand evil arts—the inevitable consequence of necessities which could not arise to the community were the unnecessary members driven to an honest, healthy, industrious occupation in neglected fields of agriculture. You judge mostly by externals, which rarely show the truth—the people in cities being chiefly learned in the art of concealing their true condition, and making the best *show* to their neighbors; while the Southern agriculturists know nothing of this art, exhibit themselves precisely as they are; use no white paint to cover old boards—no stucco to make common brick look like stone; and satisfied with the real comforts of their condition, never busy themselves in the endeavor to impose upon their neighbors with the splendors of a season which would only lead to bankruptcy.

"The dilapidated Virginia farmhouse, for example, will receive more guests, at the family table, in one month, than the marble palace in Broadway or Fifth Avenue will entertain in one year. There will be always plenty and a generous welcome, though the service be of delph and not of silver.

"That we have not towns and villages is the inevitable result of staple cultivation. *Every plantation is a village,* and where it is a large one, it will be found provided with all the essential elements of progress and performance, precisely as they are to be found in a village. Here, for example, is always a blacksmith and a carpenter, possibly a wheelwright, and frequently a shoemaker; while, in place of a hotel, for the reception of the stranger, is the mansion-house of the planter—wanting in paint, I grant—of ancient fashion, uncouth architecture—the floors, perhaps, not carpeted, and the furniture of that dark, massive mahogany which the city of New York would revolt at, but which carries to my mind an idea of the dignity of an ancient race, and that reverence for the antique which is, perhaps, too much wanting in every part of our country, except the *old states of the South.*

"This ancient mansion will be found usually with its doors thrown wide —in sign of welcome. Lest you should doubt, as you approach it, you behold the planter himself descending the old brick steps to welcome you. You will be confounded to see that his costume is neither fine nor fashionable—that he wears a great broad-brimmed white hat, exceedingly ample, which may have been manufactured for his grandfather. His coat may be of white flannel, and out at the elbows; and his pantaloons will be of domestic manufacture, homespun or nankin cotton. If you are wise enough to look below the externals, you will see, perhaps, that he has learned to despise them—at all events, you will perceive that he has sacrificed for these none of the essentials of the host, the gentleman, or the patriot. His hospitality is unimpaired by his antiquity—nay, it forms a part of it—and in the retention of the one, he has retained the other as a matter of necessity. As a gentleman, he is frank and easy of manner, unaffected in his bearing, and always solicitous of your comfort and satisfaction. He does not suffer you to perceive that he would have been better pleased that you should have admired his fine house, and passed on without tasking its hospitality. These are characteristics which must be taken as an offset to those respects which you select for censure. These, I have said, are the natural consequence of staple culture. It is the farming culture which exhibits and requires much nicety of detail. In the hands of the planter of a staple, lands are held in bodies too large to be handled minutely. It is the small plot only which you can put in bandbox condition. Lands in staple countries are of less value than labor—in farming countries, of greater value than labor. In proportion as the population becomes dense, they rise in value. But few southern planters desire a dense population. One secret of their hospitality is the extensiveness of their ranges. A wealthy planter, having from fifty to five hundred slaves, will have from a hundred to a thousand head of cattle. He kills so many beeves per annum, from four to forty, according to his *force.* That he can order a *mutton* to be slaughtered, even though but a single guest claims his hospitality, is due to his extensive tracts of field and forest. He seldom sends any of his sheep, cattle, corn, or other provisions to market. These are all retained for the wants of the homestead.

"It will not do for you, recognising the peculiar characteristics of his mode of life—their elegancies, comforts, and bounties—to cavil at deficiencies, which could only be remedied by his abandonment of habits which are grateful to the virtues, and which maintain in him the essentials of all high character—dignity and reverence."

"But there must be an end to all this hospitality. The southern planter is not prosperous. His fields are failing him—his staples are no longer valuable."

"Sufficient for the day is the evil thereof. Give us time. Let time answer your prophecy; for it is prediction—not argument, not fact—which you assert. There is no need that his hospitality should be at an end. It only needs that it should be more discriminating, and that the southern planter should steadily close his door against those who come to eat his bread only to denounce the manner in which it is made, and to sleep securely beneath his roof only to leave curses rather than prayers behind them. He must only be sure that his guest, when a stranger, is a gentleman and an honest man; and he will probably, with this modification of his hospitality, never be wanting in the necessary means for satisfying it.

"But, touching his prosperity, I hold it to be the greatest mistake in the world—examining things by just and intrinsic laws—to suppose that he is not prosperous. The southern planter does not derive from his labors so large a *money* income as he formerly did, when the culture of his great staple was comparatively in few hands. It is something different, certainly, to receive twenty cents instead of one hundred for long cottons, and six cents instead of thirty for short. But, in fact, the difference does not substantially affect his prosperity, *if he be not already in debt.* In the period of high prices for his staples, he could readily abandon farming culture to his less prosperous neighbors, leaving it to other states to supply his grain, his forage, his vegetables, his cattle, mules, and horses, for which he could well afford to pay from the excess of his income. But with his resources reduced, his policy necessarily changes, and is changing hourly, in recognition of new laws and new necessities. This change effected, his property will continue as before, though actually no great amount of money passes through his hands. His fields, that *were* failing him when he addressed them wholly to the culture of a single staple, are recovering, now that he alternates his crops, and economizes, prepares, and employs his manure. He ceases to buy grain and provisions. He raises his own hogs and cattle, and his ploughs are driven by mules and horses foaled in his own pastures. He discovers that he is not worse off now, in raising the commodities themselves, for the purchase of which he simply raised the cash before; and he further discovers that, under the present system, he learns to economize land and labor, to improve the quality of the land, and the excellence of the labor; land rises in value with the introduction of thorough tillage; and a cleanlier, more compact method of culture, increases the health of the climate as well as the prosperity of the planters. With thorough tillage he can feed his stock, and thus lessen the extent of his ranges; and this results in a gradually increasing denseness of the settlements, which are all that is necessary to rendering the state as prosperous as the individual has been."

"What do you mean by this distinction?"

"It is one that politicians do not often make, and it constitutes the grand feature in which the southern states are deficient to a northern eye. It occasions some of the difficulties in your modes of reasoning. The wealth of the state must depend mostly upon its numbers. The wealth of the individual will depend chiefly upon himself. The people of a state may be all in the enjoyment of comfort and affluence, yet the state may be poor. This is the case with all the southern states, the government of which has a sparsely settled population on which to act. Where the population is thinly planted, the roads will be inferior, the public works infrequent and of mean appearance, and the cities (which depend wholly upon a contiguous back country for support) will stagnate in visible decline, wanting enterprise and energy. The roads, the public buildings, and the cities, by which the stranger judges of the prosperity of a people, will all depend upon the population of a state. If this be large—if the soil is well covered—the powers of taxation are necessarily enlarged, without, perhaps, growing burdensome to any; but the means of life will be correspondingly diminished in the hands of the greater number. Want and poverty will trouble thousands; a few will grow rich at the expense of the rest; with the greater number, the struggle will be incessant from morning to night, to supply the most limited wants of a painful existence. But in the southern states, where the public works are few, the public buildings humble, and the cities of difficult growth or of stagnating condition the great body of the people—nay, all the people, bond and free—live in the enjoyment of plenty always, and, in most cases, of a wondrous degree of comfort.

"To illustrate this more completely by parallels: Great Britain and France are, of course, immeasurably superior, not only to the southern states of the Union, but to *all* the states, North and South, in the wonders of art, the great thoroughfares, the noble buildings, and the gigantic cities. These are erroneously assumed to be the proofs of prosperity in a nation, when it is somewhat doubtful if they can be even regarded as just proofs of its civilization. But, in Great Britain and France, millions rise every morning, in doubt where they shall procure the daily bread which shall satisfy the hunger of nature through the next twelve hours. No such apprehension ever troubles the citizen of the rural districts of the South. Rich and poor, black and white, bond and free, are all superior to this torturing anxiety; and the beggar, who in the great cities of Europe and America is as frequent as their posts, is scarcely ever to be seen, even, in a southern city—and then he is chiefly from a northern city, whence he flies to a region, of the hospitality of which (in spite of its failing fortunes) some vague rumors have reached his ears. He flies from the proud and prosperous cities of the North, seeking his bread at the hands of a people whom you profess to despise for their decline."

"With these convictions, why do you repine and complain?"

"I do neither. To do either is unmanly. That the southern people do complain, more than is proper and needful, is surely a something to be regretted; since he who pauses to complain will probably never overtake his flying prosperity. But, that there should be gloom and despondency is but natural with a people who, without positively suffering in fortune or comfort, are yet compelled, by large transitions of fortune, to contrast their present with their past. It is not that we are ruined now, but that we remember how fortunate we were before. If we compare ourselves with other people, and not with ourselves, we shall probably congratulate ourselves rather than complain."

"With your views, you are then satisfied that your people should continue rural occupations exclusively, to the rejection of manufactures?"

"By no means. I am anxious, on the contrary, that our people should embark in every department of art and trade for which they themselves or our climate may be fitted, if only that we may be perfectly independent of our northern brethren. We have abundance of water power, all over the South; we have the operatives on the spot; and we raise all the raw materials necessary for manufactures. Our water power never congeals with frost; our operatives never work short, or strike for increased wages, for we always keep them well fed and well clothed; we pension their aged; we protect and provide for their young; and, instead of being sickly at the toils we impose—puny and perishing—they are always fat and frolicsome, and always on the increase; and cotton is every day passing into more general use, as clothing for the poorer races of mankind. But, in the introduction of manufactures, I do not propose that we should neglect or abandon any of our staples: I propose that we should only employ our surplus population and lands for the purpose. There are large tracts of territory, for example, in the Carolinas, which answer for neither cotton, tobacco, nor the smaller grains. In these very regions, there is water power in abundance; and where this is not the case, there is fuel in inexhaustible abundance, for the use of steam power. I propose to increase the wealth of the state by the application of these regions to their proper use."

"But if your whole country should become manufacturing, why not? The profits of manufactures are vastly greater than those of the cotton culture. I have seen some statistics of South Carolina, where it is estimated that seven hundred operatives will realize as large a result, in working up the cotton, as a whole district of twenty-five thousand people in making the raw material. They will work up seven thousand bales, triplicating its value, while the twenty-five thousand average but a single bale to each inhabitant."

"This is the sort of statistics which delude the world. It is perhaps true that a district of South Carolina having twenty-five thousand people will send but twenty-five thousand bags of cotton to market. It is also true, perhaps, that eight hundred operatives in a manufactory will, by their labor, increase three-fold the value of eight thousand bales, making a total of market-values equal to the twenty-five thousand bales. But when the operatives have done this, they have done nothing more than feed and clothe themselves, while, in fact, the cotton-planter has sent nothing but his *surplus* crop into the market. Of the twenty-five thousand persons in agriculture, twelve thousand enjoy luxuries, as well as comforts, which are not common to the cities. They have more leisure; they enjoy more society; most of them ride on horseback, and the greater number of families keep carriage or buggy. Nothing is said of the variety of food which they command, or may command—the delights of their own homes, in their own grounds, their own gardens and firesides; and the ease, the independence and elasticity, which belong to him who lives in the air and sunshine; in exercises which are grateful; and retires from his toils at an early hour, to the enjoyments of his homestead and his sleep. But talking of sleep reminds me of supper. Captain, if my nose does not greatly err, we are in the latitude of the old North State. I have been smelling tar and turpentine for the last half hour."

Suggestions for Further Reading

The literature dealing with American intellectual history is extensive. The following list, therefore, is not intended to be definitive. Most of the works selected for inclusion in this section simply represent a cross section of some of the more important books dealing with various aspects of American intellectual development. For a more complete bibliography the reader can consult Oscar Handlin and others, eds., *Harvard Guide to American History* (Cambridge, Mass.: Harvard University Press, 1954); Library of Congress, *A Guide to the Study of the United States of America: Representative Books Reflecting the Development of American Life and Thought* (Washington, D.C.: United States Government Printing Office, 1960); and the bibliography in Merle Curti, *The Growth of American Thought* (2nd ed., New York: Harper and Brothers, 1951), pp. 801–76.

I. *General Works*

Aaron, Daniel, *Men of Good Hope: A Story of American Progressives* (New York: Oxford University Press, 1951). Contains penetrating intellectual biographies of progressives from Emerson to Veblen.

Beard, Charles A. and Mary R., *The American Spirit: A Study of the Idea of Civilization in the United States* (New York: The Macmillan Company, 1942). A study of American intellectual history that emphasizes a single theme: the idea of civilization.

Beard, Charles A. and Mary R., *The Rise of American Civilization* (New York: The Macmillan Company, 1927). A penetrating and provocative interpretation of American society from its origins.

Boorstin, Daniel, *The Genius of American Politics* (Chicago: University of Chicago Press, 1953). An attempt to explain the uniqueness of American thought by emphasizing the favorable environment within which it developed.

Bowers, David F., ed., *Foreign Influences in American Life* (Princeton, N.J.: Princeton University Press, 1944).

Burns, Edward M., *The American Idea of Mission: Concepts of National Purpose and Destiny* (New Brunswick, N.J.: Rutgers University Press, 1957). A useful historical survey of an important concept.

Cash, Wilbur J., *The Mind of the South* (New York: Alfred A. Knopf, 1941). A brilliant impressionistic interpretation of southern thought and society from its origin.

Cohen, Morris Raphael, *American Thought: A Critical Sketch* (New York: The Free Press of Glencoe, 1954). A perceptive treatment by a noted philosopher.

Curti, Merle, *The Growth of American Thought* (2nd ed., New York: Harper and Brothers, 1951). Probably the best general survey of American thought and society.

Curti, Merle, *The Roots of American Loyalty* (New York: Columbia University Press, 1946). A historical sketch of American patriotism.

Curti, Merle, *The Social Ideas of American Educators* (New York: Charles Scribner's Sons, 1935). Important for an understanding of American education.

Dorfman, Joseph, *The Economic Mind in American Civilization* (5 vols., New York: The Viking Press, 1946–1959). By far the best and most comprehensive treatment of American economic thought since the Puritans.

Dorson, Richard M., *American Folklore* (Chicago: University of Chicago Press, 1959).

Egbert, Donald D., and Persons, Stow, eds., *Socialism and American Life* (2 vols., Princeton, N.J.: Princeton University Press, 1952). Indispensable for an understanding of socialism and its influence.

Ekirch, Arthur, *The Decline of American Liberalism* (New York: Oxford University Press, 1955). A study of the decline of American liberalism, which is identified with the classical philosophical values of the Enlightenment.

Ellis, John T., *American Catholicism* (Chicago: University of Chicago Press, 1956). The best brief historical survey.

Gabriel, Ralph H., *The Course of American Democratic Thought* (2nd ed., New York: The Ronald Press Company, 1956). One of the most important and brilliant interpretations of American intellectual history.

Glazer, Nathan, *American Judaism* (Chicago: University of Chicago Press, 1957). The best brief historical survey.

Greene, Evarts B., *Religion and the State: The Making and Testing of an American Tradition* (New York: New York University Press, 1941). A useful study of the development of church-state relationships in the United States.

Hartz, Louis, *The Liberal Tradition in America: An Interpretation of American Political Thought Since the Revolution* (New York: Harcourt, Brace and Company, 1955). A stimulating study of American political thought in terms of Lockian influences.

Hofstadter, Richard, *The American Political Tradition and the Men Who Made It* (New York: Alfred A. Knopf, 1948). A discussion of the American political tradition through biographical sketches of leading figures from Thomas Jefferson to Franklin Delano Roosevelt.

Hudson, Winthrop S., *American Protestantism* (Chicago: University of Chicago Press, 1961). The best brief historical survey.

Hurst, James Willard, *The Growth of American Law* (Boston: Little, Brown and Company, 1950).

Jones, Howard Mumford, *The Pursuit of Happiness* (Cambridge, Mass.: Harvard University Press, 1953). An unusual intellectual history of a phrase made famous in the Declaration of Independence and a study of its subsequent development.

Kohn, Hans, *American Nationalism* (New York: The Macmillan Company, 1957). A useful historical survey by a leading student of nationalism.

Kraus, Michael, *The Writing of American History* (Norman, Okla.: University of Oklahoma Press, 1953). An introduction to American historical thought and practice.

Lerner, Max, *America as a Civilization: Life and Thought in the United States Today* (New York: Simon and Schuster, 1957). An all-encompassing survey and interpretation of American society.

McLoughlin, William G., Jr., *Modern Revivalism: Charles Grandison Finney to Billy Graham* (New York: The Ronald Press Company, 1959). The best general history of American revivalism.

Merriam, Charles E., *A History of American Political Theories* (New York: The Macmillan Company, 1920). An older but still useful study by an outstanding political scientist.

Mosier, Richard D., *The American Temper: Patterns of Our Intellectual Heritage* (Berkeley, Calif.: University of California Press, 1952). An interpretation of American thought through a series of successive patterns from Puritanism to pragmatism.

Mott, Frank L., *Golden Multitudes: The Story of Best Sellers in the United States* (New York: The Macmillan Company, 1947). Important for an understanding of popular American culture.

Mott, Frank L., *A History of American Magazines* (4 vols.: Cambridge, Mass.: Harvard University Press, 1938–1957). Indispensable for an understanding of intellectual developments.

Niebuhr, H. Richard, *The Kingdom of God in America* (New York: Harper and Brothers, 1937). An important history of millennialism.

Niebuhr, H. Richard, *The Social Sources of Denominationalism* (New York: Henry Holt and Company, 1929). Useful for the social origins of the various religious denominations.

Parrington, Vernon L., *Main Currents in American Thought* (3 vols., New York: Harcourt, Brace and Company, 1927–1930). One of the classic works in American history. Written from a decidedly Jeffersonian or liberal point of view.

Perry, Ralph Barton, *Puritanism and Democracy* (New York: The Vanguard Press, 1944). An important work by a noted philosopher who identified two formative elements in the American national tradition—Puritanism and the democracy of the Enlightenment.

Persons, Stow, *American Minds: A History of Ideas* (New York: Henry Holt and Company, 1958). An intellectual history in terms of a succession of minds from the Puritan mind to the neodemocratic mind.

Persons, Stow, ed., *Evolutionary Thought in America* (New Haven, Conn.: Yale University Press, 1950). A study of the influence of evolutionary theories on different disciplines.

Potter, David M., *People of Plenty: Economic Abundance and the American Character* (Chicago: University of Chicago Press, 1954). An interpretation of the American character through the concept of economic abundance.

Rossiter, Clinton, *Conservatism in America* (New York: Alfred A. Knopf, 1955). A sympathetic historical survey and analysis by a moderate adherent of the New Conservatism.

Schneider, Herbert W., *A History of American Philosophy* (New York: Columbia University Press, 1946). A good survey that attempts to relate philosophical thought to its societal environment.

Smith, Henry Nash, *Virgin Land: The American West as Symbol and Myth* (Cambridge, Mass.: Harvard University Press, 1950). A brilliant intellectual analysis of a major American theme.

Smith, James Ward, and Jamison, Albert Leland, eds., *Religion in American Life* (4 vols. to date, Princeton, N.J.: Princeton University Press, 1961–). An excellent survey of all aspects of American religion by leading authorities.

Smith, T. V., *The American Philosophy of Equality* (Chicago: University of Chicago Press, 1927). A study by a noted philosopher.

Spencer, Benjamin T., *The Quest for Nationality: An American Literary Campaign* (Syracuse, N.Y.: Syracuse University Press, 1957). An analysis of the emergence of an indigenous literary tradition.

Spiller, Robert E., and others, eds., *Literary History of the United States* (3 vols., New York: The Macmillan Company, 1948). A detailed and comprehensive history of American literature and thought since the colonial period.

Stokes, Anson P., *Church and State in the United States* (3 vols., New York: Harper and Brothers, 1950). A monumental work of encyclopedic proportions.

Sweet, William W., *The Story of Religion in America* (2nd ed., New York: Harper and Brothers, 1950). A useful general history.

Wecter, Dixon, *The Hero in America* (New York: Charles Scribner's Sons, 1941). A study of the role and symbolic importance of the hero in American society and culture.

Weinberg, Albert K., *Manifest Destiny* (Baltimore: The Johns Hopkins Press, 1935). An important intellectual history of the ideology of American expansionism.

Weisberger, Bernard A., *They Gathered at the River: The Story of the Great Revivalists and Their Impact upon Religion in America* (Boston: Little, Brown and Company, 1958). A brief general survey of American revivalism.

Wiltse, Charles M., *The Jeffersonian Tradition in American Democracy* (Chapel Hill, N.C.: University of North Carolina Press, 1935). A study of the ideology of Thomas Jefferson and its subsequent influence in American history.

Wish, Harvey, *The American Historian: A Social-Intellectual History of the Writing of the American Past* (New York: Oxford University Press, 1960). A brief history of American historiography.

Wright, Benjamin, *American Interpretations of Natural Law* (Cambridge, Mass.: Harvard University Press, 1931). An analysis of the concept of natural law and the uses to which it was put prior to the Civil War.

II. *The Puritan and Enlightenment Minds*

Adams, James Truslow, *Provincial Society 1690–1763* (New York: The Macmillan Company, 1927). A comprehensive survey of society and thought.

Adams, Randolph G., *Political Ideas of the American Revolution* (Durham, N.C.: Trinity College Press, 1922). A study of the debate over political theory leading up to the American Revolution.

Beard, Charles A., *An Economic Interpretation of the Constitution of the United States* (New York: The Macmillan Company, 1913). A classic and provocative work on the origins of the Constitution.

Becker, Carl L., *The Declaration of Independence* (New York: Alfred A. Knopf, 1922). A brilliant analysis emphasizing the Enlightenment background of the Declaration of Independence.

Boorstin, Daniel J., *The Americans: The Colonial Experience* (New York: Random House, 1958). An interpretation of colonial society and thought that emphasizes the American predilection for action over thought.

Brown, Robert E., *Charles Beard and the Constitution: A Critical Analysis of "An Economic Interpretation of the Constitution"* (Princeton, N.J.: Princeton University Press, 1956). A hostile critique of Beard's economic emphasis.

Craven, Wesley F., *The Legend of the Founding Fathers* (New York: New York University Press, 1956). A study of the founding of the body social in 1607 and 1620 and the body politic in 1776 and 1787 emphasizing also the various interpretations.

Dietze, Gottfried, *The Federalist: A Classic on Federalism and Free Government* (Baltimore: The Johns Hopkins Press, 1960). An attempt to demonstrate that the *Federalist* papers contain a coherent philosophical expression of the theory of free government.

Gaustad, Edwin S., *The Great Awakening in New England* (New York: Harper and Brothers, 1957). A useful regional study of the religious awakening beginning in the early eighteenth century.

Gewehr, Wesley M., *The Great Awakening in Virginia 1740–1790* (Durham, North Carolina: Duke University Press, 1930). A useful local study.

Greene, Evarts B., *The Revolutionary Generation 1763–1790* (New York: The Macmillan Company, 1943). A comprehensive history of society and thought.

Hindle, Brooke, *The Pursuit of Science in Revolutionary America 1735–1789* (Chapel Hill, N.C.: University of North Carolina Press, 1956). A study of the faith of the Revolutionary generation in science.

Humphrey, Edward F., *Nationalism and Religion in America 1774–1789* (Boston: Chipman Law Publishing Company, 1924). A comprehensive history of the various churches during and after the Revolution.

Koch, Adrienne, *The Philosophy of Thomas Jefferson* (New York: Columbia University Press, 1943). An exposition of Jefferson's philosophy as related to several philosophical schools of thought.

Koch, G. Adolph, *Republican Religion: The American Revolution and the Cult of Reason* (New York: Henry Holt and Company, 1933). A study of the impact of "free thought" during the Revolutionary period.

Kraus, Michael, *The Atlantic Civilization: Eighteenth-Century Origins* (Ithaca, N.Y.: Cornell University Press, 1949). A study of the interpenetration of American and European culture leading to an Atlantic civilization.

Kraus, Michael, *Intercolonial Aspects of American Culture on the Eve of the Revolution* (New York: Columbia University Press, 1928). Emphasizes the emergence of a common fund of experience among colonials prior to the American Revolution.

McDonald, Forrest, *We the People: The Economic Origins of the Constitution* (Chicago: University of Chicago Press, 1958). A detailed work that concludes by rejecting Charles Beard's interpretation of the origins of the Constitution.

Malone, Dumas, *Jefferson and His Time* (2 vols., Boston: Little, Brown and Company, 1948–1951). Covers Jefferson's career to 1792.

Maxson, Charles H., *The Great Awakening in the Middle Colonies* (Chicago: University of Chicago Press, 1920). A study of eighteenth-century revivalism.

Miller, Perry, *The New England Mind: The Seventeenth Century* (New York: The Macmillan Company, 1939), and *The New England Mind: From Colony to Province* (Cambridge, Mass.: Harvard University Press, 1953). Indispensable for an understanding of Puritanism as an intellectual movement.

Miller, Perry, *Orthodoxy in Massachusetts 1630–1650* (Cambridge, Mass.: Harvard University Press, 1933). An important volume emphasizing the early period of Puritanism in America.

Morais, Herbert M., *Deism in Eighteenth-Century America* (New York: Columbia University Press, 1934). Deals with the spread of skepticism, especially during the Revolutionary period.

Morgan, Edmund S., *The Puritan Dilemma: The Story of John Winthrop* (Boston: Little, Brown and Company, 1958). An excellent case study of an outstanding Puritan.

Morison, Samuel Eliot, *The Founding of Harvard College* (Cambridge, Mass.: Harvard University Press, 1935), and *Harvard College in the Seventeenth Century* (2 vols., Cambridge, Mass.: Harvard University Press, 1936). Indispensable for the intellectual life of colonial New England.

Morison, Samuel Eliot, *The Intellectual Life of Colonial New England* (New York: New York University Press, 1956). A highly favorable presentation of the intellectual accomplishments of the Puritans.

Murdock, Kenneth B., *Literature and Theology in Colonial New England* (Cambridge, Mass.: Harvard University Press, 1949). A useful and readable work.

Rossiter, Clinton, *Seedtime of the Republic: The Origin of the American Tradition of Political Liberty* (New York: Harcourt, Brace and Company, 1953). A work that maintains that the political theory of the American Revolution and of American society in general was a theory of ethical ordered liberty.

Savelle, Max, *Seeds of Liberty: The Genesis of the American Mind* (New York: Alfred A. Knopf, 1948). A comprehensive intellectual history of the colonial period.

Schlesinger, Arthur M., *Prelude to Independence: The Newspaper War on Britain 1764–1776* (New York: Alfred A. Knopf, 1957). A study that sheds much light on the American mind during the Revolutionary era.

Schneider, Herbert W., *The Puritan Mind* (New York: Henry Holt and Company, 1930).

Simpson, Alan, *Puritanism in Old and New England* (Chicago: University of Chicago Press, 1955).

Sweet, William W., *Religion in Colonial America* (New York: Charles Scribner's Sons, 1942). A comprehensive study.

Tyler, Moses Coit, *The Literary History of the American Revolution 1763–1783* (2 vols., New York: G. P. Putnam's Sons, 1897). A classic work that is still indispensable.

Van Doren, Carl, *Benjamin Franklin* (New York: The Viking Press, 1938). An outstanding biography.

Wertenbaker, Thomas J., *The First Americans 1607–1690* (New York: The Macmillan Company, 1927). A comprehensive survey of society and thought.

Wertenbaker, Thomas J., *The Golden Age of Colonial Culture* (2nd ed., New York: New York University Press, 1949). Cultural studies in the decades preceding the American Revolution.

Wright, Conrad, *The Beginnings of Unitarianism in America* (Boston: The Beacon Press, 1955). An intellectual history of Arminianism in New England Congregationalism.

Wright, Louis B., *The Cultural Life of the American Colonies 1607–1763* (New York: Harper and Brothers, 1957). A general survey of culture and thought.

Wright, Thomas C., *Literary Culture in Early New England 1620–1730* (New Haven, Conn.: Yale University Press, 1920). Studies the culture of New England and the literature that grew out of it.

III. *The Early National and Romantic Period*

Barnes, Gilbert H., *The Antislavery Impulse 1830–1844* (New York: D. Appleton-Century Company, 1933). An attempt to relate religion to the abolitionist movement.

Billington, Ray A., *The Protestant Crusade 1800–1860* (New York: The Macmillan Company, 1938). A study of the formative period of American nativism.

Blau, Joseph L., ed., *Social Theories of Jacksonian Democracy* (New York: Hafner Publishing Company, 1947). A convenient source book.

Bode, Carl, *The American Lyceum* (New York: Oxford University Press, 1956). An analysis of an important intellectual institution.

Bode, Carl, *The Anatomy of American Popular Culture 1840–1861* (Berkeley, Calif.: University of California Press, 1959). Useful for an understanding of popular culture.

Branch, Edward Douglas, *The Sentimental Years 1836–1860* (New York: D. Appleton-Century Company, 1934). A study that finds sentimentalism to be the key to the intellectual history of the period.

Brooks, Van Wyck, *The Flowering of New England* (New York: E. P. Dutton and Company, 1936), *The Times of Melville and Whitman* (New York: E. P. Dutton and Company, 1947), and *The World of Washington Irving* (New York: E. P. Dutton and Company, 1944). A major literary history.

Carpenter, Jesse T., *The South as a Conscious Minority 1789–1861* (New York: New York University Press, 1930). Important for an understanding of the South.

Cole, Arthur C., *The Irrepressible Conflict 1850–1865* (New York: The Macmillan Company, 1934). A comprehensive social and cultural history.

Cross, Whitney R., *The Burned-Over District* (Ithaca, N.Y.: Cornell University Press, 1950). An important case study of an area out of which came many new religious sects in the four decades prior to the Civil War.

Davies, John D., *Phrenology: Fad and Science: A 19th-Century American Cru-*

sade (New Haven, Conn.: Yale University Press, 1955). An important history of phrenology and its role in American thought and culture prior to the Civil War.

Ekirch, Arthur A., *The Idea of Progress in America 1815–1860* (New York: Columbia University Press, 1944). The evolution of the idea of progress as revealed in different institutions and areas of thought.

Fish, Carl R., *The Rise of the Common Man* (New York: The Macmillan Company, 1927). A comprehensive study of society and culture.

Frothingham, Octavius B., *Transcendentalism in New England* (New York: G. P. Putnam's Sons, 1876). A classic work still of great value.

Griffin, Clifford S., *Their Brothers' Keepers: Moral Stewardship in the United States 1800–1865* (New Brunswick, N.J.: Rutgers University Press, 1960). A useful study of philanthropic ideas.

Jenkins, William S., *Proslavery Thought in the Old South* (Chapel Hill, North Carolina: University of North Carolina Press, 1935). A history of the various arguments used in defense of slavery.

Johnson, Charles A., *The Frontier Camp Meeting* (Dallas, Texas: Southern Methodist University Press, 1955). Useful for an understanding of an important revivalist institution.

Krout, John A., and Fox, Dixon R., *The Completion of Independence 1790–1830* (New York: The Macmillan Company, 1944). A comprehensive study of society and thought.

Matthiessen, F. O., *American Renaissance: Art and Expression in the Age of Emerson and Whitman* (New York: Oxford University Press, 1941). A major work on transcendentalism.

Meyers, Marvin, *The Jacksonian Persuasion: Politics and Belief* (Stanford, Calif.: Stanford University Press, 1957).

Nye, Russell B., *The Cultural Life of the New Nation 1776–1830* (New York: Harper and Brothers, 1960). A useful general survey.

Rusk, Ralph L., *The Life of Ralph Waldo Emerson* (New York: Charles Scribner's Sons, 1949). An important biography of a major intellectual figure.

Rusk, Ralph L., *The Literature of the Middle Western Frontier* (2 vols., New York: Columbia University Press, 1925).

Smith, Timothy L., *Revivalism and Social Reform in Mid-Nineteenth-Century America* (New York: Abingdon Press, 1957). A work that not only attempts to relate religion and reform, but also points out the impact of revivalism on urban areas.

Sweet, William W., *Religion in the Development of American Culture, 1765–1840* (New York: Charles Scribner's Sons, 1952). A comprehensive survey.

Taylor, William R., *Cavalier and Yankee: The Old South and the American National Character* (New York: George Braziller, 1961). A provocative interpretation.

de Tocqueville, Alexis, *Democracy in America,* Phillips Bradley, ed. (2 vols., New York: Alfred A. Knopf, 1946). Still remains as the classic commentary on American society and institutions by one of the most perceptive and gifted of all foreign observers.

Tyler, Alice F., *Freedom's Ferment* (Minneapolis: University of Minnesota Press, 1944). A comprehensive social history of the ante-bellum decades that sheds much light on the intellectual orientation of Americans.

Index of Documents

457

Index of Names[*]

[*] Italicized numbers refer to pages of selections.

American Ideas

Source Readings in the Intellectual History
of the United States

Volume II: Dilemmas of Maturity

(1865-1962)

Part One

AMERICAN THOUGHT IN AN INDUSTRIAL AGE

$\mathcal{T}$ o the superficial observer, the acceleration in the rate of industrial growth in the last half of the nineteenth century was a clear fact that could easily be measured by the rise in productivity and the standard of living. So, too, the economic and political ascendancy of a new elite of business entrepreneurs, who almost single-handedly created vast industrial complexes, was symbolic of the times. Yet the development of an advanced industrial society brought in its wake less obvious but even more significant and disturbing changes. The phenomenal growth of cities, the rapid increase in immigration, the appearance of a modern working class, and the beginnings of industrial strife, all seemed to be undermining what men cherished most. Some Americans even questioned whether the nation's traditional and time-honored values could continue to exist in the radically new environment that was emerging. To put it another way, could the individualistic-democratic ethic of a simple agrarian society survive the advent of an urban, mechanized society where individual relationships were submerged by impersonal forces?

For the America of the late nineteenth and twentieth centuries was indeed very different, both in degree and kind, from the more simple and ordered society of an earlier era. This was so not merely because of the transition from a rural and agrarian society to an urban and industrial one. If such had been the case, perhaps men and institutions could have adapted themselves more easily to change, because their basic assumptions and presuppositions about life would have remained the same. The difficulty lay rather in the fact that the older patterns of thought no longer sufficed to meet new conditions. Increasingly, Americans found that they were unprepared to cope with the new social and economic order that was emerging. For generations they had believed in the ethic of individual responsibility, that success and achievement in this world were directly related to one's ambition, drive, and talents. In the

2

new society, however, the older morality was not merely outmoded; it seemed simply irrelevant. Upon whom, for example, could one fix responsibility for the evils of urban slums, periodic depressions, unemployment, and the amorality of large impersonal corporations? How could one still retain faith in the idea of equality of opportunity when wealth was being concentrated into fewer and fewer hands? In brief, was it possible for America to hold to its uniqueness and serve as a model for all mankind if it was increasingly torn by the same social and economic tensions that had long wracked the European world?

But the challenges and dilemmas that America faced were not solely the results of technological and industrial changes. Equally confusing were the implications raised by the novel scientific thought that accompanied the new society and supported it. Slowly but surely science began to undermine the traditional presuppositions of the synthesis of Christianity and the philosophy of the Enlightenment, upon which American society rested. In biology, for example, the reaction to the publication in 1859 of Charles Darwin's *Origin of Species* was symbolic of the newer orientation. The doctrine of the evolution of species, for which Darwin had offered an imposing array of evidence, quickly outgrew its biological definition and inevitably began to erode the older theocentric basis of Western civilization. For evolution banished the absolute and immutable by subjecting life and institutions to the flux of constant change. It even challenged the biblical story of creation, and revealed man not as a product of beneficent purpose but as a product of a blind process of natural selection. It viewed man as a member of the animal kingdom and thus removed him from the center of the physical universe, a place reserved for him in Christian cosmology. The inference drawn was that man and society were not proper objects for teleological examination, but rather could be considered more profitably from a purely naturalistic point of view. It is true that the scientific naturalists who asserted this radical viewpoint accepted the concept of natural law, and thus, outwardly at any rate, did not totally repudiate their intellectual ancestors. But the manner in which nineteenth-century science came to define natural law indicated the changes in the way men viewed themselves and their environment. The eighteenth century had looked upon Nature as orderly and rational, and the universe as an essentially harmonious machine, the masterpiece of a deity who had promulgated laws to govern its operation. The setting of human life was the fixed, geometrical order of Nature. In such a system time was of no consequence and processes operated in a cyclical fashion. The early nineteenth-century American Transcendentalists modified this mechanistic outlook by developing the concept of a transcendental Over-Soul and the idea that all men shared in a divine power and were capable of establishing rapport with it. Simultaneously, evangelical Protestantism reasserted itself, and religion and romanticism converged to play a dominant role in the social and intellectual history of the early national period.

The naturalists, on the other hand, developed a very different concept of nature and the universe. To them the universe was dynamic and changing, a place where beginnings were incomprehensible and ends irrelevant, for the natural law of organic evolution emphasized continuous flux and change. Even the intellect became a product of evolutionary forces, and was defined as the functioning of the brain and nervous system. The older philosophical distinction between mind and matter disappeared, and with it the Emersonian idea of the Over-Soul and the emphasis on natural rights and reason. Naturalists tended to reduce even morality and social phenomena to biological terms, and to insist upon the coercive power of natural law over men and society. Some extremists even posited a strict environmental determinism. Believing in the law of organic evolution, naturalists inevitably brought everything within their searching purview, including such hitherto sacred institutions as the church, family, and property. Even such varied disciplines as history, economics, psychology, sociology, anthropology, art, and literature were subjected to scrutiny.

One of the most significant by-products of evolutionary naturalism was the rise of a scientific spirit in American thought that permeated virtually every facet of society. No doubt the incorporation of man into the animal kingdom was a significant achievement. But in the long run the attack on a priori reasoning and the partial repudiation of the Christian-Enlightenment synthesis was to prove far more important. In developing what came to be known as the "science of man," the nineteenth century built a system of knowledge that rested squarely on the foundation of organic evolution. Repudiating the traditional theocentric world view in favor of a new methodological demigod, scientists sought a purely objective and rational explanation of human behavior and development. Regardless of the discipline involved, the emphasis was upon a search for the determinants of organic and cultural change.

Beginning with the imposing system of Herbert Spencer, which enjoyed its greatest popularity in America and which rested in the final analysis on the belief that, if the evolutionary process could proceed unhindered by artificial restraints, then inevitable upward progress would automatically follow, scientists began to explore the complexities of human society with a view toward explaining them in scientific terms. Implicit in their analysis was the belief that if one could understand the factors of human evolution that initiated change, one could either conform to them or else provide a positive goal and direction for their operation.

It might be supposed that Americans, because of their theistic inheritance, would have rejected outright the implications of naturalistic evolution. Such was not the case, however, largely because evolution appeared to buttress the optimistic doctrine of progress, a doctrine that had long been at the heart of the American democratic faith. After all, Darwin had traced the evolution of species from simple organisms to complex mammals. Therefore, might it not be possible to study man and society from the same frame of reference and thus discover the law of progress? Clearly, the formulation of such a law would make man the master of his own destiny, a not inconsiderable achievement, to say the least.

And so the search began. Among the first of the social sciences to adopt a naturalistic approach was anthropology. The pioneering work in this discipline was done by Lewis Henry Morgan, who published his important book *Ancient Society* in 1877. Adopting an evolutionary approach, Morgan attempted to outline a science of man and discover the factors of change by studying various cultures in their different stages of development. The appearance of a naturalistic approach in anthropology was immediately followed by similar developments in history and the other social sciences.

Within the ranks of the naturalists, however, there was no unanimity of opinion, and two opposing schools of thought soon appeared. The first, the conservative school, emphasized that progress was a function of evolutionary forces that eliminated the unfit and preserved the fit, thus leading to the appearance of newer and better organisms. Man's only choice, therefore, lay in submission to the iron law of evolution. Any attempt to intervene in human affairs, especially by resorting to governmental action, would have a deleterious rather than a favorable effect. In this camp were included such outstanding individuals as William Graham Sumner, Francis Amasa Walker, David A. Wells, E. A. Godkin, to cite only a few. The implications of this essentially conservative rationale were highly popular in an America that had embarked on a rapid exploitation of its material resources. Any individual, regardless of rank or background, could prove himself to be among the fit (usually defined in terms of wealth and income) by overcoming all obstacles and emerging the victor in the cutthroat competition of the jungle. Hence arose the ideology of the self-made man, which argued that society would benefit if individuals followed their own self-interest, since this would lead to a progressive betterment of the species.

However, a second group of naturalists, the reformers, denied the validity of such an approach. Like their conservative opponents, the reformers were evolutionists; but there was a fundamental distinction between the two groups. For the reformers insisted that man, possessing the ability to think, could direct the evolutionary process into socially desirable channels. Lester F. Ward, a leading reform evolutionist and the father of American sociology, asked in disbelief, "Is it true that man shall ultimately obtain dominion of the whole world except himself?" From the reform version of evolution flowed the liberal-progressive ethic of the early twentieth century, represented by such outstanding figures as Theodore Roosevelt and Woodrow Wilson in the political arena, and by John Dewey and Herbert Croly in philosophy. All of these men shared a common belief that it was possible for man to remold and transform nature and society by an intelligent application of the new knowledge being revealed by scientific naturalism.

The revolutionary philosophical implications of scientific naturalism did not, of course, go unchallenged. William Harris and the St. Louis school, advocates of a form of Hegelian idealism, continued to question naturalistic evolution. Among scientists, too, a bitter and acrimonious struggle ensued; and the outstanding scientist in the United States at that time, Louis Agassiz, led the attack on Darwinism on intellectual, metaphysical, and emotional grounds. Institutions of higher learning particularly felt the weight of the conflict, especially since the scientific and naturalistic outlook had not as yet replaced the older and still dominant scholastic modes of thought. By the 1880's, however, resistance to evolutionary thought within the scientific communities had all but disappeared. The inauguration of scientist Charles W. Eliot as president of Harvard in 1869 had presaged the trend, and the younger generation of students and teachers who came to maturity after the Civil War no longer questioned the validity of evolution and naturalism.

Within organized religion, on the other hand, the situation was quite different. To many ministers and laymen reared in a tradition of Christian piety, evolution raised issues and problems that threatened the very foundations of their beliefs. Here the conflict could not be so easily resolved. While it is true that liberal Protestantism sought to accommodate itself to evolution, the more fundamentalist groups, nevertheless, staked out their opposition in no uncertain terms and even went so far as to charge the scientists with atheism and materialism. Did not evolution, its opponents argued, undercut the basis of Christian cosmology by repudiating the teleological interpretation of history? Was there even room for a deity in the evolutionary hypothesis?

But the conflict that developed between traditional religion and evolutionary science was more than simply a struggle between competing beliefs and modes of thought. In a sense it was a reflection of all the problems, uncertainties, and difficulties that Americans were experiencing. At a time when men were reexamining their social and intellectual values in the light of material changes in society, organized religion, too, had to bring its own tenets under scrutiny in order to rediscover their relevance in a new and different environment. For when *Origin of Species* first appeared, the United States was still a predominantly rural nation. The rise of industrial capitalism, mechanization, and urbanization, however, confused and baffled a people accustomed to a different way of life. These social and economic changes were reflected in the cultural and intellectual transformations of the time. Just as the formulation of the American faith had originally been stated in religious terms, so the transformation of the older America raised serious doubts concerning the validity of that faith. In its widest sense, therefore, the struggle over evolution and scientific naturalism ultimately revolved around the very concept of man and society. Historically, the United States was at least in part a product of the religious foundations of Western culture. How, therefore, could Americans accept the newer scientific orientation without surrendering their religious ideals? Even more, could these religious ideals continue to subsist if they came into conflict with the hard, cold facts of science? Finally, if there existed no higher law promulgated by an omnipresent and omnipotent deity, upon what basis could a common morality acceptable to all exist? Was Christian piety and morality simply a product of a past age, to be studied only from a historical and anthropological point of view? Did it have no relevance to the present? These were some of the issues that plagued thinkers in all fields and disciplines as they attempted to bring their cosmology into harmony with naturalistic patterns and yet not go so far as to repudiate the older theism.

As a result of social, economic, and intellectual changes, Americans in the latter part of the nineteenth century were forced to reconsider, as had many generations before them, their basic assumptions and presuppositions. And as the problems of an urban, industrial society multiplied and the unity of America fragmented, individuals everywhere sought to develop a new synthesis that would provide them with an acceptable rationale.

I

Evolution and
the Rise of Naturalism

THE PUBLICATION of Darwin's *Origin of Species* in 1859 was in many respects the culmination of a whole series of intellectual and scientific innovations that were to have a profound impact upon the American mind. When combined with the higher criticism in Biblical studies and the comparative study of religion, as well as with the advances in geology, physics, and astronomy, the idea of evolution became a methodological weapon that threatened to undermine the very foundations of traditional and cherished beliefs. No longer could it be absolutely certain that man had been created by God in His image. Indeed, the entire justification of Christianity by the idea of design seemed the vestigial belief of a bygone age.

Many proponents of evolution, however, were not content merely to attack older ideas and views. Instead they proceeded to erect their own intellectual and philosophical system, which was based upon a veneration for scientific fact as the only accurate approach to knowledge. Repudiating with a vengeance the older a priori method of arriving at truth, they insisted that only the scientific method, when focused on man, society, and the physical world, would lead to real knowledge and understanding. One of the earliest products of evolution, consequently, was the emergence of a whole conglomeration of ideas that can loosely be termed "naturalism."

In the latter part of the nineteenth century, naturalistic modes of thought seemed to predominate everywhere. Arguing that complex social phenomena could be reduced to biological terms, and these, in turn, to simpler physical and mechanical terms, the naturalists laid the basis for the scientific study of man and society. Implicit in their approach was an inherent optimism, for they assumed that a better life would inevitably result once the accumulated myths, superstitions, and ignorance of past ages were replaced by objective and dispassionate knowledge. But while they accepted the idea of progress, the naturalists tended to rationalize their belief on new grounds. Whereas antebellum thinkers had found the sources of progress in Christian cosmology and the theory of individualism, the naturalists erected a scientific and, to a lesser extent, a deterministic foundation for continuous human progress, and their synthesis became symbolic of the new intellectual and ideological interests of their age.

All disciplines were to some degree influenced by the new scientific orientation. Anthropologists, for example, began to study the evolution of man and society from their most primitive beginnings, in the hope of discovering the law of progress and thus developing a true science of man. Historians also felt the impact of scientific naturalism, and several complementary and competing schools of historical thought arose. Some historians, taking their cue from biology, formulated the germ theory of institutional development which traced the historical evolution of social institutions from their earliest origins to their modern forms. Others dealt chiefly with the evolution of the social and individual organism as influenced by environmental factors. Even psychology, which had long remained within the province of philosophy and religion, began to undergo a radical transformation. Prior to Darwin psychologists had generally commenced with an acceptance of consciousness, and they had attempted to show how the mind functioned with phenomena included within the categories of knowledge and experience. To a large extent they had dealt with the metaphysical and theological problems inherent in the idea of free will, attempting to provide a place in the mind for the operation of this concept. By the end of the nineteenth century, however, psychology began to move away from its philosophical beginnings and toward the biological and physical sciences. Psychological facts began to be explained in biological and mechanical rather than in metaphysical and philosophical terms, and behaviorism and instinctivism became dominant schools in the study of mental phenomena.

Until the early part of the twentieth century, naturalists tended to be optimistic, largely because they believed that once superstition and myth were dethroned and replaced by the new demigod of science, the power that flowed from knowledge could be put to desirable uses. Certainly, at the very least, the new forms of knowledge would enable man to learn what he should not do, and thus indirectly provide a basis for continued progress. As time passed, however, some of the less likable features of naturalism began to become evident. If man were simply to be studied from a thoroughgoing biological and mechanical framework, was there any room for consciousness or free will? If man was a creature of his society and a product of its folkways, mores, and institutions, was there any room for the traditional morality and the ethic of individual responsibility which had characterized American democratic thinking in past generations? Although of fundamental importance, such questions and paradoxes as these did not appreciably trouble the early naturalistic thinkers. Not until the cataclysmic events of the twentieth century were the philosophical assumptions of the naturalists brought under searching examination.

Lewis Henry Morgan

1818-1881

Morgan, who is regarded as the father of American anthropology, was born in Aurora, New York. After being graduated from Union College in Schenectady in 1840, he studied law and later became active in politics. While still a student at college, he began to take an interest in the American Indian and eventually published a number of important monographs on the Iroquois. Influenced by Darwinian ideas, he began to broaden the scope of his researches in order to develop a comprehensive theory of social and cultural evolution, and thus to outline a science of man and the laws of progress. In his major work, *Ancient Society,* Morgan argued that the human race had evolved through three major stages of development: savagery, barbarism, and civilization. The distinguishing feature of each age was technology, which in turn determined economic development, upon which social improvement depended. Rejecting the divine origin of property, Morgan explained property in purely naturalistic terms, and he emphasized the relationship between property arrangements and social institutions. Although popular with Friedrich Engels and other Marxist thinkers, Morgan remained within the main stream of American democratic theory, because he suggested that the ultimate working out of the law of progress would result in the triumph of the democratic faith.

The following selection is from Morgan's *Ancient Society* (New York, 1877).

The great antiquity of mankind upon the earth has been conclusively established. It seems singular that the proofs should have been discovered as recently as within the last thirty years, and that the present generation should be the first called upon to recognize so important a fact.

Mankind are now known to have existed in Europe in the glacial period, and even back of its commencement, with every probability of their origination in a prior geological age. They have survived many races of animals with whom they were contemporaneous, and passed through a process of development, in the several branches of the human family, as remarkable in its courses as in its progress.

Since the probable length of their career is connected with geological periods, a limited measure of time is excluded. One hundred or two hundred thousand years would be an unextravagant estimate of the period from the disappearance of the glaciers in the northern hemisphere to the present time.

Whatever doubts may attend any estimate of a period, the actual duration of which is unknown, the existence of mankind extends backward immeasurably, and loses itself in a vast and profound antiquity.

This knowledge changes materially the views which have prevailed respecting the relations of savages to barbarians, and of barbarians to civilized men. It can now be asserted upon convincing evidence that savagery preceded barbarism in all the tribes of mankind, as barbarism is known to have preceded civilization. The history of the human race is one in source, one in experience, and one in progress.

It is both a natural and a proper desire to learn, if possible, how all these ages upon ages of past time have been expended by mankind; how savages, advancing by slow, almost imperceptible steps, attained the higher condition of barbarians; how barbarians, by similar progressive advancement, finally attained to civilization; and why other tribes and nations have been left behind in the race of progress—some in civilization, some in barbarism, and others in savagery. It is not too much to expect that ultimately these several questions will be answered.

Inventions and discoveries stand in serial relations along the lines of human progress, and register its successive stages; while social and civil institutions, in virtue of their connection with perpetual human wants, have been developed from a few primary germs of thought. They exhibit a similar register of progress. These institutions, inventions and discoveries have embodied and preserved the principal facts now remaining illustrative of this experience. When collated and compared they tend to show the unity of origin of mankind, the similarity of human wants in the same stage of advancement, and the uniformity of the operations of the human mind in similar conditions of society.

Throughout the latter part of the period of savagery, and the entire period of barbarism, mankind in general were organized in gentes, phratries and tribes. These organizations prevailed throughout the entire ancient world upon all the continents, and were the instrumentalities by means of which ancient society was organized and held together. Their structure, and relations as members of an organic series, and the rights, privileges and obligations of the members of the gens, and of the members of the phratry and tribe, illustrate the growth of the idea of government in the human mind. The principal institutions of mankind originated in savagery, were developed in barbarism, and are maturing in civilization.

In like manner, the family has passed through successive forms, and created great systems of consanguinity and affinity which have remained to the present time. These systems, which record the relationships existing in the family of the period, when each system respectively was formed, contain an instructive record of the experience of mankind while the family was advancing from the consanguine, through intermediate forms, to the monogamian.

The idea of property has undergone a similar growth and development. Commencing at zero in savagery, the passion for the possession of property, as the representative of accumulated subsistence, has now become dominant over the human mind in civilized races.

The four classes of facts above indicated, and which extend themselves in parallel lines along the pathways of human progress from savagery to civilization, form the principal subjects of discussion in this volume. . . .

The latest investigations respecting the early condition of the human race, are tending to the conclusion that mankind commenced their career at the bottom of the scale and worked their way up from savagery to civilization through the slow accumulations of experimental knowledge.

As it is undeniable that portions of the human family have existed in a state of savagery, other portions in a state of barbarism, and still other portions in a state of civilization, it seems equally so that these three distinct conditions are connected with each other in a natural as well as necessary sequence of progress. Moreover, that this sequence has been historically true of the entire human family, up to the status attained by each branch respectively, is rendered probable by the conditions under which all progress occurs, and by the known advancement of several branches of the family through two or more of these conditions.

An attempt will be made in the following pages to bring forward additional evidence of the rudeness of the early condition of mankind, of the gradual evolution of their mental and moral powers through experience, and of their protracted struggle with opposing obstacles while winning their way to civilization. It will be drawn, in part, from the great sequence of inventions and discoveries which stretches along the entire pathway of human progress; but chiefly from domestic institutions, which express the growth of certain ideas and passions.

As we re-ascend along the several lines of progress toward the primitive ages of mankind, and eliminate one after the other, in the order in which they appeared, inventions and discoveries on the one hand, and institutions on the other, we are enabled to perceive that the former stand to each other in progressive, and the latter in unfolding relations. While the former class have had a connection, more or less direct, the latter have been developed from a few primary germs of thought. Modern institutions plant their roots in the period of barbarism, into which their germs were transmitted from the previous period of savagery. They have had a lineal descent through the ages, with the streams of the blood, as well as a logical development.

Two independent lines of investigation thus invite our attention. The one leads through inventions and discoveries, and the other through primary institutions. With the knowledge gained therefrom, we may hope to indicate the principal stages of human development. The proofs to be adduced will be drawn chiefly from domestic institutions; the references to achievements more strictly intellectual being general as well as subordinate.

The facts indicate the gradual formation and subsequent development of certain ideas, passions, and aspirations. Those which hold the most prominent positions may be generalized as growths of the particular ideas with which they severally stand connected. Apart from inventions and discoveries they are the following:

I. *Subsistence,*
II. *Government,*
III. *Language,*
IV. *The Family,*

V. *Religion,*
VI. *House Life and Architecture,*
VII. *Property.*

First. Subsistence has been increased and perfected by a series of successive arts, introduced at long intervals of time, and connected more or less directly with inventions and discoveries.

Second. The germ of government must be sought in the organization into gentes in the Status of savagery; and followed down, through the advancing forms of this institution, to the establishment of political society.

Third. Human speech seems to have been developed from the rudest and simplest forms of expression. Gesture or sign language, as intimated by Lucretius, must have preceded articulate language, as thought preceded speech. The monosyllabical preceded the syllabical, as the latter did that of concrete words. Human intelligence, unconscious of design, evolved articulate language by utilizing the vocal sounds. This great subject, a department of knowledge by itself, does not fall within the scope of the present investigation.

Fourth. With respect to the family, the stages of its growth are embodied in systems of consanguinity and affinity, and in usages relating to marriage, by means of which, collectively, the family can be definitely traced through several successive forms.

Fifth. The growth of religious ideas is environed with such intrinsic difficulties that it may never receive a perfectly satisfactory exposition. Religion deals so largely with the imaginative and emotional nature, and consequently with such uncertain elements of knowledge, that all primitive religions are grotesque and to some extent unintelligible. This subject also falls without the plan of this work excepting as it may prompt incidental suggestions.

Sixth. House architecture, which connects itself with the form of the family and the plan of domestic life, affords a tolerably complete illustration of progress from savagery to civilization. Its growth can be traced from the hut of the savage, through the communal houses of the barbarians, to the house of the single family of civilized nations, with all the successive links by which one extreme is connected with the other. This subject will be noticed incidentally.

Lastly. The idea of property was slowly formed in the human mind, remaining nascent and feeble through immense periods of time. Springing into life in savagery, it required all the experience of this period and of the subsequent period of barbarism to develop the germ, and to prepare the human brain for the acceptance of its controlling influence. Its dominance as a passion over all other passions marks the commencement of civilization. It not only led mankind to overcome the obstacles which delayed civilization, but to establish political society on the basis of territory and of property. A critical knowledge of the evolution of the idea of property would embody, in some respects, the most remarkable portion of the mental history of mankind.

It will be my object to present some evidence of human progress along these several lines, and through successive ethnical periods, as it is revealed by inventions and discoveries, and by the growth of the ideas of government, of the family, and of property.

It may be here premised that all forms of government are reducible to two general plans, using the word plan in its scientific sense. In their bases the two are fundamentally distinct. The first, in the order of time, is founded upon persons, and upon relations purely personal, and may be distinguished as a society (*societas*). The gens is the unit of this organization; giving as the successive stages of integration, in the archaic period, the gens, the phratry, the tribe, and the confederacy of tribes, which constituted a people or nation (*populus*). At a later period a coalescence of tribes in the same area into a nation took the place of a confederacy of tribes occupying independent areas. Such, through prolonged ages, after the gens appeared, was the substantially universal organization of ancient society; and it remained among the Greeks and Romans after civilization supervened. The second is founded upon territory and upon property, and may be distinguished as a state (*civitas*). The township or ward, circumscribed by metes and bounds, with the property it contains, is the basis or unit of the latter, and political society is the result. Political society is organized upon territorial areas, and deals with property as well as with persons through territorial relations. The successive stages of integration are the township or ward, which is the unit of organization; the county or province, which is an aggregation of townships or wards; and the national domain or territory, which is an aggregation of counties or provinces; the people of each of which are organized into a body politic. It taxed the Greeks and Romans to the extent of their capacities, after they had gained civilization, to invent the deme or township and the city ward; and thus inaugurate the second great plan of government, which remains among civilized nations to the present hour. In ancient society this territorial plan was unknown. When it came in it fixed the boundary line between ancient and modern society, as the distinction will be recognized in these pages.

It may be further observed that the domestic institutions of the barbarous, and even of the savage ancestors of mankind, are still exemplified in portions of the human family with such completeness that, with the exception of the strictly primitive period, the several stages of this progress are tolerably well preserved. They are seen in the organization of society upon the basis of sex, then upon the basis of kin, and finally upon the basis of territory; through the successive forms of marriage and of the family, with the systems of consanguinity thereby created; through house life and architecture; and through progress in usages with respect to the ownership and inheritance of property.

The theory of human degradation to explain the existence of savages and of barbarians is no longer tenable. It came in as a corollary from the Mosaic cosmogony, and was acquiesced in from a supposed necessity which no longer exists. As a theory, it is not only incapable of explaining the existence of savages, but it is without support in the facts of human experience.

The remote ancestors of the Aryan nations presumptively passed through an experience similar to that of existing barbarous and savage tribes. Though the experience of these nations embodies all the information necessary to illustrate the periods of civilization, both ancient and modern, together with a part of that in the Later period of barbarism, their anterior experience must be deduced, in the main, from the traceable connection between the elements of their existing institutions and inventions, and similar elements still preserved in those of savage and barbarous tribes.

It may be remarked finally that the experience of mankind has run in nearly uniform channels; that human necessities in similar conditions have been substantially the same; and that the operations of the mental principle have been uniform in virtue of the specific identity of the brain of all the races of mankind. This, however, is but a part of the explanation of uniformity in results. The germs of the principal institutions and arts of life were developed while man was still a savage. To a very great extent the experience of the subsequent periods of barbarism and of civilization have been expended in the further development of these original conceptions. Wherever a connection can be traced on different continents between a present institution and a common germ, the derivation of the people themselves from a common original stock is implied.

The discussion of these several classes of facts will be facilitated by the establishment of a certain number of Ethnical Periods; each representing a distinct condition of society, and distinguishable by a mode of life peculiar to itself. The terms "Age of *Stone*," "of *Bronze*," and "of *Iron*," introduced by Danish archæologists, have been extremely useful for certain purposes, and will remain so for the classification of objects of ancient art; but the progress of knowledge has rendered other and different subdivisions necessary. Stone implements were not entirely laid aside with the introduction of tools of iron, nor of those of bronze. The invention of the process of smelting iron ore created an ethnical epoch, yet we could scarcely date another from the production of bronze. Moreover, since the period of stone implements overlaps those of bronze and of iron, and since that of bronze also overlaps that of iron, they are not capable of a circumscription that would leave each independent and distinct.

It is probable that the successive arts of subsistence which arose at long intervals will ultimately, from the great influence they must have exercised upon the condition of mankind, afford the most satisfactory bases for these divisions. But investigation has not been carried far enough in this direction to yield the necessary information. With our present knowledge the main result can be attained by selecting such other inventions or discoveries as will afford sufficient tests of progress to characterize the commencement of successive ethnical periods. Even though accepted as provisional, these periods will be found convenient and useful. Each of those about to be proposed will be found to cover a distinct culture, and to represent a particular mode of life.

The period of savagery, of the early part of which very little is known, may be divided, provisionally, into three sub-periods. These may be named respectively the *Older,* the *Middle,* and the *Later* period of savagery; and the condition of society in each, respectively, may be distinguished as the *Lower,* the *Middle,* and the *Upper Status* of savagery.

In like manner, the period of barbarism divides naturally into three sub-periods, which will be called, respectively, the *Older,* the *Middle,* and the *Later* period of barbarism; and the condition of society in each, respectively, will be distinguished as the *Lower,* the *Middle,* and the *Upper Status* of barbarism.

It is difficult, if not impossible, to find such tests of progress to mark the commencement of these several periods as will be found absolute in their application, and without exceptions upon all the continents. Neither is it necessary, for the purpose in hand, that exceptions should not exist. It will be sufficient if the principal tribes of mankind can be classified, according to the degree of their relative progress, into conditions which can be recognized as distinct.

I. *Lower Status of Savagery*

This period commenced with the infancy of the human race, and may be said to have ended with the acquisition of a fish subsistence and of a knowledge of the use of fire. Mankind were then living in their original restricted habitat, and subsisting upon fruits and nuts. The commencement of articulate speech belongs to this period. No exemplification of tribes of mankind in this condition remained to the historical period.

II. *Middle Status of Savagery*

It commenced with the acquisition of a fish subsistence and a knowledge of the use of fire, and ended with the invention of the bow and arrow. Mankind, while in this condition, spread from their original habitat over the greater portion of the earth's surface. Among tribes still existing it will leave in the Middle Status of savagery, for example, the Australians and the greater part of the Polynesians when discovered. It will be sufficient to give one or more exemplifications of each status.

III. *Upper Status of Savagery*

It commenced with the invention of the bow and arrow, and ended with the invention of the art of pottery. It leaves in the Upper Status of Savagery the Athapascan tribes of the Hudson's Bay Territory, the tribes of the valley of the Columbia, and certain coast tribes of North and South America; but with relation to the time of their discovery. This closes the period of Savagery.

IV. *Lower Status of Barbarism*

The invention or practice of the art of pottery, all things considered, is probably the most effective and conclusive test that can be selected to fix a boundary line, necessarily arbitrary, between savagery and barbarism. The distinctness of the two conditions has long been recognized, but no criterion of progress out of the former into the latter has hitherto been brought forward. All such tribes, then, as never attained to the art of pottery will be classed as savages, and those possessing this art but who never attained a phonetic alphabet and the use of writing will be classed as barbarians.

The first sub-period of barbarism commenced with the manufacture of pottery, whether by original invention or adoption. In finding its termination, and the commencement of the Middle Status, a difficulty is encountered in the unequal endowments of the two hemispheres, which began to be influential upon human affairs after the period of savagery had passed. It may be met, however, by the adoption of equivalents. In the Eastern hemisphere, the domestication of animals, and in the Western, the cultivation of maize and plants by irrigation, together with the use of adobe-brick and stone in house building have been selected as sufficient evidence of progress to work a transition out of the Lower and into the Middle Status of barbarism. It leaves, for example, in the Lower Status, the Indian tribes of the United States east of the Missouri River, and such tribes of Europe and Asia as practiced the art of pottery, but were without domestic animals.

V. *Middle Status of Barbarism*

It commenced with the domestication of animals in the Eastern hemisphere, and in the Western with cultivation by irrigation and with the use of adobe-brick and stone in architecture, as shown. Its termination may be fixed with the invention of the process of smelting iron ore. This places in the Middle Status, for example, the Village Indians of New Mexico, Mexico, Central America and Peru, and such tribes in the Eastern hemisphere as possessed domestic animals, but were without a knowledge of iron. The ancient Britons, although familiar with the use of iron, fairly belong in this connection. The vicinity of more advanced continental tribes had advanced the arts of life among them far beyond the state of development of their domestic institutions.

VI. *Upper Status of Barbarism*

It commenced with the manufacture of iron, and ended with the invention of a phonetic alphabet, and the use of writing in literary composition. Here civilization begins. This leaves in the Upper Status, for example, the Grecian tribes of the Homeric age, the Italian tribes shortly before the founding of Rome, and the Germanic tribes of the time of Cæsar.

VII. *Status of Civilization*

It commenced, as stated, with the use of a phonetic alphabet and the production of literary records, and divides into *Ancient* and *Modern.* As an equivalent, hieroglyphical writing upon stone may be admitted. . . .

Commencing, then, with the Australians and Polynesians, following with the American Indian tribes, and concluding with the Roman and Grecian, who afford the highest exemplifications respectively of the six great stages of human progress, the sum of their united experiences may be supposed fairly to represent that of the human family from the Middle Status of savagery to the end of ancient civilization. Consequently, the Aryan nations will find the type of the condition of their remote ancestors, when in savagery, in that of the Australians and Polynesians; when in the Lower Status of barbarism in that of the partially Village Indians of America; and when in the Middle Status in that of the Village Indians, with which their own experience in the Upper Status directly connects. So essentially identical are the arts, institutions and mode of life in the same status upon all the continents, that the archaic form of the principal domestic institutions of the Greeks and Romans must even now be sought in the corresponding institutions of the American aborigines, as will be shown in the course of this volume. This fact forms a part of the accumulating evidence tending to show that the principal institutions of mankind have been developed from a few primary germs of thought; and that the course and manner of their development was predetermined, as well as restricted within narrow limits of divergence, by the natural logic of the human mind and the necessary limitations of its powers. Progress has been found to be substantially the same in kind in tribes and nations inhabiting different and even disconnected continents, while in the same status, with deviations from uniformity in particular instances produced by special causes. The argument when extended tends to establish the unity of origin of mankind. . . .

It remains to consider the growth of property in the several ethnical periods, the rules that sprang up with respect to its ownership and inheritance, and the influence which it exerted upon ancient society.

The earliest ideas of property were intimately associated with the procurement of subsistence, which was the primary need. The objects of ownership would naturally increase in each successive ethnical period with the multiplication of those arts upon which the means of subsistence depended. The growth of property would thus keep pace with the progress of inventions and discoveries. Each ethnical period shows a marked advance upon its predecessor, not only in the number of inventions, but also in the variety and amount of property which resulted therefrom. The multiplicity of the forms of property would be accompanied by the growth of certain regulations with reference to its possession and inheritance. The customs upon which these rules of proprietary possession and inheritance depend, are determined and modified by the condition and progress of the social organization. The growth of property is thus closely connected with the increase of inventions and discoveries, and with the improvement of social institutions which mark the several ethnical periods of human progress. . . .

Since the advent of civilization, the outgrowth of property has been so immense, its forms so diversified, it uses so expanding and its management so intelligent in the interests of its owners, that it has become, on the part of the people, an unmanageable power. The human mind stands bewildered in the presence of its own creation. The time will come, nevertheless, when human intelligence will rise to the mastery over property, and define the relations of the state to the property it protects, as well as the obligations and the limits of the rights of its owners. The interests of society are paramount to individual interests, and the two must be brought into just and harmonious relations. A mere property career is not the final destiny of mankind, if progress is to be the law of the future as it has been of the past. The time which has passed away since civilization began is but a fragment of the past duration of man's existence; and but a fragment of the ages yet to come. The dissolution of society bids fair to become the termination of a career of which property is the end and aim; because such a career contains the elements of self-destruction. Democracy in government, brotherhood in society, equality in rights and privileges, and universal education, foreshadow the next higher plane of society to which experience, intelligence and knowledge are steadily tending. It will be a revival, in a higher form, of the liberty, equality and fraternity of the ancient gentes.

Some of the principles, and some of the results of the growth of the idea of property in the human mind have now been presented. Although the subject has been inadequately treated, its importance at least has been shown.

With one principle of intelligence and one physical form, in virtue of a common origin, the results of human experience have been substantially the same in all times and areas in the same ethnical status.

The principle of intelligence, although conditioned in its powers within narrow limits of variation, seeks ideal standards invariably the same. Its operations, consequently, have been uniform through all the stages of human progress. No argument for the unity of origin of mankind can be made, which, in its nature, is more satisfactory. A common principle of intelligence meets us in the savage, in the barbarian, and in civilized man. It was in virtue of this that mankind were able to produce in similar conditions the same implements and utensils, the same inventions, and to develop similar institutions from the same original germs of thought. There is something grandly impressive in a principle which has wrought out civilization by assiduous application from small beginnings; from the arrow head, which expresses the thought in the brain of a savage, to the smelting of iron ore, which represents the higher intelligence of the barbarians, and, finally, to the railway train in motion, which may be called the triumph of civilization.

It must be regarded as a marvelous fact that a portion of mankind five thousand years ago, less or more, attained to civilization. In strictness but two families, the Semitic and the Aryan, accomplished the work through unassisted self-development. The Aryan family represents the central stream of human progress, because it produced the highest type of mankind, and because it has proved its intrinsic superiority by gradually assuming the control of the earth. And yet civilization must be regarded as an accident of circumstances. Its attainment at some time was certain; but that it should have been accomplished when it was, is still an extraordinary fact. The hindrances that held mankind in savagery were great, and surmounted with difficulty. After reaching the Middle Status of barbarism, civilization hung in the balance while barbarians were feeling their way, by experiments with the native metals, toward the process of smelting iron ore. Until iron and its uses were known, civilization was impossible. If mankind had failed to the present hour to cross this barrier, it would have afforded no just cause for surprise. When we recognize the duration of man's existence upon the earth, the wide vicissitudes through which he has passed in savagery and in barbarism, and the progress he was compelled to make, civilization might as naturally have been delayed for several thousand years in the future, as to have occurred when it did in the good providence of God. We are forced to the conclusion that it was the result, as to the time of its achievement, of a series of fortuitous circumstances. It may well serve to remind us that we owe our present condition, with its multiplied means of safety and of happiness, to the struggles, the sufferings, the heroic exertions and the patient toil of our barbarous, and more remotely, of our savage ancestors. Their labors, their trials and their successes were a part of the plan of the Supreme Intelligence to develop a barbarian out of a savage, and a civilized man out of this barbarian.

(2)

Frederick Jackson Turner

1861-1932

Wisconsin born and bred, Frederick Jackson Turner grew to maturity near the route over which explorers and missionaries had traversed as they made their way from the St. Lawrence Valley to the Mississippi. After receiving a bachelor's degree in 1884 and a master's degree in 1888, both from the University of Wisconsin, he went to the recently founded Johns Hopkins University, where he received his doctorate.

Returning to the University of Wisconsin as a member of the faculty, Turner gained national fame as a result of his exposition of the frontier theory to explain the emergence of the American democratic individualist, and in 1910 he was called to a professorship at Harvard.

Although not a prolific writer, Turner influenced succeeding generations of American historians by applying naturalistic methods to the study of history. At Johns Hopkins he had reacted strongly against his principal instructor, Herbert Baxter Adams, who had explained the origin of American democratic institutions in terms of their evolution from the institutions of early Germanic tribes. As an alternative, Turner began to formulate his now-famous frontier theory to explain the origins of American democracy. Starting with the prevailing idea of evolution, Turner emphasized the influence of successive frontier environments upon the social organism, with the consequent creation of a new social structure. As one frontier succeeded another, each more remote from Europe and each other, a new society as well as a new type of individual resulted.

The following selection is from Turner's most famous and important writing, "The Significance of the Frontier in American History," *American Historical Association, Annual Report,* 1893.

In a recent bulletin of the Superintendent of the Census for 1890 appear these significant words: "Up to and including 1880 the country had a frontier of settlement, but at present the unsettled area has been so broken into by isolated bodies of settlement that there can hardly be said to be a frontier line. In the discussion of its extent, its westward movement, etc., it can not, therefore, any longer have a place in the census reports." This brief official statement marks the closing of a great historic movement. Up to our own day American history has been in a large degree the history of the colonization of the Great West. The existence of an area of free land, its continuous recession, and the advance of American settlement westward, explain American development.

Behind institutions, behind constitutional forms and modifications, lie the vital forces that call these organs into life and shape them to meet changing conditions. The peculiarity of American institutions is, the fact that they have been compelled to adapt themselves to the changes of an expanding people— to the changes involved in crossing a continent, in winning a wilderness, and in developing at each area of this progress out of the primitive economic and political conditions of the frontier into the complexity of city life. Said Calhoun in 1817, "We are great, and rapidly—I was about to say fearfully—growing!" So saying, he touched the distinguishing feature of American life. All peoples show development; the germ theory of politics has been sufficiently emphasized. In the case of most nations, however, the development has occurred in a limited area; and if the nation has expanded, it has met other growing peoples whom it has conquered. But in the case of the United States we have a different phenomenon. Limiting our attention to the Atlantic coast, we have the familiar phenomenon of the evolution of institutions in a limited area, such as the rise of representative government; the differentiation of simple colonial governments into complex organs; the progress from primitive industrial society, without division of labor, up to manufacturing civilization. But we have in addition to this a recurrence of the process of evolution in each western area reached in the process of expansion. Thus American development has exhibited not merely advance along a single line, but a return to primitive conditions on a continually advancing frontier line, and a new development for that area. American social development has been continually beginning over again on the frontier. This perennial rebirth, this fluidity of American life, this expansion westward with its new opportunities, its continuous touch with the simplicity of primitive society, furnish the forces dominating American character. The true point of view in the history of this nation is not the Atlantic coast, it is the Great West. Even the slavery struggle, which is made so exclusive an object of attention by writers like Professor von Holst, occupies its important place in American history because of its relation to westward expansion.

In this advance, the frontier is the outer edge of the wave—the meeting point between savagery and civilization. Much has been written about the frontier from the point of view of border warfare and the chase, but as a field for the serious study of the economist and the historian it has been neglected.

The American frontier is sharply distinguished from the European frontier —a fortified boundary line running through dense populations. The most significant thing about the American frontier is, that it lies at the hither edge of free land. In the census reports it is treated as the margin of that settlement which has a density of two or more to the square mile. The term is an elastic one, and for our purposes does not need sharp definition. We shall consider the whole frontier belt, including the Indian country and the outer margin of the "settled area" of the census reports. This paper will make no attempt to treat the subject exhaustively; its aim is simply to call attention to the frontier as a fertile field for investigation, and to suggest some of the problems which arise in connection with it.

In the settlement of America we have to observe how European life entered the continent, and how America modified and developed that life and reacted on Europe. Our early history is the study of European germs developing in an American environment. Too exclusive attention has been paid by institutional students to the Germanic origins, too little to the American factors. The frontier is the line of most rapid and effective Americanization. The wilderness masters the colonist. It finds him a European in dress, industries, tools, modes of travel, and thought. It takes him from the railroad car and puts him in the birch canoe. It strips off the garments of civilization and arrays him in the hunting shirt and the moccasin. It puts him in the log cabin of the Cherokee and Iroquois and runs an Indian palisade around him. Before long he has gone to planting Indian corn and plowing with a sharp stick; he shouts the war cry and takes the scalp in orthodox Indian fashion. In short, at the frontier the environment is at first too strong for the man. He must accept the conditions which it furnishes, or perish, and so he fits himself into the Indian clearings and follows the Indian trails. Little by little he transforms the wilderness, but the outcome is not the old Europe, not simply the development of Germanic germs, any more than the first phenomenon was a case of reversion to the Germanic mark. The fact is, that here is a new product that is American. At first, the frontier was the Atlantic coast. It was the frontier of Europe in a very real sense. Moving westward, the frontier became more and more American. As successive terminal moraines result from successive glaciations, so each frontier leaves its traces behind it, and when it becomes a settled area the region still partakes of the frontier characteristics. Thus the advance of the frontier has meant a steady movement away from the influence of Europe, a steady growth of independence on American lines. And to study this advance, the men who grew up under these conditions, and the political, economic, and social results of it, is to study the really American part of our history. . . .

At the Atlantic frontier one can study the germs of processes repeated at each successive frontier. We have the complex European life sharply precipitated by the wilderness into the simplicity of primitive conditions. The first frontier had to meet its Indian question, its question of the disposition of the public domain, of the means of intercourse with older settlements, of the extension of political organization, of religious and educational activity. And the settlement of these and similar questions for one frontier served as a guide for the next. The American student needs not to go to the "prim little townships of Sleswick" for illustrations of the law of continuity and development. For example, he may study the origin of our land policies in the colonial land policy; he may see how the system grew by adapting the statutes to the customs of the successive frontiers. He may see how the mining experience in the lead regions of Wisconsin, Illinois, and Iowa was applied to the mining laws of the Sierras, and how our Indian policy has been a series of experimentations on successive frontiers. Each tier of new States has found in the older ones material for its constitutions. Each frontier has made similar contributions to American character, as will be discussed farther on.

But with all these similarities there are essential differences, due to the place element and the time element. It is evident that the farming frontier of the Mississippi Valley presents different conditions from the mining frontier of the Rocky Mountains. The frontier reached by the Pacific Railroad, surveyed into rectangles, guarded by the United States Army, and recruited by the daily immigrant ship, moves forward at a swifter pace and in a different way than the frontier reached by the birch canoe or the pack horse. The geologist traces patiently the shores of ancient seas, maps their areas, and compares the older and the newer. It would be a work worth the historian's labors to mark these various frontiers and in detail compare one with another. Not only would there result a more adequate conception of American development and characteristics, but invaluable additions would be made to the history of society.

Loria, the Italian economist, has urged the study of colonial life as an aid in understanding the stages of European development, affirming that colonial settlement is for economic science what the mountain is for geology, bringing to light primitive stratifications. "America," he says, "has the key to the historical enigma which Europe has sought for centuries in vain, and the land which has no history reveals luminously the course of universal history." There is much truth in this. The United States lies like a huge page in the history of society. Line by line as we read this continental page from West to East we find the record of social evolution. It begins with the Indian and the hunter; it goes on to tell of the disintegration of savagery by the entrance of the trader, the pathfinder of civilization; we read the annals of the pastoral stage in ranch life; the exploitation of the soil by the raising of unrotated crops of corn and wheat in sparsely settled farming communities; the intensive culture of the denser farm settlement; and finally the manufacturing organization with city and factory system. This page is familiar to the student of census statistics, but how little of it has been used by our historians. Particularly in eastern States this page is a palimpsest. What is now a manufacturing State was in an earlier decade an area of intensive farming. Earlier yet it had been a wheat area, and still earlier the "range" had attracted the cattleherder. Thus Wisconsin, now developing manufacture, is a State with varied agricultural interests. But earlier it was given over to almost exclusive grain-raising, like North Dakota at the present time.

Each of these areas has had an influence in our economic and political history; the evolution of each into a higher stage has worked political transformations. . . .

We may next inquire what were the influences on the East and on the Old World. A rapid enumeration of some of the more noteworthy effects is all that I have time for.

First, we note that the frontier promoted the formation of a composite nationality for the American people. The coast was preponderantly English, but the later tides of continental immigration flowed across to the free lands. This was the case from the early colonial days. The Scotch-Irish and the Palatine Germans, or "Pennsylvania Dutch," furnished the dominant element in the stock of the colonial frontier. With these peoples were also the freed indented servants, or redemptioners, who at the expiration of their time of service passed to the frontier. Governor Spotswood of Virginia writes in 1717, "The inhabitants of our frontiers are composed generally of such as have been transported hither as servants, and, being out of their time, settle themselves where land is to be taken up and that will produce the necessarys of life with little labour." Very generally these redemptioners were of non-English stock. In the crucible of the frontier the immigrants were Americanized, liberated, and fused into a mixed race, English in neither nationality nor characteristics. The process has gone on from the early days to our own. Burke and other writers in the middle of the eighteenth century believed that Pennsylvania was "threatened with the danger of being wholly foreign in language, manners, and perhaps even inclinations." The German and Scotch-Irish elements in the frontier of the South were only less great. In the middle of the present century the German element in Wisconsin was already so considerable that leading publicists looked to the creation of a German state out of the commonwealth by concentrating their colonization. Such examples teach us to beware of misinterpreting the fact that there is a common English speech in America into a belief that the stock is also English.

In another way the advance of the frontier decreased our dependence on England. The coast, particularly of the South, lacked diversified industries, and was dependent on England for the bulk of its supplies. In the South there was even a dependence on the Northern colonies for articles of food. Governor Glenn, of South Carolina, writes in the middle of the eighteenth century: "Our trade with New York and Philadelphia was of this sort, draining us of all the little money and bills we could gather from other places for their bread, flour, beer, hams, bacon, and other things of their produce, all of which, except beer, our new townships begin to supply us with, which are settled with very industrious and thriving Germans. This no doubt diminishes the number of shipping and the appearance of our trade, but it is far from being a detriment to us." Before long the frontier created a demand for merchants. As it retreated from the coast it became less and less possible for England to bring her supplies directly to the consumer's wharfs, and carry away staple crops, and staple crops began to give way to diversified agriculture for a time. The effect of this phase of the frontier action upon the northern section is perceived when we realize how the advance of the frontier aroused seaboard cities like Boston, New York, and Baltimore, to engage in rivalry for what Washington called "the extensive and valuable trade of a rising empire."

The legislation which most developed the powers of the national government, and played the largest part in its activity, was conditioned on the frontier. Writers have discussed the subjects of tariff, land, and internal improvement, as subsidiary to the slavery question. But when American history comes to be rightly viewed it will be seen that slavery question is an incident. In the period from the end of the first half of the present century to the close of the Civil War slavery rose to primary, but far from exclusive, importance. But this does not justify Dr. von Holst (to take an example) in treating our constitutional history in its formative period down to 1828 in a single volume, giving six volumes chiefly to the history of slavery from 1828 to 1861, under the title "Constitutional History of the United States." The growth of nationalism and the evolution of American political institutions were dependent on the advance of the frontier. Even so recent a writer as Rhodes, in his "History of the United States since the Compromise of 1850," has treated the legislation called out by the western advance as incidental to the slavery struggle.

This is a wrong perspective. The pioneer needed the goods of the coast, and so the grand series of internal improvement and railroad legislation began, with potent nationalizing effects. Over internal improvements occurred great debates, in which grave constitutional questions were discussed. Sectional groupings appear in the votes, profoundly significant for the historian. Loose construction increased as the nation marched westward. But the West was not content with bringing the farm to the factory. Under the lead of Clay—"Harry of the West"—protective tariffs were passed, with the cry of bringing the factory to the farm. The disposition of the public lands was a third important subject of national legislation influenced by the frontier.

The public domain has been a force of profound importance in the nationalization and development of the government. The effects of the struggle of the landed and the landless States, and of the Ordinance of 1787, need no discussion. Administratively the frontier called out some of the highest and most vitalizing activities of the general government. The purchase of Louisiana was perhaps the constitutional turning point in the history of the Republic, inasmuch as it afforded both a new area for national legislation and the occasion of the downfall of the policy of strict construction. But the purchase of Louisiana was called out by frontier needs and demands. As frontier States accrued to the Union the national power grew. In a speech on the dedication of the Calhoun monument Mr. Lamar explained: "In 1789 the States were the creators of the Federal Government; in 1861 the Federal Government was the creator of a large majority of the States."

When we consider the public domain from the point of view of the sale and disposal of the public lands we are again brought face to face with the frontier. The policy of the United States in dealing with its lands is in sharp contrast with the European system of scientific administration. Efforts to make this domain a source of revenue, and to withhold it from emigrants in order that settlement might be compact, were in vain. The jealousy and the fears of the East were powerless in the face of the demands of the frontiersmen. John Quincy Adams was obliged to confess: "My own system of administration, which was to make the national domain the inexhaustible fund for progressive and unceasing internal improvement, has failed." The reason is obvious; a system of administration was not what the West demanded; it wanted land. Adams states the situation as follows: "The slaveholders of the South have bought the coöperation of the western country by the bribe of the western lands, abandoning to the new Western States their own proportion of the public property and aiding them in the design of grasping all the lands into their own hands. Thomas H. Benton was the author of this system, which he brought forward as a substitute for the American system of Mr. Clay, and to supplant him as the leading statesman of the West. Mr. Clay, by his tariff compromise with Mr. Calhoun, abandoned his own American system. At the same time he brought forward a plan for distributing among all the States of the Union the proceeds of the sales of the public lands. His bill for that purpose passed both Houses of Congress, but was vetoed by President Jackson, who, in his annual message of December, 1832, formally recommended that all public lands should be gratuitously given away to individual adventurers and to the States in which the lands are situated."

"No subject," said Henry Clay, "which has presented itself to the present, or perhaps any preceding, Congress, is of greater magnitude than that of the public lands." When we consider the far-reaching effects of the government's land policy upon political, economic, and social aspects of American life, we are disposed to agree with him. But this legislation was framed under frontier influences, and under the lead of Western statesmen like Benton and Jackson. Said Senator Scott of Indiana in 1841: "I consider the preëmption law merely declaratory of the custom or common law of the settlers."

It is safe to say that the legislation with regard to land, tariff, and internal improvements—the American system of the nationalizing Whig party—was conditioned on frontier ideas and needs. But it was not merely in legislative action that the frontier worked against the sectionalism of the coast. The economic and social characteristics of the frontier worked against sectionalism. The men of the frontier had closer resemblances to the Middle region than to either of the other sections. Pennsylvania had been the seed-plot of frontier emigration, and, although she passed on her settlers along the Great Valley into the west of Virginia and the Carolinas, yet the industrial society of these Southern frontiersmen was always more like that of the Middle region than like that of the tide-water portion of the South, which later came to spread its industrial type throughout the South.

The Middle region, entered by New York harbor, was an open door to all Europe. The tide-water part of the South represented typical Englishmen, modified by a warm climate and servile labor, and living in baronial fashion on great plantations; New England stood for a special English movement— Puritanism. The Middle region was less English than the other sections. It had a wide mixture of nationalities, a varied society, the mixed town and county system of local government, a varied economic life, many religious sects. In short, it was a region mediating between New England and the South, and the East and the West. It represented that composite nationality which the contemporary United States exhibits, that juxtaposition of non-English groups, occupying a valley or a little settlement, and presenting reflections of the map of Europe in their variety. It was democratic and nonsectional, if not national; "easy, tolerant, and contented"; rooted strongly in material prosperity. It was typical of the modern United States. It was least sectional, not only because it lay between North and South, but also because with no barriers to shut out its frontiers from its settled region, and with a system of connecting waterways, the Middle region mediated between East and West as well as between North and South. Thus it became the typically American region. Even the New Englander, who was shut out from the frontier by the Middle region, tarrying in New York or Pennsylvania on his westward march, lost the acuteness of his sectionalism on the way.

The spread of cotton culture into the interior of the South finally broke down the contrast between the "tide-water" region and the rest of the State, and based Southern interests on slavery. Before this process revealed its results the western portion of the South, which was akin to Pennsylvania in stock, society, and industry, showed tendencies to fall away from the faith of the fathers into internal improvement legislation and nationalism. . . .

It was this nationalizing tendency of the West that transformed the democracy of Jefferson into the national republicanism of Monroe and the democracy of Andrew Jackson. The West of the War of 1812, the West of Clay, and Benton and Harrison, and Andrew Jackson, shut off by the Middle States and the mountains from the coast sections, had a solidarity of its own with national tendencies. On the tide of the Father of Waters, North and South met and mingled into a nation. Interstate migration went steadily on—a process of cross-fertilization of ideas and institutions. The fierce struggle of the sections over slavery on the western frontier does not diminish the truth of this statement; it proves the truth of it. Slavery was a sectional trait that would not down, but in the West it could not remain sectional. It was the greatest of frontiersmen who declared: "I believe this Government can not endure permanently half slave and half free. It will become all of one thing or all of the other." Nothing works for nationalism like intercourse within the nation. Mobility of population is death to localism, and the western frontier worked irresistibly in unsettling population. The effect reached back from the frontier and affected profoundly the Atlantic coast and even the Old World.

But the most important effect of the frontier has been in the promotion of democracy here and in Europe. As has been indicated, the frontier is productive of individualism. Complex society is precipitated by the wilderness into a kind of primitive organization based on the family. The tendency is anti-social. It produces antipathy to control, and particularly to any direct control. The tax-gatherer is viewed as a representative of oppression. Prof. Osgood, in an able article, has pointed out that the frontier conditions prevalent in the colonies are important factors in the explanation of the American Revolution, where individual liberty was sometimes confused with absence of all effective government. The same conditions aid in explaining the difficulty of instituting a strong government in the period of the confederacy. The frontier individualism has from the beginning promoted democracy.

The frontier States that came into the Union in the first quarter of a century of its existence came in with democratic suffrage provisions, and had reactive effects of the highest importance upon the older States whose peoples were being attracted there. An extension of the franchise became essential. It was *western* New York that forced an extension of suffrage in the constitutional convention of that State in 1821; and it was *western* Virginia that compelled the tide-water region to put a more liberal suffrage provision in the constitution framed in 1830, and to give to the frontier region a more nearly proportionate representation with the tide-water aristocracy. The rise of democracy as an effective force in the nation came in with western preponderance under Jackson and William Henry Harrison, and it meant the triumph of the frontier—with all of its good and with all of its evil elements.

So long as free land exists, the opportunity for a competency exists, and economic power secures political power. But the democracy born of free land, strong in selfishness and individualism, intolerant of administrative experience and education, and pressing individual liberty beyond its proper bounds, has its dangers as well as its benefits. Individualism in America has allowed a laxity in regard to governmental affairs which has rendered possible the spoils system and all the manifest evils that follow from the lack of a highly developed civic spirit. In this connection may be noted also the influence of frontier conditions in permitting lax business honor, inflated paper currency and wild-cat banking. The colonial and revolutionary frontier was the region whence emanated many of the worst forms of an evil currency. The West in the War of 1812 repeated the phenomenon on the frontier of that day, while the speculation and wild-cat banking of the period of the crisis of 1837 occurred on the new frontier belt of the next tier of States. Thus each one of the periods of lax financial integrity coincides with periods when a new set of frontier communities had arisen, and coincides in area with these successive frontiers, for the most part. The recent Populist agitation is a case in point. Many a State that now declines any connection with the tenets of the Populists, itself adhered to such ideas in an earlier stage of the development of the State. A primitive society can hardly be expected to show the intelligent appreciation of the complexity of business interests in a developed society. The continual recurrence of these areas of paper-money agitation is another evidence that the frontier can be isolated and studied as a factor in American history of the highest importance.

The East has always feared the result of an unregulated advance of the frontier, and has tried to check and guide it. . . . But the attempts to limit the boundaries, to restrict land sales and settlement, and to deprive the West of its share of political power were all in vain. Steadily the frontier of settlement advanced and carried with it individualism, democracy, and nationalism, and powerfully affected the East and the Old World.

The most effective efforts of the East to regulate the frontier came through its educational and religious activity, exerted by interstate migration and by organized societies. . . . The New England preacher and school-teacher left their mark on the West. The dread of Western emancipation from New England's political and economic control was paralleled by her fears lest the West cut loose from her religion. Commenting in 1850 on reports that settlement was rapidly extending northward in Wisconsin, the editor of the *Home Missionary* writes: "We scarcely know whether to rejoice or mourn over this extension of our settlements. While we sympathize in whatever tends to increase the physical resources and prosperity of our country, we can not forget that with all these dispersions into remote and still remoter corners of the land the supply of the means of grace is becoming relatively less and less." Acting in accordance with such ideas, home missions were established and Western colleges were erected. As seabord cities like Philadelphia, New York, and

Baltimore strove for the mastery of Western trade, so the various denominations strove for the possession of the West. Thus an intellectual stream from New England sources fertilized the West. Other sections sent their missionaries; but the real struggle was between sects. The contest for power and the expansive tendency furnished to the various sects by the existence of a moving frontier must have had important results on the character of religious organization in the United States. The multiplication of rival churches in the little frontier towns had deep and lasting social effects. The religious aspects of the frontier make a chapter in our history which needs study.

From the conditions of frontier life came intellectual traits of profound importance. The works of travelers along each frontier from colonial days onward describe certain common traits, and these traits have, while softening down, still persisted as survivals in the place of their origin, even when a higher social organization succeeded. The result is that to the frontier the American intellect owes its striking characteristics. That coarseness and strength combined with acuteness and inquisitiveness; that practical, inventive turn of mind, quick to find expedients; that masterful grasp of material things, lacking in the artistic but powerful to effect great ends; that restless, nervous energy; that dominant individualism, working for good and for evil, and withal that buoyancy and exuberance which comes with freedom—these are traits of the frontier, or traits called out elsewhere because of the existence of the frontier. Since the days when the fleet of Columbus sailed into the waters of the New World, America has been another name for opportunity, and the people of the United States have taken their tone from the incessant expansion which has not only been open but has even been forced upon them. He would be a rash prophet who should assert that the expansive character of American life has now entirely ceased. Movement has been its dominant fact, and, unless this training has no effect upon a people, the American energy will continually demand a wider field for its exercise. But never again will such gifts of free land offer themselves. For a moment, at the frontier, the bonds of custom are broken and unrestraint is triumphant. There is not *tabula rasa*. The stubborn American environment is there with its imperious summons to accept its conditions; the inherited ways of doing things are also there; and yet, in spite of environment, and in spite of custom, each frontier did indeed furnish a new field of opportunity, a gate of escape from the bondage of the past; and freshness, and confidence, and scorn of older society, impatience of its restraints and its ideas, and indifference to its lessons, have accompanied the frontier. What the Mediterranean Sea was to the Greeks, breaking the bond of custom, offering new experiences, calling out new institutions and activities, that, and more, the ever retreating frontier has been to the United States directly, and to the nations of Europe more remotely. And now, four centuries from the discovery of America, at the end of a hundred years of life under the Constitution, the frontier has gone, and with its going has closed the first period of American history.

(3)

Oliver Wendell Holmes, Jr.

1841-1935

Born into a distinguished Boston family, Oliver Wendell Holmes, Jr. attended Harvard University but left in his senior year to serve as an officer in the Union Army. After the war he returned to Harvard, where he received a law degree in 1866. He then entered private practice and also began to teach law at Harvard. In 1882 he was named to the Supreme Judicial Court of Massachusetts and in 1899 became chief justice of that court. In 1902 he was elevated by Theodore Roosevelt to the United States Supreme Court, where he had a long and illustrious career until his retirement in 1932.

Like his contemporaries at the end of the nineteenth century, Holmes had imbibed Darwinian ideas and rejected ideas which claimed to represent a finished and therefore static reality. His approach to law was founded upon a naturalistic basis. In one of his most famous works, *The Common Law* (1881), he made the oft-quoted remark that "The life of the law has not been logic: it has been experience. The felt necessities of the time, the prevalent moral and political theories, intuitions of public policy, avowed or unconscious, even the prejudices which judges share with their fellow-men, have had a good deal more to do than the syllogism in determining the rules by which men should be governed. The law embodies the story of a nation's development through many centuries, and it cannot be dealt with as if it contained only the axioms and corollaries of a book of mathematics."

In the following selection, "The Path of the Law," *Harvard Law Review,* 10 (March 25, 1897), Holmes bluntly denied the possibility of avoiding judge-made law, and he drew a sharp distinction between law and morality, thus demonstrating the influence of naturalistic evolution upon his legal approach.

When we study law we are not studying a mystery but a well-known profession. We are studying what we shall want in order to appear before judges, or to advise people in such a way as to keep them out of court. The reason why it is a profession, why people will pay lawyers to argue for them or to advise them, is that in societies like ours the command of the public force is intrusted to the judges in certain cases, and the whole power of the state will be put forth, if necessary, to carry out their judgments and decrees. People want to know under what circumstances and how far they will run the risk of coming against what is so much stronger than themselves, and hence it becomes a business to find out when this danger is to be feared. The object of our study, then, is prediction, the prediction of the incidence of the public force through the instrumentality of the courts. . . .

I wish, if I can, to lay down some first principles for the study of this body of dogma or systematized prediction which we call the law, for men who want to use it as the instrument of their business to enable them to prophesy in their turn, and, as bearing upon the study, I wish to point out an ideal which as yet our law has not attained.

The first thing for a business-like understanding of the matter is to understand its limits, and therefore I think it desirable at once to point out and dispel a confusion between morality and law, which sometimes rises to the height of conscious theory, and more often and indeed constantly is making trouble in detail without reaching the point of consciousness. You can see very plainly that a bad man has as much reason as a good one for wishing to avoid an encounter with the public force, and therefore you can see the practical importance of the distinction between morality and law. A man who cares nothing for an ethical rule which is believed and practised by his neighbors is likely nevertheless to care a good deal to avoid being made to pay money, and will want to keep out of jail if he can. . . .

The confusion with which I am dealing besets confessedly legal conceptions. Take the fundamental question, What constitutes the law? You will find some text writers telling you that it is something different from what is decided by the courts of Massachusetts or England, that it is a system of reason, that it is a deduction from principles of ethics or admitted axioms or what not, which may or may not coincide with the decisions. But if we take the view of our friend the bad man we shall find that he does not care two straws for the axioms or deductions, but that he does want to know what the Massachusetts or English courts are likely to do in fact. I am much of this mind. The prophecies of what the courts will do in fact, and nothing more pretentious, are what I mean by the law. . . .

This is not the time to work out a theory in detail, or to answer many obvious doubts and questions which are suggested by these general views. I know of none which are not easy to answer, but what I am trying to do now is only by a series of hints to throw some light on the narrow path of legal doctrine, and upon two pitfalls which, as it seems to me, lie perilously near to it. Of the first of these I have said enough. I hope that my illustrations have shown the danger, both to speculation and to practice, of confounding morality with law, and the trap which legal language lays for us on that side of our way. For my own part, I often doubt whether it would not be a gain if every word of moral significance could be banished from the law altogether, and other words adopted which should convey legal ideas uncolored by anything outside the law. We should lose the fossil records of a good deal of history and the majesty got from ethical associations, but by ridding ourselves of an unnecessary confusion we should gain very much in the clearness of our thought.

So much for the limits of the law. The next thing which I wish to consider is what are the forces which determine its content and its growth. You may assume, with Hobbes and Bentham and Austin, that all law emanates from the sovereign, even when the first human beings to enunciate it are the judges, or you may think that law is the voice of the Zeitgeist, or what you like. It is all one to my present purpose. Even if every decision required the sanction of an emperor with despotic power and a whimsical turn of mind, we should be interested none the less, still with a view to prediction, in discovering some order, some rational explanation, and some principle of growth for the rules which he laid down. In every system there are such explanations and principles to be found. It is with regard to them that a second fallacy comes in, which I think it important to expose.

The fallacy to which I refer is the notion that the only force at work in the development of the law is logic. In the broadest sense, indeed, that notion would be true. The postulate on which we think about the universe is that there is a fixed quantitative relation between every phenomenon and its antecedents and consequents. If there is such a thing as a phenomenon without these fixed quantitative relations, it is a miracle. It is outside the law of cause and effect, and as such transcends our power of thought, or at least is something to or from which we cannot reason. The condition of our thinking about the universe is that it is capable of being thought about rationally, or, in other words, that every part of it is effect and cause in the same sense in which those parts are with which we are most familiar. So in the broadest sense it is true that the law is a logical development, like everything else. The danger of which I speak is not the admission that the principles governing other phenomena also govern the law, but the notion that a given system, ours, for instance, can be worked out like mathematics from some general axioms of conduct. This is the natural error of the schools, but it is not confined to them. I once heard a very eminent judge say that he never let a decision go until he was absolutely sure that it was right. So judicial dissent often is blamed, as if it meant simply that one side or the other were not doing their sums right, and, if they would take more trouble, agreement inevitably would come.

This mode of thinking is entirely natural. The training of lawyers is a training in logic. The processes of analogy, discrimination, and deduction are those in which they are most at home. The language of judicial decision is mainly the language of logic. And the logical method and form flatter that longing for certainty and for repose which is in every human mind. But certainty generally is illusion, and repose is not the destiny of man. Behind the logical form lies a judgment as to the relative worth and importance of competing legislative grounds, often an inarticulate and unconscious judgment, it is true, and yet the very root and nerve of the whole proceeding. You can give any conclusion a logical form. You always can imply a condition in a contract. But why do you imply it? It is because of some belief as to the practice of the community or of a class, or because of some opinion as to policy, or, in short, because of some attitude of yours upon a matter not capable of exact quantitative measurement, and therefore not capable of founding exact logical conclusions. Such matters really are battle grounds where the means do not exist for determinations that shall be good for all time, and where the decision can do no more than embody the preference of a given body in a given time and place. We do not realize how large a part of our law is open to reconsideration upon a slight change in the habit of the public mind. No concrete proposition is self evident, no matter how ready we may be to accept it, not even Mr. Herbert Spencer's "Every man has a right to do what he wills, provided he interferes not with a like right on the part of his neighbors." . . .

I think that the judges themselves have failed adequately to recognize their duty of weighing considerations of social advantage. The duty is inevitable, and the result of the often proclaimed judicial aversion to deal with such considerations is simply to leave the very ground and foundation of judgments inarticulate, and often unconscious, as I have said. When socialism first began to be talked about, the comfortable classes of the community were a good deal frightened. I suspect that this fear has influenced judicial action both here and in England, yet it is certain that it is not a conscious factor in the decisions to which I refer. I think that something similar has led people who no longer hope to control the legislatures to look to the courts as expounders of the Constitutions, and that in some courts new principles have been discovered outside the bodies of those instruments, which may be generalized into acceptance of the economic doctrines which prevailed about fifty years ago, and a wholesale prohibition of what a tribunal of lawyers does not think about right. I cannot but believe that if the training of lawyers led them habitually to consider more definitely and explicitly the social advantage on which the rule they lay down must be justified, they sometimes would hesitate where now they are confident, and see that really they were taking sides upon debatable and often burning questions.

So much for the fallacy of logical form. Now let us consider the present condition of the law as a subject for study, and the ideal toward which it tends. We still are far from the point of view which I desire to see reached. No one has reached it or can reach it as yet. We are only at the beginning of a philosophical reaction, and of a reconsideration of the worth of doctrines which for the most part still are taken for granted without any deliberate, conscious, and systematic questioning of their grounds. The development of our law has gone on for nearly a thousand years, like the development of a plant, each generation taking the inevitable next step, mind, like matter, simply obeying a law of spontaneous growth. It is perfectly natural and right that it should have been so. Imitation is a necessity of human nature, as has been illustrated by a remarkable French writer, M. Tarde, in an admirable book, *Les Lois de l'Imitation.* Most of the things we do, we do for no better reason than that our fathers have done them or that our neighbors do them, and the same is true of a larger part than we suspect of what we think. The reason is a good one, because our short life gives us no time for a better, but it is not the best. It does not follow, because we all are compelled to take on faith at second hand most of the rules on which we base our action and our thought, that each of us may not try to set some corner of his world in the order of reason, or that all of us collectively should not aspire to carry reason as far as it will go throughout the whole domain. In regard to the law, it is true, no doubt, that an evolutionist will hesitate to affirm universal validity for his social ideals, or for the principles which he thinks should be embodied in legislation. He is content if he can prove them best for here and now. He may be ready to admit that he knows nothing about an absolute best in the cosmos, and even that he knows next to nothing about a permanent best for men. Still it is true that a body of law is more rational and more civilized when every rule it contains is referred articulately and definitely to an end which it subserves, and when the grounds for desiring that end are stated or are ready to be stated in words.

At present, in very many cases, if we want to know why a rule of law has taken its particular shape, and more or less if we want to know why it exists at all, we go to tradition. We follow it into the Year Books, and perhaps beyond them to the customs of the Salian Franks, and somewhere in the past, in the German forests, in the needs of Norman kings, in the assumptions of a dominant class, in the absence of generalized ideas, we find out the practical motive for what now best is justified by the mere fact of its acceptance and that men are accustomed to it. The rational study of law is still to a large extent the study of history. History must be a part of the study, because without it we cannot know the precise scope of rules which it is our business to know. It is a part of the rational study, because it is the first step toward an enlightened scepticism, that is, toward a deliberate reconsideration of the worth of those rules. When you get the dragon out of his cave on to the plain and in the daylight, you can count his teeth and claws, and see just what is his strength. But to get him out is only the first step. The next is either to kill him, or to tame him and make him a useful animal. For the rational study of the law the blackletter man may be the man of the present, but the man of the future is the man of statistics and the master of economics. It is revolting to have no better reason for a rule of law than that so it was laid down in the time of Henry IV. It is still more revolting if the grounds upon which it was laid down have vanished long since, and the rule simply persists from blind imitation of the past. . . .

I trust that no one will understand me to be speaking with disrespect of the law, because I criticise it so freely. I venerate the law, and especially our system of law, as one of the vastest products of the human mind. No one knows better than I do the countless number of great intellects that have spent themselves in making some addition or improvement, the greatest of which is trifling when compared with the mighty whole. It has the final title to respect that it exists, that it is not a Hegelian dream, but a part of the lives of men. But one may criticise even what one reveres. Law is the business to which my life is devoted, and I should show less than devotion if I did not do what in me lies to improve it, and, when I perceive what seems to me the ideal of its future, if I hesitated to point it out and to press toward it with all my heart.

Perhaps I have said enough to show the part which the study of history necessarily plays in the intelligent study of the law as it is to-day. In the teaching of this school and at Cambridge it is in no danger of being undervalued. Mr. Bigelow here and Mr. Ames and Mr. Thayer there have made important contributions which will not be forgotten, and in England the recent history of early English law by Sir Frederick Pollock and Mr. Maitland has lent the subject an almost deceptive charm. We must beware of the pitfall of antiquarianism, and must remember that for our purposes our only interest in the past is for the light it throws upon the present. I look forward to a time when the part played by history in the explanation of dogma shall be very small, and instead of ingenious research we shall spend our energy on a study of the ends sought to be attained and the reasons for desiring them. As a step toward that ideal it seems to me that every lawyer ought to seek an understanding of economics. The present divorce between the schools of political economy and law seems to me an evidence of how much progress in philosophical study still remains to be made. In the present state of political economy, indeed, we come again upon history on a larger scale, but there we are called on to consider and weigh the ends of legislation, the means of attaining them, and the cost. We learn that for everything we have we give up something else, and we are taught to set the advantage we gain against the other advantage we lose, and to know what we are doing when we elect.

There is another study which sometimes is undervalued by the practical minded, for which I wish to say a good word, although I think a good deal of pretty poor stuff goes under that name. I mean the study of what is called jurisprudence. Jurisprudence, as I look at it, is simply law in its most generalized part. Every effort to reduce a case to a rule is an effort of jurisprudence, although the name as used in English is confined to the broadest rules and most fundamental conceptions. One mark of a great lawyer is that he sees the application of the broadest rules. There is a story of a Vermont justice of the peace before whom a suit was brought by one farmer against another for breaking a churn. The justice took time to consider, and then said that he had looked through the statutes and could find nothing about churns, and gave judgment for the defendant. The same state of mind is shown in all our common digests and text-books. Applications of rudimentary rules of contract or tort are tucked away under the head of Railroads or Telegraphs or go to swell treatises on historical subdivisions, such as Shipping or Equity, or are gathered under an arbitrary title which is thought likely to appeal to the practical mind, such as Mercantile Law. If a man goes into law it pays to be a master of it, and to be a master of it means to look straight through all the dramatic incidents and to discern the true basis for prophecy. Therefore, it is well to have an accurate notion of what you mean by law, by a right, by a duty, by malice, intent, and negligence, by ownership, by possession, and so forth. I have in mind cases in which the highest courts seem to me to have floundered because they had no clear ideas on some of these themes. I have illustrated their importance already. If a further illustration is wished, it may be found by reading the Appendix to Sir James Stephen's *Criminal Law* on the subject of possession, and then turning to Pollock and Wright's enlightened book. Sir James Stephen is not the only writer whose attempts to analyze legal ideas have been confused by striving for a useless quintessence of all systems, instead of an accurate anatomy of one. The trouble with Austin was that he did not know enough English law. But still it is a practical advantage to master Austin, and his predecessors, Hobbes and Bentham, and his worthy successors, Holland and Pollock. Sir Frederick Pollock's recent little book is touched with the felicity which marks all his works, and is wholly free from the perverting influence of Roman models.

The advice of the elders to young men is very apt to be as unreal as a list of the hundred best books. At least in my day I had my share of such counsels, and high among the unrealities I place the recommendation to study the Roman law. I assume that such advice means more than collecting a few Latin maxims with which to ornament the discourse—the purpose for which Lord Coke recommended Bracton. If that is all that is wanted, the title *De Regulis Juris Antiqui* can be read in an hour. I assume that, if it is well to study the Roman law, it is well to study it as a working system. That means mastering a set of technicalities more difficult and less understood than our own, and studying another course of history by which even more than our own the Roman law must be explained. If any one doubts me, let him read Keller's *Der Römische Civil Process und die Actionen,* a treatise on the praetor's edict, Muirhead's most interesting *Historical Introduction to the Private Law of Rome,* and, to give him the best chance, Sohm's admirable *Institutes.* No. The way to gain a liberal view of your subject is not to read something else, but to get to the bottom of the subject itself. The means of doing that are, in the first place, to follow the existing body of dogma into its highest generalizations by the help of jurisprudence; next, to discover from history how it has come to be what it is; and, finally, so far as you can, to consider the ends which the several rules seek to accomplish, the reasons why those ends are desired, what is given up to gain them, and whether they are worth the price.

We have too little theory in the law rather than too much, especially on this final branch of study. When I was speaking of history, I mentioned larceny as an example to show how the law suffered from not having embodied in a clear form a rule which will accomplish its manifest purpose. In that case the trouble was due to the survival of forms coming from a time when a more limited purpose was entertained. Let me give now an example to show the practical importance, for the decision of actual cases, of understanding the reasons of the law, by taking an example from rules which, so far as I know, never have been explained or theorized about in any adequate way. I refer to statutes of limitation and the law of prescription. The end of such rules is obvious, but what is the justification for depriving a man of his rights, a pure evil as far as it goes, in consequence of the lapse of time? Sometimes the loss of evidence is referred to, but that is a secondary matter. Sometimes the desirability of peace, but why is peace more desirable after twenty years than before? It is increasingly likely to come without the aid of legislation. Sometimes it is said that, if a man neglects to enforce his rights, he cannot complain if, after a while, the law follows his example. Now if this is all that can be said about it, you probably will decide a case I am going to put, for the plaintiff; if you take the view which I shall suggest, you possibly will decide it for the defendant. A man is sued for trespass upon land, and justifies under a right of way. He proves that he has used the way openly and adversely for twenty years, but it turns out that the plaintiff had granted a license to a person whom he reasonably supposed to be the defendant's agent, although not so in fact, and therefore had assumed that the use of the way was permissive, in which case no right would be gained. Has the defendant gained a right or not? If his gaining it stands on the fault and neglect of the landowner in the ordinary sense, as seems commonly to be supposed, there has been no such neglect, and the right of way has not been acquired. But if I were the defendant's counsel, I should suggest that the foundation of the acquisition of rights by lapse of time is to be looked for in the position of the person who gains them, not in that of the loser. Sir Henry Maine has made it fashionable to connect the archaic notion of property with prescription. But the connection is further back than the first recorded history. It is in the nature of man's mind. A thing which you have enjoyed and used as your own for a long time, whether property or an opinion, takes root in your being and cannot be torn away without your resenting the act and trying to defend yourself, however you came by it. The law can ask no better justification than the deepest instincts of man. It is only by way of reply to the suggestion that you are disappointing the former owner, that you refer to his neglect having allowed the gradual dissociation between himself and what he claims, and the gradual association of it with another. If he knows that another is doing acts which on their face show that he is on the way toward establishing such an association, I should argue that in justice to that other he was bound at his peril to find out whether the other was acting under his permission, to see that he was warned, and if necessary, stopped.

(4)

John Dewey

1859-1952

John Dewey was born in Burlington, Vermont, and attended the University of Vermont, where he received his bachelor's degree in 1879. Five years later he was awarded his doctorate from the Johns Hopkins University and then taught successively at the Universities of Michigan, Minnesota, and Chicago. In 1904 he went to Columbia University, where he remained for the rest of his career.

Dewey attempted in his writings to erect a system of logic and ethics on an evolutionary base. In doing so, he hoped to free philosophy from a sterile metaphysics and transform it into a form of social engineering. His treatment of ethical problems represented a radical departure from tradition, since he made ethical principles ancillary to the dominant social, economic, and political problems of the day. Dewey always defined an idea as essentially a plan of action, not a mirror of reality. Rejecting dualisms of any sort, he insisted that the nature and end of thought was to fulfill the purpose for which it had been brought into being, namely, to provide for the survival, growth, and better adjustment of the organism. He further maintained that the intelligent use of the scientific method was the best means of solving problems.

Probably more than any other person, Dewey was the philosopher of twentieth-century liberalism and progressivism. Hostile to all absolutisms, his instrumentalist approach had a varying social and economic content, but whatever its content it always retained a measure of social consciousness and a willingness to change as circumstances changed.

In the following selection, *The Influence of Darwin on Philosophy* (New York, 1910), Dewey described the influence of evolutionary ideas on philosophy and methods of thinking.

I

That the publication of the "Origin of Species" marked an epoch in the development of the natural sciences is well known to the layman. That the combination of the very words origin and species embodied an intellectual revolt and introduced a new intellectual temper is easily overlooked by the expert. The conceptions that had reigned in the philosophy of nature and knowledge for two thousand years, the conceptions that had become the familiar furniture of the mind, rested on the assumption of the superiority of the fixed and final; they rested upon treating change and origin as signs of defect and unreality. In laying hands upon the sacred ark of absolute permanency, in treating the forms that had been regarded as types of fixity and perfection as originating and passing away, the "Origin of Species" introduced a mode of thinking that in the end was bound to transform the logic of knowledge, and hence the treatment of morals, politics, and religion.

No wonder, then, that the publication of Darwin's book, a half century ago, precipitated a crisis. The true nature of the controversy is easily concealed from us, however, by the theological clamor that attended it. The vivid and popular features of the anti-Darwinian row tended to leave the impression that the issue was between science on one side and theology on the other. Such was not the case—the issue lay primarily within science itself, as Darwin himself early recognized. The theological outcry he discounted from the start, hardly noticing it save as it bore upon the "feelings of his female relatives."

But for two decades before final publication he contemplated the possibility of being put down by his scientific peers as a fool or as crazy; and he set, as the measure of his success, the degree in which he should affect three men of science: Lyell in geology, Hooker in botany, and Huxley in zoology.

Religious considerations lent fervor to the controversy, but they did not provoke it. Intellectually, religious emotions are not creative but conservative. They attach themselves readily to the current view of the world and consecrate it. They steep and dye intellectual fabrics in the seething vat of emotions; they do not form their warp and woof. There is not, I think, an instance of any large idea about the world being independently generated by religion. Although the ideas that rose up like armed men against Darwinism owed their intensity to religious associations, their origin and meaning are to be sought in science and philosophy, not in religion.

II

Few words in our language foreshorten intellectual history as much as does the word species. The Greeks, in initiating the intellectual life of Europe, were impressed by characteristic traits of the life of plants and animals; so impressed indeed that they made these traits the key to defining nature and to explaining mind and society. And truly, life is so wonderful that a seemingly successful reading of its mystery might well lead men to believe that the key to the secrets of heaven and earth was in their hands. The Greek rendering of this mystery, the Greek formulation of the aim and standard of knowledge, was in the course of time embodied in the word species, and it controlled philosophy for two thousand years. To understand the intellectual face-about expressed in the phrase "Origin of Species," we must, then, understand the long dominant idea against which it is a protest.

Consider how men were impressed by the facts of life. Their eyes fell upon certain things slight in bulk, and frail in structure. To every appearance, these perceived things were inert and passive. Suddenly, under certain circumstances, these things—henceforth known as seeds or eggs or germs—begin to change, to change rapidly in size, form, and qualities. Rapid and extensive changes occur, however, in many things—as when wood is touched by fire. But the changes in the living thing are orderly; they are cumulative; they tend constantly in one direction; they do not, like the other changes, destroy or consume, or pass fruitless into wandering flux; they realize and fulfil. Each successive stage, no matter how unlike its predecessor, preserves its net effect and also prepares the way for a fuller activity on the part of its successor. In living beings, changes do not happen as they seem to happen elsewhere, any which way; the earlier changes are regulated in view of later results. This progressive organization does not cease till there is achieved a true final term, a τελὸς, a completed, perfected end. This final form exercises in turn a plenitude of functions, not the least noteworthy of which is production of germs like those from which it took its own origin, germs capable of the same cycle of self-fulfilling activity.

But the whole miraculous tale is not yet told. The same drama is enacted to the same destiny in countless myriads of individuals so sundered in time, so served in space, that they have no opportunity for mutual consultation and no means of interaction. As an old writer quaintly said, "things of the same kind go through the same formalities"—celebrate, as it were, the same ceremonial rites.

This formal activity which operates throughout a series of changes and holds them to a single course; which subordinates their aimless flux to its own perfect manifestation; which, leaping the boundaries of space and time, keeps individuals distant in space and remote in time to a uniform type of structure and function: this principle seemed to give insight into the very nature of reality itself. To it Aristotle gave the name, εἶδος. This term the scholastics translated as *species*.

The force of this term was deepened by its application to everything in the universe that observes order in flux and manifests constancy through change. From the casual drift of daily weather, through the uneven recurrence of seasons and unequal return of seed time and harvest, up to the majestic sweep of the heavens—the image of eternity in time—and from this to the unchanging pure and contemplative intelligence beyond nature lies one unbroken fulfilment of ends. Nature as a whole is a progressive realization of purpose strictly comparable to the realization of purpose in any single plant or animal.

The conception of εἶδος, species, a fixed form and final cause, was the central principle of knowledge as well as of nature. Upon it rested the logic of science. Change as change is mere flux and lapse; it insults intelligence. Genuinely to know is to grasp a permanent end that realizes itself through changes, holding them thereby within the metes and bounds of fixed truth. Completely to know is to relate all special forms to their one single end and good: pure contemplative intelligence. Since, however, the scene of nature which directly confronts us is in change, nature as directly and practically experienced does not satisfy the conditions of knowledge. Human experience is in flux, and hence the instrumentalities of sense-perception and of inference based upon observation are condemned in advance. Science is compelled to aim at realities lying behind and beyond the processes of nature, and to carry on its search for these realities by means of rational forms transcending ordinary modes of perception and inference.

There are, indeed, but two alternative courses. We must either find the appropriate objects and organs of knowledge in the mutual interactions of changing things; or else, to escape the infection of change, we *must* seek them in some transcendent and supernal region. The human mind, deliberately as it were, exhausted the logic of the changeless, the final, and the transcendent, before it essayed adventure on the pathless wastes of generation and transformation. We dispose all too easily of the efforts of the schoolmen to interpret nature and mind in terms of real essences, hidden forms, and occult faculties, forgetful of the seriousness and dignity of the ideas that lay behind. We dispose of them by laughing at the famous gentleman who accounted for the fact that opium put people to sleep on the ground it had a dormitive faculty. But the doctrine, held in our own day, that knowledge of the plant that yields the poppy consists in referring the peculiarities of an individual to a type, to a universal form, a doctrine so firmly established that any other method of knowing was conceived to be unphilosophical and unscientific, is a survival of precisely the same logic. This identity of conception in the scholastic and anti-Darwinian theory may well suggest greater sympathy for what has become unfamiliar as well as greater humility regarding the further unfamiliarities that history has in store.

Darwin was not, of course, the first to question the classic philosophy of nature and of knowledge. The beginnings of the revolution are in the physical science of the sixteenth and seventeenth centuries. When Galileo said: "It is my opinion that the earth is very noble and admirable by reason of so many and so different alterations and generations which are incessantly made therein," he expressed the changed temper that was coming over the world; the transfer of interest from the permanent to the changing. When Descartes said: "The nature of physical things is much more easily conceived when they are beheld coming gradually into existence, than when they are only considered as produced at once in a finished and perfect state," the modern world became self-conscious of the logic that was henceforth to control it, the logic of which Darwin's "Origin of Species" is the latest scientific achievement. Without the methods of Copernicus, Kepler, Galileo, and their successors in astronomy, physics, and chemistry, Darwin would have been helpless in the organic sciences. But prior to Darwin the impact of the new scientific method upon life, mind, and politics, had been arrested, because between these ideal or moral interests and the inorganic world intervened the kingdom of plants and animals. The gates of the garden of life were barred to the new ideas; and only through this garden was there access to mind and politics. The influence of Darwin upon philosophy resides in his having conquered the phenomena of life for the principle of transition, and thereby freed the new logic for application to mind and morals and life. When he said of species what Galileo had said of the earth, *e pur se muove,* he emancipated, once for all, genetic and experimental ideas as an organon of asking questions and looking for explanations.

III

The exact bearings upon philosophy of the new logical outlook are, of course, as yet, uncertain and inchoate. We live in the twilight of intellectual transition. One must add the rashness of the prophet to the stubbornness of the partizan to venture a systematic exposition of the influence upon philosophy of the Darwinian method. At best, we can but inquire as to its general bearing —the effect upon mental temper and complexion, upon that body of half-conscious, half-instinctive intellectual aversions and preferences which determine, after all, our more deliberate intellectual enterprises. In this vague inquiry there happens to exist as a kind of touchstone a problem of long historic currency that has also been much discussed in Darwinian literature. I refer to the old problem of design *versus* chance, mind *versus* matter, as the causal explanation, first or final, of things.

As we have already seen, the classic notion of species carried with it the idea of purpose. In all living forms, a specific type is present directing the earlier stages of growth to the realization of its own perfection. Since this purposive regulative principle is not visible to the senses, it follows that it must be an ideal or rational force. Since, however, the perfect form is gradually approximated through the sensible changes, it also follows that in and through a sensible realm a rational ideal force is working out its own ultimate manifestation. These inferences were extended to nature: (*a*) She does nothing in vain; but all for an ulterior purpose. (*b*) Within natural sensible events there is therefore contained a spiritual causal force, which as spiritual escapes perception, but is apprehended by an enlightened reason. (*c*) The manifestation of this principle brings about a subordination of matter and sense to its own realization, and this ultimate fulfilment is the goal of nature and of man. The design argument thus operated in two directions. Purposefulness accounted for the intelligibility of nature and the possibility of science, while the absolute or cosmic character of this purposefulness gave sanction and worth to the moral and religious endeavors of man. Science was underpinned and morals authorized by one and the same principle, and their mutual agreement was eternally guaranteed.

This philosophy remained, in spite of sceptical and polemic outbursts, the official and the regnant philosophy of Europe for over two thousand years. The expulsion of fixed first and final causes from astronomy, physics, and chemistry had indeed given the doctrine something of a shock. But, on the other hand, increased acquaintance with the details of plant and animal life operated as a counterbalance and perhaps even strengthened the argument from design. The marvelous adaptations of organisms to their environment, of organs to the organism, of unlike parts of a complex organ—like the eye—to the organ itself; the foreshadowing by lower forms of the higher; the preparation in earlier stages of growth for organs that only later had their functioning —these things were increasingly recognized with the progress of botany, zoology, paleontology, and embryology. Together, they added such prestige to the design argument that by the late eighteenth century it was, as approved by the sciences of organic life, the central point of theistic and idealistic philosophy.

The Darwinian principle of natural selection cut straight under this philosophy. If all organic adaptations are due simply to constant variation and the elimination of those variations which are harmful in the struggle for existence that is brought about by excessive reproduction, there is no call for a prior intelligent causal force to plan and preordain them. Hostile critics charged Darwin with materialism and with making chance the cause of the universe.

Some naturalists, like Asa Gray, favored the Darwinian principle and attempted to reconcile it with design. Gray held to what may be called design on the installment plan. If we conceive the "stream of variations" to be itself intended, we may suppose that each successive variation was designed from the first to be selected. In that case, variation, struggle, and selection simply define the mechanism of "secondary causes" through which the "first cause" acts; and the doctrine of design is none the worse off because we know more of its *modus operandi.*

Darwin could not accept this mediating proposal. He admits or rather he asserts that it is "impossible to conceive this immense and wonderful universe including man with his capacity of looking far backwards and far into futurity as the result of blind chance or necessity." But nevertheless he holds that since variations are in useless as well as useful directions, and since the latter are sifted out simply by the stress of the conditions of struggle for existence, the design argument as applied to living beings is unjustifiable; and its lack of support there deprives it of scientific value as applied to nature in general. If the variations of the pigeon, which under artificial selection give the pouter pigeon, are not preordained for the sake of the breeder, by what logic do we argue that variations resulting in natural species are pre-designed?

IV

So much for some of the more obvious facts of the discussion of design *versus* chance, as causal principles of nature and of life as a whole. We brought up this discussion, you recall, as a crucial instance. What does our touchstone indicate as to the bearing of Darwinian ideas upon philosophy? In the first place, the new logic outlaws, flanks, dismisses—what you will—one type of problems and substitutes for it another type. Philosophy forswears inquiry after absolute origins and absolute finalities in order to explore specific values and the specific conditions that generate them.

Darwin concluded that the impossibility of assigning the world to chance as a whole and to design in its parts indicated the insolubility of the question. Two radically different reasons, however, may be given as to why a problem is insoluble. One reason is that the problem is too high for intelligence; the other is that the question in its very asking makes assumptions that render the question meaningless. The latter alternative is unerringly pointed to in the celebrated case of design *versus* chance. Once admit that the sole verifiable or fruitful object of knowledge is the particular set of changes that generate the object of study together with the consequences that then flow from it, and no intelligible question can be asked about what, by assumption, lies outside. To assert—as is often asserted—that specific values of particular truth, social bonds and forms of beauty, if they can be shown to be generated by concretely knowable conditions, are meaningless and in vain; to assert that they are justified only when they and their particular causes and effects have all at once been gathered up into some inclusive first cause and some exhaustive final goal, is intellectual atavism. Such argumentation is reversion to the logic that explained the extinction of fire by water through the formal essence of aqueousness and the quenching of thirst by water through the final cause of aqueousness. Whether used in the case of the special event or that of life as a whole, such logic only abstracts some aspect of the existing course of events in order to reduplicate it as a petrified eternal principle by which to explain the very changes of which it is the formalization.

When Henry Sidgwick casually remarked in a letter that as he grew older his interest in what or who made the world was altered into interest in what kind of a world it is anyway, his voicing of a common experience of our own day illustrates also the nature of that intellectual transformation effected by the Darwinian logic. Interest shifts from the wholesale essence back of special changes to the question of how special changes serve and defeat concrete purposes; shifts from an intelligence that shaped things once for all to the particular intelligences which things are even now shaping; shifts from an ultimate goal of good to the direct increments of justice and happiness that intelligent administration of existent conditions may beget and that present carelessness or stupidity will destroy or forego.

In the second place, the classic type of logic inevitably set philosophy upon proving that life *must* have certain qualities and values—no matter how experience presents the matter—because of some remote cause and eventual goal. The duty of wholesale justification inevitably accompanies all thinking that makes the meaning of special occurrences depend upon something that once and for all lies behind them. The habit of derogating from present meanings and uses prevents our looking the facts of experience in the face; it prevents serious acknowledgment of the evils they present and serious concern with the goods they promise but do not as yet fulfil. It turns thought to the business of finding a wholesale transcendent remedy for the one and guarantee for the other. One is reminded of the way many moralists and theologians greeted Herbert Spencer's recognition of an unknowable energy from which welled up the phenomenal physical processes without and the conscious operations within. Merely because Spencer labeled his unknowable energy "God," this faded piece of metaphysical goods was greeted as an important and grateful concession to the reality of the spiritual realm. Were it not for the deep hold of the habit of seeking justification for ideal values in the remote and transcendent, surely this reference of them to an unknowable absolute would be despised in comparison with the demonstrations of experience that knowable energies are daily generating about us precious values.

The displacing of this wholesale type of philosophy will doubtless not arrive by sheer logical disproof, but rather by growing recognition of its futility. Were it a thousand times true that opium produces sleep because of its dormitive energy, yet the inducing of sleep in the tired, and the recovery to waking life of the poisoned, would not be thereby one least step forwarded. And were it a thousand times dialectically demonstrated that life as a whole is regulated by a transcendent principle to a final inclusive goal, none the less truth and error, health and disease, good and evil, hope and fear in the concrete, would remain just what and where they now are. To improve our education, to ameliorate our manners, to advance our politics, we must have recourse to specific conditions of generation.

Finally, the new logic introduces responsibility into the intellectual life. To idealize and rationalize the universe at large is after all a confession of inability to master the courses of things that specifically concern us. As long as mankind suffered from this impotency, it naturally shifted a burden of responsibility that it could not carry over to the more competent shoulders of the transcendent cause. But if insight into specific conditions of value and into specific consequences of ideas is possible, philosophy must in time become a method of locating and interpreting the more serious of the conflicts that occur in life, and a method of projecting ways for dealing with them: a method of moral and political diagnosis and prognosis.

The claim to formulate *a priori* the legislative constitution of the universe is by its nature a claim that may lead to elaborate dialectic developments. But it is also one that removes these very conclusions from subjection to experimental test, for, by definition, these results make no differences in the detailed course of events. But a philosophy that humbles its pretensions to the work of projecting hypotheses for the education and conduct of mind, individual and social, is thereby subjected to test by the way in which the ideas it propounds work out in practice. In having modesty forced upon it, philosophy also acquires responsibility.

Doubtless I seem to have violated the implied promise of my earlier remarks and to have turned both prophet and partizan. But in anticipating the direction of the transformations in philosophy to be wrought by the Darwinian genetic and experimental logic, I do not profess to speak for any save those who yield themselves consciously or unconsciously to this logic. No one can fairly deny that at present there are two effects of the Darwinian mode of thinking. On the one hand, there are making many sincere and vital efforts to revise our traditional philosophic conceptions in accordance with its demands. On the other hand, there is as definitely a recrudescence of absolutistic philosophies; an assertion of a type of philosophic knowing distinct from that of the sciences, one which opens to us another kind of reality from that to which the sciences give access; an appeal through experience to something that essentially goes beyond experience. This reaction affects popular creeds and religious movements as well as technical philosophies. The very conquest of the biological sciences by the new ideas has led many to proclaim an explicit and rigid separation of philosophy from science.

Old ideas give way slowly; for they are more than abstract logical forms and categories. They are habits, predispositions, deeply engrained attitudes of aversion and preference. Moreover, the conviction persists—though history shows it to be a hallucination—that all the questions that the human mind has asked are questions that can be answered in terms of the alternatives that the questions themselves present. But in fact intellectual progress usually occurs through sheer abandonment of questions together with both of the alternatives they assume—an abandonment that results from their decreasing vitality and a change of urgent interest. We do not solve them: we get over them. Old questions are solved by disappearing, evaporating, while new questions corresponding to the changed attitude of endeavor and preference take their place. Doubtless the greatest dissolvent in contemporary thought of old questions, the greatest precipitant of new methods, new intentions, new problems, is the one effected by the scientific revolution that found its climax in the "Origin of Species."

(5)

John B. Watson

1878-1958

One of the founders of behavioristic psychology, John B. Watson was born in Greenville, South Carolina. Receiving an M.A. from Furman University in 1900 and a Ph.D. from the University of Chicago in 1903, he taught at the latter institution from 1904 to 1908. From 1908 to 1920 he was professor of experimental and comparative psychology at the Johns Hopkins University. In addition to publishing many works, he also edited several major psychological journals and in 1915 served as president of the American Psychological Association. In 1920, following a divorce and quick remarriage, the trustees of Hopkins demanded his resignation. After this affair Watson entered the advertising business, never again to hold an academic position.

Earlier in his career Watson had become interested in working with animals. When his studies suggested that animals learn by trial and error, he decided to investigate the human learning process in these terms. Watson's basic problem was to determine whether instincts existed, whether there were basic unlearned reactions, and above all, if man should be considered in psychology as animals. Relegating heredity to a position of minor importance, he concluded that all learning was conditioned, and consequently demanded that the concept of consciousness be eliminated from psychology. Thus the stimulus-response relationship became the basic ingredient of behavioristic psychology, and the distinction between the human and animal world all but disappeared. In one sense behaviorism was one of the most radical products of naturalism, since it led to a determinism whereby the influence of environment alone would account for human behavior and lead to a predictive and accurate science of psychology.

The following selection is from Watson's famous article, "Psychology as the Behaviorist Views It," *Psychological Review,* 20 (March, 1913), which aroused great controversy when it first appeared.

Psychology as the behaviorist views it is a purely objective experimental branch of natural science. Its theoretical goal is the prediction and control of behavior. Introspection forms no essential part of its methods, nor is the scientific value of its data dependent upon the readiness with which they lend themselves to interpretation in terms of consciousness. The behaviorist, in his efforts to get a unitary scheme of animal response, recognizes no dividing line between man and brute. The behavior of man, with all of its refinement and complexity, forms only a part of the behaviorist's total scheme of investigation.

It has been maintained by its followers generally that psychology is a study of the science of the phenomena of consciousness. It has taken as its problem, on the one hand, the analysis of complex mental states (or processes) into simple elementary constituents, and on the other the construction of complex states when the elementary constituents are given. The world of physical objects (stimuli, including here anything which may excite activity in a receptor), which forms the total phenomena of the natural scientist, is looked upon merely as means to an end. That end is the production of mental states that may be "inspected" or "observed." The psychological object of observation in the case of an emotion, for example, is the mental state itself. The problem in emotion is the determination of the number and kind of elementary constituents present, their loci, intensity, order of appearance, etc. It is agreed that introspection is the method *par excellence* by means of which mental states may be manipulated for purposes of psychology. On this assumption, behavior data (including under this term everything which goes under the name of comparative psychology) have no value *per se.* They possess significance only in so far as they may throw light upon conscious states. Such data must have at least an analogical or indirect reference to belong to the realm of psychology.

Indeed, at times, one finds psychologists who are sceptical of even this analogical reference. Such scepticism is often shown by the question which is put to the student of behavior, "what is the bearing of animal work upon human psychology?" I used to have to study over this question. Indeed it always embarrassed me somewhat. I was interested in my own work and felt that it was important, and yet I could not trace any close connection between it and psychology as my questioner understood psychology. I hope that such a confession will clear the atmosphere to such an extent that we will no longer have to work under false pretences. We must frankly admit that the facts so important to us which we have been able to glean from extended work upon the senses of animals by the behavior method have contributed only in a fragmentary way to the general theory of human sense organ processes, nor have they suggested new points of experimental attack. The enormous number of experiments which we have carried out upon learning have likewise contributed little to human psychology. It seems reasonably clear that some kind of compromise must be effected: either psychology must change its viewpoint so as to take in facts of behavior, whether or not they have bearings upon the problems of "consciousness"; or else behavior must stand alone as a wholly separate and independent science. Should human psychologists fail to look with favor upon our overtures and refuse to modify their position, the behaviorists will be driven to using human beings as subjects and to employ methods of investigation which are exactly comparable to those now employed in the animal work.

Any other hypothesis than that which admits the independent value of behavior material, regardless of any bearing such material may have upon consciousness, will inevitably force us to the absurd position of attempting to *construct* the conscious content of the animal whose behavior we have been studying. On this view, after having determined our animal's ability to learn, the simplicity or complexity of its methods of learning, the effect of past habit upon present response, the range of stimuli to which it ordinarily responds, the widened range to which it can respond under experimental conditions,—in more general terms, its various problems and its various ways of solving them,—we should still feel that the task is unfinished and that the results are worthless, until we can interpret them by analogy in the light of consciousness. Although we have solved our problem we feel uneasy and unrestful because of our definition of psychology: we feel forced to say something about the possible mental processes of our animal. We say that, having no eyes, its stream of consciousness cannot contain brightness and color sensations as we know them,—having no taste buds this stream can contain no sensations of sweet, sour, salt and bitter. But on the other hand, since it does respond to thermal, tactual and organic stimuli, its conscious content must be made up largely of these sensations; and we usually add, to protect ourselves against the reproach of being anthropomorphic, "if it has any consciousness." Surely this doctrine which calls for an analogical interpretation of all behavior data may be shown to be false: the position that the standing of an observation upon behavior is determined by its fruitfulness in yielding results which are interpretable only in the narrow realm of (really human) consciousness.

This emphasis upon analogy in psychology has led the behaviorist somewhat afield. Not being willing to throw off the yoke of consciousness he feels impelled to make a place in the scheme of behavior where the rise of consciousness can be determined. This point has been a shifting one. A few years ago certain animals were supposed to possess "associative memory," while certain others were supposed to lack it. One meets this search for the origin of consciousness under a good many disguises. Some of our texts state that consciousness arises at the moment when reflex and instinctive activities fail properly to conserve the organism. A perfectly adjusted organism would be lacking in consciousness. On the other hand whenever we find the presence of diffuse activity which results in habit formation, we are justified in assuming consciousness. I must confess that these arguments had weight with me when I began the study of behavior. I fear that a good many of us are still viewing behavior problems with something like this in mind. More than one student in behavior has attempted to frame criteria of the psychic—to devise a set of objective, structural and functional criteria which, when applied in the particular instance, will enable us to decide whether such and such responses are positively conscious, merely indicative of consciousness, or whether they are purely "physiological." Such problems as these can no longer satisfy behavior men. It would be better to give up the province altogether and admit frankly that the study of the behavior of animals has no justification, than to admit that our search is of such a "will o' the wisp" character. One can assume either the presence or the absence of consciousness anywhere in the phylogenetic scale without affecting the problems of behavior by one jot or one tittle; and without influencing in any way the mode of experimental attack upon them. On the other hand, I cannot for one moment assume that the paramecium responds to light; that the rat learns a problem more quickly by working at the task five times a day than once a day, or that the human child exhibits plateaux in his learning curves. These are questions which vitally concern behavior and which must be decided by direct observation under experimental conditions.

This attempt to reason by analogy from human conscious processes to the conscious processes in animals, and *vice versa:* to make consciousness, as the human being knows it, the center of reference of all behavior, forces us into a situation similar to that which existed in biology in Darwin's time. The whole Darwinian movement was judged by the bearing it had upon the origin and development of the human race. Expeditions were undertaken to collect material which would establish the position that the rise of the human race was a perfectly natural phenomenon and not an act of special creation. Variations were carefully sought along with the evidence for the heaping up effect and the weeding out effect of selection; for in these and the other Darwinian mechanisms were to be found factors sufficiently complex to account for the origin and race differentiation of man. The wealth of material collected at this time was considered valuable largely in so far as it tended to develop the concept of evolution in man. It is strange that this situation should have remained the dominant one in biology for so many years. The moment zoölogy undertook the experimental study of evolution and descent, the situation immediately changed. Man ceased to be the center of reference. I doubt if any experimental biologist today, unless actually engaged in the problem of race differentiation in man, tries to interpret his findings in terms of human evolution, or ever refers to it in his thinking. He gathers his data from the study of many species of plants and animals and tries to work out the laws of inheritance in the particular type upon which he is conducting experiments. Naturally, he follows the progress of the work upon race differentiation in man and in the descent of man, but he looks upon these as special topics, equal in importance with his own yet ones in which his interests will never be vitally engaged. It is not fair to say that all of his work is directed toward human evolution or that it must be interpreted in terms of human evolution. He does not have to dismiss certain of his facts on the inheritance of coat color in mice because, forsooth, they have little bearing upon the differentiation of the *genus homo* into separate races, or upon the descent of the *genus homo* from some more primitive stock. . . .

The time seems to have come when psychology must discard all reference to consciousness; when it need no longer delude itself into thinking that it is making mental states the object of observation. We have become so enmeshed in speculative questions concerning the elements of mind, the nature of conscious content (for example, imageless thought, attitudes, and Bewusseinslage, etc.) that I, as an experimental student, feel that something is wrong with our premises and the types of problems which develop from them. There is no longer any guarantee that we all mean the same thing when we use the terms now current in psychology. Take the case of sensation. A sensation is defined in terms of its attributes. One psychologist will state with readiness that the attributes of a visual sensation are *quality, extension, duration,* and *intensity.* Another will add *clearness.* Still another that of *order.* I doubt if any one psychologist can draw up a set of statements describing what he means by sensation which will be agreed to by three other psychologists of different training. Turn for a moment to the question of the number of isolable sensations. Is there an extremely large number of color sensations—or only four, red, green, yellow and blue? Again, yellow, while psychologically simple, can be obtained by superimposing red and green spectral rays upon the same diffusing surface! If, on the other hand, we say that every just noticeable difference in the spectrum is a simple sensation, and that every just noticeable increase in the white value of a given color gives simple sensations, we are forced to admit that the number is so large and the conditions for obtaining them so complex that the concept of sensation is unusable, either for the purpose of analysis or that of synthesis. Titchener, who has fought the most valiant fight in this country for a psychology based upon introspection, feels that these differences of opinion as to the number of sensations and their attributes; as to whether there are relations (in the sense of elements) and on the many others which seem to be fundamental in every attempt at analysis, are perfectly natural in the present undeveloped state of psychology. While it is admitted that every growing science is full of unanswered questions, surely only those who are wedded to the system as we now have it, who have fought and suffered for it, can confidently believe that there will ever be any greater uniformity than there is now in the answers we have to such questions. I firmly believe that two hundred years from now, unless the introspective method is discarded, psychology will still be divided on the question as to whether auditory sensations have the quality of "extension," whether intensity is an attribute which can be applied to color, whether there is a difference in "texture" between image and sensation and upon many hundreds of others of like character. . . . I believe we can write a psychology, define it as Pillsbury, and never go back upon our definition: never use the terms consciousness, mental states, mind, content, introspectively verifiable, imagery, and the like. I believe that we can do it in a few years without running into the absurd terminology of Beer, Bethe, Von Uexküll, Nuel, and that of the so-called objective schools generally. It can be done in terms of stimulus and response, in terms of habit formation, habit integrations and the like. Furthermore, I believe that it is really worth while to make this attempt now.

The psychology which I should attempt to build up would take as a starting point, first, the observable fact that organisms, man and animal alike, do adjust themselves to their environment by means of hereditary and habit equipments. These adjustments may be very adequate or they may be so inadequate that the organism barely maintains its existence; secondly, that certain stimuli lead the organisms to make the responses. In a system of psychology completely worked out, given the response the stimuli can be predicted; given the stimuli the response can be predicted. Such a set of statements is crass and raw in the extreme, as all such generalizations must be. Yet they are hardly more raw and less realizable than the ones which appear in the psychology texts of the day. I possibly might illustrate my point better by choosing an everyday problem which anyone is likely to meet in the course of his work. Some time ago I was called upon to make a study of certain species of birds. Until I went to Tortugas I had never seen these birds alive. When I reached there I found the animals doing certain things: some of the acts seemed to work peculiarly well in such an environment, while others seemed to be unsuited to their type of life. I first studied the responses of the group as a whole and later those of individuals. In order to understand more thoroughly the relation between what was habit and what was hereditary in these responses, I took the young birds and reared them. In this way I was able to study the order of appearance of hereditary adjustments and their complexity, and later the beginnings of habit formation. My efforts in determining the stimuli which called forth such adjustments were crude indeed. Consequently my attempts to control behavior and to produce responses at will did not meet with much success. Their food and water, sex and other social relations, light and temperature conditions were all beyond control in a field study. I did find it possible to control their reactions in a measure by using the nest and egg (or young) as stimuli. . . . In the main, my desire in all such work is to gain an accurate knowledge of adjustments and the stimuli calling them forth. My final reason for this is to learn general and particular methods by which I may control behavior. My goal is not "the description and explanation of states of consciousness as such," nor that of obtaining such proficiency in mental gymnastics that I can immediately lay hold of a state of consciousness and say, "this, as a whole, consists of gray sensation number 350, of such and such extent, occurring in conjunction with the sensation of cold of a certain intensity; one of pressure of a certain intensity and extent," and so on *ad infinitum*. If psychology would follow the plan I suggest, the educator, the physician, the jurist and the business man could utilize our data in a practical way, as soon as we are able, experimentally, to obtain them. Those who have occasion to apply psychological principles practically would find no need to complain as they do at the present time. Ask any physician or jurist today whether scientific psychology plays a practical part in his daily routine and you will hear him deny that the psychology of the laboratories finds a place in his scheme of work. I think the criticism is extremely just. One of the earliest conditions which made me dissatisfied with psychology was the feeling that there was no realm of application for the principles which were being worked out in content terms.

What gives me hope that the behaviorist's position is a defensible one is the fact that those branches of psychology which have already partially withdrawn from the parent, experimental psychology, and which are consequently less dependent upon introspection are today in a most flourishing condition. Experimental pedagogy, the psychology of drugs, the psychology of advertising, legal psychology, the psychology of tests, and psychopathology are all vigorous growths. These are sometimes wrongly called "practical" or "applied" psychology. Surely there was never a worse misnomer. In the future there may grow up vocational bureaus which really apply psychology. At present these fields are truly scientific and are in search of broad generalizations which will lead to the control of human behavior. . . .

The man and the animal should be placed as nearly as possible under the same experimental conditions. Instead of feeding or punishing the human subject, we should ask him to respond by setting a second apparatus until standard and control offered no basis for a differential response. Do I lay myself open to the charge here that I am using introspection? My reply is not at all; that while I might very well feed my human subject for a right choice and punish him for a wrong one and thus produce the response if the subject could give it, there is no need of going to extremes even on the platform I suggest. . . .

Will there be left over in psychology a world of pure psychics, to use Yerkes' term? I confess I do not know. The plans which I most favor for psychology lead practically to the ignoring of consciousness in the sense that that term is used by psychologists today. I have virtually denied that this realm of psychics is open to experimental investigation. I don't wish to go further into the problem at present because it leads inevitably over into metaphysics. If you will grant the behaviorist the right to use consciousness in the same way that other natural scientists employ it—that is, without making consciousness a special object of observation—you have granted all that my thesis requires.

In concluding, I suppose I must confess to a deep bias on these questions. I have devoted nearly twelve years to experimentation on animals. It is natural that such a one should drift into a theoretical position which is in harmony with his experimental work. Possibly I have put up a straw man and have been fighting that. There may be no absolute lack of harmony between the position outlined here and that of functional psychology. I am inclined to think, however, that the two positions cannot be easily harmonized. Certainly the position I advocate is weak enough at present and can be attacked from many standpoints. Yet when all this is admitted I still feel that the considerations which I have urged should have a wide influence upon the type of psychology which is to be developed in the future. What we need to do is to start work upon psychology, making *behavior,* not *consciousness,* the objective point of our attack. Certainly there are enough problems in the control of behavior to keep us all working many lifetimes without ever allowing us time to think of consciousness *an sich*. Once launched in the undertaking, we will find ourselves in a short time as far divorced from an introspective psychology as the psychology of the present time is divorced from faculty psychology.

II

Pragmatism:
An American
Philosophical Adventure

ONE OF THE EARLY FRUITS of the evolutionary hypothesis was the formulation and development of the philosophy of pragmatism, perhaps the most important and original American contribution to the Western philosophical tradition. Pragmatism itself represented a sharp break from the Spencerian deterministic version of evolution. Spencer and his followers had postulated the idea that men could do nothing but conform to the inevitable laws of human development. The pragmatists, on the other hand, elaborated a philosophical method or system based upon possibility and contingency, maintaining that it was possible for accidents or novelties to arise that were not predictable from a knowledge of their antecedents. The adherents of pragmatism wanted to avoid the extremes of a thoroughgoing naturalistic determinism as well as of a Hegelian idealism, both of which had been based on a monistic system.

Tracing its antecedents to Chauncey Wright, who published one of the earliest critiques of Spencer from a naturalistic point of view, pragmatism received its initial, overt formulation by Charles S. Peirce. Hoping to end the philosophers' prolonged disputes that could not be settled by recourse to facts, Peirce proposed what was for that time a radical notion. He held that the meaning of any conception is to be found in the practical consequences that might result from it—the sum of these consequences would thus constitute the meaning of the conception. In other words, Peirce was stressing the fact that statements or ideas had to be experimentally verifiable. He also attacked all mechanistic and deterministic hypotheses and viewed scientific laws as statements of probabilities rather than absolutes.

The implications of Peirce's originality went largely unheeded until William James and John Dewey took up where he had left off. James presented pragmatism as a method that would settle the sterile metaphysical debates that had long plagued philosophy. For, if in examining and comparing given metaphysical propositions one finds no difference in their empirical consequences, "then the alternatives mean practically the same thing, and all dispute is idle." To James the goal of pragmatism was to understand ideas by testing their theoretical as well as their practical consequences.

It remained for John Dewey, however, to elaborate the pragmatic view most fully. Dewey became the outstanding philosophical exponent of democracy, naturalism, and the scientific method. He defined an idea as the plan of action relative to the solution to a given problem. It therefore followed that the experimental approach to meaning led to an experimental or contingent theory of truth. Thus truth was defined as the hypothesis that best controls the conditions and consequences of experience at any given moment. Extended further, Dewey's instrumentalism (the name given to his approach) stood for a maximum use of free, critical, and experimental intelligence in the preservation of democracy. Rejecting the "spectator theory of knowledge," he came to regard knowledge as a part of nature, its end being not simply passive adjustment, but the manipulation of the environment to achieve desirable ends.

Pragmatism, in other words, was a frankly experimental philosophy that rejected what it regarded as the sterility of previous philosophy in favor of an approach that judged the validity of ideas by their results. Democratic in its orientation, humane and optimistic in its outlook, adventurous in spirit, it provided industrial America with a rationale that seemed to give its citizens a means of developing a new morality capable of dealing with problems that the older theistic-individualistic-agrarian ethic had not been able to do. Pragmatism put philosophy at the service of society and dissolved the "steel chain of ideas"[1] implicit in Spencerian naturalistic determinism. From a social point of view pragmatism indicated that the central issue no longer revolved around individual salvation. Rather, the paramount problem was the reconstruction of society in such a manner as to provide the individual with a collective environment that dealt with the social and economic problems of an industrialized society while maintaining a framework conducive to his self-development. In pragmatism the progressive movement of the early twentieth century was to find much of its philosophical inspiration as it set about to transform American society through a democratic collectivism.

(6)

Charles S. Peirce

1839-1914

Born in Cambridge, Massachusetts, the son of the distinguished mathematician Benjamin Peirce, Charles Peirce was graduated from Harvard in 1859. In 1861 he joined the United States Coast Survey and

1. See Eric F. Goldman, *Rendezvous With Destiny: A History of Modern American Reform* (New York, 1952), pp. 85–104.

remained with this organization for nearly thirty years. During that time he did important work in pendulum experiments, and was one of the first men to attempt to use the wave length of a light ray as a standard unit of measure.

Despite his scientific interests, Peirce always regarded himself primarily as a logician. Coming to the study of formal logic through his philosophical inquiries, he easily became America's greatest logician. He was regarded by William James as the most original thinker of his generation. Peirce invented, among other things, two new logical algebras and two new systems of logical graphs, and he was the first to give the fundamental principle for the development of the logical analysis of mathematics. He also made immensely important contributions to probability theory, induction, and the logic of scientific methodology. In philosophy Peirce was one of the key figures among the formulators of the pragmatic method.

The following selection, taken from his two articles "What Pragmatism Is," *The Monist,* 15 (April, 1905) and "Issues of Pragmaticism," *The Monist,* 15 (October, 1905), is illustrative of his philosophical approach.

Let us now hasten to the exposition of pragmaticism itself. Here it will be convenient to imagine that somebody to whom the doctrine is new, but of rather preternatural perspicacity, asks questions of a pragmaticist. Everything that might give a dramatic illusion must be stripped off, so that the result would be a sort of cross between a dialogue and a catechism, but a good deal more like the latter—something rather painfully reminiscent of Mangnall's *Historical Questions.*

Questioner: I am astounded at your definition of your pragmatism, because only last year I was assured by a person above all suspicion of warping the truth—himself a pragmatist—that your doctrine precisely was "that a conception is to be tested by its practical effects." You must surely, then, have entirely changed your definition very recently.

Pragmatist: If you will turn to Volumes VI and VII of the *Revue Philosophique,* or the *Popular Science Monthly* for November 1877 and January 1878, you will be able to judge for yourself whether the interpretation you mention was not then clearly excluded. The exact wording of the English enunciation (changing only the first person into the second) was: "Consider what effects that might conceivably have practical bearing you conceive the object of your conception to have. Then your conception of those effects is the WHOLE of your conception of the object."

Questioner: Well, what reason have you for asserting that this is so?

Pragmatist: That is what I specially desire to tell you. But the question had better be postponed until you clearly understand what those reasons profess to prove.

Questioner: What, then, is the *raison d'être* of the doctrine? What advantage is expected from it?

Pragmatist: It will serve to show that almost every proposition of ontological metaphysics is either meaningless gibberish—one word being defined by other words, and they by still others, without any real conception ever being reached—or else is downright absurd; so that all such rubbish being swept away, what will remain of philosophy will be a series of problems capable of investigation by the observational methods of the true sciences—the truth about which can be reached without those interminable misunderstandings and disputes which have made the highest of the positive sciences a mere amusement for idle intellects, a sort of chess—idle pleasure its purpose, and reading out of a book its method. In this regard, pragmaticism is a species of prope-positivism. But what distinguishes it from other species is, first, its retention of a purified philosophy; secondly, its full acceptance of the main body of our instinctive beliefs; and thirdly, its strenuous insistence upon the truth of scholastic realism (or a close approximation to that, well stated by the late Dr. Francis Ellingwood Abbot in the Introduction to his *Scientific Theism*). So, instead of merely jeering at metaphysics, like other prope-positivists, whether by long-drawn-out parodies or otherwise, the pragmaticist extracts from it a precious essence, which will serve to give life and light to cosmology and physics. At the same time, the moral applications of the doctrine are positive and potent; and there are many other uses of it not easily classed. On another occasion, instances may be given to show that it really has these effects.

Questioner: I hardly need to be convinced that your doctrine would wipe out metaphysics. Is it not as obvious that it must wipe out every proposition of science and everything that bears on the conduct of life? For you say that the only meaning that, for you, any assertion bears is that a certain experiment has resulted in a certain way: nothing else but an experiment enters into the meaning. Tell me, then, how can an experiment, in itself, reveal anything more than that something once happened to an individual object and that subsequently some other individual event occurred?

Pragmatist: That question is, indeed, to the purpose—the purpose being to correct any misapprehensions of pragmaticism. You speak of an experiment in itself, emphasizing *in itself.* You evidently think of each experiment as isolated from every other. It has not, for example, occurred to you, one might venture to surmise, that every connected series of experiments constitutes a single collective experiment. What are the essential ingredients of an experiment? First, of course, an experimenter of flesh and blood. Secondly, a verifiable hypothesis. This is a proposition relating to the universe environing the experimenter, or to some well-known part of it and affirming or denying of this only some experimental possibility or impossibility. The third indispensable ingredient is a sincere doubt in the experimenter's mind as to the truth of that hypothesis.

Passing over several ingredients on which we need not dwell, the purpose, the plan, and the resolve, we come to the act of choice by which the experimenter singles out certain identifiable objects to be operated upon. The next is the external (or quasi-external) ACT by which he modifies those objects. Next, comes the subsequent *reaction* of the world upon the experimenter in a perception; and finally, his recognition of the teaching of the experiment. While the two chief parts of the event itself are the action and the reaction, yet the unity of essence of the experiment lies in its purpose and plan, the ingredients passed over in the enumeration.

Another thing: in representing the pragmaticist as making rational meaning to consist in an experiment (which you speak of as an event in the past), you strikingly fail to catch his attitude of mind. Indeed, it is not in an experiment, but in *experimental phenomena,* that rational meaning is said to consist. When an experimentalist speaks of a *phenomenon,* such as "Hall's phenomenon," "Zeemann's phenomenon" and its modification, "Michelson's phenomenon," or "the chessboard phenomenon," he does not mean any particular event that did happen to somebody in the dead past, but what *surely will* happen to everybody in the living future who shall fulfill certain conditions. The phenomenon consists in the fact that when an experimentalist shall come to *act* according to a certain scheme that he has in mind, then will something else happen, and shatter the doubts of skeptics, like the celestial fire upon the altar of Elijah.

And do not overlook the fact that the pragmaticist maxim says nothing of single experiments or of single experimental phenomena (for what is conditionally true *in futuro* can hardly be singular), but only speaks of *general kinds* of experimental phenomena. Its adherent does not shrink from speaking of general objects as real, since whatever is true represents a real. Now the laws of nature are true.

The rational meaning of every proposition lies in the future. How so? The meaning of a proposition is itself a proposition. Indeed, it is no other than the very proposition of which it is the meaning: it is a translation of it. But of the myriads of forms into which a proposition may be translated, what is that one which is to be called its very meaning? It is, according to the pragmaticist, that form in which the proposition becomes applicable to human conduct, not in these or those special circumstances, nor when one entertains this or that special design, but that form which is most directly applicable to self-control under every situation, and to every purpose. This is why he locates the meaning in future time; for future conduct is the only conduct that is subject to self-control. But in order that that form of the proposition which is to be taken as its meaning should be applicable to every situation and to every purpose upon which the proposition has any bearing, it must be simply the general description of all the experimental phenomena which the assertion of the proposition virtually predicts. For an experimental phenomenon is the fact asserted by the proposition that action of a certain description will have a certain kind of experimental result; and experimental results are the only results that can affect human conduct. No doubt, some unchanging idea may come to influence a man more than it had done; but only because some experience equivalent to an experiment has brought its truth home to him more intimately than before. Whenever a man acts purposively, he acts under a belief in some experimental phenomenon. Consequently, the sum of the experimental phenomena that a proposition implies makes up its entire bearing upon human conduct. Your question, then, of how a pragmaticist can attribute any meaning to any assertion other than that of a single occurrence is substantially answered. . . .

Questioner: Well, if you choose so to make Doing the Be-all and the End-all of human life, why do you not make meaning to consist simply in doing? Doing has to be done at a certain time upon a certain object. Individual objects and single events cover all reality, as everybody knows, and as a practicalist ought to be the first to insist. Yet, your meaning, as you have described it, is *general*. Thus, it is of the nature of a mere word and not a reality. You say yourself that your meaning of a proposition is only the same proposition in another dress. But a practical man's meaning is the very thing he means. What do you make to be the meaning of "George Washington"?

Pragmatist: Forcibly put! A good half dozen of your points must certainly be admitted. It must be admitted, in the first place, that if pragmaticism really made Doing to be the Be-all and the End-all of life, that would be its death. For to say that we live for the mere sake of action, as action, regardless of the thought it carries out, would be to say that there is no such thing as rational purport. Secondly, it must be admitted that every proposition professes to be true of a certain real, individual object, often the environing universe. Thirdly, it must be admitted that pragmaticism fails to furnish any translation or meaning of a proper name, or other designation of an individual object. Fourthly, the pragmaticistic meaning is undoubtedly general; and it is equally indisputable that the general is of the nature of a word or sign. Fifthly, it must be admitted that individuals alone exist; and sixthly, it may be admitted that the very meaning of a word or significant object ought to be the very essence of reality of what it signifies. But when those admissions have been unreservedly made, if you find the pragmaticist still constrained most earnestly to deny the force of your objection, you ought to infer that there is some consideration that has escaped you. Putting the admissions together, you will perceive that the pragmaticist grants that a proper name (although it is not customary to say that it has a *meaning*) has a certain denotative function peculiar, in each case, to that name and its equivalents; and that he grants that every assertion contains such a denotative or pointing-out function. In its peculiar individuality, the pragmaticist excludes this from the rational purport of the assertion, although *the like* of it, being common to all assertions, and so, being general and not individual, may enter into the pragmaticistic purport. Whatever exists, *ex-sists,* that is, really acts upon other existents, so obtains a self-identity, and is definitely individual. As to the general, it will be a help to thought to notice that there are two ways of being general. A statue of a soldier on some village monument, in his overcoat and with his musket, is for each of a hundred families the image of its uncle, its sacrifice to the Union. That statue, then, though it is itself single, represents any one man of whom a certain predicate may be true. It is *objectively* general. The word "soldier," whether spoken or written, is general in the same way; while the name "George Washington" is not so. But each of these two terms remains one and the same noun, whether it be spoken or written, and whenever and wherever it be spoken or written. This noun is not an existent thing: it is a *type,* or *form,* to which objects, both those that are externally existent and those which are imagined, may *conform,* but which none of them can exactly be. This is subjective generality. The pragmaticistic purport is general in both ways.

As to reality, one finds it defined in various ways; but if that principle of terminological ethics that was proposed be accepted, the equivocal language will soon disappear. For *realis* and *realitas* are not ancient words. They were invented to be terms of philosophy in the thirteenth century, and the meaning they were intended to express is perfectly clear. That is *real* which has such and such characters, whether anybody thinks it to have those characters or not. At any rate, that is the sense in which the pragmaticist uses the word. Now, just as conduct controlled by ethical reason tends toward fixing certain habits of conduct, the nature of which (as, to illustrate the meaning, peaceable habits and not quarrelsome habits) does not depend upon any accidental circumstances, and *in that sense* may be said to be *destined;* so, thought, controlled by a rational experimental logic, tends to the fixation of certain opinions, equally destined, the nature of which will be the same in the end, however the perversity of thought of whole generations may cause the postponement of the ultimate fixation. If this be so, as every man of us virtually assumes that it is, in regard to each matter the truth of which he seriously discusses, then, according to the adopted definition of "real," the state of things which will be believed in that ultimate opinion is real. But, for the most part, such opinions will be general. Consequently, *some* general objects are real. (Of course, nobody ever thought that *all* generals were real; but the scholastics used to assume that generals were real when they had hardly any, or quite no, experiential evidence to support their assumption; and their fault lay just there, and not in holding that generals could be real.) One is struck with the inexactitude of thought even of analysts of power, when they touch upon modes of being. One will meet, for example, the virtual assumption that what is relative to thought cannot be real. But why not, exactly? *Red* is relative to sight, but the fact that this or that is in that relation to vision that we call being red is not *itself* relative to sight; it is a real fact.

Not only may generals be real, but they may also be *physically efficient,* not in every metaphysical sense, but in the common-sense acception in which human purposes are physically efficient. Aside from metaphysical nonsense, no sane man doubts that if I feel the air in my study to be stuffy, that thought may cause the window to be opened. My thought, be it granted, was an individual event. But what determined it to take the particular determination it did, was in part the general fact that stuffy air is unwholesome, and in part other *Forms,* concerning which Dr. Carus has caused so many men to reflect to advantage—or rather, *by* which, and the general truth concerning which Dr. Carus's mind was determined to the forcible enunciation of so much truth. For truths, on the average, have a greater tendency to get believed than falsities have. Were it otherwise, considering that there are myriads of false hypotheses to account for any given phenomenon, against one sole true one (or if you will have it so, against every true one), the first step toward genuine knowledge must have been next door to a miracle. So, then, when my window was opened, because of the truth that stuffy air is *malsain,* a physical effort was brought into existence by the efficiency of a general and non-existent truth. This has a droll sound because it is unfamiliar; but exact analysis is with it and not against it; and it has besides, the immense advantage of not blinding us to great facts—such as that the ideas "justice" and "truth" are, notwithstanding the iniquity of the world, the mightiest of the forces that move it. Generality is, indeed, an indispensable ingredient of reality; for mere individual existence or actuality without any regularity whatever is a nullity. Chaos is pure nothing.

That which any true proposition asserts is *real,* in the sense of being as it is regardless of what you or I may think about it. Let this proposition be a general conditional proposition as to the future, and it is a real general such as is calculated really to influence human conduct; and such the pragmaticist holds to be the rational purport of every concept.

Accordingly, the pragmaticist does not make the *summum bonum* to consist in action, but makes it to consist in that process of evolution whereby the existent comes more and more to embody those generals which were just now said to be *destined,* which is what we strive to express in calling them *reasonable.* In its higher stages, evolution takes place more and more largely through self-control, and this gives the pragmaticist a sort of justification for making the rational purport to be general. . . .

A good question, for the purpose of illustrating the nature of Pragmaticism, is, What is Time? It is not proposed to attack those most difficult problems connected with the psychology, the epistemology, or the metaphysics of Time, although it will be taken for granted, as it must be according to what has been said, that Time is real. The reader is only invited to the humbler question of what we mean by Time, and not of every kind of meaning attached to Past, Present, and Future either. Certain peculiar feelings are associated with the three general determinations of Time; but those are to be sedulously put out of view. That the reference of events to Time is irresistible will be recognized; but as to how it may differ from other kinds of irresistibility is a question not here to be considered. The question to be considered is simply, What is the intellectual purport of the Past, Present, and Future? It can only be treated with the utmost brevity.

That Time is a particular variety of objective Modality is too obvious for argumentation. The Past consists of the sum of *faits accomplis,* and this Accomplishment is the Existential Mode of Time. For the Past really acts upon us, and *that* it does, not at all in the way in which a Law or Principle influences us, but precisely as an Existent object acts. For instance, when a *Nova Stella* bursts out in the heavens, it acts upon one's eyes just as a light struck in the dark by one's own hands would; and yet it is an event which happened before the Pyramids were built. A neophyte may remark that its reaching the eyes, which is all we know, happens but a fraction of a second before we know it. But a moment's consideration will show him that he is losing sight of the question, which is not whether the distant Past can act upon us *immediately,* but whether it acts upon us just as any Existent does. The instance adduced (certainly a commonplace enough fact) proves conclusively that the mode of the Past is that of Actuality. Nothing of the sort is true of the Future, to compass the understanding of which it is indispensable that the reader should divest himself of his Necessitarianism—at best, but a scientific theory—and return to the Common-sense State of Nature. Do you never say to yourself, "I *can* do this or that as well tomorrow as today"? Your Necessitarianism is a theoretical pseudo-belief—a make-believe belief—that such a sentence does not express the real truth. That is only to stick to proclaiming the unreality of that Time, of which you are invited, be it reality or figment, to consider the meaning. You need not fear to compromise your darling theory by looking out at its windows. Be it true in theory or not, the unsophisticated conception is that everything in the Future is either *destined,* i.e., necessitated already, or is *undecided,* the contingent future of Aristotle. In other words, it is not Actual, since it does not act except through the idea of it, that is, as a law acts; but is either Necessary or Possible, which are of the same mode since (as remarked above) Negation being outside the category of modality cannot produce a variation in Modality. As for the Present instant, it is so inscrutable that I wonder whether no skeptic has ever attacked its reality. I can fancy one of them dipping his pen in his blackest ink to commence the assault, and then suddenly reflecting that his entire life is in the Present—the "living present," as we say, this instant when all hopes and fears concerning it come to their end, this Living Death in which we are born anew. It is plainly that Nascent State between the Determinate and the Indeterminate that was noticed above.

Pragmaticism consists in holding that the purport of any concept is its conceived bearing upon our conduct. How, then, does the Past bear upon conduct? The answer is self-evident: whenever we set out to do anything, we "go upon," we base our conduct on facts already known, and for these we can only draw upon our memory. It is true that we may institute a new investigation for the purpose; but its discoveries will only become applicable to conduct after they have been made and reduced to a memorial maxim. In short, the Past is the storehouse of all our knowledge.

When we say that we know that some state of things exists, we mean that it used to exist, whether just long enough for the news to reach the brain and be retransmitted to tongue or pen, or longer ago. Thus, from whatever point of view we contemplate the Past, it appears as the Existential Mode of Time.

How does the Future bear upon conduct? The answer is that future facts are the only facts that we can, in a measure, control; and whatever there may be in the Future that is not amenable to control are the things that we *shall* be able to infer, or *should* be able to infer, under favorable circumstances. There may be questions concerning which the pendulum of opinion never would cease to oscillate, however favorable circumstances may be. But if so, those questions are *ipso facto* not *real* questions, that is to say, are questions to which there is no true answer to be given. It is natural to use the future tense (and the conditional mood is but a mollified future) in drawing a conclusion or in stating a consequence. "If two unlimited straight lines in one plane and crossed by a third making the sum . . . then these straight lines *will* meet on the side, etc." It cannot be denied that acritical inferences may refer to the Past in its capacity as past; but according to Pragmaticism, the conclusion of a Reasoning power must refer to the Future. For its meaning refers to conduct, and since it is a reasoned conclusion, must refer to deliberate conduct, which is controllable conduct. But the only controllable conduct is Future conduct. As for that part of the Past that lies beyond memory, the Pragmaticist doctrine is that the meaning of its being believed to be in connection with the Past consists in the acceptance as truth of the conception that we ought to conduct ourselves according to it (like the meaning of any other belief). Thus, a belief that Christopher Columbus discovered America really refers to the future. It is more difficult, it must be confessed, to account for beliefs that rest upon the double evidence of feeble but direct memory and upon rational inference. The difficulty does not seem insuperable; but it must be passed by.

What is the bearing of the Present instant upon conduct?

Introspection is wholly a matter of inference. One is immediately conscious of his Feelings, no doubt; but not that they are feelings of an *ego*. The *self* is only inferred. There is no time in the Present for any inference at all, least of all for inference concerning that very instant. Consequently, the present object must be an external object, if there be any objective reference in it. The attitude of the Present is either conative or perceptive. Supposing it to be perceptive, the perception must be immediately known as external—not indeed in the sense in which a hallucination is *not* external, but in the sense of being present regardless of the perceiver's will or wish. Now this kind of externality is conative externality. Consequently, the attitude of the present instant (according to the testimony of Common Sense, which is plainly adopted throughout) can only be a Conative attitude. The consciousness of the present is then that of a struggle over what shall be; and thus we emerge from the study with a confirmed belief that it is the Nascent State of the Actual.

But how is Temporal Modality distinguished from other Objective Modality? Not by any general character since Time is unique and *sui generis*. In other words, there is only one Time. Sufficient attention has hardly been called to the surpassing truth of this for Time as compared with its truth for Space. Time, therefore, can only be identified by brute compulsion. But we must not go further.

(7)

William James

1842-1910

Born in New York City, William James was one of the first products of the scientific education that was emerging in America after the Civil War. Trained at Harvard's Lawrence Scientific School, he received an M.D. from Harvard in 1869 and was associated with that institution for most of his life, first as an instructor in physiology and later as a professor of philosophy. A passionate believer in free will, he opposed all deterministic philosophical systems that did not admit the factor of chance. He also dealt on many occasions with the competing claims of science and religion, attempting to erect a mode of thought that left room for both. James was a bitter foe of Spencer, largely because he was seeking an experimental approach (as Spencer was not) that emphasized active human effort operating in an unfinished world.

Not only was James an outstanding philosopher, but he also laid the foundation for the emergence of psychology as an independent discipline in America and established one of the first psychological laboratories in this country. His psychological system was based upon the active role of the self, and he was critical of those individuals who looked upon the mind as a quiet cognitive organ. Thus, the direction of James's psychological and philosophical inquiries led him to pragmatism as the basis of his scientific and philosophic systems. His emphasis on pragmatism, it must be pointed out, was not in any way related to a consideration merely of worldly success, for his use of the term "practical" did not exclude any human motive, whether aesthetic, moral, or intellectual.

The following selection is from a famous series of public lectures delivered in 1906 at the Lowell Institute in Boston and in 1907 at Columbia University, reprinted under the title *Pragmatism* (New York, 1907).

The pragmatic method is primarily a method of settling metaphysical disputes that otherwise might be interminable. Is the world one or many?—fated or free?—material or spiritual?—here are notions either of which may or may not hold good of the world; and disputes over such notions are unending. The pragmatic method in such cases is to try to interpret each notion by tracing its respective practical consequences. What difference would it practically make to any one if this notion rather than that notion were true? If no practical difference whatever can be traced, then the alternatives mean practically the same thing, and all dispute is idle. Whenever a dispute is serious, we ought to be able to show some practical difference that must follow from one side or the other's being right.

A glance at the history of the idea will show you still better what pragmatism means. The term is derived from the same Greek word πράγμα, meaning action, from which our words 'practice' and 'practical' come. It was first introduced into philosophy by Mr. Charles Peirce in 1878. In an article entitled "How to Make Our Ideas Clear," in the *Popular Science Monthly* for January of that year Mr. Peirce, after pointing out that our beliefs are really rules for action, said that, to develop a thought's meaning, we need only determine what conduct it is fitted to produce: that conduct is for us its sole significance. And the tangible fact at the root of all our thought-distinctions, however subtle, is that there is no one of them so fine as to consist in anything but a possible difference of practice. To attain perfect clearness in our thoughts of an object, then, we need only consider what conceivable effects of a practical kind the object may involve—what sensations we are to expect from it, and what reactions we must prepare. Our conception of these effects, whether immediate or remote, is then for us the whole of our conception of the object, so far as that conception has positive significance at all. . . .

There is absolutely nothing new in the pragmatic method. Socrates was an adept at it. Aristotle used it methodically. Locke, Berkeley, and Hume made momentous contributions to truth by its means. Shadworth Hodgson keeps insisting that realities are only what they are "known as." But these forerunners of pragmatism used it in fragments: they were preluders only. Not until in our time has it generalized itself, become conscious of a universal mission, pretended to a conquering destiny. I believe in that destiny, and I hope I may end by inspiring you with my belief.

Pragmatism represents a perfectly familiar attitude in philosophy, the empiricist attitude, but it represents it, as it seems to me, both in a more radical and in a less objectionable form than it has ever yet assumed. A pragmatist turns his back resolutely and once for all upon a lot of inveterate habits dear to professional philosophers. He turns away from abstraction and insufficiency, from verbal solutions, from bad *a priori* reasons, from fixed principles, closed systems, and pretended absolutes and origins. He turns towards concreteness and adequacy, towards facts, towards action and towards power. That means the empiricist temper regnant and the rationalist temper sincerely given up. It means the open air and possibilities of nature, as against dogma, artificiality, and the pretence of finality in truth.

At the same time it does not stand for any special results. It is a method only. But the general triumph of that method would mean an enormous change in what I called in my last lecture the "temperament" of philosophy. Teachers of the ultra-rationalistic type would be frozen out, much as the courtier type is frozen out in republics, as the ultramontane type of priest is frozen out in protestant lands. Science and metaphysics would come much nearer together, would in fact work absolutely hand in hand.

Metaphysics has usually followed a very primitive kind of quest. You know how men have always hankered after unlawful magic, and you know what a great part in magic *words* have always played. If you have his name, or the formula of incantation that binds him, you can control the spirit, genie, afrite, or whatever the power may be. Solomon knew the names of all the spirits, and having their names, he held them subject to his will. So the universe has always appeared to the natural mind as a kind of enigma, of which the key must be sought in the shape of some illuminating or power-bringing word or name. That word names the universe's *principle,* and to possess it is after a fashion to possess the universe itself. "God," "Matter," "Reason," "the Absolute," "Energy," are so many solving names. You can rest when you have them. You are at the end of your metaphysical quest.

But if you follow the pragmatic method, you cannot look on any such word as closing your quest. You must bring out of each word its practical cash-value, set it at work within the stream of your experience. It appears less as a solution, then, than as a program for more work, and more particularly as an indication of the ways in which existing realities may be *changed.*

Theories thus become instruments, not answers to enigmas, in which we can rest. We don't lie back upon them, we move forward, and, on occasion, make nature over again by their aid. Pragmatism unstiffens all our theories, limbers them up and sets each one at work. Being nothing essentially new, it harmonizes with many ancient philosophic tendencies. It agrees with nominalism for instance, in always appealing to particulars; with utilitarianism in emphasizing practical aspects; with positivism in its disdain for verbal solutions, useless questions and metaphysical abstractions.

All these, you see, are *anti-intellectualist* tendencies. Against rationalism as a pretension and a method pragmatism is fully armed and militant. But, at the outset, at least, it stands for no particular results. It has no dogmas, and no doctrines save its method. As the young Italian pragmatist Papini has well said, it lies in the midst of our theories, like a corridor in a hotel. Innumerable chambers open out of it. In one you may find a man writing an atheistic volume; in the next some one on his knees praying for faith and strength; in a third a chemist investigating a body's properties. In a fourth a system of idealistic metaphysics is being excogitated; in a fifth the impossibilty of metaphysics is being shown. But they all own the corridor, and all must pass through it if they want a practicable way of getting into or out of their respective rooms. . . .

You see by this what I meant when I called pragmatism a mediator and reconciler and said, borrowing the word from Papini, that she "unstiffens" our theories. She has in fact no prejudices whatever, no obstructive dogmas, no rigid canons of what shall count as proof. She is completely genial. She will entertain any hypothesis, she will consider any evidence. It follows that in the religious field she is at a great advantage both over positivistic empiricism, with its anti-theological bias, and over religious rationalism, with its exclusive interest in the remote, the noble, the simple, and the abstract in the way of conception.

In short, she widens the field of search for God. Rationalism sticks to logic and the empyrean. Empiricism sticks to the external senses. Pragmatism is willing to take anything, to follow either logic or the senses and to count the humblest and most personal experiences. She will count mystical experiences if they have practical consequences. She will take a God who lives in the very dirt of private fact—if that should seem a likely place to find him.

Her only test of probable truth is what works best in the way of leading us, what fits every part of life best and combines with the collectivity of experience's demands, nothing being omitted. If theological ideas should do this, if the notion of God, in particular, should prove to do it, how could pragmatism possibly deny God's existence? She could see no meaning in treating as 'not true' a notion that was pragmatically so successful. What other kind of truth could there be, for her, than all this agreement with concrete reality?

(8)

John Dewey

1859-1952

The following selection is from a lecture given by Dewey at Columbia University in 1908, and published in pamphlet form under the title *Ethics* (New York, 1908). [For Dewey's career see pp. 38–39.]

Since the Renaissance, moral philosophy has repeatedly reverted to the Greek ideal of natural excellence realized in social life, under the fostering care of intelligence in action. The return, however, has taken place under the influence of democratic polity, commercial expansion and scientific reorganization. It has been a liberation even more than a reversion. This combined return and emancipation, having transformed our practice of life in the last four centuries, will not be content till it has written itself clear in our theory of that practice. Whether the consequent revolution in moral philosophy be termed pragmatism or be given the happier title of the applied and experimental habit of mind is of little account. What is of moment is that intelligence has descended from its lonely isolation at the remote edge of things, whence it operated as unmoved mover and ultimate good, in order to take its seat in the moving affairs of men. Theory may therefore become responsible to the practices which have generated it; the good be connected with nature, but with nature naturally, not metaphysically, conceived, and social life be cherished in behalf of its own immediate possibilities, not on the ground of its remote connexions with a cosmic reason and an absolute end. . . .

The growth of industry and commerce is at once cause and effect of the growth in science. Democritus and other ancients conceived the mechanical theory of the universe. The notion was not only blank and repellent, because it ignored the rich social material which Plato and Aristotle had organized into their rival idealistic views; but it was scientifically sterile, a piece of dialectics. Contempt for machines as the accoutrements of despised mechanics kept the mechanical conception aloof from these specific and controllable experiences which alone could fructify it. This conception, then, like the idealistic, was translated into a speculative cosmology and thrown like a vast net around the universe at large, as if to keep it from coming to pieces. It is from respect for the lever, the pulley and the screw that modern experimental and mathematical mechanics derives itself. Motion, traced through the workings of a machine, was followed out into natural events and studied just as motion, not as a poor yet necessary device for realizing final causes. So studied, it was found to be available for new machines and new applications, which in creating new ends also promoted new wants, and thereby stimulated new activities, new discoveries and new inventions. The recognition that natural energy can be systematically applied, through experimental observation, to the satisfaction and multiplication of concrete wants is doubtless the greatest single discovery ever imported into the life of man—save perhaps the discovery of language. Science, borrowing from industry, repaid the debt with interest, and has made the control of natural forces for the aims of life so inevitable, that for the first time man is relieved from overhanging fear, with its wolflike scramble to possess and accumulate, and is freed to consider the more gracious question of securing to all an ample and liberal life. The industrial life had been condemned by Greek exaltation of abstract thought and by Greek contempt for labor as representing the brute struggle of carnal appetite for its own satiety. The industrial movement, offspring of science, restored it to its central position in morals. When Adam Smith made economic activity the moving spring of man's unremitting effort, from the cradle to the grave, to better his own lot, he recorded this change. And when he made sympathy the central spring in man's conscious moral endeavor, he reported the effect which the increasing intercourse of men, due primarily to commerce, had in breaking down suspicion and jealousy and in liberating man's kindlier impulses.

Democracy, the crucial expression of modern life, is not so much an addition to the scientific and industrial tendencies as it is the perception of their social or spiritual meaning. Democracy is an absurdity where faith in the individual as individual is impossible; and this faith is impossible when intelligence is regarded as a cosmic power, not an adjustment and application of individual tendencies. It is impossible when appetites and desires are conceived to be the dominant factor in the constitution of most men's characters, and when appetite and desire are conceived to be manifestations of the disorderly and unruly principle of nature. To put the intellectual centre of gravity in the objective cosmos, outside of men's own experiments and tests, and then to invite the application of individual intelligence to the determination of society is to invite chaos. To hold that want is mere negative flux and hence requires external fixation by reason, and then to invite the wants to give free play to themselves in social construction and intercourse is to call down anarchy. Democracy was conceivable only with a changed conception of the intelligence that forms modern science and the want that forms modern industry. It is essentially a changed psychology. The substitution, for *a priori* truth and deduction, of fluent doubt and inquiry meant trust in human nature in the concrete; in individual honesty, curiosity and sympathy. The substitution of moving commerce for fixed custom meant a view of wants as the dynamics of social progress, not as the pathology of private greed. The nineteenth century indeed turned sour on that somewhat complacent optimism in which the eighteenth century rested: the ideas that the intelligent self-love of individuals would conduce to social cohesion, and competition among individuals usher in the kingdom of social welfare. But the conception of a social harmony of interests in which the achievement by each individual of his own freedom should contribute to a like perfecting of the powers of all, through a fraternally organized society, is the permanent contribution of the industrial movement to morals—even though so far it be but the contribution of a problem.

Intellectually speaking, the centuries since the fourteenth are the true middle ages. They mark the transitional period of mental habit, as the so-called medieval period represents the petrification, under changed outward conditions, of Greek ideas. The conscious articulation of genuinely modern tendencies has yet to come, and till it comes the ethic of our own life must remain undescribed. But the system of morals which has come nearest to the reflection of the movements of science, democracy and commerce, is doubtless the utilitarian. Scientific, after the modern mode, it certainly would be. Newton's influence dyes deep the moral thought of the eighteenth century. The arrangements of the solar system had been described in terms of a homogeneous matter and motion, worked by two opposed and compensating forces: all because a method analysis, of generalization by analogy, and of mathematical deduction back to new empirical details had been followed. The imagination of the eighteenth century was a Newtonian imagination; and this no less in social than in physical matters. Hume proclaims that morals is about to become an experimental science. Just as, almost in our own day, Mill's interest in a method for social science led him to reformulate the logic of experimental inquiry, so all the great men of the Enlightenment were in search for the organon of morals which should repeat the physical triumphs of Newton. Bentham notes that physics has had its Bacon and Newton; that morals has had its Bacon in Helvétius, but still awaits its Newton; and he leaves us in no doubt that at the moment of writing he was ready, modestly but firmly, to fill the waiting niche with its missing figure.

The industrial movement furnished the concrete imagery for this ethical renovation. The utilitarians borrowed from Adam Smith the notion that through industrial exchange in a free society the individual pursuing his own good is led, under the guidance of the "invisible hand," to promote the general good more effectually than if he had set out to do it. This idea was dressed out in the atomistic psychology which Hartley built out from Locke—and returned at usurious rates to later economists.

From the great French writers who had sought to justify and promote democratic individualism, came the conception that, since it is perverted political institutions which deprave individuals and bring them into hostility, nation against nation, class against class, individual against individual, the great political problem is that reform of law and legislation, civic and criminal, of administration, and of education which will force the individual to find his own interest in pursuits which conduce to the welfare of others.

Tremendously effective as a tool of criticism, operative in abolition and elimination, utilitarianism failed to measure up to the constructive needs of the time. Its theoretical equalization of the good of each with that of every other was practically perverted by its excessive interest in the middle and manufacturing classes. Its speculative defect of an atomistic psychology combined with this narrowness of vision to make light of the constructive work that needs to be done by the state, before all can have, otherwise than in name, an equal chance to count in the common good. Thus the age-long subordination of economics to politics was revenged in the submerging of both politics and ethics in a narrow theory of economic profit; and utilitarianism, in its orthodox descendants, proffered the disjointed pieces of a mechanism, with a monotonous reiteration that if looked at aright they form a beautifully harmonious organism. . . .

Unstable equilibrium, rapid fermentation and a succession of explosive reports are thus the chief notes of modern ethics. Scepticism and traditionalism, empiricism and rationalism, crude naturalisms and all embracing idealisms, flourish side by side—all the more flourish, one suspects, because side by side. Spencer exults that natural science reveals that the rapid transit system of evolution is carrying us automatically to the goal of a perfect man in a perfect society; and his English idealistic contemporary is so disturbed by the removal from nature of its moral qualities, that he tries to show that it makes no difference, since nature in any case is known through a spiritual principle which is as permanent as nature is changing. An Amiel genteelly laments the decadence of the inner life, while his neighbor Nietzsche brandishes in rude ecstasy the banner of brute survival as a happy omen of the final victory of nobility of mind. The reasonable conclusion from such a scene is that there is taking place a transformation of attitude towards moral theory rather than mere propagation of varieties among theories. The classic theories all agree in one regard. They all alike assumed the existence of *the* end, the *summum bonum,* the final goal; and of *the* separate moral force which moves to that goal. Moralists have disputed as to whether the end is an aggregate of pleasurable state of consciousness, enjoyment of the divine essence, acknowledgment of the law of duty, or conformity to environment. So they have disputed as to the path by which the final goal is to be reached: fear or benevolence? reverence for pure law or pity for others? self-love or altruism? But these very controversies imply that there was but the one end and the one means.

The transformation in attitude, to which I referred, is the growing belief that the proper business of intelligence is discrimination of multiple and present goods and of the varied immediate means of their realization; not search for the one remote aim. The progress of biology has accustomed our minds to the notion that intelligence is not an outside power presiding supremely but statically over the desires and efforts of man, but that it is a method of adjustment of capacities and conditions within specific situations. History, as the lecturer on that subject told us, has discovered itself in the idea of process. The genetic standpoint makes us aware that the systems of the past are neither fraudulent imposture nor absolute revelations; but are the products of political, economic and scientific conditions whose change carries with it change of reflective formulations. The recognition that intelligence is properly an organ of adjustment in difficult situations makes us aware that these past theories were of value so far as they helped carry to an issue the social perplexities from which they emerged. But the chief impact of the evolutionary method is upon the present. Theory having learned what it cannot do, is made responsible for the better performance of what needs to be done, and what only a broadly equipped intelligence can do: to study the conditions out of which come the obstacles and the resources of adequate life, and to develop and test the ideas which, as working hypotheses, may be used to diminish the causes of evil and buttress and expand the sources of good. This program is indeed vague, but only unfamiliarity with it could lead one to the conclusion that it is less vague than the idea that there is a single moral ideal and a single moral motive force.

From this point of view there is no separate body of moral rules; no separate system of motive powers; no separate subject-matter of moral knowledge, and hence no such thing as an isolated ethical science. If the business of morals is not to speculate upon man's final end, and upon an ultimate standard of right, it is to utilize physiology, anthropology and psychology to discover all that can be discovered of man, his organic powers and propensities. If its business is not to search for the one separate moral motive, it is to converge all the instrumentalities of the social arts, of law, education, economics and political science upon the construction of intelligent methods of improving the common lot.

If we still wish to make our peace with the past, and to sum up the plural and changing goods of life in a single word, doubtless the term happiness is the one most apt. But we should again exchange free morals for sterile metaphysics, if we imagine that "happiness" is any less unique than the individuals who experience it; any less complex than the constitution of their capacities, or any less variable than the objects upon which their capacities are directed.

To many timid, albeit sincere, souls of an earlier century, the decay of the doctrine that all true and worthful science is knowledge of final causes seemed fraught with danger to science and to morals. The rival conception of a wide open universe, a universe without bounds in time or space, without final limits of origin or destiny, the universe with the lid off, was a menace. We now face in moral science a similar crisis and like opportunity, as well as share in a like dreadful suspense. The abolition of a fixed and final goal and causal force in nature did not, as matter of fact, render rational conviction less important or less attainable. It was accompanied by the provision of a technique of persistent and detailed inquiry in all special fields of fact, a technique which led to the detection of unsuspected forces and the revelation of undreamed of uses. In like fashion we may anticipate that the abolition of *the* final goal and *the* single motive power and *the* separate and infallible faculty in morals, will quicken inquiry into all the diversity of specific goods of experience, fix attention upon their conditions and bring to light values now dim and obscure. The change may relieve men from responsibility for what they cannot do, but it will promote thoughtful consideration of what they may do and the definition of responsibility for what they do amiss, because of failure to think straight and carefully. Absolute goods will fall into the background, but the question of making more sure and extensive the share of all men in natural and social goods will be urgent, a problem not to be escaped or evaded.

Morals, philosophy, returns to its first love; love of the wisdom that is nurse, as nature is mother, of good. But it returns to the Socratic principle equipped with a multitude of special methods of inquiry and testing; with an organized mass of knowledge, and with control of the arrangements by which industry, law and education may concentrate upon the problem of the participation by all men and women, up to their capacity of absorption, in all attained values. Morals may then well leave to poetry and to art, the task (so unartistically performed by philosophy since Plato) of gathering together and rounding out, into one abiding picture, the separate and special goods of life. It may leave this task with the assurance that the resultant synthesis will not depict any final and all inclusive good, but will add just one more specific good to the enjoyable excellencies of life.

Humorous irony shines through most of the harsh glances turned towards the idea of an experimental basis and career for morals. Some shiver in the fear that morals will be plunged into anarchic confusion—a view well expressed by a recent writer in the saying that if the *a priori* and transcendental basis of morals be abandoned "we shall have merely the same certainty that now exists in physics and chemistry"! Elsewhere lurks the apprehension that the progress of scientific method will deliver the purposive freedom of man bound hand and foot to the fatal decrees of iron necessity, called natural law. The notion that laws govern and forces rule is an animistic survival. It is a product of reading nature in terms of politics in order then to turn about and read politics in the light of supposed sanctions of nature. This idea passed from medieval theology into the science of Newton, to whom the universe was the dominion of a sovereign whose laws were the laws of nature. From Newton it passed into the deism of the eighteenth century, whence it migrated into the philosophy of the Enlightenment, to make its last stand in Spencer's philosophy of the fixed environment and the static goal.

No, nature is not an unchangeable order, unwinding itself majestically from the reel of law under the control of deified forces. It is an indefinite congeries of changes. Laws are not governmental regulations which limit change, but are convenient formulations of selected portions of change followed through a longer or shorter period of time, and then registered in those statistical forms which are amenable to mathematical manipulation. That this device of shorthand symbolization presages the subjection of man's intelligent effort to fixity of law and environment is interesting as a culture survival, but is not important for moral theory. Savage and child delight in creating bogeys from which, in concealing their origin and structure, interesting thrills and shudders may be had. Civilized man in the nineteenth century outdid these bugaboos in his image of a fixed universe hung on a cast-iron framework of fixed, necessary and universal laws. Knowledge of nature does not mean subjection to predestination, but insight into courses of change; an insight which is formulated in "laws," that is, methods of subsequent procedure.

Knowledge of the process and conditions of physical and social change by experimental science and genetic history has one result with a double name: increase of control and increase of responsibility; increase of power to direct natural change, and increase of responsibility for its equitable direction toward fuller good. Theory located within progressive practice instead of reigning statically supreme over it, means practice itself made responsible to intelligence; to intelligence which relentlessly scrutinizes the consequences of every practice, and which exacts liability by an equally relentless publicity. As long as morals occupies itself with mere ideals, forces and conditions as they are will be good enough for "practical" men, since they are then left free to their own devices in turning these to their own account. As long as moralists plume themselves upon possession of the domain of the categorical imperative with its bare precepts, men of executive habits will always be at their elbows to regulate the concrete social conditions through which the form of law gets its actual filling of specific injunctions. When freedom is conceived to be transcendental, the coercive restraint of immediate necessity will lay its harsh hand upon the mass of men.

In the end, men do what they can do. They refrain from doing what they cannot do. They do what their own specific powers in conjunction with the limitations and resources of the environment permit. The effective control of their powers is not through precepts, but through the regulation of their conditions. If this regulation is itself to be not merely physical or coercive, but moral, it must consist of the intelligent selection and determination of the environments in which we act; and in an intelligent exaction of responsibility for the use of men's powers. Theorists inquire after the "motive" to morality, to virtue and the good, under such circumstances. What then, one wonders, is their conception of the make-up of human nature and of its relation to virtue and to goodness? The pessimism which dictates such a question, if it be justified, precludes any consideration of morals.

The diversion of intelligence from discrimination of plural and concrete goods, from noting their conditions and obstacles, and from the task of devising methods for holding men responsible for their concrete use of powers and conditions, has done more than brute love of power to establish inequality and injustice among men. It has done more, because it has confirmed with social sanctions the principle of feudal domination. All men require moral sanctions in their conduct: the consent of their kind. Not getting it otherwise, they go insane to feign it. No man ever lived with the exclusive approval of his own conscience. Hence the vacuum left in practical matters by the remote irrelevancy of transcendental morals has to be filled in somehow. It is filled in. It is filled in with class-codes, class-standards, class approvals—with codes which recommend the practices and habits already current in a given circle, set, calling, profession, trade, industry, club or gang. These class-codes always lean back upon and support themselves by the professed ideal code. This latter meets them more than half-way. Being in its pretence a theory for regulating practice, it must demonstrate its practicability. It is uneasy in isolation, and travels hastily to meet with compromise and accommodation the actual situation in all its brute unrationality. Where the pressure is greatest—in the habitual practice of the political and economic chieftains—there it accommodates the most.

Class-codes of morals are sanctions, under the caption of ideals, of uncriticized customs; they are recommendations, under the head of duties, of what the members of the class are already most given to doing. If there are to obtain more equable and comprehensive principles of action, exacting a more impartial exercise of natural power and resource in the interests of a common good, it will be because members of a class can no longer rest content in responsibility to a class whose traditions constitute its conscience, but are made responsible to a society whose conscience is its free and effectively organized intelligence.

In such a conscience alone will the Socratic injunction to man to know himself be fulfilled.

(9)

Roscoe Pound

1870-

Born in Lincoln, Nebraska, Roscoe Pound attended the University of Nebraska, where he received his A.B., A.M., and Ph.D. In 1890 he was admitted to the bar, and he practiced law in Lincoln for nearly two decades while also serving as Professor and Dean of the Law Department of the University of Nebraska. In 1910 he was called to the Harvard Law School, where he remained until his retirement in 1947.

Like Oliver Wendell Holmes, Jr., Pound rejected the idea that the judge was one who simply applied the law. Instead, Pound maintained that in any given case the judge not only interpreted but also made the law. It therefore followed that the law is neither given nor fixed but is continually evolving. One of the earliest legal philosophers to interpret law from a pragmatic point of view, Pound argued that jurists shape the law to meet current necessities. Thus the law is to be judged by the result it achieves, not by the nicety of its structure nor the logic of its development from assumed first principles. But Pound's pragmatic approach did not limit his vision of the law. Pound pointed out that to describe the law as it existed was not enough, for a knowledge of what the law ought to be was equally important. Through his immensely important writings and teaching, he became a pioneer in sociological jurisprudence, a movement that attempted to relate the law to relevant social and economic issues.

The following selection, taken from "Mechanical Jurisprudence," *Columbia Law Review,* 8 (December, 1908), illustrates Pound's pragmatic approach to law.

"There is no way," says Sir Frederick Pollock, "by which modern law can escape from the scientific and artificial character imposed on it by the demand of modern societies for full, equal, and exact justice." An Australian judge has stated the same proposition in these words: "The public is more interested than it knows in maintaining the highest scientific standard in the administration of justice." Every lawyer feels this, and every thoughtful student of institutions must admit it. But what do we mean by the word "scientific" in this connection? What is scientific law? What constitutes science in the administration of justice? Sir Frederick Pollock gives us the clew when he defines the reasons that compel law to take on this scientific character as three: the demand for full justice, that is for solutions that go to the root of controversies; the demand for equal justice, that is a like adjustment of like relations under like conditions; and the demand for exact justice, that is for a justice whose operations, within reasonable limits, may be predicted in advance of action. In other words, the marks of a scientific law are, conformity to reason, uniformity, and certainty. Scientific law is a reasoned body of principles for the administration of justice, and its antithesis is a system of enforcing magisterial caprice, however honest, and however much disguised under the name of justice or equity or natural law. But this scientific character of law is a means, —a means toward the end of law, which is the administration of justice. Law is forced to take on this character in order to accomplish its end fully, equally, and exactly; and in so far as it fails to perform its function fully, equally and exactly, it fails in the end for which it exists. Law is scientific in order to eliminate so far as may be the personal equation in judicial administration, to preclude corruption and to limit the dangerous possibilities of magisterial ignorance. Law is not scientific for the sake of science. Being scientific as a means toward an end, it must be judged by the results it achieves, not by the niceties of its internal structure; it must be valued by the extent to which it meets its end, not by the beauty of its logical processes or the strictness with which its rules proceed from the dogmas it takes for its foundation.

Two dangers have to be guarded against in a scientific legal system, one of them in the direction of the effect of its scientific and artificial character upon the public, the other in the direction of its effect upon the courts and the legal profession. With respect to the first danger, it is well to remember that law must not become too scientific for the people to appreciate its workings. Law has the practical function of adjusting every-day relations so as to meet current ideas of fair play. It must not become so completely artificial that the public is led to regard it as wholly arbitrary. No institution can stand upon such a basis to-day. Reverence for institutions of the past will not preserve, of itself, an institution that touches every-day life as profoundly as does the law. Legal theory can no more stand as a sacred tradition in the modern world than can political theory. It has been one of the great merits of English law that its votaries have always borne this in mind. When Lord Esher said, "the law of England is not a science," he meant to protest against a pseudo-science of technical rules existing for their own sake and subserving supposed ends of science, while defeating justice. And it is the importance of the rôle of jurors in tempering the administration of justice with common-sense and preserving a due connection of the rules governing every-day relations with every-day needs of ordinary men that has atoned for the manifold and conspicuous defects of trial by jury and is keeping it alive. In Germany to-day one of the problems of law reform is how to achieve a similar tempering of the justice administered by highly trained specialists.

In the other direction, the effect of a scientific legal system upon the courts and upon the legal profession is more subtle and far-reaching. The effect of all system is apt to be petrifaction of the subject systematized. Perfection of scientific system and exposition tends to cut off individual initiative in the future, to stifle independent consideration of new problems and of new phases of old problems, and to impose the ideas of one generation upon another. This is so in all departments of learning. One of the obstacles to advance in every science is the domination of the ghosts of departed masters. Their sound methods are forgotten, while their unsound conclusions are held for gospel. Legal science is not exempt from this tendency. Legal systems have their periods in which science degenerates, in which system decays into technicality, in which a scientific jurisprudence becomes a mechanical jurisprudence.

Roman law in its decadence furnishes a striking example. The Valentinian "law of citations" made a selection of jurisconsults of the past and allowed their writings only to be cited. It declared them, with the exception of Papinian, equal in authority. It confined the judge, when questions of law were in issue, to the purely mechanical task of counting and of determining the numerical preponderance of authority. Principles were no longer resorted to in order to make rules to fit cases. The rules were at hand in a fixed and final form, and cases were to be fitted to the rules. The classical jurisprudence of principles had developed, by the very weight of its authority, a jurisprudence of rules; and it is in the nature of rules to operate mechanically.

Undoubtedly one cause of the tendency of scientific law to become mechanical is to be found in the average man's admiration for the ingenious in any direction, his love of technicality as a manifestation of cleverness, his feeling that law, as a developed institution, ought to have a certain ballast of mysterious technicality. "Philosophy's queerest arguments," says James, "tickle agreeably our sense of subtlety and ingenuity." Every practitioner has encountered the lay obsession as to invalidity of a signing with a lead pencil. Every law-teacher has had to combat the student obsession that notice, however cogent, may be disregarded unless it is "official." Lay hair-splitting over rules and regulations goes far beyond anything of which lawyers are capable. Experienced advocates have insisted that in argument to a jury, along with a just, common-sense theory of the merits, one ought to have a specious technicality for good measure. But apart from this general human tendency, there is the special tendency of the lawyer to regard artificiality in law as an end, to hold science something to be pursued for its own sake, to forget in this pursuit the purpose of law and hence of scientific law, and to judge rules and doctrines by their conformity to a supposed science and not by the results to which they lead. In periods of growth and expansion, this tendency is repressed. In periods of maturity and stability, when the opportunity for constructive work is largely eliminated, it becomes very marked.

"I have known judges," said Chief Justice Erle, "bred in the world of legal studies, who delighted in nothing so much as in a strong decision. Now a strong decision is a decision opposed to common-sense and to common convenience. * * * A great part of the law made by judges consists of strong decisions, and as one strong decision is a precedent for another a little stronger, the law at last, on some matters, becomes such a nuisance that equity intervenes, or an Act of Parliament must be passed to sweep the whole away."

The instance suggested in the conversation from which the foregoing extract is taken illustrates very well the development of a mechanical legal doctrine. Successive decisions upon the construction of wills had passed upon the meaning of particular words and phrases in particular wills. These decisions were used as guides in the construction of other wills. Presently rules grew up whereby it was settled that particular words and phrases had prescribed hard and fast meanings, and the construction of wills became so artificial, so scientific, that it defeated the very end of construction and compelled a series of sections in the Wills Act of 1836.

I have referred to mechanical jurisprudence as scientific because those who administer it believe it such. But in truth it is not science at all. We no longer hold anything scientific merely because it exhibits a rigid scheme of deductions from *a priori* conceptions. In the philosophy of to-day, theories are "instruments, not answers to enigmas, in which we can rest." The idea of science as a system of deductions has become obsolete, and the revolution which has taken place in other sciences in this regard must take place and is taking place in jurisprudence also. This revolution in science at large was achieved in the middle of the nineteenth century. In the first half of that century, scientific method in every department of learning was dominated by the classical German philosophy. Men conceived that by dialectics and deduction from controlling conceptions they could construe the whole content of knowledge. Even in the natural sciences this belief prevailed and had long dictated theories of nature and of natural phenomena. Linnaeus, for instance, lays down a proposition, *omme vivum ex ovo,* and from this fundamental conception deduces a theory of homologies between animal and vegetable organs. He deemed no study of the organisms and the organs themselves necessary to reach or to sustain these conclusions. Yet, to-day, study of the organisms themselves has overthrown his fundamental proposition. The substitution of efficient for final causes as explanations of natural phenomena has been paralleled by a revolution in political thought. We do not base institutions upon deduction from assumed principles of human nature; we require them to exhibit practical utility, and we rest them upon a foundation of policy and established adaptation to human needs. It has been asserted that to no small extent the old mode of procedure was borrowed from the law. We are told that it involved a "fundamentally juristic conception of the world in which all kinds of action and every sort of judgment was expressed in legal phraseology." We are told that "in the Middle Ages human welfare and even religion was conceived under the form of legality, and in the modern world this has given place to utility." We have, then, the same task in jurisprudence that has been achieved in philosophy, in the natural sciences and in politics. We have to rid ourselves of this sort of legality and to attain a pragmatic, a sociological legal science.

"What is needed nowadays," it has been said, "is that as against an abstract and unreal theory of State omnipotence on the one hand, and an atomistic and artificial view of individual independence on the other, the facts of the world with its innumerable bonds of association and the naturalness of social authority should be generally recognized, and become the basis of our laws, as it is of our life."

Herein is the task of the sociological jurist. Professor Small defines the sociological movement as "a frank endeavor to secure for the human factor in experience the central place which belongs to it in our whole scheme of thought and action." The sociological movement in jurisprudence is a movement for pragmatism as a philosophy of law; for the adjustment of principles and doctrines to the human conditions they are to govern rather than to assumed first principles; for putting the human factor in the central place and relegating logic to its true position as an instrument. . . .

With legislative law-making in the grip of the imperative theory and its arbitrary results, and judicial decision in the grip of a jurisprudence of conceptions and its equally arbitrary results, whither are we to turn? Judicial law-making cannot serve us. As things are, the cure would be worse than the disease. No court could hold such hearings as those had by legislative committees upon measures for the protection of operatives, described by Mrs. Kelley, or that recently had before the Interstate Commerce Commission as to uniform bills of lading. We must soon have a new starting-point that only legislation can afford. That we may put the sociological, the pragmatic theory behind legislation, is demonstrating every day. Legislative reference bureaus, the Comparative Law Bureau, the Conferences of Commissioners on Uniform State Laws, such hearings as the one before the Interstate Commerce Commission already referred to, hearings before legislative committees, such conferences as the one held recently with respect to the Sherman Anti-trust Law, bar-association discussions of reforms in procedure,—all these are furnishing abundant material for legislation of the best type. No such resources are open to the courts. Hence common-law lawyers will some day abandon their traditional attitude toward legislation; will welcome legislation and will make it what it should be. The part played by jurists in the best days of Roman legislation, and the part they have taken in modern Continental legislation, should convince us, if need be, that juristic principles may be recognized and juristic speculation may be put into effect quite as well by legislation as by judicial decision.

Herein is a noble task for the legal scholars of America. To test the conceptions worked out in the common law by the requirements of the new juristic theory, to lay sure foundations for the ultimate legislative restatement of the law, from which judicial decision shall start afresh,—this is as great an opportunity as has fallen to the jurists of any age. The end of a period of development by judicial decision is marked by the prevalence of two types of judges; those who think it a great display of learning and of judicial independence to render what Chief Justice Erle called "strong decisions," and those who fix their gaze upon the raw equities of a cause and forage in the books for cases to sustain the desired result. But the task of a judge is to make a principle living, not by deducing from it rules, to be, like the Freshman's hero, "immortal for a great many years," but by achieving thoroughly the less ambitious but more useful labor of giving a fresh illustration of the intelligent application of the principle to a concrete cause, producing a workable and a just result. The real genius of our common law is in this, not in an eternal case-law. Let the principles be formulated by whom or derived from whence you will. The Common Law will look to courts to develop and expound them, the Civil Law to doctrinal treatises. It is only a lip service to our common law that would condemn it to a perpetuity of mechanical jurisprudence through distrust of legislation.

III

American Individualism
and the Ideology of
the Self-Made Man

LONG BEFORE THE CIVIL WAR, the individualistic ethic had become one of the cardinal tenets of the American democratic faith. Formulated in a society unhampered by sharp feudal restrictions and articulated by a people imbued with the Protestant ethic, such a theory harmonized with the rising materialism of a nation bent on exploiting its abundant natural resources.

In the second half of the nineteenth century, however, the philosophy of individualism began to undergo a marked transformation in its intellectual and theoretical formulation. No longer was it advocated solely on religious and moral grounds, as it had been in the past. Instead, it received an impetus from the new evolutionary hypothesis, especially the version developed by Herbert Spencer.

Spencer's ideas had a special appeal to Americans, who found in them a philosophy sympathetic to the changing conditions of their society. In the first place, his imposing system, itself a product of English industrialism, provided a rationale suitable to the needs of an industrial age. Second, it seemed to rest squarely on a scientific base, built as it was on the physical law of thermodynamics and the biological notions of adaptation, selection, and evolution. Finally, it included its own version of the idea of progress, thus buttressing a faith already accepted by most Americans.

In essence, Spencer insisted that there existed a general law of organic evolution. In his view development proceeded from homogeneous to heterogeneous, from simple to complex, and from lower to higher forms. Like his contemporary Charles Darwin, Spencer utilized two ideas: Malthusian theory, which held that population would always exceed the physical ability to support itself, were it not for war, pestilence, and famine; and the notion of natural selection. He then asserted that man must conform to natural forces and could not consciously direct his own development. In fact, according to Spencer, progress could occur only if man did not attempt to impede the deterministic impact of evolution. In the final analysis, then, Spencer stood for an extreme version of laissez faire.

To a nation committed to a program of private exploitation of natural resources and the creation of a free enterprise capitalistic economy, Spencer's sociological system had an inherent attractiveness. It provided a framework by which an extreme form of individualism could be linked to a general theory of progress. It also provided an ideological and scientific justification for a conservative, laissez-faire policy. Above all, Spencer's system was in harmony with the traditional attachment of Americans to the ideals of democracy and opportunity, since any man, regardless of his rank in society, could rise as high in life as his abilities and ambitions permitted.

To be sure, not all Americans assented to the ideology of success, with its built-in acceptance of laissez faire. Nor could its adherents always agree on a precise definition of this ideology. The Spencerian version of conservative Darwinism, for example, appealed largely to intellectuals, social scientists, and educated individuals. Businessmen, on the other hand, who had neither the benefits of a formal education nor the time and ability to master the intricacies of Spencer's system, still defended laissez faire in terms derived from the Protestant ethic and the doctrines of the classical economists. Nevertheless, within broad limits, the theory of individualism and the cult of success, whatever its intellectual formulation, exerted great influence at a time when men were seeking to erect new systems of thought and mores in a changing world. Such an ideology seemed to offer fabulous rewards to those willing to test their mettle in the free and unregulated competitive arena. If the challenges were great, so too were the potential gains. And from a social point of view, society itself would ultimately be the beneficiary, since the process would ensure the progressive development of mankind to hitherto undreamed of levels.

From the Civil War to the turn of the century, this conservative faith and philosophy became the gospel of success for ambitious young Americans striving to better themselves. Even when a reaction set in, so strong was the hold of the ideology of the self-made man and the cult of success that it was destined to play an important role in subsequent decades. In our own time also, expressions of the antistate doctrine of rugged individualism in one form or another are articulated and accepted by many.

William Graham Sumner

1840-1910

Born in Paterson, New Jersey, William Graham Sumner graduated from Yale in 1863, and was ordained a minister in the Protestant Episcopal Church in 1869. His interest in social and economic matters quickly surpassed his ministerial concerns, and in 1872 he accepted a call to a newly created chair of political and social science at Yale, where he remained for the rest of his life. His fame as a scholar and teacher earned him a national reputation, as did his numerous books dealing with human society.

A disciple of Spencer, Sumner was opposed to social experimentation through governmental planning. A staunch foe of governmental regulation, he argued that such intervention could never be scientific or intelligent, and supported a laissez-faire approach based on a deterministic law of evolution. He championed big business and a sound monetary system and opposed protectionism, free silver, and inflation.

Later in life, Sumner turned from political economy to sociology. In 1906 he published *Folkways,* a book destined to have an immense influence. *Folkways* was in many ways a repudiation of some of Sumner's earlier views. In this pioneering work he maintained that individual men were ultimately governed not by reason, but by the folkways and mores of the society into which they were born and lived. Such folkways and mores, Sumner argued, were not rational creations but rather by-products of the adjustment of men to their life conditions. In other words, Sumner was positing a doctrine of cultural determinism. "The mores," he commented, "can make anything right and prevent the condemnation of anything."

The following selection is from one of Sumner's earlier works, *What Social Classes Owe to Each Other* (New York, 1883), and illustrates his philosophy during that part of his career when Spencerian elements dominated his thinking.

Certain ills belong to the hardships of human life. They are natural. They are part of the struggle with Nature for existence. We cannot blame our fellow-men for our share of these. My neighbor and I are both struggling to free ourselves from these ills. The fact that my neighbor has succeeded in this struggle better than I constitutes no grievance for me. Certain other ills are due to the malice of men, and to the imperfections or errors of civil institutions. These ills are an object of agitation, and a subject of discussion. The former class of ills is to be met only by manly effort and energy; the latter may be corrected by associated effort. The former class of ills is constantly grouped and generalized, and made the object of social schemes. We shall see, as we go on, what that means. The second class of ills may fall on certain social classes, and reform will take the form of interference by other classes in favor of that one. The last fact is, no doubt, the reason why people have been led, not noticing distinctions, to believe that the same method was applicable to the other class of ills. The distinction here made between the ills which belong to the struggle for existence and those which are due to the faults of human institutions is of prime importance.

It will also be important, in order to clear up our ideas about the notions which are in fashion, to note the relation of the economic to the political significance of assumed duties of one class to another. That is to say, we may discuss the question whether one class owes duties to another by reference to the economic effects which will be produced on the classes and society; or we may discuss the political expediency of formulating and enforcing rights and duties respectively between the parties. In the former case we might assume that the givers of aid were willing to give it, and we might discuss the benefit or mischief of their activity. In the other case we must assume that some at least of those who were forced to give aid did so unwillingly. Here, then, there would be a question of rights. The question whether voluntary charity is mischievous or not is one thing; the question whether legislation which forces one man to aid another is right and wise, as well as economically beneficial, is quite another question. Great confusion and consequent error is produced by allowing these two questions to become entangled in the discussion. Especially we shall need to notice the attempts to apply legislative methods of reform to the ills which belong to the order of Nature.

There is no possible definition of "a poor man." A pauper is a person who cannot earn his living; whose producing powers have fallen positively below his necessary consumption; who cannot, therefore, pay his way. A human society needs the active co-operation and productive energy of every person in it. A man who is present as a consumer, yet who does not contribute either by land, labor, or capital to the work of society, is a burden. On no sound political theory ought such a person to share in the political power of the State. He drops out of the ranks of workers and producers. Society must support him. It accepts the burden, but he must be cancelled from the ranks of the rulers likewise. So much for the pauper. About him no more need be said. But he is not the "poor man." The "poor man" is an elastic term, under which any number of social fallacies may be hidden.

Neither is there any possible definition of "the weak." Some are weak in one way, and some in another; and those who are weak in one sense are strong in another. In general, however, it may be said that those whom humanitarians and philanthropists call the weak are the ones through whom the productive and conservative forces of society are wasted. They constantly neutralize and destroy the finest efforts of the wise and industrious, and are a dead-weight on the society in all its struggles to realize any better things. Whether the people who mean no harm, but are weak in the essential powers necessary to the performance of one's duties in life, or those who are malicious and vicious, do the more mischief, is a question not easy to answer.

Under the names of the poor and the weak, the negligent, shiftless, inefficient, silly, and imprudent are fastened upon the industrious and prudent as a responsibility and a duty. On the one side, the terms are extended to cover the idle, intemperate, and vicious, who, by the combination, gain credit which they do not deserve, and which they could not get if they stood alone. On the other hand, the terms are extended to include wage-receivers of the humblest rank, who are degraded by the combination. The reader who desires to guard himself against fallacies should always scrutinize the terms "poor" and "weak" as used, so as to see which or how many of these classes they are made to cover.

The humanitarians, philanthropists, and reformers, looking at the facts of life as they present themselves, find enough which is sad and unpromising in the condition of many members of society. They see wealth and poverty side by side. They note great inequality of social position and social chances. They eagerly set about the attempt to account for what they see, and to devise schemes for remedying what they do not like. In their eagerness to recommend the less fortunate classes to pity and consideration they forget all about the rights of other classes; they gloss over all the faults of the classes in question, and they exaggerate their misfortunes and their virtues. They invent new theories of property, distorting rights and perpetrating injustice, as any one is sure to do who sets about the re-adjustment of social relations with the interests of one group distinctly before his mind, and the interests of all other groups thrown into the background. When I have read certain of these discussions I have thought that it must be quite disreputable to be respectable, quite dishonest to own property, quite unjust to go one's own way and earn one's own living, and that the only really admirable person was the good-for-nothing. The man who by his own effort raises himself above poverty appears, in these discussions, to be of no account. The man who has done nothing to raise himself above poverty finds that the social doctors flock about him, bringing the capital which they have collected from the other class, and promising him the aid of the State to give him what the other had to work for. In all these schemes and projects the organized intervention of society through the State is either planned or hoped for, and the State is thus made to become the protector and guardian of certain classes. The agents who are to direct the State action are, of course, the reformers and philanthropists. Their schemes, therefore, may always be reduced to this type—that A and B decide what C shall do for D. It will be interesting to inquire, at a later period of our discussion, who C is, and what the effect is upon him of all these arrangements. In all the discussions attention is concentrated on A and B, the noble social reformers, and on D, the "poor man." I call C the Forgotten Man, because I have never seen that any notice was taken of him in any of the discussions. When we have disposed of A, B, and D we can better appreciate the case of C, and I think that we shall find that he deserves our attention, for the worth of his character and the magnitude of his unmerited burdens. Here it may suffice to observe that, on the theories of the social philosophers to whom I have referred, we should get a new maxim of judicious living: Poverty is the best policy. If you get wealth, you will have to support other people; if you do not get wealth, it will be the duty of other people to support you.

No doubt one chief reason for the unclear and contradictory theories of class relations lies in the fact that our society, largely controlled in all its organization by one set of doctrines, still contains survivals of old social theories which are totally inconsistent with the former. In the Middle Ages men were united by custom and prescription into associations, ranks, guilds, and communities of various kinds. These ties endured as long as life lasted. Consequently society was dependent, throughout all its details, on status, and the tie, or bond, was sentimental. In our modern state, and in the United States more than anywhere else, the social structure is based on contract, and status is of the least importance. Contract, however, is rational—even rationalistic. It is also realistic, cold, and matter-of-fact. A contract relation is based on a sufficient reason, not on custom or prescription. It is not permanent. It endures only so long as the reason for it endures. In a state based on contract sentiment is out of place in any public or common affairs. It is relegated to the sphere of private and personal relations, where it depends not at all on class types, but on personal acquaintance and personal estimates. The sentimentalists among us always seize upon the survivals of the old order. They want to save them and restore them. Much of the loose thinking also which troubles us in our social discussions arises from the fact that men do not distinguish the elements of status and of contract which may be found in our society.

Whether social philosophers think it desirable or not, it is out of the question to go back to status or to the sentimental relations which once united baron and retainer, master and servant, teacher and pupil, comrade and comrade. That we have lost some grace and elegance is undeniable. That life once held more poetry and romance is true enough. But it seems impossible that any one who has studied the matter should doubt that we have gained immeasurably, and that our farther gains lie in going forward, not in going backward. The feudal ties can never be restored. If they could be restored they would bring back personal caprice, favoritism, sycophancy, and intrigue. A society based on contract is a society of free and independent men, who form ties without favor or obligation, and cooperate without cringing or intrigue. A society based on contract, therefore, gives the utmost room and chance for individual development, and for all the self-reliance and dignity of a free man. That a society of free men, co-operating under contract, is by far the strongest society which has ever yet existed; that no such society has ever yet developed the full measure of strength of which it is capable; and that the only social improvements which are now conceivable lie in the direction of more complete realization of a society of free men united by contract, are points which cannot be controverted. It follows, however, that one man, in a free state, cannot claim help from, and cannot be charged to give help to, another. To understand the full meaning of this assertion it will be worth while to see what a free democracy is. . . .

Social improvement is not to be won by direct effort. It is secondary, and results from physical or economic improvements. That is the reason why schemes of direct social amelioration always have an arbitrary, sentimental, and artificial character, while true social advance must be a product and a growth. The efforts which are being put forth for every kind of progress in the arts and sciences are, therefore, contributing to true social progress. Let any one learn what hardship was involved, even for a wealthy person, a century ago, in crossing the Atlantic, and then let him compare that hardship even with a steerage passage at the present time, considering time and money cost. This improvement in transportation by which "the poor and weak" can be carried from the crowded centres of population to the new land is worth more to them than all the schemes of all the social reformers. An improvement in surgical instruments or in anæsthetics really does more for those who are not well off than all the declamations of the orators and pious wishes of the reformers. Civil service reform would be a greater gain to the laborers than innumerable factory acts and eight-hour laws. Free trade would be a greater blessing to "the poor man" than all the devices of all the friends of humanity if they could be realized. If the economists could satisfactorily solve the problem of the regulation of paper currency, they would do more for the wages class than could be accomplished by all the artificial doctrines about wages which they seem to feel bound to encourage. If we could get firm and good laws passed for the management of savings-banks, and then refrain from the amendments by which those laws are gradually broken down, we should do more for the non-capitalist class than by volumes of laws against "corporations" and the "excessive power of capital."

We each owe to the other mutual redress of grievances. It has been said, in answer to my argument in the last chapter about the Forgotten Women and thread, that the tax on thread is "only a little thing," and that it cannot hurt the women much, and also that, if the women do not want to pay two cents a spool tax, there is thread of an inferior quality, which they can buy cheaper. These answers represent the bitterest and basest social injustice. Every honest citizen of a free state owes it to himself, to the community, and especially to those who are at once weak and wronged, to go to their assistance and to help redress their wrongs. Whenever a law or social arrangement acts so as to injure any one, and that one the humblest, then there is a duty on those who are stronger, or who know better, to demand and fight for redress and correction. When generalized this means that it is the duty of All-of-us (that is, the State) to establish justice for all, from the least to the greatest, and in all matters. This, however, is no new doctrine. It is only the old, true, and indisputable function of the State; and in working for a redress of wrongs and a correction of legislative abuses, we are only struggling to a fuller realization of it—that is, working to improve civil government.

We each owe it to the other to guarantee rights. Rights do not pertain to *results,* but only to *chances.* They pertain to the *conditions* of the struggle for existence, not to any of the results of it; to the *pursuit* of happiness, not to the possession of happiness. It cannot be said that each one has a right to have some property, because if one man had such a right some other man or men would be under a corresponding obligation to provide him with some property. Each has a right to acquire and possess property if he can. It is plain what fallacies are developed when we overlook this distinction. Those fallacies run through *all* socialistic schemes and theories. If we take rights to pertain to results, and then say that rights must be equal, we come to say that men have a right to be equally happy, and so on in all the details. Rights should be equal, because they pertain to chances, and all ought to have equal chances so far as chances are provided or limited by the action of society. This, however, will not produce equal results, but it is right just because it will produce unequal results—that is, results which shall be proportioned to the merits of individuals. We each owe it to the other to guarantee mutually the chance to earn, to possess, to learn, to marry, etc., etc., against any interference which would prevent the exercise of those rights by a person who wishes to prosecute and enjoy them in peace for the pursuit of happiness. If we generalize this, it means that All-of-us ought to guarantee rights to each of us. But our modern free, constitutional States are constructed entirely on the notion of rights, and we regard them as performing their functions more and more perfectly according as they guarantee rights in consonance with the constantly corrected and expanded notions of rights from one generation to another. Therefore, when we say that we owe it to each other to guarantee rights we only say that we ought to prosecute and improve our political science.

If we have in mind the value of chances to earn, learn, possess, etc., for a man of independent energy, we can go one one step farther in our deductions about help. The only help which is generally expedient, even within the limits of the private and personal relations of two persons to each other, is that which consists in helping a man to help himself. This always consists in opening the chances. A man of assured position can, by an effort which is of no appreciable importance to him, give aid which is of incalculable value to a man who is all ready to make his own career if he can only get a chance. The truest and deepest pathos in this world is not that of suffering but that of brave struggling. The truest sympathy is not compassion, but a fellow-feeling with courage and fortitude in the midst of noble effort.

Now, the aid which helps a man to help himself is not in the least akin to the aid which is given in charity. If alms are given, or if we "make work" for a man, or "give him employment," or "protect" him, we simply take a product from one and give it to another. If we help a man to help himself, by opening the chances around him, we put him in a position to add to the wealth of the community by putting new powers in operation to produce. It would seem that the difference between getting something already in existence from the one who has it, and producing a new thing by applying new labor to natural materials, would be so plain as never to be forgotten; but the fallacy of confusing the two is one of the commonest in all social discussions.

We have now seen that the current discussions about the claims and rights of social classes on each other are radically erroneous and fallacious, and we have seen that an analysis of the general obligations which we all have to each other leads us to nothing but an emphatic repetition of old but well-acknowledged obligations to perfect our political institutions. We have been led to restriction, not extension, of the functions of the State, but we have also been led to see the necessity of purifying and perfecting the operation of the State in the functions which properly belong to it. If we refuse to recognize any classes as existing in society when, perhaps, a claim might be set up that the wealthy, educated, and virtuous have acquired special rights and precedence, we certainly cannot recognize any classes when it is attempted to establish such distinctions for the sake of imposing burdens and duties on one group for the benefit of others. The men who have not done their duty in this world never can be equal to those who have done their duty more or less well. If words like wise and foolish, thrifty and extravagant, prudent and negligent, have any meaning in language, then it must make some difference how people behave in this world, and the difference will appear in the position they acquire in the body of society, and in relation to the chances of life. They may, then, be classified in reference to these facts. Such classes always will exist; no other social distinctions can endure. If, then, we look to the origin and definition of these classes, we shall find it impossible to deduce any obligations which one of them bears to the other. The class distinctions simply result from the different degrees of success with which men have availed themselves of the chances which were presented to them. Instead of endeavoring to redistribute the acquisitions which have been made between the existing classes, our aim should be to *increase, multiply, and extend the chances.* Such is the work of civilization. Every old error or abuse which is removed opens new chances of development to all the new energy of society. Every improvement in education, science, art, or government expands the chances of man on earth. Such expansion is no guarantee of equality. On the contrary, if there be liberty, some will profit by the chances eagerly and some will neglect them altogether. Therefore, the greater the chances the more unequal will be the fortune of these two sets of men. So it ought to be, in all justice and right reason. The yearning after equality is the offspring of envy and covetousness, and there is no possible plan for satisfying that yearning which can do aught else than rob A to give to B; consequently all such plans nourish some of the meanest vices of human nature, waste capital, and overthrow civilization. But if we can expand the chances we can count on a general and steady growth of civilization and advancement of society by and through its best members. In the prosecution of these chances we all owe to each other good-will, mutual respect, and mutual guarantees of liberty and security. Beyond this nothing can be affirmed as a duty of one group to another in a free state.

(11)

Andrew Carnegie

1835-1919

A literal embodiment of the "rags to riches" theme, Andrew Carnegie was born into a poor family of Scotch weavers. After migrating to America in 1848, young Andrew went to work first as a bobbin boy in a cotton mill and then as an engine tender. He quickly rose up the economic ladder, and by 1860 had become Superintendent of the Pittsburgh Division of the Pennsylvania Railroad. After the Civil War he went into business for himself, and in 1873 entered the young steel industry. By the end of the century Carnegie had become so successful that his plants were turning out the bulk of American steel. But Carnegie's interests transcended the mere amassing of a large personal fortune. A widely-read and self-educated individual, he was greatly concerned with the ethical responsibilities of the individual as well as with the workings of democracy. In 1886 he published *Triumphant Democracy* in order to demonstrate the superiority of republican over monarchical institutions.

The following selection, "Wealth," *North American Review,* 148 (June, 1889), is probably his most interesting philosophical presentation. A firm advocate of the refurbished Puritan doctrine of individualism as well as an exponent of the sanctity of private property, Carnegie believed with equal fervor that the acquisition of wealth itself was insufficient. Rather, the man of wealth had an ethical responsibility (after providing for his own family) to see that his private fortune was used for the public welfare. During his own lifetime, therefore, Carnegie gave away most of his enormous wealth for philanthropic purposes. Basically he was committed to a political theory and system of ethics that were designed to avoid social revolution while maintaining intact the older individualistic tradition in a new industrial society.

The problem of our age is the proper administration of wealth, so that the ties of brotherhood may still bind together the rich and poor in harmonious relationship. The conditions of human life have not only been changed, but revolutionized, within the past few hundred years. In former days there was little difference between the dwelling, dress, food, and environment of the chief and those of his retainers. The Indians are to-day where civilized man then was. When visiting the Sioux, I was led to the wigwam of the chief. It was just like the others in external appearance, and even within the difference was trifling between it and those of the poorest of his braves. The contrast between the palace of the millionaire and the cottage of the laborer with us to-day measures the change which has come with civilization.

This change, however, is not to be deplored, but welcomed as highly beneficial. It is well, nay, essential for the progress of the race, that the houses of some should be homes for all that is highest and best in literature and the arts, and for all the refinements of civilization, rather than that none should be so. Much better this irregularity than universal squalor. Without wealth there can be no Maecenas. The "good old times" were not good old times. Neither master nor servant was as well situated then as to-day. A relapse to old conditions would be disastrous to both—not the least so to him who serves—and would sweep away civilization with it. But whether the change be for good or ill, it is upon us, beyond our power to alter, and therefore to be accepted and made the best of. It is a waste of time to criticize the inevitable.

It is easy to see how the change has come. One illustration will serve for almost every phase of the cause. In the manufacture of products we have the whole story. It applies to all combinations of human industry, as stimulated and enlarged by the inventions of this scientific age. Formerly articles were manufactured at the domestic hearth or in small shops which formed part of the household. The master and his apprentices worked side by side, the latter living with the master, and therefore subject to the same conditions. When these apprentices rose to be masters, there was little or no change in their mode of life, and they, in turn, educated in the same routine succeeding apprentices. There was, substantially, social equality, and even political equality, for those engaged in industrial pursuits had then little or no political voice in the State.

But the inevitable result of such a mode of manufacture was crude articles at high prices. To-day the world obtains commodities of excellent quality at prices which even the generation preceding this would have deemed incredible. In the commercial world similar causes have produced similar results, and the race is benefited thereby. The poor enjoy what the rich could not before afford. What were the luxuries have become the necessaries of life. The laborer has now more comforts than the farmer had a few generations ago. The farmer has more luxuries than the landlord had, and is more richly clad and better housed. The landlord has books and pictures rarer, and appointments more artistic, than the King could then obtain.

The price we pay for this salutary change, is, no doubt, great. We assemble thousands of operatives in the factory, in the mine, and in the counting-house, of whom the employer can know little or nothing, and to whom the employer is little better than a myth. All intercourse between them is at an end. Rigid Castes are formed, and, as usual, mutual ignorance breeds mutual distrust.

Each Caste is without sympathy for the other, and ready to credit anything disparaging in regard to it. Under the law of competition, the employer of thousands is forced into the strictest economies, among which the rates paid to labor figure prominently, and often there is friction between the employer and the employed, between capital and labor, between rich and poor. Human society loses homogeneity.

The price which society pays for the law of competition, like the price it pays for cheap comforts and luxuries, is also great; but the advantages of this law are also greater still, for it is to this law that we owe our wonderful material development, which brings improved conditions in its train. But, whether the law be benign or not, we must say of it, as we say of the change in the conditions of men to which we have referred: It is here; we cannot evade it; no substitutes for it have been found; and while the law may be sometimes hard for the individual, it is best for the race, because it insures the survival of the fittest in every department. We accept and welcome, therefore, as conditions to which we must accommodate ourselves, great inequality of environment, the concentration of business, industrial and commercial, in the hands of a few, and the law of competition between these, as being not only beneficial, but essential for the future progress of the race. Having accepted these, it follows that there must be great scope for the exercise of special ability in the merchant and in the manufacturer who has to conduct affairs upon a great scale. That this talent for organization and management is rare among men is proved by the fact that it invariably secures for its possessor enormous rewards, no matter where or under what laws or conditions. The experienced in affairs rate the MAN whose services can be obtained as a partner as not only the first consideration, but such as to render the question of his capital scarcely worth considering, for such men soon create capital; while, without the special talent required, capital soon takes wings. Such men become interested in firms or corporations using millions; and estimating only simple interest to be made upon the capital invested, it is inevitable that their income must exceed their expenditures, and that they must accumulate wealth. Nor is there any middle ground which such men can occupy, because the great manufacturing or commercial concern which does not earn at least interest upon its capital soon becomes bankrupt. It must either go forward or fall behind: to stand still is impossible. It is a condition essential for its successful operation that it should be thus far profitable, and even that, in addition to interest on capital, it should make profit. It is a law, as certain as any of the others named, that men possessed of this peculiar talent for affairs, under the free play of economic forces, must, of necessity, soon be in receipt of more revenue than can be judiciously expended upon themselves; and this law is as beneficial for the race as the others.

Objections to the foundations upon which society is based are not in order, because the condition of the race is better with these than it has been with any others which have been tried. Of the effect of any new substitutes proposed we cannot be sure. The Socialist or Anarchist who seeks to overturn present conditions is to be regarded as attacking the foundation upon which civilization itself rests, for civilization took its start from the day that the capable, industrious workman said to his incompetent and lazy fellow, "If thou dost not sow, thou shalt not reap," and thus ended primitive Communism by separating the drones from the bees. One who studies this subject will soon be brought face to face with the conclusion that upon the sacredness of property civilization itself depends—the right of the laborer to his hundred dollars in the savings bank, and equally the legal right of the millionaire to his millions. To those who propose to substitute Communism for this intense Individualism the answer, therefore, is: The race has tried that. All progress from that barbarous day to the present time has resulted from its displacement. Not evil, but good, has come to the race from the accumulation of wealth by those who have the ability and energy that produce it. But even if we admit for a moment that it might be better for the race to discard its present foundation, Individualism—that it is a nobler ideal that man should labor, not for himself alone, but in and for a brotherhood of his fellows, and share with them all in common, realizing Swedenborg's idea of Heaven, where, as he says, the angels derive their happiness, not from laboring for self, but for each other—even admit all this, and a sufficient answer is, This is not evolution, but revolution. It necessitates the changing of human nature itself—a work of aeons, even if it were good to change it, which we cannot know. It is not practicable in our day or in our age. Even if desirable theoretically, it belongs to another and long-succeeding sociological stratum. Our duty is with what is practicable now; with the next step possible in our day and generation. It is criminal to waste our energies in endeavoring to uproot, when all we can profitably or possibly accomplish is to bend the universal tree of humanity a little in the direction most favorable to the production of good fruit under existing circumstances. We might as well urge the destruction of the highest existing type of man because he failed to reach our ideal as to favor the destruction of Individualism, Private Property, the Law of Accumulation of Wealth, and the Law of Competition; for these are the highest results of human experience, the soil in which society so far has produced the best fruit. Unequally or unjustly, perhaps, as these laws sometimes operate, and imperfect as they appear to the Idealist, they are, nevertheless, like the highest type of man, the best and most valuable of all that humanity has yet accomplished.

We start, then, with a condition of affairs under which the best interests of the race are promoted, but which inevitably gives wealth to the few. Thus far, accepting conditions as they exist, the situation can be surveyed and pronounced good. The question then arises—and, if the foregoing be correct, it is the only question with which we have to deal—What is the proper mode of administering wealth after the laws upon which civilization is founded have thrown it into the hands of the few? And it is of this great question that I believe I offer the true solution. It will be understood that *fortunes* are here spoken of, not moderate sums saved by many years of effort, the returns from which are required for the comfortable maintenance and education of families.

This is not *wealth,* but only *competence,* which it should be the aim of all to acquire.

There are but three modes in which surplus wealth can be disposed of. It can be left to the families of the decedents; or it can be bequeathed for public purposes; or, finally, it can be administered during their lives by its possessors. Under the first and second modes most of the wealth of the world that has reached the few has hitherto been applied. Let us in turn consider each of these modes. The first is the most injudicious. In monarchical countries, the estates and the greatest portion of the wealth are left to the first son, that the vanity of the parent may be gratified by the thought that his name and title are to descend to succeeding generations unimpaired. The condition of this class in Europe to-day teaches the futility of such hopes or ambitions. The successors have become impoverished through their follies or from the fall in the value of land. Even in Great Britain the strict law of entail has been found inadequate to maintain the status of an hereditary class. Its soil is rapidly passing into the hands of the stranger. Under republican institutions the division of property among the children is much fairer, but the question which forces itself upon thoughtful men in all lands is: Why should men leave great fortunes to their children? If this is done from affection, is it not misguided affection? Observation teaches that, generally speaking, it is not well for the children that they should be so burdened. Neither is it well for the state. Beyond providing for the wife and daughters moderate sources of income, and very moderate allowances indeed, if any, for the sons, men may well hesitate, for it is no longer questionable that great sums bequeathed oftener work more for the injury than for the good of the recipients. Wise men will soon conclude that, for the best interests of the members of their families and of the state, such bequests are an improper use of their means.

It is not suggested that men who have failed to educate their sons to earn a livelihood shall cast them adrift in poverty. If any man has seen fit to rear his sons with a view to their living idle lives, or, what is highly commendable, has instilled in them the sentiment that they are in a position to labor for public ends without reference to pecuniary considerations, then, of course, the duty of the parent is to see that such are provided for *in moderation.* There are instances of millionaires' sons unspoiled by wealth, who, being rich, still perform great services in the community. Such are the very salt of the earth, as valuable as, unfortunately, they are rare; still it is not the exception, but the rule, that men must regard, and looking at the usual result of enormous sums conferred upon legatees, the thoughtful man must shortly say, "I would as soon leave to my son a curse as the almighty dollar," and admit to himself that it is not the welfare of the children, but family pride, which inspires these enormous legacies.

As to the second mode, that of leaving wealth at death for public uses, it may be said that this is only a means for the disposal of wealth, provided a man is content to wait until he is dead before it becomes of much good in the world. Knowledge of the results of legacies bequeathed is not calculated to inspire the brightest hopes of much posthumous good being accomplished. The cases are not few in which the real object sought by the testator is not attained, nor are they few in which his real wishes are thwarted. In many cases the bequests are so used as to become only monuments of his folly. It is well to remember that it requires the exercise of not less ability than that which acquired the wealth to use it so as to be really beneficial to the community. Besides this, it may fairly be said that no man is to be extolled for doing what he cannot help doing, nor is he to be thanked by the community to which he only leaves wealth at death. Men who leave vast sums in this way may fairly be thought men who would not have left it at all, had they been able to take it with them. The memories of such cannot be held in grateful remembrance, for there is no grace in their gifts. It is not to be wondered at that such bequests seem so generally to lack the blessing.

The growing disposition to tax more and more heavily large estates left at death is a cheering indication of the growth of a salutary change in public opinion. The State of Pennsylvania now takes—subject to some exceptions—one-tenth of the property left by its citizens. The budget presented in the British Parliament the other day proposes to increase the death-duties; and, most significant of all, the new tax is to be a graduated one. Of all forms of taxation, this seems the wisest. Men who continue hoarding great sums all their lives, the proper use of which for public ends would work good to the community, should be made to feel that the community, in the form of the state, cannot thus be deprived of its proper share. By taxing estates heavily at death the state marks its condemnation of the selfish millionaire's unworthy life.

It is desirable that nations should go much further in this direction. Indeed, it is difficult to set bounds to the share of a rich man's estate which should go at his death to the public through the agency of the state, and by all means such taxes should be graduated, beginning at nothing upon moderate sums to dependents, and increasing rapidly as the amounts swell, until of the millionaire's hoard, as of Shylock's, at least

> "————The other half
> Comes to the privy coffer of the state."

This policy would work powerfully to induce the rich man to attend to the administration of wealth during his life, which is the end that society should always have in view, as being that by far most fruitful for the people. Nor need it be feared that this policy would sap the root of enterprise and render men less anxious to accumulate, for to the class whose ambition it is to leave great fortunes and be talked about after their death, it will attract even more attention, and, indeed, be a somewhat nobler ambition to have enormous sums paid over to the state from their fortunes.

There remains, then, only one mode of using great fortunes; but in this we have the true antidote for the temporary unequal distribution of wealth, the reconciliation of the rich and the poor—a reign of harmony—another ideal, differing, indeed, from that of the Communist in requiring only the further evolution of existing conditions, not the total overthrow of our civilization. It is founded upon the present most intense individualism, and the race is prepared to put it in practice by degrees whenever it pleases. Under its sway we shall have an ideal state, in which the surplus wealth of the few will become, in the best sense, the property of the many, because it is administered for the common good, and this wealth, passing through the hands of the few, can be made a much more potent force for the elevation of our race than if it had been distributed in small sums to the people themselves. Even the poorest can be made to see this, and to agree that great sums gathered by some of their fellow-citizens and spent for public purposes, from which the masses reap the principal benefit, are more valuable to them if scattered among them through the course of many years in trifling amounts.

If we consider what results flow from the Cooper Institute, for instance, to the best portion of the race in New York not possessed of means, and compare these with those which would have arisen for the good of the masses from an equal sum distributed by Mr. Cooper in his lifetime in the form of wages, which is the highest form of distribution, being for work done and not for charity, we can form some estimate of the possibilities for the improvement of the race which lie embedded in the present law of the accumulation of wealth. Much of this sum, if distributed in small quantities among the people, would have been wasted in the indulgence of appetite, some of it in excess, and it may be doubted whether even the part put to the best use, that of adding to the comforts of the home, would have yielded results for the race, as a race, at all comparable to those which are flowing and are to flow from the Cooper Institute from generation to generation. Let the advocate of violent or radical change ponder well this thought.

We might even go so far as to take another instance, that of Mr. Tilden's bequest of five millions of dollars for a free library in the city of New York, but in referring to this, one cannot help saying involuntarily, How much better if Mr. Tilden had devoted the last years of his own life to the proper administration of this immense sum; in which case neither legal contest nor any other cause of delay could have interfered with his aims. But let us assume that Mr. Tilden's millions finally become the means of giving to this city a noble public library, where the treasures of the world contained in good books will be open to all forever, without money and without price. Considering the good of that part of the race which congregates in and around Manhattan Island, would its permanent benefit have been better promoted had these millions been allowed to circulate in small sums through the hands of the masses? Even the most strenuous advocate of Communism must entertain a doubt upon this subject. Most of those who think will probably entertain no doubt whatever.

Poor and restricted are our opportunities in this life; narrow our horizon; our best work most imperfect; but rich men should be thankful for one inestimable boon. They have it in their power during their lives to busy themselves in organizing benefactions from which the masses of their fellows will derive lasting advantage, and thus dignify their own lives. The highest life is probably to be reached, not by such imitation of the life of Christ as Count Tolstoi gives us, but, while animated by Christ's spirit, by recognizing the changed conditions of this age, and adopting modes of expressing this spirit suitable to the changed conditions under which we live; still laboring for the good of our fellows, which was the essence of his life and teaching, but laboring in a different manner.

This, then, is held to be the duty of the Man of Wealth: First, to set an example of modest, unostentatious living, shunning display of extravagance; to provide moderately for the legitimate wants of those dependent upon him; and after doing so to consider all surplus revenues which come to him simply as trust funds, which he is called upon to administer, and strictly bound as a matter of duty to administer in the manner which, in his judgment, is best calculated to produce the most beneficial results for the community—the man of wealth thus becoming the mere agent and trustee for his poorer brethren, bringing to their service his superior wisdom, experience, and ability to administer, doing for them better than they would or could do for themselves.

We are met here with the difficulty of determining what are moderate sums to leave to members of the family; what is modest, unostentatious living; what is the test of extravagance. There must be different standards for different conditions. The answer is that it is as impossible to name exact amounts or actions as it is to define good manners, good taste, or the rules of propriety; but, nevertheless, these are verities, well known although undefinable. Public sentiment is quick to know and to feel what offends these. So in the case of wealth. The rule in regard to good taste in the dress of men or women applies here. Whatever makes one conspicuous offends the canon. If any family be chiefly known for display, for extravagance in home, table, equipage, for enormous sums ostentatiously spent in any form upon itself,—if these be its chief distinctions, we have no difficulty in estimating its nature or culture. So likewise in regard to the use or abuse of its surplus wealth, or to generous, free-handed cooperation in good public uses, or to unabated efforts to accumulate and hoard to the last, whether they administer or bequeath. The verdict rests with the best and most enlightened public sentiment. The community will surely judge, and its judgments will not often be wrong.

The best uses to which surplus wealth can be put have already been indicated. Those who would administer wisely must, indeed, be wise, for one of the serious obstacles to the improvement of our race is indiscriminate charity. It were better for mankind that the millions of the rich were thrown into the sea than so spent as to encourage the slothful, the drunken, the unworthy. Of every thousand dollars spent in so called charity to-day, it is probable that $950 is unwisely spent; so spent, indeed, as to produce the very evils which it proposes to mitigate or cure. A well-known writer of philosophic books admitted the other day that he had given a quarter of a dollar to a man who approached him as he was coming to visit the house of his friend. He knew nothing of the habits of this beggar; knew not the use that would be made of this money, although he had every reason to suspect that it would be spent improperly. This man professed to be a disciple of Herbert Spencer; yet the quarter-dollar given that night will probably work more injury than all the money which its thoughtless donor will ever be able to give in true charity will do good. He only gratified his own feelings, saved himself from annoyance,— and this was probably one of the most selfish and very worst actions of his life, for in all respects he is most worthy.

In bestowing charity, the main consideration should be to help those who will help themselves; to provide part of the means by which those who desire to improve may do so; to give those who desire to rise the aids by which they may rise; to assist, but rarely or never to do all. Neither the individual nor the race is improved by alms-giving. Those worthy of assistance, except in rare cases, seldom require assistance. The really valuable men of the race never do, except in cases of accident or sudden change. Every one has, of course, cases of individuals brought to his own knowledge where temporary assistance can do genuine good, and these he will not overlook. But the amount which can be wisely given by the individual for individuals is necessarily limited by his lack of knowledge of the circumstances connected with each. He is the only true reformer who is as careful and as anxious not to aid the unworthy as he is to aid the worthy, and, perhaps, even more so, for in alms-giving more injury is probably done by rewarding vice than by relieving virtue.

The rich man is thus almost restricted to following the examples of Peter Cooper, Enoch Pratt of Baltimore, Mr. Pratt of Brooklyn, Senator Stanford, and others, who know that the best means of benefiting the community is to place within its reach the ladders upon which the aspiring can rise—parks, and means of recreation, by which men are helped in body and mind; works of art, certain to give pleasure and improve the public taste, and public institutions of various kinds, which will improve the general condition of the people;—in this manner returning their surplus wealth to the mass of their fellows in the forms best calculated to do them lasting good.

Thus is the problem of Rich and Poor to be solved. The laws of accumulation will be left free; the laws of distribution free. Individualism will continue, but the millionaire will be but a trustee for the poor; intrusted for a season with a great part of the increased wealth of the community, but administering it for the community far better than it could or would have done for itself. The best minds will thus have reached a stage in the development of the race in which it is clearly seen that there is no mode of disposing of surplus wealth creditable to thoughtful and earnest men into whose hands it flows save by using it year by year for the general good. This day already dawns. But a little while, and although, without incurring the pity of their fellows, men may die sharers in great business enterprises from which their capital cannot be or has not been withdrawn, and is left chiefly at death for public uses, yet the man who dies leaving behind him millions of available wealth, which was his to administer during life, will pass away "unwept, unhonored, and unsung," no matter to what uses he leaves the dross which he cannot take with him. Of such as these the public verdict will then be: "The man who dies thus rich dies disgraced."

Such, in my opinion, is the true Gospel concerning Wealth, obedience to which is destined some day to solve the problem of the Rich and the Poor, and to bring "Peace on earth, among men Good-Will."

(12)

William Lawrence

1850-1941

Born in Boston, Massachusetts, of an old family whose roots went back to the early Puritans, William Lawrence graduated from Harvard in 1871. Later, he received his theological degree from the Episcopal Theological School at Cambridge, where he served as professor and dean from 1884 until 1893. In 1893 he was consecrated as Episcopal Bishop of Massachusetts, a position he retained until 1926. Noted for his tolerance in matters concerning both ritual and theology, Lawrence was also highly successful in raising money for his church and for Harvard.

Bishop Lawrence frequently spoke out on contemporary issues, among them the problem of wealth and morality. Denying that any conflict necessarily existed between the two, he reaffirmed the Protestant ethic with its theory of the stewardship of wealth.

The selection that follows was first delivered as an address at a dinner of the Chamber of Commerce in New York City. The text is from "The Relation of Wealth to Morals," *World's Work,* 1 (January, 1901).

There is a certain distrust on the part of our people as to the effect of material prosperity on their morality. We shrink with some foreboding at the great increase of riches, and question whether in the long run material prosperity does not tend toward the disintegration of character.

History seems to support us in our distrust. Visions arise of their fall from splendor of Tyre and Sidon, Babylon, Rome, and Venice, and of great nations too. The question is started whether England is not to-day, in the pride of her wealth and power, sowing the wind from which in time she will reap the whirlwind.

Experience seems to add its support. Is it not from the ranks of the poor that the leaders of the people have always risen? Recall Abraham Lincoln and patriots of every generation.

The Bible has sustained the same note. Were ever stronger words of warning uttered against the deceitfulness of riches than those spoken by the peasant Jesus, who Himself had no place to lay His head? And the Church has through the centuries upheld poverty as one of the surest paths to Heaven: it has been a mark of the saint.

To be sure, in spite of history, experience, and the Bible, men have gone on their way making money and hailing with joy each age of material prosperity. The answer is: "This only proves the case; men are of the world, riches are deceitful, and the Bible is true; the world is given over to Mammon. In the increase of material wealth and the accumulation of riches the man who seeks the higher life has no part."

In the face of this comes the statement of the chief statistician of our census—from one, therefore, who speaks with authority: "The present census, when completed, will unquestionably show that the visible material wealth in this country now has a value of ninety billion dollars. This is an addition since 1890 of twenty-five billion dollars. This is a saving greater than all the people of the Western Continent had been able to make from the discovery of Columbus to the breaking out of the Civil War."

If our reasoning from history, experience, and the Bible is correct, we, a Christian people, have rubbed a sponge over the pages of the Bible and are in for orgies and a downfall to which the fall of Rome is a very tame incident.

May it not be well, however, to revise our inferences from history, experience, and the Bible? History tells us that, while riches have been an item and an indirect cause of national decay, innumerable other conditions entered in. Therefore, while wealth has been a source of danger, it has not necessarily led to demoralization.

That leaders have sprung from the ranks of the poor is true and always will be true, so long as force of character exists in every class. But there are other conditions than a lack of wealth at the source of their uprising.

And as to the Bible—while every word that can be quoted against the rich is as true as any other word, other words and deeds are as true; and the parables of our Lord on the stewardship of wealth, His association with the wealthy, strike another and complementary note. Both notes are essential to the harmony of His life and teachings. His thought was not of the conditions, rich or poor, but of a higher life, the character rising out of the conditions— fortunately, for we are released from that subtle hypocrisy which has beset the Christian through the ages, bemoaning the deceitfulness of riches and, at the same time, working with all his might to earn a competence, and a fortune if he can.

Now we are in a position to affirm that neither history, experience, nor the Bible necessarily sustains the common distrust of the effect of material wealth on morality. Our path of study is made more clear. Two positive principles lead us out on our path,

The first is that man, when he is strong, will conquer Nature, open up her resources, and harness them to his service. This is his play, his exercise, his divine mission.

"Man," says Emerson, "is born to be rich. He is thoroughly related, and is tempted out by his appetites and fancies to the conquest of this and that piece of Nature, until he finds his well-being in the use of the planet, and of more planets than his own. Wealth requires, besides the crust of bread and the roof, the freedom of the city, the freedom of the earth." "The strong race is strong on these terms."

Man draws to himself material wealth as surely, as naturally, and as necessarily as the oak draws the elements into itself from the earth.

The other principle is that, in the long run, it is only to the man of morality that wealth comes. We believe in the harmony of God's Universe. We know that it is only by working along His laws natural and spiritual that we can work with efficiency. Only by working along the lines of right thinking and right living can the secrets and wealth of Nature be revealed. We, like the Psalmist, occasionally see the wicked prosper, but only occasionally.

Put two men in adjoining fields, one man strong and normal, the other weak and listless. One picks up his spade, turns over the earth, and works till sunset. The other turns over a few clods, gets a drink from the spring, takes a nap, and loafs back to his work. In a few years one will be rich for his needs, and the other a pauper dependent on the first, and growling at his prosperity.

Put ten thousand immoral men to live and work in one fertile valley and ten thousand moral men to live and work in the next valley, and the question is soon answered as to who wins the material wealth. Godliness is in league with riches.

Now we return with an easier mind and clearer conscience to the problem of our twenty-five billion dollars in a decade.

My question is: Is the material prosperity of this Nation favorable or unfavorable to the morality of the people?

The first thought is, Who has prospered? Who has got the money?

I take it that the loudest answer would be, "The millionaires, the capitalists, and the incompetent but luxurious rich"; and, as we think of that twenty-five billion, our thoughts run over the yachts, the palaces, and the luxuries that flaunt themselves before the public.

As I was beginning to write this paper an Irishman with his horse and wagon drew up at my back door. Note that I say *his* horse and wagon. Twenty years ago that Irishman, then hardly twenty years old, landed in Boston, illiterate, uncouth, scarcely able to make himself understood in English. There was no symptom of brains, alertness, or ambition. He got a job to tend a few cows. Soon the American atmosphere began to take hold. He discovered that here every man has his chance. With his first earnings he bought a suit of clothes; he gained self-respect. Then he sent money home; then he got a job to drive a horse; he opened an account at the savings bank; then evening school; more money in the bank. He changed to a better job, married a thrifty wife, and to-day he owns his house, stable, horse, wagon, and bicycle; has a good sum at the bank, supports five children, and has half a dozen men working under him. He is a capitalist, and his yearly earnings represent the income on $30,000. He had no "pull"; he has made his own way by grit, physical strength, and increasing intelligence. He has had material prosperity. His older brother, who paid his passage over, has had material prosperity, and his younger brother, whose passage my friend paid, has had material prosperity.

Now we are beginning to get an idea as to where the savings are. They are in the hands of hundreds of thousands of just such men, and of scores of thousands of men whose incomes ten years ago were two and five thousand, and are now five and ten thousand; and of thousands of others whose incomes have risen from ten to thirty thousand. So that, when you get to the multi-millionaires, you have only a fraction to distribute among them. And of them the fact is that only a small fraction of their income can be spent upon their own pleasure and luxury; the bulk of what they get has to be reinvested, and becomes the means whereby thousands earn their wages. They are simply trustees of a fraction of the national property.

When, then, the question is asked, "Is the material prosperity of this nation favorable or unfavorable to the morality of the people?" I say with all emphasis, "In the long run, and by all means, favorable!"

In other words, to seek for and earn wealth is a sign of a natural, vigorous, and strong character. Wherever strong men are, there they will turn into the activities of life. In the ages of chivalry you will find them on the crusades or seeking the Golden Fleece; in college life you will find them high in rank, in the boat, or on the athletic field; in an industrial age you will find them eager, straining every nerve in the development of the great industries. The race is to the strong. The search for material wealth is therefore as natural and necessary to the man as is the pushing out of its roots for more moisture and food to the oak. This is man's play, his exercise, the expression of his powers, his personality. You can no more suppress it than you can suppress the tide of the ocean. For one man who seeks money for its own sake there are ten who seek it for the satisfaction of the seeking, the power there is in it, and the use they can make of it. There is the exhilaration of feeling one's self grow in one's surroundings; the man reaches out, lays hold of this, that, and the other interest, scheme, and problem. He is building up a fortune? Yes, but his joy is also that he is building up a stronger, abler, and more powerful man. There are two men that have none of this ambition: the gilded, listless youth and the ragged, listless pauper to whom he tosses a dime; they are in the same class.

We are now ready to take up the subject in a little more detail. How is it favorable? The parable of my Irish friend gives the answer.

In the first place, and as I have already suggested, the effort to make his living and add to his comforts and power gives free play to a man's activities and leads to a development of his faculties. In an age and country where the greater openings are in commercial lines, there the stronger men and the mass of them will move. It is not a question of worldliness or of love of money, but of the natural use and legitimate play of men's faculties. An effort to suppress this action is not a religious duty, but a disastrous error, sure to fail. . . .

A burglar breaks into your home, awakes you, and "strikes" you for $500 which is in your safe downstairs. You expostulate: he answers that he will burn your house. But your children, you cry, will they be safe? He does not know: he wants the money. But if you give it to him, he will try the same on other people. It is against all public duty for you to yield. Again, the threat that he will burn your house; and you, miserable, conscience-stricken that you are doing a cowardly thing, and one against the safety of the public, crawl downstairs, open the safe, and hand over the cash. You have saved your house and children, but how about your duty to the public and your neighbors, as well as to yourself?

This is very much the position of the great trustees of capital, the heads of our great corporations, at the hands of the modern bandit. Shall they jeopardize the income of women and children, merchants and mechanics, and perhaps drive them into poverty? Or shall they accept the situation, yield to the threat, and trust to the authorities to seize the robber, or through an aroused public opinion so to vote, act, and legislate as to change the law and stop this modern brigandage? That some of the promoters and managers of great corporations are unscrupulous is undoubtedly true. The jail is none too good for them, if only the law would touch them. Nor have we a word of apology or justification for any man who yields to or encourages blackmail. The difficulty, however, is not a simple one. It concerns more than the directors and the politicians; it relates to the rights and liberties of the people. I do not have so much fear of the rich man in office, as I do of the poor but weak man in office and the rich man outside. Through the interplay of aroused public opinion, better legislation, and intelligent action, the relief will come. A younger generation, with its eye keen upon that danger-point, is coming to the front.

In some cities of China the houses have no windows on the street, only bare walls and the little door. The families are isolated, narrow, and selfish: there is no public spirit. When the Chinese boy returns home from his Christian Mission School, touched with the spirit of Christian civilization, his first work in bringing civilization to his home is to take a crowbar, knock a hole in the front wall, and make a window, that he may see out and the people see in. He unifies society and creates a public opinion. What is needed as our next step in civilization is to break a hole and make a window that the public may see into the great corporations and trusts and, what is just as important, that the managers may see out and recognize the sentiment of the public.

Light and action—heroic action! There are men to-day waiting and wanting to act, to throw off the shackles of the modern bandit; but they dare not alone: their trusts are too great. What is wanted is a group of men, high in position, great in power, who at great cost, if need be, will stand and say, "Thus far, up to the lines of the nicest honor, shalt thou go, and no farther."

The people have their eye upon the public service. An administration may pay political debts by pushing ignorant and unworthy men into the lower offices, but when it comes to filling positions of great responsibility the President could not, and would not if he could, appoint men less worthy than Wood in Cuba, Allen in Porto Rico, and Taft in the Philippines, men of force, intelligence, and character. Collegiate education does not insure character, but it does sift men and insure intelligence; and, as President Pritchett of the Massachusetts Institute of Technology pointed out in his inaugural address, though less than one per cent of our population are college men, yet from this very small fraction a majority of the legislative, executive, and judicial places of the General Government which have to do in any large way with shaping the policy and determining the character of the government, are chosen.

One other dark shadow, and I am done. The persistent companion of riches—luxury and an ability to have what you want. That vice and license are rampant in certain quarters is clear; that vulgar wealth flaunts itself in the face of the people is beyond question; and that the people are rather amused at the spectacle must be confessed. The theatre syndicate will turn on to the boards whatever the people want; and the general tone of the plays speaks not well for the taste and morality of the people. The strain of temptation overwhelms a fraction of our youth. But one has no more right to test the result of prosperity by the small class of the lazy and luxurious than he has to test the result of poverty by the lazy tramp.

With all this said, the great mass of the people are self-restrained and simple. Material prosperity has come apace, and on the whole it uplifts. Responsibility sobers men and nations. We have learned how to win wealth: we are learning how to use and spend it. Every year marks a long step in advance in material prosperity, and character must march in step. Without wealth, character is liable to narrow and harden. Without character, wealth will destroy. Wealth is upon us, increasing wealth. The call of to-day is, then, for the uplift of character—the support of industry, education, art, and every means of culture; the encouragement of the higher life; and, above all, the deepening of the religious faith of the people; the rekindling of the spirit, that, clothed with her material forces, the great personality of this Nation may fulfil her divine destiny.

I have been clear, I trust, in my opinion that material prosperity is in the long run favorable to morality. Let me be as clear in the statement of that eternal truth, that neither a man's nor a nation's life consists in the abundance of things that he possesseth.

In the investment of wealth in honest enterprise and business, lies our path of character. In the investment of wealth in all that goes towards the uplift of the people in education, art, and religion is another path of character. Above all, and first of all, stands the personal life. The immoral rich man is a traitor to himself, to his material as well as spiritual interests. Material prosperity is upon us; it is marching with us. Character must keep step, ay, character must lead. We want great riches; we want also great men.

(13)

Elihu Root

1845-1937

Elihu Root was descended from Puritan settlers who had migrated to America in 1639. Born in Clinton, New York, Root graduated from Hamilton College in 1865, and received his law degree from New York University School of Law in 1867. He immediately embarked upon a highly successful legal career in New York City, soon attaining a prominent place among the top rank of corporate lawyers. His associations and personal preferences drew him into the ranks of the conservative Republicans, although he himself was a moderate rather than an extreme conservative. After becoming acquainted with Theodore Roosevelt in 1886, he entered the political arena and served as Roosevelt's Secretary of War and Secretary of State, doing an outstanding job in reorganizing the War Department as well as in establishing friendly relations with Latin America. Following his years in the State Department, he served in the Senate for six years and then played an active and important role as elder statesman to the Republican party. Articulate and vocal, Root frequently expounded his brand of moderate conservatism.

The selection that follows was originally given in 1913 as one of the Stafford Little Lectures at Princeton, and is from *Experiments in Government and the Essentials of the Constitution* (Princeton, 1913).

There are two separate processes going on among the civilized nations at the present time. One is an assault by socialism against the individualism which underlies the social system of western civilization. The other is an assault against existing institutions upon the ground that they do not adequately protect and develop the existing social order. It is of this latter process in our own country that I wish to speak, and I assume an agreement, that the right of individual liberty and the inseparable right of private property which lie at the foundation of our modern civilization ought to be maintained. . . .

Now, there has been a general social and industrial rearrangement. Production and commerce pay no attention to state lines. The life of the country is no longer grouped about state capitals, but about the great centers of continental production and trade. The organic growth which must ultimately determine the form of institutions has been away from the mere union of states towards the union of individuals in the relation of national citizenship. . . .

The process of devising and trying new laws to meet new conditions naturally leads to the question whether we need not merely to make new laws but also to modify the principles upon which our government is based and the institutions of government designed for the application of those principles to the affairs of life. Upon this question it is of the utmost importance that we proceed with considerate wisdom. . . .

When proposals are made to change these institutions there are certain general considerations which should be observed.

The first consideration is that free government is impossible except through prescribed and established governmental institutions, which work out the ends of government through many separate human agents, each doing his part in obedience to law. Popular will cannot execute itself directly except through a mob. Popular will cannot get itself executed through an irresponsible executive, for that is simple autocracy. An executive limited only by the direct expression of popular will cannot be held to responsibility against his will, because, having possession of all the powers of government, he can prevent any true, free, and general expression adverse to himself, and unless he yields voluntarily he can be overturned only by a revolution. The familiar Spanish-American dictatorships are illustrations of this. A dictator once established by what is or is alleged to be public choice never permits an expression of public will which will displace him, and he goes out only through a new revolution because he alone controls the machinery through which he could be displaced peaceably. A system with a plebiscite at one end and Louis Napoleon at the other could not give France free government; and it was only after the humiliation of defeat in a great war and the horrors of the Commune that the French people were able to establish a government that would really execute their will through carefully devised institutions in which they gave their chief executive very little power indeed.

We should, therefore, reject every proposal which involves the idea that the people can rule merely by voting, or merely by voting and having one man or group of men to execute their will.

A second consideration is that in estimating the value of any system of governmental institutions due regard must be had to the true functions of government and to the limitations imposed by nature upon what it is possible for government to accomplish. We all know of course that we cannot abolish all the evils in this world by statute or by the enforcement of statutes, nor can we prevent the inexorable law of nature which decrees that suffering shall follow vice, and all the evil passions and folly of mankind. Law cannot give to depravity the rewards of virtue, to indolence the rewards of industry, to indifference the rewards of ambition, or to ignorance the rewards of learning. The utmost that government can do is measurably to protect men, not against the wrong they do themselves but against wrong done by others and to promote the long, slow process of educating mind and character to a better knowledge and nobler standards of life and conduct. We know all this, but when we see how much misery there is in the world and instinctively cry out against it, and when we see some things that government may do to mitigate it, we are apt to forget how little after all it is possible for any government to do, and to hold the particular government of the time and place to a standard of responsibility which no government can possibly meet. The chief motive power which has moved mankind along the course of development that we call the progress of civilization has been the sum total of intelligent selfishness in a vast number of individuals, each working for his own support, his own gain, his own betterment. It is that which has cleared the forests and cultivated the fields and built the ships and railroads, made the discoveries and inventions, covered the earth with commerce, softened by intercourse the enmities of nations and races, and made possible the wonders of literature and of art. Gradually, during the long process, selfishness has grown more intelligent, with a broader view of individual benefit from the common good, and gradually the influences of nobler standards of altruism, of justice, and human sympathy have impressed themselves upon the conception of right conduct among civilized men. But the complete control of such motives will be the millennium. Any attempt to enforce a millennial standard now by law must necessarily fail, and any judgment which assumes government's responsibility to enforce such a standard must be an unjust judgment. Indeed, no such standard can ever be forced. It must come, not by superior force, but from the changed nature of man from his willingness to be altogether just and merciful.

A third consideration is that it is not merely useless but injurious for government to attempt too much. It is manifest that to enable it to deal with the new conditions I have described we must invest government with authority to interfere with the individual conduct of the citizen to a degree hitherto unknown in this country. When government undertakes to give the individual citizen protection by regulating the conduct of others towards him in the field where formerly he protected himself by his freedom of contract, it is limiting the liberty of the citizen whose conduct is regulated and taking a step in the direction of paternal government. While the new conditions of industrial life make it plainly necessary that many such steps shall be taken, they should be taken only so far as they are necessary and are effective. Interference with individual liberty by government should be jealously watched and restrained, because the habit of undue interference destroys that independence of character without which in its citizens no free government can endure. . . .

The habit of undue interference by government in private affairs breeds the habit of undue reliance upon government in private affairs at the expense of individual initiative, energy, enterprise, courage, independent manhood.

The strength of self-government and the motive power of progress must be found in the characters of the individual citizens who make up a nation. Weaken individual character among a people by comfortable reliance upon paternal government and a nation soon becomes incapable of free self-government and fit only to be governed: the higher and nobler qualities of national life that make for ideals and effort and achievement become atrophied and the nation is decadent.

A fourth consideration is that in the nature of things all government must be imperfect because men are imperfect. Every system has its shortcomings and inconveniences; and these are seen and felt as they exist in the system under which we live, while the shortcomings and inconveniences of other systems are forgotten or ignored.

It is not unusual to see governmental methods reformed and after a time, long enough to forget the evils that caused the change, to have a new movement for a reform which consists in changing back to substantially the same old methods that were cast out by the first reform.

The recognition of shortcomings or inconveniences in government is not by itself sufficient to warrant a change of system. There should be also an effort to estimate and compare the short-comings and inconveniences of the system to be substituted, for although they may be different they will certainly exist.

A fifth consideration is that whatever changes in government are to be made, we should follow the *method* which undertakes as one of its cardinal points to hold fast that which is good . . . the great structure of British and American liberty has been built up generation after generation and century after century. Through all the seven hundred years since Magna Charta we have been shaping, adjusting, adapting our system to the new conditions of life as they have arisen, but we have always held on to everything essentially good that we have ever had in the system. We have never undertaken to begin over again and build up a new system under the idea that we could do it better. We have never let go of Magna Charta or the Bill of Rights or the Declaration of Independence or the Constitution. When we take account of all that governments have sought to do and have failed to do in this selfish and sinful world, we find that as a rule the application of new theories of government, though devised by the most brilliant constructive genius, have availed but little to preserve the people of any considerable regions of the earth for any long periods from the evils of despotism on the one hand or of anarchy on the other, or to raise any considerable portion of the mass of mankind above the hard conditions of oppression and misery. And we find that our system of government which has been built up in this practical way through so many centuries, and the whole history of which is potent in the provisions of our Constitution, has done more to preserve liberty, justice, security, and freedom of opportunity for many people for a long period and over a great portion of the earth, than any other system of government ever devised by man. Human nature does not change very much. The forces of evil are hard to control now as they always have been. It is easy to fail and hard to succeed in reconciling liberty and order. In dealing with this most successful body of governmental institutions the question should not be what sort of government do you or I think we should have. What you and I think on such a subject is of very little value indeed. The question should be:

How can we adapt our laws and the workings of our government to the new conditions which confront us without sacrificing any essential element of this system of government which has so nobly stood the test of time and without abandoning the political principles which have inspired the growth of its institutions? For there are political principles, and nothing can be more fatal to self-government than to lose sight of them under the influence of apparent expediency.

The American as Reformer

DESPITE THE PERSISTENCE of a strong and vocal laissez-faire conservative philosophy, there also emerged from the disorders and discontents of the new industrial age a reformist outlook that repudiated the determinism of conservatism and insisted that men could, at least in part, control their own destiny. Compounded of a blend of religious and humanitarian motives, the reformist mind provided the underpinnings of what later was to become known as the theory of the welfare state.

Like the conservatives, the reformers were faced with the problems that marked the advent of a society founded upon an industrial technology. They, too, desired to understand the nature of man and the nature of society, and thus to provide a framework that would ensure the progressive development of the species. They, too, considered themselves to be impartial social scientists and political philosophers seeking an objective explanation and understanding of events. They, too, wanted to assure the maximum development of each individual's potentiality, while at the same time taking into consideration the needs of an increasingly complex, industrialized society.

But if there were similarities, there were also significant differences. Unlike many conservatives, the reformers were distrustful of the thoroughgoing determinism of the followers of Spencer and Sumner. Demonstrating great respect for science, the historical or genetic method in economics and sociology, and a cultural analysis of social problems, they insisted that man through the use of critical intelligence could help to establish a more rational society. For did not man possess what animals lacked, namely, a reasoning faculty? And could he not, therefore, accept naturalistic evolution and direct the evolutionary process into such predetermined channels as he might consider ethically and socially desirable? In other words, the reformers maintained that science and evolution offered a positive justification for human intervention into the affairs of society. When they added this scientific justification to the older theistic outlook, with its emphasis on Christian morality, they established the basis for a philosophy of directed and conscious change.

Beneath the façade of the reform ideology lay certain basic assumptions. In the first place, most of the reformers assumed that man's environment was amenable to his control, and that science provided the method to achieve this aim. Second, they assumed not only the dignity and worth of the individual but also his social nature, which brought society into being. Third, they maintained that man was essentially a rational creature whose innate goodness had been corrupted in part by an improper environment. Finally, and above all, the reformers shared a vision of progress, compounded of a middle-class hope of neutralizing the growth of bigness, whether in labor or capital, and creating what Walter Weyl in *The New Democracy* (1912) called "a socialized democracy." Thus, a morally regenerate middle class, avoiding either the rapaciousness of a robber baron or the radicalism of a union organizer, would create a cooperative commonwealth of men working together in harmonious union, consciously directing progress toward the final perfection of man and society.

It is true that not all the reformers had precisely the same vision, nor did they necessarily justify themselves on the same ideological grounds. There were, after all, wide gulfs between men like Lester Frank Ward, Thorstein Veblen, Richard T. Ely, Henry Demarest Lloyd, Herbert Croly, and others who laid the basis for a philosophy of reform. All of them, however, in one way or another, took paths that eventually converged in the progressive movement of the first part of the twentieth century, a movement dominated by a middle-class version of the good society that would strike an equitable balance between the competing claims of the individual and of society. Theirs was a gentle and humane philosophy that envisioned a better world to come, a world dominated by moral and rational men. These reformers became pragmatists in philosophy; they attempted to develop a scientific ethical theory and apply the scientific method to moral, social, economic, and political problems alike; they interpreted institutions from an evolutionary and economic point of view; and occasionally they even voted Socialist. In the political arena they sought to destroy or regulate monopolies, to make government more representative and amenable to popular control, to provide a measure of social justice for all, and to mitigate the problems of urban life. Optimistic rather than pessimistic, they looked eagerly toward the more rational and humane society of the future, which they would help to create.

(14)

Henry George

1839-1897

Henry George was born in Philadelphia, the son of a middle-class family of English descent. He was brought up in a pious Episcopalian atmosphere, and his schooling was brief and uneventful. Leaving home at an early age, he tried his hand as a sailor, and then became a printer and newspaperman. His early career in journalism brought him in contact with the extreme poverty and social unrest that characterized many of America's urban centers. He was well read and his strongly religious upbringing aroused in him a warm sympathy for the plight of the less fortunate. Before long he was inquiring into the nature and causes of the poverty he saw about him.

In 1879 he published his most famous and important work, *Progress and Poverty*. This book influenced an amazing number of individuals who later became prominent in the progressive movement of the early twentieth century. In his work George attacked the ideology that had grown out of the conservative Darwinian analysis, arguing that it was simply a justification and rationalization of the *status quo*. Insisting that intelligence was itself a product of evolution, he maintained that it could be used to modify an environment in which progress and poverty seemed to go hand in hand. In other words, George attempted to forge a synthesis of evolutionary concepts and Christian ethics. Although his solution to the problem of poverty—the "single tax" upon the unearned increment on the value of land—was never implemented, the ideas that George advanced proved of great importance in formulating an alternative to conservative Darwinism.

The following selection is from *Progress and Poverty* (New York, 1880), fourth edition.

The present century has been marked by a prodigious increase in wealth-producing power. The utilization of steam and electricity, the introduction of improved processes and labor-saving machinery, the greater subdivision and grander scale of production, the wonderful facilitation of exchanges, have multiplied enormously the effectiveness of labor.

At the beginning of this marvelous era it was natural to expect, and it was expected, that labor-saving inventions would lighten the toil and improve the condition of the laborer; that the enormous increase in the power of producing wealth would make real poverty a thing of the past. Could a man of the last century—a Franklin or a Priestley—have seen, in a vision of the future, the steamship taking the place of the sailing vessel, the railroad train of the wagon, the reaping machine of the scythe, the threshing machine of the flail; could he have heard the throb of the engines that in obedience to human will, and for the satisfaction of human desire, exert a power greater than that of all the men and all the beasts of burden of the earth combined; could he have seen the forest tree transformed into finished lumber—into doors, sashes, blinds, boxes or barrels, with hardly the touch of a human hand; the great workshops where boots and shoes are turned out by the case with less labor than the old-fashioned cobbler could have put on a sole; the factories where, under the eye of a girl, cotton becomes cloth faster than hundreds of stalwart weavers could have turned it out with their handlooms; could he have seen steam hammers shaping mammoth shafts and mighty anchors, and delicate machinery making tiny watches; the diamond drill cutting through the heart of the rocks, and coal oil sparing the whale; could he have realized the enormous saving of labor resulting from improved facilities of exchange and communication—sheep killed in Australia eaten fresh in England, and the order given by the London banker in the afternoon executed in San Francisco in the morning of the same day; could he have conceived of the hundred thousand improvements which these only suggest, what would he have inferred as to the social condition of mankind? . . .

Now, however, we are coming into collision with facts which there can be no mistaking. From all parts of the civilized world come complaints of industrial depression; of labor condemned to involuntary idleness; of capital massed and wasting; of pecuniary distress among business men; of want and suffering and anxiety among the working classes. All the dull, deadening pain, all the keen, maddening anguish, that to great masses of men are involved in the words "hard times," afflict the world to-day. This state of things, common to communities differing so widely in situation, in political institutions, in fiscal and financial systems, in density of population and in social organization, can hardly be accounted for by local causes. There is distress where large standing armies are maintained, but there is also distress where the standing armies are nominal; there is distress where protective tariffs stupidly and wastefully hamper trade, but there is also distress where trade is nearly free; there is distress where autocratic government yet prevails, but there is also distress where political power is wholly in the hands of the people; in countries where paper is money, and in countries where gold and silver are the only currency. Evidently, beneath all such things as these, we must infer a common cause.

That there is a common cause, and that it is either what we call material progress or something closely connected with material progress, becomes more than an inference when it is noted that the phenomena we class together and speak of as industrial depression are but intensifications of phenomena which always accompany material progress, and which show themselves more clearly and strongly as material progress goes on. Where the conditions to which material progress everywhere tends are most fully realized—that is to say, where population is densest, wealth greatest, and the machinery of production and exchange most highly developed—we find the deepest poverty, the sharpest struggle for existence, and the most of enforced idleness. . . .

This fact—the great fact that poverty and all its concomitants show themselves in communities just as they develop into the conditions toward which material progress tends—proves that the social difficulties existing wherever a certain stage of progress has been reached, do not arise from local circumstances, but are, in some way or another, engendered by progress itself.

And, unpleasant as it may be to admit it, it is at last becoming evident that the enormous increase in productive power which has marked the present century and is still going on with accelerating ratio, has no tendency to extirpate poverty or to lighten the burdens of those compelled to toil. It simply

widens the gulf between Dives and Lazarus, and makes the struggle for existence more intense. The march of invention has clothed mankind with powers
of which a century ago the boldest imagination could not have dreamed. But
in factories where labor-saving machinery has reached its most wonderful
development, little children are at work; wherever the new forces are anything
like fully utilized, large classes are maintained by charity or live on the verge
of recourse to it; amid the greatest accumulations of wealth, men die of starvation, and puny infants suckle dry breasts; while everywhere the greed of gain,
the worship of wealth, shows the force of the fear of want. The promised land
flies before us like the mirage. The fruits of the tree of knowledge turn as we
grasp them to apples of Sodom that crumble at the touch. . . .

This association of poverty with progress is the great enigma of our times.
It is the central fact from which spring industrial, social, and political difficulties that perplex the world, and with which statesmanship and philanthropy and
education grapple in vain. From it come the clouds that overhang the future of
the most progressive and self-reliant nations. It is the riddle which the Sphinx
of Fate puts to our civilization, and which not to answer is to be destroyed. So
long as all the increased wealth which modern progress brings goes but to
build up great fortunes, to increase luxury and make sharper the contrast between the House of Have and the House of Want, progress is not real and
cannot be permanent. The reaction must come. The tower leans from its foundations, and every new story but hastens the final catastrophe. To educate men
who must be condemned to poverty, is but to make them restive; to base on a
state of most glaring social inequality political institutions under which men
are theoretically equal, is to stand a pyramid on its apex.

All-important as this question is, pressing itself from every quarter painfully upon attention, it has not yet received a solution which accounts for all
the facts and points to any clear and simple remedy. . . .

I propose in the following pages to attempt to solve by the methods of
political economy the great problem I have outlined. I propose to seek the law
which associates poverty with progress, and increases want with advancing
wealth; and I believe that in the explanation of this paradox we shall find the
explanation of those recurring seasons of industrial and commercial paralysis
which, viewed independently of their relations to more general phenomena,
seem so inexplicable. Properly commenced and carefully pursued, such an investigation must yield a conclusion that will stand every test, and as truth, will
correlate with all other truth. For in the sequence of phenomena there is no
accident. Every effect has a cause, and every fact implies a preceding fact. . . .

The term rent, in its economic sense—that is, when used, as I am using it,
to distinguish that part of the produce which accrues to the owners of land or
other natural capabilities by virtue of their ownership—differs in meaning
from the word rent as commonly used. In some respects this economic meaning is narrower than the common meaning; in other respects it is wider.

It is narrower in this: In common speech, we apply the word rent to payments for the use of buildings, machinery, fixtures, etc., as well as to payments

for the use of land or other natural capabilities; and in speaking of the rent of a house or the rent of a farm, we do not separate the price for the use of the improvements from the price for the use of the bare land. But in the economic meaning of rent, payments for the use of any of the products of human exertion are excluded, and of the lumped payments for the use of houses, farms, etc., only that part is rent which constitutes the consideration for the use of the land—that part paid for the use of buildings or other improvements being properly interest, as it is a consideration for the use of capital.

It is wider in this: In common speech we speak of rent only when owner and user are distinct persons. But in the economic sense there is also rent where the same person is both owner and user. Where owner and user are thus the same person, whatever part of his income he might obtain by letting the land to another is rent, while the return for his labor and capital are that part of his income which they would yield him did he hire instead of owning the land. Rent is also expressed in a selling price. When land is purchased, the payment which is made for the ownership, or right to perpetual use, is rent commuted or capitalized. If I buy land for a small price and hold it until I can sell it for a large price, I have become rich, not by wages for my labor or by interest upon my capital, but by the increase of rent. Rent, in short, is the share in the wealth produced which the exclusive right to the use of natural capabilities gives to the owner. Wherever land has an exchange value there is rent in the economic meaning of the term. Wherever land having a value is used, either by owner or hirer, there is rent actual; wherever it is not used, but still has a value, there is rent potential. It is this capacity of yielding rent which gives value to land. Until its ownership will confer some advantage, land has no value.

Thus rent or land value does not arise from the productiveness or utility of land. It in no wise represents any help or advantage given to production, but simply the power of securing a part of the results of production. No matter what are its capabilities, land can yield no rent and have no value until some one is willing to give labor or the results of labor for the privilege of using it; and what any one will thus give depends not upon the capacity of the land, but upon its capacity as compared with that of land that can be had for nothing. I may have very rich land, but it will yield no rent and have no value so long as there is other land as good to be had without cost. But when this other land is appropriated, and the best land to be had for nothing is inferior, either in fertility, situation, or other quality, my land will begin to have a value and yield rent. And though the productiveness of my land may decrease, yet if the productiveness of the land to be had without charge decreases in greater proportion, the rent I can get, and consequently the value of my land, will steadily increase. Rent, in short, is the price of monopoly, arising from the reduction to individual ownership of natural elements which human exertion can neither produce nor increase. . . .

Nothing can be clearer than the proposition that the failure of wages to increase with increasing productive power is due to the increase of rent.

Three things unite to production—labor, capital, and land.

Three parties divide the produce—the laborer, the capitalist, and the land owner.

If, with an increase of production the laborer gets no more and the capitalist no more, it is a necessary inference that the land owner reaps the whole gain.

And the facts agree with the inference. Though neither wages nor interest anywhere increase as material progress goes on, yet the invariable accompaniment and mark of material progress is the increase of rent—the rise of land values.

The increase of rent explains why wages and interest do not increase. The cause which gives to the land holder is the cause which denies to the laborer and capitalist. That wages and interest are higher in new than in old countries is not, as the standard economists say, because nature makes a greater return to the application of labor and capital, but because land is cheaper, and, therefore, as a smaller proportion of the return is taken by rent, labor and capital can keep for their share a larger proportion of what nature does return. It is not the total produce, but the net produce, after rent has been taken from it, that determines what can be divided as wages and interest. Hence, the rate of wages and interest is everywhere fixed, not so much by the productiveness of labor as by the value of land. Wherever the value of land is relatively low, wages and interest are relatively high; wherever land is relatively high, wages and interest are relatively low. . . .

In short, the value of land depending wholly upon the power which its ownership gives of appropriating wealth created by labor, the increase of land values is always at the expense of the value of labor. And, hence, that the increase of productive power does not increase wages, is because it does increase the value of land. Rent swallows up the whole gain and pauperism accompanies progress.

It is unnecessary to refer to facts. They will suggest themselves to the reader. It is the general fact, observable everywhere, that as the value of land increases, so does the contrast between wealth and want appear. It is the universal fact, that where the value of land is highest, civilization exhibits the greatest luxury side by side with the most piteous destitution. To see human beings in the most abject, the most helpless and hopeless condition, you must go, not to the unfenced prairies and the log cabins of new clearings in the backwoods, where man single-handed is commencing the struggle with nature, and land is yet worth nothing, but to the great cities, where the ownership of a little patch of ground is a fortune. . . .

We have traced the unequal distribution of wealth which is the curse and menace of modern civilization to the institution of private property in land. We have seen that so long as this institution exists no increase in productive power can permanently benefit the masses; but, on the contrary, must tend still further to depress their condition. We have examined all the remedies, short of the abolition of private property in land, which are currently relied on or proposed for the relief of poverty and the better distribution of wealth, and have found them all inefficacious or impracticable.

There is but one way to remove an evil—and that is, to remove its cause. Poverty deepens as wealth increases, and wages are forced down while productive power grows, because land, which is the source of all wealth and the field of all labor, is monopolized. To extirpate poverty, to make wages what justice commands they should be, the full earnings of the laborer, we must therefore substitute for the individual ownership of land a common ownership. Nothing else will go to the cause of the evil—in nothing else is there the slightest hope.

This, then, is the remedy for the unjust and unequal distribution of wealth apparent in modern civilization, and for all the evils which flow from it:

We must make land common property. . . .

When it is proposed to abolish private property in land the first question that will arise is that of justice. Though often warped by habit, superstition, and selfishness into the most distorted forms, the sentiment of justice is yet fundamental to the human mind, and whatever dispute arouses the passions of men, the conflict is sure to rage, not so much as to the question "Is it wise?" as to the question "Is it right?"

This tendency of popular discussions to take an ethical form has a cause. It springs from a law of the human mind; it rests upon a vague and instinctive recognition of what is probably the deepest truth we can grasp. That alone is wise which is just; that alone is enduring which is right. In the narrow scale of individual actions and individual life this truth may be often obscured, but in the wider field of national life it everywhere stands out.

I bow to this arbitrament, and accept this test. If our inquiry into the cause which makes low wages and pauperism the accompaniments of material progress has led us to a correct conclusion, it will bear translation from terms of political economy into terms of ethics, and as the source of social evils show a wrong. If it will not do this, it is disproved. If it will do this, it is proved by the final decision. If private property in land be just, then is the remedy I propose a false one; if, on the contrary, private property in land be unjust, then is this remedy the true one.

What constitutes the rightful basis of property? What is it that enables a man justly to say of a thing, "It is mine?" From what springs the sentiment which acknowledges his exclusive right as against all the world? Is it not, primarily, the right of a man to himself, to the use of his own powers, to the enjoyment of the fruits of his own exertions? Is it not this individual right, which springs from and is testified to by the natural facts of individual organization—the fact that each particular pair of hands obey a particular brain and are related to a particular stomach; the fact that each man is a definite, coherent, independent whole—which alone justifies individual ownership? As a man belongs to himself, so his labor when put in concrete form belongs to him.

And for this reason, that which a man makes or produces is his own, as against all the world—to enjoy or to destroy, to use, to exchange, or to give.

No one else can rightfully claim it, and his exclusive right to it involves no wrong to any one else. Thus there is to everything produced by human exertion a clear and indisputable title to exclusive possession and enjoyment which is perfectly consistent with justice, as it descends from the original producer, in whom it vested by natural law. The pen with which I am writing is justly mine. No other human being can rightfully lay claim to it, for in me is the title of the producers who made it. It has become mine, because transferred to me by the stationer, to whom it was transferred by the importer, who obtained the exclusive right to it by transfer from the manufacturer, in whom, by the same process of purchase, vested the rights of those who dug the material from the ground and shaped it into a pen. Thus, my exclusive right of ownership in the pen springs from the natural right of the individual to the use of his own faculties. . . .

With what other power is man by nature clothed, save the power of exerting his own faculties? How can he in any other way act upon or affect material things or other men? Paralyze the motor nerves, and your man has no more external influence or power than a log or stone. From what else, then, can the right of possessing and controlling things be derived? If it spring not from man himself, from what can it spring? Nature acknowledges no ownership or control in man save as the result of exertion. In no other way can her treasures be drawn forth, her powers directed, or her forces utilized or controlled. She makes no discriminations among men, but is to all absolutely impartial. She knows no distinction between master and slave, king and subject, saint and sinner. All men to her stand upon an equal footing and have equal rights. She recognizes no claim but that of labor, and recognizes that without respect to the claimant. . . .

If production give to the producer the right to exclusive possession and enjoyment, there can rightfully be no exclusive possession and enjoyment of anything not the production of labor, and the recognition of private property in land is a wrong. For the right to the produce of labor cannot be enjoyed without the right to the free use of the opportunities offered by nature, and to admit the right of property in these is to deny the right of property in the produce of labor. When non-producers can claim as rent a portion of the wealth created by producers, the right of the producers to the fruits of their labor is to that extent denied.

There is no escape from this position. To affirm that a man can rightfully claim exclusive ownership in his own labor when embodied in material things, is to deny that any one can rightfully claim exclusive ownership in land. To affirm the rightfulness of property in land, is to affirm a claim which has no warrant in nature, as against a claim founded in the organization of man and the laws of the material universe. . . .

The moment this distinction is realized, that moment is it seen that the sanction which natural justice gives to one species of property is denied to the other; that the rightfulness which attaches to individual property in the produce of labor implies the wrongfulness of individual property in land; that, whereas the recognition of the one places all men upon equal terms, securing to each the due reward of his labor, the recognition of the other is the denial of the equal rights of men, permitting those who do not labor to take the natural reward of those who do.

Whatever may be said for the institution of private property in land, it is therefore plain that it cannot be defended on the score of justice.

The equal right of all men to the use of land is as clear as their equal right to breathe the air—it is a right proclaimed by the fact of their existence. For we cannot suppose that some men have a right to be in this world and others no right.

If we are all here by the equal permission of the Creator, we are all here with an equal title to the enjoyment of his bounty—with an equal right to the use of all that nature so impartially offers. This is a right which is natural and inalienable; it is a right which vests in every human being as he enters the world, and which during his continuance in the world can be limited only by the equal rights of others. There is in nature no such thing as a fee simple in land. There is on earth no power which can rightfully make a grant of exclusive ownership in land. If all existing men were to unite to grant away their equal rights, they could not grant away the right of those who follow them. For what are we but tenants for a day? Have we made the earth, that we should determine the rights of those who after us shall tenant it in their turn? The Almighty, who created the earth for man and man for the earth, has entailed it upon all the generations of the children of men by a decree written upon the constitution of all things—a decree which no human action can bar and no prescription determine. Let the parchments be ever so many, or possession ever so long, natural justice can recognize no right in one man to the possession and enjoyment of land that is not equally the right of all his fellows. Though his titles have been acquiesced in by generation after generation, to the landed estates of the Duke of Westminster the poorest child that is born in London to-day has as much right as has his eldest son. Though the sovereign people of the State of New York consent to the landed possessions of the Astors, the puniest infant that comes wailing into the world in the squalidest room of the most miserable tenement house, becomes at that moment seized of an equal right with the millionaires. And it is robbed if the right is denied. . . .

We have traced the want and suffering that everywhere prevail among the working classes, the recurring paroxysms of industrial depression, the scarcity of employment, the stagnation of capital, the tendency of wages to the starvation point, that exhibit themselves more and more strongly as material progress goes on, to the fact that the land on which and from which all must live is made the exclusive property of some.

We have seen that there is no possible remedy for these evils but the abolition of their cause; we have seen that private property in land has no warrant in justice, but stands condemned as the denial of natural right—a subversion of the law of nature that as social development goes on must condemn the masses of men to a slavery the hardest and most degrading.

We have weighed every objection, and seen that neither on the ground of equity or expediency is there anything to deter us from making land common property by confiscating rent.

But a question of method remains. How shall we do it?

We should satisfy the law of justice, we should meet all economic requirements, by at one stroke abolishing all private titles, declaring all land public property, and letting it out to the highest bidders in lots to suit, under such conditions as would sacredly guard the private right to improvements. . . . .

It is an axiom of statesmanship, which the successful founders of tyranny have understood and acted upon—that great changes can best be brought about under old forms. We, who would free men, should heed the same truth. It is the natural method. When nature would make a higher type, she takes a lower one and develops it. This, also, is the law of social growth. Let us work by it. With the current we may glide fast and far. Against it, it is hard pulling and slow progress.

I do not propose either to purchase or to confiscate private property in land. The first would be unjust; the second, needless. Let the individuals who now hold it still retain, if they want to, possession of what they are pleased to call *their* land. Let them continue to call it *their* land. Let them buy and sell, and bequeath and devise it. We may safely leave them the shell, if we take the kernel. *It is not necessary to confiscate land; it is only necessary to confiscate rent.*

Nor to take rent for public uses is it necessary that the State should bother with the letting of lands, and assume the chances of the favoritism, collusion, and corruption this might involve. It is not necessary that any new machinery should be created. The machinery already exists. Instead of extending it, all we have to do is to simplify and reduce it. By leaving to land owners a percentage of rent which would probably be much less than the cost and loss involved in attempting to rent lands through State agency, and by making use of this existing machinery, we may, without jar or shock, assert the common right to land by taking rent for public uses.

We already take some rent in taxation. We have only to make some changes in our modes of taxation to take it all.

What I, therefore, propose, as the simple yet sovereign remedy, which will raise wages, increase the earnings of capital, extirpate pauperism, abolish poverty, give remunerative employment to whoever wishes it, afford free scope to human powers, lessen crime, elevate morals, and taste, and intelligence, purify government and carry civilization to yet nobler heights, is—*to appropriate rent by taxation.*

In this way the State may become the universal landlord without calling herself so, and without assuming a single new function. In form, the ownership of land would remain just as now. No owner of land need be dispossessed, and no restriction need be placed upon the amount of land any one could hold.

For, rent being taken by the State in taxes, land, no matter in whose name it stood, or in what parcels it was held, would be really common property, and every member of the community would participate in the advantages of its ownership.

Now, insomuch as the taxation of rent, or land values, must necessarily be increased just as we abolish other taxes, we may put the proposition into practical form by proposing—

To abolish all taxation save that upon land values.

As we have seen, the value of land is at the beginning of society nothing, but as society develops by the increase of population and the advance of the arts, it becomes greater and greater. In every civilized country, even the newest, the value of the land taken as a whole is sufficient to bear the entire expenses of government. In the better developed countries it is much more than sufficient. Hence it will not be enough merely to place all taxes upon the value of land. It will be necessary, where rent exceeds the present governmental revenues, commensurately to increase the amount demanded in taxation, and to continue this increase as society progresses and rent advances. But this is so natural and easy a matter, that it may be considered as involved, or at least understood, in the proposition to put all taxes on the value of land. That is the first step, upon which the practical struggle must be made. When the hare is once caught and killed, cooking him will follow as a matter of course. When the common right to land is so far appreciated that all taxes are abolished save those which fall upon rent, there is no danger of much more than is necessary to induce them to collect the public revenues being left to individual land holders. . . .

The poverty which in the midst of abundance pinches and embrutes men, and all the manifold evils which flow from it, spring from a denial of justice. In permitting the monopolization of the opportunities which nature freely offers to all, we have ignored the fundamental law of justice—for, so far as we can see, when we view things upon a large scale, justice seems to be the supreme law of the universe. But by sweeping away this injustice and asserting the rights of all men to natural opportunities, we shall conform ourselves to the law—we shall remove the great cause of unnatural inequality in the distribution of wealth and power; we shall abolish poverty; tame the ruthless passions of greed; dry up the springs of vice and misery; light in dark places the lamp of knowledge; give new vigor to invention and a fresh impulse to discovery; substitute political strength for political weakness; and make tyranny and anarchy impossible.

The reform I have proposed accords with all that is politically, socially, or morally desirable. It has the qualities of a true reform, for it will make all other reforms easier. What is it but the carrying out in letter and spirit of the truth enunciated in the Declaration of Independence—the "self-evident" truth that is the heart and soul of the Declaration—"*That all men are created equal; that they are endowed by their Creator with certain unalienable rights; that among these are life, liberty, and the pursuit of happiness!"*

These rights are denied when the equal right to land—on which and by which men alone can live—is denied. Equality of political rights will not compensate for the denial of the equal right to the bounty of nature. Political liberty, when the equal right to land is denied, becomes, as population increases and invention goes on, merely the liberty to compete for employment at starvation wages. This is the truth that we have ignored.

(15)

Lester Frank Ward

1841-1913

> The son of a mechanic, Lester Frank Ward was born in Joliet, Illinois. He served in the Union Army during the Civil War and was wounded at the battle of Chancellorsville. In 1865 he accepted a position with the Treasury Department and held that post until 1881. Meanwhile he studied at what today is George Washington University, receiving an A.B. in 1869, an LL.B. in 1871, and an A.M. in 1872. After leaving the Treasury Department, he joined the United States Geological Survey, where he made some valuable contributions to the natural sciences. Ward's fame, however, rests upon his numerous writings in the field of sociology.
>
> Drawing on his broad background in the modern sciences, Ward attempted to apply the concept of evolution to sociology. In his view of evolution, he carefully distinguished between physical or animal evolution, which was essentially purposeless, and human evolution, which could be modified by purposive action. The most significant factor in Ward's system was the existence of mind, which enabled man to pass from passive to active evolutionary processes, from physical to human or social evolution. Hence, Ward was a staunch advocate of rational and scientific planning in order to direct the evolutionary process into socially desirable channels, and he influenced several generations of young sociologists who took up where he had left off.
>
> The following selection, "Mind as a Social Factor," which appeared in *Mind,* 9 (October, 1884), is illustrative of Ward's interpretation of evolution.

☆　☆　☆　☆

Can the *laissez faire* doctrine be successfully met? That all attempts to do this have been timidly made cannot be denied. That these have been few and feeble is equally certain. While there has existed in the minds of many rational persons a vague sense of some hidden fallacy in all this reasoning, none have felt competent to formulate their objections with sufficient clearness and force to warrant pitting them against the resistless stream of concurrent science and philosophy of the nineteenth century. There has, however, been developing of late a more or less marked apprehension with regard to the possible consequences of this mode of thought. The feeling is distinct in the best minds, and to a large extent in the public mind, that the tendency of modern ideas is nihilistic. It is clear that if they become universally accepted they must work stagnation in society. The *laissez faire* doctrine is a gospel of inaction, the scientific creed is struck with sterility, the policy of resigning all into the hands of Nature is a surrender.

But this recognition is by no means proof that the prevalent opinions are false. At best it can only suggest this on the ground that true doctrines should be progressive. But this would be a *petitio principii.* Nature is not optimistic, still less anthropocentric. For aught we know, the laws of nature are such as make a recognition of strict scientific truth a positive barrier to social advancement. The argument we have been considering must be refuted, if at all, by legitimate counter-argument.

The present attempt to meet some parts of this argument is made in full consciousness of its strength as a factor in modern thought and with due deference to the great names that stand committed to it. The scientific facts which its defenders have brought to its support are, in the main, incontestable. To answer by denying these would be to abjure science and deserve contempt. The method of nature has been correctly interpreted. The doctrines of the survival of the fittest and natural selection are perfectly true doctrines. The law of competition is the fundamental law. It is unquestionably true that progress, not only in primary organic development, but also in society, has resulted from the action of this law.

After conceding all this, the attempt, notwithstanding, to stem the tide of modern scientific thought must, indeed, seem a hopeless one. At the outset it must be frankly acknowledged that if the current views are unsound the fault is not chargeable to science. If there is any defect it must lie in the inferences drawn from the facts and not in the facts themselves. To what extent, then, is the *laissez faire* doctrine, as defined and popularly accepted, an inference? If the method of nature is correctly formulated by that doctrine, wherein lies the fallacy when it is applied to man and to society? . . .

It has always been a marvel to my comprehension that wise men and philosophers, when smitten with the specious logic of the *laissez faire* school, can close their eyes to the most obtrusive fact that civilisation presents. In spite of the influence of philosophy, all forms of which have thus far been negative and nihilistic, the human animal, with his growing intellect, has still ever realised the power that is vouchsafed through mind, and has ever exercised that power. Philosophy would have long since robbed him of it and caused his early extermination from the earth but for the persistence, through heredity, of the impulse to exercise in self-preservation every power in his possession; by which practice alone he first gained his ascendancy ages before philosophy began.

The great fact, then, to which I allude is that, in spite of all philosophy, whether mythologic, metaphysical, or naturalistic, declaring that man must and can do nothing, he *has,* from the very dawn of his intelligence, been transforming the entire surface of the planet he inhabits. No other animal performs anything comparable to what man performs. This is solely because no other possesses the developed psychic faculty.

If we analyse mind into its two departments, sense and intellect, we shall see that it is through this latter faculty that these results are accomplished. If we inquire more closely into the mode by which intellect operates, we shall find that it serves as a guiding power to those natural forces with which it is acquainted (and no others), directing them into channels of human advantage. If we seek for a single term by which to characterise with precision the nature of this process, we find this in *Invention.* The essential characteristic of all intellectual action is invention.

Glancing now at the *ensemble* of human achievement, which may be collectively called civilisation, we readily see that it is all the result of this inventive process. All practical art is merely the product of successful invention, and it requires no undue expansion of the term, nor extraordinary power of generalisation, to see in all human institutions only modified forms of arts, and true products of the intellectual, or inventive, faculty.

But what is the general result of all this? An entirely new dispensation has been given to the world. All the materials and forces of nature have been thus placed completely under the control of one of the otherwise least powerful of the creatures inhabiting the earth. He has only to know them in order to become their master. Nature has thus been made the servant of man. Thus only has man succeeded in peopling the entire globe while all other animals are restricted to narrow faunal areas. He has also peopled certain portions far more densely than any other species could have done, and he seems destined to continue multiplying his numbers for a long time yet in the future. But this quantitative proof is even less telling than the qualitative. When we confine our attention to the *élite* of mankind we do not need to have the ways specified in detail by which the powers of mind have exalted the intellectual being above all other products of creation. At the present moment the most dense and the most enlightened populations of the globe occupy what are termed temperate latitudes, which means latitudes in which for from three to five months each year vegetation ceases entirely, the waters are locked in ice, and the temperature frequently sinks far below the zero of the Fahrenheit thermometer. Imagine the thin-skinned, furless animal man subsisting in such a climate. Extinguish his fires, banish his clothing, blot out the habitations that deck the civilised landscape. How long would the puny race survive? But these are not products of nature, they are products of *art,* the wages of thought—fruits of the intellect.

When a well-clothed philosopher on a bitter winter's night sits in a warm room well lighted for his purpose and writes on paper with pen and ink in the arbitrary characters of a highly developed language the statement that civilisation is the result of natural laws, and that man's duty is to let nature alone so that untrammeled it may work out a higher civilisation, he simply ignores every circumstance of his existence and deliberately closes his eyes to every fact within the range of his faculties. If man had acted upon his theory there would have been no civilisation, and our philosopher would have remained a troglodyte.

But how shall we distinguish this human, or anthropic, method from the method of nature? Simply by reversing all the definitions. Art is the antithesis of nature. If we call one the natural method we must call the other the artificial method. If nature's process is rightly named natural selection, man's process is artificial selection. The survival of the fittest is simply the survival of the strong, which implies, and might as well be called, the destruction of the weak. And if nature progresses through the destruction of the weak, man progresses through the *protection* of the weak. This is the essential distinction.

In human society the psychic power has operated to secure the protection of the weak in two distinct ways: first, by increasing the supply of the necessities of life, and, secondly, by preventing the destruction of life through the enemies of man. The immediate instrumentality through which the first of these processes is carried on is art, the product of invention. The second process takes place through the establishment of positive institutions.

It is difficult to say which of these agencies has been most effective. Both were always indispensable, and therefore all comparison is unprofitable.

Art operates to protect the weak against adverse surroundings. It is directed against natural forces, chiefly physical. By thus defeating the destructive influences of the elements and hostile forms of life, and by forcing nature to yield an unnatural supply of man's necessities, many who would have succumbed from inability to resist these adverse agencies—the feebler members of society—were able to survive, and population increased and expanded. While no one openly denies this, there is a tendency either to ignore it in politico-economic discussions, or to deny its application to them as an answer to naturalistic arguments.

If, on the other hand, we inquire into the nature of human institutions, we shall perceive that they are of three kinds, tending to protect the weak in three ways, or ascending degrees. These three successively higher means through which this end is attained are, first, Justice, second, Morality, and third, Charity. These forms of action have been reached through the development, respectively, of the three corresponding sentiments: Equity, Beneficence, and Benevolence.

All of these altruistic sentiments are wholly unknown, or known only in the merest embryo, to all animals below man, and therefore no such means of protection exist among them. They are strictly human, or anthropic. Many evolutionists fail to recognise this. Some sociologists refuse to admit it. They look about and see so much injustice, immorality and rapacity that they are led to suppose that only natural methods are in operation in society. This is a great mistake. In point of fact, the keener the sense of justice the more conspicuous the diminishing number of violations of it come to appear, and conversely, the obviousness of injustice proves the general prevalence of justice. It is the same with morality and philanthropy.

If we consider the effect of these three codes of human conduct in the direction of enabling the weaker ones to survive we shall see that it has been immense. Out of the first has arisen government, the chief value and function of which has always been and still is such protection. Great systems of jurisprudence have been elaborated, engrossing the attention of a large portion of the population of enlightened as well as of barbaric states. To say that these have been failures because often weighted with grave defects is to misinterpret history and misunderstand society. No one could probably be found to gainsay that the moral law of society has exerted a salutary influence, yet its aim is strictly altruistic, opposed to the law of the survival of the fittest, and wholly in the direction of enabling those to survive who would not survive without its protection. Finally, the last sentiment to be developed, and doubtless the highest, is so universally recognised as peculiar to man that his very name has been given to it—the sentiment of *humanity*. Yet the mode of protecting the weak arising out of this sentiment is the one that has been most seriously called in question by the naturalistic school. It must be admitted that humanitarian institutions have done far less good than either juridical or ethical institutions. The sentiment itself is of recent origin, the product only of highly developed and greatly refined mental organisation. It exists to an appreciable degree only in a minute fraction of the most enlightened populations. It is rarely directed with judgment; no fixed, self-enforcing code of conduct, as in the other cases, having had time to take shape. The institutions established to enforce it are for the most part poorly supported, badly managed, and often founded on a total misconception of human nature and of the true mode of attaining the end in view. Hence they are specially open to attack. But if ever humanitarian sentiments become diffused throughout the body politic, become the object of deep study, as have those of justice and right, it may be confidently predicted that society will prove itself capable of caring for the most unfortunate of its members in a manner that shall not work demoralisation.

In all these ways man, through his intelligence, has laboured successfully to resist the law of nature. His success is conclusively demonstrated by a comparison of his condition with that of other species of animals. No other cause can be assigned for his superiority. How can the naturalistic philosophers shut their eyes to such obvious facts? Yet, what is their attitude? They condemn all attempts to protect the weak, whether by private or public methods. They claim that it deteriorates the race by enabling the unfit to survive and transmit their inferiority. This is true only in certain cases of hereditary diseases or mental deficiencies, which should be taken account of by man because they are not by nature. Nothing is easier than to show that the unrestricted competition of nature does not secure the survival of the fittest possible, but only of the actually fittest, and in every attempt man makes to obtain something fitter than this actual fittest he succeeds, as witness improved breeds of animals and grafts of fruits. Now, the human method of protecting the weak deals in some such way with men. It not only increases the number but improves the quality.

But "government," at least, must *laisser faire*. It must not "meddle" with natural laws. The laws of trade, business, social intercourse, are natural laws, immutable and indestructible. All interference with them is vain. The fallacy here is a *non sequitur*. It may be readily granted that these laws are immutable and indestructible. Were this not the case it would certainly be hopeless to interfere with their action. But every mechanical invention proves that nothing is easier than to interfere successfully with the operation of these uniform natural forces. They have only to be first thoroughly understood and then they are easily *controlled*. To *destroy* a force is one thing, to control its action is quite another. Those who talk in this way involve themselves in the most palpable inconsistency. They must not be allowed to stop where they do. They must go on and carry their strictures to a logical conclusion. They must deny to government the right to protect its citizens from injustice. This is a clear interference with the natural laws of society. They must deny to society the right to enforce its code of morals. Nothing is more unnatural. They must suppress the healing art which keeps the sick from dying as they do among animals. Nor is this all. They must condemn all interference with physical laws and natural forces. To dam a stream must be characterised as a "vain" attempt to overcome a natural law. The wind must be left free to blow where it will, and not be forced against the fan of a wind-mill. The vapour of heated water must be allowed to float off naturally into the air and not be pent up in a steamboiler and thence conducted into the cylinder of a steam-engine. All these things and every other device of inventive man are so many attempts to "violate" the laws of nature, which is declared impossible.

What then remains of the *laissez faire* doctrine? Nothing but this: That it is useless, and may be dangerous, to attempt to control natural forces until their character is first well understood. This is a proposition which is true for every department of force, and does not involve the surrender of the whole domain of sociology after it has been demonstrated that society is a theatre of forces.

The truth thus comes forth from a rational study of nature and human society that social progress has been due only in very slight degree to natural evolution as accomplished through the survival of the fittest, and its chief success has resulted from the reduction of competition in the struggle for existence and the protection of the weaker members. Such competition, in so far as it has been permitted to operate, has tended to lower the standard of the fittest and to check advancement. It is not, of course, claimed that the natural method has ever been fully overcome. It has always operated, and still operates, powerfully in many ways. It has been chiefly in the simpler departments of physical and mechanical phenomena that the psychic, or anthropic, method has superseded it. The inventive arts have been the result. Vital forces have yielded to some extent to the influence of mind in bringing about improved stocks of animals and vegetables, and even certain social laws have come under rational control through the establishment of institutions. Still, every step in this progress has been contested. It was not enough that the intellect was feeble and ill-fitted to grapple with such problems. It was not enough that ignorance of nature's laws should cause unnumbered failures. A still stronger barrier was presented by the intellect itself in the form of positive error embodied in philosophy. As already remarked, philosophy has always been negative and nihilistic, and has steadily antagonised the common sense of mankind. It is only quite recently that there has come into existence anything like a truly *positive* philosophy, *i.e.,* a philosophy of *action*. The intellectual power of enlightened man has at length become sufficient to grasp the problems of social life. A large body of truth has been accumulated by which to be guided in their solution. Positive error in the drawing of false conclusions from established facts is now the chief obstacle. Rational interpretation has come to prevail in all the lower departments of phenomena. It is chiefly in the complex departments of psychic and social action that error still holds sway. Nothing remains to be done but to apply the established canons of science to these higher fields of activity. Here there is still competition. Here the weaker still go to the wall. Here the strong are still the fittest to survive. Here Nature still practises her costly selection which always involves the destruction of the defenceless. The demand is for still further reduction of competition, still greater interference with the operations of natural forces, still more complete control of the laws of nature, and still more absolute supremacy of the psychic over the natural method of evolution.

These ends will be secured in proportion as the true nature of mind is understood. When nature comes to be regarded as passive and man as active, instead of the reverse as now, when human action is recognised as the most important of all forms of action, and when the power of the human intellect over vital, psychic and social phenomena is practically conceded, then, and then only, can man justly claim to have risen out of the animal and fully to have entered the human stage of development.

(16)

Henry Demarest Lloyd

1847-1903

Henry Demarest Lloyd was born in New York City and was brought up in a rigid Calvinistic atmosphere, against which he later reacted. Receiving an M.A. from Columbia College in 1869, he was admitted to the New York Bar, and then became immersed in various municipal reform activities. In 1872 he joined the staff of the *Chicago Tribune* as financial editor and editorial writer. In this job he came to understand the growing problem of trusts, and began to write extensively about the problems of corporate monopoly and unethical business practices. From 1885 on he devoted all his energies to the matter of public welfare. Nine years later he published his famous work *Wealth Against Commonwealth,* a vigorous attack on monopolies, especially the Standard Oil Company. Later Lloyd took an active role in the Populist movement, and then, moving further to the left, was on the point of joining the Socialist party when he died in 1903. Throughout his career Lloyd was critical of conservative Darwinism, classical economics, and the entire theory of laissez faire. Pointing out that competition frequently resulted in monopoly, he denied that the fittest (not necessarily defined as the wealthiest) survived in an unfettered struggle for existence. The alternative facing the American people, he maintained, was either reform or revolution. He insisted, therefore, that the state was a desirable vehicle for social and economic reform, and that public ownership of monopolies was indispensable. He believed that only a Fabian socialistic approach could achieve a balance between the claims of the individual and those of society. Influenced by reform Darwinism, Lloyd played a major role in awakening the urban middle class to the problems and dilemmas of an industrialized society.

The following selection is from his *Wealth Against Commonwealth* (New York, 1894).

If our civilization is destroyed, as Macaulay predicted, it will not be by his barbarians from below. Our barbarians come from above. Our great money-makers have sprung in one generation into seats of power kings do not know. The forces and the wealth are new, and have been the opportunity of new men. Without restraints of culture, experience, the pride, or even the inherited caution of class or rank, these men, intoxicated, think they are the wave instead of the float, and that they have created the business which has created them. To them science is but a never-ending répertoire of investments stored up by nature for the syndicates, government but a fountain of franchises, the nations but customers in squads, and a million the unit of a new arithmetic of wealth written for them. They claim a power without control, exercised through forms which make it secret, anonymous, and perpetual. The possibilities of its gratification have been widening before them without interruption since they began, and even at a thousand millions they will feel no satiation and will see no place to stop. They are gluttons of luxury and power, rough, unsocialized, believing that mankind must be kept terrorized. Powers of pity die out of them, because they work through agents and die in their agents, because what they do is not for themselves.

Of gods, friends, learnings, of the uncomprehended civilization they overrun, they ask but one question: How much? What is a good time to sell? What is a good time to buy? The Church and the Capitol, incarnating the sacrifices and triumphs of a procession of martyrs and patriots since the dawn of freedom, are good enough for a money-changer's shop for them, and a market and shambles. Their heathen eyes see in the law and its consecrated officers nothing but an intelligence-office and hired men to help them burglarize the treasures accumulated for thousands of years at the altars of liberty and justice, that they may burn their marbles for the lime of commerce. . . .

Business motived by the self-interest of the individual runs into monoply at every point it touches the social life—land monopoly, transportation monopoly, trade monopoly, political monopoly in all its forms, from contraction of the currency to corruption in office. The society in which in half a lifetime a man without a penny can become a hundred times a millionaire is as overripe, industrially, as was, politically, the Rome in which the most popular bully could lift himself from the ranks of the legion on to the throne of the Cæsars. Our rising issue is with business. Monopoly is business at the end of its journey. It has got there. The irrepressible conflict is now as distinctly with business as the issue so lately met was with slavery. Slavery went first only because it was the cruder form of business. . . .

We have given the prize of power to the strong, the cunning, the arithmetical, and we must expect nothing else but that they will use it cunningly and arithmetically. For what else can they suppose we gave it to them? If the power really flows from the people, and should be used for them; if its best administration can be got, as in government, only by the participation in it of men of all views and interests; if in the collision of all these, as in democracy, the better policy is progressively preponderant; if this is a policy which, with whatever defects, is better than that which can be evolved by narrower or more selfish or less multitudinous influences of persons or classes, then this power should be taken up by the people. "The mere conflict of private interests will never produce a well-ordered commonwealth of labor," says the author of the article on political economy in the *Encyclopædia Britannica*. The failure of monarchy and feudalism and the visibly impending failure of our business system all reveal a law of nature. The harmony of things insists that that which is the source of power, wealth, and delight shall also be the ruler of it. That which is must also seem. It is the people from whom come the forces with which kings and millionaires ride the world, and until the people take their proper place in the seat of sovereignty, these pseudo owners—mere claimants and usurpers—will, by the very falsity and iniquity of their position, be pushed into deceit, tyranny, and cruelty, ending in downfall.

Thousands of years' experience has proved that government must begin where it ends—with the people; that the general welfare demands that they who exercise the powers and they upon whom these are exercised must be the same, and that higher political ideals can be realized only through higher political forms. Myriads of experiments to get the substance of liberty out of the forms of tyranny, to believe in princes, to trust good men to do good as kings, have taught the inexorable truth that, in the economy of nature, form and substance must move together, and are as inextricably interdependent as are, within our experience, what we call matter and spirit. Identical is the lesson we are learning with regard to industrial power and property. We are calling upon their owners, as mankind called upon kings in their day, to be good and kind, wise and sweet, and we are calling in vain. We are asking them not to be what we have made them to be. We put power into their hands and ask them not to use it as power. If this power is a trust for the people, the people betrayed it when they made private estates out of it for individuals. If the spirit of power is to change, institutions must change as much. Liberty recast the old forms of government into the Republic, and it must remould our institutions of wealth into the Commonwealth.

The question is not whether monopoly is to continue. The sun sets every night on a greater majority against it. We are face to face with the practical issue: Is it to go through ruin or reform? Can we forestall ruin by reform? If we wait to be forced by events we shall be astounded to find how much more radical they are than our utopias. Louis XVI. waited until 1793, and gave his head and all his investitures to the people who in 1789 asked only to sit at his feet and speak their mind. Unless we reform of our own free will, nature will reform us by force, as nature does. Our evil courses have already gone too far in producing misery, plagues, hatreds, national enervation. Already the leader is unable to lead, and has begun to drive with judges armed with bayonets and Gatling guns. History is the serial obituary of the men who thought they could drive men.

Reform is the science and conscience with which mankind in its manhood overcomes temptations and escapes consequences by killing the germs. Ruin is already hard at work among us. Our libraries are full of the official inquiries and scientific interpretations which show how our master-motive is working decay in all our parts. The family crumbles into a competition between the father and the children whom he breeds to take his place in the factory, to unfit themselves to be fathers in their turn. A thorough, stalwart resimplification, a life governed by simple needs and loves, is the imperative want of the world. It will be accomplished: either self-conscious volition does it, or the slow wreck and decay of superfluous and unwholesome men and matters. The latter is the method of brutes and brute civilizations. The other is the method of man, so far as he is divine. Has not man, who has in personal reform risen above the brute method, come to the height at which he can achieve social reform in masses and by nations? We must learn; we can learn by reason. Why wait for the crueler teacher?

We have a people like which none has ever existed before. We have millions capable of conscious co-operation. The time must come in social evolution when the people can organize the free-will to choose salvation which the individual has been cultivating for 1900 years, and can adopt a policy more dignified and more effective than leaving themselves to be kicked along the path of reform by the recoil of their own vices. We must bring the size of our morality up to the size of our cities, corporations, and combinations, or these will be brought down to fit our half-grown virtue.

Industry and monopoly cannot live together. Our modern perfection of exchange and division of labor cannot last without equal perfection of morals and sympathy. Every one is living at the mercy of every one else in a way entirely peculiar to our times. Nothing is any longer made by a man; parts of things are made by parts of men, and become wholes by the luck of a good-humor which so far keeps men from flying asunder. It takes a whole company to make a match. A hundred men will easily produce a hundred million matches, but not one of them could make one match. No farm gets its plough from the cross-roads blacksmith, and no one in the chilled-steel factory knows the whole of the plough. The life of Boston hangs on a procession of reciprocities which must move, as steadily and sweetly as the roll of the planets, between its bakeries, the Falls of St. Anthony, and the valley of the Red River. Never was there a social machinery so delicate. Only on terms of love and justice can men endure contact so close. . . .

Whether the great change comes with peace or sword, freely through reform or by nature's involuntary forces, is a mere matter of detail, a question of convenience—not of the essence of the thing. The change will come. With reform, it may come to us. If with force, perhaps not to us. But it will come. The world is too full of amateurs who can play the golden rule as an aria with variations. All the runs and trills and transpositions have been done to death. All the "sayings" have been said. The only field for new effects is in epigrams of practice. Titillation of our sympathies has become a dissipation. We shed a daily tear over the misery of the slums as the toper takes his dram, and our liver becomes torpid with the floods of indignation and sentiment we have guzzled without converting them into their co-efficients of action.

"Regenerate the individual" is a half-truth; the reorganization of the society which he makes and which makes him is the other half. Man alone cannot be a Christian. Institutions are applied beliefs. The love of liberty became liberty in America by clothing itself in the complicated group of structures known as the government of the United States. Love is a half-truth, and kissing is a good deal less than half of that. We need not kiss all our fellow-men, but we must do for them all we ask them to do for us—nothing less than the fullest performance of every power. To love our neighbor is to submit to the discipline and arrangement which make his life reach its best, and so do we best love ourselves.

History has taught us nothing if not that men can continue to associate only by the laws of association. The golden rule is the first and last of these, but the first and last of the golden rule is that it can be operated only through laws, habits, forms, and institutions. The Constitution and laws of the United States are, however imperfectly, the translation into the language of politics of doing as you would be done by—the essence of equal rights and government by consent. To ask individuals to-day to lead by their single sacrifices the life of the brother in the world of business is as if the American colonist had

been asked to lead by his individual enterprise the life of the citizen of a republic. That was made possible to him only by union with others. The business
world is full of men who yearn to abandon its methods and live the love they
feel; but to attempt to do so by themselves would be martyrdom, and that is
"caviare to the general." "We admire martyrdom," Mazzini, the martyr, said,
"but we do not recommend it." The change must be social, and its martyrdoms
have already begun.

The new self-interest will remain unenforced in business until we invent
the forms by which the vast multitudes who have been gathered together in
modern production can organize themselves into a people there as in government. Nothing but this institutionalization will save them from being scattered away from each other again, and it can be achieved only by such
averaging and concessions and co-operations as are the price of all union.
These will be gains, not losses. Soldiers become partners in invincibility by the
discipline which adopts an average rate of march instead of compelling all to
keep step with the fastest and stay with the strongest. Moralists tell men to love
each other and the right. How, by doing what things, by leaving what undone,
shall men love each other? What have the ethicals to say upon the morality of
putting public highways in private hands, and of allowing these private hands
to make a private and privileged use of them? If bad, will a mere "change of
heart," uninstitutionalized, change them?

New freedoms cannot be operated through the old forms of slavery. The
ideals of Washington and Hamilton and Adams could not breathe under
kingly rule. Idle to say they might. Under the mutual dependence of the
inside and outside of things their change has all through history always been
dual. Change of heart is no more redemption than hunger is dinner. We must
have honesty, love, justice in the heart of the business world, but for these we
must also have the forms which will fit them. These will be very different from
those through which the intercourse of man with man in the exchange of
services now moves to such ungracious ends. Forms of Asiatic and American
government, of early institutions and to-day's, are not more different. The
cardinal virtues cannot be established and kept at work in trade and on the
highways with the old apparatus. In order that the spirit that gave rebates may
go to stay, the rebate itself must go. If the private use of private ownership of
highways is to go, the private ownership must go. There must be no private
use of public power or public property. These are created by the common
sacrifices of all, and can be rightfully used only for the common good of all—
from all, by all, for all. All the grants and franchises that have been given
to private hands for private profit are void in morals and void in that higher
law which sets the copy for the laggard pens of legislatures and judges. "No
private use of public powers" is but a threshold truth. The universe, says
Emerson, is the property of every creature in it. . . .

"Human nature," "monotony," and "individuality" are the lions which
the reformer is always told will stop the way to a better world. "You cannot
change human nature." There are two human natures—the human nature of

Christ and of Judas; and Christ prevails. There is the human nature which seeks anonymity, secrecy, the fruits of power without its duties; and there is the human nature which rises against these and, province by province, is abolishing them from human affairs. Men have always been willing to die for their faith. The bad have died as bravely as the good, Charles I. with as smooth a front as Sir Harry Vane. In this readiness to die lies folded every loyalty of life. . . .

We can become individual only by submitting to be bound to others. We extend our freedom only by finding new laws to obey. Life outside the law is slavery on as many sides as there are disregarded laws. The locomotive off its tracks is not free. The more relations, ties, duties, the more "individual." The isolated man is the mere rudiment of an individual. But he who has become citizen, neighbor, friend, brother, son, husband, father, fellow-member, in one, is just by so many times individualized. Men's expanding powers of co-operation bring them to the conscious ability to unite for new benefits; but this extension of individuality is forbidden in the name of individuality. There are two individualities: that of the dullard, who submits to take his railroad transportation, his light, his coal, his salt, his reaping-machine at such prices and of such quality as arbitrary power forces upon him, and that of the shrewder man who, by an alliance of the individualities of all, supplies himself at his own price. . . .

Another great change is working in the inner mind of man, and will surely be followed by incorporation in institutions and morals and manners. The social head and heart are both being persuaded that too many are idle—rich and poor; too many are hurt in body and soul—rich and poor; too many children are "exposed," as in the old Greek and Roman market-places; too many are starving within reach of too much fertile waste; too many passions of envy, greed, and hate are raging among rich and poor. There is too much left undone that ought to be done along the whole scale of life, from the lowest physical to the highest spiritual needs, from better roads to sweeter music and nobler worship. It cannot be long, historically speaking, before all this new sense and sentiment will issue in acts. All will be as zealously pro-tected against the oppression of the cruel in their daily labor as now against oppression from invader or rioter, and will be as warmly cheered in liberty to grow to their fullest capabilities as laborers—*i.e.,* users of matter for the pur-pose of the spirit—as they are now welcomed to the liberty of the citizen and the worshipper. Infinite is the foundation of our rights. We can have all the rights we will create. All the rights we will give we can have. The American people will save the liberties they have inherited by winning new ones to be-queath.

With this will come fruits of new faculty almost beyond calculation. A new liberty will put an end to pauperism and millionairism and the crimes and death-rate born of both wretchedness, just as the liberty of politics and re-ligion put an end to martyrs and tyrants. The new liberty is identical in principle and purpose with the other; it is made inevitable by them. Those who love the liberties already won must open the door to the new, unless they wish to see them all take flight together. There can be no single liberty. Liberties go in clusters like the Pleiades.

We must either regulate, or own, or destroy, perishing by the sword we take. The possibility of regulation is a dream. As long as this control of the necessaries of life and this wealth remain private with individuals, it is they who will regulate, not we. The policy of regulation, disguise it as we may, is but moving to a compromise and equilibrium within the evil all complain of. It is to accept the principle of the sovereignty of the self-interest of the individual and apply constitutional checks to it. The unprogressive nations palter in this method with monarchy. But the wits of America are equal to seeing that as with kingship and slavery so with poverty—the weeding must be done at the roots. Sir Henry Sumner Maine says mankind moves from status to contract; from society ruled by inherited customs to one ruled by agreement, varied according to circumstances. Present experience suggests the addition that the movement, like all in nature, is pendulous, and that mankind moves progressively from status to contract, and from this stage of contract to another status. We march and rest and march again. If our society is settling down to an interval of inertia, perhaps ages long, we must before night comes establish all in as much equality and comfort as possible.

The aspirations are not new. We have had them since Plato. The knowledge of means for realizing them is not new. We have had it since Aristotle, and the history of civilization is but the record of the progressive embodiment of the ideals in institutions for the life together—sexual, social, spiritual. What is new in our moment is that mankind's accumulating forces are preparing for another step forward in this long processional realization of its best possible. Nothing so narrow as the mere governmentalizing of the means and processes of production. It is only the morally nerveless who ask government to do that which they will not rise to do. The conversion which is now working itself out within us, and perhaps is more nearly born than we suspect ("We shall not live to see slavery abolished," said Emerson, in 1859) is making itself felt on all sides of our life. In manners, in literature, in marriage, in church, in all, we see at work the saving ferment which is to make all things new by bringing them nearer to the old ideals. George Sand was revolted by the servile accent of the phrase of her day, "Madame est servie." Society has grown to the better fellowship her finer ear found wanting in these words, and is now told it is dinner, not madame or monsieur, that is served.

We are to have, of course, great political changes. We are to apply the co-operative methods of the post-office and the public school to many other common toils, to all toils in which private sovereignty has become through monopoly a despotism over the public, and to all in which the association of the people and the organization of processes have been so far developed that the profit-hunting Captain of Industry may be replaced by the public-serving Captain of Industry. But we are to have much more. We are to have a private life of a new beauty, of which these are to be merely the mechanical exhibitions on the side of politics. We are to move among each other, able, by the methodical and agreed adherence of all, to do what the words of Lamennais mean, instead of being able, as now, in most things, to afford only an indulgence in feeling them. We are to be commoners, travellers to Altruria.

We are to become fathers, mothers, for the spirit of the father and mother is not in us while we can say of any child it is not ours, and leave it in the grime. We are to become men, women, for to all about reinforcing us we shall insure full growth and thus insure it to ourselves. We are to become gentlemen, ladies, for we will not accept from another any service we are not willing to return in kind. We are to become honest, giving when we get, and getting with the knowledge and consent of all. We are to become rich, for we shall share in the wealth now latent in idle men and idle land, and in the fertility of work done by those who have ceased to withstand but stand with each other. As we walk our parks we already see that by saying "thine" to every neighbor we say "mine" of palaces, gardens, art, science, far beyond any possible to selfishness, even the selfishness of kings. We shall become patriots, for the heart will know why it thrills to the flag. Those folds wave the salute of a greater love than that of the man who will lay down his life for his friend. There floats the banner of the love of millions, who, though they do not know you and have never seen you, will die for you and are living for you, doing in a thousand services unto you as you would be done by. And the little patriotism, which is the love of the humanity fenced within our frontier will widen into the reciprocal service of all men. Generals were, merchants are, brothers will be, humanity's representative men.

There is to be a people in industry, as in government. The same rising genius of democracy which discovered that mankind did not co-operate in the State to provide a few with palaces and king's-evil, is disclosing that men do not co-operate in trade for any other purpose than to mobilize the labor of all for the benefit of all, and that the only true guidance comes from those who are led, and the only valid titles from those who create. Very wide must be the emancipation of this new self-interest. If we free America we shall still be not free, for the financial, commercial, possessory powers of modern industrial life are organized internationally. If we rose to the full execution of the first, simplest, and most pressing need of our times and put an end to all private use of public powers, we should still be confronted by monopolies existing simply as private property, as in coal-mines, oil lands.

It is not a verbal accident that science is the substance of the word conscience. We must know the right before we can do the right. When it comes to know the facts the human heart can no more endure monopoly than American slavery or Roman empire. The first step to a remedy is that the people care. If they know, they will care. To help them to know and care; to stimulate new hatred of evil, new love of the good, new sympathy for the victims of power, and, by enlarging its science, to quicken the old into a new conscience, this compilation of fact has been made. Democracy is not a lie. There live in the body of the commonalty the unexhausted virtue and the ever-refreshed strength which can rise equal to any problems of progress. In the hope of tapping some reserve of their powers of self-help this story is told to the people.

(17)

Thorstein Veblen

1857-1929

Thorstein Veblen was born on the Wisconsin frontier, the son of Norwegian parents who had migrated to America in 1847. Growing to maturity in a clannish Norwegian community, young Veblen was insulated from the mainstream of American life. He graduated from Carleton College in 1880, and after failing to get a fellowship at the Johns Hopkins University, he worked his way through Yale, receiving his Ph.D. in philosophy in 1884. Unable to secure a permanent academic position during his career because of personal difficulties and unorthodox views, Veblen moved from institution to institution, never able to find an environment that was conducive to his well-being. Yet in spite of these difficulties, Veblen became a seminal social thinker who revolutionized the study of economics and political economy.

Rejecting the deductive approach of the classical school, Veblen approached economics from an evolutionary and institutional point of view. Most of his writings, despite their apparent detachment and pretense at objectivity, were a bitter attack on the business class and its pecuniary values. Veblen, however, was always careful to make a distinction between the "engineers," or social technicians (who were interested in efficient production for the sake of society) and the businessmen (who looked upon production merely as a vehicle for making profit). Veblen elaborated his views in a number of important books, and these ideas played a major role in the intellectual development of American liberals and radicals who learned the importance of social control and planning in a business-dominated society.

The selection that follows is from Veblen's first and in many ways most important book, *The Theory of the Leisure Class* (New York, 1899).

☆ ☆ ☆ ☆

It is the purpose of this inquiry to discuss the place and value of the leisure class as an economic factor in modern life.

The end of acquisition and accumulation is conventionally held to be the consumption of the goods accumulated—whether it is consumption directly by the owner of the goods or by the household attached to him and for this purpose identified with him in theory. This is at least felt to be the economically legitimate end of acquisition, which alone it is incumbent on the theory to take account of. Such consumption may of course be conceived to serve the consumer's physical wants—his physical comfort—or his so-called higher wants—spiritual, æsthetic, intellectual, or what not; the latter class of wants being served indirectly by an expenditure of goods, after the fashion familiar to all economic readers.

But it is only when taken in a sense far removed from its naïve meaning that consumption of goods can be said to afford the incentive from which accumulation invariably proceeds. The motive that lies at the root of ownership is emulation; and the same motive of emulation continues active in the further development of the institution to which it has given rise and in the development of all those features of the social structure which this institution of ownership touches. The possession of wealth confers honour; it is an invidious distinction. Nothing equally cogent can be said for the consumption of goods, nor for any other conceivable incentive to acquisition, and especially not for any incentive to the accumulation of wealth.

It is of course not to be overlooked that in a community where nearly all goods are private property the necessity of earning a livelihood is a powerful and ever-present incentive for the poorer members of the community. The need of subsistence and of an increase of physical comfort may for a time be the dominant motive of acquisition for those classes who are habitually employed at manual labour, whose subsistence is on a precarious footing, who possess little and ordinarily accumulate little; but it will appear in the course of the discussion that even in the case of these impecunious classes the predominance of the motive of physical want is not so decided as has sometimes been assumed. On the other hand, so far as regards those members and classes of the community who are chiefly concerned in the accumulation of wealth, the incentive of subsistence or of physical comfort never plays a considerable part. Ownership began and grew into a human institution on grounds unrelated to the subsistence minimum. The dominant incentive was from the outset the invidious distinction attaching to wealth, and, save temporarily and by exception, no other motive has usurped the primacy at any later stage of the development.

Property set out with being booty held as trophies of the successful raid. So long as the group had departed but little from the primitive communal organisation, and so long as it still stood in close contact with other hostile groups, the utility of things or persons owned lay chiefly in an invidious comparison between their possessor and the enemy from whom they were taken. The habit of distinguishing between the interests of the individual and those of the group to which he belongs is apparently a later growth. Invidious comparison between the possessor of the honorific booty and his less successful neighbours within the group was no doubt present early as an element of the utility of the things possessed, though this was not at the outset the chief element of their value. The man's prowess was still primarily the group's prowess, and the possessor of the booty felt himself to be primarily the keeper of the honour of his group. This appreciation of exploit from the communal point of view is met with also at later stages of social growth, especially as regards the laurels of war.

But so soon as the custom of individual ownership begins to gain consistency, the point of view taken in making the invidious comparison on which private property rests will begin to change. Indeed, the one change is but the reflex of the other. The initial phase of ownership, the phase of acquisition by naïve seizure and conversion, begins to pass into the subsequent stage of an incipient organisation of industry on the basis of private property (in slaves); the horde develops into a more or less self-sufficing industrial community; possessions then come to be valued not so much as evidence of successful foray, but rather as evidence of the prepotence of the possessor of these goods over other individuals within the community. The invidious comparison now becomes primarily a comparison of the owner with the other members of the group. Property is still of the nature of trophy, but, with the cultural advance, it becomes more and more a trophy of successes scored in the game of ownership carried on between the members of the group under the quasi-peaceable methods of nomadic life.

Gradually, as industrial activity further displaces predatory activity in the community's everyday life and in men's habits of thought, accumulated property more and more replaces trophies of predatory exploit as the conventional exponent of prepotence and success. With the growth of settled industry, therefore, the possession of wealth gains in relative importance and effectiveness as a customary basis of repute and esteem. Not that esteem ceases to be awarded on the basis of other, more direct evidence of prowess; not that successful predatory aggression or warlike exploit ceases to call out the approval and admiration of the crowd, or to stir the envy of the less successful competitors; but the opportunities for gaining distinction by means of this direct manifestation of superior force grow less available both in scope and frequency. At the same time opportunities for industrial aggression, and for the accumulation of property by the quasi-peaceable methods of nomadic industry, increase in scope and availability. And it is even more to the point that property now becomes the most easily recognised evidence of a reputable degree of success as distinguished from heroic or signal achievement. It therefore becomes the conventional basis of esteem. Its possession in some amount becomes necessary in order to any reputable standing in the community. It becomes indispensable to accumulate, to acquire property, in order to retain one's good name. When accumulated goods have in this way once become the accepted badge of efficiency, the possession of wealth presently assumes the character of an independent and definitive basis of esteem. The possession of goods, whether acquired aggressively by one's own exertion or passively by transmission through inheritance from others, becomes a conventional basis of reputability. The possession of wealth, which was at the outset valued simply as an evidence of efficiency, becomes, in popular apprehension, itself a meritorious act. Wealth is now itself intrinsically honourable and confers honour on its possessor. By a further refinement, wealth acquired passively by transmission from ancestors or other antecedents presently becomes even more honorific than wealth acquired by the possessor's own effort; but this distinction belongs at a later stage in the evolution of the pecuniary culture and will be spoken of in its place. . . .

So soon as the possession of property becomes the basis of popular esteem, therefore, it becomes also a requisite to that complacency which we call self-respect. In any community where goods are held in severalty it is necessary, in order to his own peace of mind, that an individual should possess as large a portion of goods as others with whom he is accustomed to class himself; and it is extremely gratifying to possess something more than others. But as fast as a person makes new acquisitions, and becomes accustomed to the resulting new standard of wealth, the new standard forthwith ceases to afford appreciably greater satisfaction than the earlier standard did. The tendency in any case is constantly to make the present pecuniary standard the point of departure for a fresh increase of wealth; and this in turn gives rise to a new standard of sufficiency and a new pecuniary classification of one's self as compared with one's neighbours. So far as concerns the present question, the end sought by accumulation is to rank high in comparison with the rest of the community in point of pecuniary strength. So long as the comparison is distinctly unfavourable to himself, the normal, average individual will live in chronic dissatisfaction with his present lot; and when he has reached what may be called the normal pecuniary standard of the community, or of his class in the community, this chronic dissatisfaction will give place to a restless straining to place a wider and ever-widening pecuniary interval between himself and this average standard. The invidious comparison can never become so favourable to the individual making it that he would not gladly rate himself still higher relatively to his competitors in the struggle for pecuniary reputability.

In the nature of the case, the desire for wealth can scarcely be satiated in any individual instance, and evidently a satiation of the average or general desire for wealth is out of the question. However widely, or equally, or "fairly," it may be distributed, no general increase of the community's wealth can make any approach to satiating this need, the ground of which is the desire of every one to excel every one else in the accumulation of goods. If, as is sometimes assumed, the incentive to accumulation were the want of subsistence or of physical comfort, then the aggregate economic wants of a community might conceivably be satisfied at some point in the advance of industrial efficiency; but since the struggle is substantially a race for reputability on the basis of an invidious comparison, no approach to a definitive attainment is possible. . . .

If its working were not disturbed by other economic forces or other features of the emulative process, the immediate effect of such a pecuniary struggle as has just been described in outline would be to make men industrious and frugal. This result actually follows, in some measure, so far as regards the lower classes, whose ordinary means of acquiring goods is productive labour. This is more especially true of the labouring classes in a sedentary community which is at an agricultural stage of industry, in which there is a considerable subdivision of property, and whose laws and customs secure to these classes a more or less definite share of the product of their industry. These lower classes can in any case not avoid labour, and the imputation of labour is therefore not greatly derogatory to them, at least not within their class. Rather, since labour is their recognised and accepted mode of life, they take some emulative pride in a reputation for efficiency in their work, this being often the only line of emulation that is open to them. For those for whom acquisition and emulation is possible only within the field of productive efficiency and thrift, the struggle for pecuniary reputability will in some measure work out in an increase of diligence and parsimony. But certain secondary features of the emulative process, yet to be spoken of, come in to very materially circumscribe and modify emulation in these directions among the pecuniarily inferior classes as well as among the superior class.

But it is otherwise with the superior pecuniary class, with which we are here immediately concerned. For this class also the incentive to diligence and thrift is not absent; but its action is so greatly qualified by the secondary demands of pecuniary emulation, that any inclination in this direction is practically overborne and any incentive to diligence tends to be of no effect. The most imperative of these secondary demands of emulation, as well as the one of widest scope, is the requirement of abstention from productive work. This is true in an especial degree for the barbarian stage of culture. During the predatory culture labour comes to be associated in men's habits of thought with weakness and subjection to a master. It is therefore a mark of inferiority, and therefore comes to be accounted unworthy of man in his best estate. By virtue of this tradition labour is felt to be debasing, and this tradition has never died out. On the contrary, with the advance of social differentiation it has acquired the axiomatic force due to ancient and unquestioned prescription.

In order to gain and to hold the esteem of men it is not sufficient merely to possess wealth or power. The wealth or power must be put in evidence, for esteem is awarded only on evidence. And not only does the evidence of wealth serve to impress one's importance on others and to keep their sense of his importance alive and alert, but it is of scarcely less use in building up and preserving one's self-complacency. In all but the lowest stages of culture the normally constituted man is comforted and upheld in his self-respect by "decent surroundings" and by exemption from "menial offices." Enforced departure from his habitual standard of decency, either in the paraphernalia of life or in the kind and amount of his everyday activity, is felt to be a slight upon his human dignity, even apart from all conscious consideration of the approval or disapproval of his fellows. . . .

Abstention from labour is not only a honorific or meritorious act, but it presently comes to be a requisite of decency. The insistence on property as the basis of reputability is very naïve and very imperious during the early stages of the accumulation of wealth. Abstention from labour is the conventional evidence of wealth and is therefore the conventional mark of social standing; and this insistence on the meritoriousness of wealth leads to a more strenuous insistence on leisure. *Nota notæ est nota rei ipsius.* According to well-established laws of human nature, prescription presently seizes upon this conventional evidence of wealth and fixes it in men's habits of thought as something that is in itself substantially meritorious and ennobling; while productive labour at the same time and by a like process becomes in a double sense intrinsically unworthy. Prescription ends by making labour not only disreputable in the eyes of the community, but morally impossible to the noble, freeborn man, and incompatible with a worthy life. . . .

Conspicuous consumption of valuable goods is a means of reputability to the gentleman of leisure. As wealth accumulates on his hands, his own unaided effort will not avail to sufficiently put his opulence in evidence by this method. The aid of friends and competitors is therefore brought in by resorting to the giving of valuable presents and expensive feasts and entertainments. Presents and feasts had probably another origin than that of naïve ostentation, but they acquired their utility for this purpose very early, and they have retained that character to the present; so that their utility in this respect has now long been the substantial ground on which these usages rest. Costly entertainments, such as the potlatch or the ball, are peculiarly adapted to serve this end. The competitor with whom the entertainer wishes to institute a comparison is, by this method, made to serve as a means to the end. He consumes vicariously for his host at the same time that he is a witness to the consumption of that excess of good things which his host is unable to dispose of single-handed, and he is also made to witness his host's facility in etiquette.

In the giving of costly entertainments other motives, of a more genial kind, are of course also present. The custom of festive gatherings probably originated in motives of conviviality and religion; these motives are also present in the later development, but they do not continue to be the sole motives. The latter-day leisure-class festivities and entertainments may continue in some slight degree to serve the religious need and in a higher degree the needs of recreation and conviviality, but they also serve an invidious purpose; and they serve it none the less effectively for having a colourable non-invidious ground in these more avowable motives. But the economic effect of these social amenities is not therefore lessened, either in the vicarious consumption of goods or in the exhibition of difficult and costly achievements in etiquette.

As wealth accumulates, the leisure class develops further in function and structure, and there arises a differentiation within the class. There is a more or less elaborate system of rank and grades. This differentiation is furthered by the inheritance of wealth and the consequent inheritance of gentility. With the inheritance of gentility goes the inheritance of obligatory leisure; and gentility of a sufficient potency to entail a life of leisure may be inherited without the complement of wealth required to maintain a dignified leisure. Gentle blood may be transmitted without goods enough to afford a reputably free consumption at one's ease. Hence results a class of impecunious gentlemen of leisure, incidentally referred to already. These half-caste gentlemen of leisure fall into a system of hierarchical gradations. Those who stand near the higher and the highest grades of the wealthy leisure class, in point of birth, or in point of wealth, or both, outrank the remoter-born and the pecuniarily weaker. These lower grades, especially the impecunious, or marginal, gentlemen of leisure, affiliate themselves by a system of dependence or fealty to the great ones; by so doing they gain an increment of repute, or of the means with which to lead a life of leisure, from their patron. They become his courtiers or retainers, servants; and being fed and countenanced by their patron they are indices of his rank and vicarious consumers of his superfluous wealth. Many of these affiliated gentlemen of leisure are at the same time lesser men of substance in their own right; so that some of them are scarcely at all, others only partially, to be rated as vicarious consumers. So many of them, however, as make up the retainers and hangers-on of the patron may be classed as vicarious consumers without qualification. Many of these again, and also many of the other aristocracy of less degree, have in turn attached to their persons a more or less comprehensive group of vicarious consumers in the persons of their wives and children, their servants, retainers, etc. . . . . The leisure class stands at the head of the social structure in point of reputability; and its manner of life and its standards of worth therefore afford the norm of reputability for the community. The observance of these standards, in some degree of approximation, becomes incumbent upon all classes lower in the scale. In modern civilized communities the lines of demarcation between social classes have grown vague and transient, and wherever this happens the norm of reputability imposed by the upper class extends its coercive influence with but slight hindrance down through the social structure to the lowest strata. The result is that the members of each stratum accept as their ideal of decency the scheme of life in vogue in the next higher stratum, and bend their energies to live up to that ideal. On pain of forfeiting their good name and their self-respect in case of failure, they must conform to the accepted code, at least in appearance.

The basis on which good repute in any highly organised industrial community ultimately rests is pecuniary strength; and the means of showing pecuniary strength, and so of gaining or retaining a good name, are leisure and a conspicuous consumption of goods. Accordingly, both of these methods are in vogue as far down the scale as it remains possible; and in the lower strata in which the two methods are employed, both offices are in great part delegated to the wife and children of the household. Lower still, where any degree of leisure, even ostensible, has become impracticable for the wife, the conspicuous consumption of goods remains and is carried on by the wife and children. The man of the household also can do something in this direction, and, indeed, he commonly does; but with a still lower descent into the levels of indigence—along the margin of the slums—the man, and presently also the children, virtually cease to consume valuable goods for appearances, and the woman remains virtually the sole exponent of the household's pecuniary decency. No class of society, not even the most abjectly poor, foregoes all customary conspicuous consumption. The last items of this category of consumption are not given up except under stress of the direst necessity. Very much of squalor and discomfort will be endured before the last trinket or the last pretence of pecuniary decency is put away. There is no class and no country that has yielded so abjectly before the pressure of physical want as to deny themselves all gratification of this higher or spiritual need.

From the foregoing survey of the growth of conspicuous leisure and consumption, it appears that the utility of both alike for the purposes of reputability lies in the element of waste that is common to both. In the one case it is a waste of time and effort, in the other it is a waste of goods. Both are methods of demonstrating the possession of wealth, and the two are conventionally accepted as equivalents. The choice between them is a question of advertising expediency simply, except so far as it may be affected by other standards of propriety, springing from a different source. . . .

For the great body of the people in any modern community, the proximate ground of expenditure in excess of what is required for physical comfort is not a conscious effort to excel in the expensiveness of their visible consumption, so much as it is a desire to live up to the conventional standard of decency in the amount and grade of goods consumed. This desire is not guided by a rigidly invariable standard, which must be lived up to, and beyond which there is no incentive to go. The standard is flexible; and especially it is indefinitely extensible, if only time is allowed for habituation to any increase in pecuniary ability and for acquiring facility in the new and larger scale of expenditure that follows such an increase. It is much more difficult to recede from a scale of expenditure once adopted than it is to extend the accustomed scale in response to an accession of wealth. Many items of customary expenditure prove on analysis to be almost purely wasteful, and they are therefore honorific only, but after they have once been incorporated into the scale of decent consumption, and so have become an integral part of one's scheme of life, it is quite as hard to give up these as it is to give up many items that conduce directly to one's physical comfort, or even that may be necessary to life and health. That is to say, the conspicuously wasteful honorific expenditure that confers spiritual well-being may become more indispensable than much of that expenditure which ministers to the "lower" wants of physical well-being or sustenance only. It is notoriously just as difficult to recede from a "high" standard of living as it is to lower a standard which is already relatively low; although in the former case the difficulty is a moral one, while in the latter it may involve a material deduction from the physical comforts of life.

But while retrogression is difficult, a fresh advance in conspicuous expenditure is relatively easy; indeed, it takes places almost as a matter of course. In the rare cases where it occurs, a failure to increase one's visible consumption when the means for an increase are at hand is felt in popular apprehension to call for explanation, and unworthy motives of miserliness are imputed to those who fall short in this respect. A prompt response to the stimulus, on the other hand, is accepted as the normal effect. This suggests that the standard of expenditure which commonly guides our efforts is not the average, ordinary expenditure already achieved; it is an ideal of consumption that lies just beyond our reach, or to reach which requires some strain. The motive is emulation—the stimulus of an invidious comparison which prompts us to outdo those with whom we are in the habit of classing ourselves. Substantially the same proposition is expressed in the commonplace remark that each class envies and emulates the class next above it in the social scale, while it rarely compares itself with those below or with those who are considerably in advance. That is to say, in other words, our standard of decency in expenditure, as in other ends of emulation, is set by the usage of those next above us in reputability; until, in this way, especially in any community where class distinctions are somewhat vague, all canons of reputability and decency, and all standards of consumption, are traced back by insensible gradations to the usages and habits of thought of the highest social and pecuniary class—the wealthy leisure class.

It is for this class to determine, in general outline, what scheme of life the community shall accept as decent or honorific; and it is their office by precept and example to set forth this scheme of social salvation in its highest, ideal form. But the higher leisure class can exercise this quasi-sacerdotal office only under certain material limitations. The class cannot at discretion effect a sudden revolution or reversal of the popular habits of thought with respect to any of these ceremonial requirements. It takes time for any change to permeate the mass and change the habitual attitude of the people; and especially it takes time to change the habits of those classes that are socially more remote from the radiant body. The process is slower where the mobility of the population is less or where the intervals between the several classes are wider and more abrupt. But if time be allowed, the scope of the discretion of the leisure class as regards questions of form and detail in the community's scheme of life is large; while as regards the substantial principles of reputability, the changes which it can effect lie within a narrow margin of tolerance. Its example and precept carries the force of prescription for all classes below it; but in working out the precepts which are handed down as governing the form and method of reputability—in shaping the usages and the spiritual attitude of the lower classes—this authoritative prescription constantly works under the selective guidance of the canon of conspicuous waste, tempered in varying degree by the instinct of workmanship. To these norms is to be added another broad principle of human nature—the predatory animus—which in point of generality and of psychological content lies between the two just named. The effect of the latter in shaping the accepted scheme of life is yet to be discussed. . . . Goods are produced and consumed as a means to the fuller unfolding of human life; and their utility consists, in the first instance, in their efficiency as means to this end. The end is, in the first instance, the fulness of life of the individual, taken in absolute terms. But the human proclivity to emulation has seized upon the consumption of goods as a means to an invidious comparison, and has thereby invested consumable goods with a secondary utility as evidence of relative ability to pay. This indirect or secondary use of consumable goods lends a honorific character to consumption, and presently also to the goods which best serve this emulative end of consumption. The consumption of expensive goods is meritorious, and the goods which contain an appreciable element of cost in excess of what goes to give them serviceability for their ostensible mechanical purpose are honorific. The marks of superfluous costliness in the goods are therefore marks of worth—of high efficiency for the indirect, invidious end to be served by their consumption; and conversely, goods are humilific, and therefore unattractive, if they show too thrifty an adaptation to the mechanical end sought and do not include a margin of expensiveness on which to rest a complacent invidious comparison. This indirect utility gives much of their value to the "better" grades of goods. In order to appeal to the cultivated sense of utility, an article must contain a modicum of this indirect utility.

(18)

Lincoln Steffens
1866-1936

Lincoln Steffens was one of the major publicists of the progressive movement of the early twentieth century. He was born in San Francisco, graduated from the University of California in 1889, and went to Germany to pursue graduate work in philosophy. After returning to the United States, he became a journalist, working for such publications as the New York *Evening Post* and the *Commercial Advertiser.* The turning point in his life occurred in 1901 when he joined the staff of *McClure's Magazine,* a journal which soon began publishing his famous series of muckraking articles on municipal corruption. Steffens concluded that the process of corruption was universal. The ultimate cause was the seeking of privilege—a point of view that placed primary responsibility upon the shoulders of the business class. Nevertheless, Steffens, like other liberal and progressive reformers, maintained that reform was possible if the American people were informed of the facts. Although in later life he was to become increasingly disillusioned with democratic procedures aimed at uplifting society—an attitude which permeates the pages of his famous *Autobiography* (1931) and even led him to become an admirer of the Soviet Union and an advocate of quasi-dictatorship—in his early ca-

reer he was a true spokesman for American progressive reform and a
believer in the idea of progress.

The following selection is from the introduction to his book *The
Shame of the Cities* (New York, 1904), a collection of some of his
early muckraking articles on municipal corruption.

This is not a book. It is a collection of articles reprinted from
McClure's Magazine. Done as journalism, they are journalism still, and no
further pretensions are set up for them in their new dress. This classification
may seem pretentious enough; certainly it would if I should confess what
claims I make for my profession. But no matter about that; I insist upon the
journalism. And there is my justification for separating from the bound
volumes of the magazine and republishing, practically without re-editing, my
accounts as a reporter of the shame of American cities. They were written
with a purpose, they were published serially with a purpose, and they are
reprinted now together to further that same purpose, which was and is—to
sound for the civic pride of an apparently shameless citizenship.

There must be such a thing, we reasoned. All our big boasting could not
be empty vanity, nor our pious pretensions hollow sham. American achievements in science, art, and business mean sound abilities at bottom, and our
hypocrisy a race sense of fundamental ethics. Even in government we have
given proofs of potential greatness, and our political failures are not con-
plete; they are simply ridiculous. But they are ours. Not alone the triumphs
and the statesmen, the defeats and the grafters also represent us, and just as
truly. Why not see it so and say it?

Because, I heard, the American people won't "stand for" it. You may
blame the politicians, or, indeed, any one class, but not all classes, not the
people. Or you may put it on the ignorant foreign immigrant, or any one
nationality, but not on all nationalities, not on the American people. But no
one class is at fault, nor any one breed, nor any particular interest or group of
interests. The misgovernment of the American people is misgovernment by the
American people.

When I set out on my travels, an honest New Yorker told me honestly that
I would find that the Irish, the Catholic Irish, were at the bottom of it all
everywhere. The first city I went to was St. Louis, a German city. The next
was Minneapolis, a Scandinavian city, with a leadership of New Englanders.
Then came Pittsburg, Scotch Presbyterian, and that was what my New York
friend was. "Ah, but they are all foreign populations," I heard. The next city
was Philadelphia, the purest American community of all, and the most hopeless. And after that came Chicago and New York, both mongrel-bred, but the
one a triumph of reform, the other the best example of good government that
I had seen. The "foreign element" excuse is one of the hypocritical lies that
save us from the clear sight of ourselves.

Another such conceit of our egotism is that which deplores our politics and lauds our business. This is the wail of the typical American citizen. Now, the typical American citizen is the business man. The typical business man is a bad citizen; he is busy. If he is a "big business man" and very busy, he does not neglect, he is busy with politics, oh, very busy and very businesslike. I found him buying boodlers in St. Louis, defending grafters in Minneapolis, originating corruption in Pittsburg, sharing with bosses in Philadelphia, deploring reform in Chicago, and beating good government with corruption funds in New York. He is a self-righteous fraud, this big business man. He is the chief source of corruption, and it were a boon if he would neglect politics. But he is not the business man that neglects politics; that worthy is the good citizen, the typical business man. He too is busy, he is the one that has no use and therefore no time for politics. When his neglect has permitted bad government to go so far that he can be stirred to action, he is unhappy, and he looks around for a cure that shall be quick, so that he may hurry back to the shop. Naturally, too, when he talks politics, he talks shop. His patent remedy is quack; it is business.

"Give us a business man," he says ("like me," he means). "Let him introduce business methods into politics and government; then I shall be left alone to attend to my business."

There is hardly an office from United States Senator down to Alderman in any part of the country to which the business man has not been elected; yet politics remains corrupt, government pretty bad, and the selfish citizen has to hold himself in readiness like the old volunteer firemen to rush forth at any hour, in any weather, to prevent the fire; and he goes out sometimes and he puts out the fire (after the damage is done) and he goes back to the shop sighing for the business man in politics. The business man has failed in politics as he has in citizenship. Why?

Because politics is business. That's what's the matter with it. That's what's the matter with everything,—art, literature, religion, journalism, law, medicine,—they're all business, and all—as you see them. Make politics a sport, as they do in England, or a profession, as they do in Germany, and we'll have—well, something else than we have now,—if we want it, which is another question. But don't try to reform politics with the banker, the lawyer, and the dry-goods merchant, for these are business men and there are two great hindrances to their achievement of reform: one is that they are different from, but no better than, the politicians; the other is that politics is not "their line." There are exceptions both ways. Many politicians have gone out into business and done well (Tammany ex-mayors, and nearly all the old bosses of Philadelphia are prominent financiers in their cities), and business men have gone into politics and done well (Mark Hanna, for example). They haven't reformed their adopted trades, however, though they have sometimes sharpened them most pointedly. The politician is a business man with a specialty. When a business man of some other line learns the business of politics, he is a politician, and there is not much reform left in him. Consider the United States Senate, and believe me.

The commercial spirit is the spirit of profit, not patriotism; of credit, not honor; of individual gain, not national prosperity; of trade and dickering, not principle. "My business is sacred," says the business man in his heart. "Whatever prospers my business, is good; it must be. Whatever hinders it, is wrong; it must be. A bribe is bad, that is, it is a bad thing to take; but it is not so bad to give one, not if it is necessary to my business." "Business is business" is not a political sentiment, but our politician has caught it. He takes essentially the same view of the bribe, only he saves his self-respect by piling all his contempt upon the bribe-giver, and he has the great advantage of candor. "It is wrong, maybe," he says, "but if a rich merchant can afford to do business with me for the sake of a convenience or to increase his already great wealth, I can afford, for the sake of a living, to meet him half way. I make no pretensions to virtue, not even on Sunday." And as for giving bad government or good, how about the merchant who gives bad goods or good goods, according to the demand?

But there is hope, not alone despair, in the commercialism of our politics. If our political leaders are to be always a lot of political merchants, they will supply any demand we may create. All we have to do is to establish a steady demand for good government. The bosses have us split up into parties. To him parties are nothing but means to his corrupt ends. He "bolts" his party, but we must not; the bribe-giver changes his party, from one election to another, from one county to another, from one city to another, but the honest voter must not. Why? Because if the honest voter cared no more for his party than the politician and the grafter, then the honest vote would govern, and that would be bad—for graft. It is idiotic, this devotion to a machine that is used to take our sovereignty from us. If we would leave parties to the politicians, and would vote not for the party, not even for men, but for the city, and the State, and the nation, we should rule parties, and cities, and States, and nation. If we would vote in mass on the more promising ticket, or, if the two are equally bad, would throw out the party that is in, and wait till the next election and then throw out the other party that is in—then, I say, the commercial politician would feel a demand for good government and he would supply it. That process would take a generation or more to complete, for the politicians now really do not know what good government is. But it has taken as long to develop bad government, and the politicians know what that is. If it would not "go," they would offer something else, and, if the demand were steady, they, being so commercial, would "deliver the goods."

But do the people want good government? Tammany says they don't. Are the people honest? Are the people better than Tammany? Are they better than the merchant and the politician? Isn't our corrupt government, after all, representative?

President Roosevelt has been sneered at for going about the country preaching, as a cure for our American evils, good conduct in the individual, simple honesty, courage, and efficiency. "Platitudes!" the sophisticated say. Platitudes? If my observations have been true, the literal adoption of Mr. Roosevelt's reform scheme would result in a revolution, more radical and terrible to existing institutions, from the Congress to the Church, from the bank to the ward organization, than socialism or even than anarchy. Why, that would change all of us—not alone our neighbors, not alone the grafters, but you and me.

No, the contemned methods of our despised politics are the master methods of our braggart business, and the corruption that shocks us in public affairs we practice ourselves in our private concerns. There is no essential difference between the pull that gets your wife into society or for your book a favorable review, and that which gets a heeler into office, a thief out of jail, and a rich man's son on the board of directors of a corporation; none between the corruption of a labor union, a bank, and a political machine; none between a dummy director of a trust and the caucus-bound member of a legislature; none between a labor boss like Sam Parks, a boss of banks like John D. Rockefeller, a boss of railroads like J. P. Morgan, and a political boss like Matthew S. Quay. The boss is not a political, he is an American institution, the product of a freed people that have not the spirit to be free.

And it's all a moral weakness; a weakness right where we think we are strongest. Oh, we are good—on Sunday, and we are "fearfully patriotic" on the Fourth of July. But the bribe we pay to the janitor to prefer our interests to the landlord's, is the little brother of the bribe passed to the alderman to sell a city street, and the father of the air-brake stock assigned to the president of a railroad to have this life-saving invention adopted on his road. And as for graft, railroad passes, saloon and bawdy-house blackmail, and watered stock, all these belong to the same family. We are pathetically proud of our democratic institutions and our republican form of government, of our grand Constitution and our just laws. We are a free and sovereign people, we govern ourselves and the government is ours. But that is the point. We are responsible, not our leaders, since we follow them. We *let* them divert our loyalty from the United States to some "party"; we *let* them boss the party and turn our municipal democracies into autocracies and our republican nation into a plutocracy. We cheat our government and we let our leaders loot it, and we let them wheedle and bribe our sovereignty from us. True, they pass for us strict laws, but we are content to let them pass also bad laws, giving away public property in exchange; and our good, and often impossible, laws we allow to be used for oppression and blackmail. And what can we say? We break our own laws and rob our own government, the lady at the custom-house, the lyncher with his rope, and the captain of industry with his bribe and his rebate. The spirit of graft and of lawlessness is the American spirit.

And this shall not be said? Not plainly? William Travers Jerome, the fearless District Attorney of New York, says, "You can say anything you think to the American people. If you are honest with yourself you may be honest

with them, and they will forgive not only your candor, but your mistakes."
This is the opinion, and the experience too, of an honest man and a hopeful
democrat. Who says the other things? Who says "Hush," and "What's the
use?" and "ALL's well," when all is rotten? It is the grafter; the coward, too,
but the grafter inspires the coward. The doctrine of "addition, division, and
silence" is the doctrine of graft. "Don't hurt the party," "Spare the fair fame
of the city," are boodle yells. The Fourth of July oration is the "front" of
graft. There is no patriotism in it, but treason. It is part of the game. The
grafters call for cheers for the flag, "prosperity," and "the party," just as a
highwayman commands "hands up," and while we are waving and shouting,
they float the flag from the nation to the party, turn both into graft factories,
and prosperity into a speculative boom to make "weak hands," as the Wall
Street phrase has it, hold the watered stock while the strong hands keep the
property. "Blame us, blame anybody, but praise the people," this, the politician's advice, is not the counsel of respect for the people, but of contempt.
By just such palavering as courtiers play upon the degenerate intellects of
weak kings, the bosses, political, financial, and industrial, are befuddling and
befooling our sovereign American citizenship; and—likewise—they are corrupting it.

And it is corruptible, this citizenship. "I know what Parks is doing," said a
New York union workman, "but what do I care. He has raised my wages.
Let him have his graft!" And the Philadelphia merchant says the same thing:
"The party leaders may be getting more than they should out of the city, but
that doesn't hurt me. It may raise taxes a little, but I can stand that. The party
keeps up the protective tariff. If that were cut down, my business would be
ruined. So long as the party stands pat on that, I stand pat on the party."

The people are not innocent. That is the only "news" in all the journalism
of these articles, and no doubt that was not new to many observers. It was
to me. When I set out to describe the corrupt systems of certain typical cities,
I meant to show simply how the people were deceived and betrayed. But in
the very first study—St. Louis—the startling truth lay bare that corruption
was not merely political; it was financial, commercial, social; the ramifications
of boodle were so complex, various, and far-reaching, that one mind could
hardly grasp them, and not even Joseph W. Folk, the tireless prosecutor,
could follow them all. This state of things was indicated in the first article
which Claude H. Wetmore and I compiled together, but it was not shown
plainly enough. Mr. Wetmore lived in St. Louis, and he had respect for
names which meant little to me. But when I went next to Minneapolis alone,
I could see more independently, without respect for persons, and there were
traces of the same phenomenon. The first St. Louis article was called
"Tweed Days in St. Louis," and though the "better citizen" received attention
the Tweeds were the center of interest. In "The Shame of Minneapolis," the
truth was put into the title; it was the Shame of Minneapolis; not of the Ames
administration, not of the Tweeds, but of the city and its citizens. And yet
Minneapolis was not nearly so bad as St. Louis; police graft is never so uni-

versal as boodle. It is more shocking, but it is so filthy that it cannot involve so large a part of society. So I returned to St. Louis, and I went over the whole ground again, with the people in mind, not alone the caught and convicted boodlers. And this time the true meaning of "Tweed days in St. Louis" was made plain. The article was called "The Shamelessness of St. Louis," and that was the burden of the story. In Pittsburg also the people was the subject, and though the civic spirit there was better, the extent of the corruption throughout the social organization of the community was indicated. But it was not till I got to Philadelphia that the possibilities of popular corruption were worked out to the limit of humiliating confession. That was the place for such a study. There is nothing like it in the country, except possibly, in Cincinnati. Philadelphia certainly is not merely corrupt, but corrupted, and this was made clear. Philadelphia was charged up to—the American citizen.

It was impossible in the space of a magazine article to cover in any one city all the phases of municipal government, so I chose cities that typified most strikingly some particular phase or phases. Thus as St. Louis exemplified boodle; Minneapolis, police graft; Pittsburg, a political and industrial machine; and Philadelphia, general civic corruption; so Chicago was an illustration of reform, and New York of good government. All these things occur in most of these places. There are, and long have been, reformers in St. Louis, and there is to-day police graft there. Minneapolis has had boodling and council reform, and boodling is breaking out there again. Pittsburg has general corruption, and Philadelphia a very perfect political machine. Chicago has police graft and a low order of administrative and general corruption which permeates business, labor, and society generally. As for New York, the metropolis might exemplify almost anything that occurs anywhere in American cities, but no city has had for many years such a good administration as was that of Mayor Seth Low.

That which I have made each city stand for, is that which it had most highly developed. It would be absurd to seek for organized reform in St. Louis, for example, with Chicago next door; or for graft in Chicago with Minneapolis so near. After Minneapolis, a description of administrative corruption in Chicago would have seemed like a repetition. Perhaps it was not just to treat only the conspicuous element in each situation. But why should I be just? I was not judging; I arrogated to myself no such function. I was not writing about Chicago for Chicago, but for the other cities, so I picked out what light each had for the instruction of the others. But, if I was never complete, I never exaggerated. Every one of those articles was an understatement, especially where the conditions were bad, and the proof thereof is that while each article seemed to astonish other cities, it disappointed the city which was its subject. Thus my friends in Philadelphia, who knew what there was to know, and those especially who knew what I knew, expressed surprise that I reported so little. And one St. Louis newspaper said that "the facts were thrown at me and I fell down over them." There was truth in these flings. I cut twenty thousand words out of the Philadelphia article and then had not written half my facts. I know a man who is making a history of the corrupt construction of the Philadelphia City Hall, in three volumes, and he grieves because he lacks space. You can't put all the known incidents of the corruption of an American city into a book.

This is all very unscientific, but then, I am not a scientist. I am a journalist. I did not gather with indifference all the facts and arrange them patiently for permanent preservation and laboratory analysis. I did not want to preserve, I wanted to destroy the facts. My purpose was no more scientific than the spirit of my investigation and reports; it was, as I said above, to see if the shameful facts, spread out in all their shame, would not burn through our civic shamelessness and set fire to American pride. That was the journalism of it. I wanted to move and to convince. That is why I was not interested in all the facts, sought none that was new, and rejected half those that were old. I often was asked to expose something suspected. I couldn't; and why should I? Exposure of the unknown was not my purpose. The people: what they will put up with, how they are fooled, how cheaply they are bought, how dearly sold, how easily intimidated, and how led, for good or for evil—that was the inquiry, and so the significant facts were those only which everybody in each city knew, and of these, only those which everybody in every other town would recognize, from their common knowledge of such things, to be probable. But these, understated, were charged always to the guilty persons when individuals were to blame, and finally brought home to the people themselves, who, having the power, have also the responsibility, they and those they respect, and those that guide them.

This was against all the warnings and rules of demagogy. What was the result?

After Joseph W. Folk had explored and exposed, with convictions, the boodling of St. Louis, the rings carried an election. "Tweed Days in St. Louis" is said to have formed some public sentiment against the boodlers, but the local newspapers had more to do with that man than *McClure's Magazine.* After the Minneapolis grand jury had exposed and the courts had tried and the common juries had convicted the grafters there, an election showed that public opinion was formed. But that one election was regarded as final. When I went there the men who had led the reform movement were "all through." After they had read the "Shame of Minneapolis," however, they went back to work, and they have perfected a plan to keep the citizens informed and to continue the fight for good government. They saw, these unambitious, busy citizens, that it was "up to them," and they resumed the unwelcome duties of their citizenship. Of resentment there was very little. At a meeting of leading citizens there were honest speeches suggesting that something should be said to "clear the name of Minneapolis," but one man rose and said very pleasantly, but firmly, that the article was true; it was pretty hard on them, but it was true and they all knew it. That ended that.

When I returned to St. Louis and rewrote the facts, and, in rewriting, made them just as insulting as the truth would permit, my friends there expressed dismay over the manuscript. The article would hurt Mr. Folk; it would hurt the cause; it would arouse popular wrath.

"That was what I hoped it would do," I said.

"But the indignation would break upon Folk and reform, not on the boodlers," they said.

"Wasn't it obvious," I asked, "that this very title, 'Shamelessness,' was aimed at pride; that it implied a faith that there was self-respect to be touched and shame to be moved?"

That was too subtle. So I answered that if they had no faith in the town, I had, and anyway, if I was wrong and the people should resent, not the crime, but the exposure of it, then they would punish, not Mr. Folk, who had nothing to do with the article, but the magazine and me. Newspaper men warned me that they would not "stand for" the article, but would attack it. I answered that I would let the St. Louisans decide between us. It was true, it was just; the people of St. Louis had shown no shame. Here was a good chance to see whether they had any. I was a fool, they said. "All right," I replied. "All kings had fools in the olden days, and the fools were allowed to tell them the truth. I would play the fool to the American people."

The article, published, was attacked by the newspapers; friends of Mr. Folk repudiated it; Mr. Folk himself spoke up for the people. Leading citizens raised money for a mass meeting to "set the city right before the world." The mayor of the city, a most excellent man, who had helped me, denounced the article. The boodle party platform appealed for votes on the strength of the attacks in "Eastern magazines." The people themselves contradicted me; after the publication, two hundred thousand buttons for "Folk and Reform" were worn on the streets of St. Louis.

But those buttons were for "Folk and Reform." They did go to prove that the article was wrong, that there was pride in St. Louis, but they proved also that that pride had been touched. Up to that time nobody knew exactly how St. Louis felt about it all. There had been one election, another was pending, and the boodlers, caught or to be caught, were in control. The citizens had made no move to dislodge them. Mr. Folk's splendid labors were a spectacle without a chorus, and, though I had met men who told me the people were with Folk, I had met also the grafters, who cursed only Folk and were building all their hopes on the assumption that "after Folk's term" all would be well again. Between these two local views no outsider could choose. How could I read a strange people's hearts? I took the outside view, stated the facts both ways,—the right verdicts of the juries and the confident plans of the boodlers,—and the result was, indeed, a shameless state of affairs for which St. Louis, the people of St. Louis, were to blame.

And they saw it so, both in the city and in the State, and they ceased to be spectators. That article simply got down to the self-respect of this people. And who was hurt? Not St. Louis. From that moment the city has been determined and active, and boodle seems to be doomed. Not Mr. Folk. After that, his nomination for Governor of the State was declared for by the people, who formed Folk clubs all over the State to force him upon his party and theirs, and thus insure the pursuit of the boodlers in St. Louis and in Missouri too. Nor was the magazine hurt, or myself. The next time I went to St. Louis, the very men who had raised money for the mass meeting to denounce the article went out of their way to say to me that I had been right, the article was true, and they asked me to "do it again." And there may be a chance to do it again. Mr. Folk lifted the lid off Missouri for a moment after that, and the State also appeared ripe for the gathering. Moreover, the boodlers of State and city have joined to beat the people and keep them down. The decisive election is not till the fall of 1904, and the boodlers count much on the fickleness of public opinion. But I believe that Missouri and St. Louis together will prove then, once for all, that the people can rule—when they are aroused.

The Pittsburg article had no effect in Pittsburg, nor had that on Philadelphia any results in Philadelphia. Nor was any expected there. Pittsburg, as I said in the article, knew itself, and may pull out of its disgrace, but Philadelphia is contented and seems hopeless. The accounts of them, however, and indeed, as I have said, all of the series, were written, not for the cities described, but for all our cities; and the most immediate response came from places not mentioned, but where similar evils existed or similar action was needed. Thus Chicago, intent on its troubles, found useless to it the study of its reform, which seems to have been suggestive elsewhere, and Philadelphia, "Corrupt and Contented," was taken home in other cities and seems to have made the most lasting impression everywhere.

But of course the tangible results are few. The real triumph of the year's work was the complete demonstration it has given, in a thousand little ways, that our shamelessness is superficial, that beneath it lies a pride which, being real, may save us yet. And it is real. The grafters who said you may put the blame anywhere but on the people, where it belongs, and that Americans can be moved only by flattery,—they lied. They lied about themselves. They, too, are American citizens; they too, are of the people; and some of them also were reached by shame. The great truth I tried to make plain was that which Mr. Folk insists so constantly upon: that bribery is no ordinary felony, but treason, that the "corruption which breaks out here and there and now and then" is not an occasional offense, but a common practice, and that the effect of it is literally to change the form of our government from one that is representative of the people to an oligarchy, representative of special interests. Some politicians have seen that this is so, and it bothers them. I think I prize more highly than any other of my experiences the half-dozen times when grafting politicians I had "roasted," as they put it, called on me afterwards to say, in the words of one who spoke with a wonderful solemnity:

"You are right. I never thought of it that way, but it's right. I don't know whether you can do anything, but you're right, dead right. And I'm all wrong. We're all, all wrong. I don't see how we can stop it now; I don't see how I can change. I can't, I guess. No, I can't, not now. But, say, I may be able to help you, and I will if I can. You can have anything I've got."

So you see, they are not such bad fellows, these practical politicians. I wish I could tell more about them: how they have helped me; how candidly and unselfishly they have assisted me to facts and an understanding of the facts, which, as I warned them, as they knew well, were to be used against them. If I could—and I will some day—I should show that one of the surest hopes we have is the politician himself. Ask him for good politics; punish him when he gives bad, and reward him when he gives good; make politics pay. Now, he says, you don't know and you don't care, and that you must be flattered and fooled—and there, I say, he is wrong. I did not flatter anybody; I told the truth as near as I could get it, and instead of resentment there was encouragement. After "The Shame of Minneapolis," and "The Shamelessness of St. Louis," not only did citizens of these cities approve, but citizens of other cities, individuals, groups, and organizations, sent in invitations, hundreds of them, "to come and show us up; we're worse than they are."

We Americans may have failed. We may be mercenary and selfish. Democracy with us may be impossible and corruption inevitable, but these articles, if they have proved nothing else, have demonstrated beyond doubt that we can stand the truth; that there is pride in the character of American citizenship; and that this pride may be a power in the land. So this little volume, a record of shame and yet of self-respect, a disgraceful confession, yet a declaration of honor, is dedicated, in all good faith, to the accused—to all the citizens of all the cities in the United States.

(19)

Herbert Croly

1869-1930

A native son of New York City, Herbert Croly entered Harvard in 1886, leaving that institution several times only to return at later dates. In 1910 he finally received his bachelor's degree, which was awarded as of the class of 1890. From 1900 to 1906 he edited the *Architectural Record,* but he resigned from that post in order to write his first and most important book, *The Promise of American Life.* In 1914, with the financial backing of Willard Straight, Croly founded the *New Republic,* which quickly became one of the outstanding journals of liberal intellectuals in the United States.

Croly was in many respects one of the outstanding philosophical spokesmen for the early twentieth-century progressive movement. He maintained that in the new industrial society the older Jeffersonian liberal ideal had to be considerably modified, that liberals had to adopt Hamiltonian means of a strong central government in order to realize their Jeffersonian democratic ends. Influenced greatly by pragmatism, he insisted that all philosophies and political theories had to be considered in the light of existing realities. Croly was also a staunch believer in the idea of progress and argued that the democratic process involved constant evolution and adjustment to meet new conditions. In his eyes only a nationalistic, democratic liberalism, which involved a greater reliance upon the powers of the central government, could help to realize the promise of America. In other words, Croly hoped to harness nationalism in order to serve the general welfare. His theories influenced a whole generation of liberal intellectuals from the progressive era through the New Deal.

The selection that follows is from Croly's *The Promise of American Life* (New York, 1909).

It is . . . essential to recognize that the individual American will never obtain a sufficiently complete chance of self-expression, until the American nation has earnestly undertaken and measurably achieved the realization of its collective purpose. As we shall see presently, the cure for this individual sterility lies partly with the individual himself or rather with the man who proposes to become an individual; and under any plan of economic or social organization, the man who proposes to become an individual is a condition of national as well as individual improvement. It is none the less true that any success in the achievement of the national purpose will contribute positively to the liberation of the individual, both by diminishing his temptations, improving his opportunities, and by enveloping him in an invigorating rather than an enervating moral and intellectual atmosphere.

It is the economic individualism of our existing national system which inflicts the most serious damage on American individuality; and American individual achievement in politics and science and the arts will remain partially impoverished as long as our fellow-countrymen neglect or refuse systematically to regulate the distribution of wealth in the national interest. I am aware, of course, that the prevailing American conviction is absolutely contradictory of the foregoing assertion. Americans have always associated individual freedom with the unlimited popular enjoyment of all available economic opportunities. Yet it would be far more true to say that the popular enjoyment of practically unrestricted economic opportunities is precisely the condition which makes for individual bondage. Neither does the bondage which such a system fastens upon the individual exist only in the case of those individuals who are victimized by the pressure of unlimited economic competition. Such victims exist, of course, in large numbers, and they will come to exist in still larger number hereafter; but hitherto, at least, the characteristic vice of the American system has not been the bondage imposed upon its victims. Much more insidious has been the bondage imposed upon the conquerors and their camp-followers. A man's individuality is as much compromised by success under the conditions imposed by such a system as it is by failure. His actual occupation may tend to make his individuality real and fruitful; but the quality of the work is determined by a merely acquisitive motive, and the man himself thereby usually debarred from obtaining any edifying personal independence or any peculiar personal distinction. Different as American business men are one one from another in temperament, circumstances, and habits, they have a way of becoming fundamentally very much alike. Their individualities are forced into a common mold, because the ultimate measure of the value of their work is the same, and is nothing but its results in cash.

Consider for a moment what individuality and individual independence really mean. A genuine individual must at least possess some special quality which distinguishes him from other people, which unifies the successive phases and the various aspects of his own life and which results in personal moral freedom. In what way and to what extent does the existing economic system contribute to the creation of such genuine individuals? At its best it asks of every man who engages in a business occupation that he make as much money as he can, and the only conditions it imposes on this pursuit of money are those contained in the law of the land and a certain conventional moral code. The pursuit of money is to arouse a man to individual activity, and law and custom determine the conditions to which the activity must conform. The man does not become an individual merely by obeying the written and unwritten laws. He becomes an individual because the desire to make money releases his energy and intensifies his personal initiative. The kind of individuals created by such an economic system are not distinguished one from another by any special purpose. They are distinguished by the energy and success whereby the common purpose of making money is accompanied and followed. Some men show more enterprise and ingenuity in devising ways of making money than others, or they show more vigor and zeal in taking advantage of the ordinary methods. These men are the kind of individuals which the existing economic system tends to encourage; and critics of the existing system are denounced, because of the disastrous effect upon individual initiative which would result from restricting individual economic freedom.

But why should a man become an individual because he does what everybody else does, only with more energy and success? The individuality so acquired is merely that of one particle in a mass of similar particles. Some particles are bigger than others and livelier; but from a sufficient distance they all look alike; and in substance and meaning they all are alike. Their individual activity and history do not make them less alike. It merely makes them bigger or smaller, livelier or more inert. Their distinction from their fellows is quantitative; the unity of their various phases a matter of repetition; their independence wholly comparative. Such men are associated with their fellows in the pursuit of a common purpose, and they are divided from their fellows by the energy and success with which that purpose is pursued. On the other hand, a condition favorable to genuine individuality would be one in which men were divided from one another by special purposes, and reunited in so far as these individual purposes were excellently and successfully achieved.

The truth is that individuality cannot be dissociated from the pursuit of a disinterested object. It is a moral and intellectual quality, and it must be realized by moral and intellectual means. A man achieves individual distinction, not by the enterprise and vigor with which he accumulates money, but by the zeal and the skill with which he pursues an exclusive interest—an interest usually, but not necessarily, connected with his means of livelihood. The purpose to which he is devoted—such, for instance, as that of painting or of running a railroad—is not exclusive in the sense of being unique. But it becomes exclusive for the individual who adopts it, because of the single-minded and disinterested manner in which it is pursued. A man makes the purpose exclusive for himself by the spirit and method in which the work is done; and just in proportion as the work is thoroughly well done, a man's individuality begins to take substance and form. His individual quality does not depend merely on the display of superior enterprise and energy, although, of course, he may and should be as enterprising and as energetic as he can. It depends upon the actual excellence of the work in every respect,—an excellence which can best be achieved by the absorbing and exclusive pursuit of that alone. A man's individuality is projected into his work. He does not stop when he has earned enough money, and he does not cease his improvements when they cease to bring in an immediate return. He is identified with his job, and by means of that identification his individuality becomes constructive. His achievement, just because of its excellence, has an inevitable and an unequivocal social value. The quality of a man's work reunites him with his fellows. He may have been in appearance just as selfish as a man who spends most of his time in making money, but if his work has been thoroughly well done, he will, in making himself an individual, have made an essential contribution to national fulfillment.

Of course, a great deal of very excellent work is accomplished under the existing economic system; and by means of such work many a man becomes more or less of an individual. But in so far as such is the case, it is the work which individualizes and not the unrestricted competitive pursuit of money. In so far as the economic motive prevails, individuality is not developed; it is stifled. The man whose motive is that of money-making will not make the work any more excellent than is demanded by the largest possible returns; and frequently the largest possible returns are to be obtained by indifferent work or by work which has absolutely no social value. The ordinary mercenary purpose always compels a man to stop at a certain point, and consider something else than the excellence of his achievement. It does not make the individual independent, except in so far as independence is merely a matter of cash in the bank; and for every individual on whom it bestows excessive pecuniary independence, there are many more who are by that very circumstance denied any sort of liberation. Even pecuniary independence is usually purchased at the price of moral and intellectual bondage. Such genuine individuality as can be detected in the existing social system is achieved not because of the prevailing money-making motive, but in spite thereof.

The ordinary answer to such criticisms is that while the existing system may have many faults, it certainly has proved an efficient means of releasing individual energy; whereas the exercise of a positive national responsibility for the wholesome distribution of wealth would tend to deprive the individual of any sufficient initiative. The claim is that the money-making motive is the only one which will really arouse the great majority of men, and to weaken it would be to rob the whole economic system of its momentum. Just what validity this claim may have cannot, with our present experience, be definitely settled. That to deprive individuals suddenly of the opportunities they have so long enjoyed would be disastrous may be fully admitted. It may also be admitted that any immediate and drastic attempt to substitute for the present system a national regulation of the distribution of wealth or a national responsibility for the management even of monopolies or semi-monopolies would break down and would do little to promote either individual or social welfare. But to conclude from any such admissions that a systematic policy of promoting individual and national amelioration should be abandoned is wholly unnecessary. That the existing system has certain practical advantages, and is a fair expression of the average moral standards of to-day is not only its chief merit, but also its chief and inexcusable defect. What a democratic nation must do is not to accept human nature as it is, but to move in the direction of its improvement. The question it must answer is: How can it contribute to the increase of American individuality? The defender of the existing system must be able to show either (1) that it does contribute to the increase of American individuality; or that (2) whatever its limitations, the substitution of some better system is impossible.

Of course, a great many defenders of the existing system will unequivocally declare that it does contribute effectually to the increase of individuality, and it is this defense which is most dangerous, because it is due, not to any candid consideration of the facts, but to unreasoning popular prejudice and personal self-justification. The existing system contributes to the increase of individuality only in case individuality is deprived of all serious moral and intellectual meaning. In order to sustain their assertion they must define individuality, not as a living ideal, but as the psychological condition produced by any individual action. In the light of such a definition every action performed by an individual would contribute to individuality; and, conversely, every action performed by the state, which conceivably could be left to individuals, would diminish individuality. Such a conception derives from the early nineteenth century principles of an essential opposition between the state and the individual; and it is a deduction from the common conception of democracy as nothing but a finished political organization in which the popular will prevails. As applied in the traditional American system this conception of individuality has resulted in the differentiation of an abundance of raw individual material, but the raw material has been systematically encouraged to persist only on condition that it remained undeveloped. Properly speaking, it has not encouraged individualism at all. Individuality is necessarily based on genuine discrimination. It has encouraged particularism. While the particles have been roused into activity, they all remain dominated by substantially the same forces of attraction and repulsion. But in order that one of the particles may fulfill the promise of a really separate existence, he must pursue some special interest of his own. In that way he begins to realize his individuality, and in realizing his individuality he is coming to occupy a special niche in the national structure. A national structure which encourages individuality as opposed to mere particularity is one which creates innumerable special niches, adapted to all degrees and kinds of individual development. The individual becomes a nation in miniature, but devoted to the loyal realization of a purpose peculiar to himself. The nation becomes an enlarged individual whose special purpose is that of human amelioration, and in whose life every individual should find some particular but essential function.

It surely cannot be seriously claimed that the improvement of the existing economic organization for the sake of contributing to the increase of such genuine individuals is impossible. If genuine individuality depends upon the pursuit of an exclusive interest, promoted most certainly and completely by a disinterested motive, it must be encouraged by enabling men so far as possible to work from disinterested motives. Doubtless this is a difficult, but it is not an impossible task. It cannot be completely achieved until the whole basis of economic competition is changed. At present men compete chiefly for the purpose of securing the most money to spend or to accumulate. They must in the end compete chiefly for the purpose of excelling in the quality of their work that of other men engaged in a similar occupation. And there are assuredly certain ways in which the state can diminish the undesirable competition and encourage the desirable competition.

The several economic reforms suggested in the preceding chapter would, so far as they could be successfully introduced, promote more disinterested economic work. These reforms would not, of course, entirely do away with the influence of selfish acquisitive motives in the economic field, because such motives must remain powerful as long as private property continues to have a public economic function. But they would at least diminish the number of cases in which the influence of the mercenary motive made against rather than for excellence of work. The system which most encourages mere cupidity is one which affords too many opportunities for making "easy money," and our American system has, of course, been peculiarly prolific of such opportunities. As long as individuals are allowed to accumulate money from mines, urban real estate, municipal franchises, or semi-monopolies of any kind, just to that extent will the economic system of the country be poisoned, and its general efficiency impaired. Men will inevitably seek to make money in the easiest possible way, and as long as such easy ways exist fewer individuals will accept cordially the necessity of earning their living by the sheer excellence of achievement. On the other hand, in case such opportunities of making money without earning it can be eliminated, there will be a much closer correspondence than there is at present between the excellence of the work and the reward it would bring. Such a correspondence would, of course, be far from exact. In all petty kinds of business innumerable opportunities would still exist of earning more money either by disregarding the quality of the work or sometimes by actually lowering it. But at any rate it would be work which would earn money, and not speculation or assiduous repose in an easy chair.

In the same way, just in so far as industry became organized under national control for the public benefit, there would be a much closer correspondence between the quality of the work and the amount of the reward. In a well-managed corporation a man is promoted because he does good work, and has shown himself capable of assuming larger responsibilities and exercising more power. His promotion brings with it a larger salary, and the chance of obtaining a larger salary doubtless has much to do with the excellence of the work; but at all events a man is not rewarded for doing bad work or for doing no work at all. The successful employee of a corporation has not become disinterested in his motives. Presumably he will not do any more work than will contribute to his personal advancement; and if the standard of achievement in his office is at all relaxed, he will not be kept up to the mark by an exclusive and disinterested devotion to the work itself. Still, under such conditions a man might well become better than his own motives. Whenever the work itself was really interesting, he might become absorbed in it by the very momentum of his habitual occupation, and this would be particularly the case provided his work assumed a technical character. In that case he would have to live up to the standard, not merely of an office, but of a trade, a profession, a craft, an art, or a science; and if those technical standards were properly exacting, he would be kept up to the level of his best work by a motive which had almost become disinterested. He could not fall below the standard, even though he derived no personal profit from striving to live up to it, because the traditions and the honor of his craft would not let him.

The proposed economic policy of reform, in so far as it were successful, would also tend to stimulate labor to more efficiency, and to diminish its grievances. The state would be lending assistance to the effort of the working-man to raise his standard of living, and to restrict the demoralizing effect of competition among laborers who cannot afford to make a stand on behalf of their own interest. It should, consequently, increase the amount of economic independence enjoyed by the average laborer, diminish his "class consciousness" by doing away with his class grievances, and intensify his importance to himself as an individual. It would in every way help to make the individual workingman more of an individual. His class interest would be promoted by the nation in so far as such promotion was possible, and could be adjusted to a general policy of national economic construction. His individual interest would be left in his own charge; but he would have much more favorable opportunities of redeeming the charge by the excellence of his individual work than he has under the existing system. His condition would doubtless still remain in certain respects unsatisfactory, for the purpose of a democratic nation must remain unfulfilled just in so far as the national organization of labor does not enable all men to compete on approximately equal terms for all careers. But a substantial step would be made towards its improvement, and the road marked, perhaps, for still further advance.

(20)

Theodore Roosevelt

1858-1919

Theodore Roosevelt was born in New York City, the son of a well-to-do family. Overcoming the handicaps of physical frailty, he graduated from Harvard in 1880. Disinterested in a legal career, he turned to the writing of history, publishing numerous works as well as being honored with the presidency of the American Historical Association in 1912. Entering politics in the mid-1880's, he ran unsuccessfully as the Republican candidate for mayor of New York City. After serving as a federal civil service commissioner and as president of the New York City board of police commissioners, he became assistant secretary of the Navy under McKinley, and then won military fame during the Spanish-American War. Elected Governor of New York in 1898 and then Vice-President of the United States in 1900, he succeeded to the presidency upon the assassination of McKinley.

As President, Theodore Roosevelt emerged as one of the leaders of the progressive movement, and also helped to invigorate the office of the presidency through his espousal of a strong and active executive. From his social background and class affiliation Roosevelt had developed a sense of *noblesse oblige* and a compulsion to do good. A consummate politician, he attempted to formulate a political program that would survive the vicissitudes of American politics and yet advance progressive ideals. Like Herbert Croly, Roosevelt maintained that the historic American democratic faith, which was associated with an intense individualism, no longer sufficed to meet the problems of an industrialized society. He argued therefore that progressives had to abandon their Jeffersonian laissez-faire theory for a form of democratic collectivism. In his eyes the powers of the federal government had to be used to protect the general public as well as to regulate large-scale enterprise (which he felt was an inevitable concomitant of modern society). In brief, Roosevelt advocated a political philosophy called the New Nationalism, a philosophy that espoused the use of a strong government to achieve democratic ends through Hamiltonian, or nationalistic, means.

The following selection is from his famous speech, "The New

Nationalism," which he gave at Osawatomie, Kansas, on August 31, 1910, and is taken from *The Works of Theodore Roosevelt*, Herman Hagedorn, ed., 24 volumes (New York, 1923–1926), XIX.

We come here today to commemorate one of the epoch-making events of the long struggle for the rights of man—the long struggle for the uplift of humanity. Our country—this great Republic—means nothing unless it means the triumph of a real democracy, the triumph of popular government, and, in the long run, of an economic system under which each man shall be guaranteed the opportunity to show the best that there is in him. That is why the history of America is now the central feature of the history of the world; for the world has set its face hopefully toward our democracy; and, O my fellow citizens, each one of you carries on your shoulders not only the burden of doing well for the sake of your own country, but the burden of doing well and of seeing that his nation does well for the sake of mankind. . . .

In every wise struggle for human betterment, one of the main objects, and often the only object, has been to achieve in large measure equality of opportunity. In the struggle for this great end, nations rise from barbarism to civilization, and through it people press forward from one stage of enlightenment to the next. One of the chief factors in progress is the destruction of special privilege. The essence of any struggle for healthy liberty has always been, and must always be, to take from some one man or class of men the right to enjoy power, or wealth, or position, or immunity, which has not been earned by service to his or their fellows. That is what you fought for in the Civil War, and that is what we strive for now.

At many stages in the advance of humanity, this conflict between the men who possess more than they have earned and the men who have earned more than they possess is the central condition of progress. In our day it appears as the struggle of freemen to gain and hold the right of self-government as against the special interests, who twist the methods of free government into machinery for defeating the popular will. At every stage, and under all circumstances, the essence of the struggle is to equalize opportunity, destroy privilege, and give to the life and citizenship of every individual the highest possible value both to himself and to the commonwealth. That is nothing new. All I ask in civil life is what you fought for in the Civil War. I ask that civil life be carried on according to the spirit in which the army was carried on. You never get perfect justice, but the effort in handling the army was to bring to the front the men who could do the job. Nobody grudged promotion to Grant, or Sherman, or Thomas, or Sheridan, because they earned it. The only complaint was when a man got promotion which he did not earn.

Practical equality of opportunity for all citizens, when we achieve it, will have two great results. First, every man will have a fair chance to make of himself all that in him lies; to reach the highest point to which his capacities, un-assisted by special privilege of his own and unhampered by the special privi-lege of others, can carry him, and to get for himself and his family substantially what he has earned. Second, equality of opportunity means that the common-wealth will get from every citizen the highest service of which he is capable. No man who carries the burden of the special privileges of another can give to the commonwealth that service to which it is fairly entitled.

I stand for the square deal. But when I say that I am for the square deal, I mean not merely that I stand for fair play under the present rules of the game, but that I stand for having those rules changed so as to work for a more sub-stantial equality of opportunity and of reward for equally good service. One word of warning, which, I think, is hardly necessary in Kansas. When I say I want a square deal for the poor man, I do not mean that I want a square deal for the man who remains poor because he has not got the energy to work for himself. If a man who has had a chance will not make good, then he has got to quit. And you men of the Grand Army, you want justice for the brave man who fought, and punishment for the coward who shirked his work. Is not that so?

Now, this means that our government, National and State, must be freed from the sinister influence or control of special interests. Exactly as the special interests of cotton and slavery threatened our political integrity before the Civil War, so now the great special business interests too often control and corrupt the men and methods of government for their own profit. We must drive the special interests out of politics. That is one of our tasks today. Every special interest is entitled to justice—full, fair, and complete—and, now, mind you, if there were any attempt by mob-violence to plunder and work harm to the special interest, whatever it may be, that I most dislike, and the wealthy man, whomsoever he may be, for whom I have the greatest contempt, I would fight for him, and you would if you were worth your salt. He should have justice. For every special interest is entitled to justice, but not one is entitled to a vote in Congress, to a voice on the bench, or to representation in any public office. The Constitution guarantees protection to property, and we must make that promise good. But it does not give the right of suffrage to any corporation.

The true friend of property, the true conservative, is he who insists that property shall be the servant and not the master of the commonwealth; who insists that the creature of man's making shall be the servant and not the master of the man who made it. The citizens of the United States must effec-tively control the mighty commercial forces which they have themselves called into being.

There can be no effective control of corporations while their political ac-tivity remains. To put an end to it will be neither a short nor an easy task, but it can be done. . . .

Combinations in industry are the result of an imperative economic law which cannot be repealed by political legislation. The effort at prohibiting all combination has substantially failed. The way out lies, not in attempting to prevent such combinations, but in completely controlling them in the interest of the public welfare. . . .

The absence of effective State, and, especially, national, restraint upon unfair money-getting has tended to create a small class of enormously wealthy and economically powerful men, whose chief object is to hold and increase their power. The prime need is to change the conditions which enable these men to accumulate power which it is not for the general welfare that they should hold or exercise. We grudge no man a fortune which represents his own power and sagacity, when exercised with entire regard to the welfare of his fellows. Again, comrades over there, take the lesson from your own experience. Not only did you not grudge, but you gloried in the promotion of the great generals who gained their promotion by leading the army to victory. So it is with us. We grudge no man a fortune in civil life if it is honorably obtained and well used. It is not even enough that it should have been gained without doing damage to the community. We should permit it to be gained only so long as the gaining represents benefit to the community. This, I know, implies a policy of a far more active governmental interference with social and economic conditions in this country than we have yet had, but I think we have got to face the fact that such an increase in governmental control is now necessary. . . .

Nothing is more true than that excess of every kind is followed by reaction; a fact which should be pondered by reformer and reactionary alike. We are face to face with new conceptions of the relations of property to human welfare, chiefly because certain advocates of the rights of property as against the rights of men have been pushing their claims too far. The man who wrongly holds that every human right is secondary to his profit must now give way to the advocate of human welfare, who rightly maintains that every man holds his property subject to the general right of the community to regulate its use to whatever degree the public welfare may require it.

But I think we may go still further. The right to regulate the use of wealth in the public interest is universally admitted. Let us admit also the right to regulate the terms and conditions of labor, which is the chief element of wealth, directly in the interest of the common good. The fundamental thing to do for every man is to give him a chance to reach a place in which he will make the greatest possible contribution to the public welfare. Understand what I say there. Give him a chance; do not push him up if he will not be pushed. Help any man who stumbles; if he lies down, it is a poor job to try to carry him; but if he is a worthy man, try your best to see that he gets a chance to show the worth that is in him. No man can be a good citizen unless he has a wage more than sufficient to cover the bare cost of living, and hours of labor short enough so that after his day's work is done he will have time and energy to bear his share in the management of the community, to help in carrying the general load. We keep countless men from being good citizens by the conditions of life with which we surround them. We need comprehensive workmen's compensation acts, both State and national laws to regulate child labor and work for women, and, especially, we need in our common schools not merely education in book-learning, but also practical training for daily life and work. We need to enforce better sanitary conditions for our workers and to extend the use of safety appliances for our workers in industry and commerce, both within and between the States. Also, friends, in the interest of the working man himself we need to set our faces like flint against mob-violence just as against corporate greed; against violence and injustice and lawlessness by wage-workers just as much as against lawless cunning and greed and selfish arrogance of employers. If I could ask but one thing of my fellow countrymen, my request would be that, whenever they go in for reform, they remember the two sides, and that they always exact justice from one side as much as from the other. I have small use for the public servant who can always see and denounce the corruption of the capitalist, but who cannot persuade himself, especially before election, to say a word about lawless mob-violence. And I have equally small use for the man, be he a judge on the bench, or editor of a great paper, or wealthy and influential private citizen, who can see clearly enough and denounce the lawlessness of mob-violence, but whose eyes are closed so that he is blind when the question is one of corruption in business on a gigantic scale. Also remember what I said about excess in reformer and reactionary alike. If the reactionary man, who thinks of nothing but the rights of property, could have his way, he would bring about a revolution; and one of my chief fears in connection with progress comes because I do not want to see our people, for lack of proper leadership, compelled to follow men whose intentions are excellent, but whose eyes are a little too wild to make it really safe to trust them. . . .

National efficiency has many factors. It is a necessary result of the principle of conservation widely applied. In the end it will determine our failure or success as a nation. National efficiency has to do, not only with natural resources and with men, but it is equally concerned with institutions. The State must be made efficient for the work which concerns only the people of the State; and the nation for that which concerns all the people. There must remain no neutral ground to serve as a refuge for lawbreakers, and especially for lawbreakers of great wealth, who can hire the vulpine legal cunning which will teach them how to avoid both jurisdictions. It is a misfortune when the national legislature fails to do its duty in providing a national remedy, so that the only national activity is the purely negative activity of the judiciary in forbidding the State to exercise power in the premises.

I do not ask for overcentralization; but I do ask that we work in a spirit of broad and far-reaching nationalism when we work for what concerns our people as a whole. We are all Americans. Our common interests are as broad as the continent. I speak to you here in Kansas exactly as I would speak in New York or Georgia, for the most vital problems are those which affect us all alike. The National Government belongs to the whole American people, and where the whole American people are interested, that interest can be guarded effectively only by the National Government. The betterment which we seek must be accomplished, I believe, mainly through the National Government.

The American people are right in demanding that New Nationalism, without which we cannot hope to deal with new problems. The New Nationalism puts the national need before sectional or personal advantage. It is impatient of the utter confusion that results from local legislatures attempting to treat national issues as local issues. It is still more impatient of the impotence which springs from overdivision of governmental powers, the impotence which makes it possible for local selfishness or for legal cunning, hired by wealthy special interests, to bring national activities to a deadlock. This New Nationalism regards the executive power as the steward of the public welfare. It demands of the judiciary that it shall be interested primarily in human welfare rather than in property, just as it demands that the representative body shall represent all the people rather than any one class or section of the people.

I believe in shaping the ends of government to protect property as well as human welfare. Normally, and in the long run, the ends are the same; but whenever the alternative must be faced, I am for men and not for property, as you were in the Civil War. I am far from underestimating the importance of dividends; but I rank dividends below human character. Again, I do not have any sympathy with the reformer who says he does not care for dividends. Of course, economic welfare is necessary, for a man must pull his own weight and be able to support his family. I know well that the reformers must not bring upon the people economic ruin, or the reforms themselves will go down in the ruin. But we must be ready to face temporary disaster, whether or not brought on by those who will war against us to the knife. Those who oppose all reform will do well to remember that ruin in its worst form is inevitable if our national life brings us nothing better than swollen fortunes for the few and the triumph in both politics and business of a sordid and selfish materialism.

If our political institutions were perfect, they would absolutely prevent the political domination of money in any part of our affairs. We need to make our political representatives more quickly and sensitively responsive to the people whose servants they are. More direct action by the people in their own affairs under proper safeguards is vitally necessary. The direct primary is a step in this direction, if it is associated with a corrupt-practices act effective to prevent the advantage of the man willing recklessly and unscrupulously to spend money over his more honest competitor. It is particularly important that all moneys received or expended for campaign purposes should be publicly accounted for, not only after election, but before election as well. Political action must be made simpler, easier, and freer from confusion for every citizen. I believe that the prompt removal of unfaithful or incompetent public servants should be made easy and sure in whatever way experience shall show to be most expedient in any given class of cases.

One of the fundamental necessities in a representative government such as ours is to make certain that the men to whom the people delegate their power shall serve the people by whom they are elected, and not the special interests. I believe that every national officer, elected or appointed, should be forbidden to perform any service or receive any compensation, directly or indirectly, from interstate corporations; and a similar provision could not fail to be useful within the States.

The object of government is the welfare of the people. The material progress and prosperity of a nation are desirable chiefly so far as they lead to the moral and material welfare of all good citizens. Just in proportion as the average man and woman are honest, capable of sound judgment and high ideals, active in public affairs—but, first of all, sound in their home life, and the father and mother of healthy children whom they bring up well—just so far, and no farther, we may count our civilization a success. We must have— I believe we have already—a genuine and permanent moral awakening, without which no wisdom of legislation or administration really means anything; and, on the other hand, we must try to secure the social and economic legislation without which any improvement due to purely moral agitation is necessarily evanescent. Let me again illustrate by a reference to the Grand Army. You could not have won simply as a disorderly and disorganized mob. You needed generals; you needed careful administration of the most advanced type; and a good commissary—the cracker line. You well remember that success was necessary in many different lines in order to bring about general success. You had to have the administration at Washington good, just as you had to have the administration in the field; and you had to have the work of the generals good. You could not have triumphed without that administration and leadership; but it would all have been worthless if the average soldier had not had the right stuff in him. He had to have the right stuff in him, or you could not get it out of him. In the last analysis, therefore, vitally necessary though it was to have the right kind of organization and the right kind of generalship, it was even more vitally necessary that the average soldier should have the fighting edge, the right character. So it is in our civil life. No matter how honest and decent we are in our private lives, if we do not have the right kind of law and the right kind of administration of the law, we cannot go forward as a nation. That is imperative; but it must be an addition to, and not a substitution for, the qualities that make us good citizens. In the last analysis, the most important elements in any man's career must be the sum of those qualities which, in the aggregate, we speak of as character. If he has not got it, then no law that the wit of man can devise, no administration of the law by the boldest and strongest executive, will avail to help him. We must have the right kind of character—character that makes a man, first of all, a good man in the home, a good father, a good husband—that makes a man a good neighbor. You must have that, and, then, in addition, you must have the kind of law and the kind of administration of the law which will give to those qualities in the private citizen the best possible chance for development. The prime problem of our nation is to get the right type of good citizenship, and to get it, we must have progress, and our public men must be genuinely progressive.

(21)

Woodrow Wilson

1856-1924

Woodrow Wilson was born into a strict Presbyterian family in Staunton, Virginia. After graduating from Princeton in 1879, he studied law at the University of Virginia, and then tried, unsuccessfully, to practice law in Atlanta. Returning to academic life, he received his Ph.D. in political science and history from the Johns Hopkins University in 1886. Subsequently he taught at Bryn Mawr, Wesleyan, and Princeton. Wilson in his early writings and lectures concentrated upon analyzing the weaknesses inherent in the structure of national government. His doctoral dissertation, *Congressional Government* (1885), stressed the failure of leadership in the American political system that arose from the separation of executive from legislative leadership. After publishing many other works in history and political science, his fame was such that he was named president of Princeton University in 1902. At Princeton, he put into effect an important series of reforms, but failing to get approval for some of his ideas he turned from the academic world to politics. He began his political career as a conservative Democrat but, sensing the direction of the political winds, he moved to a more liberal position. He ran on a progressive platform and was elected Governor of New Jersey in 1910. As Governor he put through a series of reform measures that brought him national fame and, after a long, hard battle in both the preconvention and presidential campaigns, he was elected to the presidency in 1912.

Like Theodore Roosevelt, Wilson was also a progressive, though of a somewhat different variety. In espousing what he called the "New Freedom," Wilson argued that the most important task facing the American people was the destruction of special privilege, which had made the federal government a tool of selfish interests. He advocated the restoration of competition in industry. The destruction of monopoly, he believed, would automatically follow, thereby releasing the energies of the American people for the achievement of a new high level of prosperity and well-being. The objective of the New Freedom, therefore, was the preservation of free enterprise, to be achieved in part by the federal government's use of its powers to enforce competititon and to eliminate economic maladjustments. Arguing that economic freedom was a prerequisite for political democracy, Wilson also spoke in general terms about the need for social justice, though he objected to what he referred to as Roosevelt's paternalistic philosophy.

The following selections are from Wilson's campaign speeches delivered in the autumn of 1912. Their texts have been authoritatively established by John Wells Davidson in *A Crossroads of Freedom: The 1912 Campaign Speeches of Woodrow Wilson* (New Haven, 1956), and are taken from this source.

LABOR DAY SPEECH

Buffalo, New York, September 2, 1912

I believe that the greatest force for peace, the greatest force for righteousness, the greatest force for the elevation of mankind, is organized opinion, is the thinking of men, is the great force which is in the soul of men, and I want men to breathe a free and pure air. And I know that these monopolies are so many cars of juggernaut which are in our very sight being driven over men in such ways as to crush their life out of them. And I don't look forward with pleasure to the time when the juggernauts are licensed. I don't look forward with pleasure to the time when the juggernauts are driven by commissioners of the United States. I am willing to license automobiles, but not juggernauts, because if any man ever dares take a joy ride in one of them, I would like to know what is to become of the rest of us; because the road isn't wide enough for us to get out of the way. We would have to take to the woods and then set the woods afire. I am speaking partly in pleasantry but underneath, gentlemen, there is a very solemn sense in my mind that we are standing at a critical turning point in our [choice].

Now you say on the other hand, what do the Democrats propose to do? I want to call your attention to the fact that those who wish to support these monopolies by adopting them under the regulation of the government of the United States are the very men who cry out that competition is destructive. They ought to know because it is competition as they conducted it that destroyed our economic freedom. They are certainly experts in destructive competition. And the purpose of the Democratic leaders is this; not to legislate competition into existence again—because statutes can't make men do things—but to regulate competition.

What has created these monopolies? Unregulated competition. It has permitted these men to do anything that they chose to do to squeeze their rivals out and to crush their rivals to the earth. We know the processes by which they have done these things. We can prevent those processes by remedial legislation, and that remedial legislation will so restrict the wrong use of competition that the right use of competition will destroy monopoly. In other words, ours is a program of liberty and theirs is a program of regulation. Ours is a program by which we find we know the wrongs that have been committed and we can stop those wrongs. And we are not going to adopt into the governmental family the men who forward the wrongs and license them to do the whole business of the country.

I want you men to grasp the point because I want to say to you right now the program that I propose doesn't look quite as much like acting as a Providence for you as the other program looks. But I want to frankly say to you that I am not big enough to play Providence, and my objection to the other program is that I don't believe that there is any other man that is big enough to play Providence. I have never known any body of men, any small body of men, that understood the United States. And the only way the United States is ever going to be taken care of is by having the voice of all the men in it constantly clamorous for the recognition of what is justice as they see life. A little group of men sitting every day in Washington City is not going to have a vision of your lives as a whole. You alone know what your lives are. I say, therefore, take the shackles off of American industry, the shackles of monopoly, and see it grow into manhood, see it grow out of the enshackled childishness into robust manliness, men being able to take care of themselves, and reassert the great power of American citizenship.

These are the ancient principles of government the world over. For when in the history of labor, here in this country or in any other, did the government present its citizens with freedom and with justice? When has there been any fight for liberty that wasn't a fight against this very thing, the accumulation of regulative power in the hands of a few persons? I in my time have read a good deal of history and, if I were to sum up the whole history of liberty, I should say that it consisted at every turn in human life in resisting just such projects as are now proposed to us. If you don't believe it, try it. If you want a great struggle for liberty that will cost you blood, adopt this program, put yourselves at the disposition of a Providence resident in Washington and then see what will come of it. . . .

Sioux City, Iowa, September 17, 1912

There is something to do before we subscribe to great public programs of social betterment. I want to say here, as I have said elsewhere, that when it comes to a great part of the program of the third party, for example, represented by Mr. Roosevelt, I subscribe as all public-spirited men subscribe to the greater part of that program; and some very noble and public-spirited people all over the United States have been drawn to that banner because those enterprises of public justice were inscribed on that banner. But I am bound in judging of that party to ask whether the rest of the program of that party permits it to carry out that program.

Now, the illustration I want to draw with you gentlemen and ladies today is this. I am profoundly interested in the question of pure food. You know that a great deal of the food that these teeming and abundant acres in this wonderful state of Iowa produce does not come to [*us*] straight from you. It goes through a lot of intermediate processes. There, for example, are all the break-fast foods. Some man said during the coal famine a year or two ago that if the coal gave out there was at least the breakfast foods. There are so many of them and they would make very convenient fuel, some of them, because they contain a great deal besides food, they say.

The government of the United States has undertaken in recent years with the support of every man in the United States who wished the protection of the lives and energies of the people to see to it that the people of this country get what they suppose they are getting when they buy these foods; that what these foods consist of shall be on the label; that the meats which are killed in great stockyards like this—or at any rate sold in great stockyards like this—shall after they have been shipped great distances be subject to the kind of in-spection which will make it certain that they are still pure, still in such condi-tion as to furnish us with wholesome and nutritious food. But everybody now suspects, and the suspicion is based upon a great many facts that can be estab-lished by proof, that these pure food laws are not lived up to; that the inspec-tion is not always what it should be; and that a great many things are permitted to be done which nullify the pure food laws.

Let me tell you an illustration. I am not a chemist but I have lived very close to chemists a good deal of my life—quite close enough to perceive some of the odors from their laboratories—and the question of benzoate of soda has interested me very much. I suppose that most of you know that a great controversy arose because Dr. Wiley, who was in charge of the Pure Food Ad-ministration, objected to the use of benzoate of soda in certain things that were sold to you, particularly in cans for food. Now, a very nice thing oc-curred. The gentlemen who wanted to use benzoate of soda persuaded the President, Mr. Roosevelt that this was a scientific question, and therefore he should have a board of chemists to determine [*it*]. And Mr. Roosevelt picked out some of the most eminent and honest chemists in this country, headed by a personal friend of mine, the president of Johns Hopkins University. And he submitted to them this question: "Is benzoate of soda hurtful to the human stomach or to the human digestion when taken internally?" Observe that that was the only question submitted to them. And that was exactly what the people who wanted to use benzoate of soda for wrong purposes wanted to limit the inquiry to, because these gentlemen had to say that benzoate of soda in itself was not harmful to the human system, as I believe it is not. But they were not asked this question: "Can benzoate of soda be used to conceal putrefaction? Can it be used in things that have gone bad to conceal the fact that they have gone bad and to induce people to put them in their stomachs after they have gone bad?" They weren't asked that question, because if they had been they would have said, "Yes, it can be used in that way." And Dr. Wiley knew that it was used in that way.

I want to warn the people of this country to beware of commissions of ex-perts. I have lived with experts all my life, and I know that experts don't see anything except what is under their microscope under their eye. They don't even perceive what is under their nose. An expert feels in honor bound to confine himself to the particular question which you have asked him. I was approached once by a very public-spirited person who asked me if I didn't think that alcohol was poison. I said: "I don't think anything about it; I have no right to judge. I have understood that in some circumstances it is and in some circumstances it isn't. And I generally am on the safe side and don't risk it." But suppose you wanted to settle the liquor question by asking a body of experts whether alcohol was poison or not. I believe they would have to tell you that it isn't poison. But does that settle the liquor question? There are a great many things that you can take into your stomach that are not poison that will make you crazy. There are a great many things that you can take into your system which will make you very disagreeable to your families, and yet your expert would have to give them a clean bill.

The expert tariff board is very much of that character. It knows what it knows, but it doesn't know what we want to know. It knows what it inquires into but it does not answer this question: "Are the present tariff duties in the United States suitable to the present business conditions in the United States?" And when the third party proposes a permanent body of experts, it proposes a permanent postponement of tariff legislation.

Now, who wanted this expert board of chemists? The men who wanted to sell us things that weren't fit to eat. And who were they? They were representatives of some of these very special interests with which the government has been allied. And there is nobody more conversant with the conditions of his business than these very men; and there is nobody, as I know by experience, more likely to fool you with regard to the things that it will be fair to do in order to protect them from legislation which they do not desire. If you want pure food laws, therefore, make sure that you have first got an independent and courageous government. . . .

A trust is an arrangement to get rid of competition and a big business is a business that has survived competition by conquering in the field of intelligence and economy. I am for big business and I am against the trusts. Any man that can survive by his brains, any man that can put the others out of business by making the thing cheaper to the consumer at the same time that he is increasing its intrinsic value and quality, I take off my hat to and I say, "You are the man who can build up the United States and I wish there were more of you."

But the third party says that trusts have come and they are inevitable; that is the only way of efficiency. I would say parenthetically that they don't know what they are talking about because the trusts are not efficient. If I had time for another speech I could prove that to you. They have passed the point of efficiency. Their object is not efficiency, though when they sell you their stock they say it is. Their object is monopoly, is the control of the market, is the shutting out by means fair or foul of competition in order that they may control the product.

Now, the third party says these things have come to stay. Mind you, these are artificially built-up things, these things that can't maintain themselves in the market without monopoly, have come to stay, and the only thing that the government can do, the only thing that the third party proposes should be done, is to set up a commission which is to regulate them. It accepts them. It says: "We will not undertake it, it were futile to undertake, to prevent monopoly in this country, but we will go into an arrangement by which we will make these monopolies kind to you. We will guarantee that they shall be pitiful. We guarantee that they shall pay the right wages. We guarantee that they shall do everything kind and public-spirited, which they have never heretofore shown the least inclination to do; and everything that we do for pure food, everything that we do for the rectification of things that have been done wrong, hereafter, shall be done through the trusts which we ourselves regulate."

Don't you realize that is a blind alley? You can't find your way to liberty that way. You can't find your way to pure food or anything else. I am merely using pure food as an illustration. You can't find your way to social reform through the forces which have made social reform necessary. Let them first set the government free and then we will follow them or any other honest men in setting up a schedule of social reform.

Now, there are things that have to be regulated, but they are not to be regulated through the trusts. They are to be regulated by those processes, now perfectly discoverable, by which monopoly can be prevented and broken up; because these monopolies that are to be made permanent if this program goes through, these monopolies are the very things that are limiting the field of enterprise, limiting the market for labor, determining the wages of labor, determining the distribution of products throughout the country. Take one instance—the twenty-four gentlemen who constitute the directors of the United States Steel Corporation act either as presidents or vice-presidents or members of the boards of directors of more than half the railways of the United States. Now, if you want to sell steel and ship steel and are in the board of directors of a railway that is carrying steel, what do you think is going to happen? Are you going to play into your own hand or aren't you? And since you are on the inside, do you think you are going to find out how to play into your own hand or are you not? I tell you, the tentacles of these things spread in every direction, and until we have broken their inside control, the government is helpless to assist the people to righteous processes of judgment and of law.

There are two instruments that the people use in government, two voices, for after all it is what is known, what is spoken, what is believed that moves great bodies of opinion in a free country like ours. What heartens me in recent years is to see how our political audiences have grown more and more serious; how they really want to hear something said; how they really want to get some argument that they can get their teeth in and not hear buncombe, not hear rhetoric. I dare say I could build up structures of rhetoric myself, but they are too thin. I don't want to climb on them, they are too insubstantial, and the American people isn't going to be fed any longer with words. . . .

Sioux Falls, South Dakota, September 17, 1912

You say, "Well, if we are not going to legalize the trusts and control them, what are we going to do?" Well, haven't you observed how the trusts were built up? You say, "Are you going to return by law to the old-fashioned competition?" I say, "No." It is the old-fashioned competition that enabled these men to build up these combinations, because the old-fashioned competition used in the new way was this: Here is a man with some personal capital, or with some personal credit at the local bank, and he tries to set out in a little business. Here in another city is a great combination of men with millions of money at their back who come there and say: "You are a mighty little fellow and you can't come into this thing. We don't want any interlopers here. You have got only your little local market. Very well, we will cut into your little local market and sell at a loss, sell at a figure that you can't possibly sell at because everywhere else in the United States we will sell at a profitable figure, meet our losses in your locality, and we will put you out of business." That is not a fictitious, hypothetical case. That thing has happened by scores and hundreds of instances all over the United States. Now, that is competition, but what sort of competition is it?

The alternative to regulating monopoly is to regulate competition: to say that to go into a community and sell below cost for no other purpose—for it can't be the purpose of profit—for no other purpose than to squeeze out a competitor shall be an offense against the criminal law of the United States, and anybody who attempts it will have to answer at the bar of a criminal tribunal. It won't make any difference whether he is big or little, he will have to answer at that tribunal; for we have been having trials and investigations by Congress, and we know the processes of unrestricted competition by which these men have accomplished the setting up of their monopolies. If we don't know how to stop them, then the lawyers of this country have lost their ingenuity and their intelligence.

I was saying at one of the way stations where they permitted me to make a short speech this afternoon that it was a very serious thing that if a man became a candidate for office and it was discovered that at any time or place he had been counsel for a great corporation, he would have to spend the rest of the campaign explaining that away; and that after the campaign ended he wouldn't have had time enough to explain it sufficiently to get elected. Now, there is nothing dishonorable in advising a corporation, is there? Any body of men in this country doing their business legitimately is entitled to the advice of counsel and it is not dishonorable to advise them. Why are corporation lawyers therefore excluded from running for office? Because it is thought—sometimes unjustly, but universally thought—that what they have been advising their clients to do is something that has been to the detriment of the business of this country. Can you imagine any other explanation?

I know scores of lawyers who have been the intimate counsel of great corporations have never advised them to do anything illegal, but there are a great many legal things that you can do now that will put the little man out of business. That is the reason that I want to change the law, not the lawyer. I was a lawyer myself once, and you can't change a lawyer. But you can change the law. And then the whole atmosphere will clear. The lawyer will be obliged to say: "Why, my dear sirs, that is a very fine scheme; but if you follow it, you will get into the penitentiary, because you can be found out." . . .

HARTFORD, CONNECTICUT, September 25, 1912

The laws of this country have not kept up with the change of economic circumstances in this country; they have not kept up with the change of political circumstances in this country; and therefore we are not where we were when we started. We are back of the place that we were when we started. And we will have to run, not until we are out of breath, but until we have caught up with our own conditions, before we shall be where we were when we started; when we started this great experiment which has been the hope and the beacon of the world. And we would have to run twice as fast as any rational progressive program I have seen in order to get anywhere else.

I am, therefore, a progressive because we have not kept up with our own changes of conditions, either in the economic field or in the political field. We have not kept up as well as other nations have. We have not adjusted our practices to the facts of the case. And until we do, and unless we do, the facts of the case will always have the better of the argument, because if you do not adjust your laws to the facts, so much the worse for the laws, not for the facts, because law trails along after the facts. Only that law is unsafe which runs ahead of the facts and beckons to them and makes it follow imaginative programs and will-o'-the-wisps. . . .

NEW HAVEN, CONNECTICUT, September 25, 1912

The Democratic party does not stand for the limitation of powers of government, either in the field of the state or in the field of the federal government. There is not a Democrat that I know who is afraid to have the powers of the government exercised to the utmost. But there are a great many of us who are afraid to see them exercised at the discretion of individuals. There are a great many of us who still adhere to that ancient principle that we prefer to be governed by the power of laws, and not by the power of men.

Therefore, we favor as much power as you choose, but power guided by knowledge, power extended in detail, not power given out in the lump to a commission set up as is proposed by the third party and unencumbered by the restrictions of law, to set up a "constructive regulation," as their platform calls it, of the trusts and monopoly. But [*we wish*] a law which takes its searchlight and casts its illuminating rays down the secret corridors of all the processes by which monopoly has been established and polices those corridors so that highway robbery is no longer committed on them, so that men are no longer waylaid upon them, so that the liberty of individuals to compete is no longer checked by the power of combinations stronger than any possible individual can be. We want to see the law administered. We are not afraid of commissions.

It is said, with a good deal of force, I want frankly to admit, that merely to make laws and leave their application to the present courts with their present procedure is not a very likely way of reform, because the present procedure of our courts means that individuals must challenge the power that is being exerted against them, that an individual must wait until he is injured and then go to the court for redress, and that he must have money enough and courage enough to go to the court and ask for redress. For the worst of our present situation, ladies and gentlemen, is that it requires courage to challenge the power of the men now in control of our industries by resorting to any tribunal whatever. Therefore, I am ready to admit that we may have to have special tribunals, special processes, and I am not afraid, for my part, of the creation of special processes and special tribunals; but I am absolutely opposed to leaving it to the choice of those tribunals what the processes of law shall be and the means of remedy.

Therefore, the difference between the Democratic and the Republican parties, or rather between the Democratic party and those various other groups that are masquerading under all sorts of names, is that they are willing to accept the discretionary power of individuals, and we are not willing to accept anything except the certainty of law. That is the only thing that has ever afforded salvation or safety. . . .

(22)

Walter Weyl

1873-1919

Born in New York City into a lower-middle-class Jewish family, Walter Weyl imbibed that respect for learning so typical of many Jewish immigrants. After graduating from the University of Pennsylvania's Wharton School of Commerce and Finance in 1892, he went to the University of Halle in Germany for graduate studies. He continued his graduate work at the University of Pennsylvania under Simon Patton and Emery Johnson, and received a Ph.D. in economics in 1897. Deciding against an academic career, he traveled widely, making statistical surveys for the United States Bureau of Labor, as well as working closely with President John Mitchell of the United Mine Workers. By 1904 Weyl was also pursuing a journalistic career, and wrote extensively on varied social problems and issues. Sometime before 1911 he decided to write a book on American democracy, and the result was the publication in 1912 of an important contribution to progressivism, *The New Democracy.* Soon afterwards Weyl joined with Herbert Croly and Walter Lippmann to found the *New Republic,* the brilliant and provocative journal that expressed the hopes of many American liberals.

Like Croly, Weyl attempted to fashion a new philosophical basis for middle-class liberalism. Believing that the grave social and economic crisis facing America resulted from an outmoded, negative, and individualistic philosophy, he argued that only a socialized democracy would permit man to fulfill his social destiny and direct progress toward the final perfection of the human race. Essentially Weyl was attempting to preserve a middle-class democratic pragmatic liberalism by taking a middle course between nineteenth-century laissez-faire liberalism and Marxian socialism. Basic to his philosophy was the idea of a strong central government, directing progress toward moral ends.

The selection that follows is from Weyl's famous work *The New Democracy* (New York, 1912).

America to-day is in a somber, soul-questioning mood. We are in a period of clamor, of bewilderment, of an almost tremulous unrest. We are hastily revising all our social conceptions. We are hastily testing all our political ideals. We are profoundly disenchanted with the fruits of a century of independence.

Our visitors from Europe in the early days of independence were obsessed by the unique significance of our democracy. To liberty or to its excesses they ascribed all American qualities, customs, and accidents. Our native apologists laid equal emphasis upon democracy. In half-ludicrous, half-tragic orations, they acclaimed the rule of the people as the essence and import of the new Republic. America was to be the eternal land of liberty, the refuge of the world's oppressed, the mentor of Europe. The chosen people of the West were to teach the true creed of democracy, in obedience to a divine command, as explicit as that laid upon the ancient folk of Israel.

Four generations have passed since Cornwallis surrendered at Yorktown. We have survived the early days of poverty and interstate bickering. We have grown in wealth, power, and prestige. We have issued triumphantly from a great civil war, which put an end forever to chattel slavery. Our institutions have not become less popular; our patriotism, though less fervid, is perhaps deeper; our hope of equality is not quite dead.

Nevertheless, to millions of men there has come a deep and bitter disillusionment. We are no longer the sole guardians of the Ark of the Covenant. Europe does not learn at our feet the facile lessons of democracy, but in some respects has become our teacher. Foreign observers describe our institutions with a galling lack of enthusiasm, and visitors from monarchical lands applaud their native liberty, while condoling with us over our political "bosses," our railroad "kings," and our Senate "oligarchies." A swelling tide of native criticism overtops each foreign detraction.

The shrill political cries which to-day fill the air are in vivid contrast with the stately, sounding phrases of the Declaration of Independence. Men speak (with an exaggeration which is as symptomatic as are the evils it describes) of sensational inequalities of wealth, insane extravagances, strident ostentations; and, in the same breath, of vast, boss-ridden cities, with wretched slums peopled by all the world, with pauperism, vice, crime, insanity, and degeneration rampant. We disregard, it is claimed, the lives of our workmen. We muster women into dangerous factories. We enroll in our industrial army, by an infinitely cruel conscription, the anæmic children of the poor. We create hosts of unemployed men, whose sullen tramp ominously echoes through the streets of our relentless cities. Daily we read of the premature death of American babies; of the ravages of consumption and other "poor men's diseases"; of the scrapping of aged workingmen; of the jostling of blindly competing races in factory towns; of the breakdown of municipal government; of the collusion of politicians, petty thieves, and "malefactors of great wealth"; of the sharpening of an irreconcilable class conflict; of the spread of a hunger-born degradation, voicing itself in unpunished crimes of violence; of the spread of a social vice, due in numerous instances (according to the Committee of Fourteen) not to passion or to corrupt inclination, but to "the force of actual physical want." According to some critics—among whom are conservative men with a statistical bent—American democracy is in process of decay. . . .

It is in this moment of misgiving, when men are beginning to doubt the all-efficiency of our old-time democracy, that a new democracy is born. It is a new spirit, critical, concrete, insurgent. A clear-eyed discontent is abroad in the land. There is a low-voiced, earnest questioning. There is a not unreverential breaking of the tablets of tradition.

It is not merely the specific insurgent movement in Congress which occupies men's minds. That is but a symptom, but one of a hundred symptoms, of a far broader, subtler, and more general movement of revolt. Men in the Middle West, in the Far West, in the East and South; men in the factory and on the farm; men, and also women,—are looking at America with new eyes, as though it were the morning of the first day. They are using old words in strange, new senses; they are appealing to old moralities in behalf of strange, new doctrines. It is not all "talk" of congressmen, for the man who is represented is more insurgent than the man who represents him. There are millions of insurgents who have never been to Washington.

The new spirit is not yet self-conscious. It does not understand its own implications, its own alignments, or its own oppositions. It does not quite know whether to look backward or forward. It is still inchoate. It is still negative. . . .

As it becomes positive the new spirit seeks to explain itself, and in so doing to understand itself. It seeks to test its motives and ideals in their relation to American history and conditions. Is our new democracy merely the old democracy in a new coat? Is it a return to the past or a turning from the past? Is it an imported creed or a belief of native growth? Is it a high-hung Utopia or an attainable end? Is it a destruction, or a fulfillment, of the fundamental law of American development? Whence does it come? Whither does it lead? What is it and what is it to be? What does it mean, for better or worse, to the common run of us? . . .

For a long time, disliking the idea of a plutocracy, we simply denied its existence. We informed our foreign critics that our great fortunes were evanescent, accidental, due to temporary disturbances in a permanently equalizing economic process. We tried to believe that there were but three generations from shirt-sleeves to shirt-sleeves. To-day, however, the evidence is overwhelming that American fortunes do not vanish, but grow ever larger. Our plutocracy can no longer be concealed.

What is this America plutocracy? It is not, as the Century Dictionary defines plutocracy, "a class ruling by virtue of its wealth," for it is at most a class in process, and its rule is only partial, undefined, and unadmitted. Our American plutocracy is rather a more or less fluctuating group of very wealthy men, loosely united (primarily by pecuniary bonds) who, through their wealth and prestige, and through the allegiance of like-minded but poorer men, exert an enormous, if not preponderating, influence over industry, politics, and public opinion.

This plutocracy does not aspire, and dare not aspire, to personal rule. There is a tenacious political myth that our millionaires aim at the subversion of all constitutional guarantees, and at the creation of an American Empire upon the ruins of our present republic. But our over-moneyed men do not indulge such romantic and belated notions. True, an occasional millionaire succumbs to the pitiful ambition of "founding a family," and accordingly ties up his estate for a generation or two. True, there are sons and daughters and sons-in-law—young and decorative fashionables—who dislike the robustness of American life, and feebly long for those signal recognitions of leisured wealth which only royalty can confer. These facts, however, are of infinitesimal significance. Our titled marriages and our sudden appetite for heraldic quarterings are an unconscious confession, not a boast. The strident inanities, the "conspicuous waste," and the advertised idleness of a few transcendent spenders are not be dignified by an imperialistic interpretation. . . .

It is thus possible to speak of the plutocracy not only as a group of excessively wealthy men, with their business and social retainers, but also as a system of industrial organization. We may describe the plutocracy, or the plutocratic economy, as that system of industry in which a large and increasing portion of the income of society flows into great reservoirs (usually natural or legal monopolies) which are preëmpted and controlled by private corporations. The plutocratic economy is based upon a narrowing control of enlarging funds; upon a unity of command in the industrial world; upon the leadership of the large purse. Its ideal is the conquest of the world's market. Its creed is freedom of large industry from political interference. Its weapon is monopoly and large scale production.

Not only are monopoly and large scale production permanent, but they are rapidly trenching upon small scale and formerly competitive industries. The businesses in which there is a visible monopoly element are already over-powering in magnitude. A totally incomprehensible amount of capital, esti-mated, a few years ago, at thirty-one billions of dollars (par, not actual, value), represents the stocks and bonds of our railroad, public franchise, and large industrial corporations. The United States Steel Corporation alone has emitted securities which actually bring on the market over one billion of dollars. Despite prohibitory legislation, our railroads have continued to unite legally and actually. There are believed to be six compact railroad groups, each with a capital of over one billion dollars. A single group of financiers is supposed to dominate railroads with a combined capitalization of three thousand millions of dollars.

These great amalgamations are still growing. The big business concern, with a natural or artificial monopoly, or merely a short cut to the savings of the people, prospers exceedingly. It grows fat by indulging the right to levy an increasing toll upon an increasing number of millions. Secure from compe-tition (sometimes even from potential competition), the trust grows in value with the birth of each child and the advent of each immigrant. It raises prices, and each increase is immediately reflected in increased earnings, and in the issue of new capital. Not only does the public pay the increase (though not without humorous grumbling), but it allows the trusts to sell their surplus products more cheaply abroad than at home, to sell cheap abroad *for the very purpose* of selling dear at home. Though the trusts have not been uniquely responsible for the rise of prices during the last fifteen years, this rise has taken place simultaneously with a cornering of a protected market and with the absorption of an increasing proportion of the social surplus by industrial com-binations.

The trust succeeds because it is a unit. Consumers, laborers, and com-petitors, on the other hand, are many and largely unorganized. The trust can profitably employ a one-hundred-thousand-dollar man to determine when the scattered millions of consumers will stand an increase of a tenth of a cent per pound or gallon. Over its employees the trust enjoys similar advantages. A hundred mill managers are pitted against each other in a competition to secure —not necessarily the lowest paid employees—but the lowest possible, the lowest conceivable labor cost. Long hours, excessive speed, Sunday labor, night labor, the employment of women and children, the casting aside of middle-aged men, the cutting down of wages, even the running of truck stores enter into this reduction of labor cost. To preserve the advantage of unity over multiplicity, to remain one, and to keep its opponents many, the great trust usually manifests an antagonistic attitude towards labor unions. The hundred-million-dollar corporation, to rescue its honest workmen from the clutches of the walking delegate, prefers to bargain individually with each of its employees. Such bargaining between the lion and the hare—though recognized by our legal traditions as normal—usually redounds to the advantage of the lion. . . .

We are at last beginning to realize that while the "criminal record" of many of our trusts is a fact important historically and ethically, nevertheless the recognition of this fact does not teach us how in the future we must run our national businesses. We are beginning to see that we can moralize, we can socialize the trusts, and can build more wisely upon the economic tendencies of the age. This we are slowly, painfully learning. The trusts are teaching us— as we are teaching them—that the end of it all must be production on the largest scale compatible with efficiency, but a production so regulated as to ownership, stock issues, dividends, prices, wages, and profits as to safeguard the whole community. Unless we are to take the *saltum mortale* of a complete and immediate governmental ownership and operation of all large industries, we must work out a more perfect system of corporation control in the interests of society.

Against such measures of regulation, against even the creation of a state and of democratic machinery capable of such regulation, the plutocracy opposes the dead weight of its resistance. Our business magnates, to get what they could and hold what they got, have long since occupied the political positions which the democracy must gain before such regulation is entirely effective. The leaders of the plutocracy are giving direction to their pecuniary aspirations by carrying over their activities from the economic into the political field. The key to the citadel which the plutocracy has established in industry lies in the law; the law depends upon legislatures and courts; the legislatures and courts upon parties; the parties upon the powers, open and occult, which control them. To prevent the democracy, through its control of politics, from conquering the industrial field, the plutocracy enters politics. . . .

This program of the plutocracy, halting though it be, is as much superior to the negative social program of the earlier individualist as is the organization of the Standard Oil Company to that of the little companies which have been superseded. If the plutocracy were attacked by individualists alone, its arguments would avail, and its social program, like its industrial labors, would justify its existence.

But the plutocracy is also assailed by men who desire, not a return to individualism, but a progress toward democratic socialization. These opponents of the plutocracy point out its wastes, inefficiencies, and injustices, and accuse it of standing in the way of a complete harmonization of our industrial organization with our political and social aspirations.

The plutocracy's argument from prosperity is turned against itself. Who gets the prosperity? Why, after the wastes of production have been so largely eliminated, do we still suffer from overwork, child labor, sweating, industrial disease, preventable accident, slums, poverty, wretchedness? Why do wages remain low after the plutocracy has established a little order in industry? Why does an increasing inequality accompany an improved utilization of the resources of the continent?

In lessening the wastes of production, the plutocracy has increased many of the wastes of consumption. By improving industrial processes it has drawn attention to heightened inequalities of distribution. Our senseless inequalities of distribution, from our new point of view, are poor economy and low efficiency, because a gross inequality means a lessened pleasure in the consumption of wealth. A masterpiece of art in a private gallery, seen by a hundred people, gives less pleasure than would the same masterpiece in a public gallery seen by a million people. A million dollars of commodities consumed by one overrich man gives less pleasure than would the same sum added to the expenditure of ten thousand people. If the plutocracy's wiser utilization of our national resources leads only to an increasing inequality of wealth and income, the net gain to the people may be dubious.

It is exactly as though the plutocracy, with its brand-new tool, the trust, had trebled our production of coal, but had distributed the fuel so badly, over-stoking some boilers and understoking others, that the total production of heat was no greater than before. It is as though the plutocracy, boasting of its trebled production of coal, and exulting in its increased output of smoke and ashes, had failed to realize that a shivering people was demanding, not more coal, not more smoke, not more ashes, but more heat. What the people want is not wealth, but distributed wealth; not a statistical increase in the national income, but more economic satisfactions, more widely distributed.

Our new economic thought emphasizes as the industrial goal of nations, not wealth in the sense of objective values, but economic pleasures or satisfactions. The older conception measured value in terms of toil or pain involved in production, or the sheer scarcity of a desired article. If potatoes became twice as hard to get, they became twice as valuable. In this sense, our American forests are more valuable to-day, are worth more, than they were thirty years ago, because we have fewer forests and they are more easily monopolized. If to-day we could increase our deposits of coal one hundred fold, the nation (according to the earlier economics) would be poorer *because* it had more to enjoy. Much that we count as wealth is, from the point of view of the economic satisfactions of the community, not wealth at all, but its exact opposite.

Our crassly unequal distribution means not only a less effective production, but, what is worse, a comparatively pleasureless consumption of wealth. A bad distribution of wealth means a wasting of vast quantities of labor in the manufacture of unprofitable articles, and the rendering of unnecessary services. A full-grown footman devoting himself to the cultivated wants of a gold-collared puppy as clearly illustrates wasted social labor as does a man manufacturing nails by hand after machinery has been introduced, or as does a man employed in a small, ill-equipped workshop at labor which can better be done in a large, well-equipped factory.

The Achilles-heel of the Plutocratic Economy, as of the economy which preceded it, is this individualistic and objective conception of wealth. It makes the goal of our national economy the increase in articles, possessed by certain citizens and demanded by others, instead of an increase in the economic pleasure derived from a more universal, varied, and harmonious consumption. The plutocratic conception identifies wealth with gain, with the individualistic accumulation of scarce things. The plutocracy stands for "business," which is concerned uniquely with profits, and not, like industry, with production. Business means gaining money, not making things. Business destroys, when it pays to destroy, as it upbuilds when it pays to upbuild. Whether profits are secured through monopoly, adulteration, advertised poisoning, or the making of good bread and good shoes at fair prices, the end of business is the same— the maximum of profits.

For the individual man, in business against competitors, this goal of profits (within bounds of law and decency) is legitimate. For a nation the conception is self-destructive.

The social program of the plutocracy is tainted by this individualistic conception. That program is too profit-cramped, and consequently too pedantically restrained, to gain general approbation. The man on the street, though astounded at the magnitude of certain benefactions, is seldom with any deep sense of gratitude. He vaguely feels that the social program even of philanthropists is for the most part second-hand. He suspects that it comes from an outside intellectual and moral pressure, or even from an abiding sense of avertible evils to come.

These suspicions are perhaps unfounded. Yet the social ethics of the plutocracy sit somewhat awkwardly upon the victors in the great game of American profit-seeking. It is an ethic which, acknowledging no evils, proceeds to cure them; which, finding the economic world theoretically perfect in all its parts, proceeds to patch it up. The plutocrat does not come by his good intentions honestly. He is a man who instinctively worships the *status quo;* who instinctively lauds the conditions of which he is the product; who inevitably attributes the failures of others to those others' failings. If he becomes a philanthropist, or a social and political reformer, it is not so much by virtue of his philosophy as because he has a sense of order and dislikes waste. Moreover, city life and the newspaper bring home to us—and, through us, to him—poverty, illness, cruelty, and a festering wretchedness; and to all these things a growing general comfort and an increasing national wealth have made us—and him—most painfully sensitive. The cramping of the plutocratic philanthropy, however, consists herein, that the huge benefactions of multi-millionaires are seldom *intentionally* and consciously directed towards the equalization of incomes, the prevention of future inequalities, the democratization of government, or the extension of popular control over industries now given over to private exploitation. The profits of the plutocracy, even when directed to social reform, are seldom intentionally enlisted in a war against profits.

The very qualities of the plutocracy have this inevitable defect, this prenatal taint. Our business magnates, though perhaps the greatest industrial organizers in the world, are in many respects reactionary. They demand free access to the spoils of the continent. They claim the privilege (as price of their leadership) of levying a legalized tribute. By arbitrarily identifying their interests with those of the community at large, they subtly exalt their own demands above those of other social groups. They believe in docile labor. They favor business secrecy, financial absolutism, liberty of action to the industrially strong. They wish, for the sake of private profits, to rule despotically in the business field.

Because of this inability to rise above the conception of individual profits, the plutocracy finds that its own arguments, used so effectively against the individualist, are now directed against its own pretensions. As the old individualist, so, in its turn, the trust was necessary, and was tolerated. The pioneer period could not lead immediately into the period of democratic socialization, because neither we nor our businesses or governments were adjusted to such a transition. Our industry was too detailed, inchoate, multiformed; our government was too amorphous; our individualism too confident and dogmatic. Before a democracy was possible, the house must be set in order, the house industrial, political, and socio-psychological. The cleaner appointed for this necessary task of preparing the house for the owner's occupancy was our resplendent, unpremeditated plutocracy.

The task of cleaning, however, is a temporary one, and the more efficiently the cleaners work, the sooner they may be paid off and dismissed. The rapidity with which our trust builders, financiers, business engineers, and long-distance organizers are unifying our national businesses hastens their own supersession through the creation of conditions which make a still more efficient *régime* possible. The more rapidly our plutocracy, acting under the stimulus of profits, introduces the coöperative element into our businesses, the sooner will the democracy be able to adapt this coöperative element to the socialization of industry. The function of the plutocracy is to reduce chaos to order. But order is the very rock upon which democratic socialization is built. When the plutocracy shall have finished its task, it must take its booty and go.

The new democracy accepts the plutocracy's theory of the survival of the fittest civilization. It recognizes that the efficient utilization of our national resources means the wealth, bread, life of the people, and that all political aspirations must conform to this underlying economic factor. The democracy, however, instructed by its wants, interprets the word utilization in a new sense. Where the plutocracy means the greatest wealth, the democracy means the widest range of economic satisfactions. Where the plutocracy thinks of profits, the democracy thinks of recreation, leisure, a wise expenditure, and a healthful toil. Where the plutocracy emphasizes a saving in wages, the democracy emphasizes a saving in labor.

The democracy does not believe that a nation is rich because the majority owes the minority money and labor. The democracy does not wish the nation to possess that "wealth" which is merely the capitalized value of an economic rent due from the people to monopolists, but it does desire meat, potatoes, school books, public parks, and surcease from excessive toil. The democracy interprets utilization as such a production, distribution, and consumption of wealth as will give the highest excess of economic pleasure over economic pain to the largest number of people for the longest possible time. Upon this end all the industrial, political, social, and ethical ideals of the democracy converge. . . .

The new spirit is social. Its base is broad. It involves common action and a common lot. It emphasizes social rather than private ethics, social rather than individual responsibility.

This new spirit, which is marked by a social unrest, a new altruism, a changed patriotism, an uncomfortable sense of social guilt, was not born of any sudden enthusiasm or quickening revelation. It grew slowly in the dark places of men's minds out of the new conditions. The old individualism—carried to its logical sequence—would have meant impotence and social bankruptcy. Individualism struck its frontier when the pioneer struck his, and society, falling back upon itself, found itself. New problems arose, requiring for their solution slight amendments of our former canons of judgment and modes of action. In many spheres of economic life the individual began to find more profit in his undivided share of the common lot than in his chance of individual gain. On this foundation of an individual interest in the common lot, the new social spirit was laid. This egoistic interest, however, was shared by so many interdependent millions, that men passed insensibly from an ideal of reckless individual gaining to a new ideal, which urged the conservation and thrifty utilization of the patrimony of all in the interest of all.

In obedience to this new spirit we are slowly changing our perception and evaluation of the goods of life. We are freeing ourselves from the unique standard of pecuniary preeminence and are substituting new standards of excellence. We are ceasing solely to adore successful greed, and are evolving a tentative theory of the trusteeship of wealth. We are emphasizing the overlordship of the public over property and rights formerly held to be private. A new insistence is laid upon human life, upon human happiness. What is attainable by the majority—life, health, leisure, a share in our natural resources, a dignified existence in society—is contended for by the majority against the opposition of men who hold exorbitant claims upon the continent. The inner soul of our new democracy is not the unalienable rights, negatively and individualistically interpreted, but those same rights, "life, liberty, and the pursuit of happiness," extended and given a social interpretation.

It is this social interpretation of rights which characterizes the democracy coming into being, and makes it different in kind from the so-called individualistic democracy of Jefferson and Jackson. It is this social concept which is the common feature of many widely divergent democratic policies. The close of the merely expansive period of America showed that an individualistic democracy must end in its own negation, the subjection of the individual to an economically privileged class of rich men. The political weapons of our forefathers might avail against political despotism, but were farcically useless against economic aggression. The right of habeas corpus, the right to bear arms, the rights of free speech and free press could not secure a job to the gray-haired citizen, could not protect him against low wages or high prices, could not save him from a jail sentence for the crime of having no visible means of support. The force of our individualistic democracy might suffice to supplant one economic despot by another, but it could not prevent economic despotism.

To-day no democracy is possible in America except a socialized democracy, which conceives of society as a whole and not as a more or less adventitious assemblage of myriads of individuals. . . .

In two respects, the democracy towards which we are striving differs from that of to-day. Firstly, the democracy of to-morrow, being a real and not a merely formal democracy, does not content itself with the mere right to vote, with political immunities, and generalizations about the rights of men. Secondly, it is a plenary, socialized democracy, emphasizing social rather than merely individual aims, and carrying over its ideals from the political into the industrial and social fields.

Because of this wideness of its aims, the new spirit, in a curiously cautious, conservative way, is profoundly revolutionary. The mind of the people slowly awakens to the realization of the people's needs; the new social spirit gradually undermines the crust of inherited and promulgated ideas; the rising popular will overflows old barriers and converts former institutions to new uses. It is a deep-lying, potent, swelling movement. It is not noiseless, for rotten iron cracks with great sound, and clamor accompanies the decay of profit-yielding privileges. It is not uncontested, for men, threatened with the loss of a tithe of their pretensions, sometimes fight harder than the wholly disinherited. It does not proceed everywhere at equal pace; the movement is not uniform nor uninterrupted. And yet, measured by decades, or even by years, the revolution grows. . . .

I use the word "revolution," despite its fringe of misleading suggestion, because no other word so aptly designates the completeness of the transformation now in process. A social revolution, in the sense here implied, is a change, however gradual, peaceful, and evolutionary, which has for its cumulative effect a radical displacement of the center of gravity of society. Such a revolution is the substitution of a new for an old social equilibrium; a fundamental rearrangement of the relations subsisting between conflicting or allied social groups. It is a recrystallization of society on new planes. It is a new chemical union of constituent social molecules. A relatively more rapid growth of a single organ or of a single function of the social organism, a hypertrophy here, an atrophy there, may suffice to bring about a fundamental social overturn, such as we designate by the word "revolution."

This revolution, in the very midst of which we are, while believing that we stand firm on a firm earth, is a revolution not of blood and iron, but of votes, judicial decisions, and points of view. It does not smell of gunpowder or the bodies of slain men. It does not involve anything sudden, violent, cataclysmic. Like other revolutions, it is simply a quicker turn of the wheel *in the direction in which the wheel is already turning.* It is a revolution at once magnificent and commonplace. It is a revolution brought about by and through the common run of men, who abjure heroics, who sleep soundly and make merry, who "talk" politics and prize-fights, who obey alarm clocks, time-tables, and a thousand petty but revered social conventions. They do not know that they are revolutionists. . . .

The industrial goal of the democracy is the socialization of industry. It is the attainment by the people of the largest possible industrial control and of the largest possible industrial dividend. The democracy seeks to attain these ends through government ownership of industry; through government regulation; through tax reform; through a moralization and reorganization of business in the interest of the industrially weak. . . .

What the democracy desires, however, is not government ownership for itself, but merely enough government ownership, regulation, or control as may be necessary to a true socialization of industry. The democracy's goal—the socialization of industry—is a viewing of our manifold business life from the standpoint of society and not solely from that of the present beneficiaries or directors of industry. It is such a coördination of business as will permanently give the greatest happiness and the highest development to the largest number of individuals, and to society as a whole.

Socialization is thus a point of view. It is less a definite industrial program than the animating ideal of a whole industrial policy. It is a standard by which industrial conditions and industrial developments must be adjudged.

In certain industries socialization may involve a government monopoly. In others, it may mean government operation in competition with private businesses; or a government ownership with private management; or a division of the profits of private industries. Or it may involve a thoroughgoing regulation of an industry, prescribing rates, prices, services, wages, hours, labor conditions, dividends, and the internal economy in general. Or, socialization may mean a lesser regulation; or mere publicity; or encouragement; or subsidies; or legal recognition; or simply the prescribing of a minimum capital or of a preliminary training. Again, socialization may mean a deflection of the stream of wealth which flows from an industry, a deflection accomplished by tax laws, or by laws altering the conditions of conveying property. Finally, socialization may be accomplished without direct governmental regulation. How far the government shall interfere depends on the business. An insurance company, to which people who are not actuaries give money *now* that their widows may receive money fifty years hence, requires a different regulation from the business of the corner tailor, who presses your coat while you wait. . . .

Socialization considers industry as a whole. The national business is "one and indivisible"; an indissoluble union of autonomous, but linked, industries.

In emphasizing this oneness of business, socialization is doing on a large scale and from the point of view of society what the trust did on a smaller scale from the point of view of the profit-taker. Like the trust, socialization subjects rival or dissimilar businesses to the sway of a single aim. Like the trust, socialization attains unity without sacrificing variety. The trust does not always end the separate existence of constituent companies. So, under a complete socialization of our national industry, we would have thousands of separate kinds of business under different forms of ownership, management, and control, but each continuing its existence and mode of life because adapted, in the opinion of society, to contribute its share to the best progress of industry as a whole.

Like the trust, also, socialization does not end competition. The trust encourages *internal* competition. The right hand is stimulated to do better than the left, and the left to excel the right. The factory manager who attains a greater output or a less cost per unit of product than rival managers is appropriately recompensed. It is a "personally conducted" competition, which differs from the competition outside the trust (the industrial *bellum omnium contra omnes*) as the Prince Charles spaniel differs from his savage cousin, the gray wolf. Similarly, socialization relies upon competition, which educates and steels competitors, though it opposes competition which injures the contestants or others.

In actual fact socialization, in so far as it involves the actual intervention of the state, is used largely to supplement or correct competition. It is where competition is atrophied, as in the case of monopolies, or where it appears in a pathological form, as in child labor, industrial parasitism, etc., that the intervention of the state is most needed. . . .

It is probable, however, that a considerable extension of the federal government's ownership and direction of business will take place in the future. Three factors are leading in this direction. One is the increasingly evident monopoly character of many large businesses; a second is the improvement in our civil service; a third is the progressive democratization of the government. As monopoly invades business, the choice lies between government and private monopoly, instead of between government monopoly and competition. The monopoly element in the business aligns "the many" against a few insiders. As the civil service improves, moreover, the government is enabled to conduct business both honestly and efficiently. As the state becomes increasingly democratized, the people accept it as their natural representative, as opposed to an entrenched industrial oligarchy in a monopolized business. . . .

The democracy seeks a complete control over governmental machinery and processes. It seeks to break the power of a politically entrenched plutocracy, to attain to a government by the people for the people.

Without such democratic control of government there can be no permanent democratic control of industry. For, in ultimate analysis, we own our house, inherit our farm, draw our profits, or obey the factory bell by grace (or command) of the political sovereign. Bequest, inheritance, private property, free contract, are subject to law. Law is legislative enactment, executive administration, judicial interpretation. The legislature, executive, courts, are, in democratic countries, immediately or finally, actually or potentially, the creatures of poltics. They are the *genii* of the ballot box.

In attempting to secure political control, the democracy proceeds along five paths. These paths are (1) the democratic control of parties and of party nominations; (2) the democratic control of elections; (3) the democratic control of representatives already elected; (4) direct legislation by the people; (5) increased efficiency of the democratized government. . . .

The social goal of the democracy is the advancement and improvement of the people through a democratization of the advantages and opportunities of life. This goal is to be attained through a conservation of life and health, a democratization of education, a socialization of consumption, a raising of the lowest elements of the population to the level of the mass.

V

The Liberal Challenge
to Evangelical Protestantism

IN THE YEARS AFTER APPOMATTOX, Protestantism still dominated the American religious scene. For many, it constituted the basis of American society, providing an ethical code for like-mannered men to guide their actions along morally correct lines. It was true that Protestantism by no means presented a united front, for the various sects frequently came into conflict over theological and ethical problems. Yet the similarities by and large overshadowed the differences, and it was generally accepted as a truism that the Protestant vision inspired and gave meaning to the community. Certainly, the American democratic faith, no matter how defined, ultimately rested on the foundation of Protestant morality and theology.

In the latter part of the nineteenth century, however, the rapid industrialization of the nation began to pose new issues and challenges to the fabric of institutional religion. Increasingly, ministers began to find themselves hard pressed to answer the new questions within the framework of the older theology. The Protestant ethic, after all, had developed out of the idea of individual responsibility and judgment, whereby each person ultimately faced his Maker by himself without the intercession of any institutional mechanism. In turn, this ethic had evolved a philosophy based on hard work, frugality, and stewardship, qualities that were well-adapted to a materialistic society functioning in an environment of abundance. As a result, Protestantism by the mid-nineteenth century became largely a means of justifying the status quo. Even before the Civil War, for example, it had developed arguments in support of laissez faire.

The problems of an industrialized society, nevertheless, were not so easily answered within an individualistic theological framework. Consequently, the various sects set about to reconstruct their basic tenets in such a way as to retain their essential character while at the same time making them relevant to the new issues confronting their members. Yet because of social, economic, and doctrinal diversity, Protestant theologians were unable to find a common ground acceptable to all. Those ministers coming from middle- or upper-class churches tended to reflect the more conservative views of their congregations, and they were quick to reiterate the religious case for laissez faire. Henry Ward Beecher, for example, the outstanding preacher of his day and a staunch defender of evolution, even went so far as to advocate the use of naked force against striking workers. And on the whole, most Protestant churches tended to support the conservative outlook of Beecher, even if they did not always accept his theology.

A small minority of ministers, however, cognizant of the dangers facing religion if it could not provide an adequate justification for its continued existence, attempted a restatement of essentials. Developing what became known as the social gospel, these dissenting ministers focused their efforts on resolving the growing social tensions within a society in which class conflict seemed about to erupt. Insisting that religion had a vital role to play, they re-iterated their belief that the achievement of social harmony lay within the sphere of Christianity. The chief feature of the social gospel was its emphasis on the redemption of society rather than on individual salvation. To the ministers of the social gospel, it was apparent that individuals could not lead moral lives in an immoral environment. Therefore, the ministers of the social gospel be-came social and economic reformers as well as theologians. Emphasizing the potentialities for good in every individual, they sought the application of moral law to society and the substitution of cooperation for competition. Ultimately, they came to assert confidently that the ideal of the Kingdom of God could be partly attained only by those who followed in the footsteps of Jesus.

The social gospel, however, was only one manifestation of a liberalized Protestantism working to redefine the theistic basis of American society in the light of new conditions. Equally important were the efforts of those ministers who sought to show that there was no essential conflict between the new scientific naturalism and the older theism, and in this way sought to defend the relevance of Christianity. John Fiske, the philosopher-historian and cham-pion of evolution, aided their cause by identifying natural law as teleological in character and by insisting that man's spiritual evolution was the goal of all development. Others, in creating what has since been called "modernism," or "liberal Protestantism," attempted to rise above all creeds and sectarian dif-ferences to establish a universal faith based on universal evolution—a faith that would complement rather than contradict science. Essentially, the modern-ists were working toward a new synthesis of religion and politics in terms of socialized and undogmatic Christianity whose importance in a complex world would be unquestioned.

To many reared in an atmosphere emphasizing individual piety and Christian morality, however, the liberal or modernistic version of Protestant-ism constituted anathema, if not heresy. Inclined to accept the Bible as the revealed truth of God, they insisted that Protestant fundamentals remain unchanged. Viewing with alarm the rise of the city with its polyglot con-glomerations, its alien traditions, its apparent vices and corruption, and especially the intrusion of non-Protestant elements which would undermine

American homogeneity, these rural-oriented, intellectually unsophisticated, insecure individuals reacted violently against any changes that might undermine or destroy their safe, familiar world. Seeking to conserve both their faith and way of life, they were ripe for an evangelical revival that would once more reassert the older and tested beliefs. Thus the religious awakening that swept through America in the latter part of the nineteenth and early twentieth century symbolized the repudiation of the new developments in Protestantism and marked a return to the ideal of a more simplistic society based upon the twin characteristics of independence and virtue.

There were, of course, many Protestant sects that cannot be confined so easily within a liberal or conservative framework. Christian Science, for example, founded by Mrs. Mary Baker Eddy in the 1870's, was a religion based upon a conviction that matter had no real existence, and that sin, poverty, illness, pain, and death were illusions. All of these "errors" would disappear when the mortal mind entered into a harmonious relation with the Eternal Mind. Like many other novel sects in American religious history, Christian Science became popular because it appealed in part to the American sense of mysticism. Making its strongest impact among middle-class urban groups, Christian Science provided many with a sense of serenity amidst pressing social and economic tensions and offered an alternative to the materialistic values that had become dominant in American society.

In adjusting itself to a new age, therefore, Protestantism tended to divide into a number of different and sometimes conflicting elements. One group was willing to interpret essentials anew in the hope of demonstrating their relevance and importance to the problems of an industrial age. In so doing, this group laid the groundwork for a religious version of the reform impulse that constituted an integral part of the progressive movement. Another element, however, bitterly resisted change, and insisted that theological definitions and interpretations of morality remain the same. In a sense, the conflict within Protestantism was a reflection of the changes that were transforming America as it entered a new era of its history.

(23)

Dwight L. Moody

1837-1899

Born in Northfield, Massachusetts, the son of a brickmason whose ancestors had emigrated from England in 1633, Dwight L. Moody by his early twenties was a highly successful salesman. After moving to Chicago in 1856, questions of religion and human welfare began increasingly to claim his time and interest. By 1858 he had organized a sabbath school, and developed a program of evangelical services, home visitation, and social and welfare work. In 1860 he decided to devote his entire time to this work, and became an independent city missionary.

Moody was one of the outstanding evangelists of his time, and he preached his message to millions of people, both in the United States and abroad. Like his predecessor, Charles G. Finney, Moody was concerned with the salvation of the individual's soul, arguing that a truly converted Christian was free from all sin and temptations. A premillennialist, he insisted upon the weakness of unaided human endeavor and the need to concentrate upon humility. Such being the case, Moody maintained that society could be reformed only if the individual first was able to regenerate himself. Thus, to Moody, social reform was dependent on the spiritual regeneration brought about by ancillary religious revival.

The esteem in which Moody was held by millions of his countrymen derived from the simple message of hope that he brought to them. To men caught up in a period of profound social change, the Second Coming of Christ was far more reassuring than secular plans for reforming society—though the premillennial faith was for many a form of escapism from the apparently insurmountable problems of the day. Phrasing his message in the most simple terms possible, Moody caught the imagination of nonintellectual Protestant America, and he began a period of revival that was to last over a quarter of a century.

The following selection is from one of his sermons entitled "The Inspiration of the Bible," published in *Moody's Latest Sermons* (Providence, Rhode Island, 1894).

A gentleman came out to one of our meetings some time ago and said he hoped to get in that series of meetings an awakening that would last him all his life. I told he might as well try to eat enough to last him all his life. I told him he might as well try to eat enough at one time as to try to get an awakening that would last him all of his life. That is a mistake that people are making; they are running to religious meetings and they think the meetings are going to do the work. But if they don't bring you into closer contact with the word of God, the whole impression will be gone in three months. In the cx. Psalm, David prays nine times that God will quicken him according to His laws, according to His judgments, according to His precepts, according to His word. Now, if you get that kind of an awakening you have got something that is going to abide, because God's word is going to abide forever. That is substantial.

Now, another thing—you need to take the whole Bible and not a part of it. There are a great many people that are living on a few chapters and verses. They don't take the whole of the Scripture. I want to say before I forget it, that Sunday school teachers are making a woeful mistake if they don't take the whole Bible into their Sunday school classes. I don't care how young your children are, let them understand it is one book, that there are no two books—the Old Testament and the New are all one. Don't let them think that the Old Testament doesn't come to us with the same authority as the New. It is a great thing for a boy or girl to know how to handle the Bible. What is an army good for if they don't know how to handle their swords? Now, I speak very strong on this, because I was brought up in a Sabbath school that didn't have a single Bible in it. We used to have these old question books. Do you know what they are like? There are questions, and the answers are given just below; so that you don't need to study your lesson. Mother had a Bible, it was a family Bible, but she was so afraid that we would tear it that she kept it in the spare room, once in a great while we were allowed to look at it. The thing that interested me most was the family record—when Dwight was born, when father and mother were married. Those were the most interesting things to me, you know. So when I got to be a man and my beard began to come out, I was bigger then than I am now, in my own estimation. I knew it all. Oh yes! You couldn't tell me much. I was wiser than my grandfather or my great-grand-father, or all the grandsires behind me. I came down here to Boston from the country and went into a Bible class where there were a good many Harvard students. Their families belonged to the church, I suppose, and they came home to spend the Sabbath, or perhaps they came home every day. I was put into this class of young men. They handed me a Bible and told me the lesson was in John. I hunted all through the Old Testament for John, but couldn't find it. I saw the fellows hunching one another, "Ah, greenie from the country." Now, you know that is just the time when you don't want to be con-sidered green. The teacher saw my embarassment and handed me his Bible, and I put my thumb in the place and held on. I didn't lose my place. I said then that if I ever got out of that scrape, I would never be caught there again. Why is it that so many young men from 18 to 20 cannot be brought into a Bible class? Because they don't want to expose their ignorance. There is no place in the world that is so fascinating as a live Bible class. I believe that we are to blame that they have been brought up in the Sunday school without Bibles, and brought up with these quarterlies. The result is, the boys are growing up without knowing how to handle the Bible. They don't know where Matthew is, they don't know where the Epistle of the Ephesians is, they don't know where to find Hebrews or any of the different books of the Bible. They ought to be taught how to handle the whole Bible, and it can be done by Sunday school teachers taking the Bible into the class and going right about it at once. You can get a Bible in this country for almost a song now. Sunday schools are not so poor that they cannot get Bibles. Some time ago there came up in a large Bible class a question, and they thought they would refer to the Bible, but they found that there was not a single one in the class. So they went to the pews, but could not find one there. Finally they went to the pulpit and took the pulpit's Bible and settled the question. We are making wonderful progress, aren't we? Quarterlies are all right in their places, but if they are going to sweep the Bibles out of our Sunday schools, I think we had better sweep them out.

Now, a word about the whole Bible. I believe it is a master stroke of Satan to get us to doubt any portion of the Bible. If he can get us to doubt just one thing in that book he has accomplished a great point, and it is going to be the overthrow of many a man's and woman's faith. If I had the right to cut this out of the Bible and Mr. Sankey that and Mr. H. that it wouldn't be long before the whole Bible would be cut up. Once a gentleman took a Bible to his minister and said he wanted to show him the minister's Bible. The pastor said, "Why do you call it the minister's Bible? That isn't my Bible." Well, said the man, "I have sat under your ministry for some time, and when you have thrown anything out I have cut it out of the Bible." And he had got all of the Book of Job cut out, all Revelations, the Songs of Solomon, and about a third of the Bible was cut out. The minister said, "I wish you would leave that Bible with me." He didn't want the people to see the book in that condition. But the man said, "Oh, no! I have got the covers and I'm am going to hold on to them." And off he went holding on to the covers. If you were to hear some men preach, you wouldn't have anything but the covers in a few months. People say, "What, so you do with what you cannot understand?" I don't do anything with it. A man said to me once, "What do you do with what you don't understand?" "I don't do anything with it." "How do you understand it?" "I don't understand it." "Well, how do you interpret it?" "I don't interpret it." "What do you do with it?" "I don't do anything with it." "Don't do anything with it? Do you believe it?" "Yes, I believe it." Of course I do. I am glad there is a height I know nothing about in the Old Book, a length and a breadth we know nothing about. It makes the book all the more fascinating. I thank God it is beyond me. It is a pretty good proof that it came from God and not from the hand of man. You can take a chapter and read it for 365 days in the year, and always find something new in that chapter. Now, talk about believing in the New and Old Testament. What portion is there in the New Testament that you cannot find in the Old? In Matthew alone there are 100 quotations from the Old Testament. There are 89 chapters in the Four Gospels, and there are 142 quotations taken from the Old Testament.

There are 240 quotations in Revelations taken from the Old Testament. It is absurd for men to take one portion of the Bible and throw out the rest.

Another thing, there is not a thing in that Old Testament that men are cavilling about that God did not set His seal to when He was down here. Men say, "You don't believe in the story of those five cities being destroyed by fire, Sodom and Gomorrah and those three others?" Certainly. They were buying and selling until judgment came and swept them away. "And so it shall be in the coming of the Son of God." Men say, "You don't believe in the story of Elijah being fed by that widow do you?" Certainly, Christ said there were many widows in the days of Elijah, but Elijah was fed by only one widow. Why! Christ believed it, He referred to it Himself, He set His seal to it. The

Son of God believed it, and "shall the servant be above his master?" Men say "do you believe the story about the Israelites being fed on manna?" Certainly. "As Moses lifted up the serpent in the wilderness, even so must the Son of Man be lifted up." He connected that with His own cross. And then at last they look as wise as owls and say, "You certainly don't believe in the story of Jonah and the whale?" Yes, I believe in that. When I give that up I am going to give up the resurrection. As you get along in life and you have perhaps as many friends on the other side of the river as you have on this side, you will get about as much comfort out of the story of Jonah as any other story in the Bible. May God help us to hold on to it! Jesus connected that with His own resurrection. In Matthew they said thrice, "Show us a sign." And He said that the only sign should be the story of Jonah in the whale's belly. Christ believed that Jonah went into the whale's belly, and are you going to be His disciple and be wiser than He? Men say, "It is a physical impossibility for a whale to swallow a man." It says, "God prepared a great fish." That is enough. If God created a whale, couldn't He create a fish large enough to swallow a man? He can create a fish large enough to swallow the whole world at one swallow. It is astonishing how men are sneering and jeering at the idea that God couldn't do it. A friend of mine was going back to Scotland, and he heard a couple of these little modern philosophers discussing the Bible. One said, "The Bible says that Balaam's ass spoke. Now, I am a scientific man, and I have taken the pains to examine an ass' mouth, and it is so formed that it couldn't speak." He was going to toss the whole Bible over because Balaam's ass couldn't speak. My friend said he stood it just as long as he could, and finally he said, "Ah, man you make an ass and I will make him speak." The idea that the God who made the ass couldn't speak through his mouth! Did you ever hear such stuff? And yet this was one of your modern philosophers!

Then there is another class of people (and I am sorry that I am now talking to those in the church, some of your modern church members, and some that profess to be Christians) who say, "Of course I believe the Bible, but I don't believe the supernatural part." Well, now, if you are going to throw out that part, you might just as well burn it up and throw it away. There is no part of the Bible that doesn't teach supernatural things. You read that God went up from talking with Abraham. Now if that didn't take place, then the man that wrote Genesis knew he was telling a lie, and out goes Genesis. You go into Exodus and there are the ten plagues and Moses going through the Red Sea, the water coming out of the rock and all those supernatural things. Now if those things were not so the man that wrote it knew that he was telling a deliberate, wilful lie. Out goes Exodus. You go into Numbers, and there is Moses making a brass serpent, which is put onto a pole and the people are healed. If that didn't take place out goes that book. And so you can go into all the books of the Old Testament, and there is not one that hasn't something supernatural in it. You cannot touch Jesus Christ anywhere that there is not something supernatural about Him. He drops down to tell the virgin that she was to be the mother of that child, and when Christ was born there came a fire down from heaven to shout His praises. That was all supernatural. His being warned and going off into Egypt was supernatural. When He commenced His ministry there was not a day when he was not doing something supernatural. One day he speaks to the leper, and he is made whole; one day He speaks to the sea and the sea obeys Him. When He died the sun refused to look upon that scene; this old world recognized Him, and the earth reeled and rocked like a drunken man. The earth knew Him. That was supernatural. And when He burst asunder the bands of death and came out of Joseph's sepulchre that was supernatural. Christmas Evans, the great Welch preacher says, "Many reformations die with the reformer, but this reformer ever lives to carry on His reformation." Thank God we don't worship a dead Jew. Do you suppose we would have this audience here today if we were worshiping a dead Christ? Not by a good deal. If he worshiped a dead Jew we wouldn't have been quickened and given life to our souls. I thank God that our Christ is a supernatural Christ, and this book a supernatural book, and I thank God that I live in a country where it is so free that all men can read it.

Now about what Christ says about Himself. He says the Scriptures cannot be broken. Let us keep in mind that the only scriptures the apostles of Christ had was the Old Testament. The New Testament wasn't written. He means every word He says. Devil or man cannot break the word of God. Why, I would as soon doubt my own existence as to doubt that book. How any man can for one moment doubt the veracity of the Bible is a mystery to me.

Now, Christ says in one place, "Heaven and earth shall pass, but not one jot or tittle of the law shall pass until the law is fulfilled." Then, in another place, "Heaven and earth shall pass away, but my word shall not pass away." Now, I will put that as the old and new covenant. "Not one jot or tittle of the law shall pass until the law shall be fulfilled, the new covenant, and then Christ comes and adds these words, "Heaven and earth shall pass away, but my word shall not pass away." Now, notice how that has been fulfilled. There was no shorthand reporter following Him around taking down His words; there were no papers to print His sermons, and they wouldn't have printed the sermons if there had been any daily papers. The whole church and all the religious world was against Him. I can see one of your modern free thinkers standing near Him, and he hears Christ say, "Heaven and earth shall pass away, but my word shall not pass away." I see the scornful look on his face as he says, "Hear that Jewish peasant talk! Did you ever hear such conceit, such madness? He says Heaven and earth shall pass away, but His words shall not pass away." My friends, I want to ask you this question—have they passed away? Go and ask your infidels if His words have passed away. Do you know that the sun shines today on more Bibles than it has ever shone on before? Did you know that the American Bible society and the London Bible society issue 1500 Bibles every hour? Thank God the Bibles are not going out; they are just coming in! More Bibles have been printed in the last eight years than in the last 1800 years. The Bible is printed in 350 different languages—it is going to the darkest corners of the earth. "Heaven and earth shall pass away, but my word shall not pass away." Are His words passing away! No and thank God they are not going to pass away. You and I will pass away, and the world will pass away, but His word is going to live and endure. It cannot be wiped out. God broke the bands and is coming down along the ages. When they brought out the new version the American committee brought it out at the same hour as it was put out in London. It was thrown on the market on Friday morning and that would bring it out Friday afternoon. They couldn't send it to Chicago because it was so late, and so an enterprising concern set 90 different operators at work, and had the whole book telegraphed to Chicago and brought out Sunday morning. Nearly 1,900 years after Christ left the world that happened, and yet men are running around and telling us that the old book is going out! But my time is up. I will take this subject up again on Tuesday, and we will go into it deeper. I have only touched it yet. Bring your Bibles along with you, and your pencils and paper. It will be a good thing to wear out your Bibles. I don't like these gilt edged Bibles that look as if they had never been used. Don't be afraid to soil them. Bring them along with you.

(24)

William A. (Billy) Sunday

1862-1935

Billy Sunday was born in Ames, Iowa, and as a young man turned to baseball as a professional career. In 1891, however, he gave up his sports career to join the staff of the Chicago YMCA. Five years later Sunday began his independent evangelical mission.

A century of American revivalism reached its peak in Sunday's crusades, which helps to explain in part his great popularity. His revival meetings not only were run in a highly efficient manner but also were financially rewarding. And he came to be idolized by millions of Americans who heard him preach and contributed to his crusades.

Sunday's appeal stemmed from his direct message that acceptance of Christ was the only requisite for salvation. He opposed the concept of evolution, and although he was a partisan of reform, favoring civic clean-ups, moral reform, and prohibition, his individualistic approach left largely untouched the basic problems of an urbanized society. Because he championed the American individualistic tradition, he became a symbol for all those who hoped nostalgically for a simple solution through a return to an older tradition.

The following selection, taken from *Billy Sunday's Sermons in Omaha as Reported by the Omaha Daily News* (n.p., n.d., 1915?), is indicative of Sunday's theological approach.

We are reminded by this that there are in the midst of years many things that remind us that the sands in the hour glass of time are fast sifting for many of us; your hair is growing gray, your eyes are dim; it takes you longer to go a block, and you love to sit in front of the fire and doze. There is the retrospective view of life, the introspective and the prospective. If you discover anything in the introspective that has made you ashamed and disgusted with the retrospective, resolve to make the prospective better by contrast.

Away with this twentieth century tommyrot that the way to elevate the people is to mix up with them. That will not elevate them; no, you will sink in the mud as deep as they are. If you want to elevate them, you've got to live better than they do.

There are people in your city who will always suppose, because they are fools, that the only way to promote religion is for religion to move uniformly in the same old rut.

The only difference between a grave and a rut is that the grave is a little deeper than the rut, but they are both for the same purpose. Some people are afraid, scared to death to introduce innovations in religion; they are scared that God Almighty might do something out of the ordinary and arrest attention of the man who is going to hell on high gear. However sound their line of reasoning may be, the old methods are all right, science is not worth a snap of your finger, nor a picayune, unless they deliver the goods, express charges prepaid.

So, what's the nature of a revival? He was praying for a revival. As a nation we are facing the danger of the domination of the material over the spiritual; we are commercially drunk. Take a bushel of nickels and walk down the street of the average town and you can lead that grasping bunch so close to hell they can smell the brimstone and sulphur.

Hold a nickel up in front of some men's noses and they cannot see anything else. They cannot see indecency, crime or graft. All they care for is to buy and sell, and what they cannot sell they want to build a fence around it.

We have got a wonderful country; wonderful. The American advances in industry, but I am mighty sorry to say we have not had a corresponding advance in the morality and decency of the country.

Andrew Carnegie can build libraries on every street; you can build high schools in every block; you can build a university in every town, but you cannot save the people or the country without religion.

If this country has the sins of Babylon, she will go to hell like Babylon. Education will not save you; nothing will save you but the gospel of Jesus Christ.

The pursuit of money and business is pulling your men away from the church. We are facing the constantly growing danger of dominance of the material over the spiritual. This is a busy age in which we live. We have hardly time to tie our shoestrings. A fellow wakes up in the morning and rushes till night; rushes at the depot—a brakeman pokes his head into the train and yells 'twenty minutes for lunch,' and he grabs a sandwich and a cup of coffee in one hand and a cigar in the other, and then he will pay $50 to the doctor because he is full of dyspepsia.

This is the day of isms and schisms and ologies, fol-da-rols, tommyrot and heresies to lead people astray. It is an axiom that the measure of your preparation will determine the measure of your success—in religion, politics, anything else.

Doctor Booth, years ago in New York, when Moody was preaching there, said: 'Brethren, it is a disgrace that many have been sitting and carping and criticising this man. Here is a man who murders the king's English twice in every sentence and yet he has done something in this city of New York that you have not done—that is, arrest the attention of this city for one month and held it toward God's mind and God's truth for one month, and until we do that, it behooves us to pray instead of sitting in judgment on his work.'

Doctor Booth went to his study and prepared his sermon on the text: 'Come, for all things are ready,' He just had two heads, 'Come,' and 'Come now.' He got three young men who went ahead and inquired the way to God. That was three more than they had ever had before in that petrified, mildewed church.

I want to say to this audience tonight, before I forget it, that I believe that the bible is the Word of God from cover to cover. Not because I can understand it, for I cannot. Not because I understand its philosophy, speculation or theory. I cannot; wouldn't attempt it, and I would be a fool if I tried. I believe it because it is from the mouth of God, the mouth of God has spoken it.

I tell you, folks, we have got to determine now as to revival responsibility. It is never with God, never. I used to say that I can see a cloud the size of a man's hand, and I used to say there is a coming revival, but I have learned to thank God that his promises are in the present tense—n-o-w. Salvation is in the present tense. I never pray 'Save me Lord, at last, for Jesus' sake—save me now.' I am making no provision for a relapse.

Listen to me. If in your city there are sins and immorality, drunkenness and crime; if you have seduction, pandering and white slavery, and your streets are filled with staggering, reeling drunkards, and girls losing their virtue, the responsibility for that state of things is not with God, but with the citizenship of Omaha.

God puts it up to your church and your town, and if your churches are losing their power, responsibility is not with God, but with the membership of that church, of the fellow who stands in the pulpit, or both.

Political leaders will hire leaders, newspaper editors, publishers, and will spend money for voters—in order to get those who are indifferent to the political situation interested—that is nothing under the heaven but a political revival and you don't hear anybody growl about it.

In the business world, listen. In the business world men must make the market as well as the goods for the market. He must make the goods, then he goes into the market. He's got to do both. You've got all these institutions to create a demand for the product—these are business revivals; you have auto shows, they are auto revivals; you have country fairs which are nothing but revivals, where they show cows, pigs, chickens, bread, butter, horses and all the products of the farm. Then what the revival is to business, what the election is to politics, the revival is to religion; what health is to the individual the revival is to religion.

Martin Luther saved Europe from spiritual death—a spiritual revival under Martin Luther was the cause of the Reformation; nothing but a revival, and why any Lutheran will snap, snarl, growl about a revival when his church was born of a revival, I don't know.

Wesley and Whitefield saved England from the French revolution. Edwards, Finney, and Moody lifted America from degradation by revivals of their day. The prophets were all evangelists; John the Baptist, the greatest man ever born of woman, was an evangelist. The church of Pentecost was born in religion in a time of revival.

You turn up your noses at a revival when the very religion which you love was born in a time of revival. I wonder God don't knock you over. Paul was an evangelist, and whenever Paul was to preach or wherever he went they had to call out the police to protect him; he had a revival or a riot everywhere he went. You cut the day of Pentecost off of history; you cut Peter, James and Paul out of history and what you have left would not make a decent rummage sale.

Any boy can throw a stone and break a stained glass window, but it takes an artist to make one; any fool can build a fire and burn a building, but it takes a skilled mechanic to reconstruct it; a mob crucified Christ, but it took God to raise him from the dead; any fool can sneer at a revival; any fool can do that, and you are a fool if you do.

But you say by and through a revival we acknowledge we have backslidden. Well, you don't put the community in possession of any information they have not already got. You say it is temporary; so was the war, but the slaves are free today. You say it is temporary; so is rain, yet nature feels its refreshing power for weeks afterward. Exalt the evangelist; it does nothing of the kind.

The evangelist has his place in God's economy as much as the preacher. God has special men to do special work in special times. Many a man who is a success as a preacher would be the worst failure you ever looked at as an evangelist. The preacher has his place in God's economy and I have got mine. I believe God Almighty calls me to do what I am doing as much as any preacher. I could not be a pastor. I have received several invitations and have had flattering offers of salary, but if I accepted a pastorate, I would buy a round trip ticket. A revival is a conviction of sin, a conviction of sin on the part of the church.

If they wish to begin anew with their responsibilities and obligations to God, they must begin at the door of the church of God, at the house of God, not the saloons and not by the breweries and groggeries and redlight and stinking dance halls.

You men are ashamed of yourselves even now to think that you have not done more for Jesus Christ than you did. You just beat a path to the store or office and home, went to church on Sunday, and back to the store, and that is all you did, and you call that serving the Lord.

When is a revival needed? A preacher said to me in Iowa, 'I thought I had done my duty when I held up the bleeding form of Jesus Christ and dilated upon his precepts, but I find that I must talk upon sin.' You bet you must; many an old sinner isn't fit for the balm of Gilead until he is given a good old-fashioned fly blister and the currycomb of the law. And some old pachyderms will sit in their pews and one shake, like a flat-tailed sheep in the rain, one shake and they're dry.

The Spirit of God flies from the scenes of strife and discord. You might as well expect a mummy to speak and bear children; you might as well expect hell to sing the doxology. You might as well try to batter down Gibraltar, shooting green peas with a popgun, as to expect that.

A revival is needed when the worldly spirit is in the church of God. It isn't necessary to do something grossly inconsistent. A ship is all right in the sea, but all wrong when the sea is in her. The church of God is all right in the world, but all wrong when the world is in the church.

Some people come to church on Sunday morning and on Monday morning they take a header into the world and the church never sees them again until Sunday morning. They squat and take up a little space in the pew and stay there and put a little money on the plate, but you never see them again until Sunday morning. I tell you, I believe half of the church members could die and the church wouldn't lose anything of its spiritual force; it would lose them in numbers, but it wouldn't lose anything in spiritual power.

I tell you, my friends, we need a panic in religion, the world don't need informing; it needs reforming. We are going to the devil over culture clubs, as if the world needed informing. It don't need anything of the kind. There are people who go to church and go to a certain denomination because their wife goes there. They got their religion and their property in their name. They go to that church.

Look at the Sunday school. The Sunday school ought to be a constant feeder into the church. Why isn't it? Because we have Sunday school teachers who are absolutely good for nothing; they help nobody but the publishers. They don't sit down and study. They don't prepare. They go to Sunday school and try to teach, and on Monday they are at some leg show, and on Tuesday night they are at some dance, and they don't come near the church again until Sunday morning.

Men say the day of the revival is over. Fellows harp on that in the Methodist conference, in the Presbyterian meetings, in the Baptist associations, in the Congregational associations—the day of the revival is over. No, it is not. No, only with the fellow who vomits out the sentiment; but it is not over with God. The day of the revival is [not?] over.

God Almighty leaned over the battlements of heaven and looked down into the coal mines of Wales and said: 'Oh, Roberts!' and out of the depths of the coal mine came that grimy, soiled man, with dirty face, with a little lamp in his cap, and he said: 'What is it, God?' And God said, 'I want you to go and shake up Wales,' and he gave Wales the greatest revival that ever swept over this land since the days of Pentecost. There was not a college professor or preacher in Wales that God would trust with the job.

If I knew all the devils in hell and all the devils in Omaha were sitting out in the pews and sneering and jeering at me, I'd shoot God's truth into their carcasses anyway, and I propose to keep firing away at the devils until by and by they come crawling out of their holes and swear that they were never in them, but the old hides would assay for lead and tan for chair bottoms.

All that some of you church members are fit for is to help make up a crowd. You help the preacher count one more when he sends in his annual report.

I will tell you facts. Hear me. One reason why we have got these tommy-rots is because the church of God has not done her duty. I have got some thing to say about the evangelistic church.

Give us better homes. There is a great tendency to break down our homes today. Our boys and girls are going to the devil. Fathers, the trouble is you forget you are the high priest of the home; the mother forgets she represents Jesus Christ. She spends more time around the ladies' club and the literary club and other clubs, clubs which in general are all right but which, when they keep her away from home, are all wrong.

The revival is one tide from an old sea that has swept the world since Pentecost. It is not a new tide in a new sea, but an old tide in an old sea.

Give us more men for the ministry. I tell you, my friends, the church is facing a crisis in the ministry today. The young men are leaving the ministry, they are refusing to enter the ministry. Why? Because they are starved. It is a disgrace and an insult the salary they are paid.

Oh, Lord, revive thou thy works. You know that every revival that has swept this land has had two characteristics. First, it has been a revival of business men. There never has been a time when they were more willing to put their money into a campaign than now.

They are beginning to see, thoughtful business men from Maine to California and from Duluth to the gulf, that if the tidal wave of graft, intemperence, vice, licentiousness, bribery, and corruption which threatens your nation, which imperils our destiny as a nation, which threatens to overthrow our young men and young women—they are awakening to the fact that if it is to be beaten back and overthrown, it has got to be brought about by a tidal wave of religion.

They have been awakening to the fact that they have been dealing with nonessential things, and are wasting their time. Second, a revival of personal work. There has never been a time when people are more ready to work. There has never been a time when they are more ready and willing. I want every man and woman in this audience, every usher, every member of a committee, to do personal work.

I want you to pray daily, go to the neighborhood prayer meetings; come to the tabernacle; make out your prayer list; go and see your friends and neighbors and ask them to become Christians. Personal work is what counts.

Once in Canton, Ohio, a minister noticed a young man in his congregation who appeared skeptical. He talked to him and could not move him. An elder in the church asked for the young man's address and that night went to see him in a cheap boarding house. After talking until midnight they knelt down and the young man gave himself to God.

The elder next day told his minister that he had won many worldly victories, but had never felt such joy and satisfaction as when that young man accepted Jesus as his Saviour. The name of that elder was Benjamin Harrison, president of the United States.

Men of power are needed in the pulpit. When Phillips Brooks, that great Episcopal preacher, spoke, young men felt called to the ministry. I hope as a result of this revival young men will be induced to study for the ministry. Since coming to Omaha I have met five young men, converted in former meetings of mine, who are now ministers.

(25)

Theodore T. Munger

1830-1910

Born in a family that traced its roots back to the Puritans, Theodore T. Munger graduated from Yale in 1851 and from Yale Divinity School in 1855. After spending a term at the Andover Theological Seminary, he accepted a call from the Congregational Church in Dorchester, Massachusetts, and later served other New England cities as a Congregational minister.

Munger's primary concern revolved about the basic nature of religion in the changing world. While many of his contemporaries were still holding fast to the old orthodoxy, Munger was one of the pioneers in developing the "New Theology," a theology that involved a fundamental reorientation of American Protestantism. Accepting science, evolution, and historical criticism, Munger also insisted upon the importance of a theistic, though undogmatic, faith. Salvation was not simply a matter of individual regeneration, but also deeply concerned the community of which the individual was a part. Implying that Christian duty involved the application of Christianity to society itself, Munger took one of the early steps that led to the formation of the social gospel. Eventually the New Theology that he and others like Horace Bushnell created became the leaven through which American individualistic Protestantism was transformed into a more socially minded religion.

The following selection is from Munger's most famous work, *The Freedom of Faith* (Boston, 1883), wherein he attempted to define the basic elements of the New Theology.

In attempting to give some expression of the New Theology, I wish to state with the utmost emphasis that I do not speak for any party, but only describe things as I see them. And especially would I disclaim any *ex-cathedra* tone that may seem to issue from any form of words. I speak from the standpoint of the sharpest and even most isolated individuality,—for myself alone.

I will first refer to certain negative features, indicating what it is *not;* and then more fully to its positive character.

1. It does not propose to do without a theology.

It seeks no such transformation of method or form that it can no longer claim the name of a science. It does not resolve belief into sentiment, nor etherealize it into mysticism, nor lower it into mere altruism; yet it does not deny an element of sentiment, it acknowledges an element of mysticism, and it insists on a firm basis in ethics. It is the determined foe of agnosticism, yet it recognizes a limitation of human knowledge. While it insists that theology is a science, and that therefore its parts should be coördinate and mutually supporting, and an induction from all the facts known to it, it realizes that it deals with eternal realities that cannot be wholly compassed, and also with the mysteries and contradictions of a world involved in mystery and beset by contradictory forces. If it finds itself driven into impenetrable mystery, as it inevitably must, it prefers to take counsel of the higher sentiments and better hopes of our nature, rather than project into it the frame-work of a formal logic, and insist on its conclusion. It does not abjure logic, but it refuses to be held by what is often deemed logic. While it believes in a harmony of doctrines, it regards with suspicion what have been known as systems of theology, on the ground that it rejects the methods by which they are constructed. It will not shape a doctrine in order that it may fit another which has been shaped in the same fashion,—a merely mechanical interplay, and seeking a mechanical harmony. Instead, it regards theology as an induction from the revelations of God—in the Bible, in history, in the nation, in the family, in the material creation, and in the whole length and breadth of human life. It will have, therefore, all the definiteness and harmony it can find in these revelations, but it will have no more, since it regards these revelations as under a process still enacting, and not as under a finality. The modern authors whom it most consults must be regarded as holding a theology worthy of the name,—Erskine, Campbell, McLeod, Maurice, Stanley, Robertson, the Hare brothers, Bushnell; and if we enumerate its representatives among the living, we must recite the names of those who are eminent in every form of thought and in every work of holy charity.

2. The New Theology does not part with the historic faith of the church, but rather seeks to put itself in its line while recognizing a process of development. It does not propose to commit "retrospective suicide" at every fresh stage of advance. It holds to progress by slow and cosmic growth rather than by cataclysmal leaps. It allies itself even with the older rather than the later theologies, and finds in the early Greek theology conceptions more harmonious with itself than those in the theology shaped by Augustine.

3. It does not reject the specific doctrines of the church of the past. It holds to the Trinity, though indifferent to the use of the word, but not to a formal and psychologically impossible Trinity; to the divine sovereignty, but it does not make it the corner-stone of its system, preferring for that place the divine righteousness, *i.e.,* a moral rather than a dynamic basis; to the Incarnation, not as a mere physical event, for that has entered into many religions, but as the entrance into the world through a person of a moulding and redeeming force in humanity,—the central and broadest fact of theology; to the Atonement as a divine act and process of ethical and practical import—not as a mystery of the distant heavens and isolated from the struggle of the world, but a comprehensible force in the actual redemption of the world from its evil; to the Resurrection as covering the whole essential nature of man; to Judgment as involved in the development of a moral nature; to the eternal awards of conduct considered as laws and principles of character, but not necessarily set in time-relations; to human sinfulness under a conception of moral freedom; to Justification by faith in the sense of a faith that, by its law, induces an actual righteousness—a simple, rational process realized in human experience; to Regeneration and Sanctification by the Spirit as most imperative operations based on the utmost need, and on the actual presence and power of the Spirit in the life of humanity. It does not explain away from these doctrines their substance, nor minimize them, nor aim to do else than present them as revealed in the Scriptures and as developed in history and in the life of the church and of the world.

4. It is not iconoclastic in its temper; it is not pervaded by a spirit of denial, but is constructive—taking away nothing without supplying its place; it does not, indeed, find so much occasion to take away and replace as to uncover and bring to light. Believing that revelation is not so much *from* God as *of* God, its logical attitude is that of seeing and interpreting.

5. It is not disposed to find a field and organization outside of existing churches, conscious that it is building on that Eternal Foundation which alone has given strength to the church in every age. It claims only that liberty whereunto all are called in the church of Christ. It asserts that the real ground of

membership in the church is fidelity to the faith, and that this ground is not forfeited because it refuses to assent to human and formal conditions that the church has taken on, and which are not of the substance of the faith. Emphasizing as it does the headship of Christ in the visible as well as invisible church, it would retain its place in the church on the basis of its loyalty to Christ and as its all-sufficient warrant, paying small heed to a narrow, ecclesiastical logic that now confounds, and now distinguishes between, the bounds of the visible body and the breadth and freedom of Christ's church.

I pass now to the positive features of the New Theology.

1. It claims for itself a somewhat larger and broader use of the reason than has been accorded to theology. . . .

There are indeed limits to reason, and it has in it an element of faith, but so far as it goes, it goes surely and firmly; it is not a rotten foundation, it is not a broken reed, it is not a false light. It may be so sure that it can justly protest in the face of Heaven, "Shall not the Judge of all the earth do right?" It will be humble and docile and trustful, but these qualities are not abrogations of itself. It does not claim for itself the ability to measure the whole breadth and reach of truth; it does not say, I will not believe what I cannot understand, for it knows full well that human reason is not commensurate with eternal truth. But this is quite different from silencing reason before questions that have been cast upon human nature, yet are so interpreted as to violate every principle of human nature; *e.g.*, it is not called to hold its belief in God as a reasonable belief, and to accept a conception of God that throws it into a chaos of moral confusion and contradiction. To trust is a great duty; but as reason has an element of faith, so faith has an element of reason, and that element requires that the fundamental verdicts of human nature shall not be set aside. The lines on which trusting reason, or reasoning trust, proceed do not run straight into impenetrable mystery, and come back from that mystery to slay reason and wellnigh slay faith. . . .

2. The New Theology seeks to interpret the Scriptures in what may be called a more natural way, and in opposition to a hard, formal, unsympathetic, and unimaginative way.

Its strongest denial and its widest divergence from the Old Theology lie here. It holds profoundly to inspiration, but it also holds that the Scriptures were written by living men, whose life entered into their writings; it finds the color and temper of the writer's mind in his work; it finds also the temper and habit of the age; it penetrates the forms of Oriental speech; it seeks to read out of the mind and conception and custom of the writer instead of reading present conceptions into his words. In brief, it reads the Scriptures as literature, yet with no derogation from their inspiration. It refuses to regard the writers as automatic organs of the Spirit,—"moved," indeed, but not carried outside of themselves nor separated from their own ways and conceptions. It is thus that it regards the Bible as a *living* book; it is warm and vital with the life of a divine humanity, and thus it speaks to humanity. But as it was written by men in other ages and of other habits of speech, it needs to be interpreted; it is necessary to get back into the mind of the writer in order to get at the inspiration of his utterance; for before there is an inspired writing there is an inspired man, through whom only its meaning can be reached. This is a very different process from picking out texts here and there, and putting them together to form a doctrine; yet it is by such a process that systems of theology have been formed, and cast on society for acceptance. The New Theology does not proceed in such a way. . . .

3. The New Theology seeks to replace an excessive individuality by a truer view of the solidarity of the race.

It does not deny a real individuality, it does not predicate an absolute solidarity, but simply removes the emphasis from one to the other. It holds that every man must live a life of his own, build himself up into a full personality, and give an account of himself to God: but it also recognizes the blurred truth that man's life lies in its relations; that it is a derived and shared life; that it is carried on and perfected under laws of heredity and of the family and the nation; that while he is "himself alone" he is also a son, a parent, a citizen, and an inseparable part of the human race; that in origin and character and destiny he cannot be regarded as standing in a sharp and utter individuality. It differs from the Old Theology in a more thorough and consistent application of this distinction. That holds to an absolute solidarity in evil, relieved by a doctrine of election of individuals; this holds to a solidarity running throughout the whole life of humanity in the world,—not an absolute solidarity, but one modified by human freedom. It is not disposed wholly to part company with the Old in respect to the "fall in Adam" (when the Scriptures, on this point, are properly interpreted), and hereditary evil, and the like; it sees in these conceptions substantial truths, when freed from their excessiveness and their formal and categorical shapes, but it carries this solidarity into the whole life of man. If it is a fallen world, it is also a redeemed world; if it is a lost world, it is a saved world; the Christ is no less to it than Adam; the divine humanity is no smaller than the Adamic humanity; the Spirit is as powerful and as universal as sin; the links that bind the race to evil are correlated by links equally strong binding it to righteousness. It goes, in a certain manner, with the Old Theology in its views of common evil, but it diverges from it in its conceptions of the redemptive and delivering forces by ascribing to them corresponding sweep. To repeat: it does not admit that Christ is less to the race than Adam, that the Gospel is smaller than evil; it does not consign mankind as a mass to a pit of common depravity, and leave it to emerge as individuals under some notion of election, or by solitary choice, each one escaping as he can and according to his "chance," but the greater part not escaping at all. It does not so read revelation and history and life, finding in them all a corporate element, "a moving altogether when it moves at all,"—an interweaving of life with life that renders it impossible wholly to extricate the individual. It allies itself with the thought of the present age and the best thought of all ages, that mankind is moved by common forces, and follows common tendencies falling and rising together, partakers together in all good and ill desert, verifying the phrase, "the life of humanity." It believes that the Spirit broods over the "evil world" as it brooded upon the chaos of old; that humanity is charged with redemptive forces, wrought into the soul and into the divine institutions of the family and the nation, and whatever other relation binds man to man; and it believes that these forces are not in vain.

Still, it does not submerge the individual in the common life, nor free him from personal ill desert, nor take from him the crown of personal achievement and victory. It simply strives to recognize the duality of truth, and hold it well poised. It turns our attention to the corporate life of man here in the world,—an individual life, indeed, but springing from common roots, fed by a common life, watched over by one Father, inspired by one Spirit, and growing to one end; no man, no generation, being "made perfect" by itself. Hence its ethical emphasis; hence its recognition of the nation, and of the family, and of social and commercial life, as fields of the manifestation of God and of the operation of the Spirit; hence its readiness to ally itself with all movements for bettering the condition of mankind,—holding that human society itself is to be redeemed, and that the world itself, in its corporate capacity, is being reconciled to God; hence also an apparently secular tone, which is, however, but a widening of the field of the divine and spiritual.

4. This theology recognizes a new relation to natural science; but only in the respect that it ignores the long apparent antagonism between the kingdoms of faith and of natural law,—an antagonism that cannot, from the nature of things, have a basis in reality. But while it looks on the external world as a revelation of God and values the truth it may reveal; while even it recognizes in it analogies to the spiritual world and a typical similarity of method, it does not merge itself in natural science. It is not yet ready, and it shows no signs that it ever will be ready, to gather up its beliefs, and go over into the camp of natural science, and sit down under the manipulations of a doctrine of evolution, with its one category of matter and one invariable force. It is not ready to commit itself to a finite system, a merely phenomenal section of the universe and of time, with no *whence,* or *whither,* or *why,*—a system that simply supplies man with a certain kind of knowledge, but solves no problem that weighs on his heart, answers no question that he much cares to ask, and throws not one glimmer of additional light on his origin, his nature, or his destiny. It accepts gratefully the knowledge it discloses of the material universe, its laws and its processes; it admits that science has anticipated theology in formulating the method of creation known as evolution, that it has corrected modern theology by suggesting a closer and more vital relation between God and creation, and so has helped it throw off a mechanical theory and regain its forgotten theory of the divine immanence in creation. But farther than this it does not propose to go, for the simple reason that it is the end of its journey in that direction. The New Theology, like the old, refuses to merge itself in a system that is both material and finite, and therefore incapable of a moral and spiritual conception. It denies that the universe can be put into one

category, that matter is inclusive of the spiritual, or what is deemed spiritual; it denies that the material world is the only field of knowledge, and that its force is the only force acting in the world. It asserts the reality of the spiritual as above the material, of force that is other than that lodged in matter, of truth realized in another way than by induction from material facts, however fine their gradation, of an eternal existence and a human self-consciousness correlated in mutual knowledge and freedom and power. It makes these assertions on scientific grounds and as inductions from phenomena, and therefore claims for itself the possession of knowledge that is such in reality. . . .

5. The New Theology offers a contrast to the Old in claiming for itself a wider study of man.

It chooses for its field the actual life of men in the world in all their varying conditions, rather than as massed in a few ideal conditions. It finds its methods in the every-day processes of humanity, rather than in a formal logic. It deals with human life as do the poets and dramatists: it views humanity by a direct light, looks straight at it, and into it, and across its whole breadth. A recognition of human nature and life,—this is a first principle with the New Theology. . . .

6. The New Theology recognizes the necessity of a restatement of belief in Eschatology, or the doctrine of Last Things. . . .

But the New Theology does not plant its entire conception of the subject upon one word. It seeks rather to enlighten itself by the general light of the entire revelation of God; and thus it finds itself driven to such conclusions as these: namely, that every human being will have the fullest opportunity for attaining to the end of his creation as a child of God; that every human being will receive from the Spirit of God all the influence impelling to salvation that his nature can endure and retain its moral integrity; that no human being will be given over to perish while there is a possibility of his salvation. These are the very truisms of the faith, its trend, its drift, its logic, its spirit, and its letter, when the letter is interpreted under the spirit; and they are equally the demand of the human reason. . . .

Such are some of the features of this fresh movement in the realm of theology, for it can scarcely be called more than a movement, an advance to meet the unfolding revelation of God. It is not an organization, it is little aggressive, it does not herald itself with any Lo here or Lo there, it does not crowd itself upon the thought of the age, it is not keyed to such methods. It has no word of contempt for those who linger in ways it has ceased to walk in; it has no sympathy with those who have forsaken the one way. It does not destroy foundations, nor sap faith, nor weaken motives; it does not reduce the proportions of evil nor dim the glory of righteousness; it does not chill the enthusiasm of faith, nor hold it back from its mightiest effort of sacrifice. It seeks no conquest represented in outward form, but is content to add its thought to the growing thought of the world, and, if it speaks, content to speak to those who have ears to hear. It makes no haste, it seeks no revolution, but simply holds itself open and receptive under the breathing of the Spirit that has come, and is ever coming, into the world; passive, yet quick to respond to the heavenly visions that do not cease to break upon the darkened eyes of humanity.

(26)

Walter Rauschenbusch

1861-1918

Walter Rauschenbusch was born in Rochester, New York, the son of German immigrants who had fled to the United States following the abortive revolutions of 1848. He received his A.B. from the University of Rochester in 1884, and two years later graduated from the Rochester Theological Seminary. Ordained as a Baptist minister, he served for eleven years as pastor of a German church in New York City before being called to the Rochester Theological Seminary in 1897.

His New York City pastorate enabled him to see firsthand the ravages of the industrial depression that began in 1893, and also gave him the opportunity to read widely in socialist and reform literature. As a result, he turned to the task of renovating a theology that had dominated Christianity for centuries and in the process became the outstanding philosopher of the social gospel in the United States. Believing that the conditions of society frequently made men evil, Rauschenbusch insisted that a moral law be substituted for the law of the jungle and he advocated a form of revisionist socialism. The new society would be brought into existence by widening the concept of the "Kingdom of God" and applying it to the social organism. A staunch advocate of democracy, which he defined in terms of cooperation among free men of good will, Rauschenbusch held out hope and a vision of a better world to come, though by no means did he believe that the Kingdom of God could be fully realized on earth.

The following selection is from Rauschenbusch's most famous and important book, *A Theology for the Social Gospel* (New York, 1917).

The social movement is the most important ethical and spiritual movement in the modern world, and the social gospel is the response of the Christian consciousness to it. Therefore it had to be. The social gospel registers the fact that for the first time in history the spirit of Christianity has had a chance to form a working partnership with real social and psychological science. It is the religious reaction on the historic advent of democracy. It seeks to put the democratic spirit, which the Church inherited from Jesus and the prophets, once more in control of the institutions and teachings of the Church. . . .

If theology is to offer an adequate doctrinal basis for the social gospel, it must not only make room for the doctrine of the Kingdom of God, but give it a central place and revise all other doctrines so that they will articulate organically with it.

This doctrine is itself the social gospel. Without it, the idea of redeeming the social order will be but an annex to the orthodox conception of the scheme of salvation. It will live like a negro servant family in a detached cabin back of the white man's house in the South. If this doctrine gets the place which has always been its legitimate right, the practical proclamation and application of social morality will have a firm footing. . . .

In the following brief propositions I should like to offer a few suggestions, on behalf of the social gospel, for the theological formulation of the doctrine of the Kingdom. Something like this is needed to give us "a theology for the social gospel."

1. The Kingdom of God is divine in its origin, progress and consummation. It was initiated by Jesus Christ, in whom the prophetic spirit came to its consummation, it is sustained by the Holy Spirit, and it will be brought to its fulfilment by the power of God in his own time. The passive and active resistance of the Kingdom of Evil at every stage of its advance is so great, and the human resources of the Kingdom of God so slender, that no explanation can satisfy a religious mind which does not see the power of God in its movements. The Kingdom of God, therefore, is miraculous all the way, and is the continuous revelation of the power, the righteousness, and the love of God. The establishment of a community of righteousness in mankind is just as much a saving act of God as the salvation of an individual from his natural selfishness and moral inability. The Kingdom of God, therefore, is not merely ethical, but has a rightful place in theology. This doctrine is absolutely necessary to establish that organic union between religion and morality, between theology and ethics, which is one of the characteristics of the Christian religion. When our moral actions are consciously related to the Kingdom of God they gain religious quality. Without this doctrine we shall have expositions of schemes of redemption and we shall have systems of ethics, but we shall not have a true exposition of Christianity. The first step to the reform of the Churches is the restoration of the doctrine of the Kingdom of God.

2. The Kingdom of God contains the teleology of the Christian religion. It translates theology from the static to the dynamic. It sees, not doctrines or rites to be conserved and perpetuated, but resistance to be overcome and great ends to be achieved. Since the Kingdom of God is the supreme purpose of God, we shall understand the Kingdom so far as we understand God, and we shall understand God so far as we understand his Kingdom. As long as or-

ganized sin is in the world, the Kingdom of God is characterized by conflict with evil. But if there were no evil, or after evil has been overcome, the Kingdom of God will still be the end to which God is lifting the race. It is realized not only by redemption, but also by the education of mankind and the revelation of his life within it.

3. Since God is in it, the Kingdom of God is always both present and future. Like God it is in all tenses, eternal in the midst of time. It is the energy of God realizing itself in human life. Its future lies among the mysteries of God. It invites and justifies prophecy, but all prophecy is fallible; it is valuable in so far as it grows out of action for the Kingdom and impels action. No theories about the future of the Kingdom of God are likely to be valuable or true which paralyze or postpone redemptive action on our part. To those who postpone, it is a theory and not a reality. It is for us to see the Kingdom of God as always coming, always pressing in on the present, always big with possibility, and always inviting immediate action. We walk by faith. Every human life is so placed that it can share with God in the creation of the Kingdom, or can resist and retard its progress. The Kingdom is for each of us the supreme task and the supreme gift of God. By accepting it as a task, we experience it as a gift. By labouring for it we enter into the joy and peace of the Kingdom as our divine fatherland and habitation.

4. Even before Christ, men of God saw the Kingdom of God as the great end to which all divine leadings were pointing. Every idealistic interpretation of the world, religious or philosophical, needs some such conception. Within the Christian religion the idea of the Kingdom gets its distinctive interpretation from Christ. (*a*) Jesus emancipated the idea of the Kingdom from previous nationalistic limitations and from the debasement of lower religious tendencies, and made it world-wide and spiritual. (*b*) He made the purpose of salvation essential in it. (*c*) He imposed his own mind, his personality, his love and holy will on the idea of the Kingdom. (*d*) He not only foretold it but initiated it by his life and work. As humanity more and more develops a racial consciousness in modern life, idealistic interpretations of the destiny of humanity will become more influential and important. Unless theology has a solidaristic vision higher and fuller than any other, it can not maintain the spiritual leadership of mankind, but will be outdistanced. Its business is to infuse the distinctive qualities of Jesus Christ into its teachings about the Kingdom, and this will be a fresh competitive test of his continued headship of humanity.

5. The Kingdom of God is humanity organized according to the will of God. Interpreting it through the consciousness of Jesus we may affirm these convictions about the ethical relations within the Kingdom: (*a*) Since Christ revealed the divine worth of life and personality, and since his salvation seeks the restoration and fulfilment of even the least, it follows that the Kingdom of God, at every stage of human development, tends toward a social order which will best guarantee to all personalities their freest and highest development. This involves the redemption of social life from the cramping influence

of religious bigotry, from the repression of self-assertion in the relation of upper and lower classes, and from all forms of slavery in which human beings are treated as mere means to serve the ends of others. (*b*) Since love is the supreme law of Christ, the Kingdom of God implies a progressive reign of love in human affairs. We can see its advance wherever the free will of love supersedes the use of force and legal coercion as a regulative of the social order. This involves the redemption of society from political autocracies and economic oligarchies; the substitution of redemptive for vindictive penology; the abolition of constraint through hunger as part of the industrial system; and the abolition of war as the supreme expression of hate and the completest cessation of freedom. (*c*) The highest expression of love is the free surrender of what is truly our own, life, property, and rights. A much lower but perhaps more decisive expression of love is the surrender of any opportunity to exploit men. No social group or organization can claim to be clearly within the Kingdom of God which drains others for its own ease, and resists the effort to abate this fundamental evil. This involves the redemption of society from private property in the natural resources of the earth, and from any condition in industry which makes monopoly profits possible. (*d*) The reign of love tends toward the progressive unity of mankind, but with the maintenance of individual liberty and the opportunity of nations to work out their own national peculiarities and ideals.

6. Since the Kingdom is the supreme end of God, it must be the purpose for which the Church exists. The measure in which it fulfils this purpose is also the measure of its spiritual authority and honour. The institutions of the Church, its activities, its worship, and its theology must in the long run be tested by its effectiveness in creating the Kingdom of God. For the Church to see itself apart from the Kingdom, and to find its aims in itself, is the same sin of selfish detachment as when an individual selfishly separates himself from the common good. The Church has the power to save in so far as the Kingdom of God is present in it. If the Church is not living for the Kingdom, its institutions are part of the "world." In that case it is not the power of redemption but its object. It may even become an anti-Christian power. If any form of church organization which formerly aided the Kingdom now impedes it, the reason for its existence is gone.

7. Since the Kingdom is the supreme end, all problems of personal salvation must be reconsidered from the point of view of the Kingdom. It is not sufficient to set the two aims of Christianity side by side. There must be a synthesis, and theology must explain how the two react on each other. . . . The entire redemptive work of Christ must also be reconsidered under this orientation. Early Greek theology saw salvation chiefly as the redemption from ignorance by the revelation of God and from earthliness by the impartation of immortality. It interpreted the work of Christ accordingly, and laid stress on his incarnation and resurrection. Western theology saw salvation mainly as forgiveness of guilt and freedom from punishment. It

interpreted the work of Christ accordingly, and laid stress on the death and atonement. If the Kingdom of God was the guiding idea and chief end of Jesus—as we now know it was—we may be sure that every step in His life, including His death, was related to that aim and its realization, and when the idea of the Kingdom of God takes it due place in theology, the work of Christ will have to be interpreted afresh.

8. The Kingdom of God is not confined within the limits of the Church and its activities. It embraces the whole of human life. It is the Christian transfiguration of the social order. The Church is one social institution alongside of the family, the industrial organization of society, and the State. The Kingdom of God is in all these, and realizes itself through them all. During the Middle Ages all society was ruled and guided by the Church. Few of us would want modern life to return to such a condition. Functions which the Church used to perform, have now far outgrown its capacities. The Church is indispensable to the religious education of humanity and to the conservation of religion, but the greatest future awaits religion in the public life of humanity.

(27)

Edward S. Ames

1870-1958

Born in Eau Claire, Wisconsin, Edward S. Ames received his A.B. and A.M. from Drake University, a B.D. from the Yale Divinity School in 1892, and his Ph.D. from the University of Chicago in 1895. Ames spent most of his adult life as a member of the Department of Philosophy at the University of Chicago, serving as chairman until his retirement in 1935. He was also a pastor at the Church of the Disciples of Christ in Chicago from 1900 to 1940.

Author of numerous works on religion and the philosophy of religion, Ames was a leading exponent of what became known as religious modernism. Modernism, in his eyes, was the twentieth-century religion of democracy, a derivative of humanism and humanitarianism. Rejecting the idea of an incompatibility between religion and science, he started with a Jamesean study of religious experience, which he broadened into a fully empirical account of religion. Regarded as one of the most radical figures in the modernist movement, Ames's views represent the culmination of the optimistic interpretation of Protestantism that ended in the social gospel. By making good works central to religion rather than the traditional piety that had long characterized Christianity, Ames made the church an agency for the social and spiritual well-being of society as well as for the perpetuation of democratic institutions.

The following selection is from Ames' book *The New Orthodoxy* (Chicago, 1918).

There is more reasonable hope that the great historic development of religion represented by Christianity is destined to come to a new birth of power. This cannot be expected to occur, however, through a mere emotional revival of its traditional forms and doctrines. These have outlived the order of society in which they appeared and are already transcended by the leaders of religious thought still working within their domains. Such mighty social structures do not pass away at a stroke. It required centuries to build them, and they linger on in the world just as monarchies persist long after democracy has become the accepted political ideal of the world. Christianity has lived through three marked stages and, it is believed by many, is now entering upon a fourth. The first was its earliest form, in which it was a tremendously vital impulse to a higher, freer moral life among informal intimate groups, having their common bond in allegiance to the personality and inspiring message of Jesus of Nazareth. That period is directly reflected in our New Testament. Upon its pages are the fresh imprints of the vibrant, pulsing spirit of the Master. But there is little organization. It has been impossible for the most searching scholarship to find there a model for the conduct of the modern church. No fixed ritual is established. No clear and uniform body of doctrine is presented. No provision can be traced there for economic justice and social righteousness as needed by the twentieth century. But the moral aspiration and insight are there. The clear, commanding spiritual vision of Jesus shines through it as the rays of the rising sun illumine and warm the world. That record will therefore remain a source of inspiration to the end of time.

The second stage of Christianity was that known as Catholicism. It developed by the gradual extension of the faith to great numbers of communities throughout the Roman Empire and among barbarian tribes. Contact with Greek philosophy was also a great factor in formulating the conceptions of the early church. When Christianity permeated the empire it was inevitable that it should be affected by the Latin genius for organization and by the Greek power of reflective thought. The ecclesiastical institution known to us as the Roman Catholic church may truly be regarded as deriving its impetus from the gospels, its form from the Roman Empire, and its formulations of doctrine from Greek philosophy. The official authority which characterizes it is inevitably of the quality of the system on which it was patterned. This type of Christianity was arrested in its progress by the Protestant Reformation of the sixteenth century. Its fate is sealed with the death knell of monarchy and bureaucracy in all social relations—in the family, in education, and in industry. It has produced many beautiful souls. It has adorned our human world with marvelous cathedrals and pageants. It has lifted the imagination of millions from sordid and transient things to pure and lofty visions of faith. But it is not the form of religion for the modern man.

What then of Protestantism? It has now had four centuries of history. The celebration of the four hundredth anniversary of Luther's break with the Catholic church is being widely observed. He introduced great reforms which continue to exert a powerful influence. He gave the Bible to the people and made Christianity the religion of a book as it had never been before. He struck at the sharp separation of the sacred and the secular by opposing the celibacy of the clergy, by recognizing the state as an agency of God, and by dignifying common labor as having religious value. But the movement which he inaugurated became dogmatic and fixed and has not fulfilled his hopes. In Calvinism the doctrinal interest predominated and gave rise to creeds and confessions of faith which stand in the background of most of the evangelical churches today. Puritanism became austere and antagonistic to many natural and vital interests. It developed strength of conscience and determination of will, but lost breadth and the social graces and appreciation of the fine arts. Under all its differences Protestantism retained certain elements of Catholicism. It distrusted human nature; it emphasized the sacraments as essential means of grace; it clung to external authority, to the doctrines of the supernatural, and to a miraculous conversion of the natural human being in order to make him truly religious.

It is not impossible that future historians will regard Protestantism as coming to its close with the end of the nineteenth century as a vital, ascending type of religion. In that century several of the most characterisic principles of Protestantism were undermined by a larger knowledge of history and science. Protestantism was individualistic; the new order is social. It assumed the infallibility of the Bible, and that is no longer tenable. It exalted authority, and now there is no legitimate authority except that of experience. It denied that man is naturally religious, while it is commonly accepted today that man is incurably religious. We may well believe therefore that Christianity is entering upon a fourth great epoch, which has already been called by various names. It is referred to as the religion of the spirit, as social Christianity, and as the religion of democracy.

There is real need at the present time for statements of this latest form of Christianity created by the profound influences working through many agencies toward a richer life for all classes of men. What is this religion of the twentieth century? How shall we set forth the religious life as it appears in the light of the discoveries of the historians of religion, biblical students, natural scientists, and social psychologists? Let us think of ourselves as perfectly free souls, unawed by any authority over us or by any superstition within us, yet reverent toward the things which experience has taught us and eagerly in quest of clearer perceptions of the ideal possibilities of life. How does the religious life appear? How shall we understand its attitudes, its dramatis per-- sonae, its growing Bible, its changing goal, and its new drama of the spiritual life? Some persons have difficulty in thinking of the Christian life in this way, but no apologies are necessary for identifying it with the religious life at its best. Indeed, the Christian life may be regarded as just life itself at its best. . . .

First, then, reverence for life. We have come to have profound respect for the laws of nature, for the way she works, and for the possibility of co-operating with her. It is the scientific habit of mind to sit down quietly and observe the facts, to view patiently the processes in the growth of plants and animals and in the development of society in order to understand them and control them. Nothing is allowed to come between the scientist and the facts. Jesus took the same unprejudiced, impartial attitude. . . .

Religion is for him the maintenance of this attitude of respect for life. The divine order is not different in principle from that which we constantly observe. God is like a good shepherd seeking his lost sheep. He is like the father receiving back his prodigal son. The analogies of seedtime and harvest hold in the moral realm. Whoever, then, in our day has this reverence for life, respects its simple principles of industry, of generosity, of persistence, and of fidelity, possesses in this respect the Christian attitude and is to that extent and by that very fact a Christian. . . .

The second conspicuous attitude of the Christian life which I mention is love, especially love of our fellow-men. We are having a great awakening in recent years with reference to social justice. This is the phrase which we have adopted to express the development in institutions, and particularly in the state, of the attitude of consideration for our fellow-men. . . .

The third attitude of the religious life is faith. Faith is that quality by which pioneers like Abraham and the Klondike adventurers go forth into new countries. It was the attitude of Columbus. It is the forward-striving, hopeful, expectant quality. To have faith means to be willing to take some risk for a cause. It is of the essence of business enterprise and of the creative spirit in science and in art. Religious faith means to have that feeling about life as a whole. No one is able to prove conclusively that human progress will continue, but no man can get the most out of life who refuses to believe in progress and in the possibility of improving the world. In spite of all the lions in the way we must go on. In spite of human frailties and weaknesses, in spite of follies and irrationalities, in spite of selfishness and greed, in spite of false ideals and paralyzing indifference, we must go on with our task whether it is our business, our science, our politics, or our religion. They are all of a piece in this respect. Everywhere we work against difficulties and in the face of discouragements which would be heartbreaking if we thought only of them. But everywhere we keep hoping and fighting and believing that improvement is to be made. When we give up that faith, we are done with life, or at least with that particular part of it concerning which we have lost faith.

One of the striking facts in the religious experience of the modern man is that while he seems to hold sacred things more lightly than did the passing generation, yet in reality he cherishes those to which he does cling with a more vital faith. He is discovering that religion does not need to be defended and protected in order to preserve it in the world. It has a surprising depth and persistence. The rationalistic mind of the eighteenth and nineteenth centuries, which still survives here and there in societies and individuals designating themselves as rationalists, assumed that religion could not survive criticism. They supposed that religion was so inextricably bound up with superstition and supernaturalism that when these were exposed and cast aside religion itself would perish. This too has been the conviction of the extreme conservatives. They must believe the Bible "from cover to cover" or reject it all. If they should relax their adherence to miracle or prophecy they could not believe in the veracity of the teaching. There is thus a significant likeness between the extremes. They agree that one must accept all or nothing. No discrimination or qualification is approved. The Bible and the Christian religion are to be defended or rejected *in toto*.

The man of the modern mind, trained in history and in the social sciences, takes a different view. He does not indorse all that has been claimed for the Bible nor does he take it to be of equal worth in all its parts. Yet he finds in it messages of greatest value. Even contradictions, discrepancies, superstitions, and myths may be discovered without weakening the force of the moral ideals and precepts. Those things which are self-evidencing and verifiable in experience cannot be deprived of their validity because of accompanying errors or misconceptions. Religion is at last seen to be greater than the traditions which have grown up with it. It has deeper springs in human nature than have been suspected. Instead of being a delicate and tender growth it proves to be hardy and vigorous. Therefore it does not have to be sheltered and hidden against investigation and criticism. It cannot thrive at its best under patronizing influences nor at the hands of those who are unwilling to trust it to the free play of social forces. Certainly many men in our time have been surprised to realize how much more vital and satisfying their religious faith became the moment they began to view it with the same freedom and intelligence with which they regard art and politics. As with all other big human concerns, religion is at its best where it is close to life, unhindered by authority and open to reasonable, sympathetic criticism. Again and again in the history of Christianity its vital force has broken through old forms and doctrines and created new symbols and types of service. The dogma of biblical infallibility is one of the artificialities recently discarded, and the result has been the strengthening of religion. . . .

The Bible, like other vital books, grows by constant reinterpretation. This may be realized through the experience of anyone to whom it is a book of real religious value. . . .

The Bible thus attained makes a new and profound appeal to our time, for it is now a collection of writings reflecting the history of a religiously gifted people in their growth and aspirations. Within that history the prophetic utterances of the Old Testament and the words of Jesus mark the high peaks from which all the rest is surveyed and estimated. So aptly and searchingly do the social judgments of the prophets appeal to the social conscience of the present that in certain respects they seem like reformers of the twentieth century. At the same time the more adequate knowledge of Jesus has put him above all the prophets and given him a new hold upon the spiritual imagination and idealism of the best minds of the new social order. In this reconstruction of the biblical material and perspective the book has become a source of increasing inspiration and moral incentive.

The conception of Christianity as centering chiefly in another life is rapidly losing its hold. That which is coming into favor is the hope of Christianizing the social order itself, as Professor Rauschenbusch has phrased it. Here is taken into account the natural goodness and forward-moving tendency of human nature, its capacity for improvement, for measureless unselfishness, and for nobility and ideality of character beyond all calculation or present imagination. Many comparisons and contrasts between the old and the new are already familiar to popular thought. To state them in balanced sentences has the value of emphasis, though it is not without the dangers of brevity and exaggeration.

The old was static; the new is dynamic. The one sought perfection; the other seeks improvement. One was given; the other is to be gradually achieved. The first was prescribed; the second is to be progressively discovered. That goal depended on providence miraculously transforming the soul; this modern goal depends upon learning by experience as revealed in the lives of great men in the past and in scientific observation and experiment in the present. Religion then was apart from life, from the state, and from practical affairs; religion now is integral with life in all its forms. In the old days it lacked variety and the richness of individuality; in these days it is specialized and made concrete by the peculiar duties and relations given to each person by virtue of his place in society. The old had a separate unique literature; the new regards all noble literature as its medium. The traditional system had a special priesthood; the present order magnifies the priesthood of all true believers. The old attitude despised and feared the natural order which it called the world; the new loves the natural, especially in its service of social ideals. In the past there has been difficulty in using the fine arts in religion; at present they are means of the most impressive symbolization of the new spiritual values. For a long time Christ has been unreal and remote; at last he is becoming human and natural. God was the infinite veiled Being; he is now drawing near even at the risk of seeming finite. Transcendental mysticism was not difficult for the faith of yesterday; a natural, winsome mysticism throbs in the soul of today. The former ideal of the good man was the saintly soul, serene and at peace, withdrawn from the common struggle; the present ideal is of a man sinewy and full of courage, working in the midst of the human tasks, clear-headed and good-natured, conscious of far horizons, to which also his deeds have reference.

At last, then, religion has come to reckon with the fact that its highest quest is not for a supernatural order but just for natural goodness in largest and fullest measure. . . .

We are therefore confronted with the spectacle of life whose goal is not once for all set up and fixed, but which is put forward and lifted higher as we labor and aspire. The dream of the present is of a free society whose chief

aim shall be to furnish to all its members the greatest possible power of intelligence, and will, and sympathy, and capacity for social co-operation and
progress. That requires intelligence and the constant improvement of popular
education. It demands a wholesome and stimulating social atmosphere of
freest interaction and emulation for the energizing of the will. It means the
closest comradeship and the finest sympathetic imagination, such as is now
momentarily realized in times of crises, as in the Halifax disaster and in the
revelations of unselfish devotion in the trenches of the Great War.

The function of the church is to make that ideal of a free and growing
brotherhood of all mankind real to the experience and to the imagination of
men. After all this is not so different from that which it has done for the souls
of men in the past. Certainly Jesus summoned his followers into a companion-
ship of adventure and faith on behalf of fuller friendship and deeper love. It
may be said that the course of thought since the seventeenth century has been
the elaboration of the value of a society in which the individual soul could
come to its own in a kingdom of good-will. And surely modern social reformers would be satisfied if they could feel that adequate progress were being
made in the permeation of the race with the kindliness and idealism of Jesus.
That would mean the cultivation of science to understand what love really
requires us to do. It would mean better organization of the state to make the
ideals effective. It would mean better care of childhood, in whose plastic soul
lie all the possibilities of realizing the most wonderful dreams of the sages and
prophets yet to be. We cannot ignore the past nor can we be slaves to it. No
more can we merely trust everything to the future; we must anticipate it and
live in it as well as in the present. . . .

The new drama starts with man's life on the earth and with the upward
and forward tendency within it. It shows, from the earliest records, efforts
toward something better and loftier. Everywhere are temples and tombs and
the signs of uplifted hands. In and around these have flowed the intense desires
and aspirations of the unsatisfied soul of man, restless in his age-long quest.
Often mistaken as to the source of his success, always burdened with superstitions and misconceptions of himself and his world, nevertheless he has continued to follow the gleam. At last he is finding out the immediate causes of
many of his blessings and his ills. With a new joy and courage in his discovery
of scientific knowledge and power he is preparing for still greater mastery and
progress. With all of his old reverence for life and with greater zest he is not
merely *seeking* a city which hath foundations. He is building it. He does not
just sit silently listening in his worship, but he wrestles with God and, like
Jacob of old, exacts his blessing. The drama which he is enacting is one of
intense activity and profound thoughtfulness. This has quite changed the
meaning of worship. It is now no longer the contemplation of a series of
celestial events in which man beholds himself the passive recipient of divine
favor or wrath. It is rather the survey of the long path of past experience and
the memory of the heroic actors who have toiled there and the anticipation
of the further extension of that path by labor, intelligence, and unselfish de-

votion. Through it all run the realization of the magnitude of the forces involved, the incalculably great scale of the events transpiring, and the tragic character of the smallest word and deed. It is this richness and inexhaustible nature of experience which constitutes its divine quality. But the divine is no more separate and aloof. It is within and organic with the human. We surrender the old contrast of the human and the divine, not by eliminating either one to retain the other, but by insisting that life as we find it has in it the warmth and intimacy of the human and also the dynamic and the outreach of the divine. Life is in this respect all of a piece, varied and intricate, but undivided.

Part Two

AMERICAN THOUGHT IN A TROUBLED WORLD

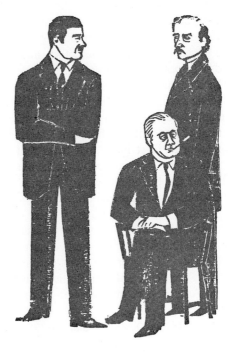

S hortly after the dropping of the first atomic bomb on Hiroshima, Norman Cousins, in an editorial in the *Saturday Review of Literature,* spoke for a generation of Americans who were fearful that the coming of peace was a prelude to the extinction of man himself. The beginning of the atomic age, he remarked prophetically, has brought less hope than fear. "It is a primitive fear, the fear of the unknown, the fear of forces man can neither channel nor comprehend. . . . It has burst out of the subconscious and into the conscious, filling the mind with primordial apprehensions."[1] Thus, the coming of a new technological age brought with it not hope and expectation but fear and foreboding. For the first time in their history Americans faced a situation where they and everything they cherished were threatened with potential destruction.

Yet the recognition of fear in the American mind was not new to 1945. Over a decade earlier, Franklin Roosevelt sought to unite the nation and stir creative response by urging that "we have nothing to fear but fear itself." At the beginning of the century observers like Henry Adams and Madison Grant were expressing at least individual fears that American society was tending toward mediocrity if not extinction. In increasing numbers Americans during the first half of the twentieth century became fearful of the new social forces affecting them both at home and abroad, of the directions in which their society was going, and of the possible loss of their republican inheritance.

The nineteenth century, as we have seen, brought the industrial revolution to America and with it profound economic and social changes. In the half century before the Civil War, the introduction of the factory system marked the beginning of America's industrialization. In the last half of the nineteenth century, the American economy greatly expanded its technological base and

---

1. "Modern Man is Obsolete," *Saturday Review of Literature,* 28 (August 18, 1945), 5.

established the basic industries and systems of national production that characterize mature industrial nations. Industrialization, urbanization, the rapid growth of the new working class, and spread of technology all reached maturity and crystallization in the 1890's, so that this decade became, as Professor Commager[2] called it, a kind of watershed that looked back to an older individualism and forward to the emergence of the New and Fair Deals. Besides these internal changes in America, events on the world scene in the twentieth century—the World Wars, the Great Depression, the struggles of the League of Nations and United Nations—made it even more difficult for Americans to retain meaning for their national existence.

The search for national meaning was complicated still further by the major intellectual currents inherited from the late nineteenth century. The evolutionary naturalism implied by Darwin's theories was extended to all human institutions, with the consequent naturalizing of such major sources of American thought as Puritanism, rationalism, and idealism. Showing that these sources did not rest on nonempirical and transcendent principles, naturalists argued that political ideals and social institutions, like the organs of an animal, must be understood as emerging within nature in man's struggle for survival. Neither transcendent, nor absolute, nor self-evident truths, America's social and moral principles were only modes of social adjustments to nature. It is significant that pragmatism, the dominant intellectual force of the first half of the twentieth century, was closely linked with evolution. Dewey in particular showed that Darwin's theory implied a view of mind and knowledge along naturalistic and pragmatic lines: ideas are interpreted as instruments for adaptation and are to be judged in terms of the quality of the results produced by the actions they direct.[3] Americans, of course, had always been a pragmatic people, distrusting abstract theory and stressing the concreteness of both beliefs and gadgets. William James, in fact, was led to characterize pragmatism as but a new name for some old ways of thinking. But, with Peirce, James, Dewey, and their many disciples, pragmatism became an explicit, self-conscious philosophy, and it was systematically applied to interpretations of all areas of human activity.

Relativism and secularism were other movements that developed in the post-Darwinian and pragmatic consciousness. Holding that truths and principles are conditioned by the cultural circumstances of the individuals proposing them, relativism owed much to evolutionary theory and went hand in hand with the adoption of developmental approaches in the sciences of man. Secularization of thought and institutions also began to affect portions of the national consciousness. This development was a normal outgrowth of other trends, for if the source of political principles was not supernaturalistic religion but nature and the struggle for survival, then both principles and

---

2. Henry Steele Commager, "The Watershed of the Nineties," *The American Mind* (New Haven, 1952), Chap. II.

3. See Dewey's essay "Charles Darwin and His Influence on Science," in his *The Influence of Darwin on Philosophy* (New York, 1910).

institutions should be cut loose from their transcendental base. Many observers of the early twentieth century pointed to a loosening of the hold of religion on the national consciousness—although Americans seemed to remain religious if not spiritual.

In their extreme form, these forces in the American mind led to expressions of skepticism and even nihilism. Skepticism cast doubt on the ability of the mind to know reality and grasp truth. The loss of virtue in the 1920's and the inability to control economic forces in the 1930's seemed to many to give experiential support to such skepticism. The attack on reason led to the cult of the irrational, with its rejection of all standards and principles in extreme cases. The "literature of revolt," with its often crushing examination of the American inheritance, gave nihilism its most forceful American expression.

Finally, America's republican system, while praised continuously through the half century, seemed to be severely threatened not only by the intellectual and literary voices of the period but also by the forces and institutions it itself had engendered. Thus, free enterprise often seemed threatened by the very persons who invoked it. Consequent upon industrialization was standardization, and the latter seemed to triumph over the individualism of the older America. Determinism mocked ideals of self-reliance; social emphases eliminated the meaning of individual guilt; and naturalism and secularism eroded the moral and religious basis of Americanism. Or so it seemed to many thoughtful persons. Perhaps the most fundamental social question of the entire period concerned the validity of the old ideas for modern and urban America.

The result of these intellectual movements and historical events was, beginning in the 1890's, the subjection of American experience to the most scrupulous examination in its history. Many persons concluded that the transcendental justifications of American experience, such as self-evident truths, natural rights, or divine sanctions, were completely unfounded. Lawyers and social scientists were finding that law—so basic in the American vision, especially the "higher law"—was not a body of fixed, eternal doctrines but was rather the rules made in the courts by very human men known as judges. Industry and technology, which promised so much in themselves and from which nineteenth-century Americans expected so much, were, as Alfred North Whitehead wrote, fulfilling the prophecies of Francis Bacon; but at the same time, "man, who at times dreamt of himself as a little lower than the angels, has submitted to become the servant and the minister of nature." Many Americans agreed with Whitehead that "it remains to be seen whether the same actor can play both parts."[4] Nineteenth-century beliefs in progress and the perfectibility of man were finding little or no basis in twentieth-century American experience. Men such as Henry Adams were linking society to the laws of physics to show the eventual decline of democratic society. By the 1950's even the American's basic character, to judge by the writings of sociologist David Riesman, had undergone fundamental change, substituting for

4. Alfred North Whitehead, *Science and the Modern World* (New York, 1925), p. 141.

the self-reliant, inner-directed man the socially oriented, other-directed man.

The idea of national mission, which in earlier chapters we have seen to be so basic to the American mind, was also subjected to re-examination, particularly as it seemed to be threatened by the national experience. To many observers the 1950's faded into history on a predominately negative note. Politicians observed what has been called a lack of national purpose; clergymen found a loss of dedication to a moral society; historians pointed to riddles and paradoxes in America's world position; and moralists decried the low standards of personal ethics. There was in many quarters a loss of commitment to historic ideals, a sense of drift resulting from the lack of clear national purpose, and a feeling that Americans were facing the future without reserves and without a clear mandate. It had not always been so in America. In fact, almost opposite characterizations had been ascribed to past generations of Americans, such as their sense of purpose, their feeling of duty, and their drive toward the future.[5]

To see these feelings as new in the American consciousness, it is only necessary to recall something of the attitudes—among them the attitude toward history—of the period that gave birth to the Declaration of Independence. The central ideas of the period were Reason and Law and their conceptual relatives. Carl Becker summarized them thus: "In the eighteenth century the words without which no enlightened person could reach a restful conclusion were nature, natural law, first cause, reason, sentiment, humanity, perfectibility (these last three being necessary only for the more tender-minded, perhaps.)"[6] Placing their trust in reason, the men of Enlightenment believed that eternal principles of right and justice could be grasped by human beings and subsequently made the platform of social criticism and reform.

Having discovered the truths of natural law—or most of them—the Enlightenment proceeded to make certain inferences about man and history. Voltaire, speaking for most of the men of the Enlightenment, observed that "History is little else than a picture of human crimes and misfortunes," and Americans accepted the theme. In this view, the past was a period of ignorance and superstition—and hence of unhappiness and misery—and consequently it was better to break with the old institutions and values in order to replace them with new and enlightened ones. The present, then, was the period of transition, the period of the establishment of an enlightened society in which history would renew itself.

Four dominant American characteristics—all of them involving an attitude toward history—developed from these assumptions. The first was the American sense of dynamism, expressed in many ways by many people, but by none better than Walt Whitman in a letter to Emerson: "Master, I am a

---

5. This and the remaining paragraphs of the introduction are based on Robert N. Beck, "America and the Hand of History," *Social Education,* 24 (May, 1960), 197–200.

6. Carl L. Becker, *The Heavenly City of the Eighteenth Century Philosophers* (New Haven, 1932), p. 47.

man who has perfect faith. Master, we have not come through centuries, caste, heroisms, fables, to halt in this land today." Second was America's sense of mission, a belief that America is an experiment for the world—is indeed the hope of the world, if only the world will accept it. Jefferson expressed this feeling perfectly when he wrote, "It is impossible not to be sensible that we are acting for all mankind." The third characteristic was the pervasive sense of America's uniqueness. "America is different," the feeling ran—so different in fact that at times she felt constrained to turn her back on the affairs of the world. Finally, there was a persistent moralism, a tendency to see the struggles of history in absolute moral terms rather than from a relativist perspective involving power politics and human passions as well as personal values.

These characteristics might be summarized in the expression "historical Puritanism." They involved an attitude toward history in many ways not unlike the Puritan attitude toward life as a whole: activism and messianism again, but also a sense of rightness with reference to the American political code, which must be used as a judge of history but is not itself considered to be historical. To be sure, America has been involved in history in many ways, but so often her involvements have been like that typified by World War I: America enters history to make the world "safe" for her particular political revelation. That the world has not wanted to accept that revelation, that it has at times resisted America's interventions as well as her preachments, has in past generations often been perplexing but seldom has disturbed her fundamental convictions. History for many Americans remained "bunk," even as they wrote and read histories by the score.

But America's historical Puritanism, it now appears, was already being eroded as the nation was called on to face the fateful events of the twentieth century. Earlier generations of Americans could remain aloof from the affairs of Europe but now Americans were forced to participate in them. The hostility and rejection that sometimes followed from America's new role in world affairs caused Americans to question their ability to act for mankind or to extend their ideals to the rest of the world. Many Americans, in fact, began to question the validity of those ideals even in their national context. Was, then, the conjunction of theory and daily experience so obvious to earlier generations no longer apparent? Was the American experience to issue in a kind of nihilism of action and purpose?

In the years that have followed this new American involvement, which has gradually eroded the tenets of historical Puritanism, many counsels have been offered. There have been the radical voices urging a basic reorientation for America and the adoption of new ideologies. Voices of conservatism have sought to recapture ideas of the past—European, American, and southern. The churches have responded to America's dilemmas by urging a return to faith, to transcendental justifications based on natural-law theory, and even to a neo-orthodoxy that attempts to synthesize biblical insights and forces in the modern world. And naturalists and liberals have sought to redefine American ideals within the context of their philosophical assumptions.

Yet, given the diversities, complexities, and alternative responses of the last half century of American history, the pattern that emerges has more unity and coherence than one might initially suspect. With some exceptions that pattern remains the American vision of Lockian liberalism and individualism. The critics of America throughout this period have been concerned less in rejecting that vision than in calling attention to the disparity between the ideal and the real. The literature of revolt, the New and Fair Deals, the symbolisms of the New Frontier of the 1960's, even the radical voices of the 1930's—all these movements testified to the continuing vitality of the American ideal, however much experience seemed to depart from it. The time has not yet come—if ever it will—to write a concluding chapter to history.

VI

Shaking of the Foundations

THE SOCIAL AND INTELLECTUAL FERMENT of the late nineteenth and early twentieth century produced a number of skeptical and pessimistic observers. Offering America new perspectives and insights into the nature of social processes, the new philosophy, pragmatism, and the new science, social science, were making inroads into the national consciousness and creating a swirl of intellectual crosscurrents that sometimes conflicted with the traditional inheritance. For many Americans, to be sure, science and pragmatism promised a great liberation, for they seemed to assure progress and to make creativity possible. Social planning and progressivism became watchwords for many Americans who believed that the phrases of Jefferson—which enjoyed a nationwide vogue in the late 1930's and 1940's—could be more fully realized by the new intellectual instruments.

Yet there were other observers who professed to see a very different picture—one indeed that was quite at variance with the traditional pattern and one that in extreme cases involved its dissolution. For example, one of the chief implications of the new social science was functionalism, or relativism, a position that viewed human ideas and institutions in particular societal settings and that denied the possibility of cross-cultural comparison. In other words, functionalists held that each culture is itself a whole, a Gestalt, and all its institutions are to be understood by reference to the culture within which they exist. Functionalism was soon applied to all areas of society— including the family, the economic system, the law, and ideologies—and it was brought to the popular consciousness by such writers as Ruth Benedict, whose *Patterns of Culture* (1934) became a scientific best seller. The analyses of the functionalists uncovered exciting and important data, but at the same time they placed in jeopardy the whole cluster of Enlightenment ideas which had served Americans in the past. Much of the recent American experience, particularly since World War II, must be understood as an attempt to overcome the eroding relativism of earlier decades.

The use of certain scientific conclusions by critics also had a disturbing effect on America. Utilizing principles taken from physics and biology, for example, Henry Adams drew not optimistic but pessimistic conclusions. Other thinkers bluntly challenged the very idea of democracy, arguing that democracy was leading America to self-destruction. Madison Grant, basing his ideas in large part upon racial premises, maintained that America's greatness was being undermined by the admission of millions of immigrants of inferior stock. Similarly, Ralph Adams Cram proclaimed that democracy reduced mankind to incapacity and led to mediocrity, both of which involved denials of human potentialities.

Thus the very foundations of American experience were being shaken. To these observations as well as to the historical events of the period, Americans were soon to address themselves. Extreme voices of protest were to be heard, proposing radical solutions to the problems at hand, but generally remaining outside the central stream of national experience. The problem of renewing a sense of national mission, however, had been clearly posed to the American people.

(28)

Madison Grant

1865-1937

Madison Grant was born in New York City of a family whose roots went back to the colonial period. He graduated from Yale in 1887 and received a law degree from Columbia University three years later. Though he carried on a legal practice, Grant very early became interested in zoology. His studies led him to write an important series of monographs on North American animals; he also played a leading role in founding the New York Zoological Society in 1895 and in the movement to preserve species threatened with extinction. Then, as a result of his zoological interests, Grant began to study ethnology. Fearing that a mixture of racial strains would prove fatal to American democracy, Grant soon became a leading propagandist in the movement to restrict immigration to this country. His ideas on the subject were summed up in his major work, *The Passing of the Great Race,* which appeared in 1916.

Reflecting the pessimism that had begun to trouble many native-born intellectuals like himself, Grant urged that the Nordic race, the ruling race of the Western world, was declining because of its mistaken belief in the power of environment to transform heredity. Heredity was all-important, he contended, and racial mixture led to racial regression. Culture was determined by race, and he warned that the Nordic race (predominantly that of Western Europe ancestry) was being threatened with hybridization and could save itself only by returning to rule by an aristocracy and by maintaining the purity of its blood, and consequently of its culture. Especially opposed to the growing tide of immigration from southern and eastern Europe that began in the late 1880's, Grant mirrored the loss of confidence in American institutions as the nation entered an era troubled by domestic and international problems.

The following selection is from *The Passing of the Great Race* (New York, 1916).

Failure to recognize the clear distinction between race and nationality and the still greater distinction between race and language, the easy assumption that the one is indicative of the other, has been in the past a serious impediment to an understanding of racial values. Historians and philologists have approached the subject from the viewpoint of linguistics, and as a result we have been burdened with a group of mythical races, such as the Latin, the Aryan, the Caucasian, and, perhaps, most inconsistent of all, the "Celtic" race.

Man is an animal differing from his fellow inhabitants of the globe, not in kind but only in degree of development, and an intelligent study of the human species must be preceded by an extended knowledge of other mammals, especially the primates. Instead of such essential training, anthropologists often seek to qualify by research in linguistics, religion, or marriage customs, or in designs of pottery or blanket weaving, all of which relate to ethnology alone.

The question of race has been further complicated by the effort of old-fashioned theologians to cramp all mankind into the scant six thousand years of Hebrew chronology, as expounded by Archbishop Ussher. Religious teachers have also maintained the proposition not only that man is something fundamentally distinct from other living creatures, but that there are no inherited differences in humanity that cannot be obliterated by education and environment.

It is, therefore, necessary at the outset for the reader to thoroughly appreciate that race, language, and nationality are three separate and distinct things, and that in Europe these three elements are only occasionally found persisting in combination, as in the Scandinavian nations.

To realize the transitory nature of political boundaries, one has only to consider the changes of the past century, to say nothing of those which may occur at the end of the present war. As to language, here in America we daily hear the English language spoken by many men who possess not one drop of English blood, and who, a few years since, knew not one word of Saxon speech.

As a result of certain religious and social doctrines, now happily becoming obsolete, race consciousness has been greatly impaired among civilized nations, but in the beginning all differences of class, of caste, and of color, marked actual lines of race cleavage.

In many countries the existing classes represent races that were once distinct. In the city of New York, and elsewhere in the United States, there is a native American aristocracy resting upon layer after layer of immigrants of lower races, and the native American, while, of course, disclaiming the distinction of a patrician class, nevertheless has, up to this time, supplied the leaders of thought and the control of capital, of education, and of the religious ideals and altruistic bias of the community.

In the democratic forms of government the operation of universal suffrage tends toward the selection of the average man for public office rather than the man qualified by birth, education, and integrity. How this scheme of administration will ultimately work out remains to be seen, but from a racial point of view, it will inevitably increase the preponderance of the lower types and cause a corresponding loss of efficiency in the community as a whole.

The tendency in a democracy is toward a standardization of type and a diminution of the influence of genius. A majority must of necessity be inferior to a picked minority, and it always resents specializations in which it cannot share. In the French Revolution the majority, calling itself "the people," deliberately endeavored to destroy the higher type, and something of the same sort was, in a measure, done after the American Revolution by the expulsion of the Loyalists and the confiscation of their lands.

In America we have nearly succeeded in destroying the privilege of birth; that is, the intellectual and moral advantage a man of good stock brings into the world with him. We are now engaged in destroying the privilege of wealth; that is, the reward of successful intelligence and industry, and in some quarters there is developing a tendency to attack the privilege of intellect and to deprive a man of the advantages of an early and thorough education. Simplified spelling is a step in this direction. Ignorance of English grammar or classic learning must not be held up as a reproach to the political and social aspirant.

Mankind emerged from savagery and barbarism under the leadership of selected individuals whose personal prowess, capacity, or wisdom gave them the right to lead and the power to compel obedience. Such leaders have always been a minute fraction of the whole, but as long as the tradition of their predominance persisted they were able to use the brute strength of the unthinking herd as part of their own force, and were able to direct at will the blind dynamic impulse of the slaves, peasants, or lower classes. Such a despot had an enormous power at his disposal which, if he were benevolent or even intelligent, could be used, and most frequently was used, for the general uplift of the race. Even those rulers who most abused this power put down with merciless rigor the antisocial elements, such as pirates, brigands, or anarchists, which impair the progress of a community, as disease or wounds cripple an individual.

True aristocracy is government by the wisest and best, always a small minority in any population. Human society is like a serpent dragging its long body on the ground, but with the head always thrust a little in advance and a little elevated above the earth. The serpent's tail, in human society represented by the antisocial forces, was in the past dragged by sheer force along the path of progress. Such has been the organization of mankind from the beginning, and such it still is in older communities than ours. What progress humanity can make under the control of universal suffrage, or the rule of the average, may find a further analogy in the habits of certain snakes which wiggle sideways and disregard the head with its brains and eyes. Such serpents, however, are not noted for their ability to make rapid progress.

To use another simile, in an aristocratic as distinguished from a plutocratic, or democratic organization, the intellectual and talented classes form the point of the lance, while the massive shaft represents the body of the population and adds by its bulk and weight to the penetrative impact of the tip. In a democratic system this concentrated force at the top is dispersed throughout the mass, supplying, to be sure, a certain amount of leaven, but in the long run the force and genius of the small minority is dissipated, if not wholly lost. *Vox populi,* so far from being *Vox Dei,* thus becomes an unending wail for rights, and never a chant of duty.

Where a conquering race is imposed on another race the institution of slavery often arises to compel the servient race to work, and to introduce it forcibly to a higher form of civilization. As soon as men can be induced to labor to supply their own needs slavery becomes wasteful and tends to vanish. Slaves are often more fortunate than freemen when treated with reasonable humanity, and when their elemental wants of food, clothing, and shelter are supplied. . . .

The continuity of physical traits and the limitation of the effects of environment to the individual only are now so thoroughly recognized by scientists that it is at most a question of time when the social consequences which result from such crossings will be generally understood by the public at large. As soon as the true bearing and import of the facts are appreciated by lawmakers, a complete change in our political structure will inevitably occur, and our present reliance on the influences of education will be superseded by a readjustment based on racial values.

Bearing in mind the extreme antiquity of physical and spiritual characters and the persistency with which they outlive those elements of environment termed language, nationality, and forms of government, we must consider the relation of these facts to the development of the race in America. We may be certain that the progress of evolution is in full operation to-day under those laws of nature which control it, and that the only sure guide to the future lies in the study of the operation of these laws in the past.

We Americans must realize that the altruistic ideals which have controlled our social development during the past century, and the maudlin sentimentalism that has made America "an asylum for the oppressed," are sweeping the nation toward a racial abyss. If the Melting Pot is allowed to boil without control, and we continue to follow our national motto and deliberately blind ourselves to all "distinctions of race, creed, or color," the type of native American of Colonial descent will become as extinct as the Athenian of the age of Pericles, and the Viking of the days of Rollo.

Henry Adams

1838-1918

Great-grandson of John Adams and grandson of John Quincy Adams, Henry Adams graduated from Harvard in 1858 and then studied law in Germany. One of the great figures in American intellectual history, Adams did not take much interest in his formal education, nor was he distinguished as a student. Rather, he found outlets for his talents by contributing to college periodicals and addressing literary societies. During the Civil War he served as secretary to his father, Charles Francis Adams, who was then ambassador to Great Britain. During these seven years in Europe, from 1861 to 1868, he read widely and was especially attracted to scientific theories. The import of these theories, he concluded, was that the American nation could never return to the absolute standards of its Puritan forebears. On his return to the United States, Adams taught medieval history for a few years at Harvard, and then devoted himself to the writing of his nine-volume *History of the United States During the Administrations of Jefferson and Madison.* This and other historical writings earned him a place among the first rank of American historians.

Following the publication of the *History,* Adams experienced a severe spiritual crisis and turned to the medieval world in search of meaning. His famous study of the mind of the Middle Ages, *Mont-Saint-Michel and Chartres,* resulted from this search. His intellectual interests at this time also became centered on social theory and he set about to discover the laws governing society. These he found in the principle of the energy available to man. Since the quantity of energy man can use is rapidly accelerating, Adams predicted that the twentieth century would be a period of swift material advance and also an era of destructive war and revolution. Man, he concluded, must learn to use this available energy productively or he will perish. Indeed, Adams was by no means certain that man would not perish.

This selection is from *The Degradation of the Democratic Dogma* (New York, 1919).

Towards the middle of the nineteenth century—that is, about 1850 —a new school of physicists appeared in Europe, dating from an Essay on the Motive Power of Heat, published by Sadi Carnot in 1824, and made famous by the names of William Thomson, Lord Kelvin, in England, and of Clausius and Helmholz in Germany, who announced a second law of dynamics. The first law said that Energy was never lost; the second said that it was never saved; that, while the sum of energy in the universe might remain constant—

granting that the universe was a closed box from which nothing could escape—the higher powers of energy tended always to fall lower, and that this process had no known limit.

The second law was briefly stated by Thomson in a paper "On a Universal Tendency in Nature to the Dissipation of Mechanical Energy," published in October, 1852, which is now as classic as Kepler's or Newton's Laws, and quite as necessary to a scientific education. Quoted exactly from Thomson's "Mathematical and Physical Papers" (Cambridge, 1882, Vol. I, p. 514), the Law of Dissipation runs thus:

1. There is at present in the material world a universal tendency to the dissipation of mechanical energy.

2. Any restoration of mechanical energy, without more than an equivalent of dissipation, is impossible in inanimate material processes, and is probably never effected by means of organized matter, either endowed with vegetable life or subjected to the will of an animated creature.

3. Within a finite period of time past, the earth must have been, and within a finite period of time to come, the earth must again be, unfit for the habitation of man as at present constituted, unless operations have been, or are to be performed, which are impossible under the laws to which the known operations going on at present in the material world, are subject.

When this young man of twenty-eight thus tossed the universe into the ash-heap, few scientific authorities took him seriously; but after the first gasp of surprise physicists began to give him qualified support which soon became absolute. . . .

Thus, at the same moment, three contradictory laws of energy were in force, all equally useful to science: (1) The Law of Conservation, that nothing could be added, and nothing lost, in the sum of energy. (2) The Law of Dissipation, that nothing could be added, but that Intensity must always be lost. (3) The Law of Evolution, that Vital Energy could be added, and raised indefinitely in potential, without the smallest apparent compensation. . . .

Down to the end of the nineteenth century nothing greatly mattered, since the actual forces could be fairly well calculated or accounted for on either principle, but schools of applied mechanics are apt to get into trouble by using contradictory methods. One process or the other acquires an advantage. The weaker submits, but in this instance, the difficulty of naming the weaker was extreme. That the Evolutionist should surrender his conquests seemed quite unlikely, since he felt behind him the whole momentum of popular success and sympathy, and stood as heir-apparent to all the aspirations of mankind. About him were arranged in battalions, like an army, the energies of government, of society, of democracy, of socialism, of nearly all literature and art, as well as hope, and whatever was left of instinct—all striving to illustrate not the Descent but the Ascent of Man. The *hostis humani generis,* the outlaw and enemy, was the Degradationist, who could have no friends, because he proclaimed the steady and fated enfeeblement and extinction of all nature's energies; but that he should abandon his laws seemed a still more preposterous idea. Never had he asserted them so aggressively, or with such dogmatic authority. He held undisputed possession of every technical school in the world, and even the primary schools were largely under his control. His second law of thermodynamics held its place in every text-book of science. The Universities and higher branches of education were greatly, if not wholly, controlled by his methods. The field of mathematics had become his. He had no serious intellectual rival. Few things are more difficult than to judge how far a society is looking one way and working in another, for the points are shifting and the rate of speed is uncertain. The acceleration of movement seems rapid, but the inertia, or resistance to deflection, may increase with the rapidity, so that society might pass through phase after phase of speed, like a comet, without noting deflection in its thought. If a simpler figure is needed, society may be likened to an island surrounded by a rising ocean which silently floods its defences. One after another the defences have been abandoned, and society has climbed to higher ground supposed to be out of danger. So the classic Gods were abandoned for monotheism, and scholastic philosophy was dropped in favor of the Newtonian; but the classic Gods and the scholastic philosophy were always popular, and the newer philosophies won their victories by developing compulsory force. Inertia is the law of mind as well as of matter, and inertia is a form of instinct; yet in western civilization it has never held its own.

The pessimism or unpopularity of the law will not prevent its enforcement, if it develops superior force, even if it leads where no one wants to go. The proof is that the law is already enforced in every field excepting that of human history, and even human history has not wholly escaped. In physics it rules with uncontested sway. In physiology, the old army of Evolutionists have suffered defections so serious that no discipline remains. . . .

The truth or the error of the three Laws of Evolution does not properly concern the teacher. No physicist can, in these days, he expected to take oath that Dalton's atoms, or Willard Gibb's phases, or Bernouilli's kinetic gases, are true. He uses for his scholars the figure or the formula which best suits their convenience. The historian or sociologist is alone restricted in the use of formulas which shock the moral sense; yet the stoppage of discussion in the historical lecture-room cannot affect the teaching of the same young men in the physical laboratory—still less the legislation of their parents at the State capital; it would merely ruin the school of history. However much to be regretted is such a result, society cannot safely permit itself to be condemned to a lingering death, which is sure to tend towards suicide, merely to suit the convenience of school-teachers. The dilemma is real; it may become serious; in any case it needs to be understood.

The battle of Evolution has never been wholly won; the chances at this moment favor the fear that it may yet be wholly lost. The Darwinist no longer talks of Evolution; he uses the word Transformation. The historian of human society has hitherto, as a habit, preferred to write or to lecture on a tacit assumption that humanity showed upward progress, even when it emphatically showed the contrary, as was not uncommon; but this passive attitude cannot be held against the physicist who invades his territory and takes the teaching of history out of his hands. Somewhere he will have to make a stand, but he has been already so much weakened by the surrender of his defences that he knows no longer where a stand can be made. As a form of Vital Energy he is convicted of being a Vertebrate, a Mammal, a Monodelphe, a Primate, and must eternally, by his body, be subject to the second law of thermodynamics. Escape there is impossible. Science has shut and barred every known exit. Man can detect no outlet except through the loophole called Mind, and even to avail himself of this, he must follow Lapparent's advice—become a disembodied spirit and seek a confederate among such physicists or physiologists as are willing to admit that man, as an animal, has no importance; that his evolution or degradation as an organism is immaterial; that his physical force or condition has nothing to do with the subject; that the old ascetics were correct in suppressing the body; and that his consciousness is sufficient proof of his right to regard Reason as the highest potential of Vital Energy. . . .

As an Organism society has always been peculiarly subject to degradation of Energy, and alike the historians and the physicists invariably stretch Kelvin's law over all organized matter whatever. Instead of being a mere convenience in treatment, the law is very rapidly becoming a dogma of absolute Truth. As long as the theory of Degradation—as of Evolution—was only one of the convenient tools of science, the sociologist had no just cause for complaint. Every science—and mathematics first of all—uses what tools it likes. The Professor of Physics is not teaching Ethics; he is training young men to handle concrete energy in one or more of its many forms, and he has no choice but to use the most convenient formulas. Unfortunately the formula most convenient for him is not at all convenient for his colleagues in sociology and history, without pressing the inquiry further, into more intimate branches of practice like medicine, jurisprudence, and politics. If the entire universe, in every variety of active energy, organic and inorganic, human or divine, is to be treated as clockwork that is running down, society can hardly go on ignoring the fact forever. Hitherto it has often happened that two systems of education, like the Scholastic and Baconian, could exist side by side for centuries—as they exist still—in adjoining schools and universities, by no more scientific device than that of shutting their eyes to each other; but the universe has been terribly narrowed by thermodynamics. Already History and Sociology gasp for breath.

(30)

Ralph Adams Cram

1863-1942

An architect and writer, Cram was born in New Hampshire and educated at Exeter High School and at Westford Academy in Massachusetts. He then studied architecture in the office of a Boston firm
for five years and served also as art critic on the Boston *Transcript*
for two years during this period. In 1886 he left for Europe, and
during his travels became especially interested in the Gothic style.
During this trip he also was converted to Anglo-Catholicism, and on
his return in 1889 he founded an architectural firm to specialize in
church buildings. Among his designs were the chapel at West Point
and the Cathedral of St. John the Divine in New York City.

For his political philosophy as well as for architecture and writing,
Cram took his inspiration from the medieval world. Arguing against
"new mechanical toys for the achieving of democracy," he scorned
such ideas as representative government, universal suffrage, and the
party system. Cram's ideal society would have been organized on the
pattern of medieval craft guilds.

The selection here is from his work, *The Nemesis of Mediocrity*
(Boston, 1917).

To-day, when men cry aloud, as never before, for guides, interpreters, leaders, there is none to answer; in any category of life, issuing out of
any nation. None, that is, that matches in power the exigency of the demand.
There are those that honestly try to lead; there are those that increasingly lead
under the grim schooling of war, slowly, painfully and towards an end still
obscure and undetermined. Arduously they struggle to build up a following, to
see the insane life of the moment and see it whole; to keep ahead of the whirlwind of hell-let-loose and direct an amazed and disordered society along paths
of ultimate safety. And always the event outdistances them, the phantasma-
goria of chaos whirls bewilderingly beyond, and either they follow helplessly
or are sucked into the rushing vacuum that comes in the wake of progressive
destruction. In the immediate necessity of war one august general after another
receives command, plays his part for a day, and disappears, marked by comparative failure if not by demonstrated incompetence. Potential reputations
break down and are forgotten, in Mesopotamia, Gallipoli, Galicia, Roumania,
the Trentino, the Carso, Champagne, the Argonne: on the North Sea, in the

Channel, through the Mediterranean. The battle fronts east, west, south, bury more than the bodies of dead soldiers, for reputations are interred with them in a quick and merciful oblivion.

Still, fate is a whimsical arbiter, whose operations are unaccountable, and any day may appear the great leaders thus far coldly refused to the desperate and death-locked armies, but there is little hope for a like mercy in statesmanship. The years just before the war were tumultuous with the petty machinations of the degenerate political and diplomatic successors of the masterly manipulators of destiny of the nineteenth century. Noble or cynical, they were leaders, these men of a dead generation: Metternich, Cavour, Disraeli, Bismarck, Gladstone, Gambetta, Lincoln, and they have left few successors, either to their glory or their infamy. Can there be honest comparison between the political leaders in Great Britain to-day and Peel, Palmerston, Gladstone, Disraeli and Salisbury, between the flotsam and jetsam of French parliamentary turbulence and Thiers, Gambetta, de Freycinet? Contrast the men now controlling the destinies of Italy with those of the epoch of the Liberation; match the present politicians of Germany with those to the front from 1870 to 1895; place in one column the members of President Wilson's Cabinet, the leaders in Congress, the Governors of the several States, and in the other the American political forces from 1860 on for the space of a generation. Whether you like them all or not, these men of an elder age, one thing you must concede, and that is their capacity and their dominance as leaders.

So one might traverse the fields of religion, philosophy, literature, art, education, matching each man who claims or is accorded priority, with those of the immediate past whose historical place is now as assured as was their acceptance during their lives. Long after the contemporary list finds "finis" written beneath, the other calendar continues until its length is greater by tenfold. Not only this, but there is unquestioned difference in quality; as between Harmsworth and Gladstone, Bryan and Cleveland, Benedict XV and Leo XIII, Wells and Emerson, Ornstein and Brahms. The leaders that once were, found their following through comprehension of their own force and dominance, those that are now, *faute de mieux,* and because there are no others to lead.

Inch by inch the valleys are being filled and the mountains brought low. More arduously the man stronger than another lifts above the level uniformity; a few still continue, lasting over from an earlier generation, but in a year or two they also will pass, and few indeed are rising to take their place. Meanwhile "the hungry sheep look up, and are not fed," for the soul of sane man demands leadership, and in spite of academic aphorisms on Equality, a dim consciousness survives of the fundamental truth that without strong leadership democracy is a menace; without strong leadership culture and even civilization will pass away.

Now as always the great mass of men look for the master-man who can form in definite shape the aspirations and the instincts that in them are formless and amorphous; who can lead where they are more than willing to follow, but themselves cannot mark the way; who can act as a centripetal force and gather into potent units the diffuse atoms of like will but without co-ordinating ability. So great is this central human instinct (which was not only the foundation of feudalism but harks back to the very beginnings of society), that when the great leader is not revealed he is invented out of the more impudent element of any potential group, assurance taking the place of competence; or optimistically assumed, the most available being dragged from his obscurity and pitched into a position, or burdened with a task, outside the limits of his ability—as he himself only too often knows.

And as the supply of leaders diminishes the more reckless becomes the desperate choice. It is perhaps not so much that men now reject all leadership as it is that they blindly accept the inferior type; the specious demagogue, the unscrupulous master of effrontery. Men follow to-day as they always have and always will, the difference lies in the quality of those that are followed. In default of the leader of the old type, the man who first saw beyond the obvious and drew others after him by force of vision and will and personal quality, the group, and the super-group which we call the mob, create their leaders in their own image, and out of their own material. . . .

Tested by every standard this leadership is now deficient both in quantity and quality. To what are we to attribute this anomalous condition? Why is it that our lack is not only appalling when compared with those periodical moments of the past when, as in the eleventh century, every nation of Europe was following leaders as amazing in number as they were commanding in ability, but even in contrast with the last quarter of the nineteenth century. This was not an epoch to which future generations will look back with any notable degree of pride, yet it left us a heritage of great names that, as I have said before, reached the number of one hundred and fifty, a count that could be increased to two hundred if the arbitrary quarter century I have chosen, during which all were still living, were extended by ten years before 1880 and by five after 1905.

The answer is simple, but it is an answer that will be rejected with practical unanimity. Democracy has achieved its perfect work and has now reduced all mankind to a dead level of incapacity where great leaders are no longer either wanted or brought into existence, while society itself is unable, of its own power as a whole, to lift itself from the nadir of its own uniformity.

"The world must be made safe for democracy" is a noble phrase, but it is meaningless without its corollary, "democracy must be made safe for the world." This latter condition does not exist. For exactly one hundred years democracy has suffered a progressive degeneration until it is now not a blessing but a menace. . . .

True democracy means three things: Abolition of Privilege; Equal Opportunity for All; and Utilization of Ability. Unless democracy achieves these things it is not democracy, and no matter how "progressive" its methods, how apparently democratic its machinery, it may perfectly well be an oligarchy, a kakistocracy or a tyranny. The three imperative desiderata named above may be achieved under a monarchy, they may be lost in a republic, the mechanism does not matter. One of the chief faults with what we call our democracy is our stolid failure to understand that there is a democratic ideal and a democratic method, that there is not necessarily any connection between the two, and that generally speaking the democratic method (unstable, constantly changing its form) is incapable of accomplishing the democratic ideal. . . .

Now for the last hundred years the world has abandoned itself to an insane devising of new mechanical toys for the achieving of democracy: representative government, the parliamentary system, universal suffrage, the party system, the secret ballot, rotation in office, the initiative, referendum and recall, popular election of members of upper legislative houses, woman suffrage, direct legislation. All have failed to obtain abolition of privilege, equal opportunity and utilization of ability, on the contrary, they have worked in the opposite direction, and so far as these three things are concerned, the peoples are worse off than they were fifty years ago, while during the same period government and society have become progressively more venal, less competent and further separated from the ideals of honour, duty and righteousness. Meanwhile so obsessed have we become by our pursuit of new devices for obtaining democracy, and by our search for nostrums to cure the ills of our constant failures, we have now wholly forgotten in what democracy consists. . . .

During the Middle Ages, when the ideal of democracy was at its highest point, and when it was most nearly achieved, it was held as incontrovertible that the purpose of political organization was primarily ethical and moral, and that its function was the achievement of righteousness and justice. Authority was from God, and the power also to enforce that authority, but both were operative only when they were used for right ends. "*La dame ne le sire n'en est seigneur se non dou dreit.*" Equally unquestioned was the fact that law was not made, but was the concrete expression of that morality, right and justice that had grown with the life of the community, exactly expressing the needs of society, and with the moral sanction of communal life behind it. "There is no King where will rules and not law" was the Mediæval conviction as opposed to the absolutism of the Renaissance first expressed in theoretical form by Machiavelli. Finally the Middle Ages asserted that Government was a solemn contract between ruled and rulers, to be broken by neither without the abrogation of the contract. Treason on the part of the sovereign was then as clearly recognized a possibility as treason on the part of the people.

This great ideal, the noblest man has yet conceived in the realm of civil law, was completely destroyed by the Renaissance, and absolutism took its place. . . .

Democracy in government and democracy in education have each played their part in the destruction of leadership and the establishing of the reign of mediocrity. There is yet a third aspect, or rather result, of the same force, which may perhaps prove in the end the most significant of all, and that is the democratization of society by the breaking down of the just and normal barriers of race, first through the so-called "melting pot" process, second through the substitution of the mongrel for the product of pure blood by reason of the free and reckless mixing of incompatible strains. From the beginning of modern democracy it has been with its adherents a cardinal point of faith that a "free country" should set no limits to immigration of any race, class or degree of cultural development. It is equally a dogma that under a true democracy there is no discrimination possible between individuals on the score of difference in race, blood or status, and that therefore no restrictions should be recognized or established which would control or limit absolute freedom of union in marital relations and the legal procreation of children.

The nineteenth century superstition, erected by the doctrinaire protagonists of "evolution," that human progress was both automatic and constant, through the acquisition of new qualities by education, the force of environment, and "natural selection," has been the scientific justification for the supposedly "democratic" principle of free immigration and free mating. Were the theory demonstrably true it would indeed negative the chief arguments for the scrupulous recognition and preservation of race values both in marriage and control of immigration. If character is determined by education and environment, and is transmitted in substance generation after generation, the question is manifestly only one of enough education, of the right kind, and distributed with sufficient generality. Mongol and Slovak, Malay and Hottentot stand on the same plane with Latin and Saxon and Celt, for it is merely a question of education, environment and continued breeding; good is cumulative, automatically transmitted, and time is the answer to all. . . .

What we confront through democracy *as it is interpreted to-day* is a degradation of the human potential through a double dissipation of energy. With no defensible standard of comparative values, all the spiritual and mental force in men is turned towards the realization of the unimportant, to which accomplishment it is given with a prodigality hardly equalled in the Middle Ages when it was lavished on the realization of the essential. Simultaneously man has been dissipating the stored-up energy of the world through his mastery of thermodynamics and his precarious dominion over electrical forces, at such a rate that physical potential has been degraded in a hundred years more than in the preceding hundred centuries. Of what becomes of this fabulous force, what the permanent contributions may be to human life, he cares little. It is sufficent for him to realize that he is the arbiter of this gigantic power, and if it is exploited and dissipated, with nothing of lasting value to show, he cares no more than any other type of spendthrift.

As Henry Adams has said, with cold irony, "Neither historians nor sociologists can afford to let themselves be driven into admitting that every gain of power—from gunpowder to steam, from the dynamo to the Daimler motor—has been made at the cost of man's and of woman's vitality." Yet the fact remains that this is true, and our present deplorable estate is partly the result of this very degradation and dissipation of energy, which has been lavished on activities totally unproductive so far as lasting benefits are concerned, and spread out over a vast area where it disappears without results.

It would seem that there is in the world at any one time only a certain amount of available spiritual energy, which may be preserved and made effectively operative through concentration, or lost through dissipation, while the physical energy, stored up out of endless ages, is limited in its original quantity, and only added to, if at all, in a very small degree. At the beginning of each new era this spiritual force is precipitated in the form of great leaders who translate it, and transmit it in available form (and directed toward productive ends) to the general mass of men. Later, the specific era having reached its meridian, the leaders pass as the prophets before them, and the force once concentrated in them, and made operative, spreads thin and ineffective, and at last is dissipated through the general mass of men. At the end the prodigal majority, having wasted its inherited substance in riotous living, falls into puerile contests and finally destroys itself, and another era takes its place in history to the accompaniment of war and anarchy. So Greece lost its leaders and squandered its intellectual heritage; so Rome dissipated its Imperial force and succumbed to barbarism; so Mediævalism played fast and loose with its spiritual capital, and so modernism is now wasting all it had inherited from these three antecedent periods, and prepares to take its place with antiquity. . . .

And if the miracle happens; if the leader comes who can shatter the Brumagem efficiency of Prussia, and so the world is saved from a fate it richly deserves, can we say that we have a better hope? Yes, if with victory comes realization of what the war means, and why it came upon us. For this realization one of two things is necessary: either such a spiritual regeneration of the great mass of people, through suffering and sorrow and privation and the bitter schooling of the trenches, that they will follow up their victory over the enemy in the field by an even greater victory over the enemy at home in religion, philosophy and society, purging a chastened world of the last folly and the last wickedness of modernism; or the coming once more of the great prophets and captains of men who alone can lead as their predecessors have always led, and so build up a new life on the ruins of an old that has passed in blood and flame and dishonour.

(31)

Charles A. Beard

1874-1948

Educated at DePauw and Columbia Universities, Beard was one of the outstanding American historians of his generation. Beard was particularly interested in exploring the relationships between economic interests and politics. He held teaching posts at Columbia and the

New School for Social Research and produced a number of major historical works. In politics he was personally aligned with progressive and liberal causes, advocating a philosophy of progressivism and social planning. Later, however, he was attacked by liberals because of his opposition to President Franklin D. Roosevelt's court-packing plan, and because of his impassioned criticism of Roosevelt's foreign policy.

Some critics of Beard have indicated that his historical work, especially his analyses of the economic factors in politics, was done in support of his political position. However, it seems likely that Beard's reputation will survive such criticism. Beard viewed the writing of history as an "act of faith," not the ascription of absolutes. Though he rejected a naive relativism, Beard contended that "the historian who writes history . . . consciously or unconsciously performs an act of faith, as to order and movement [in history], for certainty as to order and movement is denied him by knowledge of the actuality with which he is concerned." Beard in effect denied the possibility of absolute historical truth.

This selection is from Beard's presidential address to the American Historical Association, "Written History as an Act of Faith," published in the *American Historical Review*, 39 (January, 1934).

History has been called a science, an art, an illustration of theology, a phase of philosophy, a branch of literature. It is none of these things, nor all of them combined. On the contrary, science, art, theology, and literature are themselves merely phases of history as past actuality and their particular forms at given periods and places are to be explained, if explained at all, by history as knowledge and thought. The philosopher, possessing little or no acquaintance with history, sometimes pretends to expound the inner secret of history, but the historian turns upon him and expounds the secret of the philosopher, as far as it may be expounded at all, by placing him in relation to the movement of ideas and interests in which he stands or floats, by giving to his scheme of thought its appropriate relativity. So it is with systems of science, art, theology, and literature. All the light on these subjects that can be discovered by the human mind comes from history as past actuality.

What, then, is this manifestation of omniscience called history? It is, as Croce says, contemporary thought about the past. History as past actuality includes, to be sure, all that has been done, said, felt, and thought by human beings on this planet since humanity began its long career. History as record embraces the monuments, documents, and symbols which provide such knowledge as we have or can find respecting past actuality. But it is history as thought, not as actuality, record, or specific knowledge, that is really meant when the term history is used in its widest and most general significance. It is thought about past actuality, instructed and delimited by history as record and knowledge—record and knowledge authenticated by criticism and ordered with the help of the scientific method. This is the final, positive, inescapable definition. It contains all the exactness that is possible and all the bewildering problems inherent in the nature of thought and the relation of the thinker to the thing thought about.

Although this definition of history may appear, at first glance, distressing to those who have been writing lightly about "the science of history" and "the scientific method" in historical research and construction, it is in fact in accordance with the most profound contemporary thought about history, represented by Croce, Riezler, Karl Mannheim, Mueller-Armack, and Heussi, for example. It is in keeping also with the obvious and commonplace. Has it not been said for a century or more that each historian who writes history is a product of his age, and that his work reflects the spirit of the times, of a nation, race, group, class, or section? No contemporary student of history really believes that Bossuet, Gibbon, Mommsen, or Bancroft could be duplicated today. Every student of history knows that his colleagues have been influenced in their selection and ordering of materials by their biases, prejudices, beliefs, affections, general upbringing, and experience, particularly social and economic; and if he has a sense of propriety, to say nothing of humor, he applies the canon to himself, leaving no exceptions to the rule. The pallor of waning time, if not of death, rests upon the latest volume of history, fresh from the roaring press.

Why do we believe this to be true? The answer is that every written history —of a village, town, county, state, nation, race, group, class, idea, or the wide world—is a selection and arrangement of facts, of recorded fragments of past actuality. And the selection and arrangement of facts—a combined and complex intellectual operation—is an act of choice, conviction, and interpretation respecting values, is an act of thought. Facts, multitudinous and beyond calculation, are known, but they do not select themselves or force themselves automatically into any fixed scheme of arrangement in the mind of the historian. They are selected and ordered by him as he thinks. True enough, where the records pertaining to a small segment of history are few and presumably all known, the historian may produce a fragment having an aspect of completeness, as, for example, some pieces by Fustel de Coulanges; but the completeness is one of documentation, not of history. True enough also, many historians are pleased to say of their writings that their facts are selected and ordered only with reference to inner necessities, but none who takes this position will allow the same exactitude and certainty to the works of others, except when the predilections of the latter conform to his own pattern.

Contemporary thought about history, therefore, repudiates the conception dominant among the schoolmen during the latter part of the nineteenth century and the opening years of the twentieth century—the conception that it is possible to describe the past as it actually was, somewhat as the engineer describes a single machine. The formula itself was a passing phase of thought about the past. Its author, Ranke, a German conservative, writing after the storm and stress of the French Revolution, was weary of history written for, or permeated by, the purposes of revolutionary propaganda. He wanted peace. The ruling classes in Germany, with which he was affiliated, having secured a breathing spell in the settlement of 1815, wanted peace to consolidate their position. Written history that was cold, factual, and apparently undisturbed by the passions of the time served best the cause of those who did not want to be disturbed. Later the formula was fitted into the great conception of natural science—cold neutrality over against the materials and forces of the physical world. Truths of nature, ran the theory, are to be discovered by maintaining the most severe objectivity; therefore the truth of history may be revealed by the same spirit and method. The reasoning seemed perfect to those for whom it was satisfactory. But the movement of ideas and interests continued, and bondage to conservative and scientific thought was broken by criticism and events. As Croce and Heussi have demonstrated, so-called neutral or scientific history reached a crisis in its thought before the twentieth century had advanced far on the way.

This crisis in historical thought sprang from internal criticism—from conflicts of thought within historiography itself—and from the movement of history as actuality; for historians are always engaged, more or less, in thinking about their own work and are disturbed, like their fellow citizens, by crises and revolutions occurring in the world about them. As an outcome of this crisis in historiography, the assumption that the actuality of history is identical with or closely akin to that of the physical world, and the assumption that any historian can be a disembodied spirit as coldly neutral to human affairs as the engineer to an automobile have both been challenged and rejected. Thus, owing to internal criticism and the movement of external events, the Ranke formula of history has been discarded and laid away in the museum of antiquities. It has ceased to satisfy the human spirit in its historical needs. Once more, historians recognize formally the obvious, long known informally, namely, that any written history inevitably reflects the thought of the author in his time and cultural setting.

That this crisis in thought presents a distressing dilemma to many historians is beyond question. It is almost a confession of inexpiable sin to admit in academic circles that one is not a man of science working in a scientific manner with things open to deterministic and inexorable treatment, to admit that one is more or less a guesser in this vale of tears. But the only escape from the dust and storm of the present conflict, and from the hazards of taking thought, now before the historian, is silence or refuge in some minute particularity of history as actuality. He may edit documents, although there are perils in the choice of documents to be edited, and in any case the choice of documents will bear some reference to an interpretation of values and importance —subjective considerations. To avoid this difficulty, the historian may confine his attention to some very remote and microscopic area of time and place, such as the price of cotton in Alabama between 1850 and 1860, or the length of wigs in the reign of Charles II, in the pleasing but false assumption that he is really describing an isolated particularity as it actually was, an isolated area having no wide-reaching ramifications of relations. But even then the historian would be a strange creature if he never asked himself why he regarded these matters as worthy of his labor and love, or why society provides a living for him during his excursions and explorations.

The other alternative before the student of history as immense actuality is to face boldly, in the spirit of Cato's soliloquy, the wreck of matter and the crush of worlds—the dissolution of that solid assurance which rested on the formula bequeathed by Ranke and embroidered by a thousand hands during the intervening years. And when he confronts without avoidance contemporary thought about the nature of written history, what commands does he hear?

The supreme command is that he must cast off his servitude to the assumptions of natural science and return to his own subject matter—to history as actuality. The hour for this final declaration of independence has arrived: the contingency is here and thought resolves it. Natural science is only one small subdivision of history as actuality with which history as thought is concerned. Its dominance in the thought of the Western World for a brief period can be explained, if at all, by history; perhaps in part by reference to the great conflict that raged between the theologians and scientists after the dawn of the sixteenth century—an intellectual conflict associated with the economic conflict between landed aristocracies, lay and clerical, on the one side, and the rising bourgeois on the other.

The intellectual formulas borrowed from natural science, which have cramped and distorted the operations of history as thought, have taken two forms: physical and biological. The first of these rests upon what may be called, for convenience, the assumption of causation: everything that happens in the world of human affairs is determined by antecedent occurrences, and events of history are the illustrations or data of laws to be discovered, laws such as are found in hydraulics. It is true that no historian has ever been able to array the fullness of history as actuality in any such deterministic order; Karl Marx has gone further than any other. But under the hypothesis that it is possible, historians have been arranging events in neat little chains of causation which explain, to their satisfaction, why succeeding events happen; and they have attributed any shortcomings in result to the inadequacy of their known data, not to the falsity of the assumption on which they have been operating. Undiscouraged by their inability to bring all history within a single law, such as the law of gravitation, they have gone on working in the belief that the Newtonian trick will be turned some time, if the scientific method is applied long and rigorously enough and facts are heaped up high enough, as the succeeding grists of doctors of philosophy are ground out by the universities, turned loose on "research projects", and amply supplied by funds.

Growing rightly suspicious of this procedure in physicohistoriography, a number of historians, still bent on servitude to natural science, turned to biology. The difficulties and failures involved in all efforts to arrange the occurrences of history in a neat system of historical mechanics were evident to them. But on the other side, the achievements of the Darwinians were impressive. If the totality of history could not be brought into a deterministic system without doing violence to historical knowledge; perhaps the biological analogy of the organism could be applied. And this was done, apparently without any realization of the fact that thinking by analogy is a form of primitive animism. So under the biological analogy, history was conceived as a succession of cultural organisms rising, growing, competing, and declining. To this fantastic morphological assumption Spengler chained his powerful mind. Thus freed from self-imposed slavery to physics, the historian passed to self-imposed subservience to biology. Painfully aware of the perplexities encountered as long as he stuck to his own business, the historian sought escape by employing the method and thought of others whose operations he did not understand and could not control, on the simple, almost childlike, faith that the biologist, if not the physicist, really knew what he was about and could furnish the clue to the mystery.

But the shadow of the organismic conception of history had scarcely fallen on the turbulent actuality of history when it was scrutinized by historians who were thinking in terms of their own subject as distinguished from the terms of a mere subdivision of history. By an inescapable demonstration Kurt Riezler has made it clear that the organismic theory of history is really the old determinism of physics covered with murky words. The rise, growth, competition, and decline of cultural organisms is meaningless unless fitted into some overarching hypothesis—either the hypothesis of the divine drama or the hypothesis of causation in the deterministic sense. Is each cultural organism in history, each national or racial culture, an isolated particularity governed by its own mystical or physical laws? Knowledge of history as actuality forbids any such conclusion. If, in sheer desperation, the historian clings to the biological analogy, which school is he to follow—the mechanistic or the vitalistic? In either case he is caught in the deterministic sequence, if he thinks long enough and hard enough.

Hence the fate of the scientific school of historiography turns finally upon the applicability of the deterministic sequence to the totality of history as actuality. Natural science in a strict sense, as distinguished from mere knowledge of facts, can discover system and law only where occurrences are in reality arranged objectively in deterministic sequences. It can describe these sequences and draw from them laws, so-called. From a given number of the occurrences in any such sequence, science can predict what will happen when the remainder appear.

With respect to certain areas of human occurrences, something akin to deterministic sequences is found by the historian, but the perdurance of any sequence depends upon the perdurance in time of surrounding circumstances which cannot be brought within any scheme of deterministic relevancies. Certainly all the occurrences of history as actuality cannot be so ordered; most of them are unknown and owing to the paucity of records must forever remain unknown.

If a science of history were achieved, it would, like the science of celestial mechanics, make possible the calculable prediction of the future in history. It would bring the totality of historical occurrences within a single field and reveal the unfolding future to its last end, including all the apparent choices made and to be made. It would be omniscience. The creator of it would possess the attributes ascribed by the theologians to God. The future once revealed, humanity would have nothing to do except to await its doom.

To state the case is to dispose of it. The occurrences of history—the unfolding of ideas and interests in time-motion—are not identical in nature with the data of physics, and hence in their totality they are beyond the reach of that necessary instrument of natural science—mathematics—which cannot assign meaningful values to the imponderables, immeasurables, and contingencies of history as actuality.

Having broken the tyranny of physics and biology, contemporary thought in historiography turns its engines of verification upon the formula of historical relativity—the formula that makes all written history merely relative to time and circumstance, a passing shadow, an illusion. Contemporary criticism shows that the apostle of relativity is destined to be destroyed by the child of his own brain. If all historical conceptions are merely relative to passing events, to transitory phases of ideas and interests, then the conception of relativity is itself relative. When absolutes in history are rejected the absolutism of relativity is also rejected. So we must inquire: To what spirit of the times, to the ideas and interests of what class, group, nation, race, or region does the conception of relativity correspond? As the actuality of history moves forward into the future, the conception of relativity will also pass, as previous conceptions and interpretations of events have passed. Hence, according to the very doctrine of relativity, the skeptic of relativity will disappear in due course, beneath the ever-tossing waves of changing relativities. If he does not suffer this fate soon, the apostle of relativity will surely be executed by his own logic. Every conception of history, he says, is relative to time and circumstances. But by his own reasoning he is then compelled to ask: To what are these particular times and circumstances relative? And he must go on with receding sets of times and circumstances until he confronts an absolute: the totality of history as actuality which embraces all times and circumstances and all relativities.

Contemporary historical thought is, accordingly, returning upon itself and its subject matter. The historian is casting off his servitude to physics and biology, as he formerly cast off the shackles of theology and its metaphysics. He likewise sees the doctrine of relativity crumble in the cold light of historical knowledge. When he accepts none of the assumptions made by theology, physics, and biology, as applied to history, when he passes out from under the fleeting shadow of relativity, he confronts the absolute in his field—the absolute totality of all historical occurrences past, present, and becoming to the end of all things. Then he finds it necessary to bring the occurrences of history as actuality under one or another of three broad conceptions.

The first is that history as total actuality is chaos, perhaps with little islands of congruous relativities floating on the surface, and that the human mind cannot bring them objectively into any all-embracing order or subjectively into any consistent system. The second is that history as actuality is a part of some order of nature and revolves in cycles eternally—spring, summer, autumn, and winter, democracy, aristocracy, and monarchy, or their variants, as imagined by Spengler. The third is that history as actuality is moving in some direction away from the low level of primitive beginnings, on an upward gradient toward a more ideal order—as imagined by Condorcet, Adam Smith, Karl Marx, or Herbert Spencer.

Abundant evidence can be marshaled, has been marshaled, in support of each of these conceptions of history as actuality, but all the available evidence will not fit any one of them. The hypothesis of chaos admits of no ordering at all; hence those who operate under it cannot write history, although they may comment *on* history. The second admits of an ordering of events only by arbitrarily leaving out of account all the contradictions in the evidence. The third admits of an ordering of events, also by leaving contradictions out of consideration. The historian who writes history, therefore, consciously or unconsciously performs an act of faith, as to order and movement, for certainty as to order and movement is denied to him by knowledge of the actuality with which he is concerned. He is thus in the position of a statesman dealing with public affairs; in writing he acts and in acting he makes choices, large or small, timid or bold, with respect to some conception of the nature of things. And the degree of his influence and immortality will depend upon the length and correctness of his forecast—upon the verdict of history yet to come. His faith is at bottom a conviction that something true can be known about the movement of history and his conviction is a subjective decision, not a purely objective discovery.

But members of the passing generation will ask: Has our work done in the scientific spirit been useless? Must we abandon the scientific method? The answer is an emphatic negative. During the past fifty years historical scholarship, carried on with judicial calm, has wrought achievements of value beyond calculation. Particular phases of history once dark and confused have been illuminated by research, authentication, scrutiny, and the ordering of immediate relevancies. Nor is the empirical or scientific method to be abandoned. It is the only method that can be employed in obtaining accurate knowledge of historical facts, personalities, situations, and movements. It alone can disclose conditions that made possible what happened. It has a value in itself—a value high in the hierarchy of values indispensable to the life of a democracy. The inquiring spirit of science, using the scientific method, is the chief safeguard against the tyranny of authority, bureaucracy, and brute power. It can reveal by investigation necessities and possibilities in any social scene and also offerings with respect to desirabilities to be achieved within the limits of the possible.

The scientific method is, therefore, a precious and indispensable instrument of the human mind; without it society would sink down into primitive animism and barbarism. It is when this method, a child of the human brain, is exalted into a master and a tyrant that historical thought must enter a caveat. So the historian is bound by his craft to recognize the nature and limitations of the scientific method and to dispel the illusion that it can produce a science of history embracing the fullness of history, or of any large phase, as past actuality.

This means no abandonment of the tireless inquiry into objective realities, especially economic realities and relations; not enough emphasis has been laid upon the conditioning and determining influences of biological and economic necessities or upon researches designed to disclose them in their deepest and widest ramifications. This means no abandonment of the inquiry into the forms and development of ideas as conditioning and determining influences; not enough emphasis has been laid on this phase of history by American scholars.

But the upshot to which this argument is directed is more fundamental than any aspect of historical method.

It is that any selection and arrangement of facts pertaining to any large area of history, either local or world, race or class, is controlled inexorably by the frame of reference in the mind of the selector and arranger. This frame of reference includes things deemed necessary, things deemed possible, and things deemed desirable. It may be large, informed by deep knowledge, and illuminated by wide experience; or it may be small, uninformed, and unilluminated. It may be a grand conception of history or a mere aggregation of confusions. But it is there in the mind, inexorably. To borrow from Croce, when grand philosophy is ostentatiously put out at the front door of the mind, then narrow, class, provincial, and regional prejudices come in at the back door and dominate, perhaps only half-consciously, the thinking of the historian.

The supreme issue before the historian now is the determination of his attitude to the disclosures of contemporary thought. He may deliberately evade them for reasons pertaining to personal, economic, and intellectual comfort, thus joining the innumerable throng of those who might have been but were not. Or he may proceed to examine his own frame of reference, clarify it, enlarge it by acquiring knowledge of greater areas of thought and events, and give it consistency of structure by a deliberate conjecture respecting the nature or direction of the vast movements of ideas and interests called world history.

This operation will cause discomfort to individual historians but all, according to the vows of their office, are under obligation to perform it, as Henry Adams warned the members of this Association in his letter of 1894. And as Adams then said, it will have to be carried out under the scrutiny of four great tribunals for the suppression of unwelcome knowledge and opinion: the church, the state, property, and labor. Does the world move and, if so, in what direction? If he believes that the world does not move, the historian must offer the pessimism of chaos to the inquiring spirit of mankind. If it does move, does it move backward toward some old arrangement, let us say, of 1928, 1896, 1815, 1789, or 1295? Or does it move forward to some other arrangement which can be only dimly divined—a capitalist dictatorship, a proletarian dictatorship, or a collectivist democracy? The last of these is my own guess, founded on a study of long trends and on a faith in the indomitable spirit of mankind. In any case, if the historian cannot know or explain history as actuality, he helps to make history, petty or grand.

To sum up contemporary thought in historiography, any written history involves the selection of a topic and an arbitary delimitation of its borders—cutting off connections with the universal. Within the borders arbitrarily established, there is a selection and organization of facts by the processes of thought. This selection and organization—a single act—will be controlled by the historian's frame of reference composed of things deemed necessary and of things deemed desirable. The frame may be a narrow class, sectional, national, or group conception of history, clear and frank or confused and half conscious, or it may be a large, generous conception, clarified by association with the great spirits of all ages. Whatever its nature the frame is inexorably there, in the mind. And in the frame only three broad conceptions of all history as actuality are possible. History is chaos and every attempt to interpret it otherwise is an illusion. History moves around in a kind of cycle. History moves in a line, straight or spiral, and in some direction. The historian may seek to escape these issues by silence or by a confession of avoidance or he may face them boldly, aware of the intellectual and moral perils inherent in any decision—in his act of faith.

(32)

Karl Llewellyn

1893-1962

Karl Llewellyn received his A.B. from Yale University in 1915 and took his law degree at Yale Law School. He then began a distinguished teaching career at Yale, Columbia, and the University of Chicago.

Llewellyn was one of the founders of the modern school of jurisprudence known as "legal realism" or, as Llewellyn preferred to call it, "functionalism." The functionalists' position is inspired by contemporary social science. It holds that legal theory must be based on direct observation of the legal process itself and must give a complete account of all the factors in that process. Thus, legal realism inspires an empirical and factual study of the law rather than one that moves rationalistically from "higher law" principles to the resolution of cases.

The selection reprinted here is from Llewellyn's article, "On Reading and Using the Newer Jurisprudence," *Columbia Law Review,* 40 (April, 1940).

The older Jurisprudence which is current among lawyers is one which the profession did not have occasion to particularly study; a lawyer just absorbed it, largely through the fingers and the pores, as he went along. It was, and is, in essence, the homely and effective philosophy of active men about their work. And it has the solid virtues which are commonly a part of any going, working institution. The going, working institution which the philosophy seeks to reflect is not merely our rules of law, but the whole scheme of our law, our courts, our lawyers, and their work; it includes our ways of work, and the goals toward which our rules of law drive, as well as rules of law themselves. At the heart and core of that institution lies the fact that judges, and administrative officials who do not happen to be judges, are not free to do what they choose or to decide as they choose; that their action in matters which concern the rest of us is circumscribed and limited, and is guided by something independent of the individual preferences or vagaries of the judges and officials. That is a fact, it is an observable fact, it is a vital fact. In addition to that fact there is laid down in our legal system a judgment of policy, powerfully express and even more powerfully implicit. This judgment is that it is good and right that our judges and other officials should not be free to act and decide as they happen to please. The policy is one which is very dear to us; and it is a policy which needs constant vigilance lest officials, or indeed judges, overlook it. The older Jurisprudence proceeded, in consequence, to give us a rationale or doctrine which was intended to express both the fact and the policy, and which was intended to make future facts conform to the policy. In its less sophisticated form the doctrine runs that "this is a government of laws *and not* of men," and that "the rules of law determine the right decision."

As will appear in a moment, this particular phrasing of rationale or doctrine, while useful, is yet exceedingly inadequate. It wraps its words around half of the truth, and that is good; but it is also so phrased as to obscure the other half of the truth, which is not good at all. Regardless of their exactness or adequacy of phrasing, however, these particular formulations of the older Jurisprudence have a value in men's minds, and more particularly in the minds of lawyers. They have a fighting value. They are prized, they will be fought for, they will be defended from any challenge at all, because they have (without our quite knowing how) come to symbolize and indeed to embody the great and essential truth that judges are not free, nor are administrative officials. Indeed these particular formulations have come to appear to most of us (without our thinking particularly about how this has happened) as the *sole* established and available means to keep our officials and our judges reminded of our vital need that judges and officials shall not be free to decide and do as they just happen to please.

We cannot leave our judges or officials wholly free, or let them utterly loose, without chaos; that is clear. We cannot hold them down and direct them, without proper institutional machinery for holding them down and directing them; and that is clear. So much is common ground among all responsible jurisprudes, new or old. What the newer jurisprudes are worrying over is how to find a better, a more effective, a more reliable machinery for directing judges and other officials than the older rationale and doctrine have managed to give us.

For the older doctrine has not only the sturdy virtues which commonly inhere in the active man's philosophy of a going scheme of things; it has also the defects which commonly inhere in any unstudied and haphazard wisdom about a very complex human institution. Unstudied and haphazard wisdom on the lips of active men is commonly partial, it is commonly self-inconsistent, it commonly needs to have its various and variant partial expressions put down side by side, and thought through all together. The folk saws about marriage, for instance, are almost all of them rooted in deep truth—such as that man was not meant to live alone, and that marriage is a battle, and that a good woman is a pearl above price, and that it takes two to make a marriage, and that two are not enough. The trouble is that no single one of such going expressions gets its words around the whole, or even an adequate part of the truth. Similarly, the older Jurisprudence has wrestled from time to time with certain inadequacies of the two major doctrinal formulations which have been mentioned—inadequacies which affected not only full description of the actual working of our legal system but also the full expression of our legal system's judgment on what is right, needed and established policy. Thus akin to the saws of marriage there run saws of law: "Hard cases make bad law" means that in our going scheme judges pay attention to the justice of the individual case, but that they probably shouldn't, quite as much as they do. "Bad law makes hard cases" means that rules have a function beyond certainty, and that we do not like it and judges probably ought to do something about it, when the rules are merely certain and are not also just. "The law looks not to the form, but to the substance" means that courts do and should have one sharp eye out for what they see as effective justice in the case in hand, despite all building and reliance which may have rested on the rules of law. All of these expressions mean that in our system as we have it, the judge or other official does, to some (unspecified) extent, and should, to some (equally unspecified) extent, operate in ways not clearly laid down in the explicit rules of law. So that even lawyers who were troubled when Holmes stated that "General propositions do not decide concrete cases" watch judicial appointments or elections with concern because, apart from the question of character or bias, they know that the question of skill and temperament in the individual judge makes a difference both to decision and to law. . . .

What has been said can perhaps be summed up thus: the fact that judges and officials are not wholly free and must not be wholly free, divides on analysis and closer examination into two facts. The one fact is concerned with the control, the restraint, the holding down, of judges and officials; the other fact is concerned with the allowing to them of a limited degree and a limited kind of leeway, and the putting on them of a duty to exercise their uttermost skill and judgment within that leeway. Both of these facts must be seen, and both must be reckoned with, by any Jurisprudence which aims to cover the plain facts and the settled policies of our legal system. For there are two kinds of judicial or other official freedom which come in question, and the two kinds are very different. It is a fact in our legal system that judges are by no means free to be *arbitrary,* and our vital need that they shall not be free to be *arbitrary* has been caught into these rationales or doctrines about "laws and not men," and about "rules determining cases." But it is also a fact that our legal system does adjust to the individual case *and* to changes in our conditions and institutions; and that fact means that judges and other officials are free to some real degree to be *just* and *wise,* and that we have a vital need that judges and other officials shall continue to be to some real degree free to be *wise and just.* That fact happens, however, *not* to have been caught into an equally familiar, equally sharp, or equally precious rationale or doctrine. Yet it needs to be; it is no less a vital part of our legal system and of our judges' duty. There is the law, which we know as impersonal, and think of as clear; there is the right outcome, which we feel as also impersonal, and think of as hard to find, but capable of being found, and the office of the judge is to fulfill the demands of *both,* together. . . .

What I am trying to say can be almost summed up in this: that when we take a fresh look at what really goes on, then we see before us, along with our doctrines of law, and giving to those doctrines much of their meaning, the crafts of law, and the ideals and traditions of those crafts; of which judging at trial is one, and judging on appeal is another. And that to leave unstudied and almost wholly implicit the ideals and traditions of the crafts is to leave unspoken and undiscussed half of the guidance and control and soundness which lies in our actual going legal scheme of things. So that if the newer Jurisprudence, following its basic approaches of a realistic *fresh* look at what goes on, and a *sustained* effort to account for *all* of it, can open up these crafts for communicable study, it will be offering real help. . . .

But much more troublesome to understanding than any accident of any individual's phrasing, are the facts of the work and thought of lawyers at large. Lawyers think law, lawyers argue law in court. And the job of a lawyer is to show how the goal of "justice" in his case can be attained within the framework of the law. And—a point to which we shall recur in a moment, a vital point— the fact is that in a huge number of cases *there is enough leeway and give within the framework of our law* to allow of what is felt as justice being attained in the case without departing from that framework. This fact means that when a lawyer openly argues "Justice" as a major argument, instead of arguing law first and justice as showing what the "true" rule or principle or application of the law must be seen to be, then that lawyer is practically advising the court either that he has not thought the law of his case out, and made clear its bearing on his case, and so ought not to be seriously listened to; or else he is advising the court that his case really falls outside what is proper for a court to remedy. But this means, in turn, that when a lawyer is thinking about the use and work of "law", in general and in the large, it is law-in-rules which comes to his mind, and the slogans about "decision dictated by the rule of law", and "laws and not men" loom ten times as large in his mind as even the best slogan about needed change in rules, and justice in individual cases, could hope to loom. For the very changes that he urges in actual argument are urged nine times out of ten as *already* clearly "law." It is only in the particular, when the lawyer is thinking about how to shape up in some one case actually in hand, that the felt justice of his cause, the need for making the court see and feel that his client is *right,* looms large in his mind; and even then, it looms as a problem in fact, not as a problem in law.

I wish I had the skill to make this clear. For it is simple fact that when men think consciously about a problem in its general aspects—such as the problem of what rules of law do, what effect they have on courts, what effect they ought to have, and indeed, under our legal system which works on "right rules" and "true rules", what effect they must have—it is simple fact that when men start to wrestle with such a problem, they think especially about the *parts* of that problem which are intellectually hard and intellectually articulate, about the parts which call for research and careful planning, and most especially about the parts to deal with which they must resort to books and to the definite, printed word. The rest of what goes into the problem they mostly forget, or else assume; in any event they do not talk or write about it. So that the very lawyer who is most careful about the "atmosphere" of his every case, and who most deftly works each time to make the court feel justice on his side of it, to make the court want to accept his good and solid line of legal argument and reject his adversary's line of legal argument (which really, just as legal argument, is about as good and solid as his own)—that same lawyer will be telling you next day that it was the rules which decided that case; he "simply" got the court to "see" "the true" rule and its bearing. But if he is right in this, then a less skilful lawyer entrusted with the case might have lost it; and then the "true" rule would have turned out to be a different rule, at least for that case, perhaps for the whole line of cases: "settled in this State," thereafter. Indeed, it is a rare lawyer who has lost a case who does not feel that the court in deciding against him "departed" from the "clear" rule; but he does not feel that the courts make a practice of so departing—except in the cases he loses. . . .

Hence, and naturally, the newer Jurisprudence began just here, began as a lawyer's Jurisprudence, built on worry over lawyers' needs in dealing with lawyers' problems about lawyers' *individual* cases: "The prophecies of what the courts will do in fact" is language addressed to the counsellor. But the newer Jurisprudence, wherever it begins, cannot fulfill its mission if it stops with the counsellor—though I should hate to see it leave off its interest in his work. There follows at once an interest in law from the angle of the advocate and his work—an angle revealing, among other things, the extraordinary leeway which our legal system allows in the particular case for reaching *either* result contended for, and for reaching either of those results "*under law.*" There follows then, and no less, and indeed inescapably, an interest in the judge and his work. . . .

But obviously the branch of Jurisprudence which is concerned with the *judge* and the *judge's work* must see the judge in a wholly different light. A counsellor has to worry over what a judge will do, whether that doing is right or whether it is not right; right or wrong, it decides a case; right or wrong, decent or indecent, it may make or remake a rule. For a counsellor at work on counselling, what the courts *do* is thus the most important part of law; whether, I repeat, the doing is right or not. But *judges* (trial judges or appellate) cannot see law that way, nor can jurisprudes when they are working over either of the judge's functions see law that way, nor can citizens, as citizens, see law that way (though, as interested parties, they will do well to see law in fair part that way). This is not to say that the "Prediction-of-official-action" way of seeing law is a bad way or a wrong way to see law; it is to say that the prediction way is an *incomplete* way to see law. Indeed, and on the other hand, it would be an incomplete way for even a judge to see law, if he should ignore this matter of what courts will do, and sometimes do wrongly; for their doing—even wrongly—is likely to make positive law which later courts have to attend to; and what an upper court will do is what determines prospective affirmance or reversal of the court below. For all this, the branch of Jurisprudence which deals with the judge and his function must center no less upon the "just" solution than upon the solution which other courts will reach, or even that which the rules of law may seem to indicate. It must center no less upon that ideal and duty of the judge's office which requires that somehow he is to arrive at a just outcome in the case before him than upon that ideal which requires that he stay within and follow the scheme of our prevailing law.

And by revealing this double job—imposed upon him by our legal system *as* a double job—by revealing this as peculiarly the job of the judge (or indeed of any responsible administrative official) the newer Jurisprudence seems to me to get the whole matter a step further toward clarity and toward guidance. When we stop talking just about "Law" in the large and what "Law" —in the vague indefiniteness of "All Law at once"—is and does, then certainty of prediction for a counsellor can stop getting all confused with good guidance for the judge, and then the judge's peculiar problems, at trial or on appeal, come into much clearer focus. The Jurisprudence of advocacy makes clear that the rules of law as we have them do not alone provide certainty of prediction, or opposing counsel just could not make worthwhile arguments on two sides of the same case. The Jurisprudence of advocacy thus centers attention upon the need for the judge to get some guidance and help in *choosing between two tenable lines of legal argument from the authorities. Over and above the guidance and partial control given by the rules of law which we have, there is further guidance needed.* Rules giving that further guidance—rules akin to, but deeper than, our rules on use of precedent—need articulation, and are in process of getting that articulation, and of providing the further guidance which we need. And that is a problem that does not come out of hiding for sustained and articulate and rational study until we observe that the mere rules of law, in their combination, and indeed in their language, speak to the particular case so very often with a forked tongue. Any advance the newer Jurisprudence can make along this line will rather obviously advance certainty in the results of law and further the articulate rational guidance of decision—a certainty and articulate guidance which we now have less of than we need, because of our overemphasis on the rules of law alone as being *the* great factor, the *only* observable and recordable factor, and hence the *only* rationally manipulable factor, which controls judges—and other officials. . . .

The philosophy of this can be stated briefly: Legal doctrine cannot wisely attempt to achieve what is impossible of achievement. To make courts either stand still or ignore the justice of the case in hand is impossible. (It is also undesirable.) Doctrine which purports to cut down all freedom of the judge or other official is therefore unserviceable doctrine. In practice, it leads to the production and use of *de facto* leeways which *de jure* are left unmentioned; and *de facto* but unmentioned leeways are both confusing and not subject to easy control. But to merely see this and then insist that judges—and other officials—are in fact as free to move as the *rules of law now leave* them whenever they really *want* to move; or to insist that they *ought* to use all the freedom which the rules of law now leave them—either of these things is to make doctrine fit only for the super judges, the Mansfields and Marshalls, and not for the McWhirtles and McWhortles who, though good and solid men, do yet need guidance and may sometimes need control. To see just what we have, in the way of either control or guidance, is a job for realistic observation, observation of fact, of detailed fact, observation which cuts beneath formula, sustained observation. To see just what is needed, in control of freedom to be arbitrary, while leaving the necessary freedom to be just, is a job for such observation plus legal statesmanship. To formulate for practical use rules and principles which can help materially in accomplishing the desired gain in both certainty and justice, is a job for legal engineering. The task is not chimerical, because we know that there can be training for the art of advocacy; the Greeks accomplished that, and so did the Scholastics. We know, too, that there can be training for counselling; the offices "break men in," year by year. *Some* of the art of advocacy, *some* of the art of counselling, can be reduced to helpful rules and principles. Judging, too, is a craft and art of law. Well, then?

The "Well, then?" is a challenge, not a performance. The newer Jurisprudence is yet far from having worked out with clarity the relation, in the judge's actual work, of the ideal and ideological elements in our legal system to the words of the rules of law, or the relation of either of these to the going institutional practices of courts and judges. That is a plain next problem for study. The newer Jurisprudence can claim to have gotten it into the clear, to be seen as a problem. That is not too much. But what there is of it, is good.

Another problem, on which a beginning has been made, is the examination of the three major aspects of the judge, and of their relations to one another in his work. He is a *human being,* and in our system he is an American. He is a *lawyer,* and in our system he is a common-lawyer. He is a *judge,* and in our system a common-law judge of the modern American type—which is very different not only from being a Continental or English judge, but also from being merely an American, or merely a lawyer, or merely an American lawyer. Some of the older Jurisprudence is written as if a judge were practically nothing but a mechanical lawyer on a bench; some of the newer reads almost as if he were nothing but a human American in a black robe. Neither of these points of view is to be simply scorned, because there are facts under each; but no such point of view, *alone,* has value as more than a reminder that certain very real factors in the picture are never to be forgotten.

(33)

Thurman Arnold

1891-

Thurman Arnold has had a distinguished career as lawyer, teacher, and public servant. Educated at Princeton and Yale, he received a law degree from Harvard and practiced law in Wyoming until 1927. He then accepted a professorship in the Yale Law School, following which he held a series of positions in the federal government, including service as Assistant Attorney General and Associate Justice of the United States Court of Appeals. He is at present practicing law in New York City.

Politically, Arnold gave full support to the New and Fair Deals. He believed, as the selection indicates, that an elaborate mythology had grown up around American capitalism, and that this agreed-upon fiction had long ceased to reflect the reality of the American economic system. His observations strike at the heart of many of the inherited economic ideas of America.

This selection is from his best-known book, *The Folklore of Capitalism* (New Haven, 1937).

☆　☆　☆　☆

The confusion in political thinking which we have just described arose out of the gradual decay of an old legal and economic religion. The difficulty with the religion was that it had become an obstacle to the organizing ability of the American people. It was producing phobias instead of inspiration. Economic principles had become an arsenal of weapons used against new organizations instead of for them. Governmental morality had become an excuse for government not to meet obvious demands.

In a period when rational philosophies of government were necessary for our comfort, everyone was demanding a new creed; yet every new creed advanced violated the old ideals which were still sacred. This is usual in times of social change. It is one of the inevitable symptoms of progress from one form of social organization to another. The literature of the time is typical of any similar age which is experiencing a conflict between its ideals and its needs.

The most obvious conflict of 1937 was that in which the creeds accepted by respectable people described social organizations in the language of personally owned private property, when as a matter of fact the things which were described were neither private, nor property, nor personally owned. The complete failure of the language of law and economics as a means of communication of sensible ideas created the endless debate about principle and the exhortations to heed the lessons of history which we have been observing in courts, in colleges, and in the editorial pages of newspapers. Before analyzing the failure of our economic and legal language as a means of communication of practical ideas it is first necessary, at the risk of repetition, to discover why old gods always thrash around so violently before they die, and why most respectable people become so uncomfortable in the process.

The Discomfort of a Changing Mythology

The reason for this confusion which attends the growth of new organizations in society lies deep in the psychology which concerns the effects of words and ceremonies on the habits of men in groups. Men always idealize these habits and the structure they give to society. The idealizing is done by magic words which at first are reasonably descriptive of the institutions they represent. At least they represent the dreams which men have of those institutions. When the institutions themselves disappear, the words still remain and make men think that the institutions are still with them. They talk of the new organizations which have come to take the place of the old in the terms of these old words. The old words no longer fit. Directions given in that language no longer have the practical results which are expected. Realists arise to point this out and men who love and reverence these old words (that is, the entire God-fearing, respectable element of the community) are shocked. Since the words are heavily charged with a moral content, those who do not respect them are immoral. The respectable moral element of society will have nothing to do with such immorality. They feel compelled to turn the power over to nonrespectable people in order to reserve the right to make faces at them. Yet they recognize that those immoral people are doing something which has to be done. This fact can only be explained under the curious age-old concept of sin. No religion ever got along without this concept. It is useful because everyone can continue to work to abolish it, knowing full well their objective will never be reached. Thus, in these times of confusion, everyone believes that human character is disintegrating. This happens whenever the rising generation thinks differently from the old.

By this process the formulas become more important than facts. They cease to be tools and become objectives in themselves. Legal and economic literature (or whatever other ceremony is current in such times) becomes more important than life. And in the confusion which results from this conflict respectable men become angry, sad, romantic, cynical, disillusioned, last-ditch defenders of a faith. They do not become cheerful, practical technicians dealing with the facts before them.

In such times men get to talking about the decline and fall of civilization and worrying about Greece and Rome. A vast literature of explanation and exhortation pours forth. This is a symptom that the class which produces that literature is becoming uneasy and impotent and needs a great deal of printed matter in order to prove to itself that it still represents the only sound type of organization. The blame for that uneasiness is all ascribed to the immorality of a society which has perversely and sinfully become unlike the little ideal pictures which represent what a proper society should be like. At such times men predict Fascism, Communism, and all sorts of similar catastrophes. They prove this by putting it on the printed page, because they have more faith in the printed page than in the spoken word.

The result of this uneasiness may be war, or may be only a lot of oratory, poetry, and romantic economics. What happens depends on whether the kindly, tolerant, respectable elements of society are able to emerge from this mood of impotence before less kindly and tolerant people seize the reins of power. The mood does little harm if it is only a temporary escape from reality, like being in love, or mourning for the dead. Indeed, it would be a drab human race which did not shed a tear over departed institutions. Romantic lovers and inconsolable widows are both very lovely dramatizations of important ideals and the writer would not abolish them if he could. Nevertheless, it is an incontestable fact that they are hard people to put up with outside of books and when there is a job to be done.

The Mythology of Private Property in an Age of Organization

Why has the literature of law and economics become today more like a funeral service than the pep talk for salesmen which it should be to promote organization? The reason is that it is using the little pictures of private property and profit motive to describe a society which is much more like an army than the group of horse traders which it is supposed to be. Against the background of such a society the terms do not make sense. Men believe that a society is disintegrating when it can no longer be pictured in familiar terms. Unhappy is a people that has run out of words to describe what is going on.

It is obvious today that private property has disappeared. The writer, for example, owns some furniture which he can use without the assistance of any large organization, though not to the extent his parents could, because he is unable to repair it as his father was. For transportation he has an automobile, but he does not know what is going on under the hood and could not run it without a great organization to assist him. His father owned a western ranch and raised his own horses. These horses burned hay, but the hay did not come from a filling station, which in turn required a still larger organization to supply it. Yet today furniture and automobiles are the nearest we come to private property generally owned by any large group of our population.

The other things the writer "owns" are all claims to rank or privilege in an organizational hierarchy. He is a professor at the Yale Law School and hopes that Yale will feed and lodge him. He has a piece of paper from an insurance company which he hopes will induce that organization to take care of his wife if he dies. He has other pieces of paper from other organizations operating buildings and railroads and manufacturing plants which give him precarious privileges in those industrial governments. Wealth today consists in nothing any one individual can use. The standards of wealth are simply current expectations of how the individual stands with the rulers of industrial baronies coupled with a guess as to the strength of those principalities. . . .

The reason why old myths create such a problem in times when old institutions are not functioning effectively is that they induce men to act in direct contradiction to observed facts. Such conduct is of course one of the great cohesive forces of society, for when institutions are functioning effectively it is the power of superstition rather than the power of reason that holds them together. However, when the institutions have become impotent to meet social needs, these same superstitions have the effect of throwing respectable, moderate, and kindly people out of power because they cannot free themselves of the old myths long enough to be effective leaders. . . .

One of the essential and central notions which give our industrial feudalism logical symmetry is the personification of great industrial enterprise. The ideal that a great corporation is endowed with the rights and prerogatives of a free individual is as essential to the acceptance of corporate rule in temporal affairs as was the ideal of the divine right of kings in an earlier day. Its exemplification, as in the case of all vital ideals, has been accomplished by ceremony. Since it has been a central ideal in our industrial government, our judicial institutions have been particularly concerned with its celebration. Courts, under the mantle of the Constitution, have made a living thing out of this fiction. Men have come to believe that their own future liberties and dignity are tied up in the freedom of great industrial organizations from restraint, in much the same way that they thought their salvation in the future was dependent on their reverence and support of great ecclesiastical organizations in the Middle Ages. . . .

This book is not concerned with the unsolvable problem of whether America would have progressed faster or slower under some other set of myths. It does not attack the use of the corporate personality in folklore. The results have been the creation of one of the greatest productive machines that the world has ever known, and this perhaps is justification enough if anyone is interested in justifying what has happened. This book is concerned only with diagnosing the present difficulties which have come upon us now that the industrial feudalism is no longer protecting large groups of our citizens who demand security, and with trying to explain the ideological difficulties which prevent the creating of organizations which will give that protection. We cannot be practical about social problems if we are under the illusion that we can solve them without complying with the taboos and customs of the tribe. The corporate personality is part of our present religion. We must continue to refer to corporations as individuals in public discourse so long as the words have emotional relevance. Since, however, we must use the words and ceremonies, it becomes important that we be able to use them intelligently. . . .

Therefore, if one wishes to guess the social philosophy of the future, he must guess first what class will come into control of the organizations which make and distribute the goods and, second, whether the change will be violent or slow. If it is violent, a whole new set of terms will dramatize the sudden rise of the new organization to power. The old terms will flow back gradually during a period of confusion, while the new organizations fumble and fail as organizations always must fail to live up to the promises of their creed. And finally a note of positive affirmation will be heard which, like Lincoln's "Gettysburg Address," seems to link the new organizations to some heroic event in the past, to express the contradictory notions and ideals of the people, and to fill them with the pride and morale necessary for expansion.

If the rise of the new organization is slow, the terms will change their meaning, rather than be supplanted by new terms. Capitalism will become "socialistic" in a slow revolution. In a more violent one, "Capitalism" will be supplanted by "Socialism" and then in the period of stabilization "Socialism" will gradually become "capitalistic." This is what is happening in Russia. We can note today the charge being constantly made by those who were most idealistic about Socialism in Russia that the Communists are abandoning their ideals and "reverting" to Capitalism. In contrast to this we heard speeches *ad nauseam* in the last campaign that the New Deal was in devious and hidden ways making our capitalistic system socialistic. The observer who watches this process should never be alarmed about the "stupidity" of the so-called intelligent people who make speeches of this kind. It is part of the process of change in a rational world. All he needs to worry about is the character of the people who are gradually coming into power. Does he think that they are good organizers and at the same time tolerant and humanitarian? If he reaches this conclusion, he need not worry about "failure to balance the budget." All "balancing the budget" ever can mean is that an institution has achieved public acceptance of its objectives. If it has, there will never be any difficulty about balancing its budget.

(34)

David Riesman

1909-

Lawyer, educator, and social scientist, Riesman received his bachelor's degree from Harvard in 1931 and his law degree from Harvard Law School in 1934. In 1935 and 1936 he served as law clerk to Justice Brandeis, and since that time has held a number of academic positions. His work on *The Lonely Crowd* is a major study of the American character. The thesis of Riesman's study is that the national character has changed, that the older inner-directed, self-reliant individual has given way as a national type to the other-directed and socially oriented individual. In Riesman's terminology, the inner-directed person internalizes adult authority and society's standards of behavior, and judges himself and others out of his own resources. The other-directed person's character and behavior evolves from the examples of his peers and is "sensitized to the expectations" of these peers.

The selection that follows presents Riesman's thesis. It is taken from David Riesman, with Nathan Glazer and Reuel Denney, *The Lonely Crowd: A Study of the Changing American Character* (New Haven, 1950).

My concern in this book is with two revolutions and their relation to the "mode of conformity" or "social character" of Western man since the Middle Ages. The first of these revolutions has in the last four hundred years cut us off pretty decisively from the family- and clan-oriented traditional ways of life in which mankind has existed throughout most of history; this revolution includes the Renaissance, the Reformation, the Counter-Reformation, the Industrial Revolution, and the political revolutions of the seventeenth, eighteenth, and nineteenth centuries. This revolution is, of course, still in process, but in the most advanced countries of the world, and particularly in America, it is giving way to another sort of revolution—a whole range of social developments associated with a shift from an age of production to an age of consumption. The first revolution we understand moderately well; it is, under various labels, in our texts and our terminology; this book has nothing new to contribute to its description, but perhaps does contribute something to its evaluation. The second revolution, which is just beginning, has interested many contemporary observers, including social scientists, philosophers, and journalists. Both description and evaluation are still highly controversial; indeed, many are still preoccupied with the first set of revolutions and have not invented the categories for discussing the second set. In this book I try to sharpen the contrast between, on the one hand, conditions and character in those social strata that are today most seriously affected by the second revolution, and, on the other hand, conditions and character in analogous strata during the earlier revolution. . . .

My thesis is, in fact, that each of these three different phases on the population curve appears to be occupied by a society that enforces conformity and molds social character in a definably different way.

The society of high growth potential develops in its typical members a social character whose conformity is insured by their tendency to follow tradition: these I shall term *tradition-directed* people and the society in which they live a *society dependent on tradition-direction.*

The society of transitional population growth develops in its typical members a social character whose conformity is insured by their tendency to acquire early in life an internalized set of goals. These I shall term *inner-directed* people and the society in which they live a *society dependent on inner-direction.*

Finally, the society of incipient population decline develops in its typical members a social character whose conformity is insured by their tendency to be sensitized to the expectations and preferences of others. These I shall term *other-directed* people and the society in which they live one *dependent on other-direction.* . . .

A definition of other-direction. The type of character I shall describe as other-directed seems to be emerging in very recent years in the upper middle class of our larger cities: more prominently in New York than in Boston, in Los Angeles than in Spokane, in Cincinnati than in Chillicothe. Yet in some respects this type is strikingly similar to *the* American, whom Tocqueville and other curious and astonished visitors from Europe, even before the Revolution, thought to be a new kind of man. Indeed, travelers' reports on America impress us with their unanimity. The American is said to be shallower, freer with his money, friendlier, more uncertain of himself and his values, more demanding of approval than the European. It all adds up to a pattern which, without stretching matters too far, resembles the kind of character that a number of social scientists have seen as developing in contemporary, highly industrialized, and bureaucratic America: Fromm's "marketer," Mills's "fixer," Arnold Green's "middle class male child."[1]

It is my impression that the middle-class American of today is decisively different from those Americans of Tocqueville's writings who nevertheless strike us as so contemporary, and much of this book will be devoted to discussing these differences. It is also my impression that the conditions I believe to be responsible for other-direction are affecting increasing numbers of people

---

1. See Erich Fromm, *Man for Himself;* C. Wright Mills, "The Competitive Personality," *Partisan Review,* XIII (1946), 433; Arnold Green, "The Middle Class Male Child and Neurosis," *American Sociological Review,* XI (1946), 31. See also the work of Jurgen Ruesch, Martin B. Loeb, and co-workers on the "infantile personality."

in the metropolitan centers of the advanced industrial countries. My analysis of the other-directed character is thus at once an analysis of the American and of contemporary man. Much of the time I find it hard or impossible to say where one ends and the other begins. Tentatively, I am inclined to think that the other-directed type does find itself most at home in America, due to certain unique elements in American society, such as its recruitment from Europe and its lack of any feudal past. As against this, I am also inclined to put more weight on capitalism, industrialism, and urbanization—these being international tendencies—than on any character-forming peculiarities of the American scene. . . .

From bringing up children to "Bringing up Father." The typical other-directed child grows up in a small family, in close urban quarters, or in a suburb. Even more than in the earlier epoch the father leaves home to go to work, and he goes too far to return for lunch. Home, moreover, is no longer an area of solid privacy. As the size and living space of the family diminish and as the pattern of living with older relatives declines, the child must directly face the emotional tensions of his parents. There is a heightening of awareness of the self in relation to others under these conditions, especially since the parents, too, are increasingly self-conscious.

Under the new social and economic conditions, the position of children rises. They are not subjected to a period of deprivation and hardship which leads to compensatory dreams of a life of ease and pleasure. Girls are not, as they were in some earlier societies, drudges at home until, at puberty, they were suddenly given the only "capital" they were ever likely to find—that of their bodies—to live on as income, or exhaust as principal. Even boys from comfortable homes were expected until recently to hit the sunrise trail with paper routes or other economically profitable and "character-building" chores.

The parents lack not only the self-assurance that successful inner-direction brings but also the strategy of withdrawal available to many unsuccessful inner-directed types. The loss of old certainties in the spheres of work and social relations is accompanied by doubt as to how to bring up children. Moreover, the parents no longer feel themselves superior to the children. While children no longer have immediate economic value, they are less numerous, "scarcer" in relation to the number of adults: the effort is made, and it is objectively possible, to want all children who are conceived and to raise very nearly all children who are born. More is staked on every single child than in the earlier epoch when many children were not raised to maturity. In addition, apart from the fact that the children may be better Americans than the parents, in ethnic or social terms—as Jiggs's daughter is more up to date than he—there are undoubtedly other solid reasons (which I shall not go into) for the general emphasis on youth which runs through all forms of popular culture.[2]

Historical changes in the lives of adolescents can be seen most clearly, perhaps, if one looks back to those *Bildungsromane* of the nineteenth century that

---

2. This, too, is a development whose importance Margaret Mead has stressed. See *And Keep Your Powder Dry* (New York, William Morrow, 1942).

described the misunderstood youth who struggled against the harsh or hypocritical tyranny of his parents, particularly if one compares one of the best of such novels, Samuel Butler's *The Way of All Flesh,* with one of the best of our contemporary examples, for instance Lionel Trilling's short story, "The Other Margaret."[3] In Trilling's story we have a picture of a precocious young girl in the intellectual, urban, upper middle class. Margaret, who goes to a progressive school, believes that Negroes are exploited, and she resents the inferior position in the home of "the other Margaret," a Negro domestic. It is the daughter Margaret who is self-righteous, not the parents.

In the face of her criticism, buttressed as it is by the authority of the school, the parents, themselves progressive, are on the defensive. They are tense and very much concerned with what their daughter thinks—and thinks of them. Eventually, all three adults manage to destroy Margaret's illusion of the virtues of the other Margaret—the parents by reasoning; the other Margaret by bad behavior. But in the end the parents are anxious about their victory, lest it harm their sensitive child. They possess little of the certainty and security of Theobald's parents in *The Way of All Flesh.*

In this change of parental attitude the mass media of communication play a dual role. From the mass media—radio, movies, comics—as well as from their own peers, children can easily learn what the norm of parental behavior is, and hold it over their parents' heads. Thus a kind of realism is restored to the child which was his property much more simply in the societies depending on tradition-direction: the other-directed child is often more knowing than his parents—like the proverbial Harvard man, there is little they can tell *him.* . . .

In these [illustrations] I have set forth some thoughts about the middle-class world of work and play, in the hope of finding ways in which a more autonomous type of social character might develop. I cannot be satisfied that I have moved very far along these lines. It is difficult enough to consider how we may remove the barriers of false personalization and enforced privatization. It is enormously more difficult to descry, after these barriers are overcome, what in man may lead him to autonomy, or to invent and create the means that will help him to autonomy. In the end, our few suggestions are paltry ones, and we can only conclude our discussion by saying that a vastly greater stream of creative, utopian thinking is needed before we can see more clearly the goal we dimly suggest by the word "autonomy."

The reader who recalls our beginnings with the large, blind movements of population growth and economic and technological change may ask whether we seriously expect utopian thinking, no matter how inspired, to counter whatever fate for man these movements have in store. Indeed, I believe that only certain ideas will be generated and catch on, under any given socioeconomic conditions. And character, with all its intractabilities and self-reproducing

---

3. *Partisan Review,* XII (1945), 381.

tendencies, will largely dictate the way ideas are received. But despite the massed obstacles to change inherent in social structure and character structure, I believe that ideas can make a decisive historical contribution. Marx, who himself denied that ideas are very important and dismissed the utopian speculations of his predecessor socialists, himself supplied an irrefutable example of the power of ideas in history. As we all know, he did not leave the working class to be emancipated only by events. In his alternate role as propagandist, he tried himself to shape the ideological and institutional environment in which workers would live.

I think we need to insist today on bringing to consciousness the kind of environments that Marx dismissed as "utopian," in contrast to the mechanical and passive approach to the possibilities of man's environment that he helped, in his most influential works, to foster. However, since we live in a time of disenchantment, such thinking, where it is rational in aim and method and not simply escapism, is not easy. It is easier to concentrate on programs for choosing among lesser evils. We are well aware of the "damned wantlessness of the poor"; the rich as well, as I have tried to show in this book, have inhibited their claims for a decent world. But rich and poor avoid any goals, personal or social, that seem out of step with peer-group aspirations. The politically operative inside-dopester seldom commits himself to aims beyond those that common sense proposes to him. Actually, however, in a dynamic political context, it is the modest, commonsensical goals of the insiders and the "constructive" critics that are unattainable. It often seems that the retention of a given status quo is a modest hope; many lawyers, political scientists, and economists occupy themselves by suggesting the minimal changes which are necessary to stand still; yet today this hope is almost invariably disappointed; the status quo proves the most illusory of goals.

Is it conceivable that these economically privileged Americans will some day wake up to the fact that they overconform? Wake up to the discovery that a host of behavioral rituals are the result, not of an inescapable social imperative but of an image of society that, though false, provides certain "secondary gains" for the people who believe in it? Since character structure is, if anything, even more tenacious than social structure, such an awakening is exceedingly unlikely—and we know that many thinkers before us have seen the false dawns of freedom while their compatriots stubbornly continued to close their eyes to the alternatives that were, in principle, available. But to put the question may at least raise doubts in the minds of some.

Occasionally city planners put such questions. They comprise perhaps the most important professional group to become reasonably weary of the cultural definitions that are systematically trotted out to rationalize the inadequacies of city life today, for the well-to-do as well as for the poor. With their imagination and bounteous approach they have become, to some extent, the guardians of our liberal and progressive political tradition, as this is increasingly displaced from state and national politics. In their best work, we see expressed in physical form a view of life which is not narrowly job-minded.

It is a view of the city as a setting for leisure and amenity as well as for work. But at present the power of the local veto groups puts even the most imaginative of city planners under great pressure to show that they are practical, hardheaded fellows, barely to be distinguished from traffic engineers.

However, just as there is in my opinion a greater complexity of leisure response in contemporary America than appears on the surface, so also the sources of utopian political thinking may be hidden and constantly changing, constantly disguising themselves. While political curiosity and interest have been largely driven out of the accepted sphere of the political in recent years by the "crisis" mood of the press and of the more responsible sectors of public life, people may, in what is left of their private lives, be nurturing newly critical and creative standards. If these people are not strait-jacketed before they get started—by the elaboration and forced feeding of a set of official doctrines—people may some day learn to buy not only packages of groceries or books but the "larger package" of a neighborhood, a society, and a way of life.

If the other-directed people should discover how much needless work they do, discover that their own thoughts and their own lives are quite as interesting as other people's, that, indeed, they no more assuage their loneliness in a crowd of peers than one can assuage one's thirst by drinking sea water, then we might expect them to become more attentive to their own feelings and aspirations.

This possibility may sound remote, and perhaps it is. But undeniably many currents of change in America escape the notice of the reporters of this best-reported nation on earth. We have inadequate indexes for the things we would like to find out, especially about such intangibles as character, political styles, and leisure uses. America is not only big and rich, it is mysterious; and its capacity for the humorous or ironical concealment of its interests matches that of the legendary inscrutable Chinese. By the same token, what my collaborators and I have to say may be very wide of the mark. Inevitably, our own character, our own geography, our own illusions, limit our view.

But while I have said many things in this book of which I am unsure, of one thing I am sure: the enormous potentialities for diversity in nature's bounty and men's capacity to differentiate their experience can become valued by the individual himself, so that he will not be tempted and coerced into adjustment or, failing adjustment, into anomie. The idea that men are created free and equal is both true and misleading: men are created different; they lose their social freedom and their individual autonomy in seeking to become like each other.

VII

Voices of Discontent

FROM THE FOUNDING of the Republic, popular protest movements have always arisen to criticize the course of American social and economic development. In Jefferson's time, the mercantile class was the popular enemy. In Jackson's day, it was the banking power and special economic privilege. Similarly, after the Civil War, it was the large corporation and industrial entrepreneur that led to organized protest in the form of the Greenback, free silver, and labor movements, as well as the emergence of a group of reformers who hoped to eliminate the inequities and evils that existed in American society. In the 1890's the widespread agrarian unrest in the West and South found expression in populism. And in the early twentieth century the progressive and the socialist movements represented the forces of protest.

Most of these movements, despite their apparent radicalism, were within the American tradition. They did not draw very much of their inspiration from the ideologies of European discontent. Concern over the plight of the farmer and his worsening economic position had solid roots in an old agrarian tradition. The agrarian revolt of the late nineteenth century never threatened private property; it was, in fact, a movement to preserve it. The progressive movement of the early twentieth century also aimed largely at preserving the basic framework of American society by reforming its glaring defects.

In contrast to these earlier protest movements, the depression of the 1930's saw a chorus of voices proclaiming the hopelessness of American capitalism. While disagreeing violently as to proposed solutions, many people were in agreement that only a thoroughgoing reform of the basic structure of American society could alleviate the poverty, suffering, and misery of a large segment of the population.

Because of the suffering, anxiety, and despair of the 1930's, movements of the far left, such as communism, as well as those of the extreme right, including fascism, gained many converts as the depression seemed to worsen despite the efforts of the New Deal to rebuild and transform American society. Some Americans turned to the Communist party in the sincere and idealistic belief that only state ownership and control of the means of production and distribution could solve the problems of poverty and unemployment. Others, seizing upon scapegoats in the form of minority groups or radical protest movements, turned ironically to fascism in order to preserve America's cherished values.

During the 1930's, as a matter of fact, a searching critique of American society was undertaken, and various proposals were offered. As Frederick Lewis Allen pointed out in *Only Yesterday* (1940), the common denominator of all of these movements, whether of the left, center, or right, was social-mindedness—the hope of salvation not so much for individuals, but for groups and the entire nation, to be achieved through organized group action. Through the fabric of American society also ran an undercurrent of fear—fear that the promise of America had proved an illusion. In the midst of such strong tensions and social misery, it was not surprising that radical protest movements gained a large audience.

In the long run, however, Americans on the whole avoided extreme solutions, either of the right or the left. Instead they attempted to solve their problems by invoking the national power in a nondoctrinaire, pragmatic way, and this power, in turn, was used mainly to shore up and renew traditional ideals.

(35)

Charles E. Coughlin

1891-

Born in Canada, Charles E. Coughlin was ordained in the Roman Catholic priesthood in 1916 after study at the University of Toronto and St. Michael's College. In 1926 he was appointed pastor of the Shrine of the Little Flower at Royal Oak, Michigan. An effective speaker, Coughlin's nationwide radio addresses after 1930 attracted national attention and he soon had a wide following. In these talks he warned of the dangers of communism and offered in its stead a philosophy that moved steadily toward the political right. He supported Franklin Delano Roosevelt during his first two years in office but became a bitter, outspoken foe of the President thereafter. Coughlin's political and economic doctrines were expressed in his magazine *Social Justice,* which enjoyed wide circulation until it was finally barred from the mails in 1942 because of its pro-German sympathies. Father Coughlin himself in the meanwhile had been silenced by his ecclesiastical superiors.

The speech reprinted here is from *Father Coughlin's Radio Discourses, 1931–1932* (Royal Oak, Michigan, 1932).

☆ ☆ ☆ ☆

The old cry of "God give us bread" has been changed in one sense in our day to "God give us work."

Changed, said I? Most certainly. Cargoes of bananas are dumped into the Atlantic Ocean because the market is overstocked with them. Wheat fields are reduced to ashes because it does not pay to harvest them. Calves and sheep are slaughtered in the pastures because there is no gain in fattening them. Potatoes sell at fifteen cents a bushel in Michigan—hardly worth the effort to dig them. Fruit is given away for the picking of it in our orchards. Cotton is rotting in the store houses of Louisiana!

In the midst of this entire depression Almighty God, as it were, has spoken to us and said: "You have tried to get along without Me during your proud period of the nineteenth and twentieth centuries' capitalism. The lessons learned from the World War have been of no avail. The burlesquerie enacted by the Treaty of Versailles has failed to teach you and the comedy of your League of Nations which during its short expanse of existence has witnessed more wars, more upheavals and more international strife ever before in the history of the world is still unadmitted by you.

"You have rejected My principles of justice and generosity and charity. In turn I will send you a super-abundance of all things material. I will load your banks with gold. I will store your granaries with wheat. I will bless every endeavor put forth by the farmer. But in the midst of it all you are helpless because you still prefer your man made principles of legalized injustice and organized greed. Without Me you can do nothing."

My friends, in nowise are these days of pessimism. At least we have learned to face facts which is a considerable progress. Our lamp of hope has not been shattered. When the midnight of darkness comes upon us, it is then that we see more clearly the pale flickering of its tiny flame. The world speaks of the re-establishment of credit. Our own Chief Executive has done well in his promotion of it.

After all this thing called credit is more closely related to the virtue called charity than one would suspect. Slowly but surely are we determined to pursue that thin candle light of hope from this humble beginning until the full glow of the glorious morn will arrive; until hope will have matured unto its realization; until the candle flame will have burst into a sunrise!

Therefore, with honest expectancy we look forward to that happy day when the abuses which have grown around our system of capitalism will be eliminated.

The concentration of wealth in the hands of a few will no longer be tolerable. A system which produces chronic idleness for millions of our fellow citizens must be corrected. An industrial policy which does not provide for a yearly wage and for an opportunity for every willing worker to labor must be abolished. And a financial theory which does not guarantee to a depositor in a bank that he can get his money out of it as easily as he put it into it must be classified with nothing less than high brow racketeering.

International diplomacy which is builded only on the foundation of fostering international investments, caring little about the sacredness of human life and the pursuits of common happiness, must be retired. The definition of capital in terms only of gold or of silver must be rewritten until it embraces homes and farm lands and cherished possessions which are more sacred than pound sterling or metal coin.

A system of taxation which so penalizes an agriculturist or a city laborer to the extent that it is far cheaper to rent rather than to own must be remodeled. A philosophy of industrialism which looks askance upon the organization of the laborer into peaceful unions or Christian societies must be scuttled. Despotic domination over the necessities of life; unbridled competition amongst mass productionists; the fierce battle to acquire control of the State on the part of the money lords; the sophistry often choked down our throats that State ownership of public utilities is necessarily extreme socialism; the contention that the head of a State or a Government must hold his office to protect the factions of financial greed and industrial passion who elected him, caring little for the common good; in a word, man's inhumanity to man and man's effort to get along without God and His principles must be eliminated from the sphere of the civilized world.

These are the immoral elements which must be cleansed from the Augean stables of our national life even before we care to turn the corner of prosperity. Temporizers may induce a sort of new prosperity with their hypodermic needle similar to the policy of a physician who feeds the dope fiend cocaine. But today we are bent upon removing the causes which will permanently remove the renewal of these sordid effects. . . .

During these past few years we in America have been taught to regard ourselves as the chosen people of the god of materialism.

There was painted for us a panorama of resplendent prosperity. We marveled at the prodigious accumulation of wealth. We witnessed vast tracts of virgin land reclaimed from the wilderness. We beheld the utilization of steam and electricity which have become commonly adopted, and we rejoiced in the multiplication of labor saving devices whose main purpose and object was to lift the burden of labor from the hands of weary men.

Like a new god, the siren voice of American prosperity announced to the world: *"Come unto me all ye who are heavily burdened and I will refresh you."*

And why not take refuge within the embrace of those arms of wealth and power? Had not our bankers and economists portrayed for us our superiority over the rest of the world?

There were India and China, Abyssinia and Afghanistan—thousands of square miles of ancient dynasties upon whose mighty breasts were nurtured two-thirds and more of the world's population. What had these nations accomplished? Their citizens were burdened by the yoke of a so-called civilization which was reminiscent of the days of slavery, days of thankless, worthless toil.

And what for the history of America? In its short life of one hundred fifty years it had witnessed more material progress than had Asia in the past one hundred fifty centuries. Here was liberty. There was slavery. Here, labor saving inventions had lightened the toil and had improved the living conditions of everyone of our citizens. The steamship took the place of the slow sailing vessel. The railroad train and the automobile supplanted the obsolete wagon. The scythe had given way to the reaping machine; the flail, to the threshing machine.

Great turbine engines and harnessed Niagaras were throbbing night and day producing power greater than all men and all beasts of burden on the earth combined. A thousand pairs of shoes where the old time cobbler made but one spring into being; factories where under the watchful eye of a simple girl, cotton becomes cloth faster than hundreds of stalwart weavers could have turned it out with their clumsy looms; mammoth shafts and mighty anchors, motor cars and miles of concrete for them to ride upon—all of these are fabricated and manufactured with a speed and a quantity almost unbelievable.

"Behold these!" says the economist. "They are the offspring of the new god of prosperity. These are the children of progress."

"Progress" so insists the industrialist, the economist, and the international banker!

"Poetry" so speaks the jobless man in the street, the dispossessed farmer, and the ten thousand who are wincing under a system that refuses to face facts while their homes are being confiscated and their families are starving under a condition of chronic unemployment and of irrational taxation which penalizes tremendously a home owner!

Well, my friends, it is not my purpose to review for you any further this epic of American progress. Nor is it my purpose to recite for you the limitations of a so-called depression. The progress with its machinery is here to remain. The depression with its poverty is, if you will it, on the wane.

Napoleon once characterized England as a nation of shopkeepers. Were the "Little Corporal" living today perhaps he would say that America was nothing more than a nation of factory hands. As a matter of fact the United States is capable of supplying two-thirds of the machined products of the entire world. One hundred twenty million people occupied either directly or indirectly in supplying the mechanical necessities of one billion people!

As far back as the year 1914 the United States had attained leadership in manufacturing. Our methods of mass production enabled us to undersell practically every competitor.

That was the year when the factory worker's salary was raised to five dollars a day: an event that astounded the world! The Irish and the Polish peasant, the Italian and German farmer were under the impression that the streets of America were paved with gold. Five dollars a day! And this seventeen years ago!

No wonder that our factories multiplied. No wonder cities like Detroit grew from five hundred thousand to a million five hundred thousand. The world was waiting for our produce. It was our business to supply it as speedily as possible. Night and day the motors hummed. Shift followed shift. Day wages gave way to hourly wage. Hourly wages succumbed to the piece-work wage. The five dollars a day oftentimes mounted to ten and fifteen and eighteen dollars a day. America must supply the waiting world. New machines must replace the inept hands of the obsolete craftsman.

In this mad rush for efficiency and production there was scarcely a competition to be feared. Asia still dwelt in the sleep of the tenth century. Europe had not progressed beyond the early nineteenth century. South America and Africa and Australia were still in their pioneering days. We of the United States were lords of the world! . . .

Needless to say, we are confronted with perhaps the greatest moral problem of the age when we pause to face these facts. To express the problem in plain English may I put it in the form of a question: *"Under the present conditions of mass productionism is it not moral to affirm that the laborer must be guaranteed a fair, permanent and equitable wage despite the tremendous productive power of modern machinery?"* That is the question. The answer of the Catholic Church to it is a most emphatic *"Yes."*

Now associated with this thought is the unassailable and Christian theory that it is the business of government—especially a government that boasts of being of the people, by the people and for the people—to interest itself in maintaining the permanence of occupation for the ninety-six per cent of its population who belong either to the laboring or to the farming class, and to insist that the laborer is worthy of his hire. This permanence of labor is the root and basic question of all economics. This is the necessary and fundamental moral issue of our day that must be solved if our nation will endure.

No government except one that is partial and blinded will bend its major effort in caring only for the capitalist or the financier. Such efforts remind one of curing a broken leg by poulticing the head. An equal effort, at least, must be expended in guaranteeing permanent work for every man who is willing to work. What good is the wealth accumulated in the hands of a few unless their fellow citizens are living in peace and contentment? Of what use are the mass production machines unless the citizens of our nation are possessed of sufficient money to purchase the products thereof? In what nation has the right to private ownership ever been called into question except where the right to labor has been denied? Neither revolution nor banditry nor socialism thrives in a nation where there is work for the laborer who is worthy of his hire.

The right to work is as sacred as the right to own one's property. In fact the right to private ownership depends in one sense upon the right to work.

Without labor that is done by the sweat of the citizens' brows neither coal nor iron, neither silver nor gold can be fetched from the bowels of the earth. Without this labor the wheat fields will still be wild prairies and the cotton fields nothing but stamping grounds for herds of buffalo. Labor must precede capital. It is prior to it and capital depends upon it more so in that sense than labor depends upon capital.

These materials of metal and the produce of the field have from time immemorial been produced from the earth without the expenditure and assistance of so-called capital. I do not mean that labor and capital are independent of each other. I simply mean that labor must precede capital as it did in the days of the patriarchs; as it did in the days of our pioneer forefathers; and as it still does in the case of the hardy prospector and the homesteading farmer.

We have been living in an era which has been blind to this philosophy. An era which leaned towards the great immorality that labor entirely depends upon capital; and that capital must be protected at the expense of labor. As a result it has been an era bounded by the accumulation of untold wealth in the hands of the capitalists on the one side and on the other by the increase of forced idleness and starvation for the laborer. It has been an era that is forgetful of the basic law of life, the law of self-preservation.

Many eminent men among whom are Owen D. Young and Senator James Couzens, have expressed the thought that it is the business of industry or of capitalism to guarantee the care of the laboring class. In fact Mr. Young has gone further and has given expression to what many would call a radical thought when he said that industry belongs to the laborer. To use his exact words he visualized the *"day when human beings will be engaged in a particular undertaking so that they truly will be the employer buying capital as a commodity in the market at the lowest price . . . and when they will be entitled to all the profits over the cost of capital."* This is just the reversal of the conditions now existing. Today capital buys labor as if it were a commodity. At any rate, my friends, the laborer has a right to a just and a living wage. . . .

In modern times Pius XI, the leader of Catholic thought and the Head of the Catholic Faith, has said: *"Every effort, therefore, must be made that at least in future a just share only of the fruits of production be permitted to accumulate in the hands of the wealthy, and that an ample sufficiency be supplied to the workingman."*

These are not my words, my friends. They are the words of one who rules over the destiny of over three hundred million Roman Catholics. He is not a socialist nor a disciple of Karl Marx. He is the follower and representative of Jesus Christ. It is he who insists that only a just share of the fruits of production be permitted to accumulate in the hands of the wealthy. It is he who teaches the basic law of Christianity that an ample sufficiency be supplied to the workingman.

In spite of ourselves, or rather in spite of our political leaders, this depression is passing. But never more will the American workingman be content to sell his labor for a wage that is uncertain and for a remuneration that is insufficient.

This is the greatest profit which has accrued to the American laborer out of the sufferings through which he has passed. If he fails to reap the reward of his suffering and the lesson gained by his bitter experience, he needs to blame no one but himself as he continues to bear the burden of a slavery that is dressed up in the gaudy garments of liberty and prosperity.

The haphazard prosperity which we enjoyed in the days of no competition has passed. For the future there can be no other prosperity except that based upon Christian principles which are traceable to the first law of life—the law of self-preservation.

Thus, stoic complacency on the part of legislators must give way to Christian action. Actions, not words, are required! . . .

At any rate, my friends, it is childish for us as a democratic people to attribute all the ills and heartaches of our present distress to the inefficient leadership of our superiors. In this nation leaders rise from the ranks. From the humblest township official to the dignified chair of the Presidency our civil authorities have been of our own election. The laws which they write upon our books reflect the spirit of the citizens. The abuses which are perpetuated, be they social or economic or religious, have originated in the minds of the people. If bankruptcy has overwhelmed many of our principal cities it is traceable to the bankruptcy not only in things financial but in things moral which have appeared in the lives of too many of us. It is not a question so much of lack of leadership which has befallen us. It is rather a question of followership which endangers us.

Thus, we have followed unjust and immoral principles and have forsaken the ideals of the past. New definitions have come to replace the old. License which knows no law has dethroned liberty which can only exist by obedience to law. Happiness has become identified with pleasure. Thriftiness has given place to spend-thriftiness. Love has been translated into lust. Modern charity has swept aside the concept of brotherliness. Prosperity has surrendered to avarice.

Recreation has been spelled with the letters of debauchery. Patriotism has given way to internationalism. The Ten Commandments have been eliminated from our practical lives, and in their stead we have too often elected to follow the leadership and espouse the policies of the golden calf whose empire is the great wilderness.

Meanwhile, we wander aimlessly in a vicious circle, lost in the desert of depression no larger than that which encompassed the Jews of old. It is a condition in which the good must suffer with the unjust; in which the innocent must perish with the guilty. That is the price of our democracy.

(36)

John Dos Passos

1896-

Born in Philadelphia, Dos Passos graduated from Harvard in 1916, and then served as a private in the Medical Corps in World War I. His first book, *One Man's Initiation—1917* (1920), described an ambulance driver's war experiences. Then followed from Dos Passos' pen a series of literary works, most of which dealt with social issues and comprised a sensitive and critical commentary on America. He developed new literary techniques to suggest the moods and experiences of Americans as they faced changing and turbulent times. Emphasizing the confusion, waste, and loss of values in America, Dos Passos' work well illustrates the literature of social revolt.

This selection, which first appeared in *The New Republic* entitled "The American Plan: Its Rise and Fall," is from the section "Tin Lizzie" in *The Big Money,* the third volume of Dos Passos' trilogy, *U.S.A.,* published in 1936.

"Mr. Ford the automobileer," the feature writer wrote in 1900,

"Mr. Ford the automobileer began by giving his steed three or four sharp jerks with the lever at the righthand side of the seat; that is, he pulled the lever up and down sharply in order, as he said, to mix air with gasoline and drive the charge into the exploding cylinder. . . . Mr. Ford slipped a small electric switch handle and there followed a puff, puff, puff. . . . The puffing of the machine assumed a higher key. She was flying along about eight miles an hour. The ruts in the road were deep, but the machine certainly went with a dreamlike smoothness. There was none of the bumping common even to a street car. . . . By this time the boulevard had been reached, and the automobileer, letting a lever fall a little, let her out. Whiz! She picked up speed with infinite rapidity. As she ran on there was a clattering behind, the new noise of the automobile."

For twenty years or more,

ever since he'd left his father's farm when he was sixteen to get a job in a Detroit machine shop, Henry Ford had been nuts about machinery. First it was watches, then he designed a steam tractor, then he built a horseless carriage with an engine adapted from the Otto gasengine he'd read about in *The World of Science,* then a mechanical buggy with a onecylinder fourcycle motor, that would run forward but not back;

at last, in ninetyeight, he felt he was far enough along to risk throwing up his job with the Detroit Edison Company, where he'd worked his way up from night fireman to chief engineer, to put all his time into working on a new gasoline engine,

(in the late eighties he'd met Edison at a meeting of electriclight employees in Atlantic City. He'd gone up to Edison after Edison had delivered an address and asked him if he thought gasoline was practical as a motor fuel. Edison had said yes. If Edison said it, it was true. Edison was the great admiration of Henry Ford's life);

and in driving his mechanical buggy, sitting there at the lever jauntily dressed in a tightbuttoned jacket and a high collar and a derby hat, back and forth over the level illpaved streets of Detroit, scaring the big brewery horses and the skinny trotting horses and the sleek-rumped pacers with the motor's loud explosions,

looking for men scatterbrained enough to invest money in a factory for building automobiles.

He was the eldest son of an Irish immigrant who during the Civil War had married the daughter of a prosperous Pennsylvania Dutch farmer and settled down to farming near Dearborn in Wayne County, Michigan;

like plenty of other Americans, young Henry grew up hating the endless sogging through the mud about the chores, the hauling and pitching manure, the kerosene lamps to clean, the irk and sweat and solitude of the farm.

He was a slender, active youngster, a good skater, clever with his hands; what he liked was to tend the machinery and let the others do the heavy work. His mother had told him not to drink, smoke, gamble or go into debt, and he never did.

When he was in his early twenties his father tried to get him back from Detroit, where he was working as mechanic and repairman for the Drydock Engine Company that built engines for steamboats, by giving him forty acres of land.

Young Henry built himself an uptodate square white dwellinghouse with a false mansard roof and married and settled down on the farm,

but he let the hired men do the farming;

he bought himself a buzzsaw and rented a stationary engine and cut the timber off the woodlots.

He was a thrifty young man who never drank or smoked or gambled or coveted his neighbor's wife, but he couldn't stand living on the farm.

He moved to Detroit, and in the brick barn behind his house tinkered for years in his spare time with a mechanical buggy that would be light enough to run over the clayey wagon roads of Wayne County, Michigan.

By 1900 he had a practicable car to promote.

He was forty years old before the Ford Motor Company was started and production began to move.

Speed was the first thing the early automobile manufacturers went after. Races advertised the makes of cars.

Henry Ford himself hung up several records at the track at Grosse Point and on the ice on Lake St. Clair. In his 999 he did the mile in thirtynine and fourfifths seconds.

But it had always been his custom to hire others to do the heavy work. The speed he was busy with was speed in production, the records records in efficient output. He hired Barney Oldfield, a stunt bicyclerider from Salt Lake City, to do the racing for him.

Henry Ford had ideas about other things than the designing of motors, carburetors, magnetos, jigs and fixtures, punches and dies; he had ideas about sales, that the big money was in economical quantity production, quick turnover, cheap interchangeable easilyreplaced standardized parts;

it wasn't until 1909, after years of arguing with his partners, that Ford put out the first Model T.

Henry Ford was right.

That season he sold more than ten thousand tin lizzies, ten years later he was selling almost a million a year.

In these years the Taylor Plan was stirring up plantmanagers and manufacturers all over the country. Efficiency was the word. The same ingenuity that went into improving the performance of a machine could go into improving the performance of the workmen producing the machine.

In 1913 they established the assembly line at Ford's. That season the profits were something like twenty-five million dollars, but they had trouble in keeping the men on the job, machinists didn't seem to like it at Ford's.

Henry Ford had ideas about other things than production.

He was the largest automobile manufacturer in the world; he paid high wages; maybe if the steady workers thought they were getting a cut (a very small cut) in the profits, it would give trained men an inducement to stick to their jobs,

wellpaid workers might save enough money to buy a tin lizzie; the first day Ford's announced that cleancut, properlymarried American workers who wanted jobs had a chance to make five bucks a day (of course it turned out that there were strings to it; always there were strings to it)

such an enormous crowd waited outside the Highland Park plant

all through the zero January night

that there was a riot when the gates were opened; cops broke heads, jobhunters threw bricks; property, Henry Ford's own property, was destroyed. The company dicks had to turn on the firehose to beat back the crowd.

The American Plan; automotive prosperity seeping down from above; it turned out there were strings to it.

But that five dollars a day

paid to good, clean American workmen

who didn't drink or smoke cigarettes or read or think,

and who didn't commit adultery

and whose wives didn't take in boarders,

made America once more the Yukon of the sweated workers of the world;

made all the tin lizzies and the automotive age, and incidentally,

made Henry Ford the automobileer, the admirer of Edison, the birdlover,

the great American of his time.

But Henry Ford had ideas about other things besides assemblylines and the livinghabits of his employees. He was full of ideas. Instead of going to the city to make his fortune, here was a country boy who'd made his fortune by bringing the city out to the farm. The precepts he'd learned out of McGuffey's Reader, his mother's prejudices and preconceptions, he had preserved clean and unworn as freshprinted bills in the safe in a bank.

He wanted people to know about his ideas, so he bought the *Dearborn Independent* and started a campaign against cigarettesmoking.

When the War broke out in Europe, he had ideas about that too. (Suspicion of armymen and soldiering were part of the midwest farm tradition, like thrift, stickativeness, temperance and sharp practice in money matters.) Any intelligent American mechanic could see that if the Europeans hadn't been a lot of ignorant underpaid foreigners who drank, smoked, were loose about women and wasteful in their methods of production, the War could never have happened.

When Rosika Schwimmer broke through the stockade of secretaries and service men who surrounded Henry Ford and suggested to him that he could stop the War,

he said sure they'd hire a ship and go over and get the boys out of the trenches by Christmas.

He hired a steamboat, the *Oscar II,* and filled it up with pacifists and socialworkers,

to go over to explain to the princelings of Europe

that what they were doing was vicious and silly.

It wasn't his fault that Poor Richard's common sense no longer rules the world and that most of the pacifists were nuts,

goofy with headlines.

When William Jennings Bryan went over to Hoboken to see him off, somebody handed William Jennings Bryan a squirrel in a cage; William Jennings Bryan made a speech with the squirrel under his arm. Henry Ford threw American Beauty roses to the crowd. The band played *I Didn't Raise My Boy to Be a Soldier*. Practical jokers let loose more squirrels. An eloping couple was married by a platoon of ministers in the saloon, and Mr. Zero, the flophouse humanitarian, who reached the dock too late to sail,

dove into the North River and swam after the boat.

The *Oscar II* was described as a floating Chautauqua; Henry Ford said it felt like a middlewestern village, but by the time they reached Christiansand in Norway, the reporters had kidded him so that he had gotten cold feet and gone to bed. The world was too crazy outside of Wayne County, Michigan. Mrs. Ford and the management sent an Episcopal dean after him who brought him home under wraps,

and the pacifists had to speechify without him.

Two years later Ford's was manufacturing munitions, Eagle Boats; Henry Ford was planning oneman tanks, and oneman submarines like the one tried out in the Revolutionary War. He announced to the press that he'd turn over his war profits to the government,

but there's no record that he ever did.

One thing he brought back from his trip
was the Protocols of the Elders of Zion.

He started a campaign to enlighten the world in the *Dearborn Independent:* the Jews were why the world wasn't like Wayne County, Michigan, in the old horse and buggy days;

the Jews had started the War, Bolshevism, Darwinism, Marxism, Nietzsche, short skirts and lipstick. They were behind Wall Street and the international bankers, and the white slave traffic and the movies and the Supreme Court and ragtime and the illegal liquor business.

Henry Ford denounced the Jews and ran for Senator and sued the *Chicago Tribune* for libel,

and was the laughingstock of the kept metropolitan press;

but when the metropolitan bankers tried to horn in on his business

he thoroughly outsmarted them.

In 1918 he had borrowed on notes to buy out his minority stockholders for the picayune sum of seventyfive million dollars.

In February, 1920, he needed cash to pay off some of these notes that were coming due. A banker is supposed to have called on him and offered him every facility if the bankers' representative could be made a member of the board of directors. Henry Ford handed the banker his hat,

and went about raising the money in his own way:

he shipped every car and part he had in his plant to his dealers and de-manded immediate cash payment. Let the other fellow do the borrowing had always been a cardinal principle. He shut down production and cancelled all orders from the supplyfirms. Many dealers were ruined, many supplyfirms failed, but when he reopened his plant,

he owned it absolutely,

the way a man owns an unmortgaged farm with the taxes paid up.

In 1922 there started the Ford boom for President (high wages, water-power, industry scattered to the small towns) that was skillfully pricked behind scenes

by another crackerbarrel philosopher,

Calvin Coolidge;

but in 1922 Henry Ford sold one million three hundred and thirtytwo thousand, two hundred and nine tin lizzies; he was the richest man in the world.

Good roads had followed the narrow ruts made in the mud by the Model T. The great automotive boom was on. At Ford's production was improving all the time; less waste, more spotters, strawbosses, stoolpigeons (fifteen minutes for lunch, three minutes to go to the toilet, the Taylorized speedup everywhere, reach under, adjust washer, screw down bolt, shove in cotter pin, reachunder adjustwasher, screwdown bolt, reachunderadjustscrewdownreachunderadjust until every ounce of life was sucked off into production and at night the workmen went home gray shaking husks).

Ford owned every detail of the process from the ore in the hills until the car rolled off the end of the assemblyline under its own power, the plants were rationalized to the last tenthousandth of an inch as measured by the Johansen scale;

in 1926 the production cycle was reduced to eightyone hours from the ore in the mine to the finished salable car proceeding under its own power,

but the Model T was obsolete.

New Era prosperity and the American Plan
(there were strings to it, always there were strings to it)
had killed Tin Lizzie.
Ford's was just one of many automobile plants.
When the stockmarket bubble burst,
Mr. Ford the crackerbarrel philosopher said jubilantly,
"I told you so.
Serves you right for gambling and getting in debt.
The country is sound."
But when the country on cracked shoes, in frayed trousers, belts tightened over hollow bellies,
idle hands cracked and chapped with the cold of that coldest March day of 1932,
started marching from Detroit to Dearborn, asking for work and the American Plan, all they could think of at Ford's was machineguns.
The country was sound, but they mowed the marchers down.
They shot four of them dead.

Henry Ford as an old man
is a passionate antiquarian,
(lives besieged on his father's farm embedded in an estate of thousands of millionaire acres, protected by an army of servicemen, secretaries, secret agents, dicks under orders of an English exprize fighter,
always afraid of the feet in broken shoes on the roads, afraid the gangs will kidnap his grandchildren,
that a crank will shoot him,
that Change and the idle hands out of work will break through the gates and the high fences;
protected by a private army against
the new America of starved children and hollow bellies and cracked shoes stamping on souplines.

that has swallowed up the old thrifty farmlands
of Wayne County, Michigan,
as if they had never been).

Henry Ford as an old man
is a passionate antiquarian.

He rebuilt his father's farmhouse and put it back exactly in the state he remembered it in as a boy. He built a village of museums for buggies, sleighs, coaches, old plows, waterwheels, obsolete models of motorcars. He scoured the country for fiddlers to play oldfashioned squaredances.

Even old taverns he bought and put back into their original shape, as well as Thomas Edison's early laboratories.

When he bought the Wayside Inn near Sudbury, Massachusetts, he had the new highway where the newmodel cars roared and slithered and hissed oilily past (*the new noise of the automobile*),

moved away from the door,
put back the old bad road,
so that everything might be
the way it used to be,
in the days of horses and buggies.

(37)

Lawrence Dennis

1893-

After service with the American Expeditionary Force in World War I, Lawrence Dennis graduated from Harvard College in 1920. He then spent seven years in the United States Diplomatic corps, serving in Haiti, Roumania, Nicaragua, Honduras and France. He resigned in 1927 to enter the banking and brokerage fields and then, in 1930, he turned to writing. Concerned about the menace of communism as well as the apparent breakdown of American capitalism, he became convinced that fascism offered the best hope for the survival of American society. Dennis's fascism was akin to the views articulated by Hitler, Mussolini, and later Franco, but it was not simply an imitation of them. He believed that within the context of American society fascism had validity primarily in the economic field, but not in the cultural sphere where, as in Europe, fascism would result in totalitarianism. Dennis wrote a number of books and articles on political problems and edited and published two journals, *The Weekly Foreign Letter* and *Appeal to Reason.*

This selection is from an article entitled "Fascism for America," in *The Annals of the American Academy of Political and Social Science,* 180 (1935).

Conservatives like Messrs. Hoover and Ogden Mills have repeatedly warned us of the fascist danger implicit in the trends of the Roosevelt New Deal. Only this week a group of moderate socialists, rendering a report in the name of the Methodist Federation for Social Service, admonished the Nation that Senator Long, Father Coughlin, and General Johnson, all of whom either now are or recently have been supporters of the New Deal, constitute a serious fascist menace. Moderate socialists generally will be found to concur in the generalization that present trends in this country are towards fascism. As for the orthodox Communists, any one who is familiar with their current writings and utterances is aware that one of their dogmas is that the reign of a fascist antichrist is likely to be the culminating phase of the decline of capitalism and the prelude to the opening of the communist millennium. Indeed, about the only important leaders who do not openly express this fundamental agreement as to the imminence of fascism, and even as to its actuality in a modified form, are our three outstanding leaders—President Roosevelt, Senator Long, and Father Coughlin—and their followers, these leaders being charged by their conservative and liberal critics with fascist tendencies.

The Liberal Diagnosis

Now, I entirely agree with the Hoovers, the Norman Thomases, and the Communists that our three foremost political and spiritual leaders are moving in fascist directions. But I do not agree with the critics of these leaders that fascism is per se something to be feared or fought. It appears to me that prevailing social forces the world over make a fascist trend the inevitable alternative to chaos or communism. I cannot be sure at present whether our momentarily outstanding leaders will lead us on to fascism or to chaos. They are not clear in their own minds, as yet, as to ends and means. Therefore it seems to me that instead of denouncing a trend we are clearly powerless to arrest, those of us who can think and still have a chance to think out loud ought to try to clarify the issues so that the wills of the leaders and their followings may be clarified as to choices of ends and means. It is significant that I, an apologist for the authoritarian state and a critic of liberal democracy, should be trying to fix the thought of constructive minds on the analysis of present trends with a view to creating informed judgments and making enlightened choices, while the rabble of the liberal intelligentsia is largely occupied with organizing emotional demonstrations and unloosing floods of impassioned words against the fascist trend which is sweeping the world.

Now, although I agree with the diagnosis by Messrs. Hoover and Mills that we are moving towards fascism under the leadership of Messrs. Roosevelt, Long, and Coughlin, I cannot accept their prescription of a fight to preserve and reinvigorate the old system. Believing it doomed, I see no sense in fighting for it. Fighting for lost causes imposes on mankind the most futile and criminal sort of warfare. British mercantilism which was doomed in 1775, and the Southern planter system with its accompaniment of Negro slavery which was doomed by 1850, each fought on American soil two futile wars for two doomed or lost causes. Why? Well, largely because certain sincere and worthy people felt it to be a matter of duty and honor loyally to fight for a system under which they had been fairly well off.

Most of us here today, quite as much as Mr. Hoover and Mr. Mills, have been fairly well off under the liberal-capitalist system. Like all the other doomed systems of the past, it has glorious traditions which can be made to evoke dynamic responses from large numbers of people. But if it is an order doomed by the irresistible trend of prevailing social forces, why fight for it?

Every time I read an utterance of Mr. Hoover or exponents of his orthodox and traditional liberal capitalism, I think of the British loyalists of the Stuart dynasty since 1688. It is pathetic and romantic to want a boat to row you over to bonny Prince Charlie, and a constitution in distress can be almost as full of pathos as an exiled prince in distress. All that is needed now for the loyalists of the liberal American Constitution is a few good ballads. I offer this suggestion to the Republican National Committee. But I see the captains of industry, along with the realistic leaders of radical reaction to prolonged depression, climbing on the fascist band wagon.

The Communist Diagnosis

As for the communist diagnosis of the present phase of capitalist decline, particularly as to the proposition that it obviously indicates fascism in the interest of the élite of the present order, I am in substantial agreement. The Hoover conservatives say that we are going fascist and that it will be the end of liberal capitalism. To this I say "Check." The Communists say that we are going fascist because it will be the only salvation of the élite of the present order. To this I say "Double check."

With the rest of the communist thesis as to fascism, I disagree. The communist contention that any possible fascist formula will be doomed to early disaster, I find utterly unprovable. I also deny the communist assertion that any fascist formula would necessarily prove detrimental to the welfare of the people. This latter proposition, of course, raises issues of ultimate values rather than of facts, so it cannot be argued out. Naturally, I reject many of the communist values, one of the most important of which is that human welfare demands the liquidation of the élite of the old order. Liquidation, as you know, is a euphemism for experiences like being stood up before a Communist firing squad.

I find the bourgeoisie of this country too numerous and too strong to be liquidated except in one of the bloodiest and most prolonged civil wars the world has ever known. Aside from the consideration that I should not like to be liquidated, I cannot but feel that the liquidation of so large and useful a group of persons would be a greater loss to the rest of the community than the advantages any dictatorship of triumphant proletarian revolutionary leaders could possibly vouchsafe to the community.

So I am against the Marxian class struggle. I am in favor of a middle-class revolution and against a proletarian revolution. The middle-class revolution has already begun. I call it fascist. I hope it can be more productive of human values than the middle-class revolutions of England in 1648 and 1688, of America from 1776 to 1825, or of France from 1789 to 1815.

I am prepared to make a concession to the communist thesis which I cannot make to the liberal thesis. I am prepared to admit that, given a conceivable combination of circumstances and events, the radicalism of Lenin, as it might be made explicit and effective by a régime of competent, professional, power-hungry, revolutionary leaders, having a high order of military and administrative genius, could be made to work. I am unable to see how the radicalism of Adam Smith, John Locke, and John Stuart Mill, now the conservatism of Herbert Hoover, can possibly be made to work in the world of Mussolini, Hitler, and Stalin. I consider any one of the last three named leaders fitter to survive in the present struggle for existence. I would remind any who may not be clear on this point that fitness to survive is not an ethical quality.

Failure of the Present System

The reason why my money is not on the liberals and why my sympathies are not with their ideologies is due to a complex of facts implicit in the present situation and of personal preferences. I find the liberal theory and practice inadequate both to what I consider to be social requirements and to my own personal requirements. I am wholly uninterested in explanations of its failures or in prescriptions for its recovery. It has failed. It has proved inadequate. Therefore, by the inexorable law of the survival of the fittest, it is doomed.

In the present crisis of liberalism which began in 1914, the exponents, the theorists, and the practitioners of liberalism have had their innings. They and their system have failed. I cannot and do not have to prove that a new system will work better. For a new system inevitably to emerge out of the crisis of the present system, it is necessary only to have it established that the present system is inadequate. The growing ranks of the recipients of state relief and of the frustrated élite of the middle classes are going to be more and more swayed in their emotional reactions and impulses to action by the simple logic I have just stated: When a system fails or proves inadequate, a new one is indicated. There is only one argument that can defeat that logic, and that argument is turning the failure or the inadequacy of the system challenged into success and adequacy.

The liberal leaders have had their chance since 1914. They have been slipping one by one into the abyss. They have failed. The people are not interested in their excuses or sympathetic to pleas for a second chance. They have ears now only for leaders who promise a new system. New leaders will enjoy power only as long as they move in the direction of a new system. Mr. Roosevelt can hold his prestige only as long as people believe in the New Deal.

Let me emphasize the fact that we face the situation of a system which has been giving increasing signs since 1914 that it no longer works tolerably well. It came out of all the wars of the nineteenth century stronger than it went in. It is therefore nonsense to say that war is the cause of the depression or the world crisis of liberal capitalism. Liberalism won the Napoleonic wars but lost the late World War. Liberalism in England, America, and continental Europe had won innumerable wars up to 1814.

Government Financing of the System

Need I run over a bill of particulars to substantiate the proposition that the present system no longer works, and that the changes now being inaugurated in this country are not reforms calculated to restore the system to normal operating efficiency? The banks could not reopen and they could not now stay open without Government intervention. Public order could not be maintained if the state failed to increase public expenditure to provide work and relief for the growing number of the destitute and unemployed. Although surplus bank reserves are over two and a quarter billion dollars, or enough to support an expansion of commercial loans in excess of twenty billion dollars, bank loans to industry and commerce have been almost steadily shrinking during the past two years. Banks do not lend and investors do not put idle funds into new enterprises or construction because under present conditions the prospects of getting a return are not good enough.

The measure of recovery from the panicky lows of 1933 which we momentarily enjoy in the lull before the next crash is proportionate to and dependent on the amount of Government money actually being disbursed to prevent banks from being closed, to pay for labor that private enterprise will not hire, and to give money to farmers and other producers which they could not obtain in the open market. Not only the unemployed, but the banks, the railroads, agriculture, and industry are all on the dole. Profits are being obtained by certain producers through the Government financing of curtailment of production. But for this Government financing on credit of curtailment of production, prices would have continued their fall until every bank, insurance company, and large debtor in the country would have gone into insolvency.

Two things are certain: (1) The Government cannot go on financing a curtailment of production without lowering the national standard of living and without thereby increasing the violence of popular discontent; (2) the Government cannot go on financing curtailment of production, the maintenance of artificial price levels, the solvency of insolvent railroads and financial institutions, and a growing army of destitute unemployed all by the process of borrowing.

The orderly processes of the liberal-capitalist system call for adjustment of the financial difficulties through bankruptcy, mortgage foreclosures—putting the country through the legal wringer, in other words. The system calls for adjustment of market, price, and wage difficulties by letting prices and employment be determined by the free play of supply and demand without Government subsidy to production curtailment or to subsistence of the unemployed. There is not a serious-minded man in the country who would long keep his head on if he tried to put the country through the wringer of orderly capitalist readjustment. Therefore I say the system is doomed and no longer works. The plea of the conservatives for a return to the Constitution is absurd when the strict enforcement of constitutional property rights would precipitate civil war.

Every economic adjustment today rests on Government interventions in new and innumerable forms. Therefore I say we are headed towards fascism, communism, or chaos. It is not yet fascism or communism because the bases of Government intervention do not at present constitute a system which can be rationally defined or successfully maintained. In other words, the underlying scheme of Government intervention does not constitute a stable system of social administration. It seems to work only because the scheme of Government intervention now in operation is a sort of toboggan—the toboggan slide of the dollar and national credit to the vanishing point. When we hit bottom, we shall have chaos or fascism. I should like to see fascism before we hit bottom.

Briefly, there is no recovery of the orderly capitalist sort, here, in England, in France, or in Canada. There cannot be such recovery without a revival of private investment in adequate volume. There cannot be a revival of private investment in adequate volume under present conditions of closed world markets, artificial maintenance of prices, and colossal government expenditures for relief. Liberalism can stand off the final crash only as long as strong liberal governments like those of the United States, England, and France can coast along down the toboggan of inflation. But on that route, liberalism will have a one-way ride.

Liberalism in Germany survived the postwar inflationary ride only as long as the financially sound liberal countries like the United States and England could support the international financial structure. When liberalism in America, England, and France takes this last ride, there will be no other financially sound liberal countries to maintain the integrity of liberal-capitalistic institutions with the aid of foreign loans and financial arrangements. As I see it, liberalism in America is on its last ride down the dollar toboggan.

Liberalism cannot achieve a governmental pattern of intervention which can be stabilized and made permanently to work, and there's the rub. Granted this generalization which I think I have sufficiently established, we have the alternatives of some form of authoritarian state to do a job of economic or social planning, or chaos. I do not have to prove that state planning will succeed; I have only to prove that without state planning, conditions are intolerable.

Ends and Means

Broadly summarized, the issues are matters of ends and means. The ends of the liberal-capitalist state are mainly those of good policing, the protection of life and property, and the enforcement of contracts, with a little welfare in the form of education, sanitation, and traffic regulation thrown in, all on the broad assumption that individuals can best plan their economic activities without other government intervention. The ends of the authoritarian state are some sort of planned social order, made explicit and effective by the state.

There is a plan under both the liberal and the authoritarian scheme of things. But the plan of the liberal scheme of things results mostly from the play of individual and competitive initiatives in a relatively free market and field of economic choices. The plan of the authoritarian scheme of things has to result from the planning of a central authority, which must always be really a council of *persons,* charged with this function. Hence the epithet "dictatorship" attaches so easily to the planned state.

Now fascism, as a term, differs from communism, as a term, for the purposes of this discussion, largely in the following respect: The communist plan is, for the moment, whatever the Communist council of elders or cardinals of the international Communist faith, assembled in Moscow, decide and promulgate; while the fascist plan is whatever the fascist council in a given nation decides.

As yet there is no fascist council planning government intervention in this country. Consequently, any fascist plan for America which I might offer you would of necessity have to be largely the creation of my imagination. A Communist, on the other hand, could give you a plan for America fresh from the pigeonholes of the Moscow Communist Party bureaucracy. The ends of a planned society can be many and different in different societies. The means of an authoritarian state, however, are always essentially governmental. Therein communism and fascism are alike. But in this connection "governmental" must be understood as referring to everything that enters into the enterprise of achieving a centrally planned scheme of social organization. Hence, both the communist and the fascist states are properly called totalitarian.

I shall try briefly to lay down certain broad generalizations as to both ends and means of an ideal fascist authoritarian state for this country.

Public Welfare

The fundamental ends of government and public administration, whether under fascism, liberalism, communism, or any other "ism," are obviously public order and the realization of some idealized scheme of public welfare. I have little patience with those liberal, fascist, or communist critics of other political systems who assume that those systems are conceived and operated by wicked and insane leaders whose chief motivation in the exercise of political power is the gratification of irrational personal caprices at the expense of the welfare of the people they govern. Order and public welfare, I believe, are the ends of every government in operation today. But there are different schemes of maintaining order, and there are different values and hierarchies of values to make up the content of any scheme of public welfare. The ideologies and the methodologies of welfare differ.

The weakness of the liberal scheme is that it can no longer maintain order without concerning itself with economic government in ways which are admittedly incompatible with the basic tenets of liberalism. And the trouble with the liberal scheme of welfare is obviously that too many people are dissatisfied with it. Liberalism stands condemned, not of an indifference to welfare, but of failure to work out its ideologies and methodologies of welfare. As I have already stated, this amounts to saying that the liberal plan no longer works. The alternatives are chaos or an authoritarian plan. . . .

The Sphere of Control

Control, of course, is not bounded by the confines of the economic interests. The fascist state, however, is concerned mainly with effective control of capital and labor. A type of fascism could well arise to seek control in the field of cultural interests and activities not affected with important economic interest. I should deplore the growth of such a type of fascism. I am not prepared to delimit the functions of the state as the liberals are—in theories which strangely differ from practices.

Broadly stated, the individual can and should be left a large field of choices in respect to occupations, uses of leisure time, and uses of resources not required for public ends. The field in which the state has to be most authoritarian and restrictive of liberty is a field which will only affect seriously two or three thousand corporations and the five or ten thousand men who have hitherto had too much freedom of choice of policies for self-enrichment.

The point I want to stress is that so far as the millions of stockholders, bondholders, depositors, and insured having an interest in corporate affairs are concerned, fascism will not materially modify their rights or liberties, for the very good reason that, as it is, they have *de facto* no rights or liberties to be modified except the rights to sell their rights of ownership if they can find a buyer and to take what management gives them. These rights will undoubtedly be left to them.

State intervention, of course, will often penalize owners under fascism. Mistakes and rascality of management have done the same under liberal capitalism. Wherein would the right of an insuree in the Metropolitan Insurance Company have been modified if the state had told its managers that they could not put $25,000,000 into an office building in New York at a high rate of interest but that they must put that sum into slum clearance projects at a low rate of interest? There must be much state interference with corporate management under fascism, and there should be little state interference with personal habits. Economic and not sumptuary control is the need. But economic control must not mobilize cultural instruments of the control, like radio, press, school, and church, against the state. The state must have a monopoly of those uses of power which can make or break successful social planning.

This leads me briefly to speak of the problems of means under a fascist authoritarian state. The ends, as we have already seen, are order and welfare, which I would express more concretely by saying as high a standard of living as the people want to pay for with their labor and available resources. The means, however, are the more characteristically fascist features of the new system. I can only run over certain important fundamentals.

Concentration of Power

As to the political or governmental scheme of things, the keynote is concentration of power, or centralization of control. This means scrapping the principle of separation of power. Government is no longer a matter of checking and balancing or playing a game of the individual versus a state which is constantly suspected of having designs on his liberty and welfare. Individuals who have been beaten by the depression in the free market do not want liberal liberties to do things they cannot as a practical matter do, and liberal liberties for others to do things to them which the others can and actually do, and which the victims do not like to have done to them.

The liberal critics of fascism are apt to stress the question of liberty. With a curious lack of historical sense and of a sense of humor, they forget that the cry for liberty has always been the cry of the leaders of the "outs." Our liberal critics can be quite sure that any successful revolution will leave a lot of people with more liberty than they had before. Our liberal friends can also be sure that the people who want a New Deal or a new system are not entirely enchanted with their present liberties. Liberty is a word to be used by people fighting for something they do not have; it is not a good propaganda word for people to play with who are fighting to keep something they have and which their opponents are after.

Senator Long's followers really want to share other people's liberties by sharing their wealth. Every social revolution is a fight for liberty. The members of the Liberty League are on the defensive, and the leaders of the Long and Coughlin forces are on the offensive. My money is usually on the offensive. The élite of the present order can assure their leadership or liberties only by giving up the defensive and joining the offensive on the technological problems of social organization and production.

The political instrument of government must be directed by an executive council representing a mandate from the people to do a managing job. This means the end of the parliamentary or congressional system, under which governmental decisions and policies are the results of power group pressures. . . .

The Mind of the Masses

Many of the conservatives believe or seem to believe that the American people are attached to a given system and ideology. This is a delusion peculiar to the lawyers and the instructed classes. Ninety per cent of the American people have no grasp whatever of the ideological content of the system. They have not read the Federalist papers, Rousseau, Montesquieu, Adam Smith, or Blackstone. If they are moved by words or symbols, like "Constitution," "liberty," "democracy," "representative government," and so forth, it is purely a result of early emotional conditioning and the association of a given feeling with a given word, without the occurrence of any understanding process. All these words or symbols can be incanted by any demagogue committed to any enterprise. A fascist dictatorship can be set up by a demagogue in the name of all the catchwords of the present system, just as a Communist dictatorship was set up in Russia in October 1917 in the name of democracy and other catchwords of the liberals.

It is also a mistake to suppose that the American people are averse to government regimentation, or orderly organization and procedure. We are the most organized, standardized, regimented, and docile people in the world so far as the processes of mass direction and management are concerned. People who fall into this erroneous generalization about the American people fail to see that most of our government is now done by large corporations and cultural associations rather than by the state. The state can easily include the corporation and most of the cultural associations within its scheme of social control without having the masses of the people notice the difference. The $25,000-a-year vice-president of a big bank or a big university is as much the yes-man of the power hierarchy on which his job depends as any communist or fascist party official, and he has about the same liberty of basic dissent.

I am not showing a contempt but a high respect for the masses in advancing these heterodox generalizations about them. The people have too much sense to take symbols and verbalisms, like the "Constitution" and "liberty," as seriously as our educated liberals and lawyers do. Both Senator Long and Father Coughlin, in harping on the calamities of our present situation and in clamoring for changes, are in far closer harmony with the logic of mass needs than are our intellectual exponents of liberalism, or conservatism, as you may care to call it, who are invoking symbols and verbalisms not as instruments of action but as deterrents to revolutionary action. The people want public order and the elements of subsistence. Liberty with these, yes; liberty without them is nonsense.

Character of Coming Fascism

Revolutionary change is indicated. It is beginning. Its velocity and momentum will accelerate. The élite of the present order have their chance now to reform their thinking and lead the trend. Whether our coming fascism is more or less humane and decent will depend largely on the contributions our humane élite can make to it in time. There need be no acute class struggle, if the élite of the present order in both parties will but recognize that a planned economy can best be planned in the interests of the dominant élite, if it is also planned to give the masses the maximum output of human satisfactions. The larger the total product, the larger the cut for ownership and management. The problem can be that of organizing for the maximum social income as a part of organization for class advantage. It can also be a class struggle between the "ins" fighting to defend their liberties, and the "outs" fighting to capture them. It will depend largely on the decision of the "ins" during the next few months.

(38)

Twelve Southerners

1930

The new conservatism that developed in the South presented a very different reaction to changing America from those of the preceding selections. Embittered by the disappearance of the values of an agrarian society, by the dehumanizing effects of industrialization, and by the loss of southern culture, southern literary and intellectual figures spoke out to preserve and encourage an older, indigenous way of southern life. Among the spokesmen of this southern conservatism were the contributors to the volume from which the following selection is taken. They were John Crowe Ransom, Donald Davidson, Frank Lawrence Owsley, John Gould Fletcher, Lyle H. Lanier, Allen Tate, Herman Clarence Nixon, Andrew Nelson Lytle, Robert Penn Warren, John Donald Wade, Henry Blue Kline, and Stark Young.

This selection is comprised of several passages from a symposium of their views, *I'll Take My Stand: The South and the Agrarian Tradition* (New York, 1930).

☆ ☆ ☆ ☆

I

With the environment of the New World and the traditions of the Old, the South thus became the seat of an agrarian civilization which had strength and promise for a future greatness second to none. The life of the South was leisurely and unhurried for the planter, the yeoman, or the landless tenant. It was a way of life, not a routine of planting and reaping merely for gain.

Washington, who rode daily over his farms and counted his horses, cattle, plows, and bushels of corn as carefully as a merchant takes stock of his supplies, inhaled the smell of ripe corn after a rain, nursed his bluegrass sod and shade trees with his own hands, and, when in the field as a soldier or in the city as President of the United States, was homesick at the smell of fresh-plowed earth. He kept vigil with his sick horses and dogs, not as a capitalist who guards his investments, but as one who watches over his friends.

The system of society which developed in the South, then, was close to the soil. It might be organized about the plantation with its wide fields and its slaves and self-sufficiency, or it might center around a small farm, ranging from a fifty-acre to a five-hundred-acre tract, tilled by the owner, undriven by competition, supplied with corn by his own toil and with meat from his own pen or from the fields and forests. The amusements might be the fine balls and house parties of the planter or the three-day break-down dances which David Crockett loved, or horse races, foot races, cock and dog fights, boxing, wrestling, shooting, fighting, log-rolling, house raising, or corn-shucking. It might be crude or genteel, but it everywhere was fundamentally alike and natural. The houses were homes, where families lived sufficient and complete within themselves, working together and fighting together. And when death came, they were buried in their own lonely peaceful graveyards, to await doomsday together.

II

This agrarian society had its own interests, which in almost all respects diverged from the interests of the industrial system of the North. The two sections, North and South, had entered the revolution against the mother country with the full knowledge of the opposing interests of their societies; knowing this difference, they had combined in a loose union under the Articles of Confederation. Finally, they had joined together under the Constitution fully conscious that there were thus united two divergent economic and social systems, two civilizations, in fact. The two sections were evenly balanced in population and in the number of states, so that at the time there was no danger of either section's encroaching upon the interests of the other. This balance was clearly understood. Without it a union would not have been possible. Even with the understanding that the two sections would continue to hold this even balance, the sections were very careful to define and limit the powers of the federal government lest one section with its peculiar interests should get control of the national government and use the powers of that government to exploit the other section. Specific powers were granted the federal government, and all not specifically granted were retained by the states.

But equilibrium was impossible under expansion and growth. One section with its peculiar system of society would at one time or another become dominant and control the national government and either exploit the other section or else fail to exercise the functions of government for its positive benefit. Herein lies the irrepressible conflict, the eternal struggle between the agrarian South and the commercial and industrial North to control the government either in its own interest or, negatively, to prevent the other section from controlling it in its interests. Lincoln and Seward and the radical Republicans clothed the conflict later in robes of morality by making it appear that the "house divided against itself" and the irrepressible conflict which resulted from this division marked a division between slavery and freedom.

Slavery, as we shall see, was part of the agrarian system, but only one element and not an essential one. To say that the irrepressible conflict was between slavery and freedom is either to fail to grasp the nature and magnitude of the conflict, or else to make use of deliberate deception by employing a shibboleth to win the uninformed and unthinking to the support of a sinister undertaking. Rob Roy MacGregor, one of the chief corruptionists of the present-day power lobby, said that the way the power companies crush opposition and win popular support is to pin the word "bolshevik" upon the leaders of those who oppose the power-lobby program. The leaders of the Northern industrial system could win popular support by tagging their opponents as *"enemies of liberty"* and themselves as "champions of freedom." This they did. Lincoln was a politician and knew all the tricks of a politician. Seward was a politician and knew every *in* and *out*. This is true of other leaders of the "party of high ideals" which assumed the name of Republican party. Doubtless, Lincoln, Seward, and others were half sincere in their idea of an irrepressible conflict, but their fundamental purpose was to win elections and get their party into power—the party of the industrial North—with an industrial program for business and a sop of free lands for the Western farmer.

The irrepressible conflict, then, was not between slavery and freedom, but between the industrial and commercial civilization of the North and the agrarian civilization of the South. The industrial North demanded a high tariff so as to monopolize the domestic markets, especially the Southern market, for the South, being agrarian, must purchase all manufactured goods. It was an exploitative principle, originated at the expense of the South and for the benefit of the North. After the South realized that it would have little industry of its own, it fought the protective tariff to the point of nullification in South Carolina and almost to the point of dissolving the Union. In this as in other cases Southerners saw that what was good for the North was fatal to the South.

The industrial section demanded a national subsidy for the shipping business and merchant marine, but, as the merchant marine was alien to the Southern agrarian system, the two sections clashed. It was once more an exploitation of one section for the benefit of the other.

The industrial North demanded internal improvements—roads, railroads, canals—at national expense to furnish transportation for its goods to Southern and Western markets which were already hedged around for the benefit of the

North by the tariff wall. The South objected to internal improvements at national expense because it had less need of transporation than the North and
because the burden would be heavier on the South and the benefits greater for
the North—another exploitation of the Southern system. The North favored
a government-controlled bank; but as corporate wealth and the quick turnover
of money were confined to that section, such an institution would be for the
sole benefit, the South believed, of the North. There were many other things
of a positive nature which the system of society in the North demanded of the
federal government, but those mentioned will illustrate the conflict of interest
between North and South. . . .

III

And now the crisis in the South's decline has been reached.

Industrialism has arrived in the South. Already the local chambers of
commerce exhibit the formidable data of Southern progress. A considerable
party of Southern opinion, which might be called the New South party, is well
pleased with the recent industrial accomplishments of the South and anxious
for many more. Southerners of another school, who might be said to compose
an Old South party, are apprehensive lest the section become completely and
uncritically devoted to the industrial ideal precisely as the other sections of
the Union are. But reconstruction is actually under way. Tied politically and
economically to the Union, her borders wholly violable, the South now sees
very well that she can restore her prosperity only within the competition of an
industrial system.

After the war the Southern plantations were often broken up into small
farms. These have yielded less and less of a living, and it [is] said that they will
never yield a good living until once more they are integrated into large units.
But these units will be industrial units, controlled by a board of directors or
an executive rather than a squire, worked with machinery, and manned not by
farmers living at home, but by "labor." Even so they will not, according to
Mr. Henry Ford, support the population that wants to live on them. In the
off seasons the laborers will have to work in factories, which henceforth are to
be counted on as among the charming features of Southern landscape. The
Southern problem is complicated, but at its center is the farmer's problem, and
this problem is simply the most acute version of that general agrarian problem
which inspires the despair of many thoughtful Americans today.

The agrarian discontent in America is deeply grounded in the love of the
tiller for the soil, which is probably, it must be confessed, not peculiar to the
Southern specimen, but one of the more ineradicable human attachments, be
the tiller as progressive as he may. In proposing to wean men from this foolish
attachment, industrialism sets itself against the most ancient and the most
humane of all the modes of human livelihood. Do Mr. Hoover and the dis-

tinguished thinkers at Washington see how essential is the mutual hatred between the industrialists and the farmers, and how mortal is their conflict? The gentlemen at Washington are mostly preaching and legislating to secure the fabulous "blessings" of industrial progress; they are on the industrial side. The industrialists have a doctrine which is monstrous, but they are not monsters personally; they are forward-lookers with nice manners, and no American progressivist is against them. The farmers are boorish and inarticulate by comparison. Progressivism is against them in their fight, though their traditional status is still so strong that soft words are still spoken to them. All the solutions recommended for their difficulties are really enticements held out to them to become a little more coöperative, more mechanical, more mobile —in short, a little more industrialized. But the farmer who is not a mere laborer, even the farmer of the comparatively new places like Iowa and Nebraska, is necessarily among the more stable and less progressive elements of society. He refuses to mobilize himself and become a unit in the industrial army, because he does not approve of army life.

I will use some terms which are hardly in his vernacular. He identifies himself with a spot of ground, and this ground carries a good deal of meaning; it defines itself for him as nature. He would till it not too hurriedly and not too mechanically to observe in it the contingency and the infinitude of nature; and so his life acquires its philosophical and even its cosmic consciousness. A man can contemplate and explore, respect and love, an object as substantial as a farm or a native province. But he cannot contemplate nor explore, respect nor love, a mere turnover, such as an assemblage of "natural resources," a pile of money, a volume of produce, a market, or a credit system. It is into precisely these intangibles that industrialism would translate the farmer's farm. It means the dehumanization of his life.

However that may be, the South at last, looking defensively about her in all directions upon an industrial world, fingers the weapons of industrialism. There is one powerful voice in the South which, tired of a long status of disrepute, would see the South made at once into a section second to none in wealth, as that is statistically reckoned, and in progressiveness, as that might be estimated by the rapidity of the industrial turnover. This desire offends those who would still like to regard the South as, in the old sense, a home; but its expression is loud and insistent. The urban South, with its heavy importation of regular American ways and regular American citizens, has nearly capitulated to these novelties. It is the village South and the rural South which supply the resistance, and it is lucky for them that they represent a vast quantity of inertia.

Will the Southern establishment, the most substantial exhibit on this continent of a society of the European and historic order, be completely crumbled by the powerful acid of the Great Progressive Principle? Will there be no more looking backward but only looking forward? Is our New World to be dedicated forever to the doctrine of newness?

It is in the interest of America as a whole, as well as in the interest of the

South, that these questions press for an answer. I will enter here the most important items of the situation as well as I can; doubtless they will appear a little over-sharpened for the sake of exhibition.

(1) The intention of Americans at large appears now to be what it was always in danger of becoming: an intention of being infinitely progressive. But this intention cannot permit of an established order of human existence, and of that leisure which conditions the life of intelligence and the arts.

(2) The old South, if it must be defined in a word, practiced the contrary and European philosophy of establishment as the foundation of the life of the spirit. The ante-bellum Union possessed, to say the least, a wholesome variety of doctrine.

(3) But the South was defeated by the Union on the battlefield with remarkable decisiveness, and the two consequences have been dire: the Southern tradition was physically impaired, and has ever since been unable to offer an attractive example of its philosophy in action; and the American progressive principle has developed into a pure industrialism without any check from a Southern minority whose voice ceased to make itself heard.

(4) The further survival of the Southern tradition as a detached local remnant is now unlikely. It is agreed that the South must make contact again with the Union. And in adapting itself to the actual state of the Union, the Southern tradition will have to consent to a certain industrialization of its own.

(5) The question at issue is whether the South will permit herself to be so industrialized as to lose entirely her historic identity, and to remove the last substantial barrier that has stood in the way of American progressivism; or will accept industrialism, but with a very bad grace, and will manage to maintain a good deal of her traditional philosophy. . . .

IV

If anything is clear, it is that we can never go back, and neither this essay nor any intelligent person that I know in the South desires a literal restoration of the old Southern life, even if that were possible; dead days are gone, and if by some chance they should return, we should find them intolerable. But out of any epoch in civilization there may arise things worth while, that are the flowers of it. To abandon these, when another epoch arrives, is only stupid, so long as there is still in them the breath and flux of life. In our American life today good things are coming in, which we should try to understand and to share, so far as our natures allow. But it is just as obvious that good things are going out. There was a Southern civilization whose course was halted with those conventions of 1867 by which the negro suffrage in the South—not in the North—was planned, and the pillaging began. But that does not imply that this Southern civilization, once the fine flower of men's lives, is wholly dead; for the core of our humanity lies in the belief that the essence of the soul is its mockery of death. It would be childish and dangerous for the South to be stampeded and betrayed out of its own character by the noise, force, and glittering narrowness of the industrialism and progress spreading everywhere, with varying degrees, from one region to another. . . .

To arrive, then, at some conception of the end of living, the civilization, that will belong to the South, is our great, immediate problem. But in this case, as always in life, alongside a man's open course there moves a mystery, to him dark and shining at once. The mystery here is change, whose god is Mutability. In the shifting relation between ourselves and the new order lies the profoundest source for our living, I mean change in that almost mystical sense by which, so long as we are alive, we are not the same and yet remain ourselves. All things hate steadfastness and are changed, Spenser wrote, and yet, being rightly weighed:

> They are not changéd from their first estate;
> But by their change their being do dilate:
> And turning to themselves at length again,
> Do work their own perfection so by fate.
> Then over them change doth not rule and reign,
> But they rule over change and do themselves maintain.

That a change is now in course all over the South is plain; and it is as plain that the South changing must be the South still, remembering that for no thing can there be any completeness that is outside its own nature, and no thing for which there is any advance save in its own kind. If this were not so, all nature by now would have dissolved in chaos and folly, nothing in it, neither its own self nor any other.

(39)

Earl Browder

1891-

A fifth-generation American, Browder was born in Wichita, Kansas. He left school at the age of ten to help support his family. After a series of youthful jobs he became credit manager of a wholesale drug company. Learning of radical reform movements from his Populist father, Browder took part in almost all the radical working-class movements of his day.

This idealism and zeal for reform caused young Browder to join the Socialist party in 1907 at the age of sixteen. During World War I, he was sentenced to two years in prison for conspiring to oppose the draft law. The success of the Russian Revolution made a profound impression on him, but a second prison term in 1919 prevented him from taking part in the formation of the American communist movement. In 1921 Browder was invited to organize an American delegation to the first Congress of the Third International. From this beginning he started his rise within the American Communist party, becoming ultimately its national secretary and presidential candidate. His ascendency in the party ended quickly after World War II, however, and he left the communist movement to live in relative obscurity. A dedicated Marxist, Browder always stressed the importance of communism in the context of American problems and purposes.

This selection is from *The People's Front* (New York, 1938).

STRUGGLE AGAINST FASCISM AND FOR PEACE

The world is torn between two main directions of development: on the one hand stand those forces striving to maintain the rights and living standards of the masses in the midst of capitalist crisis and decay, and to maintain world peace; on the other side are the forces of fascism, striving to wipe out popular rights and throw the full burden of the crisis onto the masses, and driving toward a new world war.

The camp of fascism, of the war-makers, is mighty and menacing. It is headed by Hitler fascism, the most bloody and bestial reaction the world has ever seen. It contains Mussolini, whose hands drip with the blood of Italians and Ethiopians alike. It includes the military-fascist government of Japan, which is carving a new empire out of the body of the Chinese people. In every capitalist country its forces are organizing, backed and inspired by the monopolists of finance capital, and, where not already in power, are preparing with all energy, ruthlessness, and demagogy, to seize control of government. In the United States, this camp is headed by the dominant leadership of the Republican Party, with its allies of the Liberty League, Hearst, Black Legion, Ku Klux Klan, Coughlin, and others.

The camp of progress and peace finds its stronghold in the Soviet Union, the country of socialist prosperity. To its banner are rallying all the growing armies of those who would resist fascism and war. Relying upon its mighty strength, the French people were able to gather in the great *Front Populaire,* which threw back the first assaults of French fascism and warded off the first threat of war by Hitler, and advanced the living standards of the masses and their organized strength. Seeing in it a powerful protector, the small nations of Europe whose existence is threatened, who find less and less assistance from the great capitalist powers, turn to the firm peace policy of the Soviet Union as their reliable refuge. Even those great countries ruled by the imperialist bourgeoisie, like the U.S.A., who for their own special reasons are not ready for war, who want to maintain the *status quo,* at least for a time, must turn, even though hesitatingly, toward collaboration with the

Soviet Union. The oppressed nations look to it for inspiration and leadership. Within each capitalist country, all forces for peace, and especially the workers and farmers, are beginning to see in the policy of the Soviet Union the chief hope of peace and progress in the world.

There are voices which shout of the menace of fascism and war, even in radical and "revolutionary" phrases, but which cannot find anything to say about the mighty and growing forces for progress and peace. Such voices come from confusionists and panic-mongers, who consciously or unconsciously are the advance agents of fascism, spreading defeatism and demoralization among the masses, disarming them before the enemy.

It is possible to defeat the fascists and war-makers. It is possible to move toward progress, to maintain peace. But to do this requires that we recognize and make full use of all factors, even the smallest, that work toward this end, even temporarily. It requires a drive toward *one united international policy,* around which is rallied the growing armies of progress and peace. It requires the recognition of the role of the Soviet Union, and full utilization of this great power.

The confusionists and panic-mongers all have one common starting point for their defeatism, fatalism and hopelessness. They reject the Soviet Union as a great power for progress and peace; some of them, like the Trotskyists, are moved by definitely counter-revolutionary theories and hatreds; others, like Norman Thomas, because they are filled with doubts, reservations, hesitations, misconceptions. Wherever this influence, in whatever degree, prevails among the masses, there we have more division instead of more unity, more confusion instead of more clarity, more defeatism and demoralization instead of the growth of a militant united movement against fascism and war.

But the united People's Front is winning the masses more and more in every country. It is overcoming the demagogic slanders of the counter-revolutionists, it is dissolving the doubts and hesitations of the confused people. It must, it can, and it will win the majority of the toiling people of every country.

We will have a special report to this Convention on the detailed problems of the fight to maintain world peace, and the role of the Soviet Union and its peace policy. My report will therefore not go into the details of this subject. I must, however, before I pass on to the problems of the struggle against reaction in the United States, say just a few words about the latest historic achievements of socialism in the Soviet Union, which have made possible its rapidly enlarged role in world affairs.

The new Soviet Constitution, published in the last days, gives us some measure of the greatness of these achievements. For the first time in human history, a government can write into its basic law the guarantee to every citizen of education, work, and leisure. That is the outstanding feature of the new Constitution, which is unique, which has no counterpart or forerunner. That is the fruit of socialism, of the rule of the working class, of the First and Second Five-Year Plans for socialist industrialization, of the collectivization of agriculture, of the great Stakhanov movement for increase of socialist productivity. That is the fruit of the genius of Lenin and Stalin.

It is upon this solid foundation of working class rule and socialism that it was possible to erect the superstructure of the most complete democracy ever seen. Complete adult suffrage, beginning at the age of 18; equality of representation for all voters; guarantee of the right of self-determination of the constituent nationalities; direct election to all offices, including judiciary, by secret ballot; full guarantee of individual rights, including the rights of personal property resulting from individual labor; free speech, press and assemblage made concrete by providing the masses with printing presses, halls and possession of the streets; and freedom of worship—here, indeed, is a democracy which already, only 19 years since the revolution in a most backward country, surpasses the dreams of the great Utopians.

This is why the Soviet Union can come forward as the organizer of all the forces of progress and peace everywhere in the world.

THE ECONOMIC FOUNDATION OF DEMOCRACY

Democracy, the control of state power by the people, acting on the principle of majority rule and the delegation of power to representatives periodically chosen by election, can be historically developed only upon the foundation of an appropriate economic system.

That democracy which developed with capitalism, and which, in its purest forms, gave capitalism its highest development, was originally based upon the widespread distribution of ownership in the basic economy of the country, which was an economy of individual production, chiefly agricultural.

With the growth of commodity production, exchange, the market, division of labor, the accumulation of capital, and finally the rise of machinery, mechanical power and gigantic production units—as production took on more and more socialized forms, there took place the simultaneous process of divorcing the small owner from his property. This takes place through the normal operation of capitalist economy, accelerated always by state policy, and often by extra-legal fraud and violence. By varied and sundry means, the full development of capitalism always and necessarily means the creation of a small privileged owning class, monopoly capitalists, set over against a large wage-working class which has no ownership whatever in the means of production, and which comprises in North America the vast majority of the population.

Democracy in North America has thus been almost completely deprived of its original economic foundation. To the degree that democracy still lives under this developed capitalism, therefore, it must find for itself a new economic foundation. This is no longer possible in the form of individual ownership. All possibility of that has been destroyed beyond recall by machinery and mechanical power, making necessary large-scale mass production.

The illusion, fostered for a time by capitalist propaganda, of a democratization of capital by widespread corporate-stock ownership, was given its final death-blow by the last crisis. The only new forms by which democracy has achieved a very fragmentary and precarious economic foundation under modern capitalism, have been socialized forms—militant trade unionism, especially in its industrial form, and governmental intervention in economy under the influence of the democratic aspirations and demands.

The struggle for these new forms brings about a realignment of forces within the democracy—with the capitalists, their agents and dupes on the one side, fighting for maintenance and increase of their profits, and the producing masses on the other side, fighting for a better life at the expense of capitalist profits. This is the process that has brought the present chaos in the traditional political life of the United States and Canada.

For a time the monopoly capitalists are able to keep this struggle of the masses under their control, within certain limits, by trickery, fraud and force, by keeping the toiling masses divided and fighting among themselves instead of their common enemy. But finally, when all these resources fail them, when they see the masses uniting at last against them upon a program of social betterment at the expense of the capitalists—then the capitalists begin to destroy the democracy which in the past served them so well, but which now threatens to escape their control. They turn to fascism, the open, brutal and bloody dictatorship of finance capital, exercised by turning loose upon society the criminal underworld and declassed elements, organized and controlled by their enormous wealth, and the terrorist destruction of the organization of the people. They destroy democracy, always under the pretext that democracy is threatened with destruction at the hands of Communism, of Marxism, of Bolshevism. It is an infallible sign of the rise of fascism when, as in the United States today, such moderate democrats as President Roosevelt and John L. Lewis, who openly proclaim their allegiance to capitalism, are denounced by the Tories as "Communists."

Democracy today is destroyed in much of the capitalist world. It is fighting for its life in the remainder. It can survive under capitalism only to the degree to which there are successfully carried out such programs as those of John L. Lewis and the Committee for Industrial Organization and the economic reforms and the peace program of President Roosevelt. It will always be in danger of destruction so long as the national economy is owned and controlled by a small plutocratic capitalist class. The only final guarantee for democracy is the transfer of ownership of the national economy from the hands of the small, capitalist class into the hands of the whole people, that is, through socialism.

That is the main lesson to be drawn by us today, in the North American countries, from an examination of the achievements of twenty years of Soviet power in the Soviet Union.

The Soviet Union has been able, in a world where elsewhere democracy is on the defensive or destroyed, to make a great new democratic advance, precisely because it has taken both economic and political power out of the hands of the enemies of the people, precisely because it has given to democracy a full and complete economic foundation, one which will endure, which will not be undermined and disappear as did the individual private property. Every advance of science in the Soviet Union, every increase in production and productivity, strengthens Soviet democracy and strengthens its economic foundation.

The Soviet Union has shown the way to the final and complete guarantee of democracy, and its fullest development. And such a democracy is unconquerable. . . .

[COMMUNISM AND AMERICA'S FUTURE]

The American people have shown in many ways that they will fight against fascism. Their hatred of a fascist dictatorship is the reason why the reactionaries have clothed their reactionary program in the garb of "liberty" and "constitutionalism." That is why it is necessary for the people to make a genuine fight for freedom and liberty. By fighting to maintain and extend our democratic rights we organize and strengthen the people against reaction. They learn those deeper lessons which will eventually prepare them for that necessary reorganization of our social life which can only be achieved by taking the road to socialism.

The program which the Communist Party proposes and carries to the American people is one which by fighting for liberty will pave the way for socialism. This program to meet immediate needs is one which preserves the possibility for the American people to choose the socialist path when they think it necessary, a choice which the capitalists would deny them by fascist force and violence.

In this connection I should like to point out that it is the reactionaries who use force and violence against the people, and that the Communist Party is not an advocate of force and violence. Let me quote a resolution adopted by the Ninth Convention of the Communist Party which was held last month in New York City:

The Communist Party must smash once and for all the superstition, which has been embodied in a maze of court decisions having the force of law, that our Party is an advocate of force and violence, that it is subject to laws (Federal immigration laws, State "criminal syndicalism" laws) directed against such advocacy. The Communist Party is not a conspirative organization, it is an open revolutionary Party, continuing the traditions of 1776 and 1861; it is the only organization that is really entitled by its program and work to designate itself as "sons and daughters of the American revolution."

Communists are not anarchists, not terrorists. The Communist Party is a legal party and defends its legality. Prohibition of advocacy of force and violence does not apply to the Communist Party; it is properly applied only to the Black Legion, the Ku Klux Klan and other fascist groupings, and to the strikebreaking agencies and the open-shop employers who use them against the working class, who are responsible for the terrible toll of violence which shames our country.

We Communists believe that a strong and consistent fight for democratic rights under the conditions of decaying capitalism must ultimately lead the American people to the choice of the socialist path. In the fight against reaction the people will learn that the evils of the present system cannot be completely abolished unless a new social order, socialism, is built.

Under socialism, the United States, the richest land in the world, would be able to furnish prosperity, happiness and a rich and cultured life to all. Under socialism there would be no crisis, no poverty, no unemployment. The people would spring overnight from the kingdom of necessity and poverty to the kingdom of freedom and abundance.

We Communists maintain that the American people can and will be won for socialism. But this cannot be done by merely preaching socialism in the abstract as Norman Thomas and the Socialist Party are doing in this election. It can be done only by rallying the people to fight for their immediate and most burning needs and to organize them against their most dangerous enemies —the Liberty League, Landon and Hearst. In these struggles they will gain that determination and conviction which will lead them to abolish capitalism and establish socialism.

In waging this fight against reaction the American people are but carrying on their glorious revolutionary traditions, which are the most hallowed heritage of our people. Reactionaries of all shades attack socialism as revolutionary. But since when is revolution un-American? Our country was born and preserved in revolutionary struggles. Our people met their problems and solved them in a revolutionary way.

Today a far greater crisis confronts the American people. We Communists are confident that they will meet and solve it in the same spirit the American people solved the crises of 1776 and 1861. We Communists are proud that we can truly say that Communism is the Americanism of the twentieth century, that in the great struggles to come the Communist Party will carry forward the revolutionary traditions of the past to a higher stage, and show the American people the way to a better and more secure life in the present, and to a future of peace, freedom, happiness and prosperity for all.

VIII

The Response of
the Churches

To a people accustomed to a belief in the beneficence of divine providence and a faith in their historic mission and destiny, the momentous events that marked the twentieth century—including a world-wide depression and two global wars—were a bewildering challenge. In the midst of such a threatening world, men once more began to seek universal and unshakable standards of truth, justice, and morality to which they could hold fast.

In such an atmosphere it was perhaps not surprising that an increasing number of Americans began to examine anew the religious heritage of their society. The problem they faced, however, was not simply to restate and emphasize established religious truths. Had that been so, religion would have faced no serious crisis. But the fact was that many elements in the traditional faith of Americans seemed peculiarly outmoded and obsolete. Liberal Protestantism, for example, with its belief in the innate goodness of man, its ideal of social betterment (even utopianism), and its acceptance of a theology of immanence, appeared outdated by the monstrous evils that marked the world in these decades. Even the older fundamentalist Protestantism seemed an anachronism, especially following the failure of one of its major goals— prohibition—an objective that had promised the eradication of evil but had helped instead to spread crime and corruption in American life.

Yet the dilemmas of religion were not simply internal in nature but were intimately related to developments within American culture. For as the older individualistic ethic declined, to be replaced by a social and organizational ethic, the role and function of religion in the United States also underwent a drastic transformation. To many individuals the appeal of religion was based not so much on its intrinsic truths as on the sustenance it could provide for "the American way of life." One attended a house of worship not necessarily out of reverence for a deity and his revealed truths, but because attendance was expected. In addition, institutional affiliation provided the individual with a means of identification with a particular social grouping—an identification based increasingly on religion as the older ethnic identification declined with the end of mass immigration.

Recognizing the weakness of organized religion, virtually all religious leaders agreed on the need for a revitalized Christianity that would once again restore meaning and significance to the life of man. However, it was apparent that a simple reiteration of older themes was insufficient, and many churchmen began to seek new ways of presenting and interpreting the message of Christianity.

The quest for a theology that would provide a meaningful perspective for contemporary man became noticeable initially in Protestantism. Influenced by the crisis theology of such philosophers as Karl Barth and Paul Tillich, Protestant theologians began to undertake a searching examination of the optimistic hopes and dreams that had characterized liberal Christianity and the social gospel. Rejecting the emphasis on the innate goodness of human nature, these ministers began to resurrect the older doctrine of original sin, arguing that the dilemmas and paradoxes that mankind faced were perennial and could not be solved on a permanent basis by man. As Reinhold Niebuhr, the outstanding spokesman for Protestant neo-orthodoxy put it, the human race had little hope for redemption if it relied solely on the potentialities of human nature or the processes of history. Only a religion of grace or a gospel that held out hope of a transcendent source of redemption could bring comfort to the human spirit in its inevitable defeat in the world of nature and history. The theologians of the new orthodoxy thus propounded a religious faith that restored the transcendental significance of Christian belief. In so doing they developed a Christianity that was quite unlike that of the past—one that at times was even "post-Christian" in its sources and meanings.

Neo-orthodox Protestantism, nevertheless, was too sophisticated and intellectual a creed to have immediate effect on the lives of millions who had neither the training nor patience to master its intricacies or difficulties. Yet the need for a faith was so great that soon after the end of World War II the older evangelical-fundamentalist tradition began to reassert itself. Speaking in terms easily understood by the masses of people, evangelical ministers like Billy Graham insisted that salvation at a revival meeting not only offered man hope of divine forgiveness but also freed him from all future temptation. Thus the major prerequisite for the solution both of the problem of the individual and of national and international problems was an unreserved acceptance of Jesus. In an era when America seemed to be moving away from liberalism toward conservatism, the simple message of the evangelists struck a responsive chord in the hearts of millions who dreamed of a return to the imagined simplicities of the past.

The problems faced by Protestantism in recent decades have by no means been unique to that group alone. The Catholic Church in the United States also has had to face similar difficulties growing out of the secularization of American culture. And as Catholicism has come to maturity in the United States, it has come to accept this challenge and has tended to take a more vocal position on the moral dilemmas of our time. Since the 1930's, as a matter of fact, the Catholic hierarchy and prominent lay philosophers have embarked on a militant crusade on behalf of the Thomistic version of natural law. Insisting upon the ability of man's reason to fathom the eternal law of God, Catholics argued that the eighteenth- and nineteenth-century world had collapsed largely because of its atheism, its materialism, and its secularism that raised "progress" to the level of divine truth. Only by returning to the natural law and the traditional truths of Christianity as interpreted by the Catholic Church, they insisted, can modern man find significance and meaning in his life. Clearly, the promise, security, and serenity offered by Catholic dogma has played a major part in the resurgence of this uniquely authoritarian church in modern American society.

Despite the apparent strength of religious faith at mid-century, it is still questionable whether Christianity in any form can triumph over the increasing secularization of American life, a trend that has affected all denominations. Christianity also has been hard-pressed by critics who have attacked its supernatural beliefs and its otherworldliness, which they argue has led to a passive acceptance of evil. These critics point to the deliberate slaughter of six million Jews by a supposedly Christian nation as well as the barbarism of total warfare devised by men who claim the church's sanctions. Whether or not religion can ever again exercise the influence it has had in the past, or even become a vital force in itself rather than a means to an end—for to most Americans religion is good and desirable because it reinforces the American way of life, which is regarded as *the* ultimate good—remains for the future to answer.

(40)

Reinhold Niebuhr

1892-

One of the outstanding Protestant theologians and philosophers of our time, Reinhold Niebuhr was born in Wright City, Missouri. After studying at a theological seminary in St. Louis, he received a B.D. from Yale in 1914 and an M.A. in 1915. In the latter year he accepted a call to a struggling, working-class church in Detroit and, as a result, became interested in the problems of an industrialized society. Slowly but surely Niebuhr came to the recognition that the advocates of liberal Christianity and the social gospel had misread the nature and potentialities of man—that the liberal church, like the orthodox church, was preaching the good life in terms irrelevant to the problems of modern society. He then turned to the task of developing an outlook suitable to the contemporary world. In 1928 Niebuhr was called to Union Theological Seminary in New York City.

The leading advocate of Protestant neo-orthodoxy, Niebuhr has consistently emphasized the concept of original sin—the frank recognition of the essentially sinful and tragic nature of man. Defining original sin in terms of a historical situation that never permits a choice between absolute good and absolute evil, he rejected the notion of the perfectibility of man and the idea of progress in its eighteenth-century sense. Holding that Christianity, properly understood, has a relevance to the dilemmas of modern man, Niebuhr has attempted to formulate a more realistic philosophy that takes into account the limitations of man. He has argued that man, though capable of imposing achievements, is yet a finite being, driven by a sinful pride to claim a dignity and eminence that no man possesses and to affirm a finality for his convictions that no relative human judgment deserves. But it should be noted that while emphasizing the limitations of man, Niebuhr has always taken a liberal or radical position on social and economic issues.

The following selections are representative of Niebuhr's thinking. The first is from "The Dilemma of Modern Man," *The Nation,* 164 (February 22, 1947), and the second from *The Children of Light and the Children of Darkness: A Vindication of Democracy and a Critique of Its Traditional Defence* (New York, 1944).

We are living in an age in which our social and historical imperatives may be fairly simply defined but not easily achieved. Our task is to create and re-create community within the terms set by a technical civilization. The constant elaboration of man's technical skills has created a potential world community, but this community cannot be actualized as easily as modern men had hoped. The same technical skills have created abundance in modern industrial communities; yet these communities all suffer from great social insecurity because they find it difficult to distribute the new wealth equitably enough to guarantee harmony and stability.

In such a historical situation the average person still interprets the faith by which he lives primarily in sociopolitical terms. He has faith in this or that social objective. Usually in the United States and in the Western world generally the objective is defined as "the democratic way of life." I do not believe that such a purely political objective constitutes an adequate "faith." It may define our primary moral obligation, or at least the social dimension of that obligation, but it does not define the meaning of our existence. Any adequate sense of the meaning of life must be able to comprehend not only what we ought to do but what we are. It must explain why we are creatures who do not find it easy, or even possible, to fulfil our highest obligation.

At the present moment the popular definition of our political ideal as the "democratic way of life" hides a very great dilemma, which is also a part of the total human situation. For the world is divided between different types of "democrats," between those who would sacrifice freedom, or have already sacrificed it, for the sake of an equalitarian and collectivist democracy and those who would make no sacrifice of any freedom in the interest of justice. In the international community this cleavage may result in a world conflict between two cohorts of world-savers holding contradictory views of democracy.

In national communities it may still lead to the most tragic internecine conflicts. The truth obviously lies somewhere between these two creeds; but it is difficult to find, precisely because political creeds have been invested with a religious aura by a supposedly irreligious age. This whole development rather refutes John Dewey's hope, expressed some years ago in his "Common Faith," that men of good-will would agree on social and moral objectives, once modern culture had dissolved the irrelevant loyalties of historical religions. We have, as Americans, a particularly embarrassing position in this debate or conflict between contradictory conceptions of democracy. For America in general, and the American plutocracy in particular, has a more uncritical confidence in the organic relation between "free enterprise" and democracy than any other nation; and this type of bigotry may do more damage to the world community and the cause of justice than any religious bigotry ever did.

Even if this contradiction in the definition of our democratic objectives did not exist, it would still be impossible to define the meaning of human existence purely in terms of some social and political objective—partly because no human life can be completely contained within the bounds of the social and historical dimension of life, and partly because we do not either individually or collectively move as easily or surely toward ideal goals as past generations have assumed. Our age is secular, either non-Christian or anti-Christian, in the main outlines of its basic creed. It has disavowed the historical religious faiths partly because their symbols seem outmoded in an age of science but chiefly because modern men find the tragic view of life implicit in religion unacceptable and the old theories of redemption irrelevant. A message of redemption which offered men and nations life only through death and declared that men could be saved only through repentance seemed completely irrelevant to an age which saw history moving forward to ever more impressive elaborations of human power and freedom. There was nothing the matter with human life which historical growth could not cure.

The implicit faith of the past two centuries has hardly prepared us for the kind of frustration through which we must live in the next century or two. For we have been given the task of creating community in larger dimensions than any one or two centuries can accomplish. The frustrations of our age become pathetic rather than tragic when we have no means of either anticipating or comprehending the character of our present experiences. The one unifying element in all strands of modern culture was the idea of progress. We had faith in a redemptive history. This faith, which supposedly made all other interpretations of life completely incredible, is now progressively disclosing itself as the most incredible of all interpretations of life. This refutation of the culture of modern man by contemporary history may be regarded as the real spiritual crisis of our day.

When the atomic bomb fell upon Hiroshima it brought more than one chapter in both political and cultural history to a symbolic conclusion. It particularly concluded that chapter of Western spiritual history, beginning in the Renaissance, which regarded history as a kind of God and time as a kind of

Christ. It was an age which assumed that technical progress, which continually increased man's power over nature and freedom from natural limitations, would inevitably contribute to human welfare and happiness. It was an age which assumed that man's increased mobility and the wider range of his eyes, ears, and voice, transfigured by microscope and telescope, telegraph and radio, would inevitably lead to the enlargement of the human community. Actually mechanical advances have only created a potential, and not an actual, world community, and have meanwhile destroyed many of the organic forms of community which gave life sanity and stability in older cultures.

We have had to learn that history is neither a God nor a redeemer. The real fact is that while history solves many problems, it aggravates rather than mitigates the basic incongruities of human existence. Man is a finite and contingent creature, with some sense of universal value transcending his own existence but unfortunately inclined to endow the contingent values of his life or culture, of his truth or loyalty, with an absolute significance which it does not deserve. He thereby finds community with his fellow-men as difficult as it is necessary; particularly since his fellow-men are engaged in the same idolatrous process. Man can neither live alone, not being self-sufficient, nor easily come to terms with his fellow-men. The same instruments which extend the range of possible community also extend the range of man's impulse to domination over his fellows. Thus history pitches the drama of life on continually higher levels, but the essentials of the drama remain the same.

The fact that history is endlessly creative but not redemptive might have been more apparent to modern man had it not been for another illusion in modern culture. This other illusion is closely related to the idea of progress and is indeed frequently the basis for it. It is the illusion that the so-called "methods of science" or "impartial scientific inquiry" or "scientific objectivity" are actually the instruments by which mankind rises to higher and higher degrees of perfection. There are forms of the idea of progress which trust primarily in the extension of the evolutionary process of biology into the realm of history. But more frequently historical progress is assumed to depend upon the ability of man gradually to rise from his position as a creature of natural and historical forces to become their master. The instrument by which this is to be accomplished is science. By scientific impartiality man presumably rises from finite to universal perspectives, from interested to disinterested appraisal of problems of justice, from prejudice and passion to god-like serenity and impartiality. Science will not only unlock the mysteries of existence which have remained closed to the poetic and religious imagination and to the speculations of philosophy but will redeem man from the fragmentary and partial character of his life and actions and guarantee action of universal validity.

Sometimes it is assumed that the methods of science will make men moral merely by making them rational. Sometimes it is believed that science should be used to control the dark and irrational forces in human nature, "that the same science which has altered the face of nature can change the habits of men." Sometimes the continued egotism and irrationality of individuals are assumed, but it is believed that a "scientific" politics will be able to manage social forces as readily as man now manages the forces of nature. The end product of these illusions is the type of rationalism which dreams of setting up a world government containing scientifically tested constitutional instruments for equilibrating all the vitalities of a community of nations and for arbitrating or, if necessary, suppressing every political conflict.

A simple fact has been obscured by this cult of redemption through science. Man is a creature whose rational and vital processes are in organic unity, and there is no "scientific method" by which he can escape from the hopes, fears, ambitions, and anxieties of his own individual existence or those of his nation, civilization, or ethnic group. In all problems pertaining to the security or the meaning of his own life or the justice of his conflict with some competing life or vitality, he is never the disinterested observer but an interested participant. In so far as impartiality is possible, it is a moral and religious as much as a scientific achievement. A contrite recognition of the interested character of our views and actions must always lie behind the achievement of relative disinterestedness. The achievement involves the whole of the personality and is therefore not purely intellectual or scientific.

Modern culture has wittingly or unwittingly followed the thought of Comte, who believed that the history of the world could be divided into three ages— the theological, the metaphysical, and the scientific—and who saw the possibility of solving all human problems in the third and final stage of human development by the application of the scientific method to man's social existence. Actually the ability of science to achieve impartial and universally valid judgments rests partly upon the sharply circumscribed fields of inquiry in which science looks for causal relations and partly upon the fact that a natural science, which investigates the determined sequences of nature, is under no temptation to weigh evidence or make hazardous judgments on such imponderables as human motives.

But the wider the field of inquiry becomes, the more plainly will even the natural sciences betray themselves to be under the guidance of presuppositions, implicit or explicit metaphysical assumptions, which are not the consequence but the basis of the inquiry. If it is historical rather than biological or geological sequence which is under inquiry, there is no strictly "scientific" method of judging the motives which prompt human actions or of comparing competing vitalities in history. Every judgment of fact is also a value judgment, presupposing a norm. The norm is itself historically conditioned, and the application of the norm to the stuff of history is twice conditioned.

This fact does not invalidate the social and historical sciences or prove that they ought to be reduced to statistical proportions in order to become purer sciences. Both the logical and the analytical powers of reason remain instruments by which partial and particular points of view are corrected, and the whole stuff of historical reality is brought under examination. We must continue to seek to understand what things are and how they came to be what they are in history as well as in nature. But there is no magic in either logic or the scientific method which will coerce men or nations to subordinate the particular to the universal interest or to correct the partial by a more universal insight. Reason in history remains permanently ambiguous, being both the servant and the master of all of history's vitalities.

There is, for instance, no "scientific method" which could guarantee that statesmen who must deal with the social and political consequences of atomic energy could arrive at the kind of "universal mind" which operated in the discovery of atomic energy. Statesmen who deal with this problem will betray "British," "American," or "Russian" bias, not because they are less intelligent than the scientists but because they are forced to approach the issue in terms of their responsibility to their respective nations. Their formulation of a solution is intimately and organically related to the hopes, fears, and ambitions of nations. They must deal with history as a vital and not a rational process. As a vital process it is always something less and something more than reason. It is less than rational in so far as the power impulses of nations express themselves as inexorably as the force of a stampeding herd of cattle. It is something more than rational in so far as human beings have aspirations and loyalties transcending both impulse and prudence. Man is a heaven-storming creature whose highest ideals are curiously compounded with his immediate and mundane interests. The Marxist dream of a universal classless society, mixed with the power impulses of a Russian state and the anxieties of a precarious dictatorship, is a nice symbol of what historical reality is like. Our so-called democratic world is a little more rational; but the mixture of democratic idealism and the quest for profits of a vast American economic machine must be almost as bewildering to the outside observer as the Russian mixture.

The collective mixtures of ideals and interests are more vivid than individual expressions of human spirituality, but every individual life is governed less by prudence and rationality and more by what lies below the level of reason and rises above the level of rational calculation than a scientific culture understands. One may be grateful for the fact that poets and novelists continued to bear testimony to these dimensions of life even in a scientific age, if they dealt at all authentically with the human scene. Because man in his grandeur and in his misery, in his high aspirations and in their egoistic corruption, is and always will be a more complex creature than modern culture has understood, his history is more tragic and his redemption from self-seeking, whether individual or collective, more difficult and always less final than we have assumed.

Old cultures and civilizations, reigning oligarchies and traditional social systems and structures do not quietly yield to the logic of a new historical development. They refuse to die in bed. They take the field, ostensibly to defend their "ideals" against some new barbarism, but also to preserve established interests against new vitalities. That is why we must march through any number of world wars before we can achieve world community; and why the world community which is within the grasp of human powers will be less stable and secure than our calculating world planners can realize. History presents us with constantly enlarged responsibilities. We must meet these responsibilities if we would remain human. The Nazis have shown us the perverse consequences of any effort to turn the clock back and "return to the womb" of tribal primitivism. We must move on. But there are neither securities nor fulfilments in history in which the heart can rest.

Since we are free spirits who transcend the historical process, as well as creatures who are involved in it, we crave for some ultimate security and fulfilment. But since history remains as fragmentary and as full of contradictions as our individual life-adventures, we can have such security and fulfilment only in an ultimate sense and only by faith. The kind of faith which adequately completes the temple of meaning will also reveal that our own egotism, and that of our nation, and not merely the egotism of competitor or foe is responsible for the tragic aspects of history. Thus contrition and faith go hand in hand.

In Christian piety the devout soul always beholds itself in a double relation to Christ. The perfect love, of which the Cross is the symbol, is regarded as the final norm of human goodness and defines what man ought to be. But man also knows himself to be the crucifier of the Christ. This expresses our understanding of the fact that life can only be brought to completion by a love in which the self is not concerned for itself but only for its fellows. But we also know that as individuals and as groups we seek our own. The justice we have achieved in history is a compromise between these two impulses; and the compromise is not achieved simply by calculation and prudence. Such pity and mercy as are insinuated into the cruelties and inhumanities of human life are the fruits of the contrition, which recognizes that the egotism we abhor in others is in us also. Fanaticism is always the product of self-righteousness. Religion has produced as much fanaticism as contrition, because religion is never a good force per se, but merely the final conflict between human self-esteem and divine mercy. And the one is as frequently victorious as the other.

A secular age imagined that it could exorcise fanaticism by disavowing religion. But an age which prides itself upon its scientific objectivity has actually sunk to new levels of cruelty, for the man who knows himself to be absolutely right through the benefit of science is as cruel as those who achieved this fanaticism by religious revelation. Not only Marxist fanatics are involved in the cruelties of our age, but democratic idealists also. The ancients were certainly not more merciless to their foes than we; no one has been so merciless to a vanquished foes as we since the Assyrians. We are pitiless because we do not know ourselves to be pitiable.

A secular age thought it would be sufficient to disavow the other-worldliness of religion in order to achieve a consistent and humane sense of responsibility for the commonweal. But the disavowal of an incredible heaven led to the avowal of incredible utopias; incredible because they defined an unconditioned good amid the conditions of nature [and] history. This persistent utopianism has generated fanatical furies of our day, for if the heaven of a classless society could be established on earth, would it be worth the price which the Communists are ready to pay? It is also responsible for the alternate fits of illusion and disillusion which distract us from our historic responsibilities.

Life is never completed, either individually or collectively; and it is never completely freed from chaos or from contradictions to its essential meaning. An adequate faith must understand this quality of life; but that is impossible without an explicit or implicit belief that a divine mercy can complete what we cannot complete. Such a faith may of course be corrupted and may beguile men from their pressing responsibilities; but the alternative secular idealism also leads to deep corruptions. It tempts men to seek in others, and never in themselves, the root of human misery. And if they finally find it in themselves, their optimism gives way to despair. The mood of this century compared with the optimism of the nineteenth century looks very much like the despair which all false optimism generates. . . .

Democracy, as every other historic ideal and institution, contains both ephemeral and more permanently valid elements. Democracy is on the one hand the characteristic fruit of a bourgeois civilization; on the other hand it is a perennially valuable form of social organization in which freedom and order are made to support, and not to contradict, each other.

Democracy is a "bourgeois ideology" in so far as it expresses the typical viewpoints of the middle classes who have risen to power in European civilization in the past three or four centuries. Most of the democratic ideals, as we know them, were weapons of the commercial classes who engaged in stubborn, and ultimately victorious, conflict with the ecclesiastical and aristocratic rulers of the feudal-medieval world. . . .

Since bourgeois civilization, which came to birth in the sixteenth to eighteenth centuries and reached its zenith in the nineteenth century, is now obviously in grave peril, if not actually in *rigor mortis* in the twentieth century, it must be obvious that democracy, in so far as it is a middle-class ideology, also faces its doom.

This fate of democracy might be viewed with equanimity, but for the fact that it has a deeper dimension and broader validity than its middle-class character. Ideally democracy is a permanently valid form of social and political organization which does justice to two dimensions of human existence: to man's spiritual stature and his social character; to the uniqueness and variety of life, as well as to the common necessities of all men. Bourgeois democracy frequently exalted the individual at the expense of the community; but its emphasis upon liberty contained a valid element, which transcended its excessive individualism. The community requires liberty as much as does the individual; and the individual requires community more than bourgeois thought comprehended. Democracy can therefore not be equated with freedom. An ideal democratic order seeks unity within the conditions of freedom; and maintains freedom within the framework of order. . . .

If democracy is to survive it must find a more adequate cultural basis than the philosophy which has informed the building of the bourgeois world. The inadequacy of the presuppositions upon which the democratic experiment rests does not consist merely in the excessive individualism and libertarianism of the bourgeois world view; though it must be noted that this excessive individualism prompted a civil war in the whole western world in which the rising proletarian classes pitted an excessive collectivism against the false individualism of middle-class life. This civil conflict contributed to the weakness of democratic civilization when faced with the threat of barbarism. Neither the individualism nor the collectivism did justice to all the requirements of man's social life, and the conflict between half-truth and half-truth divided the civilized world in such a way that the barbarians were able to claim first one side and then the other in this civil conflict as their provisional allies.

But there is a more fundamental error in the social philosophy of democratic civilization than the individualism of bourgeois democracy and the collectivism of Marxism. It is the confidence of both bourgeois and proletarian idealists in the possibility of achieving an easy resolution of the tension and conflict between self-interest and the general interest. . . .

According to the scripture "the children of this world are in their generation wiser than the children of light." This observation fits the modern situation. Our democratic civilization has been built, not by children of darkness but by foolish children of light. It has been under attack by the children of darkness, by the moral cynics, who declare that a strong nation need acknowledge no law beyond its strength. It has come close to complete disaster under this attack, not because it accepted the same creed as the cynics; but because it underestimated the power of self-interest, both individual and collective, in modern society. The children of light have not been as wise as the children of darkness.

The children of darkness are evil because they know no law beyond the self. They are wise, though evil, because they understand the power of self-interest. The children of light are virtuous because they have some conception of a higher law than their own will. They are usually foolish because they do not know the power of self-will. They underestimate the peril of anarchy in both the national and the international community. Modern democratic civilization is, in short, sentimental rather than cynical. It has an easy solution for the problem of anarchy and chaos on both the national and international level of community, because of its fatuous and superficial view of man. It does not know that the same man who is ostensibly devoted to the "common good" may have desires and ambitions, hopes and fears, which set him at variance with his neighbor.

It must be understood that the children of light are foolish not merely because they underestimate the power of self-interest among the children of darkness. They underestimate this power among themselves. The democratic world came so close to disaster not merely because it never believed that Nazism possessed the demonic fury which it avowed. Civilization refused to recognize the power of class interest in its own communities. It also spoke glibly of an international conscience; but the children of darkness meanwhile skilfully set nation against nation. They were thereby enabled to despoil one nation after another, without every civilized nation coming to the defence of each. . . .

Our modern civilization, on the other hand, was ushered in on a wave of boundless social optimism. Modern secularism is divided into many schools. But all the various schools agreed in rejecting the Christian doctrine of original sin. It is not possible to explain the subtleties or to measure the profundity of this doctrine in this connection. But it is necessary to point out that the doctrine makes an important contribution to any adequate social and political theory the lack of which has robbed bourgeois theory of real wisdom; for it emphasizes a fact which every page of human history attests. Through it one may understand that no matter how wide the perspectives which the human mind may reach, how broad the loyalties which the human imagination may conceive, how universal the community which human statecraft may organize, or how pure the aspirations of the saintliest idealists may be, there is no level of human moral or social achievement in which there is not some corruption of inordinate self-love.

This sober and true view of the human situation was neatly rejected by modern culture. That is why it conceived so many fatuous and futile plans for resolving the conflict between the self and the community; and between the national and the world community. Whenever modern idealists are confronted with the divisive and corrosive effects of man's self-love, they look for some immediate cause of this perennial tendency, usually in some specific form of social organization. One school holds that men would be good if only political institutions would not corrupt them; another believes that they would be good if the prior evil of a faulty economic organization could be eliminated. Or another school thinks of this evil as no more than ignorance, and therefore waits for a more perfect educational process to redeem man from his partial and particular loyalties. But no school asks how it is that an essentially good man could have produced corrupting and tyrannical political organizations or exploiting economic organizations, or fanatical and superstitious religious organizations.

The result of this persistent blindness to the obvious and tragic facts of man's social history is that democracy has had to maintain itself precariously against the guile and the malice of the children of darkness, while its statesmen and guides conjured up all sorts of abstract and abortive plans for the creation of perfect national and international communities.

The confidence of modern secular idealism in the possibility of an easy resolution of the tension between individual and community, or between classes, races and nations is derived from a too optimistic view of human nature. This too generous estimate of human virtue is intimately related to an erroneous estimate of the dimensions of the human stature. The conception of human nature which underlies the social and political attitudes of a liberal democratic culture is that of an essentially harmless individual. The survival impulse, which man shares with the animals, is regarded as the normative form of his egoistic drive. If this were a true picture of the human situation man might be, or might become, as harmless as seventeenth- and eighteenth-century thought assumed. Unfortunately for the validity of this picture of man, the most significant distinction between the human and the animal world is that the impulses of the former are "spiritualized" in the human world. Human capacities for evil as well as for good are derived from this spiritualization. There is of course always a natural survival impulse at the core of all human ambition. But this survival impulse cannot be neatly disentangled from two forms of its spiritualization. The one form is the desire to fulfil the potentialities of life and not merely to maintain its existence. Man is the kind of animal who cannot merely live. If he lives at all he is bound to seek the realization of his true nature; and to his true nature belongs his fulfilment in the lives of others. The will to live is thus transmuted into the will to self-realization; and self-realization involves self-giving in relations to others. . . .

On the other hand the will-to-live is also spiritually transmuted into the will-to-power or into the desire for "power and glory." Man, being more than a natural creature, is not interested merely in physical survival but in prestige and social approval. Having the intelligence to anticipate the perils in which he stands in nature and history, he invariably seeks to gain security against these perils by enhancing his power, individually and collectively. Possessing a darkly unconscious sense of his insignificance in the total scheme of things, he seeks to compensate for his insignificance by pretensions of pride. The conflicts between men are thus never simple conflicts between competing survival impulses. They are conflicts in which each man or group seeks to guard its power and prestige against the peril of competing expressions of power and pride. . . .

Since the survival impulse in nature is transmuted into two different and contradictory spiritualized forms, which we may briefly designate as the will-to-live-truly and the will-to-power, man is at variance with himself. The power of the second impulse places him more fundamentally in conflict with his fellowman than democratic liberalism realizes. The fact he cannot realize himself, except in organic relation with his fellows, makes the community more important than bourgeois individualism understands. The fact that the two impulses, though standing in contradiction to each other, are also mixed and compounded with each other on every level of human life, makes the simple distinctions between good and evil, between selfishness and altruism, with which liberal idealism has tried to estimate moral and political facts, invalid. The fact that the will-to-power inevitably justifies itself in terms of the morally more acceptable will to realize man's true nature means that the egoistic corruption of universal ideals is a much more persistent fact in human conduct than any moralistic creed is inclined to admit.

Democratic theory therefore has not squared with the facts of history. This grave defect in democratic theory was comparatively innocuous in the heyday of the bourgeois period, when the youth and the power of democratic civilization surmounted all errors of judgment and confusions of mind. But in this latter day, when it has become important to save what is valuable in democratic life from the destruction of what is false in bourgeois civilization, it has also become necessary to distinguish what is false in democratic theory from what is true in democratic life.

The preservation of a democratic civilization requires the wisdom of the serpent and the harmlessness of the dove. The children of light must be armed with the wisdom of the children of darkness but remain free from their malice. They must know the power of self-interest in human society without giving it moral justification. They must have this wisdom in order that they may beguile, deflect, harness and restrain self-interest, individual and collective, for the sake of the community. . . .

The reason this final democratic freedom is right, though the reasons given for it in the modern period are wrong, is that there is no historical reality, whether it be church or government, whether it be the reason of wise men or specialists, which is not involved in the flux and relativity of human existence; which is not subject to error and sin, and which is not tempted to exaggerate its errors and sins when they are made immune to criticism.

Every society needs working principles of justice, as criteria for its positive law and system of restraints. The profoundest of these actually transcend reason and lie rooted in religious conceptions of the meaning of existence. But every historical statement of them is subject to amendment. If it becomes fixed it will destroy some of the potentialities of a higher justice, which the mind of one generation is unable to anticipate in the life of subsequent eras. . . .

Another and contrasting justification for a free society must be added. Sometimes new truth rides into history upon the back of an error. An authoritarian society would have prevented the new truth with the error. The idea that economic life is autonomous and ought not to be placed under either moral or political control is an error, for reasons which we have previously discussed. The self-regulating and self-balancing forces in economic life are not as strong as Adam Smith supposed. The propagation of this error has caused great damage in modern life. But a seed of truth was contained in the error. The intricacies of modern commerce and industry could not have developed if the medieval moral and political controls had been maintained; and even now when we know that all economic life must submit to moral discipline and political restraint, we must be careful to preserve whatever self-regulating forces exist in the economic process. If we do not, the task of control becomes too stupendous and the organs of control achieve proportions which endanger our liberty. . . .

The freedom of society is thus made necessary by the fact that human vitalities have no simply definable limits. The restraints which all human communities place upon human impulses and ambitions are made necessary by the fact that all man's vitalities tend to defy any defined limits. But since the community may as easily become inordinate in its passion for order, as may the various forces in the community in their passion for freedom, it is necessary to preserve a proper balance between both principles, and to be as ready to champion the individual against the community as the community against the individual. Any definition of a proper balance between freedom and order must always be at least slightly colored by the exigencies of the moment which may make the peril of the one seem greater and the security of the other therefore preferable. Thus even the moral and social principle which sets limits upon freedom and order must, in a free society, be subject to constant re-examination.

(41)

William F. (Billy) Graham

1918-

Born in Charlotte, North Carolina, Billy Graham was brought up a strict Presbyterian by parents who hoped that he would enter the ministry. He briefly attended Bob Jones College and then transferred to the fundamentalist Florida Bible Institute. In 1939 he enrolled at Wheaton College, another fundamentalist institution, where he received his B.A. in 1943. The following year he became associated with the Youth for Christ movement in Chicago, gaining valuable experience in revival techniques. The turning point in Graham's career came in 1949, when his tent revival in Los Angeles received national publicity. Since that time he has become America's most famous evangelist. His well-organized and well-financed revivals have attracted millions.

Graham's popularity derives essentially from his easily-understood message. Reducing faith to an all-embracing panacea for the ills of the world, he has in effect asserted that conversion produces a radical transformation in human nature. Since the sinfulness of human nature is at the root of all of man's problems, conversion is regarded as the key to peace and human happiness. Thus, mankind's problems are to be dealt with in terms of the individual; social action or collectivist solutions are futile. Consequently, Graham has criticized many features of modern society and has espoused an ultraconservative point of view in politics and economics. He has warned against deficit spending, the United Nations, the evils of big government, corruption in organized labor, and the intrusion of communists and fellow travelers into all areas of American life.

Graham's appeal has been largely to those unsophisticated people who seek a return to the imagined simplicity of the past. While Graham's and indeed the enduring influence of revivalism in general is still a debatable issue, there seems little doubt that the popularity of the movement has resulted from a spiritual void and the sense of frustration in American life.

The following selection is from Graham's *Peace With God* (New York, 1953), which has sold over half a million copies.

All humanity is seeking the answer to the confusion, the moral sickness, the spiritual emptiness that oppresses the world. All mankind is crying out for guidance, for comfort, for peace.

We are told that we live in the "age of anxiety." Historians point out that there have been few times in all history when man has been subject to so much fear and uncertainty. All the familiar props seem to have been swept away. We talk of peace but are confronted by war. We devise elaborate schemes for security but have not found it. We grasp at every passing straw and even as we clutch, it disappears.

For generations we have been running like frightened children, up first one blind alley and then another. Each time we have told ourselves: "This path is the right one, this one will take us where we want to go." But each time we have been wrong.

One of the first paths we chose was labeled "political freedom." Give everyone political freedom, we said, and the world will become a happy place. Let us select our own government leaders and we shall have the kind of government that will make life worth living. So we achieved political freedom, but we did not achieve our better world. Our daily newspapers give us reports of corruption in high places, of favoritism, of exploitation, of hypocrisy equal to and sometimes surpassing the despotism of ancient kings. Political freedom is a precious and important thing, but it alone cannot give us the kind of world we long for.

There was another very hopeful path marked "education," and many put their whole faith in it. Political freedom coupled with education will do the trick, they said, and we all rushed madly along the educational path. It seemed a bright, well-lighted, sensible path for a long time, and we traveled it with eager, expectant feet, but where has it led us? You know the answer. We are the most informed people in the history of civilization—and yet the most miserable. Our high school students know more about the physical laws of the universe than the greatest scientist in the days of Aristotle. But though our heads are crammed with knowledge, our hearts are empty.

The brightest, most inviting path of all was the one marked "higher standards of living." Almost everyone felt he could trust this one to carry him automatically into that better and more joyful world. This was felt to be the sure route. This was the "press the button and you're there" route! This was the path that led through the beautiful full-color magazine advertisements, past all the shining new cars, past the gleaming rows of electric refrigerators and automatic washing machines, past all the fat chickens cooking in brand-new copper-bottomed pots. We knew we'd hit the jackpot this time! The other paths might have been false leads, but this time we had it!

All right, look around you right this minute. At this very moment in history you see in America a country that has political freedom to an extent that is undreamed of in many parts of the civilized world. You see the greatest and most far-reaching public education system that man has ever created, and we are eulogized at home and abroad for our high standard of living. "The American way of life" we like to call this fully electrified, fully automatic, chrome-plated economy of ours—but has it made us happy? Has it brought us the joy and satisfaction and the reason for living that we were seeking?

No. As we stand here feeling smug and proud that we have accomplished so much that generations before us only dreamed about; as we span our oceans in hours instead of months; as we produce miracle drugs that wipe out some of man's most dread diseases; as we erect buildings that make the Tower of Babel seem an anthill; as we learn more and more of the mysterious secrets that lie in the depths of the sea, and peer further and further into outer space, do we lose one iota of that empty feeling within us? Do all these modern wonders bring us a sense of fulfillment, do they help to explain why we are here, do they point out what we are supposed to learn?

Or does that awful feeling persist? Does every further discovery of the magnitude of the universe comfort you or make you feel more alone and helpless than ever? Does the antidote for human fear and hatred and corruption lie in some laboratory test tube, or in an astronomer's telescope?

We cannot deny that science has given man many things he thought he wanted. But this same science has now presented us the most dreaded gift ever bestowed upon humanity. The life and future of every living being on this planet is affected by this gift of science. It stands like a somber shadow behind our waking thoughts. It stalks like a specter of horror through our children's dreams. We pretend it isn't there. We try to pretend that we haven't received this gift, that it's all a joke, and that some morning we'll wake up and find that the H-bomb hasn't really been invented and that the A-bomb has never been made—but our morning newspaper tells us different.

There are other paths, of course, and many are traveling them this very moment. There are the paths of fame and fortune, of pleasure and power. None of them leads anywhere but deeper into the mire. We are ensnared in the web of our own thinking, trapped so cleverly and so completely that we can no longer see either the cause or the cure of the disease that is inflicting such deadly pain.

If it is true that "for every illness there is a cure," then we must make haste to find it. The sand in civilization's hourglass is rapidly falling away, and if there is a path that leads to the light, if there is a way back to spiritual health, we must not lose an hour! . . .

So that is where we stand today—a nation of empty people. We have tried to fill ourselves with science and education, with better living and pleasure, with the many other things we thought we wanted, but we are still empty. Why are we empty? Because the Creator made us for Himself; and we shall never find completeness and fullness apart from fellowship with Him.

Jesus told us long ago that "Man shall not live by bread alone," but we have paid no heed. We have gone on stuffing ourselves with bread of every description. We have stuffed until we are sick.

We cannot stand the terrible emptiness of ourselves, we cannot look at the lonely desolate road that lies ahead. We are desperately weary of the hatred and greed and lust that we know are within us, but we are helpless to be rid of it and filled with something better.

Time is of the essence. The tools of total annihilation have been placed within our reach. We cannot scurry up any more false paths, we cannot explore any more unknown roads, we cannot afford to be trapped in any more blind alleys. We don't have that much time! For our generation has accomplished what other generations only *tried* to do, or dreamed of doing in their most insane moments of power and ruthlessness! We have achieved a weapon of total destruction. We are witnessing the climax of man's madness—the atom cleaved!

How the demons must have laughed as some of the most brilliant men on earth worked furiously for years to achieve this horror! The atom cleaved! Divide and conquer! Split apart, destroy, shatter, crush, crumble! He of the cloven hoof has done his work, and men have been avid to aid him. We see before us Satan's masterpiece, his clever counterfeit of the cloven tongues of divine fire. For this satanic fire and the pentecostal flames both fall from above, both are cloven, both illuminate, both instantly transform everything they touch—but with such a difference. The difference of heaven and hell!

We are living in a topsy-turvy world, where all is confusion. But you may be sure that it is confusion with a plan—Satan's plan! The Bible tells us that Satan is the great deceiver and he has devoted himself to the cause of our great self-deception and to the deceptions that lie between nations all over this world. He has led us to believe that things were getting better, when they are really getting worse. . . .

Christ came to give us the answers to the three enduring problems of sin, sorrow, and death. It is Jesus Christ, and He alone, who is also enduring and unchanging, "the same yesterday, and today and forever."

All other things may change, but Christ remains unchangeable. In the restless sea of human passions, Christ stands steadfast and calm, ready to welcome all who will turn to Him and accept the blessings of safety and peace. For we are living in an age of grace, in which God promises that whosoever will may come and receive His Son. But this period of grace will not go on indefinitely. We are even now living on borrowed time. . . .

Since you have made your decision for Christ and have begun studying the Bible, you find yourself confronted with various social obligations and problems. You have made your peace with God. You are no longer at war and at enmity with God. Sin has been forgiven. You have new horizons for your thinking—new perspectives for your life. The whole world has changed. You now begin to see others through the eyes of Jesus. Old ideas and ideals have changed. Prejudices that you once held are beginning to slip away. Selfishness that was once characteristic of you in many areas of your life has now gone. . . .

Christians, above all others, should be concerned with social problems and social injustices. Down through the centuries the church has contributed more than any other single agency in lifting social standards to new heights. Child labor has been outlawed. Slavery has been abolished. The status of woman has been lifted to heights unparalleled in history, and many other reforms have taken place as a result of the influence of the teachings of Jesus Christ. The Christian is to take his place in society with moral courage to stand up for that which is right, just, and honorable.

First: *the Christian should be a good citizen.* The Bible teaches that the Christian should be law-abiding. The Bible also teaches loyalty to country. A loyalty and love of country does not mean that we cannot criticize certain unjust laws that may discriminate against special groups. The Bible says that God is no respecter of persons. All should have equal opportunities. The government of God is to be our model.

The Bible also teaches that we are to co-operate with the government. Jesus was asked, "Is it lawful to give tribute?" Jesus set the example forever by paying taxes. It takes money to run a government and to maintain law and order. The tax dodger is a civic parasite and an actual thief. No true Christian will be a tax dodger. Jesus said, we are to "render to Caesar the things that are Caesar's." We ought to be more than taxpayers. To be simply law-abiding is not enough. We ought to seek and work for the good of our country. Sometimes we may be called upon to die for it. We are to do it gladly —as unto God. We are to be conscientious in our work as good citizens.

We should be philanthropic and give to charitable organizations that are doing good for the betterment of mankind. We should enter in to various activities such as the Community Chest, the Red Cross, the Salvation Army, and other good, constructive, and helping-hand organizations. Christians should be interested in orphanages, hospitals, asylums, prisons, and all social institutions. Jesus said, "Love thy neighbor as thyself." Think of a country without any philanthropic enterprises whatever! No one would want to live in it. We want to live where neighborly love prevails. We are to take our place in the community. Those in positions of responsibility are entitled to respect, support, and co-operation. "Let every soul be subject unto the higher powers. For there is no power but of God: the powers that be are ordained of God."

Second: *Christians should be "given to hospitality."* The Bible teaches that our homes should be open to all and that those who come in and out of our homes should sense the presence of Christ. That which God has given to us should be shared with others. In doing so God will bless and prosper our homes.

Third: *we should have the Christian attitude toward sex.* Nowhere does the Bible teach that sex in itself is a sin, although many interpreters of the

Bible would try to make it appear so. The Bible teaches that the *wrong use* of sex is sinful. For sex, the act by which all life on this earth is created, should be the most wonderful, the most meaningful, the most satisfying of human experiences. . . .

Fourth: it follows naturally that *those who take a Christian view of sex will take a Christian view of marriage.* Before you enter into a marriage, consider the real spiritual implications that make an earthly marriage binding in heaven. Little by little as we grow toward maturity, we learn to love, first our parents and our friends and later the one person who is to share our life. We have already seen how difficult this process is, for it is hate and not love that comes naturally to the unregenerate sinner. . . .

Fifth: *we are to take the Christian attitude in labor-management relationships.* The Bible says, "Whatever you do, put your whole heart and soul into it, as into work done for God, and not merely for men—knowing that your real reward, a heavenly one, will come from God, since you are actually employed by Christ, and not just by your earthly master. But the slacker and the thief will be judged by God himself, Who naturally has no distinction to make between master and man. Remember, then, you employers, that your responsibility is to be fair and just towards those whom you employ, never forgetting that you yourselves have a Heavenly Employer."

If Christ could prevail in all labor-management relations we would not have any strikes. There would not be these long drawn-out arguments in which both sides are unwilling to concede the rights of the other. Management would treat employees with generosity, and employees would be eager to put in a full day's work for their hire—for they would not only be working for their wages, they would be working for God.

The Bible teaches that there is dignity in all types of honest labor, and the Christian should be the most faithful, the most willing and efficient worker of all. He should stand out in a factory or shop as one who wants justice, but who would not stoop to take unfair advantage.

By the same token, the Christian employer should treat his employees with a respect and generosity that will become an example for other employers. A man of real Christian concepts cannot help being concerned about safety precautions, good working conditions, and the well-being of those in his employ. He will not only see his workers as "man power," but also as human beings.

Both management and labor should remember that the improved conditions and better understanding they now enjoy had their beginnings as the result of a great spiritual revival. The heritage of labor unions comes from the church and the mighty Wesleyan revivals of the eighteenth century. Social liberty for the working classes began when a Christian leader, Lord Shaftsbury, in the face of bitter family opposition, led a lifelong crusade for better working conditions, shorter hours, more pay, and fair treatment for the working man.

Had it not been for the spiritual revival of the eighteenth century, the gains that labor has made might not have been achieved, or might have been delayed until much later in our history. When some labor leaders talk of outlawing religion, disregarding God, the Bible, and the church, they should remember how much of what they have today is due to the power of the gospel of Christ.

Some labor leaders have grown haughty, proud, rich, self-satisfied, and power-seeking. Many industrialists have done the same. All of them should humble themselves before God, seek to recognize the needs of each other, their extreme dependence on each other, and above all, try to apply the Golden Rule in its most practical and realistic sense.

Sixth: *the Christian looks through the eyes of Christ at the race question* and admits that the church has failed in solving this great human problem. We have let the sports world, the entertainment field, politics, the armed forces, education and industry outstrip us. The church should have been the pace-setter. The church should voluntarily be doing what the federal courts are doing by pressure and compulsion. But in the final analysis the only real solution will be found at the foot of the cross where we come together in brotherly love. The closer the people of all races get to Christ and His cross, the closer they will get to one another. . . .

Seventh: *the Christian attitude should prevail in the matter of economics.* Jesus said a man's life does not consist in the abundance of the things which he possesses. Money is a good slave but a bad master. Property belongs in the purse or the bank but not in the heart. Wealth has its place and its power, but it is not entitled to occupy the throne or sway the scepter. Covetousness puts money above manhood. It shackles its devotee and makes him its victim. It hardens the heart and deadens the noble impulses and destroys the vital qualities of life.

Beware of covetousness in every phase and form! All of us should keep ourselves from it through vigilance, prayer, self-control, and discipline. Life is not a matter of dollars and cents, houses and lands, earning capacity and financial achievement. Greed must not be allowed to make man the slave of wealth. . . .

Eighth: *a Christian will be concerned about suffering humanity around him.* The great slum areas of your own country will become a burden to you. The poverty and suffering of thousands of people in your own neighborhood will become a concern to you. You will join with organizations and associations to help alleviate the suffering of humanity around you. Many people spend so much time in lofty enterprises that they make no contribution to suffering immediately at hand. . . .

Ninth: *the Christian has a special obligation to fellow Christians.* Fellow Christians are in a special class. We are *to have supernatural love* for them. "We know that we have passed from death unto life, because we love the brethren. He that loveth not his brother abideth in death."

We are to love our enemies. We are even to love those who persecute us and say "all manner of evil against us, falsely."

But the greatest of our human love is for those other Christians. Jesus said, "This is my commandment, that ye love one another, as I have loved you." . . .

These are just a few of the scores of things that could be mentioned that are the social obligations of the Christian. He cannot withdraw himself as a hermit and live a solitary life. He is a member of society. Therefore, the teachings of Jesus are full of our attitudes toward our fellow men.

Study the Bible, read it—and then live by it. Only then can you demonstrate to a confused world the transforming power of the indwelling Christ.

(42)

William J. Kenealy

1904-

After graduating from Boston College, William J. Kenealy earned a law degree from Georgetown University. A member of the Society of Jesus, he has taught philosophy at Boston College and also served as dean of the law school at that institution from 1939 to 1956. Since then he has taught at the law schools of Loyola University of New Orleans and Loyola University of Chicago.

Like most of his colleagues in the Catholic Church, Reverend Kenealy has taken a role in the revival of neo-Thomism in the United States. Highly critical of the school of jurisprudence stemming from Justice Oliver Wendell Holmes, Jr., the neo-Thomists have insisted that there is above man "an objective moral order" within the range of human intelligence, to which man is bound in conscience to conform. This moral order, which is God-given, is antecedent to the state, and so is universally applicable as the basis of truth and morality. The natural law is but the mandatory aspect of God's moral order.

The following selection is from a speech given by Reverend Kenealy in 1950 and reprinted as "The Majesty of the Law," *Loyola Law Review,* 5 (1950).

The majesty of the law? In what does it consist? In marble columns, or high-backed leather chairs, or black silk robes? No. These are but external symbols of an inward majesty. Does it consist, then, in that invisible force which always lurks behind the bench: the battalions of police, the regiments of soldiers, the battleships and bombing planes, which can be summoned to put teeth into a nation's laws? No. It is not force, at least, not physical force. For the true majesty of the law is more than its coercive sanction. It is a moral power, springing from a rational people's conviction that they see, enshrined in their courts, one of the few enduring elements of civilized life. It is a moral power, arising from a free people's realization that the law is the means, under Divine Providence, of enjoying in security the inalienable rights founded in their human nature by the natural law. It is a moral power, flowing from a moral people's persuasion that the administration of just human law demands their conscientious obedience, because it is their human participation in the eternal law of God. . . .

I think it would be more appropriate to say that the traditional philosophy of American law, the philosophy of the natural law, is the target of a sustained and determined attack here in our own country, and within the legal profession itself. It is an attack led by formidable antagonists. The outcome is in doubt.

In reality it is the age-old conflict between the idea of the absolute state and the idea of the natural law; between the philosophy of force and the philosophy upon which this nation was founded and to which this nation, by its most solemn covenants, is dedicated. You are familiar with the philosophy of the absolute state. Its modern name is Totalitarianism, but its name is its only novelty. It is a retrogression to ancient Caesarism: the deification of the state, upon the specious grounds of pragmatic public policy, to the annihilation of human personality. The public policy of the state is the *alpha* and *omega* of all things, the ultimate criterion of truth and the last norm of right. Human life, its origin and purpose, its dignity and value, have significance only by the yardstick of state utility. Will is substituted for reason; law becomes organized force; might becomes right. The fire of human liberty is extinguished, because there are no inalienable rights; there are no inalienable rights, because there is no natural law; there is no natural law, because there is no eternal law; there is no eternal law, because there is no God—no God, that is, but Caesar. Would you judge this philosophy by its fruits? Then behold the rotting corpses, the mangled bodies, the crippled minds, the broken hearts, the crushed liberties—the stench of physical and spiritual death—in the lands across the sea! . . .

The tragic irony of democracy is that at the very moment when our American Republic was born in a grand profession of politico-religious faith—faith in the existence of God, in the reality of His natural law, in the fact of inalienable rights beyond the reach of any government—at that very moment the foundations of that faith were already shaking in a large part of what we used to call Christendom. The young Republic had not yet attained its maturity before it was assailed and buffeted from across the sea by a maelstrom of political and social theories which pounded away at the foundations of her political philosophy. Thomas Hobbes' theory of the leviathan state laid the foundation of modern totalitarianism. David Hume's skepticism cast doubt upon the ability of the human mind to attain to any objective truth. Jean Jacques Rousseau's anti-intellectualism cast aspersions upon any rational explanation of human life. Jeremy Bentham's utilitarianism repudiated the age-old norm of morality. Emmanuel Kant drove a wedge between the legal and the moral orders. Herbert Spencer's sociological evolution cast aside fixed principles of morality and of the natural law. John Austin's jurisprudence completed the legal bridge to the modern totalitarian state. These philosophies, and the positivistic concepts of Hegel, Marx and Spengler, melted down into an amorphous philosophy of so-called realism and pragmatism—these are the ideas fighting for acceptance by our profession today.

The battle is on, make no mistake about it. Our modern legal pragmatists pooh-pooh the very notion of the natural law as a medieval fiction, which served a useful purpose in its day, but is now obsolete and never had any objective existence. To them, therefore, inalienable rights are so much metaphysical nonsense. There are no duties in conscience because morality, in its last analysis, is merely current good taste. There are no principles; there are merely prevailing formulae of expediency. Above all, there are no absolutes; no absolutes, that is, except pragmatic public policy—which means the absolute state. If it works, it's true; if it works, it's right. A rudderless philosophy which leads, logically and psychologically, to the philosophy of force. Do you think I overdraw the picture? That I exaggerate the danger?

Such alien and corrosive ideas have so far eaten their way into the fabric of modern American legal thought that even the late Mr. Justice Holmes, idol of the profession and deity of the schools could write:

> The first requirements of a sound body of law is that it should correspond with the actual feelings and demands of the community, whether right or wrong. . . . But it is clear to me that the *ultima ratio,* not only *regum,* but of all private persons is force. . . .

This was written in 1881. In 1926, forty-five years later, with the intellectual consistency characteristic of all his writings, Holmes wrote to his friend Dr. John C. H. Wu: "I don't believe that it is an absolute principle or even a human ultimate that man is always an end in himself—that his dignity must be respected, etc. We march up a conscript with bayonets behind to die for a cause he doesn't believe in. And I feel no scruples about it. Our morality seems to me only a check on the ultimate domination of force, just as our politeness is a check on the impulse of every pig to put his feet in the trough. When the Germans in the late war disregarded what we called the rules of the game, I don't see there was anything to be said except: we don't like it and shall kill you if we can. So when it comes to the development of a *corpus juris* the ultimate question is what do the dominant forces of the community want, and do they want it hard enough to disregard whatever inhibitions may stand in the way."

Now Holmes was an honest and a logical man. Believing the essence, the *ultima ratio,* of law was simply physical force, he was logical in defining law as merely "a statement of the circumstances in which the public force will be brought to bear upon men through the courts." He was logical in defining the study of law as the study of "prediction, the prediction of the incidence of the public force through the instrumentality of the courts" He was logical in sarcastically defining a right as the "hypostasis of a prophecy" a prophecy, that is, of what the courts will in fact do about it. He was logical in defining a duty as "nothing but a prediction that if a man does or omits certain things he will be made to suffer in this or that way by the judgment of the court." And he was logical in stating that "the duty to keep a contract at common law means a prediction that you must pay damages if you do not keep it— and nothing else."

This philosophy of Holmes flowed from his fundamental skepticism concerning the nature of truth, the nature of man, and the nature of human life. In his repudiation of the natural law he wrote: "I used to say when I was young that truth was the majority vote of the nation that could lick all others . . . and I think that the statement was correct in so far as it implied that our test of truth is a reference to either a present or an imagined future majority in favor of our view." Holmes was an intellectually honest man, to whom pussy-footing was an abomination. Hence he could write Sir Frederick Pollock: "I see no reason for attributing to man a significance different in kind from that which belongs to a baboon or a grain of sand." And again to Sir Frederick Pollock, when he wrote cynically: "Functioning is all there is— only our keenest pleasure is in what we call the higher sort. I wonder if cosmically an idea is any more important than bowels." With these views of life and of human nature, it is small wonder that, in 1920, he could write to his English friend: "I do think that the sacredness of human life is a purely municipal ideal of no validity outside the jurisdiction. I believe that force, mitigated so far as may be by good manners, is the *ultima ratio.* . . ." To which Sir Frederick replied: "My dear Holmes: . . . As to the sanctity of human life, I quite agree with you that there is too much fuss about it." In 1924, at the age of eighty-three, he wrote, somewhat pathetically I think, "If I were dying my last words would be: Have faith and pursue the unknown end." Two years later, he gave it as his opinion that the human personality was merely "a cosmic ganglion." And in 1929, a few years before his death, he penned this *nunc dimittis:* "I may work for a year or two but I cannot hope to add much to what I have done. I am too skeptical to think that it matters much, but too conscious of the mystery of the universe to say that it or anything else does not. I bow my head, I think serenely and say, as I told someone the other day, O Cosmos—Now lettest thou thy ganglion dissolve in peace."

So much for the philosophy of Mr. Justice Holmes! It is of tremendous importance to students of the law and to the legal profession because, as Mr. Justice Frankfurter has said, Holmes "above all others has given the directions of contemporary jurisprudence." Roscoe Pound asserted that Holmes "has done more than lead American juristic thought of the present generation. Above all others he has shaped the methods and ideas that are characteristic of the present as distinguished from the immediate past." And, according to the late Mr. Justice Cardozo: "He is today for all students of the law and for all students of human society the philosopher and seer, the greatest of our age in the domain of jurisprudence and one of the greatest of the ages."

Now Mr. Justice Holmes was indeed a great jurist, an eminent legal scholar, a fascinating stylist, a vibrant personality, and a masterful champion of many just and liberal causes—causes which deserved support from sounder premises. But I, for one, rejoice that his philosophy did not often determine his judicial decisions. I have cited his words merely for the purpose of illustrating the current trend of legal philosophy. I believe this trend constitutes a grave menace to American liberties, because it is cutting away at the foundations of American jurisprudence. I fear that, if it is not checked, it may topple the superstructure which we are proud and happy to call our American way of life. . . .

Hitler is dead and Mussolini is dead. But totalitarianism is not dead. Totalitarianism is still stalking over a major portion of God's earth, crushing the human spirit, stifling the hopes of human ambition, and repressing the inalienable rights of hundreds of millions of our fellow human beings. Only the callous can say we have liberated the smaller nations. Only the cynical can say we have secured the four freedoms everywhere. Only the blind can say that the lights of human liberty have gone on again all over the world. What American can recall without shame the fact that, even before the war ended, we deserted the very first ally to fight on our side; we abandoned, on pragmatic grounds, the heroic Polish people to a totalitarianism as ruthless and as brutal as any we fought against! And then Lithuania, Esthonia, Latvia, Yugoslavia, Hungary, weak and defenseless little peoples! Can you think, with any equanimity of the young American lads of Polish and Lithuanian and Hungarian descent who died for us? Can you think, with any complacency, of the American dead on whose "dog tags" were stamped names which sounded like Michailovich and Stepinac and Mindszenty? I cannot. I cannot, because in the lurid flame of battle I saw them go down; and I buried them at sea in the pitch blackness of night—in the Marianas, the New Hebrides, the Philippines. Yes, these, our own are dead. But totalitarianism is not dead. The wine of victory is turning to gall in our mouths; the flame of peace is flickering to ashes in our hands. Surely *this* is not the victory for which they died!

Why have we been so bitterly disappointed? Is it not because the war was a two-fold war: one of force, and one of ideas? The first, the war of physical force, resulted in victory. The arms of our enemies were laid down in surrender. But the second, the war of ideas, has hardly begun. The ideas of our enemies are still on the attack. A soldier can be shot down; but ideas are bullet-proof. This second war of ideas is even more important than the war of force. Because, in the long run, human beings are determined and governed more by ideas than by force. What are our prospects for ultimate victory in this philosophical warfare? What contribution to the struggle will be made by the legal profession, its leaders and its schools? I may be an alarmist; but I believe that our philosophic front, even today, is just about where our military front was on that fateful Sunday afternoon when the radio blared out the bombing of Pearl Harbor.

The ideological attack has caught us unprepared, confused, divided and uncertain about the essential principles of our own democracy, about the fundamental premises of our own exalted American philosophy of life and of government. Before we can hope to win the ideological war, upon which the peace and civilization of the whole world depends, we must have an intellectual and spiritual leadership convinced, united and vocal, about the true American idea of life, of law, and of government. Today we have no such conviction, no such union, no such voice. If we do not achieve such leadership in the reasonably near future, then we will lose the war of ideas. And, if that happens, American blood will be spilled again and again—or American liberty will be lost. No philosopher in history has ever pointed out another alternative between the natural law and physical force. It will be one or the other.

If man is essentially no different from "a baboon or a grain of sand"; if we are simply "cosmic ganglia"; if "functioning is all there is"; if truth is merely "the majority vote of the nation that can lick all others"; if "the sacredness of human life is a purely municipal ideal, of no validity outside the jurisdiction"; if the *"ultima ratio"* of law is simply physical force:—if these things are true, as Mr. Justice Holmes thought they were true, then we have no rational defense against the philosophy of totalitarianism; we have fought a war in vain; and American democracy is doomed to extinction. And if the thought of the legal profession and the teaching of the law schools are to follow Holmes, "the greatest of our age in the domain of jurisprudence", then our profession and our schools will play a tragic part in the disintegration of American society.

But if, on the other hand, "all men are created equal"; if "they are endowed by their Creator with certain inalienable rights" beyond the reach of any government; if all governments derive "their just powers from the consent of the governed"; if truth is something more than a counting of ballots or bullets; if ideas are worth more than bowels; if the sanctity of human life is always to be respected; if the essence of law is not mere force, but reason based upon man's moral nature:—if these things are true, as the Founders of our Republic solemnly declared, and as the philosophers of the natural law believe them to be true, then totalitarianism has no rational defense against the American philosophy of law; there was a point to World War II; and democracy will survive. And if the schools and leaders of the legal profession follow the philosophy of the natural law, rather than the philosophy of force, then they will play a glorious part in the preservation and betterment of our society.

The philosophy of the natural law is the *"philosophia perennis"*, as old as the thought of civilized man. It has been shaped by the noblest thoughts of some of the best minds in history, Sophocles, Plato, Aristotle; Cicero, Tertullian, Justinan; Jerome, Ambrose, Augustine, Albertus Magnus, Aquinas, Vittoria, Suarez, Bellarmine; Bracton, Langton, Coke, Blackstone,

Edmund Burke; James Wilson, Marshall, Chase, Story, Cooley, Kent and a host of others have contributed to its development. It is the American philosophy in the sense that, for the first time in history, a great people incorporated it expressly into the written charter of their government.

The philosophy of the natural law is not specifically Catholic, or Protestant, or Jewish. It is the philosophy which is logically antecedent to the theology of every religion. It is the philosophy of the pagan—in the classical sense of the word pagan, namely, one who worships Almighty God albeit without the benefit of supernatural revelation.

This philosophy maintains that there is in fact an *objective moral order* within the range of human intelligence, to which human societies are bound in conscience to conform, and upon which the peace and happiness of personal, national and international life depend. The mandatory aspect of the objective moral order we call the natural law. In virtue of the natural law, fundamentally equal human beings are endowed by their Creator with certain natural rights and obligations, which are *inalienable* precisely because they are God-given. They are antecedent, therefore, both in logic and in nature, to the formation of civil society. They are not granted by the beneficence of the state; wherefore the tyranny of a state cannot destroy them. Rather it is the high moral responsibility of civil society, through the instrumentality of its civil law, to acknowledge their existence and to protect their exercise, to foster and facilitate their enjoyment, by a wise and scientific implementation of the natural law with a practical and consonant code of civil rights and obligations.

The construction and maintenance of a *corpus juris,* implementing the natural law, is a perpetual and monumental task demanding the constant devotion of the best brains and the most mature scholarship of the legal profession. For the fundamental principles of the natural law, which are as universal and immutable as the human nature from which they derive, nevertheless require rational application to the constantly changing political, economic and social conditions of society. The application of the natural law *postulates* change as the circumstances of human existence change. It repudiates a naive and smug complacency in the *status quo*. It demands a reasoned acceptance of the good, and a reasoned rejection of the bad, in all that is new. It insists upon a critical search for the better. It demands an exhaustive inquiry into all the available data of history, politics, economics, sociology and every other pertinent font of human knowledge. And, of primary importance, it insists that the construction of a better *corpus juris* be made in the light of the origin, nature, purpose and limitations of the state; and in the knowledge of the origin, nature, dignity and destiny of man.

And yet in its essence, granted the existence of God, the natural law is a simple thing. It is man's participation in the eternal law of God. It implies that we know, independently of City Hall, or Baton Rouge, or Washington, or London, or Moscow—or of the Vatican, for that matter—that we are the children of God, endowed with immortal souls, destined for eternal life, bound in conscience to pursue that destiny, and possessed of inalienable rights to enable us to do so. It implies that we know, from our very nature, that some things help in attaining our end and some make it more difficult; that some acts are intrinsically right and some wrong, regardless of material consequences. It implies that human governments and human laws are instituted among us, and administered by us, to safeguard our inalienable rights and to help us attain, in human dignity, our divine destiny.

(43)

Will Herberg

1907-

Born in New York City, Will Herberg attended Columbia University, receiving his B.A. in 1927, M.A. in 1929, and Ph.D. in 1932. In his early years he became an exponent of Marxian radicalism, but the events of the 1930's shattered his hopes for a better world founded on the principles of dialectical materialism. Coming under the influence of Reinhold Niebuhr at this critical point in his life, he renounced his faith in Marxism. In so doing Herberg also became a critic of Enlightenment thought and a foe of humanistic liberalism, since the adherents of such philosophies, he argued, overestimated man's capacity for good and underestimated his propensities for evil. At present Herberg is Professor of Judaic Studies and Social Philosophy at Drew University.

Like Niebuhr, Herberg—especially in his influential book *Protestant-Catholic-Jew: An Essay in American Religious Sociology* (1955) —has employed sociological insight to reveal the shallowness of contemporary institutional religion. At the same time he has advanced his own version of existential Judaism in *Judaism and Modern Man: An Interpretation of Jewish Religion* (1951), a work that expounds a theology founded upon an absolute commitment to a transcendent God and an unshakable acceptance of man's sinful nature and his need for salvation by the interposition of divine grace.

In the following selection, "Religion and Culture in Present-Day America," Herberg has attempted to lay bare the secondary role of religion in American society, thus pointing up its vital need of a truly religious commitment and philosophy of life. The article is from Thomas T. McAvoy, ed., *Roman Catholicism and the American Way of Life* (Notre Dame, Indiana, 1960).

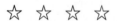

Whatever may be true about the religious situation, it certainly cannot be doubted that religion is enjoying a boom of unprecedented proportions in America today. Well over 95 per cent of the American people identify themselves religiously, as Protestants, Catholics, or Jews—an incredibly high figure by all available standards of comparison. The proportion of Americans who are church members—that is, actually on the rolls of the churches—has nearly doubled in the past half century; in the last twenty years indeed, church membership has been increasing twice as fast as population. Church and synagogue attendance is rising rapidly, Sunday school enrollment is rising even more rapidly, and religious giving has reached a formidable figure, even allowing for the inflationary devaluation of the dollar. Interest in religion and religious thinking is widespread on all cultural levels. Whatever the criterion of religiousness we take—and by religiousness I mean the "externals" of religion, using this term in a neutral sense, without prejudice— we cannot escape the conclusion that we are today witnessing an upsurge of religion without precedent in recent times.

But it is a curious kind of religion. The very same people who are so unanimous in identifying themselves religiously, who are joining churches at an accelerating rate, and who take it for granted that religion is a "very important" thing, do not hesitate to acknowledge that religion is quite peripheral to their everyday lives: more than half of them quite frankly admit that their religious beliefs have no influence whatever on their ideas in economics and politics, and a good proportion of the remainder are obviously uncertain. The very same people who distribute the Bible in vast quantities, largely by voluntary effort, are unable in their majority to give the name of one single book of the New Testament, and the showing is not very different when you take the Bible as a whole. The very same people who, four out of five, say they regard Jesus as divine, when asked to name the most important event in all universal history, place the Christ-event—the birth or crucifixion of Christ—fourteenth on the list, tied with the Wright brothers' invention of the airplane: the Number 1 event, almost without exception, is given as Columbus' discovery of America.

This is the problem: America is in the grip of a great religious boom, that is obvious; yet equally obvious, though not so easy to establish by facts and figures, is the continuing "trend toward secularism in ideas," to use Professor Handlin's phrase—it is really a trend toward secularism not only in ideas, but in attitudes and values as well. This is the problem: the religiousness of a secularist society, the "strengthening of the religious structure in spite of increasing secularization." Thinking through this paradox will take us a long way toward understanding the present religious situation in this country.

The best approach to the problem, I think, is to try to understand something of the role that religious belonging plays in the social structure and functioning of contemporary America. I will recognize that religion has its transcendent dimension, which escapes all external scrutiny and analysis; but I am deliberately limiting my inquiry at this point to those aspects that are subject to such scrutiny and analysis, and I think that these aspects are significant in the total picture. What, then, is it that strikes one about the new function of religion in the life of the American people today? It is, I think, that religion, in its tripartite form of Protestant-Catholic-Jew, is rapidly becoming the primary context of self-identification and social location in the present-day America. Let us see what this really means. . . .

The stoppage of mass immigration during the first World War, followed by the anti-immigration legislation of the 1920's, undermined the foundations of immigrant ethnicity and the immigrant ethnic group with amazing rapidity; what it did was to facilitate the emergence of third and post-third generations, with their characteristic responses and attitudes, as a decisive influence on American life, no longer threatened with submergence by the next new wave of immigration. Within the threefold American scheme of race, ethnicity, and religion, a shift took place, a shift is taking place, from ethnicity to religion as the dominant form of self-identification—as the dominant way of answering the question, "What am I? how do I differ from 'one man's family'? where do I fit in in the totality of American society?" Ethnic identifications and traditions have not disappeared; on the contrary, with the third generation, they are enjoying a lively popularity as symbols of "heritage." But now the relation between ethnicity and religion has been reversed: religion is no longer an aspect of ethnicity; it is ethnicity, or rather what remains of it, that is taken up, redefined, and expressed through religious identifications and institutions. Religion, or at least the tripartite differentiation of Protestant, Catholic, and Jew has (aside from race) become the prevailing form of defining one's identity as an American in contemporary American society.

Keeping this in mind, we can begin to understand one of the most striking facts in the religious history of this country during the past half century—the transformation of America from a *Protestant* country into a *three-religion* country. . . .

What has the transformation of America from an ethnic into a religious pluralism, and concomitantly from a Protestant into a three-religion country, meant so far as the status and character of religion in this country are concerned?

Very obviously, it has made for a boom in religious belonging. To have a "name" in American society today—to have an identity, to be able to answer the question "What am I? where do I belong?"—means increasingly to identify oneself in religious terms, as Protestant, Catholic, or Jew. These are three alternative ways of being an American. This is eminently true of the burgeoning suburban sector of American society, least true in the rural areas, and measurably true in the older urban centers. It is certainly the over-all pattern of American life. Obviously, such self-identification in religious terms engenders a new sense of belonging to one's religious community; obviously, too, it impels to institutional affiliation, characteristically expressed in terms of concern for the children: "We have to join a church (or a temple) for the sake of the children." There is profound sociological wisdom in this remark, though its theological implications may be dubious. "The church," Oscar Handlin points out, "supplies a place where the children come to learn what they are"—what kind of Americans they are. The mechanisms of other-directed conformity to which David Riesman has called attention serve to give religious belonging the compelling power it is acquiring in the pattern of suburban "sociability," but the new role of religion in this process is the result of the more basic factors I have tried to indicate in my remarks on the third generation and the transformation of America into a three-religion country.

Just as Americans are coming more and more to think of being a Protestant, being a Catholic, and being a Jew as three alternative ways of being an American, so they are coming to regard Protestantism, Catholicism, and Judaism, the "three great faiths," as three alternative (though not necessarily equal) expressions of a great overarching commitment which they all share by virtue of being Americans. This commitment is, of course, democracy or the American Way of Life. It is the common allegiance which (to use Professor Williams' phrase) provides Americans with the "common set of ideas, rituals, and symbols" through which an "overarching sense of unity" is achieved amidst diversity and conflict. It is, in a sense far more real than John Dewey ever dreamed of, the "common religion" of Americans.

Let me illustrate this point with two texts borrowed from President Eisenhower, who may, I think, be taken as a representative American really serious about religion. "Our government," Mr. Eisenhower declared shortly after his election in 1952, "makes no sense unless it is founded in a deeply felt religious faith, *and I don't care what it is.*" It is the last phrase which I have emphasized—'and I don't care what it is'—to which I want to call your attention. Of course, President Eisenhower did not mean that literally; he would have been much disturbed had any sizable proportion of Americans become Buddhists, or Shintoists, or Confucianists—but of course that never entered his mind. When he said "I don't care what it is," he obviously meant "I don't care which of the three it is—Protestantism, Catholicism, or Judaism." And why didn't he care which it was? Because, in his view, as in the view of all normal Americans, they "all say the same thing." And what is the "same thing" which they all say? The answer is given to us from the current vocabulary: "the moral and spiritual values of democracy." These, for the typical American, are in a real sense final and ultimate; the three conventional religions are approved of and validated primarily because they embody and express these "moral and spiritual values of democracy."

Let me drive this home with the second text from President Eisenhower. In 1948, four years before his election, just before he became president of Columbia, Mr. Eisenhower made another important pronouncement on religion. "I am the most intensely religious man I know," he declared. "Nobody goes through six years of war without faith. That does not mean that I adhere to any sect. (Incidentally, following the way of all flesh, he was soon to join a "sect," the Presbyterian.) A democracy cannot exist without a religious base. I believe in democracy." Here we have the entire story in a single phrase: I believe in religion because I believe in democracy! Precisely the same conviction, though expressed in a rather more sophisticated manner, was affirmed by an eminent New York rabbi not long ago. "The spiritual meaning of American democracy," he declared, "is realized in its three great faiths." Similar statements, I assure you, could be found in the pronouncements of spokesmen of the other two religious groups.

What I am describing is essentially the "Americanization" of religion in America, and therefore also its thorough-going secularization. This process is not a recent one. It began for Protestantism some time after the Civil War and proceeded apace in the latter decades of the nineteenth century. . . .

We are now, I think, in a position to penetrate the apparent paradox with which we initated this discussion, the paradox of the religiousness of a secularist society. How can Americans be so religious and so secularistic at the same time? The answer is that for increasing numbers of Americans religion serves a function largely unrelated to the content of faith, the function of defining their identity and providing them with a context of belonging in the great wilderness of a mobile American society. Indeed, for such a purpose, the authentic content of faith may even prove a serious handicap, for if it is Jewish or Christian faith, it carries a prophetic impact which serves rather to unadjust than to adjust, to emphasize the ambiguity of every earthly form of belonging rather than to let the individual rest secure in his "sociability." For this reason, the typical American has developed a remarkable capacity for being serious about religion without taking religion seriously—in which respect he is not unlike sinful human beings of all ages. His ideas, values, and standards he takes from what is so often really his ultimate commitment, the American Way of Life. He combines the two—his religion and his culture— by making the former an expression of the latter, his religion an expression of the "moral and spiritual values of democracy." Hence his puzzling pro-religious secularism, his secularistic religionism, which, looked at more closely, does not seem so puzzling after all.

From the standpoint of the man of faith, of the man who takes his religious tradition seriously, what does the picture of religion in contemporary America add up to? No simple or unequivocal answer can be given.

On the one hand, the emergence of religion as a vehicle of American belonging has made for a breakdown of anti-religious prejudice. One of the most striking features of present-day American culture is the complete absence of an Ingersoll or a Darrow, of the "village atheist" on a national scale, or for that matter, except here and there, even on a village scale. Contemporary Americans, especially the younger generation, simply cannot understand the militant atheist of yesterday; he is so remote from their mentality as to be hardly credible. The breakdown of anti-religion has contributed toward the new openness to religion that is so obvious today. Yet the religion that emerges is only too often a religiousness, or perhaps a pro-religiousness, without religion, without serious religious content, conviction, or commitment. There is great danger, as one Jewish leader recently put it, that our church or synagogue cards may hide from us the basically secularistic character of our religion. There is even danger that with the rapid spread of a contentless religiousness, the very meaning of religion in its authentic sense may be lost for increasing numbers.

There is also a positive side to the "Americanization" of religion, which sees in Protestantism, Catholicism, and Judaism three forms of being religious in the American way. To the degree that this is felt to be true, the stigma of foreignness is lifted from Catholicism and Judaism, and from such ethnic forms of Protestantism as the Lutheran. There is a new freedom and tolerance, and at least the public equality of the "three great faiths" in American life. No one who remembers what misery the taint of foreignness once brought, and what a formidable obstacle it constituted to the preservation and communication of the "non-American" faiths, will fail to be grateful for this development. But it has been purchased at a heavy price, the price of embracing an idolatrous civic religion of Americanism.

I want to express myself here very clearly, and I will do so by speaking to you as Catholics. I recently lectured to the entire student body of a well-known Catholic girls' college. In the course of my remarks, I confronted them—not in such a way as to put them on their guard, of course—with Christopher Dawson's celebrated question: "Are you Americans who happen to be Catholics, or Catholics who happen to be Americans?" Almost with one voice the girls answered, "Americans who happen to be Catholics. . . ." You appreciate the significance of the question and the answer. The question really means: "Is your ultimate allegiance and your ultimate community the Universal Church, or is it the American nation?" The answer of the girls indicated that they normally thought of themselves as primarily Americans, but of course as Americans of the "Catholic kind," just as some of their friends were Americans of the "Protestant kind," and still others Americans of the "Jewish kind." Let me assure you that I have received the same kind of response from other Catholic groups—lay groups, that is—and from Protestant and Jewish audiences as well, when the question was put to them in their own terms.

What does that mean? It means that we have in America an invisible, formally unacknowledged, but very potent religion—the religion of democracy, the religion of the American Way of Life—of which the conventional religions are felt to be more or less adequate expressions. Americans do not put it that way, in just so many words, but that is how they feel and behave. In effect, this means that they participate in an actual civic religion, very much like the civic religion of the Roman Empire in early Christian times. The authentic relation between religion and culture is subverted, of which the civic religion is the sanctification, is idolatrized by being made ultimate, which means divine. Judaism, and Christianity in its two forms, become subordinated to the culture and tend to lose all sense of uniqueness, universality, and special vocation. To the man of Jewish or Christian faith, this divinization of the American Way—even if he acknowledges, as I do, the American Way to be one of the best ways of life yet devised for a mass society—must appear as abhorrent as the ancient civic religions appeared to the Jew or Christian of those days, in spite of the fact that our own civic religion is not officially established, overtly promulgated, or enforced through persecution. . . .

The American conviction that "religion is a very good thing"—this may be taken as the second article in the American religious creed; the first is belief in God, and the third, and last, is that all really American religion is either Protestant, Catholic, or Jewish—the American conviction that religion is a very good thing, I say, means that religion is taken seriously and is endowed with a vigor and vitality that amazes foreign observers. But it also means that religion is thoroughly "functionalized," that is, converted into a tool for secular purposes. It is made to serve the sociological function of providing a form of identification and a context of belonging in a world of other-directed "sociability"; of this we have already spoken. But it is also made to serve the psychological function of conferring, on the one side, reassurance and "peace of mind," and on the other, a sense of power and achievement through "positive thinking." It is not our purpose to examine this aspect in any detail, but one thing should be noted. Just as religion on its sociological side seems to function best if it is unembarrassed with content, so religion on its psychological side easily comes to mean a contentless faith. In the one case, it may be said that Americans are religious about religion; in the other, that they have faith in faith. I appeal to you to take this description with the utmost seriousness. So eminent a religious leader as Daniel Poling quite simply describes his own conviction about faith in these words: "It was back in those days that I formed a habit which I have never broken. I began saying in the morning two words, 'I believe.' Those two words, with nothing added, . . . give me a running start for my day, for every day." Another religious leader, not a Protestant, puts it this way: "The storehouse of dynamic power on which you may draw, is *Faith.* Not religion, . . . not God, but *FAITH.*" And an advertisement in a New York paper of three eminently respectable churches is headed: "When Faith Alone Protects." In the entire ad neither God nor Christ is so much as mentioned. Church-going is recommended with the argument: "There are times in your life when faith alone protects. We all reach these times in hours of crisis which dot life's span. Regular church attendance helps you build your own personal reserve of faith." What is this but picturing God as a great cosmic public utility, and religion or church-going as a way of charging one's storage battery of faith for use in emergencies? It is hardly necessary to point out that this faith in faith, this religion of religion, is just as idolatrous as faith in a stick or stone or the religion of magical self-salvation.

Americans crave security; they are bewildered and uneasy even in their prosperity. Americans crave personal power and achievement; they are frightened at the great heteronomous forces of a mass society which threaten to grind them into nothingness. Americans crave sociability; they are terrified at the prospect of being lost in the crowd. But most of all they crave reassurance about their goals and values, which they feel called into question and threatened on every side. And so they have fashioned their religion to serve these purposes by turning it into a man-centered cult of "peace of mind," "positive thinking," and American belonging. The religion that has emerged was bitingly described by Richard Niebuhr, speaking of latter-day Protestantism, two decades ago: "A God without wrath (brings) men without sin into a kingdom without judgment through the ministrations of a Christ without a cross."

But even the more dubious forms of American religion should not be written off entirely. Even in this ambiguous structure, there may be elements and aspects—not always those, incidentally, that seem most promising to us today —which could in the longer view transform the character of American religion and bring it closer to the traditions of faith it claims to represent. Nothing is too unpromising or refractory to serve the divine will. After all, the God who is able to make the "wrath of men" to praise Him, is surely capable of turning even the superficialities, inadequacies, and perversities of contemporary religion into an instrument of His redemptive purpose.

(44)

Walter Kaufmann

1921-

German-born, Walter Kaufmann came to the United States in 1939. He received his B.A. from Williams College in 1941, and then entered military service. After the war he continued his graduate studies at Harvard and was awarded his doctorate in philosophy in 1947. Since 1947 he has taught philosophy at Princeton University.

The author of numerous works on philosophy and the philosophy of religion—including *Nietzche* (1950) and *Critique of Religion and Philosophy* (1958)—Kaufmann has emerged as one of the leading modern critics of traditional religion, especially Christianity. Insisting that theologians as well as philosophers often have deliberately avoided subjecting their opinions and beliefs to searching examination, he has attempted to point out the myths, inconsistencies, and illogical beliefs that have remained embedded in the religious heritage of Western society. He has even questioned whether traditional religion should indeed play *any* role in modern society.

In the introduction to a recent book Kaufmann remarked: "Of faith and morals, one cannot speak honestly for long without hurting feelings. Therefore, most people speak dishonestly of the most important subjects. . . . The starting point is not a set of premises that I refuse to question. This book is based not on the all-too-widespread will to believe, but on the will to be honest."[1] Kaufmann's position is probably representative of a widespread skepticism and agnosticism that has presented institutional religion with one of its most serious intellectual challenges.

---

1. Walter Kaufmann, *The Faith of a Heretic* (New York, 1961), pp. 9, 24.

The following selection is from his article "The Faith of a Heretic," *Harper's Magazine,* 218 (February, 1959). The point of view presented in this article was elaborated much more fully in his book bearing the same title, *The Faith of a Heretic* (Doubleday & Company, 1961).

When I was eleven, I asked my father: "What really is the Holy Ghost?" The articles of faith taught us in school—in Berlin, Germany—affirmed belief in God, Christ, and the Holy Ghost, and I explained to my father: "I don't believe that Jesus was God, and if I can't believe in the Holy Ghost either, then I am really not a Christian."

At twelve, I formally left the Protestant church to become a Jew. Having never heard of Unitarianism, I assumed that the religion for people who believed in God, but not in Christ or the Holy Ghost, was Judaism.

A few months after my conversation with my father, but before I left the church, Hitler came to power. Warned of the persecution that my decision might entail, I replied that one certainly could not change one's mind for a reason like that. I did not realize until a little later that all four of my grandparents had been Jewish; and none of us knew that this, and not one's own religion, would be decisive from the Nazis' point of view. My decision had been made independently of my descent and of Nazism, on religious grounds.

I took my new religion very seriously, explored it with enormous curiosity and growing love, and gradually became more and more orthodox. When I arrived in the United States in January 1939, I was planning to become a rabbi. A lot of things happened to me that winter, spring, and summer; and when the war broke out I had what, but for its contents, few would hesitate to call a mystical experience. In the most intense despair I suddenly saw that I had deceived myself for years: I had believed. At last the God of tradition joined the Holy Ghost and Christ.

Of course, I could maintain my old beliefs by merely giving them a new interpretation; but that struck me as dishonest. Ikhnaton, the monotheistic Pharaoh—as I explained in a letter to my family who were by now in England —could also have reinterpreted the traditional polytheism of Egypt, but was a fanatic for the truth. He taught his court sculptor to make life masks of people to see how they really looked, and in one of the heads which the sculptor had then done of Ikhnaton, his hunger for the truth had become stone. I had loved that head for years. Should I now do what I admired him for not doing?

You may say that Ikhnaton was wrong and that it is the essence of religion to pour new wine into old skins, reading one's current insights into ancient beliefs. But if you do this, disregarding Jesus' counsel not to do it, you should realize that you could do it with almost any religion. And it is less than honest to give one's own religion the benefit of every possible doubt while imposing unsympathetic readings on other religions. Yet this is what practically all religious people do. Witness the attitude of Protestants and Catholics toward each other. . . .

The autobiographical sketch with which I have begun may do more harm than good. Some amateur psychologists may try to explain "everything" in terms of one or two experiences; some Protestants may say. "If only he had come to *me* about the Holy Ghost!" while some Catholics may feel that it all shows once again how Protestantism is merely a way-station on the road to Hell.

This is the kind of gambit that the shut-ins pull on travelers. As if I had buried the Holy Ghost beyond recall when I was eleven, and God when I was eighteen! I merely started relatively early to concern myself with such questions—and have never stopped since. Let the shut-in explore Judaism and Protestantism, Catholicism and Buddhism, atheism and agnosticism, mysticism, existentialism, and psychology, Thomas and Tillich. Let him consult the lot and not just his own present prejudice; let him subject his thoughts about religion to the candid scrutiny of those who differ with him and to his own ever-new re-examination; let him have a host of deep experiences, religious and otherwise, and think about them. That is the ground on which a genuine conversation can take place: it need not make a show of erudition, if only it has grown out of a series of open-hearted encounters. But as long as one is content to gloat over the silver lining of one's own religion, one bars any serious conversation and merely makes the first move in a game of skill.

To an even moderately sophisticated and well-read person it should come as no surprise that any religion at all has its hidden as well as its obvious beauties and is capable of profound and impressive interpretations. What is deeply objectionable about most of these interpretations is that they allow the believer to say Yes while evading any No. The Hebrew prophets represent a notable exception. When interpreting their own religious heritage, they were emphatically not conformists who discovered subtle ways in which they could agree with the religion of their day. Nor was it their point that the cult was justifiable with just a little ingenuity. On the contrary.

Let those who like inspiring interpretations be no less forthright in telling us precisely where they stand on ritual and immortality, on the sacraments and Hell, on the Virgin Birth and Resurrection, on the Incarnation and the miracles, and on: "Resist not evil." And: "Let him who would sue you in court for your coat have your cloak, too." And: "No one comes to the Father but through Me."

If you must pour new wine into old skins, you should at least follow one of Jesus' other counsels and let your Yes be Yes, and your No, No.

When considering Christianity, it is easy to get lost in the changing fashions of thought that have been read into it or reconciled with it—from Neoplatonism (Augustine) and Aristotelianism (Aquinas) to romanticism (Schleiermacher), liberalism (Harnack), and existentialism (Tillich, Bultmann, and others). There is no room here to cross swords with a dozen apologists; in any case, dozens more would remain.

The central question about Christianity concerns Jesus Christ. If he was God in a sense in which no other man has been God, then Christianity is right in some important sense, however Christendom may have failed. To decide whether Jesus was God in some such unique sense, a philosopher cannot forbear to ask just what this claim might mean. If, for example, it does not mean that Jesus of Nazareth knew everything and was all-powerful, it is perplexing what is meant. But a large part of what most Christians mean is surely that Jesus was the best and wisest man of all time; and many Protestants mean no more than that.

Millions of Christians agree on this claim and back it up by citing Gospel passages they like; but different people pick different passages. To some, Jesus looks like St. Francis, to others like John Calvin, and to many more the way a man named Hofmann painted him. Pierre van Paassen's Jesus is a Socialist and Fosdick's a liberal, while according to Reinhold Niebuhr Jesus' ethic coincides, not surprisingly, with Niebuhr's. To use a political term: almost everybody gerrymanders, carving an idealized self-portrait from the Gospels and much less attractive straw men from the literatures of other faiths. A great deal of theology is like a jigsaw puzzle: the verses of Scripture are the pieces, and the finished picture is prescribed by each denomination, with a certain lattitude allowed. What makes the game so pointless is that not all pieces have to be used, and any piece that does not fit may be reshaped, provided one says first, "this means." That is called exegesis.

In *The Literature of the Christian Movement,* Morton Scott Enslin, one of the outstanding New Testament scholars of our time, remarks that the Jesus of the Fourth Gospel is really not very attractive, and that if it were not for the other three Gospels and the fact that most readers create for themselves "a conflate," the Jesus of St. John would lose most of his charm. Surely, the same consideration applies to all four Gospels.

Those who consider Jesus the best and wisest of men should reread the Gospels and ponder at the very least these five points.

First: Are they prepared to maintain their claim regarding the Jesus of any one of the four Gospels—and, if so, which? Or is it their point that the evidence warrants the assumption that the historical Jesus, however inadequately understood by the Evangelists, was a wiser and better man than Socrates and Jeremiah, Isaiah and the Buddha, Lao-tze and Hillel?

Secondly: Although Jesus is widely considered mankind's greatest moral teacher, the greatest Christians, not to speak of scholars, have never been able to agree what his moral teachings were. Matthew, and he alone, reports that Jesus said: "Let your Yes be Yes, and your No, No." But the four Evangelists agree in ascribing to Jesus evasive and equivocal answers to plain questions, not only those of the high priest and Pilate; and quite generally the Jesus of the New Testament avoids straightforward statements, preferring parables and hyperboles. Some of the parables are so ambiguous that different Evangelists, not to speak of later theologians, offer different interpretations. Nor have

Christians ever been able to agree on the import of the hyperboles of the Sermon on the Mount. Luther, for example, taught that Christ's commandments were intended to teach man his utter incapacity for doing good: man must throw himself on the mercy of God, believing that Christ died for our sins. On concrete moral issues, Jesus can be, and has been, cited on almost all sides. The Buddha and the Hebrew prophets were not so equivocal.

Third: One of the few things about Jesus' moral teachings that seems fairly clear is that he was not greatly concerned about social justice. This makes his ethic much less impressive than the prophets'.

Fourth: Albert Schweitzer has argued in considerable detail that this lack of concern was due to the fact that Jesus predicated his entire message on a false belief: namely, that the world was about to come to an end. If Schweitzer is right, as I think he is, Jesus was surely not the wisest of men. And can we call him the greatest moralist unless we accept his radical depreciation of *this* life and his belief in Heaven and Hell?

Finally, the Jesus of the New Testament believed, and was not greatly bothered by his belief, that God would damn and torment the mass of mankind in all eternity. According to all three Synoptic Gospels, he actually reassured his disciples:

"If any one will not receive you or listen to your words, shake off the dust from your feet as you leave that house or town. Truly, I say to you, it shall be more tolerable on the day of judgment for the land of Sodom and Gomorrha than for that town."

This is no isolated dictum; the Sermon on the Mount, for example, is also punctuated by threats of Hell.

Augustine, Aquinas, and Calvin stressed Hell, but many Christian apologists today simply ignore all such passages. A few insist that in a couple of inter-testamentary apocalypses we find far more detailed visions of Hell. They do not mention that these apocalypses would not be known today if it had not been for the esteem in which the early Christians held them. For the Jews rejected them while accepting the humane teachings of men like Hillel and Akiba. Rabbi Akiba, a contemporary of Paul and the Evangelists, taught that "only those who possess no good deeds at all will descend into the netherworld"; also that "the punishment of the wicked in Gehinnom lasts twelve months."

Of course, Jesus also stressed love, citing—or agreeing with a Pharisee who cited—Moses. But this as well as the fact that he said some lovely things and told some fine parables is hardly sufficent to establish the Christian claims about him: that much he has in common with Moses, Micah, and Hosea, with the Buddha, Confucius, and Lao-tze, to name a mere half-dozen teachers who preceded him by a few centuries.

It might be countered that the story of Jesus is the best possible symbol of love. But is it? Consider the story the way it looks to people not committed to, and prejudiced in favor of, Christianity: God caused a virgin, bethrothed to Joseph, to conceive His Own Son, and this Son had to be betrayed, crucified, and resurrected in order that all those—and only those—might be saved who should both believe this story and be baptized and eat and drink on regular occasions what they themselves believe to be the flesh and blood of this Son (or, in some denominations, merely the symbols of His flesh and blood); meanwhile, the rest of mankind suffer eternal torment, and according to many Christian creeds and teachers, they were predestined for damnation by God Himself from the beginning.

One might choose to be a Christian in spite of all this if one could intensely admire the great Christians who came after Jesus. But Peter and Paul, Athanasius and Augustine, Luther and Calvin, seem far less admirable to me, for all their admitted virtues, than Hosea and Micah, Isaiah and Jeremiah, Hillel and Akiba; or the Buddha, Socrates, and Spinoza. Maimonides, unlike Aquinas whom he influenced, did not believe in eternal damnation or that heretics should be executed. Some recent Protestant writers have been wonderfully forthright about Luther's and Calvin's shortcomings; but for candid portraits of the saints one must on the whole turn to non-Catholic writers—with at least one notable exception. In 1950, Malcolm Hay, a Catholic, published one of the most moving books of our time. *The Foot of Pride,* which is admirably frank about some of the most celebrated saints.

In an essay published in Germany in 1939—or rather in a book seized barely before publication by the Gestapo and destroyed except for about half-a-dozen copies—Leo Baeck, probably the greatest rabbi of our time, said something profoundly relevant:

A good deal of church history is the history of all the things which neither hurt nor encroached upon this piety, all the outrages and all the baseness which this piety was able to tolerate with an assured and undisturbed soul and an untroubled faith. And a spirit is characterized not only by what it does but, no less, by what it permits. . . . The Christian religion, very much including Protestantism, has been able to maintain silence about so much that it is difficult to say what has been more pernicious in the course of time: the intolerance which committed the wrongs or the indifference which beheld them unperturbed.

This thought may diminish even one's affection for St. Francis, but not one's admiration for the prophets.

The world's other religions remain. If we apply the same criteria, only two issue a real challenge to us, or at least to me: Judaism and Buddhism. I admire Genesis and Job, the Book of Jonah and the Dhammapada far above any book in the New Testament. But popular Buddhism with its profuse idolatry, its relics, and its superstitions repels me, and I have reservations even about the teachings of the Buddha. I admire much of his profound analysis of man's condition: the world has no purpose; it is up to us to give our lives a purpose; and we cannot rely on any supernatural assistance. Life is full of suffering, suffering is rooted in desire and attachment, and much desire and attachment are rooted in ignorance. By knowledge, especially of the Buddha's teachings, it is possible to develop a pervasive detachment, not incompatible with a mild, comprehensive compassion—and to cease to suffer. But consider the Old Testament and Sophocles, Michelangelo and Rembrandt, Shakespeare and Goethe: the price for the avoidance of all suffering is too high. Suffering and sacrifice can be experienced as worthwhile: one may find beauty in them and greatness through them.

Much of the appeal of Christianity is due to the fact that it contains at least intimations—but really no more than that—of this tragic ethos. But the story of Christ remains uncomfortably similar to the saga of the boss's son who works very briefly in the shop, where he makes a great point of his home and is cruelly beaten by some of his fellow workers, before he joins his father as co-chairman of the board and wreaks horrible revenge. This "happy" end makes most of the Christian martyrs, too, untragic figures. These observations may strike believers as blasphemous, but they might do well to reflect on the manner in which they pass judgment on other religions, and there may be some point in considering how one's own religion must strike those who don't accept it.

Probably the only great religion in which genuine self-sacrifice and tragedy have occupied a central place is Judaism, especially prior to the introduction of belief in any after life. Moses is the very incarnation of humane devotion, wearing himself out in the service of God and men, expecting, and receiving, no reward whatever, but finding his reward in his work. He asks God to destroy him rather than his people and intercedes for them again and again. In the prophets, from Hosea to the songs of the suffering servant, we find the same outlook.

Why, then, do I not accept Judaism? In view of all the things I do not believe, I have no wish to observe the six-hundred-odd commandments and prohibitions that define the traditional Jewish way of life, or to participate in religious services. With most so-called orthodox Jews I have much less in common than with all kinds of other people, Jews and Gentiles. Reform Judaism seems to me to involve compromise, conformism, and the wish to be innocuous. To that extent, it, too, stands opposed to the ethos of the prophets. And if a succession of great Jews should equal the boldness of the prophets, who repudiated the ritual of their day, and go a step further by also renouncing, and denouncing, all kinds of belief—would not this amount to giving up religion?

What remains if you give up the great religions? Many people think: only Communism, Nazism, and immorality. But the morality of Socrates, Spinoza, and Hume compares favorably with Augustine's, Luther's, and Calvin's. And the evil deeds of Communism and Nazism are not due to their lack of belief but to their false beliefs, even as the evils deeds of the Crusaders, Inquisitors, and witch hunters, and Luther's exhortation to burn synagogues and Calvin's decision to burn Servetus, were due to *their* false beliefs. Christianity, like Islam, has caused more wars than it has prevented; and the Middle Ages, when Europe was Christian, were not a period of peace and good will among men. Does it make sense that those who refuse to let their Yes be Yes and their No,

No—those who refuse to reject false beliefs, those who would rather stretch them and equivocate—should have a monopoly on being moral?

Renouncing false beliefs will not usher in the millennium. Few things about the strategy of contemporary apologists are more repellent than their frequent recourse to spurious alternatives. The lesser lights inform us that the alternative to Christianity is materialism, thus showing how little they have read, while the greater lights talk as if the alternative were bound to be a shallow and inane optimism. I don't believe that man will turn this earth into a bed of roses either with the aid of God or without it. Nor does life among the roses strike me as a dream from which one would not care to wake up after a very short time.

Some evils and some kinds of suffering can be abolished, but not all suffering can be eliminated; and the beauty, goodness, and greatness that redeem life on earth are inseparable from suffering. Nietzsche once said: "If you have an enemy, do not requite him evil with good, for that would put him to shame. Rather prove that he did you some good." If life hurts you, the manly thing is neither to whine nor to feel martyred, but to prove that it did you some good.

No one way is the best way of life for all. To me the *Apology* of Socrates, as immortalized by Plato in less than thirty pages, presents a challenge from which I cannot, and have no wish to, get away. Here is part of Socrates' answer to the charges of impiety and corruption of the Athenian youth, on which he was convicted and put to death:

I am better off than he is—for he knows nothing but thinks he knows, while I neither know nor think I know. . . . If you say to me, . . . you shall be let off, but upon one condition, that you are not to inquire . . . in this way any more, and that if you are caught doing so again you shall die—if this was the condition on which you let me go, I should reply: . . . while I have life and strength I shall never cease from the practice and teaching of philosophy, exhorting anyone whom I meet. . . . Are you not ashamed of heaping up the greatest amount of money and honor and reputation, and caring so little about wisdom and truth? . . . The unexamined life is not worth living. . . . If you suppose that there is no consciousness, but a sleep like the sleep of him that is undisturbed even by dreams, death will be an unspeakable gain. . . . Eternity is then only a single night.

It would be folly to wish to foist this outlook on everybody. Professors of philosophy discourage and fail a large percentage even of their graduate students and are assuredly not eager to turn all men into philosophers. In philosophy, as in religion, teaching usually involves a loss of dimension; and the Socratic fusion of philosophy and life, critical acumen and passion, laughter and tragic stature is almost unique.

One need not believe in Pallas Athena, the virgin goddess, to be overwhelmed by the Parthenon. Similarly, a man who rejects all dogmas, all theologies, and all religious formulations of beliefs may still find Genesis the sublime book *par excellence*. Experiences and aspirations of which intimations may be found in Plato, Nietzsche, and Spinoza have found their most evocative expression in some sacred books. Since the Renaissance, Shakespeare,

Rembrandt, Mozart, and a host of others have shown that this religious dimension can be experienced and communicated apart from any religious context. But that is no reason for closing my heart to Job's cry, or to Jeremiah's, or to the Second Isaiah. I do not read them as mere literature; rather, I read Sophocles and Shakespeare with all my being, too.

Moreover, I am so far quite unable to justify one of my central convictions: that, even if it were possible to make all men happy by an operation or a drug that would stultify their development, this would somehow be an impious crime. This conviction is ultimately rooted in the Mosaic challenge: "You shall be holy; for I the Lord your God am holy."

To communicate to others some feeling for man's religious quest, to arouse an aspiration in them which nothing but death can quell, and to develop their critical powers—that is infinitely more important to me than persuading anybody that Shakespeare was right when he wrote these lines:

> The cloud-capp'd towers, the gorgeous palaces,
> The solemn temples, the great globe itself,
> Yea, all which it inherit, shall dissolve:
> And, like this insubstantial pageant faded,
> Leave not a rack behind. We are such stuff
> As dreams are made on, and our little life
> Is rounded with a sleep.

I do not believe in any after life any more than the prophets did, but I don't mind living in a world in which people have different beliefs. Diversity helps to prevent stagnation and smugness; and a teacher should acquaint his students with diversity and prize careful criticism far above agreement. His noblest duty is to lead others to think for themselves.

Oddly, millions believe that lack of belief in God, Christ, and Hell leads to inhumanity and cruelty while those who have these beliefs have a monopoly on charity—and that people like myself will pay for their lack of belief by suffering in all eternity. I do not believe that anybody will suffer after death nor do I wish it.

Some scientists tell us that in our own galaxy alone there are probably hundreds of thousands of planets with living beings on them, more or less like those on the earth, and that there are about 100 million galaxies within the range of our telescopes. Man seems to play a very insignificant part in the universe, and my part is surely negligible. The question confronting me is not, except perhaps in idle moments, what part might be more amusing, but what I wish to make of my part. And what I want to do and would advise others to do is to make the most of it: put into it all you have got, and live and, if possible, die with some measure of nobility.

IX

The Conservative Stance

IN 1945 THE POWER of the German and Japanese war machines had been smashed, and Americans looked forward to an era of peace and prosperity, dominated by a concert of nations determined to see that the tragedies of the 1930's would not be repeated. Yet only a few short years later these dreams had been rudely shattered, and men were forced to face the terrifying possibility that the technology they had created might yet be used to bring about their own destruction.

But the dilemmas facing Americans at mid-century were not simply the problems of an advanced technological society. The fear of destruction was only an outward symptom of a deeper problem that ultimately concerned fundamental moral and philosophical issues. What Americans were most concerned about was their own undefined future in a world where the processes of change and transformation had been sharply accelerated and often seemed to be beyond their effective control. Ever since the days of the Puritans, Americans had enjoyed the psychological security of their firm faith in America and its destiny, a faith that revolved around a core of religious doctrines and a belief in a fundamental moral law. Indeed, the nation's history from the seventeenth through the early twentieth century seemed to offer convincing evidence that America was truly fulfilling its divine mission both in material and spiritual aspects. Because of their fortunate past, few Americans in these years appeared to be very much troubled by ideological issues. Conservatives and liberals alike, despite their wide differences, were united in an optimistic prognosis of their country's future.

The rise of Nazism and fascism in the 1930's, the worldwide threats to democracy in the 1940's, and the continued expansion of communism in the 1950's, however, forced Americans to reconsider traditional assumptions about themselves and their society. Some even attempted to formulate a new political philosophy they deemed more suited to the needs of a changing world. The result was the rise of a self-conscious conservatism.

This New Conservatism was an amalgam of many political forces and different ideological premises. It enrolled in its support those who had once had kinship with radical discontent as well as those who were concerned with maintaining the nation's great political traditions. Some who spoke out were angry young men, others were scholars of international reputation; some embraced the "radical Right" while others were "middle-of-the-roaders."

To the question, what is conservatism? there is no easy answer. The traditions of political discussion are not always consistent, and frequently in fact what is "liberal" to one generation is "conservative" to another. For Americans these terms are especially difficult, for they are lacking in a clearly defined liberal or conservative tradition, and the American electorate has seldom had an opportunity to choose officials in terms of such positions. Both conservatives and liberals have, in fact, invoked America's past and its traditions to justify and define their position. And Americans have been interested more in results than in theory. Consequently they have borrowed frequently from European sources and adapted these ideas to the American experience in a way that further blurred ideological lines and distinctions.

The conservative, one spokesman has said, "is full of harsh doubts about the goodness and equality of men, the wisdom and possibilities of reform, and the sagacity of the majority."[1] To the conservative, man is a composite of good and evil—not perfect, not perfectible. Equality has meaning only in a spiritual sense; politically, society must recognize classes and respect aristocracies. Society is a living organism, a unity, that has a status of primacy. Society cannot be static, but it must be stable, for its ideal is ordered liberty. Government is natural not artificial, good not evil. Nevertheless, government cannot serve all purposes, and it is limited in its potentialities for good. The theory of natural law becomes the basis of the limitation of government as well as of legitimate authority. Religion usually has a central role in the conservative philosophy and the conservative often assigns a prominent place in his ideal society to institutionalized religion. Finally, the conservative respects history and reveres tradition, believing them both to be man's most reliable teachers.

Such is the mood, if not the total philosophy, of the conservative. How pervasive did the conservative mood become in America? Some observers believe the new conservatism became more widespread than, for example, political choices would indicate. The search for consensus, for agreement on fundamental ideals and purposes, as well as pressures for conformity were among the forces producing an extension of the conservative mind. Adlai E. Stevenson, in the presidential campaign of 1952, observed in a speech at Columbus, Ohio, that "the strange alchemy of time has somehow converted the Democrats into the truly conservative party of this country—the party dedicated to conserving all that is best, and building solidly and safely on these foundations." The conservative sentiment he expressed was shared by wide segments of the American people.

---

1. Clinton Rossiter, *Conservatism in America* (New York, 1955), p. 17.

Peter Viereck

1916-

Born in New York City, Peter Viereck was educated at Harvard, where he received the Ph.D. degree in 1942. He then taught at several schools, including Mount Holyoke College. One of the creators of the New Conservatism, Viereck is also one of the ablest spokesmen for this conservative viewpoint. He has been influenced by a host of conservative thinkers of the past—Aristotelian, feudal, Burkean—but he writes in and for the American scene. He has also consistently opposed the "idiot conservatism" of radical right-wing groups, and has supported many social welfare programs as essential to the well-being of society.

Viereck's conservatism finds expression in many articles and in such books as *Conservatism Revisited* (1949), *The Unadjusted Man* (1956), *Conservatism: From John Adams to Churchill* (1956), and the volume from which the following selection is taken, *Shame and Glory of the Intellectuals* (Boston, 1953).

"All political systems," observed the poet Paul Valéry, "imply (and are generally not aware that they do imply) a certain conception of man, and even an opinion about the destiny of the species, an entire metaphysic." We should all try to achieve an awareness of what it is we are implying. "Metaphysically" (to use a "conservative" word despised by Enlightened Progressives), the difference between a democratic leftist and a democratic conservative is as follows: The conservative, politically descended from Burke, distrusts human nature and believes (politically speaking) in Original Sin, which must be restrained by the ethical traffic lights of traditionalism. The leftist and the liberal, descended from Rousseau, unconsciously assume the natural goodness of man—the less restrained in power the better.

If human nature were naturally good, then I would join the left-liberals and democratic socialists of the west in trusting a party power-machine to regiment a country's economy without eventually creating a political dictatorship to enforce such vast controls. Both Christianity and Dr. Freud teach a different view of human nature.

Conservatism and *liberalism,* as here used, are not clear or primary criteria for the American electoral scenes of 1952–56 (least of all while both parties are under such similarly middle-of-the-road, anti-extremist amalgams of liberal and conservative motifs as Stevenson and Eisenhower). *Conservative* and *liberal* are long-run "metaphysical" and psychological terms, not short-run practical terms. They cannot suffice to help us choose between electing a Democrat or Republican as village fire chief. In that sense they are "useless" terms of pragmatic activists. In that sense I even *intend* them to be "useless," being interested only in social and psychological speculations, not at all in political propaganda tracts for any particular party or candidate.

But in their "useless," impractical way, the terms *liberal* and *conservative* do enrich our understanding of an important split in human nature, a psychological and literary as well as political split. This is the split between those who trust the "natural goodness" of man and primarily want to release it from *outer* restraints, and those who fear his natural caveman propensities and primarily want to check them with *inner* restraints.

A sense of man's limitations—a sense of his precariousness and mystery—is the necessary corrective against megalomaniac efforts to remake the world by force. The brilliant communist atomic spy, Klaus Fuchs, wrote in his court confession that the reading of Karl Marx meant to him, above all, the overcoming of human limitations; this overweening self-assertion of man, ruthlessly remaking society regardless of moral limitations, was (he confessed) the basis of his communist faith: "The idea which gripped me most was . . . that now, for the first time, man understands the historical forces and he is able to control them, and that therefore for the first time he will be really free. I carried this idea over into the personal sphere. . . ."

There are Lenins of religion, as there are Torquemadas of atheism; both equally lack this sense of human limitation. Christianity, rightly understood, teaches it the most wisely and truly. But the formula of "Christianity or communism," high-pressured with the same techniques as a campaign for Ivory Soap instead of God, is much too pat without qualification. What about the Red Dean of Canterbury and communism's Christian "peace" fronts? The formula holds true only if you add "Christianity rightly understood," thereby opening an un-pat debate that would fill volumes. How often is Christianity understood and practiced spiritually rather than as a sociological convention? May not its spiritual ethics sometimes work through decent unbelievers (God "works in mysterious ways") while being betrayed not so much by open godlessness as by drab, leaden-eyed, uninspired lip service?

This Burkean (or today perhaps Niebuhrian) sense of human limitation and frailty, as opposed to the megalomaniac faith in limitless progress through mass-movements and material reforms, is a basic distinction between the conservative temperament and the progressive temperament. I say "temperament," not "political party" or "economic program." This Burkean sense is more basic a test of your outgrowing the illusions of liberalism than your position on the economic laws (introduced by the Republican party) against child labor or the economic laws (introduced by the Democratic party) for minimum wages. If such humane reforms, over the centuries, were a monopoly of liberalism, then who wouldn't be a liberal? What is left to debate if you beg the question by making one -ism synonymous with decency and the other with evil? What decent person today doesn't favor such laws?

No, social reform by itself is no criterion for conservative versus progressive (though the motives behind reform, whether motives of class-war-incitement or class-war-prevention, are obvious criteria). I cannot for a minute take seriously the assertions of America's superficial (merely economic) "conservatives" that they would abolish "all New Deal laws," most of which are the mildest, revolution-preventing reforms, passed by *both* parties. All that is shadow-boxing and campaign oratory. The genuine differences between the conservative and progressive outlooks on life are in the ethical and psychological realm, cutting across the lines of political party, economic class, or nationality.

There is no single shiny object to be peddled as "*the* new conservatism." That only raises the question: which kind and conserving what? Let author and reader subordinate labels to contents. I don't care what the views here presented are labeled, in case you prefer to define conservatism differently. One writer suggests, "Instead, call these views the *true* liberalism, which the totalitarian and Popular Front liberals have betrayed." Less dramatic and more pedantic than that, I'd settle for being labeled simply "a value-conserving classical humanist." What difference does it make anyway? Here is the real point: after twenty years of hackneyed liberal conformism in high places and of a cult of revolt-for-its-own-sake among writers and intellectuals, it is time to work out a more human view of humanity. And by "human" I mean a view of society based on ethics and psychology, in contrast with an ethically-relativist and psychologically-superficial view of society based on economics.

Economics, economic determinism, and their nonexistent Economic Man are superannuated Marxist-and-capitalist fads. They reflect the temporarily overwhelming impact—the impact of novelty and of crisis—made upon the nineteenth century by the industrial revolution. In America after the Civil War, this industrial impact corrupted and narrowed the broader and more idealistic conservatism of our founding fathers. Hence, the pejorative misuse of the word today; hence, the need . . . to distinguish at considerable length between the true value-conserving kind and the contemporary degenerate kind, which conserves merely economic greed. For the more independent students and younger professors, the new conservatism (in its value-conserving sense) is rapidly becoming the only escape from the stultifying standardization of their cynical, value-denying elders. . . .

Though diverse subjects have been treated in these pages, their unity is basic because it reflects two underlying themes. The one unifying theme has been negative, the other positive. Negative theme: to examine the ethical, artistic, and political dangers of the new philistinism. Positive: a humanistic conservatism to meet the danger in these three fields.

At its best, the new conservatism may be defined as the rediscovery of values. This is what makes conservatism so fresh and exciting today, unlike the earlier Colonel Blimp, as cartooned by Low. A generation of pompous,

Laski-indoctrinated leftists has intervened, a generation of Comrade Blimps, to whom conservatism is a subversive Dirty Word from the wrong side of the intellectual railroad tracks. No wonder the British Labor Government was so philistine and boring: on European unity uncreative and without Churchillian vision, in economics more skilled at afflicting the comfortable than comforting the afflicted. Conservatism is the rediscovery of tradition, the daring search for that lost Grail, the value code of Western man.

Society is in a bad way when too many people reject every ancient value in ethics and politics and art because thereby they can show off better at cocktail parties. Civilization is an infinitely fragile bundle of accumulated habits and restraints. The necessary conservative function of any generation is not just to enjoy itself but to pass on this bundle in good condition to the next generation.

Radicalism and revolt are just as valuable as conservatism so long as they really do correct social defects. But not when their insurgency accentuates, instead of corrects, social defects. In the past, when society had too much *laissez faire,* the thunder from the left was a valuable corrective to social defects. Today, when the world is afflicted by too much statism, the left accentuates, rather than corrects, social defects. Because society has changed. Today Bohemia and Left Bank and Left Wing, all the dully "daring" defiance of bourgeois conventions, have become the rheumatic jitterbugging of aging *enfants terribles.*

In the Victorian and Coolidgean ages, civilization was stuffy and stodgy, conservatism at its worst. It was dull to have only law and tradition; it was healthy and useful for obscure and surrealist poems and paintings to stir up placid reality with a nightmare art. It was healthy and useful to have the young rebel poke dull old civilization in its stuffed shirt; the *enfant terrible* served a real purpose.

Today the whole world is *terrible.* The whole world has become a surrealist painting. What was shocking in early surrealist painting was: legs and arms strewn about, buildings torn open. This contrasted with an unstrewn and untorn Victorian and Coolidgean reality. Today, however, reality is strewn all over the place. To us who were soldiers in Italy, strewn limbs and buildings became the norm. If the Babbitt is he who kowtows to fashionable conventions, then it is the wilfully obscure poet and the surrealist artist and the *enfant terrible* Greenwich Village genius who is the philistine; *he* is accentuating society's defects. The traditional moralist, the conservative in politics and in poetry, is correcting the defects. When reality is itself a nightmare, then an art which is lucid and calm and ennobling—an eighteenth-century neo-classical art—is more helpful, more original, and more exciting.

For a generation brought up not under Queen Victoria but under Princess Rita Hayworth, with not Bishop Wilberforce but Dr. Kinsey as Father Confessor, for such a generation Flaming Youth is not exciting but a bore. The only way to shock your reader in a modern non-Victorian novel—if that's what you want to do—would be to use the word "limbs" instead of "legs."

That would shock them more than all the boring four-letter words of our war novelists.

But an affectation of archiepiscopal reactionary stodginess would be just as tiresome as the present rebel stodginess. In both art and politics one pendulum extreme is as bad as the other. Why have any affectations, either reactionary or revolutionary? Why not be yourself? Integrity may be the dullest platitude in the preaching of old Polonius, but integrity is the two-plus-two that does make four. A reverence for integrity, not because it's fashionable but because it's true, such a reverence would work a moral revolution deeper and more helpful than all the shallow artistic and political and economic revolts of our panting apostles of progress. It would be a moral revolution against that inner smirk which prefers cleverness to love and prefers statistics to wisdom. . . .

Unlike the ancient conservatism of Great Britain, the young American conservatism is still primarily a cultural, ethical, and educational movement, not primarily political.

The proper start for a new American conservatism, aiming not at success but at truth, not at activism but at long-range education, is in the world of literature, the arts and sciences, intellectual history, the universities, the humanities. Starting there and slowly osmosing into more "practical" spheres of American life, such a movement will eventually affect politics and economics by raising in both parties the *level of insight* into historical and ethical processes. By being more contemplative than activist, by asking all those basic questions the activists ignore rather than by too glibly answering them, a conservative return to values will transform politics and economics indirectly. If instead it tries to start by being directly and actively political and economic, it will at best fail and transform nothing at all. At worst it will lend itself to unscrupulous material exploitation. The thoughtfulness here recommended to new conservatives is not a flight from practical action but an inner prelude to practical action. The most successful political conservatism in history, the Tory party of Disraeli and Churchill, derived to a surprising extent from sources that were almost entirely literary, like Coleridge.

Our civilization is very old, very broad; we Americans are only a very young, very small part of it. Its essentials, its truth and its beauty, together with a deep understanding of human nature, are transmitted more through the humanities than through that up-to-date journalism of the academic world, the courses in current politics, economics, and other uselessly "useful" techniques. Not that the latter are unworthy—call them the Good Housekeeping of American education—but they happen not to be the main value transmitters and insight transmitters. Values and insights are transmitted by saturating yourself in the Elizabethan and Greek plays, the Aeneid and the Song of Roland, the poetry of Dante and Hölderlin, the psychological insight of Augustine, Pascal and the nineteenth-century Russian novelists.

The American conservative can transform his country more by teaching these value transmitters, and by raising their status above the media of mass-entertainment in public esteem, than by any directly political action. (It should be evident that courses in practical technical training and in the humanities can both be happily combined, wherever economic need so dictates.)

Saturation in the value transmitters of literature is an intimately personal part of every free citizen's growth. It is achieved not by streamlined public lectures on Great Books Predigested but by lonely reverie. It is aided not at all by our mechanized and progressive "teaching aids," replete with loudspeakers, with tape-recorders, and even with thinking-brain machines for grading multiple-choice questions. There is no substitute for the traditional, even sentimental Abraham Lincoln picture of the young boy brooding alone by candlelight over the dog-eared open book. Only such daily individual reverie can think through—to its future implications—every exciting idea of the past. This does more than inane loyalty oaths and patriotic propaganda to prevent two kinds of disloyalty:

1. The constant unconscious echoing of fellow-traveler clichés in intellectual circles.

2. On a more frivolous plan, the daily cultural betrayal of our past in the mass-entertainment—the Don't Think Clubs—of the air waves and the celluloid.

Neither form of value betrayal can be compromised with even slightly. It is not enough to apologize, "I only tune in on the better programs." It is true that already today a television set can serve what its ads call "your beautiful American way of life." But only when chopped up into firewood and blazing merrily.

The new conservatism—meaning: a fresh and creative traditionalism— never admires the past passively in sterile escapism. It must daily and actively re-experience, as if for the first time, the aspirations of the past—and then fulfil them in the future. . . .

In the 1930's Edmund Wilson, agonizing over the contrast between radical ideals and Soviet realities, implored intellectuals to "take communism away from the communists." And, indeed, one of the finest achievements of the New Deal era, now drawing to a close, is that it achieved many humanitarian ideals of the so-called left without the murderous police-state practices of the far left. In the 1950's, to reverse the slogan of the 1930's, our more responsible leaders ought to take anticommunism away from the anticommunists. And to take conservatism away from the wrong—the solely economics-minded—conservatives. It will be as important to keep the present era of *pause* under humane conservatives as it was to keep the past era of *change* out of the hands of the leftist version of terrorists and thought controllers.

Youth has been called too wonderful a thing to waste on the young. Conservatism, which ought to mean the freshness and zest of rediscovery, is too wonderful to waste on the old-in-spirit. . . .

The discrediting of the Soviet fraud has made it a lot easier for intellectuals to become American traditionalists without being howled down as "reactionaries," "flag wavers," or "fascists." Recognition of the blood-stained nature of the Soviet banner makes it seem less deliciously clever to trample on the American banner at every possible occasion. This swing from the outworn poses of revolt is releasing a burst of creative new thinking.

But the same change brings new dangers as well as new blessings. In time the new traditionalism may degenerate into a new white-wash of pretentious philosophy for what has always been unpretentious: the old robber baronism of public-be-damned. At least those endearingly unshaved and candid old pirates did not try to be smoothie "philosophers" of "conservatism." Genuine giants of our dinosaur era of chaotic expansion, like crusty Commodore Vanderbilt, swashbuckling Dan Drew carelessly trailing seminaries and suicides, or old J. P. Morgan, would have puffed their black cigars scornfully at such fancy nonsense. If this white-wash takes place, then the American flag, rightly saved from the muddy boots of fellow-traveler liberals, would be saved in vain. Or is it a patriotic triumph if the dawn's early glare reveals our flag progressing from being a door mat to being a fig leaf?

Such patriots, reaping unjustified fruits from our justified revulsion against communism, now have their grand opportunity. They can now suddenly seem the Great Oaks of the American Dream instead of the parasitic vines. History itself seems beckoning us toward their comforting shade, those stalwart "un-communistic" pillars both of profit system and of God-fearingness.

But what if there be a contradiction between these two supposedly equal pillars? What if the essence of the patriotic American tradition, along with the tradition of the whole Christian-Hellenic-Judaic world, is an awareness of this contradiction between our profits and our prophets?

Lay not up for yourselves treasures upon earth . . . for where your treasure is, there will your heart be also. . . . No man can serve two masters . . . ye cannot serve God and mammon.

I have faith in American capitalism because I believe its profit system has been sufficiently modified by ethics—and because I believe it can continue to be revised peacefully, without need of socialism, when it does violate the demands of humanity. Defending it on this basis, we can create faith in our system in Europe, in India, and at home. But if we adopt the un-American principle of putting profits above humanity and ethics, we shall discredit American capitalism and aid Moscow. This will have two results, the first abroad and the second at home:

1. Abroad we will find ourselves fatally without allies, a fate not displeasing to some of the "go it alone" isolationists. In that case, the American Adam Smith will produce Cain and Abel Smith in Europe, a fratricidal destruction of the free world for Stalin's benefit.

2. More ironically, we will at home be *behaving exactly as Marxism says we behave:* namely, putting our capitalist profit motive over all religious, ethical, and cultural ties. By combating Marxism in the wrong way, we would for the first time in our history become Marxist economic determinists in our behavior.

Can anything happen that would prove Marx right? Though he was steeped in enough Western humanism to make him preferable to the Soviet terror, yet his doctrinaire Hegelianism and Prussian statism produced a dogma seemingly impossible to justify. Here is the achievement of our Old Guarders: their triumph would accomplish the dazzling feat of justifying the following passage of Marx and Engels, which our past history had gloriously disproved:

The bourgeoisie has played an extremely revolutionary role. . . . It has destroyed all feudal, patriarchal, and idyllic relationships. It has ruthlessly torn asunder the motley feudal ties that bound men to their "natural superiors;" it has left no other bond betwixt man and man but crude self-interest and unfeeling "cash payment." It has drowned religious ecstasy, chivalrous enthusiasm, and humdrum sentimentalism in the ice-water of selfish calculation. It has degraded personal dignity to the level of exchange value; and in place of countless dearly-bought chartered freedoms, it has set up one solitary unscrupulous freedom—freedom of trade.

Capitalism has many other merits but happens not to be a sacred religion. The current ambitious attempt to make it one in our textbooks is being incorrectly denounced as "fascism" by New Deal liberals and incorrectly hailed as "free individualism" by Republican conservatives. It is neither. It is a return to that Sahara of inhuman aridity: the belief in Economic Man. It is a return to the incomplete liberties—merely top-of-the-iceberg—of private economic liberty. It ignores the nine-tenths of human liberties beneath the top of the brain: the nine-tenths of imagination and art and religion. . . .

The cause of democratic socialism, opposing both fascism and communism, contains more good will than most -isms of our time. Why is most of that good will squandered without producing more than High-minded Editorials? Why, to put it cruelly, is democratic socialism ultimately a failure?

Social democracy has an attractive social program for both the masses and the intellectuals. Then why has it so frequently failed to stop either communism or fascism in Europe? Why has it failed to summon forth the energy and enthusiasm to keep itself in power firmly and long? The Weimar Republic is a classic case of such failure.

The answer is not only economic but psychological. Surely it is an obvious answer, though perhaps not normally stated in just that way. The answer is simply that an inherent inner conflict condemns all social democrats to be Hamlets. An innate schizophrenia paralyzes—(with great but rare exceptions like Reuter)—their ability to *take action* in any crisis or to stay firmly in power against aggressive enemies who know what they want.

The source of their paralyzing inner conflict is that they want incompatibles. They want economic collectivism and political individual rights at the same time. With what consequences? Their *economic* wish for collectivism requires *political* dictatorship to enforce. Their sincere *political* wish for individual liberty requires some individualism also in all the nonpolitical fields, *economics* not excluded.

But the very phrase "free enterprise"—here their conditioning makes them inflexible—the very phrase "free enterprise" horrifies all socialists and also the less moderate wing of New Dealers. Their conditioned response is to dismiss it as some Wall Street plot, some insincere propaganda slogan for selfish undemocratic interests. This it is—sometimes and superficially. But not always and not basically. Nobody is speaking of total laissez faire nor of materialistic profit worship; but basically the economy healthiest for democracy is most certainly the free market and free consumer choice, that encourager of individual diversities.

The humiliating failure of Weimar and the social democrats to prevent Germans from voting Nazi tempts one to misquote Churchill: never has so little been achieved with so much effort by so many. "But what about Scandinavia?" a socialist asks. The success of Scandinavian social democrats, insofar as it is really a success, proves my point. Where they do well, they are not democrats-plus-socialists but democrats-period. Being democratic includes social reform; "democrat" by itself already means "social-reform democrat." But social reform—Christian humanitarianism or nineteenth-century "Tory socialism"—does not at all mean the statist "socialism" of present American and European socialists.

Here I am using "socialism" not in any watered-down sense. I use it to mean a statism that socializes the economic and industrial life of the country. Socialism is a statism that nationalizes not merely a post office here, a public utility there, but the main means of production.

Full socialist control of press and radio by the government, even if indirectly via newsprint, control of most economic power by government and lack of economic power by any kind of opposition, will make democracy impossible. Impossible not in theory but in actual practice, even if sincerely maintaining every one of the outward democratic forms in theory. After becoming emperor, Augustus maintained the sovereignty of the Roman Senate in theory; did that mean Rome was still a republic?

But though democratic socialism is a contradiction, it is not one that necessarily leads to ruin. That depends on which half of the contradiction your social democrat stresses. In Europe, America can and should work with democratic socialists against communism wherever they are democrats first, as they are in the case of Reuter, Attlee, and most French and Scandinavian socialists. Europe's unsocialist socialism and America's classless, democratized capitalism are both in practice—never in theory—living in a thoroughly mixed-up economy, flexible and undoctrinaire, and doing very well, thank you.

All this does not change the fact that, in the long run, the Hamlet wavering between freedom and statism will continue to enfeeble the socialists themselves. It will also enfeeble and demoralize any country under them. In the long run they will have to face the need of shifting their position: from the outward leftist fringe of society toward the more conservative center. They will have to say quite brutally to themselves, "Come, come, no nonsense now!"

and throw out their "revolutionary" dogmas. Those dogmas are a hang-over from an earlier century, before history established beyond challenge the un-revolutionary nature of freedom. . . .

Not yet daring to breathe aloud the heresy of sobriety, some socialists tacitly have reached these centrist, mixed-economy conclusions already. Still a minority, these more reasonable souls are found with increasing frequency in England and Scandinavia; perhaps by the time of his death the wise French socialist Léon Blum had also evolved to this stage. At this stage, the ambiguous word "socialist" becomes—like Disraeli's Tory socialism or maybe Niebuhr's Christian synthesis—a sound sense of the organic ties between free individuals. It becomes a sound rebuke to the laisser-faire atomism and anarchism of the more doctrinaire capitalists, yet without crossing the fatal statist line.

But while many social democrats are democrats first, let us not optimistically overlook the fact that many others still are socialists first. The Marxist, the Bevanites, and the Schumacher wing of German socialists really "mean business" with their socialism. This does credit to their sincerity.

It does not do credit to their capacity for preserving liberties. The Achilles heel of even the wisest democratic socialists is that they recognize no statist margin, limiting the usefulness of even the wisest social legislation beyond a certain point. Instead they put their faith (that same old Rousseauistic faith) in counterbalancing the superstate by the mass-electorate, via its theoretical "democratic controls." The "natural goodness" of the Ortegan mass-man is somehow to prevent an all-powerful bureaucracy from abusing politically its excessive economic power. Well, it can't be done.

(46)

Clarence B. Randall

1891-

Born in Newark Valley, New York, Randall received the A.B. degree in 1912 and the law degree in 1915, both from Harvard University. He was then admitted to the Michigan Bar and practiced law for ten years. Subsequently, he joined the Inland Steel Company as an executive and from 1949 to 1953 he was president of the company. Since that time he has served in a number of prominent positions both in and out of government. He has turned to writing and—in his support of American capitalism, economic conservatism, and the free enterprise system—has become the spokesman of a large portion of the business community.

Randall's conservatism is focused largely on the economic sphere.

He emphasizes the central role of private capitalism in America's remarkable economic development. But, with other economic conservatives, Randall also believes that the maintenance of the system of free enterprise is a necessary condition for preserving American freedom and culture.

This selection is from *A Creed for Free Enterprise* (Boston, 1952).

Obviously, the first task to which the businessman must set himself upon trying to clarify his thinking is an understanding and proper evaluation of free enterprise itself. Here we seem to be on familiar ground. Free enterprise is our favorite theme on those rare occasions when we talk; no banquet would be complete without sonorous phrases in its praise, our advertisements proclaim it by word and picture; yet, actually, who among us so comprehends its significance that he can persuade an honest skeptic of its virtues? So often we argue only by declaration and vituperation, striving to beat down the opposition solely by the noise our voices make, without sensing that no one is listening. We do, however, thus reveal the shallowness of our understanding, and strengthen the suspicion of the public that our fervor is based solely on a selfish desire to preserve the status quo in which we are thought to be a privileged class.

Yet our record of performance is magnificent. One has only to look about in the rest of the world today to perceive that there is something very different about the economic well-being of the fortunate citizens of the United States, and that it is a difference which has saved what there is of freedom for all mankind. In two wars the American system of production has been the anchor of the free world, and today it is the sole effective deterrent to further aggression. Without it all would have been lost. Shall that lesson be lightly ignored? Shall the sneering contempt of a small group of cosmic experimenters be allowed to destroy what so many millions of men have toiled to create since the earliest days of our Republic? Every businessman in the country cries out daily for a champion who will nail these monstrous lies being put out by the enemies of his beloved free enterprise, but as for his own part in the counter crusade it sometimes turns out that "he is tied up at the moment, trying to straighten out his production schedule for the next quarter," and besides it is very hard for him to write speeches.

And therein lies our problem. No one man can do this job. And no one can be hired to do it for us. But if each man who is a part of free enterprise would come to hold the deep conviction that the perpetuation of the system itself had first priority on his talents, and if every such voice could be lifted all of the time in humble and intelligent exposition of the values of the system as the man sees them, public opinion would have to come our way overnight for the simple reason that the things we believe in are just and right. Only misunderstanding is in the way.

These things seem so clear to us that again one asks why it is that we do so badly.

First of all, curiously enough, we bog down in semantics. We, of all people, ought not to quibble over words, but we do. We quarrel with one another as to whether "free enterprise" is both complete and accurate as a description of the business system whose virtues we wish to praise. Many a monograph has been written on that subject, and much ingenuity has been employed to devise improved phrases, but I notice that none gets currency beyond that given it by the man who was the inventor. The same thing happens as to the word "democracy." Often when I have used the word "democracy" in a public address I have had to face at the close an angry citizen who has paid no attention to the substance of my argument because he has been so determined to convert me to the idea that we live in a republic. And I have a friend who simply froths at the mouth when I use the word "worker" instead of "employee" or "fellow-worker" because, he says, even the president of a company is a worker. I am impatient of these minutiae. A general audience hearing those words is not confused. Hair-splitting annoys them: they want to know what businessmen are going to do about those things. And so I say that when we contrast the proven values of free enterprise with the proven failure of socialism people know what we are talking about.

Apart from these rather sophomoric semantics, I suppose that our first and perhaps our most fundamental failure to understand the real meaning of free enterprise is to consider it synonymous with production. How we love to boast about production. I do myself. Take the steel industry, for example. In other wars, we were asked simply to divert our output from peacetime needs to armament, but when war came in Korea the new challenge was that we should carry the full normal civilian demand and yet superimpose upon that the greatest rearmament load the country has ever attempted. And in spite of the vast new capital which this required, and physical problems which taxed our resources to the limit, we have done just that. Who wouldn't be proud of such a record? And all over the country in all the great industries and in thousands of plants, both large and small, men are bursting with similar pride at the breaking of production records.

But our strength is our weakness. We have come to worship production as an end in itself, which of course it is not. We have come to give production a place of distorted importance in the scale of human values, as though it settled every question and answered every need. It is precisely there that the honest critic of our way of life makes his atttack, and finds us vulnerable.

Production, as I see it, is merely a tool to be used by society for its own advancement. To produce more and more with less and less effort is merely treading water unless we thereby release time and energy for the cultivation of the mind and spirit, and the achievement of those ends for which Providence placed us on this earth. Surely there must be for each person some ultimate value, some purpose, some mode of self-expression that makes the experience we call life richer and deeper. How forlorn it would all be otherwise. Taken collectively, the diligent and honest pursuit of those values by all thoughtful men makes the world a better place, and mankind progresses. Better production does not in itself accomplish those ends. It merely gives us more time for trying.

But with our American capacity for production thus set in its proper perspective, it justifiably stands out as a phenomenon for all the world to admire, and for us to re-examine critically in order that once fully understood the secret formula may never be lost by neglect or abandoned by default. The key to it obviously is the intelligent harnessing of the self-interest of the individual for the advancement of the common good. Throughout the countless ages that lie buried in the past, those species survived and improved in which each individual concentrated on taking care of himself. That instinct, as a force in human behavior, has eons of momentum behind it. Our wisdom lies in using it to promote the general welfare, while the fallacy of the collectivist dictator is his naive belief that it can or should be eliminated from human conduct.

However society may be organized in the political sense, the function of production remains the same. In Russia, as in the United States, the goal is the turning out of the maximum of goods and services with the minimum of time and labor in order that there may be a surplus of human effort that can be devoted to other ends. Every man must therefore be held to his task. Slave states all through the centuries have done this by the whip. Russia has added modern refinements such as blackmail, but her system is still that of the strong compelling the weak by force to work. Her industrial relations problems must obviously center around indifference, sullenness, and sabotage. In sharp contrast to this, we base our industrial philosophy upon the effectiveness of the happy man. We work hard because we work for ourselves, a primordial urge that is as much a part of our being as eating food.

Most of the occasional nonsense written in this country to decry the profit motive is either ignorance or hypocrisy: it either is failure to understand the importance of self-interest in increasing the total wealth of all the people, or just plain shutting of the eyes to the truth. For myself, I have never known a man who did not at times seek to advance his own self-interest. Professors, even those who attack our business system, vie keenly for better and bigger salaries, and clergymen want larger churches and better pay, all of which I consider to be normal and proper. Even a repulsively selfish man who knows no god but money may make tremendous contributions to society if his avarice causes him to bring into being a new or better product or produce an old one at a lower price. Just as many a necessary and useful structure may lack beauty, so may an unlovely person be useful to society. A horse with a very evil disposition can nevertheless pull the farmer's plow. So the secret of free enterprise is that we harness the natural instinct of each man to serve himself, and rely on other natural forces to see that as he serves himself he serves society.

Foremost among these forces is competition. In the management of a business the sharp bite of honest, aggressive competition is the automatic corrective that safeguards the public from extortion. No man can be said to be making too much profit if many others are trying to beat him at his own game and none can succeed. The larger his profit, the greater will be the number of those who will try and the greater the chance that they will succeed. Those who pursue him hotly have many points of attack—quality, design, service, and above all price—and he redoubles his effort as they approach because he knows that today's profit may be tomorrow's loss. He is spurred both by hope of gain and fear of loss, and never for a moment can he relax his effort. He spends his life actually producing the most that he can for the common good. How could there be a better formula than that for bringing about continuously the maximum of effort by all of the people? How can it be possible that in the long run the collective effort of nations ruled by force, where each member of society goes to his task reluctantly and without hope, will match that of free men going joyously about their tasks because they are permitted to help themselves as they add to the total wealth?

But it all hinges on the operation of the free market. No modern nation in this socially conscious world will long permit selfishness to go unrestrained, and if it is not held in check by competition because the free market has been interfered with, the people will assert themselves and take away the privileges of free enterprise by collective action. In the steel industry that means nationalization. In other words, the free market as created by honest competition is an indispensable part of the free enterprise system, and if as businessmen we desire to perpetuate the privileges we must accept with full integrity the correlative obligations and responsibilities. We will not be permitted to accept the one and reject the other. Free enterprise is not a hunting license. We must not exploit self-interest and at the same time handcuff the policeman whom society has established in the form of competition.

But not all American businessmen yet see this clearly. There are still those who make the telephone call to their competitor before announcing a new price; still those who hesitate to enter a new market until their doing so has been cleared with the rest of the industry; still those who describe a trade association that quietly polices prices as "constructive." Such men have no business philosophy and no understanding of the way of life they seek to save. Daily they put expediency and short-term profit above principle and survival. Their conduct brings the whole system into disrepute, and it is high time that they learned that our public has never been so sensitive to lack of honesty as it is today. Curiously enough, such men are often naive to the point of denouncing government for suspending natural economic laws through the imposition of wage and price controls, although exercising privately themselves the right to suspend the free market. All that is needed is a little straight thinking and some old-fashioned character to put a stop to such practices; and they would stop overnight if we could make it clearly understood that free enterprise itself is at stake.

To document that statement, all that is required is to look overseas. With us our economy is still dynamic, creative, and vigorous; still bursting at the seams with new ideas, new products, and better methods; still displaying flashes of genius and breath-taking concepts; still daring to take great risks; still lighting the age-old fires of ambition in the eager minds of young men. But in Europe the economy is torpid and sick, kept alive for the most part by blood transfusions from the healthy arteries of our industry. Over there the young men seek security and have a depressing sense of fatalism about the future. They doubt whether there is anything they can do about themselves in particular or the world in general. Among the older businessmen are many who are very wise, and many who often seem to have a clearer understanding of the world in which they live than their counterparts among us, but there is a lack-lustre look in their eyes. They are defensive, sensitive to criticism, and more proud of what has been than of what is to be. Their spirit is not that of the risk-taking entrepreneur, but of the conservator of what their fathers and grandfathers have passed on to them.

These are, of course, generalizations, to which there are brilliant and heartening exceptions, as I should be the first to admit. The new Margam plant of the Steel Company of Wales, for example, is one of the finest steel-producing units in the world, admirably engineered and aggressively managed; the soon to be completed wide continuous sheet steel rolling mill of Sollac in the north of France will equal the best of ours in efficiency and will give light manufacturing in central Europe a tremendous stimulus; and few enterprises anywhere have more competent staff or more alert management than Holland's small but vigorous steel company. An American could learn much from any one of those operations. And when it came to shrewd world-wide merchandising he would do well to have a look at postwar Arbed in Luxemburg, the largest steel company in that interesting country and the largest company anywhere outside the United States.

But the characteristic of European businessmen as a class as distinguished from Americans is their complacency, their timidity, and their instinctive looking to each other and to government for protection against the rude shocks of the contemporary world. And the thing that they fear most is price competition. Almost to a man they are cartel-minded, and it seems to me to be a sound inference that their unwillingness to face honest, vigorous price competition is the cause of their technological backwardness. Their ingenuity has gone not into thinking up ways of beating their competition by lowering prices or entering new markets, but into ways of persuading their competitor that it would be unsocial for him to do either. And in this they have usually had the full support of their government. It is no coincidence, therefore, in my opinion, that those countries which are now turning to the United States for so-called technical assistance are those in which there have been no traditions of real competition and no laws against restraint of trade and monopolistic practices worthy of the name. And much as I admire many of the present leaders of the British steel industry, I am bound to say that in my opinion their rejection of price competition, their instinct for collectivism, and their willingness to accept government control in exchange for the right to agree on prices laid the foundation upon which it was easy for a hostile government to carry out nationalization. All of which brings me back once more to the deep conviction that an honest free market is the very essence of free enterprise and that we cannot hope to deny the one and preserve the other.

But the businessman who is earnestly seeking to think through his own personal philosophy about free enterprise must go one step further and reflect upon the nature of freedom itself. I have always been unhappy at the suggestion that freedom can be expressed in the plural. Rather it seems to me it is a concept that is indivisible and sole. There are no "freedoms": there is simply freedom, and it runs as the breath of life through every phase of the American tradition. In fact, it is America.

Those daring spirits who conquered our wilderness and founded our cities and wrote our laws and began our businesses were men who broke away. No man would turn his back on the land of his fathers and the place of his birth unless he felt within himself a desire so great that it was simply irresistible. That common desire which our successive waves of immigrants from the older countries all felt was simply to live their own lives. They asked no security, and looked only to the strength of their arms and the keenness of their minds to meet their needs. But they had deep respect for each other, and assumed that their neighbors would behave as they did.

It was of such forebears that American free enterprise was born, and such is its spirit. We propose to drive as hard as we can toward our own ends but we know that we must stop short of injuring others or the whole scheme will have to be abandoned. We rely on the conscience of the individual to guide business conduct toward the general welfare. This is the responsibility side of freedom that distinguishes it from license. It is the democratic tradition because it is a self-imposed restraint instead of one that is external, as in the totalitarian states. But it is obviously subject to abuse by those who do not understand, or worse still, by that small but evil minority of men who understand and consciously ignore conscience. And in any state, when men abuse freedom there has to be law. Society has no other way of preserving itself from those who will not play the game. The proliferation of laws restricting freedom of action may be taken as an indication that more and more people either do not understand the social obligations of freedom, or lack the moral courage to do what they know is right. And when it is the business community at which the laws are aimed, it may be a sign that free enterprise is dying because it is not understood by those who practice it.

Whether or not this is a correct analysis of our business system is of little moment. But that each American businessman owes it to himself and to the system of which he is a part to make his own analysis would seem to be clear. It is a time for heart searching and action. The march toward socialism and nationalization is on. We who would reverse that trend must recognize that this is so, and then accept day-to-day responsibility for doing something about it. But for our acts to be effective, we must first have understanding.

(47)

Russell Kirk

1918-

Russell Kirk, born in Plymouth, Michigan, did his undergraduate work at Michigan State University and his graduate work at Duke. He has taught political science at Post College, Long Island University. In addition to his teaching duties, Kirk has become, through his writings and lectures, one of the leading right-wing spokesmen for the New Conservatism, a movement motivated by a desire to find a measure of stability and security in terms of past tradition.

Bitterly critical of the ethical relativism of liberals and their supposed inability to distinguish and fight against totalitarian challenges, Kirk, in *The Conservative Mind* (1953), attempted to define the New Conservatism in terms of a divinely inspired natural law, a conviction that orders and classes were indispensable to society, a belief that property and freedom were inseparably entwined, and a frank recognition that reform—as distinguished from change—frequently led to a "devouring conflagration." Arguing further that modern secular liberalism, because of its superficial approach to morality and its tendency to make man the measure of all things, prepared the ground for the advent of the disasters of the twentieth century, Kirk and other conservatives have attempted to expound a conservative ideology suitable to American society.

The following selection is from Kirk's article, "What is the Republic?" *National Review,* 3 (February 2, 1957).

Conservatism is not an ideology; but conservatism does possess a body of principles, a framework of concepts which endures after the controversies of the hour have faded out of memory. One of the most important of those concepts is the idea of the Republic.

The word "republic" means public things, the commonwealth, the general welfare as expressed in political forms. The idea of the Republic lies at the root of American conservative thought. We have not known monarchy since 1776, and we always have been suspicious of "pure democracy"—that is, of government by the masses, without constitutional checks, protection for minorities, and representative institutions. Our government, as Calhoun said, "is, of course, a Republic, a constitutional democracy, in contradistinction to an absolute democracy; and . . . the theory which regards it as a government of the mere numerical majority rests on a gross and groundless misconception."

The purpose of the collectivist state is to abolish the classes, voluntary associations, and private rights, swallowing all these in the blur of the "general will" and absolute equality of condition—equality, that is, of everyone except the administrators of the state. The purpose of our Republic, on the contrary, has been to reconcile classes, protect voluntary associations, and nourish private rights. We do not recognize any "general will," but only the opinions of private citizens and legitimate groups. We do not seek equality of condition, but only equality of legal rights—the classical principle of justice, "to each his own."

We never have fallen, most of us, into the error that "commonwealth" means "collectivism." Our common freedom and our common prosperity have been nurtured by a salutary neglect of the notion of an absolute central sovereignty. This original conservative cast of our politics has not departed from among us. Unenchanted by the fallacy that the will of the majority is the will of God, we have sustained a Republic marked by sound security against the will and the appetite of temporary and irresponsible majorities.

Our Republic, in short, has been a complex of private and local liberties. Its great merit has been not equality, but freedom. Yet there are signs that public affection for this Republic, and understanding of it, are diminishing in our day. Sometimes we seem nearly to have arrived at the condition in which Cicero found the Roman Republic in his time: when, he wrote in *The Republic,* the Roman commonwealth seemed like an ancient painting, its colors faded and no skilled restorer to be found. Well, it is not too late for us to restore; and the intelligent conservative does more than cling to what has survived of an ancient order: he also rebuilds.

The conservative endeavors to conserve certain great and ancient things. He endeavors to conserve the religious and moral traditions that make us more than beasts. He endeavors to conserve the legacy of Western civilization, the wisdom of our ancestors, that makes us more than barbarians. And he endeavors to conserve that civil social order, political and economic, which has been developed through the trials of many generations, and which confers upon us a tolerable measure of justice and order and freedom. In the present age, the conservative is particularly sedulous to conserve freedom. We stand in no immediate peril of material want or of anarchy. But we are in danger, almost imminently, of a loss of freedom that would make us less than truly human. The modern conservative, therefore, tends to emphasize the claims of liberty, though in another age he might need to emphasize the claims of charity and duty. But if he is true to his own principles, he does not forget that every freedom is married to a responsibility.

The great contest in the modern world is not between two theories of economics, "socialism" and "capitalism," as Bernard Shaw tried to convince us. Rather, the real struggle is between traditional society, with its religious and moral and political inheritance, and collectivism (under whatever name), with its passion for reducing humanity to a mere tapioca pudding of identical producers and consumers. There is far more to this struggle than questions

of profits and wages. But nowadays we are menaced by an economic collectivism which, if triumphant, would put an end not merely to a free economy,
but to freedom of every description. Therefore it is worthwhile to say a little
about the necessity for economic freedom.

Without a free economy, freedom of any sort is most difficult to maintain.
The Republic is more important than any especial economic domination; yet
the Republic cannot endure without an economy substantially free. There are
two principal reasons why—given the conditions prevalent in modern America, and the political institutions that are ours—a free economy is essential
to the preservation of freedom in general: to intellectual freedom, to civil
liberties, to representative government, to freedom of private action. The first
of these is that men and women can enjoy external freedom only if they are
subject to no single, absolute master for their subsistence. The second of these
is that ordinary integrity requires ordinary rewards, and that in a collectivistic
economy (whether called "capitalistic," or "socialistic," or what you will)
the old motive to integrity, the ancient reasons for responsible conduct, are
lacking.

First, a few words about the former reason. Men and women must eat.
If they are dependent upon a solitary power or a solitary individual for their
subsistence, they are slaves. They can act in any external respect only upon
the sufferance of that master. If that master is the state, they have no alternative employment; they must obey, or live on air; and the state, because of its
impersonality, can be a harder master, more devoid of charity and generosity,
than any medieval lord.

To say that the "democratic" state would not deprive anyone of liberty
is to play upon words. The democratic state, like any other, is directed by individuals, with all the failings to which humanity is heir, especially the failing
of the lust for power. To suppose that the mass-state would be always just
and generous toward its slaves is to suppose that there would exist, upon all its
levels, a class of philosopher-kings superior to human frailty, purged of lust
and envy and petty ambition. But in modern America we have no such class
to draw upon; indeed, often we seem to be doing what we can to abolish that
sense of inherent responsibility and high honor which compensates a patriarchal or feudal society for its lack of private liberty. It is more probable, as
George Santayana suggests, that we would be the subjects of a host of squalid
oligarchs, devoid of the high sense of responsibility. The Republic would
have perished.

And a few words about the second reason. Most people do not act, and
cannot, out of a regard for the general welfare. In any economy, our indolence
and selfishness require incentives. Some few persons always will act out of
altruism; but they will not be numerous enough to sustain a modern economy,
once the old incentives of advancement, profit, and acquisition of property
are gone. This sad truth already has flashed upon the minds of the more serious
socialists in England, dismayed at the flaws in their own creation, and has

led to ominous talk among them of "new incentives"—"the stick as well as the carrot."

For the conserving of freedom of any sort, then, the economy must be free in considerable measure. I repeat that much of the popular discussion of economic questions is obsolete, because it is founded, especially in America, upon the assumption that we still are living in a nineteenth-century condition characterized by the pressure of population upon food-supply. But the real problems of the twentieth century are different from those of the nineteenth, often especially in the economic sphere, and are in some respects more difficult to approach. Our conservative task is to reconcile personal freedom with the claims of modern technology, and to try to humanize an age in which Things are in the saddle. The triumph of technology, though it has solved for the time being, here in America, the ancient problem of material want, has created new problems. But we need not march on, as if propelled by some ineluctable destiny, toward a complete collectivization of economic life, the exploded ideal of the nineteenth-century socialists.

We can no longer afford to bow before ideology. Thinking is a painful process; but only by thought can ideology be kept in check; no ideologue ever was beaten on his own ground, except by another ideologue. It is vain to appeal to a theoretical "freedom" of the nineteenth century. It is worse than vain to suppose that, by simply repeating the words "freedom," "democracy," and "progress," we can reconcile a system of impersonal economic consolidation with the ancient personal liberties of our civilization. The person whom Mr. Sidney Hook calls the "ritualistic liberal" seems to think that all we have to do to keep our freedom is to complain constantly and irresponsibly that our freedom is being lost. Yet many of these same ritualistic liberals applaud the very economic and social processes that are reducing the domain of freedom. I hope that conservatives will do something more than this.

We cannot afford merely to drift with the current of events, applying the pragmatic solution of considering every case simply upon its own passing merits. Present policies tend directly toward the establishment of an economic collectivism, under one name or another, inimical to the Republic. Certain measures of taxation, for instance, most conspicuous in Britain but differing only in degree in America, operate to destroy private enterprise in the old sense, to abolish the inheritance of property and the sense of responsibility that accompanies inheritance, and to substitute, in the long run, state compulsion for the ancient motives to integrity. Little serious thought seems to be given to the consequences, for one thing, of continuing inheritance taxes at their present rate; yet they now constitute confiscation, and are a levy upon capital, not a voluntary contribution out of income toward the maintenance of the Republic. A society as rich as ours can afford to tolerate rich men and women —and can afford to encourage, indeed, the bequest and inheritance of large properties.

No social institution does more to develop decent leadership and a sense of responsibility than does the inheritance of large properties, and of the duties that accompany those properties. Tocqueville, observing a century and a quarter ago the American hostility toward inherited wealth, remarked that great fortunes confer benefits of many sorts upon the whole of society—in leadership, in the encouragement of the arts, in the support of letters, in the nurture of novel undertakings; while a multitude of petty competences, rags to riches and back to rags in one generation, encourages only arrogance and the expenditure of wealth in evanescent display and creature comforts. I am not suggesting that the remedy for all our ills lies in repealing the inheritance-tax; I am merely saying that we need to think through such problems as this afresh, and to do our thinking free from the slogans of the ideologues.

And if inherited wealth brings some measure of responsibility to a commonwealth, so do the old disciplines of thrift, self-advancement, and personal ownership. Some of the more intelligent Americans, in every class and occupation, now are aware of the menace of irresponsibility in economic life, which soon communicates itself to political life: the irresponsibility of the salaried managers of vast corporations, of civil servants vested with brief authority upon which there is small check, of labor-union officials who may have risen to a high place principally through the arts of the demagogue. A Republic does not endure forever upon the moral and social capital of an earlier time. A sense of responsibility is produced by hard lessons, by private risk and accountability, by a humane education, by religious principle, by inherited rights and duties. A Republic whose leaders are the flies of a summer cannot expect to obtain ordinary integrity without the old motives to integrity; it will turn, in desperation, to the hero-administrator, the misty figure somewhere at the summit—and, in the end, that hero-administrator no longer will be found.

It is not only the process of economic consolidation and the operation of positive law that diminish the sense of responsibility guarding ordered freedom in the Republic. Other measures, more technological than directly political, operate to make man into a machine-server, with a great deal of idleness but little true leisure, free in the sense that no one oppresses him directly, but servile in the sense that he has been deprived of the old interests and hopes in life: failing to come to man's estate, he remains a perpetual child. In our present equilibrium, here in America, we may seem to have given a large measure of economic prosperity to the mass of men and women, at small cost in freedom. But I am thinking of what this Republic, and all the world, may be fifty years from now.

Not being high-school debaters, conservatives do not possess facile and simple solutions to all these discontents. They merely say that the first step toward curing a malady is to diagnose it correctly. I suggest that we must find our happiness in work, or not at all; and that servile work, however economically profitable, is irreconcilable with social freedom. With John Henry Newman, in his reply to Sir Robert Peel more than a century gone, I am not offering any new ideology; I am merely appealing to those principles of morals and politics which have been known to mankind for a great while. "I am proposing no measures, but exposing a fallacy, and resisting a pretense. Let Benthamism reign, if men have no aspirations; but do not tell them to be romantic, and then solace them with glory."

Freedom, after all, is a romantic aspiration, earnestly desired by only a minority of men and women. (Romantic aspirations, I may add, are what make life worth living.) Only a small minority, too, feel clearly the call of responsibility. But, that freedom and that responsibility gone, the habitual freedom and the security of the great mass of men and women must slip away too, in the economic sphere as in the political. There are some among us who do not desire to be solaced with the glories of *Brave New World*. Political economy had its beginnings in the work of philosophers who, whatever their deficiencies, were concerned primarily with the extension of freedom. Political economy is far gone in decay when it becomes no better than an apology for the reduction of men and women to a condition of prosperous servility.

The success of the American Republic, and the preservation of our old liberties, have been achieved in considerable part by our aversion, here in America, to divorcing theory from prudence. No other society ever had problems so complex as ours; but no society before our age ever had such a wealth of learning available, and such an economic margin, to aid in the solving of problems. The analysis of the real meaning of freedom, and the examination of the nature of responsibility, are available to us Americans at the slight cost of a little of our idle time. Yet many of us seem to prefer to wander, thoughtless, into a devil's sabbath of whirling machinery, presided over by a commissar.

Liberals and radicals offer us no solution to our grand difficulties; they either are content to drift with the current of events, or urge us actually to row faster down the stream which they call Progress, but which the conservative knows to be Decadence. The Liberals and the radicals have forgotten the meaning of the Republic. But conservatives, who were not born yesterday, know that men and women have free will. A Republic dies only when its citizens have neglected the wisdom of their ancestors and the methods of right reason. There are more conservatives left among us than there were good men left in Sodom; and I think that, God willing, the conservatives will yet prevail.

One of the most eloquent of American conservative thinkers was a woman, Agnes Repplier. Miss Repplier was not inclined to exchange the reality of the American Republic for some Utopia of the collectivists. Loving her country, she wrote, "If patriotism becomes an emotion too expansively benevolent to make men willing to live and die for something concrete like a king or a country, we shall have nothing left to fall back upon but sexual love, which is a strong individual urge, but lacks breadth and scope of purpose. It burned Troy; but it did not build Rome, or secure the Magna Carta, or frame the Constitution of the United States." Love of the Republic shelters all our other loves. That love is worth some sacrifice.

(48)

Walter Lippmann

1889-

Born in New York City, Lippmann graduated from Harvard College and then spent a year doing graduate study there in philosophy. Lippmann thought of becoming a teacher but decided instead to turn to writing. He then entered upon a long and distinguished career as editor, author, and columnist. Over the years he has developed a reputation as one of America's most important political commentators.

At Harvard, Lippmann espoused socialist ideas, and early in his career he associated himself with many liberal and radical causes. One of his first posts was that of associate editor of the *New Republic.* But the debacle of Versailles forced Lippmann to reconsider his fundamental assumptions. His subsequent disillusionment with liberal ideas found partial expression in his book *Public Opinion,* published in 1922. In the years that followed, Lippmann gradually adopted more conservative ideas, if not the whole mantle of conservatism. Of special importance is Lippmann's support of the resurgence of the natural-law theory of society.

This selection, which discusses the theory of natural law, is from *The Public Philosophy* (Boston, 1955).

☆   ☆   ☆   ☆

I should say that I am a liberal democrat and have no wish to disenfranchise my fellow citizens. My hope is that both liberty and democracy can be preserved before the one destroys the other. Whether this can be done is the question of our time, what with more than half the world denying and despairing of it. Of one thing we may be sure. If it is to be done at all, we must be uninhibited in our examination of our condition. And since our condition is manifestly connected with grave errors in war and peace that have been committed by democratic governments, we must adopt the habit of thinking as plainly about the sovereign people as we do about the politicians they elect. It will not do to think poorly of the politicians and to talk with bated breath about the voters. No more than the kings before them should the people be hedged with divinity. Like all princes and rulers, like all sovereigns, they are ill-served by flattery and adulation. And they are betrayed by the servile hypocrisy which tells them that what is true and what is false, what is right and what is wrong, can be determined by their votes.

If I am right in what I have been saying, there has developed in this century a functional derangement of the relationship between the mass of the people and the government. The people have acquired power which they are incapable of exercising, and the governments they elect have lost powers which they must recover if they are to govern. What then are the true boundaries of the people's power? The answer cannot be simple. But for a rough beginning let us say that the people are able to give and to withhold their consent to being governed—their consent to what the government asks of them, proposes to them, and has done in the conduct of their affairs. They can elect the government. They can remove it. They can approve or disapprove its performance. But they cannot administer the government. They cannot themselves perform. They cannot normally initiate and propose the necessary legislation. A mass cannot govern. . . .

Where mass opinion dominates the government, there is a morbid derangement of the true functions of power. The derangement brings about the enfeeblement, verging on paralysis, of the capacity to govern. This breakdown in the constitutional order is the cause of the precipitate and catastrophic decline of Western society. It may, if it cannot be arrested and reversed, bring about the fall of the West. . . .

There is a principle which, if it can be applied deeply enough, gets at the root of the disorder of modern democracy. It is that though public officials are elected by the voters, or are appointed by men who are elected, they owe their primary allegiance not to the opinions of the voters but to the law, to the criteria of their professions, to the integrity of the arts and sciences in which they work, to their own conscientious and responsible convictions of their duty within the rules and the frame of reference they have sworn to respect.

The implied principle may be defined in other terms by saying that while the electors choose the ruler, they do not own any shares in him and they have no right to command him. His duty is to the office and not to his electors. Their duty is to fill the office and not to direct the office-holder. I realize that, as I have stated it, the principle runs counter to the popular view that in a democracy public men are the servants (that is, the agents) of the people (that is, of the voters). . . .

We are living in a time of massive popular counter-revolution against liberal democracy. It is a reaction to the failure of the West to cope with the miseries and anxieties of the Twentieth Century. The liberal democracies have been tried and found wanting—found wanting not only in their capacity to govern successfully in this period of wars and upheavals, but also in their ability to defend and maintain the political philosophy that underlies the liberal way of life.

If we go back to the beginnings of the modern democratic movements in the eighteenth century, we can distinguish two diverging lines of development. The one is a way of progress in liberal constitutional democracy. The other is a morbid course of development into totalitarian conditions. . . .

Although the two ways of evolution appear to have the same object—a society with free institutions under popular government—they are radically different and they arrive at radically different ends.

The first way, that of assimilation, presumes the existence of a state which is already constitutional in principle, which is under laws that are no longer arbitrary, though they may be unjust and unequal. Into this constitutional state more and more people are admitted to the governing class and to the voting electorate. The unequal and the unjust laws are revised until eventually all the people have equal opportunities to enter the government and to be represented. Broadly speaking, this has been the working theory of the British movement towards a democratic society at home and also in the Commonwealth and Empire. This, too, was the working theory of the principal authors of the American Constitution, and this was how—though few of them welcomed it —they envisaged the enfranchisement of the whole adult population.

The other way is that of the Jacobin revolution. The people rise to power by overthrowing the ruling class and by liquidating its privileges and prerogatives. This is the doctrine of democratic revolution which was developed by French thinkers in the eighteenth century and was put into practice by the Jacobin party in the French Revolution. In its English incarnation the doctrine became known as Radicalism. In America, though it had its early disciples, notably Tom Paine, not until the era of the Founding Fathers was over, not until the era of Andrew Jackson, did the Jacobin doctrine become the popular political creed of the American democracy. . . .

Of the two rival philosophies, the Jacobin is almost everywhere in the ascendant. It is a ready philosophy for men who, previously excluded from the ruling class, and recently enfranchised, have no part in the business of governing the state, and no personal expectation of being called upon to assume the responsibilities of office. The Jacobin doctrine is an obvious reaction, as de Tocqueville's observation explains, to government by a caste. When there is no opening for the gradualness of reform and for enfranchisement by assimilation, a revolutionary collision is most likely.

The Jacobin doctrine is addressed to the revolutionary collision between the inviolable governing caste and the excluded men claiming the redress of their grievances and their place in the sun. Though it professes to be a political philosophy, the doctrine is not, in fact, a philosophy of government. It is a gospel and also a strategy for revolution. It announces the promise that the crusade which is to overthrow the ruling caste will by the act of revolution create a good society.

The peculiar essence of the dogma is that the revolution itself is the creative act. Towards the revolution as such, because it is the culmination and the climax, all the labor and the sacrifice of the struggle are to be directed. The revolutionary act will remove the causes of evil in human society. Again and again it has been proved how effective is this formula for arousing, sustaining and organizing men's energies for revolution: to declare that evil in society has been imposed upon the many by the few—by priests, nobles, capitalists, imperialists, liberals, aliens—and that evil will disappear when the many who are pure have removed these few who are evil. . . .

We live long enough after the new gospel was proclaimed to have seen what came of it. The post-revolutionary man, enfranchised and emancipated, has not turned out to be the New Man. He is the old Adam. Yet the future of democratic society has been staked on the promises and the predictions of the Jacobin gospel.

For the Jacobin doctrine has pervaded the theory of mass education in the newly enfranchised mass democracies. In America and in most of the newer liberal democracies of the Western world, the Jacobin heresy is, though not unchallenged and not universal, the popular and dominant theory in the schools. . . .

The Jacobin doctrine does not solve this problem of mass education—as it does not solve or even throw light upon the problem of how to construct and govern the utopian society which is to exist when the revolution has taken place. What it does is to provide an escape from these unsolved problems. It affirms that in politics the state will wither away and then there will be no problems of how to govern it. . . .

In the Jacobin gospel of the eighteenth century, and even in the Marxist gospel of the nineteenth century, the new man would be there when the artificial garments were removed—when once he was emancipated by the revolutionary act from the deformation imposed upon him by the clergy, the nobility and the bourgeoisie. A hundred years later the new man was nowhere in sight. So the early and softer gospel gave way to a later and infinitely harder one. The new man and the new heaven on earth demanded the remaking of pre-Leninist and pre-Hitlerian man. The decrees of history as revealed to Marx, and the decrees of nature as revealed to Hitler, had to be carried out.

But in order to do that, the human species had first to be transformed—or failing that, exterminated. Destiny called upon the mortal god to make surviving mankind "an active unfailing carrier," as Hannah Arendt says, "of a law to which human beings would otherwise only passively and reluctantly be subject."

In the eyes of its devotees, this is not an inhuman and satanic doctrine. It is above and beyond humanity. It is for the superman that its gospel announces. The ruthlessness, the arbitrariness, the cruelty are not monstrous wickedness. They are natural and necessary, predestined like the fall of a sparrow, in the sublime construction of the earthly paradise. . . .

To speak of a public philosophy is, I am well aware, to raise dangerous questions, rather like opening Pandora's box. . . .

The founders of our free institutions were themselves adherents of this public philosophy. When they insisted upon excluding the temporal power from the realm of the mind and the spirit, it was not that they had no public philosophy. It was because experience had taught them that as power corrupts, it corrupts the public philosophy. It was, therefore, a practical rule of politics that the government should not be given sovereignty and proprietorship over the public philosophy.

But as time went on, there fell out of fashion the public philosophy of the founders of Western institutions. The rule that the temporal power should be excluded from the realms of the mind and of the spirit was then subtly transformed. It became the rule that ideas and principles are private—with only subjective relevance and significance. Only when there is "a clear and present danger" to public order are the acts of speaking and publishing in the public domain. All the first and last things were removed from the public domain. All that has to do with what man is and should be, or how he should hold himself in the scheme of things, what are his rightful ends and the legitimate means, became private and subjective and publicly unaccountable. And so, the liberal democracies of the West became the first great society to treat as a private concern the formative beliefs that shape the character of its citizens.

This has brought about a radical change in the meaning of freedom. Originally it was founded on the postulate that there was a universal order on which all reasonable men were agreed: within that public agreement on the fundamentals and on the ultimates, it was safe to permit and it would be desirable to encourage, dissent and dispute. But with the disappearance of the public philosophy—and of a consensus on the first and last things—there was opened up a great vacuum in the public mind, yawning to be filled. . . .

I believe there is a public philosophy. Indeed there is such a thing as the public philosophy of civility. It does not have to be discovered or invented. It is known. But it does have to be revived and renewed.

The public philosophy is known as *natural law,* a name which, alas, causes great semantic confusion. This philosophy is the premise of the institutions of the Western society, and they are, I believe, unworkable in communities that do not adhere to it. Except on the premises of this philosophy, it is impossible to reach intelligible and workable conceptions of popular election, majority rule, representative assemblies, free speech, loyalty, property, corporations and voluntary associations. The founders of these institutions, which the recently enfranchised democracies have inherited, were all of them adherents of some one of the various schools of natural law.

For over two thousand years, says Barker, European thought has been acted upon by the idea that the rational faculties of men can produce a common conception of law and order which possesses a universal validity. This conception was first formulated as a theory by Zeno and the Stoics. It was absorbed by the Roman lawyers, was adopted by the Christian fathers, was reestablished and reworked by Saint Thomas Aquinas, and in a new formulation, after the Renaissance and Reformation, it provided the philosophy of the English Revolution of 1688 and of the American Revolution of 1776. The long life of this idea and, above all, the recurring revival of the idea in all ages, would seem to indicate that it reflects a wide and recurring human need—that it is involved with practical questions of policy in the face of recurring political problems. . . .

They are the laws of a rational order of human society—in the sense that all men, when they are sincerely and lucidly rational, will regard them as self-evident. The rational order consists of the terms which must be met in order to fulfill men's capacity for the good life in this world. They are the terms of the widest consensus of rational men in a plural society. They are the propositions to which all men concerned, if they are sincerely and lucidly rational, can be expected to converge. . . .

As the bitter end has become visible in the countries of the total revolution, we can see how desperate is the predicament of modern men. The terrible events show that the harder they try to make earth into heaven, the more they make it a hell.

Yet, the yearning for salvation and for perfection is most surely not evil, and it is, moreover, perennial in the human soul. Are men then doomed by the very nature of things to be denied the highest good if it cannot be materialized in this world and if, as so large a number of modern men assume, it will not be materialized in another world?

The answer to this question is known. It can be had by recognizing the difference between the realm of existence where objects are materialized to our senses, and the realm of essence, where they are present to the mind. I am using the ambiguous but irreplaceable word "essence" as meaning the true and undistorted nature of things. The understanding of our relation to these two realms of being is exceedingly difficult to communicate, so difficult that, as a matter of fact, it has remained an esoteric wisdom.

Yet if there is a way out of the modern predicament, it begins, I believe, where we learn to recognize the difference between the two realms. For the radical error of the modern democratic gospel is that it promises, not the good life of this world, but the perfect life of heaven. The root of the error is the confusion of the two realms—that of this world where the human condition is to be born, to live, to work, to struggle and to die, and that of the transcendent world in which men's souls can be regenerate and at peace. The confusion of these two realms is an ultimate disorder. It inhibits the good life in this world. It falsifies the life of the spirit. . . .

In the traditions of civility, the prevailing view has been that the two realms are inseparable but disparate, and that man must work out his destiny in the balance, which is never fixed finally between the two. . . .

I believe that the public philosophy can be revived, and the reconnaissance which we have made has been a demonstration that when it is applied to such central concepts as popular sovereignty, property, freedom of speech, and education, the public philosophy clarifies the problems and opens the way towards rational and acceptable solutions. The revival of the public philosophy depends on whether its principles and precepts—which were articulated before the industrial revolution, before the era of rapid technological change, and before the rise of the mass democracies—depends on whether this old philosophy can be reworked for the modern age. If this cannot be done, then the free and democratic nations face the totalitarian challenge without a public philosophy which free men believe in and cherish, with no public faith beyond a mere official agnosticism, neutrality and indifference. There is not much doubt how the struggle is likely to end if it lies between those who, believing, care very much—and those who, lacking belief, cannot care very much. . . .

I do not contend, though I hope, that the decline of Western society will be arrested if the teachers in our schools and universities come back to the great tradition of the public philosophy. But I do contend that the decline, which is already far advanced, cannot be arrested if the prevailing philosophers oppose this restoration and revival, if they impugn rather than support the validity of an order which is superior to the values that Sartre tells each man "to invent."

What the prevailing philosophers say about religion is not itself, in Tillich's terms, religion as an ultimate concern of worship and of love. But if the philosophers teach that religious experience is a purely psychological phenomenon, related to nothing beyond each man's psychic condition, then they will give educated men a bad intellectual conscience if they have religious experiences. The philosophers cannot give them religion. But they can keep them away from it.

Philosophers play the same role in relation to the principles of the good society. These require, as we have seen, the mastery of human nature in the raw by an acquired rational second nature. In the literal sense, the principles of the good society must be unpopular until they have prevailed sufficiently to alter the popular impulses. For the popular impulses are opposed to public principles. These principles cannot be made to prevail if they are discredited, —if they are dismissed as superstition, as obscurantism, as meaningless metaphysics, as reactionary, as self-seeking rationalizations.

The public philosophy is in a large measure intellectually discredited among contemporary men. Because of that, what we may call the terms of discourse in public controversy are highly unfavorable to anyone who adheres to the public philosophy. The signs and seals of legitimacy, of rightness and of truth, have been taken over by men who reject, even when they are not the avowed adversaries of, the doctrine of constitutional democracy.

If the decline of the West under the misrule of the people is to be halted, it will be necessary to alter these terms of discourse. They are now set overwhelmingly against the credibility and against the rightness of the principles of the constitutional state; they are set in favor of the Jacobin conception of the emancipated and sovereign people.

I have been arguing, hopefully and wishfully, that it may be possible to alter the terms of discourse if a convincing demonstration can be made that the principles of the good society are not, in Sartre's phrase, invented and chosen—that the conditions which must be met if there is to be a good society are there, outside our wishes, where they can be discovered by rational inquiry, and developed and adapted and refined by rational discussion.

If eventually this were demonstrated successfully, it would, I believe, re-arm all those who are concerned with the anomy of our society, with its progressive barbarization, and with its descent into violence and tyranny. Amidst the quagmire of moral impressionism they would stand again on hard intellectual ground where there are significant objects that are given and are not merely projected, that are compelling and are not merely wished. Their hope would be re-established that there is a public world, sovereign above the infinite number of contradictory and competing private worlds. Without this certainty, their struggle must be unavailing.

(49)

Friedrich A. von Hayek

1899-

Hayek is one of the few foreign-born thinkers included in this volume. Nevertheless, he merits inclusion because the position he has developed is an important one in the Western community of nations, and is attractive to many Americans.

Born in Vienna, Hayek received his doctorate from the University of Vienna in 1923. Shortly thereafter, he settled in England, where he taught at the University of London. He became a naturalized British citizen in 1938. In 1950 he went to the University of Chicago as professor of social and moral science.

Hayek's political and economic views are clearly not in agreement with those of modern liberals. He maintains—in the spirit of the dominant trends of nineteenth-century social thought—that individual liberty is the most precious of political values. At the same time, he believes that conservatives can learn valuable lessons from the liberal's valid criticisms of conservatism. Searching for a name for his position, he accepts "Whiggism" as perhaps the best descriptive term he can find—though he notes that earlier generations might well have used the term "liberal" to designate his views.

The selection here is from the Postscript "Why I Am Not a Conservative" to his book *The Constitution of Liberty* (Chicago, 1960).

At a time when most movements that are thought to be progressive advocate further encroachments on individual liberty, those who cherish freedom are likely to expend their energies in opposition. In this they find themselves much of the time on the same side as those who habitually resist change. In matters of current politics today they generally have little choice but to support the conservative parties. But, though the position I have tried to define is also often described as "conservative," it is very different from that to which this name has been traditionally attached. There is danger in the confused condition which brings the defenders of liberty and the true conservatives together in common opposition to developments which threaten their different ideals equally. It is therefore important to distinguish clearly the position taken here from that which has long been known—perhaps more appropriately—as conservatism.

Conservatism proper is a legitimate, probably necessary, and certainly widespread attitude of opposition to drastic change. It has, since the French Revolution, for a century and a half played an important role in European politics. Until the rise of socialism its opposite was liberalism. There is nothing corresponding to this conflict in the history of the United States, because what in Europe was called "liberalism" was here the common tradition on which the American polity had been built: thus the defender of the American tradition was a liberal in the European sense. This already existing confusion was made worse by the recent attempt to transplant to America the European type of conservatism, which, being alien to the American tradition, has acquired a somewhat odd character. And some time before this, American radicals and socialists began calling themselves "liberals." I will nevertheless continue for the moment to describe as liberal the position which I hold and which I believe differs as much from true conservatism as from socialism. Let me say at once, however, that I do so with increasing misgivings, and I shall later have to consider what would be the appropriate name for the party of liberty. The reason for this is not only that the term "liberal" in the United States is the cause of constant misunderstandings today, but also that in Europe the predominant type of rationalistic liberalism has long been one of the pacemakers of socialism.

Let me now state what seems to me the decisive objection to any conservatism which deserves to be called such. It is that by its very nature it cannot offer an alternative to the direction in which we are moving. It may succeed by its resistance to current tendencies in slowing down undesirable developments, but, since it does not indicate another direction, it cannot prevent their continuance. It has, for this reason, invariably been the fate of conservatism to be dragged along a path not of its own choosing. The tug of war between conservatives and progressives can only affect the speed, not the direction, of contemporary developments. But, though there is need for a "brake on the vehicle of progress," I personally cannot be content with simply helping to apply the brake. What the liberal must ask, first of all, is not how fast or how far we should move, but where we should move. In fact, he differs much more from the collectivist radical of today than does the conservative. While the last generally holds merely a mild and moderate version of the prejudices of his time, the liberal today must more positively oppose some of the basic conceptions which most conservatives share with the socialists. . . .

Before I consider the main points on which the liberal attitude is sharply opposed to the conservative one, I ought to stress that there is much that the liberal might with advantage have learned from the work of some conservative thinkers. To their loving and reverential study of the value of grown institutions we owe (at least outside the field of economics) some profound insights which are real contributions to our understanding of a free society. However reactionary in politics such figures as Coleridge, Bonald, De Maistre, Justus

Möser, or Donoso Cortés may have been, they did show an understanding of the meaning of spontaneously grown institutions such as language, law, morals, and conventions that anticipated modern scientific approaches and from which the liberals might have profited. But the admiration of the conservatives for free growth generally applies only to the past. They typically lack the courage to welcome the same undesigned change from which new tools of human endeavors will emerge.

This brings me to the first point on which the conservative and the liberal dispositions differ radically. As has often been acknowledged by conservative writers, one of the fundamental traits of the conservative attitude is a fear of change, a timid distrust of the new as such, while the liberal position is based on courage and confidence, on a preparedness to let change run its course even if we cannot predict where it will lead. There would not be much to object to if the conservatives merely disliked too rapid change in institutions and public policy; here the case for caution and slow process is indeed strong. But the conservatives are inclined to use the powers of government to prevent change or to limit its rate to whatever appeals to the more timid mind. In looking forward, they lack the faith in the spontaneous forces of adjustment which makes the liberal accept changes without apprehension, even though he does not know how the necessary adaptations will be brought about. It is, indeed, part of the liberal attitude to assume that, especially in the economic field, the self-regulating forces of the market will somehow bring about the required adjustments to new conditions, although no one can foretell how they will do this in a particular instance. There is perhaps no single factor contributing so much to people's frequent reluctance to let the market work as their inability to conceive how some necessary balance, between demand and supply, between exports and imports, or the like, will be brought about without deliberate control. The conservative feels safe and content only if he is assured that some higher wisdom watches and supervises change, only if he knows that some authority is charged with keeping the change "orderly."

This fear of trusting uncontrolled social forces is closely related to two other characteristics of conservatism: its fondness for authority and its lack of understanding of economic forces. Since it distrusts both abstract theories and general principles, it neither understands those spontaneous forces on which a policy of freedom relies nor possesses a basis for formulating principles of policy. Order appears to the conservatives as the result of the continuous attention of authority, which, for this purpose, must be allowed to do what is required by the particular circumstances and not be tied to rigid rule. A commitment to principles presupposes an understanding of the general forces by which the efforts of society are co-ordinated, but it is such a theory of society and especially of the economic mechanism that conservatism conspicuously lacks. So unproductive has conservatism been in producing a general conception of how a social order is maintained that its modern votaries, in trying to construct a theoretical foundation, invariably find themselves appealing almost exclusively to authors who regarded themselves as liberal. Macaulay, Tocqueville, Lord Acton, and Lecky certainly considered themselves liberals, and with justice; and even Edmund Burke remained an Old Whig to the end and would have shuddered at the thought of being regarded as a Tory.

Let me return, however, to the main point, which is the characteristic complacency of the conservative toward the action of established authority and his prime concern that this authority be not weakened rather than that its power be kept within bounds. This is difficult to reconcile with the preservation of liberty. In general, it can probably be said that the conservative does not object to coercion or arbitrary power so long as it is used for what he regards as the right purposes. He believes that if government is in the hands of decent men, it ought not be too much restricted by rigid rules. Since he is essentially opportunist and lacks principles, his main hope must be that the wise and the good will rule—not merely by example, as we all must wish, but by authority given to them and enforced by them. Like the socialist, he is less concerned with the problem of how the powers of government should be limited than with that of who wields them; and, like the socialist, he regards himself as entitled to force the value he holds on other people.

When I say that the conservative lacks principles, I do not mean to suggest that he lacks moral conviction. The typical conservative is indeed usually a man of very strong moral convictions. What I mean is that he has no political principles which enable him to work with people whose moral values differ from his own for a political order in which both can obey their convictions. It is the recognition of such principles that permits the coexistence of different sets of values that makes it possible to build a peaceful society with a minimum of force. The acceptance of such principles means that we agree to tolerate much that we dislike. There are many values of the conservative which appeal to me more than those of the socialists; yet for a liberal the importance he personally attaches to specific goals is no sufficient justification for forcing others to serve them. I have little doubt that some of my conservative friends will be shocked by what they will regard as "concessions" to modern views that I have made in Part III of this book. But, though I may dislike some of the measures concerned as much as they do and might vote against them, I know of no general principles to which I could appeal to persuade those of a different view that those measures are not permissible in the general kind of society which we both desire. To live and work successfully with others requires more than faithfulness to one's concrete aims. It requires an intellectual commitment to a type of order in which, even on issues which to one are fundamental, others are allowed to pursue different ends.

It is for this reason that to the liberal neither moral nor religious ideals are proper objects of coercion, while both conservatives and socialists recognize no such limits. I sometimes feel that the most conspicuous attribute of liberalism that distinguishes it as much from conservatism as from socialism is the view that moral beliefs concerning matters of conduct which do not directly interfere with the protected sphere of other persons do not justify coercion. This may also explain why it seems to be so much easier for the repentant socialist to find a new spiritual home in the conservative fold than in the liberal.

In the last resort, the conservative position rests on the belief that in any society there are recognizably superior persons whose inherited standards and values and position ought to be protected and who should have a greater influence on public affairs than others. The liberal, of course, does not deny that there are some superior people—he is not an egalitarian—but he denies that anyone has authority to decide who these superior people are. While the conservative inclines to defend a particular established hierarchy and wishes authority to protect the status of those whom he values, the liberal feels that no respect for established values can justify the resort to privilege or monopoly or any other coercive power of the state in order to shelter such people against the forces of economic change. Though he is fully aware of the important role that cultural and intellectual elites have played in the evolution of civilization, he also believes that these elites have to prove themseves by their capacity to maintain their position under the same rules that apply to all others.

Closely connected with this is the usual attitude of the conservative to democracy. I have made it clear earlier that I do not regard majority rule as an end but merely as a means, or perhaps even as the least evil of those forms of government from which we have to choose. But I believe that the conservatives deceive themselves when they blame the evils of our time on democracy. The chief evil is unlimited government, and nobody is qualified to wield unlimited power. The powers which modern democracy possesses would be even more intolerable in the hands of some small elite.

Admittedly, it was only when power came into the hands of the majority that further limitation of the power of government was thought unnecessary. In this sense democracy and unlimited government are connected. But it is not democracy but unlimited government that is objectionable, and I do not see why the people should not learn to limit the scope of majority rule as well as that of any other form of government. At any rate, the advantages of democracy as a method of peaceful change and of political education seem to be so great compared with those of any other system that I can have no sympathy with the anti-democratic strain of conservatism. It is not who governs but what government is entitled to do that seems to me the essential problem.

That the conservative opposition to too much government control is not a matter of principle but is concerned with the particular aims of government is clearly shown in the economic sphere. Conservatives usually oppose collectivist and directivist measures in the industrial field, and here the liberal will often find allies in them. But at the same time conservatives are usually protectionists and have frequently supported socialist measures in agriculture. Indeed, though the restrictions which exist today in industry and commerce are mainly the result of socialist views, the equally important restrictions in agriculture were usually introduced by conservatives at an even earlier date. And in their efforts to discredit free enterprise many conservative leaders have vied with the socialists. . . .

What I have said should suffice to explain why I do not regard myself as a conservative. Many people will feel, however, that the position which emerges is hardly what they used to call "liberal." I must, therefore, now face the question of whether this name is today the appropriate name for the party of liberty. I have already indicated that, though I have all my life described myself as a liberal, I have done so more recently with increasing misgivings—not only because in the United States this term constantly gives rise to misunderstanding, but also because I have become more and more aware of the great gulf that exists between my position and the rationalistic Continental liberalism or even the English liberalism of the utilitarians.

If liberalism still meant what it meant to an English historian who in 1827 could speak of the revolution of 1688 as "the triumph of those principles which in the language of the present day are denominated liberal or constitutional" or if one could still, with Lord Acton, speak of Burke, Macaulay, and Gladstone as the three greatest liberals, or if one could still, with Harold Laski, regard Tocqueville and Lord Acton as "the essential liberals of the nineteenth century," I should indeed be only too proud to describe myself by that name. But, much as I am tempted to call their liberalism true liberalism, I must recognize that the majority of Continental liberals stood for ideas to which these men were strongly opposed, and that they were led more by a desire to impose upon the world a preconceived rational pattern than to provide opportunity for free growth. The same is largely true of what has called itself Liberalism in England at least since the time of Lloyd George.

It is thus necessary to recognize that what I have called "liberalism" has little to do with any political movement that goes under that name today. It is also questionable whether the historical associations which that name carries today are conducive to the success of any movement. Whether in these circumstances one ought to make an effort to rescue the term from what one feels is its misuse is a question on which opinions may well differ. I myself feel more and more that to use it without long explanations causes too much confusion and that as a label it has become more of a ballast than a source of strength.

In the United States, where it has become almost impossible to use "liberal" in the sense in which I have used it, the term "libertarian" has been used instead. It may be the answer; but for my part I find it singularly unattractive. For my taste it carries too much the flavor of a manufactured term and of a substitute. What I should want is a word which describes the party of life, the party that favors free growth and spontaneous evolution. But I have racked my brain unsuccessfully to find a descriptive term which commends itself.

We should remember, however, that when the ideals which I have been trying to restate first began to spread through the Western world, the party which represented them had a generally recognized name. It was the ideals of the English Whigs that inspired what later came to be known as the liberal movement in the whole of Europe and that provided the conceptions that the American colonists carried with them and which guided them in their struggle for independence and in the establishment of their constitution. Indeed, until the character of this tradition was altered by the accretions due to the French Revolution, with its totalitarian democracy and socialist leanings, "Whig" was the name by which the party of liberty was generally known.

The name died in the country of its birth partly because for a time the principles for which it stood were no longer distinctive of a particular party, and partly because the men who bore the name did not remain true to those principles. The Whig parties of the nineteenth century, in both Britain and the United States, finally brought discredit to the name among the radicals. But it is still true that, since liberalism took the place of Whiggism only after the movement for liberty had absorbed the crude and militant rationalism of the French Revolution, and since our task must largely be to free that tradition from the overrationalistic, nationalistic, and socialistic influences which have intruded into it, Whiggism is historically the correct name for the ideas in which I believe. The more I learn about the evolution of ideas, the more I have become aware that I am simply an unrepentant Old Whig—with the stress on the "old."

To confess one's self an Old Whig does not mean, of course, that one wants to go back to where we were at the end of the seventeenth century. It has been one of the purposes of this book to show that the doctrines then first stated continued to grow and develop until about seventy or eighty years ago, even though they were no longer the chief aim of a distinct party. We have since learned much that should enable us to restate them in a more satisfactory and effective form. But, though they require restatement in the light of our present knowledge, the basic principles are still those of the Old Whigs. True, the later history of the party that bore that name has made some historians doubt where there was a distinct body of Whig principles; but I can but agree with Lord Acton that, though some of "the patriarchs of the doctrine were the most infamous of men, the notion of a higher law above municipal codes, with which Whiggism began, is the supreme achievement of Englishmen and their bequest to the nation"—and, we may add, to the world. It is the doctrine which is at the basis of the common tradition of the Anglo-Saxon countries. It is the doctrine from which Continental liberalism took what is valuable in it. It is the doctrine on which the American system of government is based. In its pure form it is represented in the United States, not by the radicalism of Jefferson, nor by the conservatism of Hamilton or even of John Adams, but by the ideas of James Madison, the "father of the Constitution."

I do not know whether to revive that old name is practical politics. That to the mass of people, both in the Anglo-Saxon world and elsewhere, it is today probably a term without definite associations is perhaps more an advantage than a drawback. To those familiar with the history of ideas it is probably the only name that quite expresses what the tradition means. That, both for the genuine conservative and still more for the many socialists turned conservative, Whiggism is the name for their pet aversion shows a sound instinct on their part. It has been the name for the only set of ideals that has consistently opposed all arbitrary power.

It may well be asked whether the name really matters so much. In a country like the United States, which on the whole still has free institutions and where, therefore, the defense of the existing is often a defense of freedom, it might not make so much difference if the defenders of freedom call themselves conservatives, although even here the association with the conservatives by disposition will often be embarrassing. Even when men approve of the same arrangements, it must be asked whether they approve of them because they exist or because they are desirable in themselves. The common resistance to the collectivist tide should not be allowed to obscure the fact that the belief in integral freedom is based on an essentially forward-looking attitude and not on any nostalgic longing for the past or a romantic admiration for what has been.

The need for a clear distinction is absolutely imperative, however, where, as is true in many parts of Europe, the conservatives have already accepted a large part of the collectivist creed—a creed that has governed policy for so long that many of its institutions have come to be accepted as a matter of course and have become a source of pride to "conservative" parties who created them. Here the believer in freedom cannot but conflict with the conservative and take an essentially radical position, directed against popular prejudices, entrenched positions, and firmly established privileges. Follies and abuses are no better for having long been established principles of policy.

X

The Restatement of Liberalism

To THE DEGREE that the conservative mood gained in strength and importance, the older pragmatic, secular, democratic liberalism that had played such an important role in American life and thought since the 1880's came increasingly under attack. Vernon L. Parrington, the author of a classic history and defense of the American liberal tradition, caught the beginnings of the newer mood of disillusionment and doubt when he wrote shortly before his death in 1929:

> Liberals whose hair is growing thin and the lines of whose figures are no longer what they were, are likely to find themselves today in the unhappy predicament of being treated as mourners at their own funerals. When they pluck up heart to assert that they are not yet authentic corpses, but living men with brains in their heads, they are pretty certain to be gently chided and led back to the comfortable armchair that befits senility. Their counsel is smiled at as the chatter of a belated post-Victorian generation that knew not Freud, and if they must go abroad they are bidden take the air in the garden where other old-fashioned plants—mostly of the family *Democratici*—are still preserved. [1]

And yet Parrington himself was unwilling to abandon his liberal faith, so strongly did he believe in its validity. As he concluded: "Yet it is perhaps conceivable that our current philosophy—the brilliant coruscations of our younger intelligentsia—may indeed not prove to be the last word in social philosophy. Perhaps—is this *lèse-majesté*—when our youngest liberals have themselves come to the armchair age they will be smiled at in turn by sons who are still cleverer and who will find their wisdom as foolish as the wisdom of 1917 seems to them today."[2]

Parrington proved to be a wiser prophet than he perhaps realized, for the in the 1930's and afterwards it became fashionable to accuse liberals of espousing a shallow optimism based on the faulty premise of the innate goodness of man. The liberal belief in reason, science, and critical intelligence as weapons in the construction of a better world was not founded on historical reality, these critics argued, and they went so far as to contend that the liberal vision of progress had proved a disastrous illusion, which had left mankind unpre-

1. Vernon L. Parrington, *Main Currents in American Thought* (New York, 1930), vol. III, p. 401.
2. *Ibid.*, p. 413.

pared to cope with such evils as Nazism and communism. The attack on liberalism was widespread and drew sustenance from such varied sources as Protestant neoorthodoxy as well as fundamentalism, Catholic neo-Thomism, and others who advanced various forms of philosophical and political conservatism. Indeed, many who had once been associated with the liberal philosophy and liberal causes demonstrated a hostility born of disillusionment toward the older ideological underpinnings of their faith.

But despite the sharpness of the conservative attack, liberalism in one form or another is still perhaps the prevailing belief of a majority of Americans. And defenders of liberalism continue to insist that their philosophy, with certain modifications, still can and should play a vital and important role in American life. These modern liberals refuse to speak in terms of absolutes. They are critical of the revival of a prescriptive interpretation of natural law and theories of original sin, and they are opposed to a community of fixed hierarchies. They maintain that liberalism and democracy—defined in terms of science, critical intelligence, tolerance, and a belief in the possibility of progress—still possess an attractiveness that other philosophies lack. Democratic liberalism, they have argued, is the one system that by rejecting authoritarian absolutes (whether religious, political, or intellectual) provides its own self-correctives. In the tradition of John Dewey, many liberals have continued to fight for an ideology they deem worthy of defense. Often they have accepted as valid some of the criticisms levied against the older liberalism—especially its utopian optimism and its reluctance to confront the totalitarian challenges of the 1930's and afterwards—and have attempted to reformulate the liberal philosophy by introducing a greater degree of realism and by pointing out the danger of accepting a view of man that omits a recognition of his potential for evil.

Whether or not American liberalism, however defined, can continue to exist among the vicissitudes and dangers of the modern world remains an unanswered question. Daniel Bell, himself active in numerous liberal causes during the New Deal, spoke for a whole generation of disillusioned liberals and radicals whose hopes were shattered in the gas chambers of Dachau and Auschwitz and on the leveled streets of Nagasaki and Hiroshima when he remarked that "Ours, a 'twice-born' generation, finds its wisdom in pessimism, evil, tragedy, and despair."[3] In seeking the explanation for the inadequacy of liberalism, Bell concluded that

In the end, the generation failed. Not because the idealistic impulses became exhausted; this is the inevitable trajectory, perhaps, of any radical generation. Not because events had belied the predictions; this is a healthier America. But because this may well have been the *last* radical generation for a time—the last because it was the first that tasted power and became corrupt. (Yet it is not only that power corrupts, for, as Alex Comfort once said, corrupt men seek power.) But the seed of the corruption was the *hubris* of the "possessed." Generous of impulse,

---

3. Daniel Bell, *The End of Ideology: On the Exhaustion of Political Ideas in the Fifties* (Glencoe, Ill., 1960), p. 287.

it sought the end of injustice, but in the single vision the dogmatism grew hard and the moral sense cynical, so that, when reality proved the vision false, all that was left was the hardness, or the despair.[4]

And yet, as a leading exponent of the liberal philosophy has remarked in an eloquent defense of liberalism, "Our disappointments are real. But they are real because our powers are great and our expectations legitimately high."[5]

(50)

Franklin Delano Roosevelt

1882-1945

Franklin Delano Roosevelt was born at Hyde Park, New York, and was educated at Groton, Harvard, and Columbia Law School. Early in his career he entered politics, serving as New York state senator (1910–1913), Assistant Secretary of the Navy (1913–1920), and governor of New York (1929–1933). He was elected President in 1932, holding that office until his death in 1945 soon after beginning his fourth term in office.

Throughout his presidency Roosevelt was a highly controversial figure, worshiped by some and hated by others. Aristocratic in his origins, he was a democrat by inclination and conviction, never losing faith in the validity of American ideals. Assuming office during the depths of the depression when the very fabric of society was threatened with dissolution, Roosevelt brought to the presidency an optimism that he communicated to his fellow Americans and a frank willingness to experiment in social and economic matters. Conservative in the sense that he hoped to preserve the basic framework of American society, Roosevelt was instrumental in bringing about a tremendous expansion in the role and power of the federal government. Yet Roosevelt always remained true to American traditions, affirming his basic belief in the validity of democratic procedures to solve contemporary problems. In many ways his New Deal was a union of the theory of the general welfare state with a political pragmatism designed to implement this theory through the democratic process.

The following selection is from Roosevelt's famous address before the San Francisco Commonwealth Club during the campaign of 1932, reprinted in *The Public Papers and Addresses of Franklin Roosevelt* (New York, 1938), vol. I.

4. *Ibid.*, pp. 291–292.
5. Charles Frankel, *The Case for Modern Man* (New York, 1955), p. 209.

The issue of Government has always been whether individual men and women will have to serve some system of Government or economics, or whether a system of Government and economics exists to serve individual men and women. This question has persistently dominated the discussion of Government for many generations. On questions relating to these things men have differed, and for time immemorial it is probable that honest men will continue to differ.

The final word belongs to no man; yet we can still believe in change and in progress. Democracy, as a dear old friend of mine in Indiana, Meredith Nicholson, has called it, is a quest, a never-ending seeking for better things, and in the seeking for these things and the striving for them, there are many roads to follow. But, if we map the course of these roads, we find that there are only two general directions.

When we look about us, we are likely to forget how hard people have worked to win the privilege of Government. The growth of the national Governments of Europe was a struggle for the development of a centralized force in the Nation, strong enough to impose peace upon ruling barons. In many instances the victory of the central Government, the creation of a strong central Government, was a haven of refuge to the individual. The people preferred the master far away to the exploitation and cruelty of the smaller master near at hand.

But the creators of national Government were perforce ruthless men. They were often cruel in their methods, but they did strive steadily toward something that society needed and very much wanted, a strong central State able to keep the peace, to stamp out civil war, to put the unruly nobleman in his place, and to permit the bulk of individuals to live safely. The man of ruthless force had his place in developing a pioneer country, just as he did in fixing the power of the central Government in the development of Nations. Society paid him well for his services and its development. When the development among the Nations of Europe, however, had been completed, ambition and ruthlessness, having served their term, tended to overstep their mark.

There came a growing feeling that Government was conducted for the benefit of a few who thrived unduly at the expense of all. The people sought a balancing—a limiting force. There came gradually, through town councils, trade guilds, national parliaments, by constitution and by popular participation and control, limitations on arbitrary power.

Another factor that tended to limit the power of those who ruled, was the rise of the ethical conception that a ruler bore a responsibility for the welfare of his subjects.

The American colonies were born in this struggle. The American Revolution was a turning point in it. After the Revolution the struggle continued and shaped itself in the public life of the country. There were those who because they had seen the confusion which attended the years of war for American independence surrendered to the belief that popular Government was essentially dangerous and essentially unworkable. They were honest people, my friends, and we cannot deny that their experience had warranted some measure of fear. The most brilliant, honest and able exponent of this point of view was Hamilton. He was too impatient of slow-moving methods. Fundamentally he believed that the safety of the republic lay in the autocratic strength of its Government, that the destiny of individuals was to serve that Government, and that fundamentally a great and strong group of central institutions, guided by a small group of able and public spirited citizens, could best direct all Government.

But Mr. Jefferson, in the summer of 1776, after drafting the Declaration of Independence turned his mind to the same problem and took a different view. He did not deceive himself with outward forms. Government to him was a means to an end, not an end in itself; it might be either a refuge and a help or a threat and a danger, depending on the circumstances. We find him carefully analyzing the society for which he was to organize a Government. "We have no paupers. The great mass of our population is of laborers, our rich who cannot live without labor, either manual or professional, being few and of moderate wealth. Most of the laboring class possess property, cultivate their own lands, have families and from the demand for their labor, are enabled to exact from the rich and the competent such prices as enable them to feed abundantly, clothe above mere decency, to labor moderately and raise their families."

These people, he considered, had two sets of rights, those of "personal competency" and those involved in acquiring and possessing property. By "personal competency" he meant the right of free thinking, freedom of forming and expressing opinions, and freedom of personal living, each man according to his own lights. To insure the first set of rights, a Government must so order its functions as not to interfere with the individual. But even Jefferson realized that the exercise of the property rights might so interfere with the rights of the individual that the Government, without whose assistance the property rights could not exist, must intervene, not to destroy individualism, but to protect it.

You are familiar with the great political duel which followed; and how Hamilton, and his friends, building toward a dominant centralized power were at length defeated in the great election of 1800, by Mr. Jefferson's party. Out of that duel came the two parties, Republican and Democratic, as we know them today.

So began, in American political life, the new day, the day of the individual against the system, the day in which individualism was made the great watchword of American life. The happiest of economic conditions made that day long and splendid. On the Western frontier, land was substantially free. No one, who did not shirk the task of earning a living, was entirely without opportunity to do so. Depressions could, and did, come and go; but they could not alter the fundamental fact that most of the people lived partly by selling their labor and partly by extracting their livelihood from the soil, so that starvation and dislocation were practically impossible. At the very worst there was always the possibility of climbing into a covered wagon and moving west where the untilled prairies afforded a haven for men to whom the East did not provide a place. So great were our natural resources that we could offer this relief not only to our own people, but to the distressed of all the world; we could invite immigration from Europe, and welcome it with open arms. Traditionally, when a depression came a new section of land was opened in the West; and even our temporary misfortune served our manifest destiny.

It was in the middle of the nineteenth century that a new force was released and a new dream created. The force was what is called the industrial revolution, the advance of steam and machinery and the rise of the forerunners of the modern industrial plant. The dream was the dream of an economic machine, able to raise the standard of living for everyone; to bring luxury within the reach of the humblest; to annihilate distance by steam power and later by electricity, and to release everyone from the drudgery of the heaviest manual toil. It was to be expected that this would necessarily affect Government. Heretofore, Government had merely been called upon to produce conditions within which people could live happily, labor peacefully, and rest secure. Now it was called upon to aid in the consummation of this new dream. There was, however, a shadow over the dream. To be made real, it required use of the talents of men of tremendous will and tremendous ambition, since by no other force could the problems of financing and engineering and new developments be brought to a consummation.

So manifest were the advantages of the machine age, however, that the United States fearlessly, cheerfully, and, I think, rightly, accepted the bitter with the sweet. It was thought that no price was too high to pay for the advantages which we could draw from a finished industrial system. The history of the last half century is accordingly in large measure a history of a group of financial Titans, whose methods were not scrutinized with too much care, and who were honored in proportion as they produced the results, irrespective of the means they used. The financiers who pushed the railroads to the Pacific were always ruthless, often wasteful, and frequently corrupt; but they did build railroads, and we have them today. It has been estimated that the American investor paid for the American railway system more than three times over in the process; but despite this fact the net advantage was to the United States. As long as we had free land; as long as population was growing by leaps and bounds; as long as our industrial plants were insufficient to supply our own needs, society chose to give the ambitious man free play and unlimited reward provided only that he produced the economic plant so much desired.

During this period of expansion, there was equal opportunity for all and the business of Government was not to interfere but to assist in the development of industry. This was done at the request of business men themselves. The tariff was originally imposed for the purpose of "fostering our infant industry," a phrase I think the older among you will remember as a political issue not so long ago. The railroads were subsidized, sometimes by grants of money, oftener by grants of land; some of the most valuable oil lands in the United States were granted to assist the financing of the railroad which pushed through the Southwest. A nascent merchant marine was assisted by grants of money, or by mail subsidies, so that our steam shipping might ply the seven seas. Some of my friends tell me that they do not want the Government in business. With this I agree; but I wonder whether they realize the implications of the past. For while it has been American doctrine that the Government must not go into business in competition with private enterprises, still it has been traditional, particularly in Republican administrations, for business urgently to ask the Government to put at private disposal all kinds of Government assistance. The same man who tells you that he does not want to see the Government interfere in business—and he means it, and has plenty of good reasons for saying so—is the first to go to Washington and ask the Government for a prohibitory tariff on his product. When things get just bad enough, as they did two years ago, he will go with equal speed to the United States Government and ask for a loan; and the Reconstruction Finance Corporation is the outcome of it. Each group has sought protection from the Government for its own special interests, without realizing that the function of Government must be to favor no small groups at the expense of its duty to protect the rights of personal freedom and of private property of all its citizens.

In retrospect we can now see that the turn of the tide came with the turn of the century. We were reaching our last frontier; there was no more free land and our industrial combinations had become great uncontrolled and irresponsible units of power within the State. Clear-sighted men saw with fear the danger that opportunity would no longer be equal; that the growing corporation, like the feudal baron of old, might threaten the economic freedom of individuals to earn a living. In that hour, our antitrust laws were born. The cry was raised against the great corporations. Theodore Roosevelt, the first great Republican Progressive, fought a Presidential campaign on the issue of "trust busting" and talked freely about the malefactors of great wealth. If the Government had a policy it was rather to turn the clock back, to destroy the large combinations and to return to the time when every man owned his individual small business.

This was impossible; Theodore Roosevelt, abandoning the idea of "trust busting," was forced to work out a difference between "good" trusts and "bad" trusts. The Supreme Court set forth the famous "rule of reason" by which it seems to have meant that a concentration of industrial power was permissible if the method by which it got its power, and the use it made of that power, were reasonable.

Woodrow Wilson, elected in 1912, saw the situation more clearly. Where Jefferson had feared the encroachment of political power on the lives of individuals, Wilson knew that the new power was financial. He saw, in the highly centralized economic system, the despot of the twentieth century, on whom great masses of individuals relied for their safety and their livelihood, and whose irresponsibility and greed (if they were not controlled) would reduce them to starvation and penury. The concentration of financial power had not proceeded so far in 1912 as it has today; but it had grown far enough for Mr. Wilson to realize fully its implications. It is interesting, now, to read his speeches. What is called "radical" today (and I have reason to know whereof I speak) is mild compared to the campaign of Mr. Wilson. "No man can deny," he said, "that the lines of endeavor have more and more narrowed and stiffened; no man who knows anything about the development of industry in this country can have failed to observe that the larger kinds of credit are more and more difficult to obtain unless you obtain them upon terms of uniting your efforts with those who already control the industry of the country, and nobody can fail to observe that every man who tries to set himself up in competition with any process of manufacture which has taken place under the control of large combinations of capital will presently find himself either squeezed out or obliged to sell and allow himself to be absorbed." Had there been no World War—had Mr. Wilson been able to devote eight years to domestic instead of to international affairs—we might have had a wholly different situation at the present time. However, the then distant roar of European cannon, growing ever louder, forced him to abandon the study of this issue. The problem he saw so clearly is left with us as a legacy; and no one of us on either side of the political controversy can deny that it is a matter of grave concern to the Government.

A glance at the situation today only too clearly indicates that equality of opportunity as we have known it no longer exists. Our industrial plant is built; the problem just now is whether under existing conditions it is not overbuilt. Our last frontier has long since been reached, and there is practically no more free land. More than half of our people do not live on the farms or on the lands and cannot derive a living by cultivating their own property. There is no safety valve in the form of a Western prairie to which those thrown out of work by the Eastern economic machines can go for a new start. We are not able to invite the immigration from Europe to share our endless plenty. We are now providing a drab living for our own people.

Our system of constantly rising tariffs has at last reacted against us to the point of closing our Canadian frontier on the north, our European markets on the east, many of our Latin-American markets to the south, and a goodly proportion of our Pacific markets on the west, through the retaliatory tariffs of those countries. It has forced many of our great industrial institutions which exported their surplus production to such countries, to establish plants in such countries, within the tariff walls. This has resulted in the reduction of the operation of their American plants, and opportunity for employment.

Just as freedom to farm has ceased, so also the opportunity in business has narrowed. It still is true that men can start small enterprises, trusting to native shrewdness and ability to keep abreast of competitors; but area after area has been preempted altogether by the great corporations, and even in the fields which still have no great concerns, the small man starts under a handicap. The unfeeling statistics of the past three decades show that the independent business man is running a losing race. Perhaps he is forced to the wall; perhaps he cannot command credit; perhaps he is "squeezed out," in Mr. Wilson's words, by highly organized corporate competitors, as your corner grocery man can tell you. Recently a careful study was made of the concentration of business in the United States. It showed that our economic life was dominated by some six hundred odd corporations who controlled two-thirds of American industry. Ten million small business men divided the other third. More striking still, it appeared that if the process of concentration goes on at the same rate, at the end of another century we shall have all American industry controlled by a dozen corporations, and run by perhaps a hundred men. Put plainly, we are steering a steady course toward economic oligarchy, if we are not there already.

Clearly, all this calls for a re-appraisal of values. A mere builder of more industrial plants, a creator of more railroad systems, an organizer of more corporations, is as likely to be a danger as a help. The day of the great promoter or the financial Titan, to whom we granted anything if only he would build, or develop, is over. Our task now is not discovery or exploitation of natural resources, or necessarily producing more goods. It is the soberer, less dramatic business of administering resources and plants already in hand, of seeking to reestablish foreign markets for our surplus production, of meeting the problem of underconsumption, of adjusting production to consumption, of distributing wealth and products more equitably, of adapting existing economic organizations to the service of the people. The day of enlightened administration has come.

Just as in older times the central Government was first a haven of refuge, and then a threat, so now in a closer economic system the central and ambitious financial unit is no longer a servant of national desire, but a danger. I would draw the parallel one step farther. We did not think because national Government had become a threat in the 18th century that therefore we should abandon the principle of national Government. Nor today should we abandon the principle of strong economic units called corporations, merely because their power is susceptible of easy abuse. In other times we dealt with the problem of an unduly ambitious central Government by modifying it gradually into a constitutional democratic Government. So today we are modifying and controlling our economic units.

As I see it, the task of Government in its relation to business is to assist the development of an economic declaration of rights, an economic constitutional order. This is the common task of statesman and business man. It is the minimum requirement of a more permanently safe order of things.

Happily, the times indicate that to create such an order not only is the proper policy of Government, but it is the only line of safety for our economic structures as well. We know, now, that these economic units cannot exist unless prosperity is uniform, that is, unless purchasing power is well distributed throughout every group in the Nation. That is why even the most selfish of corporations for its own interest would be glad to see wages restored and unemployment ended and to bring the Western farmer back to his accustomed level of prosperity and to assure a permanent safety to both groups. That is why some enlightened industries themselves endeavor to limit the freedom of action of each man and business group within the industry in the common interest of all; why business men everywhere are asking a form of organization which will bring the scheme of things into balance, even though it may in some measure qualify the freedom of action of individual units within the business.

The exposition need not further be elaborated. It is brief and incomplete, but you will be able to expand it in terms of your own business or occupation without difficulty. I think everyone who has actually entered the economic struggle—which means everyone who was not born to safe wealth—knows in his own experience and his own life that we have now to apply the earlier concepts of American Government to the conditions of today.

The Declaration of Independence discusses the problem of Government in terms of a contract. Government is a relation of give and take, a contract, perforce, if we would follow the thinking out of which it grew. Under such a contract rulers were accorded power, and the people consented to that power on consideration that they be accorded certain rights. The task of statesmanship has always been the re-definition of these rights in terms of a changing and growing social order. New conditions impose new requirements upon Government and those who conduct Government. . . .

I feel that we are coming to a view through the drift of our legislation and our public thinking in the past quarter century that private economic power is, to enlarge an old phrase, a public trust as well. I hold that continued enjoyment of that power by any individual or group must depend upon the fufillment of that trust. The men who have reached the summit of American business life know this best; happily, many of these urge the binding quality of this greater social contract.

The terms of that contract are as old as the Republic, and as new as the new economic order.

Every man has a right to life; and this means that he has also a right to make a comfortable living. He may by sloth or crime decline to exercise that right; but it may not be denied him. We have no actual famine or dearth; our industrial and agricultural mechanism can produce enough and to spare. Our Government formal and informal, political and economic, owes to everyone an avenue to possess himself of a portion of that plenty sufficient for his needs, through his own work.

Every man has a right to his own property; which means a right to be assured, to the fullest extent attainable, in the safety of his savings. By no other means can men carry the burdens of those parts of life which, in the nature of things, afford no chance of labor; childhood, sickness, old age. In all thought of property, this right is paramount; all other property rights must yield to it. If, in accord with this principle, we must restrict the operations of the speculator, the manipulator, even the financier, I believe we must accept the restriction as needful, not to hamper individualism but to protect it.

These two requirements must be satisfied, in the main, by the individuals who claim and hold control of the great industrial and financial combinations which dominate so large a part of our industrial life. They have undertaken to be, not business men, but princes of property. I am not prepared to say that the system which produces them is wrong. I am very clear that they must fearlessly and competently assume the responsibility which goes with the power. So many enlightened business men know this that the statement would be little more than a platitude, were it not for an added implication.

This implication is, briefly, that the responsible heads of finance and industry instead of acting each for himself, must work together to achieve the common end. They must, where necessary, sacrifice this or that private advantage; and in reciprocal self-denial must seek a general advantage. It is here that formal Government—political Government, if you chose—comes in. Whenever in the pursuit of this objective the lone wolf, the unethical competitor, the reckless promoter, the Ishmael or Insull whose hand is against every man's, declines to join in achieving an end recognized as being for the public welfare, and threatens to drag the industry back to a state of anarchy, the Government may properly be asked to apply restraint. Likewise, should the group ever use its collective power contrary to the public welfare, the Government must be swift to enter and protect the public interest.

The Government should assume the function of economic regulation only as a last resort, to be tried only when private initiative, inspired by high responsibility, with such assistance and balance as Government can give, has finally failed. As yet there has been no final failure, because there has been no attempt; and I decline to assume that this Nation is unable to meet the situation.

The final term of the high contract was for liberty and the pursuit of happiness. We have learned a great deal of both in the past century. We know that individual liberty and individual happiness mean nothing unless both are ordered in the sense that one man's meat is not another man's poison. We know that the old "rights of personal competency," the right to read, to think, to speak, to choose and live a mode of life, must be respected at all hazards. We know that liberty to do anything which deprives others of those elemental rights is outside the protection of any compact; and that Government in this regard is the maintenance of a balance, within which every individual may have a place if he will take it; in which every individual may find safety if he wishes it; in which every individual may attain such power as his ability permits, consistent with his assuming the accompanying responsibility.

All this is a long, slow talk. Nothing is more striking than the simple innocence of the men who insist, whenever an objective is present, on the prompt production of a patent scheme guaranteed to produce a result. Human endeavor is not so simple as that. Government includes the art of formulating a policy, and using the political technique to attain so much of that policy as will receive general support; persuading, leading, sacrificing, teaching always, because the greatest duty of a statesman is to educate. But in the matters of which I have spoken, we are learning rapidly, in a severe school. The lessons so learned must not be forgotten, even in the mental lethargy of a speculative upturn. We must build toward the time when a major depression cannot occur again; and if this means sacrificing the easy profits of inflationist booms, then let them go; and good riddance.

Faith in America, faith in our tradition of personal responsibility, faith in our institutions, faith in ourselves demand that we recognize the new terms of the old social contract. We shall fulfill them, as we fulfilled the obligation of the apparent Utopia which Jefferson imagined for us in 1776, and which Jefferson, Roosevelt and Wilson sought to bring to realization. We must do so, lest a rising tide of misery, engendered by our common failure, engulf us all. But failure is not an American habit; and in the strength of great hope we must all shoulder our common load.

(51)

Lewis Mumford

1895-

A native of New York City, Lewis Mumford attended the City College of New York, Columbia, and New York University, although he never received an academic degree. For most of his career he has been one of America's most important social critics. His major work has been a multivolumed study of the philosophy of civilization, of which five books have been published (*Technics and Civilization, The Culture of Cities, The Condition of Man, The Conduct of Life, The City in History*), all of them concerned with the weaknesses and disintegrations of modern society.

In the classical humanist tradition, Mumford has argued persuasively and effectively for a greater degree of rational planning in our urban society, pointing out with brilliant insights the disintegrative tendencies inherent in most of our cities and the threat this poses to our culture.

The following selection was written by Mumford in 1940 when he resigned as an editor of the *New Republic*. This move was occasioned by his disillusionment with those pragmatic liberals who, he felt, would not take a firm stand against the menace of Nazi totalitarianism. In this article he argued against pragmatic liberalism as a political philosophy for Americans, and offered instead his own version of the liberal philosophy. The text is from "The Corruption of Liberalism," *New Republic,* 102 (April 29, 1940).

☆ ☆ ☆ ☆

As an economic creed, liberalism was undermined by imperialism and monopoly before the nineteenth century closed. But as a personal and social philosophy, liberalism has been dissolving before our eyes only during the past decade. The liberal lacks confidence in himself and in his vision of life. He has shown in every country where the attacks on liberalism have been forceful that he either does not possess stable convictions, or that he lacks the insight and the courage that would enable him to defend them. Continually hoping for the best, the liberal remains unprepared to face the worst; and on the brink of what may turn out another Dark Ages, he continues to scan the horizon for signs of dawn. . . .

The Romans used to say that the worst results come about through the corruption of what is good; and one may say this about the present state of liberalism. But the defects of liberalism are not due to isolated mistakes of judgment that individual liberals have made; they are due to fatal deficiencies that go to the very roots of liberal philosophy. Unfortunately, liberalism's weaknesses are so debilitating that they not merely undermine its own will-to-survive, but they may also give up elements in a longer human tradition, on whose maintenance our very civilization depends.

Liberalism is a very mixed body of doctrine. So it is important that, in discussing its errors, we should detach its essential and enduring values from those which have characterized a particular age, class or group. . . .

Now the universal elements in liberalism, the moralizing elements, are the real objects of the fascist attacks. These universal elements arose long before modern capitalism: they were part of the larger human tradition, embodied in the folkways of the Jews, in the experimental philosophy of the Greeks, in the secular practices of the Roman Empire, in the sacred doctrines of the Christian Church, in the philosophies of the great post-medieval humanists. The Marxian notion that ideas are always the shadows of the existing economic institutions runs bluntly against facts precisely at this point. For although a culture forms a related organic whole, a residue is left in each period and place which tends to become part of the general heritage of mankind. This residue is relatively small in amount but infinitely precious; and no single class or people can create it or be its sole keeper.

The effort to equate Manchester liberalism with the humanist traditions of personal responsibility, personal freedom and personal expression is sometimes shared by the defenders of capitalistic privilege; that is the gross fallacy of those who try to tie together private capitalism and "the American way." But these notions are false, whether held by the absolutists of private property or by the absolutists who would challenge the regime of private property. The most important principles in liberalism do not cling exclusively to liberalism: what gives them their strength is their universality and their historic continuity. Confucius, Socrates, Plato, Aristotle, testify to them no less than Jefferson and Mill. Liberalism took over this humanist tradition, revamped it, and finally united it to a new body of hopes and beliefs that grew up in the eighteenth century.

This second element in liberalism, which seems to many people as important as the first, rests upon a quite different set of premises. Liberalism in this sense was symbolically a child of Voltaire and Rousseau: the Voltaire who thought that the craft of priests was responsible for the misery of the world, and the Rousseau who thought that man was born naturally good and had been corrupted only by evil institutions. It was likewise a by-product of the inventors and industrialists of the period, who, concentrating upon the improvement of the means of life, thought sincerely that the ends of living would more or less take care of themselves.

This pragmatic liberalism, which I shall here distinguish from the ideal liberalism, was vastly preoccupied with the machinery of life. It was characteristic of this creed to overemphasize the part played by political and mechanical invention, by abstract thought and practical contrivance. And accordingly it minimized the role of instinct, tradition, history; it was unaware of the dark forces of the unconscious; it was suspicious of either the capricious or the incalculable, for the only universe it could rule was a measured one, and the only type of human character it could understand was the utilitarian one. That there are modes of insight into man and into the cosmos which science does not possess, the liberal did not suspect; he took for granted that the emotional and spiritual life of man needs no other foundation than the rational, utilitarian activities associated with the getting of a living. Hence, finally, liberalism's progressive neglect of the fields of esthetics, ethics and religion: these matters were left to traditional thinkers, with the confident belief that they would eventually drop out of existence, mere vestiges of the race's childhood. On the whole most liberals today have produced no effective thought in any of these fields; and they live, as it were, on the debris of past dogmas and buried formulations. Unconscious, for example, of the sources of their ethical ideas, they pick up more or less what happens to be lying around them, without any effort at consistency or clarity, still less at creativeness: here a scrap left over from childhood, there a fragment of Kant or Bentham, or again a dash of Machiavelli, pacifist Quakers one moment and quaking Nietzscheans the next.

In short, it is not unfair to say that the pragmatic liberal has taken the world of personality, the world of values, feelings, emotions, wishes, purposes, for granted. He assumed either that this world did not exist, or that it was relatively unimportant; at all events, if it did exist, it could be safely left to itself, without cultivation. For him men were essentially good, and only faulty economic and political institutions—defects purely in the mechanism of society—kept them from becoming better. That there might be internal obstacles to external improvement seemed to him absurd. That there was as large a field for imaginative design and rational discipline in the building of a personality as in the building of a skyscraper did not occur to him. Unfortunately, immature personalities, irrational personalities, demoralized personalities are as inevitable as weeds in an uncultivated garden when no deliberate attempt is made to provide a constructive basis for personal development.

Behind this failure to establish, on a fresh basis, a normative discipline for the personality was a singular optimism—the belief that it was not needed. Did not liberalism imply an emancipation from the empty institutional religion, from the saws, precepts, moralizings of the past? Did this not mean that "science," which confessedly despised norms, would eventually supply all the guidance necessary for human conduct? Such was the innocence of the liberal that those who were indifferent to ethical values thought of themselves as realists. They could hardly understand William James when he called emotionality the *sine qua non* of moral perception. But the fact was that the most old-fashioned theologian, with a sense of human guilt and human error, was by far the better realist. Though the theologian's view of the external world might be scientifically weak, his view of the internal world, the world of value and personality, included an understanding of constant human phenomena— sin, corruption, evil—on which the liberal closed his eyes.

Pragmatic liberalism did not believe in a world where the questions of good and evil were not incidental but of radical importance. Its adherents thought that they would presently abolish the evils inherent in life by popularizing anesthetics and by extending the blessings of the machine. They did not believe in the personal life. That was outmoded. Esthetic interests, moral discipline, the habits of contemplation and evaluation, all this seemed mere spiritual gymnastics: they preferred more physical exercises. By activity (busy work) pragmatic liberals kept their eyes manfully on the mere surface of living. They did not believe that any sensible man would, except when he made his will, face the more ultimate facts of existence. For them, the appraisal of death was a neurotic symptom; happily, science's steady advances in hygiene and medicine might postpone further and further that unpleasant occasion itself. . . .

Is it any wonder, then, that pragmatic liberalism has been incapable of making firm ethical judgments or of implementing them with action? Its color-blindness to moral values is its most serious weakness today; hence it cannot distinguish between barbarism and civilization. Indeed, it is even inclined to pass a more favorable verdict on barbarism when it shows superiority in material organization. Refusing to recognize the crucial problem of evil, those who follow this creed are incapable of coping with the intentions of evil men: they look in vain for merely intellectual mistakes to account for the conduct of those who have chosen to flout man's long efforts to become civilized. Evil for the pragmatic liberal has no positive dimensions: he conceives it as a mere lack of something whose presence would be good. Poverty is an evil, because it indicates the lack of a good, namely riches. For this kind of liberal, the most heinous fact about a war is not the evil intentions and purposes that one or both sides may disclose: it is mainly the needless waste of material, the unbearable amount of human suffering, the premature deaths.

Lacking any true insight into these stubborn facts of human experience— corruption, evil, irrational desire—liberals also fail to understand that evil often lies beyond purely rational treatment, that a mere inquiry into causes, mere reasonableness and sweetness in one's attitude, may not only fail to cure an evil disposition but may aggravate it. Now, unfortunately, there are times when an attitude of intellectual humility and sympathy is entirely inappropriate to the press of a particular situation. There are times when active resistance or coercion is the only safeguard against the conduct of men who mean ill against human society. The alternative to coercion is what the religious call conversion, salvation, grace, on the part of the offender. That, too, is essentially a pre-rational process, not hostile to reason, but proceeding by a short cut into an area that reason cannot directly touch. Liberals tend to minimize the effectiveness of both coercion and conversion, both force and grace; but it is hard to point to any large and significant social change in which both elements did not play a part.

Coercion is, of course, no substitute for intelligent inquiry and no cure in itself for anti-social conduct. But just as there are maladies in the human body which call for surgery rather than diet—though diet, if applied at an early stage, might have been sufficient—so there are moments of crisis in society when anti-social groups or nations that resist the ordinary methods of persuasion and compromise must be dealt with by coercion. In such moments, to hesitate, to temporize, only gives the disease a deeper hold on the organism; and to center one's efforts upon changing the mind of one's opponent, by opposing reason to his irrationality, and to overlook the elementary precaution of depriving him of his weapons for attacking one, is to commit a fatal offense against the very method one seeks to uphold.

The liberal's notion that reasoning in the spirit of affable compromises is the only truly human way of meeting one's opponent overlooks the important part played by force and grace. And his unctuous notion that evil must not seriously be combated because the person who attempts to oppose it may ultimately have to use physical force, and will become soiled by the act of fighting, is a gospel of despair. This belief is the core of his defeatist response to Nazism; it means in practice turning the world over to the rule of the violent, the brutal and the inhuman, who have no such fine scruples, because the humane are too dainty in their virtue to submit to any possible assault on it. Now the dangers are real: force *does* brutalize the users of it; when blood is spilt, anger rises and reason temporarily disappears. Hence force is not to be used daily in the body politic, like food or exercise; it is only to be used in an emergency, like medicine or the surgeon's knife. Fascism is barbarous, not because it uses force, but because it *prefers* force to rational accommodation: it deliberately turns mental and physical coercion into human nature's daily food. . . .

The essential moral weakness of liberalism, which I have only glanced at here, is coupled with a larger weakness in the liberal philosophy. Along with liberalism's admirable respect for rational science and experimental practice, goes an overvaluation of intellectual activities as such, and an undervaluation of the emotional and affective sides of life. In the liberal theology, emotions and feelings have taken the place of a personal devil. Now as every good psychologist knows, and as Count Korzybski has ably demonstrated, emotions and feelings, associated with the most devious and remote body processes, are involved in all thought. Reason and emotion are inseparable: their detachment is a practical device of limited use. Thought that is empty of emotion and feeling, that bears no organic relation to life, is just as foreign to effective reason as emotion that is disproportionate to the stimulus or is without intellectual foundations and references. The body, the unconscious, the pre-rational are all important to sound thought. But because the liberal has sought no positive discipline for emotion and feeling, there is an open breach between his affective life and his intellectual interests. His first impulse in any situation is to get rid of emotion because it may cause him to go wrong. Unfortunately for his effort to achieve poise, a purely intellectual judgment, eviscerated of emotional reference, often causes wry miscalculations. The calmness and sangfroid of Benes was perhaps his most serious weakness during the long period before the Munich crisis; ominously, it repeated the self-defeating mood of Bruening, in the days preceding his removal. Instead of priding himself on not being "carried away by his emotions," the liberal should rather be a little alarmed because he often has no emotions that could, under any conceivable circumstances, carry him away. . . .

Closely allied with the liberal's emotional anesthesia is his incurable optimism—a wrinkled smile left over from the eighteenth century, when, in the first flush of confidence, the possibilities of human advance seemed boundless. This optimism belonged to a constructive and expanding age: in its inception, it was a healthy reaction against the moldering institutions and precedents of the past. But it has become an unfortunate handicap in a period when destructive forces are gaining the upper hand, and when, in the approaching stabilization of population and industry, the malevolence of the human will, on the part of the propertied classes, may at critical moments—as already in Germany and Italy—give unlimited power to those who represent barbarism. Destruction, malice, violence, hold no temptation for the liberal; and in the kindness of his heart, he cannot bring himself to believe that they may viciously influence the conduct of any large part of mankind. The liberals could not understand that the gift of Czecho-Slovakia to Nazi Germany could not appease Hitler: that one might as well offer the carcass of a dead deer in a butcher store to a hunter who seeks the animal as prey—the meat being valued chiefly as a symbol of his prowess. And that is why the talk of mere economic adjustments that would enable the fascist states to live at peace with the rest of the world is muddled nonsense; it assumes, contrary to fact, that fascism springs out of rational motives and pursues concrete utilitarian ends. The bad arrangements of the peace of Versailles did not by themselves create fascism, nor will the best results of a magnanimous peace conference be able at once to wipe out its destructive impulses and undermine its irrational philosophy. Unfortunately it is not in Ricardo or Marx or Lenin, but in Dante and Shakespeare and Dostoevsky, that an understanding of the true sources of fascism are to be found.

Economic explanations reflected a reality in the nineteenth century; they disguise a reality—the claim to barbaric conquest—today.

During the last ten years, the optimism of the liberals has remained unshaken. The incurable tendency of the liberal is to believe the best about everybody: to hope when there is no reason to hope, and to exhibit the nicest moral qualms, the most delicate intellectual scruples, in situations that demand that he wade in and coarsely exert his utmost effort. We now face a world that is on the brink, perhaps of another Dark Age; and because a Dark Age is not included in the liberal chronology, liberalism glibly refuses to accept the evidence of its sense. Like the sun-dial, it cannot tell time on a stormy day. So, habitually, the pragmatic liberals brand those whose eyes are open to the human devastation around them as "hysterical," "mystical," "having concealed fascist tendencies," or—taking a leaf from the Hitlerites—as "warmongers."

Now one must remember that liberalism has two sides. There is an ideal liberalism, deeply rooted in the example and experience of humanity: a doctrine that commands the allegiance of all well disposed men. And there is a transient doctrine of liberalism, the pragmatic side, which grew up in the eighteenth century out of a rather adolescent pride in the scientific conquest of nature and the invention of power machinery: this is the side that emphasizes the utilitarian aspects of life, that concentrates on purely intellectual issues, and that, in its exclusive concern for tolerance and "open-mindedness" is ready to extend its benevolent protection to those who openly oppose the very purposes of civilization. What is important in ideal liberalism are elements like the great Roman notion of *Humanity,* united in the pursuit of freedom and justice, embracing all races and conditions. This ideal is radically opposed at every point to the autarchy advocated by the fascists; and it is no less opposed to the isolationism, moral and physical and political, advocated by most American liberals—a passive milk-and-water version of the fascist's contemptuous attitude toward the rest of the human race. . . .

To achieve a new basis for personal development and communal action, the liberal need not abandon his earlier concern for science, mechanism, the rational organization of society. But he can no longer regard the world that is embraced by these things as complete or all-sufficient. The world of political action must transcend that of the Economic Man: it must be as large as the fully developed human personality itself. No mere revision of Marxism, no mere ingenious political program with a few socialistic planks added or taken away, no attempt to make five disparate economic systems produce profit in a community where new social motives must take the place of dwindling or absent profits—none of these shallow dodges will suffice. What is demanded is a recrystallization of the positive values of life, and an understanding of the basic issues of good and evil, of power and form, of force and grace, in the actual world. In short: the crisis presses toward a social conversion, deepseated, organic, religious in its essence, so that no part of personal or political existence will be untouched by it: a conversion that will transcend the arid pragmatism that has served as a substitute religion. For only the living—those for whom the world has meaning—can continue to live, and willingly make the fierce sacrifices and heroic efforts the present moment demands.

(52)

Carl L. Becker

1873-1945

One of the outstanding American historians of his generation, Carl Becker was born in Lincoln Township, Blackhawk County, Iowa. After he received his B.A. and his doctorate from the University of Wisconsin, Becker taught at various colleges and universities before he moved to Cornell University in 1917, where he spent the rest of his academic career.

The author of many important historical and philosophical works, including *The Declaration of Independence* (1922) and *The Heavenly City of the Eighteenth Century Philosophers* (1932), Becker early in his career addressed himself to the problems inherent in the writing of history. Reacting against both scientific history and the positivist approach to the reconstruction of the past, Becker sought to find a new basis for historical knowledge. He emphasized the distinction between history and science, and frankly asserted that the historian could not escape the perspective of his own society—a fact that made impossible the writing of objective history and science. Bringing to the writing of history a pragmatic skepticism, his own researches led him to question fixed and absolute definitions of truth, including some of the "glittering generalities" associated with Enlightenment liberalism. After all, Becker asked, had not liberty fostered plutocracy and had not equality led to conformity?

Despite his rejection of fixed and absolute values, Becker was too shrewd an observer of contemporary events not to recognize the menace presented by totalitarianism during the 1930's. By the early 1940's, therefore, he had begun to make his peace with the modern liberal democratic philosophy descended from the Enlightenment. In returning to the virtues of the Enlightenment and rejecting the skepticism that seemed to flow from his pragmatic relativism, Becker was in essence shoring up the foundations of a liberal democratic philosophy and way of life.

The following selection is from Becker's *Modern Democracy* (New Haven, Conn., 1941).

☆ ☆ ☆ ☆

The liberal democratic faith, as expressed in the works of eighteenth and early nineteenth-century writers, is one of the formulations of the modern doctrine of progress. . . .

The eighteenth century was the moment in history when men first fully realized the engaging implications of this resplendent idea, the moment when, not yet having been brought to the harsh appraisal of experience, it could be accepted with unclouded optimism. Never had the universe seemed less mysterious, more open and visible, more eager to yield its secrets to common-sense questions. Never had the nature of man seemed less perverse, or the mind of man more pliable to the pressure of rational persuasion. The essential reason for this confident optimism is that the marvels of scientific discovery disclosed to the men of that time a God who still functioned but was no longer angry. God the Father could be conceived as a beneficent First Cause who, having performed his essential task of creation, had withdrawn from the affairs of men, leaving them competently prepared and fully instructed for the task of achieving their own salvation. In one tremendous sentence Rousseau expressed the eighteenth-century world view of the universe and man's place in it. "Is it simple," he exclaimed, "is it natural that God should have gone in search of Moses in order to speak to Jean Jacques Rousseau?"

God had indeed spoken to Rousseau, he had spoken to all men, but his revelation was contained, not in Holy Writ interpreted by Holy Church, but in the great Book of Nature which was open for all men to read. To this open book of nature men would go when they wanted to know what God had said to them. Here they would find recorded the laws of nature and of nature's God, disclosing a universe constructed according to a rational plan; and that men might read these laws aright they had been endowed with reason, a bit of the universal intelligence placed within the individual to make manifest to him the universal reason implicit in things and events. "Natural law," as Volney so clearly and confidently put it, "is the regular and constant order of facts by which God rules the universe; the order which his wisdom presents to the sense and reason of men, to serve them as an equal and common rule of conduct, and to guide them, without distinction of race or sect, toward perfection and happiness." Thus God had devised a planned economy, and had endowed men with the capacity for managing it: to bring his ideas, his conduct, and his institutions into harmony with the universal laws of nature was man's simple allotted task.

At all times political theory must accommodate itself in some fashion to the prevailing world view, and liberal-democratic political theory was no exception to this rule. From time immemorial authority and obedience had been the cardinal concepts both of the prevailing world view and of political and social theory. From time immemorial men had been regarded as subject to overruling authority—the authority of the gods, and the authority of kings who were themselves gods, or descended from gods, or endowed with divine authority to rule in place of gods; and from time immemorial obedience to such divine authority was thought to be the primary obligation of men. Even the Greeks, who were so little afraid of their gods that they could hobnob with them in the most friendly and engaging way, regarded mortals as subject to them; and when they lost faith in the gods they deified the state as the highest good and subordinated the individual to it. But the eighteenth-century world view, making man the measure of all things, mitigated if it did not destroy this sharp contrast between authority and obedience. God still reigned but he did not govern. He had, so to speak, granted his subjects a constitution and authorized them to interpret it as they would in the supreme court of reason. Men are still subject to an overruling authority, but the subjection could be regarded as voluntary because self-imposed, and self-imposed because obedience was exacted by nothing more oppressive than their own rational intelligence.

Liberal-democratic political theory readily accommodated itself to this change in the world view. The voice of the people was now identified with the voice of God, and all authority was derived from it. The individual instead of the state or the prince was now deified and endowed with imprescriptible rights; and since ignorance or neglect of the rights of man was the chief cause of social evils, the first task of political science was to define these rights, the second to devise a form of government suited to guarantee them. The imprescriptible rights of man were easily defined, since they were self-evident: "All men are created equal, [and] are endowed by their Creator with certain inalienable rights, among which are life, liberty, and the pursuit of happiness." From this it followed that all just governments would remove those artificial restraints which impaired these rights, thereby liberating those natural impulses with which God had endowed the individual as a guide to thought and conduct. In the intellectual realm, freedom of thought and the competition of diverse opinion would disclose the truth, which all men, being rational creatures, would progressively recognize and willingly follow. In the economic realm, freedom of enterprise would disclose the natural aptitudes of each individual, and the ensuing competition of interests would stimulate effort, and thereby result in the maximum of material advantage for all. Liberty of the individual from social constraint thus turned out to be not only an inherent natural right but also a preordained natural mechanism for bringing about the material and moral progress of mankind. Men had only to follow reason and self-interest: something not themselves, God and Nature, would do whatever else was necessary for righteousness.

Thus modern liberal-democracy is associated with an ideology which rests upon something more than the minimum assumptions essential to any democratic government. It rests upon a philosophy of universally valid ends and means. Its fundamental assumption is the worth and dignity and creative capacity of the individual, so that the chief aim of government is the maximum of individual self-direction, the chief means to that end the minimum of compulsion by the state. Ideally considered, means and ends are conjoined in the concept of freedom: freedom of thought, so that the truth may prevail; freedom of occupation, so that careers may be open to talent; freedom of self-government, so that no one may be compelled against his will. . . .

The liberal-democratic revolution has been so far betrayed, the ideal so imperfectly portrayed in the course of events, that its characteristic features cannot easily be recognized in any democratic society today. . . .

Stated in general terms the essential reason is that the idea of liberty, as formulated in the eighteenth century, although valid enough for that time, has in one fundamental respect ceased to be applicable to the situation in which we find ourselves. In the eighteenth century the most obvious oppressions from which men suffered derived from governmental restraints on the free activity of the individual. Liberty was therefore naturally conceived in terms of the emancipation of the individual from such restraints. In the economic realm this meant the elimination of governmental restraints on the individual in choosing his occupation, in contracting for the acquisition and disposal of property, and the purchase and sale of personal services. But in our time, as a result of the growing complexities of a technological society, the emancipation of the individual from governmental restraint in his economic activities has created new oppressions, so that for the majority of men liberty can be achieved only by an extension of governmental regulation of competitive business enterprise. It is in the economic realm that the traditional idea of liberty is no longer applicable; in the economic realm, accordingly, that the discord between democracy as an ideal and democracy as a going concern is most flagrant, most disillusioning, and most dangerous. . . .

Such, in broad outline, are the circumstances that may serve to explain the profound discord between democracy as an ideal and as a reality. In terms of the ideal there should have emerged from the liberal-democratic revolution a relatively simple society of free, equal, and prosperous citizens, fraternally coöperating to effect, by rational discussion and mutual concession, the common good. In fact there emerged an extremely complex society in which highly intricate and impersonal economic forces, stronger than good will or deliberate intention or rational direction, brought about an increasing concentration of wealth and power in the hands of the fortunate few, and thereby nullified, for the majority of the people, many of those essential liberties which provide both the theoretical justification and the necessary conditions for the practical success of democratic institutions.

This discord, long since perceived by the discerning, has in our time become so flagrant that in many countries the ideal has been abandoned as an illusion. In these countries new social philosophies now prevail which maintain that the attempt to apply the principles of individual liberty, not only in the economic but in the political and the intellectual realm, was a fundamental error, and is responsible for the social and international conflicts which now bewilder and distress the world.

To accept this view implies the end of democratic institutions as we know them, and the renunciation of that faith in the worth and dignity of the individual which we have cherished even if we have not always justified it in action. I do not accept this view. I believe that in the long run it will prove mistaken—fatal to any way of life that can rightly be called civilized. But I also believe that if the democratic way of life is to survive we must give to the traditional concept of freedom a more positive content. The traditional concept of individual liberty is essentially negative. The freedom it emphasizes is freedom from constraint, and indeed from a particular kind of constraint, that is to say, governmental constraint. In the economic realm the result of freeing the individual from governmental constraint is that today far too many people are always in danger of losing those positive goods without which freedom from governmental constraint is of no value. What the average man now needs is the opportunity to acquire by his own effort, in an occupation for which he is fitted, the economic security which is essential to decent and independent living. This opportunity has now disappeared for something like a quarter of the working population. In my opinion it can only be restored, if at all, by such governmental regulations of our economy as may be necessary to enable private economic enterprise to function effectively and for the common good.

If then the democratic way of life is to survive we must distinguish the kinds of individual freedom that are essential to it from those that are unessential or disastrous. Broadly speaking, the kinds that are essential are those which the individual enjoys in his intellectual and political activities; the kinds that are unessential are the relatively unrestrained liberties he has hitherto enjoyed in his economic activities. The distinction is comparatively easy to make in theory, but will be extremely difficult to effect in practice. Not the least of the difficulties arises from the fact that in the traditional ideology the freedom of the individual in the political, the intellectual, and the economic realms are so intimately associated that they seem to stand or fall together. The result is that any proposal to regulate by governmental authority the system of free economic enterprise is sure to be opposed on the ground that if the system of free economic enterprise cannot be maintained the other freedoms of democracy, freedom of thought and political freedom, must in the end be abandoned also. Whether this is true can only be determined by the event. Whatever the event may be, the difficult but essential task which confronts all democratic societies today may be formulated as follows: how in practice to curtail the freedom of the individual in economic enterprise sufficiently to effect that equality of opportunity and of possessions without which democracy is an empty form, and at the same time to preserve that measure of individual freedom in intellectual and political life without which it cannot exist. . . .

Those political and intellectual trends I have discussed and discriminated under the terms Liberal-Democracy, Socialism, Communism, and Fascism. The differences between them, both as ideological systems and as going concerns, are obvious and important; but underneath their differences we can note, in respect to what they propose to do and are doing to solve the problem of the distribution of wealth, an interesting and significant similarity. It is a similarity of direction: all these systems are carrying us, with or without our consent, toward an extension of governmental regulation of economic enterprise.

That this is the direction is evident. In all liberal-democratic countries, for the last hundred years, there has been a steadily increasing amount of such regulation of economic enterprise. Both Communism and Socialism propose to make the regulation complete by abolishing private property in the means of production, and the Communist regime in Russia has already accomplished this object. Fascism, no less than Communism, proposes to subordinate the individual to the state; and in the principal Fascist countries, although private property in land and capital has not been formally abolished, the national economy has been so far subjected to governmental direction that free economic enterprise has virtually disappeared. Like it or not, the complexities of a highly integrated technological civilization are carrying us in a certain direction, that is to say, away from freedom of the individual in economic enterprise and toward an extension of social control. This is therefore the direction which, in democratic as well as in other countries, the transformation of the problem of the distribution of wealth will surely take.

The question that chiefly concerns us is whether the necessary social regulation of economic enterprise can be effected by the democratic method, that is to say, without a corresponding social regimentation of opinion and political freedom. Can the possessors be sufficiently dispossessed and the dispossessed be sufficiently reinstated without resort to violence—to revolution and the temporary or the permanent dictatorship. The Communists say no—sooner or later the revolution. The Fascists say no—the totalitarian state is the only solution. They may of course be right. It is futile to suppose that democracy must survive because it accords with the law of nature or some transcendent increasing purpose. Nor can we dismiss the rise of dictatorship in half the world as a temporary aberration brought to birth by the ingenuity of sinister or psychopathic individuals. Common men, when sufficiently distressed, instinctively turn to the inspired leader; and dictatorship in our time, as in past times, is the normal price exacted for the failure of democracy to bind common men by their hopes and fears. The survival of democratic institutions thus depends, not upon the attractiveness or logical consistency of theories of government, but upon the possibility of effecting, by the pragmatic democratic method, a sufficient equalization of possessions and of opportunity to provide common men with what they will consent to regard as tolerable. . . .

It is as essential that the minority should voluntarily submit to the measures taken as it is that the majority should voluntarily approve them. Democratic government rests upon the principle that it is better to count heads than it is to break them. The principle is a good one, but unfortunately men will not, under certain conditions, so regard it. By and large the principle works well enough so long as the issues to be decided do not involve those interests which men will always fight for rather than surrender. By and large, democratic government, being government by discussion and majority vote, works best when there is nothing of profound importance to discuss, when the rival party programs involve the superficial aspects rather than the fundamental structure of the social system, and when for that reason the minority can meet defeat at the polls in good temper since it need not regard the decision as either a fatal or a permanent surrender of its vital interests. When these happy conditions disappear democratic government is always in danger.

The danger has already proved fatal in many countries. It exists, although it may not prove fatal, even in those countries where the democratic tradition is most strongly intrenched. For in these countries too the insistent problem of the distribution of wealth is beginning to involve those fundamental class interests which do not readily lend themselves to friendly discussion and mutual concession. The flagrant inequality of possessions and of opportunity is creating an ever sharper differentiation between the beneficiaries of private property in the means of production and the masses whose present circumstances and future prospects depend less upon individual character and talent than upon the hazards of the business cycle. Accompanying this differentiation there has been and is going on a confused but persistent realignment of political parties: on the Right, conservative parties representing the beneficiaries of the system of free enterprise; on the Left, radical parties representing the poor and the dispossessed. As the divergence between Right and Left becomes sharper and more irreconcilable, moderate and conciliatory parties tend to disappear, and the rival party programs of the extreme groups, no longer confined to the superficial aspects of policy within the framework of the traditional system, are increasingly concerned with the validity of the assumptions on which the system rests. Underlying the question of the equitable distribution of wealth is the more fundamental question of the validity of the institution of private property as a means of effecting it. The present power of the possessing classes rests upon the institution of private property; the present distress of the masses is somehow involved in it. If the present discords should be prolonged and intensified, the danger is that the masses will turn to revolution rather than submit to a system which fails to relieve them, that the classes will welcome forcible repression rather than surrender a system which guarantees their power. . . .

When we consider the problem of preserving democratic institutions broadly, from both the national and the international point of view, we seem to be helplessly caught in a vicious circle. We know that democratic institutions are threatened by social discords within the nations, and still more by war between them. We know that if we could avoid war it would be much easier to resolve our social discords, and that if we could resolve our social discords it would be much easier to avoid war. If we could do either of these things without the other, the future of democracy would be fairly secure; if we could do both of them it would be altogether so. Yet we know that social discords are a major cause of war, and that war is the one thing that will make it impossible, if anything does, to resolve our social discords. It is in such situations that reason succumbs to force, in such situations that dictators flourish and democracy declines.

It is possible that the crisis which confronts the modern world involves something more serious even than the collapse of democratic institutions. The contradictions in the capitalist system may be no more than symbols of a discord more profound—the discord between the physical power at our disposal and our capacity to make a good use of it. It is obvious at all events that the history of the last two centuries presents us with a disturbing paradox: whereas the application of reason to the mastery of the physical world has proceeded with unanticipated success and mounting optimism, the persistent effort to shape the world of human relations to humane and rational ends has been so far unavailing that we are oppressed with a sense of frustration and defeat.

Long ago it was said that man can more easily take a city than govern himself. Never was the saying more true than now. Never before has the intelligence of man placed so much material power at his disposal: never before has he employed the power at his disposal for the realization of purposes more diverse or more irreconcilable. The hand of man is subdued to what it works in, and the mind admires what the hand can accomplish. Modern man is therefore enamored of mechanical force. Fascinated by the esthetic precision and sheer power of the instruments he has devised, he will use them for doing whatever by their aid can be done, in the confident expectation that what can be done with such clean efficiency must be worth doing. Thus the machines we have invented tend to enslave us. Compelling us to use them on their own terms, and to adjust our conduct to their virtues and limitations, they somehow generate social forces which, being too complex and too intangible to be easily understood, shape our lives to ends we do not will but cannot avoid.

In times past certain civilizations, long established, brilliant and prosperous and seemingly secure against mischance, slowly decayed and either disappeared altogether or were transformed past recognition and forgotten. What has happened many times in the history of mankind may happen again. There are no barbarian hosts without the gates, but there are plenty of potential barbarians within them. It is then within the range of possibility that the flagrant discord between the mechanical power at man's disposal and his capacity to make good use of it is carrying the world into another period of widespread and chronic confusion in which democracy will everywhere succumb to dictatorship, reason to naked force, and naked force prove to be the prelude to another dark age of barbarism.

I do not say that this will happen. I do not think it will. But it is futile to suppose that it cannot happen, futile to rely upon the saving grace of some transcendent increasing purpose (a law of nature, or dialectic of history, or totalitarian state) to bring us in spite of ourselves to a predestined good end. For the solution of our difficulties the only available purposes are our own, the only available intelligence such as we can command. If then democracy survives, if civilization in any tolerable form survives, it will be because, in some favored parts of the world the human mind remains unshackled and, aided by time and fortunate circumstances, proves capable of subordinating the unprecendented material power at its command to the achievement of rational and humane ends. More obvious now even than in the seventeenth century is the truth of Pascal's famous dictum: "Thought makes the whole dignity of man; therefore endeavor to think well, that is the only morality." The chief virtue of democracy, and in the long run the sole reason for cherishing it, is that with all its defects it still provides the most favorable conditions for the maintenance of that dignity and the practice of that morality.

(53)

Sidney Hook

1902-

Born in New York City, Sidney Hook received his B.S. from the City College of New York and his M.A. and Ph.D. from Columbia University. In 1927 he joined the department of philosophy and later became chairman of the graduate division of philosophy and psychology at New York University. He served also as president of the American Philosophical Association.

A student and disciple of John Dewey, Hook has been an ardent advocate of the pragmatic philosophy as a means of clarifying contemporary social, cultural, and political problems. A prolific writer of books and articles on determinism and dialectical materialism, he has also been a frequent commentator on contemporary issues. He has consistently defended democracy against its critics, and has dealt with the difficult problem involved in granting freedom to those individuals and groups who would destroy it in the event they attain power. Critical of metaphysical speculation, Hook has argued effectively for a pragmatic, secular, democratic liberalism as a way of life.

The following selection, "Naturalism and Democracy," appeared in Yervant H. Krikorian, ed., *Naturalism and the Human Spirit* (New York, 1944). In it Hook describes the possible justifications of democracy, and concludes by rejecting any idealistic philosophy and by reaffirming the validity of the pragmatic tradition.

We now come to the problem which is of primary concern to philosophers. What are the grounds upon which acceptance of democracy in contradistinction to other modes of social life can be justified? So far as I can see, there are four generic types of justification which have been or can be offered.

The first asserts that the rational foundation of democratic belief consists in a set of supernatural religious truths in the sense that there can be no intelligent ground for choosing between democracy and other forms of society which does not logically commit us to some kind of theology.

The second asserts the same thing about metaphysics understood as a theory of "reality." Usually these two approaches go hand in hand.

The third maintains that the choice of democracy is a nonrational preference rooted in the constitution of our natures and brought to flower by nurture and education.

The fourth affirms that the belief in democracy is an hypothesis controlled by the same general pattern of inquiry which we apply to any scientific hypothesis, but referring to different subject matter, that is, our evaluations.

1. *Democracy and religion.* Does democracy as a way of life rest upon belief in supernatural religious truths in the sense that if the latter are denied, the former must necessarily be denied? It is becoming increasingly fashionable to maintain this. Were historical considerations relevant here, I think it could be conclusively established that the great institutional religions, with the possible exception of some forms of Protestantism, have tended in fact to support theocratic forms of government. Nor is this surprising if the Kingdom of Heaven be taken as a model or inspiration for the Kingdom of Earth. Whoever heard of a democratically organized Paradise? Walt Whitman in heaven would meet with the same fate as Lucifer, but for different reasons. Not only is the notion of a democratically organized heaven blasphemous, but the proposal to reform along democratic lines a hierarchically organized church would lead to excommunication. If we examine the actual behavior which has been sanctified by the maxim: "Render unto Caesar what is Caesar's and to God what is God's," we will discover that historical, institutional religion has always been able to adapt itself to any form of government or society which will tolerate its existence.

But our concern is not with historical questions, fascinating as they are, but with the logic of the position. We must consequently rephrase the question to read: Does belief in democracy logically rest upon any theological propositions in the sense that the denial of the second entails the denial of the first? And for this discussion I shall take as illustrative of theological propositions the two cardinal propositions of natural theology, namely, "God exists" and "Man has an immortal soul." To assert that whoever has no grounds for affirming the existence of God and immortality has no grounds for affirming the validity of democracy is to claim that the former are at least necessary conditions of the latter. I shall argue that they constitute neither necessary nor sufficient conditions.

a. Before examining this claim, let us note the tremendous risk it involves. Were those who advance it ever compelled to admit that these theological propositions are indemonstrable or false, they would have to surrender their belief in democracy. But this, I submit, very few of them are prepared to do. They would search for other reasons and grounds. Like those who would make the validity of moral judgments dependent upon the existence of God and immortality, the theological defenders of democracy shift from a problem in which, although difficult, it is possible to reach an agreement on the basis of some empirical evidence, to one in which the nature of the terms and sphere of discourse makes such agreement much more difficult. Confirmed democrats, it seems to me, are much more convinced of the validity of the democratic ideal than they are of the theological propositions upon which it presumably depends. They would no more exonerate from the obligation of accepting the democratic ideal an atheist or agnostic who pleads that he has no reason to believe in God and the hereafter than they would exempt him from the obligation of living honestly.

b. Aside from the difficulties of establishing God's existence, how can we get from the fact of his existence to the desirability of the democratic way of life? None of the attributes of God, save the moral attributes, can serve as a premise justifying one way of life rather than another. And if the moral attributes of God can serve as premises, necessary or sufficient, for the democratic way of life, it is only because *we* regard them as worthy, that is, as truly moral. Obviously any theology which makes God's power the justification or source of his goodness is worse than useless for purposes of deriving democracy. The attribution of moral qualities to God is an expression of what we think his qualities ought to be. And this is a problem of precisely the same order as that which we are called upon to answer when we ask for the grounds of our democratic allegiance.

c. The situation is the same if we grant that human beings have immortal souls. In what way is this a necessary or sufficient presupposition of democracy? The brotherhood of man may be a theological fact as it is a biological fact, but what makes it wrong for Cain to kill his brother Abel and right, under certain circumstances, for us to kill Cain is a moral principle which can no more be derived from theology than from biology—unless, of course, the moral principle is one of the premises of our theological (or biological) system. In this case we are no further along than we were when we raised the question about the democratic way of life. In passing it should be observed that belief in the immortality of the soul can be, and has been, used (in the Hindu doctrines of *samtra* and *karma*) to sanctify the tightest system of antidemocratic social stratification the world has ever seen.

2. *Democracy and metaphysics.* The problem of the metaphysical foundation of democracy is more difficult because of varying conceptions of metaphysics. By "metaphysics" I shall understand the discipline designated by the term "ontology" or any theory of "being *überhaupt.*" The evidence seems to me to be overwhelming that there is a definite historical connection between the social movements of a period and its dominant metaphysical teachings; furthermore, I am prepared to defend as a historically true proposition that systems of idealistic metaphysics, because of the semiofficial roles they have played in their respective cultures, have been more generally employed to bolster antidemocratic social movements than systems of empirical or materialistic metaphysics. Whether there is *always* an intrinsic personal or psychological relation between a philosopher's metaphysics and his ethics or politics is a more difficult question, but one which seems to me to require an answer in the negative. More germane to our present concern is my contention that there

is no necessary logical connection between a theory of being or becoming and any particular theory of ethics or politics. Stated more accurately, it seems to me demonstrable that no system of metaphysics *univocally* determines a system of ethics or politics. There may be certain facts about man and nature which might have a bearing upon our judgment about what social system is of the highest worth, but, as I shall argue later, these are facts concerning which the empirical sciences are qualified to report without benefit of metaphysics.

Two species of metaphysics are most often invoked in behalf of democracy. One asserts that the value of democracy or the values from which it may be derived are "grounded in reality," a phrase which is interpreted to mean that the universe "justifies" or "guarantees" both the validity and the ultimate supremacy of basic human ideals. I must confess that it is difficult for me to understand this view except as a shamefaced kind of theology. However that may be, there is no agreed-upon denotation of *the* universe. There are many universes. Nor is there any one basic human ideal, but there are many human ideals which are often in conflict with one another, even though they all invoke the universe as a ground of their validity and as a guaranty of their triumph. Finally, and most important, no matter what character the universe is alleged to have, no matter what the nature of the far-off event toward which it is moving, no matter who wins or loses, nothing logically compelling in the way of judgment follows unless *we* have already morally evaluated the character of events. For most metaphysics the very word "reality" is an implicit value term. To be sure, history may be conceived as a struggle between the Prince of Darkness and the Prince of Light, but the latter is so named because he carries *our* moral flag.

The second metaphysical view to which resort is often made is at the same time a kind of rejoinder to our position. It distinguishes between a metaphysical realm of being and a metaphysical realm of values and grounds the democratic way of life in the latter. Just as the spectrum of colors is there to be beheld by all who are not color blind and would still be there even if man's ancestors had climbed no higher than the mole in the tree of evolution, so the spectrum of values is there to be beheld by all who are not value blind and would still be there even if human beings had never existed at all. The view that colors would still be there even if human beings had no eyes is not without its difficulties. But they do not begin to compare in difficulty with the view that values are essentially unrelated to an evaluator and his interests. Santayana has quite aptly remarked of this doctrine that there is much sense in saying that whiskey "is pervaded as it were, by an inherent intoxication, and stands dead drunk in its bottle."

The subject is vast, but it is enough to show that this view is question-begging in precisely the same way as other theological and metaphysical derivations. The existence of these absolute norms is presumably certified or authenticated at some point by an act of immediate intuition. If the testimony of the intuition is construed not merely from what individuals *say* they intuit but also from the conduct that flows from their intuition—and conduct counts more in any moral scheme than mere words—then it is clear that individuals intuit or "see" *different* values. The "great" visions are not all compatible with one another in what they command, not to mention the visions that we do not call great. Which visions are the authentic ones? Prior to every conclusion that these are the objective values of all eternity, or even of all time and existence, is the assumption that *this* is the trustworthy seer. In a dispute between two men, one of whom asserts that the other is color blind and the other that the first is "just seeing things," there are definite ways of determining who is right. In a dispute between two seers whose immediate intuitions report conflicting news about the nature and hierarchy of absolute values, there is no rational way of reaching a consensus. The true prophet cannot be distinguished from the false by invoking absolute values whose validity depends upon a prior assumption of the reliability of prophetic testimony. The complacency with which some writers have cut the Gordian knot by introducing reference to the intuitions of "the best people" or "the most cultured people" or "the saving remnant" is evidence either of parochialism or of snobbery.

The record of human error and cruelty shows what ghastly consequences often result from the conviction that one's moral insight cannot possibly be wrong and that it needs no further justification than its own incandescent purity. No more than a solipsist can make plausible on his own assumptions the existence of another solipsist, can an absolutist find a rightful place for another absolutist who disagrees with him. Absolutists face each other over an abyss which cannot be bridged even by their weapons of war.

3. *Democracy and preferences.* The view that an acceptance of democracy is an expression of a preference does not carry us far until the kind of preference is indicated. A preference may express a passing whim or a deep natural bent; it may be impulsive or reflective. Preferences are rooted in our natures. Their forms, occasions, and objects are supplied by education, that is, broadly speaking, by social habits and intelligence. But either our natures can be changed, or the educators can be re-educated. If neither is possible, then the fact of moral choice becomes unintelligible. If we can offer no justification of a preference except that it is ours, obviously no point of intellectual or moral issue is raised; nor, a fortiori, can any be settled by the trial of arms. If we offer a justification of a preference, it will take one of the generic forms already discussed or about to be discussed.

4. *Democracy as a hypothesis.* When democracy is taken strictly as a form of political government, its superiority over other forms of government can be established to the extent to which it achieves more security, freedom, and cooperative diversity than any of its alternatives. If we test the workings of political democracy by Paul's scheme of virtues or by Nietzsche's, we may perhaps reach another conclusion. So long as there is no dispute about observable effects and so long as we raise no question about the moral ideals by which we evaluate these effects, we have clear sailing.

But, as has already been made plain, by democracy as a way of life we mean a way of organizing human relationships which embodies a certain complex of moral ideals. Can these ideals be treated as hypotheses? The conventional reply has always been that no moral principle can be regarded as a hypothesis, for we must already have certain knowledge of what is good before we can evaluate the consequences of acting upon it. If any position is question-begging, surely this seems to be.

Were this a symposium on value theory, I would devote all my time to developing the general theory of moral ideals as hypotheses. But here I can only barely indicate that the notion is not viciously circular. A moral ideal is a prescription to act in a certain situation or class of situations in determinate ways that will organize the human needs and wants involved so as to fulfill a set of other values which are postulated as binding in relation to the problem in hand. No more than in other cases of inquiry do we start with an empty head. The cluster of values we bring to the situation is the result of prior experience and reflection. *They are not arbitrarily postulated.* The consequences of acting upon the hypothesis may lead us to challenge a postulated or assumed value. This in turn can become the subject of a similar investigation. Terminal values are always related to specific contexts; there is no absolute terminal value which is either self-evident or beyond the necessity of justifying itself if its credentials are challenged. There is no vicious infinite regress involved if we take our problems concretely and one at a time. Nor is the procedure narrowly circular. For if after a long history of raising and solving moral problems we postulate as a value in solving a later problem a value which had itself to be certified in an earlier problem, this would testify to the presence of a fruitful set of systematically related values in the structure of our moral behavior. New values would emerge or be discovered in the course of our attempt to act upon our ideals and from the necessity of mediating the conflict between the postulated values as they bear on concrete human needs in specific situations.

I should like, however, to make the general position take form out of the discussion of the theme before us. That theme is: *Why should we treat individuals of unequal talents and endowments as persons who are equally entitled to relevant consideration and care?* Short of a treatise, I can state only the reasons, without amplification of the concrete needs of the social situation which democracy seeks to meet and the institutional practices by which it must meet them.

1. This method of treating human beings is more successful than any other in evoking a maximum of creative, voluntary effort from all members of the community. Properly implemented, it gives all persons a stake in the community and elicits a maximum of intelligent loyalty.

2. It enlarges the scope of our experience by enabling us to acquire insight into the needs, drives, and aspirations of others. Learning to understand how life is organized by other centers of experience is both a challenge and a discipline for our imagination. In aiding the growth of others, we aid our own growth.

3. The willingness to understand another man's point of view without necessarily surrendering to it makes it more likely that different points of view

may negotiate their differences and learn to live peacefully with one another. A democratic community cannot be free from strife in a world where inequalities will always exist, but its ethics, when intelligently acted upon, makes more likely the diminution of strife or its transference to socially harmless forms than is the case when its principle of equality is denied. The consequences are less toadying, less fear, and less duplicity in the equalitarian community than there are in the non-equalitarian society.

4. In nurturing the capacities of each individual so that they may come to their greatest fulfillment we can best share our existing stores of truth and beauty and uncover new dimensions in these realms. How can anyone dedicated to the values of science and art consistently oppose a policy which maximizes the possibility of the discovery and widest dispersion of scientific truths and artistic meanings?

5. Regard for the potentialities of all individuals makes for less cruelty of man toward man, especially where cruelty is the result of blindness to, or ignorance of, the needs of others. A community organized along democratic lines is guilty of cruelty only at those points where it has failed to live up to its own ideals. A totalitarian community is systematically insensitive to the personal needs not only of members of the outlawed scapegoat group but also of the majority of its subjects who are excluded from policy-making discussions. At best, there is no way of determining these personal needs except by the interpretation of the dictator and his experts who act on the fateful dogma that they know the true interests of their subjects better than the subjects themselves. At worst, the dictator assumes not only that he speaks for his subjects but that in some mystic way he feels and thinks for them too. Despite the great limitations—limitations from the point of view of their own ideals—under which the nineteenth- and twentieth-century democracies of the Western world suffered, I think it is indisputable, on the evidence, that by and large their social life, in so far as this was the consequence of policy, displayed less cruelty than the social life of any other historical period.

6. Reasonableness of conclusions, where attitudes and interests conflict, depends upon the degree of mutual consultation and free intellectual communication between the principals involved. The democratic way of life makes possible the widest forms of mutual consultation and communication. Conclusions reached by these processes have a quality that can never be found where conclusions are imposed by force or authority—even if they are our own. Let me illustrate what I mean by taking as an example an enterprise represented by a community of scholars, let us say the American Philosophical Association. Who among us, desirous as we may be of the possibility of philosophical agreement, would forego the methods of public discussion, criticism, argument, and rejoinder for a philosophical consensus imposed by a Gestapo or a G.P.U., even if by a strange quirk of affairs it was *our* philosophic position that the goon squads of orthodoxy sought to make the way of salvation? Who among us, knowing that outside the threshold of our meetings there stood an individual of foreign country, color, or faith, capable of making

a contribution to our deliberations, would not open the door to him? These are not rhetorical questions framed to discover philosophical fifth columnists. They are designed to show that the procedures of critical discussion and discovery, which are pre-eminently exhibited in the work of a scientific community, take for granted that national, racial, or religious origins are irrelevant to the logic of the method by which reasonable conclusions are reached. Democracy as a way of life differs from its alternatives in that it makes possible the extension of this method of reaching reasonable conclusions from the fields of professional science and philosophy to all areas of human experience in which genuine problems arise.

There are other grounds that may be offered in justification of democracy as the most adequate social philosophy for our times. Every one of them, like the foregoing, postulates implicitly or explicitly values or desiderata. But I repeat: these postulates are ultimate only for the problem in hand. They may require justification. When we undertake such justification, we have undertaken a new inquiry into a new problem. Much is assumed on the basis of previously tested evidence: nothing is logically begged.

There are two important consequences of approaching democracy in this way. The first is that we avoid the temptation, which is rapidly gaining vogue, of making democracy absolutely valid in and for itself. There are many today who write as if they believe that democracy should prevail even though the heavens fall and say in so many words that "to question the validity of democracy is to disbelieve in it" and that we can meet the blind fanatical faith of fascism only with a faith in democracy which is at least just as fanatical. This temptation, it seems to me, must be avoided, because, by counterposing subrational dogma to subrational dogma, we prepare the ground for an acceptance of a "might makes right" morality. Secondly, those who make of democracy an absolute value, which requires no justification but its inherent rightness, tend to identify this absolute democracy with whatever particular democratic *status quo* exists. On the other hand, the natural tendency of those who cannot distinguish between social philosophies on the ground of their inherent rightness is to test a social philosophy by the social institutions in which it is embodied. They are, therefore, more attentive to the actual workings and effects of democracy, more historical minded, and less likely to gloss over existing imperfections.

To those who say that human beings will not fight wholeheartedly except for certainties, and emphatically not for a hypothesis which is only probable, the reply must be made that this empirical proposition is highly dubious. Men have fought and do fight vigorously for causes on the basis of preponderant evidence. Vigorous action, indeed, is only desirable in troubled situations when we have first decided what *is* intelligent action. And intelligent action does not result when we assume that our ideas or ideals simply cannot be wrong. That both intelligence and resoluteness are compatible is clear in fields as far apart as military science and medicine. Once it is decided that the chances of one military action are relatively better than another or once it is decided that an operation gives a patient a better chance of surviving than no operation, wisdom demands that the best warranted alternative be pursued with all our heart and all our soul. Let us remember that when we are called upon to fight for democracy we are not asked to fight for an ideal which has just been proposed as a *merely possible* valid ideal for our times; we already have considerable evidence in its behalf, the weight of which, unfortunately too often, is properly evaluated by some critics only when democracy is lost or imperiled.

(54)

Morris Raphael Cohen

1880-1947

Born in Minsk, Russia, Morris Cohen came to the United States at the age of twelve. After receiving his B.S. degree from the City College of New York in 1900 and his Ph.D. from Harvard University in 1906, he returned to City College until his retirement in 1938. At City College he helped to shape the thinking of several generations of students, many of whom subsequently achieved prominence in their own right. Cohen gained a reputation as one of America's most prominent philosophers, and received many professional honors, including election as president of the American Philosophical Association in 1929.

The embodiment of the spirit of intelligent and critical dissent, Cohen was never associated with any party or cult. Although his writings touched on many other subjects, legal philosophy was his specialty. In fact, Cohen spent most of his career in a search for an adequate philosophical basis for justice, for, as he saw it, any commentator on the law as it existed also had the duty to formulate a philosophy of what the law ought to be. Consequently, Cohen attempted to apply pragmatism in such a way as to justify metaphysical speculation, and his legal philosophy sought a reconciliation of naturalism and idealism.

The following selection, taken from a collection of his essays entitled *The Faith of a Liberal* (New York, 1946), illustrates Cohen's conception of liberalism as a way of life.

To affirm a faith in liberalism may seem quixotic at a time when the word "liberalism" is commonly associated either with an outmoded individualistic theory of economics or with a political trend that shuns clear thinking and seems to offer a special haven to those mushy-minded persons who, rather than make a definite choice between Heaven and Hell, cheerfully hope to combine the best features of each. But liberalism and liberal civilization may be conceived more generously. For my part I prefer to think of the liberal temper as, above all, a faith in enlightenment, a faith in a process rather than in a set of doctrines, a faith instilled with pride in the achievements of the human mind, and yet colored with a deep humility before the vision of a world so much larger than our human hopes and thoughts. If there are those who have no use for the word "faith" they may fairly define liberalism as a rationalism that is rational enough to envisage the limitations of mere reasoning.

Liberalism is too often misconceived as a new set of dogmas taught by a newer and better set of priests called "liberals." Liberalism is an attitude rather than a set of dogmas—an attitude that insists upon questioning all plausible and self-evident propositions, seeking not to reject them but to find out what evidence there is to support them rather than their possible alternatives. This open eye for possible alternatives which need to be scrutinized before we can determine which is the best grounded is profoundly disconcerting to all conservatives and to almost all revolutionaries. Conservatism clings to what has been established, fearing that, once we begin to question the beliefs that we have inherited, all the values of life will be destroyed. The revolutionary, impressed with the evil of the existing order or disorder, is prone to put his faith in some mighty-sounding principle without regard for the complications, compromises, dangers, and hardships that will be involved in the adjustment of this principle to other worthy principles. Revolutionaries and reactionaries alike are irritated and perhaps inwardly humiliated by the humane temper of liberalism, which reveals by contrast the common inhumanity of both violent parties to the social struggle. Liberalism, on the other hand, regards life as an adventure in which we must take risks in new situations, in which there is no guarantee that the new will always be the good or the true, in which progress is a precarious achievement rather than an inevitability. . . .

Liberalism has been viewed historically as that philosophy which regards the exercise of human energy as in itself a good, which becomes evil only when it becomes self-defeating. It is opposed to the view that regards the natural desires of the flesh as inherently evil and justified only under certain restricted and properly sanctioned conditions. Liberalism is thus a reaction against all views which favor repression or which regard the denial of natural desires as in itself a good.

Liberalism so conceived is concerned with the liberation of the mind from the restraints of authoritarianism and fanaticism. As opposed to the policies of fear and suppression, based on the principle that nature is sin and intellect the devil, the aim of liberalism is to liberate the energies of human nature by the free and fearless use of reason. Liberalism disregards rules and dogmas that hinder the freedom of scientific inquiry and the questioning of all accepted truths. Prophets, priestly hierarchies, sacred books and sanctified traditions must submit their claims to the court of human reason and experience. In this way mankind wins freedom from superstitious fears, such as that of magic or witchcraft, and from arbitrary and cruel restraints on human happiness. Liberalism in general thus means the opening up of opportunities in all fields of human endeavor, together with an emphasis on the value of deliberative rather than arbitrary forces in the governance of practical affairs. . . .

We are now entering into the world arena, and the question is no longer that of the special type of liberal civilization which once existed in the United States, but whether any type of liberal civilization can exist in our America. Liberal civilization has existed in many forms in many nations. What is its essence? Here again it is safer to indicate realities and let the result coin its own definition.

Liberal civilization came to the fore in Europe in the middle of the eighteenth century. It was a movement which banished the Inquisition, abolished the despotic power of kings, and broke up the system of censorship and of political and economic privilege in relation to taxation, trade, and obedience to oppressive laws. It was necessary to wage a long fight before monopoly privileges were taken away from the old aristocracy. The movement to extend education to everybody came to full force only in the nineteenth century. It was the nineteenth century that saw the removal of limitations on the suffrage as well as those on holding public office: property qualifications, religious affiliations, and the like. The liberal movement was directed to the wiping out of such restraints. The emancipation of women and their final admission to the privilege of the suffrage has occurred within our own day.

If a formula is necessary for all this, I would suggest that liberalism means a pride in human achievement, a faith in human effort, a conviction that the proper function of government is to remove the restraints upon human activity. The philosophy back of that is summed up in two great faiths or beliefs: the belief in progress, and the belief in toleration. I think those are the two fundamental ideas of liberalism.

The idea of progress can hardly be understood unless we have in mind the ideas against which the idea of progress was a reaction. The people who were in favor of progress had some definite objective. They were opposed to the old attitude which we associate with Calvinism, but which existed even in large sections of the Catholic Church, as well as in non-Christian groups. This was the view that human nature is profoundly and radically sinful and corrupt. Therefore human beings cannot be trusted to fulfill their natural inclination. Nature is sin. To indulge our natural impulses is sinful. That is an idea which is easily recognized; it has not yet died.

As a consequence of the idea that the human flesh is corrupt and our nature sinful, there was the necessity of relying upon authorities and magistrates, rules and blue laws. The excessive regulation of life by governments, such as we had in some of the Puritan colonies, was a natural consequence of that belief.

The belief in progress was a reaction against such a point of view. The believers in progress said: "No, human flesh is not originally corrupt. To be sure, man commits sins and crimes. You cannot deny that. But that is due to the bad institutions under which we live. If you could only wipe out the evil institutions under which man has lived, human nature would assert itself." This is the idea that underlies almost all of Shelley's writings—an idea that he got from God-win.

There is something very beautiful and noble about that idea. There are, to my knowledge, few parallels in human history to the nobility of Condorcet in the shadow of the guillotine. He was hiding in a garret in Paris; his life was hanging on a thread; and yet he was writing a marvelously enthusiastic sketch of the progress of the human race, anticipating for the human race an indefinite advance towards perfection.

The only fit parallel that I can find to the nobility of that act is Socrates discussing the immortality of the soul, just before drinking the hemlock, or Jesus saying, "Father, forgive them, for they know not what they do," during the crucifixion.

The idea of progress took root as a creed of hope and a fighting faith. In the course of time, however, progress came to be a shibboleth for a fatalistic optimism or meliorism. The notion that man inevitably progresses through the centuries came to claim the support of science under the name of evolution. But there is no evidence in science or history for the assumption that human nature is bound to become perfect as it develops in time.

There is no proof that human history is a simple straight line upward and onward, and there can be no such proof. For one thing, there are no clear meanings that can be assigned to the terms "upward" and "onward." Upward, of course, was a very definite idea under the old Ptolemaic astronomy. But under modern conditions one has to define "upward" with regard to standards. Unfortunately, people who talk glibly about progress and evolution generally have no very definite conception of any final goal or standard, or even of any definite direction. . . .

Belief in gradual and inevitable progress becomes more and more difficult to maintain, in the face of the carnage and destruction of two world wars and the failure of two victories to achieve the high objectives upon which so many wartime hopes were pinned. The kind of liberalism that was associated with this faith in progress through piecemeal cumulative reform has little appeal today and may well have less tomorrow. But is the liberal attitude necessarily dependent upon confidence in the inevitable success of our efforts? Many stout champions of the liberal cause have been frank to admit their inability to predict the future. Why can we not risk our lives in struggles of uncertain outcome? I am inclined to think that the faith in progress which is essential to the liberal attitude is not a faith in the inevitability of progress but rather a faith in its possibility.

That faith requires us to admit that we do not already possess the absolute truth. Such an admission runs counter to the religious, political, or economic convictions of many men and women. But it may be that the same catastrophes and failures which are destroying the faith in inevitable and gradual progress may also undermine the absolutisms that block the development of a liberalism fitted to the problems of our American future. . . .

Liberalism can move forward, like science, because it embraces self-correcting principles which permit the correction of error and partial truth without an overthrow of the system that makes such correction possible. Like science, liberalism is based on the faith that other human beings can carry forward, by rational methods, the gains that we have won in human understanding. The faith of the liberal, as of the scientist, grows out of a deep humility which recognizes the limitations of mortal finitude and acknowledges the impossibility of any individual's attaining correct answers to all the problems that he faces. But this humility is combined with a hope that, through rational communication and collaboration among individuals, a living body of common thought may be created which will more adequately answer the problems of an age or society than can any individual, whether he be a scientist or a dictator. In the long run, liberal democracy may outlast any form of dictatorship because the strength of a liberal democracy is not bounded by the prowess of any one man or party. The strength of liberalism lies in the fact that it enables each of us to rise above the limitations of our hereditary class prejudices and to contribute toward a body of *ideas and aspirations in action* that may incorporate more understanding than is vouchsafed to any single mortal. In the end, there is no way in which people can live together decently unless each individual or group realizes that the whole of truth and virtue is not exclusively in its possession. This is a hard lesson to learn, but without it there can be no humane civilization.

Let us take the other great belief of liberalism: the belief in tolerance. This is very closely connected with scientific method. Unless one has a certain amount of skepticism in one's system, one cannot possibly believe in tolerance. What does tolerance mean? Tolerance means that we shall give our enemies a chance. If we are secure and we know that our enemies cannot hurt us, we may be willing to give them a chance. But suppose that we believe in a certain sacred truth—say the truth of the Messiah, or the truth of a certain economic order, or the truth of certain constitutional doctrines—and some scalawag preaches that these are not true. Shall we be tolerant to untruth? That seems to me to be the crux of the whole question of liberalism. The true liberal has a certain amount of skepticism. The true liberal, being impressed with scientific method, says: "Certainly we should, for, although I am convinced that what I believe to be the truth is the truth, the other man may have something to say which I haven't heard yet, or the other man may have a point of view which is worth investigating. On the whole, in the conflict of opinions, more truth will thus come out than if there is suppression."

This attitude involves a number of things which are generally not recognized. It involves not only a certain amount of skepticism in our own fundamental conviction, but a certain amount of detachment which very few people have. It is a rare gift to be able to be tolerant in that sense, because if we are pressed, if the enemy has the sword at our throats, we are not tempted to play fair and play according to the rules. We will do anything in our power to kill our assailant—or, at any rate, to get the sword away. And in general, people are not tolerant under stress, in periods of great passion, in periods of compulsion. Tolerance is a virtue that seems to thrive only in a certain leisure, in a certain cultivation. The people who show it best are the philosophers, because they thrive on diversity; or scientists, who also thrive upon the skepticism that is inherent in scientific methods. . . .

The hasty conclusion that liberalism is dead has been given currency by the passionate and uncompromisingly ruthless war spirit, common to Communists and Fascists. But I do not believe that liberalism is dead, or that it has outlived its day. There still seems to me enough human reason left to which to appeal against reckless fanaticism.

Fanaticism is prone to belittle the gains that have come to mankind from the spirit of free inquiry, free discussion, and rational accommodation. So long as human beings lack omniscience, society can only suffer serious loss when one group suppresses the opinions and criticisms of all others. Liberalism, conceived as the spirit of free inquiry, free discussion, and rational accommodation, can continue to appeal to the conscience of men as long as the world offers visible proofs of the blindness of all illiberal power philosophies.

Liberalism, so conceived, may take forms very different from those with which the word has been traditionally associated in the popular mind. Traditionally, liberalism has been conceived as a form of individualism. Liberalism in economics has been associated with opposition to collective controls over production and distribution. In politics liberalism has been historically associated with the supremacy of individual rights. Neither of these beliefs has a very bright future. . . .

My own belief is that increased governmental participation in our economic life is desirable and necessary if we are to avoid the greater evils of economic anarchy and corporate despotism. And such an approach to the problem of economic controls can be made entirely within the framework of liberalism. I do not challenge the right of those who oppose this tendency to invoke the name of liberalism. Liberals may disagree with each other on all kinds of vital issues. But if liberal individualists and liberal collectivists disagree with each other they do not need to resort to guns to settle their differences. Like scientists they can argue and exchange evidence and arrange crucial experiments; and, though these methods cannot be relied upon to produce immediate unanimity on all issues, they do, in the long run, bring substantial agreement on most issues which have been examined in a scientific spirit over a considerable period. And the problems that have been thus solved, whether in the field of mathematics or in the field of penology, are more likely to stay solved than those settled by guns. . . .

There remains the inevitable question: Is it worth while to try to perpetuate liberal civilization? Perhaps most people, if pressed to state their real attitude, would say it is not. For liberal civilization, after all, is based upon (or can be expressed in) the Greek motto: "What is important is not life, but the good life." Many of our current opinions seem to me to be contrary to that. They seem to assume that life as such is more important than the good life. That seems to me the real issue, and one of the most fundamental issues we can face. The reasons that lead the Catholic Church to condemn birth-control; the reasons that make so many lovely, sentimental people condemn the death penality for criminals—all these reasons seem to me to go upon the assumption that life as such is sacred, and the human beings must not lay their hands upon the gates of life and death. If you really believe that, then the question of liberalism is a minor matter. The important thing is: "Keep your hands off from the gates of life and death."

The real liberal takes a very different attitude. He believes that life is important only as the condition or opportunity for the good life, and prefers not to live at all if he must live as a slave or in degradation.

History has no end, and I do not pretend to be able to predict the future. But I do think it worth while to reiterate my general disbelief in the doctrine that history is just one continuous line of progress onward and upward; or even in the more ancient view of Aristotle, the Hindus, Vico, and Nietzsche, that history is a series of repeatable cycles. I accept neither of these views because I do not believe history is as simple as that. In fact, I do not believe that if we take the whole complex of history we can form any adequate symbol for it. What we can do is to consider certain phases of it.

Suppose we stood outside of the earth and actually saw its motion. It would appear even more irregular than that of the other planets. We obtain some clarity by decomposing the concrete reality into elements. So it is, I think, with regard to history. We have to decompose the various elements which enter into history, and trace each one of them separately. When we do that it seems to me that we have to fall back upon a general view which may be called the polarity of nature, i.e., the two-sidedness of things. In the physical realm there is always action and reaction. There is no one force acting, but always many forces acting in opposite directions. So, in life, there is growth and decay. In human history there are ups and downs. There are periods of flowering and periods of decay. There is no use, it seems to me, in thinking that any one movement of history, or of human life, will continue forever.

So I come back to the notion of Goethe—that if you could say to one moment, "O stay, thou art so fair," that would be the end.

(55)

Arthur M. Schlesinger, Jr.

1917-

Born in Columbus, Ohio, the son of a distinguished American historian, Arthur Schlesinger, Jr., graduated from Harvard in 1938. The following year his honors thesis was published under the title *Orestes*

A. Brownson: A Pilgrim's Progress. While a Junior Fellow at Harvard, he wrote *The Age of Jackson* (1945), for which he received a Pulitzer Prize. To date he has also published three volumes of a multi-volume work on the New Deal entitled *The Age of Roosevelt.*

Approaching the study of history from a liberal framework, Schlesinger has seen American history as alternating between periods of liberal reform and conservative consolidation, with social conflict the generating force behind this cycle. Not only has he championed the forces of liberal reform in his historical studies, but he has taken an active role in political affairs. He served first as an advisor to Adlai E. Stevenson during the presidential campaigns of 1952 and 1956, and then became a member of John F. Kennedy's administration as a special assistant to the President.

Schlesinger has been deeply concerned with preserving liberal democratic values against their many detractors. He is thoroughly familiar with the criticisms levied against American liberalism from the progressive era through the New Deal. Consequently, Schlesinger has worked to revive liberal theory in order to make it a functional philosophy that recognizes the darker side of man's nature, and yet preserves the idea of man as the master of his own destiny who is able, within certain limits, to direct the course of society and to promote the well-being of members of that society. To develop a more realistic ideology, he has attempted to synthesize the theory of original sin as expounded by Reinhold Niebuhr with the older democratic liberalism, thus providing a philosophy relevant to the challenges of contemporary life.

The following selection is from Schlesinger's *The Vital Center: The Politics of Freedom* (Boston, 1949).

Western man in the middle of the twentieth century is tense, uncertain, adrift. We look upon our epoch as a time of troubles, an age of anxiety. The grounds of our civilization, of our certitude, are breaking up under our feet, and familiar ideas and institutions vanish as we reach for them, like shadows in the falling dusk. Most of the world has reconciled itself to this half-light, to the reign of insecurity. Even those peoples who hastily traded their insecurities for a mirage of security are finding themselves no better off than the rest. Only the United States still has buffers between itself and the anxieties of our age: buffers of time, of distance, of natural wealth, of national ingenuity, of a stubborn tradition of hope.

A nation which has made a religion of success ought to find it hard to acclimate itself to the middle of the twentieth century. For frustration is increasingly the hallmark of this century—the frustration of triumphant science and rampant technology, the frustration of the most generous hopes and of the the most splendid dreams. Nineteen hundred looked forward to the irresistible expansion of freedom, democracracy and abundance; 1950 will look back to totalitarianism, to concentration camps, to mass starvation, to atomic war. Yet for the United States the world tragedy still has the flickering unreality of a motion picture. It grips us as we see it; but, lingering over the familiar milk-shake in the bright drugstore, we forget the nightmare in the resurgence of warmth and comfort. Anxiety is something we hear about. It is not yet part of our lives—not of enough of our lives, anyway, to inform our national decisions. . . .

Since progressives, on the whole, create our contemporary climate of opinion, the impression exists that the present perils to free society result exclusively from the failure of the conservatives. In a sense, this is true—in the sense that the conservatives have had the power, notably in the period between the wars, and have failed to use it intelligently. Yet one reason for their failure, as D. W. Brogan has reminded us, is the failure of their critics, whose hearts were in the right place, but whose heads were too often "muddled, full of sentiment, empty of knowledge, living on slogans and clichés, unwilling to realize how complicated is the modern world and that the price of liberty is eternal intellectual vigilance." Compared with the conservatives, the progressives were indeed innocent; but is innocence enough?

During the years of plutocratic stagnation, why did not progressivism have strong faith and lucid purposes? And, in the cases where progressives were sure of their diagnosis and of their remedy, why has that certitude now vanished? Let us concede at once the relative superiority in practice of left-wing governments—at least of the pragmatic left, though not of the doctrinaire left. The New Deal government of Franklin D. Roosevelt, for all its confusions and defects, kept its eye more steadily on the ball than any other government of our time, conservative, socialist, Communist or fascist. Yet history has discredited the hopes and predictions of doctrinaire progressivism about as thoroughly as it has those of conservatism. The progressive "analysis" is today a series of dry and broken platitudes, tossed out in ash-heaps (where they are collected and dusted off by the editors of the liberal weeklies).

What is the progressive? The defining characteristic of the progressive, as I shall use the word, is the sentimentality of his approach to politics and culture. He must be distinguished, on the one hand, from the Communist; for the progressive is soft, not hard; he believes himself genuinely concerned with the welfare of individuals. He must be distinguished, on the other, from the radical democrat; for the progressive, by refusing to make room in his philosophy for the discipline of responsibility or for the danger of power, has cut himself off from the usable traditions of American radical democracy. He has rejected the pragmatic tradition of the men who, from the Jacksonians to the New Dealers, learned the facts of life through the exercise of power under conditions of accountability. He has rejected the pessimistic tradition of those who, from Hawthorne to Reinhold Niebuhr, warned that power, unless checked by accountability, would corrupt its possessor.

The type of the progressive today is the fellow traveler or the fellow traveler of the fellow traveler: see the Wallace movement or (until fairly recently) the columns of the *New Republic* and the *Nation*. His sentimentality has softened up the progressive for Communist permeation and conquest. For the most chivalrous reasons, he cannot believe that ugly facts underlie fair words. However he looks at it, for example, the USSR keeps coming through as a kind of enlarged Brook Farm community, complete with folk dancing in native costumes, joyous work in the fields and progressive kindergartens. Nothing in his system has prepared him for Stalin.

This is not a new breed in American history. A century ago, after Jacksonian democracy had split over the slavery question, one wing of northern Jacksonians under Martin Van Buren went into the Free Soil Party. The other wing refused to turn against the South. Many of this pro-southern group retained a Jacksonian desire for social reform; they certainly held no brief for slavery; yet as men implicated in the industrial evils of the north, who were they, they would cry, to pronounce judgment on the social system of the South? "The only difference between the negro slave of the South, and the white wages slave of the North," as one member of this group put it, "is, that the one has a master without asking for him, and the other has to beg for the privilege of becoming a slave. . . . The one is the slave of an individual; the other is the slave of an inexorable class."

The members of this group were known as Doughfaces—that is, "northern men with southern principles." The infiltration of contemporary progressivism by Communism had led to the same self-flagellation, the same refusal to take precautions against tyranny. It has created a new Doughface movement—a movement of "democratic men with totalitarian principles."

The core of Doughface progressivism is its sentimental belief in progress. The belief in progress was the product of the Enlightenment, cross-fertilized with allied growths, such as science, bourgeois complacency, Unitarianism and a faith in the goodness of man. It dispensed with the Christian myths of sin and atonement. Man's shortcomings, such as they were, were to be redeemed, not by Jesus on the cross, but by the benevolent unfolding of history. Tolerance, free inquiry and technology, operating in the framework of human perfectibility, would in the end create a heaven on earth, a goal much more wholesome than a heaven in heaven. . . .

Optimism gave the progressives a soft and shallow conception of human nature. With the aggressive and sinister impulses eliminated from the equation, the problem of social change assumed too simple a form. The corruptions of power—the desire to exercise it, the desire to increase it, the desire for prostration before it—had no place in the progressive calculations. As a result, progressivism became politically inadequate: it could neither persuade nor control the emotions of man. And it became intellectually inadequate: it could not anticipate nor explain the tragic movements of history in the twentieth century. Ideologies which exploited the darker passions captured men by appeals unknown to the armory of progressivism. . . .

Conservatism in its crisis of despair turns to fascism: so progressivism in its crisis of despair turns to Communism. Each in a sober mood has a great contribution to make to free society: the conservative in his emphasis on law and liberty, the progressive in his emphasis on mass welfare. But neither is capable of saving free society. Both, faced by problems they cannot understand and fear to meet, tend to compound their own failure by delivering free society to its totalitarian foe. To avoid this fate, we must understand as clearly as possible the reasons for the appeal of totalitarianism. . . .

As organization towers higher and higher above him, man grows in forlornness, impotence and fear. As monopoly or state capitalism enlarges its power, the outlets in economic enterprise dwindle. Man longs to escape the pressures beating down on his frail individuality; and, more and more, the surest means of escape seems to be to surrender that individuality to some massive, external authority. Dostoievsky remarks, "Man is tormented by no greater anxiety than to find some one quickly to whom he can hand over that gift of freedom with which the ill-fated creature is born." The psychological stigmata of the fugitives from freedom, Erich Fromm finds in his remarkable analysis, are the strivings for submission and for domination, the losing of self in masochism or sadism.

The totalitarian state, which has risen in specific response to this fear of freedom, is an invention of the twentieth century. It differs essentially from old-style dictatorship, which may be bloodly and tyrannical but yet leaves intact most of the structure of society. Totalitarianism, on the contrary, pulverizes the social structure, grinding all independent groups and diverse loyalties into a single amorphous mass. The sway of the totalitarian state is unlimited. This very fact is a source of its profound psychological appeal. On an economic level, it seeks to supply the answer to the incoherence and apparent uncontrollability of industrial society. On the political and psychological level, it holds out hope of allaying the gnawing anxieties; it offers institutional outlets for the impulses of sadism and masochism. As a system of social organization, it purports to invest life with meaning and purpose. Against the loneliness and rootlessness of man in free society, it promises the security and comradeship of a crusading unity, propelled by a deep and driving faith. . . .

The independent left everywhere in the world has been in a state of moral paralysis at least since 1917. The commanding personality of Lenin and the unanswerable fact of the Russian Revolution gave Western radicalism a fatal complex of inferiority. Under the spell of that complex, the left committed itself to the long and corrupting enterprise of accepting in the Soviet Union crimes much worse than those it attacked in its own countries. Just as the left gained moral strength when it protested against Amritsar or the judicial murder of Sacco and Vanzetti, so it lost moral strength when it kept its silence before the anonymous victims of the Soviet despotism. . . .

If the distinguishing moral commitment of the new radicalism is its faith in freedom and the unconditional rejection of totalitarianism, the distinguishing political commitment is its belief in the limited state. The Soviet experience has caused a revaluation of the politics of Marxism—a revaluation which questions in particular the total concentration of all political and economic power in the apparatus of the single-party state. For the Soviet experience has proved, if it has proved anything, that concentration of power creates classes whatever the system of ownership—classes under Communism as well as under capitalism. Who whom? remains the crucial question; and in every system, as history has finally taught us, the tendency of the ruling class toward oppression can be checked only by the capacity of the other classes for resistance.

And resistance requires essentially an independent base from which to operate. It requires privacy, funds, time, newsprint, gasoline, freedom of speech, freedom of assembly, freedom from fear; it requires resources to which its own access is secure and which remain relatively inaccessible to the ruling class. Resistance is possible, in short, only when the base is clearly separate from the state. Under a system of total state ownership, the sinews of resistance are doled out to the opposition only by the charity of the ruling class. . . .

The failure of nerve is over. The new radicalism need not invoke Marx at every turn in the road, or point its prayer-rug every morning to Moscow. It has new confidence in its own insights and its own values. It has returned in great part to the historic philosophy of liberalism—to a belief in the integrity of the individual, in the limited state, in due process of law, in empiricism and gradualism. Man in its estimate is precious but not perfect. He is intoxicated by power and hence most humane in a society which distributes power widely; he is intimidated by industrialism and thus most secure in a society which will protect him from want and starvation. We conclude with Pascal: "Man is neither angel nor brute, and the unfortunate thing is that he who would act the angel acts the brute."

As the old order crumbles through the world, we know that any path which can preserve peace and freedom is narrow and hazardous. Our instruments must be as precise as possible, our analysis as dispassionate, our conclusions as honest and objective as we can make them. One false step may plunge the world into atomic war or deliver it into totalitarian darkness. The new radicalism seeks to fight for honesty and clarity in a turbulent and stricken society, to restore a serious sense of the value of facts, of the integrity of reason, of devotion to truth. Its final success will depend upon its immediate success in shaping the policy of the only one of the two great powers accessible to it: the United States. . . .

Today, finally and tardily, the skeptical insights are in process of restoration to the liberal mind. The psychology of Freud has renewed the intellectual's belief in the dark, slumbering forces of the will. The theology of Barth and Niebuhr has given new power to the old and chastening truths of Christianity. More than anything else, the rise of Hitler and Stalin has revealed in terms no one can deny the awful reality of the human impulses toward aggrandizement and destruction—impulses for which the liberal intellectual had left no room in his philosophy. The conceptions of the intellectual are at last beginning to catch up with the instincts of the democratic politician.

When the challenge of Communism finally forced American liberals to take inventory of their moral resources, the inventory resulted in the clear decision that freedom had values which could not be compromised in deals with totalitarianism. Thus America found itself reaching much the same conclusion as the non-Communist left of Europe. In the years after the Second War Americans began to rediscover the great tradition of liberalism—the tradition of Jackson and Hawthorne, the tradition of a reasonable responsibility about politics and a moderate pessimism about man. . . .

The people as a whole are not perfect; but no special group of the people is more perfect: that is the moral and rationale of democracy. Consistent pessimism about man, far from promoting authoritarianism, alone can inoculate the democratic faith against it. "Man's capacity for justice makes democracy possible," Niebuhr has written in his remarkable book on democratic theory; "but man's inclination to injustice makes democracy necessary."

The image of democratic man emerges from the experience of democracy; man is a creature capable of reason and of purpose, of great loyalty and of great virtue, yet also he is vulnerable to material power and to spiritual pride. In our democratic tradition, the excessive self-love which transforms power into tyranny is the greatest of all dangers. But the self-love which transforms radicalism from an instrument of action into an expression of neurosis is almost as great a danger. If irresponsible power is the source of evil, and irresponsible impotence, the source of decadence, then responsible power—power held for limited terms under conditions of strict accountability—is the source of wisdom. . . .

The fight on the part of the "humble members of society" against business domination has been the consistent motive of American liberalism. Far from importing subversive European ideas when he renewed this theme, Franklin Roosevelt was only returning to the political doctrine of the hallowed past. Nor is there anything specifically Marxist about class conflict. "As far as I am concerned," Marx himself wrote, "the honour does not belong to me for having discovered the existence either of classes in modern society or of the struggle between the classes. Bourgeois historians a long time before me expounded the historical development of this class struggle." "To limit Marxism to the teaching of the class struggle," added Lenin, "means to curtail Marxism—to distort it, to reduce it to something which is acceptable to the bourgeoisie. A Marxist is one who *extends* the acceptance of the class struggle to the acceptance of the *dictatorship of the proletariat*." It is precisely this extension which American radicalism has refused to make.

The problem of classes is this: Class conflict is essential if freedom is to be preserved, because it is the only barrier against class domination; yet class conflict, pursued to excess, may well destroy the underlying fabric of common principle which sustains free society.

I cannot imagine a free society which has eliminated class conflict. So long as there is inequality in the distribution of property and variety in the nature of economic interests, so long will politics center on economic issues; and so long the insurgency of the discontented will provide the best guarantee against the tyranny of the possessors.

Yet this conflict must be kept within bounds, if freedom itself is to survive. The differences among classes in a capitalist democracy are often wide and bitter; but they are much less impassable than the differences between capitalist democracy and authoritarianism; and sometimes in the heat of the battle the warring classes tend to forget their family relationship. It is perhaps fortunate for the continuity of the American development that the Civil War came along to heal the social wounds opened up in the age of Jackson; that one world war closed the rifts created by the New Freedom and another those of the New Deal. But external war is an expensive means of making antagonistic classes suddenly realize how much their agreement outweighs their differences. . . .

The lesson of the experiments with democratic socialism is plainly that the state should aim at establishing conditions for economic decisions, not at making all the decisions itself. It should create an economic environment favorable to private business policies which increase production; and then let the free market carry the ball as far as it can. Keynes, not Marx, is the prophet of the new radicalism.

The function of the state, in other words, is to define the ground rules of the game; not to pitch, catch, hit homers or (just as likely) pop up or throw to the wrong base. The state may acquire total economic power for the most benevolent of motives; but benevolence is no guarantee of wisdom. The danger of the total planner is, first, that his almost inevitable blunders may convulse the entire economy, and, second, that in a panic-stricken effort to cover up his blunders he may multiply his controls till they destroy the initiative and free movement of men and finally the free play of political criticism.

The state can do a great deal to set the level of economic activity by policies which at once will be stable enough to create an atmosphere favorable to private investment and adequate consumption and effective enough to prevent economic breakdown. Keynes and his followers have pointed out the great resources of fiscal and monetary policy. When a sag in spending or in demand threatens the economy, then the government through tax reduction and compensatory spending can maintain high levels of employment and production. Taxation and subsidies can be potent means of directing private investment to under-developed industries and regions; and a whole range of general incentives can be used to draw labor and capital into socially beneficial undertakings. . . .

Free society cannot survive unless it defeats the problems of economic stagnation and collapse. But economic success can only create the conditions for the survival of freedom; it can make no guarantees. The preservation of freedom requires a positive and continuing commitment. Specifically the maintenance of the United States as a free society confronts the American people with an immediate responsibility in two areas in particular: civil rights and civil liberties. . . .

World destiny has belatedly thrust upon the United States the necessity for having a real foreign policy—a policy, that is, which exists in terms of day-to-day operations, not in terms of Fourth of July oratory. Webster's reply to Hülsemann served too long as the model for American diplomacy: "The power of this republic at the present moment is . . . of an extent in comparison with which the possessions of the House of Hapsburg are but as a patch on the earth's surface." Americans today, both conservative and liberal, still tend to think of foreign policy in terms of such ringing defiances of European tyrants—foreign policy as a means of expressing sentiments, in other words, not of influencing events. . . .

A little American efficiency, accompanied by a policy of support for native progressive movements, would go far to counter the appeal of the Russian revolutionary spirit in the undeveloped areas. We have to accept the fact that we must apply this efficiency selectively in Asia. The reconstruction/containment formula stretches our resources in Europe alone, and we can hardly undertake a program of comparable scope for all the peoples of Asia and Africa. We must choose our spots—Japan, perhaps, the Philippines, Indonesia, India, Israel, Turkey—concentrate on exporting technology rather than commodities, and seek to make those nations the leaders of a progressive Asian civilization along democratic lines. A confused and mistaken policy has lost us the battle in China. But, if we learn from the Chinese failure, we may be able to help build a pro-democratic alternative to Communism in the other crucial areas of the Orient. We must pursue our Asian objectives with as much determination as we have pursued our objectives in Europe. Europe's mighty industrial capacity undoubtedly gives it top priority in the Soviet plan of expansion; but, in the long run, the loss of either Europe or Asia would be fatal to the democratic position.

The present design of our foreign policy, then, is to carry out the reconstruction/containment policy in Europe and to develop some more complex and limited equivalent in the underdeveloped lands. These policies cannot succeed, however, unless the United States itself does things we have not done in the past. First, we must stay out of a depression and thereby show the world that our strength is solid and stable. Second, we must revise our commercial expectations, reduce our tariffs and open our gates wide to foreign goods. Our efforts to increase production through the world will have little effect in ending the dollar gap unless we are willing to accept foreign goods in exchange for our own. Third, we must reform our own racial practices—not only repeal such insulting symbols as the Oriental exclusion laws, but demonstrate a deep and effective concern with the racial inequities within the United States. Fourth, we must not succumb to demands for an anti-Soviet crusade or a preventive war, nor permit reactionaries in the buffer states to precipitate conflicts in defense of their own obsolete prerogatives. . . .

Through this century, free society has been on the defensive, demoralized by the infection of anxiety, staggering under the body blows of fascism and Communism. Free society alienates the lonely and uprooted masses; while totalitarianism, building on their frustrations and cravings, provides a structure of belief, men to worship and men to hate and rites which guarantee salvation. The crisis of free society has assumed the form of international collisions between the democracies and the totalitarian powers; but this fact should not blind us to the fact that in its essence this crisis is internal.

Free society will survive, in the last resort, only if enough people believe in it deeply enough to die for it. However reluctant peace-loving people are to recognize that fact, history's warning is clear and cold; civilizations which cannot man their walls in times of alarm are doomed to destruction by the barbarians. We have deeply believed only when the issue of war has reduced our future to the stark problem of self-preservation. Franklin Roosevelt read the American people with his usual uncanny accuracy when he named the Second War, not the "war for freedom," but the "war for survival." Our democracy has still to generate a living emotional content, rich enough to overcome the anxieties incited by industrialism, deep enough to rally its members to battle for freedom—not just for self-preservation. Freedom must become, in Holmes's phrase, a "fighting faith."

Why does not democracy believe in itself with passion? Why is freedom not a fighting faith? In part because democracy, by its nature, dissipates rather than concentrates its internal moral force. The thrust of the democractic faith is away from fanaticism; it is toward compromise, persuasion and consent in politics, toward tolerance and diversity in society; its economic foundation lies in the easily frightened middle class. Its love of variety discourages dogmatism, and its love of skepticism discourages hero-worship. In place of theology and ritual, of hierarchy and demonology, it sets up a belief in intellectual freedom and unrestricted inquiry. The advocate of free society defines himself by telling what he is against: what he is for turns out to be certain *means* and he leaves other people to charge the means with content. Today democracy is paying the price for its systematic cultivation of the peaceful and rational virtues. "Many a man will live and die upon a dogma; no man will be a martyr for a conclusion."

Democracy, moreover, has not worn too well as a philosophy of life in an industrial age. It seemed more solid at the high noon of success than it does in the uncertainties of falling dusk. In its traditional form, it has presupposed emotional and psychological stability in the individual. It has assumed, much too confidently, that the gnawing problems of doubt and anxiety would be banished by the advance of science or cured by a rise in the standard of living. The spectacular reopening of these problems in our time finds the democratic faith lacking in the profounder emotional resources. Democracy has no defense-in-depth against the neuroses of industrialism. When philosophies of blood and violence arise to take up the slack between democracy's thin optimism and the bitter agonies of experience, democracy by comparison appears pale and feeble.

Yet it seems doubtful whether democracy could itself be transformed into a political religion, like totalitarianism, without losing its characteristic belief in individual dignity and freedom. Does this mean that democracy is destined to defeat, sooner or later, by one or another of the totalitarian sects?

The death pallor will indeed come over free society, unless it can recharge the deepest sources of its moral energy. And we cannot make democracy a fighting faith merely by exhortation nor by self-flagellation; and certainly not by renouncing the values which distinguish free society from totalitarianism. Yet we must somehow dissolve the anxieties which drive people in free society to become traitors to freedom. We must somehow give the lonely masses a sense of individual human function, we must restore community to the industrial order. . . .

The essential strength of democracy as against totalitarianism lies in its startling insight into the value of the individual. Yet, as we have seen, this insight can become abstract and sterile; arrogant forms of individualism sometimes discredit the basic faith in the value of the individual. It is only as far as that insight can achieve a full social dimension, so far as individualism derives freely from community, that democracy will be immune to the virus of totalitarianism. . . .

Democracy requires unremitting action on many fronts. It is, in other words, a process, not a conclusion. However painful the thought, it must be recognized that its commitments are unending. The belief in the millennium has dominated our social thinking too long. Our utopian prophets have always supposed that a day would come when all who had not worshiped the beast nor received his mark on their foreheads would reign for a thousand years. "And God shall wipe away all tears from their eyes; and there shall be no more death, neither sorrow, nor crying, neither shall there be any more pain: for the former things are passed away." . . .

So we are forced back on the reality of struggle. So long as society stays free, so long will it continue in its state of tension, breeding contradiction, breeding strife. But we betray ourselves if we accept contradiction and strife as the total meaning of conflict. For conflict is also the guarantee of freedom; it is the instrument of change; it is, above all, the source of discovery, the source of art, the source of love. The choice we face is not between progress with conflict and progress without conflict. The choice is between conflict and stagnation. You cannot expel conflict from society any more than you can from the human mind. When you attempt it, the psychic costs in schizophrenia or torpor are the same.

The totalitarians regard the toleration of conflict as our central weakness. So it may appear to be in an age of anxiety. But we know it to be basically our central strength. The new radicalism derives its power from an acceptance of conflict—an acceptance combined with a determination to create a social framework where conflict issues, not in excessive anxiety, but in creativity. The center is vital; the center must hold. The object of the new radicalism is to restore the center, to reunite individual and community in fruitful union. The spirit of the new radicalism is the spirit of the center—the spirit of human decency, opposing the extremes of tyranny. Yet, in a more fundamental sense does not the center itself represent one extreme? while, at the other, are grouped the forces of corruption—men transformed by pride and power into enemies of humanity.

The new radicalism, drawing strength from a realistic conception of man, dedicates itself to problems as they come, attacking them in terms which best advance the humane and libertarian values, which best secure the freedom and fulfillment of the individual. It believes in attack—and out of attack will come passionate intensity.

Can we win the fight? We must commit ourselves to it with all our vigor in all its dimensions: the struggle within the world against Communism and fascism; the struggle within our country against oppression and stagnation; the struggle within ourselves against pride and corruption: nor can engagement in one dimension exclude responsibility for another. Economic and political action can help restore the balance between individual and community and thereby reduce one great source of anxiety. But even the most favorable social arrangements cannot guarantee individual virtue; and we are far yet from having solved the social problem.

The commitment is complex and rigorous. When has it not been so? If democracy cannot produce the large resolute breed of men capable of the climactic effort, it will founder. Out of the effort, out of the struggle alone, can come the high courage and faith which will preserve freedom.

(56)

B. F. Skinner

1904-

Born in Susquehanna, Pennsylvania, B. F. Skinner received his bachelor's degree from Hamilton College in 1926 and a Ph.D. from Harvard five years later. Between 1933 and 1936 he held one of the prized appointments as a Junior Fellow at Harvard. After teaching at the Universities of Minnesota and Indiana, he returned in 1948 to Harvard as professor of psychology.

Widely known for his experiments in the control of behavior, Skinner has also dealt with the difficult problem of the relationship between democracy, science, and ethics. Holding steadfastly to the validity of the scientific approach in the study of the individual as well as of society, he has insisted that such knowledge could be used to evolve a community marked by peace and order, peopled by brave, healthy, intelligent, and happy individuals. In 1948, he published a utopian novel, *Walden Two,* in which he sketched out in detail his ideal, to be achieved through scientific control and manipulation of human beings.

Although skeptical of particular answers to the dilemmas posed by ethical questions, Skinner has remained loyal to the pragmatic tradition of John Dewey. He is a supporter of the view that the scientific method provides the only means for the discovery of truth, including ethical truth. In this sense he is within the democratic liberal tradition and a foe of those philosophers and theologians who would erect systems that deprive man of effective control of his own destiny.

The following selection is from Skinner's article "Freedom and the Control of Men" in *The American Scholar*, 25 (Winter, 1955–1956); this article was also reprinted in his book *Cumulative Record: Enlarged Edition* (New York, 1961).

The second half of the twentieth century may be remembered for its solution of a curious problem. Although Western democracy created the conditions responsible for the rise of modern science, it is now evident that it may never fully profit from that achievement. The so-called "democratic philosophy" of human behavior to which it also gave rise is increasingly in conflict with the application of the methods of science to human affairs. Unless the conflict is somehow resolved, the ultimate goals of democracy may be long deferred.

Just as biographers and critics look for external influences to account for the traits and achievements of the men they study, so science ultimately explains behavior in terms of "causes" or conditions which lie beyond the individual himself. As more and more causal relations are demonstrated, a practical corollary becomes difficult to resist: it should be possible to *produce* behavior according to plan simply by arranging the proper conditions. Now, among the specifications which might reasonably be submitted to a behavioral technology are these: Let men be happy, informed, skillful, well behaved and productive.

This immediate practical implication of a science of behavior has a familiar ring, for it recalls the doctrine of human perfectibility of eighteenth- and nineteenth-century humanism. A science of man shares the optimism of that philosophy and supplies striking support for the working faith that men can build a better world and, through it, better men. The support comes just in time, for there has been little optimism of late among those who speak from the traditional point of view. Democracy has become "realistic," and it is only with some embarrassment that one admits today to perfectionistic or utopian thinking.

The earlier temper is worth considering, however. History records many foolish and unworkable schemes for human betterment, but almost all the great changes in our culture which we now regard as worthwhile can be traced to perfectionistic philosophies. Governmental, religious, educational, economic and social reforms follow a common pattern. Someone believes that a change in a cultural practice—for example, in the rules of evidence in a court of law, in the characterization of man's relation to God, in the way children are taught to read and write, in permitted rates of interest, or in minimal housing standards—will improve the condition of men: by promoting justice, permitting men to seek salvation more effectively, increasing the literacy of a people, checking an inflationary trend, or improving public health and family relations, respectively. The underlying hypothesis is always the same: that a different physical or cultural environment will make a different and better man.

The scientific study of behavior not only justifies the general pattern of such proposals; it promises new and better hypotheses. The earliest cultural practices must have originated in sheer accidents. Those which strengthened the group survived with the group in a sort of natural selection. As soon as men began to propose and carry out changes in practice for the sake of possible consequences, the evolutionary process must have accelerated. The simple practice of making changes must have had survival value. A further acceleration is now to be expected. As laws of behavior are more precisely stated, the changes in the environment required to bring about a given effect may be more clearly specified. Conditions which have been neglected because their effects were slight or unlooked for may be shown to be relevant. New conditions may actually be created, as in the discovery and synthesis of drugs which affect behavior.

This is no time, then, to abandon notions of progress, improvement or, indeed, human perfectibility. The simple fact is that man is able, and now as never before, to lift himself by his own boot straps. In achieving control of the world of which he is a part, he may learn at last to control himself. . . .

Designing a new cultural pattern is in many ways like designing an experiment. In drawing up a new constitution, outlining a new educational program, modifying a religious doctrine, or setting up a new fiscal policy, many statements must be quite tentative. We cannot be sure that the practices we specify will have the consequences we predict, or that the consequences will reward our efforts. This is in the nature of such proposals. They are not value judgments—they are guesses. To confuse and delay the improvement of cultural practices by quibbling about the word *improve* is itself not a useful practice. Let us agree, to start with, that health is better than illness, wisdom better than ignorance, love better than hate, and productive energy better than neurotic sloth. . . .

With a world of their own making almost within reach, men of good will have been seized with distaste for their achievement. They have uneasily rejected opportunities to apply the techniques and findings of science in the service of men, and as the import of effective cultural design has come to be understood, many of them have voiced an outright refusal to have any part in it. Science has been challenged before when it has encroached upon institutions already engaged in the control of human behavior; but what are we to make of benevolent men, with no special interests of their own to defend, who nevertheless turn against the very means of reaching long-dreamed-of goals?

What is being rejected, of course, is the scientific conception of man and his place in nature. So long as the findings and methods of science are applied to human affairs only in a sort of remedial patchwork, we may continue to hold any view of human nature we like. But as the use of science increases, we are forced to accept the theoretical structure with which science represents its facts. The difficulty is that this structure is clearly at odds with the traditional democratic conception of man. Every discovery of an event which has a part in shaping a man's behavior seems to leave so much the less to be credited to the man himself; and as such explanations become more and more comprehensive, the contribution which may be claimed by the individual himself appear to approach zero. Man's vaunted creative powers, his original accomplishments in art, science and morals, his capacity to choose and our right to hold him responsible for the consequences of his choice—none of these is conspicuous in this new self-portrait. Man, we once believed, was free to express himself in art, music and literature, to inquire into nature, to seek salvation in his own way. He could initiate action and make spontaneous and capricious changes of course. Under the most extreme duress some sort of choice remained to him. He could resist any effort to control him, though it might cost him his life. But science insists that action is initiated by forces impinging upon the individual, and that caprice is only another name for behavior for which we have not yet found a cause.

In attempting to reconcile these views it is important to note that the traditional democratic conception was not designed as a description in the scientific sense but as a philosophy to be used in setting up and maintaining a governmental process. It arose under historical circumstances and served political purposes apart from which it cannot be properly understood. In rallying men against tyranny it was necessary that the individual be strengthened, that he be taught that he had rights and could govern himself. To give the common man a new conception of his worth, his dignity, and his power to save himself, both here and hereafter, was often the only resource of the revolutionist. When democratic principles were put into practice, the same doctrines were used as a working formula. This is exemplified by the notion of personal responsibility in Anglo-American law. All governments make certain forms of punishment contingent upon certain kinds of acts. In democratic countries these contingencies are expressed by the notion of responsible choice. But the notion may have no meaning under governmental practices formulated in other ways and would certainly have no place in systems which did not use punishment.

The democratic philosophy of human nature is determined by certain political exigencies and techniques, not by the goals of democracy. But exigencies and techniques change; and a conception which is not supported for its accuracy as a likeness—is not, indeed, rooted in fact at all—may be expected to change too. No matter how effective we judge current democratic practices to be, how highly we value them or how long we expect them to survive, they are almost certainly not the *final* form of government. The philosophy of human nature which has been useful in implementing them is also almost certainly not the last word. The ultimate achievement of democracy may be long deferred unless we emphasize the real aims rather than the verbal devices of democratic thinking. A philosophy which has been appropriate to one set of political exigencies will defeat its purpose if, under other circumstances, it prevents us from applying to human affairs the science of man which probably nothing but democracy itself could have produced.

Perhaps the most crucial part of our democratic philosophy to be reconsidered is our attitude toward freedom—or its reciprocal, the control of human behavior. We do not oppose all forms of control because it is "human nature" to do so. The reaction is not characteristic of all men under all conditions of life. It is an attitude which has been carefully engineered, in large part by what we call the "literature" of democracy. With respect to some methods of control (for example, the threat of force), very little engineering is needed, for the techniques or their immediate consequences are objectionable. Society has suppressed these methods by branding them "wrong," "illegal" or "sinful." But to encourage these attitudes toward objectionable forms of control, it has been necessary to disguise the real nature of certain indispensable techniques, the commonest examples of which are education, moral discourse, and persuasion. The actual procedures appear harmless enough. They consist of supplying information, presenting opportunities for action, pointing out logical relationships, appealing to reason or "enlightened understanding," and so on. Through a masterful piece of misrepresentation, the illusion is fostered that these procedures do not involve the control of behavior; at most, they are simply ways of "getting someone to change his mind." But analysis not only reveals the presence of well-defined behavioral processes, it demonstrates a kind of control no less inexorable, though in some ways more acceptable, than the bully's threat of force. . . .

The methods of education, moral discourse, and persuasion are acceptable not because they recognize the freedom of the individual or his right to dissent, but because they make only *partial* contributions to the control of his behavior. The freedom they recognize is freedom from a more coercive form of control. The dissent which they tolerate is the possible effect of other determiners of action. Since these sanctioned methods are frequently ineffective, we have been able to convince ourselves that they do not represent control at all. When they show too much strength to permit disguise, we give them other names and suppress them as energetically as we suppress the use of force. Education grown too powerful is rejected as propaganda or "brainwashing," while really effective persuasion is decried as "undue influence," "demagoguery," "seduction," and so on.

If we are not to rely solely upon accident for the innovations which give rise to cultural evolution, we must accept the fact that some kind of control of human behavior is inevitable. We cannot use good sense in human affairs unless someone engages in the design and construction of environmental conditions which affect the behavior of men. Environmental changes have always been the condition for the improvement of cultural patterns, and we can hardly use the more effective methods of science without making changes on a grander scale. We are all controlled by the world in which we live, and part of that world has been and will be constructed by men. The question is this: Are we to be controlled by accident, by tyrants, or by ourselves in effective cultural design?

The danger of the misuse of power is possibly greater than ever. It is not allayed by disguising the facts. We cannot make wise decisions if we continue to pretend that human behavior is not controlled, or if we refuse to engage in control when valuable results might be forthcoming. Such measures weaken only ourselves, leaving the strength of science to others. The first step in a defense against tyranny is the fullest possible exposure of controlling techniques. A second step has already been taken successfully in restricting the use of physical force. Slowly, and as yet imperfectly, we have worked out an ethical and governmental design in which the strong man is not allowed to use the power deriving from his strength to control his fellow men. He is restrained by a superior force created for that purpose—the ethical pressure of the group, or more explicit religious and governmental measures. We tend to distrust superior forces, as we currently hesitate to relinquish sovereignty in order to set up an international police force. But it is only through such counter-control that we have achieved what we call peace—a condition in which men are not permitted to control each other through force. In other words, control itself must be controlled.

Science has turned up dangerous processes and materials before. To use the facts and techniques of a science of man to the fullest extent without making some monstrous mistake will be difficult and obviously perilous. It is no time for self-deception, emotional indulgence, or the assumption of attitudes which are no longer useful. Man is facing a difficult test. He must keep his head now, or he must start again—a long way back.

Those who reject the scientific conception of man must, to be logical, oppose the methods of science as well. The position is often supported by predicting a series of dire consequences which are to follow if science is not checked. A recent book by Joseph Wood Krutch, *The Measure of Man,* is in this vein. Mr. Krutch sees in the growing science of man the threat of an unexampled tyranny over men's minds. If science is permitted to have its way, he insists, "we may never be able really to think again." A controlled culture will, for example, lack some virtue inherent in disorder. We have emerged from chaos through a series of happy accidents, but in an engineered culture it will be "impossible for the unplanned to erupt again." But there is no virtue in the accidental character of an accident, and the diversity which arises from disorder can not only be duplicated by design but vastly extended. The experimental method is superior to simple observation just because it multiplies "accidents" in a systematic coverage of the possibilities. Technology offers many familiar examples. We no longer wait for immunity to disease to develop from a series of accidental exposures, nor do we wait for natural mutations in sheep and cotton to produce better fibers; but we continue to make use of such accidents when they occur, and we certainly do not prevent them. Many of the things we value have emerged from the clash of ignorant armies on darkling plains, but it is not therefore wise to encourage ignorance and darkness.

It is not always disorder itself which we are told we shall miss but certain admirable qualities in men which flourish only in the presence of disorder. A man rises above an unpropitious childhood to a position of eminence, and since we cannot give a plausible account of the action of so complex an environment, we attribute the achievement to some admirable faculty in the man himself. But such "faculties" are suspiciously like the explanatory fictions against which the history of science warns us. We admire Lincoln for rising above a deficient school system, but it was not necessarily something *in him* which permitted him to become an educated man in spite of it. His educational environment was certainly unplanned, but it could nevertheless have made a full contribution to his mature behavior. He was a rare man, but the circumstances of his childhood were rare too. We do not give Franklin Delano Roosevelt the same credit for becoming an educated man with the help of Groton and Harvard, although the same behavioral processes may have been involved. The founding of Groton and Harvard somewhat reduced the possibility that fortuitous combinations of circumstances would erupt to produce other Lincolns. Yet the founders can hardly be condemned for attacking an admirable human quality.

Another predicted consequence of a science of man is an excessive uniformity. We are told that effective control—whether governmental, religious, educational, economic or social—will produce a race of men who differ from each other only through relatively refractory genetic differences. That would probably be bad design, but we must admit that we are not now pursuing another course from choice. In a modern school, for example, there is usually a syllabus which specifies what every student is to learn by the end of each year. This would be flagrant regimentation if anyone expected every student to comply. But some will be poor in particular subjects, others will not study, others will not remember what they have been taught, and diversity is assured. Suppose, however, that we someday possess such effective educational techniques that every student will in fact be put in possession of all the behavior specified in a syllabus. At the end of the year, all students will correctly answer all questions on the final examination and "must all have prizes." Should we reject such a system on the grounds that in making all students excellent it has made them all alike? Advocates of the theory of a special faculty might contend that an important advantage of the present system is that the good student learns *in spite of* a system which is so defective that it is currently producing bad students as well. But if really effective techniques are available, we cannot avoid the problem of design simply by preferring the status quo. At what point should education be deliberately inefficient?

Such predictions of the havoc to be wreaked by the application of science to human affairs are usually made with surprising confidence. They not only show a faith in the orderliness of human behavior; they presuppose an established body of knowledge with the help of which it can be positively asserted that the changes which scientists propose to make will have quite specific results—albeit not the results they foresee. But the predictions made by the critics of science must be held to be equally fallible and subject also to empirical test. We may be sure that many steps in the scientific design of cultural patterns will produce unforeseen consequences. But there is only one way to find out. And the test must be made, for if we cannot advance in the design of cultural patterns with absolute certainty, neither can we rest completely confident of the superiority of the status quo. . . .

Far from being a threat to the tradition of Western democracy, the growth of a science of man is a consistent and probably inevitable part of it. In turning to the external conditions which shape and maintain the behavior of men, while questioning the reality of inner qualities and faculties to which human achievements were once attributed, we turn from the ill-defined and remote to the observable and manipulable. Though it is a painful step, it has far-reaching consequences, for it not only sets higher standards of human welfare but shows us how to meet them. A change in a theory of human nature cannot change the facts. The achievements of man in science, art, literature, music and morals will survive any interpretation we place upon them. The uniqueness of the individual is unchallenged in the scientific view. Man, in short, will remain man. (There will be much to admire for those who are so inclined. Possibly the noblest achievement to which man can aspire, even according to present standards, is to accept himself for what he is, as that is revealed to him by the methods which he devised and tested on a part of the world in which he had only a small personal stake.)

If Western democracy does not lose sight of the aims of humanitarian action, it will welcome the almost fabulous support of its own science of man and will strengthen itself and play an important role in building a better world for everyone. But if it cannot put its "democratic philosophy" into proper historical perspective—if, under the control of attitudes and emotions which it generated for other purposes, it now rejects the help of science—then it must be prepared for defeat. For if we continue to insist that science has nothing to offer but a new and more horrible form of tyranny, we may produce just such a result by allowing the strength of science to fall into the hands of despots. And if, with luck, it were to fall instead to men of good will in other political communities, it would be perhaps a more ignominious defeat; for we should then, through a miscarriage of democratic principles, be forced to leave to others the next step in man's long struggle to control nature and himself.

Morton White

1917-

A native son of New York City, Morton White received a B.S. from the City College of New York in 1936 and his M.A. and Ph.D. in philosophy from Columbia University in 1938 and 1942, respectively. After teaching at Columbia and the University of Pennsylvania, he went to Harvard in 1948 as a professor of philosophy.

The author of a number of philosophical studies and inquiries, including *The Origins of Dewey's Instrumentalism* (1943) and *Toward Reunion in Philosophy* (1956), White has been concerned with preserving the values associated with the pragmatic democratic liberalism of twentieth-century America. In 1949, as a matter of fact, he published *Social Thought in America,* a critical though highly sympathetic analysis of five important intellectual figures (John Dewey, Oliver Wendell Holmes, Jr., Thorstein Veblen, Charles A. Beard, James Harvey Robinson) who had contributed much to the liberal philosophy. Admitting that at mid-century the views of these men were coming more and more under attack by the adherents of the right as well as by numerous theologians, White insisted nevertheless that these early twentieth-century liberals had provided a sound foundation on which to erect a social and political ideology. White has been sharply critical of detractors of liberalism, particularly Reinhold Neibuhr and Walter Lippmann—the former for emphasizing the doctrine of original sin and the latter for going back to the Aristotelian-Thomistic version of natural law.

The following selection is from an abridged version to the "Epilogue for 1957" of *Social Thought in America,* which appeared under the title "Original Sin, Natural Law, and Politics" in *Partisan Review,* 23 (Spring, 1956).

I will consider the views of two distinguished critics of the liberal tradition: Reinhold Niebuhr, the most democratic and courageous opponent of secular liberalism on the American scene, and Walter Lippmann, who has bemoaned the disappearance of "The Public Philosophy" in a vein distinctly antithetical to the outlook of Dewey and Holmes. In criticizing Lippmann and Niebuhr I mean to align myself spiritually with Dewey and Holmes, even though I am not always prepared to defend the actual letter of their texts. I do not share Niebuhr's faith, nor do I admire his Hegelian way of dealing with contradictions; I cannot accept the historical inevitability of sin which is such an important part of his view; I deplore Lippmann's revival of the ancient and obscure theory of essences and natural law. And, in general, it seems to me a sad commentary on the thought of 1956 that two of our most popular social thinkers can produce nothing more original or natural than original sin and natural law as answers to the pressing problems of this age.

Niebuhr, Dewey and Human Nature. It has been maintained that Niebuhr's reflections on human nature have provided a new generation of liberals with insights that transcend the limitations of Dewey. On the one hand Dewey is pictured as a disciple of the Enlightenment, confident of the intrinsic goodness of human nature, one of the latter-day *illuminati* who see man everywhere in the chains of ignorance and who hold that scientific knowledge will usher in a millennial era of social happiness through democratic planning. On the other hand Niebuhr is seen as a shrewd Pauline, aware of man's selfishness, and his inevitable incapacity to free himself from the effects of original sin through his own unassisted efforts. Supplied with this more accurate picture of human nature, Niebuhr is supposed to see the folly of placing too much trust in any central group of social planners, while Dewey, it is argued, was ineffectually innocent, a child of light in Niebuhr's biblical phrase, but unable to illuminate this wicked world of gas chambers and mushroom clouds. Niebuhr becomes the symbol of tough, Christian realism, while Dewey represents soft-headed, complacent, dreamy secular liberalism.

What we must consider, then, is the relation between Dewey's and Niebuhr's views of human nature, the grounds offered for them, and their political consequences.

Dewey is presumably a child of light, but what is a child of light in Niebuhr's view? He is defined by contrast to children of darkness "who know no law beyond their will and interest." By contrast "those who believe that self-interest *should* be brought under the discipline of a higher law could then be termed 'the children of light' "; the children of light "may thus be defined as those who *seek* to bring self-interest under the discipline of a more universal law and in harmony with a more universal good." [My italics.]

Surely there is nothing wrong with being a child of light, then. To believe that one should bring self-interest under a more universal law and in harmony with a more universal good, is to act morally; and surely the effort to act morally is not being attacked by Niebuhr. One can hardly believe that he opposes the effort to bring self-interest under law, in spite of his grotesquely false statement that "nothing that is worth doing can be achieved in our lifetime." Therefore one seeks for a more plausible explanation of what he means.

As we push on we see that Niebuhr may escape absurdity, but only at the expense of making it silly to say that Dewey is a child of light and at the risk of making the whole distinction between the two kinds of children useless. In the last analysis Niebuhr may mean by a child of light either (a) one who thinks that it is *easy* to bring self-interest under law, or (b) one who thinks that we can bring self-interest *completely* under a higher law, that we will reach a time when men will *always* act so as to give only limited weight to their own desires. But on either view of a child of light, it is preposterous to suppose that Dewey is a child of light and doubtful to suppose that the contrast between children of light and children of darkness can illuminate the ideological struggles of our time. It is almost ridiculous for Niebuhr to present his own version of the Christian view as the only one to navigate between idiotic optimism and equally idiotic pessimism, as if all rationalists and naturalists said that men were gods, while their extreme opponents maintained that they were devils, and only Niebuhr knew the middle way.

To get back to Dewey and his position in Niebuhr's scheme. Dewey has never supposed that the way to social happiness would be *easy,* nor has he ever said that a time would come when *all* human action would be morally right and all tensions resolved. . . .

It must be said in Niebuhr's behalf that there is an awful lot in Dewey's writing which suggests that the way to a better society *is* easy. For it is true that Dewey in his later writings tended to identify the intelligent solution of a social problem as one that dispenses with the use of force, and therefore seemed to imply that it was never desirable to apply force. If Niebuhr criticizes Dewey on this count, I can understand Niebuhr, but I reject another aspect of Niebuhr's attack on Dewey's attitude toward intelligence. Once we distinguish between the relatively specific conclusion that all political problems can be solved without the appeal to force, and the more general philosophical thesis that no conclusion about the ways of achieving certain ends should be arrived at except by the use of intelligence or scientific method, we see a far more profound issue between Dewey and Niebuhr. In other words, if one identifies the use of intelligence with the use of absolutely peaceful methods, one is accepting a dubious thesis within political technology itself, but if one identifies the use of intelligence with the use of what is commonly called scientific method in the evaluation of judgments of political technology, one can only ask: What other ways are there? One must remember, of course, that we are thinking of political technology as the discipline in which we ask about the best ways of achieving certain social and political ends, and that the answers to such questions take the form of statements to the effect that a certain kind of action is most likely to achieve a certain kind of result.

Human Nature and Politics. So far, I see no reason to think of Niebuhr as having demolished or replaced Dewey as a social or political philosopher. But we have not yet dealt with what is thought to be Niebuhr's chief distinction: his deeply "realistic" vision of man's state by comparison with Dewey's supposedly idle dreams. What can we say about this contrast after our earlier conclusions about Dewey's relations to the children of light?

Here it seems necessary to say, as one must so frequently say when one is bound by neither formula nor prejudice, that the differences which Niebuhr magnifies so dramatically and misleadingly are differences in degree of emphasis on the part of thinkers who see that man is not perfect. Some think that the resolution of social tension is extremely difficult and some are more optimistic; in short, there are disputes as to how heavenly earth can be. But can this bare, unqualified, banal dichotomy, if it is the real dichotomy between the children of light and the children of darkness, help us divide the intellectual or political globe in an interesting way? All we have here is the recognition that men are somewhere between the serpent and the dove, and while Niebuhr puts us closer to the serpent, Dewey puts us closer to the dove. But the serious question for political action is "How close?" in either case. Niebuhr's more recent reflections lead him to answer: "Too close to the serpent to allow for successful central planning," and for this reason some of our younger liberals who reject socialism in favor of Keynesianism now think of Niebuhr as one of the deepest political thinkers in America: for example, Arthur Schlesinger, Jr.

It should be remembered, however, that Niebuhr has not always held his present political position. He defended socialism in his earlier work, when he held the same Pauline and Augustinian doctrine of man. What has happened since then is that Niebuhr's skepticism about man's power to help himself has deepened; Niebuhr has learned things about man and society which were not previously encapsulated in the view of man he inherited from Augustine and Paul. That view is consistent with a variety of political positions, and it's absurd to suppose that Niebuhr only recently began to wake up to "implications" that he should have seen in his salad days. Niebuhr saw Stalin, Hitler, Mussolini, and Franco in operation, and this, more than any theological speculation about man, must have brought home to him the dangers of limiting political freedom. In this respect he is like Dewey and all human beings who learn by experience. It is therefore absurd to say that while Niebuhr has a theory which permits him to see that man is not perfect, Dewey is tied to a philosophy preventing him from seeing the same obvious fact. The difference between Niebuhr and Dewey must be put in more concrete terms and once we put it in this way we shall be leaving relatively empty "theories of human nature" for the solid ground of politics.

The contemporary liberal's fascination with Niebuhr, I suggest, comes less from Niebuhr's dark theory of human nature and more from his actual political pronouncements, from the fact that he is a shrewd, courageous, and right-minded man on many political questions. Those who applaud his politics are too liable to turn then to his theory of human nature and praise it as the philosophical instrument of Niebuhr's political agreement with themselves. But very few of those whom I have elsewhere called "atheists for Niebuhr," follow this inverted logic to its conclusion: they don't move from praise of Niebuhr's theory of human nature to praise of its theological ground. We may admire them for drawing the line somewhere, but certainly not for their consistency.

Historical Inevitability and Original Sin. Precisely because of the emergence of Niebuhr as an influence on so many distinguished liberals of the present generation, there is a greater need for some of Dewey's methodological exhortations. Dewey is committed to the use of empirical methods in discovering what man is or is not likely to achieve, while Niebuhr is, in the last analysis, a devotee of the a priori road that begins with a theology based on faith. Furthermore, Niebuhr is committed to a view of history which in its own way is as rigid as any promulgated by Marx or the more dogmatic theorists of the

Enlightenment. Niebuhr constantly speaks of "the perennial and persistent character of human egotism in any possible society," "the vast forces of historical destiny," "inexorable historical developments," and of social conflict as an "inevitability in human history," in a way that leaves him open to all the arguments so powerfully deployed by Isaiah Berlin in his essay, *Historical Inevitability*.

It is true that Niebuhr often shows a fondness for citing historical evidence in support of his conclusions; he says, for example, that the doctrine of original sin "emphasizes a fact which every page of human history attests." But such evidence as he does offer is surely not enough to establish the thunderous statement that man *cannot* conquer his selfish interests to the point of establishing a planned society. His dark view of man's estate is, in his own mind, a corollary of his doctrine of original sin and that is a view of man which, as he says in his *Nature and Destiny of Man,* transcends the canons of rationality. If history should fail to support his view, or if it should at any moment appear to go against it, Niebuhr's attitude toward his own doctrine would not be seriously affected, since his own conviction rests on faith. In this respect it resembles all of the interpretations of history, like Augustine's and Hegel's, which are demolished in Berlin's essay. But the matter should stand differently with those of Niebuhr's admirers who have not yet been persuaded of the theology underlying Niebuhr's reflections on history. How can those who are sober historians and who reject the pretensions of inevitability and necessity that they find in Toynbee or Marx, react to the block historical universe that Niebuhr portrays when he speaks of inexorable historical developments, vast forces of historical destiny, and inevitability in human history?

From Kierkegaard to Hegel. I have said little about the details of Niebuhr's theology, except to point out that it rests on faith and that it implies the inevitability of sinfulness in history. And although there is hardly space for dealing with the labyrinth of Niebuhr's theology, it is desirable to say something, however brief, about the inevitability of sin in Niebuhr's view, if only to remind some of his more agnostic admirers once again of what he says in his more theological writings. It is to Niebuhr's credit that he recognizes that "the Christian doctrine of sin in its classical form offends both rationalists and moralists by maintaining the seemingly absurd position that man sins inevitably and by a fateful necessity, but that he is nevertheless to be held responsible for actions which are prompted by an ineluctable fate." . . .

Niebuhr says that none of this is to be taken "literalistically," though one should suppose that it is to be taken literally. He criticizes literalistic distortions of Christian doctrine, such as the view that we inherit corruption. This is connected with Niebuhr's belief that we are not doomed to sin by *natural* causes, with his opposition to the Pelagian notion that original sin is a force of inertia in nature, and with his constant rejection of the view that man's *finitude* is solely responsible for his sinning. All of this Niebuhr expresses by saying that "evil in man is a consequence of his *inevitable though not necessary* unwillingness to acknowledge his dependence, to accept his finiteness and to admit his insecurity," and so it is important to say a few words on this contrast between the necessary and the inevitable, especially in the light of what was said earlier about Niebuhr's views on history.

The problem of necessity is one of the most difficult philosophical problems, and therefore one can never be sure of understanding even what the most clear-headed philosophers say on this subject. But there is a usage according to which what happens necessarily happens inevitably. Thus Webster, when he explains the meaning of "inevitable," quotes Burke as saying: "It was inevitable; it was necessary; it was planted in the nature of things." That is to say, we sometimes take "inevitable" and "necessary" as interchangeable, even if as philosophers we are not altogether sure of what they mean. What, then, does Niebuhr want to bring out by distinguishing them? So far as I can see, that we do not sin necessarily in the sense of being determined by what he calls *natural* or physical causes, because we transcend nature. But Niebuhr says that we cannot avoid sinning. His point is that we are driven to sin, not by physical events, but by other things which are equally beyond our control. Niebuhr is therefore free to demarcate a certain kind of unavoidable act, namely that which is caused physically, and call it a *necessary* one, while he calls another kind of unavoidable act—the kind produced by our finitude, freedom, and lack of faith—*inevitable*. The important point is, however, that he believes (a) that we commit certain evil acts which are unavoidable, and (b) that we are morally responsible for them, that is, subject to blame for them.

Now there have been philosophers who have tried to make the inevitability of an act consistent with praising or blaming it. And there are others, like Mr. Berlin in the essay I have cited, who think that inevitability and blame are incompatible. But Niebuhr is a very different kind of thinker. He agrees that there is a contradiction between them but, in his Hegelian and Whitmanesque way, accepts it. The doctrine of original sin, he says, "remains absurd from the standpoint of a pure rationalism, for it expresses a relation between fate and freedom which cannot be fully rationalized, unless the paradox be accepted as a rational understanding of the limits of rationality and as an expression of faith that a rationally irresolvable contradiction may point to a truth which logic cannot contain. Formally there can be, of course, no conflict between logic and truth. The laws of logic are reason's guard against chaos in the realm of truth. They eliminate contradictory assertions. But there is no resource in logical rules to help us understand complex phenomena, exhibiting characteristics which seem to require that they be placed into contradictory categories of reason." Some readers may appreciate what Niebuhr means when he adds that "loyalty to all the facts may require a provisional defiance of logic, lest complexity in the facts of experience be denied for the sake of a premature logical consistency," but how long does he want us to wait? With such a modest remark Niebuhr may disarm even some of the most logically hardened of his readers, but he can't help making them wince when he calls on Hegel's dialectic in his defense: "Hegel's 'dialectic' is a logic invented for the purpose of doing justice to the fact of 'becoming' as a phenomenon which belongs into [*sic*] the category of neither 'being' nor 'non-being.' The Christian doctrine of original sin, with its seemingly contradictory assertions about the inevitability of sin and man's responsibility for sin, is a dialectical truth which does justice to the fact that man's self-love and self-centredness is inevitable. . . ." How easy it is for the extremes to meet and what an irony of history it is that a follower of Kierkegaard—the great enemy of Hegel—should have to appeal to Hegel to save himself at the most vital point in his argument.

Enter Lippmann and Locke. In turning from the thought of Niebuhr to the recent writing of Walter Lippmann we find a similar preoccupation with human deficiency, selfishness, and ineptitude, only this time the fault is said to lie not in power-mad leaders who plan us into totalitarianism but rather with the people, the masses who have secured so much power over government and turned statesmen into lackeys. In one respect, therefore, Lippmann and Nie-buhr appear at opposite poles of the social thinking that has gained prominence since the work of Dewey and Holmes went into eclipse. Lippmann fears the masses and Niebuhr fears the leaders, so that while Niebuhr has replaced Dewey as the hero of some liberals who have abandoned socialism, Lippmann has come to replace Justice Holmes as the hero of the more conservative young men. The Augustinian doctrine of original sin in Niebuhr is neatly matched by the Thomistic concept of natural law in Lippmann.

The doctrine of natural law is one of the oldest and most debated doctrines in the history of moral and political philosophy. It is the central theory of the Catholic Church on moral and political matters; it was adopted by John Locke; it influenced the language and thought of the Declaration of Independ-ence; it was rejected by Dewey, Holmes, and Veblen; it has recently been re-vived by many thinkers who, like Lippmann, cannot bear the absence of a set of moral principles which are universally binding, certain, rationally estab-lished by the inspection of universals, essences, or meanings, depending on which outmoded epistemology or ethics is adopted. . . .

Mr. Lippmann is eager to revive the notion of self-evident natural law and to put it in the hands of wise statesmen who will not be so tied to the de-mands of the people. Presumably with the approval of Mr. Mortimer J. Adler, who is thanked in the preface of *The Public Philosophy* and who has expressed similar views in a less winning way, Mr. Lippmann chastises positivist pro-fessors who have subverted natural law through a refusal to recognize that there is a realm of essences in addition to a realm of existence. It is ironical, therefore, that positivists like Rudolf Carnap have in recent times been the most active defenders of the notion of analyticity (the sister notion of self-evidence, as we have seen) as well as supporters of the view that meanings and universals exist. Positivists, of course, have used the notions of analyticity and meaning quite differently. They are mainly interested in showing that mathe-matical propositions are analytic, that is to say, true by virtue of the meanings of their component terms, and they vehemently (and laudably) deny that the principles of morality may be so viewed. But it is certainly wrong to say, as

Lippmann does, that all of them deny the existence of the universals or meanings which are so essential for the philosopher of natural law.

In opposition to Lippmann, Locke, Aquinas, and the positivists, to say nothing of a vast number of the other philosophers like Bertrand Russell and G. E. Moore in some of their writings, I think that the notion of an analytic statement, the notion of a self-evident statement as conceived by Aquinas and Locke, and the meanings so dear to all of them and Lippmann, are first of all obscure in themselves and secondly incapable of sustaining the philosophical load which has been put upon them. I shall concentrate on the significance of this contention for the doctrine of natural law, though I can at best outline only part of my view here.

Very few philosophers have taken the existence of meanings, conceived as universals, for granted. The usual pattern of philosophical argument is to assume that the reader believes in the existence of physical objects—the tables and chairs of epistemology books—but that he is too dull to see that universals like the attribute of being a table also exist. And so it is frequently pointed out that we couldn't understand the general word "chair" unless it had a meaning quite distinct from every individual chair in the universe. In this way the existence of meanings construed as properties of things is supposedly proven. But then a new move must be made, for the ordinary man has a rather limited conception of existence; in other words he uses the word "exists" narrowly, as applying only to physical objects which exist in space and time, and this won't do.

Having begun with a tolerance and a garden-variety understanding of the word "exist," the ordinary man has now been led to the point where he must see that there are at least two meanings of "exist" and that this is the solution to the problem of understanding. But can any one suppose that this postulation of Platonic meanings really illuminates the notion of understanding? We think immediately, and rightly so, of dormitive virtues "explaining" why opium puts people to sleep.

The situation is even worse when we examine Lippmann's introduction of essences. The Platonic theorist of understanding has the comparatively easy job of showing how understanding is *possible,* whereas Lippmann must show that a belief in self-evident principles of natural law is *necessary.* In other words, the philosopher who offers the theory of understanding outlined above can at least assume that the man he is trying to persuade understands *some* words, and after having found out what those words are, the philosopher may begin to crank his machines and grind out his universals in order to "explain" how the understanding the man has is possible. But a theorist of natural law will frequently have to face people who don't believe that there are self-evident moral principles to begin with. How can he get the machinery rolling then? Where can he begin? What premises can the theorist of natural law start with? Surely it is not self-evident that *there are* self-evident principles of natural law and therefore we must be shown that there are.

It may be said in reply that the theorist of natural law *can* deal with the man who has not quite made up his mind, the man who is at most doubtful about whether there are self-evident principles of morality. But this is *par excellence* a situation in which the philosopher of natural law appeals to things which are at least as dubious and at least as obscure as that which is to be defended or explained. Does Lippmann suppose that he is likely to persuade such a doubtful man that there are essences which if properly unpacked make the truth of moral principles evident? Even if he were to accomplish the first bit of required persuasion—that is to say, even if the public should be persuaded of the existence of essences—Lippmann will fail to show them that the principles of political morality are self-evident statements about men in which, as Aquinas says, "the predicate is contained in the notion of the subject," or logically deducible therefrom. . . .

We all have deep moral convictions: we firmly believe certain moral principles which we try to act on to the best of our ability. They make up, along with others, the foundations of our whole structure of belief; they constitute our terminal beliefs. We want them to be consistent with each other and to fit in harmoniously and simply with other, less confidently held beliefs; we want this structure to mesh with experience and feeling. But individuals and societies have surrendered many beliefs which they once accepted as terminal, and some of these beliefs are moral beliefs. What, then, is the purpose of inventing a mysterious realm of essence *of which* our terminal beliefs are supposed to be true? Wouldn't it be saner to recognize that we all have our ultimate convictions at any moment, that they are not absolutely immune to change (though we can resolve, at our own peril, to make them permanently immune), that some people adopt the same beliefs as terminal and others don't? Who are the people we get along with? Very often the people with whom we have a great deal of agreement on these fundamental beliefs. Who are the people we quarrel with? Very often those with whom we don't share these beliefs. The point is that we and those whose lines end up at the same terminal shouldn't need the kind of mutual encouragement that comes from inventing a realm of essences beneath (or above) the terminal: and those who go in different directions are the last people in the world who are likely to use essences in the same way even if they agreed that such things existed.

(58)

Richard Hofstadter

1916-

Born in Buffalo, New York, Richard Hofstadter, after graduating from the University of Buffalo, received his Ph.D. from Columbia University in 1942. He taught at various institutions of higher learning, and re-

turned to Columbia in 1946 as a professor of American history. He has produced several important and influential historical works, including *Social Darwinism in American Thought 1860–1915* (1944), *The American Political Tradition and the Men Who Made It* (1948), and *The Age of Reform* (1955)—the latter winning him the Pulitzer Prize.

Hofstadter is one of the leading intellectual historians in the United States. His approach to the study of American history is from a decidedly liberal or progressive framework. Despite his evident sympathies, however, he has also been a sharp and subtle critic of the progressive tradition, pointing out its excessive moralism, its occasional lapses in the direction of isolationism and racism, and its opportunism. Hofstadter himself has been ideologically homeless; he has not advanced any alternative ideology to the liberal faith. His partial disillusionment has, nevertheless, not made him merely a passive spectator. He is critical of much of the current thought that passes for conservatism.

As the following selection indicates, Hofstadter characterizes much of the so-called contemporary conservatism as a pseudo-conservatism, which reflects the "authoritarian personality" and in fact involves a basic rejection of the fundamental principles of American society. It is taken from "The Pseudo-Conservative Revolt," *The American Scholar,* 24 (Winter, 1954–1955).

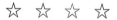

There is, however, a dynamic of dissent in America today. Representing no more than a modest fraction of the electorate, it is not so powerful as the liberal dissent of the New Deal era, but it is powerful enough to set the tone of our political life and to establish throughout the country a kind of punitive reaction. The new dissent is certainly not radical—there are hardly any radicals of any sort left—nor is it precisely conservative. Unlike most of the liberal dissent of the past, the new dissent not only has no respect for nonconformism, but is based upon a relentless demand for conformity. It can most accurately be called pseudo-conservative—I borrow the term from the study of *The Authoritarian Personality* published five years ago by Theodore W. Adorno and his associates—because its exponents, although they believe themselves to be conservatives and usually employ the rhetoric of conservatism, show signs of a serious and restless dissatisfaction with American life, traditions and institutions. They have little in common with the temperate and compromising spirit of true conservatism in the classical sense of the word, and they are far from pleased with the dominant practical conservatism of the moment as it is represented by the Eisenhower Administration. Their political reactions express rather a profound if largely unconscious hatred of our society and its ways—a hatred which one would hesitate to impute to them if one did not have suggestive clinical evidence.

From clinical interviews and thematic apperception tests, Adorno and his co-workers found that their pseudo-conservative subjects, although given to a form of political expression that combines a curious mixture of largely conservative with occasional radical notions, succeed in concealing from themselves impulsive tendencies that, if released in action, would be very far from conservative. The pseudo-conservative, Adorno writes, shows "conventionality and authoritarian submissiveness" in his conscious thinking and "violence, anarchic impulses, and chaotic destructiveness in the unconscious sphere. . . . The pseudo-conservative is a man who, in the name of upholding traditional American values and institutions and defending them against more or less fictitious dangers, consciously or unconsciously aims at their abolition."[1]

Who is the pseudo-conservative, and what does he want? It is impossible to identify him by class, for the pseudo-conservative impulse can be found in practically all classes in society, although its power probably rests largely upon its appeal to the less educated members of the middle classes. The ideology of pseudo-conservatism can be characterized but not defined, because the pseudo-conservative tends to be more than ordinarily incoherent about politics. The lady who, when General Eisenhower's victory over Senator Taft had finally become official, stalked out of the Hilton Hotel declaiming, "This means eight more years of socialism" was probably a fairly good representative of the pseudo-conservative mentality. So also were the gentlemen who, at the Freedom Congress held at Omaha over a year ago by some "patriotic" organizations, objected to Earl Warren's appointment to the Supreme Court with the assertion: "Middle-of-the-road thinking can and will destroy us"; the general who spoke to the same group, demanding "an Air Force capable of wiping out the Russian Air Force and industry in one sweep," but also "a material reduction in military expenditures"; the people who a few years ago believed simultaneously that we had no business to be fighting communism in Korea, but that the war should immediately be extended to an Asia-wide crusade against communism; and the most ardent supporters of the Bricker Amendment. Many of the most zealous followers of Senator McCarthy are also pseudo-conservatives, although there are presumably a great many others who are not.

The restlessness, suspicion and fear manifested in various phases of the pseudo-conservative revolt give evidence of the real suffering which the pseudo-conservative experiences in his capacity as a citizen. He believes himself to be living in a world in which he is spied upon, plotted against, betrayed, and very likely destined for total ruin. He feels that his liberties have been arbitrarily and outrageously invaded. He is opposed to almost everything that has happened in American politics for the past twenty years. He hates the very thought of Franklin D. Roosevelt. He is disturbed deeply by American participation in the United Nations, which he can see only as a sinister organization. He sees his own country as being so weak that it is constantly about to fall

---

1. Theodore W. Adorno et al., *The Authoritarian Personality* (New York, 1950), pp. 675–76. While I have drawn heavily upon this enlightening study, I have some reservations about its methods and conclusions. For a critical review, see Richard Christie and Marie Jahoda, eds., *Studies in the Scope and Method of "The Authoritarian Personality"* (Glencoe, Illinois, 1954), particularly the penetrating comments by Edward Shils.

victim to subversion; and yet he feels that it is so all-powerful that any failure it may experience in getting its way in the world—for instance, in the Orient— cannot possibly be due to its limitations but must be attributed to its having been betrayed. He is the most bitter of all our citizens about our involvement in the wars of the past, but seems the least concerned about avoiding the next one. While he naturally does not like Soviet communism, what distinguishes him from the rest of us who also dislike it is that he shows little interest in, is often indeed bitterly hostile to such realistic measures as might actually strengthen the United States vis-à-vis Russia. He would much rather concern himself with the domestic scene, where communism is weak, than with those areas of the world where it is really strong and threatening. He wants to have nothing to do with the democratic nations of Western Europe, which seem to draw more of his ire than the Soviet Communists, and he is opposed to all "give-away programs" designed to aid and strengthen these nations. Indeed, he is likely to be antagonistic to most of the operations of our federal government except Congressional investigations, and to almost all of its expenditures. Not always, however, does he go so far as the speaker at the Freedom Congress who attributed the greater part of our national difficulties to "this nasty, stinking 16th [income tax] Amendment."

A great deal of pseudo-conservative thinking takes the form of trying to devise means of absolute protection against that betrayal by our own officialdom which the pseudo-conservative feels is always imminent. The Bricker Amendment, indeed, might be taken as one of the primary symptoms of pseudo-conservatism. Every dissenting movement brings its demand for Constitutional changes; and the pseudo-conservative revolt, far from being an exception to this principle, seems to specialize in Constitutional revision, at least as a speculative enterprise. The widespread latent hostility toward American institutions takes the form, among other things, of a flood of proposals to write drastic changes into the body of our fundamental law. Last summer, in a characteristically astute piece, Richard Rovere pointed out that Constitution-amending had become almost a major diversion in the Eighty-third Congress.[2] About a hundred amendments were introduced and referred to committee. Several of these called for the repeal of the income tax. Several embodied formulas of various kinds to limit non-military expenditures to some fixed portion of the national income. One proposed to bar all federal expenditures on "the general welfare"; another, to prohibit American troops from serving in any foreign country except on the soil of the potential enemy; another, to redefine treason to embrace not only persons trying to overthrow the government but also those trying to "weaken" it, even by peaceful means. The last proposal might bring the pseudo-conservative rebels themselves under the ban of treason: for the sum total of these amendments might easily serve to bring the whole structure of American society crashing to the ground.

As Mr. Rovere points out, it is not unusual for a large number of Con-

---

2. Richard Rovere, "Letter from Washington," *New Yorker,* June 19, 1954, pp. 67–72.

stitutional amendments to be lying about somewhere in the Congressional hoppers. What is unusual is the readiness the Senate has shown to give them respectful consideration, and the peculiar populistic arguments some of its leading members have used to justify referring them to the state legislatures. While the ordinary Congress hardly ever has occasion to consider more than one amendment, the Eighty-third Congress saw six Constitutional amendments brought to the floor of the Senate, all summoning simple majorities, and four winning the two-thirds majority necessary before they can be sent to the House and ultimately to the state legislatures. It must be added that, with the possible exception of the Bricker Amendment itself, none of the six amendments so honored can be classed with the most extreme proposals. But the pliability of the senators, the eagerness of some of them to pass the buck and defer to "the people of the country," suggests how strong they feel the pressure to be for some kind of change that will give expression to that vague desire to repudiate the past that underlies the pseudo-conservative revolt.

One of the most urgent questions we can ask about the United States in our time is the question of where all this sentiment arose. The readiest answer is that the new pseudo-conservatism is simply the old ultra-conservatism and the old isolationism heightened by the extraordinary pressures of the contemporary world. This answer, true though it may be, gives a deceptive sense of familiarity without much deepening our understanding, for the particular patterns of American isolationism and extreme right-wing thinking have themselves not been very satisfactorily explored. It will not do, to take but one example, to say that some people want the income tax amendment repealed because taxes have become very heavy in the past twenty years: for this will not explain why, of three people in the same tax bracket, one will grin and bear it and continue to support social welfare legislation as well as an adequate defense, while another responds by supporting in a matter-of-fact way the practical conservative leadership of the moment, and the third finds his feelings satisfied only by the angry conspiratorial accusations and extreme demands of the pseudo-conservative.

No doubt the circumstances determining the political style of any individual are complex. Although I am concerned here to discuss some of the neglected social-psychological elements in pseudo-conservatism, I do not wish to appear to deny the presence of important economic and political causes. I am aware, for instance, that wealthy reactionaries try to use pseudo-conservative organizers, spokesmen and groups to propagate their notions of public policy, and that some organizers of pseudo-conservative and "patriotic" groups often find in this work a means of making a living—thus turning a tendency toward paranoia into a vocational asset, probably one of the most perverse forms of occupational therapy known to man. A number of other circumstances—the drastic inflation and heavy taxes of our time, the dissolution of American urban life, considerations of partisan political expediency—also play a part. But none of these things seem to explain the broad appeal of pseudo-conservatism, its emotional intensity, its dense and massive irration-

ality, or some of the peculiar ideas it generates. Nor will they explain why those who profit by the organized movements find such a ready following among a large number of people, and why the rank-and-file janizaries of pseudo-conservatism are so eager to hurl accusations, write letters to congressmen and editors, and expend so much emotional energy and crusading idealism upon causes that plainly bring them no material reward. . . .

What I wish to suggest—and I do so in the spirit of one setting forth nothing more than a speculative hypothesis—is that pseudo-conservatism is in good part a product of the rootlessness and heterogeneity of American life, and above all, of its peculiar scramble for status and its peculiar search for secure identity. Normally there is a world of difference between one's sense of national identity or cultural belonging and one's social status. However, in American historical development, these two things, so easily distinguishable in analysis, have been jumbled together in reality, and it is precisely this that has given such a special poignancy and urgency to our status-strivings. In this country a person's status—that is, his relative place in the prestige hierarchy of his community—and his rudimentary sense of belonging to the community— that is, what we call his "Americanism"—have been intimately joined. Because, as a people extremely democratic in our social institutions, we have had no clear, consistent and recognizable system of status, our personal status problems have an unusual intensity. Because we no longer have the relative ethnic homogeneity we had up to about eighty years ago, our sense of belonging has long had about it a high degree of uncertainty. We boast of "the melting pot," but we are not quite sure what it is that will remain when we have been melted down.

We have always been proud of the high degree of occupational mobility in our country—of the greater readiness, as compared with other countries, with which a person starting in a very humble place in our social structure could rise to a position of moderate wealth and status, and with which a person starting with a middling position could rise to great eminence. We have looked upon this as laudable in principle, for it is democratic, and as pragmatically desirable, for it has served many a man as a stimulus to effort and has, no doubt, a great deal to do with the energetic and effectual tone of our economic life. The American pattern of occupational mobility, while often much exaggerated, as in the Horatio Alger stories and a great deal of the rest of our mythology, may properly be credited with many of the virtues and beneficial effects that are usually attributed to it. But this occupational and social mobility, compounded by our extraordinary mobility from place to place, has also had its less frequently recognized drawbacks. Not the least of them is that this has become a country in which so many people do not know who they are or what they are or what they belong to or what belongs to them. It is a country of people whose status expectations are random and uncertain, and yet whose status aspirations have been whipped up to a high pitch by our democratic ethos and our rags-to-riches mythology. . . .

Status problems take on a special importance in American life because a very large part of the population suffers from one of the most troublesome of all status questions: unable to enjoy the simple luxury of assuming their own nationality as a natural event, they are tormented by a nagging doubt as to whether they are really and truly and fully American. Since their forebears voluntarily left one country and embraced another, they cannot, as people do elsewhere, think of nationality as something that comes with birth; for them it is a matter of *choice,* and an object of striving. This is one reason why problems of "loyalty" arouse such an emotional response in many Americans and why it is so hard in the American climate of opinion to make any clear distinction between the problem of national security and the question of personal loyalty. Of course there is no real reason to doubt the loyalty to America of the immigrants and their descendants, or their willingness to serve the country as fully as if their ancestors had lived here for three centuries. None the less, they have been thrown on the defensive by those who have in the past cast doubts upon the fullness of their Americanism. Possibly they are also, consciously or unconsciously, troubled by the thought that since their forebears have already abandoned one country, one allegiance, their own national allegiance might be considered fickle. For this I believe there is some evidence in our national practices. What other country finds it so necessary to create institutional rituals for the sole purpose of guaranteeing to its people the genuineness of their nationality? Does the Frenchman or the Englishman or the Italian find it necessary to speak of himself as "one hundred per cent" English, French or Italian? Do they find it necessary to have their equivalents of "I Am an American Day"? When they disagree with one another over national policies, do they find it necessary to call one another un-English, un-French or un-Italian? No doubt they too are troubled by subversive activities and espionage, but are their countermeasures taken under the name of committees on un-English, un-French or un-Italian activities?

The primary value of patriotic societies and anti-subversive ideologies to their exponents can be found here. They provide additional and continued reassurance both to those who are of old American ancestry and have other status grievances and to those who are of recent American ancestry and therefore feel in need of reassurance about their nationality. Veterans' organizations offer the same satisfaction—what better evidence can there be of the genuineness of nationality and of *earned* citizenship than military service under the flag of one's country? Of course such organizations, once they exist, are liable to exploitation by vested interests that can use them as pressure groups on behalf of particular measures and interests. (Veterans' groups, since they lobby for the concrete interests of veterans, have a double role in this respect.) But the cement that holds them together is the status motivation and the desire for an identity. . . .

Such status-strivings may help us to understand some of the otherwise unintelligible figments of the pseudo-conservative ideology—the incredibly bitter feeling against the United Nations, for instance. Is it not understandable that such a feeling might be, paradoxically, shared at one and the same time by an

old Yankee-Protestant American, who feels that his social position is not what it ought to be and that these foreigners are crowding in on his country and diluting its sovereignty just as "foreigners" have crowded into his neighborhood, and by a second- or third-generation immigrant who has been trying so hard to de-Europeanize himself, to get Europe out of his personal heritage, and who finds his own government mocking him by its complicity in these Old-World schemes?

Similarly, is it not status aspiration that in good parts spurs the pseudo-conservative on toward his demand for conformity in a wide variety of spheres of life? Conformity is a way of guaranteeing and manifesting respectability among those who are not sure that they are respectable enough. The nonconformity of others appears to such persons as a frivolous challenge to the whole order of things they are trying so hard to become part of. Naturally it is resented, and the demand for conformity in public becomes at once an expression of such resentment and a means of displaying one's own soundness. This habit has a tendency to spread from politics into intellectual and social spheres, where it can be made to challenge almost anyone whose pattern of life is different and who is imagined to enjoy a superior social position—notably, as one agitator put it, to the "parlors of the sophisticated, the intellectuals, the so-called academic minds."

Why has this tide of pseudo-conservative dissent risen to such heights in our time? To a considerable degree, we must remember, it is a response, however unrealistic, to realities. We do live in a disordered world, threatened by a great power and a powerful ideology. It is a world of enormous potential violence, that has already shown us the ugliest capacities of the human spirit. In our own country there has indeed been espionage, and laxity over security has in fact allowed some spies to reach high places. There is just enough reality at most points along the line to give a touch of credibility to the melodramatics of the pseudo-conservative imagination.

However, a number of developments in our recent history make this pseudo-conservative uprising more intelligible. For two hundred years and more, various conditions of American development—the process of continental settlement, the continuous establishment in new areas of new status patterns, the arrival of continuous waves of new immigrants, each pushing the preceding waves upward in the ethnic hierarchy—made it possible to satisfy a remarkably large part of the extravagant status aspirations that were aroused. There was a sort of automatic built-in status-elevator in the American social edifice. Today that elevator no longer operates automatically, or at least no longer operates in the same way.

Secondly, the growth of the mass media of communication and their use in politics have brought politics closer to the people than ever before and have made politics a form of entertainment in which the spectators feel themselves involved. Thus it has become, more than ever before, an arena into which private emotions and personal problems can be readily projected. Mass communications have aroused the mass man.

Thirdly, the long tenure in power of the liberal elements to which the pseudo-conservatives are most opposed and the wide variety of changes that have been introduced into our social, economic and administrative life have intensified the sense of powerlessness and victimization among the opponents of these changes and have widened the area of social issues over which they feel discontent. There has been, among other things, the emergence of a wholly new struggle: the conflict between businessmen of certain types and the New Deal bureaucracy, which has spilled over into a resentment of intellectuals and experts.

Finally, unlike our previous postwar periods, ours has been a period of continued crisis, from which the future promises no relief. In no foreign war of our history did we fight so long or make such sacrifices as in World War II. When it was over, instead of being able to resume our peacetime preoccupations, we were very promptly confronted with another war. It is hard for a certain type of American, who does not think much about the world outside and does not want to have to do so, to understand why we must become involved in such an unremitting struggle. It will be the fate of those in power for a long time to come to have to conduct the delicate diplomacy of the cold peace without the sympathy or understanding of a large part of their own people. From bitter experience, Eisenhower and Dulles are learning today what Truman and Acheson learned yesterday.

These considerations suggest that the pseudo-conservative political style, while it may already have passed the peak of its influence, is one of the long waves of twentieth-century American history and not a momentary mood. I do not share the widespread foreboding among liberals that this form of dissent will grow until it overwhelms our liberties altogether and plunges us into a totalitarian nightmare. Indeed, the idea that it is purely and simply fascist or totalitarian, as we have known these things in recent European history, is to my mind a false conception, based upon the failure to read American developments in terms of our peculiar American constellation of political realities. (It reminds me of the people who, because they found several close parallels between the NRA and Mussolini's corporate state, were once deeply troubled at the thought that the NRA was the beginning of American fascism.) However, in a populistic culture like ours, which seems to lack a responsible elite with political and moral autonomy, and in which it is possible to exploit the wildest currents of public sentiment for private purposes, it is at least conceivable that a highly organized, vocal, active and well-financed minority could create a political climate in which the rational pursuit of our well-being and safety would become impossible.

Daniel Bell

1919-

Daniel Bell was born in New York City and attended the City College of New York, receiving his B.S. in 1938. He has had a varied career, serving as a staff writer and later as editor on *The New Leader,* and as labor editor of *Fortune Magazine* from 1948 to 1958. Besides his career in journalism, he taught at the University of Chicago and then went to Columbia University as a professor of sociology. He is also the author of numerous historical and sociological works.

During the 1930's Bell was active in many liberal and radical causes. But by the end of that decade, as events began to reveal the superficiality and even the dangers of contemporary "isms," he began to retreat from the world of ideology. His book, *The End of Ideology* (1960), a collection of essays published by Bell during the 1950's, is a penetrating revelation of the transformation and decline of the older liberal faith. Bell's comments reflect his progressive disillusionment with the world of ideology, which he came to feel could no longer serve as a guide for human improvement. Although his disenchantment omits pessimism and he side-steps some of the conservatively oriented implications of his own position, Bell's work stands as an example of the dilemma facing many liberals who have lost their ideological faith but who have not been able to find a viable substitute. Thus Bell insists that criticism of the existing order is indispensable, but at the same time he repudiates all philosophical grounds upon which to base such a criticism. In a certain sense his hesitations represent the indecisiveness of the American people toward the future as they enter the decade of the 1960's.

The following selection is from Bell's book *The End of Ideology: On the Exhaustion of Political Ideas in the Fifties* (Glencoe, Ill., 1960).

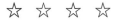

There have been few periods in history when man felt his world to be durable, suspended surely, as in Christian allegory, between chaos and heaven. In an Egyptian papyrus of more than four thousand years ago, one finds: ". . . impudence is rife . . . the country is spinning round and round like a potter's wheel . . . the masses are like timid sheep without a shepherd . . . one who yesterday was indigent is now wealthy and the sometime rich overwhelm him with adulation." The Hellenistic period as described by Gilbert Murray was one of a "failure of nerve"; there was "the rise of pessimism, a loss of self-confidence, of hope in this life and of faith in normal human effort." And the old scoundrel Talleyrand claimed that only those who lived before 1789 could have tasted life in all its sweetness.

This age, too, can add appropriate citations—made all the more wry and bitter by the long period of bright hope that preceded it—for the two decades between 1930 and 1950 have an intensity peculiar in written history: world-wide economic depression and sharp class struggles; the rise of fascism and racial imperialism in a country that had stood at an advanced stage of human culture; the tragic self-immolation of a revolutionary generation that had proclaimed the finer ideals of man; destructive war of a breadth and scale hitherto unknown; the bureaucratized murder of millions in concentration camps and death chambers.

For the radical intellectual who had articulated the revolutionary impulses of the past century and a half, all this has meant an end to chiliastic hopes, to millennarianism, to apocalyptic thinking—and to ideology. For ideology, which once was a road to action, has come to be a dead end.

Whatever its origins among the French *philosophes,* ideology as a way of translating ideas into action was given its sharpest phrasing by the left Hegelians, by Feuerbach and by Marx. For them, the function of philosophy was to be critical, to rid the present of the past. ("The tradition of all the dead generations weighs like a nightmare on the brain of the living," wrote Marx.) Feuerbach, the most radical of all the left Hegelians, called himself Luther II. Man would be free, he said, if we could demythologize religion. The history of all thought was a history of progressive disenchantment, and if finally, in Christianity, God had been transformed from a parochial deity to a universal abstraction, the function of criticism—using the radical tool of alienation, or self-estrangement—was to replace theology by anthropology, to substitute Man for God. Philosophy was to be directed at life, man was to be liberated from the "specter of abstractions" and extricated from the bind of the supernatural. Religion was capable only of creating "false consciousness." Philosophy would reveal "true consciousness." And by placing Man, rather than God, at the center of consciousness, Feuerbach sought to bring the "infinite into the finite."

If Feuerbach "descended into the world," Marx sought to transform it. And where Feuerbach proclaimed anthropology, Marx, reclaiming a root insight of Hegel, emphasized History and historical contexts. The world was not generic Man, but men; and of men, classes of men. Men differed because of their class position. And truths were class truths. All truths, thus, were masks, or partial truths, but the real truth was the revolutionary truth. And this real truth was rational.

Thus a dynamic was introduced into the analysis of ideology, and into the creation of a new ideology. By demythologizing religion, one recovered (from God and sin) the potential in man. By the unfolding of history, rationality was revealed. In the struggle of classes, true consciousness, rather than false consciousness, could be achieved. But if truth lay in action, one must act. The left Hegelians, said Marx, were only *littérateurs.* (For them a magazine was "practice.") For Marx, the only real action was in politics. But action, revolutionary action as Marx conceived it, was not mere social change. It was, in its way, the resumption of all the old millennarian, chiliastic ideas of the Anabaptists. It was, in its new vision, a new ideology.

Ideology is the conversion of ideas into social levers. Without irony Max Lerner once entitled a book "Ideas Are Weapons." This is the language of ideology. It is more. It is the commitment to the consequences of ideas. When Vissarion Belinsky, the father of Russian criticism, first read Hegel and became convinced of the philosophical correctness of the formula "what is, is what ought to be," he became a supporter of the Russian autocracy. But when it was shown to him that Hegel's thought contained the contrary tendency, that dialectically the "is" evolves into a different form, he became a revolutionary overnight. "Belinsky's conversion," comments Rufus W. Mathewson, Jr., "illustrates an attitude toward ideas which is both passionate and myopic, which responds to them on the basis of their immediate relevances alone, and inevitably reduces them to tools."

What gives ideology its force is its passion. Abstract philosophical inquiry has always sought to eliminate passion, and the person, to rationalize all ideas. For the ideologue, truth arises in action, and meaning is given to experience by the "transforming moment." He comes alive not in contemplation, but in "the deed." One might say, in fact, that the most important, latent, function of ideology is to tap emotion. Other than religion (and war and nationalism), there have been few forms of channelizing emotional energy. Religion symbolized, drained away, dispersed emotional energy from the world onto the litany, the liturgy, the sacraments, the edifices, the arts. Ideology fuses these energies and channels them into politics.

But religion, at its most effective, was more. It was a way for people to cope with the problem of death. The fear of death—forceful and inevitable— and more, the fear of violent death, shatters the glittering, imposing, momentary dream of man's power. The fear of death, as Hobbes pointed out, is the source of conscience; the effort to avoid violent death is the source of law. When it was possible for people to believe, really believe, in heaven and hell, then some of the fear of death could be tempered or controlled; without such belief, there is only the total annihilation of the self.

It may well be that with the decline in religious *faith* in the last century and more, this fear of death as total annihilation, unconsciously expressed, has probably increased. One may hypothesize, in fact, that here is a cause of the breakthrough of the irrational, which is such a marked feature of the changed moral temper of our time. Fanaticism, violence, and cruelty are not, of course, unique in human history. But there was a time when such frenzies and mass emotions could be displaced, symbolized, drained away, and dispersed through religious devotion and practice. Now there is only this life, and the assertion of self becomes possible—for some even necessary—in the domination over others. One can challenge death by emphasizing the omnipotence of a movement (as in the "inevitable" victory of communism), or overcome death (as did the "immortality" of Captain Ahab) by bending others to one's will. Both paths are taken, but politics, because it can institutionalize power, in the way that religion once did, becomes the ready avenue for domination. The modern effort to transform the world chiefly or solely through politics (as contrasted with the religious transformation of the self) has meant that all other institutional ways of mobilizing emotional energy would necessarily atrophy. In effect, sect and church became party and social movement.

A social movement can rouse people when it can do three things: simplify ideas, establish a claim to truth, and, in the union of the two, demand a commitment to action. Thus, not only does ideology transform ideas, it transforms people as well. The nineteenth-century ideologies, by emphasizing inevitability and by infusing passion into their followers, could compete with religion. By identifying inevitability with progress, they linked up with the positive values of science. But more important, these ideologies were linked, too, with the rising class of intellectuals, which was seeking to assert a place in society.

The differences between the intellectual and the scholar, without being invidious, are important to understand. The scholar has a bounded field of knowledge, a tradition, and seeks to find his place in it, adding to the accumulated, tested knowledge of the past as to a mosaic. The scholar, qua scholar, is less involved with his "self." The intellectual begins with *his* experience, *his* individual perceptions of the world, *his* privileges and deprivations, and judges the world by these sensibilities. Since his own status is of high value, his judgments of the society reflect the treatment accorded him. In a business civilization, the intellectual felt that the wrong values were being honored, and rejected the society. Thus there was a "built-in" compulsion for the free-floating intellectual to become political. The ideologies, therefore, which emerged from the nineteenth century had the force of the intellectuals behind them. They embarked upon what William James called "the faith ladder," which in its vision of the future cannot distinguish possibilities from probabilities, and converts the latter into certainties.

Today, these ideologies are exhausted. The events behind this important sociological change are complex and varied. Such calamities as the Moscow Trials, the Nazi-Soviet pact, the concentration camps, the suppression of the Hungarian workers, form one chain; such social changes as the modification of capitalism, the rise of the Welfare State, another. In philosophy, one can trace the decline of simplistic, rationalistic beliefs and the emergence of new stoic-theological images of man, e.g. Freud, Tillich, Jaspers, etc. This is not to say that such ideologies as communism in France and Italy do not have a political weight, or a driving momentum from other sources. But out of all this history, one simple fact emerges: for the radical intelligentzia, the old ideologies have lost their "truth" and their power to persuade.

Few serious minds believe any longer that one can set down "blueprints" and through "social engineering" bring about a new utopia of social harmony. At the same time, the older "counter-beliefs" have lost their intellectual force as well. Few "classic" liberals insist that the State should play no role in the economy, and few serious conservatives, at least in England and on the Continent, believe that the Welfare State is "the road to serfdom." In the Western world, therefore, there is today a rough consensus among intellectuals on political issues: the acceptance of a Welfare State; the desirability of decentralized power; a system of mixed economy and of political pluralism. In that sense, too, the ideological age has ended.

And yet, the extraordinary fact is that while the old nineteenth-century ideologies and intellectual debates have become exhausted, the rising states of Asia and Africa are fashioning new ideologies with a different appeal for their own people. These are the ideologies of industrialization, modernization, Pan-Arabism, color, and nationalism. In the distinctive difference between the two kinds of ideologies lies the great political and social problems of the second half of the twentieth century. The ideologies of the nineteenth century were universalistic, humanistic, and fashioned by intellectuals. The mass ideologies of Asia and Africa are parochial, instrumental, and created by political leaders. The driving forces of the old ideologies were social equality and, in the largest sense, freedom. The impulsions of the new ideologies are economic development and national power.

And in this appeal, Russia and China have become models. The fascination these countries exert is no longer the old idea of the free society, but the new one of economic growth. And if this involves the wholesale coercion of the population and the rise of new elites to drive the people, the new repressions are justified on the ground that without such coercions economic advance cannot take place rapidly enough. And even for some of the liberals of the West, "economic development" has become a new ideology that washes away the memory of old disillusionments.

It is hard to quarrel with an appeal for rapid economic growth and modernization, and few can dispute the goal, as few could ever dispute an appeal for equality and freedom. But in this powerful surge—and its swiftness is amazing—any movement that instates such goals risks the sacrifice of the present generation for a future that may see only a new exploitation by a new elite. For the newly-risen countries, the debate is not over the merits of Communism—the content of that doctrine has long been forgotten by friends and foes alike. The question is an older one: whether new societies can grow by building democratic institutions and allowing people to make choices—and sacrifices—voluntarily, or whether the new elites, heady with power, will impose totalitarian means to transform their countries. Certainly in these traditional and old colonial societies where the masses are apathetic and easily manipulated, the answer lies with the intellectual classes and their conceptions of the future.

Thus one finds, at the end of the fifties, a disconcerting caesura. In the West, among the intellectuals, the old passions are spent. The new generation, with no meaningful memory of these old debates, and no secure tradition to build upon, finds itself seeking new purposes within a framework of political society that has rejected, intellectually speaking, the old apocalyptic and chiliastic visions. In the search for a "cause," there is a deep, desperate, almost pathetic anger. The theme runs through a remarkable book, *Convictions,* by a dozen of the sharpest young Left Wing intellectuals in Britain. They cannot define the content of the "cause" they seek, but the yearning is clear. In the U.S. too there is a restless search for a new intellectual radicalism. Richard Chase, in his thoughtful assessment of American society, *The Democratic Vista,* insists that the greatness of nineteenth-century America for the rest of the world consisted in its radical vision of man (such a vision as Whitman's), and calls for a new radical criticism today. But the problem is that the old politico-economic radicalism (pre-occupied with such matters as the socialization of industry) has lost its meaning, while the stultifying aspects of contemporary culture (e.g., television) cannot be redressed in political terms. At the same time, American culture has almost completely accepted the avant-garde, particularly in art, and the older academic styles have been driven out completely. The irony, further, for those who seek "causes" is that the workers, whose grievances were once the driving energy for social change, are more satisfied with the society than the intellectuals. The workers have not achieved utopia, but their expectations were less than those of the intellectuals, and the gains correspondingly larger.

The young intellectual is unhappy because the "middle way" is for the middle-aged, not for him; it is without passion and is deadening. Ideology, which by its nature is an all-or-none affair, and temperamentally the thing he wants, is intellectually devitalized, and few issues can be formulated any more, intellectually, in ideological terms. The emotional energies—and needs—exist, and the question of how one mobilizes these energies is a difficult one. Politics offers little excitement. Some of the younger intellectuals have found an outlet in science or university pursuits, but often at the expense of narrowing their talent into mere technique; others have sought self-expression in the arts, but in the wasteland the lack of content has meant, too, the lack of the necessary tension that creates new forms and styles.

Whether the intellectuals in the West can find passions outside of politics is moot. Unfortunately, social reform does not have any unifying appeal, nor does it give a younger generation the outlet for "self-expression" and "self-definition" that it wants. The trajectory of enthusiasm has curved East, where, in the new ecstasies for economic utopia, the "future" is all that counts.

And yet, if the intellectual history of the past hundred years has any meaning—and lesson—it is to reassert Jefferson's wisdom (aimed at removing the dead hand of the past, but which can serve as a warning against the heavy hand of the future as well), that "the present belongs to the living." This is the wisdom that revolutionists, old and new, who are sensitive to the fate of their fellow men, rediscover in every generation. "I will never believe," says a protagonist in a poignant dialogue written by the gallant Polish philosopher Leszek Kolakowski, "that the moral and intellectual life of mankind follows the law of economics, that is by saving today we can have more tomorrow; that we should use lives now so that truth will triumph or that we should profit by crime to pave the way for nobility."

And these words, written during the Polish "thaw," when the intellectuals had asserted, from their experience with the "future," the claims of humanism, echo the protest of the Russian writer Alexander Herzen, who, in a dialogue a hundred years ago, reproached an earlier revolutionist who would sacrifice the present mankind for a promised tomorrow: "Do you truly wish to condemn all human beings alive today to the sad role of caryatids . . . supporting a floor for others some day to dance on? . . . This alone should serve as a warning to people: an end that is infinitely remote is not an end, but, if you like, a trap; an end must be nearer—it ought to be, at the very least, the labourer's wage or pleasure in the work done. Each age, each generation, each life has it own fullness. . . ."

Suggestions for Further Reading

The literature dealing with American intellectual history is extensive. The following list, therefore, is not intended to be definitive. Most of the works selected for inclusion in this section simply represent a cross section of some of the more important books dealing with various aspects of American intellectual development. For a more complete bibliography the reader can consult Oscar Handlin and others, eds., *Harvard Guide to American History* (Cambridge, Mass.: Harvard University Press, 1954), Library of Congress, *A Guide to the Study of the United States of America: Representative Books Reflecting the Development of American Life and Thought* (Washington, D.C.: United States Government Printing Office, 1960), and the bibliography in Merle Curti, *The Growth of American Thought* (2nd ed., New York: Harper and Brothers, 1951), pp. 801–876.

I. General Works

Aaron, Daniel, *Men of Good Hope: A Story of American Progressives* (New York: Oxford University Press, 1951). Contains penetrating intellectual biographies of progressives from Emerson to Veblen.

Beard, Charles A. and Mary R., *The American Spirit: A Study of the Idea of Civilization in the United States* (New York: The Macmillan Company, 1942). A study of American intellectual history that emphasizes a single theme: the idea of civilization.

Beard, Charles A. and Mary R., *The Rise of American Civilization* (New York: The Macmillan Company, 1927). A penetrating and provocative interpretation of American society from its origins.

Boorstin, Daniel, *The Genius of American Politics* (Chicago: University of Chicago Press, 1953). An attempt to explain the uniqueness of American thought by emphasizing the favorable environment within which it developed.

Bowers, David F., ed., *Foreign Influences in American Life* (Princeton, N.J.: Princeton University Press, 1944).

Burns, Edward M., *The American Idea of Mission: Concepts of National Purpose and Destiny* (New Brunswick, N.J.: Rutgers University Press, 1957). A useful historical survey of an important concept.

Cash, Wilbur J., *The Mind of the South* (New York: Alfred A. Knopf, 1941). A brilliant impressionistic interpretation of southern thought and society from its origins.

Cohen, Morris Raphael, *American Thought: A Critical Sketch* (New York: The Free Press of Glencoe, 1954). A perceptive treatment by a noted philosopher.

Curti, Merle, *The Growth of American Thought* (2nd ed., New York: Harper and Brothers, 1951). Probably the best general survey of American thought and society.

Curti, Merle, *The Roots of American Loyalty* (New York: Columbia University Press, 1946). A historical sketch of American patriotism.

Curti, Merle, *The Social Ideas of American Educators* (New York: Charles Scribner's Sons, 1935). Important for an understanding of American education.

Dorfman, Joseph, *The Economic Mind in American Civilization* (5 vols., New York: The Viking Press, 1946–1959). By far the best and most comprehensive treatment of American economic thought since the Puritans.

Dorson, Richard M., *American Folklore* (Chicago: University of Chicago Press, 1959).

Egbert, Donald D., and Persons, Stow, eds., *Socialism and American Life* (2 vols., Princeton, N.J.: Princeton University Press, 1952). Indispensable for an understanding of socialism and its influence.

Ekirch, Arthur, *The Decline of American Liberalism* (New York: Oxford University Press, 1955). A study of the decline of American liberalism, which is identified with the classical philosophical values of the Enlightenment.

Ellis, John T., *American Catholicism* (Chicago: University of Chicago Press, 1956). The best brief historical survey.

Gabriel, Ralph H., *The Course of American Democratic Thought* (2nd ed., New York: The Roland Press Company, 1956). One of the most important and brilliant interpretations of American intellectual history.

Glazer, Nathan, *American Judaism* (Chicago: University of Chicago Press, 1957). The best brief historical survey.

Greene, Evarts B., *Religion and the State: The Making and Testing of an American Tradition* (New York: New York University Press, 1941). A useful study of the development of church-state relationships in the United States.

Hartz, Louis, *The Liberal Tradition in America: An Interpretation of American Political Thought Since the Revolution* (New York: Harcourt, Brace and Company, 1955). A stimulating study of American political thought in terms of Lockian influences.

Hofstadter, Richard, *The American Political Tradition and the Men Who Made It* (New York: Alfred A. Knopf, 1948). A discussion of the American political tradition through biographical sketches of leading figures from Thomas Jefferson to Franklin Delano Roosevelt.

Hudson, Winthrop S., *American Protestantism* (Chicago: University of Chicago Press, 1961). The best brief historical survey.

Hurst, James Willard, *The Growth of American Law* (Boston: Little, Brown and Company, 1950).

Jones, Howard Mumford, *The Pursuit of Happiness* (Cambridge, Mass.: Harvard University Press, 1953). An unusual intellectual history of a phrase made famous in the Declaration of Independence and a study of its subsequent development.

Kohn, Hans, *American Nationalism* (New York: The Macmillan Company, 1957). A useful historical survey by a leading student of nationalism.

Kraus, Michael, *The Writing of American History* (Norman, Okla.: University of Oklahoma Press, 1953). An Introduction to American historical thought and practice.

Lerner, Max, *America as a Civilization: Life and Thought in the United States Today* (New York: Simon and Schuster, 1957). An all-encompassing survey and interpretation of American society.

McLoughlin, William G., Jr., *Modern Revivalism: Charles Grandison Finney to Billy Graham* (New York: The Ronald Press Company, 1959). The best general history of American revivalism.

Merriam, Charles E., *A History of American Political Theories* (New York: The Macmillan Company, 1920). An older but still useful study by an outstanding political scientist.

Mosier, Richard D., *The American Temper: Patterns of Our Intellectual Heritage* (Berkeley, Calif.: University of California Press, 1952). An interpretation of American thought through a series of successive patterns from Puritanism to pragmatism.

Mott, Frank L., *Golden Multitudes: The Story of Best Sellers in the United States* (New York: The Macmillan Company, 1947). Important for an understanding of popular American culture.

Mott, Frank L., *A History of American Magazines* (4 vols., Cambridge, Mass.: Harvard University Press, 1938–1957). Indispensable for an understanding of intellectual developments.

Niebuhr, H. Richard, *The Kingdom of God in America* (New York: Harper and Brothers, 1937). An important history of millennialism.

Niebuhr, H. Richard, *The Social Sources of Denominationalism* (New York: Henry Holt and Company, 1929). Useful for the social origins of the various religious denominations.

Parrington, Vernon L., *Main Currents in American Thought* (3 vols., New York: Harcourt, Brace and Company, 1927–1930). One of the classic works in American history. Written from a decidedly Jeffersonian or liberal point of view.

Perry, Ralph Barton, *Puritanism and Democracy* (New York: The Vanguard Press, 1944). An important work by a noted philosopher who identified two formative elements in the American national tradition—Puritanism and the democracy of the Enlightenment.

Persons, Stow, *American Minds: A History of Ideas* (New York: Henry Holt and Company, 1958). An intellectual history in terms of a succession of minds from the Puritan mind to the neodemocratic mind.

Persons, Stow, ed., *Evolutionary Thought in America* (New Haven, Conn.: Yale University Press, 1950). A study of the influence of evolutionary theories on different disciplines.

Potter, David M., *People of Plenty: Economic Abundance and the American Character* (Chicago: University of Chicago Press, 1954). An interpretation of the American character through the concept of economic abundance.

Rossiter, Clinton, *Conservatism in America* (New York: Alfred A Knopf, 1955). A sympathetic historical survey and analysis by a moderate adherent of the New Conservatism.

Schneider, Herbert W., *A History of American Philosophy* (New York: Columbia University Press, 1946). A good survey that attempts to relate philosophical thought to its societal environment.

Smith, Henry Nash, *Virgin Land: The American West as Symbol and Myth* (Cambridge, Mass.: Harvard University Press, 1950). A brilliant intellectual analysis of a major American theme.

Smith, James Ward, and Jamison, Albert Leland, eds., *Religion in American Life* (4 vols. to date, Princeton, N.J.: Princeton University Press, 1961–   ). An excellent survey of all aspects of American religion by leading authorities.

Smith, T. V., *The American Philosophy of Equality* (Chicago: University of Chicago Press, 1927). A study by a noted philosopher.

Spencer, Benjamin T., *The Quest for Nationality: An American Literary Campaign* (Syracuse, N.Y.: Syracuse University Press, 1957). An analysis of the emergence of an indigenous literary tradition.

Spiller, Robert E., and others, eds., *Literary History of the United States* (3 vols., New York: The Macmillan Company, 1948). A detailed and comprehensive history of American literature and thought since the colonial period.

Stokes, Anson P., *Church and State in the United States* (3 vols., New York: Harper and Brothers, 1950). A monumental work of encyclopedic proportions.

Sweet, William W., *The Story of Religion in America* (2nd ed., New York: Harper and Brothers, 1950). A useful general history.

Wecter, Dixon, *The Hero in America* (New York: Charles Scribner's Sons, 1941). A study of the role and symbolic importance of the hero in American society and culture.

Weinberg, Albert K., *Manifest Destiny* (Baltimore: The Johns Hopkins Press, 1935). An important intellectual history of the ideology of American expansionism.

Weisberger, Bernard A., *They Gathered at the River: The Story of the Great Revivalists and Their Impact upon Religion in America* (Boston: Little, Brown and Company, 1958). A brief general survey of American revivalism.

Wiltse, Charles M., *The Jeffersonian Tradition in American Democracy* (Chapel Hill, N.C.: University of North Carolina Press, 1935). A study of the ideology of Thomas Jefferson and its subsequent influence in American history.

Wish, Harvey, *The American Historian: A Social-Intellectual History of the Writing of the American Past* (New York: Oxford University Press, 1960). A brief history of American historiography.

Wright, Benjamin, *American Interpretations of Natural Law* (Cambridge, Mass.: Harvard University Press, 1931). An analysis of the concept of natural law and the uses to which it was put prior to the Civil War.

II. *Industrial and Modern America*

Aaron, Daniel, *Writers on the Left: Episodes in American Literary Communism* (New York: Harcourt, Brace and Company, 1961). The great depression of the 1930's and the rise of literary Marxism.

Abell, Aaron I., *American Catholicism and Social Action* (Garden City, N.Y.: Hanover House, 1960). A study of the emergence of the Catholic version of a socialized gospel.

Abell, Aaron I., *The Urban Impact on American Protestantism 1865–1900* (Cambridge, Mass.: Harvard University Press, 1943). Important for an understanding of the impact of industrialization on religion.

Auerbach, Morton, *The Conservative Illusion* (New York: Columbia University Press, 1959). A historical study of conservatism that analyzes the New Conservatism in great detail from a hostile point of view.

Bremner, Robert H., *From the Depths: The Discovery of Poverty in the United States* (New York: New York University Press, 1956). Emphasizes the changing definition and interpretations of poverty.

Brooks, Van Wyck, *The Confident Years: 1885–1915* (New York: E. P. Dutton and Company, 1952), and *New England: Indian Summer 1865–1915* (New York: E. P. Dutton and Company, 1940). Part of the author's detailed and important study of the writer in America.

Buck, Paul H., *The Road to Reunion 1865–1900* (Boston: Little, Brown and Company, 1937). A cultural and intellectual study of the aftermath of the Civil War.

Cargill, Oscar, *Intellectual America* (New York: The Macmillan Company, 1941). An important work in the history of American ideas and foreign influences.

Carter, Paul A., *The Decline and Revival of the Social Gospel: Social and Political Liberalism in American Protestant Churches 1920–1940* (Ithaca, N.Y.: Cornell University Press, 1956). A brief analysis of the social gospel after the First World War.

Chugerman, Samuel, *Lester F. Ward: The American Aristotle* (Durham, North Carolina: Duke University Press, 1939). An analysis of the father of American sociology.

Commager, Henry S., *The American Mind: An Interpretation of American Thought and Character Since the 1880's* (New Haven, Conn.: Yale University Press, 1950). A useful general survey of American intellectual history since the end of the nineteenth century.

Cremin, Lawrence A., *The Transformation of the School: Progressivism in American Education, 1876–1957* (New York: Alfred A. Knopf, 1961). An excellent survey of basic issues and ideas in American education.

Cross, Robert D., *The Emergence of Liberal Catholicism in America* (Cambridge, Mass.: Harvard University Press, 1958). An important study of the nature of American Catholicism in the latter part of the nineteenth century.

Curti, Merle, ed., *American Scholarship in the Twentieth Century* (Cambridge, Mass.: Harvard University Press, 1953). A study of the evolution of American scholarship in such fields as history, the social sciences, and others.

Destler, Chester M., *American Radicalism 1865–1901* (New London, Conn.: Connecticut College, 1946). Contains important insights for the student of American intellectual history.

Dorfman, Joseph, *Thorstein Veblen and His America* (New York: The Viking Press, 1934). The most comprehensive biography of Veblen available.

Faulkner, Harold U., *The Quest for Social Justice 1898–1914* (New York: The Macmillan Company, 1931). A comprehensive study of society and thought.

Filler, Louis, *Crusaders for American Liberalism* (New York: Harcourt, Brace and Company, 1939). Useful biographical studies illuminating early twentieth-century progressivism.

Fine, Sidney, *Laissez Faire and the General-Welfare State: A Study of Conflict in American Thought 1865–1901* (Ann Arbor, Mich.: University of Michigan Press, 1956). A comprehensive intellectual history emphasizing the emergence of a coherent body of thought opposed to conservative Darwinian thinking.

Forcey, Charles, *The Crossroads of Liberalism: Croly, Weyl, Lippmann, and the Progressive Era 1900–1925* (New York: Oxford University Press, 1961). An intellectual analysis of three major progressive philosophers.

Foster, Frank H., *The Modern Movement in American Theology* (New York: Fleming H. Revell Company, 1939). A useful general introduction.

Furniss, Norman F., *The Fundamentalist Controversy 1918–1931* (New Haven, Conn.: Yale University Press, 1954). A good monograph on the history of Protestant fundamentalism in the twentieth century.

Ginger, Ray, *Altgeld's America* (New York: Funk and Wagnalls Company, 1958). An intellectual history of Chicago at the turn of the century that illustrates many of the important intellectual movements.

Goldman, Eric F., *Rendezvous With Destiny: A History of Modern American Reform* (New York: Alfred A. Knopf, 1952). A well-written work that is comprehensive in its coverage.

Gurko, Leo, *The Angry Decade* (New York: Dodd, Mead and Company, 1947). A study of the literature of the depression decades of the 1930's.

Handlin, Oscar, *Race and Nationality in American Life* (Boston: Little, Brown and Company, 1950). Useful essays illustrating various aspects of American social and intellectual history.

Herberg, Will, *Protestant-Catholic-Jew: An Essay in American Religious Sociology* (Garden City, N.Y.: Doubleday and Company, 1955). Probably the best critique of the American religious scene at mid-century.

Higham, John, *Strangers in the Land: Patterns of American Nativism 1860–1925* (New Brunswick, N.J.: Rutgers University Press, 1955). The best and most complete history of American nativism and racism available.

Hoffmann, Frederick J., *The Twenties* (New York: The Viking Press, 1955). An illuminating literary history of the 1920's.

Hofstadter, Richard, *The Age of Reform: From Bryan to F.D.R.* (New York: Alfred A. Knopf, 1955). A sociological analysis of American reform in the twentieth century, somewhat debunking in its orientation.

Hofstadter, Richard, *Social Darwinism in American Thought 1860–1915* (Philadelphia: University of Pennsylvania Press, 1944). Indispensable for an understanding of American intellectual history from the Civil War to the First World War.

Hopkins, Charles H., *The Rise of the Social Gospel in American Protestantism 1865–1915* (New Haven, Conn.: Yale University Press, 1940). Important for an understanding of the emergence of liberal Protestantism.

Jordy, William H., *Henry Adams: Scientific Historian* (New Haven, Conn.: Yale University Press, 1952). A study of Adams' pessimistic views of history.

Kazin, Alfred, *On Native Grounds* (New York: Reynal and Hitchcock, 1942). A major work in literary and intellectual history.

Kirkland, Edward C., *Dream and Thought in the Business Community 1860–1900* (Ithaca, N.Y.: Cornell University Press, 1956). A study of the businessman, emphasizing the diversity of types.

McCloskey, Robert G., *American Conservatism in the Age of Enterprise* (Cambridge, Mass.: Harvard University Press, 1951). An analysis of the thought of William Graham Sumner, Stephen J. Field, and Andrew Carnegie.

May, Henry F., *The End of American Innocence: A Study of the First Years of Our Own Time 1912–1917* (New York: Alfred A. Knopf, 1959). A valuable intellectual history emphasizing the breakdown of the older unity of American thought prior to the outbreak of the First World War.

May, Henry F., *Protestant Churches and Industrial America* (New York: Harper and Brothers, 1949). A work illustrating the impact of industrialism on American Protestantism.

Meyer, Donald B., *The Protestant Search for Political Realism 1919–1941* (Berkeley, Calif.: University of California Press, 1960). A detailed history of the reaction against the older social gospel and the emergence of Protestant neo-orthodoxy.

Miller, Robert M., *American Protestantism and Social Issues 1919–1939* (Chapel Hill, N.C.: University of North Carolina Press, 1958). A study of the social attitudes of American Protestantism on such varied issues as civil liberties, race relations, war, and the merits of the contending economic philosophies.

Moore, Edward C., *American Pragmatism: Peirce, James, and Dewey* (New York: Columbia University Press, 1961). A philosophical analysis of the three major pragmatist thinkers.

Nevins, Allan, *The Emergence of Modern America 1865–1878* (New York: The Macmillan Company, 1927). A comprehensive study of society and thought.

Newman, William J., *The Futilitarian Society* (New York: George Braziller, 1961). A hostile examination of American conservatism at mid-century.

Noble, David W., *The Paradox of Progressive Thought* (Minneapolis, Minnesota: University of Minnesota Press, 1958). A history of progressive ideology emphasizing certain intellectual weaknesses.

Paul, Arnold M., *Conservative Crisis and the Rule of Law: Attitudes of Bar and Bench 1887–1895* (Ithaca, N.Y.: Cornell University Press, 1960). Useful for an understanding of the legal mind and American conservatism.

Perry, Ralph Barton, *The Thought and Character of William James* (2 vols., Boston: Little, Brown and Company, 1935). The definitive biography of a leading philosopher.

Prothero, James W., *The Dollar Decade: Business Ideas in the 1920's* (Baton Rouge, La.: Louisiana State University Press, 1954). Emphasizes the extreme conservatism of American businessmen during the 1920's.

Quint, Howard H., *The Forging of American Socialism: Origins of the Modern Movement* (Columbia, S.C.: University of South Carolina Press, 1953). By far the best history of American socialism at the end of the nineteenth century.

Resek, Carl, *Lewis Henry Morgan: American Scholar* (Chicago: University of Chicago Press, 1960). An illuminating study of a major figure in American social science.

Riesman, David, and others, *The Lonely Crowd: A Study of the Changing American Character* (New Haven, Conn.: Yale University Press, 1950). An important analysis of the American character structure at mid-century.

Schlesinger, Arthur M., *The Rise of the City 1878–1898* (New York: The Macmillan Company, 1933). A pioneering comprehensive analysis of society and thought.

Schneider, Herbert W., *Religion in 20th Century America* (Cambridge, Mass.: Harvard University Press, 1952). Good for an understanding of religious intellectual thought.

Slosson, Preston W., *The Great Crusade and After 1914–1928* (New York: The Macmillan Company, 1931). A comprehensive survey of society and thought.

Spitz, David, *Patterns of Anti-Democratic Thought* (New York: The Macmillan Company, 1949). An illuminating critique of American anti-democratic thought in the twentieth century.

Starr, Harris, E., *William Graham Sumner* (New York: Henry Holt and Company, 1925). The most comprehensive study of Sumner.

Strout, Cushing, *The Pragmatic Revolt in American History: Carl Becker and Charles Beard* (New Haven, Conn.: Yale University Press, 1958). An important intellectual analysis of two major historians who reflected many of the intellectual currents of the twentieth century.

Wecter, Dixon, *The Age of the Great Depression 1929–1941* (New York: The Macmillan Company, 1948). A comprehensive study of society and thought.

White, Edward A., *Science and Religion in American Thought: The Impact of Naturalism* (Stanford, Calif.: University of California Press, 1952). Important for intellectual history at the end of the nineteenth century.

White, Morton, *Social Thought in America: The Revolt Against Formalism* (New York: The Viking Press, 1949). An important comparative study of Dewey, Veblen, Holmes, Beard, and Robinson, emphasizing the antiformal elements inherent in their thinking.

Wiener, Philip P., *Evolution and the Founders of Pragmatism* (Cambridge, Mass.: Harvard University Press, 1949). A crucial work on the origins of pragmatism.

Wilkins, Burleigh T., *Carl Becker* (Cambridge, Mass.: M.I.T. Press, 1961). An intellectual biography of an important historian.

Wyllie, Irvin G., *The Self-Made Man in America: The Myth of Rags to Riches* (New Brunswick, N.J.: Rutgers University Press, 1954). An important intellectual history of a major American myth.

Index of Documents

487

Index of Names*

Abel, 423
Abbot, Francis E., 58
Abraham, 199, 221
Acheson, Dean, 470
Acton, Lord (John E. E. Dalberg-Acton), 390, 392–393
Adam, 211
Adams, Charles Francis, 239
Adams, Henry, 228, 230, 234, *239–242*, 247, 256
Adams, Herbert Baxter, 21
Adams, John, 134, 239, 393
Adams, John Quincy, 23, 239
Adler, Mortimer J., 460
Adorno, Theodore W., 463–464
Agassiz, Louis, 6
Akiba Ben Joseph (Rabbi), 351–352
Alger, Horatio, 467
Allen, Charles H., 105
Allen, Frederick L., 276
Ambrose, St., 338
Ames, Edward S., *218–225*
Ames, James B., 36
Amiel, Henri F., 71
Aquinas, St. Thomas, 338, 349, 351–352, 384, 461–462
Arendt, Hannah, 383
Aristotle, 41, 63, 69, 136, 327, 338, 407, 435
Arnold, Thurman, *264–268*
Athanasius, St., 352
Attlee, Clement, 366
Augustine, St., 209, 338, 349, 351–353, 362, 457–458
Augustus, 366
Austin, John, 33, 37, 335

Bacon, Francis, 70, 230
Baeck, Leo, 352
Bancroft, George, 250
Barker, Ernest, 384
Barth, Karl, 313, 440
Beard, Charles A., *248–257,* 454

Beck, Robert N., 231
Becker, Carl L., 231, *413–421*
Beecher, Henry Ward, 194
Beer, Theodor, 52
Belinsky, Vissarion, 473
Bell, Daniel, 396–397, *471–477*
Bellarmine, Roberto Cardinal, 338
Benedict XV (Pope), 244
Benedict, Ruth, 234
Benes, Eduard, 411
Bentham, Jeremy, 33, 37, 70–71, 335, 408
Benton, Thomas H., 26–28
Berkeley, George, 66
Berlin, Isaiah, 458–459
Bernouilli, Daniel, 241
Bethe, Hans A., 52
Bigelow, Melville M., 36
Bismarck, Otto E. L. von, 244
Blackstone, William, 297, 338
Blum, Léon, 367
Bonald, Louis Jacques Maurice de, 388
Booth, William, 203
Bossuet, Jacques B., 250
Bracton, Henry de, 37, 338
Brahms, Johannes, 244
Brandeis, Louis D., 269
Bricker, John, 464–466
Brogan, Denis W., 437
Brooks, Phillips, 207
Browder, Earl, *305–311*
Bruening, Heinrich, 411
Bryan, William Jennings, 244, 286
Buddha, 350–352
Bultmann, Rudolph, 349
Burke, Edmund, 24, 339, 358, 390, 392, 459
Bushnell, Horace, 208–209
Butler, Samuel, 272

Caesar, Julius, 18
Cain, 423
Calhoun, John C., 21, 374
Calvin, John, 350–353

* Italicized numbers refer to pages of selections.

489